China

Guide

Travel Guides to Planet Earth!

CRITICAL ACCLAIM FOR RUTH LOR MALLOY'S *CHINA GUIDE*
– *New, revised, 11th edition* –

"The most comprehensive and practical of the many recent books I've seen. An up-to-date, informative guide to China travel."
Loren Fessler, author of *China* and *Chinese in America*

"This hefty book is packed with facts, maps, and terrific tips on everything from accidents to earthquakes, toilets to tipping. (A) first-rate history of the awakening giant, Malloy answers most questions a novice traveler might have."
Paul King, *The Toronto Star*

"This guide may be the best once-over-lightly look at China ... it not only covers destinations, restaurants, hotels and shopping, but also gives you a passing acquaintance with useful aspects of Chinese culture."
Keith Graham, *The Atlanta Journal/The Atlanta Constitution*

"For my money, this is the best book on the market. "
Lorraine Williams, *The Budget Traveler*

"I use your guidebook as my sole reference when planning all different aspects of my tours to China (I lead several tours there each year). Your book has been a tremendous help to me and is the most readable and useful one out there, as far as I'm concerned."
Wendy Abraham, *Jewish Historical Tours of China*

About the Author

Ruth Lor Malloy is a Canadian of Chinese ancestry. She has been a travel writer, conference organizer, social worker, freelance photographer, wife and mother, and author of guide books to China since 1975. Ruth has also published a novel set in China. She travels frequently to China for fun as well as research, and has lectured on Yangtze River cruise ships and escorted North American tour groups.

Ruth's home is in Toronto, but she has also lived in Hong Kong, Philippines, Thailand, Kazakhstan and India.

She updates and expands on selected information in this book on her website: *www.china-travel-guide.com*. There she can answer your questions, inform you of new bargains, and publish travel reports from other recent travelers.

Open Road -
Travel Guides to Planet Earth!

Open Road Publishing has guide books to exciting, fun destinations on four continents. As veteran travelers, our goal is to bring you the best travel guides available anywhere!

No small task, but here's what we offer:

• All Open Road travel guides are written by authors with a distinct, opinionated point of view – not some sterile committee or team of writers. Our authors are experts in the areas covered and are polished writers.

• Our guides are geared to people who want to make their own travel choices. We'll show you how to discover the real destination – not just see some place from a tour bus window.

• We're strong on the basics, but we also provide terrific choices for those looking to get off the beaten path and experience the country or city – not just see it or pass through it.

• We give you the best, but we also tell you about the worst and what to avoid. Nobody should waste their time and money on their hard-earned vacation because of bad or inadequate travel advice.

• Our guides assume nothing. We tell you everything you need to know to have the trip of a lifetime – presented in a fun, literate, no-nonsense style.

• And, above all, we welcome your input, ideas, and suggestions to help us put out the best travel guides possible.

China

Guide

Travel Guides to Planet Earth!

Ruth Lor Malloy

Open Road Publishing

Open Road Publishing

We offer travel guides to American and foreign locales. Our books tell it like it is, often with an opinionated edge, and our experienced authors always give you all the information you need to have the trip of a lifetime. Write for your free catalog of all our titles.

**Open Road Publishing
P.O. Box 284, Cold Spring Harbor, NY 11724
E-mail: Jopenroad@aol.com**

11th Edition

Front cover photo©2002 by Jeannine Krawczyk Photography, Chicago. The image is from The Mountain That Flew From Afar, Hangzhou, China. Back cover photo courtesy of Ruth Lor Malloy. Hong Kong maps are based on maps courtesy of Hong Kong Tourism Board.

All prices, schedules, and details are subject to change. We will not be held responsible for any such fluctuations, or other experiences, that travelers may encounter during their visit.

China Guide

Contents

List of Illustrations

Bodhisattva   32
The Eight Buddhist Emblems of Happy Augury   33
The Attributes of the Eight Taoist Genii   39
The Dragon of Heaven   128
Symbols of the Intellectual Elite   129
The Eight Precious Things   129
Two Variations of Shou   130
The Fu   130
Five Bats Surrounding Shou   130
Scepter, Writing Brush, & Uncoined Silver   131
The Three Fruits   131
Prunus, Orchid, Bamboo, & Peony   131
Peach Blossom, Lotus Flower, Chrysanthemum, & Narcissus   132
How to Use Chopsticks   165

Sidebars

Maps

Sidebars

Sidebars

14

China Guide

Many people are responsible for this book: travelers who took the time to share their experiences and impressions, expatriate residents in China who talked of the problems and joys of living there, business travelers on airplanes, and fellow tourists in hotel elevators, Yangtze cruise ships, and trains. Among these have been Jean Ash, Kevin van der Laan, Alan and Debbie Hurvitz, Elizabeth Stone, Nikki Denley, Queena Lee, Shirley Thomas and Carol Waters.

Thanks go also to Ray and Nida Cranbourne, Murray and Dodi Fromson, Saul and Alison Lockhart, Ralph and Laine Loveland, Lo Ging Lei, Richard and Alison Wong and Xu Manhua for their hospitality as well as assistance.

I am particularly grateful to those who traveled with me on Concepts East and IST tours whose reactions I could get immediately, and who helped decide by their comments and illnesses, the restaurants and hotels to include, and the warnings to make. Especially valuable were Bob Isaacson, Virginia Stearns, Mei Li Stearns Isaacson, and Phyllis M. Stearns and their world of Chinese adoptions, and iron and steel mills. Then there was Caroline Walker who forced me to take an (ugh) overnight bus, taught me more about altitude sickness, and opened archaeological doors.

I want the readers of my website, especially Joyce Werking who sent many questions, to know that they helped direct the way this book was written. They wanted specifics, prices, the reliability of Chinese travel agents, and schedules. They wanted to avoid crowds and to plan their own trips. They suggested travel agents who helped them.

Many travel agents in China have been generous in their help. I chose to mention some by name with their cities. These were very helpful to me and I expect they will be useful to you too. In addition, there's been Michael Sun of GZL International Travel Service (Guangzhou), Song Rui in Xi'an, and Yang Wu and Alice Xiaofan Yuan of CYTS Head Office.

A special thank-you goes to the China National Tourism Administration, the China Tourist Office in Toronto, the Hong Kong Tourism Board, and the Macao Government Tourist Office. Air China and China Southern provided trans-Pacific flights without which I couldn't do research, and I could not have escorted tours without the support of Yue Chi of Asia Adventures in Toronto.

The provincial and municipal tourism offices mentioned in my book also deserve my gratitude. Many officials wrote long letters and endured hours of questioning. Many provided guides and transportation. Extra special was Mr. He Xiaozu of the Gansu Tourism Administration.

There's also the Canadian Embassy in Beijing and Consulates in Chongqing, Guangzhou, Hong Kong and Shanghai, and the Canada-China Business Council.

For their help in making complicated travel arrangements, I would like to thank Ms. Xiao Dong Feng of Air China in Vancouver, Irene Emory of Bass Hotels & Resorts, Jeff Ruffalo of China Southern Airlines, Zhang Cong of CITS Huangshan, Karisa Lui and Stephen Wong of the Hong Kong Tourism Board, Daniella Wu of Hyatt International Hotels, Daniel Lai of Marriott, Patricia Goh of Meritus Hotels, Lesley Yu of Orient Royal Cruises, David Huang of Yunnan Overseas Travel Corporation, Marion Darby, Ellen Levy and Judy Reeves of Shangri-La Hotels, and Stella Chan of Zenith Hotels. Thanks too to Paul Chu whose China Travel Service in Vancouver paid for one of my hotels.

For translations, I am indebted to Kalina Huang, and for guiding me around Song Tang Mao and Denny Ip. For proof reading, a great deal of help came from Elaine Melnick but the mistakes are mine. I am especially grateful to Lin Feng for his suggested changes.

Hotels whose assistance also made the research possible were in **Beihai**: Shangri-la; **Beijing**: Holiday Inn Lido, China World Hotel, Harbour Plaza, Holiday Inn Chang An West, Holiday Inn Downtown, JCMandarin, Jianguo, Kerry Centre, New World Courtyard Marriott, Novotel Peace, Shangri-La, St. Regis, State Guest House;

Changsha: Grand Sun City; **Chengdu**: Crowne Plaza; **Chongqing**: Harbour Plaza, Holiday Inn, Marriott; **Dali**: Golden Flower JinHua; **Dunhuang:** Grand Sun Hotel; **Fuzhou:** Hot Spring Hotel; **Guangzhou**: China Hotel, Holiday Inn, White Swan; **Guilin**: Bravo, Fubo, Sheraton; **Haikou:** Mandarin, Huandao Tide;

Hangzhou: Shangri-la, Holiday Inn; **Hefei:** Holiday Inn, Novotel Hefei; **Hong Kong**: Island Shangri-La, Kowloon Hotel, Kowloon Shangri-La, The Peninsula, Regal Airport Hotel, The Salisbury YMCA; **Jinan**: Sofitel; **Kunming**: Harbour Plaza, Holiday Inn;

Lanzhou: New Century, Xilan International Hotel; **Lijiang**: Jade Dragon Garden Hotel; **Liuzhou**: Jingdu Hotel; **Macau**: Hyatt Regency; **Nanjing:** Shangri-La Dingshan, Crowne Plaza; **Nanning**: Majestic Hotel; **Putuoshan**: Putuoshan Hotel; **Qingdao:** Hai Tian, Holiday Inn, Huiquan Dynasty, Shangri-La; **Qinhuangdao**: Gloria Resorts; **Sanya:** Cactus, Gloria Resort, Pearl River Garden, Resort Horizon, Sun Sea Sky Hotel;

Shanghai: Crowne Plaza Yin Xing, Four Seasons, Hilton Shanghai, JC Mandarin, Marriot Hongqiao, Portman Ritz-Carlton, Pudong Shangri-la, Renaissance Yangtze, Regal International East Asia Hotel, Renaissance Yangtze; **Shantou:** International Hotel; **Shenzhen:** Shangri-La, Landmark Hotel; **Suzhou**: Sheraton, Gloria Plaza, Bamboo Grove Hotel; **Taishan:** Garden Hotel; **Taiyuan:** Shanxi Grand Hotel; **Tianjin:** Hyatt Regency, Sheraton; **Turpan**: Turpan Hotel; **Urumqi:** Holiday Inn, Hoi Tak; **Wuhan:** Holiday Inn Riverside, Holiday Inn Tian An, Shangri-La;

Xiamen: Holiday Inn Crowne Plaza, Marco Polo; **Xi'an**: Grand New World, Shangri-La Golden Flower, Sheraton, Xi'an Garden; **Xinglong:** Kangle Garden Resort ;

Yangshuo: Country Cottage, West Street; **Yantai**: Shandong Pacific; **Yinchuan**: International Hotel; **Zhaoqing**: International Youth Hostels; **Zhengzhou:** Sofitel, Crowne Plaza, Holiday Inn; **Zhongdian:** Gyalthang Dzong Hotel; **Zhuhai**: Harbour View Hotel; Wuxi: SheratonWuxi Hotel & Towers.

My appreciation also goes to my editor Jonathan Stein for his guidance, patience and support. Most of all, this book would not have been possible without the cooperation of my family, especially my husband Michael Malloy. To all go my thanks and the thanks of our readers.

Chapter 1

introduction

China is a fascinating place, a historically and culturally rich country. A visit is a pleasant learning experience. In this 11th edition, I've updated this guide to bring you the real China once again. I'll take you to all the great destinations plus hundreds more you haven't heard about. I'll lead you to terrific hotels and home stay with families, to good restaurants and temples and interesting things to do.

I'll take you along the length of the Great Wall, steer you to a fun camel ride along the romantic Silk Road, show you where to bicycle among the beautiful mountains of Guilin and guide you along China's great rivers and dramatic gorges. I'll take you strolling through the backstreets and alleys of Beijing, Shanghai, and Guangzhou, and steer you to my favorite birdwatching spots. For sheer beauty, China is hard to beat. It has some of the world's most spectacular and little known natural scenery.

In Beijing, wander the Forbidden City and marvel at the majestic Summer Palace and the intriguing Temple of Heaven. What did it all mean? In Shanghai, stroll along the Bund and ride the ancient stand-up ferry to Pudong. In Xi'an, take in the incredible terracotta army (nearly 2,200 years old) and the magnificent city wall. Dine on China's famous banquet food – where else can you get culinary delights shaped like phoenixes, swans, and rabbits?

You'll also find hundreds of pages of travel advice, money-saving tips, and trip planning ideas. You'll get frank information about hotels, guides and travel agents. There's special advice for business people and Overseas Chinese. You'll find important place names and dishes in Chinese and English. I've even given leads to finding a job. So go west – across the Pacific to China for the trip of a lifetime!

Chapter 2

Yes, you must visit China. You've got to see what it has to offer. It's too big a country to ignore. It has the world's largest population and one of the oldest civilizations. It has had thousands of years to develop a variety of multi-splendored cultures, some so different you won't associate them with China.

For the sightseer, China has fantastic international-class attractions. It has scenes of great beauty, challenges for the adventurer, and places for the vacationer to relax.

Visit its ancient monuments, palaces, and tombs and temples. Raft its river gorges and climb its mountains. Hike through primitive forests, past varieties of trees once eaten by dinosaurs. Enjoy festivals of sweet and juicy *lichis* and dancing dragons; worship at smoky temples with burning incense and prostrating pilgrims. Meet China's many different minorities. Take photos of curved temple roofs silhouetted against golden red sunsets. Capture on film the misty look of mountain paintings seen on aged scrolls.

Shop or just enjoy looking at antiques, carved gilded beds, inlaid chests, porcelain, jades, cloisonne, carpets, cashmere and silk. Consider everything from up-to-date stainless steel cutlery to silk gowns covered with beads and sequins. I'll show you how you can save half or more of the price you'd pay at home.

Sample China's great food with its endless variety and styles of cooking. It ranges from bland to fiery hot, chicken and prawns, camel humps and scorpions! I'll take away the mystery and teach you how to order - and how to eat the Chinese way.

See where people lived 6000 years ago, where they made pottery and buried their dead. Puff your way up the

Great Wall that 2200 years ago was linked together for over 6000 kilometers, or meditate in China's classical gardens. Search for traces of foreign influence – Marco Polo, Jesuit missionaries, Jewish refugees, Muslim traders and Mongol invaders. Trace the development of Buddhist art.

Feel wonder at the functioning mountain-top monasteries, cities full of 19th-century European architecture, creepy tombs, and eerie caves. Get a tan on a beach or be pampered by China's growing number of international class resorts. Golf at its international class clubs. Get treated with Chinese herbal medicines, acupuncture or *qigong*. They just might work for you and it's cheaper than in America.

Discover terraced mountains, gothic cathedrals, and pagodas. Look for the world's highest mountains, jeep through the desert, hot-air balloon over the Yellow River. Gallop horses on China's prairies and make friends with the hospitable natives.

Find out about one of the world's fastest growing economies, China's rite of passage as she resists yet tries to join the world community, as she moves from feudal thinking beyond communist quotas to free-market capitalism. See how the post-September 11 economy is affecting it. Look for surviving pockets of the primitive and exotic. Look for the soul of the great modern cities with their subways and superhighways. You can still find aspects of its exotic past. Relax at nightclubs, discos, karaoke bars and in jacuzzis, and enjoy the convenience of international direct-dial telephones, credit cards, cellular-phones, and fiber optics.

In **East China**, look for traces of the old maritime trade, the hybrid temples with fancy eaves, and the great adventurers who sailed to Africa, saved Taiwan from the Dutch, and fought pirates. Look for the schools and hospitals, monuments built by successful migrants to Southeast Asia and foreign missionaries. Go to the silk cities with their museums, to the tranquil beauty of West Lake, and discover the legacy of the Song dynasty. Plan your trip to include a re-enactment of an emperor's ritual worship at the temple of Confucius.

Marvel at the annual kite festival in Weifang. And enjoy bustling Shanghai with its European architecture, its shopping, and three of the best museums in the country, one of them exclusively on sex.

Search for traces of Chiang Kai-shek and first president Sun Yat-sen in the Nationalist capital of Nanjing. Consider charming Yangzhou where Marco Polo was an official. Enjoy the old garden city of Suzhou, and Huangshan Mountain, the favorite of landscape painters. Look for the China of American author Pearl S. Buck and read her beautifully-written novels.

In **North China**, explore Beijing, the nation's capital, and gasp at the magnificence of the 15th-century Forbidden City palace. Walk where emperors and their families rode bicycles and played badminton. Go to the Ming and Qing imperial tombs, summer palaces, and fly a kite in Tiananmen Square.

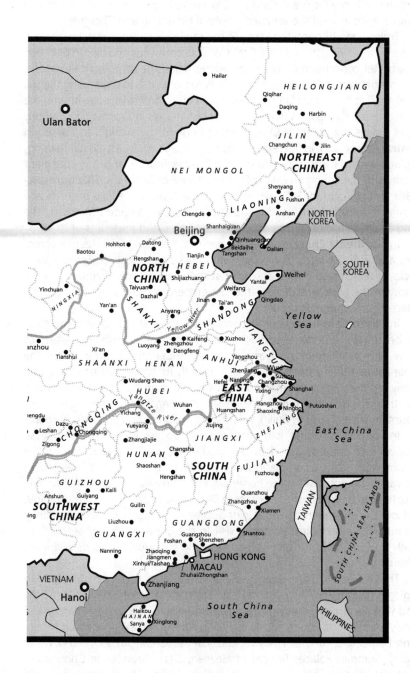

Further north, see the great Yungang Cave Temple and the incredible Hanging Temple. Hike around the temples of Wutai Mountain and Chengde.

Trek or ride through the Mongolian grasslands with their vast vistas and horse herds. If you can, visit the Great Wall at both ends and also in between for a better conception of its immense length and the centuries it still spans.

In **Northwest China**, follow Marco Polo from oasis to oasis along the Silk Road, thrill at the vibrant Sunday market and question the veiled women in the Uygur city of Kashgar. Admire the Buddhist murals in Dunhuang's famous caves where the oldest existing printed book in the world was found. In **Central China**, bask in the refined culture of the Song dynasty in old Kaifeng, applaud a martial arts display beside the Shaolin Temple, and enjoy the giant buddhas in the Longmen caves. Try to conceive of life in the Shang dynasty (16th to 11th century B.C.) when they made those incredible bronzes and sacrificed humans to the gods. And don't miss the Terracotta Warriors, the Tang and Han tombs, the temples, dance shows, and museums of Xi'an.

In **Northeast China**, ride behind one of the endangered steam locomotives and look for signs of Japanese and Russian occupation. Spy on great flocks of red-crested cranes and thrill at the sparkling ice sculpture festival. Follow in the footsteps of Puyi, the last emperor of China, his Manchurian palace and Communist prison.

In **South China**, pay your respects to a 2000-year old noblewoman and her beautiful lacquerware and silks, and inspect the ancestal homeland of many Chinese migrants to North America, Britain and Australia. Visit the hyper-active trading port of Guangzhou with its museums, pagodas, and family temples. Enjoy the miniatures of China's main tourist attractions and the theme park of China's minorities in Shenzhen. Cruise the lovely mountain-lined Li River in Guilin, visit minority villages, and botanical gardens.

In **Southwest China**, join a tour to Miao, Bouyei, Bai, Dong and Tibetan villages. Get water-splashed in the traditional way and look for former headhunters. Relax as dramatic scenery floats by on a Yangtze River cruise, and race a dragon boat in the hometown of its inspiration. Examine the fine sculptures of Buddha and ancient life in Dazu, trek in the forests of Jiuzhaigou, and look for endangered pandas in or outside of Chengdu. Climb sacred Emei Mountain or make a less stenuous visit to the great Buddha at Leshan. Go south and up to Tibet for one of the world's unique, isolated, and lively cultures.

The UNESCO World Heritage Sites are Great Wall, Forbidden City, Mogao Grottoes (Dunhuang), Museum of the Terracotta Warriors, Peking Man Site, Mountain Resort and Outlying Temples in Chengde, Temple, Cemetery and Family Mansion of Confucius, Ancient Building Complex in Wudang Mountains, Potala, Old Town of Pingyao, Classical Gardens in Suzhou, Old Town of Lijiang, Summer Palace, Temple of Heaven, Dazu Grottoes in Chongqing, three natural sites in Wulingyuan, Jiuzhaigou Valley, Huanglong scenic and

The Best of China
The Best...

Beach: Yalong Bay in Sanya, Hainan
City walls: Nanjing and Xi'an
Cleanest cities: Dalian, Weihai, Xiamen and Zhuhai
Confucian experience: Qufu
Cruises: Yangtze Gorges and the Li River, Guilin
Gardens (Classical): Beijing, Suzhou, Hangzhou, Yangzhou
Imperial palaces: Forbidden City; Summer Palace (Beijing); Shenyang
Imperial tombs: Ming (Beijing), Qing (Zunhua) and Tang (Xi'an)
Mosques: Xi'an and Kashi
Mountain for scenery: Huangshan
Mountain for climbing: Qomolangma (Everest, in Tibet)
Museums: Beijing, Chengdu, Shanghai, Xi'an, Zhengzhou
Museum (dinosaurs): Zigong (Chengdu)
Museum (Neolithic): Xi'an
Museum (kite): Weifang
Nature Reserves: Jiuzhaigou (Chengdu) and Zhangjiajie (see Changsha) for wilderness; Wolong near Chengdu for pandas; Hong Kong for birds and pink dolphins; Bird Island near Xining, Poyang Lake near Jiujiang, and Qiqihar near Harbin for cranes; Hefei for 8000 alligators.
Panda-watching: Chengdu
Shopping (general, arts and crafts): Shenzhen, Shanghai and Beijing
Markets for antiques: Beijing, Shanghai, Tianjin, and Zhongshan (furniture)
Market for silks: Hangzhou
Market for pearls: Suzhou
Shopping for minority crafts: Tibet, Yunnan, Guizhou.
Temples (Buddhist): Tibet, Suzhou, Hangzhou, Chengde, Beijing
Temples (caves): Datong, Dazu, Dunhuang, Luoyang
Temple (kung fu): Shaolin (Zhengzhou), Wudangshan
Tomb figures: Xi'an

The Largest ...
Monument: the Great Wall
Statues: Hong Kong (new), Macau (new), Wuxi (new),Sanya (new), Leshan (ancient)

The Most ...
Romantic places: Hong Kong, Macau, Hangzhou, Guilin and the Yangtze River.
Exotic experiences: Lhasa in March, minority festivals in Guizhou, Yunnan, Xinjiang, Inner Mongolia, and Tibet
Interesting small cities: Chengde, Dali, Guilin, Kaifeng, Kashgar, Lhasa, Lijiang, Quanzhou, Qufu, Suzhou, Taishan, Turfan, Xigaze, Yangzhou, Zhaoqing
Important 'Crouching Tiger, Hidden Dragon' sites: Huangshan, Wudangshan, Turfan.
Steam locomotive locations: Northeast China

Historic Interest Area, four cultural and natural sites on Mount Taishan, Mount Huangshan, Wuyi Mountain, Mt. Emei, Leshan Giant Buddha, One cultural landscape in Lushan National Park.

Keep reading and I'll help get you to all of these and more!

How To Use This Book

More than 1,000 destinations are open to foreign visitors. Listed here are the most important. Mentioned under these headings, especially those of the provincial capitals, are minor destinations that you might also like. The list here is grouped by regions along traditional Chinese lines so you will know what else is close by to see.

Chinese characters for tourist sites and dishes are listed in Chapter 25. Many restaurants don't have menus in English. You can point to the characters.

Don't jump to the conclusion that a temple founded in 1250 A.D. means the buildings are over 700 years old. The buildings may have been rebuilt recently. In a country that has had many upheavals, air raids, and revolutions, it's amazing that so many great monuments have survived to this day. Many are UNESCO Heritage Sites.

For shoppers, listed are items produced locally which tend to be cheaper than elsewhere. Hours given for stores and tourist sites are approximate and subject to change. Those in summer are about an hour later than those in winter. Telephone first if in doubt. Schools, villages, and factories are basically the same in the whole of China, and these are not mentioned in every destination unless there is something unusual about them. Please visit schools, villages, and factories wherever possible to give your trip more depth about the people.

China is now producing a great deal of travel literature of its own. Do supplement the information here with what is available in China, especially more detailed maps and tourist handouts from your hotel. Ask the concierge to write your destination in Chinese characters for taxi and bus drivers. Do not consider any guidebook as your only source of information. A guidebook should stimulate your interest, give you good background, and point you in the right direction. So ask many questions while you are in China.

As anyone who has been to China knows, you get seven different answers to the same question if you ask seven different people. Getting solid information has been difficult, even simple telephone numbers. Quoting hotel prices is almost impossible too as they fluctuate according to demand and season. I have tried to mention the range of recent discounts off the published prices so you will know what to ask for.

Names

There is some redundancy in names, such as Lu Shan Mountain, (*shan* means mountain). This is for people who don't know Chinese, and such names are commonly used in English. It may appear cumbersome to put in the *pinyin*, the English, and the Chinese characters for place names, but in China some people will use the Chinese name and others will use the English. You might think they are talking of two different places. The multiple names listed are to help avoid confusion.

Sources differ frequently as to historical dates and events, and English translations of site names. Names like Han, Song, Ming, and Qing refer to dynasty, as 'in the Ming,' with Mongol the same as Yuan, and Manchu the same as Qing. It would help if you learned the names and general dates of the major dynasties.

The words "Guest House" and "Hotel" are interchangeable and do not imply quality. The words "monastery" and "temple," and "Moslem" and "Muslim" are also interchangeable.

Prices are quoted in U.S. dollars or "Y" Chinese yuan unless otherwise specified.

Spellings & Telephone Numbers

In 1979, China adopted the *pinyin* system of romanizing its language based on the Beijing pronunciation. Thus "Peking" became Beijing. The old spellings can still be found in old books and are still used occasionally in China. I have tried to use the *pinyin* spelling but on some occasions the old Wade-Giles for historical people. The old and new names of major cities and dynasties are in Chapter 7.

Another confusing area has been whether words like Hong Qiao should be together as one or separated into two words. The tendency now is to combine place names into one word even though they can be very long. Shijiazhuang, for example, would be easier to pronounce if separated into Shi Jia Zhuang, but is found written both ways.

Avoid confusing the provinces Hunan and Henan, Jiangxi and Jiangsu, Shaanxi and Shanxi, Hubei and Hebei, and the cities Jilin and Jinan.

There is still no standard translation for important place names; for example, Lingyan Si in Jinan has been translated Magic Cliff or Intelligent Rock Temple in different pieces of Jinan tourist literature.

As for telephone numbers, I have listed more than one at times because sources differed. Try both. Failing that, ask an English-speaker from CITS (China International Travel Service), your hotel telephone operator, business center, or an embassy for an up-to-date one.

Miscellaneous

I have tried to make the information in this book as accurate as possible. The situation in China is so fluid that changes will have taken place by the time you visit. When in doubt, ask your hotel or guide. And should you find things different, please let me know so I can make a mention on my website **www.china-travel-guide.com**. This website is periodically updated, and contains a lot of information not in this book.

The travel agencies listed here should be able to help you, especially those with a contact name. As far as I can tell, those mentioned here are reliable, but a mention in this book is not necessarily a recommendation. Just be aware that going directly to agents in China, is cheaper than going through a travel agent outside. And if these Chinese agents fail to help you, please let me know.

I have given several options. Not all agents will answer within the promised 48 hours. Not all e-mail addresses will work because the government is cracking down on servers who do not monitor outgoing e-mail. And government offices only seem to accept faxes during their office hours (when you're asleep). Some websites are only in Chinese. Those marked with English might give you a notice "to display language characters properly, you need..." You can "cancel" that and read the English anyway.

Finally, to avoid having to carry a book as heavy as this, you might want to cut out the pages you think you'll need in China, and staple each section. Carrying the Beijing chapter around Beijing is a lot easier than carrying the whole book around the city.

Have a great trip!

Chapter 3

itineraries

I recommend that visitors concentrate on one area of China at a time. It's a big country with much to offer! You can spend at least five days sightseeing in Beijing alone – and you'll see in the Beijing and Shanghai chapters extensive day-to-day itineraries.

However, if you think you'll never see China again and want to cover the highlights in 18 days, try Beijing, Xi'an, Shanghai, Suzhou or Hangzhou, the Yangtze River cruise, Kunming or Guiyang, Guilin, and exit via Hong Kong. You should include Shanghai, China's most cosmopolitan city, to balance rural impressions like the Yangtze valley. You have to include Chongqing, and Wuhan or Yichang, because that's where you get the Yangtze River cruise boat.

This itinerary is an enlightening introduction with a wide variety of sights to see and includes the Terracotta Warriors, classical gardens, big cities, quiet towns, the Grand Canal, good temples, ancient mummies, and an introduction to China's minorities. It also includes the Great Wall, Forbidden City, and Summer Palace. But you go at a hectic pace and fly a lot. Many travel agents offer this kind of tour.

I'm all for tours by road because China's countryside is so interesting. In five days from Shanghai, you can drive to Hangzhou, then see Shaoxing, 1000 Island Lake, and onward to Huangshan, one of the most gorgeous mountains in the country. In between are charming villages and farms, as yet relatively untouched by modern skyscrapers.

Shandong province is pleasant and some visitors do a tour that covers the tiny hometown of Confucius, a medium-sized city, a sacred and unique mountain under

UNESCO protection, an ancient capital, the largest sea port and former foreign colonized city. In eight days, seven nights, you can do Beijing, Jinan, Tai'an, Qufu, Suzhou, Shanghai.

Henan province also has variety: the Shang dynasty relics at Anyang, the Song dynasty capital of Kaifeng, the Song tombs, the cave-temple statues at Luoyang, the *kung fu* Shaolin Temple and a lot of pleasant countryside in between. This can be done by car in a week. For more details, see Zhengzhou.

People can fly on long weekends out of Hong Kong for a relaxing holiday in Guilin, or shopping in Shanghai, Tianjin or Beijing. From Shanghai, you can visit the temples of Ningbo, or do a pilgrimage to Putuoshan in three days. From Beijing, you can take the train and spend a weekend visiting Buddhist temples and the summer palace in Chengde or the Great Wall at Qinhuangdao.

In the cooler weather, I would also head out of Macau or Hong Kong for Guangdong province, nothing spectacular but interesting and enlightening: Zhongshan for the delta countryside and Dr. Sun Yat-sen's house, Taishan the ancestral home of early Chinese-American immigrants, Foshan for the Ancestral Temple, Zhaoqing for charming mountain scenery, Guangzhou for the Cantonese food, and Shenzhen for the theme parks. China Travel Service offers four-day tours to some of these destinations, and you can stay longer in Shenzhen and do the theme parks on your own before returning to Hong Kong.

You could also head for Yalong Bay for a few days of sun and beach.

Most of the above suggestions tend to concentrate on South, East and North China. One of my favorite areas for scenery and interesting costumes is in the Southwest and includes Guiyang for Kaili and Huangguoshu, and Kunming for Lijiang, Dali and Zhongdian. The hotels here are not as nice but you can visit minority villages and meet real weavers and embroiderers. An itinerary like this can take ten days. If you want to see Tibet, an ancient culture clinging to the roof of the world, that's another four to six days at least. These are especially good in summer to avoid the heat of the lowlands.

There's also the Silk Road, especially for people who have already done classical China. You can spend more time in imperial Xi'an. Don't miss Jiayuguan with its fortress at the western end of the Great Wall, the best of the cave temples in Dunhuang, the earthen ruins in Turpan, more cave temples in Kuqa, the mummies, and the Sunday market in Kashgar. Then there's the new highway across the Taklamakan desert. Forget Urumqi except to go in and out. You can do this in 10 days too.

If you're into nature hiking, there's Wuyi (Fuzhou), Zhangjiajie (Changsha), and Jiuzhaigou (Chengdu).

For detailed itineraries in Beijing and Shanghai, see Chapters 14 and 15.

Chapter 4

Land

China extends from Mongolia and Siberia in the north and to Kazakhstan, Kyrgyzstan, Afghanistan, Pakistan, India and Nepal in the west and south west. In the south it borders Bhutan, Bangladesh, Myanmar, Laos and Vietnam. And on the east, it touches only North Korea.

Its east coast is washed by the Yellow Sea, the East China Sea and the South China Sea. It also considers Taiwan and the Paracel Islands part of China. It is 9.6 million square kilometers, the world's third largest country.

China has 23 provinces, five autonomous regions, four administrative municipalities, and two Special Administrative Regions, Hong Kong and Macau.

If you keep in mind that Beijing is the same latitude as Philadelphia, Guangzhou the same as Havana, and Urumqi in the far west is a four-hour flight from Beijing to its east, you get a feeling for the vastness of the country. Its northernmost tip is as far north as James Bay in Canada.

China extends upwards too, with the highest mountains in the world, and downwards to the second lowest body of water. It has vast deserts and fertile valleys, great prairies, evergreen forests and rubber plantations. It is big and varied.

People

China has 1.2 billion people, 22% of the earth's population living on 7% of the earth's arable land. That she has done so much with so little is a credit to Chinese pragmatism and ingenuity. The official language is **Mandarin Chinese** or putong hua. This is taught in all the schools. You will also hear the distinctive Shanghai, Fujian, and Guangdong (Cantonese) languages, and hundreds of minor languages and dialects. Most people, however, use a common written language.

China has 56 different ethnic groups. The majority are Han. Eight percent of the population are members of 55 other nationalities. These 96 million people live in areas totaling half of China, including strategic areas near its borders. Yunnan province for example has 26 different nationalities. Although they are usually less educated and poorer, the varied cultures of these minorities are rich, meaningful, and fascinating.

A nationality doesn't necessarily settle in one location. Often sub-branches are spread over several provinces, with different costumes and dialects; for example, the Miao are found in Guizhou, Hunan, Yunnan, Guangdong, Guangxi, and Sichuan. Miao women in Guizhou wear pleated skirts and in Hunan wear trousers. The color and designs of their headdress also varies.

During festivals and market days, most minorities, especially women, wear their distinctive costumes, which many decorate with fine embroidery, and, sometimes, heavy silver jewelry. Hairstyles could indicate marital status and have historical meaning.

The festivals of the nationalities are worth experiencing. The **Dai** celebrate a water-splashing festival similar to that in neighboring Thailand and Burma. The **Kazakhs** have a horse racing festival, the **Yi** a torch festival, the **Tibetans** celebrate the Great Prayer Festival, and so on. Mongolians have colorful sporting meets, with distinctive wrestling, horses, and archery. Facilities for tourists in minority areas are still modest but not impossible.

China's Government

First and foremost, the government is Communist. Sometimes it's easy to forget that in today's capitalist atmosphere. Jiang Zemin is President of China and General Secretary of the Communist Party. The Prime Minister is Zhu Rongji, and Chairman of the National People's Congress is Li Peng. Officially at the top of the government is the National People's Congress. In 2002, many of these leaders will change.

The State Council is the executive organ accountable to this congress and is similar to a cabinet. The Communist Party now is trying to re-enter almost every facet of life, after pulling back in the mid-to-late 1980s. It blamed the 1989 student demonstrations on the lack of political education of the people. But many Communist Party members seem to be afflicted now with money fever too – at least until the next campaign against corruption. At press time, people seem very casual about politics.

Religion

After atheistic Communism took over China, it discouraged religions. The Cultural Revolution later destroyed many religious buildings and harrassed its adherents. Since the late 1970s, the government has again allowed recognized religious bodies to openly practise and has been helping reconstruct religious buildings. Today you will see worshippers in most temples, mosques and churches. There has been a revival also of superstitions.

Although the Chinese constitution says that all Chinese citizens have freedom of belief, implementation remains uneven. Today, in some provinces, there is interference in Christian church affairs by 'leftist cadres.' Generally, however, these recognized religions are flourishing, as you can see. Unregistered groups like Falun Gong have a lot of troubles. To find out more, consult Amnesty International. But try to visit a church service during your visit to judge the situation yourself.

China's great traditional religions are Taoism, Buddhism, and Confucianism, although in some sense, Confucianism is more of an ideology or philosophy. Taoism and Confucianism are uniquely Chinese. Buddhism came later. Islam and Christianity are more recent imports. Ancestor worship and animism are ancient folk religions.

Decide for yourself if what you see is religion or superstition. Chinese people are pragmatic, worshipping whatever gods might answer their prayers. If a friend prayed successfully to one god for a baby boy, then other barren women would try that god too. It is not unusual for the same person to have his children baptized as Christians, burn incense to a deceased grandfather, and then retire to contemplate in a Taoist or Buddhist monastery. The same person may support several different temples and churches at the same time.

Religions have been encouraged, tolerated, and persecuted throughout Chinese history. In the early Tang, some emperors ordered the killing of Buddhists, while other emperors encouraged Buddhism and financed the construction of temples.

Ancestor Worship

Ancestor Worship involves praying to departed ancestors as you would pray to Buddha or a saint. You take care of them with incense and offerings and they take care of you. You worship your ancestors in gratitude for your life.

There used to be at least one ancestral temple (miao) for every village, since each village was comprised of people with a common ancestor. Here they informed the ancestors of important family events like births and marriages. Many families kept a family history book. The Red Guards destroyed many of these books and family tablets during the Cultural Revolution. When you go to a village, ask about this temple. In ancestral temples, tablets with the names of the ancestors were kept in neat rows and worshipped with burning incense, gifts of food, and ceremonial bowing at least twice a year.

Animism & Other Religions

There are temples to the city god. Fishermen worship the Goddess of Heaven, **Tian Hou** or **Mazu**. (See Quanzhou.) In villages, look for incense burned at the foot of sacred trees and in tiny shrines for the earth god.

Buddhism

Buddhism arrived in China from India. **Gautama**, the founder, was an Indian prince, born in the sixth century B.C., who was brought up confined to a palace. When he was 29, he saw the suffering of the outside world for the first time and forsook his wealth and family. For six years, he traveled in search of life's meaning. He found it, became known as Buddha (the awakened or enlightened one) and then preached his ideas for 45 years: the **Four Noble Truths** and the **Noble Eightfold Path** to nirvana. The circles on top of Buddhist stupas and pagodas are in the same numbers: four and eight.

Buddha taught that the source of all suffering is selfish desire, and one must stop all desire. Some sects believe in asceticism. The Chinese, Mongolians, and Tibetans generally follow the **Mahayana** school of faith and good works, and believe Buddha is divine and can answer prayers – even though Buddha never asked people to petition or worship him.

You will see people in temples, smoking incense in hand, nodding to the statues or kowtowing on the floor, asking for favors, without regard for the extinction of all desire. Achieving **nirvana** is the aim of all forms of Buddhism, accomplished by ending the continuous cycle of reincarnation through the extinction of the self. Today, China has more than 3,600 Buddhist temples open for worship with over 30,000 monks and nuns.

Bodhisattva

Buddhist temples come in two basic varieties, of which there are infinite variations. First are **Chinese Buddhist temples**, surrounded by windowless walls, which frequently have four fierce-looking, larger than life-size, human-type guardians after the first gate. Each temple might have different names for these. Inside the first hall, visitors are greeted by the fat, laughing Buddha, **Maitreya**, or in Chinese, Mi Lo Fu. He is the Buddha still-to-come. Behind him is **Wei Tou**, the military bodhisattva, the armed warrior who guards the Buddhist scriptures. Wei Tou is probably comparable to the Indian god Indra.

Central in the main hall is the **Buddha** (known also as Sakyamuni or Prince Siddhartha Gautama). Also in this hall are usually statues or paintings of

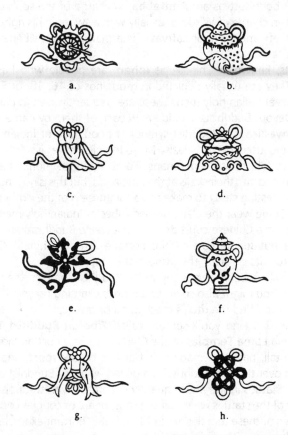

The Eight Buddhist Emblems of Happy Augury

a. The wheel of the law
b. The conch shell
c. The state umbrella
d. The canopy
e. The lotus flower
f. The covered vase
g. The pair of fishes
h. The endless knot

bodhisattvas, known in Chinese as *pusas*. These are saints who have gained enlightenment but have come back to the world to help other people attain it too. A favorite bodhisattva is Avalokita, known in China as **Guanyin** (Kwan Yin, Kuan Yin), or the Goddess of Mercy. Guanyin may have several heads and arms and may be carrying a vase or a child. She is usually behind Sakyamuni, facing north.

Guanyin started out as a male god in China until about the 12th century, when his followers preferred to worship him as a woman. He is still sometimes depicted as male. Said one guide, 'Men believe he is male and women believe she is female.'

Other bodhisattvas are **Amitabha**, in charge of the souls of the dead, **Manjusri**, in charge of Wisdom, usually with a sword in his right hand and a lotus in his left, and the bodhisattvas of Pharmacy, Universal Benevolence, and the Earth.

Arhats, known in Chinese as **lohan**, are people who have achieved nirvana. They are usually depicted in groupings of 16, 18, or 500, and are based on real Indian holy men. These are frequently seen in paintings or as statues. Devout Buddhists should know each of them by name.

The swastika is a Buddhist symbol of good luck, of Indian origin, later inverted and used by the Nazis. Most temples have live fish and turtles. Full-time Buddhists are vegetarians. Some Buddhist monks had pieces of incense burned into their skulls at their initiation, but this is no longer required.

An interesting study to make as you sightsee is of the clothing carved on Buddhas. Some wear the plain, draped robes of Indian holy men, others the fancy, feminine Chinese court dress with jewelry. Buddhism arrived in China from India, but Buddhist art in China became distinctly Chinese. Can you date a statue from its clothes? The fatness of its face?

You will probably see many more Buddhist temples than Taoist and Confucian. You might also see robed monks chanting prayers if your timing is right. Do you find the rituals mechanical or mystical?

The second kind you'll see are called **Tibetan Buddhist Temples** by Tibetans and **Lama Temples** by the Chinese. Usually built on mountainsides, they have tall, narrow windows, flatter less ornate roofs, and are usually decorated over the main door with a gilded wheel of Buddhist doctrine and two deer. Statues inside are frequently decorated with turquoise and coral, and many of the statues wear pointed caps, or are of couples copulating. The best known of these temples are in Tibet, but important examples are also in Beijing, Chengde, Qinghai, and Gansu.

These temples are expressions of the Tibetan and Mongolian form of Buddhism, into which have been injected elements of the early Tibetan religion called **Bon**.

Many Tibetan Buddhists believe that the Dalai Lama, who is considered both the temporal and religious head of Tibetan Buddhism, is a reincarnation of Avalokita or Guanyin, or the god Chenrezi. The religion's peaceful and wrathful aspects are reflected in the murals and statues of these temples. Tibetan Buddhism is also divided into sects, the main ones being the meditative Yellow Sect and the esoteric Red Sect.

Note: The Chinese government refers to Tibetan Buddhism as 'Lamaism' and their temples as 'Lama' temples or 'lamaseries,' but the Tibetans themselves do not. See also Lhasa and Chengde.

Cave Temples with frescoes and Buddhist statues were first built in India and spread with the Silk Road into China. Caves have always been conducive to meditation. One gets a feeling of security, like being back in a mother's womb. **Dunhuang** is the greatest for its paintings. The two at **Lanzhou** are noted for their strikingly dramatic sites and the richness of their sculpture. Important for carvings are also **Datong** and **Luoyang**.

Other cave temples listed as protected historical monuments by the State Council are at Anxi and Linxia in Gansu; Handan in Hebei; Turpan, Baichen, and Kuqu in Xinjiang; Guangyuan, Leshan, and Dazu in Sichuan; Jianchuan in Yunnan; Gongxian in Henan; Guyuan in Ningxia; and Hangzhou in Zhejiang. I highly recommend the book Bones of the Master, A Journey into Secret Mongolia, by George Crane. This is a delightful account of a 1996 trip by a hedonistic American poet and a Chan Buddhist monk to find and properly bury the bones of the monk's master.

Christianity

Christianity arrived in full force with its missionaries in the latter part of the 19th century. The treaties after the **Opium War** in 1842 forced China to accept them. Because of backing by foreign powers, Chinese Christians tended to be an elite group, at times successfully appealing to their foreign protectors if they got in trouble with Chinese law. This caused much resentment. Christian Churches were most frequently built in western architecture with gothic windows, and many Roman Catholic churches look like transplants from Europe.

Some foreign missionaries closed their eyes to ancestor worship so they could claim converts. Many Chinese questioned the exclusivity of Christianity.

Dr. Sun Yat-sen, the father of the Chinese republic, was a Christian, but as a Chinese nationalist he criticized missionaries as lackeys of foreign imperialists. Many Chinese misunderstood the motives of missionaries. Some of these fears led to such incidents as the **Tientsin Massacre** (see Tianjin). The Chinese attacked missionaries more because of nationalism than religious hostility.

Missionary schools influenced some Chinese Communist leaders. Mao Zedong once edited the Christian-sponsored Yale-in-China Review. Zhou Enlai admired the ideals and the work of the YMCA and YWCA.

In 1950, the hysteria of the Korean War led the Chinese to consider westerners, including many missionaries, as 'enemy aliens.' They accused them of spying and sabotage and jailed many; after all, Americans and Canadians were killing Chinese soldiers in Korea, including Mao's son.

The Communists felt that foreign imperialism was linked to the Chinese Christian dependence on foreign missionaries. After 1949, the Communists encouraged Christian churches to cut their ties with their foreign mentors and Protestants set up the **Three-Self Patriotic Movement**. The Catholic Church, however, officially opposed the rulers of new China. Most of the bishops not jailed fled. When those Catholic leaders who remained nominated new bishops to meet the pastoral needs of more than 100 vacant dioceses, the Vatican ignored these nominations. When Chinese leaders went ahead with consecrations, Rome regarded them as irregular.

The situation has improved now. Having missed Vatican II, some priests still celebrate the Mass in Latin for older Catholics, but young priests are being trained to celebrate in Chinese. Many consecrations are now recognized (unofficially) by Rome.

During the **Cultural Revolution**, the Red Guards destroyed and closed churches and temples as part of the movement against the 'Four Olds.' Many church buildings became apartments, factories and warehouses. The Catholic Cathedral in Guangzhou was used for storage.

In 1978-79 after the Cultural Revolution, the government encouraged the rebuilding of temples and churches, returned deeds to congregations and paid overdue rents. It had to relocate the people and factories who had taken over the buildings. Some Christians had actually continued to tithe even while the churches were closed and later brought these treasures to their newly-opened gathering places.

Over 8000 Protestant churches and over 20,000 meeting points across China are flourishing with over 12 million Protestant Christians and 15 to 25 million enquirers. Thirteen seminaries and Bible Schools are open. A few churches have to open Saturdays as well as Sundays to accommodate worshippers. Some Christians worship corporately in their homes.

While some foreigners have questioned the authenticity of the 'state-recognized' versus the 'house' Christians, most Chinese believers do not think they are different. It may be a matter of convenience. Some Christians attend both the small family fellowships and the large general congregations. Leadership training is the major challenge for the burgeoning congregations of often semi-literate Christians in the countryside. In 1988, two Protestant bishops were installed. It was the first such event since 1955.

Foreigners wanting to contact Protestant groups should ask for the **China Christian Council** or **Three-Self Patriotic Movement**. Catholics should ask for the **Chinese Catholic Patriotic Association**. Don't let the word Patriotic bother you. It doesn't sound as chauvinistic in Chinese. You should also consult your own church or national church organizations. When you get to China, worship with the Chinese and please do not disturb the service with a camera, or by being late or leaving early.

Chinese Christians, particularly those in isolated places, will probably be delighted to have you join them. Please don't be overly generous. The Chinese want to be self-reliant. Donations with no strings attached can be made to the **Amity Foundation**, a Christian-inspired people's organization devoted to health, education, and welfare projects for all Chinese, not just Christians.

Recently, a group of foreigners was arrested and deported for proselytizing. A Hong Kong man was imprisoned for smuggling in thousands of Bibles to an unrecognized sect. You can ask Christians in China how they feel about this and if they want missionaries. The United Bible Society has given a modern press to the Amity Foundation, which is helping the Protestant churches publish their own literature. Since 1981, the China Christian Council has printed over 10 million Bibles.

Figures are hard to get but there are at least 4.5 million registered Catholic Christians, 1,000 large Catholic churches, and 10,000 chapels. Over eleven seminaries are now open and about 12 convents with 200 women under formation. Reuters estimates eight million Catholics have ties to Rome and are therefore illegal.

Ties between the Vatican and China seemed to be improving until the Vatican celebrated the canonization of 120 Catholics killed prior to Liberation on China's national day. The Chinese government considered these Catholics imperialists and "bullies" and the coincidence an affront. The Vatican has diplomatic relations with Taiwan and not with Beijing.

Confucianism

Confucian temples used to be in every sizable community in China, at one time about 2,680 of them, now dwindled in number down to about 300. For a history and description of Confucianism, see Qufu.

Confucius was worshipped because his teachings supported the stratification of society, with the emperor and elder males on top. He was officially worshipped during the spring and autumn equinoxes. Try to imagine the burning incense and the muffled clang of gongs, as slow, rhythmic processions of officials in long red gowns and caps arrived, each man to kowtow, head to the ground, in deepest reverence. They left offerings of food and wine on the altar. Musicians played ritual bells. Such ceremonies still take place in Qufu for tourists.

Confucian temples did not usually have statues, but simply tablets with the names of ancestors written on them. The walls were red. The south gate was usually left unbuilt until a son from the town passed the difficult examinations and became a Senior Scholar. Only a Senior Scholar and the Emperor could enter by the south gate. No women were considered for the examinations, but if Chinese opera plots are to be believed, some did successfully take them disguised as men.

Was Confucianism a religion or a philosophy? This question is frequently debated. While Confucius himself skeptically rejected the supernatural, Chinese people did and, in some cases, still do consider him a god. He is among the Taoist deities too. But he was primarily a teacher of ethics, of 'right conduct,' and good, stable government. Many Confucian temples now are only museums because Confucianism no longer has imperial patronage. The largest temples are in Beijing and Qufu.

Taoism

Taoism (Daoism) was founded 1800 years ago by a sage named **Lao Zi** (Lao Tzu), whose message was conveyed to the world by a disciple named Mencius. It preaches that everything exists through the interplay of two opposite forces: male-female; positive-negative; hot-cold; light-dark; heaven-earth; yang-yin, etc.

Taoists try to achieve harmony out of the conflict of these forces through the Tao or the Way. Taoism is closer to nature than other religions. Its saints have found enlightenment after spending years meditating in caves. Over the years, it has been diluted by superstitions like charms, spells, ghosts, and nature spirits. Taoism was most popular in the Tang and Song, but declined in the Ming. Its most famous monasteries are in Beijing, Chengdu, Huashan, and Wudangshan.

Taoist temples have statues of Taoist gods, among whom are **Guanyin** and **Confucius**. You can identify other gods and saints by the symbols they carry.

The **Eight Taoist Genii** (Immortals or Fairies) were originally eight humans who discovered the secrets of nature (see illustration on next page). They lived alone in remote mountains (one of them in a cave at Lushan), had magic powers and could revive the dead. They are usually found together on a vase or in one painting, or as a set of eight porcelain pieces. Chung Li-chuan carries the fan to revive the spirits of the dead, Lu Tung-in the supernatural sword, Li Tieh-kuai the staff, Tsao Kuo-chiu the castanets, Lan Tsai-ho the flower basket, Chang Kuo the bamboo tube, Han Hsiangtzu the flute, and Ho Hsien-ku the lotus flower. Two are women.

In the center of the dual **Yin-Yang**, the principles of being are surrounded by the eight **Trigrams of Divination**. The Eight Trigrams represent eight animals and eight directions. At eleven o'clock are the three unbroken lines of heaven; then clockwise, clouds, thunder, mountains, water, fire, earth, and wind. These are used in fortune telling. You may have heard of the **I Ching**, which uses these trigrams.

Many Taoist temples are now museums. Taoists after all are meditators and want to get away from people. See Wudangshan. And look for the 1983 book *The Wandering Taoist* by Deng Ming Dao.

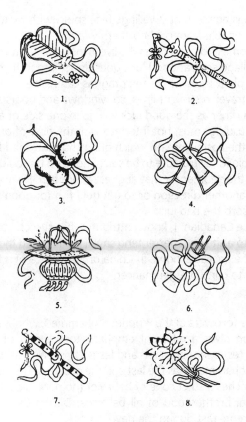

The Attributes of the Eight Taoist Genii

1. The fan
2. The sword
3. The pilgrims' staff & gourd
4. The castanets
5. The flower baskets
6. The tube and rods
7. The flute
8. The lotus flower

Feng Shui

Geomancy, once suppressed by Chairman Mao, is making a comeback, influenced by its success in Hong Kong. Feng means wind and shui means water. It is geomancy, the placing of graves, dwellings, doors and furniture in harmony with the forces of nature. **Feng shui** is related to Taoism. It is more an art or pseudo-science than a religion. In some cases it makes practical sense since its teachings advise that dwellings face south with mountains behind them to protect people from cold northern winds.

Good luck comes from dragons who live in mountains, and it is best to site a structure or village so that good luck goes down into it. If you don't have mountains, you plant trees where the dragons can reside.

Spirits only travel in straight lines, so windows and doors should not be in line with each other as the good luck will go in one side of a building and out the other. Buildings must not interfere with the flow of *qi*, as in *qigong* or *taiqi* (taichi), the cosmic breath which brings harmony and health.

It is preferable for a structure to be surrounded on three sides by running water. If it isn't, the geomancer may suggest a fountain. He might tell you to hinge a door in another direction or to get gold fish for good luck with one black one to absorb the bad luck.

One Chinese-Canadian I know attributes his success to moving his brother's grave to a site with better feng shui. He smuggled the bones out of Hong Kong to the ancestral home in China on the advice of a fortune teller, and was careful to consult a geomancer.

Islam

Muslims are followers of the Prophet Mohammed, who was born in 570 A.D. This religion gives a different emphasis to the god of Judaism and Christianity. Old Testament prophets and Jesus Christ are considered honored prophets, but Mohammed was the last and the greatest. The holy book is the Koran, which teaches a strict code of behavior (no pork, alcohol, idols, etc.), and the universal brotherhood of all believers. During the holy month of Ramadan, adherents fast during the day.

Islam arrived in China in 652 A.D. during the Tang Dynasty, with Arab and Persian traders who settled in Guangzhou, Quanzhou, Hangzhou, Yangzhou and along the Silk Road. During the 13th century, Kublai Khan brought Moslem soldiers, artisans, and officials to China to work for him. Approximately 10 million Chinese Moslems are known today as **Hui**, but **Uygurs**, **Kazakhs**, **Kirgiz**, **Uzbeks**, etc., are also Moslems, a total of about 17 million followers of Mohammed. Mosques are always open afternoons on Friday, the holy day.

Islamic mosques are architecturally of two varieties. Those with rounded, onion-like domes and minarets, are mainly in northwest China. Other mosques look like Chinese temples, with curved roofs and ornate dragons and phoenixes (in spite of the prophet's teachings against making images).

In either style, visitors always remove their shoes before entering the great hall. There is a place for washing hands and feet before prayers. The main building is the Great Hall, which is decorated with Arabic writing, arches, and flower motifs. Moslems pray five times a day, facing the holy city of Mecca in Saudi Arabia.

Moslems can pray anywhere, but the devout usually pray in a mosque if they can. Note the prayer rugs with designs woven into them indicating the direction in which to kneel. Carpets made in Moslem areas deliberately do not have images of animals or objects on them. Note also the disproportionate number of women worshippers, and in some mosques, separate sections for women.

a
s
h
o
r
t
h
i
s
t
o
r
y

Chapter 5

Earliest Times

The ancestors of human beings lived in China 8,000,000 years ago. Archaeologists found the remains of Ramapithecus man in Lufeng in Yunnan province. Yuanmou Man lived 1,000,000 years ago and Lantian Man, 600,000 to 700,000 years ago.

The famous **Peking Man** is a mere youngster. He's only 400,000 to 500,000 years old. About 20,000 to 30,000 years ago, Liuchiang Man lived in Guangxi, near Guilin. Hotao Man lived in Inner Mongolia, and Upper Cave Man back in Zhoukoudian. Other milestones are the **Lungshan Culture** and **Yangshao Culture** in Henan of 5,000 to 7,000 years ago. (See Xi'an's Banpo Museum.)

Dynasties date from about 2000 B.C. and overlap because different dynasties controlled different parts of China at the same time. Eastern and Western usually refer to periods of the same dynasty with different capitals.

The **Xia** dynasty usually dates from about the 21st to 16th centuries B.C. and marks the beginning of the slave system. It is known for irrigation and flood control work, a rudimentary calendar, the earliest form of writing (about 2300 B.C.) and the earliest bronzes. Some archaeologists place its capital in Henan province.

The **Shang** (16th to 11th centuries B.C.) had the earliest glazes, wine, and silk. It developed ritual bronze casting to a high art and even had carved jade handles on swords and spears. A famous Shang relic is an ivory cup inlaid with jade. It had iron and used cowry shells for money. This culture traded outside of China and developed writing and ancestor worship. They communicated with the gods by cracking tortoise shells and began the first cities: Zhengzhou and Anyang.

The **Western Zhou** (11th century to 771 B.C.) and the **Eastern Zhou** (770 to 249 B.C.) welded bronze and produced the first lacquer. They used copper coins and crossbows and lived in walled cities, developed elaborate rituals and music using jade instruments, and further developed ritual bronze vessels in profusion.

Confucius lived in the **Spring and Autumn Period** (770 to 476 B.C.). Warring states fought for power. Confucius preached a return to the Zhou rituals and tried to stabilize society by insisting on obedience to emperors, fathers, husbands, and older brothers. This was the beginning of feudalism. This period had cylindrical tile sewer pipes, iron implements and oxen for plowing, and a form of steel. They used metal spade-shaped coins, chopsticks, and had a knowledge of mathematics, astronomy and medicine.

The **Warring States** (47 to 221 B.C.) was a transitional period to feudalism. Master Sun produced his famous book The Art of War, praised as recently as a few years ago by General Norman Schwartzkof. During this period, Mencius promoted Taoism. The silent Mohists flourished. The first large scale irrigation and dams included erosion control. People used iron farm tools and manure for fertilizer. They mined and produced salt. Doctors first diagnosed diseases through feeling the pulse. Scientists wrote the first books on astronomy, and used magnets.

Emperor Qin (221 to 206 B.C.) unified China for the first time, and started building the Great Wall and the Terracotta Army. He standardized weights, measures, writing, and currency. He developed a strict legal code. His dynasty had the first clay burial figures, highly developed medicine and agriculture. But he is infamous for burning most historical records and for executing scholars.

The **Eastern and Western Han** (206 B.C. to 220 A.D.) had the water wheel, windmill and the first seismograph. They produced the first plant-fiber paper and a water-powered bellows for smelting and the first important Chinese medical text, and used general anesthesia in surgical operations, acupuncture and moxibustion. Its astrologers produced the first armillary sphere and discovered that moonlight comes from the sun. During its reign, Szuma Chien wrote China's first history book. And burying rich people in jade suits was fashionable. Emperor Han Ming-ti ordered the first Buddhist temple built in Luoyang in 68 A.D.

The **Silk Road** (2nd century B.C. to 14th century A.D.) connected China to India, Western Asia, and even Rome with trade routes along which the Chinese exported silk, tea, iron and steel, peach and pear trees, and the knowledge of paper making and deep-well digging. They received grapes, pomegranate and walnut trees, sesame, coriander, spinach, the Fergana horse, alfalfa, Buddhism, Nestorianism, and Islam. The main stops in China west from Xi'an were Lanzhou, Wuwei, Dunhuang, then north through Turpan or south through Ruoqiang. Arab and Persian traders settled in Xi'an and Yangzhou.

During the **Three Kingdoms** (220 to 265 A.D.), people managed to develop a water pump, celadon, and ships big enough to carry 3000 men, as well as fight great battles. The **Western and Eastern Jin** (265 to 420) followed, then the **Southern and Northern Dynasties** (420 to 589). During these periods the Chinese developed the first arched stone bridge, the widespread use of celadon, and two crops a year. The **Northern Wei** dynasty started the construction of the Buddhist cave statues at Luoyang and Datong.

The **Sui** (581 to 618) built the 2,000 kilometer-long Grand Canal, had ships up to 70 meters long, and an arched stone bridge still in use today in Zhaoxian county, Hebei.

Chinese Civilization Flourishes

The **Tang** (618 to 907) was one of China's most prosperous and culturally developed dynasties. This era produced three-color and snow-white porcelains, inlaid mother-of-pearl, gold and silver, wood-block printing, fine silk, and woven feathers. They used an adjustable curved-shaft plow and made an attempt at land reform. The Tang was the most prosperous period of the Silk Road era, but merchants also traded by sea. They opened a special office for foreign trade in Guangzhou, where Arab traders built a mosque.

Buddhism entered Tibet during this dynasty from Nepal and China. Later, Chinese monks took Buddhism to Japan and Korea. (Kyoto is modeled on Xi'an). The Chinese monk Hsuan Tsang went to India (629-645) to obtain the Buddhist sutras. Chinese travelers also went to Persia, Arabia, and Byzantium. Tang poets are still the most respected. Look for fat women's faces in paintings and sculptures. They are most likely Tang.

The **Five Dynasties** (907 to 960) was a transitional warring period. The Liao (916 to 1125) controlled Inner Mongolia and part of southern Manchuria. It invaded China and occupied Beijing and built an extant 66.6-meter wooden pagoda in Ying Xian, Shaanxi.

The **Northern and Southern Song** (960 to 1279) was a prosperous and culturally-developed period. It had the first paper money, moveable type, compass, gunpowder, and rocket-propelled spears. It made fine porcelains and red lacquer and improved on the use of acupuncture and moxibustion. It made progress in mining and metallurgy. Hangzhou, then known as Qinsai, was the largest, richest city in the world according to Marco Polo.

The **Western Xia** (1038-1277) controlled today's Gansu and western Inner Mongolia. During the **Jin** (1115 to 1234) the first western missionaries were recorded. Franciscan friars arrived in Inner Mongolia. The Jin captured Beijing and controlled Kaifeng, the Wei River valley, Inner Mongolia, and northwestern China.

The **Yuan** or Mongols (1271 to 1368) had a water clock and improved cotton spinning and weaving. They gave us the famous blue-and-white, the underglaze red porcelain, and cloisonne. They controlled all of today's China and areas north and east including Moscow, Kiev, Damascus, Baghdad, and Afghanistan. From 1275-92, **Marco Polo** visited and served in the court of Kublai Khan.

The **Ming** (1368 to 1644) imported corn, potato, tobacco, peanuts, sunflower, and tomatoes from America. They refined the blue-and-white porcelain and added colors and had sea links with Malacca, Java, Ceylon, and East Africa. The Chinese Emperor lent Macau to the Portuguese, and the first Christian missionary, **Matteo Ricci** of the Society of Jesus, lived in Macau and then in Beijing. The Dutch colonized Formosa (Taiwan) until 1662.

The **Qing** (1644 to 1911) is noted for some of the best porcelains. It had to cope with foreign incursions. Cheng Chengkung (**Koxinga**), drove the Dutch from Taiwan. Qing forces expanded into Russia, Korea, Vietnam, Burma, and Sikkim, but later lost a great deal of territory. The British introduced opium as a narcotic. During this dynasty, the first U.S. trading ship, Empress of China, arrived in Guangzhou, the first British mission met the emperor (at Chengde), and the first Protestant missionary, Robert Morrison of Britain, arrived. American missionary work started in 1830.

In 1839, China attempted to stop the opium trade. It burned 20,000 chests near Guangzhou, more than half a year's trade. This resulted in the **Opium War** (1840 to 1842). Britain needed to sell China opium to balance trade. British forces with French help seized a few cities along the coast and threatened Nanjing. The Chinese gave in, ceding Hong Kong island to Britain and opening to foreign trade Guangzhou, Xiamen, Fuzhou, Ningbo, and Shanghai. This was the beginning of the foreign exploitation of China, and the establishment of "foreign concessions" in Shanghai. Countries with concessions included Germany, Italy, Japan, Belgium, Russia and the United States. About this time, in 1848, Chinese emigration to America and Australia started.

The Decline of the Dynasties

The **Taiping Heavenly Kingdom** (1851 to 1864) was a rebellion against the Manchus led by a Christianity-inspired Cantonese who believed himself the younger brother of Jesus Christ. Starting in 1851 in Guangxi, this became the largest peasant movement in Chinese history. At one time the rebels occupied most of China. They established a capital at Nanjing for eleven years and were defeated in part by a foreign mercenary army led by British officer Charles Gordon, known as Chinese Gordon, who was later killed in the Sudan.

The **Second Anglo-Chinese War** (1856 to 1860) was also known as the Arrow War. It ended after the sacking of Beijing, the burning down of the Summer Palace, and more unequal treaties for China, including the ceding of Kowloon to the British. In 1870, China started to send thirty students a year to the United States to study. Students also went to Britain and France.

During the latter half of the 19th century, the French took Vietnam (then a tributary state of China) and Japan seized Taiwan, the Pescadores, and the Liaoning peninsula from China. In 1898, Britain leased the area north of Kowloon and about 235 islands around Hong Kong for 99 years. The Chinese reacted with tragic incidents like the Tientsin Massacre of French missionaries. It was during this turn-of-the century period that the **Empress Dowager Tzu Hsi** kept the **Kuang Hsu Emperor** under house arrest for defying her. He had passed various reforms to modernize China.

In 1899, the United States declared that foreign powers should not cut up China into colonies and all nations should be free to trade with China. Only Britain bothered to reply, but for a while China looked to the United States as its only foreign friend. Then in 1900 came the **Boxer Rebellion**, also known as the Rebellion of the Society of the Righteous and Harmonious Fists, a reaction, at times encouraged by the Empress Dowager, against increasing foreign domination. The Boxers attacked foreigners and Chinese Christians.

Foreign powers, including the Americans, responded by capturing Beijing, sacking it, and forcing another humiliating treaty on China. Then the Japanese invaded southern Manchuria. The Empress Dowager died in 1908 and was succeeded by two-year-old **Pu-yi**, the last emperor of China.

The Republic

On October 10, 1911, the first victory of **Dr. Sun Yat-sen's republican revolutionaries** followed an accidental explosion in one of their bomb factories in Hankou. Dr. Sun became president of the Chinese republic with its capital at Nanjing. But the new country suffered a lot of growing pains and external problems. Outer Mongolia, with Russian help, declared independence from China. In 1913, **Yuan Shih-kai** was elected president. Then Japanese troops took over the naval base at Qingdao and won its infamous Twenty-one Demands. Many Chinese protested. They protested more after Yuan proclaimed himself emperor.

The republic was saved when Yuan died of a heart attack, but warlords gained control of the country. World War I ended with the Japanese keeping its gains in China and western powers retaining their pre-war concessions.

The May 4, 1919, student demonstrations against the Versailles Treaty marked the beginning of the nationalistic and cultural upsurge known as the **May Fourth Movement**, the training ground for many Communist revolutionaries.

On July 1, 1921, the Chinese Communist Party was founded in Shanghai with Russian Communist help, although the Soviets preferred to support Sun Yat-sen. Dr. Sun agreed to cooperate with Russian and Chinese Communists and sent **Chiang Kai-shek** to Moscow for military training. Mikhail Borodin and General Vassily Blucher arrived as advisers. Dr. Sun could not be sure of help from Britain and America. On March 12, 1925, he died of cancer in Beijing.

In 1926, Generalissimo Chiang Kai-shek and Soviet supplies led the **Northern Expedition** in a successful attempt to unify China, wrest control from the warlords, and fight the unequal treaties. In 1927, the Northern Expedition took Nanjing and Chiang tried to purge Communists in Shanghai. **Chou En-lai** escaped and went on to found the Chinese Red Army which attempted to take Changsha. Ill-prepared, it withdrew to Jiangxi where the Communists established the first Chinese soviet, distributing land to the peasants in the area. The next year the Nationalists took Beijing and renamed it Peiping (Northern Peace).

In 1931, the Japanese invaded Manchuria and set up a puppet government under Pu-yi called Manchukuo. Chiang accepted a humiliating truce in 1933 while continuing to attack the Communists on Jinggang Shan with a 'scorched earth' policy. On October 16, 1934, the Communists, aware they could no longer hold their base on Jinggang Shan, started out with 80,000 troops on the **Long March**. They arrived three months later in Xunyi, Guizhou. **Mao Tse-tung** took over as leader of the march and they decided on northern Shaanxi as their goal, the only Communist base big enough. In addition, they could fight the Japanese invaders in that area.

From Xunyi, the march continued in spite of Nationalist bombs and troops. The major battles were fought at Loushan Pass (February 1935) and Luting suspension bridge over the Tatu River. Edgar Snow gives a good account of the march in his book *Red Star Over China*. Some of the important battles have been immortalized in ivory or porcelain. The Long March was joined by other Communist armies and ended in northern Shaanxi in 1935, a journey of 12,500 kilometers. The original marchers were reduced to 8,000, including 30 women. The Communists moved to Yan'an in 1937.

The Communists fought against the Japanese while the Nationalists tried to eliminate the Communists. In 1936, Chiang was kidnapped by one of his own officers at Huaqing Hot Spring and forced into a wartime coalition with the Communists against the Japanese, in what is known as the **Xi'an Incident**.

The Japanese War & Civil War

On July 7, 1937, the killing of Japanese soldiers near Beijing set off the 1937-45 war between Japan and China, during which Japan occupied most of urban China. Chiang moved his capital to Hankou and finally to Chongqing while the western powers remained neutral. Many warlords with their private armies rallied to fight the Japanese but were destroyed.

Although the Nationalists blocked supply routes, the Communist armies waged guerrilla warfare against the Japanese, engaged in political and economic work among peasants, and developed strategy, discipline, and plans for the takeover of the rest of China.

In 1938, the Canadian surgeon **Dr. Norman Bethune** joined the Communist Eighth Route Army and died the following year of blood poisoning while operating without antiseptics. Because of his skills at improvisation and selfless devotion to duty, Bethune later became a Chinese national hero. (See Shijiazhuang.)

The United States entered the war after Japan's attack on Pearl Harbor in 1941. It increased aid to Chiang and tried to reconcile Mao and Chiang against the Japanese.

The Japanese were defeated in 1945. China got most of her territory back, including Taiwan and the Pescadores. Outer Mongolia and Manchuria were placed under the Russian sphere of influence. The **Chinese civil war** continued though, especially in Manchuria. US President Harry Truman ended aid to the Nationalists to avoid American involvement in the civil war.

The Communists advanced and eventually won because of severe inflation, Nationalist corruption, the breakdown of law and order, mass Nationalist troop defections, and the Communists' success in winning the hearts and minds of the peasants.

The Mao Years

On October 1, 1949, known as **Liberation Day**, Chairman Mao proclaimed the birth of the **People's Republic of China** from the Gate of Heavenly Peace, Tiananmen, in Beijing. Later Chiang and loyal troops and officials fled to Taiwan. Refugees flooded Hong Kong. The Communists tried but failed to take the offshore islands of Matsu and Quemoy across from Taiwan.

For the next decade the Communists, with Russian help, tried to rebuild the nation and put their ideals into practice. They started trials by peasants of landlords and executed about two million people. They attempted to "remold" intellectuals. They divided the land among the peasants, 0.15 to 0.45 acres each.

In 1950, the **Korean War** began with North Korea invading South Korea. Chinese forces joined the North after the United Nations and South Koreans counterattacked north of the 38th Parallel (the border between the two Koreas) and China felt threatened. The Chinese jailed and expelled many foreign missionaries, teachers, and scholars as imperialist spies. China accused the United States of using poison gas and germ warfare and circulated maps showing American bases surrounding China. The Americans began an embargo which ended many years after the war ended, in the 1970s.

China started to use Hong Kong and Macau as trading centers and sources of foreign exchange. In 1950, Britain recognized China. In 1949-50, China took **Tibet**. In 1955, the Chinese suppressed a rebellion there and in 1959, the **Dalai Lama** fled to India.

During 1956-57, Mao, in an effort to incorporate intellectuals into the revolution, began the **Hundred Flowers Movement**: "Let a hundred flowers bloom together, let a hundred schools of thought contend." Mao believed the overwhelming majority of intellectuals supported the revolution and communism, and encouraged intellectuals to speak freely about the bureaucracy. Intellectuals did not respond and about a year later the Communist Party began its own efforts to clean up the bureaucracy. Once started, the intellectuals participated fully. However, the attacks were so severe that within five weeks the Movement ended and the **Anti-Rightest Campaign** began, aimed at the intellectuals.

The **Great Leap Forward** (1958-60) was a failed economic plan that led to the death of millions of people. Mao was convinced that food production could be substantially increased by reorganizing people into communes. Unfortunately, the communes were reporting increases in production when production was actually decreasing. Initial efforts to report the bad news were not well received by Mao, and the devastating program continued until 1960.

In 1961, Mao accused the Russians of being revisionists, giving in to capitalism and to "nuclear blackmail." China rejected Russia's offer of nuclear weapons in exchange for bases in China. China and Russia divorced in 1960 when **Nikita Khrushchev** ordered the end of all Soviet aid. Russian advisers left and the Chinese insisted on repaying Russian military aid immediately.

These years, 1959 to 1962, were a difficult period for China. In addition to the repayments, the country endured 'natural calamities.' Liu Shao-chi became president while Mao continued as Communist Party Chairman. India asserted control of disputed border territory. China sent a punitive invasion force into India and then announced a ceasefire and withdrew.

In 1963, China started to supply Hong Kong with fresh water. In 1964, it exploded a nuclear bomb at the Lop Nor testing grounds in Xinjiang. That same year **Chiang Ching**, Mao's wife, started a campaign to make culture serve the revolution and abolished traditional Peking opera. Later she allowed only eight operas to be performed, all written by revolutionary committees. In 1965, an article instigated by Mao in a Shanghai newspaper introduced the **Great Proletarian Cultural Revolution** to the public for the first time. The next year, activists put up the first important 'Big Character Poster' at Beijing University, and Chairman Mao felt that people were forgetting the aims of the revolution. He swam the Yangtze River at Wuhan (nine miles) to show he was still powerful and in charge.

Mao taught that workers and peasants were the basis of the Chinese revolution. Many party cadres were re-educated in 'correct' political thinking by learning to respect and love physical labor. Doctors swept floors to help them identify with the masses and understand their problems. Corruption was punished harshly.

The first of many **Red Guard** rallies in Tiananmen Square in support of Chairman Mao was held August 18, 1966. Schools closed so that students named Red Guards could travel and learn to make revolution. They rode free on trains, slept in school dormitories and were fed by municipalities. They traveled the country taking part in revolutionary movements against the Four Olds: the elimination of old ideas, culture, customs, and habits. They destroyed religious statues, buildings and ancestral tablets. They changed the names of streets and parks from old dynastic names to 'The East Is Red' (Dong Fang) and 'Liberation' (Jiefang), stripped some women of their tight western trousers and cut off long 'bourgeois' hair. They also attacked elements of foreign influence, and any obstacles to completing the course of the revolution.

They denounced **Deng Xiaoping** and in 1968 deposed President Liu, who died shortly afterward. The Cultural Revolution became very violent and led to riots even in Hong Kong and Macau. The schools re-opened in 1969. Fellow peasants and workers chose which student should study in university. They based eligibility on the completion of at least two years of manual labor, how well you knew Maoist theory, and how enthusiastic and selfless you were in serving the people.

The next year, China launched its first satellite. In 1971, the United States table tennis team and US Secretary of State **Henry Kissinger** visited China and paved the way for American recognition of China and the visit of President **Richard Nixon** in 1972. China took the United Nations seat occupied by Taiwan, and Canada resumed diplomatic relations.

Deng Xiaoping was rehabilitated in 1973, and became a vice-premier. In 1974 China asserted control of the Paracel Islands as one million Soviet troops ringed its northern border. In January 1976, Premier Chou En-lai died and Deng Xiao-Ping became acting premier. Chou supporters put wreaths in Tiananmen Square in his honor. Chiang Ching, Mao's wife, ordered the removal of the wreaths. A clash ensued and Mao blamed Deng, who once again fell into disfavor.

Not long after, a massive earthquake shook North China centering on the city of Tangshan and was believed by many to foretell the death of Mao Tse-tung a few months later. **Hua Guo-feng** succeeded him and arrested the **Gang of Four** who were blamed for many of the country's ills. The Four were Chiang Ching, Mao's widow, and three leaders from Shanghai. Deng was rehabilitated again and resumed his previous posts. The following year, posters advocating personal freedoms and democracy appeared on **Democracy Wall**, but this experiment didn't last very long at all.

In 1979, the U.S. and China resumed full diplomatic relations. Tensions between China and Vietnam were worsening in the late 1970s, and China went to war in 1979 owing to what Beijing termed Vietnamese 'armed incursions' into China.

The Deng Xiao-Ping Era

In 1980, **Zhao Ziyang** became premier. Leaders tried to improve living standards and eliminate "left deviation, that is, the over-rigid and excess control of the economic system, the rejection of commodity production, and the mistaken attempt to transfer prematurely the ownership of all enterprises to the state."

Under the orders of Deng Xiao-ping, they began an economic reassessment and encouraged foreign investment. They banned Democracy Walls.

The Communists had started out with a land-to-the-peasants program, then collectivization, communes, and finally private plots. During the Cultural Revolution, they abolished private plots, then reinstated and encouraged them later. In the 1970s, it was apparent that even that system was not meeting the needs of the people.

The New Economic Policies

In the early 1980s, an economy largely based on the family replaced the communes. Most counties adopted the Responsibility System, whereby rural inhabitants rent land or machines. The government receives an agreed share of the produce while villagers keep or sell the surplus. Anybody can also make money from handicrafts, livestock, and vegetables for their own gain. This system still exists and you will see the results in 'free markets.' Families and collectives have opened hotels, restaurants, and factories. It would seem that China has almost come around full circle, with the government replacing the feudal landlords. But has it?

Under the new economic system, the market, not the government determines what is grown. Many peasants have been working furiously and are making more money then ever before. China is undergoing another revolution. For the first time, rural China is earning less than 50% of its income from agriculture and many rural inhabitants are making more than salaried city dwellers.

The revolutionary slogans of nationalistic self-sufficiency and personal sacrifice of the nineteen fifties and sixties have given way to international cooperation and modernization. Some people are getting richer faster than others. The new economic policies also include encouraging foreign investment. The leadership has successfully attracted foreign capital with tax breaks and business infastructure, roads, railways and harbors. Factories, office blocks and hotels have proliferated everywhere. Most areas have IDD telephones and new airports. Beijing, Hangzhou, and Shanghai have video telephone services. In the early 2000's, China seemed to have more mobile telephones than anywhere else in the world.

The progress is uneven; some previously booming cities have lost their steam because of poor leadership but Pudong has recently built the tallest building in the world.

The leadership denounced the Cultural Revolution and the Communist Party booted out thousands of leftists. They started encouraging intellectuals to contribute to modernization and are now considering entrepreneurs for membership – a contradiction indeed.

Record harvests and an increase in cash crops encouraged the new economic policies. The leadership ordered all state-owned companies to make a profit and pay taxes. Foreign exchange reserves hit a record high, and China went on an importing spree. Factories became independent and made their own production and marketing decisions. President Ronald Reagan visited, and US-China relations warmed. Deng proclaimed a one-country, two-systems policy in dealing with Taiwan and Hong Kong.

The Communist Party spelled out its plan for 'socialism with Chinese characteristics.' It joined the Asian Development Bank. Some government-owned factories were allowed to issue stock. For the first time since Liberation (1949), a factory declared bankruptcy and a stock market opened (in Shanghai). The government announced that all new factory workers would be under limited instead of life-time assignments. The government also started a federal unemployment insurance and pension scheme.

In 1987, student demonstrations for more freedom led to the resignation of leaders advocating 'bourgeois liberalization.' This included the Communist Party general secretary. University students were forced to take courses in Marxist-Leninist theories, trips to the countryside and factories, and military training.

As a result of demonstrations for independence by Tibetans in Lhasa, China closed Tibet to all foreign tourists except for prepaid tours. Taiwan permitted its citizens to visit the mainland. Many tearful reunions took place between family members who had not seen each other since 1949. Mail, telegram, and telephone service also resumed.

In the late 1980s, previously suppressed individualism surfaced. The press printed real news, not just government-approved news. For students, the new attitudes extended to politics and demonstrations. The leadership, once benevolent on many levels, became nepotistic and corrupt with lavish state spending on banquets, foreign cars, and overseas trips. If Mao were alive, he probably would have started another Cultural Revolution. Inflation started getting out of control.

In 1989, the Panchen Lama, the second highest Tibetan Buddhist leader, died and more demonstrations for independance took place in Lhasa. The Dalai Lama offered a compromise: China would oversee its foreign affairs and keep troops in Tibet in exchange for religious and cultural autonomy. He was awarded the Nobel Peace Prize.

In Beijing, the death of Hu Yao-bang set off **student demonstrations** and hunger strikes that continued relatively unopposed for a month and a half. The students asked for the end of government corruption and a say in student government. They shouted defiant foreign slogans. Demonstrations centered in Tiananmen Square in Beijing, but took place in other towns and cities as well. Plans for the historic visit of Soviet President Mikhail Gorbachev were thwarted because of the students. The leadership was divided on how to react.

What emerged was a reversion to old ways. Like a traditional, autocratic Chinese father who 'lost face' in front of a guest and realized his authority was disintegrating, the Chinese leadership regressed to brute force. An estimated 300 to 3000 people were killed in Tiananmen Square on **June 4**: innocent bystanders, unarmed demonstrators, civilians, soldiers and some rioters. Over 450 military, police, and public vehicles were alleged by the government to be destroyed. Student leaders were arrested.

The government said those killed were 'ruffians and criminal elements taking advantage of the turmoil.' It said the students needed political education and sent some to the army. It set students and workers to studying the government's version of the 'counter-revolutionary rebellion.' Shanghai and Beijing executed 'rioters.' It arrested a youth for trying to place a wreath in the square and jailed a number of people for 'counter-revolutionary crimes.'

Around the world, thousands of protesters marched, especially in Hong Kong. Some foreign governments imposed economic sanctions. Some of the student leaders took refuge in foreign missions. The most prominent was

Democracy & Human Rights

Democracy movements are not new. Writing criticisms and complaints in public places has occurred in China for centuries and especially during the Cultural Revolution, when they were used to attack capitalist roaders (but not to criticize the government).

Late in 1978, the writing of big character posters on Democracy Walls flourished unhindered. Four months later, this right was restricted. Criticism of socialism, the dictatorship of the proletariat, party leadership, and the ideas of Marx, Lenin, and Mao were taboo.

In 1979, foreigners could visit Democracy Walls, talk with anyone and accept leaflets. But later, some Chinese were arrested and charged with passing state secrets to foreigners. In December 1979, however, wall posters were curtailed. In September 1980, these rights were deleted from the constitution.

In 1989, a million people supported student demonstrations for democracy in Beijing, and more elsewhere in the country. They were brutally suppressed. If you want more information on this subject, and on political rights in general, contact **Amnesty International**, **Asia Watch**, and the **US State Department**.

astrophysicist Fang Lizhi, who lived for almost a year in the US Embassy before being allowed to leave for the U.S.

Tourism almost stopped. The World Bank suspended all loans but later resumed them. Some foreign businesses withdrew. Countries abroad gave preferential treatment to Chinese refugees and made it easier for Chinese students to stay. Because of these actions and the awarding of the Nobel Peace Prize to the Dalai Lama, China accused foreign governments of interfering in its internal affairs. Amnesty International said at least 500 people were executed for offenses related to the demonstrations and for counter-revolutionary activities.

By late 1990, China was relatively back to normal, the press dull and obedient. Foreign businesses came back. International sanctions were lifted. The economy continued to grow, especially in the countryside, and China had an international trade surplus. Martial law was lifted in Beijing and Lhasa. Inflation was held down to 2%, compared to 17% in 1989. Twelve Catholic bishops were arrested because of secret Vatican ties. Beijing's Asian Games was an organizational success, but did not attract the large numbers hoped for.

China implemented a five-day work week and cut back on free health care and subsidies to state corporations. The United States accused China of using forced prison labor for exports and demanded the protection of intellectual property rights. Still, China achieved an international trade surplus with the United States. The nation was experiencing double digit economic growth rate.

China Today

From about 1992 until 1997, the country was booming. China continued to buy airplanes and cars from the United States and its overheated economy triggered inflation and subsequent economic controls. The government announced a staff cutback of 25% and kept trying to get rid of highly subsidized state enterprises.

The collapse of the Gouhou Dam in Xinjiang region killed 242 people and President Jiang Zemin ordered the Chinese press to print positive news. The government forbade officials from going into business or practicing nepotism. They were forbidden from trading in stocks or accepting gifts of money. But as they have for thousands of years, many officials bypassed the rules. The government announced that over 60% of China's 500 cities was short of water.

In the mid-1990s, China arrested, sentenced, and then released Chinese-American Harry Wu, a former prisoner who was determined to enlighten the world about conditions in China's prisons. He was deported and then-US First Lady Hilary Clinton attended the United Nation's Women's Conference in Beijing along with about 30,000 other women.

China strongly protested visits of the Taiwan president to the United States, even though these were private. It felt threatened by the Taiwan elections. The United States continued to object to the violation of intellectual property rights and human rights. A conflict between the government and the Dalai Lama about the reincarnation of the Panchen Lama threatened any reconciliation on Tibet.

But during this time, China bought American cars, factories, electric generators, subway and railway cars and airplanes. Canadians were hired to design shopping malls.

In 1997, **Hong Kong** returned to Chinese rule; a couple of years later Macau followed. An economic recession in the rest of Asia stopped China's growth and started a price war in its hotels. China vowed not to devalue its currency. It started monitoring messages sent over electronic mail and arrested a server for giving mailing lists to democracy rights organizations abroad. In 1998, the worst floods in decades caused much damage along the Yangtze River. The government continued its efforts to close down factories that were not productive.

China has since been progressing into the 21st century. It has increased the speed of many of its trains, completed many expressways, worked on the trans-China superhighways, new nuclear power plants, airports, and ship ports. The controversial **Three Gorges Dam** across the Yangtze River has been on schedule and should finish in 2009. Having developed much of the country, it is now concentrating on improving its western provinces – Gansu, Ningxia, Tibet, and Xinjiang.

The growing middle and upper classes have shown an increased appetite for consumer goods from abroad. China has joined the **World Trade Organization** which lead to some interesting questions for visitors to ask. Is this membership good or bad for China? For the little people? The proletariat? The multinationals?

There are opportunities to sell foreign-made products to the Chinese. And foreign travel agencies, department stores, as well as restaurants have opened in China.

Many conflicts still exist with the U.S, especially the bombing of the Chinese embassy in Belgrade, and the emergency landing of a U.S. reconaissance plane on Hainan Island. After September 11, 2001, China supported the U.S. in its fight against terrorism but felt that the U.S. needed to consult more with the United Nations before taking action. It objected to the U.S. failing to implement previously negotiated disarmament and nuclear weapons treaties, the arming of Japan, and its sale of warships to Taiwan. It objects to the U.S taking too big a role in Asian affairs and U.S. interference in its internal affairs, its treatment of "evil cults."

Many Americans feel China is using the anti-terrorism campaign as an excuse to oppress its own enemies, "ethnic separatists, religious extremists, terrorists, and the Falun Gong. For China's position on these issues, see its website: *www.china-embassy.org/eng/.*

In 2002, President George W. Bush visited China and President Jiang is expected to visit the U.S. In spite of the surface friendship, ask yourself as you travel around, is war between these two powers inevitable? Also ask yourself, will China go bankrupt? Is it spending more than it's earning?

Recently China was chosen to be the site of the 2008 summer Olympics, and won the right to the play-offs of the World Cup Soccer, two big feathers in its cap. Many people speak freely with foreigners now. I suggest you use discretion in advocating democracy, human rights, and the western point of view, unless you want to be booted out of the country. With care, there are many questions for you to ask: What about social security? Free health care? What is being done about AIDS, and illegal drugs? Legal rights? What is the effect of satellite television? China's 20 million Internet users? How is the government regulating these sources of foreign information?

But be careful what you send by e-mail. It could be monitored.

China's Dynasties

The names of the dynasties below are given two ways: the first word is spelled using pinyin transliteration; the word in parentheses is the old spelling.

Xia (Hsia)	c. 21st-16th century B.C.
Shang (Shang)	c. 16th-11th century B.C.
Western Zhou (Chou)	c. 11th century-771 B.C.
Spring & Autumn Period	770-476 B.C.
Warring States Period	475-221 B.C.
Qin (Chin)	221-206 B.C.
Western Han (Han)	206 B.C. - A.D. 24
Eastern Han (Han)	25-220
The Three Kingdoms	220-265
Wei (Wei)	220-265
Shu (Shu)	221-263
Wu (Wu)	222-280
Western Jin (Tsin)	265-316
Eastern Jin (Tsin)	317-420
Southern/Northern Dynasties	420-589
Southern Dynasties	420-589
Song (Sung)	420-479
Qi (Chi)	479-502
Liang (Liang)	502-557
Chen (Chen)	557-589
Northern Dynasties	386-581
Northern Wei (Wei)	386-534
Eastern Wei	534-550

Western Wei	535-556
Northern Qi (Chi)	550-577
Northern Zhou (Chou)	557-581
Su (Sui)	581-618
Tang (Tang)	618-907
Five Dynasties	907-960
Liao (Liao)	916-1125
Song (Sung)	960-1279
Northern Song (Sung)	960-1127
Southern Song (Sung)	1127-1279
Western Xia (Hsia)	1038-1227
Jin (Kin)	1115-1234
Yuan (Yuan)	1271-1368
Ming (Ming)	1368-1644
Hongwu (Hung Wu)	1368-1399
Jianwen (Chien Wen)	1399-1403
Yongle (Yung Lo)	1403-1425
Hongxi (Hung Hsi)	1425-1426
Xuande (Hsuan Teh)	1426-1436
Zhengtong (Cheng Tung)	1436-1450
Jingtai (Ching Tai)	1450-1457
Tianshun (Tien Shun)	1457-1465
Cheng Hua (Cheng Hua)	1465-1488
Hongzhi (Hung Chih)	1488-1506
Zhengde (Cheng Teh)	1506-1522
Jiajing (Chia Ching)	1522-1567
Longqing (Lung Ching)	1567-1573
Wanli (Wan Li)	1573-1620
Taichang (Tai Chang)	1620-1621
Tianqi (Tien Chi)	1621-1628
Chongzhen (Chung Chen)	1628-1644
Qing (Ching)	1644-1911
Shunzhi (Shun Chih)	1644-1662
Kangxi (Kang Hsi)	1662-1723
Yongzhen (Yung Cheng)	1723-1736
Qianlong (Chien Lung)	1736-1796
Jiaqing (Chia Ching)	1796-1821
Daoguang (Tao Kuang)	1821-1851
Xianfeng (Hsien Feng)	1851-1862
Tongzhi (Tung Chih)	1862-1875
Guangxu (Kuang Hsu)	1875-1908
Xuantong (Hsuan Tung)	1908-1911

planning your trip

Chapter 6

When to Go

The best weather is May-June and September-October, but you could run into crowds and delays. You could also try late April. In November, go to Beijing first and then move south. Guangzhou, Guilin, Hong Kong and Hainan are wonderful in November and December.

Try to avoid the seven-day holidays because of the crowds, inflated prices and closed offices. These are around the lunar new year (late January or early February), May First Labor Day, and National Day October first. Travel for the new year is especially difficult in Guangzhou and Fujian, as hotels and trains are full of Overseas Chinese visitors, and some tourist attractions are closed. Avoid Guangzhou during the trade fairs and any other cities with big events. Go to Lhasa in March when the days are warm, the nomads are on pilgrimages, and few other tourists are around. Avoid Lhasa in the summer when tourists outnumber costumed Tibetans.

The hottest time of the year is usually July and early August. Head then for wonderful Yunnan – Lijiang, Dali and Zhongdian. Almost all hotels, most tourist buses and some taxis are air-conditioned. Put mountain or seaside resorts at the end of a hot tour. During April-May and through the summer, rain and high humidity make south China (including Guangzhou and Guilin) quite oppressive, but the greenery is lush and beautiful. Inner Mongolia and the Silk Road have sandstorms in spring and autumn. Avoid mountain areas, the Yangtze Gorges and outdoor sights in the rainy season because of floods or landslides.

Again, China extends from the same latitudes as James Bay in Canada to Cuba. Beijing is at almost the same latitude as Philadelphia, and Guangzhou as Havana. Take altitude into account: the higher, the colder, especially at night.

Winter in North China begins in mid-November and extends to late February and the air is very dry. The Spring Festival/lunar new year is frequently the coldest time. Air pollution is particularly bad in winter as coal is used for fuel. But most tour agencies and hotels give discounts.

Wise tourists who are healthy and not afraid of the cold could plan trips in the winter even in the north. Newly-fallen snow transforms any city into a wonderland and makes red pavilions and curved gold roofs intensely beautiful. It also makes roads slippery and traffic slow-moving. Hotels are not usually crowded then (except for conventions.)

It is important to remember that the Chinese do not heat their buildings (like museums and palaces) as warmly as we do even though it can be cold. South of the Yangtze these have no heat at all. But most tourist hotels three stars and up are heated. Some low-priced hotels are not. If the cold bothers you, go only to the tropics. Even in Guangzhou, you might need a top coat and a sweater at that time of year.

Movies to Get You Ready for China!

You can borrow videos of tourist attractions from Chinese missions. Check your neighborhood video store. Look for Academy Award winner **Crouching Tiger, Hidden Dragon** (if only for the scenery and choreography), and nominees **Ju Dou** and **Raise the Red Lantern** by director Zhang Yimou. Then there's **Farewell My Concubine** and **Red Sorghum**, the last four tragedies.

If you can only see one movie, see **Shower** about changing attitudes and life styles in today's China. It is much lighter than most of the movies here. There's also **China: The Panda Adventure** (Imax Theatres) with a happy ending. Also funny are **Eat, Drink, Man, Woman**, and the **Wedding Banquet**, both Taiwan-made and set in Taiwan.

Other Tragedies are **Xiu Xiu**, set in Tibet during the Cultural Revolution; **The Story of Xinghua**, a woman bought by a husband she detests and who lives near the Great Wall; **In the Mood for Love** is set in Hong Kong in 1962 and is typical of the middle class of that era.

Good foreign-made movies are **The Sand Pebbles** (although filmed in Taiwan), **The Last Emperor** (with great shots of The Forbidden City), and **Bethune, The Making of a Hero**. **The First Emperor** (shown on the museum circuit), is short but excellent, especially if you're going to Xi'an. Even if you're not going to teach and have no interest in kung fu, see **Iron and Silk**. For Tibetan films, see theTibet chapter.

Other Things to Consider When Planning

If you are interested in visiting schools, factories, and offices, avoid vacations, holidays and weekends. If you want to see a festival, consider those dates.

Now that China has a five-day work week, business hotels are not full on Friday and Saturdays nights and prices are softer then. Do not expect business appointments on weekends. Cheaper tourist hotels and popular tourist attractions however are busier on weekends with China's growing number of domestic tourists. Avoid the Forbidden City, and the Badaling Great Wall on weekends.

What to Pack

Clothing & Luggage

Sightseers should dress for comfort with good walking shoes. Sneakers are ideal. White is not practical in China's polluted air; besides, it is the color of mourning, so brighten it up. Bring sunscreen, and a sun hat or buy a cheap one there.

You might feel compelled to dress up for dinner in five-star hotels and for a captain's banquet on Yangtze cruise ships. But you don't have to. Chinese people are generally informal. Recently, banquets in Shanghai had printed invitations specifying lounge suits but no one was sent away who didn't wear one.

From mid-November to late March, north China, including Beijing, is bitterly cold. I even froze in Beijing one May; two sweaters and a top coat were barely enough. Many of the cheaper hotels are not well heated. A hot water bottle will help keep you warm in cheaper hotels.

A jogging suit is ideal for lounging and sleeping on trains. Take along a coat, long underwear, heavy slacks, thermal socks, and warm boots. Do as the natives do: plan on layers of clothing and a windbreaker top. If you have to, you can buy a down coat (half US prices), fleece-lined Gore-Tex jacket (Y180 at the Silk Market), and wool or silk long johns (Y100 for bottoms) in China. If you are also traveling to warmer climes or need room in your luggage for purchases, you could take old clothes you can discard when no longer useful.

The rainy season is March to May in the south, with rain or drizzle almost every day. After it starts getting hot, a trench coat will feel like a sauna. You can buy cheap umbrellas there.

All of lowland China is hot in July and August, so bring cotton clothing. Shorts are common on women now, but tops should be more modest. Most Chinese women wear trousers and loose-fitting blouses, and, increasingly, skirts. Men wear slacks and white shirts even in offices though the trend depending on their position, is towards business suits if they work in offices.

The new, with-it generation has been dressing more colorfully. Many young people have dyed red hair. Jeans are in style. Modern young women wear tights and even miniskirts.

Older Chinese women don't dress elegantly except in the wealthiest levels of society. The Chinese like to see foreign women wearing Chinese dress, but try not to look like restaurant staff with slinky brocade gowns. They also like to see the latest styles from abroad.

If you are invited to dinner, you can ask your host if what you have on is all right. Should men wear ties? Women should not overdo makeup or you'll have other people wondering if your eyelashes and hair are real – especially in isolated areas that see few foreigners. Younger Chinese women are into makeup. Sure, take your heels but go easy on the jewelry. The current style with the younger set is three-inch soles.

At less formal banquets, many Chinese men and women wear loose-fitting shirts and trousers. Some might be coming from work or arriving by bicycle. Chinese officials do not usually bring their spouses to banquets, but this is changing slowly at the upper levels.

Wearing cosmetics, jewelry, and bright colors (except for children) was considered self-indulgent, bourgeois, and counter-revolutionary from 1949 until recently. Doing so led to assault, hours of interrogation and even imprisonment during the Cultural Revolution. It is understandable why the older generation hesitates about changes. For business, dress as you would in your own country to show respect.

Laundry is done in one day at most hotels if in by 8 am. All hotels three stars and up in big cities have dry cleaning. The Chinese do an adequate job, but if your dress is special, the average hotel could ruin it. It would be wise to wash delicate clothes like silk underwear yourself. Some hotels provide clothes lines in bathrooms.

I usually pack wash and wear clothes. Most of my travel wardrobe is from **Tilley's** in Toronto, *Tel. 416/441-6141 or www.tilley.com*. It has socks and panties that dry overnight and wonderful skirts and fake silks that don't need ironing and can be worn to cocktail parties.

Your luggage should have a lock and will probably have to endure a lot of punishment. Some bags have been left out in the rain and I sometimes take a large garbage bag to protect the contents. Your bags should have your name, telephone number, and address outside and inside, and something like a wide ribbon to identify it on an airport luggage belt.

Free luggage allowance: If you're going in a group tour, you're usually allowed one or two suitcases. You should also have a carry-on bag for overnight train rides (your big bag may not be accessible), and airplanes (in case your checked luggage is delayed or lost).

China's domestic airports are sometimes strict about the weight limit on checked bags. For first class it's 40 kg, 30 kg for business class, and 20 kg for economy class. For discounted fares it's 20 kg first class and 15 kg economy. Economy class carry-on bags should not exceed 20 x 40 x 55 cm and five kg. I once argued that I had arrived on an international flight and showed my

Don't Count on Porters

Porters and trolleys are available in some but not all train stations and airports. In train stations, independent travelers should be prepared to carry their own bags, perhaps up and down a flight of steps, to a taxi. We've had people laughing at us – two women struggling with bags – and no offer to help. Consider a set of luggage wheels. Porters from hotels can help put bags onto trains, but in some cities, no one can meet individuals at your train car to help carry your bags. Guides can meet groups.

In some places, notably the train from Luoyang to Xi'an, porters insist that luggage be locked. If you can't get a lock, they will sell you one – cheap. It might fall apart en route so it's best to take your own lock.

ticket, and didn't have to pay for overweight. On another occasion, in Xi'an which guides say is notorious about overweight luggage, we had to pay considerably for the extra. Guilin is another strict airport.

Air China allows two pieces of luggage on trans-Pacific flights. Each bag should not exceed 32 kg and the sum of the height, width and length no more than 158 cm or 62" in first and executive class, and less in economy. Carry-on bags should fit under the seat. The sum of the width, height and depth should not exceed 45" or 115 cm.

A weight limit of 35 kg usually applies on trains; in 1998 we were caught twice and had to pay! But once when the U.S. president had arrived that day in China, my American friend didn't have to pay.

Toiletries

Four- and five-star hotels give away free shampoo, conditioner, and soap. Most hotels will probably give you toothbrushes, soap, and a few other goodies like combs. China has international brand soaps, toothpaste and shampoo. The lemon shampoo is acceptable. Handy-wipes for cleaning hands are good too. Take your favorite sanitary napkins or tampons.

Short-wave Transistor Radios

During the 1989 turmoil, in the days following June 4, *China Daily* mentioned nothing of the tanks and killings. Shortly afterwards, CNN and foreign newspapers were censored. Sometimes some but not all news websites get blocked. One never knows. Many hotels have news in English and CNN. Hotels are supposed to do their own censoring. But as the government owns part of the satellite, in case of emergency, do take a short-wave radio. See Chapter 7, *Emergencies & News*.

PLANNING YOUR TRIP 63

Photography

You can buy Kodak and Fuji print film but usually only 100 ASA. Ektachrome is getting more common. It is best to bring your own. Be sure to take extra batteries, flash cubes, video tapes, and Polariod film. You don't want to spend time looking for these.

Personal video cameras are allowed. Use of commercial video cameras requires permission. Video cassettes might be erased by airport x-ray machines, so pack them in lead pouches. If declared, your cassettes could be seized and screened with a charge, but I haven't heard of this happening lately. Officials are looking for pornography and religious materials. If you don't have any, your tapes should be returned in hours or weeks.

To avoid x-rays of camera film at airport security, ask for a hand inspection. Multiple exposures to x-rays can adversely affect them.

Maps & Books

You can usually get a free detailed map in English at four and five-star hotels. For wandering around on your own without a guide, take a Chinese-English phrase book or electronic dictionary.

Medicines, Vitamins, & Goodies

Take what you need. Exact equivalents may be hard to find. Chinese traditional medicines are frequently effective, so if you're adventurous, you might try them. Many hotels and cruise ships have doctors. With Chinese painkillers, you might experience strange mood changes. A few pharmacists in big cities can fill Western prescriptions, but don't count on it except in Beijing and Shanghai. Take two batches of essential medicines. Keep one on you, and one in your luggage in case one set gets lost.

Take Pepto-Bismol tablets (mild) and Immodium (serious) in case of diarrhea or upset stomach. Ask your doctor about Diamox for altitude sickness for Tibet. If you're bothered by pollution or dust, take a nose mask (or buy a cheap silk scarf in China).

Please consult a knowledgeable doctor about malaria. The danger is only in Hainan and the tropics close to the Laotian and Myanmar borders. For these infected areas, take long sleeves and trousers for after dark (when these mosquitoes bite), and a good repellent. If you have flu-like symptoms after being bitten, tell your doctor to check for malaria. It can be fatal.

Take a few snacks and if you need more, buy them in China. Some hotels and ships provide bottled water. All have free boiled water.

Gifts

Gifts are not essential, but you may want to give them to friends, or exceptional service people. Cash is becoming the norm. What are good gifts? Anything not made in China is usually acceptable. Some people give novelties like refrigerator magnets or unusual ball-point pens. You can give candy, postcards, Italian silk ties, cosmetics, souvenir playing cards, baseball caps, t-shirts, pins, or picture books with scenes of your country. Something for children like coloring books or books in English is great. For breaking the ice with children, take a bag of balloons or tiny cars.

You don't have to take gifts to schools, and certainly not to factories and communes. But schools do not usually receive any compensation for the disruption caused by visitors. If you want to leave a souvenir of your visit, give general gifts like books, frisbees, and pictures that everyone can enjoy. Giving to a few individuals may upset the others.

Since people everywhere are studying English and other foreign languages, books are a great idea. China is short of teaching materials in English. Guides, of course, would prefer cash, but you might also want to leave them magazines such as Vogue or People, your used guide book, or music tapes. If you are going to Lhasa, Tibetans appreciate photos of the Dalai Lama, but passing these out may be construed as interference in an internal dispute by the Chinese authorities. If you are visiting foreign residents in China, ask what gifts they would like. They can usually get everything there now.

Photocopies & Addresses

Make copies of the first important pages of your passport, your Chinese visa, and birth certificate (or certificate of citizenship) are essential. These are in case you lose your passport and should be kept separate from it. You should have extra passport photos. It is also helpful to have photocopies of plane tickets, travelers check receipts, and credit cards. You should have the telephone numbers of your credit card companies so you can stop payment in case of loss. If your prescription medicines can be mistaken for illegal drugs, take a copy of your prescriptions. Some people print up address stickers for post cards, e-mail addresses and emergency government and family addresses. You should send a copy of your address and itinerary to your country's consulate if you're staying three months and more, and leave a copy for your family or friends.

Take telephone and e-mail addresses of your friends, the travel agent who organized your tour, and the travel agents in China who are supposed to take care of you. You should also have telephone and e-mail addresses of your insurance company, which can offer advice.

Packing for Business

Business cards are essential for business people, preferably in Chinese on the back. It is good to take a one-page introduction in Chinese of your company (if possible). A few hotels print cards within 24 hours.

Officials dealing with Japan and Hong Kong have been accepting television sets and condos! Some have asked shamelessly for computers and 'Benzes.' There is no guarantee that an expensive gift will get you what you want. The danger is that from time to time, campaigns rage against corrupt officials who use their positions for personal gain. Chinese jails aren't nice. Chinese legal rights aren't the same. The government has executed people for accepting bribes.

Usually, inviting an official to a banquet to celebrate a deal, or to thank especially helpful people, is sufficient. Modest corporate gifts like agenda books and lighters are fine. Some Chinese appreciate hard liquor, like Chivas Regal. The tendency is now for wine. People are more concerned about health.

If you are traveling with a laptop, be aware that most hotel room safes are not big enough to hold them. You might want to take along a computer lock and a universal electrical adapter, found in travel stores. Most hotels have safe deposit boxes at the reception desk.

You should be able to access the e-mail sent to your home address directly into your computer easily when you're in China. Some top hotels have computer valets who know how to do this.

Money & Travel Costs

For valuables, it's a good idea to take a money belt and neck safe (a small purse worn under the clothes suspended by a cord around the neck). Fanny packs worn on the outside of your clothes can be slashed. Take mainly travelers' checks as a precaution against theft. While many ATMs are in China, not all of them work and they could cost you $2 to $10 per transaction. Take also a couple hundred US dollars in cash in relatively new bills, no larger than fifties, and preferably smaller for shopping and tips if you want.

If you're on a prepaid tour you only have to worry about incidentals like airport taxes (Y50 for domestic and Y90 for international), bicycle rentals, shopping, overweight luggage, a massage, barber or hairdresser, a round of drinks at a bar, postage stamps, long-distance telephone calls home, laundry, and unexpected emergencies. Then there are tips; some tour operators suggest US$6 a day for guides and drivers.

If you're not on a prepaid trip, take your credit card (most hotels three stars and up accept Visa, MasterCard and American Express) and travelers checks. Four and five

Exchange Rate

You'll note that prices in this book, as in China, are listed with a "Y" before the number, as in Y100. This tells you that the cost is 100 yuan. The 2002 rate of exchange is **8.3 yuan to one US dollar**, so divide the yuan price by 8.3 to get the dollar equivalent. I have a link to a foreign exchange website at my site: www.china-travel-guide.com.

star hotels can book flight tickets and most will charge this to your account, payable by credit card. A few travel agents and Chinese airlines now accept credit cards. But most do not.

Because of the fear that Chinese currency will be devalued, many Chinese are collecting US cash. Take this for shopping in small bills. You get better prices. The bills should not be old, worn nor torn.

Prices differ. Hotels in big, busy cities like Beijing and Shanghai are just as expensive as New York City. Hotels in smaller towns like Guilin and Suzhou are much cheaper. Food in restaurants outside of hotels is cheaper. In street markets you can eat well for less than Y10 a meal if you have to and want to.

Laundry prices and quality depend on the quality of the hotel but if you're watching your pennies, take wash and wear. My website lists sample laundry prices. Telephone calls from hotels can add up. Take more money than you think you need. It will cost you time and money if your bank has to send you more.

Essential Information & Government Help

If you're worried about civil unrest, floods, travel advisories, or need any help, telephone the **U.S. State Department** in Washington, D.C., *Tel. 202/ 647-5225 or 202/647-3000*, or consult any American consulate abroad (American Citizens' Services).

State Department travel information publications are available online at *http://travel.state.gov*. You can receive copies of information publications by sending a self-addressed, stamped envelope to **Overseas Citizens Services**, *Room 4800, Department of State, Washington, DC 20520-4818*. (Write the name of the requested country or countries on the envelope.) You can also find Consular Information Sheets and Travel Warnings at the 13 regional passport agencies and at U.S. embassies and consulates abroad. The information can also be accessed through an airline or travel agent's computer reservation system.

Canadians should telephone the **Ministry of Foreign Affairs**, *Tel. 800/ 267-6788 or fax-back 800/575-2500 or online at http://www.dfait-maeci.gc.ca*. Other numbers include *Tel. 800/561-8868 and 800/267-8376*). For bulletins: *www.voyage.gc.ca/consular_home-e.htm*. On working abroad, call *613/ 944-4000*. For immunization requirements look up Health Canada: *http:// hwcweb.hwc.ca/hpb/lcdc/osh/travel/index.html*.

For help when abroad, the Canadian Commission Hong Kong website is *http://www.canada.org.hk*. See also Beijing, Chongqing, Guangzhou, and Shanghai. Canadians should call Consular Services, Foreign Affairs, 24 hours a day. If an embassy or consulate is closed, call collect *613/996-8885 or toll free at 800/387-3124, E-mail: sos@dfait-maeci.gc.ca*.

See also websites listed under individual cities throughout this book.

Helpful Websites in English

Note: some of the airline websites below sometimes have special discounts for web visitors only. Addresses do not include punctuation. See also Practical Information under each city.

- **Air Couriers**: *http://www.aircourier.org*. You can only take carry-on luggage but you might be able to get a return fare to Hong Kong for $150 to $495.
- **Business Information**: *http://www.chinavista.com, www.cbw.com* and *http://www.chinaonline.com*
- **Books and periodicals on China**: *www.chinabooks.com*
- **Chinese Business World's Air Travel Guide for China**: *http://www.cbw.com/tourism/airline/airguide.htm*. This can be a little out of date but it will help you anyways.
- **Chinese language courses**: *www.ocrat.com*
- **Cultural Background**: *http://www.chinapage.org/china.html*. This site has a few maps, music, poetry, and history.
- **Foreign Ministry of China**: http://www.fmprc.gov.cn. This official website gives you China's point of view.
- **Journeywoman** (for women looking for traveling companions): *www.journeywoman.com*
- **Lunar-Western Calendar Conversion Chart**: *http://umunhum.stanford.edu/~lee/chicomp/lunar.html*
- **Maps of China and many Chinese cities**: *www.china-travel-guide.com/chinamap2.htm*
- **News** (Chinese sources in English): *www.chinadaily.com.cn, www.peopledaily.com.cn*, and *www.xinhua.org*. See also Chapter 7, Emergencies:how to get news.
- **Oriental-List**: recent travelers, residents in China and travel book writers share their experiences and answer questions. Be prepared for seven or eight items a day. To subscribe, e-mail: *oriental-list@list.xianzai.com*
- **Prices & Discounts**: among the many discount travel websites, try Travelocity at *http://www.travelocity.com* or Orbitz at *http://www.orbitz.com*

China National Tourist Offices

U.S. Website: *www.cnto.org* (English). China Website: *www.cnta.com* or *www.cnta.gov.cn* — English button is in the top right hand corner. This site has maps, lists of travel agents, descriptions of destinations, temperatures, provincial maps, etc. You can get brochures and questions answered from the China National Tourist Offices. Their branches include:

- **New York**, *350 Fifth Avenue, Suite 6413, Empire State Building, New York, NY 10118. Tel. 212/7609700. Fax 212/7608809. E-mail: cntony@aol.com;*
- **Los Angeles**, *333 West Broadway, Suite 201, Glendale, CA91204. Tel. 818/5457507. Fax 818/5457506*

- **Toronto**, *480 University Avenue, Suite 806, Toronto, Ontario, Canada M5G1V2. Tel. 416/599-6636. Toll free: 866/599-6636, Fax 416/599-6382. E-mail: cnto@tourismchina-ca.com*
- **London**, *4 Glentworth St., London, NW1 5PG, UK. Tel. 0044-20-79359787. Fax. 0044-20-74875842*
- **Singapore**, *7 Temasek Boulevard, # 12-02 Suntec Tower One, Singapore 038987. Tel. 0065-3372220. Fax 0065-3380777*
- **Sydney**, *19th Floor, 44 Market Street, Sydney, NSW2000, Australia, Tel. 0061-2-92994057. Fax 0061-2-92901958*
- **Hong Kong,** *Asia Tourism Exchange Center Limited, 13th Floor, Tower A, 14 Xinwenhua Center, Science Museum Road, Tel. 00852-27325801. Fax 00852-27217154*

Customs

It is easier to get customs information before you leave your home country than in China. Find out what you cannot take back. Customs have confiscated dried beef and pork. The US allows no fruit unless canned or dried, but Agriculture Canada allows tropical fruit like fresh mangoes, that are not grown in Canada. Dried medicinal herbs are okay. Certain animal products are forbidden or restricted. For example, both Canada and the US allow no ivory, crocodile, alligator, leopard, or tiger products, as these are endangered.

Many countries allow duty-free coin and stamp collections, antiques (over 100 years old), and 'works of art' (one-of-a kind, not factory-made copies). Be sure to get a certificate of proof when you buy. The red wax seal on an antique is China's proof that the item is allowed out of the country.

Before you leave, register valuable items you will be bringing back with your own Customs, especially if they look new. You will need serial numbers, or you could carry an appraisal report for jewelry with photo, bill of sale, or Customs receipt (if applicable). This is to avoid hassles on your return. You don't want to pay duty on possessions you've had for years.

In the **United States**, you can obtain the booklet *Know Before You Go* from the US Customs Service, Department of the Treasury, Washington, DC 20229. Americans are allowed a duty-free exemption of $400 on accompanied baggage every 30 days after a 48 hours absence. You pay 10% on the next $1000 worth of goods. This includes a maximum of 200 cigarettes (one carton) and one liter (33.8 fl.oz.) of alcohol. Tax rates vary. For example, the tax rate on carvings from Hong Kong is lower than on carvings from China. You can mail gifts worth US$50 or less, but the receiver cannot accept more than one duty-free parcel in one day. You should tell US Customs if you are carrying over $10,000 in cash. Get US Customs travel information at *www.customs.ustreas.gov/travel/travel.htm*.

Canadian Customs now give a duty-free personal exemption for residents of Canada of $750 after seven days absence. Over that, you pay about

15%. This limit might be extended soon so ask before you leave Canada. You may send duty-free gifts from abroad of no more than $60 in value each but they must have a gift card enclosed.

Certificates of Origin, obtained at some Friendship Stores and factories, could mean a much lower duty rate on silk, for example. For more detailed information, contact your local customs office or the InfoCentre, Department of Foreign Affairs and International Trade, *125 Sussex Drive, Ottawa, K1A 0G2, Tel. 800/267-8376, or 613/944-4000*. Ask for the booklet *Bon Voyage But..* You can also call *800/461-9999* for automated information, or call *613/993-0534*.

Be aware that certain items are restricted from entering Canada. If you are considering importing meat or dairy products, plants, weapons, vehicles, exotic animals or products made from their skins or feathers, contact your local Customs Border Services Office of the Canada Customs and Revenue Agency *(http://www.ccra-adrc.gc.ca)* or the Canadian Firearms Centre *(http://www.cfc.gc.ca)* beforehand for guidance.

Health Precautions

Consult a travel clinic for updating your **immunization** record especially tetanus. You are not required to have any immunizations as a requirement for entering China, unless you've been in an African yellow fever area six days prior to your arrival in China. Long-term travelers should ask about Encephalitis B and Hepatitis B.

Some North American travel doctors are recommending immunization against typhoid, tetanus, polio, and Hepatitis A, good protection if you are going to rural areas off the tourist track. A health certificate is required for people going to reside in China for over a year and includes an AIDS test. Get one before you leave home.

In south China, malaria pills are recommended for malarial areas. Most tourists do not have to worry about this, but those going off-the-beaten-track to Hainan Island or areas of China bordering Laos, Burma, and Vietnam should consider it. Consult US travel advisories before you get to China.

Be warned about the poisonous lead level in some glazes. Do not eat or drink regularly out of Chinese ceramics, especially yellows, until you have them checked.

Because of the heavy air pollution in Chinese cities, people who are susceptible to respiratory ailments such as asthma and allergies, should take air filtering masks to wear. They should also head for its marvelous country-side. See Adventure and Eco-tourism.

For more details, see Chapter 7, *Basic Information*.

Passports & Visas

You will, of course, need a **passport** valid for the duration of your trip and probably six months afterwards. Give yourself plenty of time to get a copy of your birth certificate, photos, and sponsors. US applications are on the web at *http://travel.state.gov/passport_services.html* and you can also get forms at your local post office.

You can get a **tourist visa** from any Chinese consulate in five working days. If you're in a hurry, it can be done in less for more money. You can also get a much cheaper visa in one working day (or in less if you pay more) at the Chinese visa office in Hong Kong or at the border in some Chinese cities like Haikou, Sanya, Shenzhen, Zhongshan and Zhuhai. Under some conditions, your tour group of five or more can enter Shanghai and get a visa at either airport. Individual travelers can stay 24 hours without even a transit visa because it has two international airports. A frequent traveler should think about a multiple-entry visa. See my Hong Kong chapter.

For a prepaid group tour of nine or more, travel agents can obtain one visa but you have to enter and leave China together. You should ask for a separate visa if you want to leave on your own.

Transit visas are not necessary if you stay less than 24 hours inside the transit lounge of the airport. You must have a visa for your next stop, and a confirmed plane reservation out. In an emergency, visas can be obtained at some ports in China.

Travelers to Tibet need to be on a prepaid tour even for one person, and travel agents can arrange this. See Chengdu and Lhasa. If you want to book this in China after you get there (cheaper), do not mention Tibet on your visa application form. If you do, the consulate will insist that you get a permit for Tibet before you go.

Hong Kong and Macau also have different requirements.

A Visa Application Form requires one photo, the usual information, and the name of your host unit in China. The host can be CITS, the Chinese agency organizing your trip, the hotel where you have a confirmed reservation, or a friend in China who has invited you.

If you are visiting relatives or friends you will need their name(s), nationality, occupation, place of work, and relationship to you. In case of unexpected delays, ask for a few more days in China than you think you need.

Your visa will admit you to any international airport or seaport in China, and to any of the cities currently open to foreign visitors within the time limit mentioned. Your hotels will take care of the formalities with Public Security. If you're staying with friends, you have to register with Public Security too within 24 hours.

A one-month visa for example is good for one month from the day you enter China, not from the day you get a visa. If need be, travel agents can help you extend your visa after you get to China.

If You Have a Chinese or Hong Kong Passport

If a U.S. or Canadian citizen of Chinese ethnic origin who is also a Chinese or Hong Kong citizen goes to China on a Hong Kong or Chinese passport, he or she is seen by the Chinese government as a Chinese national. The foreign government cannot help in the event of trouble.

Visas are good for most of China. You may need to get an alien travel permit later in China to go off-the-beaten track like border areas. Ask a travel agent there.

To get a visa, you can apply directly yourself to a Chinese consulate, sending your passport, photos and application by pre-paid return courier. You can ask a travel agent to do it for a fee. Line-ups at consulates for visas can be long.

If you arrive in China without a visa, you will probably be sent back on the same plane to where you came from. Your carrier will be fined as it is supposed to check your passport before letting you on the plane. You might be fined as well. However, I have only heard of one person arriving without a visa, and I think our guide at the airport bribed the immigration officer who allowed the culprit entry. But please don't count on it.

You may need visas for other countries in which you will be traveling Get as many visas as you require before you leave home. You should be sightseeing rather than waiting in consulates.

Chinese Missions

The Chinese Embassy in the **US** is located at *2300 Connecticut Avenue, NW, Washington, DC 20008, Tel. 202/265-9809. Fax 202/324-4055. E-mail: webmaster@china-embassy.org. Website: china-embassy.org/eng/.* For areas of Chinese consulates, click on *cnto.org* and then "visa."

To contact consulates:
• *100 West Erie Street, Chicago, IL 60610. Tel. 312/803-0098, Fax 312/803-0122*
• *3417 Montrose Blvd., Houston, TX 77006. Tel. 713/524-4311, Fax 713/524-8466.Website: http://www.chinahouston.org*
• *443 Shatto Place, Los Angeles, CA 90020, Tel. 213/807-8018, Fax 213/380-1961. Website: http://www.chinaconsulatela.org*
• *520 12th Avenue, New York, NY 10036, Tel. 212/502-0271, Fax 212/502-0245. Website: http://www.nyconsulate.prchina.org/eng/index.html*
• *1450 Laguna Street, San Francisco, CA 94115, Tel. 415/928-6931, Fax 415/563-4861. Website: http://consulatesf.webchina.org*

In **Canada**; *Ottawa: 515 St. Patrick Steet, K1N 5H3. Tel. 613/789-3434. Fax 613/7891911. Calgary: 1011 6th Ave. S.W., Suite 100, AB T2P 0W1. Tel. 403/2643322. Fax: 2646656; Toronto: 240 St. George Street, M5R 2P4. Tel:416/9647260. Fax 3246468; Vancouver: 3380 Granville Street, V6H 3K3. Tel. 604/7347492. Fax 604/7370154.*

The embassy's website in Canada is: *www.chinaembassycanada.org*; in the U.K. it's: *http://www.chinese-embassy.org.uk.*

Hotel Reservations

Reservations are recommended during high tourist season, festivals, or trade fairs. Definitely have a hotel booked at least for your first night. Your travel agent or airline can reserve rooms or you can do it yourself on the web or through hotel chains in North America. For example, for the Holiday Inn in Beijing, phone Holiday Inn's toll-free number or the Holiday Inn nearest you. You can also contact your hotels directly in Chinese if it's not a four or five-star hotel. The time in Beijing and the rest of China is on the home page of my website, www.china-travel-guide.com. Hotels should give you a confirmation if asked.

You can also use hotel toll-free numbers to get an idea of prices and specials and then compare these with what travel agents have to offer. Cheaper hotels do not usually accept reservations. If you are traveling prepaid, make sure you are carrying the relevant vouchers and the telephone number of your travel agent in case something goes wrong.

Some of the major cities like Beijing and Shanghai have hotel representatives at the international airport who can tell you if a room is available. You can haggle if you want as they might get commissions for snaring you.

Some travel agents in North America or China have booked blocks of rooms in many Chinese hotels at wholesale rates. These are usually cheaper. Only about two per cent of guests pay the published hotel rates in China. Save your money for something else.

Medical & Travel Insurance

Do not assume that your medical insurance coverage at home will take care of all your medical expenses abroad. It might only cover a percentage. It certainly will not cover "evacuation" on a private plane with medical staff.

If you pay for your travel through some credit cards, you automatically get travel insurance. Do check the terms. Ask about evacuation insurance if you are going off the well-beaten tourist track. **AEA/SOS International** has clinics and doctors in Beijing and other cities around China for this and other emergency medical help. *Tel. (U.S. and Canada) 800/523-8930, Website: www.intsos.com, E-mail: webmaster@intsos.com.*

Check prices and conditions also with **Access America**, *Tel. 800/244-9421; P.O. Box 11188, Richmond, VA 23236-4949.* There is **Blue Cross** at www.bluecross.com; **Ingle Life/Heath**, *Tel. 800/216-3588*, and **Liberty Health Ease** at *www.cover-me.com*. If you pay for medical treatment abroad, make sure you get receipts.

How Should You Go? Package Tour or Solo?

A prepaid group or customized individual tour is the most convenient, but individual travel has become easier, more popular, usually cheaper, and tailored to your own pace. Making arrangements for individual travel can be time-consuming and frustrating.

Prepaid Tours

Just book with a good travel agent and most of your problems are solved. You can choose a set tour with other people (cheaper) or have one custom-made. The fewer people you have, the more expensive the rate per person will be.

If you just want an introduction to China, a general interest tour is ideal. See Chapter 3. Figure out what areas interest you and call a lot of travel agents. If you want to visit schools, factories, or hospitals, take a special-interest or Friendship Association tour. Or make sure schools, factories, or hospitals are included in your tour.

You can customize your tour – five vs four or three star hotels. See Mini-tours below. Most group tours are flexible; you can avoid most of the group activities. However, deviation means more money. If you get sick and spend another night in the same hotel, the hotel probably charges individual not group rates.

Tour groups can be fun if you have the right people. But a tendency does develop to regard the Chinese as 'them' as opposed to 'us.' As soon as group members start joking about the 'natives,' you've crossed the line and become a group tourist. If you are visiting China to meet the people and learn about the country, make an effort to break free. Venture out into the streets alone. Lounge in parks, especially on Sundays. A lot of students are waiting to practice their English on you. You might even be invited to someone's home.

Tour groups tend to get you up and out by 8:30am-9am daily and you might not see your hotel room until 9pm that night. You won't have a chance to relax before dinner. You usually eat breakfast in your hotel but other meals in different restaurants around town, usually close to the last museum or zoo of the day. Organizers try to save money by not driving you back and forth to your hotel.

Questions for Prepaid Tours with Set Itineraries

How many of your desired destinations are offered? How many days will you have in each place? How many people are in the group? How old? Sexes? Will you be asked for tips for guides and drivers in each city? Airport taxes?

Do you have an international guide? National guide? What happens if your plane is canceled or your guide doesn't meet you? Ask about refunds if you are stuck in an airport for a day.

What is the price? Why is it different from another organizer with the same cities and number of days? Usually the price includes visa fee, group transportation (from your home airport or your first point in China?), hotel accommodation (double or single occupancy?), one, two or three meals a day, sightseeing, group transfers, and admission tickets to tourist attractions and cultural events. Will you be traveling with a guide or interpreter? Are the trains soft or hard class?

Price quotes do not usually include passport fees, excess baggage, medical, and other personal expenses. Nor do they include expenses for itinerary changes or prolonged tours 'due to unforeseen circumstances.' Ask about those 'unforeseen circumstances.' These could include plane cancellations, overbooking, missed connections, illness, or accident. Who pays for these inconveniences? Will you be expected to pay on the spot? Ask about health, evacuation, and cancellation insurance. What are the benefits? What language will the guide speak? What refund do you get if the tour is partly canceled? What hotels do you get? (Check the hotels in this book to see if those are what you want.) What happens if the tour operator goes out of business?

On the Yangtze cruise, are shore excursions included in the price?

All tours are subject to changes in itinerary by the Chinese, so don't blame your travel agent entirely. Prices, too, are subject to change.

Cruising to China
Cruise lines include Cunard, EuroLloyd, Pearl Cruises, Princess and Royal Viking. You usually pay extra if you want a guided tour at ports of call. See also Yangtze Gorges.

Mini-packages
Travel agents offer packages that could include only travel tickets, transfers, hotel accommodations, and breakfast. You sightsee on your own or book sightseeing tours locally. It is an ideal compromise for business people and those who want to do their own thing. In some but not all cities, you can join a relatively inexpensive local tour, but times are not necessarily at your convenience.

Independent Traveling
Many foreigners have traveled in China happily and successfully on their own. Some backpackers have loved it, not minding dormitory accommodations and delays. Travelers with bigger budgets have an easier and more comfortable time. Your four or five-star hotel can meet your plane or train if

requested. You can join a group tour or hire a taxi for sightseeing and hire a guide whenever you need one.

On-your-own traveling is not as easy in China as in Europe. If you can't speak Chinese, however, you can get around with this guide book. The Chinese are usually sympathetic and helpful to lost and bewildered foreigners.

Time-Shares

An increasing number of hotels and resorts have signed up with RCI, a time-share outfit, in such cities as Beijing, Guilin, Hangzhou, Kunming, Qingdao, Sanya, Shanghai, Tianjin, Wuhan and Wuxi. Go to *www.RCI.com* for more details.

Special Requests

Chinese travel agents are willing and eager to accommodate you, but they are not always able to.

Put your special request to several travel agents at home and in China. Those at home will have to contact China anyway. The best way to communicate is by fax. E-mail is not always reliable but it is becoming more so. If you call China, it helps to have a Mandarin speaker with you to do the talking.

Scientists can contact the Foreign Affairs Department of the Chinese Academy of Sciences. Mountain climbers should contact the Chinese Mountaineering Association and travel agents. School groups should contact CYTS. Sports teams wanting to play Chinese teams, or individuals wanting a ski package or parachuting should try China International Sports Travel Service. For religious groups, consult the national headquarters of your own church, synagogue or mosque first, before you talk with a travel agent.

If you want to drive your own car into China, contact China Sports Travel in Beijing, China Nature International Travel in Urumqi or CTS in Xi'an.

Overseas Chinese – The "Roots" Route

An Overseas Chinese is anyone with a Chinese surname, face, or the address of a relative and/or an ancestral village in China. There are no special discounts now for Overseas Chinese. CTS is the most experienced agency for Overseas Chinese. They can help find your relatives and tell you what gifts you can take them duty-free.

It is permissible to live with relatives in China or have relatives stay with you in your hotel. You can take part in special camps and seminars offered by the Overseas Chinese Association in some counties in Guangdong province. See Taishan. These are great introductions to China and the area. Courses could be on language, painting, medicine, music, dance - and are in English.

You could write the Overseas Chinese Association or travel agent in your county for information, or try a Chinatown travel agent, a family association, or a county association. You can probably find these in any large Chinatown in America. A Chinese consulate might have information.

Again, if you enter China on a Chinese passport, you are considered Chinese and subject to Chinese laws, not the laws of your country of citizenship.

Before you go, Overseas Chinese should start collecting the names of relatives, particularly of ancestors, born in China. The name of your ancestral village is essential if you want to visit it. Be aware that many villages have changed their names, but in China, you might find an older person who remembers it. Usually you refer only to your father's family. No one cares about maternal lines! The names should help people in your village place you. The welcome is better if they can establish a connection than if they can't. The names, of course, should be written in Chinese.

Take as much documentation as you can: a letter in Chinese from your family association, your father's or grandfather's old passport, and a map of where they lived in the village.

Friendship Associations

These associations the world over can give information on China and some sponsor their own study tours. Some entertain visiting Chinese delegations and students, teach English, collect books in English for China, show Chinese movies, and provide lecturers on China. They are a good introduction to the country. The Cultural Affairs Office at a Chinese mission can usually give addresses:

In the US, contact **USCPFA**, *New York Chapter, 122 West 27th Street, 10th floor, New York, NY 10001-6227. Tel/Fax 212/989-5152. Contact: Irving Zuckerman, 215 Park Row, New York, N.Y. 10038. Tel/Fax 212/267-5358. E-mail: izuckerman@aol.com. For tours, contact Barbara H. Cobb, 496 Ellenwood Drive, Nashville, TN. 37211. Tel. 615/833-9512.*

In Canada, it's the **Federation of Canada-China Friendship Associations**, *1344 Hutchison Avenue, Prince George, B.C., V2M 5J8, Tel/Fax 250/562-1655.*

In England, look up the **Great Britain-China Centre**, *15 Belgrave Square, London, SW1X 8PS, Tel. 44(0)7235-6696, Fax (0)20 7245-6885. E-mail:contact@gbcc.org.uk. Web: www.gbcc.org.uk.*

Business Travel

China's membership in the World Trade Organization will change procedures. Businesspeople should contact the trade or commercial office at a Chinese diplomatic mission, your mission in China, and your government's department of trade. There are also China Trade Councils. These will all probably tell you to contact a Chinese trading corporation, some of whom have representatives in North America. If the Chinese are interested, they will send you an invitation that will give you a visa. The best introduction is to join a trade mission organized by your country. You can also get a tourist visa and investigate business possibilities directly yourself. No one I've negociated with has ever asked to see a business visa.

If you have an organization in China make your travel arrangements, you should tell your host the quality of the hotel you want. It is embarrassing for a host to make changes after you arrive since he or she probably booked through an old school chum.

See also *Business* in Chapter 7.

Scholarly Exchanges and Study Opportunities

In the United States, contact the **Council for International Exchange of Scholars**, *3007 Tilden Street NW, Suite 5L, Washington DC. Website: www.iie.org/cies/*. In Canada, contact a Chinese consulate *(http://www.china-embassy.org/)*. Some North American universities, colleges, states, provinces, and cities organize exchanges.

'Self-supporting' foreign students are accepted at some universities in China. You can apply directly to addresses from the Internet or from the Education Office at a Chinese mission. Academic credits may not be equivalent. Tuition depends on the school and has been about $1600 to $2500 for a Masters program, with living expenses $2.50 to $7 a day. Living conditions may not be comfortable.

Visiting as a Foreign Expert

Specialists and professionals can give lectures or demonstrations to their Chinese counterparts if invited to do so. Don't expect anything more than a 'thank you' and maybe a tax write-off for part of your expenses.

Working in China

Foreign commercial companies offer the highest salaries and usually the best living conditions. Get a list of North American companies with offices in China through the **U.S. or Canada-China Business Council** and contact them before you leave home. The U.S. council's website is: *www.uschina.org/*. The Canada-China Business Council has been advertising for interns. Its website is: *www.ccbc.com*.

Many jobs are advertised in English on websites: *www.zhaopin.com* and *www.chinahr.com*. There's also *www.xianzai.com* in Beijing and Shanghai.

You can find advertisements for jobs in *China Daily* and the *South China Morning Post*. If you're in Hong Kong on a Friday, the Post has a huge section and there's a giveaway distributed in the MTR.

The Canadian Executive Service Organization sends retired Canadian scholars (mainly scientists) and technical experts to China. It aims to transfer

Canadian expertise to businesses, communities, and organizations to help them achieve their goals of economic self-sufficiency.

Hong Kong and China are eager for teachers of English. You can contact the **Chinese Educational Association for International Exchange**, *37 Damucang Hutong, Beijing, or the Foreign Experts Bureau, Friendship Hotel Beijing, 100873 or P.O. Box 300, Beijing, 100086.* For job applications, it could be faster to write directly to the Office of the President or the Foreign Affairs Office of the school where you wish to teach; the Foreign Experts Bureau is primarily a central clearing house. The Bureau is looking for people to work in universities, newspapers, publishing houses, and other cultural institutes.

If you are an experienced teacher, ask around, anyone who speaks English, even a travel agent, a hotel manager, or any college or university. If you speak English and have any idea about teaching, you could ask any hotel or a tourism school if it wants an English teacher or other staff. China has many private schools too, desperate for teachers of English.

Talk with business people about job possibilities. Good English-speaking secretaries are in short supply. But check out work regulations and income tax first. Local hires might be paid Chinese-level salaries, which isn't much.

China hires foreign language teachers on one to two year contracts. The great need is for English language teachers and also teachers of middle-level technology and managerial skills. There have been more than 9000 foreign teachers a year working in China.

Long-term experts usually have at least a Masters and three years' teaching experience. They should receive a contract, transportation and home leave. The stipend ranges from Y1000 to Y1200 a month, not much. Be aware that 30% to 50% of your salary can be taken out of China in foreign currency. Some experts receive free accommodation, medical care, etc. Their salary is frequently ten times that of local teachers, so no complaints, please.

Foreign teachers (not experts) are usually locally hired and do not get the same benefits. Some money-strapped colleges have hired native English-speakers without any teaching qualifications who just drop by. (See Fuzhou). They give only room and board. Some foreigners teach and study part-time. See Beidaihe, Suzhou, and Zhuhai. These short term teaching jobs can let you stay longer and get a deeper experience of the country. I taught English for a month in a hotel, a wonderful experience. Managers and principals are happy to hire on the spot because they don't have to go through the bureaucratic hassles of getting permission to hire someone.

Read *Dear Alice: Letters Home from American Teachers Learning to Live in China* edited by Phyllis L. Thompson and published by the Institute of East Asian Studies, U.C.-Berkeley in 1998. See also *River Town* by Peter Hessler who taught English for two years in 1996.

Short term courses

Many travel agencies, tourism offices and even hotels offer courses in cooking, martial arts, acupuncture, and other Chinese arts, but primarily for groups. Several colleges and universities offer six-to-eight-week Chinese language courses. It's best to start learning before you go to China, and expect polishing from a short course.

Traveling as a Guest

Lucky you. Do be aware that local residents and even government corporations may not know all the attractions you might want to see. One visitor to Shenyang desperately wanted to find the locomotive museum, but local friends had never heard of it. Another guest wasted hours waiting for the host's car. It would have been more efficient to take a taxi.

Tell your hosts what you want to do in advance and what kind of accommodations you would like. Offer to pay. Give them plenty of time to make arrangements. And don't expect them to be as efficient as a travel agency. Delays are inevitable and much time wasted with formalities.

Adopting a Child

This is usually done through agencies based in your home country. In China you are in a tour group with other new parents and tours and hotels are all arranged, babies in tow. There is usually no time to sightsee on your own. U.S. citizens usually pick up a child in one city, and then spend time in Guangzhou at the U.S. consulate there with the red tape.

The best support group is **Families with Children From China** at: *www.fwcc.org/.* This wonderful site is full of information and links to everything you need. It's got up-to-date regulations, descriptions of the cities in China where the children are from, and chapters in many North American cities. At the **U.S. Consulate**, the Adopted Children Immigrant Visa Unit phone is *81888911, Fax 81883000, E-mail: GuangzhouA@state.gov.*

Wheelchair-confined Travelers

Only a few hotels have been set up for people in wheelchairs with wider bathroom doors and bars near toilets. A lot of helpful hands are available, however, and many hotels have ramps. Most of

Your Very Own Customized Tour

If money is no object, you might also be interested in a tour customized only for yourself, your family and your friends. Some travel writers like myself have organized trips for clients for a fee and in some cases accompanied them around China, making sure everything is okay. Write to me via my website: *www.china-travel-guide.com* if you are interested.

these are in top-of-the-line expensive hotels however. If such facilities are crucial to your visit, contact the hotels to make sure a room is available for you. See Yangtze Gorges.

Choosing a Prepaid Tour

You should consult an agent with good contacts in China. In dealing with North American travel agents, consider the following. How long have they been sending people there? How many people did they send last year? If the answer is more than three years, and in the hundreds, you should be okay. The Chinese do their best for agents they know well and trust.

It's best to book everything in advance in high tourist season. The cheapest tours are probably through Chinatown agencies. Surf the web.

You can use any of the experienced agents below. And yes, you might save money organizing your own tour group but it's not easy. The more people you have, the cheaper it is. But there are also a lot of headaches as flight schedules, prices and the people you count on change their plans without warning.

The following agencies have all been in business a long time, especially China Travel Service in the United States and Canada. Most can book Chinese domestic flights, ferry, and train tickets. They can reserve and ticket charter flights between Hong Kong and China. They can reserve hotels with discounted rates in major cities.

These agencies and those listed below can book tours, mini-packages, join-in tours, and special interest tours for individuals or groups. A few can book the trans-Siberian train. All tour agents can probably book international tours like China and Vietnam, or China and Hong Kong. Phone them and compare services and prices.

Prepaid travelers booking through a travel agent usually have to pay the full price of the tour prior to their arrival in China. You may have to pay extra at the end of your trip. If there are to be additional expenses, you are usually

Get It in Writing!

If you are traveling without a guide, and your travel agent at home says you can pick up your plane ticket in China, or that your hotel room has been paid, just be sure you get it in writing. I have gone to CITS in China to pick up tickets and they never heard of me. The tickets were later found under the code number of the tour group I was leading, or my nationality. I have seen guests arguing in hotels because the hotels had no record of payment. The traveler has to pay and then collect refunds from travel agents at home.

consulted during the trip. For example, flights delayed by weather might mean an option of paying for an additional day or cutting out another part of the tour. Many travel agencies cover small additional costs themselves rather than antagonize their clients. On the other hand, you might get some money back. Near the top of the line for group tours is Abercrombie and Kent. Among the big operators is Pacific Delight, which can do both individual travel and groups.

In the US

Abercrombie & Kent, Inc., *1520 Kensington Road, Oak Brook, IL 60523-2141, Tel. 630/954-2944. Toll free: 800/323-7308. Fax 630/954-3324. Web: www.abercrombiekent.com.*

China Focus, *870 Market Street 1215, San Francisco, CA 94102, Tel. 415/788-8660, 800/868-7244, 888/688-1898. E-mail: info@chinafocustravel.com. Web: www.chinafocustravel.com.* Expect four-star hotels.

China Travel Service (USA), Inc. *San Francisco Main Office, 575 Sutter Street, L/F, San Francisco, CA 94102. Tel. 415/ 352-0388 , Fax 415/ 352-0399; Toll-Free: 800/899-8618; E-mail: melody@chinatravelservice.com or info@chinatravelservice.com. Website: www.chinatravelservice.com. Los Angeles Branch Office / USCTS Building, 119 South Atlantic Blvd., Suite 303, Monterey Park, CA 91754. Tel. 626/457-8668. Fax 626/ 457-8955. E-mail:usctsla@aol.com.* For the Guangzhou Export Commodities Fair.

Elderhostel, *11 Avenue de Lafayette, Boston, MA 02111-1746. Tel. 877/ 426-8056. Fax 877/426-2166. Web: www.elderhostel.org. E-mail: registration@elderhostel.org.* In 2002, it is offering approximately 30 programs in China for adults over 55.

GAT China Vacations, *Main Office, 2512-2514 Huntington Drive, San Marino, CA 91108. Tel: 800/877-1565. Local: 626/285-3777. Fax: 888/868-0593. Local: 626/291-2287. E-Mail: info@grand-travel.com. Website: www.GAT@grand-travel.com.* Consolidator for China Southern Airlines.

Hidden Treasure Tours, *162 W. Park Ave 2nd Fl., Long Beach, New York 11561. Tel. 516/670-9232. Fax 516/432-0544. 1-888-889-9906. E-mail: hiddentour@aol.com. Website: www.hiddentreasuretours.com.* Steve Powers organizes Tibet trips led by local staff and Nepal-based western guides.

Intourist USA, *12 South Dixie Highway, Lake Worth, Florida, 33460, Tel. 561/585-5305 or 800/556-5305, Fax 561/582-1353. E-mail: info@intourist-usa.com. Website: www.intourist-usa.com.* For the trans-Siberian railway from Moscow to Beijing.

Pacific Delight Tours, Inc., *205 East 42nd Street, Suite 1908, New York, 10017. Tel. 800/221-7181, Fax 212/818-1780. E-mail:*

pdt@pacificdelighttours.com. Web: www.pacificdelighttours.com. It has sales offices also in Los Angeles, Seattle, Minneapolis and Florida, and one to come in Chicago. In 2001, it sent over 12,000 passengers to China.

In Canada

If the Canadian dollar is low, tours from Canada might be cheaper. Some experienced Canadian travel agencies are:

Sitara International, Inc., *Suite #206 - 8678 Greenall Avenue, Burnaby, B.C., V5J 3M6. Tel. 604/264-8747. Fax 604/264-7774. Toll Free USA & Canada: 1/800/888-7216. E-mail: sitara@sitara.com. Website: www.sitara.com.* Specializes in travel between Pakistan, China, and Central Asia, and has offices in Pakistan.

Asia Adventures and Study Tours, *455 Avenue Road, Suite 300, Toronto, Ontario, M4V 2J2. Tel. 416/322-6508. Fax. 416/322-0541. E-mail: info@asiaadventures.ca. Website: www.asiaadventures.ca.* Ask for Yue Chi. It offers a comprehensive range of adventure, cultural and educational programs that include a Sichuan cooking school, summer programs for children, Silk Road tours, and self-drive safaris from Beijing to Lhasa.

China Travel Service (Canada) Inc., *556 West Broadway, Vancouver, B.C., V5Z 1E9, Tel. 604/872-8787, 800/663-1126. Fax 604/873-2823. E-mail: chinatl@max-net.com.* Ask for Paul Chu.

Conference World Tours, *4141 Yonge Street Suite 402, Toronto, Ontario, M2P 2A8. Tel. 416/221-6411. Fax 416/ 221-5605. Toll-Free 1-800-387-1488 Canada or USA E-Mail conference@vision2000.ca. Website: www.conferencetours.com.* This agency has a luxury train tour on the Silk Road.

Tour East Holidays, *1033 Bay Street, Suite 302, Toronto, M5S 3A5, Tel. 416/929-0888, 800/667-3951. Fax 416/929-8295. E-mail: tour@toureast.com. Web: www.toureast.ca. Also 101-1014 Homer Street, Vancouver, B.C., V6B 2W9, Tel. 604/683-2828, 800/818-1885, Fax 683-3682.* Good flight prices.

Knowledgeable Travel Agents in other Countries

Note: China Travel Service also has branches in Bangkok, Berlin, Frankfurt, Kuala Lumpur, London, Manila, Paris, Seoul, Singapore, Sydney, and Tokyo.

Australia: *Helen Wong's Tours, Level 17, Town Hall House, 456 Kent Street, Sydney, N.S.W.2000, Tel. 2/92677833, 800/252760, Fax 2/ 92677717. E-mail: hwtaus@helenwongstours.com; web: www.helenwongstours.com.*

Kazakhstan: *Central Asia Tourism Corporation, 537, Seyfullina Street, Almaty, 480012, Tel. 7-3272-501070, Fax 3272-501707. E-mail:*

catfvk@online.ru. Contact: Folke and Christina von Knobloch. E-mail: fvk@centralasiatourism.com. Website: www:centralasiatourism.com.

Travel Agents in China

If you want to deal directly with China and save yourself a lot of money, Chinese travel agents are listed under the different cities. The head offices of the main competing travel agencies are listed under Beijing. All travel agencies listed in this book are legally qualified to deal with foreign travelers but the person who answers your telephone call or e-mail might not know very much. The best person might be out-of-town. I suggest you contact two or three of those listed and deal with the one that answers you within 48 hours (except for weekends and holidays.) I would choose one with the best English who anticipates your questions. If the spelling is poor, it means they don't care about fine details. If they answer with just "Andy" or "Bill" and no address, telephone number, and agency name, it also means they are sloppy.

In organizing my own tours, I have dealt with a dozen or so agencies. Most have been reliable. I usually pick an agent in my first Chinese city to book the rest of my flights and even hotels. This could save about $50 a flight for the same flight booked in North America. It could also save you on hotel prices as a travel agent in Xi'an for example would have contracts with hotels in Xi'an for prices below the "walk-in" discounts listed in this book. (You might also want to check prices with hotels directly but be aware of travel agent service fees.) Most travel agents do not yet accept credit card payments, but they do accept bank transfers with U.S. or foreign banks. Many are willing to wait until you arrive to be paid the balance in cash. (They can cancel plane tickets and hotel rooms if you don't show up.)

Usually the best travel agency for English-speaking foreigners is China International Travel Service in each city, but in some cities, China Travel Service or the Overseas Travel Corporation are best. You should be okay with most of the agents listed in my book. When you contact them, tell them where you got their name. And do tell me if you're happy with them or not, so I can tell other readers.

You can also contact all convenient China-bound airlines, get a quote from its major consolidators, and see if your own travel agent can match it. These are agents who buy large groups of tickets at cheaper rates and sell them at cheaper rates. There may be restrictions of various sorts with them.

For individual travelers, can the agent advise you what to do if your guide doesn't meet you at the airport? Would the agent know the prices and quality of cheaper hotels? Does the city have tour groups you can join on the spot? The cost of taxis?

Making Reservations

Book as much of your itinerary as possible beforehand in high season, preferably two months or more in advance. Some sailing dates on the Yangtze have been booked a year in advance. You pay nothing at first to make a reservation and can always cancel later. You can buy flight schedules for all airlines at airports in China and usually free from a Chinese airline abroad. The best website with Chinese schedules is: *www.flychina.com*. *E-mail: info@flychina.com*.

Says Wei Wu of the OTC in Guilin, "Hot lines like Guilin-Shanghai or Beijing have discounted tickets for each flight but obtaining these tickets may not be easy. Night flights are still in the trial period and subject to change without prior notice." Be aware of lower baggage allowances with discounted fares.

If you want one of the cheaper seats, you should check with a Chinese travel agent at least six months in advance.

If you can't get the flight you want, book a later flight and try 'stand-by' after you get there. I was once 16th in line for stand-by out of Shanghai and managed to get on my desired flight, but you never know. If stand-by doesn't work, you still have the flight you booked.

If your trip co-incides with big events like the Olympics, you should try two years in advance.

You can book bus tours from Pakistan, ferries from Japan and Korea, and trains from Europe. As for the trans-Siberian railway, see the Beijing chapter for Monkey Business Infocenter who can handle either direction, You should start asking travel agents about these at least two months in advance.

Getting to China
By Air

Airlines do not fly all routes daily so give your agent a list of stops you want to make before and after China, and how long you want to spend in each place. Suggest several options.

You can fly direct, with one or two stops from many countries to China. You can fly to Beijing and Shanghai from Brussels, Chicago, Los Angeles, New York, Paris, San Francisco, Seattle, Tokyo, Vancouver, etc. There are many flights from Europe and flights to Guangzhou from Ho Chi Minh City, Los Angeles, Melbourne, etc. You can also enter China at Urumqi, Harbin and Kunming.

For people who want to surf the net themselves and try to save money, among the many airlines flying to mainland China westward from North America are: **Air Canada** (*www.aircanada.ca*), **Air China** (*www.airchina.com.cn*, about 11 hours non-stop from Vancouver to Beijing), **China Eastern** (15 hours from Chicago), **China Southern** (*www.et-china.com* and see Guangzhou, Chapter 20), **Japan Airlines** (*www.jal.co.jp via Japan*), **Korean Airlines** (*www.koreanair.com via Seoul*), **Northwest** (*www.nwa.com/*, including non-stop from Detroit), and **United** (*www.ual.com/*). Even more fly to Hong Kong whose flagship airline **Cathay Pacific** has a branch called **Dragonair** that flies to many cities in China. Some of these give specials on their website: *www.cathaypacific.com.*

Simpler is trying *www.travelocity.com*, *www.expedia.com*, *www.flightcentre.ca* (Canada) or *www.flightcenter.com* (U.S.) and click on "For Further Enquiry." It charges no service fee and guarantees the cheapest flights. These three can give you their best deal on any airline.

Ask your agent if the international flights are nonstop. Do you care? Can you sit in a tight economy class seat for 14 hours? (I would suggest you get an aisle seat, or bulk head or emergency exit seat which have a little more leg room and more ease in getting up to stretch. You can also aim for a seat at the back which is more likely to have empty seats you can grab so you can lie down completely flat. If you want to see the movies, ask for that too. Some monitors could be too far away. Some airlines like Cathay Pacific and China Southern have monitors in economy class for every seat.

Is there an extra charge for stopovers? A day in Tokyo to visit your niece? You've always wanted to see Kyoto! Is going via Hong Kong cheaper? Check a few travel agents for packages. Maybe it's better for you via Europe, or Bangkok or Singapore. How about going on to Australia? How about around-the-world fares? How long are the flights? Vancouver to Beijing is 10.5 hours on Air China.

If you want to know schedules and prices of some China domestic flights, try *www.FlyChina.com*. For China Southern, China's largest airline, click on: www.et-china.com. There's also *TravelSky.com* which is only in Chinese. If you're concerned about frequent flyer points ask about those too. China Southern frequent flier miles can be added to Delta Sky Miles in some cases. If you are concerned about air safety, click on *www.faa.gov/apa/traveler.htm*, *www.aviation-safety.net* or *Airsafe.com*.

Finnair flies from New York to Helsinki in a little over seven hours, and then Helsinki to Beijing in about eight. You can break up a long plane trip with a stop there. Or you can take it in one big dose. Northwestern's Detroit-Beijing flight is 14 hours. China Southern flies non-stop Los Angeles to Guangzhou in 15 hours and back in 11 hours. Cathay Pacific has been offering free companion tickets if you pay full fare on first and business class between certain cities and under certain conditions.

Regular charter flights are organized by China Travel Service and China International Travel Service. These are "charters" because of a technicality in aviation regulations. They fly regularly and are okay, but travel agents aside from CTS and CITS abroad cannot usually book them.

Via Central Asia

Travel from Kazakhstan, Kyrgyzstan, and Uzbekistan into China is possible but the rules keep changing. For flights, check with Central Asia Travel in

Almaty. By air, the Kazakh flights are not reliable. Chinese airlines fly between Almaty and Urumqi twice a week and should be fine. Tashkent also has flights twice a week with Urumqi.

Sometimes land borders gets closed unexpectedly for days. A public bus goes between Bishkek and Kashi in summer. Travel agents in Kashi can give you days and prices.

Trains from Almaty leave Kazakhstan at least once a week and arrive in Urumqi about 36 hours later of which 10 hours is spent at the border changing wheels. Central Asia Travel (Almaty) can usually book just about everything.

The Euro-Asia Land Bridge is a railway line that runs from Rotterdam to Lianyungang on China's east coast. There are daily trains from Moscow to Almaty. You enter China from Almaty (Kazakstan) close to Urumqi.

Via Hong Kong

Many travelers enter China through Hong Kong. The train from here to Beijing is comfortable. Buses, ferries and trains go to many places in south China. Travel agents here have a high degree of expertise and many have direct connections with individual tourism officials in China. Hong Kong is also loaded with professional China watchers, China-related banks, and experienced business people who can give advice in English. See Hong Kong, Shenzhen and Guangzhou.

Via Korea

There are flights but also ferries between South Korea or Japan and China. Ports are Qingdao, Weihai and Tianjin. Between Inchon and Tianjin it's a 758 km trip done in about 28 hours. Do not expect a fancy cruise ship. These are cargo/passenger ferries. You can fly from Pyongyong in North Korea to Dalian, Shenyang and Beijing, but you can also cross the Yalu River at Dandong in Liaoning province and then take a train to Beijing.

Via Macau

Macau has an international airport and flight connections with a growing number of Chinese cities among them Chongqing, Fuzhou, Guilin, Haikou, Kunming, Shanghai, Xiamen, and Xian. You can also cross the border on foot or bus. See Macau.

Via Mongolia & Siberia By Train

An international train arrives from Ulan Bator. Contact Monkey Business Information in Beijing.

Via Nepal

You can get Nepalese visas easily at the border or at the airport on arrival for about $30 for 60 days or $50 for a 60-day multiple entry (recommended if you're going to Tibet and back). August is usually the busiest month and should be avoided if possible. The Chinese embassy is open Mondays, Wednesdays and Fridays if a visa is not included in your package tour.

China Southwest Airlines/Air China flies new 757's between Kathmandu and Lhasa. Flights have been pretty reliable and are scheduled on Tuesdays, Thursdays and Saturdays from April first to the end of November and only Tuesdays and Saturdays in winter. For views of Mt. Everest, sit on the left side from Kathmandu.

You can also go by road to Lhasa from Kathmandu, but because of rains between June 15 and September 15, there are treacherous landslides on both sides of the border. Porters on the Nepal side can carry luggage over the slides for about $10-$20 each. They have been known to disappear around corners, so keep up with them. Be prepared to hike several hours yourself in rugged countryside.

From Kathmandu to the border is 114 km (four hours or more). From Zhangmu at the border, travelers switch to landcruisers and buses ordered in advance for a rugged 800 to 900 km to Lhasa. See Tibet and Lhasa for Nepalese travel agents or Hidden Treasure Tours in the U.S. for arrangements.

The most expensive tours usually get the best buses. Although the two governments have signed an agreement allowing buses from each side to cross the border, no scheduled bus service has started yet. From here to Lhasa can take three days if you sightsee. My thanks to Steve Power of Hidden Tours for helping with this information.

Via Pakistan

Recent events in Afghanistan might affect arrangements for you to travel this route. Consult your country's travel advisories.

Pakistan and Chinese airlines both have had flights between Urumqi and Karachi and Islamabad. You can also go by land. Sitara International in Vancouver is the expert on this spectacular route. You can usually get Chinese visas in Islamabad in three working days if all papers are in order.

The Karakorum Highway and border posts at Sust (Pakistan) and Tashkurgan (China) are usually open May 1 to October 31 but the rains in July and early August frequently set off landslides, and snow might block the pass early May and late October.

From Islamabad in Pakistan, you can try to fly to Gilgit (Pakistan). Be prepared for delays especially mid-May to July of one or two days because of weather. You can also try to fly from Islamabad to Skardu with less chance of delay. From here the drive to Gilgit is about five hours.

The alternative is road from Islamabad to Gilgit, a beautiful drive with overnight at Besham (six hours from Islamabad), or at Chilas (nine hours from Islamabad and three hours from Gilgit). It is amazing. Think Himalayas and Pamirs. If you can, you should fly one way and drive one way for the view.

Sitara Travel in Pakistan (see above under Travel Agents & Tour Operators) can help arrange transportation. The weather is most reliable in September and October.

From Gilgit, a public bus leaves about 9am taking about six hours (189 miles) to the border. There are two Government of Pakistan vehicles that take passengers between Sust (Pakistan checkpost) and Tashkurgan/Taxkorgan where the Chinese immigration is done. CITS Kashi can meet you with a vehicle at the border if you want to pay more. Passengers can stay the night at the Pamir Hotel in Taxkorgan. From there to Kashgar it takes six hours on a good 179 km road. If you have the opportunity, stop at Karakuli Lake at the foot of the Muztaghata mountain. There are some yurts. Public mini-buses are available from Taxkorgan but don't budge until full. Individuals have successfully hitchhiked. Women have traveled alone on this route safely, though I wouldn't do it myself.

The altitude at Taxkorgan is about 3200 meters or over 9000 feet, almost the same as Lhasa so read up about altitude sickness. The highest point on the road is over 5000 meters at Khunjerab/Kunjirap Pass. The temperature ranges from -4 C to 30 C in summer.

Besides the scenery, the advantage of this route is its proximity to what used to be Gandhara, the area between today's Peshawar and Taxila in Pakistan. Chinese pilgrims went there in the Tang dynasty to learn about Buddhism. Here are ruins of great monasteries, the influence of Alexander the Great, and superb collections of Greco-Indo art in museums once curated by Rudyard Kipling's father.

Via Southeast Asia

The Vietnam-China border is open and you can take a train to Nanning and depending on the day, onward to Beijing. You should take advantage of being in this remote area of Guangxi to see its ethnic minorities. Tours can be picked up at the border. You can also go by passenger ship from Haiphong in Vietnam to Fangcheng in Guangxi province, 131 miles, and about 10 hours away. See Nanning, Beihai and Kunming.

It is difficult to go into China from the Lao border by land. You can fly into Kunming from Bangkok, Vientiane, and Yangon (Rangoon).

Myanmar (Burma) has now opened border points at Mong La (87 km and five hours by land from Kengtung) and Muse (124 km and four hours drive from Lashio). You must have both Myanmar and China visas. Travel agents can arrange a Myanmar car to the border, and a Chinese car to meet you on the other side. Be prepared to tip border officials. You can also fly to Kengtung.

Via Russia

From Moscow, the Chinese train to Beijing has been leaving Tuesdays and goes through Irkutsk, Ulan Bator, Erlian and Datong, before arriving in Beijing on Mondays. The Russian train has been leaving Saturdays and goes through Irkutsk, Manzhouli, Harbin, Shenyang to Beijing. The routes are the same for both trains until Ulan-Ude near Lake Baikal, but the Russian one continues for 12 hours via Harbin to Beijing.

Moonsky Star Ltd. (Hong Kong, with a sister travel agency called Monkey Business Infocenter in Beijing) can give you current detailed information. It says that there are four- and two-bed sleepers. The Chinese hard-class is very dirty. Take your own food, especially for the Mongolian sector.

You will need visas for most countries on the route. Russian Railways say that the Chinese train is 'irresponsibly' overbooked and 'does not allow any mid-trip interruptions or boardings during May-September.. If you wish to stop enroute, you should plan your trip using local trains..'

It also says that the Chinese trains have downgraded confirmed reservations, allowed too many people into the compartments, and passengers pass the time drinking. Some cars do not have heat in winter. I have heard the same about the Russian trains. US sources say the Chinese soft-class train is better.

Via Taiwan

At press time, there were no ferry services between Taiwan and China. Travelers from Taiwan usually go to China via Hong Kong or Macau. This could change any day.

Border Formalities

Have your passport and entry forms ready for inspection. You may or may be given a Health form to complete. You get these from your plane or look for them upon arrival at Immigration. You have to present your passport, pick up your luggage, and pass through Customs in your first Chinese city. Airports have luggage carts. Give yourself plenty of time between planes. If you are taking in any large duty-free gifts to China necessitating a stamp on a receipt, have that and a completed Customs form ready too.

People with nothing to declare do not have to fill a Customs form. If you declare recorded videotapes upon entry, you may be delayed as Customs officials screen them. If you have any trouble, just say they're for personal use. Chances are, your bags will not be searched.

Changing Money on Arrival

Every airport arrival hall, Bank of China, and every hotel three stars and higher can sell you Chinese currency. Keep your receipts for changing money back before you leave. You are allowed to change back half of what you changed in the first place.

Keep your Baggage Declaration (if any) and your Departure Card in a safe place. You might need them on the way out.

You are allowed duty-free items for your own personal use. Forbidden are fire arms, ammunition and explosives, materials like books and video tapes "detrimental" to China's politics, economy, culture and ethics, poisonous drugs, narcotics and opium, morphia, heroin, etc., diseased animals, plants and their products, unsanitary foodstuffs and Chinese currency over Y6000.

Getting to Your Hotel

If you neglected to make hotel reservations, or otherwise need help, look first to see if there is a CITS branch or hotel representative in the arrival hall. If not, telephone the tourist hotline, CITS, CTS, or one of the hotels listed in this book.

Top hotels have vehicles that can meet you upon arrival if you let them know when and on what you are arriving. In some cities, aggressive touts might compete for your fare and grab your bags. Usually there are cheaper taxis lined up in order outside. Insist on using the meter or settle on a price before you get in. Take down the odometer reading if there's no meter. No taxi should charge more than Y2.50 per kilometer. Consult the distance from the airport to the hotel as listed in this book. Most taxi drivers are honest, but you never know.

There is also an airport bus to the downtown office of the CAAC-affiliated airline from which you can get a taxi. It is cheap.

Now That You've Arrived, Don't Forget...

Keep your passport handy for registering at hotels, buying travel tickets, checking in at most airports, applying for an alien travel permit, and changing money. Carry around a copy of your passport and your visa. Keep the original locked up in a safe deposit box or in a pouch around your neck. You should carry identification at all times. If you are staying in China over three months or there is reason for an evacuation or worried parents, register with your embassy or consulate. If you lose your passport after registering, it's easier to get a new one.

Adjust your watch. All of China is in the same time zone.

Making Connecting Flights

Consult your cabin crew before you arrive, more than one person, as to where to go. At the terminal, look for the information desk. International passengers do have to go through immigration and customs formalities before boarding domestic flights. Usually the international and the domestic terminals are close together, but Shanghai has two international terminals, over an hour from each other.

Leaving China

Some airlines do not require that you reconfirm your flight at least 72 hours before departure. But do ask. You can telephone the airline yourself or your hotel can do it, usually for free. While Air China says you can reconfirm international flights by telephone, my own experience has been different. If you telephone, get a reservation number so you can locate your reservation later.

Make sure your visa has not expired or you will be detained and fined. See Emergencies in the Basic Information chapter.

If your flight is early in the morning, book transport and breakfast the night before. Some airports have restaurants that open about 7am. Be prepared to pay the Y90 airport tax required for all international flights, including those to Hong Kong.

You can buy foreign currency back before or after Customs clearance if you have your foreign exchange receipts. You need to complete a departure form for immigration when you leave China.

Your next big hurdle is Customs in your own country. Have your list of purchases and receipts handy. If you know the rate of duty, list the goods with the highest rate first on your declaration form. Report unaccompanied luggage so they will be exempted too. Show your Certificates of Origin if you have any. The onus of proof that an article is an 'antique' or 'work of art' and therefore free of duty, is on the owner of the goods. A Customs officer might not accept your certificate or receipts. Depending on the country, you probably have the right to appeal any decision.

basic information

Chapter 7

Air & Noise Pollution

You might be affected by polluted air. Recently, the National Environmental Protection Agency said the cities with the cleanest air were Shenzhen, Xiamen, Hefei, Zhuhai, Fuzhou, Nanning, Dalian, Chongqing, Wuhan, Hangzhou, Shanghai, Nanjing and Shenyang, in descending order with Shenzhen the cleanest. The cities with the dirtiest unacceptable air, in order, are Qingdao, Tianjin, Guangzhou, Zhengzhou and Beijing, with Beijing the worst. China Daily publishes a weekly air index of 31 cities. On particularly bad days, Shanghai for one tells its elderly to stay indoors. For the meaning of the air-pollution index, see Beijing.

China is trying to do something about its pollution: no-smoking areas, no coal-burning or polluting factories downtown, and compulsory car washing in some cities. Many cities are building expressways to eliminate congestion and fumes. Traffic from outside is restricted during the day.

For your own sake, make sure you use air-conditioned vehicles and don't be proud, wear a nose mask – even if you're the only one. You might have to start to tour early (like 8am) to avoid the rush hour. You can visit small cities and the countryside instead, which are interesting and have much cleaner air.

Development means a lot of construction noises too, and you should avoid hotels in the process of renovating if you expect to spend time there during the day. You might also notice that some cities have banned the honking of horns.

For China's Air Pollution Index, see Beijing.

Barbers & Hairdressers

The best are in hotels and every hotel seems to have a beauty salon. The quality of work, even in a three-star, is not bad but you might wonder about the hygiene at that level.

Beggars

Yes, there are a few. Use your own discretion. As I have in New York City, I would ask them why they have to beg, and then decide whether to give. Or take them to the closest restaurant and give them a meal. Or ignore. Beggars in China do not look on the verge of starvation, not even the badly deformed.

Bookstores

Stores with a selection of books in English are usually in major hotels (like Beijing's Holiday Inn Lido and Shanghai's Jinjiang Hotel), and Friendship Stores (like Beijing's and Shanghai's). Some department stores have them. The best selection is in **Foreign Languages Book Stores** in Beijing and Shanghai. Don't expect much in smaller cities. Bookstores in hotels should also have the *International Herald Tribune, Asian Wall Street Journal, Time, Newsweek,* and Hong Kong's *South China Morning Post.*

Books in English

To help get immersed in old (and new) China, read **Romance of the Three Kingdoms** while sitting on a cliff at Zhenjiang, overlooking the Yangtze, at the place where the widow of Liu Pei pined for her husband. Read **A Dream of the Red Chamber** while relaxing in the courtyard of one of the reproductions of the setting. Read **Pilgrimage to the West** on a trip along the Silk Road. Translations of these books are cheaper in China, and if you have the time, will add immeasurably to your experiences there. Read **The Wandering Taoist** while sitting on top of Huashan.

A Dream of the Red Chamber (also known as Dream of Red Mansions) paints a vivid and convincing picture of how the rich (and their servants) lived during feudal times. Any Chinese over 35 years of age should know this story, the family's connection with the imperial court, and its decline during the Qing dynasty. The plot might move too slowly for Western readers, who probably will have trouble also remembering the Chinese names. The sexual encounters are mentioned, and some are surprising, but they are not fully described. Attendants dressed as the characters inhabit the Red Chamber reproductions, known also as Daguan Yuan (Grand View Garden) in Beijing and Shanghai.

Business

Trading with China is not like trading with other countries. As one trade official put it, "If you want to play in the Chinese sand pile, you have to play by Chinese rules."

These rules are much too complicated to put into a travel guide. There are lots of books, business guides, and experienced people to give advice. But to get you started: Trading with China is done primarily through foreign trading corporations, a list of which you can obtain from a Chinese mission. Joint ventures are negotiated through the Ministry of Foreign Trade and Economic Cooperation (MOFTEC). An increasing amount of business is now done with private companies.

Do not expect decisions to be made as quickly as elsewhere. You may need two or three visits as an introduction to show the sincerity of your interest. On the other hand, in one factory, the managers dawdled long enough to take me and several of their buddies to lunch at company expense, more a treat for themselves than for me.

Take a pile of your business cards, preferably with a Chinese translation on the flip side. It would also be helpful to take a one-page introduction of your company in Chinese. Exchanging cards with both hands is now part of the ritual when people meet for business. Talk to people in your embassy or government department of foreign trade and commerce. See also Commercial Disputes below.

Business Hours

Office hours are usually 8:30am-4:30 or 5:30pm with lunch 11:30am or 12-1:30 or 2pm. China has a five-day work week. Store hours vary with each city and are usually open 9:30 or 10am until 9:30 or 10pm daily including holidays.

Children - Taking the Kids

I took my five-year-old for a five-week visit, my seven-year-old to visit relatives, and my nine-year-old on a group tour. I even took a reluctant teenager on an eight destination tour. I was glad I did, but then, this depends on the child. A year later, the teenager went back to China on her own with her school to work on a commune!

I did not use a baby sitter because the children accompanied me to evening movies and theatrical performances. They liked the dance dramas, the acrobats, and puppets. The younger children did find the traditional operas boring except for the amazing fighting scenes.

I would not take a child just to be left with a Chinese-speaking baby sitter unless the child understood Chinese. On one trip, at communes and factories, many willing hands kept them amused while grown-ups talked. The children were interested in seeing how things were made. Guilin, with its caves, mountains, and boat trip was ideal. They would love the Shenzhen theme parks.

The Chinese love children and are intrigued by those different from their own. You do have to protect children with blond hair and blue eyes, for instance, from being overly fondled. Tour-bus drivers bought mine popsicles, and pinched cheeks. In restaurants they disappeared with waiters to be shown off to the cooks.

Two of them became sick with bad colds, but doctors took care of them. They were well in a couple of days, missing only one day of the tour. Two lived with relatives. The seven-year-old had a ball learning how to bring up water from an open well, washing his own clothes by hand, and tending a wood fire. It took a while to adjust to the smelly outhouses, but he managed. The neighborhoods where we lived with family were full of other children, and in spite of initial shyness and the language barrier, they made friends. Strangers on the street and in buses would stop and try to talk to them. Barriers of formality melted right away, and I'm not the only one who has gotten a room in an overcrowded hotel because my child was very tired.

Food was a problem. The young ones lived only on scrambled eggs and *cha siu bow* (barbecued pork buns). Hamburgers and milk are now easier to find. Baby food in jars for infants and disposable diapers are in Friendship Stores. Most hotels do not charge for children sharing their parent's room. Most hotels can arrange for babysitters.

Civil Disturbances

If there is any possibility of unrest in China, check with your country's mission for advice. You should let your consulate know where to find you.

Commercial Disputes

In cases of commercial disputes, the authorities have seized the passports of the foreigners involved, especially those of Chinese origin, until the dispute is settled. A commercial dispute could be the non-payment of a hotel bill by your credit card company. Contact your embassy.

Complaints

The China National Tourism Administration is directly under the State Council, China's cabinet. It oversees tourism in China, regulating prices and quality of hotels, restaurants, guides, and some travel agencies. For complaints regarding travel agencies organizing tours from abroad, contact the Quality Supervisory Bureau addresses of the tourism bureau. Travel agents should know the numbers. You might get a refund if warranted. These bureaus have the power to punish or take away licenses. This authority may not work perfectly, but they should help you. Give as many details as you can: venue, date, people and amount of money involved.

Contacting You in an Emergency

Your family has your itinerary. Your travel agent has given them the telephone numbers of your hotels. But no one at your hotel speaks English and your next scheduled trip to American Express' Client Mail isn't for a week.

The best way to contact you in China in an emergency is to phone the State Department in Washington, or Foreign Affairs in Ottawa, for help and advice. See Chapter 6. You can also telephone your country's mission in China. A Chinese-speaking officer can phone the hotel and ask you to phone home. Go through your travel agent, the people who booked your itinerary, or the cruise company of your Yangtze ship. This book also has addresses for ships in Chongqing, Wuhan and Yangtze Gorges.

Your family could put an advertisement in *China Daily* too but this only reaches the main cities.

Electricity

Chinese appliances are 220 volts and have either two-, or more commonly, three-pronged plugs (with straight or slanted prongs). Most hotel bathrooms have transformers for electric razors with North American two-prong plugs. Power outages are not common in hotels three stars and up, many of which have their own generators.

Embassies & Consulates

Foreign embassies are in Beijing; some consulates are in Chengdu, Chongqing, Guangzhou, Kunming, Shanghai, and Shenyang.

Emergencies

Chances are these things won't happen, but just in case, here are some things to do. In case of earthquakes, flood, plane crashes, and other such events reported by the media at home, do contact your friends and family at home to tell them you are all right, that the floods were a thousand km away. They could be bothering your embassy needlessly about your safety.

Credit cards: If lost, telephone your credit card company collect as soon as possible or you'll be charged for any purchases after date of loss. Hopefully, you will have made a photocopy of the number.

Deaths: Someone should contact the relevant embassy, which in turn tries to get in touch with next-of-kin and take charge. The mission can make arrangements for the repatriation of remains. Goods belonging to the deceased and death certificates might be released to next-of-kin only after the bills are paid.

Medical Emergencies

Generally for medical emergencies, taxis are quicker to get than ambulances. In Beijing and some other large cities, however, if you telephone 120 and inform the dispatcher that the patient has had a heart attack, the ambulance should arrive with a defibrillator. 120 is also used for ambulances in many other cities.

For a medical problem while in your hotel, try "Reception," "Assistant Manager," or the attendant on your floor. Some attendants sleep in a room close to the service desk. Many hotels have doctors during the day or on call. As a precaution, always get the room number of your guides.

Facilities for treating emergencies in China are not as sophisticated as in many other countries but Beijing and Shanghai have Western doctors. Do not expect elaborate life-support equipment, or to be up walking the day after a broken hip.

The Chinese do not store O-negative blood in their blood banks because Chinese people do not have it. In case of very serious ailments, contact your country's mission for help and advice. A medical evacuation by air even from nearby Guangzhou to Hong Kong could cost about $25,000. Consider evacuation insurance.

Demonstrations: Don't be afraid of them. They are usually orderly except in Tibet, where demonstrators and bystanders have been shot without warning by police. If a policeman asks you to move on and not take photos, please obey or accept the consequences. During the 1989 democracy demonstrations, foreigners were treated with respect by the students and caution by the military. I don't know of any foreigners hurt.

Earthquakes: The main danger is collapsing buildings. If you can't get outside into the open, away from falling debris, dive under a desk, table, bed, or take shelter in a doorway. As soon as the shaking stops, usually after a few seconds, rush outside by the stairway (not the elevator).

Expired visas: You can get an extension from the Foreign Affairs Department of the Security Police in five working days in any city. If you pay more, you can get it sooner. Travel agents can help you for a fee. See Passports below.

Hostile crowds: The May 1985 soccer riot in Beijing proved that this could happen. Anyone looking like the victorious Hong Kong Chinese were threatened and abused. If you think you're surrounded by hostile people, try smiling. Chances are they're just curious or even jealous. Ignore them or try to make friends. Speak to individuals quietly, in English if you don't know

Chinese. Someone may understand. Above all, act friendly and cool. Shouting obscenities is counterproductive. Call for the police. Apologize if you need to. If someone is drunk, just leave.

Law-breaking: If you are accused of breaking a Chinese law, contact your country's mission. Do not expect the rights that you would have in your own country, like bail, but you might see a lawyer. Minor violations could mean detention and deportation. An American once fell asleep while smoking and set fire to a hotel. Ten people died and he was sentenced to 18 months imprisonment and ordered to pay compensation. Some foreign travelers have wandered into restricted areas and been detained by the police, questioned impolitely, and put on the next bus out. Journalists should get permits before interviewing students and reporting on activities in universities. You might be put in jail and deported — or nothing might happen.

Someone in one of my tour groups took a cloth laundry bag from a hotel. The manager was very officious and accusative, not the least bit friendly any more.

Just don't do anything illegal! China has relations with Interpol. Illegal possession of drugs could mean seven years imprisonment. If in doubt, ask.

How to get news and what to do: U.S. citizens, look for your embassy's telephone numbers and e-mail addresses under Beijing, Chengdu, Guangzhou, Hong Kong, Shanghai, and Shenyang. Canadian citizens, look for yours under Beijing, Chongqing, Hong Kong, and Shanghai. British citizens should contact their Foreign & Commonwealth Office. See Beijing. Citizens of other countries should contact their own embassies.

Let your embassy know where to find you in case of evacuation. During the Tiananmen violence, Canada and the U.S. chartered planes to fly citizens home.

In the event of an emergency, don't skimp on money. Contact a hotel where the staff speak your language and can help you. Talk to your China travel agents.

There are many ways to keep abreast of the news – if you want to do so. Recommended hotels with CNN, the all-news station, are mentioned in my book. Internet services are mentioned under our *Practical Information* section for each city and you can get Yahoo.com or Hotmail.com. Most hotels also provide internet service. Among other websites with up-to-date news are *www.scmp.com, www.nytimes.com, www.latimes.com, torstar.com, www.guardian.co.uk, www.cnn.com,* and *www.news.bbc.co.uk.* Some of these sites, and CNN, could be blocked from time to time but not all of them at the same time.

Many five-star hotels also subscribe to the *International Herald Tribune, South China Morning Post, USA Today, The Straits Times,* and the *Asian Wall Street Journal.* Copies are usually found in Business Centers.

E-mailing friends at home might be your only source of information as your embassy's telephone lines will be busy, and news websites could be inaccessible.

But you must not let an obsession with news at home spoil your trip. If there's something important and you really need to know the news, your guides will probably tell you. And they can help you do something about it.

See also "Photocopies and Addresses" in Chapter 6.

Money problems: If you run out, ask your embassy to cable home for some, or telephone collect. It usually takes five banking days. **Western Union** can transfer US dollars brought to one of its outlets for a 0.5% fee. The sender has to have your passport number. Western Union is not available in every Chinese city yet. It is however in Beijing, Dalian, Hangzhou, Nanjing, Qingdao, Shanghai, Urumqi, and Xi'an. Its hotline in China is *Tel. 10/63184313*.

Borrow if you can from fellow travelers. Your credit card can get you cash advances with a 4% or so service charge, or some cards can get you free check cashing from the Bank of China or American Express. Away from big cities, cash advances might take hours to clear with questions like, "What is your mother-in-law's first name?" Some airlines take credit cards. You can ask your hotel for a cash advance to be paid for with your bill on your credit card. Embassies might give small emergency loans, but very reluctantly.

Any Visa card with a logo can access any of 1,700 ATMs in China. Shanghai alone has 700 for cash withdrawals. American Express offices are in Beijing, Guangzhou, Shanghai and other cities. But they don't always work.

Passports: If lost or stolen, talk to your guide or hotel. Get a certificate from the Public Security Bureau saying it's been lost, and contact your country's mission. This certificate acts as a temporary identification that will get you to a city with your consulate. You should have a photocopy of your passport number. If you are staying in China a long time (US citizens over six months, Canadians over three months), it is always good to register with your country's mission. You will be able to get a new passport a lot easier if yours is lost. Missing passports are so common, CITS has a package that includes two trips to Public Security with a guide and car. You should be able to do it on your own however.

If you are traveling with a guide, your escort might have your passport number. You need a passport to travel in China, leave China, and get a hotel room.

For a new passport, you need evidence of citizenship, like a birth certificate, and photos. Your embassy could give you a temporary passport within one or two hours if you have the proper papers. With this document you can get a Chinese visa so you can leave China.

Losing a passport creates a lot of trouble and additional expense. It could mean staying a couple of extra days or leaving your tour group. Guard yours carefully.

Police: In most cities, the emergency number is 110.

Safe deposit boxes: You'll find these in many hotel rooms, and you should use them. You program them with a code you choose yourself. Just don't wait until the last minute to get your valuables out in case you can't get the box open. Usually one manager in the hotel has the ability to open them and it could take time to find him.

Theft: Pickpockets operate even in daytime. Do not leave purses or briefcases unattended. Hotels have safe deposit boxes. Cheaper hotels have more chance of theft. Always use the peephole in your hotel room door before opening it to strangers. If in doubt, phone Reception. If something of yours is missing from your room, notify the management. If you need a police report so you can claim insurance, go to the Public Security Bureau. Recent travelers in Xian found it took them 3.5 hours to register the loss of a walkman.

Traffic accidents: If your car accidentally injures anyone, do what you should in your own country. Attend to the injured. Otherwise, stay where you are. Do not get involved in arguments. Wait for the police to arrive. The police will take statements, and if you are found to be in any way responsible as the driver or even as a passenger (were you distracting the driver?), you may be liable for a fine or payment for damages. The fine would remunerate the family of the injured, or deceased for the rest of his productive years. There is a standard formula. If the accident is serious, contact your country's mission.

Travelers checks: If lost, take your receipts to the Bank of China. For American Express, contact their offices in China. It has courier refunds.

Typhoons: This Cantonese word meaning big wind denotes a hurricane or tropical cyclone. These may hit China anywhere along its east coast from April to November. They usually last for a maximum of three days and you should stay inside substantial buildings on high ground with bottled water to drink and some food. The danger is falling debris, strong winds, rain and floods. Airports will probably be closed. Typhoon Signal One is a warning, and Ten is a direct hit.

Endangered Species

China and many other countries are parties to the Convention on International Trade in Endangered Species of Wild Fauna and Flora (CITES). Any species or products of a species on its lists could be seized by the Customs Department of the signatories, unless you have a permit. Get details from your government wildlife service or Customs.

Locally, however, Chinese officials are relaxed about restricting the sale and eating of some endangered or threatened species, like the giant salamander. Coats of spotted cats have been found for sale in Friendship Stores. But China has executed the killers of pandas.

The problem is knowing what is or is not on the list, and what is fake. When in doubt, don't eat or buy products made from any wild animals, especially spotted cats, alligators, and birds. But some deer, game, birds, bears, and snakes for example, are grown commercially and can be eaten.

Among the other Chinese species listed by the Convention are: Himalayan argali, Tibetan brown bear, golden cat, dhole (wild dog), gibbons, Przewalski's horse, langur, macaque, and wild yak. Among the birds are the relict gull, crested ibis, and some varieties of cranes, storks, pheasant, and egrets. Avoid parts of elephants, crocodiles, tortoises, and marine turtles. You will need a permit to export live specimens of all parrots, monkeys, cats (except domestic), hawks, eagles, falcons, tortoises, boas, pythons, iguanas, and some song birds, cobras, lizards, fish, butterflies, corals and mollusks. Also all orchids and all cacti and many other flora are protected.

There are rules about traveling with exotic pets, and permits must be obtained prior to departure. Contact the **U.S. Federal Wildlife Permit Office**, *Tel. 703/358-2104*, or the **Canadian Wildlife Service**, *Tel. 819/997-1840*, if you have any questions.

The authority allowed to issue CITES permits in China is **The People's Republic of China Endangered Species of Wild Fauna and Flora Import and Export Administrative Office**, *Ministry of Forestry, Hepingli, P.O. Box 100714, Beijing, Tel. 64214180 or 64229944*. Branches are also in Chengdu, Fuzhou, Guangzhou, Shanghai, Tianjin, and Hong Kong.

Gardens & Parks

Relaxing in a Chinese garden is different from rushing through on a guided tour. Go back to one you especially like and just sit and absorb. A Chinese garden is not just a park or something attached to a building. It is an art form, the world in miniature, with mountains, water, plants, and buildings – a three-dimensional Chinese painting you can enter to try to experience infinity.

Gardens were built for a leisurely lifestyle in which poetry, philosophical contemplation, and the beauty of nature were of the utmost importance. Imagine living here! The ugly world of poverty and injustice was kept outside the high walls.

Take your time exploring. Look at the integration of the buildings with nature, the pinpointing of places of particular beauty by unusually-shaped windows and moon gates. Absorb the tranquillity of the water. Look at the reflections. Think of poetry. The meaning of life. A garden takes time – infinite time.

Gambling

Gambling has been illegal here, but it's gradually coming back to the mainland. There have been state lotteries for decades. In the last few years, horseraces have started again, at first with prizes like cartons of cigarettes, but lately, with real cash. Casinos are planned. Hong Kong has had its Jockey Club for over 100 years. Macau is becoming more like Las Vegas. But China is not the place for gamblers.

Gifts

Never give a pet dog as a gift. In Beijing, registering one costs Y5,000 for the first year, and Y2,000 each subsequent year. It might end up in the stewpot. See also Weddings below, and Hospitality, and What to Bring.

Glossary of Terms & Abbreviations

An asterisk throughout this book (*) indicates that a site is genuine and under the protection of the national government.

arhats - Buddhists who have attained Nirvana.

bodhisattvas - Buddhist saints who attained Nirvana but returned to help others.

CAAC - formerly China's only airline. Now it oversees all Chinese airlines. It is used here collectively for former CAAC regional airlines.

cadre - in Chinese *kanpu*, meaning core element. Any person who plays a leadership role in the Party.

CITS - China International Travel Service.

CTS - China Travel Service.

dagoba - similar to an Indian stupa, a bell-shaped tower under which is buried a Buddhist relic or the ashes of a monk.

feng-shui - also known as geomancy. It is the placing of graves, dwellings, doors and furniture in harmony with the forces of nature.

Food Street - term usually used for Chinese fast food or snack restaurant.

guanxi - connections

HK - Hong Kong

JV - joint venture; a business arrangement involving several parties. This is most frequently used in international ventures.

lohan - the Chinese word for arhat, or Buddhist saint

Manchu - the group from northeast China who ruled China under the dynasty name Qing.

Mongol - the group from north China who ruled China under the dynasty name Yuan.

neolithic - pertaining to the Stone-Age period in which man developed pottery, weaving, and agriculture, and worked with polished stone and metal tools.

penjing - the art of growing miniature trees and plants. Similar to Japanese bonsai.

PLA – People's Liberation Army.

pinyin - the official system of romanizing the Chinese language.

pusa - the Chinese word for bodhisattva or Buddhist saint, who is on a higher level than lohan.

qigong - Chinese yoga. Health and healing through breathing exercises, massage, and magnetism.

RMB - ren min bi: peoples' money, one of the terms used to refer to Chinese currency.

stele - a large stone tablet used to commemorate an event, a life, or an important piece of writing.

taiji or **taichi** - Chinese shadow boxing.

Wade-Giles - the most commonly used of the old systems of romanizing the Chinese language.

WC - water closet. Toilet.

wok - a large, round pan for cooking.

work unit - every salaried worker belongs to one of these.

X - telephone extension.

Guides

Guides have to pass an examination. Training is on the job, usually learned by accompanying an experienced guide for several months. But some agencies have been so short-handed that guides with little English and no training have been used. The Department of Education is responsible for staff training, and prospective guides should spend four years learning a language, Chinese history, geography, and art history. Guides must pass an exam before they can wear an official badge with their photo.

If you are on a group tour of several cities, you might get a national guide who stays with you and makes sure that you get your planes and your luggage, and all goes smoothly. At each city you also get a local guide and, at some attractions, an on-the-spot guide.

For most visitors, your Chinese escorts will be the only Chinese people you can get to know well. Ask them lots of questions about life in China. Guides are open about discussing their salaries. Some might tell you they get no salaries and depend on tips. It could be true.

Please be patient when a guide is speaking English. If it is painful to listen to, ask for another guide. If you can't get a better one, you have to decide if the poor guide you have is better than no guide at all.

Confusion over numbers is a common translation problem. The Chinese think in terms of ten thousands rather than thousands. Do not mistake sixteen for sixty or seventeen for seventy. Ask your guide to write down important figures for you. When you are using an interpreter, speak slowly and simply, preferably one sentence at a time.

Remember that guides are not scholars. Their knowledge of traditional Chinese culture is frequently limited to memorizing a set spiel.

Don't Be at the Mercy of Your Local Guide

It is very important to take a list of what you want to do and see. Usually your itinerary is set but if there's something important you must do, you might be able to work it in on your own. Sometimes, the national guide or escort, is available to help.

If you joined a tour to see the Terracotta Warriors and the local guide is hurrying you through, say no, you want to spend more time there.

If you don't like your guide, ask for another.

Guides do not usually eat with you. At mealtimes, you can find them at a staff table. They might stay in your hotel overnight. It is good to know where they can be reached, especially if you can't speak Chinese.

If any of them greets you with "It's my birthday today but I wanted to help you out so I came" or some such, don't believe it.

Do be aware that some guides have to take you shopping, even if you don't want to. China's travel agencies have been hit hard by competition. Because they tend to book tours six months to a year in advance, their profit margins get shrunk by inflation by the time the groups arrive with payment. In order to break even, they have been taking a share of the tips given to guides and drivers, making contracts with tourist stores, and taking a percentage of sales. They may have to take their groups to restaurants of poorer quality. Talk it over with your travel agent at home or head for upmarket tours.

One guide broke into tears and said she would lose her job if she didn't take our group to a particular factory! As a tour escort, I've even thought of paying money to the guide not to take us to a factory. But that solution is ridiculous. With one group, the national guide tried to explain the situation to the group, and offered us other goodies to entice us to go to the factory. We got unscheduled stops in return. See also Tourism Realities below.

Health & Medical Concerns

China is among the healthiest and cleanest countries in Asia but there have been reports of typhoid, malaria, plague, and rabies, usually in isolated rural areas far off the tourist routes. (A few cases of rabies have shown up in Shanghai however.) Venereal diseases are back, and like elsewhere, HIV positives are growing in number. One hears occasionally of encephalitis, hepatitis, cholera, and intestinal parasites. Avoid wading in lakes and rivers in central China's Yangtze River area because of schistosomiasis.

You can find out about these and malaria areas from the World Health Organization or your travel clinic. Malaria only occurs in Hainan and the tropical parts of Yunnan province. It is spread by mosquitos, usually after dark. Use the net above your bed, or ask for one. You should use mosquito repellents, and wear long sleeves and pants when you go out at night. Check for malaria if you have flu-like symptoms within a year afterwards.

Chinese medical facilities are good for common ailments. Many Overseas Chinese go to China for acupuncture, qigong, and even western medical treatment. If you are sick, you will probably be given a choice of western or traditional Chinese medicine, or both. Chinese herbal medicines are frequently effective, but my son had to be bribed with lots of candy to drink his herbal tea, because it tasted so awful.

Outside of a few clinics in big cities, Chinese medical facilities might look grubbier than those in the West. A consultation at a hotel clinic is usually cheap or free, with medicines extra. Usually these doctors can handle most simple ailiments.

If you complain about your health too much, you might get a doctor even if you don't request one. Most tour organizers state emphatically that tours to China are rugged. They are not for invalids or people with respiratory or heart conditions because of the climbing, the dust and air pollution. The Chinese are especially nice to older people, but older or frail people should take precautions.

Some North American prescriptions and western doctors are available at international clinics in Beijing, Nanjing, and Shanghai and other cities. These are expensive if you have no insurance. Some Chinese pharmacies might have western patent medicines. But don't count on it.

If you are hospitalized, you might have to take your own mug, plate, towel, soap, and a friend. The staff and other patients may not speak English. Standards are not the same as in America. In one of the best hospitals in Beijing, beds were only changed once a week.

Remember, a prepaid group tour is usually strenuous with a packed schedule, unless the whole group agrees to a slower pace. Most hotels but not all restaurants have elevators. Things can be easier for pay-as-you-go individual travelers who can do things at their own speed. If you're not in good health, don't travel there.

Chinese hospitals are adequate, and some doctors have western training and excellent western standards especially in Beijing and Shanghai. Most facilities are at least 30 years behind what you're used to.

Holidays, Fairs, & Festivals

These are the official Chinese holidays:

January 1	(offices closed for five days plus weekends)
Spring Festival/New Year	the date depends on the lunar calendar around the end of January or early February (offices closed for five days plus weekends)

May 1	Labor Day (offices closed for five days plus weekends)
October 1-2	National Day, celebrating the founding of the PRC in 1949

In addition, the following are celebrated with special programs, but offices and schools are open:

March 8	International Working Women's Day
March 12	Tree-planting day, South China
April (first Sunday)	Tree-planting day, North China
May 4	Youth Day (May 4th Movement)
June 1	Children's Day
July 1	Founding Day of The Communist Party of China
August 1	Founding Day of the Peoples' Liberation Army
September 10	Teachers Day
September 27	World Tourism Day; celebrated by different cities in turn.

To calculate approximate lunar dates on the western calendar, see Lunar Calendar below.

The Chinese also celebrate several other traditional holidays. The **Lantern Festival** starts the last day of the Spring Festival. The **Dragon Boat races** commemorate the untimely death of an upright official. (See Zigui and Yueyang.) The **Mid-Autumn Festival** celebrates the most beautiful full moon of the year.

Check with travel agents about the dates of festivals around the time of your visit like Weifang (for the kite festival), Kunming (for the Water-splashing Festival and Third Moon Market), and Guiyang for festivals of the nationalities. Be aware that the dates for some festivals might not be decided until the last minute, especially in Tibet. On the other hand, festivals might be canceled without much warning. See also my website for some festival dates.

Some festivals are just an excuse to sell something, but most are colorful and exotic. Bring lots of film. People dress in their best. Many festivals are punctuated with fireworks, dragon dances, competitions, courtship rituals, parades, pageants, thousands of dancing school children, and special banquets. Some are genuine folk festivals, religious celebrations, and horse and camel markets and, as such, are not organized for tourists. Arrangements for these should improve with experience and time but tourism might ruin the spontaneity.

Some festivals are so well organized, tourists travel with police escorts quickly from place to place, without a chance to stop and take photographs.

Do book a tour for a festival with a travel agency because festivals attract tens of thousands of people. As one of the crowd, you won't see much unless you're well over six feet tall. If a travel agency has organized something, you should be able to get a good seat and at least a place to sleep.

Information for Tourists

Beijing, Guangzhou and Shanghai have tourist handouts and maps distributed in hotels, bars and restaurants frequented by foreigners. See Practical Information under those cities. Several cities and provinces and regions have tourist offices and travel agents where free literature is available. Addresses are also in this book.

Consider your hotel your friend. The better quality the hotel, the more information it can give you. Hotels, four-stars and up, are usually the best sources. Try assistant managers, concierges, business centers, or public relations. Some hotels organize their own tours. Hotel telephone operators and business centers can usually find telephone numbers for you. Many hotels give out free maps. Ask them to write destinations for you in Chinese so you can go where you want.

North American Sales Managers of travel agencies usually speak English. Branches in hotels only want to sell tours and clerks might not speak it.

China has been producing a large number of maps and guidebooks in English. You can get some for free from China Tourist Offices. They are very detailed. Jinan's, for example, shows Taishan Mountain and diagrams of the Confucian Family Mansion and Confucian temple. Many maps list major hotels, tourist attractions, restaurants, stores, and important telephone numbers. Information desks have opened at some airports.

Many tourist attractions have inexpensive, knowledgeable on-site human guides paid by the hour. A few speak English. Some tourist attractions also have unofficial freelance guides, who may know very little and speak poor English. Test their knowledge first and decide on a price beforehand. Try Y20-Y30 an hour for your group, not per person. .

Some diplomatic missions have libraries with books about China. The US consulates have current travel advisories with up-to-date information on travel risks. Consulates should also have important addresses like those of doctors and pharmacies.

Fellow travelers are great. Most love to share their experiences. They can tell you what was worthwhile to visit and what was not. Don't be shy about asking.

Foreign residents are also great. If you invite foreign students and experts to dinner, they should be able to give you a lot of good tips, such as where you can buy cheap name brands, and a good tailor. Contact these people at the expat hangouts listed in major cities.

Languages of China

In Shanghai they speak Shanghainese; in Shantou, Hainan, and Taishan, they speak dialects of Cantonese; in Fujian, they speak Fukienese. Most of the

55 national minorities have their own distinctive languages or dialects. But the whole country knows putonghua or Mandarin, based on Beijing pronunciation. Many of the older officials speak Russian. Younger ones might speak English. A few people speak French.

Chinese is not all that hard to understand. Listen carefully as it is spoken because tones are very important and a wrong tone could change the meaning of a word. Some words recur frequently. Ask what these mean. You probably know some Chinese already. Shanghai means above the sea – Shang is above. When you get to Beijing, you will hear about Beihai Park, North Sea Park. Hai again is sea. As for Bei, also found in Beijing, it means north. Beijing is Northern Capital. Jing is the same jing as in Nanjing, Southern Capital.

Other words that you will probably encounter:

ang = nunnery
binguan = guesthouse
can guan = restaurant
si = temple
da lu = avenue
dong = east
fan dian = hotel or restaurant
ge = small pavilion
guan = pass
he = river
hu = lake
jiang = river
jie = street
ling = tomb
lou = multi-storied pavilion big enough for people to live in
lu = road
men = gate
miao = temple, usually ancestral or Confucian
quan = spring (of water)
sha = sand
shan = mountain
si = temple
ta = pagoda
tang = temple
ting = tiny pavilion
xi = west
xian = county
yuan = garden
zhong = middle or central
zhou = city state (smaller than a province; larger than a city)

Phonetic Guide to Chinese

To pronounce Chinese letters, learn the following phonetic alphabet showing pronunciation with approximate English equivalents. Letters in the Wade-Giles system are in parentheses. The following is in putonghua:

a (a), a vowel, as in far

b (p), a consonant, as in be

c (ts), a consonant, as in ts in its

ch (ch), a consonant, as in ch in church, strongly aspirated

d (t), a consonant, as in do

e (e), a vowel, as er in her, the r being silent; but ie, a diphthong, as in yes and ei, a diphthong, as in way

f (f), a consonant, as in foo

g (k), a consonant, as in go

h (h), a consonant, as in her, strongly aspirated

i (i), a vowel, two pronunciations

  1) as in eat

  2) as in sir in syllables with the consonants c, ch, r, s, sh, z and zh

j (ch), a consonant, as in jeep

k (k), a consonant, as in kind, strongly aspirated

l (l), a consonant, as in land

m (m), a consonant, as in me

n (n), a consonant, as in no

o (o), a vowel, as in aw in law

p (p), a consonant, as in par, strongly aspirated

q (ch), a consonant, as ch in cheek

r (j), a consonant pronounced as r but not rolled, or like z in azure

s (s, ss, sz), a consonant, as in sister; and sh (sh), a consonant, as sh in shore

t (t), a consonant, as in top, strongly aspirated

u (u), a vowel, as in too, also as in the French u in tu or the German umlauted u in Muenchen

v (v), is used only to produce foreign and national minority words, and local dialects

w (w), used as a semi-vowel in syllables beginning with u when not preceded by consonants, pronounced as in want

x (hs), a consonant, as sh in she

y used as a semi-vowel in syllables beginning with i or u when not preceded by consonants, pronounced as in yet

z (ts, tz), a consonant, as in suds and zh (ch), a consonant, as j in jump

Laundry

Most hotels three-stars and above will do your laundry and dry cleaning if you get it to them by 8am. It should be done the same day by 6pm. Many also have express service. Check my website: www.china-travel-guide.com for laundry prices.

Learn About China

To get the most out of your trip, read before you go. There is a dizzying list of good books on China. The more you know, the more you'll learn and enjoy. A statue may be striking, but it is more meaningful if you know it's the 'warrior woman,' made famous in American literature by Maxine Hong Kingston. A building in a park in Lhasa becomes the movie theater built by Heinrich Harrer where the German refugee showed the young Dalai Lama his first movies. Many books are listed with individual cities throughout this guide.

Learn Some Chinese

It is best to learn Mandarin which is understood all over China. But your friends or relatives could speak a local dialect in their home. They should however understand Mandarin.

The same Chinese characters are understood throughout China. The characters used today have been simplified since 1950. Make sure that your teacher gives you the new script and the pinyin romanization.

The level of English is improving daily, but is still poor. Take a phrase book. I don't speak much Chinese and sometimes travel alone and have a good time even without an interpreter. The Chinese try very hard to understand attempts to communicate. Draw pictures and try charades. Make friends with potential interpreters. And remember the more you try to speak Chinese, the more friends you'll make, and the more you'll enjoy China. If you can, ask someone to teach you numbers because you need to hear the tones. Reading numbers will help in museums. You only have to learn ten; the rest are combinations. When someone asks you to help with English, ask for help with your Chinese.

Some key phrases are:

hello!	*ni hao?*
how are you?	*ni hao?*
goodbye	*zai jian*
thank you	*xie xie*
I'm sorry	*dui bu qi*
how much?	*duo shao qian?*
good	*hao*
no good	*bu hao*
restaurant	*canting, fandian*
hotel	*binguan, fandian, dajiudian*

toilet	*cesuo*
east	*dong*
south	*nan*
west	*xi*
north	*bei*
middle	*zhong*
street	*jie*
avenue	*dajie*

Leaving Luggage

How do you cope with purchases in China? Is there an alternative to lugging them around the country and paying excess baggage?

This is no problem if you are going to be in the same city twice. Leave purchases with friends, hotels, or airport baggage checkrooms to be picked up later. If you did a lot of shopping in Shanghai and are leaving from Guangzhou in a week, one possibility is sending a package EMS (Express Mail Service) from a post office or DHL courier to your hotel in Guangzhou. It should arrive on time. You can also mail small packages home. It just takes a lot more time. See Postal Service below.

Looking Up Chinese Citizens

Yes, you can visit friends and relatives in China, even while on a group tour or business trip. Give yourself at least 30 days for an answer by mail. Ask for their telephone and fax numbers so you can contact them when you arrive. Chinese friends and relatives should also be able to take time off with pay to visit and even sightsee with you. Inform guides if you want to take time off from the planned schedule to go off with them. Local Chinese can go to your hotel without any problem except after 11pm.

Some local people may feel uneasy about entering a hotel, particularly a fancy one. Many are glad to see inside and brag to their friends that they ate there or at least had a photograph taken inside. If they are reluctant, you could arrange to meet in a restaurant, a park, or their home. You could take them on sightseeing trips with your tour group (for a fee). This will give you time to visit without missing the attractions.

Your chances of going to the home of a friend will depend on the political climate at the time. It could also depend on how embarrassed some Chinese are about the modesty of their lodgings or whether they can afford a taxi or elaborate meal for you. So do not insist if local Chinese friends hesitate. Doctors make less than $100 a month.

Overseas Chinese have a freer time talking with Chinese citizens. Chinese people generally are not open to discussing their deepest feelings, problems or sex life. It took six months of living together before one Chinese roommate confided to me how unhappy she was about her parents.

China does go through occasional xenophobic periods; your Chinese friends might get into difficulty if they meet you. Immediately after the 1989 Tiananmen troubles, many Chinese intellectuals were fearful of contacting foreign friends. And in 2002, e-mail was being monitored.

Lunar Calendar

In the Chinese lunar calendar, the year consists of 12 months of 29 or 30 days each. Every three or so years, an extra month is added. The year starts on the second new moon following the winter solstice, which could be any time between January 21 and February 20 on the western calendar. In 2002, it's February 12; in 2003, it's February 1; and in 2004, it's January 22. To calculate approximate lunar dates on the western calendar, click on web: *www.umunhum.stanford.edu/~lee/chicomp/lunar.html.*

Marriage

It could take about one month but it is possible for a foreigner to marry a Chinese citizen. Permission has to be given by the work unit of the Chinese spouse and in some cases compensation paid before permission is granted to leave the country. The government might want to be repaid for education in return for a contracted number of years of work. Consult your country's mission about the implications.

Money & Banking

Major credit cards are accepted at top hotels, many of the medium-priced hotels in big cities, some top restaurants, and many tourist stores. American Express seems to be the most useful, with its free emergency check-cashing service and its ability to pay for Chinese airplane tickets. But Visa can access more ATMs and seems to be accepted in more places. You can buy airplane tickets with a credit card from only a few foreign airlines, like Dragonair, Air Canada, Finnair, JAL, Northwest, United, and Lufthansa. With an American Express card, you can purchase travelers checks at the Bank of China.

Be aware that:

• Counterfeit bank notes have been circulating. Money exchanged at hotels and banks are not usually a problem, but money given as change has been. Counterfeits have been as small as Y10 notes. To detect them, hold bills up to the light. You should be able to see watermarks, pictures unseen when lighted from the top. Always carry lots of small change to avoid getting change.

• Cash advances cost about 4% and could take a few minutes or hours to get. You might be able to convince your hotel to charge a cash advance as well as your hotel expenses to your credit card.

- Personal checks are not generally accepted, but some can be cashed at the Bank of China with some credit cards. You could also try your embassy or hotel.
- It takes five banking days to cable money to China, assuming everyone knows his job and has your passport number.
- Payment can also be made to some travel agencies through bank transfers.
- Cash brings a slightly lower foreign exchange rate than travelers checks.
- Credit card fraud is common. Always be aware of where your card is. Make sure only one impression is made. Never leave a card in the hotel lobby's safe deposit box. Always ask for the card's impression back, the one made when you checked into the hotel as a deposit.

The Hong Kong Bank, Royal Bank of Canada, and Bank of America have branches in China but not always for retail business. This is changing, so check with your bank before you go. Most foreign bank branches are in Shanghai or Shenzhen.

Foreign Currencies & Exchanging Money

In early 2002, the US dollar was worth about 8.28 Chinese yuan, the Canadian 5.2 yuan, and the Hong Kong dollar 1.06 yuan. The US dollar was worth $7.8 Hong Kong, and $4.9 Canadian. My website has a link to a currency converter: *www.china-travel-guide.com*.

It is best to take US dollars in cash but I have never had problems with Canadian travelers checks. Among the foreign travelers checks also accepted are: Australian, Austrian, Belgian, British, Danish, French, German, Hong Kong, Japanese, Malaysian, Dutch, Norwegian, Singaporean, Swedish, and Swiss.

You can change money at border points, government tourist stores, the Bank of China, and major hotels. You can buy back 50% of the foreign currency you originally sold if you can present your exchange receipts.

Before you go to isolated places like Xigaze, Jing Hong and Kaili, ask about money changing. Frequently, this is only done there in banks, not open on Sundays, early mornings, or evenings. Get enough changed before you go. Some four- and five-star hotels in big cities can change money almost 24 hours a day. A small service charge is added every time you exchange money both in hotels and at the bank. There's no big difference in rates between the two. You will probably need your passport number or hotel room number to change money at the hotels. Clerks sometimes accept a photocopy.

In Guangdong province near the Hong Kong border, Hong Kong cash has been accepted in stores and by street peddlers. However, using foreign currency is illegal. Local Chinese value Hong Kong and US dollars because of inflation and because some people are going abroad and need it. Peddlers everywhere, even in far-off Tibet, accept US dollars in cash eagerly.

Local currency is called *renminbi* (RMB) – peoples' money. The Chinese dollar, known as the *yuan* (or *kuai*) equals 10 *jiao* or 100 *fen*. Yuan notes are in denominations of 100, 50, 20, 10, 5, 2, and 1. The smaller jiao notes are 5, 2, and 1. The coins are 5, 2, and 1 fen, and Y1.

Although prices are quoted in foreign currencies, you must pay for tourist hotels in Chinese currency. See also Hong Kong and Macau.

Museums

China has recently opened some very exciting museums: you must not miss the Shanghai Museum, the Shanghai History Museum, and the Museum of Ancient Chinese Sex Culture. Titles are in English and the displays are great. Provincial museums in Zhengzhou and Xi'an are also exceptional. So is the Shu Museum in Chengdu and the Han museum in Guangzhou. Most other museums however can be deadly dull if you don't do it right. I have seen people hurrying past pieces without batting an eyelash that set my heart pounding.

You will get much more out of a Chinese museum: (1) if you read something about Chinese history first (for a quick course see Chapter 4); (2) if you take a knowledgeable guide; and (3) if you are eager to learn things like the date of the earliest pottery, weaving, writing, money, etc. It might excite you even more to compare these with the earliest in your civilization. Try to figure out how and why things were made. Trace their development.

China is so rich in archaeology that most cities have good collections. It's just the displays that are unimaginative. Museums are lessons in history, collections of exquisite art, and links with humans who came before you. The problem for foreigners is that many museums do not have titles in English. If you don't have a guide and have learned your Chinese numbers, at least you could look up the dates and get a general idea of the period and what the relic might be. Each gallery is usually labeled with a dynasty name and/or a date and is usually set up chronologically from primitive to revolutionary times.

Some museums have booklets in English. Some museums have been built over archaeological sites, a most intriguing idea. You stand where you know people stood 6,000 years ago and look at the remains of their children. The skeletons are still there, excavated and protected by glass. If you are at all psychic, you might feel some ancient vibes in a situation like this.

Bronzes are not as well known abroad as Chinese porcelains or paintings. The museums in China are full of these ceremonial vessels, easily dismissed as uninteresting. They are, in fact, very special, the product of a highly developed technology with no peer anywhere else in the world at that time. Where else over 3000 years ago has anyone cast 800 kilograms of molten bronze into a one-piece bell? Just think of the logistics of doing it. Did they use cranes? How many finished bells had to be melted again when they did not produce the correct tone? Did anyone get beheaded for the mistake?

And then to bury the result! The economy must have been pretty solid to support this kind of extravagance. Or did the masses have to suffer for it?

Bronzes are uncensored history books cast in metal. The earliest script was inscribed on them, like a family Bible, recording family names and important dates. Later, historical events were recorded on them.

The shapes of ritual bronzes were based originally on everyday utensils. No one seems to know if the bronzes themselves were used in daily life. They were usually found in tombs buried with the dead for the use of the spirits.

The Chinese cast this alloy of tin and copper from molds. The oldest surviving bronzes are from the Shang and maybe the Xia dynasty, and one can trace the development of the art in China's well-stocked museums; the shapes of the legs, the decorations, the type of script. Even if you can't read Chinese, at least you can see the differences in style from dynasty to dynasty. Bronzes were fashionable until the Han, after which the art died out. (See Provincial Museum under Wuhan.)

Some guides are steering tourists away from the revolutionary sections of museums, thinking they may not be interested. Do tell them if you are. It is good to see China's version of historic events. It may differ from what you have always heard. For this reason, Chinese history from 1840 on should be of tremendous interest. Did British soldiers really sack and rape in every city they captured? Was the captain of the British ship Amethyst acting cowardly or heroically? Did the missionaries deserve to be thrown out of China? Why do the Communists glorify the Christian-inspired Taipings and the fanatical Boxers? Was the Long March a cowardly or heroic act? Was the Great Leap Forward a mistake? Was the Cultural Revolution a mistake without any redeeming features?

Music & Chinese Opera

Music lovers can find classical and contemporary Chinese and Western music. Among the best Chinese orchestras are the Shanghai Chinese Orchestra, Hong Kong Chinese Orchestra, Peking Central Folk Orchestra, Beijing Central Philharmonic Orchestra, and China Broadcasting Symphony Orchestra.

Among the most famous contemporary Chinese composers are Chou Wen-Chung (USA), Luo Jing-jing (Shanghai), Tan Dun (Beijing, who won an Oscar for the Crouching Tiger Concerto in 2001), Ma Sitson (USA), and Ju Hsiaosong (Beijing).

Also look for programs or cassettes that include popular compositions like the erhu concerto Manjianghong; The Butterfly Lovers for orchestra and violin; Reflections of the Moon on Two Lakes, an erhu concerto; Lady General Mu Kweiying, an orchestral work converted from Chinese opera.

The erhu, banhu, gaohu, and zhonghu are stringed instruments held upright and played with a bow. The pipa and liuqin look and sound like mandolins, the ruan more like a banjo. The yangqin is like a dulcimer played with bamboo mallets. Other Chinese instruments are the guqin, sheng, bamboo flute, and zheng.

Cui Jian is China's top pop singer.

Traditional Chinese Opera should be experienced at least once. It is very popular with older people and is sung in its own classical language. Your guide might not understand it without the subtitles in Chinese. The jabbering in the audience is usually a discussion of what is going on. Beijing has shorter performances for foreigners in comfortable theaters, with subtitles in English.

To the uninitiated, traditional Chinese opera can be dull, with its many long monologues, high-pitched singing, and sluggish action. The villain is always known at the beginning. The performance usually takes three hours, and the percussion instruments especially are loud, as if to elevate the audience to a higher level of consciousness – but not as high as at a rock concert.

Chinese opera dates from the Yuan and blossomed into one of the most popular entertainment forms during the Ming. For a largely illiterate population, operas were courses in history. They were performed at major festivals, weddings, funerals, birthdays and promotions for human and ghostly guests.

China has many forms of traditional opera. The most popular are Beijing and Qunqi. Qunqi has more dancing movements and more melodic, mellow tunes. The Shaoxing opera company has only female singers. In the old days, some operas went on for weeks, people came and left as they pleased, chatted with friends, ate and drank. The crack of watermelon seeds and the sipping of tea blended with the music, which spectators also sang if the tune was familiar. In addition to shouting approval and clapping, one also growled and swore when actors were less than perfect. You must see the Chinese movie *Farewell My Concubine* about opera performers.

The stories are usually ancient, so a knowledge of history helps. They are also based on classic literature, like *The Dream of the Red Chamber* or *Pilgrimage to the West*. Some are based on modern history. Two books, published in China, should be helpful: Latsch's *Peking Opera as a European Sees It* and Wu's *Peking Opera and Mei Lanfang*. Mei Lanfang was the greatest female impersonator. It is common to have a man play a woman's role.

The makeup might bewilder you. A white face shows a treacherous but dignified person and a white patch on the nose indicates a villain. Red is for loyalty and sincerity; black, honesty and all-around goodness; yellow, impulsiveness; gold and silver for demons and gods. It is always fun to watch the actresses in love scenes expressing themselves with delicate and reserved gestures. Note how they excitedly carry their tune to a higher and higher pitch within one breath.

Usually the fighting scenes, if any, are breathtaking and graceful, like ballet. Cymbals and hollow wooden knockers punctuate the action. The audience frequently applauds a musician, especially the one playing the stringed erhu. Usually a good opera singer tries to keep his own erhu player for life. The costumes are handmade and artfully embroidered, depending on the character played.

The singing takes some getting used to. It can sound like screeching and whining. But it takes many years of training to achieve such perfection. Settings are usually simple and symbolic. The acting, too, is symbolic, and Chinese audiences know what every gesture, every move of the eyebrow means.

Among the symbols: an old man and a girl with an oar are on a boat; a man lifting up his foot as he exits is stepping over the high threshold of a door; crossed eyes mean anger; walking with hands extended in front means it's dark; a man holding a riding crop means he's riding a horse, or sometimes he is a horse. You should be able to tell the difference! A particularly well-executed swing of long hair (anguish) or prolonged trembling (fear) will elicit gasps of appreciation and applause.

Two bamboo poles with some cloth attached represent a city wall or gate. A chariot is two yellow flags with a wheel drawn on each. A couple of poles on either side of an actor is a sedan chair. A hat with two long, dangling pheasant or peacock feathers is worn by a high military officer, usually a marshal; a hat with wobbling wings out to the sides just above the ears belongs to a magistrate. Generals have flags matching their costumes and are mounted like wings on their backs. The flags are distributed to identify imperial messengers.

After the performance, you may want to go backstage to see everything up close, and makeup being removed.

Nightlife & Recreation

Just about anything you might want to do can be found now in China. This runs the gamut from typical western activities, such as the symphony and discos, acrobats and opera, to more uniquely Asian activities like karaoke (you sing with a video). Most movies are in Chinese. Look for historical dramas so you can see costumes and architecture, like The Three Kingdoms and The Dream of the Red Chamber.

Chinese television consists primarily of documentaries, travelogues, kung fu action thrillers, and tearjerkers. It also has news, sports, boring political speeches, and educational broadcasts, such as language lessons.

Chinese acrobats are usually very entertaining. Also offered are song and dance shows and sports competitions. I highly recommend exhibitions of wushu, a traditional martial art, and variety shows like the Lao She Tea House in Beijing, where you can appreciate talent in spite of language differences.

Most tour groups will be taken to one or two cultural presentations. If you want to go to more, you can on your own. They are very cheap – usually Y10-

Y60. Tickets should be booked in advance through your hotel or travel agent. You can also go to the theater yourself, just like home.

Dance parties, discos and karaoke are more fun if you get up and participate. Dances are organized in public parks (7pm to whenever). Because people are shy, you will find men dancing with other men, and women dancing with each other. But many couples dance too. The music is a melange of fox trots, waltzes, tangos, cha-cha, and rock. In some places, you can take your own cassettes.

Night markets are opening up all over where weather permits, for clothes and for some great cheap food.

Nightclubs and North American-type bars have opened, some with live entertainment in the big cities. The best bars are in hotels but many small decent bars have opened. Just be wary of bars where hostesses sit down and drink with you and then bill you excessively for their drinks. Many hotels now have gyms, bowling alleys, and lighted tennis courts. Huge, magnificent "swim worlds" are in unexpected places like Harbin and Shenyang. Ice skating rinks are in Beijing, Hong Kong, Chongqing and Tianjin.

Hotel coffee shops, bars, and many stores stay open late. Massages are great. By law, men massage men and women massage women, but it doesn't always work out that way. Beijing, Guilin, Wuhan, and Xi'an are among the cities with dinner theaters.

In Beijing and Shanghai, there's jazz, good dramas, and a lot to do. Look for Western performers too. In many cities, batches of seats are reserved for foreigners. You might be able to get some of these at your hotel service desk and travel agent.

With many foreigners now living and working in China, activities foreigners like to do have now been organized. Many cities now have a Hash House Harrier group, a drinking club with a running problem. Joining a weekend run is not just a good way to get exercise, but an opportunity to meet resident foreigners and English-speaking, westernized Chinese. On Friday evenings, many local foreigners get together to celebrate TGIF (Thank God It's Friday). They are good sources of information though they tend to be cliquish. Foreigners have organized just about everything from Frisbee tournaments to alpine skiing and camping on the Great Wall.

The days of going to bed at 9pm because there's nothing to do are disappearing in the big cities.

To get information on these activities, look up the Xianzai's websites in Beijing or Shanghai. Contact your consulate or foreigners working in hotels for locations and telephone numbers.

Nursery Schools

Many tours schedule visits to nursery schools or children's palaces, which are always entertaining and charming. Count on at least one hour. In some nursery schools, visitors are involved in some of the children's games. In all nursery schools you will have a performance of songs and dances, and maybe get a briefing with an opportunity to ask questions.

Nursery school songs are a good indicator of the current political atmosphere. At one time the children were singing songs about shooting down American planes. Recently, we found a five-year-old girl doing a sexy dance. Of course we voiced objections to her teachers! In more advanced schools, you may be expected to read an English lesson.

Overseas Chinese

Do not hesitate to look up relatives (if you have any) in China. You can learn more about China from your relatives than from any tour. It won't be the same but it will be a deeper kind of experience. I am the third generation of my family to live in Canada. The first time I met my family in China, they pointed out a long-forgotten photograph on the wall of my Canadian family taken 20 years before. My aunt knew everyone by name. Until I started planning a trip to China, I didn't know she existed.

In her home, I saw how a six-course meal could be cooked in one wok in one hour. I learned how politeness smoothes over a multitude of sins, all ignoring my embarrassing encounter with a naked grown-up nephew who was bathing behind a screen in the kitchen; there was nowhere else to bathe. On the streets they pointed to the strange-looking foreigners, my fellow North Americans who had then just started to invade Xinhui. I didn't learn much about the history of the city, but I sure learned a lot about Chinese people and myself.

I think people of Chinese ancestry in particular should visit China. If you feel this bicultural conflict as many of us do, it would be good to explore the Chinese part of your roots. If nothing else, it will help you understand your parents, your grandparents, or your great-grandparents. It might even help you understand yourself.

In my father's village in Taishan, I was shocked to learn he had been born in a mud house. I found the watch towers where he used to look out for bandits, and imagined him riding the water buffalos. My grandfather's grave was a simple mound. I had expected something more elaborate, considering the money my father sent back to the village.

I highly recommend a visit to your ancestral village, if you can find it. Even if you have no relatives there, at least you can look around and see how you would have lived if your ancestors had not emigrated. If you do find relatives, you might find your name, if you're male, in a family history book.

Don't be concerned if you don't have money to take expensive presents. People outside China send back presents to family partly to show off. They also send them because they feel a strong family obligation. Sure they'll ask you to pay for schooling and to help your cousin emigrate to the US. If you can help them, do. If you can't, don't. Getting to know your relatives and learning about China are much more important than a few dollars. You might just want to treat them to dinner at a restaurant, a nice gesture, especially if you're staying with them.

Photography

China is now like most other countries regarding photographs. Over twenty years ago, I couldn't even take a photo of my five-year-old on a public boat. Today you can take pictures everywhere except inside police stations and prisons, military installations, and certain museums. Flash photography damages relics. Museums charge a fee or confiscate your film. Out of courtesy, please ask people if you can photograph them close up. Would you like someone to stick a camera in your face without permission? You might find in China people wanting to pose their children beside you for their cameras.

If your camera breaks down, look for a Kodak agent, who might be able to repair it for you. China has lots of camera stores. If you want to buy film in China, there's Kodak and Fuji. The Kodak boxes for 100 ASA print film are entirely in Chinese. Do not buy from peddlers who leave the film in the sun. Aim for air-conditioned stores. It is not easy to buy film with speeds higher than 100. Try the Beijing Friendship Stores or specialized photo stores.

Postal Services

These are generally reliable and airmail takes seven to ten days to North America. Hotels can provide stamps but for mailing packages you need a real post office. Only international post offices can dispatch parcels overseas. Some hotels can send packages for you but you have to pay a service charge and the taxi fare to and from the international post office. In addition, you probably have to have your package sewn up in white cloth or sealed in regulation boxes after Customs inspection. You have to fill out forms in triplicate. A few post offices provide boxes. Customs inspect all packages, even those sent inside China. Registration and insurance are cheap and recommended if you have someone in the city to follow up should packages get lost.

Surface mail to North America can take six weeks to three months. Airmail can take a week to 10 days. Letters mailed in China to Chinese addresses must have an envelope with red squares at the top for the postal code. It must also be a regulation size. Ask the post office if it needs to be addressed in Chinese and the clerk might put Chinese on it for you. Consult your hotel's business center if you have a problem.

For North America, stamps for an airmail postcard costs Y4.20. A letter of up to 100 gms Y20.80. For 100-250 gms Y39.80 to North America. Registration costs an additional Y6.50. Prices might have gone up lately, so ask.

Post offices are usually open 8:30am to 6pm on weekdays, and some are closed Saturday afternoons. All are closed on Sundays. Express Mail Service (EMS) from post offices takes three days to the United States and is cheaper than Courier service. You can book courier services through hotel business centers or directly with DHL, UPS, TNT, or OCS. These take only documents.

As for mailing letters to you from home, chances are you'll be home before mail can get to you. If you're in China a long time, you could schedule regular mail pick-ups at your embassy. American Express has client mail service in several cities like Beijing and Guangzhou.

If you expect to receive faxes in your hotel, give your room number as part of your address to correspondents. And keep asking for incoming messages at the front desk or business center.

Warning: Many travelers have found that postcards left with money for hotel staff to mail don't arrive. This happens all over the world. It is best to glue the stamps on yourself. Do be aware that some stamps don't have glue on the back. If you want to save money, carry the cards back home and mail them from home. They will probably get there more quickly.

Saving Money

Those who want to save money need time, and shouldn't care about the highest available standards of cleanliness and comfort. The more expensive the hotel, the higher the cost of other services like laundry and food.

Public Safety

Chinese safety standards are casual except where a lot of foreigners are concerned. We urge you to avoid the average amusement park ride since these are primarily for locals. But I have only heard of one cable car accident involving a foreigner. A tourist at the Great Wall was in a car when it stopped for the night. Trying to attract attention, he fell out.

Yes, you can go out at night alone on the streets but not to places that are deserted. It's probably safe but one never knows. Recently there have been reports of people being drugged by "friends" and then robbed. Passports as well as cash are much in demand.

A mother and cute child have been used to distract victims while an accomplice grabs their bag. An English-speaking youth has taken a foreigner to a restaurant where he was grossly over-charged. Many woman in bars have invited themselves to the table of a foreigner. Her drink is only tea but the victim gets a bill for several hundred yuan. When he protests, several men appear and threaten him.

Just don't let your guard down.

Chinese-managed hotels with the same star ratings as international hotels are usually cheaper, and usually not as good. Avoid services offered by hotels, especially tempting room mini-bars. But ask your hotel about reconfirming or booking flights. They just might do it for free.

All Holiday Inns discount 20% off the published rate for persons 65 years and over. It also gives 10% off food and beverages. Sheraton gives seniors' discounts, and cheaper room prices if booked in advance. Look into special hotel packages, especially in winter.

At each hotel ask to look at the cheaper rooms. They could be all right.

Reception clerks tend to think all foreigners want the top quality rooms. Rooms on the uppermost floors and with the best views are usually more expensive. Tell the clerk you're a student (if you have your card), or a foreign expert (even if you've just given one lecture). Ask if the hotel has CAA, AAA or seniors' discounts. Anything! Ask for the Sales Manager who is in a position to give the biggest discounts. Many hotels have dorms with up to 30 or 40 beds in a room for about Y35 a bed and up. Try hostels. Share rooms with friends, as most rooms cost the same for one or two guests.

Hotels in big cities are more expensive, so stay away from the center of the city. Find a room in small town hotels and commute. Or take anything you can get for the first night, and then look around.

On telephone calls home, ask your family to call you in your hotel room. Rates are cheaper from North America. Avoid hotel e-mail services. They usually charge over Y60 an hour. Look for cyber cafes, or China Telecom offices where e-mail is cheaper. I've tried to mention the cheaper ones.

Book hard-class trains or take buses or ferries between cities. You might not mind it. Express buses are getting better – almost like home. Avoid travel agents. If you have to use them, use travel agents associated with hotels that cater to backpackers. Their services are usually cheaper.

Do not assume that the Chinese are giving you anything free. Always ask, "What is the charge?"

Eat in bun or noodle shops or at market stalls. These cost less than hotel restaurants and some are clean. One backpacker spent two and a half months eating cheaply at market stalls and never got sick. But others aren't so lucky, so stick to well-cooked food and avoid tap water and raw vegetables. China has a lot of food stores now with cheap, decent looking cooked foods on sale. I've taken paper bowls to China to be filled at street markets. No worries.

Travel with Chinese friends. Avoid tourist restaurants. Invite one of the young people trying to practice English on you to take you to a restaurant where ordinary people eat. Foreign hitchhikers have traveled around China successfully, sleeping in hostels for local Chinese (after much persistent pleading), sometimes for less than Y2 a night. (Take your own bedding and you won't be surprised by bedbugs.)

Stay with friends or relatives. Courtesy demands you take them presents, but this could be anything from cookies to a refrigerator.

Travel during low tourist season. The south is pleasant in the wintertime.

Backpackers should be able to manage on $15 a day for a bed in a dorm, food, and local transportation, especially now that International Youth Hostels have opened.

Take public transportation for short trips instead of taxis. Rent a bicycle.

Ask your hotel service desk or CITS if there is a tour you can join. Try to round up other individual travelers to go with you on the same tour. This lowers the rate you have to pay. Four people sharing a taxi might be cheaper than taking a bus tour. Write ahead to Panda Tours and ask for a discount for four people.

You might try to hitch free rides with tour groups. While you're at a tourist attraction or hotel, ask other foreigners if you can get a ride with them. They usually don't mind.

Do your own laundry or take it outside your hotel to be done. At the Holiday Inn Lido in Beijing, you don't pay a service charge if you leave your laundry at a store in the building. If laundry is too expensive, buy underwear and tee shirts, and dress shirts at street markets instead.

Security

Pilfering in hotel rooms is possible so lock your valuables away. Strong padlocks and fancy luggage tags have disappeared between hotels on flights, though usually nothing else is missing. You should watch your purse and wallet in crowded areas. Like elsewhere in the world, take the usual precautions.

Double lock doors at night. Memorize the fire escape map on the door. Do not allow strangers into your hotel room. But generally, do not worry. You can go out safely at night.

China is safer than many places in the US. If emergencies erupt again, please feel confident that in 1989, tour guides acted professionally. They avoided danger and got their guests out of China safely. In late 2001, they made a special effort to help stranded travelers.

US Citizens Services in Guangzhou which covers southern China says there is very little crime, except for pickpocketing, mostly around the Guangzhou railway station, and in Yangshuo at the end of the Li River trip from Guilin.

Smoking

There is more awareness of the hazards of cigarette smoking. A growing number of hotels have non-smoking areas in restaurants, elevators, and some floors. Smoking is forbidden in airport waiting rooms and on some trains and all domestic flights. A smoking room is set aside at airports for addicts. China has the most smokers in the world and 4.4 million Chinese die of smoking-related illnesses a year.

Social Situations

Does Yes Mean YES? Well, usually. Cultural differences do create misunderstandings. For example, a memorandum of understanding in trade means that negotiations can begin in earnest. It does not mean, as many foreigners have sadly discovered, that a contract has been signed.

If a Chinese nods and says yes, yes, he could be just trying to please you. He may not understand a word you are saying. So be wary. Ask a question that requires a full sentence in answer. For the same reason, a Chinese might give you dates and spellings and swear they are right. But what he means is that it is the best information he has and if you press him, he will check.

Chinese people are very polite in their personal relationships with friends or business acquaintances. They try not to hurt feelings. If you make a mistake, the very polite ones will not point it out to you. If you do something they do not like, they might ask someone senior to talk to you about it.

But Chinese people may not seem polite at times, especially in crowds, or clerks in government stores. But if someone introduces you properly, most Chinese will prove to be extremely hospitable and helpful. The shop girl who ignores you is probably afraid of you or is unfulfilled by her job. Don't take it personally.

Once I caught my knee in the door of a crowded bus and got a bad bruise. At the time, my cousins laughed while I felt like crying. It was their way of reacting to embarrassment. Just don't feel offended.

Does No Mean NO? Well, sometimes. You will have to judge for yourself when a negative decision can be challenged.

You might hear "mei you." It means "there isn't any." It basically means please disappear, but when you don't, something has to be done. Some foreigners have challenged it at airline offices by standing firm, smiling, asking for the manager, and refusing to budge until they got a ticket.

By protesting to a hotel clerk who said there was no room, I did get a bed in a dorm. This does not mean you should try to argue every time you are told it is not possible, or that your safety cannot be guaranteed. It could mean: (1) language is a problem and they do not understand your request; (2) they don't want to be bothered trying; (3) they don't want too many people going there, but if you insist, they'll let you go; (4) there is genuine concern for your safety; (5) you really aren't allowed to go.

Arguing is an art too. Do not lose your temper or you've lost the battle. Suggest an alternative.

Note: Sometimes a 'no' answer is a 'no.' Sometimes 'no' should be answered with "How much will it cost?" or "Would Y10 help?"

Ask Questions: An official of the Overseas Chinese Travel Service once told me the only advice he had for visitors was, "Ask questions." It is good advice. The Chinese do not volunteer much information. So when in doubt, ask!

Applause: You could be greeted by applause as a sign of welcome at institutions and cultural performances. It might even happen on the streets. Applaud back.

Criticisms and Suggestions: You may be asked for these. If you have any, do give them. It will help improve services. Mention that the bathroom floor is filthy. Ask the attendant to clean it. If an attendant has been particularly helpful, write it down. She may get a bonus.

Good Manners: While it may be fashionable to be late elsewhere in Asia, this is not so in China, where groups of children may be outside in the rain waiting for your car so they can applaud as you arrive. Traditionally, Chinese conversations, even business conversations, start out with something innocuous: a discussion of the weather or a painting on the wall. A friendly mood is set first. Then comes the business.

Chinese people may not be polite in crowds. They may surround your bus and stare at you. But it is their country. Also, when using an interpreter, don't forget to look at the person with whom you are actually conversing. When giving out business cards, use both hands and stand, with the writing facing the receiver. Do not put cards received immediately into your pocket. Read them carefully first and maybe make some comment about them.

Chinese Hospitality: This can be very lavish and people may go into debt to show how happy they are to see you. It is always appropriate to take a gift when you go to a Chinese home. Presents or money for the children are fine (about Y20 each) if you are a relative or a close friend. Otherwise, it is insulting. Wine, fruit or candy is acceptable. If you have time for a return banquet, that would be the easy way out.

If you are accompanied by Chinese friends or relatives, avoid buying anything in a store because they may want to pay for it. The salary range for most people is quite low. Chinese don't have to pay exorbitant medical bills when sick, most pay no income tax, and rent is low. But people have to save a long time to buy what you wouldn't think twice about buying. Hospitality may demand that you be given a gift. Suggest something inexpensive if you are asked.

I have visited many homes – of peasants, officials, workers, and professional people. By western standards, most are crowded. Poorer families might share a kitchen and bathroom with other families. In only rare cases will there be room for overnight guests, especially in the cities.

In rural areas, you might have to sightsee on foot or on the hard back ends of bicycles if your hosts cannot afford any other means of transportation. It is a real adventure!

If You're Invited to a Wedding: In old China, a gift of money in a red packet was the accepted thing to give. Money is still much appreciated. But gifts to help set up a new household are more frequently given now: porcelain tea sets, video players, and bed covers (preferably red, for happiness). In some places, giving a clock is bad luck. It implies a time limit on the marriage.

Wedding invitations usually mean a banquet, but do ask. You can say something like: "I've never been to a Chinese wedding before. Tell me what to expect." Budget Y200 for a gift to casual acquaintances, more for business colleagues.

Weddings have become big business. Wedding stores have sprung up renting out elaborate costumes for photographs with expensive make-up artists to help.

Names and Forms of Address: "Attendant" is the best translation for all service personnel like waiters, room boys, and chambermaids. If you have to get their attention, you can call them "fu wu yuan." Ask people what they want to be called. Some have names in English.

Relatives are referred to and called by their relationship to you, like Second Aunt Older Than My Father, or Fifth Maternal Uncle of My Grandfather's Generation, both one word in Chinese. Your relatives will tell you what to call them.

Chinese put surnames first. Chou En-lai would be Premier Chou. You rarely address a person by his given name, except children or relatives.

Guanxi: This means relationships, influence, pull, or connections, and are an important part of Chinese life. Schoolmates, teachers, relatives, workmates - people who know each other well have a stronger and longer hold on each other than in the West. Guanxi is related to merit and to helping each other. Strangers are politely accepted, but with reservation, until they have proved themselves trustworthy, friendly, and useful. But this custom isn't fair to capable people without connections.

Flirting: You will probably embarrass older Chinese people if you indulge in too much display of affection in public, even with your own spouse. Older Chinese will be embarrassed. Friendly embraces are unusual even upon greeting a Chinese friend of long standing. The younger generation is more understanding. You will also embarrass Chinese people if you lose your temper with anyone.

Joking about Politics and Sex: Many visitors are warned not to make fun of sex or politics, particularly Chinese politics. With the older generation, to joke about sex is embarrassing. Sex is very private. To joke about politics or even to argue about it is to show lack of sensitivity. Politics is taken very seriously in China. People are put into jail because of it, lose their jobs, and spend long hours in meetings discussing political implications. Some young people, however, might find such humor refreshing and I have heard some tell hilarious (and perhaps dangerous) political jokes in public.

Political Questions: Don't be afraid. If it is done in the right spirit, both the Chinese and you can learn a lot. Political discussions can get heated. If you succeed in convincing them, it wont be because of shouting and red faces.

If they look uncomfortable with the question, don't pursue it. They may be under a lot of pressure to give the correct political answer and they may not know it. The better you know a person, the franker an answer you will get. And no answer is also an answer, if you know what I mean.

Warning: If a young Chinese woman is walking with a Caucasian man, many Chinese assume she is a prostitute. Prostitution is illegal and the police have been known to wait and watch so they can catch couples in bed. It is illegal to be a customer.

Spellings: Names of People

Pinyin	Wade-Giles
Bainqen Lama	Panchen Lama
Cixi	Tzu Hsi (Tsu-hsi, Qing Empress Dowager)
Deng Xiaoping	Teng Hsiao-ping
Feng Yuxiang	Feng Yu-hsiang (general)
Guan Yu	Kuan Yu (Three Kingdoms)
Guo Moruo	Kuo Mo Ruo
Hua Kuofeng	Hua Guo-feng (former Party chairman)
Jiang Jieshi	Chiang Kai-shek
Jiang Qing	Chiang Ching (widow of Mao Tse-tung)
Lin Biao	Lin Piao
Liu Shaoqi	Liu Shao-chi (former president)
Mao Zedong	Mao Tse-tung
Sun Yixian	Sun Yat-sen (father of republican China)
Xuan Zhang	Hsuan-tsang (Tang dynasty monk)
Yuan Shikai	Yuan Shih-kai (2nd president of China)
Zhong Shan	Chung Shan (honorific name of Sun Yat-sen)
Zhou Enlai	Chou En-lai (former premier of China)
Zhu Yanzhang	Chu Yuan-chuan (first Ming Emperor)

Spitting

Campaigns in some cities have taken place against the unhealthy and disgusting habit of spitting in public, a reflection of rural society. Fines in Beijing have averaged Y42 and have been successful in curtailing, but not eliminating it. The Chinese believe that swallowing phlegm is unhealthy.

Symbols

You will see these everywhere; in palaces, temples, pagodas, museums, fancy restaurants, gardens, parks, on dishes, windows, and screens. Knowing what they are will help you recognize bits of Chinese culture even in North America in Chinese restaurants.

The Chinese Dragon is said to have the head of a camel, the horns of a deer, the eyes of a rabbit, the ears of a cow, the neck of a snake, the belly of a frog, the scales of a carp, the claws of a hawk, and the palm of a tiger. It has whiskers and a beard and is deaf. It is generally regarded as benevolent but is also the source of thunder and lightning. The five-clawed variation was once reserved exclusively for the emperor. The flaming ball represents thunder and lightning, the sun or the moon, or the pearl of potentiality. It is frequently surrounded by clouds.

The Dragon of Heaven

The cloud design is most usually blue and depicted in the lower border of a rich man's gown, in a traditional opera costume, or in an antique portrait.

The scepter is commonly about half a meter long and made of metal, stone, bone, or wood. It is like a magic wand and is given as a gift, a symbol of good wishes for the prosperity and longevity of the recipient. The larger ones are found in museums.

The lion is not native to China. The design is unique to China because the craftsmen never saw a real one. Lions are often seen in front of buildings as protectors either playing with a ball (male) or a kitten (female). They are considered benevolent. The ball is said by some to represent the imperial treasury or peace. Others say it is the sun, a precious stone, or the Yin-yang. Seen also on festive occasions as a costume for dancers, the lion is sometimes confused with the Fo dog, which is usually blue with longer ears.

The phoenix is said to resemble a swan in front, a unicorn behind, with the throat of a swallow, the bill of a fowl, the neck of a snake, the tail of a peacock, the forehead of a crane, the crown of a Mandarin duck, the stripes of a dragon, and the back of a tortoise. Its appearance is said to mean an era of peace and prosperity. It was the symbol used by the empresses of China and is often combined in designs with the dragon.

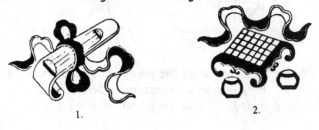

The intellectual elite was associated with these four symbols:
1. The harp 2. The chess board 3. The books 4. The paintings

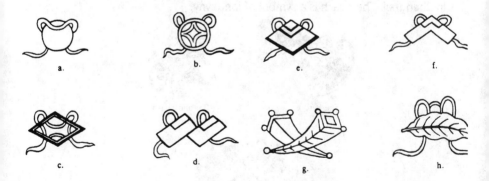

The eight precious things:
a. the pearl; b. the coin; c. the rhombus (victory); d. the books;
e. the paintings; f. the musical stone of jade (blessing);
g. the rhinoceros-horn cups; h. the artemisia leaf (dignity)

1.

2.

**These are only two of the many variations often seen.
There is even a teapot in the Shou design.**
1. the round Shou 2. the long Shou, both meaning long life

Below is one of the many variations of the character for happiness. Sometimes it is circular and doubled, especially prominent at weddings.

The Fu (happiness)

The word for bat in Chinese is fu. So is the word for happiness. A bat is thus a symbol of happiness. These are everywhere: on the walls and ceilings of the Forbidden City and on the ceiling of the restaurant of the Peace Hotel in Shanghai. The peach is a symbol of longevity.

The bat

Bat and peach

Five bats, surrounding the character Shou

When five bats are combined with the longevity character, they mean the five great blessings: happiness, wealth, peace, virtue, and longevity.

Scepter, writing brush, & uncoined silver
Together, these are a symbol of success.

The three fruits
The three fruits are fragrant fingers of Buddha, peach, and pomegranate. Together they mean happiness, longevity, and male children.

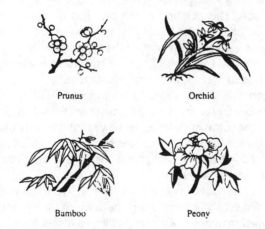

Prunus   Orchid

Bamboo   Peony

The prunus or plum blossom symbolizes beauty; the orchid, fragrance; bamboo is an emblem of longevity, and the peony means wealth and respectability.

Peach blossom

Lotus flower

Chrysanthemum

Narcissus

These are featured singly or combined in a set of four: the peach blossom represents spring, the lotus flower is summer, chrysanthemum is autumn, and narcissus is winter. Frequently, there is only one of each of these on a four-panel screen.

Other common symbols are the crane (longevity), the stag (longevity and prosperity), and the lotus (purity and perfection). The Buddha is usually seated on a lotus.

Among the many strange beings are the two at the top two corners of many temple roofs, tails pointing to the sky. This is a carp turning into a dragon, symbolic of a scholar turning into a magistrate. There is also the unicorn, known as qi-lin, with the body of the musk deer, the tail of an ox, the forehead of a wolf, and the hoofs of a horse. The male has a horn, the female does not. It is a good, gentle, and benevolent creature.

The wooden fish, a red object found in most Buddhist temples, is a clapper, used for beating time while the monks chant the sutras. Some say that monks dropped the sutras in water as the holy scriptures were being brought from India. A fish ate the sutras, so it was beaten to force it to regurgitate. Others say if you don't beat the fish, there will be an earthquake. I think it's used to keep the monks awake.

The tortoise, usually seen with a giant stele on its back, is one of the four supernatural animals, the others being the phoenix, the dragon, and the unicorn. Real ones are frequently kept at Buddhist temples, for they are sacred, an emblem of longevity, strength, and endurance.

Telephone, Telecommunications, & E-mail

You should be aware that telephone, fax, and e-mail communications could be monitored. E-mail providers have had to sign agreements stating no one is sending anything illegal. Many providers who were not legally registered have recently been closed down.

Not all mail gets answered, so if you're booking a room in a hotel, you could say that if you don't hear from the hotel, you are going to assume that there's no room.

E-mail is very popular. To send and receive e-mail while you're traveling, just register for free with *www.hotmail.com* or *www. yahoo.com*. Use their POP mail feature to access the mail sent to your home computer. Cyber cafes and bars are everywhere, usually near or in China Telecom offices and around universities.

I cannot emphasize too much that people staying in China for any length of time and trying to get around on their own without a guide, should buy a mobile telephone. Mine was second hand and cost Y800 through a trusted travel agent and included quite a bit of air time. You might be able to get a similar no frills Nokia for less now. This is much cheaper than leasing one and you can use it any place in the world aside from North America. You can call anywhere in China and overseas.

This mobile has been extremely valuable in telling people I'll be late for appointments and in trying to tell taxi-drivers where to go.

Most local telephone calls from hotels have been free, but top hotels in the big cities, are charging Y1 to Y2 a call. Hotel business centers charge Y2 a call. Public telephones range from Y0.05 to Y2.00, cheaper with phone cards.

Many local Chinese now have private telephones. Those that don't might share a telephone with everyone else in their building. You need a Chinese-speaker to reach them. Each village has at least one telephone in the village office. You can leave a message asking your friends to telephone you at your hotel. Be sure to give your room number.

Direct dial is much faster (20 seconds) than operator-assisted calls, which might take from three minutes to a couple of hours (in remote towns). Dialing direct from your hotel room is the easiest but one of the more expensive ways to communicate abroad from China. The operator can tell you what numbers to dial to access your country. You pay a three-minute minimum and a service charge.

Most hotels have card phones in their lobbies. These telephones are also on the streets, in shopping centers, railway stations, and in telecommunications offices. This might not be the cheapest way to call North America but there is no service charge and no minimum. You can buy phone cards from the hotels or the telecommunications offices in set denominations. You use the card until you no longer have a balance. The cost of the call is automatically deducted.

You can also telephone abroad by dialing one of the local numbers below and connecting immediately with an American or Canadian operator. You can then charge the call to your own telephone calling card, or "collect." Some hotels charge a service fee if you call these numbers from your room, but if you call from a public telephone, it is cheaper.

Calling Card Access Numbers & Country Codes
    For the US, AT&T is 108-11, MCI is 108-12, and Sprint is 108-13. For Bell Canada, dial 108-186. Some hotels also have "USA Direct" or "Canada Direct" telephones in their lobbies where you push one button and you connect with an American operator. This doesn't work for Canada because you're then asked which language you want, and there's no button to press for that.
    China's telephone country code is **86**. Some other country codes are:

Australia - 61	Malaysia - 60
Canada - 1	Philippines - 63
Hong Kong - 852	Singapore - 65
India - 91	Thailand - 66
Japan - 81	United Kingdom - 44
Macau - 853	United States - 1

    Don't forget the time difference. China has forbidden "Call-Back" telephone calls, but you can telephone your own family and have them phone you. This is about the cheapest way to make trans-Pacific telephone calls. Make sure you give them your hotel room number.
    A few hotels and business centers like the Portman Ritz-Carlton in Shanghai have call forwarding and conference call facilities. You can lease cellular phones through business centers in some hotels but it's much cheaper to buy.
    Faxes sent overseas are expensive from both hotels and telecommunication offices because they charge a three-minute minimum. It is best to find a friend with a fax machine so you only pay for the amount of time you use. One page usually takes less than one minute. It is cheaper to send a fax to China from North America than to send one from a hotel in China to another city in China.
    If you are touring during the day and want to leave a message with someone in the same city during office hours, send a fax from your hotel. Local faxes are reasonably priced and shouldn't have a three-minute minimum.
    Many Chinese turn off their fax machines at night, making it difficult for business calls to reach them from North America.
    Some cities have videophones. Try the telecommunications office on Nanjing Dong Road, near the Peace Hotel in Shanghai.

Time Zones
    All of China is in the same time zone. Beijing is 13 hours ahead of New York and Toronto. Please make adjustments for standard and daylight savings time.

Tipping

This is officially forbidden. However, guides and drivers do expect and accept tips and make more money than doctors, university professors, and government officials. First and foremost, you don't have to tip anyone unless you want to. That is the nature of tipping.

You should tip in hotels only for services above the call of duty. Do not tip the attendant who fixes your broken toilet. That is his duty. Avoid tipping in hotels that add a percentage for service. While staff may not necessarily get the service charge, you have paid for their services. In some hotels, tips are accepted as a token of friendship and shared among the staff.

A suggested tip for a bell man is Y5 to Y10 a load and for a porter at the train station Y2 to Y10. As for tour guides and drivers, tip only those who have been exceptionally good, and no more than Y16 per day for the national guide, and Y24 per day shared by the local guide and driver. Cruise ships suggest you put $5 to $6 per day per guest into a box, on top of a 15% service charge. This tip is split among all Chinese service staff including cooks, and other behind-the-scene personnel.

Miserable hours have been wasted in tour groups arguing about tips and gifts. Sometimes tour groups just pass around an envelope on the bus to the airport for the driver and local guide. Sometimes, tour organizers include tips as part of the price of the tour.

Asking for tips is strictly forbidden. A few attendants in newly opened hotels will refuse tips. Please thank them profusely. Such purity of spirit should be encouraged. You could perhaps give them a modest souvenir instead and send a letter of commendation to the hotel manager praising them. As for guides, they expect tips and recently have had to share them. Some have had to give a set amount to their travel agencies whether they receive money or not. But this is not your problem.

Toilets

You are out shopping. Nature calls. What do you do? Expensive department stores and malls usually have decent toilets. If you can, head for the closest tourist hotel, barge in as if you were staying there, and use its facilities. Don't expect Western toilets except in tourist hotels or on the well-beaten foreign tourist path. The Chinese toilet is the squatting kind over a hole in the ground. These are difficult for people with poor knees. There is usually no place to hang up purses. Toilets are best in your own hotel room.

Some public toilets, especially those in less developed areas, stink unbearably. Foreigners could dab perfume or Tiger Balm under their noses. Sometimes it is better for people traveling by road to stop behind a bush to fertilize the fields. This is certainly better than sharing toilets with writhing maggots. In smaller communities you may find a container of earth or a bucket of water for covering or flushing, but such is well off the tourist track.

Tourism Realities

Going on a group tour doesn't eliminate all problems. But it does mean someone else has to deal with them, and that someone else should find you a clean toilet. Shortages of trained, experienced staff with a good command of English plague all sectors of the industry because it has expanded too quickly. Recent group tourists have complained of inexperienced guides, although most are excellent.

Weights & Measures

For metric conversions, visit: *http://www.sciencemadesimple.com/ conversions.html.*

China uses both the metric system and the Chinese system:

1 gong-jin (kilogram) = 2.2 pounds
1 jin or gun (catty)   = 1.33 pounds = .604 kg
1 dan (picul)   = 100 catties = 133 pounds or 60.47 kg
1 mi (meter)   = 39.37 inches
1 gong li (kilometer) = .6 mile = 1 km
1 li (Chinese mile)   = .3106 mile = 1/2 km
1 mu   = .1647 acres
1 hectare   = 2.471 acres = 10,000 square meters
100 hectares   = 247.1 acre = 1 sq. km
259 hectares   = 1 sq. mile
1 squre meter   = 10.764 square feet
1 square feet   = .0929 square meters

Kilometer-Mile Conversion Tables

To convert kilometers to miles, multiply by 6 and divide by 10.

Miles	Kilometers	Kilometers	Miles
1	1.6093	1	.621
2	3.2186	2	1.242
3	4.8279	3	1.863
4	6.4372	4	2.484
5	8.0465	5	3.105
6	9.6558	6	3.726
7	11.2651	7	4.347
8	12.8744	8	4.968
9	14.4837	9	5.589
10	16.093	10	6.21

Metric Conversions

Centigrade (Celsius)		**Fahrenheit**
-40°		-40°
-20°		-4°
0°	Freezing Point	32°
10°		50°
20°		68°
30°		86°
40°		104°
50°		122°
60°		140°
70°		158°
80°		176°
90°		194°
100°	Boiling Point	212°

To convert Fahrenheit to Celsius subtract 32, multiply by five, and divide by nine. To convert Celsius to Fahrenheit multiply by nine, divide by five, and add 32.

–*Charts prepared by Linda Malloy*

Chapter 8

Air Travel

China's air safety record and service have improved considerably since the early 1990s. Northwest Airlines has been helping to train Chinese pilots and the US Federal Aviation Administration has been helping China overhaul the industry, from installing radars to training personnel. On routes between main cities, your flights will probably be on new planes.

You should be able to buy a timetable at the airport. If you have a choice of flights, choose the shortest flying time. You are more likely to get a newer plane with bigger seats. Aim for the earliest flights of the day. Delays become compounded as the day progresses.

If you want to know schedules and prices of some China domestic flights, try *www.FlyChina.com*. For **China Southern**, China's largest airline, click on *www.et-china.com*. Your hotel should also be able to help.

You can usually buy tickets at airports, airline offices, hotel business centers, and travel agents. The first two do not charge a service charge. The business center might not charge its own guests. Travel agents certainly will add a fee.

Tickets have to be paid for by noon, the day before departure. All domestic reservations have to be reconfirmed before noon two days before the flight if the ticket was not bought in the city of departure. Check with your travel agent.

Give yourself extra time to get to the airport in rain or snow. Check-ins start 1.5 hours before departure for domestic flights and two hours for international flights. Check-in ends 30 minutes before flight time. Prepare to pay either a domestic (Y50) or an international airport tax

(Y90). You might want to pay additional personal accident or baggage insurance at the check-in counter.

It is very difficult to get accurate flight departure information over the telephone and sometimes even after you arrive at the airport. If a flight is late, insist on a progress report; if very late, free food. Be sure to confirm delays with more than one official before you decide to go back into town.

Most planes are booked from the front. There may not be room for all the carry-on bags, so try to get there early. Planes have been known to leave early and of course sometimes late.

Carry some snacks and a good book. Airport waiting rooms have an information desk with a clerk who might know some English. Some have electronic monitors showing flight numbers. Because boarding announcements are not always audible, check frequently. You could look out the window for your plane. The plane number is painted on the fuselage and should be mentioned on your boarding pass. You could also look for other people with the same color boarding pass and try out your Mandarin. Many Chinese people take a friendly interest in foreign travelers and will tell you when to board the flight.

Some airports have a room for smokers. Meal announcements are usually not in English, so keep your eyes on fellow passengers if you're delayed. Be prepared to walk to your plane no matter what the weather.

Until recently, **CAAC** was the only airline operating domestically in China. Then it was broken up into regional subsidiaries and many other new airlines were born. **China Southern**, **China Eastern** and **Air China** became the largest.

Today, the airlines are being reorganized again and these three airlines will take over the others by 2004. Their IATA codes are:
• Air China (Beijing) – CA
• Northeast Airlines (Shenyang) – CJ
• Northwest China Airways (X'ian) – WH
• China Southern Airlines (Guangzhou) – CZ
• Southwest Airlines (Chengdu) – SZ
• China Eastern (Shanghai) – MU
• Xiamen Airlines (Xiamen) – MF
• Xinjiang Airlines (Urumqi) - XO

If you are flying with a Chinese airline from North America, you should be able to make domestic reservations through your carrier, or through China Travel Service. It is much cheaper to book flightsby e-mail through a travel agent based in China.

Most domestic flights have only economy class. Hot food has been served on some flights, but food is usually cold, edible and unconventional; for example, Southwest Airlines' box lunch had shrimp chips, sponge cake, plain

China Travel Guidelines

When you're traveling around China, follow these rules and your travels will be a lot easier:

Whenever you go anywhere alone, carry the name of your hotel in Chinese.

If you are traveling without a guide between cities, take the telephone numbers of your travel agents in both places. If your flight is canceled, at least you can telephone for help.

Always carry lots of small change for shopping and expenses.

Among your highest priorities upon arriving in a new place is to arrange your out-bound travel.

If you are traveling overnight by train or by ferry (not a luxury tourist ship), take your own mug, soap, chopsticks, and towel.

Always carry toilet tissue with you.

And be aware that a cancellation fee is always charged when you make changes in travel arrangements.

roll, spicy beef jerky, and sausage in pastry which would have been better hot, but it was okay; Take your own snacks. If any domestic airline is responsible for unscheduled overnight stopovers, hotel accommodation should be arranged by the carrier free of charge. (But you might have to insist.)

Booking airplane tickets is not always easy and you may have to try to fly stand-by. Because many travelers book more than one flight in order to insure a seat, keep trying. Rumor has it that front seats are saved until the last minute for VIPs.

Flying China's Friendly Skies

China is buying many new planes, opening convenient booking offices, and building or expanding airports.

Some planes are small and uncomfortable (especially for big foreigners). A few have broken seat belts and luggage bins that fall open. Cabin crews are not always careful about safety checks, but civil aviation keeps improving. You can book return flights and a whole itinerary now in major cities.

If any domestic airline cancels your flight, you'll get a full refund. If a passenger asks for a refund between two and 24 hours before flight departure, the cancellation fee is 10%. If you fail to cancel before flight time, there is no refund. Refunds can only be made at the place of purchase or a place approved by CAAC. Full refunds on international tickets are made if you cancel before check-in time.

Foreign airlines also fly to China but have no domestic services.

Airline Miscellany

Check for up-to-date information but in the past, no babies under 10 days of age and no pregnant women almost due were allowed to fly. An infant under two not occupying a separate seat and accompanied by an adult is charged 10% of the adult fare. Children two to 12 are charged 50%-65% of the adult fare.

If a checked bag is lost, the compensation will not exceed Y40 per kilogram. If you want more, you should buy luggage insurance beforehand.

Some Chinese airlines operate international flights similar to other international airlines, but with minimal services. Flights have cheap headsets, alcoholic drinks in first class, beer in economy, and some movies in English.

No smoking is allowed on flights under six hours. Helicopter service is available in some cities depending on demand.

Bus Travel

Highway buses can be more dangerous than trains, but are frequently faster, and go more often. Try to aim for the biggest and newest ones, Volvos, Mercedes, and Daewoos. Bus companies are not going to trust their most expensive vehicles to hotshot drivers, and in a confrontation with a much smaller car, the big guy usually wins. Most of these have toilets and video monitors.

Air-conditioned buses and mini-buses speed along many routes, some of the big ones are two-tier for almost horizontal sleeping. Ask about the kind of bus you will be taking because the small, hard-seated ones are very cheap, overcrowded and have little luggage space except on the roof or your knees. They leave when full, stop and start frequently, and can be uncomfortable for big foreigners, especially if you have to stand. I have heard horror stories of windows impossible to close in freezing weather, and carbon monoxide poisoning because of bad maintenance.

China has acquired some modern sleeper buses but old ones with dirty sheets and blankets are still operating. None have toilets; drivers stop beside the road, a real problem for women. So check your bus before you commit yourself. And if you have lots of luggage, buy two seats.

The main problem with buses are traffic jams getting in and out of cities and onto expressways. The problem with international buses is having to haul your luggage out and into two Customs posts and back out again. You should book your trip ahead of time so you will know exactly where the terminal is. I once showed up at a bus station to find one of three buses that day canceled. Fortunately, a resourceful taxi driver telephoned the hotel where he had picked me up, got the receptionist to translate, and took me to another station. I got the last seat on a bus just about to pull out.

Take your own food. Many big buses give out bottled water, have an attendant, but stop at dumpy restaurants. With a busload of travelers, you can't expect service immediately. As soon as the driver is finished eating, the bus leaves. Toilets are usually primitive with long line-ups.

CYTS and CTS (HK) have tours by tourist bus in Fujian and Guangdong, a great and comfortable way to see the country. Jiangsu also has a week-long coach tour.

Ferries & Tour Boats

China has some real antiques crossing harbors and rivers. They are cheap, but avoid them if they look too crowded and tippy. Most fatal accidents on ferries have recently been blamed on overloading and drunken crews. See Yangtze Gorges for ferries along the Yangtze, Wuxi for ferries along the Grand Canal, and Hong Kong for ferries to China. See also Qingdao, Tianjin, and Weihai for ferries to Korea and Japan. On overnight ferries, do take your own mug, soap and towel.

Hitchhiking

Backpackers have hitched rides with truck drivers. On-your-own tourists in isolated spots like Dunhuang have been able to get rides on tour buses. It's a matter of luck. If you have connections with foreign experts, etc., you might be able to use staff cars.

One way to hitchhike is to wait at the door of your hotel. Stop anyone getting into a vehicle and ask for a ride. Or you can go out to the main road and try to wave vehicles down. You could have a note in Chinese asking for a free ride or you could offer to pay for the ride. Always ask beforehand for the price. Hitchhikers have been treated to meals by hospitable drivers. I was once picked up by the police and treated to a banquet. They even refused cigarettes.

As a precaution, hitchhikers should make a record of the vehicle's license number. And avoid drunk or suspicious-looking drivers as you would in North America.

Train Travel

China has a vast network of railways, linking every provincial and regional capital (except Lhasa) to Beijing. A railway line to Lhasa is currently under construction. Railway lines have been burgeoning and many are being electrified. Diesel is replacing steam. Service has improved, with many new air-conditioned express tourist trains. In the past few years, train speeds have increased.

Train tickets can be bought through hotels or travel agencies (usually for a service fee), or at the railway station. In Beijing for a small service fee, you can avoid the hassles at the station by buying at the Novotel Peace Hotel or other railway outlets. Stations have ticket windows provided for foreigners but clerks have limited English. Lineups can be long, especially for hard class.

You can only buy tickets four days in advance. Travel agencies can usually reserve soft class train tickets a week in advance. It is cheaper but riskier to buy tickets for the same or next day at train stations especially around holidays. Seasoned travelers say the best time to queue for day train tickets is just before lunch. When the clerks return half an hour later, you'll be first in line. Scalpers around train stations and in some coffee shops can buy tickets for you with a big markup. While this is illegal, everybody does it; but some scalpers

All Aboard the Iron Rooster!

China is buying better passenger trains, and improvements have started to show. Some travel agents have chartered air-conditioned coaches for their clients. A luxury train trip along the Silk Road is organized by Conference World Tours, and China Express Railway Service. See Chapter 6 and Chapter 14 (Beijing) for addresses and phone numbers.

might not be seen again. You pay upon receipt. Travelers have boarded trains using platform tickets and then bought tickets from the conductor on the train. This, however, is risky, as space may not be available.

Hard & Soft Class

Trains are classified as special express, regular, and suburban. Passengers usually have a choice of hard and soft-class seats or berths. The most comfortable are in the middle of a coach, away from noise and wheel vibrations. State your preference when you buy.

Prepaid tourists usually travel soft-class berth, which can be almost the same price as going by plane. The berths are the height of bourgeois comfort if you have air-conditioning. Compartments usually have lace curtains, a table with lamp, an overhead fan, and sleeping spaces with bedding and towels for four people on two upper and two lower bunks. An overhead loft stores large suitcases.

It is best to take a small overnight bag too if you are sleeping on the train. Most group luggage is stored at one end of the car and may not be accessible.

Ask the conductor to lock your door when you go to the dining car. The plug for the fan (if you have one), and the switch for the loudspeaker are frequently under the table. Dining-car food is edible, simple, and, on some trains, surprisingly good. Passengers usually give their orders to a steward beforehand and are notified when their food is ready.

Six people share one compartment of hard-class berths in the same amount of space as soft-class. Berths are padded and tiered in threes, the middle berth being the best.

Hard-class is noisy and dirty, with other passengers smoking, frequently clearing throats and spitting on the floor. You cannot turn off the loudspeaker, which starts at 6am. Sheets and warm blankets are provided, but if you get on between terminals, these may have been used.

Passengers can eat in the dining car or buy food from vendors on the train or at each station. Bring your own cups of instant noodles. Steaming hot water is available in each car. Hard-class seats are very crowded. Accommodations can be upgraded after the train is underway if space is available. The conductor is usually in the middle coach.

The Hong Kong-Beijing train is great, beautiful and comfortable. If you are travelling alone first class, ask for a compartment for two. Chances are you'll have it all to yourself.

Train Basics

To find out about departure times, ask at three-star and up hotels. Schedules are in Chinese. China Tourist Offices abroad have had a time table in English, but everything was changed in late 2001 and early 2002. Give yourself plenty of time to find your train. Platforms are not marked in English, but the train number is posted. The destination of each coach should be marked on its side in pinyin. Expect train stations to be very crowded with people sleeping on the floors overnight. Expect people to push and shove. Do protect small children.

Like travel on overnight ferries, men and women are assigned compartments without regard to sex, even in soft-class. If this arrangement bothers you, ask for another compartment. The Chinese are used to such travel. Tourist groups usually sort themselves out. I have never heard of sexual harassment on a train in China, so don't feel nervous.

To protect valuables, do not use your purse as a pillow. Things have been stolen that way. Put your valuables in a money belt around your waist or around your neck under your clothes. Tie your camera to your arm.

Toilets look like they've been hosed down and not scrubbed. You might want to use a disinfectant. On coaches reserved for foreign tour groups, you can be sure of toilet paper and soap (in a common soap dish). Soft-class passengers on some tourist trains now have a choice of western toilet seats or a squat. Usually it's a squat.

A washroom in each car offers several sinks usually with running water. Many prepaid tourists wait until they arrive at their hotels before washing. However, sometimes on arrival early in the morning, hotel rooms have not been vacated, and tourists are taken sightseeing instead.

Most coaches on express trains are air-conditioned. No smoking is allowed but this is not enforced unless you complain. Baggage might be checked for inflammable and dangerous articles and weight. Luggage is frequently pushed in and out of train windows to a waiting guide because it's easier than hauling it. On some trains, the dining car becomes a disco or karaoke bar at night.

Do not discard your ticket. You might be asked for it again at the exit gate of your arrival station, but then again you might not. That's the way China is. Regulations and enforcement keep changing. Round trip train tickets cannot usually be booked. So consider booking the next leg of your train journey immediately upon arrival.

On some international trains like Hong Kong-Beijing, you also have to haul your luggage out and into the Customs House and back at borders.

Getting Around Town & Country

Bicycles & Motorcycles

These can be rented from hotels and bicycle-rental shops. Some rented bicycles have fallen apart. Check everything at the shop. You will probably have to leave a deposit or some identification, but do not leave a passport. Clerks have accepted old student cards, expired drivers licenses, anything with a photo. Guard your receipt.

Always park in a supervised parking lot, otherwise your bicycle may disappear. Make a note of the license number and where you left it. Put on some colored tape or a tag so you can find it quickly again among hundreds of identical bicycles. Most cities have bicycle lanes, and some have streets forbidden to bicycles.

If you are staying for any length of time, you might want to buy a bicycle and sell it when you leave.

Officially all bicycles should have bicycle licenses, but most foreigners have had no trouble without one. Some people have taken their own bicycles into China. (To ship a bicycle by train means having to go to the train station a day ahead of time and, at the other end, spending time finding it.) Spare parts for foreign makes are a problem.

You can take a group tour by motorcycle or bicycle, but these tours are not cheap. A truck carrying spare parts follows behind and picks up tired bikers.

Some adventurous bikers have traveled from town to town on their own. Please be aware of the problems. Roads might not be paved. If you get into an accident, you might not be able to communicate. You might secure only substandard accommodations. You might need alien travel permits for some areas. Check about licenses if you want to travel by motorcycle. Police do hassle motorcyclists.

For safety's sake, do not travel alone. If you do, let me know of your experiences.

Motorscooter Rickshaws

For two people or more, these are cheaper than taxis and can take lots of luggage, but they're not comfortable. They swerve and bounce. Prices are often fixed and paid in advance.

Bicycle Rickshaws (san-lien che)

Built for two, these cost very little in rural areas and a lot in tourist areas. You can only go short distances. Please consider the driver and get off and walk up steep slopes. Bicycle rickshaws are ideal for leisurely sightseeing in places like Suzhou and skirting traffic jams in Beijing (though taxis might be cheaper). Please don't ride them in heavy motorized traffic since they can be dangerous. Agree on a price in advance, especially in tourist towns. Make sure the price is for the ride, not for each person.

Be careful about your belongings as thieves on bicycles have been known to grab purses and cameras from these.

Taxis

You can get moderate-priced taxis outside tourist hotels, railway stations, airports, passenger-ship quays and places frequented by visitors. You can ask someone to telephone for a taxi, and you can also flag down a taxi on the street in most cities.

If taxis are not easy to find and you have several stops to make, it's better to hire one by the half-day or full day. You can also pay by the meter (or odometer) with a charge for waiting. Always agree on the price before you go. Usually you need not pay for a meal for a driver if you are near his home base, but you might invite him to a meal if you are a long way from his home. Restaurants and hotels have sections for staff if you don't want to eat together.

If you need a taxi early in the morning or for a full or half day, it is best to make a reservation at the taxi stand the night before. Taxi companies and travel agents also have buses for larger groups.

Not all taxis have meters, but hotels should know prices. While most drivers are honest, a few have added imaginary waiting time in Chinese to the receipts, or charged higher rates. If you feel cheated, don't pay, and ask cheerfully for someone to call a policeman. If you have already paid, get a receipt, take the driver's name and license number, and complain to the manager, dispatcher, or to the local tourism administration. Ask your consulate for advice. Some cities have a taxi complaint office. Letters to China Daily have resulted in penalties for drivers and apologies from taxi companies.

Another ploy is to pay what you consider the proper fare, get out, and leave. If the driver follows you, negotiate a settlement. Some drivers charge extra because they have to pay the touts who bring them customers. Try to avoid the middleman.

Some travelers have been greeted at railway stations and airports by a pack of touts grabbing at their bags, a frightening experience indeed, especially if you don't know what these strangers are doing. There is usually a line of legitimate taxis with meters waiting outside.

You can hire a taxi to take you from city to city, but you have to pay the fare back to the driver's base. Ask ahead of time for the price and distance. In isolated regions, ask if you need an alien travel permit. The problem is military zones.

Public Tourist Buses

These are available frequently near the railway stations in several cities like Suzhou and Shanghai. They go to tourist attractions in nearby cities and might have a commentary in Chinese. They are a good bargain if you take along a guide book. It's best to take your own lunch to save time and make sure you know when the next bus is coming along or going back. Make sure you agree on a price before you hop in.

Self-drive Cars

Generally, you have to be a registered resident in China to get a driver's license in China. You need a medical certificate and your own driver's license translated into Chinese. There is a written test and you are allowed to bring your own translator. You can't use an international license to drive in China.

But – some travel agents can make arrangements to drive your own car into China from Hong Kong or Central Asia. It might cost you up to $1,000 and a lot of time to get permission. You can drive a jeep with a tour group on the Silk Road. China International Sports Travel in Beijing and CTS in Xi'an have organized car rallies from Paris to Beijing.

Getting Around Cities

Public City Buses

Most of these are usually oppressively overcrowded, especially during rush hour and Sundays. But they are cheap. Recently, new air-conditioned buses have appeared, charge more (Y6 or Y7), and these are fine. Hotel personnel can tell you which bus to take and armed with your destination in Chinese, you should have an adventure asking people for help along the way. Some cities have bus maps in English. Fellow passengers are usually friendly and helpful.

Some public mini-buses have set routes. They are more expensive than most larger public buses but cheaper than taxis, and you do get a seat. In Beijing, Chengdu, Hangzhou, Nanjing, Shanghai and other tourist cities, there are now large public tourist buses going to major tourist sites. Another bus comes along about 30 minutes later to pick you up again for another spot. As in all crowded places, beware of pickpockets.

Shuttle Buses

Shuttles are available at a few hotels. You can take them to airports, Friendship Stores, and a few tourist attractions.

Subways

You can use subways in Beijing, Guangzhou, Shanghai and Tianjin and maps in English are available. Other cities are building subways. Walk down the stairs, pay about Y2 or Y3, and choose your platform. Signs are in pinyin; in Shanghai, they're also in English. If you avoid rush hour, they are a great way to get around.

Walking

Something has to be said about walking because of all the bicycles and cars: crossing streets can be dangerous! Try to let a native upstream run interference. Cross at lights after looking behind you and right and left. Some cities have overpasses and underpasses, so please use them.

Checklist for Solo Travelers

• Fax or e-mail your hotel before you arrive to arrange transportation if necessary, giving them your flight number or train and coach numbers. Someone at your destination should hold up a sign with your name or the hotel's name on it. Most hotels charge for picking you up but some have free scheduled shuttle buses. If you have less than a day, you could also ask the hotel or a travel agency to reconfirm or book the next stages of your travel.

• Consult your hotel travel service or a travel agency about the next leg of your trip, reconfirming plane tickets or booking train tickets.

• For your day of departure, book transportation and if there are no porters, ask if the driver can carry your luggage to the train platform or check-in counter. If the driver cannot and you have loads of luggage, ask the hotel to help you. The hotel might send a bellman with you and you only need to pay a tip.

Chapter 9

shopping

Shopping in China is great for many things, but it's not as cheap as it used to be.

China, which already sells more to the U.S, than it buys, wants to keep selling to the world. Its market includes its own increasingly sophisticated and wealthy shoppers. It has to produce international class goods at competitive prices but also a lot of goods for the proletariat.

You can find great bargains in the street markets and good quality for a wide variety of merchandise, but you can also find a lot of lower quality wares. Shopping in China is still a challenge, a rewarding experience for those with a good eye for bargains.

China has always made some fine arts and crafts: hand-knotted carpets, watercolor paintings, fine embroidery, porcelain, cloisonne, stone carvings, and feather pictures. Chinese stores and markets have been offering marvelous silks, cashmere, and pearls. It is now also great for modern goods like leather handbags, briefcases, and name-brand cameras. You can find mechanical toys, stuffed animals, dolls, computers, and cellular phones. It still has antiques, reproductions of antiques, and historical souvenirs at good prices.

The most important things to remember are:
• If you want bargains, you have to do your homework and you have to take time. You have to know prices in North America and you have to compare those with prices here in more than one shop. Keep good notes.
• If you only have time for tourist shops, you have to expect high prices but you can haggle there.

- As a general rule, the more Chinese shoppers there are in a shop, the better the prices. If foreign tourists are the only customers, beware.
- Merchants think foreigners are rich, and expect you to pay high prices. When you play by Chinese rules, they suddenly realize you're human too. And it's amazing. They warm up to you. They respect you.
- Haggling is the custom. Merchants know they make you feel good if you get a discount so they put up the prices. You've got to haggle.
- Shops are everywhere. They are at almost every popular tourist attraction but don't assume from the location that they're all tourist traps. Prices in some shops here could actually be reasonable.

Haggling

The chance of getting discounts is better on the Chinese mainland than in Hong Kong. Dickering over prices is imperative particularly in privately-run stores and markets, unless you want to pay three or four times the going rate. You can also haggle in department stores, airport stores, and museum stores. Just ask for a manager who can make such decisions. Aim for the owners, not the salaried clerks.

The secret is to **know prices**, not to show any enthusiasm for the thing you want to buy, and not to buy the first thing you see. In markets, many stalls sell the same items. If you are asked what you want to pay, suggest a ridiculously low amount: a quarter of the seller's first price. Then walk away pretending you are not interested. You might share a laugh with the dealer. The seller might counter with hand motions for you to give a higher bid, and you could come up a bit if interested. Start to move away again and look at the same thing in the next stall. It is a guessing game. The seller is trying to decide how badly you want it, and you are trying to decide the bottom line for the seller.

The best time for you to haggle is when you're the first customer of the day, no other customers are around, and when the merchant wants to go home. Pretend you're a foreign resident, not a tourist. Make them think you will come back again and again. When you think you have bargained as low as possible, then pull out your US cash and say, "How much is it if I pay in US dollars?" At that point, you might get another 5% off.

On the other hand, if the merchant doesn't budge even after you've walked away, make a note of the store's location. If you still want that item after looking around and finding nothing else like it, go back and ask for a lower price. The merchant may or may not come down and you have to make a difficult decision.

• Quality and prices are higher in Hong Kong where clothes are more fashionable.
• If you don't have the time or energy to haggle, shop in the Friendship Store or hotel stores. They speak the best English.

Antiques: Hong Kong offers the best quality because prices are higher there. But China, the source, has a lot. Dealers in China have to trust you before they close their doors and show you the real old stuff, some of it perhaps stolen. Officially, antiques made between 1795 and 1949 are not allowed out of the country unless they have a red wax seal on them. Only a few stores are allowed to sell anything for export made before 1795. The exception is Hong Kong where they can export anything.

Customs officials rarely search the bags of departing visitors to enforce this rule. But an alert officer might spot the shape of a large vase in a suitcase being x-rayed. I know they did catch one foreigner trying to take out old porcelain and confiscated the pieces until she returned to take them to the Arts Objects Clearance Office. Arts Objects offices are very difficult to find however but any good antique store should be able to help you.

The best, and most fun, antique shopping for knowledgeable or adventurous shoppers are the weekend street markets in Tianjin, Shanghai and Beijing: old clocks, watches, cricket boxes, porcelains, bird cages, curtain holders, silver jewelery, stone carvings, embroidery, and even Qing army boots. Antique markets also can be found sometimes in temples, museums, near other kinds of markets, bird and fish markets, or by themselves. Many cities now have daily markets with fixed stalls in multi-storied buildings (gu dong). See Zhongshan for furniture.

Antique stores run by the government are more reliable but expensive and frequently over-priced. Some won't budge on prices but a lot will. Many are found in museums and tourist attractions like the Forbidden City and Summer Palace. They buy their wares from the markets. Some antique stores are contracted to private dealers so haggling can be productive. Only antiques in government stores are guaranteed.

Baby toys: Avoid stuffed animals unless you're sure of what's inside. They could be stuffed with dirty materials. Avoid baby toys unless you know there's no lead in the paint. Check for bells and removeable buttons and eyes that babies could swallow. Chinese safety standards are not as strict as those in North America.

Beanie Babies: China makes a lot of counterfeits. Check the Beanie Baby website. They range from Y12 in the markets to around Y50 in the Friendship Store in Beijing. US Customs allows only small quantities for personal use in spite of copyright violations.

Ceramics: Some of these have been found to contain lead glazes. If you plan to consume food and drink out of them regularly, do test them for lead.

Clothing: The bargains are in the street markets. The best styles and quality are in Hong Kong but Beijing and Shanghai are getting right up there too. Some locally-made brands are very good: Giordano and Bossini for sportwear for example. But you'll see the likes of Victoria's Secret, L.L. Bean, and North Face too. I've bought name brand hiking boots too.

An American "size nine" doesn't mean a thing in China. If you are buying for yourself, you should try on clothes for size. If you are buying clothes for someone else, you should have their measurements. Wool and cotton will probably shrink if washed in hot water. Do not believe labels. Sometimes they're genuine overruns; sometimes they really don't belong. Check the quality carefully and decide for yourself.

Clothing and other items imported from elsewhere for sale in China are, of course, cheaper in the country of origin. Some of what you see may have been made in Hong Kong or Taiwan. Big international name brands are not bargains as they're aimed at the local market.

Styles can be behind the West or ahead of it. Because it makes clothes ordered by foreign manufacturers, China's goods get onto the local market before it gets abroad. Young people are wearing styles that will show up in America six months later.

Cruise ship stores: These have very limited variety, are highly overpriced but frequently have a sale towards the end of the cruise.

Department stores (shang chang) and malls: Prices are reasonable to expensive with good variety. Look for sales. Department Stores frequently have arts and crafts too. Look for good buys in embroidered jackets, clothing, gloves, silks, down coats, furs, novelties, etc. Prices, styles, and qualities are frequently better than in the Friendship stores.

Exchanges: Do not expect exchanges except in government stores and department stores. Guard your receipts.

Factory stores: Every arts and crafts factory has a showroom where visitors can buy what is made, but prices are usually higher than elsewhere. If you can't get a 40%-50% discount, look for stores around the immediate neighborhood which just might sell the same things, but at cheaper prices. Some showrooms are open all the time; others are open by appointment only. Aim for factories that have overruns from export orders. They should be made to Western tastes.

Friendship Stores: These are government stores originally set up for foreigners but now like any other modern department store. At least one Friendship Store serves every city. Prices are about the same or slightly higher than other Chinese stores, but the goods are of better quality and some items are unavailable elsewhere. Government stores have a reputation for honesty. If you ask, clerks usually tell you if it's real or fake. The standard of English is usually higher than other stores. At least some signs are in English.

In addition to arts and crafts, the larger Friendship Stores have textiles, television sets, watches, bicycles, sewing machines, lace, silk jewelry bags, cosmetics, herbal medicines, food, jewelry, thermos bottles, camera film, cameras, jackknives, flashlights, cashmere sweaters, silk blouses, cigarettes and wine – just about everything. Friendship Stores have locally-made goods for sale too.

The best Friendship Stores are in Beijing and Shanghai and they both take credit cards. The Beijing Friendship Store delivers goods to your hotel, takes telephone orders, and ships. It guarantees its goods.

If customers have solid evidence of misrepresentation, you should be able to get your money back. You can also try to appeal to the tourism bureau for mediation and a copy of its list of approved stores. Even in some of these shops, you can get a 10% discount if you ask. If you want to buy a lot, you might get a higher discount.

At government stores, clerks tend to ignore you. At private stores, they are aggressive. But private stores usually discount more.

Hotel stores: Stores in fancy joint-venture hotels are not cheap, but you can find some of the best clothing styles, fabrics, and antiques there. In three-star hotels, you might also be able to find a few clothes with name brands like Oleg Cassini, Victoria's Secret, and Land's End. But sizes and color ranges are limited. Hotels popular with Japanese visitors, like the Garden in Shanghai, have excellent quality and high priced goods, one-stop shopping for the top of the market.

Fakes & Reproductions

Learn how to tell fakes from real antiques. Some merchants will tell you the truth. Others can't because they don't know. Going to museums and factories should help you learn.

Rub a pearl on the front of your tooth. If it feels gritty, it's real. If it's smooth, it's fake. As for "antiques" look around. Antiques are usually one of a kind. If other stalls are selling the same thing, it's probably a reproduction. Look closely inside translucent stones. Glass is warmer than stone and has circular bubbles inside. To test for 100% silk, take a few threads and burn it. Silk will not leave a residue but polyester will.

For real hand embroidery, just look for different-sized stitches, and stitches in different directions. The smaller the stitches, the better. For antique embroidery, look for muted colors.

Reproductions can make good gifts too – if the quality is good and the prices are fair.

If in doubt in a market, assume all "antiques" are fake and offer prices accordingly. Offer Y20 to Y50 and see what happens.

Jade: The Chinese word for jade is "yu" and means any hard stone, usually green. It can be carnelian (red jade), soap stone, serpentine, or whatever. The western definition of "jade" is jadeite or nephrite. Chinese people will sometimes label these harder stones "high quality" jade, and the rest "low quality" jade.

Do be aware that some so-called jades can be doctored. If you look carefully, you might suspect a thin imperial green jade piece on top of a low quality piece with a band of green glue in between. The join is covered by a gold setting. In a couple of years, the glue will dry out and your ring will look terrible. Hong Kong has been doing this for decades. China is doing this now. Check everything carefully.

Live plants, birds, and animals: These are usually not allowed into your country without certificates. These are not easily obtainable outside your country. You have to research this before you leave home.

Markets: Markets with lots of similiar shops or stalls, either indoors or out, have the cheapest prices and sometimes have great quality. You have to be extremely careful but these might have genuine name brands and real jade carvings. Markets sell everything— fruits and vegetables, clothes, antiques, curios, pets, flowers and handicrafts. With no changing rooms, people buying jeans have to try them on over their own trousers. They could be seconds, or factory overruns. The colors might run, some clothing will shrink. Check the zippers, everything, carefully.

Minority handicrafts: It is usually more meaningful to buy handicrafts (usually embroidery or batik) directly from the maker in her village. Walk into any minority village, and someone will probably show up with something to sell. Prices are best there. A good embroidered jacket from the Miao nationality costing $60 in a Kaili village would probably sell in New York City for a couple of hundred dollars. If you can't get to a village, look for a peddler.

Consider laundering problems before you buy. Some ethnic skirts could lose their pleats, and the paper lining of applique jackets and baby blankets from Xi'an might disintegrate if washed.

Packing and Shipping: Few stores can crate and ship goods for you. Some hotels can help. Ask before you buy. See Postal Service above. In some cases, the local US consulate might be able to help you if the goods shipped to you are not what you ordered. If you expect to buy fragile porcelains, take your own bubble wrap to the market.

Painted-inside balls: These are a variation of an old art form. Getting the right perspective on a curved surface takes a lot of skill. Prices for these depend on whether it's glass or crystal (more expensive), and the fineness of the work.

Pirated compact discs and recordings: These could be of good or poor quality. They can be purchased in street markets, and at railway stations. If your Customs Service catches these, however, they will be confiscated. The same goes for pirated computer programs. Hong Kong could fine you.

Receipts: Save these so you can argue with Customs officials in your own country, or get a refund or exchange. Receipts are usually in Chinese with English numerals, so make a note on it of what each refers to at the time you buy. Put on tags of your own too to remind you where you bought it, how much you paid, and what it is. To help prove to your own Customs people that it's a duty-free antique, you have to get an official-looking receipt from the store stating its age.

Snuff bottles: Bottles for snuff, usually with an ivory spoon, is a 250-year old art. Old and unusual ones are collector's items, the most valuable made of carved pink coral and amber decorated with lacquer and pearl. Many are made of Peking glass. Since early in the 19th century, they were painted on the inside surface, an art that continues to this day. Obviously, those pieces are meant for show, not use.

Tailors: They are not as organized as in other places in Asia, like Hong Kong. But they are cheap! Don't bother having clothes tailored here unless a tailor is recommended by Western friends and you have a picture or sample of what you want made. See Crowne Plaza Hotel in Shanghai for a tailor who makes suits for the hotel's Western staff and should be good.

Taxes: China does not have taxes on sales.

Tour guides: Many guides take you shopping to stores where they get commissions. But your guides should also be able to get you discounts, good discounts, like 15% if you're in a group. Dont expect guides to be on your side in markets; some have been scolded for telling tourists the price is too high.

Videos and slides: of Chinese tourist attractions are available. Be sure you buy videos tapes labelled NTSC, not PAL. Otherwise they cannot work with North American machines.

Warnings: Peddlers at stalls, especially at the Great Wall, have been known to wrap up a cheaper T-shirt than the one you chose. Always check before you leave. This could also happen in stores. Keep a close watch.

Wholesale Markets: These are also good places to purchase gifts. Groups of silk factories have banded together to form one such market in Hangzhou. Groups of sweater manufacturers have done the same outside of Ningbo. In Guilin all the merchandise displayed in the tourist markets can be bought at the tourist wholesale market, open to everyone. The Pearl Market in Suzhou is wonderful. Prices and selection are generally good.

How to Choose

Before you go to China, learn about quality in museums and prices in Chinatown stores. If you are a serious shopper, plan your trip so you can see how a favorite craft is made. Locally-made crafts are listed under each destination in this book.

In the factory, you can study how the pieces are made and what makes a good piece. Will the wood or lacquer crack in dry, centrally heated houses?

You should handle some of the best pieces. Feel the weight and the surface texture. Compare these with ordinary quality goods. For reproductions, study the originals in nearby museums. Remember also that handmade articles are each different - of course! So before you buy, check carefully, not just for flaws, but for the rendering that you like best.

Generally speaking, consider (1) the amount of work involved in the production – the finer and more intricate something is, the better; (2) good proportions, lines, balance, and color; (3) how closely it represents what it is supposed to represent; (4) the quality of the material – will it chip? Rip? and (5) whether it will be a joy forever, or will you easily tire of it? (Primitive art does not have to be well proportioned or intricate.)

Crafts can also be made-to-order, but most Chinese factories are not set up for easy ordering. These of course take a lot of time. The most difficult part is getting the craftsperson to understand exactly what you want.

Most general tours include at least one handicraft factory and always one Friendship or Arts and Crafts store in every city. Many cities also have handicraft institutes where new crafts are developed and craftspeople are trained.

If you are more interested in handicrafts than temples, it is best to take an individual or special-interest tour. On a regular tour, the average tourist will be back on the bus waiting while you're still talking about the iron content in glazes.

Buying Something Cheap & Uniquely Chinese

China has a good variety of novelties, things distinctively Chinese to take back to your nieces, nephews, and bridge buddies. These are relatively cheap and easy to carry. Unique are porcelain sherds made into small pendants, embroideries, pearls, silk bags shaped like little children, silk scarves and ties, hand-painted wooden ducks, small peasant paintings, and fancy Uyger daggers for letter openers. You can buy hand-painted T-shirts and chops with rubber stamps both made by artists in hotel lobbies with the names of your friends. Cheap souvenir pins with pandas or the names of tourist sites are available. Thimbles, chopsticks, nail clippers, pill boxes and bracelets are made in cloisonne. Dough figurines in plastic cases of lovely ladies or opera figures cost Y15 each. In markets, you can pay Y20 for stone rollers (that help get rid of wrinkles and cool the skin). These have been marked at Y400 on some cruise ships! Expandable stone bracelets have cost Y6 in street markets, though I did pay Y25 each for "amber."

Posters, postcards, and comic books are fun and cheap, and so is a map of the world showing China in the center, or of Canada and the US in Chinese characters. Look for colored paper-cuts for glueing on windows or walls. Scroll pictures are easy to carry. How about Mao caps and buttons? Now that green tea is considered health-giving, people should appreciate gifts of it. Not all Chinese tea is green however so read labels.

Other suggestions: porcelain sherd boxes that can be stood up for display; cute tea pots in unusual shapes, and hand-stitched quilts (in American styles). Also typical are lace tablecloths (others shrink in hot water) or batik table cloths. Cork carvings are traditional and pretty and can be tiny enough to pack. Look for framed pictures of two-sided embroidery, horn or root carvings, and carved balls within balls.

There's all kinds of lacquerware, bamboo, and feather craft. Zhejiang province has multi-colored Qingtian stone carvings. Acupuncture dolls are about ten inches high and come with genuine acupuncture needles and an instruction booklet (in Chinese) for friends interested in it. Acupuncture posters are found in bookstores. Think about exercise balls for older arthritic people though they can be very heavy.

There are children's story books in English or books of Chinese characters. If you're in a foreign language bookstore, you'll find a great many books in English (cheap), all printed in China. Book lovers must visit Liulichang in Beijing to look at samples of fine Chinese printing and art books. The Shanghai Museum has a good selection of books in English.

Some museum reproductions are quite good and not too expensive. Check out the retail store in any museum you visit, especially the Shanghai Museum.

Consider Chinese kites. You can hang them on the wall if you don't fly them. Cloth wall hangings of Chinese zodiac animals are best from Beijing and Lanzhou. Xi'an's are not as good. Cheap tiger slippers for babies from Xi'an are cute. Vests with appliques have been a hit with tourists in Xi'an, where they are cheaper than elsewhere in China.

Furs, cashmere sweaters, down coats, and leather jackets are bargains, but please don't buy any endangered species. A Hong Kong furrier said the quality of the tanning of a lot of Chinese skins is not very good and might later stink when wet, so check items carefully. We've had no trouble with fur hats.

Mythological & Historical Subjects in Arts & Crafts

- Poet Shi Yung of the late Spring and Autumn Period has a knot on top of his head and a sword at his back.
- Wei Tou is the guardian of Buddhism and of the Goddess of Mercy.
- Guan Yin was originally a god, but in recent sculpture, always the Goddess of Mercy. She is depicted with children, or carrying a cloud duster (like a horsetail whip), or with many heads and arms, or with a vase.
- Princess Wen Chen was the Chinese princess who married a Tibetan king and took Buddhism to Tibet.

- Li Shi-zen was the Ming dynasty author of the classic book on medicinal herbs. He is shown carrying herbs in a basket and a hoe.
- God of Longevity is an old man with a peach.
- God of Wealth is a well-dressed man with a scepter.
- Laughing Buddha or Maitreya is fat and jolly and sometimes is surrounded by children or standing alone with raised arms.
- Eight Taoist Genii - see Taoism in Chapter 4.
- Fa Mu-lan is the famous woman general who inspired Maxine Hong Kingston's *The Woman Warrior*, and is now a Disney heroine.
- Characters from classical Chinese novels: *Water Margin*, *The Dream of the Red Chamber*, *Pilgrimage to the West*.

Chapter 10

China, which will be hosting the **2008 Summer Olympics** and qualified to play World Cup Soccer in 2002, is sports-crazy. The favorite spectator sport is **soccer** and probably the most popular participatory sport is **billiards**, which you see everywhere. Soccer is a passion and like elsewhere it has deteriorated into fights among spectators. The season in Beijing is May to October; in the south it's all year round. In Shanghai it's played at Hong Kou Stadium; in Beijing it's at Workers' Stadium near City Hotel. Just follow the cheering.

The favorite traditional sport at which the Chinese excel is **ping-pong**. It is less popular than billiards, and the national tournament is usually in May. Another traditional sport is **kung fu**. Martial arts have been practised since the Tang dynasty, especially at Shaolin Temple and Wudangshan, The latter was the home of the heroes of *Crouching Tiger, Hidden Dragon*. For Chinese martial arts in Beijing, look for announcements of demonstrations in tourist give-aways. The most important place is of course near Shaolin Temple where students at the government school give demonstrations and tens of thousands of youngsters take courses. Xi'an has the world famous national champion Zhao Chang Jun and Bruce Lee's coach has a school in Beijing. See "Dengfeng."

The sport taking the most space in recent years has been **golf**, but few Chinese actually play; the courses are mainly for foreigners especially Japanese. You can make arrangements to play through the top hotels, or telephone golf courses directly yourself. Good courses are in Zhongshan, Tianjin, Shenzhen, Shanghai, Beijing and a growing number of cities. China Tourist offices should have brochures and maps of courses. See also *http://user.hk.linkage.net/~klaus/golf/sinogolf.html.*

Many sports now emerging are new to China. There's **hot-air ballooning** and **gliding** in Anyang, and gliding in Jiayuguan. China International Sports has hot-air balloon tours over the Great Wall, and along the Silk Road and there are international competitions. It made arrangements for a British team to float over Mount Everest. Beijing has paragliding and hang-gliding. See *http://sportschina.com.*

Mountain climbers can attack over 60 peaks, including Qomolangma (Everest). **Rock climbing** should become more popular now that several hotels, Hong Kong's Salisbury YMCA, recreation centers, and the Chinese University of Geology have tread walls or climbing walls.

Skiing has been slow in developing but there are now at least four public resorts and one training resort (Jilin province). The best and most famous is at Yabuli in Heilongjiang province, which hosted the 1996 Asian Winter Games. See Harbin.

Adventurers might be interested in a US company that's advertising snow boarding, bicycling and skiing in China. Except for Yabuli, it seems to take clients to places with no lifts. However, if you're interested, it's China Ski Corporation, *2049 Crestvue Circle, Golden, CO 80401. Tel. 303/432-8166. E-mail: info@chinaski.com, Website: www.chinaski.com.* But I can't recommend it yet.

Heilongjiang and Jilin provinces have **ice hockey** teams and expatriates in Beijing are forever looking for hockey players.

American **football** has not developed much of a following. The Agricultural University has had a team. **Baseball** stadiums are in Chengdu, Lanzhou, Shanghai and Guangzhou. **Rugby** has been developing so well that Chinese teams have participated in Hong Kong's prestigious Rugby Sevens and done well. International teams have played in Shanghai. Beijing has an annual **Cricket Sixes** in the autumn with Chinese and expatriate teams. The Heineken Open **tennis** competitions brought Andre Agassi, Rainer Schuettler, Irakli Labadze and Michel Kratochvil to Shanghai in 2001. Most major hotels have courts. Visit *www.heinekenopenshanghai.com.* Hong Kong hosts the Salem Open. The **Beijing marathon** is run during the Spring Festival and there's nothing to stop you from running with it. Shanghai has a world class **squash** court.

Basketball is growing in importance and American coaches have been working with Chinese teams. Get a look at the Sports Bar at the Gloria International Hotel in Beijing where you can throw baskets before drinks. The Kerry Center in Beijing has an indoor basketball court. **Bowling** is big and has the same rules as in North America. The biggest is the Workers Bowling Centre near Workers' Stadium with 100 alleys.

Sailboarding is only in Qinhuangdao and Sanya. Sanya has the most **water sports**, among them water polo, scuba diving, para-sailing and sailing. Qingdao is hosting the sailing at the 2008 Olympics. Whitewater rafting is in the upper reaches of the Yangtze River in Sichuan and Qinghai, and in Yanqing County in Beijing. Many groups bring their own rafts, but China Sports can supply tents and bags.

Horseracing in Hong Kong is famous. The mainland is starting to develop some tracks and the sport is expected to grow. Look for events at the Beijing Country Horse Racing Club. The club house is not comfortable unless there have been improvements since this book went to press. You have to sit on concrete steps. A board displays the odds and the same twenty horses race each time. It's at Mapo, Shunyi County, *Tel. 69441499*. Just don't expect Happy Valley.

For those who want to play against Chinese teams, contact China International Sports Travel Service in Beijing, *http://www.sportstravel.com.cn*. On a less formal basis, contact your embassy or consulates, or the physical education departments of international schools in China. Some foreigners who live in China organize their own sports teams and are always looking for volunteers for ultimate frisbee or skiing.

The bulletin boards of supermarkets frequented by foreigners, such as those in the China World Hotel or the Holiday Inn Lido in Beijing, could have notices too. See major cities about the Hash House Harriers ("a drinking club with a running problem").

For **bodybuilding machines**, your best bet is a good hotel. The China World in Beijing has enough to harden a battalion. It also has indoor tennis courts. In Shanghai, the Portman Ritz-Carlton has an excellent health club, the Regal International has the most tennis courts, and the Regal East Asia Hotel has rooms opening onto games at the Shanghai Stadium.

China has both professional and amateur sports. Professionals play with sponsored clubs like the Chinese Basketball Association (CBA). Only amateurs can take part in the Olympics – but these athletes are trained by the government. Kung fu is not an Olympic sport yet.

China International Sports Travel can make arrangements for most sports, competitions, importing equipment, the Beijing Marathon, and the international bicycle meet around Qinghai Lake. It can arrange airplanes, hot air balloons, oxygen, and mountaineering. It claims that it can get permits faster than directly through the Mountaineering Association. It has 20 branches around the country and promises to answer e-mails "at once." See the Beijing chapter for the address.

If you want to make conversation with people you meet in China, ask them about the best football team. Shanghai's Shenhua were national champions in 2000 and in 2001. The best ping-pong players are Kong Ling Hui and Wang Nan who won gold in the 2000 Olympics. A top diver is Fu Ming

Xia, four times gold metal winner in the last four Olympics. Basketball star Wang Zhi Zhi has been playing in the U.S. in the NBA.

See also *http://sportschina.com*, and for connections with the expatriate community, see Xianzai Beijing and Xianzai Shanghai in each city.

Ecotourism

China is making a good attempt at developing nature reserves and national forests, with places to hike, bicycle, raft, and breathe fresh air. Unfortunately, in some places it is over-building and attracting too many tourists. These have caused UNESCO to threaten withdrawl of heritage status. See Zhangjiajie for Wulingyuan.

It is building an international class national park in Yunnan province near Lijiang and Zhongdian with American help. China has over 66 biosphere protection zones and nature reserves, at least fourteen of which are members of UNESCO's Man and the Biosphere Program.

Of the destinations mentioned in this book, these UNESCO programs are accessible from Changchun (Mt. Changbai), Chengdu (Wolong Panda Reserve, Jiuzhaigou), Fuzhou (Mount Wuyi), Kunming (Xishuangbanna), Yangtze Gorges (Shennongjia), and Zhaoqing (Mt. Dinghu).

For nature reserves, see Xining for Qinghai Lake's Bird Island, and Harbin for the Zhalong Nature Preserve near Qiqihar with its red crested cranes. Chengdu is central for pandas. Look up Wuhan for attempts to save river dolphins, Yichang for sturgeon, and Hefei for alligators.

Considered World Heritage Sites by UNESCO are Mt. Taishan (see Jin'an), Mt. Huangshan Scenic Area (see Hefei), Wulingyuan Scenic Area (see Changsha), Jiuzhaigou Scenic Area (see Chengdu), and Mt. Lushan Scenic Area (see Yangtze Gorges).

You might want to add a couple days to your visits to Guilin for the Longsheng Hot Springs National Forest Park. There's Dalian for the tiny Benxi National Forest Park (and cave), Datong for Mount Wutai National Forest Park, and Fuzhou for Wuyi Mountain.

Major botanical gardens are in Beijing, Chengdu (near Dujiangyan), Guangzhou, Guilin, Nanjing, Jinghong (see Kunming), Lushan, Shenyang, Turpan, Wuhan, and Zhaoqing. There are many others besides. Flower festivals are all over the country, peonies in Luoyang, and camellias in Kunming. Yunnan province also has the world's biggest rhododendron tree on the Burma Road.

All these areas have hiking opportunities. There's also the Huangguoshu Waterfall and the Kaili area near Guiyang, and many others.

For tame rafting, there's Wuyi, Zhangjiakou/Wulingyuan and Shennongjia above. For serious white water rafting, mountain climbing and skiing, see Sports above.

For trekking by camel, contact travel agents in the Silk Road cities, and Hohhot in Inner Mongolia. For bicycling, see China International Sports Travel for tours. Very popular for cycling on your own is Yangshuo near Guilin.

Accommodations are modest, and serious ecologists will question some of its practices, but China's efforts should be encouraged and enjoyed. You yourself can help plant trees in Zhengzhou and pick up trash on the Great Wall. China is very aware that these areas should be kept clean. Huangshan is a good example with laundry carried by porters to be washed at the base of the mountain. However, at spectacular Huangshan, there's no place where tourists can quietly meditate or watch a sunrise without groups of noisy tourists spoiling the experience.

The China National Tourism has published two booklets, *Ecotour Highlights*, and *China's National Forest Park*, which are available from China Tourist Offices.

Ride with Genghis Khan!

Travel agents like China International Sports Travel can organize **one-week camel treks** in the Taklamakan Desert or take you riding with those most famous of horsemen, the Mongols.

food & drink

Chapter 11

Background to Chinese Cuisine

The infinite number of Chinese dishes, flavors, textures, and methods of cooking makes eating here exciting. The most famous cooking styles are Beijing, Cantonese, Shanghai, and Sichuan. There are also vegetarian and minority foods. Try the local food. Cantonese is best in Guangdong; Szechuan (Sichuan) in Sichuan.

Chinese food is usually chopped up in thin, bite-size pieces, making knives unnecessary at the dinner table. The thinness is for quick cooking, using a minimum of fuel. Chinese food can also appear whole, like fish or pork hocks, but these can be easily separated by chopsticks. When poultry is cooked whole, it is chopped up before appearing at the table. Sometimes the bones are splintered so the food inside the bones can be reached. Do be careful.

Chinese ingredients reflect the many periods of famine in Chinese history. Everything possible is eaten; nothing is wasted, not even chicken feet, duck tongues, jellyfish, and sea slugs – all famous delicacies.

The Chinese food served to most prepaid groups is usually adequate. If you want to eat better, you can pay more for better restaurants. If food is important, take a gourmet tour.

Restaurants in China

Until recently, restaurants were generally dumpy and tacky, a reflection of revolutionary attitudes. The new economic policies mean many new or renovated eating places, some very striking joint ventures in the gaudy Hong Kong style, and you can even find Starbucks coffee.

The bottom stick is held firmly by the base of the thumb and the knuckle of the ring finger. The top stick is the ONLY one that is moved and is held by the thumb and the index and middle fingers. The tip of the top stick should be brought toward the tip of the bottom one. Keep the tips even.

How to Use Chopsticks

International-class hotels import ingredients and executive chefs. Some families and factories have also started restaurants with better food and service than state-run establishments.

The current make-a-profit-or-quit policy has forced improvements everywhere. Provincial and city-state tourism administrations are regulating restaurants. They should have a list of those fit for foreign tourists, and if you have a complaint, contact the local tourism administration. Each restaurant should have a plaque that says it's been approved.

Foreigners can be put into private dining rooms in restaurants if they wish. These are usually cleaner with less smoke than eating with the masses, and could cost more. Many state-run restaurants receive guests at 6pm and then rush you out at 8:30 or 9pm so the staff can go home. If you want to linger, choose a privately-owned or hotel restaurant.

The days are long gone when you could trust waitresses to give you a correct bill. Hold on to the menu. Check the items, prices, and total.

Ordering Food

Menus in restaurants for foreign visitors are usually in English and Chinese and a la carte. Some restaurants have a fixed menu too which you don't usually see. You have to ask. The fixed menu is served to tour groups, who need not worry about ordering. Individuals can order this too for an easy way out. Food on the fixed menu is relatively inexpensive and you get more variety for one or two people; just say *feng fan* or *bao chan*. Menus change every day.

Gourmets avoid fixed menus and buffets because the food is not freshly cooked. But buffets, with their large number of different dishes, are good introductions. If you like a particular dish, ask the name so you can order it again.

Every restaurant has its specialties. These are probably more expensive and are sometimes not worth it. In Ningbo, they included red blood-raw clams which I couldn't eat! Aim also for local or regional dishes like fresh seafood if you're near an ocean. (Top-quality restaurants and hotels everywhere get seafood flown in and charge a lot more.) Meals in the countryside are usually excellent because the vegetables go from the garden to the wok.

It is best to eat with a large group of people to get a greater number of courses. Ten is ideal for a table, and you may get a private room thrown in. When ordering, two people should order three courses plus a starch; five people should order six courses plus a starch or two. Choose only one of poultry, fish, beef, pork, or vegetable. This will give you variety and abundance. If you find you are getting too much, order less next time.

If you need more courses, start the rounds again. If you've already chosen chicken, choose duck or goose. Vary tastes and textures: sweet, pepper-hot, salty, steamed, deep-fried, poached, boiled, roasted, baked in mud – the choice is endless.

Don't feel that every meal should be a banquet. The danger in China is overeating.

For popular restaurants, it is always best to reserve a table and even order meals ahead by telephone, especially for banquets. Restaurants for the masses won't take reservations. Ask your hotel's service desk to make reservations for you, telling the restaurant how much you want to pay but also approving the dishes suggested. One restaurant suggested bears' paws, a local delicacy and an endangered species, which no one ate. Most of the cost went into that one dish!

Elaborate Banquet Dishes

These should be ordered at least 24 hours ahead of time and a hefty charge is levied if you cancel.

Don't look for chop suey, chow mein with crispy noodles, or fortune cookies - those are Chinese-American dishes. China has fried noodles, but they are not the same. But with the new economic policies, anything could show up! And be aware that some wild animals used by the Chinese as food are, or may soon be, on the endangered species list. Please avoid them. Tell your host in advance that you don't want them.

Special Diets

If you have special food preferences, let your guide know. For an upset stomach, order rice congee, which is rice cooked to a gruel consistency and flavored with salted egg, fermented bean curd, or whatever. Congee is easy on the stomach. Avoid fried dishes, spices, and dairy products. Eat dry crackers, arrowroot biscuits, and apple sauce.

If you have cankers in the mouth, try hung pean (chrysanthemum tea). It comes already sweetened in one-cup packages and is an old Chinese remedy.

People on general-interest tours should not expect special diets. Salt-free and diabetic diets are impossible. Chinese cooking uses more salt than Western cooking. You could, however, go on a special tour for people with the same restrictions. Vegetarians usually manage on a general tour. Vegetarian restaurants exist, but are not on the daily tourist route. Muslim restaurants also exist but so far there is no kosher cooking except in Hong Kong, but do look at Beijing and Shanghai in this book.

Desserts

Foreigners on tours will be offered fresh or canned fruits. If you're in Guangdong in May or June, ask for fresh lichees - or buy them in markets. Look for pomelo, especially in Guilin or Sichuan. It's a sweet grapefruit with a thick rind. Try Hami melon on the Silk Road. China also has ice cream, sweet red beans, sweet almond paste, and deep-fried crystallized apples and bananas. Aside from fruit, the Chinese do not have much of a tradition for desserts.

To be absolutely safe, eat only ice creams like Bud's, Wall's, Movenpick's and Haagen-Dazs.

Beverages

Most prepaid meals for foreigners include soft drinks, beer, and tea. Canned fruit juice, wine and liquor cost extra. Coca-Cola and Pepsi have bottling plants in China. In some cities you can get coconut water, almond juice or good reconstituted juices. Laoshan is the most famous mineral water but others are also good.

Tsingdao beer is the favorite. It is made with barley, spring water, and hops from a German recipe. Five Star Beer has been designated by the government for state banquets. Local beers are usually good. Locally-brewed foreign beers like San Miguel are increasingly available. Moslem restaurants don't serve alcohol.

The Chinese consider the following three liquors to be the best: Mao tai, made from sorghum and wheat yeast, very potent and usually served in tiny goblets; Fenjiu, mellow and delicate flavor from Shanxi province; Wuliangye, five-grain spirit from southern Sichuan, with a fragrant and invigorating flavor.

Dairies have opened, but outside big cities, you only get UHT, powdered or canned milk. If you're uncertain of the pasteurization, order milk hot. It'll probably arrive sweetened. In Tibet you can get yak butter tea and in Yunnan, there's crispy fried goat's cheese.

Chinese Wines

Foreign wines are very expensive; the Chinese version is cheaper. **Dynasty's White Riesling** and **Rose** are good. **Huadong Qingdao Chardonnay** (the product of an Australian joint venture) and **Dragon Seal's Cabernet Sauvignon** (a French joint venture) are popular.

Dry red **Cabernet Sauvignon by Vinitalia** is worth trying, a Sino-Italian joint venture from Hangzhou. Xinjiang produces **Lanlou** red and white, outstanding table wines worth trying. **Great Wall** has both a red and white, light, lively and sparkling. **Chateau St. Pierre** is an American wine bottled here, red and sweet with a little sparkle. You can get foreign wines with meals mainly in the top hotels, and you can buy wines in supermarkets.

Drinking tea is an art in China. Some springs are famous for their tea-making qualities. If you go to Hangzhou, try long jing tea there. A favorite tea in hot weather is po li. Keemun is good in the wintertime and when you've had greasy food. Lu an should help you sleep. Oolong is the most common tea in south China, while most foreigners like jasmine. Jasmine is said to heat the blood and should be balanced at the same meal with po li or pu er.

Every Chinese has a personal list of the four most famous green teas. Long jing (dragon well), yun wu (mist of the clouds), mao hong (red straw), and bi lu chuen (green spring) are probably among the most popular.

Breakfasts

Foreign tour groups in one- and two-star hotels usually receive Western breakfast with greasy eggs. You also get lightly toasted bread, coffee, and fruit or canned juice. Four-star-and-up hotels now have Western buffets or mixed Western and Chinese buffets.

You can opt for Chinese breakfasts if enough people in the group want them. Chinese breakfasts differ regionally: dim sum or rice congee with peanuts, pickles, salt, or 1000-year-old eggs in south China; in the north, you could get lots of different buns, or 'oil sticks,' which are like foot-long doughnuts, deep-fried and delicious, but hard to digest. You dip these in hot soy milk. In Shanghai, you might get gelatinous rice balls with sugar inside, or baked buns with sweet bean paste inside. They are great!

Western Food

Most low-star tourist hotels serve Western food, but it is rarely as good as Chinese except in four- and five-star hotels. Bread is sometimes cut thick and is usually white. Sometimes it is one Chinese meat-and-vegetable course with bread instead of rice. Good to excellent Western food is available in four-star and up international hotels. Some of these hotels also have delicatessens where you can buy cold cuts and cheese. Some restaurants in Northeast China have Russian food.

Local Chinese prefer Chinese food and have rejected invitations to Western meals because of "too much meat" or the lack of familiarity with knives, forks, and foreign table manners.

Courtesies

Group tours should be punctual at meals as the food is usually ready on time. Meals are served family-style and the dishes may be sitting on the table getting (ugh!) cold.

Guests of honor are traditionally given seats where they face the door. Left-handed people should sit where they can avoid clashes with right-handed chopsticks.

Many restaurants distribute damp towels at the beginning of meals to refresh guests as well as to clean. You can wipe faces, hands, and backs of necks with them. Sometimes towels are distributed also during the meal, and always at the end.

If you pass tea or bowls or calling cards, to be polite, use both hands and bow.

Chinese food is usually served on large platters, which ideally arrive one at a time. The food comes hot off the wok at the peak of perfection to be eaten immediately.

In families, diners pick what they want with chopsticks which are great for reaching across tables, keeping fingers clean, and hitting naughty children. Outside of families, use serving spoons. After guests express admiration for the beauty of the food, Chinese hosts put the best morsels on the plates of the people around them. You could do this, too, after the first round. Since you put your own chopsticks into your mouth, you should use the other end for serving. The host usually invites guests to start eating. Groups of friends can declare a moratorium on such formalities and have everybody dig in. Hei fai means 'Raise chopsticks!'

Slurping, or even burping, indicates that you are rude. If you don't have enough room on your dish for bones and other discards, just leave them neatly on the table itself. Less-polished Chinese will spit them onto the floor!

If you want a tiny plate of hot chili condiment to spice up a bland dish, ask for *la jiang*.

In very fancy restaurants, an attendant distributes every course and guests do not help themselves. Individual plates are removed and replaced with clean ones after most courses. The host usually invites guests to start eating.

Giving a Banquet

Hosting a feast is the accepted and most important way to return hospitality or to show gratitude for a favor. If your guide persists in refusing your invitation to eat with you, he may relent and join you the day before you leave as a farewell gesture.

You may want to throw a banquet for some of your Chinese colleagues and people who have been helpful. Discuss your guest list with one of the Chinese involved so you won't offend anybody important by leaving them out. Discuss spouses and times and seating arrangements, but don't be offended if spouses don't show up. The venue is important because some restaurants are more prestigious than others.

Even-numbered days are more auspicious than odd-numbered days. Restaurants may be busier with wedding parties then.

Toasting & Banquets

Chinese people do not like to drink alone. Toasting at banquets is a complicated art, and you are not expected to know the finer points. Just do what you do at home. Stand up, give one or two sentences, make sure everybody is joining you, and drink. Gan bei! means 'Empty your glass!'

The first toaster is usually the host, who gets the ball rolling. A frequent toast is to the friendship of the people of your country and China, and the health of friends and comrades present. You can tell a funny story and then talk about your sadness about leaving China and the new friends you have made, and meeting again in your country.

Toasts might continue all evening, and so might the meal, or at least until the restaurant turns out the lights. If the banquet is extremely large, the host might circulate to all the tables, drinking toasts at each one. On smaller, less formal occasions, the Chinese may want to drink you under the table. Be alert; they may be putting tea in their own glasses. You may want to try that yourself after awhile.

I have been to banquets where I didn't touch a drop of liquor. I can't get mao tai past my nose - it's so strong. Chinese hosts are not usually offended if you toast with tea or soft drinks. If you don't want to drink liquor, mumble something about a medical problem, like an allergy. Try to divert your fellow diners. Try exchanging songs - but no drinking ones. It may be the only occasion when you'll hear the national anthem of China. You can turn your cup or glass upside down to signal to the waiter that you've had enough.

If you want to stop eating and your host keeps piling food onto your plate, just lay down your chopsticks. Thank him politely but don't eat anymore. Your host shouldn't feel insulted.

Recently, as an austerity measure, the lavishness of top-level state banquets was curtailed officially to four courses and a soup, and the length limited to one and a half hours. This might be the beginning of a trend, but then again, it might not. Banquets are part of the culture.

Eating with the Locals

You can eat quite well for comparatively little money if you're willing to try food stalls and restaurants for the masses. The standard of cleanliness and speed of service are not generally as high as in restaurants for tourists. The cigarette smoke may be suffocating. It is customary to share tables with other diners in busy restaurants.

Payment is made when you order (so you can't stomp out impatiently). Some finicky eaters take their own chopsticks and spoons to places like this, but as far as I can see the dishes are scalded, and if the food is freshly cooked, there should be no problems. The soup sterilizes the utensils (you hope), but you can also rinse them yourself with steaming tea.

Hot pot is ideal in places like this for the same reason. With no menus in English, do remember to take along Chapter 25 of this book and point.

Fast Food Stalls & Cafeterias

These are recent innovations and are multiplying quickly. Some serve instant noodles. A knowledge of Chinese isn't necessary; you can point.

Outdoor night markets are an adventurous attraction for gourmet as well as budget travelers. Make sure the food is steaming hot and the utensils are scalded or eat directly from the pot. Avoid uncooked sauces and condiments.

Sometimes I take my own paper bowls and disposable chopsticks and get food straight off the grill or steamer. It's great, and oh, so cheap. Sometimes in Beijing, you can get steaming hot sweet potatoes, filling enough for breakfast for a yuan.

Food Streets

Food streets are usually managed by hotels so are cleaner and more foreigner-oriented. The food is usually light and prices are reasonable: noodles, fried rice, side orders of barbecued duck, cuttle-fish, etc.

Eating Precautions

To avoid an upset stomach and intestinal parasites, do not drink water out of faucets. Most bottled drinks are fine, but make sure the seal isn't broken. Steer clear of ice, popsicles, ice cream (except for foreign brands), watermelon, and other fruit. Don't eat anything raw unless it's imported, or carefully washed and peeled. Animal and human manure is used in China as fertilizer. Local people have developed immunities.

Be careful on ferries and small boats. Dishes are frequently washed in river water and are not always scalded carefully afterward. Some people take disinfectants like tincture of iodine. Two drops in a liter of water kills all germs in 20 minutes. When cooking your own food, as in Mongolian Hot Pot, be careful that the utensils you use on raw meat or fish are not the same utensils you put into your own mouth. Sterilize utensils in the hot pot.

Other Tips

The secret of eating a Chinese meal is finding out first how many courses you will be getting. Banquet meals usually have a copy of the menu on the table. If there are 12 courses, take no more than one-twelfth of what you would usually eat in a meal from each plate; otherwise, you will be too full to eat the later dishes. Also, take your time. You can't rush through a big meal. Some famous banquets have taken days.

Fish is the last formal course in some places. If you happen to be eating with superstitious fishermen, don't turn a fish over to get at the flesh on the other side. It means their boat will turn over!

Think about "Chinese restaurant syndrome." Its symptoms are an increased pulse and a tight feeling around the sinuses. This 'syndrome' is a result of the large amount of Monosodium Glutamate (MSG or Ajinomoto) in Chinese food. Cooks in China use a little, but not much. You can say , "Wo bu

Here's the Best Way to Eat ...

Mantou: the plain steamed roll. Either take bites while holding with chopsticks or fingers, or break apart and stuff pieces with bits of meat. You can also dip it in sauces. **Jiao zi** are small stuffed ravioli-like pastries, steamed or fried; **bao zi** are steamed dumplings and may have beans or meat and vegetables inside. The names get confusing.

White rice: served in bowls. Put the bowl up to your mouth and shove the rice in with chopsticks. More genteel people might want to pick up chunks with chopsticks.

1000-year-old eggs: you usually have to either acquire a taste or close your eyes and think of something else; they are best eaten with pickles and are delicious.

Shrimp with shells left on: take a bite of half, then, with your teeth and chopsticks, squeeze out the meat. You could use your fingers to shell them. Cooking shrimp in their shells retains most of the yummy flavor.

Two-and three-foot long noodles: lean over your bowl and pick up a few noodles with chopsticks. Put the noodles in your mouth, biting off pieces and leaving the rest temporarily in your bowl. Don't worry about slurping. The Chinese enjoy long noodles because they symbolize longevity.

Ice cream: ask for a spoon.

yao wei jin." I don't want MSG.

Among the beauties of a Chinese meal is the variety. If you don't like one thing, you might like something else. On prepaid tours, you might want to talk with your escort about the overabundance of food when meat for the common man is so limited - if this bothers you.

Menus in English are by translators, not public relations people. Some dishes may sound absolutely terrible, but are really very good. Don't let a name like 'frog oil soup' throw you.

Dried preserved fruit is delicious, but do not eat too many at a sitting. They are full of preservatives.

Health restaurants have dishes made from Chinese herbal medicines with lots of ginseng, sea horses, deer antlers, and things best left unmentioned. Some foods are known to combat high blood pressure; other foods are good for pregnant women. These are indeed for the adventurous eater because of their unusual flavors, and they can be very delicious.

If you invite your poor relatives to dinner, be sensitive that a meal in a tourist restaurant is a real treat. Normally, they cannot afford it. Since they get little meat, do order more for them. Do encourage them to take the leftovers home. They may be too polite to ask.

Regional Cuisines

For specific dishes, see also Chapter 25, Glossary of Chinese Characters.

Beijing (or Peking or Northern) cooking is light and salty with few sauces but lots of garlic, leeks, and scallions. It has flour-made buns, rolls and meat dumplings. Food is baked, steamed, roasted, fried, or boiled in soup. In winter, be sure to try hot pot.

Cantonese (or Guangdong or Southern) style has crisp vegetables quickly fried in peanut oil and is somewhat sweet with starch in the sauces. It uses a lot of oyster sauce or fish sauce in cooking, or poured over boiled vegetables. A few dishes could be dog, monkey, and snake. (Please, no pangolin and other endangered species!) *Dim sum* are those small fried or steamed Cantonese pastries served at breakfast or lunch and are ordered from a menu (classier), or chosen from a trolley brought to your table. The trolley attendant can take off any cover for you to see inside. The most famous dim sum restaurant is the Panxi Restaurant in Guangzhou. But it's great in most other restaurants in the province. Chicken feet, known as Phoenix feet, are delicious! Honest!

Fujian cooking has lots of seafood and light soups, suckling pig, and non-fat spring rolls. You may recognize Filipino dishes like *lumpia* and *lechon*, originally from this province. It is similar to Cantonese with some unique dishes.

Mongolian Barbecue is not really Mongolian or even traditional Chinese. This form of cooking, where you put slices of meat, vegetables, and any number of sauces into a bowl and have someone cook it for you on a large inverted wok, seems to be of recent Taiwanese origin. Restaurants are found more in North America than in China where I can only name one – in Shanghai. There are some real Mongolian restaurants in Beijing, but they cook in another way.

Muslim cooking is found in Xinjiang, Ningxia, and Gansu, but also in Beijing and Xi'an, anywhere there is a large Muslim population. It is primarily lamb or mutton. Muslims do not eat pork and are not supposed to drink alcohol. This food can be very spicy hot but not always.

Among its most popular dishes are: *Ghosh nan*, which is like a pizza with ground meat on top and sometimes with sesame seeds. One can be a full meal; *kabob* is usually ground mutton mixed with egg, or a small stick of barbecued meat; *lagman/latiaozi* is noodles with tomatoes, green peppers, meat, potatoes; *manta* is dumpling (with no soup), like *jiao tze*; *nan* is a flat, baked bread; *pilou* is pilaf/pilau rice with dried fruit, mutton, carrots, and onions; *tonor kabob* is a large stick with barbecued meat spiced with cumin and red pepper.

Shanghai cooking from eastern China is similiar to that of Suzhou, Yangzhou, and Wuxi. It is cooked longer in sesame oil, neither sweet nor salty. It can be very ornamental. *Borscht* is on the menu of many Shanghai restaurants because of the White Russians who once lived in Shanghai. Look for crab in November.

Some **Sichuan (Szechuan)** dishes are highly spiced, peppery hot, and oily. Formal banquet cooking is more bland. Smoked duck with camphor and tea flavor and many other dishes are not spicy hot.

Vegetarian cooking has had a long tradition in China and was first documented 2000 years ago. It developed with Buddhism, which forbids its adherents from killing animals, and restaurants are frequently found near Buddhist temples. Distinctively Chinese are dishes that imitate meat in taste, texture, and looks. While this does not encourage reverence for life as taught by Buddha, it does make it easier for some Buddhists to become vegetarian. Many of the dishes are made of soy bean and could use a lot of monosodium glutamate.

Chapter 12

hotel basics

Abbreviations & Hotel Jargon

These are the abbreviations relevant to hotels, accommodations, and Chinese government travel services:

BBC – British Broadcasting Corporation with regular world news

BC - Business center or hotel office capable of selling tickets, sending faxes, and offering a secretary for hire

CITS - China International Travel Service

CNN – The major English–language news station from the US

Credit Cards - American Express, Visa, MasterCard, and sometimes Diners

CTS - China Travel Service

CYTS - China Youth Travel Service tours

Executive Floor - A section set aside for higher paying guests usually with complimentary breakfast, a lounge, concierge service, cocktails, and other services

HBO – Home Box Office, an English language movie channel

Http – the first letters of a website

IDD – International Direct Dial

Renovated – means major improvements.

Star TV – a Hong Kong channel offering, sports, entertainment, and/or music channels in English

Tourist Hotlines — telephone numbers set up to help with any problems, emergency translating, or complaints of tourists

Wide twin - twin beds at least 53" wide each

Y - Yuan (Chinese currency)

All dollar prices given in this book, unless otherwise noted, are in US dollars. Again, **1$US=Y8.3**. Payment should be in Chinese currency.

Some Generalities About Mainland Hotels

The hotels mentioned here are the top hotels in each city and the best hotels in each price category for North Americans. I have also chosen them for location, convenience to downtown and to tourist attractions. Hotel ratings such as "three-star," "'four-star," etc., indicate the government's rating system, with five the highest quality. Most hotels have singles, doubles, and suites. Those of the lowest one- and two-stars might have dormitories of three or more beds to a room as well. In a few cases, the "best" hotels in a city may not be very good.

New Chinese-managed hotels might be very beautiful at first, but they can deteriorate quickly. In many Chinese-managed hotels, total renovations are

International Hotel Chains in China & Their North American Toll-Free Numbers

If you read about an interesting hotel in your destination city, phone its representative here in North America for prices and reservations:

Courtyard by Marriott: *Tel. 800/321-2211, 800/468-3571*
Gloria Hotels: *Tel. 800/821-0900 Utell*
Hilton International: *Tel. 800/445-8667*
Holiday Inns Worldwide: *Tel. 800/HOLIDAY*
Hyatt International Corporation: *Tel. 800/233-1234*
Intercontinental: *Tel. 800/327-0200*
ITT Sheraton and St. Regis: *Tel. 800/325-3535*
Leading Hotels of the World: *Tel. 800/223-6800*
Marriott Corporation: *Tel. 800/228-9290, 468-3571*
New Otani: *US Tel. 800/421-8795; Canada Tel. 800/273-2294.*
Novotel: *Tel. 800/221-4542, Tel. 800/NOVOTEL (668-6835)*
Radisson Hotels: *Tel. 800/333-3333*
Regal Hotels International: *Tel. 800/222-8888*
Ramada International: *Tel. 800/468-3571*
Renaissance Hotels & Resorts: *Tel. 800/468-3571*
Ritz-Carlton: *Tel. 800/468-3571*
Shangri-La International: *Tel. 800/942-5050*
Sofitel: *Tel. 800/221-4542*
Steigenberger: *Tel. 800/223-5652; http://www.srshotels.com.*
The **International Youth Hostel Federation** can be reached at *www.iyhf.org.*

made every three to four years, but in the meantime, soft drinks and spit get hopelessly ground into beautiful wool carpets. Foreign-managed hotels try to practice perpetual maintenance. See also Hong Kong and Macau.

Hotels Today

Travelers today have the benefit of good old-fashioned capitalistic competition. Big international hotel management chains are in every possible city. This has led to sub-categories. Four-star international chain hotels are usually better and more expensive than four-star local hotels.

Pleasing visitors has become important! In the 1960s, tourists used to be happy with a boring room and private bath, and then, later, an air-conditioner, refrigerator, and television set. Today's visitors expect spotless carpets, non-smoking rooms, coffee makers, and an in-room safe. Tomorrow's visitors will probably want a computer in every room and high-speed internet access. Many hotels have imported foreign managers to raise their standards.

Be aware that hotel rooms are frequently classified from standard/moderate, to superior, and up to deluxe. "First class" is usually below superior.

Brand-new hotels may not have all their services available, but at least the rooms will be in pristine condition and prices low. There is a tendency for Chinese partners to insist on a "soft" opening. You might find annoying a lot of daytime hammering.

It is my experience that most hotels four-stars and higher should respond with a fax to a request for a reservation if so asked. Some have in-room safes and satellite television in English. The quality of most is usually satisfactory for all but very fussy North Americans. Those of three-stars might be a little worn with stained carpets, and might not be acceptable to discriminating Americans. Usually there's an assistant manager on duty who speaks English. But even in four-star hotels, carpets on lower floors can look dirty.

Hotel Star Ratings

Government assessments are an indication of design, equipment, hygiene, maintenance, management, service quality, and facilities (but not location). To qualify for a rating, hotels must also receive letters from satisfied guests. Star ratings are sometimes given for political reasons.

Each of the following items begets a certain number of points. Each star rating has a minimum number of points. Three stars does not mean that every hotel so graded has special guestrooms for wheelchaired people, for example. (They might only have one wheelchair.)

Local or provincial governments hand out one- to three-star ratings but the national government must approve four- and five-stars ratings. Only hotels fully opened for one year are formally rated, and a plaque should be prominently displayed. Each successively higher rating incorporates the best criteria of the ratings below it.

Foreigners are not supposed to stay in a hotel with less than one star because the standards are terrible – but many do. The criteria are roughly:

One-Star hotels must have air-conditioning, coffee shop, dining room, and at least 20 guest rooms, cleaned daily. Of these, 75% must have private baths. They must have central heating, a lobby with information and reception desk, postal service, and 12-hour a day hot and cold running water.

Two-Star hotels must have at least 20 guest rooms, 95% with private baths, 50% with telephones, and 16 hours of hot and cold running water. Western and Chinese breakfast must be offered.

Three-Star hotels must have at least 50 beautifully-decorated guest rooms with dressing table, desk, drawers, and closet and a carpet or wood floor. There should be a bedside control panel; 24-hour cold and hot water; and 110/220V outlet. Telephones should be in every room with international direct dial (IDD), mini-bar and refrigerator, color television sets, in-house movies, music; writing materials. Expect sunproof curtains; and bed turn-down service.

They must have single rooms and suites, Western and Chinese dining rooms (with English-speaking attendants, and the last order no earlier than 8:30pm), 16-hour coffee shop, banquet hall or function room, buffet breakfast and bar service (until midnight), and 18-hour room service.

They must also have elevator service, public telephone and washroom, equipment and service for disabled people, disco or karaoke, massage, beauty parlor, barber, bookstore, reading room, 12-hours a day foreign exchange, safe deposit boxes, store, camera film developing, fax and telex services, luggage storage, 24-hour laundry and drycleaning, wake-up calls, shoe polishing, and access to taxis. They should be able to mend articles of everyday use for guests. They should accept major credit cards. They must have an emergency electricity supply for public areas, medical services, 16-hour a day doorman, and message service. On duty 24-hours a day should be a luggage porter, checkroom service, guest reception, and managers on call. An assistant manager should be in the lobby 18 hours a day. There should be a price list, tourist map (English-Chinese), flight and railroad timetables available. *China Daily* should be available.

Four-star hotels should have luxurious and spacious sound-proof rooms, low-noise toilets, and hair dryers. They should have guest and service elevators, background music, health club, swimming pool, sauna, business center, greenhouse, 24-hour doorman, reservations accepted through fax/telex, 24-hour room service, and onward reservations in China for guests. A guest reception and assistant manager should be available in the lobby 24 hours a day. Laundry should be returned by next day.

The restaurants in four-star hotels should provide two kinds of Chinese food with the last order no earlier than 9pm. Bar service should be available to 1am. There should be a 24-hour coffee shop and a breakfast and dinner buffet. A clinic should be on-site. A business center with photocopying, typing and translation services should be available, as should a ticketing agency with city tours and babysitting services.

Five-star hotels are usually palatial with huge lobbies. The hardware and food in some match the best of New York but the English won't be as good. Still, service and English should be the best available, especially in the international chain hotels.

No-Star Hotels

These can be very dirty, with public hole-in-the-floor toilets, no English, heat or air- conditioning.

Don't be surprised if attendants snarl at guests, are reluctant to carry luggage, answer bells, or give any type of service. A few might be fire traps with stairways locked or blocked. Few have good bedside reading lamps. But there are no-star hotels where the staff is sweet and helpful where you'll be pleasantly surprised.

Many inns in some tourist places like Lijiang, Pingyao and Yangshuo have no stars, and are clean and adequate. In some tourist cities, families are opening their homes to foreign guests for about Y100 a night, or free in exchange for English lessons. Look at Pingyao and Zhuhai.

One- & Two-Star Hotels

These can be acceptable sometimes. An attendant might go to the bank for money changing, or take telexes to the post office. Some will send someone to get plane tickets, or hail a taxi. You can frequently borrow adapters (for electric razors), portable electric heaters, fans, hair-dryers, and irons. Some also have in-house television (in Chinese).

Most have shower curtains, hand or low shower heads, and one day laundry service. The air-conditioning and heat might not be adequate. Many have low-wattage bedside reading lamps. But the carpets will be stained and badly laid. A few of these hotels might have roaches, but I have never experienced bed bugs. A few might also have smelly and clogged public toilets, and poor plumbing in the rooms.

Sometimes gates are locked after 11pm and while most hotels over three stories have elevators, sometimes these are turned off at night. In either case, make a loud noise and wake someone up.

Western breakfast selections might be limited to greasy fried eggs, orange juice, toast, and coffee. The Chinese breakfast would probably be better.

Attempts to make reservations by fax or letter might just end up in a pile of unclaimed mail. Few staff, if any, can read English. Just take a chance and show up, or telephone on arrival. Some hotels charge the guest if the hotel has to fax back. This is understandable, considering the cost of faxes and the low room rate.

In some of these hotels, standards might differ according to floors. Foreigners are usually given the best and most expensive rooms.

Top Hotels
Some of these hotels have their own fleets of Mercedes limousines or buses that make regular runs to the airport or city center. At least two hotels have Rolls Royces. Many have executive floors with concierges, free continental breakfasts, and fast check-in. Many have magnificent ball rooms and lobbies and cater to foreign business people on expense accounts. They have the best Western food, and probably the best Chinese food in town, and the most luxurious breakfast buffets. Some leave chocolates on your pillow, or a rubber ducky on your bathtub, nice little touches that bring a smile.

The danger of a luxury hotel, in China as elsewhere, is its great economic disparity with the life of the ordinary citizen. The cost of one night in such a hotel could be the equivalent of several months income. If you go to learn about China, you'll have to make a great effort to do so if you stay in a luxury hotel.

What to Expect
Air-conditioning and heat: All starred tourist hotels have these, but the quality varies according to cost. Once the heat is turned on for the winter, it takes three days in some hotels to switch back to air-conditioning. If there is a sudden heatwave, you might find your hotel too hot. You could ask the attendant to open the windows, but in some hotels, they can't be opened. It would be best to change to another room, out of the sun.

Beds: These are usually firm and good. Rooms for standard groups usually have twin-size beds. Some beds are too short and narrow for tall foreigners. Top hotels have duvets and feather pillows.

Check-out time: usually noon with 50% of the room rate charged if you stay until 6pm.

Chinese customs: While some hotels may look like North American hotels, don't be surprised to find staff sleeping in the lobby, and occasionally on the dining room tables.

Discounts: You should always try for one, especially if you know the occupancy rates are low. Sample dialogue: "What discount are you giving today? But it's a weekend. Don't you think it should be 20%? 50%? Okay, but how about including breakfast?" "Can I speak with the sales manager, please?"

Keys: There are different systems. In the lower ranks, you might not get a key at all. An attendant will open and lock your door for you Soviet-style. At the other end of the scale, you might get a customized electronic key system that makes a record of the comings and goings in your room. If something goes missing, security should know the time it happened.

In many hotels, the key card also activates the electricity, an energy saving device. However, if two people are in a room and one wants to read and then sleep while the other goes bar-hopping, there might be a problem with the lights. Many hotels only give one key card. So stick a comb or folded paper in the key card slot by the door.

Locks: Even some three-star hotels do not have double locks on their guestroom doors. An attendant could barge in on you at any time after a token knock. A rubber doorstopper helps.

Prostitution: Yes, it does exist, even in the best of hotels. You might get strange telephone calls from women at night, a knock on your door, or hear loud laughing in the hallways. It is of course illegal but hard to control. You can complain to the management. Be aware that some five-star hotels intercept all telephone calls to their guests so you won't be so bothered.

Security: Most top hotels have excellent security. You don't usually see anyone but hotel guests and staff on guest room floors. And you might notice security cameras. No unregistered guests can stay in rooms after 10 or 11pm. (This is not always enforced in poorly-managed hotels.) Hotel thefts are rare, especially in the four-stars and up international hotels, but don't leave tempting valuables unlocked and in sight. Use the safe deposit boxes. Pilfering by hotel staff is rare but it happens. Items taken recently have included perfume, sweaters, shoes, flashlights, cigarettes, and film. If you are on a lower floor, make sure your windows are locked.

Smoke alarms: These are usually in every room. Fire extinguishers should be on every floor, and fire hoses on higher floors. Most rooms have fire exit maps in English on their doors.

Sports: Hotels at all levels could have bicycles for rent, ping pong, badminton, and billiards. Attendants at swimming pools are not necessarily trained lifeguards, and you should supervise your own children. Also, personally check the cleanliness of a pool. Many hotels have imported fitness equipment. And you can ask about taiji/taichi groups you can join at 6am in the parks. Some hotels have aerobics, morning bicycle tours, and jogging maps.

State Guest Houses: These can be palatial, some suites used by queens with large gardens and lots of privacy. Rooms are frequently big with high ceilings. The service, service facilities, and maintenance, however, are usually poor.

Suites: Some of the top hotels have fancy two-story duplexes, or studios. Even medium-range hotels might have incredible luxury suites with gold-plated fixtures, antiques, and jacuzzis.

Surcharges: Even Chinese-managed hotels add a service charge of five to 20% on rooms, telephone calls and meals. Part of this could be a municipal tax.

Telephones: In most hotels three-stars and up, the telephone operator should speak English. If you're in a cheaper hotel where no one speaks English, you can make local calls by first pushing '0' or '9'. If it is not a dial phone, tell the operator "wai xian" (why she-an). To ask for the service desk, where there just might be someone who speaks English, say "fu wu tai" (foo woo tie). To get other rooms in most hotels, just dial the room number unless otherwise specified.

Not all hotels will have IDD capability in every guest room. You might have to call the operator or go to a desk in the lobby. If there is no IDD, you can still call from your room. You might have to book the call at the service desk, and pay a service charge beforehand. Or an attendant might come knocking on your door afterwards. It could take hours.

There is usually a service charge, even for collect calls not completed. You might want to ask the rate first. For more information, see Chapter 7.

Tipping: See Chapter 7.

University Hostels: These are included because they are inexpensive, and because these give you opportunities to meet and interact with students. Some universities have new, good hostels. Others are dirty and run-down.

Water for Drinking: Top hotels now give free bottled water. In addition, hot, boiled water is available in thermoses in all hotels, either in the room, or free on request. Sometimes, there is a flask for cooling. Don't drink water out of the tap, not even in the top hotels.

Some hotels have electric kettles that turn themselves off upon boiling. This does not give enough time to kill all the bacteria. Do not use the non-potable water in these devices. Many hotels also provide ice cubes, hopefully made of boiled water.

Workmanship: This could be bad. You can't expect people who have never seen a western bathroom to know that paint shouldn't be slopped on top of marble, nor bare holes left in bathroom floors.

Hotel Chains: The top international chains are the Crowne Plaza, Hilton, Hyatt, Kempinski, Marriott, Meritus, Okura, Peninsula, Regal, Renaissance, Ritz-Carlton, Shangri-La, Sheraton and Sofitel. I would also recommend the Courtyard by Marriott, Holiday Inn, Novotel, and SAS. The Gloria and Zenith have a range of hotels from three- to five-stars. Days' Inn is opening some cheaper hotels. Silk Road Hotel Management Co. Hong Kong has some very interesting hotels on the Silk Road, most in Chinese architecture. The International Youth Hostel Federations has opened several hostels which are recommended for backpackers. Some have standard rooms which are okay for budget travelers too.

Of the Chinese-managed groups, the Jin Jiang runs the gamut from the pretentious Jin Jiang Tower (Shanghai) and the very good Kunlun (Beijing) down to modest hotels with peeling wallpaper and poor service. The China Friendship Tourist Hotel Group ranges from one or two good properties down to poor ones. Huating is so-so.

Hotel Prices

You should not have to pay the prices published in this book. Most hotels give discounts all year round. 'Walk-in' discounts can range from 10% to 50% of the published price. Corporate discounts have been up to 60% if your company has signed a contract guaranteeing a minimum number of rooms per year. Sheraton hotels give 'Suresavers' with 30% saving if booked 30 days in advance. It also has weekend specials. Also see Saving Money in Chapter 7.

It is almost meaningless to print prices because they keep changing and are negotiable. For the latest prices for hotels belonging to international chains, use the North American toll-free numbers above or contact the hotel itself. Prices for rooms booked by travel agents might be even cheaper (plus service charge). There's also the web, or you could telephone the sales manager at the hotel directly. You have to do some homework for your bargains.

China's system of awarding stars to hotels gives some indication of price, but a four- star in Beijing is much more expensive than a four-star in Guilin. Prices published here are maximums.

best places to stay

Chapter 13

The hotels listed here are those I particularly like. For more details and prices, look up the full review in the hotel's respective destination chapter.

Guangzhou Favorites

The **White Swan** has a magnificent atrium garden, and a great location on historic Shamian Island beside the Pearl River and next to the US Consulate. I like sitting in its coffee shop and watching the river traffic go by, and I like its good quality shops. I like wandering around almost car-free Shamian Island, a quiet oasis away from the crowded city. But the hotel is close enough to walk to the very special, very exotic Qingping Market.

I also like the **China Hotel** because of its service, food and English. It's so convenient to everything. You can walk to many tourist attractions and the train station. The other preferred hotel is the **Garden**, because of its magnificent lobby and its proximity to stores, and restaurants with which it is joined by a convenient overpass. No risking my life crossing busy streets here. I like its cheaper food street, its buses with Hong Kong, and downtown check-in for China Southern Airlines.

Gloria International Hotels

Gloria International Hotels are not consistently the top of the market, but they have some pretty good ones. I especially like its hotel in **Harbin**, the **Gloria Inn**. It is such a jewel because of its location. The inn is right on the Songhua River, on a "walking street," a real plus. If you follow the river to the right, there is one of the largest, most exotic street markets in China. Away from the river is the city's main shopping area surrounded by old Russian buildings. The hotel itself is modest, but clean. It has the basics, only three stars, and the price is right. There's also the **Gloria** in Qinhuangdao. This is also basic and modest, but it's almost in the shadow of the Great Wall. The location is wonderful.

The **Gloria Resort** in **Sanya, Hainan Island** is in a beautiful tropical setting. It is set amid franjipani trees and bougainvillea bushes, and right on a white-sand beach. Its free- form pool goes under bridges, and I'm looking forward to trying its barbecue. Its Chinese food was so great, we didn't want to try anything else. You can rent all kinds of equipment like sailboards and scuba now. Its presidential villa is one of the most tastefully decorated in China.

Harbour Plaza Hotels

The Harbour Plaza chain is new and growing. I've only seen two and especially like the **Harbour Plaza Chongqing** because of its location right downtown on a "walking" street, close to shops, offices, and the ferry pier. In the past, I've hated shopping in Chongqing because of traffic-congested streets. But now it's great.

I also like the **Harbour Plaza** in **Kunming** because of the minority textiles in the lobby, the service, and the superb location near Green Lake.

Holiday Inns

I usually count on Holiday Inns to be clean and well managed, with good Western food and good English. Four-star prices are lower than five. I love the one in **Urumqi** because up to now, it's been pretty well the only hotel on the Silk Road with real Western standards. Going there after the dust of the Gobi Desert, and cruddy hotels elsewhere, is like going home for a while. I love the setting of the **Holiday Inn Riverside** in **Wuhan.** You can walk down to the cruise ships and along the Yangtze River, and go next door to some exotic buildings.

I have been drawn to the **Lido** in **Beijing** because it has every possible service I need— a post office, Bank of China, a Hong Kong drug store (but no pharmacy), and a real supermarket – all under the same roof. It has cheaper Chinese restaurants and a street market in the neighborhood. The rooms are big, unpretentious, and comfortable; the twin beds are doubles and I can spread my work out on one. If I happen to be there for Thanksgiving, I know I can get a turkey dinner. I can also get great Thai food in a luxurious Thai setting. It has 25 television channels and every guest gets a *Herald Tribune* as well as *China Daily*. It also has a book shop, deli and a laundry shop. It is also easy to remember the Chinese name, "Lido Fandian," for taxi drivers.

There always seems to be a Lido representative at the airport and no need to wait in the taxi line. Its shuttle bus goes frequently downtown and back. It's only 20 minutes to the Friendship Store. After a couple of nights there, I feel recharged and ready to go back to places with no international news, and no weather reports.

Hong Kong Favorites

To choose the best hotel in Hong Kong is a struggle, a toss-up between the **Peninsula**, the **Grand Hyatt**, and the **Island Shangri-la**.

At the Peninsula, my junior suite was marvelous, huge, decorated in rich Indian prints, with more telephones than I could count. It had a fax machine, a giant desk, and a thermometer reading outside temperature. It also had a magnificent bathtub flush to a window, where you can soak and enjoy the view. The sight of the harbor from the living room – it was the 16th floor – especially with its 19th century Bombay telescope, was worth the long flight across the Pacific. The telescope was permanently set up and strategically located to catch just about anything in the harbor, from tiny pilot boats to giant cruise ships, from little junks to navy cruisers. The view was so stunning with all the lights I didn't want to close the curtains.

The Grand Hyatt has the same great roof-top garden as the Renaissance Harbour View and the same marvelous view of the harbor. But it is a more beautiful hotel, more luxurious, and of course, more expensive. I had high tea here, Devonshire cream and the whole bit. I don't think England could have done better.

The Island Shangri-la is mentioned below under the Shangri-la Hotels section. **The Salisbury YMCA**, has been a favorite since my first trip to Hong Kong in 1961, the place to stay when a company expense account is not picking up the tab. But it's not only the price. The Y has a million-dollar location next door to the Peninsula, and this time I found the food and service vastly improved. It's got the only laundromat found so far in a hotel in town. There's a great gym and pool, and you can now also make a reservation by e-mail or fax.

Marriott International

This U.S. chain has some excellent hotels and I especially like the one in **Chongqing** for its service and location. I'm looking forward to seeing its new hotel in **Shanghai** on my next trip, close to pedestrian Nanjing Road and the Shanghai Museum.

New World Hotels

I like the **Grand New World Xi'an**, its lobby warmed by an amazing carpet, and punctuated by giant statues, ministers of the Qin emperor. It has a decent food street, especially enjoyed because you don't have to go far to save money. It is inside the city wall and convenient to the Grand Mosque and market, and it now has this interesting new Buddhist temple behind it.

Shangri-La Hotels

The Shangri-La Hotels are an Asian-based chain. My favorite is the **Island Shangri-La** in Hong Kong because it's so beautiful, with its multi-storied Chinese landscape painting and its profusion of Venetian chandeliers and art work. Its location is ideal too, so handy to everything, including one of Hong Kong's best parks and shopping malls. It is close to the metro, trams, a walk to the ferries and the British relics of the city.

I also like the **China World Hotel** in **Beijing** for its beautiful lobby and good location on Jianguomenwai. The China World is a self-contained world, a convenience desperately needed when time is short. It too has a good supermarket, a good bakery, a deli, a gym, and several places to reconfirm plane tickets. It has a wide range of restaurants in the complex including one where you can get a quick, cheap lunch. And there's a cyber cafe nearby. No one needs to go outside at all. It has more stores than the Lido but it doesn't have its park. It is a quick drive to Tiananmen Square and the antique market. But it's a lot more expensive. You're paying for a very luxurious and palatial hotel, a marvelous lobby lounge, good rooms and service. You're paying for a downtown location, and a very spacious and private hotel setting, within walking distance of offices, the very special Silk Market, and department stores. In Beijing I also like the **Shangri-La** and the **Kerry Center Hotel** too.

If I rave about Shangri-La Hotels, it's because they are excellent. The service and the food are usually superb and lavish. Their locations are usually the best. The **Pudong Shangri-La** has one of the best situations in Shanghai, in relatively uncrowded Pudong, right near the waterfront. From there is one of the best views of the lights on Shanghai's historic Bund.

The Shangri-La in **Hangzhou** is a favorite because of its quiet garden setting. I've liked it even before it was taken over by the Shangri-La people. You can just walk out the door, past the trees, across the road, and there's lovely West Lake. I like to walk early in the morning and the lake, especially at dawn, has a magical quality about it. Out onto the nearby causeway with water on either side, you can see the morning sun, a rosy one on my last trip, peeking out from behind strings of weeping willow branches, bare in winter. And if I stand in the right spot, you can frame the sun under a deeply-curved Song-dynasty roof while the mist hides the line of modern skyscrapers on the tranquil horizon. You can breathe deeply as everything seems to blend together in a living, classical Chinese painting.

One time when I was there, a group of white-haired seniors on bicycles came charging along, yelling for people to get out of the way. They wanted to speed up so they could ride over the humpback bridge without having to stop and walk up. It was so unexpected and fun, it made me want to live in Hangzhou when I retire.

The hotel itself is romantic, old in a nice way, quiet, warm, not marred by glitz. The rooms are bigger than its rival, the Dragon; the atmosphere is more classy but simple and not pretentious. The lake is an extension of the hotel's garden.

I could continue raving about other Shangri-Las too. They are all beautiful, a fusion of East and West, with good locations, good rooms, and fine service. I like them all.

If you pay the full rate at any Shangri-La, you get free airport limousine transfers, laundry, breakfast, local telephone calls, long-distance calls at cost, and late 6pm check-out.

Sheraton Hotels

I don't like big, brassy hotels with giant chrome pillars. So, no matter how good the service and the rooms, I have avoided the Great Wall Sheraton in Beijing. But recently however, Sheraton has been opening some marvelous new hotels. I think **St. Regis** in **Beijing** is one of the most beautiful in the country. The service and location off Jianguomenwai are great too.

But the Sheraton in **Suzhou** takes the cake. It is built in Chinese style, not gawdy stereotypical Chinese palace style, but quiet Suzhou Song and Ming dynasty garden style. It even has an adaptation of maze-like courtyards in which you can get very lost. It too is one of the most beautiful in the country. And its location inside the city moat, surrounded by history, is excellent.

Silk Road International Hotels

This new Hong Kong chain has been opening or taking over some hotels with real Chinese flavor. I'm anxious to see the hotel across the street from the Tibetan Buddhist Monastery in **Xining** (Qinghai province) because it looks like part of that monastery. Its hotel in **Dunhuang** is like a fortress and is outside of town in the desert. You can see the desert sunrise and sunset from its grounds. Its hotel in **Beijing** is also in old courtyard style but much smaller.

Zenith

Zenith also has a range of properties from five-star down to three. The one I like best is the **Harbour View** in **Zhuhai**, because the service and food are good and it's right on the ocean.

Chapter 14

beijing

The capital of China – **Beijing** – is surrounded by Hebei province and is on the northern fringe of the North China plain. It is 180 km west of the sea and about 44 meters above sea level, with mountains to the north, west, and east. The population is about 12 million (7 or 8 million urban) and 3 million "floaters" or unregistered migrants. At least 500,000 people have cars and there are 8 million bicycles.

The best time to visit is autumn. High tourist season is September 15 to November 15, and March 1 to June 1. It is at almost the same latitude as Philadelphia with similiar temperatures. The hottest days are in July and August, up to 38°C; the coldest are in January and February, down to -20°C, sometimes with snow. Sand storms occasionally blow from December to late March, and sometimes into May and even August. The winter air is heavily polluted and very dry. The annual precipitation is 683 millimeters, usually from June to August. There's a chronic water shortage which should be alleviated in the future by diverting water from the Yellow and Yangtze Rivers.

In 2001, Beijing was named host for the 2008 Summer Olympic Games. In the years leading up to the Games, don't expect to get around this city with ease as roads get widened, two new subways and a light rail system get built, and whole neighborhoods get demolished and recon-structed. Restaurants and bars will disappear and hopefully reappear elsewhere. If you are going to spend any length of time in this city, do get yourself a mobile telephone so you can inform people you're going to be late, or you're lost and please tell the taxi driver how to get there.

This warning is to prepare you for the worst, but not to deter you from a visit as Beijing strives to become "a modern city with an ancient flavor." Guides and drivers should have figured out ways to get around as painlessly as possible by the time you get there. I hope. Construction plans include the refurbishing and opening of additional heritage sites like the home of Matteo Ricci, the remarkable 16th century Jesuit missionary from Italy. The air should get progressively cleaner towards 2008 and the taxi drivers should have learned their 300 phrases in English.

Note: If the air quality index is below 100, all is well. If it's between 200 and 300, it's medium pollution. If it's over 300, it's heavy pollution and people are advised to stay indoors. You could carry a scarf or mask to cover your nose if you think the air will bother you. Beijing is doing a lot to eliminate air pollution, limiting motor vehicles inside the city, and switching to natural gas inside the Fourth Ring Road. It has been exiling polluting factories to the far suburbs.

Arrivals & Departures
By Air
Beijing is about a four hour flight west of Tokyo, three hours north of Guangzhou or Hong Kong, and 1 1/2 hours northwest of Shanghai. It has air links with 81 Chinese cities and at least 45 foreign cities.

If you're flying into Beijing, be aware that fog might delay flights in winter. The "left luggage" storage room at the airport is not open 24 hours. Taxis from the airport downtown should cost Y60-Y90.

Public "A" Airbuses ply between the main Beijing Railway Station and the airport every 20-30 minutes for about Y16. A1 stops at the Hilton, A2 at the Lufthansa Center, Kempinski, Landmark, Great Wall Sheraton and Huadu Hotels. A4 goes to the Swissôtel and Beijing Asia Hotel, and A6 goes to the Beijing International Hotel and Wangfujing. For information, Tel. 65265019.

At the airport also, each airline has a ticket booth where you can reconfirm and buy tickets. It is a good place to compare prices and look for discounts. Beijing to Shanghai costs about Y1030, and to Chongqing Y1400. Beijing to Lhasa costs Y2040, and to Guangzhou Y1510. Beijing to Xi'an costs Y960, and Kunming Y1600 or Y1670 depending on the airline. Ask about discounted red-eye specials. You can probably get flights to Shanghai without a reservation.

In the departure level also, exchange rates differ slightly between the China Construction Bank and the Bank of China. These banks are side by side. You can get a cash advance with a Visa card. These banks are open 9am to 4:30pm weekdays, and 9am to 6pm on Saturdays and Sundays. A clinic is open 7am to 9pm, and a hospital is open 24 hours. The post office sells IP and IC telephone cards, and foreign newspapers as well as stamps. It is open 6:30am to 8pm. For **general airport inquiries**, call *64563604*.

Among the airlines servicing Beijing are:

• **Aeroflot**, *Tel. 65002980, 65002412*

- **Air Canada**, *Tel. 64682001, Fax 64637906, 64634048*
- **Air China**: the booking office for all Chinese airlines is at 15 Chang'an Xi Avenue, west of the Telegraph Building (clock tower) and Zhongnanhai gate, *Tel. 66017755*. For domestic flights, *Tel. 66013336;* for international flights, *Tel. 66016667;* for the information counter at the airport, *Tel. 26892689 x 2580, 64663698*
- **Air France**, *Tel. 65881388, 65051818. Fax 65881389*
- **Air Macau**, *Tel. 65158988. Fax 65159979*
- **Alitalia**, *Tel. 65610378. Fax 65056654*
- **All Nippon Airways**, *Tel. 65053311. Fax 65909175*
- **Austrian Airlines**, *Tel. 64622161/4, Fax 64682166, 64622166*
- **British Airways**, *Tel. 65124070, Fax 65123637*
- **Dragonair**, *Tel. 65182533, Fax 65183455, 65054347*
- **Finnair**, *Tel. 65127180, Fax 65127182*
- **Japan Airlines**, *Tel. 65130888. Fax 65139865*
- **Kazakh Airlines**, *Tel. 65126688*
- **KLM Royal Dutch**, *Tel. 65053505. Fax 65055506*
- **Korean Airlines**, *Tel. 65050088, 65051047. Fax 65051049*
- **Lufthansa**, *Tel. 64654488. Fax 64653223*
- **Malaysian Airlines**, *Tel. 65052681-3. Fax 65052680*
- **Mongolian Airlines**, *Tel. 65079297. Fax 65077397*
- **Northwest**, *Tel. 65053505, Fax 65051855*
- **PIA**, *Tel. 65051681-4, Fax 65052257*
- **Qantas**, *Tel. 64674794, 64673337, Fax 6451098*
- **SAS**, *Tel. 65183738, Fax 65183736*
- **SIA**, *Tel. 65052233, Fax 65051178. Web: Http://www.singaporeair.com*
- **Thai International**, *Tel. 64608899. Fax 64606990*
- **United Airlines**, *Tel. 64631111. Fax 64635634*

By Train

Beijing is at least a 28-hour high-speed trip north of Hong Kong and 19 hours northwest of Shanghai. It can also be reached by train from Ulan Bator (Mongolia), and, beyond that, from Moscow. Rail links are with every provincial and regional capital except Lhasa.

Tickets can be booked 30 days in advance on the Beijing Through Train from Hong Kong which leaves on alternate days. The train departs from Hung Hom Station in Kowloon at 3:00pm and arrives at Beijing West at 6:58pm the following day. Consult *http://www.kcrc.com* for schedules and fares, which are roughly HK$508 to HK$1039.

The high-speed deluxe train from Shanghai with two people sharing a compartment costs Y900 per person.

The new West Beijing Railway Station is in southwest Beijing on Lianhuachi Dong, 6.7 km from Tiananmen Square, *Tel. 63216263, 63216253*. It has been the terminal for all trains going through the city of Zhengzhou, including those from Hong Kong. The old east Beijing Station, near the Beijing International Hotel, has been the terminal for three international lines (Trans-Siberian, Mongolia, and North Korea) and trains from Shanghai and Inner Mongolia. For train inquiries, *Tel. 6554866, 65776851, 65129525.*

If you're planning on traveling to Russia by train, do contact Monkey Business Info for travel tips and tickets. The Chinese train (#3) leaves Beijing on Wednesdays at 7:40am via Datong. The Russian train (#19) leaves on Saturdays at 11:10pm via Shenyang and Harbin. They take about seven days to reach Moscow. You can buy tickets also at China International Travel Service (Beijing International Hotel). See Practical Information below.

Train Prices
The Novotel Peace Hotel supplied these prices in Chinese yuan in late 2001 for the following Chinese cities. "X" means the frequency per day for express trains. It charges a Y5 service fee for bookings. You can book tickets here three days before departure e.g. tickets for Sunday cannot be bought before the preceding Thursday. Do ask for the name and address of the train station.

	Soft Berth	Hard Berth	Hard Seat	
Hefei	Y400	263	143	
Zhengzhou	264	175	94	4X
Wuchang	429	281	154	2X
Changsha	529	345	191	1X
Guangzhou	705	458	253	3X
Shenzhen	720	467	257	1X
Kunming	890	578	320	1X
Chengdu	642	418	231	2X
Chongqing	545	348	181	2X
Urumqi	1006	652	363	1X
Yichang	486	319	175	1X
Xi'an	417	274	150	1X

By Bus
A 1300 km expressway runs between Beijing and Shanghai and goes through Tianjin, Jinan, Tai'an, Linyi, Zhenjiang, Wuxi, and Suzhou. You can also take buses to many other neighboring cities. You can get long distance buses at the Zhagongkou bus terminal.

Orientation
Beijing is the most important place to visit in China. It is the nation's capital and it has a 3,000-year history, beginning in the Western Zhou dynasty, when it was known as **Ji** (Chi). Its most impressive historical monuments date from

the 13th century A.D. The museums here have the best collections in China, the temples among the most impressive. The palaces are the biggest and most elaborate. For most Chinese people, visiting Beijing has been and still is a lifetime ambition and many are now able to do it.

The **Liao** (916-1125 A.D.) were the first to build a capital here. They called it Nanjing, Southern Capital, as distinct from their old capital farther north in Manchuria. The name was changed again to **Yanjing** (Yenching) in 1013. In 1125, the Jin, a Tartar dynasty, overthrew the Liao and enlarged the city, calling it **Zhongdu**, Central Capital. The Mongols (Yuan) under Kublai Khan overthrew the Jin and built a new capital called **Dadu** (Ta Tu). In 1368 the Ming drove out the Yuan and established its capital at Nanjing in 1409, with Beijing, then called **Peiping Fu**, as an auxiliary capital.

Beijing became the main capital again in 1421 (Ming) and continued as the Qing capital into the early 1900s. In 1860, it was invaded by foreign troops, mainly English and French. The foreigners completely destroyed the Yuanmingyuan Palace. The Boxers took over in 1900 and laid siege to the Foreign Legation section, but were repelled by an international military force while the Qing Empress Dowager fled temporarily to Xi'an. In 1928, the Nationalist government moved its capital to today's Nanjing, and Beijing became **Peiping** (Northern Peace). The Japanese held it from 1937 to 1945. When the Communists took over in 1949, it regained its old name and former position as capital of the nation.

During imperial times, no structures taller than the Forbidden City were allowed. Fortunately, Beijing escaped the Pacific War relatively intact. In 1959, ten massive buildings were completed for the tenth anniversary of the founding of the People's Republic. Built in the heavy, plain Soviet style, these included the Great Hall of the People, the Museums of History and the Revolution, and the Palace of the Minorities. They are period pieces now.

Beijing is centered around the **Forbidden City** and **Tiananmen Square**. The old legation area is east of the square, between the Beijing, Xinqiao, and Capital Hotels. The few remaining European buildings there reflect that period of its history. The Chinese city was south of the Qianmen Gate on the southern edge of Tiananmen Square. Do note that the north-south meridian is in a straight line through the Drum Tower and Bell Tower, right through the middle of the Forbidden City.

Beijing is circled by four concentric ring roads without stop lights. Second Ring Road, which the No. 2 metro line follows, has several names: Andingmengdong St., Chaoyangmennan, Fuchengmennan St., Xizhimennan St., and Deshengmenxi St. Third Ring Road is Sanhuan Zhong, Dong, Bei, Xi or Nan, depending on the locations – central, east, north, west or south. There is talk of this road becoming Olympic Boulevard. Fourth Ring Road is the next circular road outside of it and is Sihuan as in Beisihuandong Lu (North Fourth

Ring East Road). A fifth ring road is being constructed and should be finished before 2007.

Beijing now consists of ten districts and nine counties. Chaoyang District is the Central Business District. Rural villages raise the famous force-fed Beijing ducks. Over 2000 factories, mainly in the suburbs, produce iron and steel, mine coal, make machines, basic chemicals and petroleum, electronics, and textiles.

The people of Beijing speak **Mandarin** (putong hua), the official national language, but they twirl their tongues more and go heavy on the "r's." They are predominantly **Han**, but you will see flat, wide Mongolian and Manchu faces too. Beijing people tend to be reserved compared to other Chinese. Don't be put off by this, for they are warm and friendly once they get to know you.

Getting Around Town

You need at least six hectic days to cover the important attractions in Beijing. If you have more time, do it leisurely. The easiest way to get around is by taxi except for traffic jams. The fastest is by metro.

Bicycle rickshaws are cheap but only used for short distances. You have to decide on a price before you hop aboard. About Y10 is fair for one kilometer and these can frequently get around traffic jams. You can rent bicycles at some hotels, among them the Palace and Song He Hotels.

Large public tour buses, You 1 to You 18 with tickets from Y30 to Y60, go to the Great Wall at Mutianyu, Simatai, and other tourist areas. Tour buses 1 to 5 follow regular routes to major tourist attractions. Tour Bus 1 goes from Qianmen to the Badaling Great Wall and the Ming Tombs.

Express air-conditioned buses ply the city for a few yuan every five to ten minutes. Good for visitors is No. 801 from Liangmaqiao near the Kempinski to Qinghua and Beijing universities, and the Summer Palace. There's also the frequent and comfortable No. 808 from the northwest side of the Beijing Railway Station past Xidan, the Beijing Exhibition Centre, the zoo, Xiyuan Hotel, Carrefour shopping mall, the Olympic Hotel, the National Library, Friendship Hotel, Cyber Tower, and Modern Plaza Computer City. Its terminal is at the back gate of the Summer Palace (Yi He Yuan), a 1 1/2 hour trip for Y6. Regular buses 1, 4, 37, 52 and 57 link Tiananmen Square with the Friendship Store, the Silk Market, and the Jianguo, Jinglun and China World hotels. Check all these buses the day before your trip to make sure they're still operating.

For detailed up-to-date information in English, phone the **Beijing Tourism Hotline**, *Tel. 65130828.*

Many individual travelers use public transport successfully if they have the time. Just avoid rush hours especially 7:30am-9am and 4pm-7pm. Public buses and subways operate from 5am-11 or 11:30pm and cost Y3. Bus and subway maps are available in many hotels.

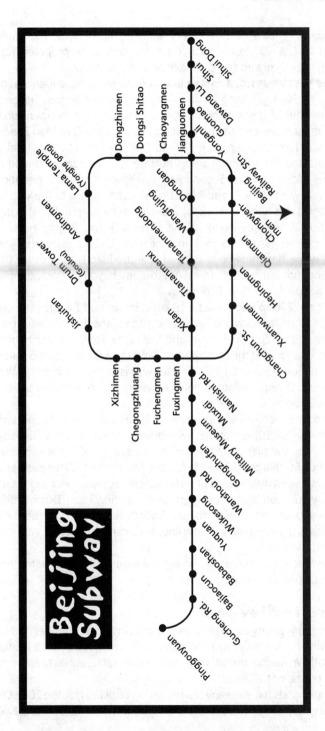

Subway trains operate every three-eight minutes and stations are marked with a "D" inside two concentric circles. Be prepared for people pushing their way into the carriages before you get out.

The **east-west no. 1 metro line** goes from Pingguoyuan station in the west along Fuxing, Chang'an and Jianguomenwai Avenues. "Pingguoyuan" is on the front of trains going west, and "Shui Dong" is on trains going east. Important stations on this line from east to west are Guo Mao Zhan at Third Ring Road. From here you can walk to Traders, China World Hotel, Jianguo Hotel and the Silk Market from its north exit. Jianguomen Station is across from the Gloria Hotel on Second Ring Road, south of the International Post Office, and west of the Friendship Store. You can change to the loop line here.

Dongdan is about a block west of the Beijing International Hotel and its youth hostel. Wangfujing is at the Oriental Plaza, Beijing Hotel and the important Wangfujing Avenue. Tiananmendong is at the east end of Tiananmen Square while Tiananmenxi is at its west end. Xidan is the exit for the CAAC office and Xidan shopping street. At Fuxingmen, you can change to the loop line or get off for CITS or Parkson's.

The **no. 2 loop line** makes a 16-km circle around Tiananmen Square and the Forbidden City following Second Ring Road (and the old wall), and reaches near the Beijing Zoo (Xizhimen) and the Lama Temple (Yonghegong). The Qianmen station is at the south end of Tiananmen Square. Some stations have no destination signs in English. The subway is being expanded with a north-south line to Olympic Village. A light rail system is planned to link the city center with the airport.

Taxis are plentiful and available 24 hours a day. The cheapest are those marked with Y1.20, sometimes with drivers who don't know the city. These cost Y10 for the first five km, then Y1.20 every additional kilometer. Taxis marked Y1.60 charge Y10 for the first five km, then Y1.60 for every additional. There have been attempts at orderly taxi lines at the airport and train station, but in the end, you have to be aggressive in getting a taxi. Do not fall for touts who ask you where you want to go in English. It is best to join the taxi queues. Avoid roads marked with a yellow line. Taxis can't stop there. And make sure the meter is running.

See *Practical Information* for **sightseeing tours** from hotels and travel agencies.

Where to Stay

There are plenty of hotel rooms, except in late September and October, and during trade shows and conferences. Hotels have direct telephone lines and booths at Beijing airport's international arrival terminal. Many hotels have shuttle buses, not all free.

Some hotels have already started taking bookings for the 2008 Olympics, but many say they won't know prices until a year or so before. Olympic

Stadium and Village will be in the north of the city. Sporting events will be all over the city.

Beijing has a lot of good hotels now. Below are those I recommend because of quality and location. They include cheaper and lower quality ones for budget travelers.

The most luxurious and classy hotel with top services is the St. Regis. The China World and Shangri-La are not quite as lavish, but they are also tops for service and quality. These are followed by the Kempinski, the Great Wall and Palace. This order will probably change as hotels are redecorated and services upgraded. The new Grand Hyatt should be up there too.

The best of the four-star hotels are the Holiday Inn Lido, the Jianguo, and Traders. Up and coming is the Harbour Plaza. The Song He is the best three-star hotel because of its central location and tolerable standards. The best for backpackers are the two Youth Hostels.

Prices listed here are in US dollars or Chinese yuan. Check my website: www.china-travel-guide.com for current exchange rates. The published rates listed are subject to change, negotiations, a 10% to 15% surcharge and Y6 tax per bed per day. Some hotels have recently discounted 10%-60% off these published prices even during high tourist season. Local telephone calls range from free to two yuan. Some hotels have in-room safes only in suites or executive floors; safes are mentioned if they're in every room.

Hotels here are all international quality except for the cheapest ones, with money exchange, credit card service, business centers, beauty salons, western coffee shop, and international direct dial. The top hotels can organize theme parties for groups. The best sports facilities are at the Kerry, Holiday Inn Lido, China World, and Kempinski. Because traffic jams downtown are endemic, do consider a hotel close to the places you need to visit.

A Crowne Plaza Beijing North is scheduled to open in late 2002, 10 km north of the Beijing Asian Games Village, close to Olympic Village and towards the Great Wall. It should have 593 rooms (including apartments) and be great for conferences and weekends out of the city. If you want the experience of "old Beijing," do look at the three-star Bamboo Garden Hotel, the Lu Song Yuan and the Haoyuan Binguan.

The following are roughly in order of location, the highest prices first in each area, and the areas closest to Tiananmen first. See also Chapter 13, China's Best Places to Stay.

Around the Forbidden City & Tiananmen Square

The best location for tourists and some business people is near Tiananmen Square. The Grand Hotel here is the only hotel with traditional Chinese rooms. It's the closest hotel to the Forbidden City. The Beijing Hotel next to it is of lesser quality and has recently been renovated with an unusual décor that takes some getting used to.

Around the corner is Wangfujing Avenue, now partly a pedestrian street with its mix of modern chrome-plated shopping malls, the old Catholic church, and a couple of tiny old stores with latticed wooden fronts. Outdoor cafes, grass and real flowers make this a pleasant spot in warm weather. Nearby, and also within walking distance of the Forbidden City, are several hotels. The Palace is the best of the lot here. The Crowne Plaza is second, the Grand is third and the Beijing fourth. Next and a long way behind are the Tianlun Dynasty, Novotel Peace, Wangfujing Grand, Prime, Song He and Day's Inn roughly in order of quality. The Haoyuan, in this area which up to now has been a real, old-style Beijing inn, is planning renovations in 2002. You might want to look at it later in the year.

The five-star quality Grand Hyatt Beijing opened too late to be reviewed for this book but it has the second best location in town across from the Beijing Hotel in the huge glass-sided Oriental Plaza—if you like that glitzy kind of place. Because of Hyatt's reputation, I would rate it provisionally right after the Palace near the top even though I have yet to see it.

Oriental Plaza

The **Oriental Plaza** (Dong Feng Guang Chang), is a half-kilometer long and 200-meter wide office-apartment-hotel-shopping complex with two floors of supermarkets, shops with upmarket brands, Tony Roma's Restaurant, Schlotzsky's Deli, and a four-screen cineplex. It has three floors of underground parking (1,800 vehicles), and is promoted as the biggest commercial development in Asia. It has its own subway entrance and is home to the **Grand Hyatt Beijing**.

Further from the Forbidden City, south of the old Legation section and east of Tiananmen Square are the Capital, the New World Courtyard, and the Novotel Xinqiao in that order of quality, with the Capital best and closest to Tiananmen, and the Courtyard a close second for quality. The Xinqiao and New World are in a very crowded, traffic-congested neighborhood about one kilometer from the south end of the square. The New World Courtyard looks good but the Novotel Xinqiao might catch up with it. Novotel took over its management in 2001. The Courtyard and the Novotel Xinqiao have the advantage of being very close to the Chongwenmen metro stop. The Jianguo Qianmen Hotel is the only hotel in this group that is west of Tiananmen Square.

Unless otherwise mentioned, hotels here are about 30-35 km from the airport, two-three km from Beijing Railway Station and 8-10 km from the Beijing West train station. This area is also near Beijing municipal government offices, good restaurants, and traffic jams. Count on a 40-minute drive from the airport during the day.

THE PALACE HOTEL (Wangfu Fandian), *8 Goldfish Lane (Jinyu Hutung), Wangfujing Street, 100006. Five stars, Tel. 65592888, Fax 65129050. E-mail: info@peninsula.com or tph@peninsula.com. Website www.peninsula.com. $300-$400 for rooms, and $400-$3600 for suites. It has been discounting 30-40% off this rate.*

Built in 1989, the Palace has 17 stories and 530 classy rooms with safes, molded ceilings, and CNN, BBC and CNBC. Nice touches are its bathroom panic buttons, thermometers for exterior temperatures, and bathroom heat lamps. It has duplex suites, non-smoking and executive floors. Its room service and pressing service are available 24 hours. In the building is a Bank of China. The breakfast buffet is Y160, lunch is Y170, and dinner Y180. Especially good is its Cantonese restaurant. It has a year-round 25-meter-long indoor pool, 22-machine gym, spa, and aerobics and yoga classes. It has at least two Rolls Royces and bicycles for hire. Piaget should have its first China store here soon. I saw signs of wear but its lobby has since been refurbished. Managed by the Peninsula Group.

GRAND HOTEL BEIJING (Gui Bin Lou Fandian), *35 Chang'an Dong Avenue, 100006. Five stars, Tel. 65137788, 65130057. Fax 65130048, 65130050. E-mail: sales@mail.grandhotelbeijing.com.cn. Website: www.grandhotelbeijing.com. $200-$300 for rooms, $330-$2700 for suites. It has been discounting 20-40%.*

This is the most beautiful part of the Beijing Hotel complex and is separately managed. Built in 1989-90, this 10-story hotel has 218 large rooms with safes, CNN, Star TV and HBO. It has a 24-hour business center, small indoor pool, small gym and sauna. Its small dark lobby contrasts with its beautiful seven-story atrium with amazing zodiac reproductions from the Yuanmingyuan Palace. Cantonese, especially good Sichuan, and French food are available. The breakfast buffet costs $16. For a view of the Forbidden City, try the 10th floor bar at sunset on a clear day. A member of the Leading Hotels of the World.

CROWNE PLAZA BEIJING (Wang Guan Jia Re Jiudian), *48 Wangfujing Avenue, 100006. Five stars, Tel. 65133388, Fax 65132513. E-mail: hicpb@public3.bta.net.cn. Website: www.crowneplaza.com/hotels/pegwf. $200-$280 for rooms. $388-$1500 for suites. It has been discounting 40 to 50%.*

Built in 1991 with major renovations in 1999, this nine-story hotel has 383 rooms, in-room safes, executive and non-smoking floors. Rooms are 26 to 28 square meters. It has CNN, HBO, a 24-hour business center, and an art gallery. Its eighth floor rooms have computers. It also has a grill room, American, Cantonese and French food, and an airy eight-story atrium coffee shop. It rents out bicycles and has a steam bath, tanning machine, and 10 gym machines. Its indoor pool is 12.5 meters long. Its driveway is too small for big tour buses.

DYNASTY HOTEL (Tianlun Fandian), *50 Wangfujing Street, 100006. Five stars, Tel. 65138888, Fax 65245553, 65137866. E-mail: tianlun@tianlunhotel.com. Website: www.tianlunhotel.com. $200-$230 for rooms. $260-$1800 for suites. Ask for a discount.*

Built in 1991-92 and renovated in 1999, this nine-story, 408-room hotel has in-room safes, dirty carpets, CNN and pay television. Rooms are 22-38 square meters. It has a bake shop, Sichuan, Cantonese and Huaiyang restaurants, and a cheaper basement food street open 11:30am to 9:30pm. There's a gym, 15-meter indoor pool, bowling and tennis. Its 2500-square meter, seven-story high European-style atrium with fountain and "sidewalk" restaurant is breathtaking. There's an antique shop.

PRIME HOTEL BEIJING (Hua Qiao Da Sha), *2 Wangfujing Avenue, 100006. Five stars but looks like a four, Tel. 65136666, Fax 65134248. E-mail: sales@phb.com.cn. Website: www.primehotel.com (English). $200-240 for rooms, $320-$1500 for suites and includes breakfast. It has been discounting 20 to 30%.*

This was the Overseas Chinese Hotel in the 1960s. It is on the same street as the back gate of the Forbidden City, about a 15 minute walk. It has 10 stories and 402 rooms, mostly 35 to 42 square meters. It has CNN, an executive floor and non-smoking rooms. There are Chinese, Italian, Mexican, and Cantonese restaurants. There's a gym with 10 machines where I saw a guest running in bare feet – not very hygienic, and a small indoor pool and bicycles for hire. It looks worn and the grouting was moldy, but it has big in-room safes.

GRAND HYATT BEIJING, *1 Chang An Dong Avenue, 100738. Tel. 85181234, Sales Fax: 85186288. E-mail: grandhyattbeijing@hyattintl.com. Website: www.hyatt.com. This 591-room hotel in the Oriental Plaza opened in 2001 and has been offering special introductory room rates of $138 (single) and $158 (double) including complimentary buffet breakfast.*

Rooms have all-marble bathrooms, genuine goose-down duvets, and original works of art. They have high-speed modem lines and video-on-demand. Its 24-hour Grand Café has Italian, French and Beijing cuisine, and an open kitchen. High tea is available in its Fountain Lounge and its Noble House Chinese restaurant looks like a Chinese nobleman's courtyard mansion. It also has a patisserie. There's a gym, spa pools, and 50-meter long indoor pool with underwater music and "virtual sky."

CAPITAL HOTEL (So Du Dajiudian), *3 Qianmen Dong Street, 100006. Four stars, Tel. 65129988, Fax 65120321, 65120309. E-mail: capital.bch@meritus-hotel.com. $180-$288 for rooms and $320-$2,000 for suites. It has been discounting 20 to 50%.*

First built in 1989 with major renovations finished in mid-1996, this 22-story hotel has 326 large rooms, CNN and HBO, and in-room safes. Rooms average 38 square meters. It has two executive floors, four bowling lanes,

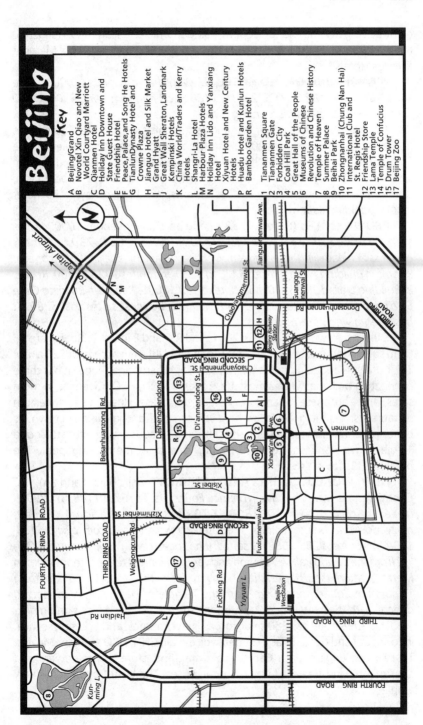

Beijing

Key

A Beijing/Grand
B Novotel Xin Qiao and New
   World Courtyard Marriott
C Qianmen Hotel
D Holiday Inn Downtown and
   State Guest House
E Friendship Hotel
F Peace,Palace,and Song He Hotels
G TianlunDynasty Hotel and
   Crowne Plaza
H Jianguo Hotel and Silk Market
I Grand Hyatt
J Great Wall Sheraton,Landmark
   Kempinski Hotels
K China World/Traders and Kerry
   Hotels
L Shangri-La Hotel
M Harbour Plaza Hotels
N Holiday Inn Lido and Yanxiang
   Hotel
O Xiyuan Hotel and New Century
   Hotels
P Huadu Hotel and Kunlun Hotels
R Bamboo Garden Hotel

1 Tiananmen Square
2 Tiananmen Gate
3 Forbidden City
4 Coal Hill Park
5 Great Hall of the People
6 Museums of Chinese
   Revolution and Chinese History
7 Temple of Heaven
8 Summer Palace
9 Beihai Park
10 Zhongnanhai (Chung Nan Hai)
11 International Club and
   St. Regis Hotel
12 Friendship Store
13 Lama Temple
14 Temple of Confucius
15 Drum Tower
17 Beijing Zoo

eight-piece gym and indoor pool. It has Cantonese, Italian, and Hangzhou restaurants, and 24-hour room service. It can seat 400 banquet-style. Member Meritus Hotels.

WANGFUJING GRAND HOTEL, *57 Wangfujing Avenue, 100006. Five stars, Tel. 65221188, Fax 65223816. $180-$260 for rooms, and $300-$1800 for suites. It has been discounting 50%.*

This hotel looks like a four-star and its standards are slipping. Some floors however were renovated in 2001. This has the second best hotel view of the Forbidden City. Built in 1996, it has 14 stories, 227 rooms, CNN, and in-room safes. Rooms are 24.7 square meters. There's an executive floor, Italian, Korean, Sichuan and Cantonese restaurants, an 11-piece gym, 20-meter indoor pool and sauna.

BEIJING HOTEL (Fandian), *33 Chang'an Dong Avenue, 100004. Five stars, Tel. 65137766, Fax 65137703 (sales), 65137307. E-mail: business@chinabeijinghotel.com.cn. Website: www.chinabeijinghotel.com.cn. Rooms in Building A range from $220 to $280 and suites $420-$8000. Rooms in Building B are $290-$480, and suites $590-$8000. Rooms in Building C are $220 and $230. A suite is $320. In Building E, business suites cost $280. It has been giving 20% discounts.*

Building A was renovated in 2001, and B,C and E in 2000. Rooms are 36 to 50 square meters. Every room has broad-band internet access for $20 a day. This hotel has added a pool, bowling, squash, billiards and tennis. It has three connecting buildings with almost 1000 rooms, CNN, HBO, Cinemax, in-room safes, and Cantonese, Shanghai, Sichuan, Japanese, Huaiyang and western restaurants. It is the only place where you can get Tangjia cuisine in town. Its banquet room can seat 800 at tables. It has a famous acupuncturist, a good 15-piece gym, squash, tennis, bowling, and a 25-meter long pool. The breakfast buffet is Y45.

NEW WORLD COURTYARD MARRIOTT (Xinshijie Fandian), *3C Chongwenmenwai, Chongwen District. Four stars, Tel. 67181188, 67088013 (reservations), Fax 67081808, 67088031 (reservations). E-mail: nwcyados@Mailbox.rol.cn.net. Website: www.courtyard.com/bjscy. $188-$198 for rooms, $288-$588 for suites. It has been giving 40% discounts. One km from the Beijing Railway Station and very convenient to the Chongwenmen Metro Station (south exit), it is 40 km from the airport, 1.5 km from Tiananmen Square, and 2 km from the Temple of Heaven. It is connected directly with the New World Department Store which has an ice skating rink.*

This 1998 hotel has 280 small rooms, in-room safes, and ticketing service, indoor pool and gym. It has a garden, voice-mail, CNN, HBO and Star Movies. There is an English pub, Cantonese restaurant, store, office towers and apartments, and free city/airport shuttle buses. The buffet breakfast is very ample.

NOVOTEL XINQIAO HOTEL (Fandian), *2 Dong Jiao Min Xiang Street, 100004. Four star tower, Tel. 65133366, Fax 65125126, 65128902. E-mail: xinqiao@public2.bta.net.cn. Website: www.accorhotels-china.com/beijing. $156 for rooms, and $240-$359 for suites. It has been discounting 20-40%.*

Built in 1954 and expanded in 1998, this six- and 14-story hotel has a total of 400 rooms with CNN. Some rooms have small bathrooms. It has bicycles for hire, and in-room safes, Cantonese, Shandong and Japanese food. It has good, reasonably priced dim sum, and natural hot spring water. It is generally acceptable except for the maintenance and English, which are expected to improve because Novotel took over in 2001.

NOVOTEL PEACE HOTEL (Heping Binguan), *3 Jinyu Hutong, Wangfujing Avenue, 100006 (across from the Palace Hotel). Four stars, Tel. 65128833, Fax 65126863, 65266989. E-mail: novotelp@163bj.com. Website: www.accorhotels-china.com/beijing. Rooms in its four-star east building cost $110-$180 and suites $250-$750. It has been discounting 30-40% and charging $88 for an executive club package (including one hour's free e-mail).*

Built in 1952, this hotel finished refurbishing all 344 rooms in 1999, and a few in 2001. Rooms in its east wing are 32 square meters and have almost floor to ceiling windows. It has some non-smoking rooms, a small indoor pool and gym, carpet stains, and CNN. There's a room safe. We found the breakfast buffet good, the work of its French chef who cooks authentic Western food. Accor Hotels.

JIANGUO QIANMEN HOTEL (Fandian), *175 Yongan Road, Xuanwu District, 100050. Three stars aiming for four. Tel. 63016688, Fax 63013883. E-mail: sales@shtj.com.cn. It is 3 km southwest of Tiananmen, 7 km from the Beijing train station, and 36 km from the airport.*

This 410-room hotel was renovated in 2000. Rooms now have safes, kettles and CNN. It is the home of the Li Yuan Beijing Opera and is close to Liulichang antique market. Jianguo International Hotels.

BEIJING SONG HE HOTEL (Song He Dajiudian), *88 Dengshikou, Dongcheng District 100006. Three stars, Tel. 65138822, Fax 65139092. E-mail: sales@songhehtl.com. Website: www.songhehtl.com. $90-$110 for rooms, $200 for suites. It has been discounting 20%. It is east of the Tianlun Dynasty Hotel.*

The best rooms are above the tenth floor. Built in 1992, this hotel has 310 rooms with safes, minibars, and bad grouting. Some floors were renovated in 2001. It has CNN, two movie channels in English, western, and Cantonese restaurants, low hall ceilings and dirty carpets. The breakfast buffet is about Y58. Lots of restaurants are in the neighborhood. It changes travelers' checks, accepts credit cards and rents out bicycles. Its dinner buffet is Y68 and it charges Y2 a minute for e-mail.

DAYS INN TIANRUI (Tianrui Jiudian), *15 Bai Shu Hutong, Dong Cheng, 100006. Tel. 65266699, Fax 65244828. E-mail: trpublic@tianrui.com.cn.*

Website: www.tianrui.com.cn or Daysinn.com. This is on a quiet, residential lane a block east of the north side of the Catholic Church on Wangfujing Ave. It is south and east of the Tianlun Dynasty Hotel and 1.2 km from the Forbidden City. This 64-room hotel accepts credit cards but can't change money. Rooms are $80, suites are $128-$328. It has been offering 30% discounts.

Standard rooms here have large twin beds, mini-bars, and showers (no tubs). They have no room safes, and no television channels in English. It has a sauna and massage, but no gym and no pool. The standard of English is poor to non-existent but Tom Tian, Housekeeping Department Manager, speaks a little English. His B.P. is 1278285233. It's clean except for the hall carpets, the location is great, and the staff is friendly. Opened in 1997, it joined Days' Inn, the North American chain in 1999. It charges Y35 for a Western breakfast, and Y20 for a Chinese breakfast.

Jianguomenwai

This is the second-best location, especially for business people but also for shoppers and tourists. It is about four km east of Tiananmen Square on Jianguomenwai Avenue, which is the same street as the Forbidden City. On the southwest side of Jianguomenwai from west to east, bunched together are the Gloria Plaza, and New Otani Hotels, the Beijing Tourism Tower, Scitech Building, and the Scitech Hotel. On the north side spread out west to east for about two km are the Beijing International Club, and behind it the St. Regis Hotel, C.I.T.I.C. Building, Friendship Store, Guiyou Department Store, Silk Alley, Starbucks, Jianguo and Jinglun Hotels.

Next are the China World and Traders Hotels in the China World Trade Center (CWTC) at Dongsanhuan (Third Ring Road). The Kerry Center is a block north of Traders' Hotel. In this area, the best hotels are the St. Regis, China World, and Kerry. The China World is in the process of making major renovations.

The western part of this less crowded area is within walking distance of the United

China World Trade Center

The **China World Trade Center** (CWTC) is a city in itself with hotels, an arcade, apartments, offices and shops. It has exhibition and conference centers, and airline offices, CITS, and Bank of China (open 9am-5pm). It has a cyber cafe, German bakery, deli, coffee shops, restaurants, Baskin-Robbins ice cream, and Pizza Hut. For business people, it has couriers and a print shop. It also has a supermarket (open 9am-9pm), an indoor ice skating rink, and fitness center. It is about 27 km from the airport, 3 km from the Beijing Railway Station, and 20 km from the West Railway Station. All other hotels in this area are closer to these stations.

States embassy, Ritan Park, and the international post office. The Beijing International Hotel is between Tiananmen/Wangfujing and the Jianguomen Hotels. It is walking distance to the Beijing Railway Station and is a nice compromise but Tiananmen is still a half-hour walk away. A good deal here for backpackers is its Youth Hostel.

ST. REGIS BEIJING HOTEL (Beijing Guoji Ju Le Bu Fandian), *21 Jianguomenwai Avenue, 100020. Five star standard, Tel. 64606688, Fax 64603299. E-mail: beijing.stregis@stregis.com. Web: www.stregis.com/ beijing. $300-$450 for rooms, $400-$4000 for suites. It has been giving 20-40% discounts. The buffet breakfast costs $22, lunch Y188, and dinner Y195.*

This 1997-98 hotel has 273 spacious rooms and suites with big bathrooms, tubs and separate shower stalls. Rooms have walk-in wardrobes, safes, CNN and in-house movies. They also have data ports and butler service (in black tails), light clothes pressing on arrival, and wake-up tea or coffee. This boutique hotel has Western, Asian, Italian, Japanese and Cantonese restaurants, and 24-hour room service. It has a 24-hour business center. The furnishings are Asian and Western, classical and current, a mix of styles put together with considerable flair. Look carefully at the details, even at the handmade paper under the Chinese calligraphy. Its spa has a 25-meter long pool and hot spring water. Starwood Hotels and Resorts.

CHINA WORLD HOTEL (Zhong Guo Da Fandian), *1 Jianguomenwai Avenue, Da Bei Yao, 100004. Five stars, Tel. 65052266, Fax 65050828, 65053165. E-mail: cwh@shangri-la. Web: www.Shangri-La.com. $250 and $335 for rooms, $320 and $2900 for suites.*

Built in 1990, this 21-story hotel should be renovated in stages in 2002 and 2003. It will have 716 rooms with good-size desks, CNN, high-speed internet access, and safes big enough for laptops. Rooms are 38 and 44 square meters and larger. It has or will have non-smoking, executive and higher quality Premier class floors. In the complex, there is a deli and bake shop, eight bars and restaurants including Cantonese, Western and Japanese restaurants, and Expresso Bar (with Y35 lunch). Its Aria Bar and Grill offers a choice of 100 wines, and has an open kitchen, steaks, seafood, and entertainment Its two ballrooms can seat 1000 and 500 people banquet style. Facilities include one of the best gyms in Beijing, squash, sauna, steam bath, indoor tennis, golf simulator, and pool. Its lobby hosts a concert of classical music Sundays from 4 to 6pm.

The China World executive floor recently offered about 25 different choices and a wide variety of fruit and juices for breakfast. Its coffee shop offers even more. Managed by Shangri-La International Hotels and Resorts.

THE KERRY CENTRE HOTEL BEIJING (Jia Li Fandian), *1 Guang Hua Road, 100020. Five-star standards. Tel. 65618833. Fax 85299977. E-mail: hbkc@shangri-la.com. Web: www.shangri-la.com. Rooms range from $230 to $300, and suites from $350 to $2000. Ask about discounts. This 1999 hotel* *is aiming for the more casual, I.T. generation of business travelers. It is next door to two office buildings with shopping malls, British and Singapore diplomatic offices, a supermarket, clinic, bars and restaurants.*

The marble in the Kerry's lobby is an amazing bright yellow, spectacular when lit from behind. Its walls are galleries of modern art. The 8-foot-wide desks in the guest rooms are obviously for work. Rooms each have a wireless keyboard, high-speed internet access and swivel chairs on rollers. The lighting is obscenely luxurious. Room telephones have hands-free and hold buttons. Some higher rooms have air purifiers. Its gym is the best in town; its pool is 35 meters long. It has 72 top-of-the-line exercise machines, and women's boxing classes. Its grand ballroom can seat 1000 at a sit-down banquet. The service is generally eager, the staff friendly. For its restaurants, see below.

JIANGUO HOTEL (Fandian), *5 Jianguomenwai Avenue, 100020. Four stars, Tel. 65002233, Fax 65958108, 65010539. E-mail:sales@hoteljianguo.com. Website: www.hoteljianguo.com. $220-$280 for rooms, and $330-$400 for suites. It has been discounting 20-40%.*

Built in 1982 with Mediterranean-style architecture and courtyard garden, this 469-room hotel has exemplary standards. It has duplexes. Its rooms are 30 square meters and have two data ports. It is 4 stories with a 9-story tower, and has a 24-hour business center and room service. Its singles are not all king-size (fortunately), and its televisions receive CNN, HBO and BBC. It has an executive floor with complimentary use of a computer and printer. There's a fine French restaurant (see below), American bistro, Cantonese food, and gourmet food/bake shop. It also has Japanese, German and Italian food and a barbecue. The buffet costs $10-$12 for breakfast, Y92-Y118 for lunch, and Y148-Y188 for dinner. It has a five-piece gym, 15-meter year-round indoor pool and bicycles to rent. The lobby lounge has a relaxing cozy atmosphere where you can people-watch. Jianguo International Hotels.

HOTEL NEW OTANI CHANG FU GONG HOTEL (Chang Fu Gong Fandian), *26 Jianguomenwai Avenue, 100022. Five stars, Tel. 65125555, 65125711 (Sales), Fax 65125346, 65139810. E-mail cfg@cfgbbj.com. Website: www.cfgbj.com (English). Y1530-Y1870 for rooms, and Y2550-Y5525 for suites. It has been discounting 20-30%.*

Opened in 1990, this 24-story hotel has executive floors, 500 rooms with hand showers, low bathroom ceilings and molded plastic sinks. Rooms are 32 to 36 square meters. It has CNN, HBO and Cinemax, Japanese and continental restaurants. It has a narrow indoor pool, lighted tennis court, and a good 16-piece gym. Housekeeping and maintenance need work but it gives good discounts and renovates five floors every year. Managed by New Otani International.

JINGLUN HOTEL (Jinglun Fandian), *3 Jianguomenwai Avenue, 100020. Four stars, Tel. 65002266, Fax 65002022. E-mail: jinglun@public3.bta.net.cn. Website www.jinglunhotel.com. $180-$220 for rooms, $230-$260 for suites. It has been discounting 20-30%. The breakfast buffet costs $12.*

Built in 1984, this 12-story glitzy hotel has 659 rooms with small bathrooms, wide twin beds and safes. Rooms are 29 square meters. It has the Aeroflot office, an indoor pool and gym. It also has a clinic, Japanese, Cantonese and snake restaurants. The pedestrian and taxi access here is unpleasantly crowded, and this hotel needs some refurbishing which should be done soon with data ports in rooms. It is otherwise well maintained and managed by Nikko Hotels International. Mongolian Airlines is next door.

TRADERS HOTEL (Guo Mao Fandian), *1 Jianguomenwai Avenue, 100004. Four stars,. Tel. 65052277, Fax 65050818. Website: www.Shangri-La.com. $170-$240 for rooms and $290-$580 for suites. It has been giving a 35% discount on rooms. Ask about its WTO package.*

Built in 1989, with a west wing added in 1998, this 567-room hotel has non-smoking rooms, in-room safes, and CNN. Guests can use facilities like the pool and tennis courts at its big sister China World Hotel next door. This comfortable, well-managed hotel has good service and high standards, its own small fitness center, and offices. Rooms have data ports and small safes. Two executive floors should be added soon. Managed by Shangri-La Hotels and Resorts.

GLORIA PLAZA HOTEL (Kai Lai Dajiudian), *2 Jianguomennan Avenue, 100022. Four stars, Tel. 65158855, Fax 65158533. $160 and $190 for rooms.*

Built in 1992, this hotel has 423 large rooms and suites, and executive floors. Rooms are 32 to 36 square meters with data ports. Rooms on the west side have a great view of the old Qing observatory. Some rooms have safes, but all get CNN and HBO. There is a 24-hour business center and room service. It has Korean barbecue, international, European and Cantonese seafood restaurants. Its 13-piece gym also has a good view, and it has a 17-meter long indoor pool, sauna, and an amazing sports bar where you can shoot baskets. You can also play its electronic games for free. The carpets are a little stained but being replaced. Gloria International Hotels.

BEIJING INTERNATIONAL HOTEL (Beijing Guoji Fandian), *9 Jianguomennei Avenue, 100005. Five stars, Tel. 65126688, Fax 65129972, 65129961. E-mail: info@bih.com.cn. Website: www.bih.com.cn. $160-$220 for rooms, $280-$1000 for suites. It has been discounting 20 to 45% on standard rooms. 28 km from the airport, 0.5 km from the Beijing Railway Station, and one block from the Dong Dan subway station.*

Built in 1987, this 29-story hotel has 1008 large rooms with huge windows, Shanghai and Cantonese food, Hangzhou noodle shop, a revolving restaurant, and 24-hour room service. Rooms are 28 square meters. It has CNN, HBO, an executive floor, and several travel services. There's tennis, bowling, a 21-piece gym and a 20-meter-long heated indoor pool and sauna. It has lots of shops, a supermarket, and Siberian Airlines. A refurbishment of its 6th to 19th floors was made in 2001. Executive rooms have high speed internet access. Carpets need work. Its ballroom can accommodate 500 at a sit-down banquet. It has a youth hostel on the premises.

SCITECH HOTEL (Saite Fandian), *22 Jianguomenwai Avenue, 100004. Four stars, Tel. 65123388, Fax 65123542, 65123543. E-mail: sthotel1@sun.sw.com.cn. Rooms are 18 square meters, and cost $120, while suites cost $160-$500. It has been discounting 20%.*

Built in 1991, this 15-story, 294-room hotel has small bathrooms and beds, in-room safes, CNN and HBO. It has a Cantonese restaurant, 24-hour room service and business center, 16-piece gym, indoor pool and tennis. Guests can use the sports equipment in the Scitech Club next door. It has two executive and two non-smoking floors.

BEIJING YOUTH HOSTEL *(affiliated with the International Youth Hostel Federation) is on the grounds of the Beijing International Hotel, 9 Jianguomennei Avenue, 100005. E-mail: info@bih.com.cn. Tel. 65126688 X 6145 or 6146, Fax 65229494. Website: www.iyhf.org. It's in an 11-story building north and east of the main hotel building.*

Members of the IYHF get discounts. Rooms are clean but have no private baths. The public bathrooms are okay. This hostel has air-conditioning, 24-hour hot water, and a laundry room. Dorms for four or six people cost Y90 per bed. You can get cafeteria food in a building across the courtyard. It has internet service. A cheaper internet bar is across the street. See also Zhaolong Hotel below.

Further Away But Still Within Third Ring Road

The Jing Guang Hotel is about two km due north of the China World Trade Center. A little further west and north near Beijing Workers' Stadium, the Sanlitun markets, and lots of bars and restaurants, are the City and the Zhaolong hotels. These are still central and close to embassies and restaurants. Of these the Jing Guang is the best, then the Zhaolong and finally the City. A youth hostel is attached to the Zhaolong.

JING GUANG NEW WORLD HOTEL (Jing Guang Zhong Xin), *Jing Guang Centre, Hu Jia Lou, Chao Yang Qu, 100020. Five stars, Tel. 65978888, Fax 65973333. E-mail: jghef@ht.rol.cn.net. Website: www.newworldhotels.com. $200-$300 for rooms, and $460-$1300 for suites. It has been discounting 30-40%. It is 5 km from the Beijing Railway Station, 25 km from the airport, and 7 km from the Forbidden City.*

Built in 1990, this hotel has good standards, and 446 guest rooms. Rooms are 30-40 square meters and safes are only in its two executive floors. It has a non-smoking floor, CNN, and HBO. There's a food street, Cantonese, Japanese, and Korean restaurants, deli, and 24-hour room service. It has a 16 meter-long indoor pool, steam bath, jacuzzi, and a 20-piece gym. Renovations to rooms should start in 2002. A Marriott Hotel.

ZHAOLONG HOTEL (Fandian), *2 Congti Bei (Workers Stadium) Road, Chaoyang District, 100027. Four stars, Tel. 65972299, Fax 65972288. E-mail: zlh@zhaolonghotel.com.cn. Y1290-Y1550 for rooms, Y2800-Y8800 for suites. It has been discounting 30 to 50%.*

This 1985 hotel has 19 storys, 259 rooms and small bathrooms. Rooms are 25 square meters. It has a year-round indoor pool and gym, and serves Western, Cantonese, and Taiwanese food.

The **ZHAOLONG YOUTH HOSTEL** is part of the Zhalong Hotel. (See also the Beijing International Hotel). From the front door of the hotel, go towards Third Ring Road and turn right. A double room costs Y70 per person. A six-person dorm costs Y60 per person. This hostel has a laundromat and a kitchen. It has six floors, a television room, lockers, heat and air-conditioning, and 24-hour hot water, but no elevator. Its e-mail is Y20 for 30 minutes. Cheaper restaurants are within walking distance. The website is *www.iyhf.org.*

CITY HOTEL BEIJING (Cheng Shi Binguan), *4 Gongti Dong Road, Chaoyang District, 100027. Three stars, Tel. 65007799, Fax 65008228, 65007668. E-mail: sales333@263.net. This whole area might be torn down so double-check before you attempt to book here after 2002. Rooms are Y1000-Y1100, suites Y1400-Y3700 and apartments Y750-Y1200. It has very pretty rooms with HBO and CNN, safe, and some dirty carpets. There are electric hand driers in the rooms.*

This 1989 hotel has 85 big rooms and 135 studios and apartments. It has a shuttle bus, small gym, Cantonese and hot pot restaurants. It's a bit scruffy and modest but comfortable and used to English speakers. Managed by Chains International (Hong Kong).

The Old Beijing Hotels

Of the three here, the Bamboo Garden is best. They are all within Second Ring Road, the Haoyuan close to Wangfujing Avenue. They are listed separately because their attraction is their link to social history, not to comfort and services.

BAMBOO GARDEN HOTEL (Zhu Yuan Binguan, or Kang Sheng's Villa), *24 Xiaoshiqiao Alley, Jiugulou Avenue, Xicheng District, 100009. Three stars. Tel. 64032229. Fax 64012633. E-mail: bbgh@bbgh.com.cn and website: www.bbhg.com.cn. Rooms are Y380 and Y580. It accepts travelers checks, cash, and international credit cards and is northwest of the Drum Tower, the area of the hutong tours.*

This beautiful garden villa is more reminiscent of gracious old Beijing than the tiny courtyard houses seen on those tours. It was the home of a Qing minister of posts, and the garden of a famous eunuch. It was recently the home of Kang Sheng, one of the infamous Gang of Four. If you eat here, at the nearby Kaorouji Restaurant, or at the Li Family Restaurant nearby, you're in another era. Rooms are in Chinese style but it has television channels in

English. Its 40 rooms each have two data ports, poor grouting and no in-room safe. Its tea house charges Y80 to Y200 for a pot of woolong but its Western breakfast is only Y40. Its back building is new. A hotel car picks up passengers at the airport for Y120. There's a Chinese and a western restaurant, dance hall, laundry, massage, sauna and travel agency. The staff is friendly with little English.

LU SONG YUAN HOTEL (Binguan), *22 Banchang Hutong, Kuan Street, Dongcheng District, 100009. Two stars, Tel. 64040436, 64011116, Fax 64030418. E-mail: lsyhotel@263.net. Website: webmaster@the-silk-road.com. No credit cards. $35-$75 for rooms. Two dorms with six beds each at $10 with CNN but no windows. North of the Art Gallery. You can reach this hotel by buses #104, 108, 113, and 2, plus a short walk. It has 31 rooms. It gives 10% discounts to IYHF members and is close to downtown.*

The Lu Song Yuan does not have the garden space of the Bamboo Garden. It offers Western breakfasts and Beijing food. Silk Road International Hotels.

HAOYUAN BINGUAN, *53 Shijia Hutong (Lane at 148 Dongsiei Street), 100010, Tel. 65125557, Fax 65253179. Y600-Y1000 for rooms. Website: www.women.org.cn/womenorg/hao/index.htm. It has been discounting 10%. This inn now has signs in English on both Dongsi Nan Avenue, and Chaoyangmen Nan Avenue.*

Built in 1984, the Haoyuan has 19 rooms, some with private baths and none with television in English. It is clean but in need of maintenance. It has few services and little English. But it is charming and in traditional Beijing courtyard style. After renovations in 2002 it should be able to change travelers checks and serve breakfast but it takes no credit cards and is operated by the All-China Womens' Federation.

The Great Wall-Kempinski-Kunlun-Hilton cluster & SAS

This area is further out in the northeast, about 9 km from the Beijing Railway Station, and about 24 km from the airport. It is about 15 km from the West Beijing railway station and is on Third Ring Road. Hotels here are the Kempinski, Great Wall Sheraton, Hilton or Kunlun, Landmark Towers, Huadu and Jianguo Inn in descending order of preference and all are within walking distance of each other. This group is relatively close to three diplomatic areas, including the Australian and Canadian embassies, and the Agricultural Exhibition Centre. An interesting flower supermarket is behind the Landmark.

The SAS is about two kilometers northwest of this cluster, at the International Exhibition Center and inside Third Ring Road.

You should consider staying at the Kempinski, Landmark or Great Wall Hotels if you are going on foot frequently to the Lufthansa Centre. This center has the Youyi Shopping Centre, the offices of Thai Airways, Lufthansa, Air Canada, United, Asiana, and Qantas airlines, an international medical office, and the South African Embassy. Heavy traffic might threaten guests going there from other hotels and an overpass to the south makes for a long walk.

KUNLUN HOTEL (Fandian), *2 Xin Yuan Nan Road, Chaoyang District, 100004. Five stars, Tel. 65903388, Fax 65903158. E-mail: kunlunht@public3.bta.net.cn or kunlun@public.bta.net.cn. Website: www.hotelkunlun.com. $260-$310 for rooms and $440-$2800 for suites. It has been discounting 20-50%. All rooms should be refurbished before 2003.*

Built in 1986-88, this 29-story hotel has 900 rooms with large safes, CNN, and data ports. Rooms are 33-50 square meters. It has a revolving restaurant, Japanese, Korean, Vietnamese, Shanghai, and Cantonese restaurants, and 24-hour coffee shop. Its ballroom can accommodate 550 people at a sit-down banquet. It has a 14-meter-long indoor pool, gym, outdoor tennis and a shuttle bus. Its staff is friendly, lively and helpful. This is a good, dependable hotel with a play room for children, cigar store, real post office, and golf shop. My only problem was finding someone before 7:30am who spoke English. At 8am, it was okay. Get a look at its very elegant second floor Shanghai Restaurant. Managed by the Jin Jiang Group.

KEMPINSKI HOTEL (Yan Sha Zhong Xin, Kai Bin Si Ji), *Beijing Lufthansa Centre, 50 Liangmaqiao Road, Chaoyang District, 100016. Five stars, Tel. 64653388, Fax 64563366. E-mail: khbcres@public.east.cn.net. Website: www.kempinski-beijing.com. In North America, Tel. 800/426-3135. $230-$290 for rooms, $350-$2500 for suites. It has been discounting 30-50%.*

Built in 1992, this well-run 18-story hotel has 530 rooms with small safes, CNN, CNBC and HBO, and executive and non-smoking floors. It has eight handicapped rooms. All suites have executive floor benefits. It has Bavarian, and Italian restaurants and its own brewery. Service is good and its ballroom seats 1600 banquet style. It has a 16 meter-long indoor pool, solarium, two gyms, and lighted tennis courts. It should have renovated floors 5 to 16 in 2001 with data ports. A Lufthansa hotel. Leading Hotels of the World.

BEIJING HILTON INTERNATIONAL (Xi Er Dun Fandian), *1 Dongfang Road, 100027. Five stars, Tel. 64662288, Fax 64653052, 64672970. E-mail: reserve@hiltonbeijing.com.cn or hilton@hiltonbeijing.com.cn. Website: www.hilton.com. $230 to $310 for rooms. Presidential suite $1500.*

Built in 1993, this 25-story, 363-room hotel has executive floors, in-room safes and in-house movies. All rooms have charming Japanese windows, CNN and HBO, data ports, and separate shower stalls as well as tubs. It has 24-hour room service and a business center, Cantonese, Shanghai, Japanese, and American fusion cuisine. There's an elegant cigar bar, a 13-meter long indoor pool, squash, outdoor lighted tennis court, 33-piece gym, and bicycles for hire. Non-smoking rooms are available.

GREAT WALL SHERATON HOTEL (Changcheng Fandian), *10 Dongsanhuan Bei Road, Chaoyang District, 100026. Five stars, Tel. 65905566, Fax 65905398, 75905222. Website: starwood.com/Sheraton. $220-270 for* *rooms and $350-$2400 for suites. It has been discounting 30%. Opened in 1984, the Great Wall has been upgrading its guest rooms, a three-year winter project to be finished in 2002. This 21-story hotel has its own private garden and 1007 rooms with CNN, BBC, and HBO. Its standard rooms are 30.6 square meters. Every room has two data ports and a large safe. It has executive and non-smoking floors. Its business center, coffee shop, room service and money exchange never sleep. Its buffet breakfast is lavish and includes 21 kinds of toppings for congee, probably a record. It has a daily barbeque May-October and it can seat 800 people at tables for a banquet.*

The Great Wall also has Air China and CITS offices. You can exercise in its indoor pool, Clark Hatch health club, and two outdoor tennis courts. This hotel can arrange champagne and hors d'oeuvres at sunset on the Great Wall as you listen to an adventurer speak about running the whole length of it. It is active in a program to clean up the litter, usually in June. (Contact Joyce Li extension 2202 or 2121).

RADISSON SAS HOTEL (Huang Jia Fandian), *6A Beisanhuan Dong Road, Chaoyang District, 100028. Four stars, Tel. 64663388, Fax 64653186, 64653183. E-mail: sales.beijing@radissonsas.com; Website: www.radissonsas.com. Rooms are $170 to $210. Presidential suite $800. It has been discounting 30% and giving seniors' rates. It is 20 km from the airport and 10 km from Tiananmen, and adjacent to the China International Exhibition Center (CIEC) in the north of the city. It is within walking distance of a Carrefour mall and a few restaurants, disco, and two McDonald's. It takes eight minutes by taxi to Sanlitun bar street.*

Built 1992-93, this 15-story hotel should finish a total renovation in 2002. It has 374 rooms, most about 28 square meters. Some desks have no drawers but all rooms have safes and trouser press machines. It has executive floors and non-smoking rooms. There's CNN and Star Movies with speakers in its relatively large bathrooms, a grill room, and Cantonese food. For sports, there's a 17-meter-long indoor pool, outdoor tennis court, 2 squash courts, and a 9 piece gym. This hotel is very clean, bright and cheerful.

BEIJING LANDMARK TOWERS (Liangmahe Fandian), *8 Dong Sanhuanbei Road, Chao Yang District, 100004. Next door to the Great Wall Sheraton Hotel. Four stars, Tel. 65906688, Fax 65900537. E-mail: sales@landmarktowers.com. Website: landmarktowers.com. Standard rooms are $160 and business suites $180-$220. It has been giving 20-40% discounts in low season.*

This 1990 hotel has 15 stories, 472 rooms and 240 apartments. It is charming but the air inside smells of food. It is otherwise okay. It has Cantonese, Shanghai, Sichuan, and Korean restaurants, and the Hard Rock Cafe. It has CNN, HBO and CNBC, web-tv in some rooms, a small indoor pool, gym and sauna. Rooms are 25, 38 or 50 square meters with laptop-sized safes. SRS World Hotels.

HUADU HOTEL (Fandian), *8 Xinyuan Nan Road, Chaoyang District, 100027. Three stars aiming for four, Tel. 65971266, 65001754, Fax 65971218.*

*E-mail: hdfd@huaduhotel.com.cn. Website: www.huaduhotel.com.cn. Y758-
Y888 for rooms and Y1168 for suites. It has been giving a 20% discount.*
Built in 1982, this six-story, 500-room hotel has in-room safes. It is grubby,
badly managed, and the air is stuffy. It lacks signs in English, has 40 watt bulbs,
but has kettles, in-room safes, CNN and Star TV. The English isn't bad for a
three-star but it can be a problem. It is adequate for budget travelers if you get
a good discount. The Western breakfast buffet costs Y50. It expects to open
a swimming pool and Air China office soon. Kingdom International Hotels.
JIANGUO INN, *8 Xinyuan Nan Road, Chaoyang District, 100027. Tel.
65971866. This modest but clean 87 room inn has a good location between
the Huadu and Kunlun Hotels. It charges Y292 with no discounts.*
It has 24-hour hot water, air-conditioning, a café and business center.
English is lacking but what can you expect? It's cheap. It is not related to the
Jianguo International Hotels.

The Holiday Inn Lido/Harbour Plaza Cluster
This northeast cluster is in a residential area near big parks, about 14 km
from the Beijing Railway Station and 25 km from the Beijing West railway
station. It is 15 km from Tiananmen, and 15 km from the airport. The hotels
are within walking distance of each other, restaurants, and bars, and four
kilometers from the Kempinski-Great Wall cluster. The closest subway stop is
Dongzhimen on the No. 416 bus line. The Lido has more services.
HOLIDAY INN LIDO (Lido Fandian), *Jichang Road, Jiang Tai Road,
100004. Four stars, Tel. 64376688, Fax 64376237, 64376540. E-mail:
info@lidoplace.com. $140-$180 for rooms, $180-$1150 for suites. Senior's
discount on request. Walk-in guests have been getting 40% discounts. Its
summer package including breakfast has been $99. If you can't find its booth
at the airport, look for a man in a green jacket at door No. 5, first floor, arrival
wing.*
Across from Lido Park with its childrens' playground, this 1984-85, five-
story hotel has 720 spacious rooms. Its standard twin beds are wide but you
need a flashlight to read directions for its laptop-sized in-room safe. It has an
executive floor, CNN and HBO. Its business center, clinic and coffee shop never
sleep. There's a post office, Bank of China, and travel service counter.
The buffet breakfast costs about Y110. There's also a yummy pizzeria, deli
and pub, Cantonese restaurant, and especially good Thai and German
farmhouse food. Its Texan Bar & Grill is as authentic as you can get in China.
See Where to Eat below. This hotel has non-smoking areas, bicycles for hire,
bowling, a gym, and a year-round 14-meter-long indoor pool. Japanese,
German and international schools are on the premises as are a supermarket,
Watson's "drug store" (no pharmacist), Baskin-Robbins and a Starbucks.

This is Asia's largest Holiday Inn and growing. The downtown shuttle bus is free and its airport shuttle is hourly (on the hour) from the airport from 9am to 10pm for Y20. The Lido Club next door has squash, golf, four indoor tennis courts, and heated indoor pool. Restaurants and a curio and clothes market are across the street.

HARBOUR PLAZA HOTEL (Haiyi Jiuduan), *8 Jiang Tai Xi Road, Chao Yang District, 100016. Four stars, Tel. 64362288, Fax 64361818 or 64376310 (Sales). E-mail: hpbjpr@public.fhnet.cn.net. Website: www.harbour-plaza.com/hpbj. $140-$240 for rooms, and $380-$600 for suites. It has been discounting 30 to 40% on some rooms and offering an executive club package for $95. It has a free downtown shuttle, a weekend antique market shuttle (Y30), and an airport shuttle (Y25). It has been a 10-minute taxi ride via Fourth Ring Road from the China World Trade Centre.*

Built in 1990 as the Grace Hotel, and managed by Hutchison Whampoa since 1997 (a great improvement), this attractive 17-story hotel has 370 rooms and executive and non-smoking floors. Rooms are 19, 28 and 40 square meters and have CNN, BBC and HBO. Its executive floor breakfast buffet is very adequate and includes made-to-order eggs and cappuccino. Its regular breakfast is even more lavish. Its buffet dinner costs Y105. Its luxurious all-you-can-eat dim sum, available 11:30am-2:30pm is Y90-Y100 including tea. It has reflexology and massage service. It will be adding a sauna and steam bath soon but no pool.

West Beijing

Hotels here are further from the airport but closer to the West Beijing Railway Station. Both the Holiday Inn Downtown and the State Guest House are within a few minutes walk of shopping and the west exit of the Fuchengmen metro stop and only five km from the Forbidden City. They are also five km from Beijing West railway station, and a few meters from Second Ring Road in a growing financial street with bank headquarters and computer companies. The State Guest House is newer, more luxurious and beautiful and has been very good value for money. The Holiday Inn is further west just off the east-west metro line. The Beijing Telecom and Media Centre are within one kilometer of Beijing West Railway Station.

HOLIDAY INN CHANG AN WEST BEIJING (Chang Feng Jia Re Jiu Dian), *66 Yong Ding Road, Haidian District, 100039. Four star standards, Tel. 68132299, and Fax 68280066. E-mail: hichanganw@sohu.com. Website: www.holiday-inn.com. It is a 15-minute drive to the Financial District, and close to two big sports stadiums. It is about 37 km from the airport, 12 km. from Tian An Men Square (same metro line), and 16 km from the Summer Palace. Rooms range from $140 to $180, and suites $180 to $1150. Its introductory package was Y368 for a standard room and breakfast. This 248-room hotel is a 10-minute walk from Wukesong metro stop and is in a* residential neighborhood. Exit from the north-west end of the station and walk west about three blocks on Fuxing Avenue. Turn right on Yong Ding.

Rooms are 30 to 50 square meters. It has 10 service apartments and two office floors. Rooms have a large in-room safe, and should have high-speed internet access now. They offer CNN, HBO, and data ports; some are non-smoking, and some for wheel-chair travelers. Its ballroom can accommodate 250 guests banquet style. Its buffet breakfast costs Y50. It offers Hong Kong-style Western food and seafood. It has bowling and an 18-meter long pool. Its nine-piece gym has a punching bag that's good for frustrated business people, and it has a cross-bow range.

STATE GUEST HOUSE HOTEL (Guo Bin Fandian), *9 Fuchengmenwai Road, Xicheng District, 100037. It is aiming at five-star standards, Tel. 68005588, Fax 68005888. E-mail: nfo@stateguesthotel.com. Website: www.stateguesthotel.com. This 502-room hotel has rooms ranging from $139 to $259, and suites $259 to $5000. It has been discounting 10 to 30%. Its special opening rate was $88.*

This hotel opened in 2000 as a Radisson, and became independent in 2001. Its ballroom seats 400 guests banquet style and it can do video-conferencing. It has 24-hour room service and a 24-hour coffee shop. It also has a Cantonese restaurant, a Manhattan bar and grill, and a roof garden with real seven-meter high banyan trees. Its rooms are 26 to 54 square meters with high speed internet access, speaker phones, CNN and small desks. It has executive floors. Its three-story high atrium lobby has real palm trees, gold trim, and Corinthian pillars. The gym has 19 good machines and staff can give a chiropractic massage. No one is allowed to swim in its indoor 16-meter long pool without a cap, fortunately. Reservations through Steigenberger/ SRS.

HOLIDAY INN DOWNTOWN, *98 Beilishi Road, Xichengqu, 100037, Four stars. Tel. 68338822, Fax 68340696. E-mail: downtown@public.east.cn.net. Website: www.basshotelschina.com. $130-$205 for rooms, and $230-$265 for suites. It has been discounting 25-50%.*

This small, friendly hotel is comfortable and unpretenious. It is good value for money. It has 346 rooms, a small indoor pool, small gym, a coffee shop, and a Japanese restaurant. Rooms are 30 to 34 square meters. It is next to Isetan department store and Kenny Roger's Roasters Restaurant.

BEIJING TELECOM HOTEL (Beijing Dian Xin Fandian) *6, Shifangyuan, Haidian District, 100036. Five stars, Tel. 63901166, Fax 63901273. Website: www.bth.telehotels.cn.net. This hotel is across the road from the train station and reached by an underpass near the main door of the station. You can telephone for a bellman to help you at 63902100 for Y100 but it's cheaper to take a taxi. Rooms cost $140-$160 and suites $230-$1800.*

This hotel's 328 rooms have Star TV, 33 international channels (but no CNN), and broadband access. It has safes, but poor grouting. It has simulta-neous translation systems and high-definition conference video-phones. There's an indoor pool and gym, and it can pick you up at the airport in a Red Flag (Hong Qi) stretch limo. It serves European, Korean and Chinese food.

MEDIA CENTRE (Meidiya Zhongxin), *11B Fuxing Road, 100038. Three stars, Tel. 68514422, Fax 68516288, 68515240. E-mail mediaf@public.bta.net.cn. Website: www.mediacenter.com.cn. Just west of the Millenium Museum and one km north of the Beijing West train station, this hotel is west of the Military Museum metro stop. Y430-Y830 for rooms and Y760-Y1780 for suites. It has been giving 20% discounts.*

This 11-story, 253-room hotel with apartments, has in-room safes, CNN, medium-sized beds, and mini-bars. Rooms are 27 and 29 square meters. Its 7th and 9th floors have computers. A Japanese joint venture, it has Cantonese, Sichuan, and Japanese food, a health club and billiards. Its Media Centre has satellite transmission, equipment leasing, and television production services. English might be a problem but this is one of the best deals in town if you ask for a stronger light bulb. It only has 25 watt ones. Its buffet breakfast is Y50.

HARMONY HOTEL *59, Suzhou Hutong, Youtong Street, Xicheng District, 100005. Tel. 6528-5566, Fax 6559-9011. Rooms have been Y280 in this cheap, clean hotel.*

The Northwest Hotels

The Shangri-La, Xiyuan, and New Century Hotels are 35-38 km from the airport, about 15 km from Beijing Railway Station and about 7-11 km from Beijing West Station The Third Ring Road has made these hotels and the Friendship Hotel quickly accessible from the city center (15-20 minute drive) and the airport. The Shangri-La is the best here, then the Xiyuan. The New Century was having a serious renovation in 2001 so should be good too. These three are within walking distance of each other and the zoo, the Temple of the Great Bell, Beijing Art Museum, the Negotiations Building, and a Pizza Hut. Across from the Xiyuan are also the Carrefour mall and two bars. The Dinosaur Museum and Planetarium are nearby.

The Friendship Hotel is north of here, about four km from the Shangri-La. These are the closest hotels in this book to Beijing, Qinghua and other major universities, Yuanmingyuan, the Summer Palace, and Western Hills. Boat tours go in summer on the nearby canal to the Exhibition Center, the Qing emperors' old route.

SHANGRI-LA HOTEL (Shang Gorilla Fandian), *29 Zizhuyuan Road, 100089. Five stars, Tel. 68412211, Fax 68418006. E-mail: slb@shangri-la.com. Website: www.Shangri-La.com. $200-$260 for rooms. $300-$1300 for suites. It has had a $175 special. This hotel is in a residential area across the road from the Beijing Art Museum and close to countryside, wooded hills, Holstein cows, pagodas, and peach trees. It is also near an industrial area. It is a 20-minute drive to the botanical garden and 30 minutes to the Fragrant Hills and is good for conferences.*

This hotel opened in 1987 with 657 spacious rooms, the smallest 34 square meters. It has offices, an executive floor, a 720-square meter grand ballroom, and conference facilities. It has a non-smoking floor, 24-hour business center, CNN, HBO, CNBC, voice mail, and in-room safes. You can choose from its delicatessen, Cantonese, Continental, Nishimura Japanese, and Italian restaurants. It has great pastry too. It can seat 450 at a banquet. There is indoor tennis, a 15-meter-long indoor heated pool, basketball, 18-piece gym and squash, and its own garden. The breakfast buffet costs about Y150. This classy hotel displays Chinese paintings in its elevators and its pool area is highlighted with stained glass. A 22-piece orchestra plays classical western music for high tea, 3pm on Sundays. I've tried the massage. It's great. Managed by Shangri-La International Hotels and Resorts.

BEIJING NEW CENTURY HOTEL (Xinshiji Fandian), *6 Southern Road, Capital Gym, 100044. Five stars, Tel. 68492001, Fax 68491103. E-mail: bc@newcenturyhotel.com.cn. Website: www.newcenturyhotel.com.cn. $80-$280 for rooms, and $130-$2000 for suites. This 32-story hotel was seriously renovated in 2001 and 2002. It is across the street from the Capital Gymnasium which should be used during the 2008 Olympics.*

This 1992 hotel has 720-rooms with CNN and HBO, broadband internet access, safes and 24-hour room service. It has small rooms with stained carpets. It has a 24-meter long indoor pool, steam bath, a modern, 22-piece gym, bowling, and lighted indoor tennis. Rooms are 28 and 42 square meters. It has Western, Japanese, Sichuan and Cantonese food and snacks, and 24-hour room service. ANA Hotels International.

XIYUAN HOTEL (Fandian), *1 Sanlihe Road, 100044. Four stars. (Maybe five stars in 2002.) Tel. 68313388, Fax 68314577. E-mail: xyhotel@public3.bta.net.cn. Tel. in North America 800/821-0900. $109-$169 for rooms, and $145-$1000 for suites. It has been discounting 40% off of this.*

The Xiyuan boasts a main 26-story building with 705 spacious rooms, one Muslim floor, two non-smoking and three executive floors, and 10 four-story villas. This old hotel with garden now has in-room safes, in-house videos, CNN and Star TV, and 24-hour room service. It serves German beer, and has good Moslem, Japanese and Korean, Shandong and Sichuan restaurants. It also has a revolving restaurant and a fast food restaurant. There's a small heated pool, steam bath, and a health club. The breakfast buffet costs Y98.

FRIENDSHIP HOTEL (Youyi Binguan), *3 Baishiqiao Road, 100873. Four stars. Tel. 68498888, Fax 68498866. E-mail:fhtjcn@public.3.bta.net.cn. $100-$137 for rooms, $157-$199 for suites. Rooms have been discounted to $56-$94. 35 km to the airport, 16 km to Beijing Railway Station, and 10 km to the Beijing West Railway Station. It is in a residential suburb close to the Third Ring Road Bei San Huan exit. You can walk to Bai Shi Qiao (high tech area) and two shopping malls. The closest metro stop is Gongzhufeng.*

Built in 1954 for Soviet experts, this is currently home for many foreign teachers. Services are also geared to short-term guests. It has five- and six-story buildings set in a huge garden. Building One is the best with an executive floor. Building Three has baby sitting service and rooms for the disabled. Building Five is old. Its 26 restaurants have Russian-style, Cantonese, Western and Sichuan food. It has indoor and outdoor pools, gym, tennis, bowling, golf driving range, and a track. It arranges hiking tours. It has a total of 1900 rooms, most small to medium sized with small baths, and each with safes and BBC. Its brass could be better polished and its bulbs are only 40 watts, but it's okay.

Airport Hotel

The most convenient major hotel to the airport (three km away) is the fancy Beijing Sino-Swiss Hotel. This hotel is good even for a two-hour stop between planes, or an unexpected overnight. It has good food, English, and services. It is especially good for children and could be considered a resort. You might also want to consider the Holiday Inn Lido above.

BEIJING SINO-SWISS HOTEL (Guo Du Da Fandian), *Xiao Tianzhu Village, Shunyi District. P.O. Box 6913, 100621. Four stars. Tel. 64565588, Fax 64561588, 64561355. E-mail: executive.office@sino-swisshotel.com. Website: www.sino-swisshotel.com. Rooms are $130-$225. A three-hour transit room costs $25. A day-use room costs $45 between 6am and 6pm. While a taxi could charge Y60-Y80 to downtown Wangfujing, the Sino-Swiss provides free airport (10 minutes) and downtown shuttle buses (25 minutes). Its airport shuttle is at car park D109 opposite international arrival exit gate 5.*

This four-story hotel is in a small village with tiny stores, public bars and restaurants across the street. It is a few meters off the main airport road and is ideal for conferences. (It can manage up to 550 people.) Built in 1990, it has 12 stories with 408 rooms, half of them with bare wooden floors, a plus because the carpets are a little stained. (Renovations however should be completed the end of 2002.) The hallways however are narrow. Rooms are 28 to 35 square meters. It offers CNN, BBC, in-house movies, and non-smoking floors. You can choose between a Chinese, Mongolian, Japanese, Italian, and Swiss restaurant (with cheese fondue and choice of 30 grappa wines).

It claims Beijing's largest indoor pool. It has squash, tennis, and acupressure and therapeutic massages. There's a 14-piece gym, a golf-putting range, activities for children on weekends, and a camel named Amanda. Breakfast buffet $12. Chinese breakfast $7. They are planning an executive floor and it has an airport monitor in its lobby.

Other Locations

Crowne Plaza Beijing North is scheduled to open in late 2002 10 km north of the Beijing Asian Games Village, close to Olympic Village and towards the Great Wall. It should have 593 rooms (including apartments) and be great for conferences and weekends out of the city.

Where to Eat

Beijing is a gourmet's delight with excellent food from all over the country and the world. So far, I've come across six hotels offering over 100 different foreign wines. These are the China World, Great Wall Sheraton, Hilton, Jianguo, Kempinski, and Palace, and there's probably more. The Courtyard Restaurant has a list of about 200 imported wines.

Dress codes are not mandatory anywhere, but you really should get dressed up for high level government and diplomatic functions, restaurants in top hotels, the Great Hall of the People, or the China Club (which has sharp-dressing Hong Kong members.) Even then, Justine's at the Jianguo Hotel just says "no shorts."

Quality is consistently good in these hotels, but you can find cheaper gems too. Many tour groups say the best meal is the home-cooked one prepared for the Hutong Tours by the occupant of one of the houses. And you might find something incredibly tasty in a street market.

See chapters 11 and 25 on Food on Mongolian and Beijing dishes.

Prices listed are subject to change and restaurants in hotels add a 10-15% service charge.

BEIJING FOOD

It's always enlightening to try the local cuisine. Beijing food is much like Shandong's, but influenced by Manchu and Mongol imperial tastes. It is usually salty (as opposed to sweet) and is not highly spiced. Sauces are used less frequently than in Cantonese cooking. Everyone must try Peking duck at least once! The best part is the crispy skin, which is dipped in sweet, dark brown hoisin sauce, seasoned with fresh green onion, and then wrapped in a thin pancake. You eat it by hand.

Peking Duck (Kaoya Dian)

QUANJUDE KAOYA DIAN RESTAURANT, *13 Shuaifuyuan, east of Wangfujing, Tel. 65253310, 65228384. Fax 65251642. E-mail ofisher@sina.com. It's open 11am-3pm and 4:30pm-9pm. This is part of the most famous duck restaurant chain. Another branch is at 158 Qianmen Nan Avenue, Tel. 65112542. Open 10:30am-9:30pm.*

For eight people, the Quanjude suggests two Peking ducks at Y168; salted beef for Y60; mushrooms and pine nuts for Y16; chicken with cashews Y28; shelled prawns with chili oil Y115; duck soup free; braised abalone with cabbage Y120, and fruit Y100. This restaurant has clean white table cloths, charming Chinese style ambience and bright chandeliers. It has four floors, the fourth with an open kitchen. A Western toilet is on the second floor.

Many other restaurants offer cheaper Peking ducks. Cheaper, just as succulent (some say it's better) and towards the Shangri-La Hotel in the west of town is the **Jiu Hua Shang**, on *Gong Ti Dong Men, Hai Dian Qu, 55*

Zengguang Avenue, Haidian District, Tel. 68483481 or 68414518. It's open 11am to 2pm, and 5pm to 9pm and accepts no international credit cards. The sign outside says Ziyu Hotel in English and it's to the right as you drive into the courtyard. Its door has pictures of ducks. It costs Y88 for one duck, Y50 for a half. Mushrooms and asparagus cost Y58, braised shell fish Y26, and shrimps with cashew nuts Y48. These are enough for a party of five. This restaurant is not as big and fancy as the Quanjude but if food and prices are more important to you, this is it.

There's also the **King Roast Duck** near McDonald's, *24 Jianguomenwai, Tel. 65156908.*

Qing Imperial Food

LI JIA CHAI (Li Family Restaurant), *11 Yangfang Hutong, De Nei Avenue. Have your driver or hotel telephone 66180107 for reservations and directions. The Li Jia Chai is very difficult to find, unless a sign has now been posted outside the gate. It could cost Y400-Y600 per person. No credit cards.*

Located across the lake from Soong Ching-ling's residence, this tiny restaurant is in a courtyard dwelling in a lane full of tiny traditional houses. But it has great imperial cooking and classy table settings, a special and exotic experience especially when Mr. Li talks about the different dishes and his grandfather who cooked in the Qing court. A reservation should be made a few days in advance but give it a last-minute try anyway.

FANG SHAN RESTAURANT *in Beihai Park, is along the lake by the White Dagoba at 1 Wenjin Street, Xicheng District, inside the South Gate. Tel. 64011879. Open 11am-1:30pm and 5pm-7:30pm. It accepts credit cards.*

The cooks in this unique restaurant were taught by the Empress Dowager's cooks. Unfortunately the food here isn't as good as it used to be, but it's still worth a try for its historic lakeside setting.

Mongolian

For all these popular restaurants, you should make reservations in advance on weekends. Mongolian hot pot which you cook yourself at your table in soup is famous and everywhere in winter. Mongolian barbecue where you select the raw ingredients and sauces, and then have someone else cook them for you on a huge inverted wok is not really Mongolian and is rare in China.

For Mongolian food in a relatively authentic setting, you can eat in a gher (yurt) at the **Sino-Swiss Hotel** (see *Where to Stay* above), and at the **Swissôtel**, *Hong Kong Macau Center, Dong Si Shi Tiao Li Jiao Qiao, Tel. 65012288, open 5:30pm-10pm.* Reservations are required. Popular hot pot restaurants are also at *7 Taiping Qiao Avenue, website: www.koufaju.com.cn.* There's the **Beijing Neng**, *5 Taiping Qiao Avenue, Tel. 6601-2560 and open*

9:30am to 2:00am. No credit cards. Famous Mongolian restaurants are the Donglaishu and the Kaoroji.

DONGLAISHUN RESTAURANT, *5/F, Sundong Plaza, 198 Wangfujing Avenue, Tel. 65280932. Open 11am-2pm and 5pm-9:30pm.*

Great hot pot.

KAOROJI RESTAURANT, *14 Di'anmenwai Avenue, Tel. 64045921, 64042554.*

Located near the Drum Tower and by Houhai Lake, the Kaoroji is famous. This Moslem restaurant was founded in 1848 on this very spot near the 500-year old Yinding stone arch bridge. It has tender succulent barbecue. (Ask the restaurant for its historical brochure.)

Cheap, Traditional Beijing Food

At the opposite end of the scale are onion and sesame buns hot out of the oven, or steaming hot sweet potatoes in their jackets cooked in huge bins on the street for Y1-Y2 each. A typical breakfast is deep fried oil sticks (like long donuts) dipped in soy milk and found in street stalls and tiny canteens. Look also for *jiao zi* meat dumplings, either steamed or boiled in soup. Take your own chopsticks and bowl if the hygiene turns you off. Avoid the outdoor night food market on Jinyu Hutong and Wangfujing because there are no seats, and it's too crowded. It's pickpocket heaven.

For a little more comfort, walk to the **Sun Dong An Plaza** on the corner near this market and go down to the basement. Here at the base of the escalators you can find demonstrations of old crafts, and a real tea house with old-style performances of magicians and musicians. The tea house charges a Y10 entrance fee, Y20 for tea and Y6 for watermelon seeds. During the National Day holidays, the place was full of stalls selling traditional-style pastries, candies, and many crafts. Permanent are pastry stores, and a collection of food stalls where you can point at what you want. While these can be crowded, you might at least find somewhere to sit. I've only tried a bowl of noodles there but I'd go back there again to try something else because it all looks fascinating.

For the Romantic

Some foreigners celebrate their weddings with dinner on a boat in Kunming Lake at the **Summer Palace**, or enjoy picnic suppers under a full moon at the **Ming Tombs** or **Great Wall**. Catering can be done by any top hotel—or take some snacks.

OTHER CUISINES

Superb food is available in the top hotels but there are also a lot of good restaurants.

Around the Forbidden City, Tiananmen Square, & Wangfujing Avenue
Food in the Grand, Palace, and the Novotel Peace should be considered.
HANWOORI KOREAN RESTAURANT. *Korean. Novotel Peace Hotel, 3 Jinyu Hutong, Wangfujing Avenue (across from the Palace Hotel), Tel. 65128833 X 6605, 6607. Open 11am-2:30pm and 5pm-10pm. It takes credit cards.*
This is a good Korean restaurant with the same menu as its sister restaurant, the Sorobal in the Lufthansa Centre (listed below). For cheaper Korean restaurants, there's the Wudaokou District. Ask for the Xiong Jia Restaurant near the Xi Jiao Hotel.
COURTYARD RESTAURANT, *95 Donghuamen Avenue, Tel. 65268883, 65268880. Open 6pm-10pm. Drinks only 10pm-1am. Accepts credit cards.*
The food here is a fusion of East and West. It's near the East Gate of the Forbidden City. Champagne costs Y78 a glass and wine Y45. Entrees in this pleasant, modern restaurant are Y120-Y195, appetizers Y55-Y90, and soups Y35-Y55.
GREEN TIANSHI VEGETARIAN RESTAURANT, *57 Dengshikou St., Tel. 65242476, 65242349. E-mail: friend@GreenTianshi.com or Crystal@GreenTianshi.com. Website: GreenTianshi.com. Open 10am-10pm.*
This lovely restaurant takes credit cards and has no MSG. Imitation Peking Duck costs Y220, grilled steaks Y68, and sweet and sour fish Y90. The menu is in Chinese and English. It allows no smoking, alcohol, eggs nor meat.
HONG KONG FOOD CITY, *Cantonese. 18 Donganmen Avenue, just west of Wangfujing near the night food market, Tel. 65136668. It is open 11am-3am and takes credit cards.*
If you are desperate for Cantonese food and can't afford the dim sum in the hotels, give this a try though it might be better to wait until you get to Guangzhou or Hong Kong.
The **DA SHANGYUAN RESTAURANT** is a tour group restaurant, but we like it and it's easy to find. From the back gate of the Forbidden City, go left and cross the street. It is on the corner. The food is good and the toilets clean.
SCHLOTZSKY'S DELI, *Oriental Plaza, corner of Wangfujing and Chang'an Avenue. Tel. 85186810, Fax 85186811. Branches also in the China World and Third Ring Road West (Tel. 62161651).*
Very American. Sandwiches, pizza and brownies.

Jianguomenwai
Especially good hotel restaurants are in the St. Regis, China World, and Jianguo Hotels.
DANIELLI'S, *St. Regis Hotel, 21 Jianguomenwai Avenue, Tel. 64606688. Open 11:30am-2:30pm and 6pm-10:30pm.*
This is an excellent Italian restaurant. Try the *spaghetti al arogosta* Y165, crab soup with seafood and scallops scented with sambuca Y65, and an

antipasto of deep fried calamari with chili garlic mayonnaise Y140. The St. Regis' Celestial Court restaurant has all-you-can-eat Cantonese dim sum for Y108.

JUSTINE'S, *Jianguo Hotel, 5 Jianguomenwai Avenue, Tel. 65002233 X 8039, open 6:30am-9:30am, 12 noon-2:30pm, and 6pm-10pm.*

With draperied ceiling, and maroon-and-gold striped chairs, this restaurant offers some of the best European food in the city. It has a Y99 business lunch which is free if it isn't served within an hour. Its appetizers range from Y148-Y198, salads Y70-Y112, soups Y68-Y75, fish Y178-Y225, meat Y172-Y255, flambe dishes Y265-Y398, and desserts Y60-Y85. Its popular goose liver on glazed apple and cognac soaked blackberries is Y139.

SUMMER PALACE, *Cantonese. China World Hotel, 1 Jianguomenwai Avenue, Tel. 65052266. 11:30am to 2:30pm (2:15pm last order) and 6pm to 10:30pm (10pm last order). Monday to Friday) dim sum set lunch Y88. Lunch and dinner set menu ranging from Y300 to Y1000 per person.*

Popular dishes are sauteed diced beef with black pepper sauce Y80 (small), braised superior shark's fin with saffron Y480, and sauteed baby octopus with crisp garlic and black beans Y78 (small).

TRADERS HOTEL COFFEE SHOP, *1 Jianguomenwai Avenue, Tel. 65052277 is behind the China World Hotel.*

It has a good international lunch buffet for about Y138 and a daily dim sum buffet for Y68 It's half-price for ladies on weekends.

SAMPAN RESTAURANT, *Cantonese, etc. Gloria Hotel, 2 Jianguomennan Avenue, 100022. Tel. 65158855. Credit cards. It is open 11:30am-2pm; 5:30pm-10pm.*

The Sampan has braised shark's fin with shredded chicken Y148; combo platter appetizers Y88; hot-and-sour soup Beijing-style Y28 per person; sauteed mixed seafood with macadamia nuts Y98; pan-fried boneless duck with lemon sauce Y68; beef steak Cantonese-style on sizzling platter Y68. The dim sum is good.

THE TAJ PAVILION. *Indian. China World Trade Centre. Its door is on the south side and can be easily seen from Jianguomenwai Avenue. L128 West Wing Office Block. Tel. 65055866, 65052288 X 80116. Fax 65055866.*

I was told by several people that it had the best Indian food in town. I can only vouch for the paneer pesharwari, which was very good with generous chunks of cheese. Samosas were Y28, pakoras Y26, kebabs Y32, and raita Y15. Chicken tikka costs Y50, tandoori prawns Y120, butter chicken Y75 and mutton Dahiwalla Y68. Plain nan is Y10 and lassi Y15. It is open 11:30am-2:30pm and 6:30pm-10:30pm and accepts credit cards.

GOLDEN SIAM LOTUS THAI RESTAURANT, *China World Shopping Mall, SB124A, 1, Jianguomenwai Avenue, Tel. 65055386 and 13501033889. This is within sight of the Pizza Hut in the West Wing office building.*

It charges Y20 and Y30 for tea, Y30 for a juice, and Y15 or Y25 for a beer. Salads range from Y28 to Y48, spring rolls are Y25 and Y40, barbecued pork

Y48, and curries Y48 to Y68. Its rice crackers with shrimp dip (*Kao Tang Na Tang*) at Y38 and Y58, are especially good. Pad Thai is Y48. It has a menu in English with photos.

BLEU MARINE RESTAURANT-BAR. *French. 5 Guang Hua Xi Road, a block north of the Gui You Department Store, Tel. 65006704. It is open Monday-Saturday from 11:30am-10:30pm, or whenever. It accepts credit cards.*

This restaurant is charming and casual with comfortable captains chairs. Its set lunch costs Y80 for two courses, or Y100 for three. It has a great appetizer with nuts and wonderful sweet chicken liver, a huge helping that was too much for one person. Entrees are Y40-Y75, fish Y85-Y138, meat Y75 and Y85, and desserts Y35-Y45.

RISTORANTE PIZZERIA ADRIA II, *this branch is north of the Gui You Department Store, on 14 Dong Da Qiao Road. Tel. 65006186.*

This place is popular for Italian food. It's part of a chain. An order of prosciutto e funghi pizze costs Y62, pizza Bolognese Y66, and pizza quattro formaggi Y72. Also popular are Spaghetti alla Carbonara for Y52 and costata senza osso al whisky for Y118. Free delivery for orders over Y150 and less than four kilometers away. Ask for its wine list.

OMAR KHAYYAM INDIAN RESTAURANT, *Indian. Asia-Pacific Building, 8 Ya Bao Road, Tel. 65139988 X 20188/20203. Open daily 11:30am-2:30pm and 6pm-10:30pm. It accepts credit cards.*

This restaurant has cooks from North India. Reservations are recommended on weekends or for big groups. Chicken tikka costs about Y55; tandoori chicken Y25, Y50 and Y95; palak paneer Y55; roganjosh Y69; and mutton vindaloo Y76. The food is good. Beer costs Y12-Y25.

XIAO WANG'S HOME RESTAURANT, *in an alley west and south of the Kerry Center and north of the Jinglun Hotel. Telephone for directions: 65913255, 65943602.*

This restaurant made its reputation with large servings and cheap home-style Chinese food beside the Scitech Hotel. With its move, prices have now gone up but the food is still good, the *jiao zi* delicious. The crispy rice dish serves four.

AH WEN'S SHANGHAI RESTAURANT, *2, Guang Hua Dong Road towards the Hangwei Building Tower. Tel. 65918032. Website: www.5eat.com. Open 11:00am-2:30pm, and 5:30pm-10pm.*

Next door to Xiao Wang's on this alley, an interesting looking restaurant yet to be tested but the juicy meat buns sound delicious for Y8-Y16 a plate.

SAMMIE'S, *a few stores to the east of the Silk Market at 65 Dong Da Qiao Road, Tel. 65958708. Website: www.beijingsammies.com. It is open 7:30am-midnight.*

Sammie's has great sandwiches and freshly-made coffee. You can order food on line and have it delivered. Coffees cost Y8 to Y20 and sandwiches Y20 and Y25.

All Sammies and baked goods are half price after 9pm. For delivery and catering, *Tel. 65068838.*

SCHLOTZSKY'S DELI, *Unit 206, Second Floor, China World Tower 2, Chao Yang Dist., Tel. 65050806. Fax 65050827.*
American food.

PIZZA HUT, *outside the Friendship Store is open about 10:30am-10:30pm. Tel. 65017768 or 65324121. Website: www.pizzahut.com.cn.*

A nine-inch pizza ranges from Y45-Y55, a 12 inch from Y65-Y85. Drinks are Y8 to Y29. Tiramisu costs Y15, and peach and mango cheese cake Y15 a piece.

BASKIN-ROBBINS, *at the Friendship Store sells donuts and ice cream and has been open 24 hours. Tel. 65018864.*

It charges Y10 for a cone and Y4-Y10 for a hot pastry.

HAAGEN-DAZS CAFE, *between the Friendship Store and the St. Regis Hotel on Ritan Road.*

You can get more than just ice cream here.

Ritan Park & Full Link Plaza

XIHE YA JU RESTAURANT, *at the northeast corner of Ritan Park (west side). Sichuan, Cantonese, etc. Moderate, Tel. 65941915, 65067643. It's open 11am-2pm and 5pm-10pm and accepts credit cards.*

This cute little café with multi-colored checked table cloths is very popular with foreigners. One section is air-conditioned with plastic grapes and gourds. Among its most popular dishes are Angel ham duck soup for Y98, Cantonese steamed fish for four people for Y200, and Xihe garlic pork ribs for Y32. It has a menu with photos.

SHANGHAI GOURMET, *4/F Full Link Plaza, 18 Chaoyangmenwai Avenue, Chaoyang District. Tel. 65881863, Fax 65881861. Website: www.sshgourmet.com.*

NYC MUSIC KITCHEN, *Shanghai and Sichuan. Moderate. 4/F, Full Link Plaza, Tel. 65881791/1793. It's open 11am-midnight. Happy Hour is 5pm-7pm, two for one.*

This modern-looking cafe has a disc jockey playing mainly US pop music. Live jazz, rock, and pop music are offered regularly on some evenings. Popular dishes include steamed mini-shrimp dumplings for Y25, pan-fried bun with pork filling for Y16, minced meat ball and cabbage in clay pot Y42, and roasted baby back ribs with scallions for Y45.

Further Away But Still Downtown

The City Hotel-Zhaolong Hotel-Sanlitun area has very casual and moderate-priced dining. See also bars with food in this area in the *Nightlife & Entertainment* section below.

BERENA'S BISTRO, *6 East Sports Stadium Road is open 11:30am-midnight, Tel. 65922628, Fax 65062702. Close to Frank's Place and the City Hotel, Berena's is a moderately-priced Cantonese and Sichuan restaurant favored by foreigners. Open 11am-midnight.*

THE DEN, *near the City Hotel at 4A Gongti East Road.*
This lively nightspot has good food too. See *Nightlife* below.

METRO CAFÉ, *Italian. 6 Gong Ti Xi Lu (by Workers Gymnasium), Tel. 65527828. Orders from 11:30am-12:00 midnight. Last dinner order at 10:20pm. It accepts credit cards.*

This restaurant has freshly-made pasta and reasonable prices, served in an attractive patio garden with fountain in summer. It's known for its lasagne bolognese for Y65, fettuccine with chicken and pepper cheese sauce for Y65, and Y35-45 Caesar salad. Manager Marvin Lau is from Hawaii.

FRIDAY'S, *American. 19 Dong Sanhuanbei Road, one block south of the Zhaolong Hotel on the west side of Third Ring Road, Tel. 65975314, Fax 65975240. E-mail: tgif@public.cmit.cn.net. It is open 11am-midnight, and takes credit cards.*

This, the first restaurant of this Dallas chain in China, has great ribs for Y65 a half rack or Y88 for full. It also has fajitas, fried mozzarella, and buffalo wings, nachos, hamburgers, soup and salad, and loaded potato skins. The waiters dress in cute costumes and it has tiffany lamp shades, striped red and white plastic table cloths and Rock Hudson movie posters.

LIU FEN ZHENG RESTAURANT, *on the east side of Nanxinhua Street about three buildings south of where the buses and taxis stop for Liu Li Chang, the old arts and antique street. The restaurant is just south of the overpass.*

Al Fresco Dining in Beijing

Summer is patio time especially along Jianguomenwai where hotels have tables on the street in front. Also prolific and informal is the former Sanlitun Market (whose clothing stalls were removed because they were "too messy." We beg to differ of course. That market was lots of fun.) Notable along this stretch of Sanlitun Road, has been **Bella's Bake Shop** which has been good especially for cinnamon buns and cookies. *Tel. 64168785 and open 8am-midnight.* Try also the **Side By Side Cafe**, *number 54, Tel. 64164191, open 9am-2am.* Also recommended is **Serve the People Restaurant**, *north of Bella's, Tel. 64173449, 84517489, 64153242,* where you can get an American breakfast for Y35 and Thai food.

You can also relax on the patio beside the **Holiday Inn Lido** and on the pedestrian part of **Wangfujing Avenue**.

Outside are two two-meter-high plaster figures of bowing waiters in tiger slippers. It is open 10:30am-10:30pm.

This is a little noodle shop, modest and grubby, but it's decorated with an old Victrola, giant Chinese opera masks, and 1920s movie posters. The menu is in English. At Y8 for a bowl of noodles, it can't afford to replace its cracked dishes very often and clean up its greasy floor. But the main attraction besides the good food is its waiters who chant words of welcome as each group of customers enter, a custom also being revived in other noodle restaurants in the city as well.

Great Wall-Kempinski-Kunlun area

LOUISIANA RESTAURANT, *Fusion. Expensive. Beijing Hilton, 4 Dong Sanhuan Bei Road, 1 Dongfang Road, Tel. 64662288, 64674754. It's open 11am-2pm; 6pm-10:30pm.*

This restaurant has a marvelous blend of Pacific Northwest, Creole, and Asia-Pacific cooking. The menu changes frequently so there's always some variety introduced by guest chefs like Claus Mayr and Charles Saunders. It also matches local and foreign wines to each dish. Popular are the winter squash bisque, and gumbo soups. Highly recommended is the rack of lamb smoked with coffee beans, after marinating in sugar cane juice. Also great is the butterfly Norwegian salmon. Or try the tender supremo of free-range chicken with mango sauce. The most popular dessert is the Mud Bug.

SEASONS RESTAURANT, *International. Expensive. Kempinski Hotel, Beijing Lufthansa Centre, 50 Liangmaqiao Road, Tel. 64653388. It accepts credit cards.*

This has a great Sunday champagne brunch (11:30am-3pm) for Y245 including champagne and beer. Its daily buffet lunch is Y170 and dinner Y180. Try other restaurants here too like the PAULANER which has a Y65 net lunch special. It is open from 11am to 1am. Its sausages cost Y45 to Y76 and Paulaner beer Y33 to Y80.

FLO, *2/F Rainbow Plaza, 16 East Third Ring Road, Tel. 65955139. 11am-2pm, 6pm-11pm.*

Highly recommended, authentic French food, near the Great Wall Hotel. It has a French chef and serves genuine French oysters, imported from France. Expensive but worth it.

SHANGHAI RESTAURANT, *Kunlun Hotel, 2 Xin Yuan Nan Road. Tel. 65903388. Open 11:30am-2pm, and 5:30pm-9:30pm. It accepts credit cards.*

Designed in Louis XIV style, this restaurant is worth visiting for the décor as well as the food. Moderate prices. Popular are braised hairy beans, bean curd skin rolled with fungus, crystal shrimps, stir-fried shredded eels, braised Mandarin fish with pine nuts, and sauteed eggplant in spicy sauce. Believe me, these taste better than they sound.

The Cantonese restaurant in the Kunlun is also good for lemon chicken, bean soup, and sweet and sour pork.

SCHILLER'S 1, *opposite the Kempinski Hotel. Maybe. Tel. 64619276, Fax 6619276, 64619276. E-mail: office@schillers.com.cn. It is open 7am -1am daily. Happy Hour: 5pm-7pm daily.*

This is one of the oldest Western restaurants in town and it serves burgers, spaghetti and other popular Western-style dishes like deep-fried cheese roll (6 pieces for Y45 an order), "Rouladen" – beef roll German style for Y60, and Hungarian goulash for Y45. For "Weizen," its locally-made German white beer, it's Y30 a bottle. For its other branches see *www.schillers.com.cn*. Schiller-2 serves German food and beer along with its regular fare. Schiller's-3 has a live band and B.B.Q buffet on weekends.

THE RED BASIL THAI RESTAURANT, *Thai. Moderate. Sanyuan Dong Qiao, Third Ring Bei Road, northwest and across the street, one block north from the Hilton. A sign above the trees in front says "Thai Restaurant." Tel. 64602339, Fax 64673120. It is open daily 11:00am-2pm, and 5:30pm-10pm (last order).*

This restaurant has amazing Thai cooking. We really liked the kai hor bei teoy, balls of marinated chicken with pan dan leaf for Y50. The yum woon san talay is a spicy glass noodle salad for Y60; tom yum koong, spicy and sour soup with fresh prawns for Y50; and sweet golden egg yolk silk thread, an edible cloth of egg for Y25. Thai ice tea was Y20, and fresh coconut Y50. Singha beer was Y50. The food, hurrah, had no MSG. The management is related to that of the Grand Lijiang Hotel in Lijiang.

SORABOL KOREAN RESTAURANT, *Korean. Basement of the You Yi Shopping Center, Lufthansa Center, 50 Liangmaqiao Road, Tel. 64651845. Open 11am-2:30pm, and 5pm-9:30pm daily. It accepts credit cards. Moderate.*

You can get good boolgahlbi or marinated short ribs, or boolgogi (marinated beef) or haemool pahjuhn (spring onion and seafood pancake). This restaurant is part of a chain of good Korean restaurants. While you're in the basement, there's a bake shop and edible snacks in the supermarket next door for the budget-minded.

ADRIA RISTORANTE PIZZERIA CAFE, *Italian. Moderate. 16 Xinyuan Street, north of the Capital Mansion. Tel. 64600896. It is open 11am-11pm.*

This has the best pizza in town, some would say in Asia. It has green and white table cloths with red napkins. Pizza costs Y48 to Y70.

Holiday Inn Lido/Harbour Plaza/airport area

BOROM PIMAM THAI RESTAURANT, *Thai. Moderate to expensive. Holiday Inn Lido, Jichang Road, Jiang Tai Road, Tel. 64376688. It is open 11:30am-2pm and 6pm-10pm, and accepts credit cards.*

This outstanding restaurant in traditional Thai-style, is worth the trip out from downtown. It is another romantic setting, a place for lovers. You can sit on the floor or on chairs. Soups cost Y33-Y45; salads Y33-Y60; noodles and rice Y37-Y60; fish and seafood Y55-Y170; curries Y45-Y45-Y58.

TEXAN BAR & GRILL, *Tex-Mex. Moderate. Holiday Inn Lido, Jichang Road, Jiang Tai Road, Tel. 64376688. Credit cards accepted.*

The nachos were crispy and deep-fried. Its blade steak (Y55) had been marinated with Mexican spices and a sweet sauce, a recipe chef Jeff Wei had learned in Australia. It was great. The burrito was not like Taco Bell's but was good. The sweet corn on the cob had been shipped frozen from the U.S. and was soft and uninteresting as a result. (Local corn would have been worse; it's tasteless.) The T-bone steak costs Y58, tenderloin Y78, rib eye Y68, and sirloin Y65 – each per 100 grams, and served with potato wedges with Cajun spices. Their pork ribs with spicy tomato wedges and sour cream cost Y85. Pecan pie with ice cream is Y33.

SINO-SWISS HOTEL, *near the airport.*

The coffee shop at lunch time offers salads for Y40 and Y50, Zurcher Geschnet zeltes for Y55 and Y110, Australian beef tenderloin Y160, udon noodles Y75, and soups for Y30-Y40. The salad bar was Y45.

HOME AWAY FROM HOME (Xian Shi, Lido Zhong Ma Dui Mien), *Beijing. Moderate. Across the street from the Lido's main entrance. Tel. 64360023.*

In this modest family-run restaurant, good were the barbecued sliced chicken at Y22, sauteed shredded chicken with red pepper for Y28 (a little oily), and stir-fried broccoli for Y18. This is everyday fare – nothing special, but at least it'll fill you up. The menu is in Chinese and English. But it's not worth making a special trip from downtown to eat here.

Near the Northwest Hotels

NISHIMURA RESTAURANT, *Rabatayaki Japanese. Shangri-La Hotel, 29 Zizhuyuan Road, Tel. 68412211. Accepts credit cards.*

This restaurant offers sushi, grilled vegetables on skewers, steak and onions. Rabatayaki is Japanese peasant food, where the shaved dried fish wiggle like worms. Try the delicious sampler that arrives in a lacquer box. Good were the chicken yakatori (Y20 for two sticks), a half order of cold noodles for Y30, teppanyaki for Y150, sushi Y120, and a vegetable salad for Y30. The atmosphere is casual. Try also the **Shang Palace** in this hotel, which is exceptional too.

MOSLEM RESTAURANT, *very moderate. Ground floor, Xiyuan Hotel, 1 Sanlihe Road, Tel. 68313388. Credit cards accepted.*

Try the sauteed lamb kidney for Y48, the barbecued mutton or chicken shashlik for Y8 a piece, the boiled mutton dumplings in soup for Y26, the pan-fried beef with onion in a bun for Y5 each, and the fried minced mutton wrapped in egg for Y38.

Moslem Fare

For Moslem food, it has been **Uygurville**, a street market with cheap food and great shishkebobs, meat on skewers, and nan bread. Also known as **Xinjiang Village** (Xinjiang Cun), it's on Baiwanzhuang Xi Road, Ganjiakou which is north and west of the Holiday Inn Downtown, and south of the Xiyuan Hotel. It might not be clean so if you eat there, be careful. Kebobs straight from burning coals should be okay. No one speaks English. The soups and stews can be very spicy hot and great.

Cat Calls & Whistles

Beijing is no longer the quiet, puritanical city of the pre-1980s where you arrived at restaurants at 6pm and had to leave by 9pm. There are a lot of fun restaurant-bars, like **Henry J. Bean's** *in the West Wing Building, China World Trade Center, Tel. 65052266 X 6569 (open Sunday-Thursday 11:30am-1:30am, and Friday-Saturday 11:30am-1:30am).* There you might find juggling bartenders, waitresses dancing on table tops, and similiarly-inspired customers–if the mood is right. Live music daily except Sunday. Chicken quesadillas with salsa, sour cream and guacamole, and brownies with real whipping cream. Huge servings.

Very popular is the **Afanti** or A-fun-ti where guests are crowded together into long tables (check your exits in case of fire). The food and entertainment are Uighur from Xinjiang province, and great. A couple 30-minute shows highlight a dancer, her floor-length hair waving wildly as she twirls in high heels amid whistles and cat calls. She also throws caps into the audience to a heavy tambourine beat and lively middle eastern music. But I went alone and found myself at a ring-side table. It's a lot more fun with friends who end up dancing on the tables. The menu could include a whole sheep, salad, and mutton shashlik or Arabian sweets. Afanti is at *Jia 2 Hou Guai Bang Alley, Chaonei Street, Dong Cheng District. This is an alley off of Chao Nei Avenue and west of Bei Xiao Jie and Second Ring Road. Tel. 65272288, 65251071 for directions and for show times. It is open 11:30am-10 or 11pm. A full meal costs Y80, Y180, or Y260 each if 10 people are together, beverages extra. It accepts credit cards. Many hotels distribute its card. E-mail: afunti@afunti.com.cn. Website: www.afunti.com. It takes credit cards.*

The **Daijiacun** (Dai Village) **Restaurant** is more subdued, but cooks could kill live snakes at your table–if you want. Dai minority women cheerfully dance between tables. They also invite customers to join them. The food is good: bacon cooked in bamboo, spicy hot stewed fish in coconut, roast beef on hot stone, and bamboo rice. *Open 11:30am-2pm, and 4:30pm-9:30pm. It's at the west gate of factory 3501, Guandongdian Nanjie, Chaoyang, north of the China World. Ask a Chinese speaker to phone for reservations and performance times. Prices are moderate. Tel. 65942455, 65089186.*

More reliable is the **Xiyuan Hotel** above and the **Xinjiang Autonomous Region Beijing Office**, at North Gan Jia Kuo, where there are three decent Moslem restaurants in this big courtyard. None, except the Xiyuan, however, have menus in English, so you have to point.

See Moslem section in the *Food & Drink* chapter.

Cheaper Food

If you want a snack to fill you up, fast-food Cantonese restaurants are in the basements of the **Jing Guang New World Hotel** (pork dumplings, noodles and congee), and the **Tianlun Dynasty Hotel** (Gourmet Bazaar, open 11:30am-2pm; 5:30pm-9:30pm). Shopping malls also have fast food restaurants.

Bake shops are all over. Hotels like the **Kempinski** and **Holiday Inn Lido** have good delis. The Kempinski deli is open from 7am to 11pm, and its fresh fruit juice costs Y45, sandwiches Y30-Y34, quiche Y24, and ham and cheese croissant Y24.

Grocery shops everywhere sell dried noodles in just-add-water cups, cookies and biscuits. One of the branches of **Deli France**, the Hong Kong company, is on the second floor of the Sun Dong An Plaza. **McDonald's** are everywhere. One is across the street from the zoo. There's also **KFC** and **Pizza Hut**.

See also *Nightlife & Entertainment* below and *Cheap Beijing Food* above.

Seeing the Sights

I have arranged this section as a six or seven day plan. This is a very heavy schedule and you have to squeeze your shopping and strolling into the evenings. You really need two leisurely weeks, and then some. Don't miss the **Beijing Opera**, the **acrobats**, the **Lao She Tea House**, and the **pandas**. See something of modern Beijing: the **China World Trade Center's** maze of stores, and take a ride on the subway. Visit the **Blue Zoo** and relax in a pub or a tea house. Take advantage of the cheaper prices or unique opportunities for extraordinary cultural events like Turandot performed in the Forbidden City (under the baton of Zubin Mehta) or the Three Tenors, or the Johann Strauss Orchestra of Vienna. Beijing isn't just ancient relics. It's a world class, cosmopolitan city.

For tours and tour buses, see *Practical Information* below. Most museums are open between 9am and the last entry time of 4pm daily, but hours keep changing and are longer in summer. If an exact time is essential, call the museum or the **24-hour Tourism Hotline**, *Tel. 65130828*.

DAY ONE

Tiananmen Square is 98 acres and great for kite-flying in the spring. Try to imagine 1966 at the beginning of the Cultural Revolution, when a million school children filled this square, chanting slogans and waving Chairman Mao's little red book of quotations. The father of Communist China stood in front and acknowledged the screams and cheers of the youngsters. Besides giving them a vacation from school, he also gave them a mandate to travel around the country on the trains with room and board in each city, all free.

Unfortunately, the Cultural Revolution had a serious downside as well, with many people killed and persecuted throughout the country. It was in effect a civil war.

It will be hard for many foreigners to forget the much televised, idealistic young students demonstrating nonviolently for democracy in early 1989. An estimated 300 to 3,000 people were killed in or around the square in what the Chinese government calls "the quelling of the counter-revolutionary rebellion." Chinese government accounts of the turmoil and Western sources do not agree, as you might expect.

The square is bounded on the north by Tiananmen Gate and on the west by the Great Hall of the People. On the east is the Museum of the Chinese Revolution and the Museum of Chinese History, and on the south you can't miss the imposing Qianmen Gate. In the center, from the north to south, are the Monument to the People's Heroes and Chairman Mao's Memorial Hall. The portrait of Chairman Mao on Tiananmen Gate is changed every year on October 1.

Let's start with **The Great Hall of the People**, also known as People's Congress Hall, China's parliament, *Tel. 66801188*. It is open to tourists 8:30am-3pm when not used for meetings. Built in 1959, the Great Hall measures 171,800 square meters. Three main sections include a 5000-seat banquet hall, a three-story, 10,000-seat auditorium, and lounges in the style of each of the provinces. To some observers, the People's Congress is merely a rubber-stamp group of representatives. To others, it is a forum for the opinions of citizens.

Magnificent, beautiful Qianmen Gate to the south has a **folk museum**. To the south of that is **Dazhalan**, the old Chinese shopping area where you can still get cloth shoes.

The Gates of Beijing

Beijing's gates are marvelous. Each had a very specific purpose; for example, night soil could only go through **Andingmen** in the north, and prisoners to be executed plodded through the west gate, **Xuanwumen**. Departing soldiers marched through another of the north gates even if they had to fight in the south. The impressive **Deshengmen** (Victory Gate) can be climbed. A couple of the gates now house serious art galleries.

In the **Monument to the People's Heroes**, the sculptures represent the burning of the opium and the Opium War, 1840-42; the Taiping Heavenly Kingdom, 1851-64; the Revolution of 1911; the May 4, 1919 demonstration against the Versailles Treaty and for the New Cultural Movement (calling for literature in the colloquial rather than the generally incomprehensible classical language); the May 30, 1925 Incident in Shanghai, a protest against foreign powers in China. Look also for the August 1, 1927 uprising in Nanchang and the Anti-Japanese War, 1937-45.

In April 1976, during the Qingming (Ching Ming) festival, when the dead are honored, attempts by the Gang of Four to remove wreaths brought by private citizens in memory of Premier Zhou Enlai were resisted by pro-Zhou supporters at this monument. Hundreds were wounded and thousands arrested. This protest is now referred to as the April Fifth Movement against the Gang of Four, and encouraged pro-Zhou politicians like Deng Xiaoping to attempt to overthrow them. In 1989, this monument was central to the student demonstrators.

The **Chairman Mao Memorial Hall**, *Tel. 65132277*, is a mausoleum built in 1977 and houses the remains of China's revolutionary leader. The hours keep changing but you should be able to visit between 8:30am-11:30am daily except Sundays. It's also open some afternoons. The simple white building, with 44 granite columns and glazed yellow trim, is 33.6 meters high and 105 meters square.

The visit takes less than 30 minutes. As a token of respect, visitors are advised not to wear bright colors, especially red, but I've never seen anyone stopped. No cameras or purses are allowed. You first enter the North Hall where there is a seated, three-meter-high marble statue of the leader. Then, quietly, two by two, you enter the Central Hall where Chairman Mao (1893-1976) lies in state.

The **Museum of Chinese History**, *Tel. 65128321*, open 9am-4pm, has the best of China's artefacts but it has only a few titles in English. Books with photos of the collection might be a good souvenir and help you identify pieces. The museum is divided into four sections: primitive society, slave society, feudal society, and semi-colonial-semi-feudal society. You can walk through without absorbing much in an hour, it is so large. You need at least a half day to do it justice. Please take it in short doses. The entrance to the museum is opposite the Great Hall of the People. The history museum is to the right.

Relics here date from 1.7-million-year-old pre-human teeth to 1911. They include a model of the cave where the Peking Man was found. Also on display are a 14th-century B.C. ivory cup inlaid with jade, a Shang bronze wine vessel with four protruding ram's heads, and a Western Zhou sewer pipe with the head of a tiger. Intriguing, too, are a model of a Warring States irrigation system, tomb figures galore, and a model of a first-century B.C. wheel used to operate a bellows to melt iron. Here, too, is the Flying Horse of Gansu, which people around the world waited many hours to see when it was exhibited abroad. No queues here!

There is also a model of a 1700-year-old drum chariot with a figure of a child on top, always pointing south, and another miniature drum chariot with a figure that beats a drum every 500 meters, a Yuan water clock, and some Yuan rockets attached to spears. I can only whet your appetite. It is best to take a friend who reads Chinese—unless things have changed recently.

Tiananmen (Gate of Heavenly Peace) is the second most famous structure in China. From its high balcony the imperial edicts were read, and this is where, on October 1, 1949, Chairman Mao Zedong (Mao Tse-tung) proclaimed the People's Republic of China. It is a symbol of old and new China. The country's leaders frequently appear here on national days to review the parades and festivities. It was built in 1651 and stands 33.7 meters high. The rostrum where Chairman Mao stood is open to tourists for a fee.

Through the gate under Chairman Mao's portrait and to the left is **Zhongshan Park**, the memorial park to Dr. Sun Yat-sen. To the right is **Working People's Cultural Park**. These two parks are great for an early morning walk because of the magnificent walls, towers, gates, moats, and pavilions, and also because of the people limbering up for the day. You might hear some very beautiful voices resound off the walls from very shy singers hiding behind bushes and screens. Where else can they practice without neighbors complaining?

In the square between the two parks is a tiny white marble pavilion looking much like a Japanese lantern. In imperial times, if an official made a serious error, his black gauze cap was placed inside and he was taken out to be executed at the Wumen in front of the palace. Commoners were executed at the marketplace seven km southwest of here near the Qianmen Hotel.

The Forbidden City

The **Gu Gong** or **Imperial Palace** (also known as **Palace Museum** or **Forbidden City**), *Tel. 65132255*, is open and costs about Y40. No one is admitted after 3:30pm. Visitors usually enter by the Wumen (Meridian Gate) inside the Tiananmen Gate and head north. An Acoustiguide, recorded by British actor Roger Moore, giving details about a limited area, is recommended for travelers without guides for additional payment. You can photograph exteriors with still or video cameras, but not interiors. You can also enter from the north gate but most use the south. A toilet is at the south entrance to the left as you enter.

The Gu Gong was the home and audience hall of the Ming and Qing emperors. Many buildings here are as the Qing left them, minus relics now in the National Palace Museum in Taiwan. You can see the queue of the Last Emperor Pu Yi, which he cut off himself, his bicycle, and his cricket box. To walk at a leisurely pace from one end to the other takes about 30 minutes, but to explore it thoroughly takes at least a full day, some would say a week. Tour groups usually whiz through the center, following the north-south axis, the center of the world. If you want to see it all, and the side chambers are all worth seeing, see the center first, and then go back for the east chambers, following the signs to the important exhibits. Then see the west-side exhibits.

The **Forbidden City** was originally built from 1406 to 1420 as the palace of the Ming emperors. It lies on more than 720,000 square meters (178 acres) of land and has over 8600 rooms. The surrounding imperial red wall is over 10 meters high. Only imperial palaces were allowed to have yellow ceramic roofs. (Commoners could only use gray.)

Toward the end of the Qing, 280,000 taels of silver were needed annually to maintain the palace, the money collected in taxes and rents from 658,000 acres of royal estates. Two thousand ladies-in-waiting and 3,000 eunuchs served here. Some eunuchs became more powerful than the self-indulgent emperors. Sacked by foreign powers in 1900, the Forbidden City was restored and now maintains a permanent staff of painters and carpenters so that every 20 years all the buildings are renewed.

The Forbidden City is divided into two major sections: the outer palace (for business) and the inner residential courts. Directly inside the Meridian Gate at the south entrance are the five marble bridges "like arrows reporting on the emperor to Heaven." The River of Gold below is shaped like a bow. Note the gates; red was used only for important structures. Each has 81 studs - nine times nine, an imperial number. Seven layers of brick line the courtyards so no one could tunnel in from below. Note the well-worn white squares, on each of which a royal guard stood whenever the emperor ventured past.

Throughout the palace, huge cauldrons of water stand ready for possible fires. On the north side, beneath the cauldrons, are air vents that fan fires set in winter to keep the water inside from freezing. Note the lack of hiding places for possible assassins.

The first building is the **Taihedian** (Tai Ho Tien; **Hall of Supreme Harmony**), the most stately of all the buildings. It is surrounded by incense burners, 18 bronze ones representing the then 18 provinces, and others in the form of a stork (longevity) and a dragon-headed tortoise (strength and endurance). Note the copy of an ancient sundial and the small openings in the side of the pavilion to allow air to circulate inside. This building was used for major ceremonies.

Imagine the area in front of the Hall covered with silk-gowned ministers and officials kneeling in rows, their heads to the ground while smoke poured from incense burners and musicians played on the balcony. Can you see the child emperor being carried by a palanquin above them to the highly carved throne? If you can't, try to see the Chinese historical movie *Power Behind the Throne* and the American movie *The Last Emperor*.

Each of the 18-meter-high cedar pillars was made from one piece of wood. Each of the floor tiles took 136 days to bake, after which it was immersed in oil for a permanent polish. The bricks are solid, about 5 inches thick and 18 inches square. The base and throne are carved sandalwood.

The second building on the north-south axis is the **Zhonghedian (Hall of Complete Harmony)**, used by the emperor to receive his ministers, to rest, and to dress before he entered the Taihedian. The two Qing sedan chairs here were for traveling within the palace. The braziers were for heat and the four cylindrical burners for sandalwood incense. Note the imperial dragon symbols on the ceiling.

The **Baohedian (Hall of Preserving Harmony)**, the most lavish of these halls, was for imperial banquets and, during the Qing, the re-testing of the top scorers in the national examinations. Behind this hall, between the stairways, is a giant carving of dragons from one piece of marble, 16.5 meters by 3 meters and weighing about 250 tons. Anyone caught touching this imperial symbol was executed. The carving and the timbers were brought here in winter by sliding them over ice made from water out of wells especially sunk for the occasion. Nothing was too extravagant for the representative of Heaven!

A photographer is stationed between two of the large pavilions and can take photos of you or your group in the morning, and deliver them and a booklet as ordered to your restaurant or hotel for about Y60 each. These are quite good and you don't pay until delivery.

Several buildings on both sides of these main halls were used for study, lectures, a library, and even a printing shop. Beyond this third hall are the Inner Courts, the three main buildings, similar to the three in the outer palace; the **Qianqingong (Hall of Heavenly Purity)** where the emperors used to live, and where deceased emperors lay in state.

Cixi (Tzu Hsi), the infamous Empress Dowager, received foreign envoys in the **Jiaotaidian (Hall of Union)**. Women were not allowed in the outer palace. The **Kunninggong (Palace of Earthly Tranquility)** was a residence in the Ming and a shrine in the Qing. One of the Qing emperors used its eastern room as a bridal chamber.

East of the Kunninggong is a hall where clocks from all over the world are exhibited, gifts from foreign missions. In the back of the inner court is the **Imperial Garden**, where you can find a snack bar. The imperial family sipped tea, played chess, and meditated in this beautifully designed but tiny garden. Can you imagine living in this crowded space with little or no grass?

Then, continuing northward, you arrive at the back gate where tour groups usually meet their buses, poor things, because they miss out on a lot. But you're not finished yet. Retracing your steps to the entrance of the inner court, turn left (east) at the Qianqinggong, past the washrooms and the Nine Dragon Screen, and then turn left again.

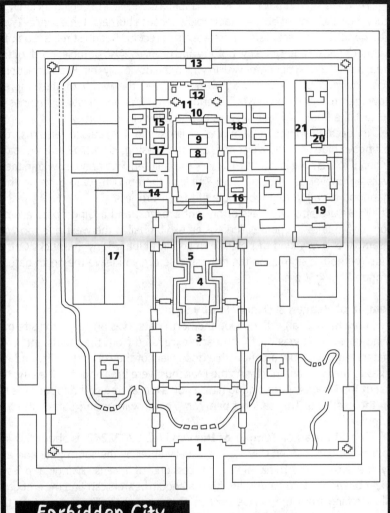

Forbidden City Palace Museum

1 Wumen Gate
2 Tianhemen Gate
3 Taihedian Hall
4 Zhonghedian Hall
5 Baohedian Hall
6 Qianqingmen Gate
7 Qianqinggong Palace
8 Jiaotaidian Hall
9 Kunninggong Palace
10 Imperial Garden
11 Thousand Autumn Pavilion
12 Qinandian Hall
13 Shenwumen Gate
14 Yanxindian Hall
15 Chuxiugong Palace
16 Hall of Bronzes
17 Hall of Ceramics
18 Hall of Arts & Crafts of the Ming
   & Qing Dynasties
19 Hall of Paintings
20 Hall of Jewelry
21 Qianlong Garden

Here are several pavilions with exhibitions well worth seeing including a stunning collection of gold artifacts, bells, incense burners, table service (with jade handles), and scepters. There are also precious Buddhist relics. Look for paintings and antique jewelry, pottery and bronzes. Also notable, north of this area, is the 12-inch diameter well in which the obviously-thin Pearl Concubine was drowned by a eunuch after she incurred the wrath of the Empress Dowager in 1900. You pay a Y5 entry fee and Y2 for plastic overshoes to protect the floors. A clean toilet is near the jewelry exhibit.

In each building, look at the ceilings and the palace lanterns, the distinctive blue Manchu cloisonné, and the Western clocks. Where were the imperial toilets? the kitchens? Think of the children who grew up within these walls and never set foot outside! Think of the eunuchs who gave up their manhood for a job that would benefit their families!

There are also two halls of ancient bronzes, and a Qing opera exhibit. Some have titles in English. There is an exhibit hall in the west side too with a sample of every kind of porcelain made in China. A tiny Starbucks Coffee shop (without a sign) is on the right side before you leave the north gate. It is open 8am-4:30pm.

Temple of Heaven & Other Nearby Sights

Jingshan (Coal) **Hill**, outside the north gate, was originally the site of a Ming coal pile. It was built with earth excavated from the moats and is 43 meters high. It is now a park with a good view of the Forbidden City and the lakes to the west and north. As the Manchus were breaking into the city, the last of the Ming emperors hung himself on a locust tree at the foot of the hill on the east side. This park is open 7am-7pm in winter and 5am-9:30pm in summer.

The ***Tiantan** or **Temple of Heaven**, *Tel. 67022242*, is about five km south of the Forbidden City. People usually enter by the south gate and exit by the east gate. Think of the processions of incense-swinging priests, spear-bearing palace guards, and the palanquin bearers carrying the emperor, all marching from the palace unseen by anyone else. Setting eyes on the emperor was another crime punishable by death.

The temple is set in the middle of a 667-acre park with many pine and cypress trees, some over 500 years old. Give yourself at least 20 minutes for a quick look, an hour for a more thorough tour. The Temple of Heaven was built in the same period as the Forbidden City (1420). It was used a couple times a year when the emperor, bearing all the sins of the Chinese people, humbled himself before Heaven and performed the rituals calculated to bring good harvests. The temple has two concentric walls, both round at the north and straight at the south, heaven being round and earth square, or didn't you know?

To the south is the **Imperial Vault of Heaven**, originally built in 1530 and rebuilt in 1752. In this building without horizontal beams were stored the tablets of the gods of heaven, the wind god, the rain god, etc. Sacrifices were made on the circular Sacrificial Altar on the winter solstice. The surrounding wall has a strange echo effect. You can hear people talking softly beside it from an unusual distance — but not if a lot of noisy people are around. Also count the number of stone slabs on the floor, staircases, and balustrades. They are in multiples of nine.

The raised, 360-meter passage between the main buildings is the **Red Stairway Bridge**. To the north is the famous **Qinandian (Hall of Prayer for Good Harvests)** with triple eaves and 38 meters high. The four central columns represent the four seasons. Around these four are two rings of 12 columns each, the inner symbolizing the 12 months and the outer the 12 divisions of day and night. Here, the emperor performed the rites on the 15th day of the first moon of the lunar calendar. Beside this hall is a musical instrument exhibit.

DAY TWO
The Hutong Tour

Before the 1970s, the whole of Beijing consisted mainly of tiny courtyard houses which have almost disappeared. This tour was created by a photographer obsessed with recording the old architecture and trying to save it. His privately operated company now has at least 50 bicycle rickshaws and drivers. While blankets are provided in cold weather, we do recommend this tour only when it's warm and dry.

The three-hour tour leaves twice a day about 100 meters west of the north entrance to Beihai Park. Look for tricycles with maroon canopies. It goes past a lake to the **Drum Tower** (open 8:30am-4pm) on the north-south axis with 69 high stairs. Here is a good view, one decrepit 13th century Yuan dynasty drum and 25 reproductions you can bang for Y5 in addition to the Y20 admission fee. Five times a day for 20 minutes there's a drum concert. From there you go to the old Yinding /Silver Ingot Bridge and one of the courtyard houses. We had tea with a 78-year old Communist cadre, then went to the other extreme to Prince Gong's digs where we chuckled about the piece of the Great Wall he had built to remind him of his Manchu past. This mansion was originally built by a Ming eunuch in the southern style in 1776-1785.

Prince Gong's Mansion is at 23 Lu Yin Street and can be visited even if you're not on a tour. It is open 8:30am-4pm daily. It was owned at one time by the great-uncle of the last emperor. Go for the pretty garden, the theatre, and the traditional style buildings. Tours get a demonstration of a Chinese tea ceremony, which is not as elaborate as that of the Japanese.

Some tours then go for lunch in a home, and try to make *jiao zi* dumplings. The delicious home-cooked meal and opportunity to talk with ordinary Beijing inhabitants is frequently one of the highlights of a tour. Did you know garbage is collected there three times a day? and the postman comes twice a day?

Contact: any travel agency or the **Beijing Hutong Tourist Agency**, *26 Di An Men Xi Avenue, Xi Cheng, 100009, Tel. 66159097, Fax 64002787. Website: www.hutongtour.com.* Tours leave about 8:50am and 1:50pm.

Next head over to **Beihai Park** (North Sea Park), open 7:30am-4pm, only a few blocks west of Coal Hill. If you are short of time, just look for the Baita Shan (White Dagoba Hill) and then the Nine Dragon Screen (1756) on the opposite side of the lake. While the whole area is a historic site protected by the State Council, these are the highlights of this big, 168-acre park full of intriguing old buildings, the Jingxinzhai (Serenity Study), winding paths, and interesting rocks that could take a half day to explore. Rowboats are for hire and, in the winter, ice skating on the lake is an exotic experience (but bring your own skates).

The **Fang Shan Restaurant** has a great setting. It is near the White Dagoba and serves the same fancy, delicate dishes (well, almost!) once presented to the Empress Dowager. In the 10th century (Liao), an imperial residence was built here. In the 12th century (Jin), auxiliary palaces were constructed here and a lake excavated, the earth used to build the artificial hills and the ***Round City** at the southern edge. During the Yuan, the Qionghua Islet was expanded and the palace of Kublai Khan, no longer standing, was made the center of the city.

Also on the islet, the 35.9 meter-high, bell-shaped **White Dagoba** was first constructed in 1271. The current stupa was built in 1731. Noteworthy is Kublai Khan's 3000-liter jade liquor container (1265) and the Jade Buddha in Chengguang Hall in the Round City on the mainland, by the White Dagoba causeway.

The **Nine Dragon Screen** on the north side of the lake is of glazed brick and is five by 27 by 1.2 meters. Successive dynasties added buildings to Beihai, but this park was also looted by the foreign powers in 1900.

Zhongnanhai, south of Beihai, has not been generally open to the public because it contains the residences and offices of China's leaders. Very special tour groups have successfully requested a visit. The Qing Guangxu (Kuang Hsu) emperor, who attempted to make modern reforms, much to the displeasure of the Empress Dowager Cixi, was imprisoned here during the winters when he was not at the Summer Palace. The historically important Pavilion of Purple Light, and Fairy Tower were recently repaired. The South Gate, brilliant red and fancy, is on Chang'an Avenue west of the Tiananmen, too prominent to miss.

DAY THREE

The Summer Palace, Temple of the Azure Clouds, Temple of the Sleeping Buddha, and Fragrant Hill are all within 10 km of each other, 20-30 km northwest of Tiananmen. Because of traffic jams, avoid this area on week-ends.

The **Summer Palace** or **Yiheyuan** (Garden of Cultivating Peace) is about 15 km from downtown and was opened to the public in 1925, Tel. 62881144. It can be reached on public buses 808 from the northwest side of the Beijing Railway Station. A visit to this 717-acre garden usually takes a couple of hours. It is three-quarters water. Originally built in the 12th century, it was expanded in 1750 for the 60th birthday of Emperor Qianlong's mother and burned in 1860 by the British-French army. It was rebuilt by the Empress Dowager Cixi (Tzu Hsi) on the occasion of her 60th birthday (1895) and financed with funds meant for the Chinese navy. It was badly damaged by the foreign powers in 1900; the existing buildings were restored in 1903.

The imperial court lived here every year, when possible, from April 15 to October 15, receiving diplomats and conducting business in the **Renshoudian** (**Hall of Longevity and Benevolence**). Empress Dowager Cixi, who was the power behind the throne from 1861 to 1908, lived in this hall near the Deheyuan (Grand Stage) where she could indulge in her passion for theatri-cals. The stage floor is hollow so that ghosts could emerge from it. The **Grand Stage** is now a separate museum requiring an additional fee. It contains Cixi's jewelry and dinnerware, and wax figures of Cixi and imperial concubines. Attendants are in Qing palace costumes. In the exhibition hall behind the stage is the 1898 automobile given to the emperor by General Yuan Shikai.

Twenty-eight ladies in waiting, twenty eunuchs, and eight female officials waited on the Empress Dowager. For lunch, she was offered at least 128 courses daily.

In the **Hall of Jade Ripples**, to the south of the main entrance, she kept the Guangxu (Kuang Hsu) emperor imprisoned every summer from 1898 to 1908 after he tried unsuccessfully to institute reforms to modernize China and to take his rightful power back. Note the walls around the compound. The rooms here and elsewhere are furnished as they were then.

The **Long Corridor** extends 728 meters along the lake to the famous **Qingyan (Marble) Boat** whose second floor is actually wood. There are 1,400 paintings here; some guides say 10,000, a spectacular display. To the north up the hill are the Hall of Dispelling Clouds, the Tower of Buddhist Incense, and the Temple of the Sea of Wisdom where the empress used to hold her birthday celebrations and religious services. The **Xiequyuan (Garden of Harmonious Interests)** was designed like the Jichangyuan (Garden) in Wuxi. Also on the hill is a Tibetan-style Lama Temple. Across Kunming Lake is a 17-arch bridge and, on an island, the Dragon King Temple.

Visitors usually enter by the east gate and walk to the marble boat and onwards to the west gate. Or you can take a boat back the way you came and end up at the east side again near the 24-arch bridge. The boat trip costs about Y4 per person and gives another view of the palace.

Northwest of the Summer Palace are the **Botanical Garden** and the **Temple of the Sleeping Buddha (Wofusi,** or Temple of Universal Spiritual Awakening). Do not expect to rush through any of these temples as there's a lot of walking. The Sleeping Buddha was first built in the Tang and reconstructed in the Yuan, Ming, and Qing. The lacquered bronze Sakyamuni, which was cast in 1320 (Yuan), is 5.33 meters long and weighs 54 tons. The Buddha here is giving his last words to his disciples before his transition. Because he is barefoot, successions of emperors have presented the statue with 11 pairs of huge hand-made cloth shoes on display in the same room.

The **Biyunsi (Temple of Azure Clouds)** is less than a kilometer from the Fragrant Hill Hotel but it is a kilometer from the parking lot, and open 8am-4:30pm. It is more important than the Sleeping Buddha because of its stunning collection of religious statues and the Diamond Throne Pagoda. The Biyun was first built in the Yuan as a nunnery. During the Ming, it was the burial place for powerful eunuchs. In 1748, Emperor Qianlong ordered built the Hall of Five Hundred Arhats and the Diamond Throne (or Vajra Throne) Pagoda. The 508 gilded, wooden Buddhist saints are life-size and strikingly beautiful, each different, and protected by dirty glass.

In 1925, the body of Dr. Sun Yat-sen lay in state at this temple until the completion of his mausoleum in Nanjing. A tiny museum is at the spot. The unique 34.7-meter Diamond Throne Pagoda consists of five small pagodas in the Indian style and some excellent carvings.

Xiang Shan (Fragrant Hill) Park is open roughly 7:30am-5:00pm, *Tel. 62591155.* It was a 150-hectare (384 acre) hunting ground for many emperors. A 20-minute chairlift to the top of the mountain now gives a spectacular view of the area, especially in autumn, when the air is less dusty and some leaves are red. The highest peak here is 557 meters.

If time permits on the way back to town, glimpse the **Yuanmingyuan ruins,** open 7am-7pm, *Tel. 2551488.* This Garden of Clear Ripples was built in an area full of bubbling springs and was used as an imperial resort from the 11th century. A major palace was built here in 1690 and later rebuilt as the favorite palace garden of Emperor Qianlong, with buildings copied from Suzhou, Hangzhou, and Yangzhou. Sacked by Anglo-French forces in 1860 (after Qing forces tortured their envoys), it was partially repaired only to be destroyed again in 1900. The foreigners wanted to punish the emperor for the siege of the legations.

The few remains of this Garden of Gardens and Palace of Palaces can be glimpsed in 20 minutes if you enter the correct gate. Enough remains of the marble archways of the Evergreen Palace to show the influence of the European missionaries who helped design it. Since the imperial families favored the Yuanmingyuan over the Imperial Palace, they kept their most precious treasures and books here. The 1860 burning took 2 days and is documented in a good Chinese-made movie, *The Burning of the Summer*

Palace. One of the best accounts in English is Garnet J. Wolseley's Narrative of the War with China in 1860. A small exhibition near the entrance tells the story. The maze and some other buildings have been reconstructed.

DAY FOUR

Some people prefer to take their own box lunch to the ***Great Wall** even though restaurants are available. For an excursion to the Great Wall, *Tel. 63011864*, see *The Great Wall* excursion section later in this chapter. Remember, Badaling is not the only place to see this impressive site, nor is it the best. If you are on a prepaid tour, you can still ask your guide a couple of days ahead of time, and you might be able to go instead to Mutianyu. This is much less crowded and less commercial.

The **Ming Tombs (*Shisan Ling)**, are among the most famous sights in China. Open daily, the tombs are usually combined with a trip to the Great Wall at Badaling another 30 km beyond them. The Tombs are about a 60-km, 1-hour drive northwest of Tiananmen and cost about Y40 for Dingling and Y35 for Changling.

These 13 imperial tombs were built from 1409 to 1644 and spread over 40 square kilometers. Each tomb consists of a Soul Tower, a Sacrificial Hall, and an underground palace where the bodies were placed. Approaching from the south, you can see a big, carved white marble archway, erected in 1590, beyond which are the Great Red Gate, ornamental pillars, and the Tablet Pavilion. The **Sacred or Spirit Way** has 24 stone animals (lions, unicorns, camels and elephants), 12 larger-than-life-size humans (military officers and government officials), and a few enterprising hawkers (also an old China tradition) selling furs, porcelain, and carved and gilded wooden pieces. Because of its association with funerals, few Chinese visit this kilometer-long walk. Gardeners here are not allowed to use machines. Noise would disturb the spirits.

Two of the tombs are set up for visitors: **Changling** is the biggest and earliest but you cannot enter it. Its museum there has a gold crown, headdresses, jade belt and other items found in the tombs.

Dingling has been excavated and can be entered. It is the tomb of the 13th Ming Emperor Wanli, who ruled for 48 years, from age 10. The tomb was begun when he was 22 years old. It took six years and cost eight million taels of silver to build. *Tel. 60761196*. This underground palace consists of three halls, the central one with passages to annex chambers, totaling 1195 square meters. Each marble door weighs four tons and was closed from the inside by propping two large stone poles against them. Note the two triangular depressions in the ground inside the door where the poles rested. Note also the blue and white porcelain jars with the dragons, which were half filled with oil when the tomb was opened. The oil was burned to create an oxygen-free vacuum inside. In the central hall are three marble thrones, two for the empresses, one for the emperor, all real. Note the Five Altar Pieces and the porcelain lamp. The rear hall has the three coffins and plaster replicas of 26 chests.

Many tourists have lunch near the Ming Tombs at the 1200-seat **Yulong Friendship Restaurant**, in Deng Zhuang, Changping, *Tel. 6974-5731, 6974-5732*. This is very close to the Badaling Expressway and west of the Changping Ming tomb. It is best to make a reservation and order in advance. I've had deep-fried fish, hot-sour soup, chicken slivers, chicken with peanuts, sweet and sour pork, and spring rolls with barbecue sauce, all good. To get to the restaurant, you have to go through a huge souvenir store which has a demonstration of how cloisonné is made inside the door to the left as you enter. The selection was good but prices were higher than the markets.

You could also take lunch at the nearby and expensive **Beijing International Golf Club**, *Tel. 60762288, 69746388*. Some tour groups go to the not-too-bad **Nine Dragon Palace Restaurant** (note: there's a pay toilet here). The setting on a reservoir is lovely, and the deep-fried tomatoes and fries are good, but otherwise don't expect much. It is two km south of the gate to the Spirit Way.

If you have time, you should also wander around the other tombs, which are not repaired and are usually free of tourists. Enjoy the rural beauty. These others have not been opened because of the high cost of careful archaeological work. Besides, no one knows where the entrances are because their builders were executed and no records have survived. The exterior of the tombs and the Great Wall are best seen at dusk, when one feels the presence of ghosts. Seeing weeds growing on imperial terraces and birds making nests on once glorious beams is a good time to reflect on life and death.

DAY FIVE

Head for the furthest first. The **Arthur M. Sackler Museum of Art and Archaeology** is at Beijing University, *Tel. 62501667, 62751667*. You can go to the west gate and bear left once inside. It's the other side of the pond. Buses 801 and 332 go by. The Sackler contains 14 galleries from Paleolithic to Ming from the university's own collection: 1100 year old silver chopsticks, and an ancient bronze rabbit. It is worth the trip to see these, and this beautiful 100 year old university that was involved in the Tiananmen demonstrations.

Next is the **Da Zhong Si**, the **Temple of the Great Bell** with its 6.75 meter tall bell. The oldest bell here is 2400 years old. The temple is at 31A Beisanhuan Xi Road, Haidian District, *Tel. 62550843* and it should be open 8:30am-4:30pm. Of this temple's 40 different ancient bells, the most spectacular was cast during the reign of Emperor Yongle (1403-1425 A.D.) in a clay mold and weighs 46.5 tons. How did they bring it here without a crane and truck? In 1733, the Chinese slid it on ice in winter or on wheat shells in summer and put it on a mound. After attaching the bell onto beams, they dug out the mound and built the hall around it. The 220,000 handsome Chinese characters on it are Buddhist scriptures and prayers.

Other bells were used for religious ceremonies to drive away worldly worries and attract the attention of the gods. Some bells here announced the time of day and the closing of the city gates. Some were used in music rituals. (See also Wuhan.) Look for the exhibit on how the bells were made.

Do visit the **Beijing Art Museum** in the exotic 16th century Wanshou temple complex across the road from the Shangri-La Hotel. It has 18 larger-than-life arhats or saints, Tibetan statues, and multi-colored shoushan stone carvings. It has imperial seals and robes, paintings, pottery, jades, and Buddhas–a small but beautiful collection worth making a trip out here to see. It is closed on Mondays, has titles in English, and costs about Y10. *Tel. 68413382, 68413379.*

The **Beijing Zoo** is across the main street from the Xiyuan Hotel, *Tel. 68314411*, and should be open 7:30am-5pm or 8am-6pm daily. The pandas are near the main entrance to the left. The zoo also has a huge aquarium with 800 species of saltwater fish, 500 species of fresh water fish and sea mammals. It should have 50,000 specimens. Also near the Xiyuan Hotel are the **Planetarium**, 138 Xizhimenwai Avenue, *Tel. 68352453*, and the **Dinosaur Museum**.

The **Blue Zoo ocean aquarium** is at Worker's Stadium (South Gate), *Tel. 65913397, 65913398 ext, 1178, Fax 65935262, E-mail: market@public.bta.net.cn.* It has been open 9am to 8pm. This is a New Zealand joint venture. A 120-meter clear, acrylic tunnel allows 6000 sharks, rays, sturgeons, and other creatures to swim over and beside you as you pass by on a moving sidewalk. The sharks are fed by a human in scuba gear twice a day and also on request. Staff give lectures for no extra charge (English on request). Adults pay about Y75, children under 18 years Y50, family of three Y150, and kids under one meter are free.

DAY SIX

The ***Yonghegong (Lama Temple)** is spectacular. It is open roughly 8:30am-4pm, and may be closed Mondays, *Tel. 64074951, 64041408*. The entrance fee is Y20, plus Acoustiguide in English. Count on spending at least 40 minutes here. First built in 1694, this Mongolian-Tibetan temple is at the Yonghegong subway exit. Beautifully renovated, it reveals pavilion after pavilion of increasingly impressive figures, the largest in the back hall 18 meters high. This last Buddha was carved from one piece of sandalwood from Tibet and the temple was built around it.

The steles are incised with Han, Manchurian, Mongolian, and Tibetan script. The statues in the main halls resemble those in most Buddhist temples, but some statues wear the pointed Himalayan caps and white Tibetan scarves, a gift of respect. The buildings on either side have the more typical Tibetan demons, human skulls, and tankas. You pay extra to enter two exhibition halls inside. One is on revolutionary history. The other shows the treasures given as tribute to Qing Emperor Qianlong and should not be missed. No one may burn incense inside this temple, a good precaution against fires.

The Yonghegong was built in 1694 as an imperial residence for Emperor Yongzheng, then still a prince. It was transformed into a temple in 1744 during Emperor Qianlong's reign, part of his attempt to unite the Han, Manchu, Mongol, and Tibetan peoples into one country. He also took a Uygur princess into his court, one of his favorite empresses. For more on Tibetan Buddhism, see also Lhasa and Chengde. Prayer wheels are on sale.

The **Shudian (Capital Museum)**, in the old Yuan dynasty Confucius Temple, is almost across Yonghegong Avenue from the Lama Temple. It is at 3-13 Guozijian Street, Dongcheng District, *Tel. 64012118*, and is open daily 9am-4pm, except perhaps on Mondays. It is the second largest Confucian temple in China. The exhibits on Beijing history, Qing armor, and the stone drums are worth seeing. Look for maps and relics of the old Yuan city too.

The **Sports Museum** is hard to find and it's a long way from downtown. It is in the huge National Olympic Sports Centre (O-lim-pi-ke ti-yi-zhong-xin) in the north part of most maps. No signs in English have been outside. Sports fan should persist. The museum is on the west side of Andingmen Road (which might be Anil Road there), and is across from the KMK Hotel. The building has a peak like a mountain and can be seen from the east gate, only about 100 meters away. *Tel. 64912233 X 479 or 13641364699, Fax is 64912167*. It is open 8:30am-4:30pm daily and costs Y5. (Ask for Mr. Chen Jing).

The museum is small, but it has a gallery with ancient sports pictures on porcelain bowls, or as scroll paintings or engravings. A Tang dynasty polo game shows players on those fat horses. Male athletes in gowns play a Song dynasty football game. Ceramic acrobats do their stuff, and an enlargement of the famous Song dynasty painting of Kaifeng shows people wrestling and swinging. Athletes raced dragon boats during the Spring and Autumn Period – before dragon boats honored Qu Yuan. (See Zigui.) Look for the 5000-year-old ceramic balls. In a second gallery are recent sports trophies, historical photos, and gold medals. About one-third of the exhibits had titles in English.

If you have more time and interest, Beijing has over one hundred museums with more being opened every day. Listed here are only the most prominent.

WALKS

You might begin with the area north of the Xinqiao Hotel and south of the Beijing Hotel for the old European architecture. This foreign legation area was under siege during the Boxer uprising from June 13, 1900. On June 20, most foreign diplomats and missionaries and 2,000 Chinese Christian refugees took shelter in the British Legation until the International Relief Force arrived on August 13. That British Legation building has been torn down to make way for a housing project. But many of the old buildings are still there, some now used by the Beijing Municipality and the Communist Party.

Walk around the Forbidden City and in the two parks in front of it. This area is full of old houses with antique doors, carvings, grinding stones used as steps, and fancy, carved stone door hinges. These crowded courtyards are fascinating. The names of the alleys evoke another age: Nai Zi Hutong (Wet Nurse Lane) was where the new mothers who nursed the imperial babies lived. Flower Lane was for those who hand made all the silk flowers for the imperial ladies. There were also Goldsmith Lane, Laundry Lane, and Bowstrings Lane.

Nightlife & Entertainment

There's a lot of good stuff here: opera, ballet, symphony orchestras, movies, art exhibitions, martial arts and bars. Beijing's large expatriate community is a market for many activities and have themselves introduced many sports and clubs. Consult your consulate, tourist handouts or the Xianzai Beijing e-mail newsletter below for events and times. The web sites under Practical Information can also give you the latest information on exhibitions, concerts, ballet, jazz, and acrobatic shows, and ice hockey matches.

Many hotels have a box of cards with maps and addresses in Chinese for some of the following. In some cases, the card merits discounts.

For traditional Chinese arts, a good introduction to Beijing Opera is the pleasant **Li Yuan Theater** in the Qianmen Hotel, 175 Yongan Road, just south of Liulichang antique street, *Tel. 63016688 X 8860*. Performances are held every evening at 7:30, usually with English titles to help you understand the plot. Real opera is longer and can be boring. This is a short introduction with just excerpts. Prices are Y30, Y90, Y120 and Y150. You don't have to take a tour. You can do it by yourself. The ticket office at the hotel is open 9am-8pm.

For a traditional Chinese variety show, there's the delightful **Lao She Tea House (Lao She chaguan)** in the Da Wan Cha Building, third floor, 3 Qianmen Xi Avenue, 50 meters west of Kentucky Fried Chicken at the south end of Tiananmen Square, *Tel. 63036830*. No credit cards. At about 7:40pm, it offers 100 minutes of Beijing's top talent, including opera singers, magicians, cross-talk, and comedy acts that require no language to enjoy. Go at 5pm for dinner if you want. About Y40-Y120 includes snacks, and Y60-Y200 includes dinner. Reserve two days in advance.

Every second Friday at 7:30pm, **Cherry Lane** shows good Chinese movies with English subtitles at the Sino-Japanese Youth Exchange Centre, 40 Liangmaqiao Road, *Tel. 65004466 X 103*. The film maker is frequently present to answer questions. This costs about Y50 per person. For information, *Tel. 65224046, 64615318/9, Fax 65224047. Website: www.cherrylanemovies.com.cn.*

The 95-minute show put on by China's **National Acrobatic Troupe** is as good as Shanghai's, with more artistry, creative lighting, good costumes, and less muscle. It's not the same old stuff; it's developed the art of plate spinning to new heights, and barrel spinning is now child spinning. Book through your hotel or at the Tiandi Theatre in the Poly Plaza (near the Hong Kong and Macau Centre), *Tel. 65023984*. The box office is open 9am-6pm. This nightly show begins about 7:30pm. The cheaper seats get only bottled water and peanuts. This troupe toured the US twice in 1997. Performances might not be daily so ask.

Some hotels like the **Swissôtel** and **China World** have concerts in their lobbies on Sunday afternoons, not the quietest places to listen. For complete relaxation, there are massages. A famous massage chain is the Tian He Lian Ge. Most hotels can provide massages even in your room. You can also watch the fish swimming at the Blue Zoo. The larger hotels have cocktail lounges with live music.

Beijing's Jazz & Classical Hot Spot

If you're tired of things Chinese, Beijing also has other fare. The second floor of the **Sanwei Book Store** has live, smoke-free jazz, the same good group every Friday evening at about 8:30pm. It has live classical music on Saturday evenings. The admission is about Y30. This tiny book store is on a side street across the street south from the Cultural Palace of the Nationalities on Fuxingmennei Avenue, *Tel. 66013204*.

In the Jianguomenwai area

One of the more popular hotel bars among foreigners is **Charlie's Bar** at the Jianguo Hotel. **Salsa Cabana** in the Kempinski Hotel has Latin music. You can shoot baskets at the **Sports Bar** at the Gloria Hotel. Many pleasant, small, privately-run Chinese bars have also opened, but have also been periodically closed for prostitution or drugs.

Watering Holes Frequented By Foreigners

MEXICAN WAVE RESTAURANT, *Guang Hua Xi Road, Dongdaqiao Xie Street, Tel. 65063961*.

This is one block behind the Gui You Department Store, open 11am-2am and is usually packed after 11pm because it has a good bar. It has moderate prices but it's not famous for its food. This is where the Hash House Harriers hang out on Sundays at 4pm. It takes credit cards.

THE JOHN BULL PUB, *44 Guang Hua Road, next to the Brazilian and British Embassies and behind the International Post Office, Tel. 65325905, is open daily 10:30am-1am, weekends to 1:30am. Major credit cards are accepted. E-mail: jb@unet.net.cn.*

Fish and chips, and steak and kidney pie are Y90 each. It has Guinness, Kilkenny and Tetley beers, Yorkshire pudding, and bangers and mash. You'll find it difficult to believe you're in China.

Sanlitun Area

There are three groups of restaurants and bars here. Embassies have been warning about pickpockets and prostitutes especially on the two Sanlitun bar streets.

THE DEN, *4A Gongti East Road, Tel. 65926290. E-mail DEN@263.net. Website: www.den.com.cn*

This is a good restaurant as well as lively nighttime bar. You'll find people in their twenties and thirties, guest DJs from abroad, and singalongs, liveliest around midnight. This is in the same block as the City Hotel. Salads range from Y22-Y35, hot dishes Y35-60, pasta Y28, and pizza Y40-Y60. It has patio tables and the food is especially good.

FRANK'S PLACE, *East Sports Stadium Road, Tel. 65072617, 65891985, is near the City Hotel and is American-owned.*

Hamburgers are Y40 and considered by some the best in town. Pizza is Y40-Y55. Hotdogs Y30-Y50. A club sandwich is Y45. A good bake shop, Bella's, is next door.

South of Gongrentiyuchang Bei Avenue, and a couple of blocks behind Frank's Place and the City Hotel on Dongdaqao Xie Street, are several other restaurants and bars, a favorite area for foreigners and Chinese alike.

MINDER'S CAFE, *near the above corner, No. 1 Houpingfang, Xinyi Building, Nan Sanlitun, Tel. 65006066, E-mail: shaiming@public.east.cn.net.*

This has a casual pub atmosphere, and good steaks, sandwiches, burgers, and spaghetti. It has a band every evening and serious darts on Thursday evenings. Open 11am to whenever, its happy hour is 2pm-8pm and it has a disco on weekends after midnight. Filet mignon is Y98, osso bocco Y72, and chili con carne Y35.

DURTY NELLIES IRISH PUB,*on the same lane as Minder's Cafe, at 12 Nan Sanlitun, Tel. 65022808. It is open 12 noon-1:30am on weekdays and 2:30am on weekends and accepts credit cards.*

It has Guinness and Kilkenny, as well as Chinese beers for Y25. It has stews, steak and roasts on Sunday, a Belgian chef, and at least one Irish person on hand at all times. There's Irish music, darts, and paintings of Michael Collins and Oscar Wilde on the walls. A live band plays on weekends.

NASHVILLE, *14 East Building, Dongdaqiao Xie Street, Tel. 65024201. Same alley as Durty Nellies. It accepts Visa and American Express cards.*

Come here for country music, blues, and rock and roll. The house band plays nightly from 9:30pm with no cover charge. The food is Western, barbecues, kebobs and sausages.

HIDDEN TREE, *also on the same alley as Durty Nellies, and a little further south. Tel. 65093642.*

It serves Belgian beer. Monkey Business Infocenter which books the trans-Siberian train has an office upstairs.

LOFT, *4 Worker's's Stadium North Road, Tel. 65017501.*
This former warehouse houses the biggest bar in town. It has funky lighting, dark colors, and lots of live trees indoors. It's a good place to hang-out but the music, food and service are uninspiring.
Then on Sanlitun North, there's another group of bars favored by local imbibers.

In the Kempinski-Great Wall Sheraton Area
HARD ROCK CAFE, *in the Landmark Arcade next to the Great Wall Sheraton Hotel, 8 Dongsanhuan Bei Road, Tel.65906688 X 2571. E-mail: andrewho64@hotmail.com. It accepts credit cards.*
The Hard Rock has great fries and hot fudge brownies (Y38) but the rest is not exciting for the price. (Hainan chicken rice is Y70, cheeseburgers Y73, and rib eye steak Y170.) It is open Sunday through Thursday 11:30am-2am; Friday and Saturday 11:30am-3am. Last dinner served at 10:30pm. No happy hour. This is one of the best discos, very noisy after 10:30pm and expensive.
PAULANER BRAUHAUS, *in the Kempinski Hotel, Lufthansa Centre, 50 Liangmaqiao Road, Tel. 64653388 X 5731, open 11am-1am. It accepts credit cards. See Where to Eat section above.*
This is a boutique brewery with huge shining beer vats, long tables, and benches. It has good food, too, like half-grilled pork knuckles with sauerkraut and roast potatoes, and Nuernberger sausage with sauerkraut and mashed potatoes.

Other Locations
Out towards the Xiyuan Hotels are two more bars for locals:
SEA SAIL BAR, *141 Xiwai St., close to Carrefour, is between the Capital Gymnasium and Beijing Exhibition Centre, Tel. 68316187.*
It charges Y20 for soft drinks, Y30 for Heineken and a local band plays. It takes no credit cards, and attracts the 20 to 30 year old crowd with a mix of Chinese and Western popular music.
JIN WAN BA DIAN BAR, *54 Zhong Guan Cun South Avenue, Tel. 88361531.*
Not far from the Sea Sail Bar, this place seems to be open 24 hours with a live band at 9:40pm and is said to be noisier and livelier. Beer costs Y30 and sodas Y20.

Sports & Recreation
The weekly cyber-newsletter *Xianzai Beijing* is mainly for foreigners living in Beijing but it should be helpful to the sports-minded visitor. A recent edition calls for ice hockey players, and offers contact addresses for paragliding and bungee jumping, rock climbing and horse racing. For a free subscription see Practical Information below. And look at tourist handouts.

The **Hash House Harriers** are not really sports people. They are "a drinking club with a running problem." Running with this group of friendly fun lovers is a good way to meet Beijing residents. They have their own website: *www.beijinghhh.com*. Contact Alastair Ferguson, *Tel. 138-0104-8963; 6505-3355 ext. 2955, or Rick Rhead 138-0111-1104; 6437-6763*. Once a week Hashers in Beijing meet to have a run, some beers, and an "after the run" meal. The run can be as serious as you want and lasts about five miles, or about one hour. Meals are at the Mexican Wave Restaurant, beside Guanghua Road Primary School, *Tel. 6506-3961*. See above.

The **Beijing International Golf Club** is at Shisanling, Changping County, *Tel. 60762288, 69746388, Fax 60761111*. It's the best for golf and has a remarkable setting near the Ming Tombs. It also has squash courts, pool, a huge fitness center and aerobics room. For the **Hua Tang Golf Club**, *Tel. 61593932*. For the **Shun Yi Country Club**, *Tel. 69401111*. Major hotels can arrange.

Many hotels have bowling. **Gongti 100** at 6 Gongti Xi Road near Workers' Stadium has 100 lanes and is open 24-hours, *Tel. 65522688*. Outdoor ice skating at the Summer Palace or Beihai Park is an old tradition and the China World has a rink. The Australian, British and Indian embassies should know about cricket. The Gloria Hotel has a huge **Sports City Cafe** with batting cage, basketball hoop, and darts.

Festivals

The **Beijing Marathon** is open to everyone. It is held annually in mid-October and travel agents can make arrangements. The week before and after the lunar new year, a **temple fair** takes place at the Temple of the Earth, the Ditan. The **Golden Autumn Festival** is at the Yuanmingyuan. Look for **dragon boat races** in June and kite-flying contests in the spring.

Shopping

Beijing is a great place to shop because its large international community demands high-quality goods at competitive prices. Locally-made are cloisonné, silk, dough figurines, lacquerware, chops, jade carvings, pearls, filigree jewelry, and carpets. The factories are essentially tourist traps because prices are higher than in the stores — even if you haggle. You should first go to the Friendship Store and make notes of what things cost and then aim for less.

The most popular with tourists for incredible bargains, is the crowded **Xiushui Free Market/Silk Alley** (open 9am-6:30pm daily) between the Jianguo Hotel and Friendship Store on Jianguomenwai. This is the best such market in China. Here are mainly clothes, ties, scarves, cashmere sweaters, linens, name-brand Gore-Tex jackets, and also crafts from all over the country. These are fashionable export-quality overruns and seconds, Calvin Klein's and North Face, so look goods over carefully. There are also 100% polyester ties labeled "100% silk," to be avoided. A name brand Gore-Tex jacket with fleece lining shouldn't cost more than Y160.

Also for Gore-Tex, sports shoes and boots, souvenirs, bed spreads, table cloths, and casual clothes – try the market across the street from the main entrance to the Holiday Inn Lido. A few stalls are between the Palace Hotel and Wangfujing Avenue. There's the **Yabao Lu Market** in the Russian section at 16 Chaoyangmenwai Street. It's huge and mainly wholesale with signs in Russian. *Tel. 6599-3516*. Open 9:30am-6pm.

For one-stop souvenir shopping at the cheapest prices, go to the **Hongqiao Market (a.k.a. Pearl Market)** in the building with the traditional Chinese roof across the street and east of the Temple of Heaven on Tiantan Dong Road. The third floor has tiny antique stores, reasonably priced fresh-water pearls, cloisonné, and crafts wholesale, and you should check qualities carefully and haggle. There are also antique and curio stalls here. It is open 8:30am-7pm, *Tel. 67117429 or 67117499*. Some merchants have credit card service, and other merchants can use these for a Y10 fee.

For silk, a reliable, well organized, but expensive place with good variety is the four-story **Yuan Long Silk Store** just north of the Temple of Heaven at 55 Tiantan Road, *Tel. 67022288, Fax 67012854*. There, a man's short robe costs Y199, a rich looking man's brocade smoking jacket costs Y600, a pair of men's pajamas cost Y495, and long john's Y145. Plain heavy silk textiles 110 cm-wide were marked at Y180 a meter, 90 cm-wide Shantung costs Y72, and 75 cm-wide brocade costs Y88 a meter. A coffee shop is on the fourth floor for tired companions.

There's also **Zhang's Textiles** for embroidery at NB140B1 floor, in the China World Shopping Mall, China World Trade Center, *Tel. 65056201*. *Website: www.zhangstextiles.com*. Also in the CWTC at B1EN102 is Shang Hai Xu with gorgeous silk dresses and a tailor, but no one seems to speak English there.

Of the department stores, good is the **Lufthansa Friendship Shopping City (Youyi Yensha Shang Cheng)** at 52 Liang Ma Qiao Road, *Tel. 64651188*. It is beside the Kempinski Hotel and north of the Great Wall Sheraton. The Jianguomenwai area has the *Gui You Department Store (Gui You Dasha), Tel, 85629105*. It is open 9:30am to 9:30pm.

The **Friendship Store** on Jianguomenwai Avenue between the International Club and Jianguo Hotel, shouldn't be avoided entirely. You can find things there you can't elsewhere and without the crowds. There are furs, down coats, cashmere sweaters, silk underwear and textiles, groceries, books in English, cloisonne, stone carvings, wines, carpets, antiques, and even fresh flowers. The Friendship Store can reset jewelry and develop photos, and a tailor here does a reasonable job in three weeks. A directory in English is on the ground floor. Like most other department stores, this one takes credit cards.

Wangfujing Avenue, Beijing's main traditional shopping street on the east side of the Beijing Hotel, is very crowded. This area is in the process of being transformed from an area of interesting little shops with latticed wooden store fronts, to an expensive, modern shopping area with giant malls and goods like anywhere else in the world. The **Sun Dong An Centre** sells the likes of Montagut Paris, Burberry's, Ports International and Esprit. The Foreign Languages Book Store is at 235. There's also the **Beijing Department Store** (on the west side, *Tel. 65126677*).

Visit factories only to see how things are made and to study quality. Some tours on the way to the Great Wall stop at the cloisonné factory, the **China Beijing North Suburbs Industrial Art Factory**, Ding Fu Huang Zhuang, Shahe, *Tel. 69732942, 69737417*. It is 20 minutes south of the Ming Tombs, open 8am-6pm, and takes major credit cards. Do get a look at the manufacturing process. It's interesting.

A pearl factory is also on the way to the Great Wall, its wares cultured in the Miyun Reservoir. You get only the opening of one mussel, a come-on for this over-priced store.

The telephone number of the **Jade Carving factory** is *67128899*, and the **Beijing Arts and Crafts Wood Carving Factory** is *67110006*.

For antiques, the best bargains are at the weekend **Ghost/Dirt Market** on Panjiayuan Road, two blocks west of Second Ring Road, behind the Le You Hotel, west and north of the imposing Henan Building. Private dealers lay goods out on tables under a huge roof. Go early (about 5:30am on a weekend) for the best selection and smaller crowds. The place is jammed at 10am and dealers start to pack up about 3pm. This street market is full of reproductions and fakes, ethnic textiles, stone carvings, wood carvings, porcelains, etc. but people with a good eye can find real treasures especially if they haggle well and don't mind being hassled and pushed and subjected to cigarette smoke. No credit cards nor receipts available. Permanent stalls are here too and open daily 9am-6pm.

Collections of other small private dealers are at the **Beijing Curio City (Guwanchung)**, behind the Duty-Free Store, the west side of Hua Wei Qiao Bridge, Dongsanhuan, open 9:30am-6:30pm. It has escalators and three stories of shops: curios, pearls, furniture, jewelry, silver, paintings, and embroideries. *Tel. 67747711*.

For upmarket antiques, the **Shangri-La** and **Grand Hotels**, **Summer Palace** and **Forbidden City** have good stores. The Friendship Store also has some good pieces. For large Buddhas, look in the shop at the back of the Ghost Market. Owners of stalls everywhere will sometimes close their doors and produce some illegal Tang or Song dynasty pieces. The **Huaxia Antique Store** is at 293 Wangfujing Avenue, and open 9am-7pm. This government store has lots of porcelains, carvings, rugs, etc. and you can get an official red wax seal and receipt for purchases. It is more reliable than the markets.

The largest collection of stores selling real antiques, reproductions and fakes, and arts and crafts, is **Liulichang** (on both sides of Xuanwumen Wai Avenue), the main street where the buses stop. It is open roughly 10am-5:30 or 6pm, later in summer. This is more expensive and has better goods generally than the markets and stalls and is less crowded. It also has art books (mainly in Chinese). You could spend hours poking around.

In 1277, artisans made glazed tiles here. In the Qing, it was a market with 140 shops selling the same sort of arts it does today, including reproductions of paintings, the Dunhuang murals, bronzes, and porcelains. In the old days, some of the merchandise was stolen from the Forbidden City and other wealthy homes. Small shops are also next to, and behind, the Rong Bao Zhai art store on the west side at No.64. Try **Xie Yan Fang** at No.3 with great embroideries and old books at reasonable prices. *Tel. 63017979*, and **Kui Jin Ge** at No. 115 for porcelain, wood toggles, and gold jewelry, *Tel. 63017979*. Prices here could be better than the Friendship Store if you haggle. The **Beijing Cultural Relics Store** at 64 Liulichang Dong Street, *Tel. 63033848*, is allowed to sell pre-Qing relics.

Get the Red Wax Seal of Approval!

If your antiques are expensive, they need a **red wax seal for export**. Ask your store to get one before you buy.

Copies of traditional Chinese painting abound in every tourist spot by the ton. Famous local contemporary art is now worth collecting as many Chinese artists are commanding six-figure-prices for their works. You might want to start collecting lesser known artists now and hope they will become famous. Already well known internationally are Fang Lijin and Cai Guoqing. Important are Qi Zhilong, Su Xinping, Wang Yuping, Sui Jianguo, Lu Ping, Zhang Hongbo, Wan Huangxiang, and Qi Zhilong. Consider local Beijing artists Sun Gang Hua, Huang Gang, and Zeng Fan Zhi.

The **Red Gate Gallery**, Watchtower, Dongbianmen, Chongwenmen is a serious artist enclave. It is privately run by Brian Wallace with a stable of 22 artists. The postal address is *Beijing International Post Office, Box No. 9039, Beijing, 100600. Tel. 65251005 or 65275080, Fax 65824236, E-mail: redgate@eastnet.com.cn, Website: www.redgategallery.com.*

For a look at what today's artists are doing, visit *www.Chinese-art.com.*

Excursions & Day Trips

See separate entries in this guide for Beidaihe, Chengde, Datong, Qinhuangdao, Shanhaiguan, and Shijiazhuang for overnight trips nearby. Zunhua with its Qing imperial tombs and Tianjin can be day trips.

THE GREAT WALL
(Wanlichangcheng; 10,000 li-long wall)

The length of ***The Great Wall** has been officially given as 12,700 Chinese li, or 6,350 km (3,946.55 miles) long from Jiayuguan to Shanhaiguan. Some scholars, however, add another 1,040 km all the way to the Yalu River on the Korean border. The length depends on what you measure, as there are many offshoots and parallel walls. The Wall is in various states of repair.

The best time to see the wall is in the afternoon after most of the tourists have left. Stay to see the sunset if you can. The autumn is especially good when the air is clearer and red leaves add interest to photos.

Orientation

The Great Wall was first built in shorter pieces in the fifth century B.C., as a defensive and boundary wall around the smaller states of Yen, Chao, and Wei. The first Qin emperor (221-206 B.C.), who unified China for the first time, linked up and extended the walls from Liaoning in the east to Gansu in the northwest as protection from other nomadic tribes. The wall was subsequently repaired and extended by succeeding dynasties, especially the Ming.

Originally built by slave labor, it has been called the world's longest graveyard because many of its builders were buried where they fell. It was designed in places to allow five horsemen or ten soldiers to march abreast in some places along the top. It was almost a superhighway, considering the rough mountain terrain. A system of bonfires communicated military information to the emperor at a speed considered rapid for that period.

Visiting the Wall

The Great Wall is most frequently visited at ***Badaling** but tours now go to other places as well. (See *Practical Information*.) Badaling is about 75 km (one hour) by expressway northwest of Beijing. It and the two Ming Tombs are open about 8am-4:30pm, *Tel. 69121383*. It is extremely crowded. Avoid weekends and early mornings. Most tourists leave Beijing by tourist buses between 8am-9am. To avoid crowds, arrive later or go elsewhere.

Tours range in price and a taxi could be cheaper for four friends. See *Getting Around Town* above.

Badaling is about 1000 meters above sea level. Here the wall averages 7.8 meters in height, is 6.5 meters wide at the base, and 5.8 meters wide at the top. Watchtowers are located every few hundred meters. Note the giant rocks and bricks of uniform size, the gutters, and the waterspouts. You can walk, and in some places climb, for several hundred meters in either direction or you can take a cable car which is a long way from the main entrance, back by the bus parking lot. Skateboarding on the wall has been allowed, but is not recommended when it is thick with people, which is most of the time.

A shaggy Bactrian camel and pony for photographing are available. Taking a box lunch is recommended, especially in pleasant weather, so you can spend more time at the Wall.

Also of note is the gate in the center of **Juyongguan (Chuyungkuan Pass)**, about 10 km south of Badaling which you pass on the way. It is built of finely-carved marble and called ***Guofie (Cloud Terrace)**. Originally the base of a tower built in 1345 (Yuan), the walls have carved Buddhas, celestial guardians, and the text of a Buddhist sutra in Sanskrit, Tibetan, and four other languages. Tours do not usually stop here except by request and it is considerably steeper than Badaling.

A 3-km-long section of the Great Wall is at **Mutianyu**, 70 km northeast of Beijing in Miyun County, *Tel. 69626505*. It is beautiful with more rugged hills than Badaling. A 720-meter-long Swiss-built cable car can take you from the parking lot uphill to the base of the Wall. Another cable car can take you back. Each costs about Y35 one way. This is in addition to the entry fee of Y50.

You'll find a very steep section about 90 km from Beijing at **Huang Ya Pass**. You can go by road from Beijing to Chengde following the Wall with stops at Simatai and Jinshan Ling.

Simatai, 140 km from Beijing is spectacular. At Jinshan Ling (150 km from Beijing and 110 km from Chengde), there is camping but bring your own tent. Officials here say you can see the lights of Beijing from the top but it's not an easy climb.

An 850-meter section is open in **Jixian County**, 60 km northeast of Tianjin but closer to Beijing, and two sections are available near **Datong**. The Great Wall has also been restored and opened to visitors at 3,000-year-old **Shanhaiguan** (with cable car), over 40 km north from Beidaihe, and about 30 km from Qinhuangdao in the east. The tower was built in 1381. Nearby, at Old Dragon Head, the Great Wall meets the sea and there's a Gloria Hotel within a kilometer of it.

In west China, you can see the Wall in Ningxia close to **Yinchuan**, and in Gansu at ***Jiayuguan**, its western terminus where it is much narrower but still fascinating.

People interested in hiking the whole length of the Great Wall should visit: *www.wildwall.com/*. Briton William Lindesay was the first known foreigner to walk its entire length alone. You can e-mail him at *wildwall@public.netchina.com.cn*. CITS in Qinhuangdao helped to organize a Japanese group who also walked the whole length.

See separate listings under Qinhuangdao, Jiayuguan, Yinchuan, Dunhuang, and Tianjin, for more details.

Practical Information
Beijing Marathon. October. *Website: www.cits.net/cits30.htm (English)* or *Tel. CITS at 66011122 ext. 6156.*

Beijing Tourism Administration, *Beijing Tourism Tower, 28 Jianguomenwai Avenue, 100022, Tel. 65158844 X 3313, Fax 65158223. E-mail: lhx1618@sina.com. Website: www.bjta.gov.cn (Chinese). For information, maps, and brochures.*
Business Hours: for offices 8:30am to 4:30pm or 5:30pm with lunch 12 to 1:30pm or 2pm. Store hours on Wangfujing about 9am-8:30pm or 9pm. China Post, Holiday Inn Lido 8:30am-5:30pm Monday-Friday. 8:30-12pm on Saturday. Bank of China at Holiday Inn Lido. Monday-Friday, 9am-4:30pm. Saturday-Sunday closed. Bank of China at Beijing's Capital Airport. 9am-4:30pm weekdays, and 9am-6pm on Saturdays and Sundays.

China National Tourism Administration, *Division of Europe & Americas, Dept. of Marketing & Promotion, 9A Jianguomennei Avenue, 100740, Tel. 65201430, Fax 65122851.* For brochures. It is best to go to China Tourist Offices abroad. See Chapter 6.

Cellular Phone Rentals: PhoneRent (Yi Guang S&T Ltd), *4/F Golden Bridge Building, A1 Jianguomenwai Avenue, Tel. 65866665, Fax 65060820.* Ask for Bruce Zhao or Even Li.

Embassies (Da She Guan): It is very difficult to impossible to get **visas** elsewhere in China to go to neighboring countries. You should get these visas before you arrive at their land borders. Best get them before you leave home. It takes a lot of time here. Always take your passport when you go to any embassy. Below are addresses and contact information for major embassies:
• **Australia**, *21 Dongzhimenwai Street, Sanlitun, 100600, Tel. 65322331, Fax 65323101*
• **Canada**, *19 Dongzhimenwai Avenue, Chao Yang District, 100600, Tel. 65323536, Fax 6532-5544. E-mail: bejing-cs@dfait-maeci.gc.ca/. Monday-Friday, 8am-5pm. Websites: www.canada.org.cn, http://www.voyage.gc.ca or http://voyage.dfait-maeci.gc.ca/destinations/menu_e.htm.* For emergency assistance after hours, call also Department of External Affairs and International Trade in Ottawa toll-free at *10800-1400125* or use the services offered by Canada Direct.
• **Denmark**, *San Li Tun, Dong Wu Jie 1. Tel. 6532 2431/32, Fax 6532 2439. E-mail: bjsamb@bjsamb.um.dk. Office hours: 9am-5pm*
• **France**, *3 Sanlitun Dong Road, Chao Yang District, Tel. 65321331, 65324841*
• **Germany**, *17 Dongzhimenwai Avenue, Chaoyang District, Tel. 65322161. Website: www.deguangzhou.org/*
• **Israel**, *China World Trade Center, Tel. 65052970, 65050328*
• **Japan**, *7 Ritan Road, Jianguomenwai, Tel. 65322361*
• **Kazakhstan**, *9, Dong 6 Road, Sanlitun, Tel. 65326182*
• **Mongolia**, *2 Xiushui Bei Jie, Tel. 65321203, Fax 5325045.* Not open daily. Phone for hours. Accepts only US$ for visas.
• **Myanmar** (Burma), *6 Dongzhimenwai Avenue, Tel. 65321425, Fax 65321344*
• **Nepal**, *1, Xiliujie, Tel. 65321795, Fax 65323251*

- **Netherlands**, *4 Liang Ma He Nan Road, 100600, Tel. 65321131, Fax 65324689*
- **New Zealand**, *1 Ritan Dong Er Street, Chaoyang District, 100600, Tel. 65322731, Fax 65324317*
- **Pakistan**, *Dongzhimenwai, Tel. 65322504*
- **Philippines**, *23 Xiu Shui Bei Street, Jianguomenwai, 100600, Tel. 65321872*
- **Poland**, *1 Ritan Road, Jianguomenwai, 100600, Tel. 65321235, Fax 65323761. Not open daily, mornings only.*
- **Russian Federation**, *Dongzhimen Bei Zhong Street, Number 4, 100600 (Not open daily), Tel. 65321381, 65324851*
- **South Korea**, *3 Dong Si Jie, Tel. 65320290, Fax 65320141*
- **Thailand**, *40 Guanghua Road, Tel. 65321903, Fax 65321745, 65321748*
- **UK**, *11 Guanghua Road, Jianguomenwai, 100600, Tel. 65321961, Fax 65321937. Website: www.fco.gov.uk/travel*
- **US**, *3 Xiushui Bei Street (Chancery), 100600, Tel. 65323831. American Citizen Services, 2 Xiushui Dong Street, 100600 (northeast of the Jianguomenwai Friendship Store), Tel. 65323431, Fax 65324153. Open Monday through Friday, except holidays, between 8:30am-12noon and 2pm-4pm. E-mail: amcitbeijing@state.gov. Website: www.usembassy-china.org.cn or www.travel.state.gov. For after-hour emergencies, Tel. 65321910 or 1391082-5917. Public Affairs Section, 17 Guang Hua Road, 100600, Tel. 65321161, Fax 65322039. US Customs Service, 31 Technical Club Companies Ltd., 15 Guanghua Road, 100020, Tel. 65002392, Fax 65003032. See also Chengdu, Guangzhou, Shanghai, and Shenyang.*
- **Vietnam**, *32 Guanghua Road, Jianguomenwai, Tel. 65321155, 65325720*

Fire, Tel. 119
Internet Services, try one of the following:
- **Sparkice** is in the China World Trade Center in the building to the right as you enter from Jianguomenwai. It is on the same level as the main entrance of the China World Hotel and the first hour has been free. *Tel. 20010815. It is open 24 hours. Its website is: www.icafe.com.cn.* They charge Y8 for a soft drink.
- **Qian Yi Internet Café**, *southeast corner of Tiananmen Square, Old Railway Station Shopping Mall 3/F, Tel. 67051722, Fax 67051632. Website: www.qianyi-wb.com.* Take the metro to Qianmen. Look for the clock tower (with no clock) in the gray and white striped building nearby. This is open 9:30am to 10pm. It charges about Y20 an hour. Tea costs Y5. English is spoken.
- there's a cheaper internet bar across the road from the Beijing International Hotel.

Medical Concerns, for minor ailments, consult your hotel. For more serious problems:

• **Ambulance**, *telephone 120*. Ambulances are equipped with defibrillators.
• For the **International First Aid Center** (Gi Jou Chong Xin), *near KFC on Qianmen, Tel. 65255678, 66014336.*
• For a **local hospital**: **Xiehe Hospital** (also known as Capital Hospital or Peking Union Medical College Hospital), the Foreigners' Clinic is at *53 Dongdanbei Avenue, 6/F, Tel. 65295296. The Emergency Room entrance is at No. 1 Shuaifuyuan Hutong, behind the hospital. Tel. 24 hours 65295284 (in Chinese only).* This hospital is behind the Palace Hotel downtown.
• For **international medical service**, foreign doctors and higher prices: the **International Medical Center**, *Lufthansa Center, Suite 106, has a pharmacy, dental and medical office. Its 24-hour service telephone is 64651561-63, Fax 64651984.*
• For **women and children**, there's the **Beijing United Family Health Center**, *2 Jiangtai Road, Chaoyang District, 100016, Tel. 64333960, Fax 64333963. E-mail: bjunited@bjunited.com.cn. Website: www.beijingunited.com. (English). It's near the Holiday Inn Lido.*
• For **emergency medical services** including death and evacuation, try **Asia Emergency Assistance** (AEA), *Building C, BITIC Leasing Center, 1 North Road, Xing Fu San Cun, Chaoyang District, 100027, Tel. 64629100 (24 hours), Fax 64629111. Website: www.internationalsos.com.* It has a pharmacy and makes house calls. Maps are available in the collection of business cards in many hotel lobbies.
• For **emergency medical services**, contact the **MEDEX Assistance Corporation**, *Regus Office 19, Beijing Lufthansa Center, No. 50 Liangmaqiao Road, 100016. For its 24-hour Alarm Center, Tel. 64651264, Fax 64651269.*
• **Vista Clinic**, *Kerry Center Shopping Mall, 1 Guanghua Road, Chaoyang District, 100020. Tel. 85296618, Fax 85296615. Website: www.vista-china.net.* This private clinic with one American doctor, and a team of English-speaking local doctors includes an ophthalmologist and dentist. It offers psychological counseling, sports medicine, and traditional Chinese medicine. It is a partner of the Peking University Medical College. A consultation costs Y380. A flu shot costs Y125. It operates 24 hours.

Police, *Tel. 110*; Foreigners' Section of the Beijing Public Security Bureau, *Tel. 65255486, 65253102. Open weekdays 8:30am-11:30am, and 1:00pm-5:00pm.* Extensions of visas take one week, or double the price for express service. *It is half a block north of the East Gate to the Forbidden City at 85, Bei Chi Zi Avenue, Tel. 65253102.* CITS has a visa extension package.

Religious Services in English: A non-denominational Christian group has church services in English at the **Sino-Japanese Youth Exchange Center**,

40 Liangmaqiao Road, near the Kempinski Hotel. Tel. 64386536 for informa-tion. Proof of foreign citizenship needed. There's also the **Congregation of the Good Shepherd**, *Capital Club Athletic Center, next to the Capital Mansion, Tel. 65954558, 64155276.* The **Canadian embassy** has been hosting a Catholic mass in English on Sunday evenings, *Tel. 65323536.*

Shabbat Services are held on Friday evenings at 7pm in the third floor ballroom of the **Capital Club Athletic Center**, *Capital Mansion, 6 Xinyuan Nan Road, Chaoyang District, near the Hilton and Sheraton Great Wall Hotels. Tel. 64672225. Website: www.sinogogue.org.*

Taxi: Capital Taxi Co., *Tel. 64616688.*

Telephone Operators: *information Tel. 114; long-distance information 116; overseas operator Tel.115; time Tel. 117; weather Tel. 121.*

Trans-Siberian Trains: Monkey Business Infocenter specializes in this train and related tours. It is above the Hidden Tree Bar at *12 Dong Da Qiao Xie Street, Nan San Li Tun, Chao Yang District, 100027 until 2003. Tel. 65916519, Fax 65916517. E-mail: MonkeyChina@compuserve.com. Website: www.monkeyshrine.com. It's open Monday to Saturday from 10am to 7pm; and Sunday from 4pm to 8pm.* Ask for Chris Stanley and Andy Jones, who say the best train is the Chinese, not the Russian one. You should book one month in advance for May to September. **CITS** has a brochure on this train and can also make bookings. *Located in the Beijing International Hotel, Tel. 65126688 X 1758, Fax 65120503. Website: www.ctn.com.cn (Chinese). E-mail: tianwei@cits.com.cn*

Tourist Complaints, Supervisory Bureau of Tourism Quality of Beijing Municipality, *Room 1001, Beijing Tourism Building, 28 Jianguomenwai Street, 100022, Tel. 65130828 (24 hours), Fax 65158251, 65158255.*

Tourism Hotline, 24 hours, *Tel. 65130828.* Questions, complaints, and compliments.

Travel Agents, check these for good hotel discounts, and cheaper city tours:
• **BTG International Travel & Tours (BTG Tours),** *4/F Minzu Hotel, No. 51 Fuxingmen Nei St., 100031, Tel.66014466 X 414, Fax 66012077, (its headquarters will move in 2002 or 2003). Website: www.btgtours.com,* This travel service group is a combination of several existing travel services with branches around China. Foreign travel agents and individual travel-ers may contact **BTG Overseas Travel**, *Tel. 66014849, Fax 66063062, or E-mail: botccn@public.bta.net.cn.* Once in China, they can also get in touch with **CITS Beijing**, *Beijing Tourism Building, No.28 Jianguomenwai Ave., 100022 or any of its offices in Beijing, Tel. 65150515, 65158562 (round the clock service), Fax 65158603, or E-mail: citsbj@public.bta.net.cn. The Beijing Tourism Tower ticket office on Jianguomenwai is open 8:30am-11:30am, and 1:30pm-5pm. Tel. 65158566.* For Outbound tickets, contact Christine, **BTG Outbound Tour Department,** Tel. 75239139, 65239146. For join-in day tours, try **Dragon Tours** to the Great Wall at Badaling section every day (Y330). The Forbidden City-

Temple of Heaven-Tiananmen tours have been every Tuesday, Thursday and Saturday (Y320). The Summer Palace- Lama Temple-Panda Tours every Monday, Wednesday and Friday (Y300). The Forbidden City-The Temple of Heaven-The Summer Palace-Tiananmen Square Tours every Monday, Wednesday, Friday and Sunday (Y360). Mutianyu (Great Wall) every Tuesday, Thursday and Saturday (Y230). It also can arrange rickshaw tours, Peking opera, Chinese acrobatics and Beijing Cultural City events. Free hotel pickup and reservations at: Jianguo Hotel, Scitech Hotel, Kunlun Hotel, Landmark Hotel, Radisson SAS, Wangfujing Grand Hotel and Jinglun Hotel.

- **China Hualong International Travel Service**, *European and North American Dept., 4/F, Beijing International Hotel, Tel. 65129043/65254703 X 8018, 8021, Fax 65124448. E-mail: hualong@public.fhnet.cn.net. Website: www.welltravel.com*. Ask for Helene Song. This is for city and Great Wall tours. Tours to Simatai are Y380 and Jinshanling Y450. A tour to Mutianyu is Y260 and Huanghua is Y320 but are not daily.
- **China International Sports Travel,** *4/F, Weitu Mansion, C3 Longtan Road, Chongwen District, 100061, Tel. 67117366, Fax 67117363. Website: www.cist-china.com (English) or www.CISTonline.com. E-mail: yuanxiaoge@262.net or cist@china.com*. Ask for Mr. Yan Xiao Ge who speaks English and is very helpful.
- **China International Travel Service Head Office,** *Room 711, CITS Building, 103 Fuxingmennei Avenue, 100800, Tel. 66053632, Fax 66012021. E-mail:xiemz@cits.co.cn, chuxia@cits.com.cn or aibin@cits.com.cn. Website: www.cits.net*. I have worked with this agency on three different occasions with tour groups and it has been wonderful. Contact Ms. Xie Mengzhu or Ai Bin for tours.
- **China Travel Service Head Office,** *China Travel Service Tower, North American Department, 2 Dong Beisanhuan, 100028, Tel. 64622288, 64612577, Fax 64612570, 64612556.* Special packages for the Olympics are planned. Mini-packages with your choice of hotel, guaranteed departures. "We will hold the reservation until we can't find you at the airport," said Zhang Tao, Sales Manager *(zt.oz@ctsho.com or ext. 6415).*
- **China CYTS Tours Holding Co., Ltd** is a publicly-owned travel agency which can book travel tickets, hotel reservations and organize tours around China for groups and individual travelers. It has over 60 branches around China, and is developing adventure travel packages. It ranks the second among Chinese tour companies. Its head office address: *23 C Dong Jiao Min Xiang, 100006, Beijing. Tel. 65243388, Fax 65211350.* Contact the North American Department, Deputy General Manager, Mark (Wang Liang), *E-mail: markwl@cytsonline.com. Tel. 65135122, Fax 65135137. Website: www.CYTSonline.com (Chinese). E-mail: webmaster@cytsonline.com or hotline@cytsonline.com.*

- **Happy Holiday Travel Service**, *Room 2223, Wujing Hotel, A15 Workers' Stadium Dong Road, Chaoyang District, Tel. and Fax 65013829, Tel. 65013637. Ask for Lucy Guan. E-mail: happyday@public.bta.net.cn.*
- **Helen Wong's Tours**, *Room 3040/3041, Beijing International Hotel, 9, Jianguomennei Avenue, 100005, Tel. 65254385, 65126688 X 3040, 3041, Fax 65257667. E-mail: hwtpek@public3.bta.net.cn. Website: hwtaus@helenwongstours.com.* Contact Sam Chen. This is the first wholly Australian-owned tour company in China. It can book hotels, tours and has its own guides.
- **Hualong International Travel Service**, *4/F, Beijing International Hotel, 9 Jianguomennei, 100005, Tel. 65126688 X 7808, Fax 75129553. E-mail BYHA@elong.com.*
- **Jing Hua Hotel** provides a group tour to the Great Wall at Simatai for Y80. This is considerably cheaper than any other tour, and leaves at 8am and returns at 5 or 6 pm. It offers transportation only and no guide. *Tel. 6722-2211 X 3359. The Jing Hua Hotel is at Xi Luo Yuan Nan Lu, Yongdingmenwai, 100077, Tel. 67222211.* Take the 17 bus from the Temple of Heaven. It is almost due south of this temple at Third Ring Road South.
- **Panda Tours**, which operates city and Great Wall tours can be reached at *98 Beilishi Road, Western District, Holiday Inn Downtown, Tel. 68036963, or Fax 68037044. E-mail: bjpanda@public.bta.net.cn. Website:www.chinaonlinetravel.com/pandatours/pandabeijing.htm.* They should give a 10% discount on tours for two people or more. Write ahead to: Wu Zengguang.

Vehicle Rental Services: *Yundao Car Rental, Auto Building, 44 Guanghua Road, Chaoyang Dist., Tel. 65326328/6. Fax 65928714.* Ask for Ms. Song Chunying. A Santana rents for Y350 for 8 hours/100km a day. Try also: **Shouqi Automobile Leasing Co.**, *62 Huayan Beili, Asian Games Village, Tel. 62058881, Fax 62328637. E-mail: sqzl@mail.sqzl.com.cn.* Ask for Mr. Liu Lin.

Websites & Tourist Information. You can read current and past editions of the helpful weekly and e-mail newsletter *Xianzai Beijing* by visiting them online at *www.xianzai.com*. It has a wealth of information about bargain airfares, restaurant specials, jobs, and used furniture and appliances for sale. It also lists sports opportunities, A.A. contacts, Hash House Harriers, current festivals, and orientation for newcomers.

Other helpful websites include *www.beijingnews.com.cn gives news, www.beijingscene.com/ and www.metronet.com.cn/*.

Look for tourist handouts like *METROzine, Beijing Journal, Around Beijing* and *City Weekend*. The latter is very helpful with addresses in Chinese and English and its website is *www.cityweekend.com.cn*. (English) These are distributed in hotels and expat hangouts like the San Wei Bookstore and Mexican Wave Café.

Chapter 15

Shanghai has been blossoming in the new millennium. Plan on at least three or four full days here if you're sightseeing. You must visit the new history museum under the Oriental Pearl Tower in Pudong with its realistic, life-like, life-size dioramas and take a ride up the tower to see the view. You should go to Pudong on a dinky little ferry and enjoy the lights coming onto the famous old European buildings of its waterfront Bund. You must walk through the neighborhood of Xintiandi which has been tastefully reconstructed in old Shanghai architecture. It is one of the most beautiful and successful fusions of traditional culture and modernity in China.

The Shanghai Museum with the best Chinese collection in the world can't be missed either. Then there's M on the Bund, a restaurant in one of those old European buildings with the best view of Shanghai's signature architecture and great food. I urge you to also see the Jade Buddha Temple or Jing'an Temple because these are both functioning temples, not museums. Also on the must-see list is the Yuyuan Garden, and a tastefully executed sex museum, where young couples go to learn how to perpetuate the species from historical pictures on porcelain.

To see the inside of one of the old houses and learn about the father of modern China, visit the Sun Yat-sen house. Then there's the Shanghai Stock Exchange. You should visit one of the water towns near Suzhou or Hangzhou, where the architecture hasn't changed in centuries. Then there's the old Jesuit basilica on top of a hill outside of town and another bit of modern history – the old Jewish ghetto where refugees from the Holocast lived. In the evening take in a performance at the Grand Theatre –

the exterior looks so ethereal in the dark. And of course, listen to the famous "jazz" band from the 1920s at the Peace Hotel.

These are just the highlights. There's much more.

Shanghai is mainland China's second largest city, its busiest port and an industrial city making Volkswagen and Buick cars, electronics, telecommunications equipment, iron and steel, home appliances, and petrochemicals. It is an important trading city and has China's major stock market. Think of it as China's New York.

Shanghai straddles the **Huangpu River** and reaches the Yangtze River on China's east coast, about 28 km from its Bund or downtown waterfront. It borders on Jiangsu and Zhejiang provinces and is due west of the southern tip of Japan. The urban population is approximately 9.48 million. The greater Shanghai area has at least 14.6 million people plus 4 million "floaters." Its population density is about 50,000 people per sq km, another world record. It covers roughly 120 km north-south, and nearly 100 km east-west.

The hottest temperature is 35°C in July and August; the coldest is minus 5°C in January and February. Most of its 1200 mm of rain falls May-September. It is about the same latitude as Jacksonville, Florida. Its natives speak a dialect unlike that of Beijing and more akin to that of Hangzhou and Suzhou, only faster.

History

This municipality, directly under the control of the central government, began 6,000 years ago as a tiny fishing village. It celebrated its 700th birthday as a city in 1991. It became a port in the 16th century. By 1840 its population was 500,000. Two years later, the British seized it, and although the Chinese paid a $300,000 ransom to keep it from being sacked, British soldiers and Chinese thieves severely looted it.

The Treaty of Nanking of that year opened Shanghai to foreign trade and settlement. This led to its partition into British, French, and later Japanese concessions, which are still reflected in its downtown architecture. The British concession became the International Settlement and foreign rule continued until the 1940s. Each of the concessions had its own tax system, police, courts, buses, and electrical voltage. A criminal could escape justice simply by going from one administration to another.

Shanghai thrived as a port, trading principally in silk, tea, and opium. Most of the foreign trade was British, and one-fifth of the opium reached China in fast American ships. From 1853 to 1855, the Small Sword Society controlled the walled Yuyuan section of Shanghai. This was a Cantonese-Fukinese secret society that wanted to restore Ming rule and prohibit opium. It was helped in its struggle by some foreign seamen, but many other foreigners supported the Manchus who regained the city. In 1860, the Taiping Heavenly Kingdom tried unsuccessfully to take Shanghai. In 1915 students and workers demonstrated here against the Twenty-One Demands of Japan. And in July 1921, the first Congress of the Communist Party of China met secretly here.

In 1925, a worker striking for higher wages was killed at a Japanese factory. This led to a demonstration by workers and students in the International Settlement, during which the British police killed several demonstrators. A rash of nationwide anti-imperialist protests followed. In April 1927, Chiang Kai-shek ordered a massacre of the Communists here, and Chou En-lai barely escaped with his life. The late 1920s was the golden age of Shanghai.

In 1932, Shanghai resisted a Japanese attack for two months and then made a truce. China appealed to the League of Nations and the United States, neither of whom did anything to help. Japan attacked again in August 1937. The Nationalists fought back for three months before retreating to Nanjing and later to Chongqing. The movie and book *Empire of the Sun* is set in this period and parts were shot in Shanghai. The Japanese stayed until 1945 and in May 1949, the Communists took the city. During the Cultural Revolution, it was the scene of many intense political struggles, especially in January 1966.

Today Shanghai is a boom town, but look carefully. Many of its huge new high-rise nickelodeon buildings and fancy single-family houses are empty. Many of its old 19th century neighborhoods have been torn down. It has been experiencing double-digit economic growth and its average per capita income of about Y11,000 is one of China's highest. It is the "dragon's head" of the burgeoning Yangtze River basin.

Shanghai is building the largest container port in the world with 52 berths, a 20-year project. By 2004, it hopes to have trains to Beijing in three hours running 500 km/hour. It's bidding for international meetings. It's building the biggest exhibition center in China, a German joint venture. There is talk also of 10 light rail lines and eleven subway lines. Shanghai is ambitious. It wants to surpass Hong Kong.

At the same time, it is increasing its green spaces. The city has 24-hour video cameras monitoring air pollution. No one can burn coal within the city. It is building a natural gas pipeline from China's western Xinjiang region. Its air is better than that of Beijing and Guangzhou.

Shanghai is pleasant because the people are outgoing and lively, and eager to learn. Shanghainese have been known for over a century for their quick wit, business talents, and efficiency. Today, parts of Shanghai are reminiscent of Manhattan or Paris. Its cosmopolitan heritage is reflected in its architecture and in the relative sophistication of many of its citizens. Its fashions and standards for products and services are the result of its longer, more concentrated periods of dealing with fussy foreigners. Its shopping is the best in the country.

It is a big, very crowded city that is more redolent of trade, commerce, and industry than it is of ancient Chinese culture. Many visitors think Shanghai can be missed, but as a contrast to other parts of China you should at least look

Good Books to Prepare for Shanghai

Try Noel Barber's **The Fall of Shanghai**; Pan Lin's **In Search of Old Shanghai**; and especially Sterling Seagrave's **The Soong Dynasty** – a very readable and revealing book about the Soongs, sons-in-law Gen. Chiang Kai-shek and Dr. Sun Yat-sen, son TV Soong (reluctant premier and finance minister), and their Soviet, gangster, and wealthy Christian, American and Chinese friends. For the Cultural Revolution, there's **Life and Death in Shanghai** by Nien Cheng. For Shanghai today, read Pamela Yatsuko's **New Shanghai: the Rocky Rebirth of China's Legendary City**. This is a serious book on the economics of the city, its politics, history, and vices. Ms. Yatsuko, who worked here as a journalist from 1995 to 1998, reveals how the Shanghai Museum was built, and writes of Shanghai's artists and homosexuals, its Western investors and government control.

at it. Feel its vibrancy. It is the most livable and exciting city now for foreigners in China.

In 2001, Shanghai hosted the Asia Pacific Economic Cooperation Forum. Delegations of world leaders occupied its five-star hotels. Radio and television stations broadcasted English lessons daily and hotel staff had to pass examinations in it. Whole neighborhoods, streets, one tunnel and some offices and stores were closed during the talks. The arrangements contributed to the Forum's success and Shanghai grew even more sure of its place in the world. It is now aiming to bid for the 2010 EXPO.

Arrivals & Departures

Shanghai is joined to other parts of China by air, land, and water. If you are traveling by car, be aware that between 4-7pm, Shanghai restricts the number of motor vehicles entering and leaving the city.

By Air

Shanghai is about a two-hour flight northeast of Hong Kong and less than two hours southeast of Beijing. It has been linked by air with at least 74 other cities including Los Angeles, Macau, New York, Osaka, Paris, San Francisco, Seattle, Seoul, Tokyo, and Vancouver.

Shanghai has two international airports. The original plan was to gradually shift international flights from Hongqiao to the newer **Pudong International Airport**, a process that could take until 2005 to complete. In early 2002, flights from North America, Europe and Australia have been landing in Pudong. Flights from Macau, Cambodia, Singapore, Thailand and the Philippines tend to fly into **Hongqiao**. Flights from Japan and domestic flights are split between Hongqiao and Pudong.

Visitors trying to save time and money should consider using Hongqiao Airport instead of Pudong if they have a choice. Hongqiao is closer to the hotels and a taxi could cost a quarter of the Pudong price to downtown. Many hotels have free shuttles from Hongqiao but not from Pudong. Very helpful has been the Travel Service Centre where you can book and reconfirm flight tickets without paying a service fee.

From Hongqiao also, buses go directly to Hangzhou, Suzhou, Nanjing, Wuxi, etc. The bus terminal is at the domestic arrivals level after you leave the baggage-claim area.

Luggage storage at Hongqiao airport is open 6am to 9:30pm, and costs from Y5 to Y20 per piece per day. The maximum is 30 days. Most telephones at the airports need cards to operate, which you can buy in shops here and elsewhere. The ATMs in the arrivals' lounge of both airports should work with MasterCard, Cirrus, Visa and Plus, but they were not working during my visit. There are banks.

Airport authorities have been trying to encourage travelers to use Pudong International Airport with discount air fares, some as high as 30% off. It is 30km from downtown Shanghai, *Tel. 38484500*. Important signs are in English. It has a pharmacy, first aid station, Watson's drug store, a tea shop, convenience store, police station, and Bank of China. Stores sell toys and a few books in English. Restaurants have entrees in the Y50-Y80 range. At Cholon Restaurant, dumplings cost Y25. The arrivals level has a business center, but no mobile phone rentals. Luggage storage opened from 6am to the last flight. For information, call *38484500*.

Buses between Pudong and Hongqiao airport leave every 15 to 30 minutes between 6am and 9pm and cost about Y30 from Pudong but free from Hongqiao. The trip takes 90 minutes. Buses go downtown between 5:30am and 6am to 8pm or 9pm and fares range from Y40 to Y90. A downtown check-in terminal is being built in Jingan but won't be finished for a couple of years.

Foreigners, with some exceptions, can spend up to 48 hours in Shanghai without a valid visa if they have a visa and confirmed flight ticket to their next destination. *Website: www.shanghai.gov.cn/visa-e/Index.htm (Chinese only)*

Major airlines include:
- **Aeroflot**, *Tel. 62798033*
- **Air Canada**, *Tel. 63758899, Fax 63758386. E-mail: shatocp@uninet.com.cn*
- **Air China**, *Tel. 63277888, 62692999*
- **Air France**, *Tel. 63606688. Airport 62688899 X 5325*
- **Air Macau**, *Tel. 62481110*
- **All-Nippon Airways**, *Tel. 62797000, 64723000*
- **Ansett Australia Airlines**, *Tel. 64155209*

- **CAAC/China Eastern Airlines**, *200 Yan'an Xi Road, Tel. 62475953 for domestic, 62472255 for international, Fax 6276761. Ticketing offices in many hotels. Airport information, Tel. 62683659, 62688918, 62537664*
- **Dragonair**, *Tel. 62798099, 62798128, Fax 62797189. Airport 62558899 X 5307*
- **Japan Airlines**, *Ruijin Building, Tel. 64723000*
- **Korean Airlines**, *Equatorial Hotel, Tel. 6275000, 62786000*
- **Lufthansa**, *Tel. 62481100*
- **Malaysian Airlines**, *Tel. 62798607*
- **Northwest Airlines**, *Shanghai Center, Tel. 62798607, 62798088; airport Tel. 62558899 X 5319*
- **Qantas**, *Tel. 62798660, 62798128, Fax 62798650*
- **Shanghai Airlines**, *Tel. 62550550, 62688558*
- **Singapore Airlines** *(SIA), Tel. 62891000*
- **Swissair**, *Tel. 63758211, 62797381*
- **Thai Airways**, *Tel.62487766, 62797175*
- **United Airlines**, *Tel. 62798009. At airport, Tel. 62558899 X 5304*
- **Virgin Atlantic**, *Tel. 53534600*

By Train

Shanghai has four train stations. It's best to use the main railway station. The others are for commuters. At the main station, you can walk directly to the subway without coming up for air and vice versa. At press time, the train from Hangzhou took three hours, and from Suzhou one hour. The train from Guangzhou took about 24 hours. The fastest train from Beijing took 14 hours. These times should decrease in 2002 because trains will be going faster.

You can book tickets at the **Foreigners' Ticket Office in the Shanghai Railway Station**, *Tel. 63179090*. It is on the right as you enter and is open 7:25am to 7:25pm. If you have a problem with the language, walk over to the Holiday Inn ticket office where you can ask questions and order tickets in English. You can also buy tickets through any travel agents for a fee and they'll be delivered to your hotel. See *Practical Information* below.

By Bus

From the Hongqiao airport terminal, buses have been leaving several times daily for Nanjing, Suzhou: (Y50); Wuxi (Y75) and Hangzhou (Y85). Unfortunately there's no English here. See Chapter 25.

An important bus terminal is beside **Shanghai Stadium, Staircase 5**. (Take exit 1 from the Shanghai Stadium metro station.) This has a schedule in English and Mr. Wu, No. 0058, speaks English. He is there daily except Wednesday and Thursday. This station is home to 10 different tourist buses for the city and neighboring areas. It also has bus tours with Chinese guides only. It has several buses daily to the Jinling Hotel in Nanjing (for about Y95),

Wuxi (Y39), and Hangzhou. *Tel. 64265555, 64266455. Website: www.interrainbow.com (Chinese only).*
A **Long Distance Bus Station** is a few blocks south of the Shanghai Railway Station at the corner of Hengfeng and Hanzhong Roads across from the Zhao An Hotel. From here buses leave for the likes of Hefei (every three hours), Ningbo (every 20 minutes), Suzhou, (every 40 minutes), Wuhan (once a day), and Wuxi (once an hour).

By Ship
The advance ticket office for passenger ships is at 1 Jinling Dong Road. The **Shiliupu Passenger Terminal** is at 111 Zhongshan Road, south of the Bund (to Putuoshan). The Gongping Road Passenger Terminal is at 60 Gongping Road. The telephone number for all three is *63261261.*

Orientation
The city is divided by the Huangpu River. Pudong means "east of the Huangpu River." The older part of Shanghai is Puxi or "west of the Huangpu River." Streets running east-west downtown are usually named after cities and those running north-south after provinces. Elevated expressways help you get around the city quickly. One of these, the six-lane Inner Ring Road, is 48 km long and takes 36 minutes to circle. Along with the east-west expressway and the north-south expressway, this is like a misshapen pizza roughly cut into four pieces. The expressway between the airports is part of this system. These elevated expressways are frequently the longer, more expensive, and fastest ways to go places.

Getting Around Town
Major hotels give out free maps. Guides and join-in tours are available through travel agencies and hotels. Taking a taxi might be cheaper for three or more people than taking a tour bus. Chapter 25 of this book has a list of the important tourist attractions in Chinese and English. Many tourist magazine handouts available in hotels, bars, and tourist restaurants have lists of restaurants and sites in English and Chinese.

By Public Bus
Air-conditioned Bus 938 goes from Hongqiao Airport to Pudong but takes about two hours. It goes by the Xijiao Guest House and the Marriott Hong Qiao, and stops across the street from the Hua Ting Guest House before it goes over the bridge to Pudong. The Number 505 goes from People's Square, past the Hilton, Sheraton Grand Hotel, Zoo, Nikko Longbai Hotel to the airport. Bus 911 from the Marriott Hong Qiao Hotel ends up on Huaihai Road, and Bus 57 at Jingan.

A good bus is 925 which goes from the Shanghai Museum in People's Square (renmin guan chang) along Zhong Shan Xi Road past the Equatorial and Hilton hotels out past the Hongqiao hotels and the Marriott Hongqiao. Taxis are hard to get at the Museum and this could be your only choice.

The double-decker Number 911 goes past the Isetan Department Store, the Crowne Plaza and then to the Hongqiao airport. Ordinary buses are incredibly crowded but air-conditioned buses are comfortable and not so crowded. Mini-buses ply fixed routes and seats are guaranteed.

By Public Tour Bus

Every good hotel lobby should have a rack with literature from the Shanghai tourist bureau including a handy card with the tourist bus routes.

Outside the Shanghai Stadium (Staircase Five) towards the Hua Ting Hotel, within half a block east of the Shanghai Stadium Metro Station is a terminal for tourist buses. *Tel. 64265555, 64266455. Website: www.interrainbow.com (Chinese only).* Fares are generally in the Y2-Y12 price range. Relatively comfortable buses leave every 30 minutes to an hour, usually between 6:30am and 5pm.

Route No. 1 goes to Sheshan and Song Jiang. Route Nos. 2 and 6 go to Jia Ding. Route No. 3 goes to Pudong. Route 4 goes to the zoo, Zhujiaqiao and Grand View Garden. Route No. 7 is a historical and cultural tour that includes Dr. Sun Yat-sen's residence. Route No. 8 includes the Jingan Temple, the Bund and Nanjing Road Pedestrian Street. These are especially convenient for places outside of town, a cheap way to see the countryside. Make sure you know the time of the last return bus. Consult the Tourism Hot Line below if necessary.

A **hop on-hop off tourist bus** also leaves every 45 minutes to an hour from the side door of the Garden Hotel on Mao Ming Road, Monday-Friday 9am-4:15pm and Saturday-Sunday 8:45am-5:45pm. For Y18 a day, these will take you to the Shanghai Museum, the Oriental Pearl TV Tower in Pudong, Yaohan/New Age Department Store, Nanpu Bridge (bus stop 251), Yuyuan Garden, the Bund, Shanghai Museum and back to the Jin Jiang Hotel. You might want to take this bus without stopping as a good overall introduction to the city and then go back to spend more time in places that interest you.

By Metro (di tie) & Light Rail (qiang gui)

Look for the logo, a circle with two mountain peaks or "M" inside. You pay Y3 to anywhere in the system. You get a card from a machine or human to put into the turnstile on the way in and out. If you avoid rush hours, you can usually get a seat. Signs in the metro are in English and Chinese.

The 14-km **No. 1 line** starts from the Shanghai Railway Station with stops at Han Zhong Road, Xin Zha Road, People's Park (Nanjing Road, Shanghai Museum, Grand Theatre, Flower and Bird Market. This is the closest stop to the Bund in Puxi and you can change to No. 2 metro line here without paying

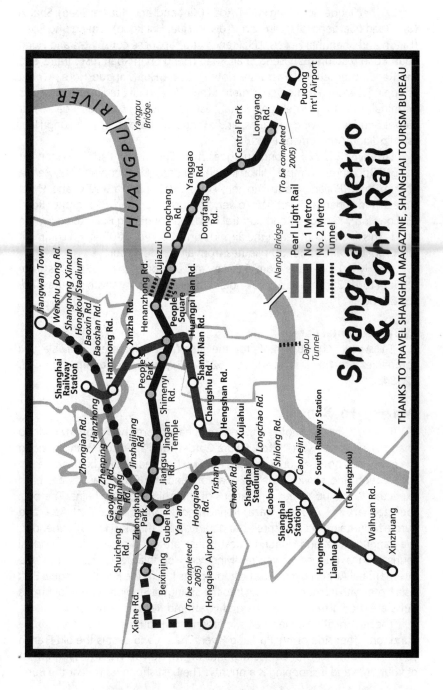

Shanghai Metro & Light Rail

THANKS TO TRAVEL SHANGHAI MAGAZINE, SHANGHAI TOURISM BUREAU

extra). Then it goes to Huang Pi Nan Road (Xintiandi and Huaihai Road), Shanxi Nan Road (Garden Hotel, Jin Jiang Tower, Huai Hai Road), Chang Shu Road (Hilton and Shanghai Hotels, US, French and Japanese consulates and Heng Shan Road restaurants), Heng Shan Road (Heng Shan Road restaurants and the Regal International East Asia Hotel), Xu Jia Hui (Jianguo Hotel, Orient Shopping Centre, Pacific Department Store), Shanghai Stadium (Tourist Bus Terminal, Hua Ting Hotels and Regal East Asia Hotel), Cao Bao Road (near carpet and jade-carving factories, and Mongolian barbecue), Xin Long Hua, and Jin Jiang Amusement Park.

Line No. 2 is 22 km long and goes from Zhongshan Park with stops at Jiangsu Rd., Jingan Temple (Hilton Hotel), Shimenyi Rd., People's Park, Henan Zhong Road (Pujiang Youth Hostel), Lujiazui (Shangri-La and Grand Hyatt Hotels and Oriental Pearl TV Tower, Dongchang Road, Dongfang Road (Holiday Inn), Yanggao Road, Central Park and Longdong Road to Longyang Road. This line will not reach the airports until 2004 or 2005 at which time it will probably take about 50 minutes from airport to airport.

Line No. 1 operates from 5:30am to 10:20pm. Line No. 2 runs from 5:55am to 10:28pm, and at peak hours trains arrive every seven minutes. *Tel. 63189188.*

By Taxi & Rental Car

Taxis cost Y10.80-Y14.40 for the first three kilometers. Reliable taxi companies are the **Dazhong**, *Tel. 62188888*, and **Friendship Taxi**, *Tel. 62584584.*

Where to Stay

The best five-star hotels for English speakers are the Portman, Pudong Shangri-La, Grand Hyatt, Hilton, Okura Garden, and Sheraton Grand. Among the many new hotels to open in 2002 are two that should also be near the top for location and service. The JW Marriott and the Four Seasons are both expected to live up to the reputations of their high-quality chains. The best four-stars are the Crowne Plaza, Renaissance, Sofitel, Regal East Asia, and Purple Mountain. The best three-star downtown is the City Hotel. Further out, the Jianguo Hotel and Huating Guest House are good choices for individual tourists on a budget. If you're flying via Hongqiao Airport, there's the International Airport Hotel. The best for sports fans is the Regal Shanghai East Asia Hotel with its rooms opening into the Shanghai Stadium. Great for fitness buffs are the Portman, Hilton, Grand Hyatt and Regal International.

The best location for leisure travelers and some business people is near the Bund, on either side of the Pu Jiang River. The second best is the old French concession area. This of course depends on where you want to spend most of your time and if shopping is a priority. The best shopping is near the Bund

(Nanjing Road) and French Concession (Huaihai Road). Shopping malls are all over the city now.

Hotels have been full only in late September and October or during a conference or trade show. The low season, when prices are soft, is from late November or December to mid-March. July-August is the not-quite-so-busy "shoulder season." Because of the five-day work week, haggle on weekends.

The top hotels here have international-class services like credit cards, beauty salons, coffee shops with Western food, foreign exchange, and business centers. English is usually good in the five-star hotels, but only in a few four and three stars. Hotels listed here are considered good for service, location and English. If you want a feeling of the old Shanghai of the foreign concessions, do consider the Garden, Peace, and Jin Jiang Hotels – all of which have some 1920s ambiance. Of these, the first choice is the Peace because of its location on the Bund. Also below are some cheaper hotels for budget-minded people.

Prices here are in US dollars or Chinese RMB yuan. They are subject to change, negotiation, and a 10 or 15% surcharge. Discounts off the published rates have ranged from 20% to 60% depending on the season. Hotels charge about Y1 for local telephone calls and an excessive amount for e-mail. See below for cheaper Internet Cafes. Hotels here are listed according to location, roughly in ascending order away from the Bund except for Pudong which is at the end. Within each area, the most expensive is first, the cheapest last.

The Bund/Waterfront/East Nanjing Road Area

The best location for visitors and some business people is near and along the Bund. This area is also 30 minutes drive from Hongqiao Airport by expressway, and 50 minutes from Pudong airport.

In Puxi, the hotels here are closest to People's Square metro stop and within 50 meters to 3 km of the Bund. A pedestrian tunnel, vehicular tunnel and ferry connect them with Pudong. Roads and sidewalks are very congested. The Art Museum, bird and fish market, the Grand Theatre, Shanghai Museum, Friendship Store, and Nanjing Road shopping are close. The view of Pudong at night is spectacular.

Until I have a chance to see the Four Seasons or JW Marriott, the Sofitel is my first choice and the Peace Hotel second here. The Central is attractive but looks too much like a temple to the money god. The Sofitel is the most convenient to Nanjing Road shopping and the subway. Rooms are smaller than those at the Peace. Both are close to the Bank of China, post office, the Friendship Store, foreign language book store, and Bund.

All but the Ocean Hotel are within five km of the railway station. The Ocean is about nine km from the railway station and is nearest to the Yangpu Bridge. The city is building a waterfront walkway from near the Ocean Hotel to the Bund, three km west, due in 2002 or 2003.

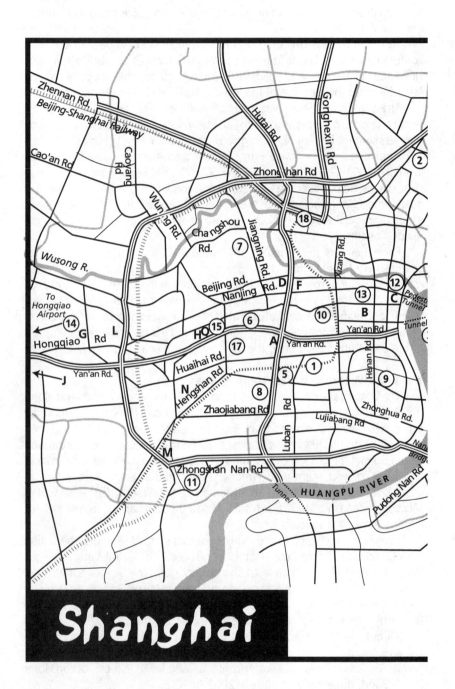

Shanghai

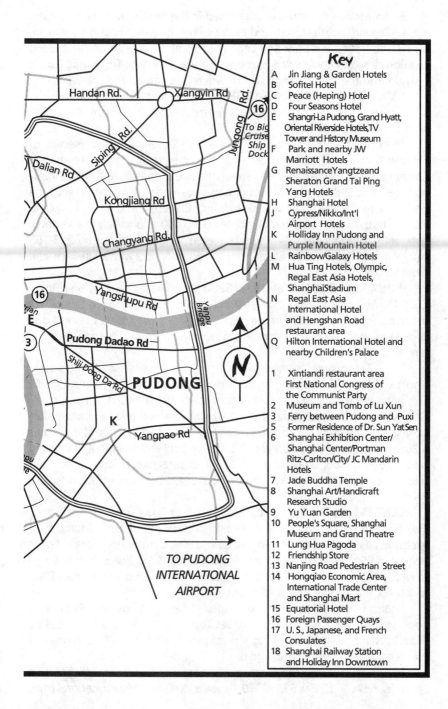

Handan Rd.
Xiangyin Rd
16
To Big
Cruise
Ship
Dock
Dalian Rd
Siping Rd.
Jungong Rd.
Kongjiang Rd
Changyang Rd.
Yangshupu Rd
16
3
E
Pudong Dadao Rd
Yangpu Bridge
Shiji Dong Da Rd
PUDONG
N
K
Yangpao Rd

TO PUDONG
INTERNATIONAL
AIRPORT

Key

A Jin Jiang & Garden Hotels
B Sofitel Hotel
C Peace (Heping) Hotel
D Four Seasons Hotel
E Shangri-La Pudong, Grand Hyatt, Oriental Riverside Hotels, TV Tower and History Museum
F Park and nearby JW Marriott Hotels
G Renaissance Yangtze and Sheraton Grand Tai Ping Yang Hotels
H Shanghai Hotel
J Cypress/Nikko/Int'l Airport Hotels
K Holliday Inn Pudong and Purple Mountain Hotel
L Rainbow/Galaxy Hotels
M Hua Ting Hotels, Olympic, Regal East Asia Hotels, Shanghai Stadium
N Regal East Asia International Hotel and Hengshan Road restaurant area
Q Hilton International Hotel and nearby Children's Palace

1 Xintiandi restaurant area First National Congress of the Communist Party
2 Museum and Tomb of Lu Xun
3 Ferry between Pudong and Puxi
5 Former Residence of Dr. Sun Yat Sen
6 Shanghai Exhibition Center/ Shanghai Center/Portman Ritz-Carlton/City/ JC Mandarin Hotels
7 Jade Buddha Temple
8 Shanghai Art/Handicraft Research Studio
9 Yu Yuan Garden
10 People's Square, Shanghai Museum and Grand Theatre
11 Lung Hua Pagoda
12 Friendship Store
13 Nanjing Road Pedestrian Street
14 Hongqiao Economic Area, International Trade Center and Shanghai Mart
15 Equatorial Hotel
16 Foreign Passenger Quays
17 U. S., Japanese, and French Consulates
18 Shanghai Railway Station and Holiday Inn Downtown

Budget travelers should be interested in the Pacific Luck, YMCA, Aster House/Pujiang/Youth Hostel, and E-Hotel. Their locations near the Bund are fantastic but service is poor and English very limited. The YMCA has a good location close to People's Park but the service is slow too. The Pacific Luck is next door to the Public Security office where you can extend your visa.

JW MARRIOTT HOTEL SHANGHAI, *399 Nanjing Xi Road, 200003. Five star standards. E-mail: shanghaijwdom@marriott.com Website: www.marriott.com.*

This hotel is across the street from People's Square at the intersection of Nanjing Xi Road and Huangpei Bei Road. It is near the Shanghai Art Museum, flower market, and the pedestrian street. It is due to open in 2002 with a lobby on the 37th to 39th floors, 342 rooms, non-smoking floors, voice mail and data ports. There's a California grill, casual, and Chinese restaurants, and cigar lounge. Its ballrooms can accommodate 200 to 400 respectively at a sit-down banquet. Its rooms are 38-40 square meters, and executive studios 56-65 square meters. It has a 25-meter indoor and outdoor pool with a sun-deck, and a health club.

FOUR SEASONS HOTEL SHANGHAI (*Si Ji Jiu Dian), 500 Weihai Road, 200041. Five star standards. Tel. 62568888. Fax 62565678. E-mail: for information eva.ho@fourseasons.com. E-mail: for reservations chorkiang.lee@fourseasons.com. Website: www.fourseasons.com/shanghai (English). 2002.*

This 37-story hotel is three blocks from the Shimenyi Road metro stop. Rooms are $315 with an opening discount of about 40%. This hotel has a 24-hour business center, concierge and room service. It has Chinese and Japanese restaurants, steak and seafood grill, and alternative cuisine (healthy foods). Its ballroom can seat 530 at a formal banquet. It has a 26-piece gym and spa, plunge pools, indoor pool and whirlpool, sauna and steam rooms. Rooms average 39 to 61 square meters and have three telephones, safes, and speaker phones. Four Seasons Hotels and Resorts, Asia Pacific.

CENTRAL HOTEL SHANGHAI, *555 Jiujiang Road, 200001. Four stars. Tel. 53965000, Fax 53965188. E-mail: chbc@centralhotelshanghai.com. Website: www.centralhotelshanghai.com. 1999. Conveniently located right behind the Sofitel Hotel, one block from Nanjing Dong Road. Rooms range from $160 to $190 and are 30 to 33 square meters. Suites range from $300 to $1200. It has been giving 45% discounts.*

Rooms offer CNN and HBO, and safes. It has non-smoking floors but no pool. Some rooms have "Internet TV Set Top Box." There's a 24-hour coffee shop, bowling, billiards, and an eight-piece gym. Staff have spiffy uniforms and the décor is bright with yellow gold.

PEACE HOTEL (Heping Fandian), *20 Nanjing Dong Road, 200002. Five stars. Tel. 63216888, Fax 63290300. E-mail: sales@shanghaipeacehotel.com.*

Website: www.shanghaipeacehotel.com (English). $120-$250 for rooms, $320-$350 for suites. It has been discounting 45%.

Built in 1929 and renovated in 1997, the 11-story North Building has 260 rooms, many with walk-in closets, televisions in bathrooms, and 30 and 40 square meters. It has an executive floor, non-smoking rooms, CNN, and a famous Sichuan-Cantonese-Shanghai restaurant, and a French restaurant. Do ask Public Relations for a tour and don't miss the charming Indian suite, Victor Sassoon's own tower apartment, the Lalique glass, and the glamorous old ballroom. Sassoon made his money from real estate and opium. The famous 1920s jazz band still plays off-key daily from 8pm, more corn than music. All these make up for the musty odors, the deteriorating grouting, the poor gym, the difficulty of parking for tour buses outside, and the so-so breakfast.

Its South Building is across Nanjing Road. Rooms in this 1906 building have been beautifully renovated in Victorian style with 20th century safety features and in-room safes. It re-opened in 1998, has six stories, 100 rooms about 35 square meters, and a good view of the river. It is worth a look. Jin Jiang International.

OCEAN HOTEL (Yuan Yang Binguan), *1171 Dong Da Ming Road, 200082. Four stars. Tel. 65458888, Fax 65458993. E-mail: oceansal@online.sh.cn. Website: www.oceanhotel-sh.com. $110 to $180 for rooms and $280 for suites. It has been discounting 30%. Next to a department store, old Jewish ghetto and close to a post office. Two km from the International Port.*

Built in 1988, this 28-story building has 370 rooms and executive floors. Its standard rooms are 24 square meters and were renovated in 2001. Rooms have data ports and safes. It has a 24-hour business center, CNN, a health club but no pool. There's a Japanese restaurant and a revolving restaurant with good Western food.

HOTEL SOFITEL HYLAND SHANGHAI (Hailun Binguan), *505 Nanjing Dong Road, 200001. Four stars. Tel. 63515888, Fax 63514088. E-mail: sofitel@hyland-shanghai.cn. Website: accorhotels-china.com. Rooms start at $108 and suites $150. It has been discounting 10-20%.*

Built in 1993, this compact, modern hotel has 30 stories, 389 rooms, and good service. It has CNN and HBO, in-room safes, high-speed internet access, and executive and non-smoking floors. It has international, Western and Cantonese food. You can watch the activity on Nanjing Road from the comfort of its Brauhaus 505 restaurant. It has its own brewery and 24-hour room service. There's a 15-piece gym with an Alpha 33 relaxation pad but no pool.

PARK HOTEL (Guoji Fandian), *170 Nanjing Xi Road, 200003. Four stars. Tel. 63275225, Fax 63276958. E-mail: sales@hotmail.com. Website: www.parkhotel.com.cn. $80-$170 for rooms, $180-$600 for suites including tax and service charge. It has been discounting 10-20%. Near People's Square* *subway station, this is one of the best locations for Nanjing Road shopping and People's Park.*

Built in 1934 and renovated 1999, this 24-story, 217-room hotel has small baths, safes, CNN, HBO, and Beijing and continental food. Rooms are 20 to 28 square meters. English might be a problem. A Jin Jiang Hotel.

PACIFIC LUCK HOTEL (Jing Fu Yun Dajiudian), *299 Wusong Road, 200080. Three stars. Tel. 63259800, Fax 63259709, 53259725. E-mail: plhotel@online.sh.cn. This 160-room hotel is in a Chinese neighborhood with cheap but adequate restaurants nearby, a movie theatre, and a department store. It is a ten minute walk to the Friendship Store and the Bund. Rooms are Y680 and Y770. Suites are Y1000-Y1200. It has been discounting 30%.*

It has CNN, a new gym, Cantonese food, and accepts credit cards. Its breakfast buffet costs Y38, a few dishes were chipped and English is a problem.

YMCA HOTEL (Qian Nian Hui Binguan), *123 Xizang Nan Road, 200021. Three stars. Tel. 63261040, Fax 63201957. E-mail: ymcahtl@isdnnet.sta.net.cn. Website: www.ymcahotel.com. $55-$82 for rooms, $145-$300 for suites, and $15 per bed in a dormitory. It has been giving 25% discounts and accepts credit cards.*

Built in 1929 with 11 stories, this hotel has 165 worn rooms and a 24-hour coffee shop. Rooms are 14 to 24 squares meters. English could be a problem. There are dirty carpets, poor grouting and no non-smoking rooms. Budget travelers only. Jin Jiang International Management.

E-BEST HOTEL SHANGHAI, *687 Dong Daming, 200080. Tel. 65951818, Fax 65957400. E-mail: ebest@public6.sta.net.cn or rsv@ebest-hotel.com. Website: www.ebest-hotel.com. It is about two kilometers north of the Bund. Y188 for a double and Y268 for a twin.*

This 70 year old, six-story pink hotel was built in 1929, and most recently renovated in 1999. It has 189 rooms that range from 14 to 26 square meters. English might be a problem. Don't expect too much at that price. It offers only Chinese breakfasts. Its roof garden has a view of the Huangpu River.

ASTER HOUSE HOTEL/PUJIANG HOTEL (Pujiang Fandian), *15-17 Huang Pu Road, 200080. Tel. 63246388, Fax 63243179. One star. Y120-Y350 for rooms (not all with private bath), Y55 per bed in dormitory. Take bus 928 or subway no. 2 from the railway station and get off at Henan Road. It is a 10-minute walk and is across the street from the Seagull Hotel.*

This 116-room hotel was founded in 1846 as O'Richard's Hotel, Shanghai's first. It was moved here in 1857 and renamed the Astor House Hotel, then the Pujiang Hotel. It should be a museum, rather than a favorite backpacker hotel. Its beautiful dark wood paneling, wooden floors, and its marvelous hallway make it look like a period movie set. It has a Chinese restaurant with white linen tablecloths and air-conditioning. English could be a problem. Check the fire exits.

Part of this hotel is the **Shanghai Youth Hostel** linked to the International Youth Hostel Federation. (www.iyhf.org). Food is no cheaper than in other local restaurants. For Y20 you could get a lunch of meat and vegetables, with fried noodles or rice, plus drink. Rooms are generally small. Its travel agent was not helpful and the laundry machine was broken. Guests usually use the internet at a nearby hotel.

By the Railroad Station

HOLIDAY INN DOWNTOWN (Guang Chang Chang Cheng Jia Ri Jiou Dian), *Plaza Wing, 285 Tian Mu Xi Road, 200070. Four star standard. Fax 63543019. Great Wall Wing, 585 Heng Feng Road, 200070. Fax 63543019. These two wings are on the same street, separated by the road from the train station. The telephone number is 63538008. E-mail: hidtsha@public8.sta.net.cn. Website: www.holiday-inn.com. Rooms are Y830-Y1620, and suites Y1330-Y3280. It has been giving up to 40% discounts.*

This 465-room hotel was opened in 1995, and taken over by Holiday Inn in 1999, and renovated until early 2002. It has 20 and 14 stories. It has an executive club and non-smoking rooms and its gym is small. Rooms are 26.to 30 square meters with data ports, CNN and safes. Its executive floor has international newspapers in English. Its business center has a computer with a camera eye. There is also a China Eastern Airline office. The breakfast buffet costs Y78. The better section is the Great Wall with its business center and Western coffee shop.

This hotel is very conveniently located south of the Shanghai Railway Station. Go out the main door of the station and straight towards the street ahead. Just before the overpass, on the right is a KFC which is attached to the Great Wall Wing; on the left is the Plaza Wing. If arriving by subway, take the Number Three exit and the first left at street level. This neighborhood is crowded, busy, fascinating and dirty, 17 km. (20 minutes) from Hongqiao Airport, and 45 minutes from Pudong International Airport by road.

The Old French Concession Area

This popular hotel area is about 13 km from the Hongqiao airport, 50 km from the Pudong airport, four km from the railway station, and six km from the Bund. It is a pleasant residential, diplomatic, and tourist shopping area full of restaurants and bars and near Huaihai Road and its big department stores.

The Jin Jiang and Garden Hotels are close together and within walking distance of shopping, the Shanxi Road subway stop, and Huaihai Road. The Hilton and Shanghai Hotels are together near the Children's Palace, and are closest to the US Consulate. The Portman Ritz-Carlton (in the Shanghai Centre), City and JC Mandarin surround the Shanghai Exhibition Center with its tourist stores and restaurants.

The Shanghai Center is an important international business center with offices and apartments. It has one of the theatres of the Shanghai acrobats, Hard Rock Cafe, and United, Thai, Qantas, Dragonair, and Northwest airlines, DHL, travel agents, Canadian consulate, supermarket, and Watson's drug store You can walk to the Jingansi Temple and its metro station. These three groups are within three km of each other. An expressway goes right by the Hilton.

The best hotels here are the Portman Ritz-Carlton, Hilton, and Garden (in spite of its plastic soap dishes), all aiming for excellence.

A taxi costs about Y50 from Hongqiao airport to the JC Mandarin Hotel, and around Y200 from Pudong airport.

THE PORTMAN RITZ-CARLTON (Po Ter Man Jiu Dian), *Shanghai Centre, 1376 Nanjing Xi Road, 200040. Five stars. Tel. 62798888, Fax 62798800. E-mail: reservation@portman.com.cn. Website: www.ritzcarlton.com. $300-$380 for rooms and $480-$3800 for suites. Ask about its luxurious Romance of Shanghai and Presidential Bike Pack packages. It is 1.5 km from the Shanxi Nan subway stop. Nearby are CITS, Plaza 66, CITIC Square and West Gate Mall.*

Opened in 1990, this hotel was taken over by Ritz-Carlton in 1998. Since then, it has been undergoing major renovations and improved its service. It has 50 stories and 564 huge rooms with at least three telephones each and non-smoking floors. Rooms are 27 (or more) square meters and all have voice mail, CNN, HBO, NBC and safes. Its executive club floors require a special key card for elevator access. There is Cantonese, American, and Japanese restaurants all with dress code: smart casual, no shorts. For its Italian restaurant, see below. It has one of the largest health clubs in the city: indoor tennis, squash, aerobics, a 50-piece gym, and kick boxing, pilates and taiji classes. There's an indoor-outdoor lap pool. Ask about its "bath menu" and "fitness kit" and Deng Xiao Ping's boat for parties. Its "technology butler" is available to solve computer problems. The Portman offers a wonderful snack (water, croissants and yogurt) for guests flying out as an alternative to airline food.

OKURA GARDEN HOTEL SHANGHAI (Huayuan Fandian), *58 Maoming Nan Road, 200020. Five stars. Tel. 64151111, Fax 64158866. E-mail: garden@online.sh.cn. Website: www.gardenhotelshanghai.com. $250-$465 for rooms and $550-$3000 for suites. Set in a large 28,000 square meter garden, this hotel is 100 meters from the closest metro stop, Shanxi Nan Road.*

Opened in 1990, the classy Garden incorporates the 1926 Cercle Sportif with its marvelous old ball room into its building. It has 34 stories, 500 rooms each with safes, three telephone jacks, HBO and CNN, and gleaming white bathtubs. It has non-smoking and executive floors, a classy-looking business center, voice mail, and 24-hour room service. It has international newspapers in English and rooms are 29 to 36 square meters. There's a 25-meter long pool under a retractable roof, good 15-piece gym, and lighted outdoor tennis court. It has Chinese, Japanese and continental food and its breakfast buffet costs Y168 (including service). It has parking for 240 cars. Hotel Okura management. Member of Leading Hotels of the World.

SHANGHAI HILTON INTERNATIONAL (Jingan Dajiudian), *250 Hua Shan Road, 200040. Five stars. Tel. 62480000, Fax 62483848. E-mail: shhilton@public.sta.net.cn. Website: www.hilton.com. $230-$290 for rooms, $600-2200 for suites. Two blocks from the Jingansi metro station and ten minutes walk to the Changshu Road metro station which are on different metro lines.*

Built in 1988, this 43-story hotel has 772 rooms, each with at least three telephones, BBC, CNBC and HBO. Rooms are 37-39 square meters. It has Western, Italian, Cantonese, teppanyaki, and Sichuan restaurants. Its buffet breakfast costs Y166 in its coffee shop and Y135 in its Shanghai Express. You can also get a sandwich in its deli for Y36-Y39. Its express lunch is Y50. The Atrium Café is open 24 hours and its ballroom can seat 350 guests banquet-style. The Hilton has a beautiful spa with ozone-enriched air, a 15-meter indoor pool, 36-piece gym, lighted outdoor tennis, and squash. It has non-smoking and four executive floors, a classical Chinese garden indoors and outdoors with waterfall. Its business center has international newspapers in English and its clinic is open 24 hours. Its concierge can book tickets for the Shanghai Acrobats or soccer games. The hotel can book a whole train car for groups to Suzhou, and cater it with food and open bar.

SHANGHAI JC MANDARIN (Jing Cang Wen Hua), *1225 Nanjing Xi Road, 200040. Five stars. Tel. 62791888, Fax 62791822. E-mail: mandarin.sjm@meritus-hotels.com. Website: www.jcmandarin.com. $220-$290 for rooms, $410-$1490 for suites. It has been giving 20-40% discounts.*

Opened in 1990 and renovated in 2000, this 30-story hotel has 600 rooms each with three telephone jacks, HBO, safes, and contact-free key card system. Deluxe rooms are 36 square meters. It has non-smoking and executive floors, continental cuisine, a patisserie, and especially good Cantonese cuisine. Its seafood buffet costs Y168. Its ballroom can accommodate 500 at a sit-down banquet. It has a clinic, tennis, squash, and a 20-piece gym, an all-weather pool, sauna, Jacuzzi and steam room. There's also a playroom for children and a book store. A marvelous lacquer painting of Ming Admiral Cheng Ho dominates the lobby. Managed by Meritus Hotels and Resorts.

JIN JIANG HOTEL (Jin Jiang Fandian), *59 Mao Ming Nan Road, 200020, Tel. 62582582, Fax 64725588. E-mail: jinjiang@public2.sta.net.cn. Website: www.jinjianghotelsshanghai.com. In its five-star Cathay and Grosvenor buildings, it's $155-$165 for rooms and $195-$3000 for suites. Its three-star building is $100 for rooms and $140-150 for suites. It has been discounting 30%.*

First built in 1929, this hotel has 505 rooms, HBO, CNN, and a famous Sichuan restaurant. Its Cathay Building is good with big rooms and a pool and gym. Its Grosvenor building has a classy art deco lobby, and is all suites. Its grubby south building, the Jinnan is three-stars, and has dirty carpets, The Jin Jiang has a good book store, crafts store, boutiques, and supermarket. As a historical hotel, the Peace is more interesting, and the Garden across the road much better. A good Indian restaurant is in the compound. It is working on a convention center, health center, and bowling. English might be a problem

CITY HOTEL (Chen Shi Jiu Dian), *5-7 Shanxi Nan Road, 200020. Three stars going on four. Tel. 62551133, Fax 62550611, E-mail: reserve@cityhotelshanghai.com. Website: www.cityhotelshanghai.com. $110-$130 for rooms, $235 for suites. Walking distance to the Shanghai Centre.*

Built in 1988-89, this 259-room hotel has data ports, soft beds, CNN, 40-watt bulbs, and no safes. Rooms are 18 to 20 square meters. It has executive floors and popular Sichuan and Shanghai restaurants. The buffet breakfast is $9. There are international newspapers in English, an indoor pool and a good 12-piece gym.

SHANGHAI HOTEL (Binguan), *505 Wulumuqi Road, 200040. Three stars. Tel. 62480088, Fax 62481056. E-mail: shotelc@online.sh.cn. Y738-Y1288 for rooms, Y1888-Y3888 for suites. It has been discounting 10% and including breakfast.*

Built in 1983, and renovated in 1997, this modest hotel has 23 stories and 562 rooms. Rooms are 18 square meters. It has Western, Chaozhou and Japanese food, a gym, Jacuzzi, CNN and Star Movies. Huating Group.

Shanghai Stadium Metro Area

This is a convenient location for soccer fans and individual travelers near a tourist bus terminal, and a metro stop. The Hua Ting Hotel and Towers, Regal East Asia, Jianguo Hotel, and Hua Ting Guest House are in this area. These are in order of quality with the Hua Ting Hotel and Towers the best. They are also close to an elevated highway. There are two relatively good shopping areas nearby, restaurants, the Shanghai Gymnasium, the 80,000-seat soccer stadium, and a little further away, the Cao He Jing High Tech park. This area is about 12 km from the Hong Qiao Airport and about 15 km from the train station. The Hongqiao Development Zone is six km away.

HUA TING HOTEL AND TOWERS (Hua Ting Binguan No.1), *1200 Caoxi Bei Road, 200030. Five stars. Tel. 64391000, Fax 64390130. E-mail: huating@huating-hotel.com. Website: www.huating-hotel.com. $215-$330 for rooms, and $305-$1800 for suites. It has been offering 40% discounts. Take exit 5 from the Shanghai Stadium metro stop.*

Built in 1986, this 26-story hotel has 770 spacious rooms with large beds, voice mail and CNN, and Japanese, executive, and non-smoking floors. It has a 12.5-meter, year-round indoor pool, 11-piece gym, bowling and tennis, Cantonese, Sichuan, Shanghai, Japanese, Continental, and Asian food. There's a popular 24-hour American sit-down deli and a good shopping center.

Buffets are Y128 for breakfast, Y128 for lunch, and Y178 for dinner. Its ballroom seats 800 at a sit-down banquet. Its business center has international newspapers in English.

REGAL SHANGHAI EAST ASIA HOTEL (Foo Hao Dong Ya Jiudian), *666-800 Tian Yao Qiao Road, Xu Hui District, 200030. Four stars. Tel. 64266888, Fax 64265888. E-mail: rseah.info@regal-eastasia.com. Website: www.regal-eastasia.com. $160-$240 and $260-$650. Ask about a discount. E-mail: rseah-c@online.sh.cn. This is part of the Shanghai stadium.*

This 1997 hotel has 350 rooms with data ports, CNN, CNBC, and HBO. Guests in some rooms above the 10th floor can see into the stadium and have to pay extra if there's a game. It has non-smoking and executive club rooms, Japanese, Chinese and Western restaurants. The breakfast buffet costs Y88. Its 12th floor Sports Bar also has a view of events inside the stadium. The concierge should have a schedule of games and of the tour buses outside. It has aerobics, steam room, whirlpool and a 21-piece gym. Guests can use some of the facilities in the stadium, like the track, if available.

JIANGUO HOTEL (Binguan), *439 Caoxi Bei Road, 200030. Four stars. Tel. 64399299, Fax 64399714, 64398588 (reservations). E-mail: shjgbc@online.sh.cn. Website: www.jianguo.com. Y1100-Y1500 for rooms, Y2600-Y5600 for suites. It has been discounting 20-30%. Eleven km from the airport and eight km from the railway station. It is very close to the Xujiahui metro stop, four department stores, two computer malls, and across the street from the Jing Xuan Hotel and Catholic church.*

This hotel is within one kilometer of the Hua Ting Hotel towards the Orient Shopping Centre. Opened in 1991 and renovating executive floors in 2001, it has 23 stories and 473 rooms, most about 20 square meters. Guests can borrow a web-tv, and its in-room safe can fit a laptop. It has an eight-piece gym, CNN and HBO, Cantonese, Shanghai, Chaozhou and French food, and a 24-hour coffee shop. Some carpets are a little dirty, but it should be renovating soon. English might be a problem. Its business center has international newspapers in English. Shanghai New Asia Group

HUA TING GUEST HOUSE SHANGHAI (Hua Ting Binguan No. 2), *2525 Zhong Shan Xi Road, 200030. Three stars. Tel. 64391818, Fax 64390322. Reservation Fax: 64390416. E-mail: HTGHMO@sh163e.sta.net.cn. Y680 for rooms. Y1020-Y1300 for suites. It has been discounting 35%. This is not to be confused with its neighbor, the Hua Ting Hotel and Towers.*

Built in 1987, this 149-room hotel renovated all rooms recently. It has 17 stories and 149 rooms. There are non-smoking rooms, rooms with broadband internet access, CNN and HBO. Its standards and prices are not as high as its sister hotel next door. Guests here can use facilities next door but must pay cash.

In-Between Hotels

CROWNE PLAZA YINXING (Yin Xing Jia Re Jiudian), *400 Panyu Road, 200052. Four stars. Tel. 62808888, Fax 62803353. E-mail: cpsha@crowneplaza.com.cn. Website: www.cpshanghai.com (English). $210-$310 for rooms, and $400-$800 for suites. 15 km from the airport, 9 km from the railway station, and 5 km from the Hongqiao area. It is between the French Concession area and the Hongqiao area and 1.8 km from the Xu Jia Hu metro stop. This is the best hotel for the Shanghai film and television festivals theatre next door. It's in a residential neighborhood with supermarket, small restaurants, and an internet bar.*

Built in 1991-92, this hotel has 26 stories and 496 rooms, most of them 31 square meters. Rooms have safes, CNN, BBC, and HBO. It has executive and non-smoking floors, and rooms for wheelchair travelers, a good gym, good size indoor pool, steam bath, sauna, squash, and tennis. The lobby lounge offers international newspapers in English. It has Cantonese, Sichuan, Japanese, and international food, and 24-hour room service. Its bar claims the longest happy hour in town 11am-7pm. Children have a playground with free nanny service at lunch and for some kids, free food. An ATM is in the lobby. It has two video rooms and a video library. Ask about special rates for teens and seniors.

REGAL INTERNATIONAL EAST ASIA HOTEL, *516 Hengshan Road, 200030. Five stars. Tel. 64155588, Fax 64452755. E-mail: rieah@regal-eastasia.com. Website: www.regal-eastasia.com. $250-$340 for rooms and $700-$5000 for suites. It has been discounting 30 to 40%. This hotel is in a pleasant residential area, about a five minute walk to the Heng Shan Road metro stop and the Hengshan Road bars and restaurants. It is between the old French Concession area and the Shanghai Stadium.*

This 1997 hotel has 300 big rooms. It also has CNN, HBO and in-room safes, non-smoking rooms and executive floors. It looks good and is included primarily because of its eight outdoor and two indoor tennis courts with 1200-spectator seats. It also has a 25-meter heated pool, 12-lane bowling alley, golf simulator, squash, kung fu classes, and a 21-piece gym with a Versa Climber. It is ideal for athletic business people and tennis players. The buffet breakfast costs Y150. The English is good. The lunch buffet costs Y120, and dinner Y175. Its business center subscribes to the South China Morning Post. A Regal International Hotel.

Near the Hongqiao Exhibition Centre

The Hongqiao Development Zone (HQDZ) is the best location for hotels if you're involved with exhibitions there. It is less than 10 km from Hongqiao Airport and about 12 km from the train station and from the Bund. The closest subway stop is about three km away at Changning Road on No. 2 line. This area has a couple of exhibition centers, including the Shanghai Mart, for big trade shows. It also has some major government offices, luxury apartments, a recreation center, two department stores, a few consulates, restaurants, and several hotels: Sheraton Grand Tai Ping Yang (top), the Renaissance Yangtze Shanghai, then the Galaxy, and the Rainbow in that order of quality with the Sheraton best. In the neighborhood is Friends of the Earth Park, which is open daily at 6am and is good for joggers. It is beyond 18 lanes of traffic from the Renaissance, but there's an underpass. In addition to the Hongqiao area, this zone is close to restaurants and a giant department store in Gubei.

Towards the airport from here is a government guest house, the site of the Heineken Open (tennis), the zoo, antique furniture stores, the Marriott Hongqiao Hotel, and a growing number of expensive single-family houses. Airport buses leave every 30 minutes from the Renaissance Yangtze.

SHANGHAI MARRIOTT HONGQIAO, (Wanhao Hongqiao Dajiudian), *2270 Hongqiao Road, 200336. Five star standards. Tel. 62376000, Fax 62376275. E-mail: hkres@marriott.com. Website: www.marriotthotels.com. For North American reservations, Tel. 1-800/221-9290. $230-$300 for rooms; $400-$2500 for suites. It has been discounting 55%. This 315-room, eight-story hotel was opened in 2001. It is only three km from the Hongqiao airport but 55 km (about 45 minutes if non-stop) from the Pudong airport. In 2001, a taxi cost about Y35 from downtown, but cheap public buses outside are frequent. Bus 938 from the Hongqiao airport's domestic terminal goes by the door. Look for the Marriott and the Agricultural Exhibition Centre on the right side. For shopping in Gubei two km away, see Shopping below.*

Rooms have data ports, speaker phones, CNN, voice-mail and VOD. They have safes and are 32 to 35 square meters. It has non-smoking rooms, wheelchair enabled rooms, an executive floor, and international periodicals in English. Its breakfast buffet costs Y118, lunch Y128 and dinner Y138 in its 24-hour Atrium Café. There's a sports bar and a Manhattan steak house. Its ballroom can seat 600 at tables It has a good 23-piece gym, medium-sized year-round indoor pool and outdoor lighted tennis court.

SHERATON GRAND TAI PING YANG HOTEL, (Tai Ping Yang Da Fandian), *5 Zunyi Nan Road, 200336. Five stars. Tel. 62758888, Fax 62755420. E-mail: sheratongrand@uninet.com.cn Website: www.sheratongrand-shanghai.com. $210-$310 for rooms and $468-$2888 for suites. It has been giving 20-50% discounts.*

Opened in 1992 as a Westin hotel, this classy property became a Sheraton in January, 2002. It has 27 stories and 496 spacious rooms with safes, voice mail, a rubber ducky in the bathtub, and BBC, NBC, and HBO. All rooms have a swivel chair and an executive desk with three electrical outlets, and were renovated in 2001. It has non-smoking and executive floors with international newspapers in English. Club Level floors (22/F-26/F) require keycard access in the elevators. Expect especially good Italian and Japanese food, an English pub, deli, and 24-hour room service. Its dinner buffet costs Y158 and it can seat

500 people banquet style. There's a dress code and mobile telephone restriction in its food and beverage outlets. It has a good 21-piece gym and a small outdoor pool.

RENAISSANCE YANGTZE SHANGHAI HOTEL, (Yangtze Jiang Da Jiudian), *2099 Yan'an Xi Road, 200336. Four stars going on five. Tel. 62750000, Fax 62750750. Opened in 1990-91, this 34-story hotel upgraded its facilities in 2001. It is next to a super-highway.*

Its 570 rooms with data ports and safes, CNN and HBO, are mostly 28 square meters. It has non-smoking and executive floors, a gym, a spa, and small, year-round pool. It has Asian, Sichuan, Chaozhou and some of the best Cantonese food in town. Its ballroom seats 500 banquet style. It also has Cadillac limousines. Its business center subscribes to international newspapers in English and rooms receive five television channels in English. Its Western buffets are now Y128 for breakfast and Y168 for dinner. Its set Chinese breakfast is Y55-Y70. Dim sum in its Food Pavilion ranges from Y10-Y20 per basket.

GALAXY (Ying He Binguan), *888 Zhongshan Xi Road, 200051. Four stars. Tel. 62755888, Fax 62750039. E-mail: bc@galaxyhotel.com. Website: www.galaxhotel.com. $160-$200 for rooms and $260-$1000 for suites. It has been discounting 30%.*

Built in 1990, this hotel has 35 stories and 685 rooms with soft beds, CNBC, and 40-watt bulbs. Rooms are 16.5 square meters and have in-room safes above the 23rd floor. It has two lobbies, Cantonese, Sichuan and Korean food, a gym and bowling. No pool. Its breakfast buffet costs Y85. English might be a problem. Jin Jiang Group.

RAINBOW HOTEL (Hongqiao Binguan), *2000 Yan'an Xi Road, 200051. Four stars, Tel. 62753388, Fax 62757244 (reservations), 62753736 (guests). E-mail: info@rainbowhotel.net or rainbow@public.sta.net.cn. Website: www.rainbowhotel.net or www.cbw.com/hotel/rainbow. $150-$170 for rooms, $300-$600 for suites. It has been discounting 50%.*

Built in 1988, this 30-story hotel has 630 rooms, narrow halls and beds, and small bathrooms. It is clean and adequate with 40-watt bulbs, CITS airline ticket desk and Asiana airlines. It has non-smoking rooms, 24-hour room service, a small pool and old-style gym. Rooms are 20 square meters. Its buffet breakfast costs Y78, lunch Y68 and dinner Y68. English might be a problem. Jin Jiang Group.

The Airport-Cypress Hotels Area

These hotels are within two km of the airport and 19 km of the railway station. The closest to the airport is the International Airport Hotel. While it has fewer services, it looks cleaner and more cheerful. Both have co-operated with frequent shuttle buses from the airport.

CYPRESS HOTEL (Long Bai Fandian), *2419 Hongqiao Road, 200335. Four stars. Tel. 62688868, Fax 62681878, 62688007. E-mail:*

sales@cypresshotel.com. Website: www.cypresshotel.com. $140-$240 for rooms and $260-$400 for suites.

Built in 1982 and renovated in 1996, this hotel has six stories and 149 rooms, most about 15 square meters. They offer CNN and HBO. It is set in a vast garden. It has a China Eastern booking office, book store and recreation center with indoor pool, 13-machine gym, bowling, tennis, and squash. There's a lovely patio cafe, German food, smartly uniformed bell men, and flight monitors. It has non-smoking rooms. Book through SRS Reservations.

SHANGHAI INTERNATIONAL AIRPORT HOTEL (Guoji Ji Chang Binguan), *2550 Hongqiao Road, 200335. Three stars, Tel. 62688866, Fax 62688393, 62689455. E-mail: siahotel@online.sh.cn. Website: www.siah.com. $78-$120 for rooms. $224 for suites. It charges Y180 for a room for two hours. It is a five-minute walk from Hongqiao airport. A free airport shuttle bus is on request.*

Built in 1988, this hotel has eight stories and 308 small rooms with data ports. This transit hotel also has CNN, massage, and teppanyaki. Its buffet breakfast is Y88. Its internet costs Y20 for 30 minutes. There's no pool, no safe box, and no health club. There's a China Eastern ticketing office, flight departure monitors and free check-in for some China Eastern flights. A Japanese joint-venture (Chalon).

The Suburbs

The Novotel is better for long-staying guests and too far out for tourists. In spite of the Botanical Garden next door, the air isn't much better than downtown.

NOVOTEL SHANGHAI YUAN LIN (Yuan Lin Binguan), *201 Bai Se Road, Xuhui District, 200231. Three stars. Tel. 64701688, Fax 64700008. Reservations e-mail: asiapac.res@accor-hotels.com. Website: www.accorhotels-china.com/yuanlin. About $100-$120 for rooms. It is 15 km from Hongqiao airport, one hour from Pudong airport, 17 km from the railway station, and 16 km from the Bund. Free access to the Botanical Garden next door.*

Built in 1990, this six-story, 183-room hotel has a once-a-day shuttle bus to Xujiahui metro station (otherwise a Y38 trip by taxi to Nanjing Road), two non-smoking floors, CNN, and Star TV. It has an indoor pool, gym and tennis, and 40 Canadian-made villas.

Pudong

One of the best places to stay now for tourists is in Lujiazui near the Huangpu River. The setting is good and not crowded, the air is better, and the view of the Bund is great. Lujiazui is about 40 km/40-50 minutes by road from Pudong International Airport and 30km/25-30 minutes from Hong Qiao Airport.

The Shangri-La and the Grand Hyatt are the top hotels here with the best service, location, and English. The Grand Hyatt, currently the world's highest hotel, is exciting and overwhelming. The Shangri-La is more relaxing with equally great service. The Oriental Riverside is very good and was central to the top-level APEC meeting in 2001. (George W. Bush, Jean Chretien and other Asia-Pacific leaders were there.) All three are within walking distance of each other on or near the Huang Pu River. They are also steps from the Lujiazui metro station (two stops from People's Square), a vehicular tunnel and the quaint Yanan Road ferry. See "Pudong" below.

The pedestrian tunnel from the Bund exits close to the door of the Oriental Riverside/ International Convention Centre. There's also a large square full of good restaurants and bars nearby, and the new Super Brand Mall, the largest in Asia, should be partially open soon. And of course there's the Oriental Pearl Tower with the city's great History Museum.

The other hotel grouping in Pudong here (Purple Mountain and Holiday Inn Pudong) is near No. 2 line's Dongfang Road metro stop, two stops southeast of Lujiazui and within walking distance of shopping. This area is 35 km from the Pudong airport and 25 km from Hongqiao airport. The Novotel is by itself about a five-minute drive east of the Lujiazui metro stop.

GRAND HYATT, Jin Mao Tower, *88 Century Boulevard, 200121. Five stars. Tel. 50471234 or 50491234, Fax 50491111. E-mail: info@hyattshanghai.com. Website: www.shanghai.hyatt.com. Rooms are $320-$380 and suites $510-$4500. It has been discounting 44%.*

This amazing hotel has 555 guest rooms, all with views, and it extends from Reception on the 54th floor to the 87th floor. It has seven executive floors and 20 "grand rooms" with a 180-degree view. It has the world's highest bar, the highest gym, and the highest swimming pool. Its top is at an altitude of 420.5 meters, arrived at in less than one ear-popping minute. Look at the interior view from the top of its 33-story atrium. You can use a running machine and watch the ships below. Its lap pool is 16 meters long with a bird's eye panorama.

Rooms average 30 to 40 square meters. Each has an inter-active television with internet access, wired and wireless broadband connections, two telephone lines, voice mail and digital telephone. Each bathtub is either against a window or has a view. The bathrooms are huge with heated mirrors, glass sinks, and transparent scales. The business center never sleeps and provides a 24-hour technology concierge to help with computer problems. It also has video conferencing.

There are 12 classy restaurants and bars, some of which have different levels so every diner can see the Bund or Yangtze River. You have a choice of Cantonese, Japanese, Shanghai, and Western food. The Chinese restaurant has silver-tipped, cherry wood chopsticks and. 130 different labels are on its wine list. The Grand Café has an open kitchen with a lunch buffet at Y168, and dinner at Y188. High tea is Y88. A good meal could cost you Y300-350 per person, not including drinks. The hotel recommends that you reserve three days in advance for a window seat.

PUDONG SHANGRI-LA HOTEL (Pudong Shang Gorilla), *33 Fu Cheng Road, Pudong, 200120. Five stars. Tel. 68828888, Fax 68826688. E-mail: slpu@shangri-la.com. Website: www.shangri-la.com. $250-$370 for rooms and $490-$3500 for suites. It has been giving 40% discounts. (See China's Best Places to Stay.) This is next to the Huangpu Riverside Garden, the new super-mall, and is the closest of the riverside hotels to the ferry.*

This superb 1998 hotel has 606 large rooms, mostly 39 to 41 square meters. Rooms have data ports, kettles, safes, executive work desks, and CNN. It has high-speed internet access in its executive club or, on request. There's 24-hour room service, Japanese and Chinese restaurants, and an amazing entertainment center with metal menus and a different view of the world. Its popular, pillar-less grand ballroom can seat at least 1200 people at tables for banquets. Its buffet costs Y150 for breakfast or lunch, and about Y185 for dinner. It has a 20-piece 24-hour gym, a 20-meter-long indoor pool, tennis, Jacuzzi and steam bath. There is a world-class view of the Bund from its two-story high coffee shop, its lounge, ball room, pool, running machines, and Bund-side rooms. Its business center has international newspapers in English. It displays hundreds of paintings.

ORIENTAL RIVERSIDE HOTEL SHANGHAI AT THE SHANGHAI INTER-NATIONAL CONVENTION CENTER, *2727 Riverside Avenue, 200120. Five stars. Tel. 50370000, Fax 50370045, 50370999. Website: www.shicc.net. E-mail: hotel@shicc.net or sales@shicc.net. Look for the "SHICC" sign at the top of the building. It was first opened in 1999, became the Barcelo Grand in 2000, and in 2001, it was renamed the Oriental Riverside. Its 260 rooms range from $210 to $260, and suites from $360 to $3000. It has been giving 50% discounts.*

Most of the rooms in this 10-story hotel have views of the Bund and the Huangpu River. They are 30-35 square meters. Its large lobby has a copy of a Qin bronze chariot, European sculptures, and a Bank of China ATM. All rooms have separate shower and bath, safe, voice mail, data ports, CNN and HBO. Desks are small; windows are floor to ceiling and it has an executive floor. Its grand ballroom is the largest in Asia and able to accommodate 3000 at a sit-down banquet. It has simultaneous translation facilities for 10 languages. There are French and Chinese restaurants, and the breakfast buffet and lunch buffet are $15 each. Facilities such as the health club look good: 12-piece gym, mini-golf, indoor pool, and bowling. It has two outdoor tennis courts. Reserve through SRS.

PURPLE MOUNTAIN HOTEL (Zi Jin Shan Dajiudian), *778 Dongfang Road, Pudong New Area, 200122. Four star, Tel. 68868888, Fax 68868800. E-mail: pmhotel@prodigychina.com or shpmhd@online.sh.cn. Website: www.purplemountainhotel.com. $180-$220 for rooms, $280-$2880 for*

Pudong

Tourists should not ignore **Pudong**. Business people, of course, have already found it. Pudong is between the Huangpu River and the mouth of the Yangtze River. It is across the Huangpu from the famous Bund. In 1990, this community south and east of old Shanghai was nothing but rice fields and villages. The national government gave it first priority for economic development and you can see the results today. It is booming even now. Its major investors are from Hong Kong, Japan and the United States. Its annual growth rate in some areas has reached 30% to 50%. Its population is at least 1.6 million. Pudong hopes to exceed Hong Kong in importance.

You can get to Pudong by two vehicular tunnels (one more is planned), one pedestrian tunnel (two more are planned), two bridges, or by any of seven ferries. The best **ferry** for tourists is from the **Dong Chang Road Ferry Terminal** (Dong Chang Lu Ma Tou) near Yan'an Dong Road and the Bund. It disembarks about 300 meters south of the Shangri-La Hotel. The ferry operates 24 hours and costs Y1 for a return trip, payable on the Puxi side, a nice reminder that all is not glitz and high prices in this burgeoning city. The trip is short and passengers stand. The river here is only 360 meters wide.

The ferry and nearby **Huangpu Riverside Garden** are highly recommended for seeing the lights on the Bund. The ferry operates 24 hours a day every 20 minutes. The 647 meter-long pedestrian tunnel goes between Nanjing Dong Road (across from the Peace Hotel) near the statue of Mayor Chen Yi to the Oriental Riverside Hotel and Oriental Pearl TV Tower in five minutes. You sit in cars and watch a weird light show for Y20 one way, Y30 return. Children are charged half-price. On the Pudong side, it exits just outside the door of the Oriental Riverside Hotel. It operated Monday through Thursday from 9am to 9:30pm, and from Friday to Sunday from 9am to 10:30pm. There is an elevator for wheel-chair people and an escalator.

The metro should soon link the two airports. Pudong International Airport is the largest airport in China. Pudong already has Asia's biggest department store (Yaohan/New Age/Babaiban), its highest television tower, the world's tallest building, and the Shanghai Stock Exchange. Hotels like the Shangri-La can arrange visits to the Stock Exchange or you can telephone *68808888*. It's at 528 Pudong Nan Road.

Pudong is a planned city with lots of open park space, and hotels here are 30 minutes drive from either airport.

suites. *Price includes a good breakfast buffet. Discounts have been 30%-40%. It is also within walking distance of local restaurants and is close to the New Age shopping center and a cheap internet bar. (See below.)*

This 46-story, 400-room hotel is between the Holiday Inn and the Inter-Continental Hotel. It has an airport shuttle bus, CNN, CNBC, and a 24-hour coffee shop. The service is good. There's a delicatessen and a good convenience store with a microwave. The view is great and when it's not foggy or smoggy, you can see the Huangpu River and the Jin Mao Tower. It has a four-lane bowling alley with shoe rentals and an eight-machine gym. Its business center offers recent editions of international periodicals in English.

HOLIDAY INN PUDONG SHANGHAI (Pudong Jia Ri Jiudian), *899 Dong Fang Road, Pudong, 200122. Four stars. Tel. 58306666, Fax 58305555. E-mail: hipudong@public6.sta.net.cn. Website: www.holiday-inn.com. $180-$240 for rooms and $240-$1,200 for suites.*

This 1998, 32-story, 320-room hotel has room safes, three executive floors, and room data ports. Rooms are 30-32 square meters and some have internet TV with keyboards. It has airport shuttle service, 24-hour room service, non-smoking floor, and seven floors of office space for rent. Enjoy its Irish pub, Chinese, Mediterranean, and Shanghai food. Its ballroom can seat 500 banquet style. There's a gym, aerobics room, Jacuzzi, steam room and indoor pool. Its Deli Corner has apple pie, Black Forest cake, and lemon meringue pie. Its breakfast buffet has been Y88, lunch Y88, and dinner Y88. Rooms receive CNN, NBC, MTV, HBO, and National Geographic.

NOVOTEL ATLANTIS (Hai Shen Nuofute Dajiudian), *728 Pu Dong Avenue, 200120. Four stars. Tel. 50366666, Fax 50366677. E-mail: novotela@online.sh.cn. Website: www.accorhotels-china.com/atlantis. Elsewhere contact any Accor/Novotel Reservation Service. This 2000 hotel is on the 30th to 50th floors of a 50-story office tower with 300 parking spaces and a good view of the harbor. Rooms are $160-$220 and suites $240-$1800. Its discount has been about 40%.*

Rooms in this hotel are mainly 28 to 33 square meters. Its 303 rooms have voice mail, two data ports, safes, and some have interactive web TVs. It has four executive floors, non-smoking rooms, and a ladies floor. There's a heated 25-meter long indoor pool, aerobics room, and a good gym. Its revolving restaurant has a good-looking fine-dining room with Art50, a gallery of contemporary Chinese or western paintings. Its coffee shop is open 24 hours and on weekends has a children's corner. Its breakfast buffet costs Y68, its dinner buffet costs Y158 and it has a cigar bar. Its fun pub is called Hot Stock, but its monitors have drink rather than stock prices. It has a delicatessen with French pastries, and a Mediterranean restaurant. The décor is Scandinavian with nautical touches. An Accor Hotel.

Where to Eat

Every hotel, four-stars and up, should be able to lay on a great Chinese banquet but if you want to impress anybody, take them to the Pudong Shangri-La, Portman Ritz-Carlton, or Grand Hyatt. These same three hotels are also tops for Western food. The JC Mandarin and Renaissance Yangtze are exceptional for Cantonese. Best, and also prestigious, among the Western or fusion restaurants are M on the Bund and T8 in Xintiandi. Many restaurants no longer serve just Shanghai, Cantonese or Western food. They offer a mixture of styles on the same menu and plates.

Districts with rows of interesting restaurants are on Heng Shan Road, in Xintiandi (more trendy and Western) in a wide price range, and around the Jin Jiang and Okura Garden Hotels.

The following groupings are roughly in order of distance from the Bund although Pudong is a separate section.

Shanghai Cuisine

The local food is sweeter, lighter and prettier than other Chinese cuisines. It has a delicate consistency. See Chapter 11 and 25. See also Pudong below.

MEILONGZHEN, *Nanjing Xi Road, 22 Lane 1081, Tel. 62566705, about 100 meters east of the JC Mandarin Hotel.*

This is the old-tried-and-true. It is especially good for the famous hairy crabs in November and dumplings, moderate prices, and is open 11am-2pm and 5pm-9:30pm

LU BO LANG RESTAURANT, *10 Wen Chang Road, (18 meters south of the Seven-Bend Bridge near Old Town Temple and Starbucks), Yuyuan Garden, Tel. 63550500, 63554408. Open 7am-10am, 11am-1:45pm, and 2pm-4:30pm. Afternoon tea 5pm-10pm. It accepts credit cards.*

This famous restaurant is great for typical Shanghai snacks. You can get a sample of 12 different dumplings and cakes, enough for a light lunch. The service however is slow.

NANXIANG STEAMED BUNS RESTAURANT, *85 Yuyuan Garden Road. Open 7am-5:30pm and 6pm-8pm. Tel. 63554206.*

This famous restaurant only serves steamed buns and they are delicious. Its specialty is crab buns. Go to its second floor and ask for its set menu "tao chan" for Y60 unless you don't mind waiting a long time.

HONGQIAO REN JIA ("Hongqiao Household"), *2 Zunyi Road, Tel. 62330200, 62743563. Open 9:30am to 10:30pm daily. No credit cards.*

This is within sight of the Sheraton Grand Hotel and is very popular with locals, noisy and modest. The menu is in English and Chinese with red flags beside its most popular dishes and red chilies beside the few spicy ones. Dumplings (crab and pork) were delicious for Y28. They charged Y2 extra for tea, and Y2 for the unordered peanuts and beans on the table. Opened in 1998, it has rattan furniture and smells of Chinese wine. Among its popular dishes are green crab in liquor Y58, marinated pork Y22, pomfret with lemon sauce Y18, duck with soya sauce Y25, and frog with Chinese tea Y28. Beer was about Y10. Other dishes on its extensive menu included donkey meat, and sushi. The fried king prawns were Y25 and were delightful.

Other Chinese Cuisines

PHOENIX AND DRAGON RESTAURANT, *Chinese. 8/F, Peace Hotel, 20 Nanjing Dong Road. Tel. 63216888, Fax 63290300, 63297979.*

Its convenient and historical location on the Bund is the main attraction. There's also a good view of Pudong but the windows are small. The menu is good and the food a mix of styles. Roast Cantonese duck is Y56 and Y112. Smoked pomfret in Shanghai soy sauce Y76 and Y152. Diced chicken with cashew nuts in hot sauce Y50 and Y100. Sliced crocodile Sichuan style Y150. It uses MSG in many dishes.

PEACH GARDEN RESTAURANT. *Cantonese. JC Mandarin Hotel, 1225 Nanjing Xi Road. Tel. 62791888, Fax 62791822.*

The dim sum includes deep-fried yam dumplings (lacy and crispy on the outside, and gooey inside), steamed rice rolls with dough fritters Y18, steamed dumpling with minced pork Y20, Shanghai style crab meat dumplings in superior soup Y34, and classic shrimp dumplings Y30. Chefs add "a little" MSG.

FU RONG ZHEN SICHUAN RESTAURANT, *Crowne Plaza Hotel, 388 Panyu Road, Tel. 62808888. Accepts credit cards.*

This Sichuan restaurant has had perfect dan-dan noodles. It has better Sichuan food than some restaurants in Chongqing. Try the sliced pork with garlic sauce, deep-fried shrimp with chili sauce, tea-smoked duck with dumpling, shredded chicken with Sichuan sauce, or boiled beef with chili and onions. You can request different degrees of hot spices.

DYNASTY RESTAURANT, *Cantonese. Renaissance Yangtze Hotel, 2099 Yan'an Xi Road, 200336. Tel. 62750000, Fax 62750750.*

The Dynasty is open for lunch and dinner. The Yangtze also has a cheaper food "pavilion" where you can get a good set Cantonese breakfast for Y55 or Y70, dim sum from Y8 to Y22 a basket, noodles Y22 to Y28, and congee Y5 to Y32.

TIE MU ZHEN. *Mongolian barbecue. Qing Xiang Co, 33 Chao-Bao Road, Tel. 64360126, 11am-2pm and 5pm-8pm. This is south of the Hua Ting Hotel. You should make reservations. Credit cards accepted.*

This is a favorite with tourist groups and it's not authentically Chinese. But how can you go wrong with barbecue when you pick your own ingredients and sauces? Prices are moderate for individuals but cheap for groups of 10 or more. You might not enjoy its factory-like atmosphere, noise, and noon-hour line-ups, nor the over-priced up-market shopping that is next door.

Foreign Cuisines

Try any of the top hotels. The Sheraton Grand and Hilton have great Italian restaurants and a choice of over 100 wines, mostly French in the Sheraton Grand's Giovanni's restaurant, Tel. 62758888. The Giovanni also has good US sirloin steak with arugula and fine herbs for Y136, and grilled US beef tenderloin for Y149. The grill room in the Garden Hotel is great. So is the Manhattan Steak House in the Marriott Hongqiao and Palladio in the Portman Ritz-Carlton.

Restaurants here are listed geographically from the Bund almost to the airport. See also geographical groupings. M on the Bund is a place for anniversaries and popping the question.

M ON THE BUND 7/F, *Continental. No. 5 The Bund, (entrance on Guangdong Road), Tel. 63509988, Fax 63220099. Website: www.m-onthebund.com. Credit cards accepted.*

The setting is magnificent at this restaurant. You must be here at dusk to watch the lights come on. Bring a camera. You can dine on its terrace (if you make a reservation on time and the weather cooperates). The food is wonderful. One of us ate a warm salad of smoked goose breast and orange segments tossed in a plum sauce for Y178. Another had hot house-smoked salmon with Dutch cucumber salad for Y174. A third ordered slowly-baked, salt-encased selected leg of lamb with roasted root vegetables for Y168, and a fourth had crispy suckling pig for Y148. All these dishes lived up to its reputation as one of the best restaurants in Shanghai. It was pretty special.

PALLADIO, *Italian. The Portman Ritz-Carlton Hotel, Shanghai Centre, 1376 Nanjing Xi Road, Tel. 62797188.*

Its mozzarella comes direct from Italy and it has over 130 wines and liqueurs, mostly Italian. Popular there are: pan fried goose liver on soft polenta Y120, squid ink risotto with gold leaf Y100, and pan-fried cod Y178. Its pesto had green olives, basil, olive oil, garlic, pine nuts, salt, pepper, and Pecorino cheese and was out of this world. Its outstanding goose liver was served with a glass of Gewurztraminer wine vinegar, a delicious and interesting novelty to help digestion. Dessert can be a light, hot chocolate pudding with caramelized orange and caramel ice cream Y70. Coffee or tea was Y40. If you're not too busy eating, look at the antique Italian décor and the staff uniforms designed by Stefano Ricci.

THE HARD ROCK CAFÉ, *American. Shanghai Centre, Suite A05 & 110, 1376 Nanjing Xi Road, 11am-2am, Sunday-Thursday, and 11am-3am Friday-Saturday. Tel. 62798133.*

The Hard Rock here seems to be better than in Beijing. It has reasonably-priced set lunches, burgers, pizzas and tee-shirts.

MALONE'S AMERICAN CAFÉ, *near the Shanghai Centre, 257 Tong Ren Road, Tel. 62472400.*

You can't get any more American than this place.

TONY ROMA'S, *American. Shanghai Centre, Tel. 62797129. Open 11am-10:30pm. Credit cards.*
Expensive-but-worth-it ribs but also burgers, sandwiches and salads.
ATRIUM CAFÉ, *Shanghai Hilton Hotel, 250 Hua Shan Road, Tel. 62480000.*
Good food, and live band.
MANHATTAN STEAK HOUSE, *Shanghai Marriott Hongqiao, 2270 Hongqiao Road. Tel. 62376000, Fax 62376275. E-mail: hkres@marriott.com. Open 5:30pm-10:30pm.*

A New York Caesar salad costs Y45, spinach salad Y30, oysters Rockefeller Y105, Manhattan clam chowder Y47, prime rib roasted on the bone Y175-Y198-Y238, a New York strip steak Y188, a large T-bone Y318, New York cheesecake Y38, and baked Alaska Y40.

Xintiandi

You must at least walk through this neighborhood. To get there while avoiding traffic jams, take the metro to Huangpi Nan Road station. Once there, you start asking for Xintiandi, Tai Cang Lu and Madang Lu. A good place to meet friends is in front of, or in, Starbucks. The best restaurant here is T-8. While you're in this area, drop in at **Xavier** for innovative scarves, jewelry, feathered hats, and purses. *Tel. 63287111, Fax 63287333.*

LATINA RESTAURANT, *Brasilian and barbecue. Xintiandi Plaza, Lane 169 Taicang Road, Bldg. 18-20. Tel. 63203566. E-mail: latina@prodigycn.com.* Churrasco and soup, rice and fries Y68. Dinner buffet Y98.

LUNA, *Western. 15,16, 25 Lane 169, Tai Cang Road. Tel. 63361717. Fax 63361777. Takes credit cards. Live music evenings.*

We loved the pizza here, but some of our friends didn't. Soups were Y28-32. (The pumpkin soup was special., Middle Eastern with cumin and coriander. Good also was the green pea with mint yogurt.) Salads are Y35-Y38, appetizers Y38-Y67, pizza Y50-Y68, pastas Y48-Y67, and main courses Y55-Y68. Desserts: crepe Moroccaine (dates, cinnamon and orange) Y35, and Catalan crème brulee (soft egg custard with caramelized brown sugar) Y32. They were all as good as they sound.

KABB, *American. House 5, North Block, Tai Cang Road. Tel. 33070798.*

T8 RESTAURANT BAR AND CLUB, *Western and Asian fusion. 8 Xintiandi North Part, Lane 181 Tai Cang Road. Tel. 63558999. Fax 63114999. This is on a narrow alley but there are signs. Lunch is 11:30am to 2:30pm except on Tuesdays. Dinner is 6:30pm to 10:30pm with the last drink at midnight. It takes credit cards.*

The furnishings are modern Japanese, dramatic and tasteful. You can watch the cooking. One of us had citrus and black pepper blinis, sugar-cured salmon, with avocado salsa and egg yolk caviar dressing. The other had the Sichuan seared king prawns, garlic cream, mixed cress and crab spring roll.

There was also slow-cooked lamb and Sichuan pie, yellow curry coriander bisque and onion jam. They were very good, and not overly expensive.

Near the Jin Jiang and Garden Hotels

TANDOOR, *Indian. 59 Mao Ming Nan Road (in the Jin Jiang Hotel, Food Street), Tel. 64725494, 62582582 X 9301. It is open 11:30am-2pm and 5:30pm-10:30pm.*

This is a beautiful looking restaurant, in tasteful Indian style. Prices are moderate. Appetizers Y38, soup Y38-Y40, barbecue Y60-Y95, meat Y70-Y95, vegetable curries Y58, breads Y12-Y18, rice Y50-Y75, side dishes Y20 and desserts Y40.

BAR 1931 RESTAURANT, *Asian. 112 Mao Ming Nan Road, Tel. 64725264. Open 11am-2am. No credit cards.*

This pleasant cozy little place tries to duplicate the ambience of the 1930s with old Shanghai posters, shoes for bound feet, and an old Victrola. It has color-coordinated table settings. The menu was Asian. Deep-fried duckling slice Beijing-style was Y55, cold noodles with Japanese sauce Y35, and Yuyuan Garden fried dumpling eight pieces for Y28. It's a nice quiet place for a drink.

C'EST LA VIE *(sanlewei faguo canting), French. 207-4 Mao Ming Road at Fuxing Road, Tel. 64159567. E-mail sanlewei@hotmail.com. Open 6:30pm-11:30pm. Closed on Sunday. (Other times on request.) Credit cards accepted.*

This is a very charming auberge with superb food. Popular in autumn has been the chestnut soup for Y45 and goose liver trilogy appetizer for Y145. Main courses are served with five kinds of vegetables and you should consider the pan-fried duck breast for Y140 or poached red snapper filet for Y140. For dessert you have a choice of five which could include the homemade choux pastry stuffed with homemade ice cream topped with chocolate sauce for Y55. You can choose from 50 French wines. It has a menu in English.

SANDOZ PORTUGUESE RESTAURANT, *Portuguese and Macanese food. 207 Mao Ming Nan Road, Tel/Fax 64660479. 11:30am-11pm. Credit cards accepted.*

Curried crab Y108, cod Y83, baby back ribs Y88, and African chicken Y52. It has a good reputation.

HAZARA, *Indian, No. 4 Building, Ruijin Guest House, 118 Ruijin Road. Tel. 64664328. Accepts credit cards. Open 5:30pm-10:30pm Sunday-Thursday, and to 11pm Friday and Saturday.*

This restaurant in Indian shamiana décor has carved wooden pillars and wicker chairs. Some consider it the best Indian food in town. Among its popular dishes are: Punjabi samosas Y53, raan e hazara (lamb) Y173, and dhaal hazara (lentils) Y88.

FACE, *Northern Thai. No. 4 Building, Ruijin Guest House, 118 Ruijin Road. Tel. 64664328. E-mail lanna@uninet.com.cn. Accepts credit cards. The Face bar is open noon to 2am daily with a happy hour 5-8pm. Lan Na Thai is open*

11:30am to 2:30pm daily, and 5:30pm to 10:30 (last order on Sunday to Thursday) and to 11pm (Friday and Saturday).

Among its popular dishes are tod man goong (prawn cake) Y55, tom yam goong (prawn soup) Y50, and pla kaow sam rod (fried grouper with sweet and spicy sauce) Y140.

Heng Shan Road

Restaurants and bars here are roughly between the Heng Shan Rd. and Changshu Rd. metro stations. They offers a wide variety of national cuisines. During warm weather, tables move out into its patios and balconies.

A THOUSAND AND ONE NIGHTS RESTAURANT, *Middle Eastern. 4 Heng Shan Road, Tel. 64731178, 64738289. WEBSITE: www.1001nights.com.cn. It is open 11am-2am, and a belly dancer performs 7:30pm-11pm daily.*

Among its appetizers, tabouli costs Y40-Y80, hummus Y25-Y50, falafel Y25, fried kibbeh (lamb and pine nuts) Y35, and kabobs (minced lamb barbecue) Y48. Pita is Y5 for three pieces, and Tushka is Y48. Fresh juices are Y10-Y25, and Arabic coffee Y20. The décor, the cook and boss are Syrian.

MR. STONE, *Australian. 2/F, No. 4, Heng Shan Road. Tel. 6473666, Fax 64739672. Saturday to Thursday 11:30am-11:30pm. Friday 11:30am-12:30 midnight. Accepts credit cards.*

You cook your own U.S. or Australian steak on a 400 C stone. For Y168 you get a top grade sirloin with salad, soup, bread, fruit or coffee. 750ml of Australian wine costs Y345 and French Y548. It also has Spanish, South African, Italian and California wines. Live music flows 7-10pm.

BOURBON STREET, *Cajun/Creole. 191 Hengshan Road, Tel. 64457556. E-mail: sfc@uninet.com.cn.*

This claims the longest bar in Shanghai, and home-cooking by a Baton Rouge chef. There is also a walk-in humidor for cigar smokers and Cuban cigars are available. Happy hour is 4-8pm. Cajun gumbo is Y30-Y55, jambalaya Y75, shrimp creole Y65, and Louisiana crab cakes Y40.

SASHA'S, *Fusion. House 11, 9 Dong Ping Road (at Heng Shan Road), Tel. 64746166, Fax 64746170. Credit cards accepted. Open 6pm-11:30pm, with bar 10am-2am.*

Sasha's setting is as interesting as its menu. Built in the 1920s for a Jewish taipan, the house was also lived in by Chiang Kai-shek and owned by his in-laws the Soong's. Jiang Qing, Chairman Mao's widow, also used it for her theatricals. The bar is on the ground floor; the main dining room is on the second. The food has unusual flavors and tastes good. Starters are Y55-Y72, soups Y40-Y78, salads and pastas Y58-Y105, main courses Y128-Y240, grill Y200-Y240 and desserts Y50-Y110. There's a long wine list – including French, Spanish, Australian, Italian, and Californian. The wooden-latticed interior with white marble table tops is unusual and charming.

COCHINCHINA, *Vietnamese, Block 11, 889 Julu Road near Chang Shu Road, Tel. 64456797. Open 11am-11pm. Reservations recommended.*

It has a patio and balcony. This is one of the restaurants in a row of beautiful old mansions. The interior has been done in gracious 19th century colonial Indo-Chinese style and should be visited for the setting if not for the food. It accepts credit cards. Its mixed Vietnamese appetizer is Y98, king prawn sour soup Y38, mango chicken salad Y48, chicken curry with French bread Y50, steamed whole fish topped with aromatic herbs Y98, salt and pepper soft shelled crab Y98, and fried banana with vanilla ice cream Y28.

SIMPLY THAI, *5-C Dong Ping Road, Tel. 64459551, fax 54560972. Open 10:30-2:30, and 6pm-10:30pm. It serves afternoon tea 2:30pm-4:30pm for Y35. Credit cards accepted and reservations needed on weekends.*

You can choose different chili levels. Tom yam soup is Y38, phad si you gai for two is Y48, Thai papaya salad Y40, green curry kang kiaw wan Y48, and thod mun pia fried fish cake Y48. The atmosphere is very modest and casual.

Pudong

Food at the Hyatt and the Shangri-La has been great. Try also the Novotel. You can get cheaper and almost as good in the Lujiazui food corner between the Hyatt and the Shangri-La Hotels.

SHANG PALACE, *Cantonese. Shangri-La Pudong Hotel, 33 Fu Cheng Road, Pudong, Tel. 68828888.*

All Shang Palaces in this Hong Kong hotel chain have superb and expensive Cantonese cooking. Try the barbecued meat combo, hot-sour soup, pan-fried chicken, braised Shanghai cabbage, and stir-fried sliced beef with peaches and vegetables. It accepts credit cards.

XIAO NAN GUO RESTAURANT, *Shanghai-Cantonese. No. 2, 17 Yinchengxi Rd., Lujiazui Food Corner, on the street closest to the Shangri-La Hotel. Tel. 58877000. Accepts Visa cards. Open 11am-2pm and 5pm-9pm (last order).*

Braised bean curd with crab Y48, fried shrimp Y88, spicy Sichuan chicken Y28, and noodles Y15-Y25. It is very popular, has moderate prices and photos of dishes on its menu. Waiter Tong Jie speaks English.

ALI BABA'S DONER KEBAB, *Middle Eastern. Shop 57, Building 5, Lujiazui Food Corner, 17 Yin Cheng Xi Road. Tel. 50541411.*

Nan, thin slices of barbecued lamb, baklava (honey pastries) and raki! Prices are moderate and the ambience simple. Credit cards accepted.

FOOD LIVE, *Asian. Basement. Jin Mao Tower, 88 Century/Shiji Dadao Boulevard. Tel. 50471234 or 50491234.*

Great for cheap food is the basement of the Grand Hyatt where you can get Hyatt-supervised food like Cantonese barbecued duck and pork with rice, cold vegetables and a soft drink for about Y21. Other stalls have Hainan chicken, fried chicken, noodles and congee, with entrees ranging from Y10 to Y20. Toilets are pretty good too.

Cheaper Eats & Fast Food

Most department stores and some office buildings have food courts. My favorite is the basement of the Jin Mao Tower in Pudong above. There's a **Delifrance** in Central Plaza at 381 Huai Hai Zhong Road, *Tel. 53825171.* No cards. Look in *Where to Stay* for hotels with delicatessens. Bake shops are everywhere.

Pizza Hut is in the Gubei Carrefour Mall, see "Shopping." It will deliver within three kilometers. *Tel. 68671100.* **Subway** is in the Sincere Building basement next to the Sofitel on 479 Nanjing Pedestrian Street, *Tel. 63220570.* It is open 9am-11pm. It has sandwiches for Y15-Y30, and soda and chips for Y25. Noodle and dumpling restaurants are cheap. Supermarkets and convenience stores are everywhere, some with microwaves. You won't starve.

Seeing the Sights

Refer to the map on pages 274-275 for major sights in this section.

The riverside embankment known as **The Bund** and its neighboring 19th century European buildings are Shanghai's signature. Tell taxi drivers "Zhongshan Dong Lu." It starts where Suzhou Creek flows into the Huangpu River and then goes south to Jinling Road, a distance of about 1500 meters.

The Bund is busy with sightseers and taiji people mornings and evenings, but it was even more active between the mid-19th and mid-20th centuries when 240 foreign banks flourished here. Look at the grandeur of the Bank of China's lobby and the Greek columns of the Customs House. Look into the Pudong Development Bank, which used to be the Hongkong and Shanghai Bank building. It has some marvelous 1923 mosaic murals of London, New York, and Paris, cities where the bank also had branches. Historical plaques are posted outside important buildings. You can also ask the Peace Hotel public relations department for a tour.

The elevated walkway beside the river is being extended north for three kilometers, and south beyond Yan'an Road. If you walk from the Peace Hotel to Yan'an Road, you can go on about the same distance to Yuyuan Garden. For historical reasons, you might want to visit Huangpu Park, the oldest and smallest park in the city. It is at the junction of Suzhou Creek and the Huangpu River, across the bridge from Shanghai Mansions. Created in 1868 by the British, and next to the Suzhou and Huangpu Rivers, this once displayed the infamous sign 'No Dogs and Chinese Allowed.'

The best time to see the Bund is late afternoon so you can stay to see the lights paint the buildings on both sides of the river. They come on from about 7pm until 10pm depending on the season. The best place to see them is from the restaurant M on the Bund. You might also want to take the ferry from the

Your Choice of Views

To see the whole city at a glance, you have to get above the forest of skyscrapers. The observation platform at the **Jin Mao Tower** is higher than that at the Oriental Pearl Tower. If you don't want to also see the History Museum, the Jin Mao view is cheaper. Its Observation Deck is at 340.1 meters and costs Y50 for an adult and Y25 for students. This is open 8:30am-9pm daily and is at 88 Shiji Avenue, *Tel. 50475101. E-mail: tour@jinmao88.com.* These two competing towers are a five minutes walk from each other in Pudong. See also Grand Hyatt Hotel above.

The **Oriental Pearl Television Tower** (Dongfang Ming Zu), 2 Lane 504 Jujiazui Road. *Tel. 58791888, 58827333,* open 8am-9:30pm. Y70. At 468 meters, it has been the tallest such structure in Asia and the third highest in the world but the observation deck is only at 263 meters. You can see this tower as you look east on Nanjing Road. It has an elevator, hotel rooms, revolving restaurant and a bar as well. In its basement is the **Shanghai History Museum**.

You can also get a free view by taking the elevator to the lobby of the Grand Hyatt.

south end of the Bund to Pudong, walk north to the riverside park or any of the hotels there, and then return by metro or pedestrian tunnel.

Shanghai History Museum, Oriental Pearl Tower, *Tel. 58791888X80444.* Open 8am-9:30pm. Expect to pay Y70 even though you might not want to go up the tower. In 2001, there weren't any separate tickets. This exciting museum is down one flight of stairs. Keep asking for "bo wu guan" and look for a hallway off the circular room downstairs. An Acoustiguide costs Y30. The city began as a village 6000 years ago. Shanghai County was born in 1291. The museum has models of farmers, blacksmiths, and merchants. Its herb store smells authentic. Its European inhabitants are sympathetic, not caricatures. You see movies of people projected in proper scale onto models of alleys, a brilliant technique. You can compare a scale model of the buildings on the Bund in the 1930s to the Bund today. You should look for yourself in a movie of old Shanghai amid old mansions. Most signs are in English.

The excellent **Shanghai Museum**, with one of the world's best collections of Chinese antiquities, is in People's Square, 201 Renmin Avenue, 200003, *Tel. 63270276, Fax 63728522.* It is open Monday through Friday, 9am-5pm, no admissions after 4pm; and Saturdays 9am-8pm, with no admissions after 7pm. Admission is Y60 which includes a recommended "Acoustiguide," Y20 otherwise. You have to leave your passport or a Y400 deposit for an Acoutiguide. From the outside, this five-story building looks like a giant Chinese bronze with four huge handles, its shape symbolizing that heaven is round and earth is square. The exhibits are well lit and signs are in English and Chinese, galleries full of marvelous bronzes, Buddhist statues, fine porcelains, paintings, minority costumes, and furniture. Look for the Tibetan skulls and demon masks, the polished mirrors, and Qianlong's jade wine goblet. Nearby in the square is the **Grand Theatre**, especially beautiful at night. Underneath People's Square is the **Hong Kong Mall** (Di Tie Shang Cheng), with decent clothes shopping, supermarket, bakery, and tourist information.

If you like temples, visit the **Jade Buddha Temple**, 170 Anyuan Road, Puto District, *Tel. 62663688*. It is open daily, 8am-5pm, but closed for lunch at noon. This is a good introduction to Buddhist temples, but nearby Suzhou has better, older and less crowded ones. The Jade Buddha Temple was built in 1882 in the southern outskirts of Shanghai. It was bodily moved to Shanghai in 1918 and now occupies about two acres in the western part of the city. Many monks live in this temple, and you might hear them reading the scriptures.

In the first hall, a 2.6-meter-high, gold-faced Wei Tuo, the military protector of the Buddhist scriptures, menacingly greets visitors. On each side are two temple guardians. The three largest figures inside the next parallel building are Sakyamuni (center), to his right the Amitaba Buddha (with lotus), and the Yuese Buddha, carrying the Buddhist wheel of law. Along the sides are the 20 guardians of heaven. Guanyin is centered behind the three main Buddhas. Note the very thin Sakyamuni, above, paying homage, and the 18 arhats or saints.

On the second floor the seated 1.9-meter-high Jade Buddha, carved from one piece of white jade in Burma, was brought to China in 1882. The shelves on both sides of the room contain 7240 volumes of Buddhist scriptures, printed in the Qing 200 years ago. In another building is a Reclining Buddha, also of white jade.

There's also the **Jingan Temple**, 1686 Nanjing Xi Road, *Tel. 62566366*. Open 7:30-4:45. This is close to the Hilton Hotel and is a real, functioning temple too. It can be full of worshippers, candles burning in front of photographs of the recently deceased. Please respect the feelings of the mourners. It was first built in 246 AD. The current buildings are Qing dynasty. Xintiandi was opened in 2001 and constructed with strong elements of "shikumen" architecture, so typical of old Shanghai. It's best to walk there in the evening to enjoy the lights on the buildings. It is one of the most beautiful and successful fusions of traditional culture and modernity in China. It offers upscale boutiques, bars and restaurants and is close to the site of the First National Congress of the Communist Party, an interesting and ironic contrast. For directions, see Xintiandi under *Where to Eat* above.

The **Museum of Ancient Chinese Sex Culture** is at 1133 Wu Ding Road, *Tel. 62301243. Website: www.7cv.com (in Chinese only)*. This unusual museum is open 10am to 6pm daily and the entrance fee is Y30. It covers over 5000 years of cultural history in a tasteful way. It has over 1200 objects collected by Prof. Liu Dalin. These include objects of worship, esoteric Tibetan statues, porcelain couples performing sex acts (for educational purposes), and ancient erotic paintings. There is also a 3000 or 5000 year old artificial penis. (Sources at the museum differ.)

The ***Yuyuan Garden**, Yuyuan Road, *Tel. 63260830*, is a major tourist attraction. Open daily, 8:30am-4:30pm, Y20. Should you see it if you are also going to the gardens of Suzhou? It depends on how much time you have and how much you like gardens. This one is pretty good, but it is crowded in the mornings. It was originally laid out between 1559 and 1577 by a financial official from Sichuan and now covers 20,000 square meters.

The top of Rockery Hill was until recently the highest point in the city from which you could see the Huangpu River nearby. Five dragons top the wall that winds around the garden. Look for their heads. Note the unusually-shaped doors, and of course, the lovely moon gates. The south side of the garden was for aristocratic women, kept out of sight of all but family members.

About 100 years ago, part of the garden became the 98-shop **Yuyuan Market**, once the busiest in the city and still bustling. Its recently built Chinese-style architecture helps make this a fun place to visit. In the market you can buy buttons and silk ribbons, hair clips, vests and beautiful European-type dolls. You can watch jiao zi and other Chinese dumplings being made. It is a good place for souvenirs. **Lao Jie** or Old Street is a pedestrian mall with a fantastic antique market, especially on weekends. Take a peek at the old **Huxin Ting Tea House**, *Tel. 63736950*, the most famous tea house in the city and learn about this Chinese institution. Count the number of local women here.

At least four **water towns** with old architecture are near Shanghai and Suzhou. A visit is a wonderful contrast to the glass walls and crowds of Shanghai. You can get short boat rides on canals in them all. My first recommendation would be Wuzhen if you want to see demonstrations and people in period dress. My second would be Zhujiajiao because it's more interesting than Tongli. I would not recommend Zhouzhuang village. It's too commercial, expensive, and touristy.

Wuzhen in north Zhejiang province has narrow streets and canal boat rides, but it also has demonstrations of wine-making and fabric-dyeing. It is a two-hour drive from Shanghai and 1.5 hours from Hangzhou. This is a reconstructed village but it's not obnoxiously commercial. People are friendly and wear period costumes. The entry ticket allows you into a temple, and to watch demonstrations. There's also a puppet performance, and bed museum. Take a picnic lunch if you want. Buses go from Shanghai Stadium.

At 1000-years old, **Zhujiajiao** village in Qingpu County. *Tel. 59242771*, is especially interesting because of its museums. It is full of well-maintained old houses, shops, 16th century moon bridges, and a museum of farm tools. There are also narrow alleyways, old tea houses, and a private garden made in 1912, whose owner sent his three daughters to Canada. The local specialty is steamed sticky rice in bamboo leaves, great for picnics. It also makes bamboo baskets. People are very friendly and seem happy to be photographed. You can get here by taking No. 4 tourist bus from Shanghai Stadium. The office is 100 Gongyuan Road, Qingpu, 201700, *Tel. 21/59732890 or 59242771, Website: www.zhujiajiao.com (English).*

Tongli is close to Suzhou and is charming and not developed for tourists. We dropped in at a kindergarten there, and visited some homes. The natives were very friendly and the contact with old China was real, not a theme park. Travel agents can make arrangements.

Shanghai's Jewish History

Jews in Shanghai? Yes, there have been three main migrations. A handful of Sephardic Jews arrived from west Asia in the mid-1800s. These were the Kadoories, Hardoons, and Sassoons, who invested in much of Shanghai's real estate.

Then came White Russian Jews, refugees from the Communist revolution who arrived in the early 1920s. The third and latest group came to escape Hitler's Europe in the late 1930s. The 19,000 or so who reached Shanghai were mainly from Poland, Germany, and Austria. They were encouraged to stay by the then Japanese rulers even though Japan was an ally of Germany. The Japanese incorrectly thought they could borrow large sums of money from them. This group arrived with only their clothing, choosing Shanghai because it was the only place that would take them. Earlier migrants and Jews from other parts of the world helped them.

There were also Jews from Russia who arrived via Harbin. In 1943, the Japanese forced all Jews into Hongkou district. They endured US bombs and a few married Chinese people.

After the war, most discovered they had no families in Europe. With the communization of China, they left for other parts of the world. The last of the resident Shanghai Jews died in the 1980s.

Part of the **Ohel Moshe Synagogue**, built in 1927, is now a museum organized by the district government. A good sign in English points to two rooms with a few relics and photos. Located on the second floor of 62 Chang Yang Road in Hongkou District, *Tel. 65120229, and 65416312*; open 9am-4:30pm Monday to Friday. It is behind the Ocean Hotel, where a memorial plaque (in English and Hebrew) also sits in a nearby park. Ask for guide Wang Fah Liang, a neighborhood resident who can tell you in English about the area.

Shanghai Walks

Downtown Shanghai is too crowded and the air too polluted for much walking, but there's the **Nanjing Pedestrian Street**, **The Bund**, and **Lao Jie** near Yuyuan Garden. People's Park doesn't have much greenery. You can also head for an air-conditioned urban mall. In the suburbs are the Botanical Gardens and the zoo. There's interesting hiking on the hill around the **Basilica** in She Shan.

The **Roman Catholic Basilica** (Xu Jia Hui, She Shan), Zao Xi Bai Road, *Tel. 57651651, 57813349*, is high on a hill beside the Academy of Science's Observatory and a visit there could take four hours. You can take bus No. 1 from Shanghai Stadium for the 45-minute ride to "She Shan." It is comfortable with reclining seats and good air-conditioning. On the way, the bus might slow down while the conductor offers the same ride for Y2. Never mind. If you had to take a taxi, it would cost several hundred yuan.

There are two possible stops at She Shan. After the Jinjiang Floating World theme park, you should see cable car cables over the road and the Forest Hotel. Holler for a stop, and look for the Cable Car station. If you miss this stop, then get off at the next stop which says "She Shan." Be aware that buses go almost every hour so ask for the next couple of departure times.

Ask people for "She Shan" and follow the resulting pointed fingers, up 100 stairs, and then a 20-minute walk past a huge netted aviary to a cable car terminal. Hop onto the cableway (Y18) and 10 minutes and one stop later, you should see the magnificent church which makes the trip worthwhile. Another climb of about 50 stairs gets you there.

The basilica looks incongruously European. The Jesuits built the observatory in the 1860s and the basilica in the 1920s. A Jesuit seminary is still at the base of the hill and it has a tiny **guest house**, *Tel. 57651651, 57651521*. Stations of the cross line the driveway up and pilgrimages take place in May. It has had confessionals and mass every evening at 7 pm. The interior is simple. I thought of Gregory Peck playing a China-based priest in "The Keys of the Kingdom."

The former **residence of Dr. Sun Yat-sen**, 7 Xiangshan Road, is in the old French Concession, and open 9:30am-11am and 2pm-4:30pm. *Tel. 64372954*. Once inside, you are back in the 1920s. The house was bought by Chinese-Canadians for the father of republican China for 16,000 pieces of silver. Dr. Sun lived here with his wife intermittently from 1920 to 1924, just before his death of cancer in 1925. His widow, Soong Ching-ling, lived in the house until 1937, when the war forced her to move to Chongqing.

Besides the antiques, there are some old photographs, a 1920 China train map, Sun's medical instruments, clothes, and glasses. Dr. Sun was in charge of railways for a short time after he resigned as president. The house contains his library: a 1911 Encyclopedia Britannica, biographies of Bismarck, Cicero, Lincoln, and Napoleon in English, books in Japanese, and ancient works in Chinese. No photos are allowed.

Soong Ching-ling was the sister of Mme. Chiang Kai-shek. She eloped with the already-married Dr. Sun and was virtually disowned by her wealthy Christian father, up to that point one of Dr. Sun's strongest supporters. She was tolerated by her family and her powerful in-laws, although she was outspoken in her opposition to their exploitation of China. She was, after all, the widow of the widely respected father of the country. She chose to remain in China after Liberation, and worked to promote the welfare of children. See also Nanjing and Zhongshan for more about Dr. Sun.

The **Shanghai Stock Exchange** was founded in 1990. A visit will give you some indication of the vast scope of China's capitalism. Unfortunately the guides speak poor English and give a murky description but you can see its immense trading floor. Ask for its booklet. It's at 528 Pudong Nan Road, 200120, *Tel. 68808888, 68806146, Fax 68803459. E-mail: qli@sse.com.cn.* Open 9am-11:30am and 1pm-5pm, weekdays. Hotels like the Shangri-La Pudong can also arrange visits.

Travel agents are also offering one-day join-in tours to Suzhou, Hangzhou, Yangzhou and Wuxi. See also Putuoshan and Ningbo for interesting overnight trips.

Nightlife & Entertainment

Tourist and expat giveaways are full of sports and entertainment events. See Practical Information below for websites with listings of performances and competitions.

Shanghai has high standards of international music, art, and drama, a contribution of its many immigrants particularly the Jews. No one should miss Shanghai's magnificent and imposing **Grand Theatre** in People's Square next to the Shanghai Museum. It is meant to look like an eagle about to take off, and is lit up at night. It claims the largest stage in the world. Your hotel concierge should be able to get tickets. You can get one-hour tours of the theater from 9am-11:30am, and 1pm-4:30pm for Y50, *Tel. 63276562, 63868686 ext. 3303.* Recent performers were Luciano Pavarotti, the Moscow Ballet, the Norwegian Jazz Band and the Cairo Opera Theatre Ballet Co. It has three theaters, the largest seating 1800 people, and the smallest 250. It has three restaurants and is at the People's Square metro stop. *Tel. 63875480.*

For everybody, the **Shanghai Acrobatic and Magic Troupe** is a fun show with magicians, sword-swallowing, juggling and sometimes performing pandas. One of the acts I saw was dangerously thrilling. The trapeze artists performed over the audience without a net. New also was a Mongolian with a fancy whip act. The Shanghai Acrobats have been performing at the Shanghai Centre Theatre (1376 Nanjing Xi Road), and the Lanxing Theatre (57

Mao Ming Nan Road) but not every night. Y30-Y60. There's also **Shanghai Circus World** at 2266 or 2666 Gong He Xin Road, *Tel.66527550, 56653646* for Y50–Y280. Travel agents and hotel concierges can arrange tickets for a fee.

The best evening walk is the promenade between the Shangri-La Pudong Hotel and the Huangpu River when the Bund lights are on sometime between 7pm and 10:30pm. This does not always happen at the same time every night. The park costs Y5 and is less crowded than the Bund.

For sheer relaxation, try a massage in your hotel.

The Bar Scene

The best bars are in the hotels: **Charlie's** at the Crowne Plaza has a Filipino band. There's **Hyland 505**, second floor, Hyland Sofitel Hotel, 505 Nanjing Dong Road, *Tel. 63515888*. This has a Happy Hour 6pm-8pm daily, a mini-brewery and pub with darts, pool and live entertainment. And don't forget **B.A.T.S.** at the Shangri-La. Thursday night is Ladies Night and Friday and Saturday no cover for Ladies. Happy Hour is 6pm-8pm nightly. The **Portman Ritz-Carlton** has had an American jazz trio.

You usually don't have to be overly cautious in these hotel but be on your guard elsewhere. If I left out places where prostitutes might show up, you wouldn't see any bars listed. Be careful about scams too. In some bars you'll pay unreasonably high prices for hostesses to drink with you. Be careful about pickpockets and purse snatchers.

The following bars have been recommended by my women friends, both Chinese and American. You can also go bar-hopping in Xintiandi or Hengshan Road.

PEACE HOTEL, *20 Nanjing Dong Road. Tel. 63216888.*

The famous Peace Hotel jazz band is a Shanghai institution. Musicians play 1930s music off-key with a beat that inspires dancing. Don't expect Oscar Peterson. Reservations are needed in high tourist season.

KABB (Kathleen's American Bistro Bar), *House 5, North Block, Xintiandi, 181 Taicang Road, Tel. 33070798.*

JUDY'S TOO, *176 Mao Ming Nan Road, Tel. 64731417.*
Good lively dancing there.

MALONE'S AMERICAN CAFE, *near the Portman, 257 Tong Ren Road, Tel. 62472400*
Usually lively with sports on television. It's moderately priced.

O'MALLEY'S IRISH PUB, *42 Tao Jiang Road is near the US Consulate, Tel. 64370667. E-mail: omalleys@public.sta.net.cn. It accepts credit cards.*

There's a real fireplace and an Irish manager here. Live Irish music plays 8:30pm Irish-time to midnight daily except Sunday. Foreigners, not just Brits, hang out here, even though it's somewhat expensive. There's a garden, and specials like roast lamb for Y110. Guinness and Kilkenny is Y65 a pint or Y40 a half-pint. No Happy Hour. Bangers and mash Y95, O'Malley's burger Y95, fish and chips Y130, and Irish Stew Y140.

CALIFORNIA CLUB, *2, Gaolan Road, Fuxing Park, Tel. 63180785.* Hong Kong-run and lively.

BABYLON, *191 Hengshan Road, (see Where to Eat above), Tel. 64457556.* A live band performs at 9pm.

Sports & Recreation

The tourist and expat giveaways below under Practical Information can tell you about bungee jumping, kick boxing, karate and aikido training. **Hash House Harriers** can be found through its website: *www.shanghaihhh.com.* This is the drinking club with a running problem, fun for walkers as well as runners, and is a good place to meet local Chinese and foreign residents. **American Citizen Services** also has a list of clubs for long-stay expatriates to join. *Website: www.xianzai.com.*

At least six golf courses are in Shanghai, 12 within an hour of the city. Among the best is the 18-hole **Shanghai International Golf Club** in Hongqiao, *Tel. 59241969, Fax 59728520.* Hotels like the Sheraton Grand Hotel can make arrangements. There's also the 18-hole **Tomson Golf Club** at 1 Long Dong Da Dao, Pudong, *Tel. 58338888.* **Shanghai Links** is good and is at Lingbai Road, Pudong, *Tel. 58975899.* Hotels like the Pudong Shangri-La can arrange for you to play there.

Popular are motor-driven go-carts. Some operate to 2am and there are separate ones for kids and adults. There's a place at the Shanghai Stadium. The **Xian Xia Tennis Centre** near the Xijiao Guest House hosts the annual Heineken tennis championships *(www.heinekenopenshanghai.com)* which has attracted Michael Chang and Goran Ivanisevic. You can play there too. It's at 1885 Hongqiao Road, *Tel. 62626720.* See also the Regal International East Asia Hotel above.

Shopping

Shanghai is the best place in China (outside of Hong Kong) for selection and quality, and time should be set aside to shop if interested. Produced in the city are jade, ivory and whitewood carvings, lacquer ware, needlepoint tapestries, silks, carpets, embroideries, gold and silver jewelry (especially filigree), artificial flowers, painted eggs, reproductions of antique bronzes, and such proletarian articles as jogging suits, bedroom slippers, winter jackets, heavy tee-shirts, gloves and fake Beanie Babies. Shopping in factories is usually more expensive than in department stores but do visit factories to see how crafts are made and to learn about good quality.

You'll find most places cheaper than Hong Kong for China-made clothes, crafts and antiques. Shopping in the international departure lounge at the airport even is actually quite good; it has a few books and magazines in English, clothes, arts and crafts, and the usual duty-free items.

Antiques and curios: If you don't trust your judgment, head for the expensive antique shops and get a certificate for antiques. In markets just assume everything's a reproduction or fake, and haggle accordingly. I usually offer Y30 for everything and laugh and frequently pay just that for wonderful antique carvings and stone statues. I've also paid Y40 for stone bowls with metal trim (over Y400 in hotel stores), and for a string of pearls.

The best bargains in antiques is at the Saturday and Sunday morning **Fuyou Market** which is no longer on Fuyou Road but one block away on Fang Bang Zhong Road and Henan Nan Road on Lao Jie Old Street. It is in a building which opens at 9am-6pm weekdays, and 5am-6pm on weekends, with weekend merchants on the fourth floor. *Tel. 63281796.*

The next best market (for possible bargains) is the basement of the **Old Town Gods' Temple Market** in the Hua Bao Building, 265 Fong Bang Zhong Road, Yuyuan Garden, *Tel. 63557011, 63559999.* This is open 9:30am-6:30pm daily. Then there's the semi-outdoor **Dongtai Antique Market**, around 54 Dong Tai Road (near Xizang Road) which is open 9am-6pm. It has about 200 shops. If you have problems finding it, telephone Tom Tang, one of the vendors, at *63080117.* He speaks English. The market is open 11am-5pm daily. It's near the site of the First National Congress of the Communist Party.

Guides are reluctant to take you to these markets partly because they don't get any commissions. But the markets are fun; you can find tiny shoes for bound feet, old silver jewelry with real kingfisher feathers, and cricket boxes - things you see in museums.

For the top-of-the-line antiques and for people who would rather pay extra and avoid crowds, look at the **Shanghai Antique & Curio Store** for antiques guaranteed by the government. It's at 192-246 Guangdong Road, *Tel. 63212864, Fax 63216529.* Other antique shops are in the area. There's the **Antiques and Curio Branch, Friendship Store**, 694 Nanjing Xi Road, *Tel. 62539549.* Several antique stores are between the Hilton and the Shanghai Hotels on Hua Shan Road. Especially good is the **Kuo Yue Cha Artware shop** in the Hilton itself on the second floor with good quality stone carvings, porcelain and jade – and negotiable prices.

For **antique furniture** and reproductions try Antique Alley around 1438 Hongqiao Road towards the airport from the Sheraton Grand and Renaissance. There are several shops and workshops here and you should be able to ship purchases at horrendous prices. *Tel. 62199229.* Try the **Wanbo Furniture Shop**, 1426 Hongqiao Road, *Tel. 62089581, or 13901884044.* There's also the **Zhong Zhong Antique Furniture Store**, 28 Hong Xu Road, *Tel. 64064066, Fax 64064065. E-mail: zhongcom@sh163d.sta.net.cn.*

Art: Shanghai has lots of galleries for serious not tourist art. You can see works of important contemporary artists at the website of the very important

Shanghart at *www.shanghart.com; E-mail : shanghart@shanghart.com*. It is best to inform this gallery of your interest before you visit so it can show you a wide selection. Its store usually has little on hand. Shanghart's website contains over 2000 works by 30 artists, photos of some artist's studios, and its Suzhou creek warehouse. It is at 2A Gaolan Road, 200020, *Tel 63593923, Fax 63594570.*

Every two months a different artist or group is highlighted at **Art50**, a gallery of contemporary Chinese or western paintings at the top floor of the Novotel Atlantis Hotel in Pudong. A serious gallery is in the Shanghai Center (Ignore the tourist art. There's really a good gallery there.)

Arts and Crafts: Serious souvenir shoppers should check out the reasonable prices first at the **Arts and Crafts Shopping Centre**, 190-208 Nanjing Xi Road (next to the Park Hotel), *Tel. 63276530, E-mail: sharts@public.sta.net.cn*. This is open 10am-9pm. Jewelry is on the ground floor and crafts on upper floors. Here you can buy silver or cloisonné chop sticks, silk, tee shirts, quilts, clothes, shoes, gloves, ties, children's dresses, carpets, cloisonné, yard goods and furniture. Across the road is a KFC.

Check also the Friendship Store for moderate prices and stores in and around the Old Town Gods' Temple in Yuyuan Garden for cheaper quality and prices. The Shanghai Museum has some good reproductions. For reasonable prices, look also in department stores.

Arts and Crafts factories: Carpets – **Shanghai General Carpet Factory**, 25 Caobao Road, *Tel. 64361713*. There's also the **Shanghai Jade Carving Factory**, 33 Caobao Road, *Tel. 64362660*. Both are near the Caobao Road metro stop.

Books: The best for books in English is the **Foreign Language Book Store** at 390 Fuzhou Road, 200001, *Tel. 63223200*. Open 9am-5:30pm. It will mail books and has a branch in Pudong named the Shanghai Book Trader. They take credit cards. The Jin Jiang and Cypress Hotels, and the Friendship Store also have books in English. For art books look in the Shanghai Museum. There's also the top floor of the **Shanghai Book City** at 465 Fuzhou Road, *Tel. 63522222*. The **Shanghai Art Bookstore** is on the third floor, 42 Hua Shan Road, *Tel. 62487476*. Most art books are in Chinese and relatively cheap.

Carpets: In addition to the above, good carpet selections are in the Arts and Crafts Shopping Center and the Friendship Store.

Clothes: the **Xiangyang/Huating Market** is at 999 Huai Hai Zhong Road (at Xiangyang Road) half a block from the Shanxi Nan Road metro stop. This is Shanghai's equivalent of the Beijing Silk Market. Its 300 or so booths have better quality factory overruns and seconds than other street markets. Look for great buys on silk shirts, boots, jeans, jackets, purses, watches (with Mao waving his hand), CDs, and backpacks.

At the other end of the price range is **Maison Mode**, 1312 Huaihai Zhong Road, *Tel. 64310100*, near the Garden Hotel. It sells international name brands, and is expensive and free of crowds.

Friendship Store, other Department Stores and Malls: The Friendship Store is at 40 Beijing Dong Road, *Tel.53080600* and open 9:30am-10pm. It is two blocks north of the Peace Hotel, and is one of the largest in China. It can crate and ship purchases. Prices are higher than other department stores but it has a good variety of lacquerware, cinnabar, eggs, peasant paintings, cloisonné, teapots, old porcelain shard boxes, pearls, musical instruments, ordinary stone carvings, painted silk screens, calligraphy, cross-stitch, antique embroidery, and dough figures.

Nanjing Dong Road has the best general shopping. It is a pleasant pedestrian mall with an electric train for tired shoppers. Its many department and specialty stores are open here about 9:30am to 10pm. A favorite is the moderately-priced **New World** at 2 Nanjing Xi Road, *Tel.6358888*. This is beside the circular overpass opposite the proletarian **Number One Department Store**, *Tel. 63588888, 63223344*. Nanjing Road is where tourists from all over the world shop. (Some maps have lists of stores and I found the concierge at the Sofitel Hotel helpful in locating a place to get a watch battery. The Shanghainese themselves shop along **Huaihai Road,** a very long street with denser crowds. Good there with moderate prices is **Parkson Department Store** at 918 Huaihai Zhong Road, near the Shan Xi Nan Road metro stop, *Tel. 64158818*.

Many shopping malls and department stores in other areas have proliferated. A favorite is the moderate-to-expensive **Meilongzhen Plaza/ West Gate Mall** at 1038 Nanjing Xi Road, *Tel. 62721111, 62187878*. It is open 9:30am-10pm and has curios, sporting goods, clothes, toys, cosmetics, art gallery, music cd's, optical store, jewelry, Watson's drug store, Isetan department store and travel agent. It also has a bakery, a wine shop, and a Haagen- Dazs ice cream parlor.

Gubei is out towards the airport and near the Hong Qiao hotels. You can buy just about everything there including Haagen-Dazs ice cream, suitcases, groceries and Pashmina shawls. The **Carrefour Gubei Shopping Center** with 80 small shops is at 268 Shuicheng Nan Road, *Tel. 62098899*. It is open 8:30am to 10pm daily and takes Visa credit cards. It has an ATM and taxis are plentiful. Pearl stores are also in the neighborhood. There is also shopping and decent restaurants near the Hongqiao Exhibition Centre, Sheraton and Renaissance hotels, four km. away from Gubei.

The **Orient Shopping Center** is at 8 Caoxi Road, *Tel. 64870000*, open 10am-9pm near the Jianguo and Hua Ting Hotels. Three other department stores and two computer malls are near by.

Musical Instruments. A small store is at 114 Nanjing Dong Road. Try the department stores or the Shanghai Piano Co., 369 Yunnan Road at Nanjing Road.

Pearls. **Amy's Pearls**, 56 Gubei Nan Road (near the airport), *Tel. 62753954. Mobile: 13916313466. E-mail: Pearlsbyamy@hotmail.com. Website: www.amy-pearl.com.* Open 9am-7pm. Custom designs. Freshwater, Tahitian, and sea-water pearls. Wholesale and retail. Reasonable prices. In the same area is **Julie's Pearls**, 106 Gubei Nan Road. *Tel. 62086576. Mobile 13962182888.* Open 8am-10pm. Downtown there's **Shanghai Traveling Goods Building**, 2/F, 558 Nanjing Dong Road. You might also visit Suzhou, an hour's drive away, for cheaper prices and its incredible Pearl Market.

Pharmacies and drug stores. Check with the international medical providers in Practical Information below. **World Link Medical Centre** should have Western medicines. It's in the Shanghai Centre, 1376 Nanjing Xi Road, *Tel. 62797688* (24 hours). **Watson's** is a Hong Kong "drug store" chain with patent medicines. It has branches in the Shanghai Center and Meilongzhen Plaza, but no pharmacist. For Chinese medicines, try the Lao De Ji Dispensary at 51 Nanjing Dong Road, the Friendship Store, or **Shanghai No. 1 Pharmacy** at 616 Nanjing Dong Road, *Tel. 63224567.* There's also the **Jinjiang Drug Store** at 8586 Huaihai Zhong Road, *Tel. 64372900* (24 hours).

Photography. The **Guan Long Photo Store** can fix cameras, has a wider variety of films and camera batteries. It's near the Peace Hotel at 180 Nanjing Dong Road at Jiangxi Zhong Road, *Tel. 63218699.* Most hotels, department stores, and the Friendship Store have cameras and film.

Silk: A good selection is in the Friendship Store, and Arts and Crafts Shopping Center but markets and stores in Suzhou and Hangzhou have more variety. See especially the Silk Market in Hangzhou.

Silk embroidery: rank badges, framed specimens, lotus shoes, and clothes are at **Zhang's**, Suite 202A Shanghai Centre, 1376 Nanjing Xi Road, *Tel/Fax 62798587. Website: www.zhangstextiles.com. E-mail: mason@zhangstextiles.com.*

Supermarkets are everywhere, especially in malls and department stores. Best for foreigners are those in the Friendship Stores, Shanghai Center and the Jin Jiang Hotel.

Tailors might take two weeks to three months to make anything. Hotels can recommend.

Practical Information

ATMs: Money machines are in the Citibank outside the Peace Hotel, and on the sixth floor of the Union Building near the Bund and Yan'an Dong Road. You can get cash from your Visa card at most branches of the Bank of Reconstruction. Many are around the city. Unfortunately, not all ATMs work all the time. People who work in the Shanghai Center say that the ATM there usually functions. It is next to The Market and the tailor shop and takes many international cards.

Business Hours: Most offices are open five days a week; some offices 8:30am-5pm, or 9am-5:30pm. Lunch time goes from 11:30 or 12 noon to 1 or 1:30pm.

Consulates: Hours are usually Monday to Friday, about 8:30am-5pm. If you are traveling independently, it is a good precaution to register with your country's mission. In the event of a lost passport, replacement should be faster. Should there be an emergency, you will be notified.

• **Australia**, *Tel. 64334604, Fax 64376669*
• **Canada**, *Tel. 62798400, Fax 62798401, Suite 604, West Tower, American International Centre at the Shanghai Centre, 1376 Nanjing Xi Lu, Shanghai 200040, E-mail: shngi@dfait-maeci.gc.ca/ or info@shanghai.gc.ca. Website: www.canada.org.cn or www.shanghai.gc.ca. Emergency Services, Dept. of Foreign Affairs and International Trade, Tel. 10800-1400-125.*
• **Denmark**, *Tel. 62090500, Fax 6209 0504. E-mail: gkldksh@uninet.com.cn. Website: www.dk-embassy-cn.org/shanghai/index.html. Office hours: 9am-4:30pm.*
• **France**, *Tel. 64377414, Fax 64377073, 64339437*
• **Germany**, *Tel. 64336953, Fax 64714488, 64714448. Website: www.deguangzhou.org/*
• **Israel**, *Tel. 62098008, Fax 62098010*
• **Italy**, *Tel. 64716980/89/91/96, Fax 64716977. E-mail: conitsha@public4.sta.net.cn*
• **Japan**, *Tel. 62780788, Fax 62788988*
• **Korea**, *Tel. 62196417, Fax 62196918*
• **New Zealand**, *Tel.64711127, Fax 64310226*
• **Poland**, *Tel. 64334735, 64330417*
• **Russian Federation**, *Tel. 63242682, Fax 63069982*
• **Singapore**, *Tel. 64370776, Fax 64334150*
• **Switzerland**, *Tel. 62700519, Fax 62700522*
• **UK**, *Tel. 62797650, Fax 62797651*
• **US**, *1469 Huaihai Zhong Road, 200031. Passport required for identification before entry. Tel. 6433-6880. American Citizen Services, Tel. 64336880 X 247, X 293, Fax 64375173, 64711148. Open 8:30am-11:30am or 12pm, and 1 or 2pm-4 or 4:30pm, Monday through Friday.*

Cruise ship lines: Regal China Cruises, *Room 1104, No. 2, Lane 257, Dalian Xi Road, 200081. Tel. 65080103. Fax 65221894.*
Emergencies:
• **Ambulance**, Tel. 120,
• **Fire**, Tel. 119,
• **Police**, Tel. 110

Flight Prices & Schedules

A good website for current flight prices and schedules in China is: *www.flychina.com*. Approximate prices are: Shanghai to Beijing Y1030, Chengdu Y1440, Chongqing Y1340, Dalian Y970, Guilin Y1190, Haikou Y1480, Harbin Y1560, Hohhot Y1230, Kunming Y1670, Taiyuan Y1090, Tianjin Y930, Urumqi/Wulumuqi Y2390, Wuhan Y740, Xiamen Y880, Xi'an Y1150. If you are trying to save money and can book in advance, ask about night flights which could be cheaper. Some travel agents charge a Y30 service fee to book tickets.

Internet Bars: There are a lot, but many have been closed recently by the government. On the same street as the Holiday Inn Crowne Plaza and less than a block away is **Yi Xian Tong**, Gong Zhong Dian Nao Wa at 198 Fahua Zhu Road, *Tel. 62821003*. This has at least three dozen computers, some of them hooked up to the web for twenty-four hours. It charges Y7 to Y10 an hour. This is near the Bubble Tea and Coffee Shop. Three blocks from the Purple Mountain Hotel in Pudong is an internet service with about 14 computers at Y5 an hour. It's at Wei Fang 4 Cun 484, *Tel. 68670776*. There also the ground floor of the Shanghai Library which is free but expect long queues. It's at 1555 Huaihai Dong Road, *Tel. 64455555*, open 8:30am-8pm.

Medical Concerns:

• **Hong Qiao Medical Center**, *Manderine City, Unit #30, 788 Hong Xu Road, Tel. 64055788*

• **Hua Shan Hospital**, *12 Wulumuqi Zhong Road, Foreigners' Clinic, 19/F, Tel. 62483986*

• **International SOS Pte Ltd**, *Shanghai Representative Office, 555 Xu Jia Hui Road, 11C, Guangdong Development Bank Tower, 200023. Administration Tel. 62959951, Fax 63901428. Alarm Center, Tel. 62950099. Alarm Center. Fax 63901428.* Clinic and evacuation.

• **Sino-Canadian Dental Clinic**, *Ninth People's Hospital, 7/F, main building, 639 Zhi-Zhao Ju Road, Tel. 63774831 X 5279*

• **World Link Medical Center** (US and expatriate doctors; imported vaccines), *Shanghai Center, 1376 Nanjing Xi Road, Suite 203, Tel. 62797688. If you are a member, Tel. 7pm to 8am 62797699.*

Public Security Bureau, beside the Pacific Luck Hotel (Jing Fu Yun Dajiudian), a kilometer north of the Bund at 299 Wusong Road. It takes a week to extend a visa but you can get express service for a higher fee.

Taxi Complaints, *Tel. 63216611*

Telecommunications Telegram and Telephone office, 30 Nanjing Dong Road, near the Peace Hotel. This has videophone and card phones.

Tourist Information & Complaints

Shanghai Municipal Tourism Administration, 2525 Zhong Shan Xi Road (in Hua Ting Guest House), 200030, *Tel. 64391818 extensions 2414, 2309, 2311*. They have a handy free map of the metro and light rail system. On the flip side is a map with tour bus routes. These cards are available in major hotels or from one of the 22 Shanghai Tourist Info Offices. One is in the Hongqiao Airport (International Arrivals), *Tel. 62688899 ext. 56750* or People's Square Metro Station ("in the lobby of ticket inspection"), *Tel. 64381693. Its website: www.tourinfo.sh.cn* has sketch maps, addresses of its 22 information centers (not all with English speakers), and addresses and hours of its tourist attractions. I did find an English-speaker in its People's Square office. *E-mail: webmaster@tourinfo.sh.cn*. It can book tickets and accept complaints but the **Shanghai Tourism Quality Control Office's telephone number** is *64393615. E-mail: shatqso@stn.sh.cn*.

Tourist handouts: Magazines like *Quo*, *That's Shanghai,* and *Shanghai Talk* are free at many of the hotels and expatriate hangouts. They have lots of helpful information on restaurants, bars, events, kick-boxing and bungi jumping.

Train prices: trains are increasing their speeds again in 2002. Information on schedules was not available at press time. The easiest way to learn about prices and schedules is by e-mailing a travel agent in your departure city.

For an idea of some prices, Beijing – the super fast train with two people sharing a deluxe compartment costs Y900 per person. Soft sleeper is Y685 and hard sleeper Y396. Shanghai to Changsha soft sleeper, Y427. Chengdu soft sleeper Y770. Chongqing soft sleeper Y754. Fuzhou soft sleeper Y417. Guangzhou hard and soft sleeper Y584 to Y792. Hangzhou Y60-Y110. Suzhou Y40 to Y110. Departures are frequent. Reservations are only needed on weekends.

Travel Agencies:
• **Great West Travel**, *Suite 6600, Shanghai Centre, 1376 Nanjing Xi Road, 200040. Tel. 62798489. Fax 62798488. E-mail: grtwest@public.sta.net.cn.* Ask for Coco Tang or Rachel Wang. This is a small, efficient agency.
• **Shanghai China International Travel Service**, *CITS Building, 1277 Beijing Xi Road, 200040, (behind the Shanghai Centre). Tel. 62898899, Fax 62893018. For America, Australia and Asia Division, Room 609, Tel. 62890025, Fax 62893018. E-mail: baoyp@scits.com with copy to Tony Q. Chen: tonycq@scits.com.* Ask for Bao You Pei who helped this book a lot. Ticket booking office, ground floor, *Tel. 62894510,* open 8:30am-

11:30am and 1pm-5pm. Offices also at *66 Nanjing Road (near the Peace Hotel), Tel: 63234067, and 2 Jinling Dong Road, Tel. 63238770, Fax 63238759. Individual Travel Division, Tel. 62892512, Fax 62897838. Head office, 2 Jinling Dong Road, 200002 (near Yan'an Road and the Bund), Tel. 63238748.*

• **China Shanghai Spring International Travel Service**, *1558 Ding Xi Road, 200050, Tel. 62520000 X 187, 62101493, Fax 62523734. E-mail: springtour@china-sss.com. Open daily 9am-9pm.* Ask for Sally Shao, Sales Manager who helped this book a lot, or Ken Chen (Chen Kun), Manager, European and American Dept., *Tel. 62520000X187, or 62514510.* Ken was our guide once and is very good. *Website: www.china-sss.com.* No service charges for issuing a train ticket. Charges however for delivery.

• **Shanghai China Travel Service**, *881 Yan'an Zhong Road, 200040 (domestic tours), Tel. 62478888, Fax 62475521, 62792281.* Contact Mr. Sun Quan, Sales Manager, Europe and America Department, *Tel. 62794414, 62478888X221, Fax 62792281. E-mail: sunq@scts.com. Website: www.scts.com.*

• **CYTS Tours**, *2 Heng Shan Road, 200031, Tel. 64331826, Fax 64733349. E-mail: cyts@public.sta.net.cn.*

Websites: Shanghai government's site is *www.sh.gov.cn.* It is in English, but its travel information, hotels and events are out of date. It is worth a visit for other information however.

Websites for tourist information: in English, the best website is *www.xianzai.com.* You don't have to subscribe. You can see current and past editions immediately. The site lists performances of concerts, plays, films, dance, operas, everything. It also reviews new restaurants.

Good and current is: *www.Shanghai-ed.com.* You can ask this site questions about Shanghai.

Another helpful and current website is: *www.thatsshanghai.com.*

I found dates slow to access at *www.shanghaitalk.net.*

There's *www.shanghabc.com* especially for people moving to Shanghai, and it lists cultural events. The website *www.Chinanow.com* is not updated regularly but it is helpful also on Beijing, Chengdu, Nanjing and Kunming.

At *www.expatsh.com*, there are places to rent, consulates, restaurant reservations (but no reviews), and links to newspapers in Australia, U.S., and Canada. During the APEC forum, it listed streets that would be closed.

e
a
s
t

c
h
i
n
a

Chapter 16

Fuzhou
(Foochow)

The capital of Fujian province, on the east coast across the straits from Taiwan, **Fuzhou** is an important coastal city especially for business people and those with relatives here. It is on the way to the mountain resort of Wuyi, a UNESCO World Heritage site. Fujian has been in the news recently as the home of "boat people," who risked their lives trying to enter the U.S. and Canada illegally. These adventurers come from towns in the north of the province with a tradition of emigration. As you look around the cities listed here, ask yourself if people here need to spend thousands of dollars to leave.

This is one of my favorite provinces because it is different from the rest of China and yet very Chinese and very pleasant. It is easy and cheap to get around on good buses. The weather is subtropical and most of the province is mountainous and beautiful. The only problem is that very little English is understood here. The Southern Fujian dialect is distinct, neither Cantonese nor Mandarin. This language is spoken also by the majority on Taiwan only 150 km. away. But people are friendly and lots of help is available.

Arrivals & Departures

Flights arrive from Hong Kong, Macau, and 39 other Chinese cities. Flights with Macau connect directly with those from Taiwan. Currently only cargo ships arrive directly from Taiwan, but hopefully this will change soon. The international airport is modern and gleaming, almost a quarter-kilometer long, and waiting for an influx of visitors from Taipei some day. A left-luggage room and hotel booths are outside the arrival hall. The airport is forty minutes (50 km), southeast of the city.

Buses take up to four hours from Xiamen. A very convenient and not-so-crowded bus station is beside the Minjiang Hotel. Look for the sign "Zhong Lu Da Ba Shou Piao Chu," *Tel. 7551443, 7608848.* Buses also go from here every 20 to 30 minutes to Shantou, Shenzhen (12 hours and faster than train), Guangzhou (12 hours), and major cities in Fujian. There are no buses to Shanghai but there's an overnight train taking about 17 hours. It's better to fly.

Orientation

Fuzhou is a 5000-year-old city. In the Tang dynasty, it was expanded to include three hills and the waterfront Bund. Opened to foreign trade in 1842 because of the Opium War, Fuzhou had British and American dockyards, and factories for making tea bricks. It was once home to about 10 foreign consulates. The old British Community Church is still a church. Across the street is the Hua Nan Women's College which is looking for native English-speakers to teach English in return for room and board.

The city is also noted for its hot springs. It became the provincial capital in 1949. Prominent is a statue of Lin Zexu (Lin Tse-Hsu), 1785-1850, the minister born here who destroyed the opium in 1840 outside of Guangzhou. The population is 1.5 million urban, four million total. The Min River runs through town from Wuyi. The hottest temperature is 39°C in July and August; the coldest, -0.8°C in February. Most rain falls May and June.

Where to Stay

Hotels here are not great but they are adequate. You won't find anything close to Beijing's Kunlun Hotel. At one of these, a female visitor knocked at my door at 3am, note in hand, but this could happen anywhere. Fuzhou hotels add a 10 to 15% service charge and all but the University Guest House accept credit cards. The Lakeside Hotel has the best standards for English-speaking tourists and is near the government guest hall. The Foreign Trade Center Hotel and the Hot Spring Hotel are downtown, close to the Foreign Trade Center, have hot spring water and are convenient to shopping. The three-star Min Jiang Hotel is near them in this area of banks and stock companies which is about three kilometers from city center. A supermarket is next to the Hot Spring Hotel.

HOT SPRING HOTEL (Quan Dafandian), *218 Wusi Zhong Road, 350003. Five stars, Tel. 7851818, Fax 7835150. E-mail: hshfz@pub1.fz.fj.cn. Website: www.hshfz.com (English). Rooms have ranged from Y988 to Y1380. Suites have been Y1780 to Y10888. It has been giving 40% discounts. Four km from the railway station.*

Built in 1986, and renovated in 1998, this 16-story, 311-room hotel has a large outdoor pool open May 1 to October 1. It has a garden, nine-piece gym with some German equipment, tennis, and bowling. Standard rooms are large with balconies, CNN and European television, small closets, and no drawers, but it has an executive floor. It has a Japanese and a French restaurant, night club, 500-seat banquet hall, and 20-seat cinema. The elevator carpets are dirty and stains were on bedroom carpets. It has had two foreign staff teaching English.

LAKESIDE HOTEL (Xihu Dajiudian), *158 Hubin Road, 350003. Five stars, Tel. 7839888, Fax 7836585. Email: info@lakeside-hotel.com. www.lakeside-hotel.com" Website: www.lakeside-hotel.com (English). Rooms have been Y950-Y1398 and suites Y1700-Y8808. Its Dynasty suites are two-story. It has been giving 25% discounts, and included breakfast. It is five kilometers from Dong Jie Kou city center and three km from the railway station.*

Built in 1988 and renovated in 1998, the Lakeside has 22 stories and 436 rooms with safes and big desks. It also has a decent eight-piece gym, disco, small outdoor pool, tennis, Japanese and Cantonese restaurants. Even-numbered rooms have a lakeview. It has non-smoking rooms and executive floors, CNN, Australian TV, and BBC and VOD. It carries the South China Morning Post. I found some of the room carpets and all the elevator carpets dirty but staff assured me they would be cleaned. Its ballroom has a big screen and closed circuit television and holds 300 guests banquet style.

FUJIAN FOREIGN TRADE CENTER HOTEL (Wai Mao Zhong Xing Jiudian), *73 Wusi Road, 350001. Five stars. Tel. 7523388, Fax 7550358 (Sales) or 7564841 (Reservations). Email: ftchotel@public.fz.fj.cn or tichotel@public.fz.fj.cn. Rooms have been Y838-Y1030 and suites Y1467-Y1886. It has been giving 50-60% discounts and has apartment suites with kitchens. It is three kms from the railway station.*

Built in 1985 and next door to the Foreign Trade Center, this seven-story, 323-room hotel has attractive rooms, 20-meter-long pool, tennis, book store, and conference hall. Its 1996 south section is better with 32 square meter rooms. It has two non-smoking floors, in-room safes, CNN and BBC. It serves French, Japanese, Cantonese, and Fujian food. Elevator carpets were dirty.

MIN JIANG HOTEL (Binguan), *Wusi Road, 350001. Three stars. Tel. 7557895, Fax 7551489. E-mail: mjht@pub2.fz.fj.cn. Rooms have been Y400-Y660 and suites Y980-Y1980. It has been giving 40% discounts, is 3.5 km from the railway station and across the street from the Bank of China.*

This China Travel Service hotel has 412 rooms, Cantonese and Huaiyang cuisines. There's television from Australia, France, Hong Kong, CNBC, but no CNN. It has VOD. Its lobby has a marvelous stone carving of horses, like ocean waves, and it has been building an extension and renovating some guest rooms. No English.

The **GUEST HOUSE OF FUZHOU UNIVERSITY** (Fuzhou Da Xue Zhao Dai Suo), *Tel. 7893374,* is to the right as you leave the main entrance of the West Temple. Look for a three-story green and white tile building with a sign in

English. Rooms have private showers, toilets, televisions, and telephones but no air-conditioning and no heat. They are small and grubby, no one speaks English but they are very cheap.

Homestays

CITS can arrange for teenage groups on educational tours to stay in local homes temporarily for about $15 per night each (group rate).

Where to Eat

The best food is in the hotels. A chain of **Fu Restaurants** has been serving okay fast food at moderate prices: sizzling beef, steamed shrimp, spinach soup with mushrooms (hu guo tang), and fried oysters with eggs (hai li jian). It's not bad for fast food.

You can get Fujian food at the **Bafang Yuan Restaurant**, 82 Dong Da Road, *Tel. 7556134, or 7557993.* This is across from the Dong Hu Hotel. We had crab on sticky rice with pea pods, mashed yu (yam) with nuts, sesame, sugar, oil and dried pear, and three soups - all good. Prices were moderate.

Seeing the Sights

Fuzhou was first built in the 9th century and bombed by the Japanese in 1941. Some of its buildings are 20th century, but it is worth a visit for its elegant architecture. Fuzhou has some impressive buildings. Its high court looks like the Brandenburg Gate from the upper floors of the Lakeside Hotel, a wonderful vantage point. The city has a new aquarium. Do look at the very impressive **West Temple (Xi Chan Si),** not far from downtown on Yang Ziao Road. Deeply carved dragons slither up its pillars. Look for its 1000-arm Goddess of Mercy and its 33 incarnations of Guan Yin. It currently has 100 monks. If you're lucky you might see worshippers releasing caged birds. Its Buddhas are huge. There's a 1000-year-old banyan tree, a Black Pagoda which you can't climb, and a 63-meter-high 15-story White Pagoda which you can. It also has Tang dynasty litchi/lichee trees, and an expensive and dirty vegetarian restaurant. The grounds are open from about 7am to 6pm.

The **Shoushan Stone Carving factory** is wonderful if you like stone carvings. It used to carve chops for the Qing emperors who valued its yellow color. This stone has many different colors, each worked into the designs. Its showroom is an art gallery of fine stone and ivory carvings and is about three kilometers from the West Temple. It is open 8:30am to 11am and 1:30pm to 4:30pm, Monday to Friday, and is at 229 Liu Yi Zhong Road, *Tel. 3362978, Fax 3352196.*

In one day, you can also visit **Gushan (Drum Hill)** which is topped by a huge drum-shaped boulder at least 969 meters high and is 10 km east of the city, open 7 or 7:30am-6pm. Here is the **Yongquan Si (Surging Spring Temple)** which was founded in 908 A.D. and has a white jade Buddha. Monks chant twice a day. The **Qianfo Taota (Thousand-Buddha Pottery Pagoda)** and the **Shuiyun Ting (Water and Cloud Pavilion),** east of the Yongquan Si are both from the Song dynasty. Views from the 18 caves west of the temple are famous.

Especially worth a visit is the **Memorial Hall of Lin Zexu,** the native son who destroyed the 20,000 chests of opium. It is a small shrine to the national hero who is known also as a calligrapher and a poet. Lin was one of the first Qing officials to take an interest in things foreign. Because the British attacked as a result of Lin's actions, the emperor exiled him to far-off Xinjiang.

Nightlife & Entertainment

There's a disco and bowling at the **Hot Springs Hotel** and a night food market and dancing near May 1 Square. Travel agents can arrange for you to use the **Wusi Road Sports Centre**. Fuzhou has four golf courses. The Festival of Goddess Mazu is held in April and May on Meizhou Island in Putian City, 108 km south.

Excursions & Day Trips

Xiamen is the most developed for tourists in the province, with good hotels. Quanzhou has wonderful old architecture and unique temples and museums. Fuzhou has less to offer tourists.

Wuyi is 460 km from Fuzhou and is a place for hiking and leisurely bamboo rafting down the winding jade-green Min River, a short trip. It's for getting away from city noises and air pollution, but not necessarily from noisy holiday-makers. Its highest mountain is 717 meters. It is in the northwest side of the province, divided into two parts, a normal town, and a tourist area with hotels, a 60 sq km scenic area, and a 570 sq km United Nations Biosphere Reserve. The airport is in between, 14 km away from the town, and about 11 km from the tourist area. The total population is 218,000.

It is very cold in winter, sometimes with snow, hot in summer, and humid all year round. The best time to go is autumn. Over 200 mm of rain falls each month in April, August and September.

The easiest way is to fly from any of 18 Chinese cities or Hong Kong. The scenic way is by air-conditioned train for about $12. Trains from Fuzhou leave once a day about noon. Trains also go every other day from Xiamen. You can go by road in about six hours along the beautiful Min River, past terraced hills growing jasmine flowers, sugar cane and rice. CTS charges $160 a car.

Hotels are basic, a step above camping. Staff English is generally poor. The Wuyi Mountain Villa is the best. Travel agents say the two-star Post and Telecom Hotel are okay. (Xingcun Town, Tel. 5262988, Fax 5262666.)

WUYI MOUNTAIN VILLA, *Wuyi Palace, 354302. Three stars. Tel. 5251888, Fax 5252567. CITS charges $45 for individual guests.*

This hotel, owned by CTS Fujian, is set in a large garden. Its 112 rooms are in connected two- and three-story buildings. It claims the largest presidential suite in China (700 sq meters). Standard rooms have soft beds, heat, and air-conditioning. It gives demonstrations of the local tea-making ritual, an 800 year old art.

About Wuyi Tea

The first cup clears your thirst.
The second cup calms you down.
The third cup helps you use all your wisdom.
The fourth cup starts you sweating,
And all your troubles leave your body.
The fifth cup makes your skin smoother.
The sixth cup makes you feel clean and immortal.
The seventh cup makes your soul float.
–ancient Ming poem

Seeing Wuyi

There's a 9.5 km relaxing rafting trip that takes 90 minutes to glide past 18 curves, from the Xingcun Town Ma Tou port. It's a Song dynasty-designed raft for six people. It costs Y300 a raft or Y50 per person. Some raftsmen tell jokes in Mandarin as well as stories about the rocks ("two copulating turtles"). You pass caves with 3800-year-old coffins in the fourth curve, and if you're lucky, you see birds. The raft stops at Ancient Street, with its Song architecture, near Great King Peak in town.

You should also climb the 800 steps up to 409-meter-high Tianyou (Heavenly Tour) Peak which is open all year round. Sedan chairs are available but they don't go up the side with the best view which is narrow and precarious. On top is a temple inspired by a famous high-ranking official Peng Zu who retired here with his two sons, thousands of years ago.

Wuyi produces black mushrooms, bamboo shoots, cloud's ears, local wine, and Wuyi tea. Shops are down the hill and across from the Jade Maid Hotel. China Travel Service, Wuyi Palace, 354302, *Tel. 5255846.* Contact Jacques Zhong (who can speak French). CITS' telephone is *5303808, Fax 5302161.* The telephone code is 599.

Practical Information

China International Travel Service Fujian, *7/F Lippo Tianma Plaza, 1 Wuyi Bei Road, 350001, Tel. 3370065, 3370070. North America department Tel. 3370110, Fax 3370077, 3370076. E-mail: fujicits@public.fz.fj.cn.* Ask for Ms. Hsu Fan or Manager of the Sales Department. Mr. Xu Xingtang.

CTS, Fujian Branch, *116 Wusi Road, 350001, Tel. 7615705, 7539219, Fax 7553983, 7535110. E-mail: fjcts1@pub3.fz.fj.cn.* Its ticket office is at 128 Wusi Road. Ask for Linda Lai, Sales Manager, who has been extremely helpful.

Fujian Provincial Tourism Bureau, *1, Daying Street, Dong Da Road, 350001, Tel. 7559379, Fax 7538758.* Ask for Sophie Cheng Yu-Fei.

Hours: Offices 8am-5pm (some until 6pm); stores, 8am-9pm.

Telephone code: 591

Xiamen

(Hsiamen, Amoy)

Xiamen is on the southeast coast of Fujian (Fukien) province, over 200 km across the straits from Taiwan, but just 2.5 km from one of Taiwan's offshore islands. It is important because it is one of the cleanest cities in China, well-run and very pleasant. Traffic jams are rare, city buses are modern and efficient, and bicycles are few. Even the few motorcyclists wear helmets! Fines are imposed for littering. Officially, no spitting is allowed, and only natural gas is used for fuel. The air is clean.

Xiamen is the ancestral home of millions of Overseas Chinese now living in other parts of Asia, a port city, and an important trading city. Over 2000 joint-venture companies operate here but no heavy industries or factories are allowed downtown. It is charming (like Hong Kong used to be), with some old architecture, and lots of parks. Its Gulanyu Island is a gem.

Xiamen was the home base of General Zheng Chenggong (known as Koxinga), who repelled the Manchu invaders and then rid Taiwan of the Dutch in 1662. Xiamen was a minor trading port when the British seized it in 1839. In 1842, the Treaty of Nanking allowed foreigners to build residences and warehouses here. For many years, especially in the late 1950s, both explosives and propaganda shells were lobbed onto Xiamen from Kinmen in Taiwan.

Today Xiamen has a 131 sq-km Special Economic Zone. Dell Computers, Kodak, Lucent Technology, and Microsoft are among the many international companies with projects here. The urban population is 550,000, the total 1.2 million. Local people speak the Xiamen or Fukienese dialect in addition to Mandarin. The hottest weather descends in July and August when the temperature soars to 38°C for a couple of weeks; the coldest is in February, when it could dip to -4°C. The annual precipitation is about 1206 mm, mainly from May to July.

Arrivals & Departures

You can no longer reach Xiamen by sea. It is a 1.5-hour flight southwest of Shanghai and one hour flight northeast of Guangzhou. It is linked by air with 51 other Chinese cities and by direct flights with Bangkok, Hong Kong, Kuala Lumpur, Macau, Manila, and Singapore. Its airport is one of the largest in China because Xiamen will be the major gateway from Taiwan when direct travel is resumed. It is on the north tip of Xiamen Island and takes about 25 minutes downtown by taxi.

You can get to Xiamen by train but many of these routes are painfully long. From Shanghai, for example, it could take over 24 hours. From Fuzhou, it's 15 hours by train. The bus from Fuzhou is much faster and takes less than four hours. You can also reach Xiamen by air-conditioned express bus in nine hours from Shenzhen, and in 1.5 hours from Quanzhou. It should soon take only four hours from Shantou.

Xiamen has many bus companies and can pick up passengers near hotels, but it could take an hour of several stops before your bus heads out of the city. Travel time is shorter if you leave from the main bus terminal. Wu Chu Bus Station is near the front entrance of the railway station and has frequent departures. Signs are only in Chinese. CITS charges Y100 for a transfer that includes transportation from a hotel and a guide to make sure you get on the right bus.

Orientation

Downtown is 131 sq. km Xiamen Island, where most of these hotels and the Gulangyu ferry are located. To any other place on this island, it's no more than a 30-minute drive. Taxis cost Y8 for three km. An 18-km expressway around the island should be finished in 2002. Zhongshan Road the main shopping area is near the ferry pier. Many of its colonial buildings still hang over the sidewalks in the charming old way, giving a nice feeling of history.

Where to Stay

The Mandarin is the only five-star hotel and it's opulent and good but isolated. If you want to be downtown near the action, look at the others. The three-star Lujiang Hotel has a special location on the waterfront near the Gulangyu ferry pier. It's got lovely old architecture. Gulangyu has a modest resort hotel. The hotels here, four-stars and up, have international standards, beauty salons, night clubs or discos, foreign exchange and credit card services. Hotels add 7%-15% service charge to the following prices which should be discounted.

XIAMEN MANDARIN HOTEL (Yue Hua Jiudian), *Huli District, 361006. Five stars. Six km from the airport and 20 minutes from downtown. Tel. 6023333, Fax 6021035. E-mail: mandarin@public.xm.fj.cn. Website: www.xmmandarin.com. About $180-$300 for rooms, $360-$700 for suites, and $580-$12000 for villas. It has been discounting 50% if reservations are made in advance. Its newest Hai Yu Building is the executive club with hi-tech facilities. The grounds are so big, you need a golf cart to get around quickly.*

Built in 1984, this 287-room complex is set on a hill with its own garden. It is very modern, sparkling clean, and well maintained. It has buildings of three and seven stories, and 14 villas. They have non-smoking rooms. Rooms are 45 to 50 square meters. There is a conference center, health club (new in 2002), pool, tennis, and free shuttle bus downtown. Rooms have safes, CNN, HBO, VOD, and broadband internet access. It serves French, Japanese, Sichuan, and Cantonese food and can seat 450 banquet style. The reception area is in the Tian Feng Hall. A Famous Hotel Club.

HOLIDAY INN CROWNE PLAZA HARBOURVIEW (Jiari Haijin Dajiudian), *12-8 Zhen Hai Road, 361001. Four stars aiming for five stars. Tel. 2023333, Fax 2036666. E-mail: reservation@hi592.com. Website: www.china.sixcontinentshotels.com (English). 15 km from the airport, four from the railway station, 0.6 km from the ferry pier, and close to shopping and the ferry. $160-$260 for rooms and $350-$820 for suites. It has been discounting 40% except during trade fairs. Weekends are cheaper than weekdays.*

Built in 1992, this 22-story, 349-room hotel has CNN, in-room safes, non-smoking rooms, and executive floors. Rooms are about 28 square meters with VOD and broadband internet access. It has Italian, Japanese, Western, and Chinese restaurants and 24-hour room service. Its banquet room can seat 550 at tables. There's a small outdoor pool, good gym, foot massage parlor and clinic. It houses the offices of Silk Air, American Express, ANA, and Malaysian Airlines. It renovated its lobby and suites in 2001.

THE MARCO POLO HOTEL, *8 Jianye Road, Hubin Bei, Yuandang New Urban District, 361012. Four-stars. Tel. 5091888, Fax 5092888. E-mail: xiamen@marcopolohotels.com. Website: www.marcopolohotels.com. $160-$225 for rooms and $250-$980 for suites. It has weekend packages and has been discounting 20%-50%. It is near government offices, Bank of China, the Trade Centre, Yuandang Lake, and city hall.*

With seven stories (one is executive), this luxury hotel has 350 rooms (including disabled and non-smoking). Rooms have safes, voice mail, eight television channels in English and broadband internet access. Its business center has international newspapers in English. Available is a good gym, sauna, and 24-hour room service, a 16-meter pool and tennis. There's a Japanese and Western restaurant. Its eight-story atrium has a waterfall, lounge, and Filipino band. Its complimentary shuttle goes to the airport 14 times a day. A Hong Kong joint venture.

LUJIANG HOTEL (Binguan), *54 Lujiang Road, 361001. Three stars, Tel. 2022922, Fax 2024644. E-mail: lujihtl@public.xm.fj.cn. Website: www.fjta.com/xmlujiang or www.xmlujiang.fjta.com. (Chinese only with photos.) Rooms have been Y410-Y700, and suites Y830-Y1360. It has been giving 30% discounts.*

Built in 1989, this six-story, 153-room hotel had major renovations in 1998. It has large rooms, Sichuan, Cantonese, Chaozhou, health-giving, and continental food. There's an American breakfast but no buffet for Y25. Its Chinese breakfast costs Y15 but you don't get coffee. It has IDD, satellite television, mini-bar and refrigerator, but the grouting is moldy, there's no CNN, and no in-room safe. It has an open roof-top patio with a good view of Gulangyu's neon lights. English could be a problem.

GULANGYU VILLA, *14 Gusheng Road, 361002. Three stars. Tel. 2060160, 2063280, Fax 2060165. E-mail: glvhotel@public.xm.fj.cn. Rooms have been Y360-Y550, and suites Y880, and it has been giving 20% discounts.*

This pretty 75-room hotel is on a swimming beach on the south shore in the western part of Gulangyu Island. It is relatively near the Arts and Crafts School and Gulang Rock. Rooms have balconies, only showers, no tubs, and are air-conditioned. There's a coffee room and Chinese restaurant. It also has a business center, IDD, conference room, and spacious grounds bordering its beach. It is managed by China Travel Hotel Management Services H.K. but I could find no one who spoke English.

QINDAO HOTEL (Jiudian) , *8 Lu Jiao Road, Tel. 2066668. Fax 2066688. Y235 to Y320. Suites are Y620. No discounts.*

This two-star 42-room guest house is about 200 meters to the left as you leave the main ferry pier on Gulanyu Island. It is beyond the station for renting electric cars, and has a Chinese restaurant, air-conditioning, satellite television, ticketing office, and international direct dialing facilities. I could find no one who could speak English. Rooms are clean but with peeling plaster. The Gulangyu Villa Hotel is better but this is okay if you're desperate for a bed on the island.

Where to Eat

Fijian food is much like Cantonese, and heavy on fresh sea foods, of course, with some distinctive dishes. The Fujianese tend to have more than two soups at a banquet. See Chapter 25 for recommended local dishes.

XIAMEN SHUYOU SEAFOOD RESTAURANT, *North Hubin Road, Tel. 5098888.*

This is close to the Marco Polo Hotel with moderate prices. Its private rooms have their own toilets.

LUJIANG HOTEL, *54 Lujiang Road, Tel. 2022922X709.*

This hotel has an interesting medicinal banquet on the sixth floor. Someone should be around who can explain in English each dish's effect on your body. The banquet is delicious and different with cashews, beancurd, celery, bamboo shoots, dangui (osmanthus flower) and fish. Tiny red goujizi berries are to brighten the eyes. Manyu fish should heal wounds and "dispel the water in the body." Bamboo, meat and pancreas of squid, are good for the breath. A menu in English is available.

The best Western food found is in the **Marco Polo Hotel** and the **Holiday Inn Crowne Plaza**. (I didn't have a chance to eat at the Mandarin but it has European chefs.) The coffee shop in the MarcoPolo charges Y45 for a Caesar salad, Y75 for a prawn cocktail, Y50 for tortilla chips with guacamole and spicy tomato salsa, Y88 for pork chops, and Y145 for a 220gm imported prime sirloin steak. Among the most popular dishes at the Crowne Plaza's Portofino Italian Restaurant are Pizza Margarita Y 42.00, Tournedos Alla Rossini Y168.00, and Tiramisu Y38.00.

There's also a clean, huge **Pizza Hut** with a great view of Gulangyu, on the 24th floor of the Haibin Building at 53 Lu Jiang Road to the left on the waterfront road as you leave the Lujiang Hotel and cross Zhongshan Road. Tel. 2033876. It is open 24 hours. Spaghetti has been Y25 to Y28; onion rings Y8; a 6" pizza Y23 to Y29; a 9" Y42 to Y49.

Seeing the Sights

Public bus #18 goes from Xiamen University to Jimei for Y5. #28 goes from Xiamen University to the National Exhibition Centre on Qian Pu Road for Y1. #67 goes from the harbor near the Lujiang Hotel to Tong An (movie city) for Y6.

The 1,000-year-old Nan Putuo (**South Putuo) Temple** is named after the home of the Goddess of Mercy. Most of the current buildings are recent, but the tablets, scrolls, sculptures, bells, etc., are from the Song and Ming. Famous is the stunning, three-faced, multi-armed statue of Guanyin. A festival is held here New Year's Eve. Behind the temple is Five Old Men Peaks, which you can climb for a good view of the Taiwan Straits. At its foot is the Overseas Chinese Museum, Fongchaon Hill, outlining the contributions of natives who emigrated overseas.

Special is the Ronguang Treasures Museum in the old **Hulisan Fort (**Bo Wu Yuan). It is one km south of Xiamen University. Take no. 17 bus from the railway station. It goes every 15 minutes. It's open 7am-6pm daily, Tel. 2099603. This museum has 4,600 fascinating rocks with natural pictures on them. Look for Emperor Qianlong's pet rock. These were collected by seven generations of a Singapore family. There's also an exhibit of fire arms, ranging upwards from 11 cm long, and including a 12th century cannon, believed to be the oldest in the world. A bonus here is a view of Taiwan's Kinmen which you can see through its powerful binoculars.

Jimei, 2.83 sq km, is worth an hour and is 15 km north of downtown. A 2.8-km causeway connects it with Xiamen Island on the road to Quanzhou. Eighty percent of its 23,000 people have relatives abroad.

On Jimei is a monument built by Overseas Chinese philanthropist, Tan Kah Kee, who made his money from rubber, rice, and pineapples in Singapore. Turtle Garden, built in 1950, is an encyclopedia in stone, full of pictures of what Mr. Tan wanted to teach people about the world outside China: factories, machinery, exotic animals, Chinese literature, history, and culture. His elaborate, horseshoe tomb has pictures of his life.

Nearby is the huge Jimei Middle School, one of many he financed. Here, Overseas Chinese students from all over the world come to study. For those curious about the man, a tiny museum is nearby.

See the Islands

Gulangyu (Drum Wave) Island is 1.7 hilly square kilometers, seven minutes across the 'Egret River' by ferry from Xiamen Island every five to 15 minutes. The Gulangyu population is about 15,000. Formerly the foreign ghetto with 14 consulates, its houses are currently being transformed into multi-storied resorts and apartments. It is a wonderful place to live, so close to downtown and yet so idyllic. It has a couple of swimming beaches. Dadeji is relatively close to the ferry pier. There's also Gangzi Hou or the Moon Garden.

The island is decorated profusely with frangipani, flame trees, and heavily-scented plants. Gulangyu is a car- and bicycle-free resort area, great for children and relaxing. It is cleaner and more prosperous-looking than Hong Kong's outlying islands to which it bears some resemblance.

There are electric carts that can take you on a tour for Y30. I took one to the Gulang Villa Hotel and it took two different routes, one through a long tunnel, and on the way back, up into the hills, a good opportunity to see the whole place. The dominating statue is of Koxinga. Gulangyu has two small museums, two churches (one from 1882), a temple, and a concert hall. Many music lovers live here and you might hear Bach and Verdi floating on the evening breeze. There's an Underwater World for Y70.

Everyone must climb or take the cableway up 90-meter-high **Riguang Yan (Sunlight Rock)** for the view and the story of two devoted egrets, the male killed by a greedy, unromantic goshawk. Also here is the Lotus Flower Nunnery (Sunshine Temple), the camp where Koxinga stationed his men, and Zheng Chenggong Memorial Hall, with souvenirs of his life, and a history written by a Dutchman about the fall of Taiwan/Formosa. The city museum is nearby.

If you want to walk to Shuzhuang Garden, designed in the late 1890s, take the road past the Concert Hall and People's Stadium. The island also has a piano museum. There's a map.

The adventurous might want to hire a boat from a fisherman or travel agent for a tour of the harbor, and see the Taiwan-held island of **Kinmen** a little closer. A couple of years ago, the first ship in 52 years arrived legally from the Taiwan offshore island of Kinmen/Quemoy. Unfortunately, it's been only one way so far. Visits from China to Kinmen are still illegal. When this route from China to Kinmen opens, it should be easy to visit the bunkers and the big guns which fired on Xiamen in the 1960s and to see the world's biggest amplifier.

Nightlife & Entertainment

During the **moon festival** in the autumn, people buy cakes in different shapes. The bigger the pancake, the bigger the wished-for fortune. Four hundred years ago, Koxinga started the popular local dice game of Bobian during the festival because his troops from Xiamen were homesick. A night market has been from about 6pm-10:30pm on Ding An Road. You can also try the **Arcadia Disco Pub**, Building N, Bailuzhou, Tel. 5088888 ext. 3788, 1766.

Xiamen has three golf courses, one of which is an 18-hole course designed by Greg Norman. The Mandarin has tennis. The Marco Polo has aerobic lessons. Dongshan Island Resort, four hours' drive south of Xiamen, is the best resort in the province.

Shopping

Locally made are Caiza silk figures, lacquer thread-decorated vases, colored clay figures, and bead embroidery. You may want to try the yupi peanuts, the gongtang crisp peanut cakes, dried longan fruit, and preserved olives. Locally grown are longan, litchis, oolong tea, and sugarcane. The main shopping street is near ancient Zhongshan Road, rebuilt in its original style. It is hard to park, but look for the white sign with green characters indicating a taxi or bus stop.

You should be able to buy commodities from Taiwan on Da Deng Dao Island, near Kinmen. It has over 200 stores. The main shopping street with big fancy department stores is Zhongshan Road.

Excursions & Day Trips
QUANZHOU

Quanzhou, a 1.5 to two hours' journey by road north of Xiamen, and a little over three hours south of Fuzhou, has always been a favorite. The closest airport is in Xiamen. Its urban population is 500,000, its total 7,280,000.

This city is unique in what it has to offer tourists, and even as it modernizes, it is still one of a kind. Its old apartment buildings and cottages are being torn down and replaced with new buildings, each district in its own distinct architecture. The designs incorporate traditional Chinese touches like curved eaves and roof tiles. The area around the mosque copies the archway from the gate of that building. Because glass skyscrapers are forbidden, Quanzhou is one of the best looking cities in China.

Quanzhou was considered one of the two largest ports in the world by Marco Polo, who knew it as Zaiton or Citong. Today it is one of the 24 cities protected by the State Council as a historical monument. But it's more than just architecture. It has some unique religious relics.

The two hotels here add a 10-15% service charge and take credit cards and travelers checks. The best hotels are now the Quanzhou Hotel and then the Overseas Chinese Hotel.

QUANZHOU HOTEL (Fandian), *22 Zhuang Fu Lane, 362000. Tel. 2289958, Fax 2182128. E-mail: quzhhtl@pub1.qz.fj.cn. Website: www.quanzhouhotel.com. Its four-star 13-story Nan Xin Building has 20 square meter rooms with safes and costs $110. Suites are $150-$1500. Its six-story, three-star Dong Hui Building has 18 square-meter rooms that cost Y468. Suites range from Y1300 to Y2633. It has been giving 30% discounts but not on its presidential suite which has its own sauna, jacuzzi, and karaoke. Renovations were made in 2001.*

This hotel has 295 rooms, non-smoking floors, and CNN. It has 12 bowling alleys, massage, and it charges Y40 for the use of both its pool and gym. The indoor pool is 20 meters long, is year-round and heated. The gym is small; the tennis court is lighted. Its hot pot costs Y48 and the breakfast buffet Y46. It serves continental, Cantonese, Hunan, and Fujian cuisine.

OVERSEAS CHINESE HOTEL, *Baiyuan Road, 362000. About a three star. Tel. 2282192, Fax 2284612. E-mail: hqds@public.qz.fj.cn. Website: www.overseaschinesehotel.com (Chinese). It is opposite the Workers' Cultural Park (Gong ren wen hua) and beside a couple of street markets (clothes and food), with lights and noise almost all night. It accepts credit cards, but no travelers checks. The Bank of China is close by. Rooms are Y350-Y580 and suites are Y460-Y2460. It has been giving at least 25% discounts.*

The lobby and two executive floors were renovated in 2001. It has 234 rooms 18 to 50 square meters, not including bath. They have large desks, safes, clean carpets, and CNN, a pool, tennis court, and five-piece gym.

Seeing Quanzhou

Among the unusual sights here is the **Kaiyuan Temple**, one km northwest of the Overseas Chinese Hotel. It dates from the Tang. The main hall has 100 heavy stone Greek-type columns, Indian touches, and gaudy bird-women musicians/servants. Look also for the 1000-armed, 1000-eyed Guanyin. Note the corners of the roof, the curled swallow tails, and the lively dragons that are distinctively southern Fujian. The two pagodas here are 48 and 44 meters high.

The **Quanzhou Maritime Museum** has unusual relics for China. It's at Donghu Road, Fengze Region, Tel. 2100561. The ancient Indian artifacts are from the home of an obviously wealthy Indian merchant and includes a 1.2 meter-high statue of the god Vishnu. It also has a statue of Mani, which looks like the one in the Caoan Temple, and could be a reproduction. Sources differ. Its label says that Manichaeanism had "elements of Jain, Christian and Buddhism." Mention is made of a Ceylonese prince, Shi Gong Xian, who arrived here in 1459, but virtually nothing is written of him. The museum is open 8am to 5:30pm daily, and also has models of junks and sampans and relics of Nestorian Christianity and Islam. Look for the Franciscan tombstone with a cross. There are remains of a 13th-century ship, 24-meters long, found in Quanzhou Bay.

The ***Qingjing** (**Grand Mosque**) on Tushan Street is half a kilometer from the Overseas Chinese Hotel. It is one of the few mosques in eastern China with west Asian architecture. Parts are ruins but the rest is still used for worship. Historical explanations are in English. One sign lists the surnames of the Moslem families here.

Old God Rock is four km from the city. This five-meter high stone statue of the God of Longevity or Laotze, the founder of Taoism, is 600 years old.

Caoan Temple is the last Manichaean temple in China of a minor but interesting religion, with a Persian prophet who became the god, Mani. The temple is 25 km. outside the south gate of the city, and very modest and small. The road there is bad for three kilometers, and no English sign helps illiterates in Chinese. But there is a notice in English on the gate which explains that the religion was started in the third century B.C. and came to China in the seventh century. It was brought by Uighur troops who were hired by the first Ming emperor as mercenaries. This temple was first built in 1339 A.D. The statue of Mani here was carved in the Yuan dynasty. At one time, St. Augustine was an adherent. My guide knew nothing about the religion, or the carved rock god inside, 1.5 meters tall with lightening and energy emanating from his body. Sources seem to agree that the statue of Mani here is really old. I found one worshipper, the woman caretaker. I don't think she knew how unique she was.

Local travel agents said to see **Chong Wu**, an old fishing village that is a 45-minute taxi ride from Quanzhou. It is off the main highway and difficult to get to by public bus.

The **Tomb of Zheng Chenggong (Koxinga)** is at Nan'an, about 25 km northwest of Quanzhou.

The hometown of the **sea goddess Mazu** or **Tianhou**, who is worshipped by fisherfolk in 1,500 temples around the world, especially in Hong Kong, Macau, and Taiwan, is on Meizhou Island, near the city of Putian. It is about 88 km from Quanzhou. Mazu was originally a woman named Lin Mo or Lin Mazu who lived from 960 to 987 A.D. and is credited with saving members of her own family and later other fishermen from shipwreck.

Yongding is a six-hour drive from Xiamen. Here are the "tu lou," the square or round clay villages (thought at one time by American intelligence to be missile sites). Actually, these three-story "tou lou" structures are in typical Hakka architecture, the front doors of each home facing inwards to the village central square. They were built this way for mutual protection and probably to control the families. Roads to Yongding are not great and tours usually spend two days. The villages organize typical Hakka programs. See travel agents.

CTS's Sales Manager Jacking Cai (Cai Jian Jing) has been very helpful for this book. His office is in the Overseas Chinese Hotel, Baiyuan Road, 362000. *Tel. 2226987, 2985687, Fax 2282366. E-mail: ctsqz@pub2.qz.fj.cn or caiwww@pub1.qz.fj.cn.*

A street of **internet bars** is to the right as you leave the Overseas Chinese Hotel. Turn at the second left at a store that says "Come on," in English near the Industrial Commercial Bank of China. There are 15 bars on Hou Cheng Street, and some are open 24 hours. They charge Y4 an hour.

Quanzhou's **telephone code** is 595.

Practical Information

Internet Café, *230-232 Hubin Nan Road, across from the Min Nan Hotel. Operated by China Telecom. Tel. 5155167 and 5155169.* It's open 24 hours and costs Y7 an hour.

China Travel Service, *70 Xin Hua Road. Tel. 2024286, 2079408, 2042206, Fax 2031862.* Contact: Ms Doris Liu.

CITS, *15/F of the Zhenxing Building, Tel. 2231259, Fax 2231260, 5145063. E-mail: CITSXM@public.xm.fj.cn.* Contact Nancy Chen, International Dept. Manager or Linda Deng (Deng Lin), Tour Dept. Manager.

Telephone Code: 592

The Grand Canal

The oldest and longest in the world, the **Grand Canal** was built in the Sui dynasty (581-618 A.D.) and originally extended 1,794 km from Hangzhou to Beijing, an inland shipping route safe from seafaring pirates.

Today, visitors can still take tour boats on parts of the canal for an intimate look at life on the water. The water is dirty and the trip can be noisy. However, that was the way it was 1500 years ago! At individual cities along the route, you can visit parts of the canal. **Wuxi** has a 36.5-meter-long, two-storied "dragon boat" with flashing eyes. Tours also cruise near **Suzhou**.

Hangzhou

(Hangchow)

Visitors flock to **Hangzhou**, the capital of Zhejiang province, because of beautiful West Lake. Hangzhou also has temples, gardens, tea, museums, herbal medicines, and its history as the capital of the Southern Song dynasty. It has the largest silk market in the country. But essentially the visit is to experience this lake, by boat, on foot, or above from the hills. It is spectacular.

Arrivals & Departures

Located 140 km southwest of Shanghai, Hangzhou is best reached from there by two-hour or so express trains leaving about six times a day. Important to know is that its new Hangzhou Railway Station is for trains terminating in the city. The old train station is now the Hangzhou East Railway Station and is a stop for trains passing through. When you buy a ticket, ask about this. In addition, if you are going to Shanghai from Hangzhou, make sure your ticket is for the main Shanghai station, not the Shanghai south station. Otherwise you will end up in a suburban station with no taxis. Insist on "Express" and "new station to new station."

An express roadway runs between Hangzhou and Shanghai, and by the end of 2002, an expressway linking Hangzhou with Suzhou should take cars 1.5 hours by road. Hangzhou has air connections with Hong Kong and 37 Chinese cities. Shanghai's Hongqiao airport is 90 minutes by road from Hangzhou and there are no flights between Shanghai and Hangzhou.

Orientation

Hangzhou is on the **Qiantang River** at the southern end of the Grand Canal, on the east coast of China. Founded over 2,200 years ago in the Qin, it began to prosper as a trading center after that important canal was completed in 610. It was the capital of the tiny state of Wuyueh (893-978), at which time the first dikes forming the lake were built. After 1127, it became the capital of the Southern Song dynasty.

The best book giving a detailed picture of the city from 1250 to 1276 is Jacques Gernet's *Daily Life in China on the Eve of the Mongol Invasion*, essential for visitors who want to know a lot of history, to compare life then with now, and to look for old ruins. The city was seized by the Mongols under Kublai Khan in 1279 and visited by Marco Polo the next year when it was known as Kinsai. The Venetian explorer raved about it, then the largest and richest in the world, its silks and handicrafts much in demand in China and abroad.

Hangzhou has been a famous resort for centuries, attracting painters, poets, and retired officials as well as tourists. It is also a major industrial city producing chemicals, steel, pharmaceuticals, and electronics. Villages here grow the famous Longjing (Dragon Well) tea, and silk worms. Today Zhejiang province produces one-third of China's silk.

Tourists spend most of their time around West Lake, and on Hefang Street which has been reconstructed in Ming and Qing dynasty architecture. The modern commercial city and train stations are east of the lake. One of the main shopping areas is around Wuling Square near the Radisson Hotel. The business and financial center, and soon department stores, are near or around Wushan Square.

A pedestrian street is being constructed on Hefang Street near the Medicine Museum in Ming and Qing Dynasty architecture. The new Qun Huang Ge tower, on top of the hill within sight of its entrance at the southern end of Yanan Nan Road, is near the site of the old Song dynasty palace and has a good view of the lake.

The coldest weather is in January, a little below -10°C; the hottest is in July, with highs of 37°C. The annual precipitation is about 1452 millimeters, mainly May-June. The population of greater Hangzhou is 6.5 million, and of urban Hangzhou 3.7 million. The air is better than many other cities and the atmosphere is more relaxed

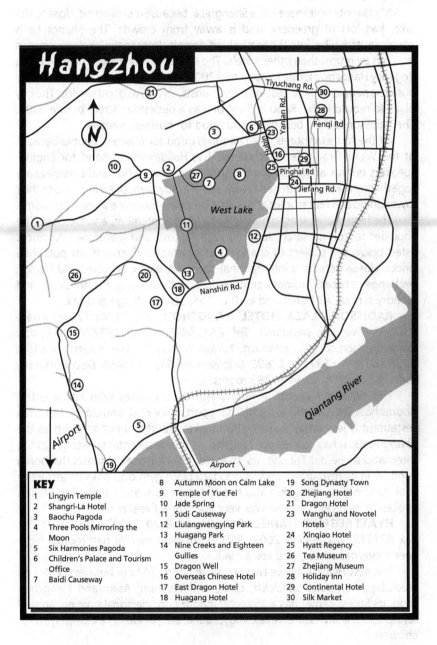

Hangzhou

West Lake

Qiantang River

Airport

Airport

Tiyuchang Rd.

Yanan Rd.

Fenqi Rd.

Pinghai Rd.

Jiefang Rd.

Nanshin Rd.

KEY

1 Lingyin Temple
2 Shangri-La Hotel
3 Baochu Pagoda
4 Three Pools Mirroring the Moon
5 Six Harmonies Pagoda
6 Children's Palace and Tourism Office
7 Baidi Causeway
8 Autumn Moon on Calm Lake
9 Temple of Yue Fei
10 Jade Spring
11 Sudi Causeway
12 Liulangwengying Park
13 Huagang Park
14 Nine Creeks and Eighteen Gullies
15 Dragon Well
16 Overseas Chinese Hotel
17 East Dragon Hotel
18 Huagang Hotel
19 Song Dynasty Town
20 Zhejiang Hotel
21 Dragon Hotel
23 Wanghu and Novotel Hotels
24 Xinqiao Hotel
25 Hyatt Regency
26 Tea Museum
27 Zhejiang Museum
28 Holiday Inn
29 Continental Hotel
30 Silk Market

Where to Stay

My favorite hotel here is the Shangri-La, because it's romantic, close to the lake, has lots of greenery, and is away from crowds. The Shangri-La is convenient for hikes into the hills behind it and is closer to the lake's causeways (but not by much) than other hotels. The service is very good. The new Hyatt Regency Hangzhou is due to open mid-2002, should have the best location for business people and the best view for tourists, as well as good service. The city plans to rebuild Hubin Road in front of it as a pedestrian street before 2006. The Radisson is third best here, and good for business people.

Of the four-star hotels, the Dragon is good for business people because of the World Trade Center close-by. The Holiday Inn is good for English-speakers but it's about 2.5 km from the lake. The Haihua and Lakeview are together by the lake. Both need work and are only mentioned because of their lower prices and fantastic locations. The Lakeview has some three–star rooms.

The high tourist season here is April, May, September, and October. The shoulder season is March, June through August, and November. All prices listed below are subject to change and substantial discounts off published prices. Hotels here have international standards with credit card and foreign exchange services, business centers, IDD, coffee shops, health clubs, and laundry service. All hotels add a 10 or 15% service charge and tax.

RADISSON PLAZA HOTEL HANGZHOU, *333 Ti Yu Chang Road, 310006. Five star standards. Tel. 85158888, Fax 85157777. Website: www.radisson.com/hangzhoucn. 1.5 km from West Lake. Rooms are $190-$250 and suites $315 to $3600. Duplexes are $420 to $465. Discounts have ranged from 26% to 54%. 283 rooms.*

This hotel has executive floors, and duplex suites with kitchenettes. Rooms have 24-hour movies, CNN, data port, voice mail, and clocks. Its Italian restaurant is less classy and its Y98 breakfast buffet is not as lavish as the Shangri-La's. It has conference facilities. Its business center subscribes to the International Herald Tribune. Its 15-meter pool entertains guests through a window in its restaurant, and its good 20-piece gym overlooks its attractive roof garden. Its health club also has a steam room and sauna. The English spoken at its reception desk was very poor for a five-star hotel.

HYATT REGENCY HANGZHOU, *28 Hubin Road, 310006. Tel. 87131234, Fax 87131818. Opening 2002. 368 rooms with marble bathrooms, high-speed internet access, and voice mail.*

This new Hyatt will have two executive floors, 24-hour business center on weekdays, computer specialist, clinic, and Western, Asian and Hangzhou food. Its fitness center has a 25-meter indoor pool, personal training, lighted tennis court, acupressure, reflexology, sauna, etc., as well as a Camp Hyatt for children.

SHANGRI-LA HOTEL HANGZHOU (Shang Gorilla Fandian), *78 Beishan Road, 310007. Five stars, Tel. 87977951, Fax 87073545. $180-$360 for rooms, $330-$1000 for suites. Discounts are on its Website: www.shangri-la.com. E-mail: slh@mail.hz.zj.cn. This hotel is on the north shore of West Lake. The best view of the lake is from its East Building executive floor. Its lake view is otherwise blocked by historic 300-year old camphor trees. It is 7km from Hangzhou Railway Station.*

Rooms are 33 to 58 square meters. Its recently-renovated East Building has 156 rooms. Its Main Building dates from 1956 and has six stories, 199 rooms with smallish bathrooms and is more convenient to its store and restaurants. These two buildings are joined by a covered walkway. It also has three villas, a total of 387 rooms. There's a business center, broadband internet access, a historic 500-seat theater, satellite television, and Italian and Cantonese restaurants. The breakfast buffet costs Y152. It has a good 20-piece gym, boating, bicycles, and a 33-meter-long pool. The hotel has been under Shangri-La International management since 1985.

See also Chapter 13, *Best Places to Stay*.

LAKEVIEW HOTEL HANGZHOU (Wanghu Binguan), *2 West Huancheng Road, 310006. Four stars. Tel. 87078888, Fax 87073027. E-mail: whhotel@wanghuhotel.com or sales@lakeviewhotelhz.com. Website: www.wanghuhotel.com. Y980-Y1280 for rooms Y1600-Y3600 for suites. It has been discounting 40%. Economy rooms are Y250-Y500.*

This hotel has 410 rooms, most 20 square meters. It has an executive floor, CNN, CNBC, health club and pool, and Cantonese and Sichuan restaurants. It has a second building with two and three-star rooms. Economy rooms have dirty carpets, CNN, kettles, no tubs, just showers, no refrigerators, and no elevator service. You can get a cheap and good pedicure here.

HOLIDAY INN HANGZHOU, *289 Jianguo Bei Road (at Fengqi), 310003. Four star standards, Tel. 85271188, Fax 85271199. E-mail: hihz@mail.hz.zj.cn. Website: www.holiday-inn.com. Y900-Y1500 for rooms and Y2300-Y6688 for suites. It has been discounting 20-50%. It is 10 km from Jian Qiao airport, and four km from Hangzhou Railway Station, in a residential district near the new financial and trading district. It is also 500 meters from the Silk Market, and close to several antique stores.*

This hotel has 294 rooms, three executive floors, non-smoking floors and rooms for the physically challenged. Rooms have safes, CNN, CNBC, and HBO, and irons, and are 28 square meters. There is a 15-meter long year-round indoor pool, and 23-piece gym. It has a delicatessen, Cantonese, Western, and international restaurants, and conference facilities. Live snakes and turtles, on display, are among the special dishes in its Chinese restaurant. There's a play area for children. It charges no service fee for booking tickets for guests.

DRAGON HOTEL (Huang Long Fandian), *7 Shuguang Road, 310007, next to the World Trade Center. Four stars, Tel. 87998833, Fax 87998090. E-*

mail: dragon@mail.hz.zj.cn. Website: www.dragon-hotel.com. 34 km from the airport, seven km from the railway station. Five minutes walk to Dragon Cave. Y600-Y890 for rooms, Y1200-Y5000 for suites.

Built in 1987-88 with most rooms renovated in 1998, this six-, seven and nine-story hotel has 525 spacious rooms, most with small baths, CNN, HBO, and CNBC. It has a gym, lighted outdoor tennis courts, bicycles, and a 25-meter outdoor pool. It has a beautiful inner courtyard garden, and airport shuttle service. Its ballroom seats 350 people banquet style. The buffet breakfast is $10.

HAI HUA (Hai Hua Dajiudian), *298 Qingchun Road, 310006. Four stars. Tel. 87215888, Fax 87215108. Rooms are $67-$140, and suites $250-$780. It has been discounting 45%.*

Opened in 1997 and no longer a Novotel in 2002, this hotel has 247 rooms ranging from 26.8 to 34 square meters, 25- and 40-watt lamb bulbs, and maybe CNN. It has a steam room, a 13-meter heated indoor pool, four-piece gym, massage, and dance hall. Its breakfast buffet costs Y80. The carpets were stained.

Where to Eat

Hangzhou claims "beggar's chicken" as its own. The first was made with lotus leaves and mud from West Lake. The lake fish is very bony. The food and ambiance in the hotels are generally good.

LOU WAI LOU RESTAURANT, *30 Gushan Road, Tel. 87969023, 87969682. E-mail: louwailou.com@pub.zjpta.net.cn. It is near the Shangri-La Hotel. It takes only Chinese credit cards and cash, and is open 10am-2:30pm, and 4pm-9:30pm. It is accessible by boat.*

This 1848 restaurant is famous. It does put MSG in its food so tell them if you don't want it. It has four big dining rooms, and a terrace overlooking the lake. Its most beautiful room is the Russian dining room with a fancy chandelier. Its beggar's chicken is Y89, West Lake fish in sweet and sour sauce Y35, Su Dong pork Y5 each, and water shield soup Y25 for a big bowl. It has a limited menu in English and a brochure with helpful photos. There are two Western toilets.

HU QING YU TANG (MEDICINE) RESTAURANT, *across from the Traditional Medicine Museum, 88 Da Jin Lane, Wu Shan, Tel. 87025896, 87025922. It is open 8am to 8pm and takes only Chinese credit cards.*

Founded in 1873 and serving "healthy food," it has a booklet in English with photos of dishes that are meant to prevent and treat diseases. You need a scientific dictionary to understand some of the ingredients like radix angelicae sinensis and fructus lycii. Staff can explain what each dish is supposed to do – like "invigorating vital energy, tonic therapy, strengthening the bones and muscles." Think of it as adventurous eating. Much of it tastes good too. It serves regular Hangzhou food as well with dishes from Y6 to Y68. Its Western toilet is clean.

The **Food Street** on the ground floor of the **Wang Hu Hotel** serves fast Hangzhou, Guangdong and Sichuan food and it isn't bad. Its deep-fried duck was Y36, custard with minced pork Y16, fried pork liver with leek Y15, fried asparagus with garlic sauce Y18, and baked beggar's chicken Y88. The won ton was Y7, soft drinks Y8, and beer Y8 to Y25. It has vegetables growing in boxes which you can order. You can try its well-reputed top floor restaurant too.

PEPPINO'S, *Shangri-La Hotel, 78 Beishan Road, Tel. 87977951.*

For Italian food, there's Peppino's, whose executive chef is French but it has visiting Italian chefs. It also has a good supply of Cuban cigars. The menu is changed four times a year but this will give you an idea of what's available. The suberb goose liver came with puff pastry, black truffle, mushrooms, parsley and wine sauce for Y75. Cream of mushroom soup had a poached egg, two kinds of mushrooms, onions, and pesto for Y35. The double lamb chops with a choice of sauces and garnish was Y170. The T-Bone steak was Y160. For dessert there was tiramisu for Y55, and apple tart for Y45. There's no MSG and it uses real Italian ingredients.

THE OAK, *at the Holiday Inn, Tel. 85271188.*

Steaks range from Y140 to Y180, soup Y30, and grilled beef burgers Y78. It's at 289 Jianguo Bei Road (at Fengqi),

PIZZA HUT, *by the lake at 15 Hubin Road. Tel. 87016029.*

Expect a queue outside at mealtimes. A nine inch costs Y45-Y55, and a 12 inch Y65-Y85.

Seeing the Sights

The city now has air-conditioned tourist buses to the major attractions. From the Lingyin Temple, No. 1 connects with Yanan Xin Cun near Wulin Square in city center and No.4 goes to the Song Dynasty town. A one-day city tour can cost from Y240 to Y650 each depending on the number of people booked. You don't have to take a tour to see the most important attraction here. Just get a map and a bicycle. You can also hire your own boat.

Xihu (West Lake), is a 5.6-sq km lake, linked to the Qiantang River. It was first dredged under the orders of the famous Song poet, Su Dong Po, then mayor. It is now 15 km in circumference, with an average depth of 1.8 meters. Lotus flowers bloom from late June through August, great carpets of green with pink globes. In the spring and autumn, the mist floats over the water. Fireworks explode in October.

Paths go up the hill behind the Shangri-La Hotel for a great view. You go out the main door of the Shangri-La and make a right. After the Yue Fei Temple make another right and go up the stairs to the right. You can walk along the ridge northeast to Baochu Pagoda, a 1 1/2 hour round trip.

Visitors with only one day to spend in the city could take a boat ride with stops at various famous sites. Take in the **Pagoda of Six Harmonies, Lingyin Temple, Jade Spring,** and a **silk factory**. You can hire boats at different places around the lake. The best times to see the lake itself is in the mist, in the moonlight, or just at sunrise before the sun makes strong shadows. One of the favorite spots for viewing the lake, especially during the harvest moon, is at **Pinghuqiuyue (Autumn Moon on Calm Lake Pavilion)** at the southeastern end of Gu Shan (Solitary Hill). But don't expect to be alone.

On an islet is the **Wenlan Ge (Pavilion for Storing Imperial Books)**, built in 1699 (Qing), and one of the seven imperial libraries. This one was especially built to store the *Sikuzhunsu*, a 33,304 volume Chinese encyclopedia ordered by Emperor Qianlong. It took 10 years to copy it by hand. The stone Chamber to the Three Venerables (Han San Lao Hui Zi) here was carved in 52 A.D. The island has the provincial museum, *Tel. 87971177*, open 8:30am-4:30pm) and a good restaurant, the Lou Wai Lou.

The famous **Zig-Zag Bridge** is on the islet Xiaoyingzhou (Three Pools Mirroring the Moon) and can be reached only by boat. Did you know that bad spirits can only move in straight lines? Stand on the bridge here and nothing can harm you. This islet was first constructed in 1607 (Ming) with mud cleared from the lake. Look for the "island in a lake and the lake in an island."

During the Moon Festival, candles light up the small pagodas, thus creating "Three Pools Mirroring the Moon."

The **Liuhe Ta *(Pagoda of Six Harmonies)**, Zhijiang Road, *Tel. 86591364, 87038911, 86082980*, is on the north bank of the Qiantang River. Open about 6:30am-5:30pm. Built in 970 A.D., it is 59.89 meters or 13-stories tall, octagonal, and made of brick and wood. It can be climbed for a good view. West of this temple is the shallow and clear Nine Creeks and Eighteen Gullies.

Seeing Hangzhou on Wheels

You can rent a bicycle from a hotel then toodle along the 1.8 km, 1,000 year old Baidi Causeway with stops at the Autumn Moon on Calm Lake Pavilion, Wenlan Ge (next to the Zhejiang Provincial Museum), Xiling Seal Engraver's Society, Tomb and Temple of Yue Fei, and Jade Spring. Leaving the lake, go to Lingyin Temple. Turn back to the Yue Fei Tomb and then south onto Sudi Causeway. Follow Nan Shan and then Hubin roads. Stop to enjoy Liulanwenying Park if only for its name, which means Park to See the Waving Willow and Hear the Singing of the Birds.

Another beautiful bicycle tour, says the Shangri-La, is to Longjing Village (5 km from the Shangri-La), down to Nine Creeks and Eighteen Gullies on cobblestone roads, through the Longjing Tea Plantations, and back.

The **Lingyin (Soul's Retreat) Temple**, One Fa Yun Si Nong, Te/. 87968665. Open about 7:30am-4:30pm. Entry to the park is Y20, and to the temple an additonal Y15. Lingyin is nine km from the city, west of West Lake. Founded in 326 A.D., its Celestial King's Hall and 33.6-meter-high Buddha Hall are all that is left of the original 18 pavilions and 72 halls. Lingyin at one time housed 3000 monks. The seated Sakyamuni inside is 19.6 meters high. The temple guardian behind the Four Celestial Kings was carved from camphor wood during the Song. Lingyin is still one of the largest and most magnificent temples in China. It has a new hall with 500 life-size arhats and a very cheap, dirty, and simple vegetarian restaurant with no English.

Across from Lingyin temple is ***Feilaifeng (Peak that Flew from Afar)**, named by an Indian monk after a similar-looking Indian peak that must have flown here! The 380 carvings along the narrow, hilly trails are from the Five Dynasties to the Yuan.

It could take three or four days to cover all the important spots in Hangzhou at leisure. The 45-meter-high **Baochu (Precious Stone Hill) Pagoda** is on a 200-meter-high hill north of the lake. It was first built in 968 to pray for the safe return of the unjustly arrested Qian Hongchu, a successful effort. The pagoda was last reconstructed in 1933.

The ***Tomb and Temple of Yue Fei**, Te/. 87969670, is at the northwest corner of the lake, next to the Shangri-La Hotel. It is open 6:30am-6:30pm and charges Y20. He was a famous Song general who was unjustly executed in 1142. Public reaction forced a retrial 20 years later that reversed the verdict. A temple was built with statues of his four accusers kneeling for forgiveness before his grave. These four are spat on even today.

Yue Fei was also a calligrapher and poet who came from a family that valued patriotism. His mother tattooed his back with four characters to remind him of his duty to his country. His son was murdered on the day of Yue Fei's death. Their tombs are together but only contain their clothing. An exhibition hall illustrates Yue Fei's battles.

At the **West Lake Longjing (Dragon Well) Tea Co.**, Longjing Road, Te/. 87962219, you can see the famous tea growing on hillsides. It is usually picked in late March or early April. Connoisseurs of good tea pay fabulously high prices for the best of the harvest, the most tender leaves hand-picked before the spring rain. The quantity is also limited because only a few villages have the proper soil and water.

The **Jade Spring** is on Yugu Road, off the northwest corner of the lake, within walking distance of the Shangri-La Hotel. It is for goldfish and flower lovers, as multi-colored ornamental fish are bred here. It is inside the 200-hectare **Hangzhou Botanical Garden**, Te/. 87961908, which has 3700 species of plants, including 120 varieties of bamboo.

A cable car runs 8am-5pm between Beigao Feng (North Peak) and near the Lingyin Temple, giving a good view of the lake. You can also drive up

Wushan Hill, east of the lake, the highest spot in the city. This has an 800-year-old camphor tree and the ruins of the former Song palaces, trashed by the Mongols. At 6am it is full of taiji and disco people.

There are many interesting museums, all with signs in English. Among them is the **Tea Museum** which has good exhibits and is open daily 8:30am-4:30pm all year, *Tel. 87964221, 87068136*. It's four km from the Shangri-La past the Xihu Guest House west of the lake.

The **Silk Museum**, just south of the lake, has the oldest weaving machines in China, ancient silks and Ming and Qing court robes. It also has a silk fragment from 2715 B.C. It is open 8:30am-4:30pm. *Tel. 87071843*.

The **Hu Qing Yu Tang Museum of Traditional Chinese Medicine** on He Fan and Dajingxiang Streets, *Tel. 87815209, 86992277*, should be seen for its beautiful old wood-panelled building as well as its exhibits, one of the two most famous herbal medicine stores in the Qing. Open 8am or 8:30am-5pm Monday to Friday, it closes for lunch from 11am-12noon and has titles in English. It is across from the Medicine Restaurant.

Interesting is **Song Dynasty Town** with demonstrations of Song weaving, pottery-making, puppetry, and pony rides. You do get some feeling for the architecture of the period, but I didn't like the children who kept jumping on the suspension bridge. It's at 148 Zhijiang Road, 310008, *Tel. 87090470, 87321785, Fax 87090471*. Y50. Open 8am-9:30pm, April-November with shorter hours in winter, and with many show times.

Ask about the special events like the marathon race in October, international boat festival (September), the annual China Silk Culture Festival late October, the traditional medicine festival in May, and New Year's Eve.

Nightlife & Entertainment

The Shangri-La has had a jazz band. The **Paradise Disco** (TIANTANG RENJIAN) is in the World Trade Center, 15 Shuguang Road, *Tel. 87990888*. The **Stargate Disco** in the Hyatt Regency Shopping Plaza, 126 Pinghai Road, *Tel. 87131234* is good.

Romance is taking a boat on the lake after dark under a full moon on a warm summer evening with the one you love. Head for Three Pools Mirroring the Moon, or Su Causeway and Bai Causeway and expect to pay about Y240 for two hours.

Relax in a tea house. You don't go there to eat. You go here to talk, nibble preserved fruit, fish, seeds and nuts, and drink tea—all day if you want. The easiest to find is the **Hupanju Cha Lou** at 23 Hubin Road. It's open 7:30am-1am and accepts Visa cards. It is on the lake near the Hai Hua and Lakeview/Wanghu Hotels with curved Chinese roofs. Its 120 different kinds of teas range from Y30 to Y5000. A demonstration of tea ceremony costs Y80. Staff can tell you which tea to drink to lose weight or fight insomnia. Toilets are clean.

Then there's **Starbucks** at 333 Yiyuchang Road, *Tel. 35067159*.

Sports & Recreation

Hotels have packages for the **West Lake Golf CLub**. Its 36 holes were designed by Jack Nicklaus.

Shopping

This province is known for silk textiles, woven silk pictures, satin, brocades, silk parasols, lace, mahogany and boxwood crafts. It also produces fresh water pearls, longquan celadon, sandalwood fans, woven bambooware, distinctive Tianzhu chopsticks, and stone and wood carvings. Look for the incredible multi-colored pyrophylite stone carvings from Qingtian. Most valuable are the translucent ones with many colors. The Dragon Hotel has some magnificent Qingtian carvings in its lobby.

Hangzhou also makes some fancy scissors that are useful souvenirs. Now that green tea is fashionable for health, a package should be a welcome gift at home. Loose leaves are better quality than tea bags.

The main shopping areas are **Jiefang Road** and **Yan'an Road**. For a local department store, try the **Hangzhou Department Store** on Jiefang Road, *Tel. 85158800*.

For silk fabric and garments, check out prices and quality in the department stores, the Silk Museum, or the **Hangzhou Silk Store** at 1 Hubin Road, *Tel. 87028963, 87020733*. Then visit the **Hangzhou Sichou Shichang** (wholesale silk market). It's at 253 Xinhua Road, *Tel. 85152901*. It is open daily 8am or 8:30-6pm with three blocks of shops full of overruns and seconds from many of the local silk factories. Prices are great but better if you haggle. Wonderful scarves streaked with gold thread cost Y10 (small) and Y65 (large) at **Si Tai Si Jin**, at number 3-1 on the shorter sidestreet. Tel. 85193547. The same larger scarves were in a hotel shop for Y250. Silk by the meter ranges from Y58 to Y85. A heavy weight satin silk sleeveless tank top was about Y40, men's dress shirt Y75, and panties for Y18. "Washable silk" in Chinese is "Ke Shui Xi Sichou."

The **Du Jin Sheng Silk Factory** is at No. 519 Feng Qi Road, 310006, *Tel. 87064420*. Call to let them know you are coming to see the process.

Lots of tea pots are for sale in the Tea Museum. **Wushan Road** (Wushan Yeshi) is a good place for serious antiques. It has about five stores. Try the **Siu Shu Keung** at Number 118, *Tel. 87060926*, for ancestral portraits (at one-third Hong Kong prices), jade, and porcelain. In the evening from 7pm-10pm, this road turns into a curio market.

The government **Cultural Relics Company** at 90 Dongpo Road just east of the lake, *Tel. 87013447*, has good quality but prices are a little high. It gives export seals.

Excursions & Day Trips

For Ningbo (about 168 km or 2 1/2 hours southwest) and Shaoxing (about 58 km or 1 1/2 hours southeast), see below. For Huangshan (200 km west), see separate listings.

Between Hangzhou and Huangshan is the 30-year-old **1,000 Island Lake (Qian Dao Hu)**, a two-day trip with an overnight at the lake. This largely undeveloped lake is 580 sq km, very pretty and pristine. Mountains rise up to 200 meters. On its 1078 islands are a couple of temples. One island has 200 wild, free-roaming monkeys. Another has a thousand snakes in pits (a worthwhile 30-minute stop). From the hotel, you can take a ferry to Anhui province on the other side of the lake and then go by road to Huangshan.

Wuzhen is a reconstructed 1000-year-old village with citizens in period costume and demonstrations of wine making and puppets. It is considered the best of the water towns and is in north Zhejiang province, a two-hour drive from Shanghai and 1.5 hour drive from Hangzhou. This village is not overly commercial and people are friendly. The entry ticket allows you into a temple, and to watch demonstrations. There's a bed museum, and a boat ride. See "water towns" under Shanghai. Buses going from the Stadium in Shanghai are cheaper than hiring a taxi from Hangzhou.

The **Tidal Bore of the Qiantang River** is most spectacular in early October. In 1974 it reached a height of nine meters, but it is not usually that dramatic. You can be seen it in nearby Haining or Xiaoshan (Tidal Wave Watching Resort). Travel agents can arrange.

Practical Information

Hours: offices, 8:30am-5 or 5:30pm with lunch about 11:30am-1:30pm, Monday to Friday; stores daily 9am-8 or 9pm; banks 8:30am-5pm five days a week; most temples open daily from 8:30am-5:30pm, museums 9am-4 or 4:30pm daily. Some parks close at 6pm.

Travel agents & Tourism Offices:
• the **Holiday Inn** here charges Y20 to book a train seat and Y40 to book a sleeping berth. It charges its guests nothing to book a plane ticket.
• **China Hangzhou Overseas Tourist Co.**, *3/F Yaojiang Tower, 239 West Lake Road, Tel. 87709821, 87709770 (operator), Fax 87709772, 87709771. E-mail: otchzfjp@mail.hz.zj.cn, otctravel@mail.china.com.* Ask for Daniel Xu, Manager, Incoming Tours Dept. who gave me a lot of help. *Tel. 13606500335.* This agency charges Y200 a day for a guide plus expenses, $5 to book a hotel room or flight.
• **CITS Zhejiang**, *1 Shihan Road, 310007, Tel. 85157361, 85215526, Fax 85156576. E-mail: zjcitsat@mail.hz.zj.cn.* Ask for Lin Shu Sen, Director, English Department Sales. It charges $10 to book a flight or hotel. For a guide in Hangzhou for two to five people, it charges $30 for eight hours. It also charges $5 for booking a flight or hotel room.

• **Hangzhou Tourism Bureau**, *484 Yanan Road, Tel. 85165224, Fax 85152645. E-mail hljtc@mail.hz.zj.cn.*
• **Zhejiang Provincial Travel and Tourism Bureau**, *1 Shihan Road, Hangzhou, 310007. Brochures available. Contact Mr. Xu Peng, Tel 87054468. Fax 85156429. Or Mr. He Shi Yuan, Tel. 87054458.* Tourist complaints, contact Supervisory Bureau of Tourism Quality of Zhejiang Province, *Tel. 85156631, 85158831, Fax 85156429.*

Internet cafés: Many are on Wensan Road near the I.T. shops.
Telephone code: 575.
Tourist Complaints: *Tel. 85171292*

Ningbo
(Ningpo)

Ningbo is on the Zhejiang coast south of Shanghai. With an urban population of 1.240 million people, it is known for its great ship builders and prominent business people. It also has some important archaeological and historical sites.

Arrivals & Departures

Ningbo can be reached by train (in about 1.5 hours) or two hours by road from Hangzhou. It can also be reached by express bus from Shanghai and Hangzhou. It is linked by plane with about 29 Chinese cities and Hong Kong. From Shanghai it's a 30-minute flight, a convenient weekend trip.

Orientation

The Ningbo area was settled at least since 4800 B.C. and some scholars now claim the cradle of Chinese civilization was here, and not the Yellow River. Records were first made in the Spring and Autumn Period (700-476 B.C.). It has been a major port since the Tang. Ice-free, it was made a treaty port, open to foreign trade and residence in 1842. After 1860, a French military detachment was stationed here.

If you have only one day, see Hemudu, the library and the two temples to the east. From Ningbo, Putuoshan could be a two-day trip.

Where to Stay & Eat

Hotels here have international services like credit cards, business centers, and international direct dial telephones. Add 15% surcharge to prices.

CITIC NINGBO HOTEL, *One Jiangdong Bei Road. Five stars. Tel. 87757888, Fax 87334739. CITS charges $58.*

XIN YUAN HOTEL, *188 Jiefang Nan Road, 315000. Four stars. Tel. 87321818, Fax 87294439.*

Seeing the Sights

The ***Tianyige Library**, completed in 1561 (Ming to Qing) is half a kilometer from the Asia Garden Hotel. It still has more than 300,000 books, 80,000 of which are from the Ming. Scholars can see these books upon request. The library is worth visiting for its simple elegance and its peaceful, tastefully-designed gardens. It was the blueprint for the other seven imperial Qing libraries.

At the entrance to the library is a sign that says something like "This is not an amusement park. No fun inside. Keep out." Don't be intimidated by the blunt Ningbo manner. Note also the conversations of the man-in-the-street, which might sound like intense, bitter arguing.

Both the **Tiantong Temple** (35 km), and the **Ayuwang (King Asoka) Temple** (30 km) are east of the city in rural hill country. The Ayuwang was founded in the third century and has relics of Sakyamuni (Buddha) in its highest hall. The Tiantong Temple is one of the largest temples south of the Yangtze, with over 700 halls and over 100 monks. The Tiantong has sent many teachers to Japan and consequently attracts many Japanese visitors. It is the second holiest shrine of the Zen or Chan sect. Zen Buddhist statues are supposed to have deepset eyes looking at their noses as the nose safekeeps one's heart to avoid temptation. See if you can find any. Better still, try crossing your eyes when you feel tempted to sin.

The **Hemudu site** is west of the city in Yuyao County about 90 minutes by road in the flourishing countryside. It has a small but good museum with signs in English. Displayed are a still playable 6-7,000-year-old bone flute, rice, plough shares, weaving, inlaid-bone and wood carvings, and jade ornaments.

The ***Bao Guo Temple**, built in 1013 (Northern Song), is the oldest extant wooden structure south of the Yangtze, and is in Yuyao, 20 km north of the Asia Garden Hotel. Unlike other temples, which have large beams for support, this one uses many small ones.

Excursions & Day Trips

Putuo Shan, another of my favorite places, is the home of **Guanyin (Kuan Yin)**, the Goddess of Mercy, and is one of the **Four Sacred Buddhist Mountains**. It has been a pilgrimage place for worshippers of this goddess since the early 10th century. If the weather is good, you can take a bus from the Shiliupu Quay (Number 16 pier) just south of the Bund in Shanghai (30 minutes) and then a hoverferry from Lu Tiao Gang/Luchaogang. The bus-ferry combination costs Y155-Y185. From Ningbo, it's a one hour bus to Ningbo port, and then a one-hour 10 minute ride in a bigger boat (Y57) which leaves every hour. Expect to pay an entry fee upon arrival at the island.

The air in Putuo Shan is clean and the scenery beautiful. Buddhist temples with a goddess as the central deity make this place very interesting and the religious art is outstanding. The architecture is old, and you're in another, earlier tranquil world. The place is full of carved gateways, flagstone roads, and stone stairways. The island is only about 10 km. long and now has over 20 monasteries and nunneries. It has 3000 to 4000 inhabitants of whom about 1000 are monks and nuns. You can get around by minibus or taxi. Buses cost Y2 to Y8 but it's best to walk. If you've planned only a one-day tour here, you are missing out on the walks, religious processions and ceremonies. Three days are better.

The hotels are adequate if you're not fussy. In summer and on weekends, do make a reservation. The best is the Putuoshan Hotel:

PUTUOSHAN HOTEL, *93 Meichen Road, Putuoshan, Zhoushan, 316107. Tel. 580/6092828 or fax 6091818. E-mail: htpts@mail.zsptt.zj.cn. Website: www.putuoshanhotel.com (English). It is about a kilometer from the ferry pier near the center of town. The hotel's mini-van meets all ferries. This 168-room hotel is about four stars. Rooms cost Y730-Y1,888, and suites Y1588-Y3888. It has been giving 10% to 30% discounts in low season and charges a flat Y20 service charge per night per room.*

This hotel has the best English. Its business center has e-mail service and ferry tickets for sale. It is air-conditioned and generally clean, but I found carpets stained, bathrooms moldy and no television in English. It accepts credit cards and changes only cash. There's a coffee shop, a Chinese restaurant, and a vegetarian restaurant with good food.

XILEI XIAOZHUANG HOTEL, *nearby at 1 Xiang Hua, 316107, beside Puji Temple. Tel. 580/6091515 or 6091812 X 501, 55, or 545, Fax 6091023.*

The second best hotel is this 153-room three-star. It's about Y200 cheaper than the Putuoshan Hotel but early morning gongs might disturb your sleep.

The cleanest restaurants are in the Putuoshan Hotel. The temples offer vegetarian lunch for cheap. Several okay restaurants are in town, three of them across from the Putuoshan Hotel.

Buy a map (from the ferry terminal in Shanghai). There are very few signs in English. Temples on Putuoshan give free admission to seniors over 60. Important to see are the Puji Temple, a 10 minute walk from the Putuoshan Hotel and is the largest temple here. At 4:15am, you can go to watch the monks chant and beat gongs until 6am in a dramatic, exotic setting. Worshippers burn paper money. No flash photos allowed.

Bus 1 takes you from town center to the main ferry quay (ma tou) and then south to the big statue of Guan Yin. From there you can walk to the Don't-Want-to-Go Temple, Purple Bamboo Temple, and the Guan Yin Footprint Temple. Bus 2 goes to the same ferry quay, the big statue, and then north to the Fayu Temple (second largest). From Fayu you can get another bus to the ropeway up to the Hui Ji Temple. Not to be missed are the nunneries, Western

Paradise Hill (Xi Shan Fa Jie), above the hotels. At the **Yuan Tong Nunnery** is the most beautiful statue of the goddess.

The beaches here have fine golden sand and are adequate for swimming in summer. At the north end of the best **100 Step Beach** (Bay Bu Shad) is the **Sunrise Pavilion (Chao Yang Ge)** with a marvellous collection of Guan Yins carved in wood, well worth a visit.

At the stop in the south, the **Don't Want to Go Temple (Bu Kun Qi Guan Yin)** is the oldest and most important here. It is small and by the sea, just below the much larger **Purple Bamboo Temple (Putuo Zi Zhu Ling)**. This temple commemorates the visit of a Japanese monk in 916 A.D. with a statue of the goddess as he attempted to return to Japan with her. Continuous storms prevented him from doing so and the Chinese believe Guan Yin wanted to stay in Putuoshan. Hence, they consider this her home.

The 33-meter high copper **Guan Yin** was finished in 1997. From here it's only a few steps to the Guanyin Footprint Temple where you can see the goddess' double-human size print on a rock by the sea. She jumped from Lokha Island nearby which you can see with its tower about 10 km. away.

At the top of the cableway is the Qing dynasty **Fayu Temple**, the only one not dedicated to the goddess. Its central figure is Sakyamuni, the Buddha. but there is no view from the top. Hopefully you can see processions of monks going to the beach for ceremonies. Festivals are on Guan Yin's birthdays (January 19, June 19 and September 19 in the lunar calendar). The website www.putuoshan.net/lyzn.html is partly in English.

CITS Putuo Shan is at 25 Wenhua Road, Ding Hai District, Zhongshan City, 316000, *Tel. 580/6091183, 2024931, Fax 2027342, 2024931, E-mail should be pcits@mail.csptt.zj.cn.* Ask for Mr. Yao.

Practical Information

Ambulance, *Tel. 120*

Ningbo China Travel Service, *5/F Golden Dragon Hotel, Ningbo 315010, Tel. 87307998, Fax 87329429.*

Ningbo Overseas Tourist Corporation Co., *3 Lane 5, Xinchangchun Road, 315010, Tel. 7262681, Fax 7286856.*

Ningbo Travel and Tourism Bureau, *35 Changchun Road, Yinhe Building 3, 315012, Tel. 87303141, Fax 87291266. Website: www.travel.nb.gov.cn (English).*

Police, *Tel. 110*

Telephone Code: 574

Website: *http://www.zjonline.com.cn/ehzzj/route.htm.*

Shaoxing
(Shaohsing)

You go to **Shaoxing** to get a feel of old traditional China. It is a 2-3000 year-old town, best known for its wine. It's 30 years behind other cities. It was the birthplace of China's most famous pre-Liberation writer, Luxun (Lu Hsun). Some of his stories, notably The Story of Ah Q, were set in this town, and a highly recommended but very sad 1982 movie was made of the Ah Q novella here. Literary types should pay a visit to his former residence and the Luxun Memorial Hall.

Shaoxing was the capital of the State of Ye during the Spring and Autumn period. The "tomb" of Emperor Yu, the third century B.C. Xia dynasty founder, is in the south suburbs at the base of Mt. Kuaiji. No one knows if the remains of this pioneer in irrigation are actually here in Yuwang Miao Temple. In any case, he died in Shaoxing during a visit. The name Shaoxing means "gathering place," for example, of the people celebrating the miraculous engineering feats of Emperor Yu.

Shaoxing is famous throughout China for its distinctive opera. It is less formal, full of emotion, action, and audience-pleasing lyrics, gorgeous costumes, and flashy sets. All parts are played by women.

Arrivals & Departures

Shaoxing is 60 km from Hangzhou by train or road, three hours from Ningbo. It is 65 km from the closest airport in Hangzhou.

Orientation

Shaoxing is attractive because it still has many houses, streets, canals, and boats from centuries ago. Much time can be spent walking around in this time warp. Changes have been made however: the addition of a local television station and the lovely sycamore and plane trees lining the streets. The Second Hospital was the former mission hospital.

Shaoxing today is the capital of one of the ten most prosperous small counties in China, its wealth based on textiles. The urban population is 591,000, the total 4,327,000. Don't miss the **Wine Festival** if you're here in September.

Where to Stay & Eat

These hotels take credit cards, have international direct dial phones, air-conditioning, and are subject to 10% surcharge and discounts. The best is the International.

XIANHENG HOTEL, *680 Jiefang Road, 312000. Four stars, Tel. 8068688, Fax 8051028. E-mail: xianheng@public.sxptt.zj.cn. Y380-Y560 for rooms,* and Y600-Y6800 for suites. It is 48 km from the airport, 4 km from the railway station and 3 km from the pier. This 22-story hotel has 236 rooms.

SHAOXING INTERNATIONAL HOTEL (Guoji Fandian), *100 Fushan Xi Road, 312000, Tel. 5166788, Fax 5166778. Four stars. Y380-Y680 for rooms, Y800-Y6600 for suites.*

This is near Fushan Hills in a western suburb, an eight-minute drive from the train station and 50-minute drive from the airport.

SHAOXING HOTEL (Binguan), *9 Huanshan Road, 312000. Three stars. Tel. 5155888, Fax 5155565. It's 67 km from the airport and three km from the railway station. About Y300-Y550 for rooms and Y3800 for suites.*

It has traditional late Ming garden-style architecture. The dining hall is an old family temple.

Seeing the Sights

If you want to visit **East Lake**, **Yuwang Miao**, **Lang Ding (Orchid Pavilion)**, **Luxun's home and museum**, **Qiu Jin's home,** and stroll about the town, you need at least two full days. You could also ask about the story of the scholar writing with a brush made of mouse whiskers. Tours can visit a home for the aged.

Shaoxing is known for its **lovely canals** and lake, alive with boats of all descriptions. Especially striking are its distinctive foot boats, the oars worked by foot. Do take a lake boat trip through its canals, and into caves cut out of the lake's quarried cliffs to see the hanging gardens. You can also glide under some of its 3,000 stone-arched bridges to old temples and the market, a good way to see the city.

Also of interest are the **Orchid Pavilion**, dating back to the fourth century, and the **Shen family garden**, which commemorates the meeting between Song dynasty lovers. The home of the early 20th century female revolutionary Qiu Jin is open as a museum. Premier Chou En-lai, though born in Jiangsu province, was brought up in this city and you can visit his house.

You can take another boat trip near ancient Keqiao, 12 km from Shaoxing, pulled in the old way by two men along part of a five-km long stone towpath to a 800-year-old stone bridge. Travel agents can also arrange a demonstration of Shaoxing opera on board.

Shopping

Shaoxing wine, brewed with two thousand years of experience, is a "must purchase" item. You can savor a sample at the **Xian Heng Wine Shop**, 44 Luxun Road, named after a Luxun short story. Other locally-made items include lace, felt hats, paper fans, silk, porcelain, bambooware, and ink stones. The Shaoxing Antique Store is on Jiefang Nan Road.

Practical Information

Shaoxing Overseas Travel Corporation, *Tel. 5116517, Fax 5126698.*
E-mail: sxotc@mail.sxptt.zj.cn.
Shaoxing International Travel Agency, *Tel. 5128428, Fax 5126324*
Telephone Code: 575.

Hefei

(Hofei)
   Hefei is the capital of Anhui (Anhwei), a province mostly on the north bank of the Yangtze River. Its only international class tourist destination is marvelous **Huangshan Mountain** and its neighborhood. This mountain is the inspiration for Chinese landscape painters, poets, and mystics and is a UNESCO Heritage Site. Anhui does have a lot of traditional culture and architecture, Three Kingdom's and early Ming dynasty history. Hefei was once famous for its tea and silk.

Arrivals & Departures

   Flights from 22 cities and Hong Kong are available now. There's also train service from Beijing (11 hours), Nanjing (six hours), and Shanghai (nine hours). Hefei is connected by expressway to Nanjing, a 185 km trip taking two to three hours (faster than train), and to Shanghai six hours (faster than train). About 26 buses a day arrive from Nanjing at the Mingguan Road bus station, one of many bus stations.

Orientation

   In the province live Han, Hui, She, and 12 other nationalities. Because of its strategic location, numerous battles were fought here in the ancient past. Hefei's tourist attractions can be squeezed into one day. It would take a week to see the province. Hefei's urban population is 800,000, the total about two million. The coldest weather in January is -5°C; the hottest in July and August is 39°C.

Where to Stay

   These three downtown hotels are close to the park and the river around the old city. All are well located for pleasant walks and exercise. The best is the Holiday Inn, then the Novotel and thirdly the Anhui Hotel. The international chains have better service and English. The Anhui Hotel looked older and rundown in comparison. The five-star Zenith Grand Park Hotel (Ming Zhu) is too far out in the economic zone to be useful for tourists. Hotels here add a 15% service charge, have business centers, beauty salons, accept credit cards, and make foreign exchange.

HOLIDAY INN HEFEI (Gujing Jia Ri Jiu Dian), *1104 Changjiang Dong Road, 230011. Five stars expected in 2002. Tel. 4291188, Fax 4291166. E-mail: hihfe@mail.hf.ah.cn. Website: www.holiday-inn.com/hefeichina.*

This 1998 hotel is close to Xiaoyaojin Park, Hefei's largest, three km from the railway station, six km from the hi-tech industrial zone, and 12 km from the international airport. Y920-Y1000 for rooms, Y1500-Y7800 for suites. It has been discounting 45% and included breakfast.

This 338-room hotel has an indoor pool, gym, steambath, and jacuzzi. It also has CNN, CNBC and HBO, Korean, Cantonese and Western food, in-room safes, and a free airport shuttle. It has three executive floors.

NOVOTEL HEFEI (Ya Gao Qi Yun Shan Zhuang), *199 Wuhu Road, 230001. Applying for four stars. Tel. 2887777, Fax 2884341. E-mail: info@novotel-hefei.com. Website: www.accorhotels-asia.com. Ten km from the airport. Close to the Bao Zheng Memorial Temple. $95-$150 for rooms and $180 for suites. The discounted rate for walk-ins is $45-$65. Suites are $90-$120 and include breakfast. Airport transfers are complimentary.*

This 246-room hotel was opened in 1998 and seriously refurbished in 2001. All rooms have high-speed internet access, CNN, and safes. There is an executive floor and non-smoking floors, Sichuan, Cantonese, Anhui, continental, Asian and French food. It offers a weekend dim sum buffet for Y28. Every Saturday afternoon and Wednesday evenings, it has an "English Saloon" for speaking English, a great opportunity for visitors to meet local people. The dinner buffet is Y58. Noodles in its Noodle-Stop shop range from Y8-Y13. An Accor Hotel.

ANHUI HOTEL (Fandian), *18 Meishan Road, 230022. Tel. 2811818, Fax 2817583. Located 12 km from the airport, and 10 km from the railway station. Four stars. Y660-Y980 for rooms, and Y930-Y5880 for suites. In off-season, standard rooms have been Y338-Y450 including breakfast.*

This 305-room hotel has non-smoking floors, CNN and Star Plus, in-room safes, and Cantonese and Western cuisine. North rooms in summer had a view of an island with 1000 egrets.

Where to Eat

Anhui specialties are fresh-water crabs and locally-produced Gujing Gongjiu wine, once sent as tribute to the Ming emperors. Try cured Mandarin fish, stewed turtle, Fulizi braised chicken, Wenzhenshan bamboo shoots, and sesame cakes. Dishes are somewhat salty and slightly spicy hot with thick soups.

For good local food, try the **Shu Wang Huo Guo** at 153 Mei Shan Road, *Tel. 2847888.* Also recommended for local and Cantonese food are any **Jin Man Lou Restaurant** which have excellent service and reasonable prices. One is at 147 Meishan Road, *Tel. 2844777.* Another is **Da Fu Hao** at 2 Meishan Road, *Tel.2816000.*

Lots of snack bars with delicious crustaceans are everywhere in spring and summer. For Western and Cantonese food there are the Holiday Inn and Novotel.

Seeing the Sights

If you have a half day, do a city tour. If you have a full day, go to Fengyang. The charm of this province is its old architecture and its countryside but the best part is in the south over three hours away around Huangshan. Fengyang has history. Taxis start at Y5 for the first three km.

In Hefei, **Xiaoyaojin Park** is near the center of the city. During the Three Kingdoms period 1700 years ago, General Zhang Liao of the State of Wei fought against General Sun Quan (Sun Chuan) of the State of Wu. The site is now a park with three islets, on one of which is the tomb and statue of General Zhang.

The **Tomb of Lord Bao** (999-1062) was rebuilt in 1985. In a quiet garden in the center of the city between the Holiday Inn and the Novotel, it is open 8am-6pm daily, *Tel. 2887011.* An exhibition hall with wax figures in beautiful period costumes has signs in English outlining his honesty which included condemning the husband of the emperor's daughter. In another case, he ruled against the emperor's mother. Signs, however, neglect to mention if he kept his job. The tomb itself is entered through a dark tunnel below, which was full of mosquitos in June.

The **Mingjiao Temple** on Huaihe Road is close to the Holiday Inn, and open daily from 7am-6pm, *Tel. 2656284.* You can have eight monks chant prayers for you. They regularly chant at 4am and 6am daily. Destroyed in the 19th century during the Taiping War, this temple was rebuilt by General Yuan Hongmo of the Taiping Heavenly Kingdom.

The **Anhui Provincial Museum** has the most complete 2-300,000-year-old skeleton of homo erectus hexianensis, and 4-5000-year-old jadeware, both the oldest found so far in China. You might recall that China announced in summer 1999 that it had found evidence of the ancestors of humans older than Richard Leakey's in Africa. These were in the southern part of Anhui. The museum does not have these yet, but do keep looking for them. Skeptical local archaeologists said that China is always making such claims, but let's keep an open mind. This museum also has a reproduced Eastern Han Tomb, real early porcelains and celadons, and titles in English.

The Provincial Museum is on 268 Anqing Road, *Tel.2824655* and is open 8:30-10:30am, 3-5pm, daily except Mondays and Thursday afternoons.

Shopping

Pears, pomegranates, grapes, kiwi fruit, and herbal medicines are grown in the province. Local products include candied dates, tea, bamboo mats, and iron pictures. Hefei is also noted for its four scholarly treasures: Xuan writing brush, Hu ink stick, She ink slab and Xuan paper. Try the **Hefei Department**

Store, 124 Yangtze Road or the **Shang Zhi Du Department Store** on Suzhou Road. The **Chenghuangmiao shopping center** was built in the Ming style and surrounds the 900-year-old Town God's Temple. It has lots of antiques and curios for sale.

Excursions & Day Trips

Near **Bengbu** in Fengyang County, on the railway line between Beijing and Shanghai, and 169 km by expressway from Hefei, is the ancestral home of the first Ming emperor, who proclaimed it a royal city. Among the Ming tombs here are Tang He's, one of the Ming dynasty founders. The ***ruins of the Imperial City of the Middle Capital**, and stone inscriptions at the Imperial Mausoleum, are under State Council protection. If you are seriously interested, bring your own interpreter. No one speaks English there.

Zhu Yuanzhang (Chu Yuan-chang), who became the first Ming emperor, came from a very poor family. For a while he was a beggar. After becoming emperor, he wanted to honor his parents. He built a tomb for them even though their bodies were lost. The tomb had to be bigger than his own in Nanjing. It has 32 pairs of stone animals and officials, more than any other imperial Sacred Way in China. The sculptures are original and in good repair.

The **Ming Huangling tomb** is seven km outside this tiny county town and surrounded by corn fields. You have to hire a car to get there; there are no public or tour buses. Zhu also constructed a double wall around this town. The huge Drum Tower, originally built in 1376 and rebuilt in 1999 on the original base, is in the center. At 42 meters high, this drum tower is bigger than the Tiananmen Gate in Beijing. A museum should be in the drum tower now.

Jiuhuashan (Mt. Jiuhua), is one of the **Four Buddhist mountains**. It is 220 km south of Hefei. It can be combined with a trip to Huangshan if you have at least four days. It has over 90 Ming and Qing temples, 6,800 Buddhas which were untouched by the Red Guards, and 99 peaks. Motor vehicles can drive up to 608 meters. There is a 1350-meter-long cable car to Tiantai Temple. In Baisui Gong (Buddhist Mummy Hall), there is a 380-year-old gold-plated monk. About 680 monks and nuns live in 93 temples. In Qiyuan Temple and Dabeilou, visitors can hear chanting in the morning. Most of the important temples are no more then two kilometers from Ju Long Hotel.

A temple fair is on the 30th day of the seventh lunar month for 10 days. The coldest mean temperature in January is -3˚C. The hottest mean temperature is 18˚C in July. The best hotel is the three-star **Julong Hotel**, Jiuhua Street, Qingyang County, 242811. *Tel. 5011368, 5011227, Fax 5011022.* It is on the mountain, and accepts credit cards.

CITS is on Jiuhua Street, Jiuhua Mountain, Qinyang County, 242811. *Tel. 5011318, Fax 5011202. E-mail: feiyzh@mail.hf.ah.cn.* Ask for Fei Ye Chao, general manager. For **China Travel Service**, *Tel. 5011588, Fax 5011587.* For cable car information, *Tel. 5011719.* The telephone code is 566.

Huangshan City, in Tunxi, is made up of several districts one of which, Tunxi, has the airport, the railway station, the best hotels, and some of its ancient relics. Tunxi is a one to two hour drive from this famous mountain. Flights arrive from Hong Kong and from 13 other cities. Flights from most Chinese cities are infrequent so it's hard to fit a visit here into a tight itinerary. The most frequent flights are from Shanghai with two or three departures a day. Guangzhou has several flights a day but not daily. Other cities might have two or four flights a week. By train from Beijing it takes 23 hours, from Shanghai it's about 11 hours, and from Guilin every other day, it's about 24 hours.

In downtown **Tunxi** close to the Huangshan International Hotel, is Old Street with antique and curio stores, old architecture, museums, gilded wood carvings, and real cockroaches in plastic. Tunxi is also over an hour's drive to Yixing County with its heritage villages which can be visited on the way to or from the mountain. You can get a superb lunch there in one of the elegant old Huizhou style mansions if you book ahead of time. The 800-year-old **Hong Cun village** is one of two UNESCO heritage villages, and some of the scenes from the popular movie *Crouching Tiger, Hidden Dragon* were shot there. (Remember the fighters flitting over a pond.) It has a moon bridge, narrow streets, water wheel, and houses with fire walls, ornate wood carvings, and murals.

Another heritage village is **Xidi** which is over 940 years old and has 124 Ming and Qing style houses. The **Tangyue Archways**, *Tel. 559/6573333*, can be interesting for those wanting to learn about Chinese traditions and values. They are beside China's only hall for women in Shexian (five km from Tunxi).

The Huangshan International Hotel is the best hotel in the whole area. The Guomei is newer. No hotel has CNN. CITS charges $50 a room for the Huangshan International, ($60 for Oct 1 to 7). For the Guomai Hotel, it's $45 generally, and $55 for high season.

HUANGSHAN INTERNATIONAL HOTEL (Guoji Dajiudian), *31 Huashan Road, Huangshan City, 245000. Tel. 2526999, Fax 2512087. E-mail: hsihotel@mail.ahwhptt.net.cn. Website: www.huangshanintlhotel.com. Four stars. 201 rooms. This is only a 12-minute drive from the airport and two km from the railway station. It accepts credit cards and travelers checks. Rooms are $80 and suites range from $150 to $700.*

The food here is especially good and overabundant. (We had to tell them to bring half portions.) It has television only in Chinese, in-room safes and a small gym. A CTS Hotel.

HUANGSHAN GUOMAI HOTEL *is one km. from the railway station and eight km. from the airport. It takes credit cards, and is at 25 Qianyuan Nan Road, 245000, Tel. 2351188, Fax 2351199. E-mail: hsgmhotl@mail.hs.ah163.net.*

Travel agents: **CITS** can be reached through *zhangcong@chinahuangshan.com*, *citseu@huangshanguide.com. Website: www.huangshanguide.com*. Its website is full of photos, maps (that need enlarging), and links to Huangshan travel agents.

Contact Zhang Cong who speaks English and helped this book a lot. His telephone is *559/2526184 (Office), 2523198 (Home). His mobile is 13013126690*. He can arrange home stays with local families.

Huangshan Municipal Tourism Administration, *63 Yan'an Road, Fax 2514019, 2511850 for brochures.*

Tunxi's telephone code: 559.

Wuhu, in the southeastern part of the province, is where the Qing-yi River joins the Yangtze. On the railway line between Nanjing and Hefei, it is the main foreign trading river port for the province and the fourth largest port on the Yangtze. It also produces silk and those lovely pictures made of forged iron, usually painted black. Its **Alligator Breeding Center** (8,000 alligators) is in Xuan Chen, near Wuhu.

Practical Information

E-mail service has been Y9 an hour on the second floor of the main post office (You Zhen Building), on Changjiang Road, open 8am-7pm.

Hours: offices 8 or 8:30am-5 or 6pm, lunch 12-2pm. Bank of China, 8am-5pm.

Hefei Telephone Code: 551

Huangshan Scenic Area

Located in southern Anhui province, **Huangshan Mountain** is one of China's top ten tourist attractions, a national scenic area, and a UNESCO World Heritage site. Climbing the mountain has been described by one writer as "walking into an unending Chinese landscape painting."

The coldest month is January, with a low of -6°C; the warmest is July, with a high of 20°C. The annual precipitation is 1600 mm, mainly from June to September.

The Huangshan Tourism Development has managed the scenic area since 1996. It is a company listed on two stock exchanges, 49.5% is owned by the city of Huangshan, and it is very well run. Over 500 workers pick up trash, even if visitors throw it over the edge of a cliff, said Scott our guide. Porters carry all laundry down the mountain to be washed. They have to carry everything, food, construction materials and furniture up.

On the other hand, visitors have increased to over a million a year, and hotels to at least 12, and the quality has been deteriorating. Hotels have been catering largely to tourist groups content with three-star accommodation and dormitories. Visitors all want to see the sunrise from the same traditional spots, and go from scenic spot to scenic spot, making lots of noise and pushing people out of the way to take photos of themselves against the scenery. As a result, there are few places where people can sit and soak in the changing beauty in peace and solitude. But all is not hopeless. You can take side-trails. If you can afford it, the mountain-view rooms in the VIP Hall of the Beihai Hotel are above the crowds. And if you head for the new scenic spot, Fantastic, near the top of the Taiping cable car, you can get away from most of the rabble. In addition, the hotels are now replacing dormitories with standard rooms.

In spite of the crowds, the incredible scenery is worth the effort. You are above cloud level, and sometimes you get a sea of clouds below you with peaks poking up through them. Sometimes clouds set off the horizontal 400 year old pines sticking out of the crags. Clouds appear about 208 days a year, mainly in the spring. You can't get this effect on a quick one or two day tour unless you're very lucky. And if it rains, you're out of luck. For non-photographers, one or two days on top is enough.

Arrivals & Departures

Huangshan Scenic Area is one of the districts of Huangshan City and is 320km southwest of Shanghai. It is 5-6 hours by road from Hefei. The closest airport and railway station is in Tunxi about 68 km. away by road. Huangshan can also be reached by road from Hangzhou via 1,000 Island Lake if you have your own vehicle, an interesting excursion. (Huangshan CITS charges about $150 for a van). See Tunxi above.

Where to Stay & Eat

During low tourist season, CITS charges $100 a room including service charge for any of the three hotels suitable for foreigners: the Beihai, Xihai, and Shilin. In high season, it's $150 per room. A buffet breakfast is an additional $10 per room. You should leave most of your luggage at a hotel at the base and take only what's needed for the mountain top. Porters can be very expensive and if it's raining, your luggage might get wet.

Some hotels on the top do not change travelers' checks, but there's a Bank of China. Some are air-conditioned or have television in English. Some have heat. All add a 10% surcharge.

The altitude at the mountain-top hotels is at least 1500 meters or over 4500 feet. English at the main three-star hotels is miniscule. During the August and September dry season, water in all hotels could be rationed. The high tourist seasons are the May 1 and October 1, seven-day holidays. Laundry prices are about double what you pay elsewhere and you get it back next day. Again, everything has to be carried up by porter, the resort's unsung heroes.

All hotels can lend heavy jackets to their guests free of charge. You can buy cheap plastic rain coats for about Y8 and cheap wooden walking sticks too. The best hotel is the Xihai. The best view from a hotel, and of the sunrise, is from the Beihai. These three hotels take credit cards.

BEIHAI (North Sea) HOTEL, *242709. Three stars, Tel. 5582555, Fax 5581996. It is half a kilometer walk, including a 340-meter uphill climb, from the cable car terminal.*

This 224-room hotel was opened in 1958 and expanded in 1996 and 2001 and has a great view, especially from its Jin She VIP hall and room No. 6608 (Y1280 net). A dance hall should be finished now. Rooms are 14 and 18 square meters. Those in the Jin She building are 20 square meters. A bed in a dormitory with no lockers costs Y50 to Y100. The breakfast buffet is Y40; the lunch and dinner Y80. It has 24-hour hot tap water. Cheaper rooms are adequate but not luxurious.

XIHAI (West Sea) HOTEL (Dajiudian). *Xihai Scenic Area, 242709, Tel. 5588987, 5588888, Fax 5588988. E-mail: hsxhhotel@mail.hs.ah163.net. Website: www.hsxihaihotel.com. Three stars. Rooms are Y850 to Y1280, the higher price in peak season. Suites all year round are Y1730-Y5888. It has 500 beds in dormitories for Y85 each and has been discounting 20%.*

The 1988-built West Sea has 142 rooms. At 1600 meters, it is a half hour (one km) climb from the top of the Yanggu cable car and 15 minutes from the upper Taiping Station. Its restaurant charges for pork chops Y90, beef stroganoff Y90, frogs Y121, and hamburger Y70. Coffee in its lobby bar is Y30 to Y48; tea Y10 to Y20; beer Y15 to Y20, and water Y6. The Xihai serves better coffee and better American breakfast than the others.

SHILIN HOTEL (Dajiudian), *Beihai Scenic Area, 242709. Three stars. Tel. 5584040, Fax 5581888. E-mail: ksnfdhs@mail.ahwhptt.net.cn. Website: www.shilin.com. (English) Rooms are about Y850 to Y1280. It is a half hour's walk from both the Taiping and Yungu cable stations.*

This 142-room hotel has mainly Asian guests. Rooms are 18 square meters, have showers (no tubs), 24-hour hot tap water, and pay movies. Some of the Shilin's buildings are being upgraded, its cheaper dormitory buildings being replaced with 20-square meter, standard rooms, each with a terrace, bathtub, shower, and good view. It was opened in 1998 and has e-mail. It says it will be hiring people who speak English. Its buffet breakfast is Y80. It has a sauna for Y100 but no Jacuzzi.

Seeing the Sights

The standard tour is three days and three nights, with one or two nights on the mountain top. There's time to see a heritage village and Old Street too.

Huangshan Scenic Area is 154 sq. km with 72 peaks, three cableways and 45 km of paved paths. The top hiking area allows no vehicles. Smoking is only permitted inside the hotels. None of the hotels have swimming pools nor gyms. ("The mountain is the gym.")

It is not really a plateau. Even after you get to the top with the cable cars, there's still a lot of climbing up and down. The center is around the Beihai Hotel, the Bank of China and one tiny store. Hotels are scattered. You eat in far-from luxurious hotel restaurants. Directional signs are in English. If you get yourself a map in English, you can do everything on your own.

The end of April is the most beautiful time, and hiking is good to the end of October. Winter is also beautiful with wizened trees laden with snow. All cable cars operate from 6:30am to 4pm daily except during high winds and electrical storms. Be prepared to wait in line at the bottom in high season even though you have a reservation. The ride and the use of the V.I.P. waiting room cost Y81 one way at the Taiping. (Other passengers pay Y66 and wait longer. This is the closest cableway to Tunxi.

The 2800-meter-long Yungu cable car on the east slope leaves from near the Cloud Valley Hotel and makes the ascent in eight minutes. Its top station is about a 20-minute walk uphill to the Beihai Hotel. Beyond that is another ten minutes walk to the Xihai Hotel or Shilin Hotel.

If you go on foot, you have a 2.5-3 hour climb up 15,000 stone steps but you can hire a sedan chair. A sedan chair from the top of the Yungu cable car to the Beihai Hotel costs about Y300 (prices are fixed) plus a tip of about Y50 for each carrier. (If you don't tip, you risk unpleasant pestering.) Porters were satisfied with Y20 to carry a small bag plus a tip of Y10.

The highest **Lotus Flower Peak** rises to 1864 meters. To reach the base of the final ascent to the top means climbing 800 stone steps cut into a 60-70 degree angle cliff, nose almost to rock. One section of the second highest peak, **Tian Du (Heavenly Capital Peak)**, is 1,830 meters and has a ridge less than a meter wide called Carp's Backbone. Although iron chain railings are there to assure the unsure, some people resort to crawling to get across. This is just to say that Huangshan is both for the strong and adventurous, as well as the average tourist. It is challenging in places, but in others, it's as easy as going into any public park. Paths are mostly paved.

Practical Information

For travel agents, see Tunxi, above.
Telephone code: 559.
Website: *www.huangshanguide.com*

Jinan

Jinan, the capital of Shandong province, is an industrial center producing trucks, textiles, and paper, and has been famous primarily for its springs, its Buddhist temples, and its proximity to Linzi, Taishan mountain and Qufu. Jinan is primarily for business people, an economic boom-town based on minerals, agriculture and trade. It used to have a unique tourist attraction but a lowering water table due to over-use has emasculated its once famous springs beyond repair. Only one still exists and tourists no longer are encouraged to see it. For some tourists, Jinan, with the area's only five-star hotel, is the base for day trips to Qufu and Taishan and is the closest airport to these major tourist sites.

Jinan was settled more than 5000 years ago by the neolithic Dawenkou and Longshan peoples. It dates from the sixth century B.C., when it was the gate city to the state of Qi and the starting point of the ancient Qi Great Wall. It was named Jinan, meaning south of the Ji River, a name it has kept even though that river dried up centuries ago.

Jinan was a busy commercial center during the Tang, and Marco Polo spoke favorably of its garden atmosphere and its thriving silk industry. It has been the provincial capital since the Ming.

The climate is temperate. The hottest in late July to early August is 33°C; the coldest in January, -10°C. The annual precipitation is about 700 millimeters, mainly in July and August. The urban population is 2.4 million, the total 5 million.

Arrivals & Departures

Jinan is at the junction of the Beijing-Shanghai and the Qingdao-Jinan railways. It takes five hours from Beijing. Jinan can also be reached by plane from Hong Kong and 40 other cities. The airport is 40 km from town. Express buses to Qingdao (4 to 4.5 hours) and Yantai (5.5 hours) leave hourly from the South Bus Terminal, *Tel. 2984344, 2984345*. It is almost due south of Beijing about 400 km by expressway and 15 km from the south shore of the Huanghe (Yellow River).

Where to Stay

Hotels here add a 10 or 15% service charge. The best hotel is indisputably the Sofitel but the new five-star Crowne Plaza as yet unseen should be up there too. The four-star Zhonghao Grand Hotel and the Yuquan Simpson Hotel are good. The Minghe is a good three-star. The following prices are subject to change, discounts and 10% service charge. Hotels here have IDD, business centers, coffee shops, good beds and accept credit cards.

SOFITEL SILVER PLAZA JINAN (Sofite), *66 Luoyuan Avenue, 250063. Five stars, Tel. 6068888, Fax 6065666. E-mail: sofires@public.jn.sd.cn (reservations) or sofitel@jn-public.sd.cninfo.net. Website: www.accorhotels-asia.com. It is located in the downtown financial and commercial district, south of Daming Lake, and adjacent to the Silver Plaza, Jinan's largest shopping mall. Rooms are $100-$120, suites $150-$200, and apartments $340. It has been discounting 35% and in winter, charging $68 including breakfast.*

This 326-room, 49-story hotel was opened in 1999. Rooms are 26 and 32 square meters and it has non-smoking floors, ladies' rooms and suites. All rooms have two telephone lines, panic button, safe, CNN and HBO. It has Japanese, Mediterranean, French, Cantonese and Shandong restaurants. Its revolving restaurant and lounge has a dance floor and band. Its fine Western restaurant has an open barbecue, grill, French food, and a choice of 80 wines. Its ballroom and vestibule can seat up to 800 guests banquet-style. There's a wine and cigar lounge. The breakfast buffet has especially good pastries. Its health club is high-tech, has a heated year-round indoor pool and offers reflexology.

GUI HE CROWNE PLAZA, *3 Tian Di Tan Street, 250011. Tel: 6029999, Fax 6023333. E-mail: cpguihejinan@luneng.com. It has 306 rooms with rates similar to the Sofitel.*

Its restaurants serve Cantanese, Japanese, Korean and Italian foods and it has a gym and swimming pool.

ZHONGHAO GRAND HOTEL (Zhonghao Dajiudian), *165 Jiefang Road, 250013. Four stars. Tel. 6968888, Fax 6993200, 6968899. E-mail: zhonghaohotel@sina.com. This 1998, 343-room hotel accepts credit cards. Rooms are Y780 and Y1180; suites are Y1280 to Y6680 and it has been discounting 40%. It is in a residential area and its staff speaks a little English.*

This hotel has a 24-hour coffee shop with Y38 breakfast buffet, free with room. There are dirty carpets, bowling alley, 18-meter-long heated indoor pool, steam room, jacuzzi and sauna. It also has a small gym with good equipment.

YUQUAN SIMPSON HOTEL, *68 Luoyuan Avenue, 250011. Four stars. Tel. 6938888, Fax 6934993. E-mail: yqbc@jn-public.sd.cninfo.net. Website: www.yuquan.com.cn (English). It is 35 km from the airport and five km from the railway station.*

This hotel has 300 rooms, complimentary baby-sitting, Western, Shandong, Cantonese, Korean, and Japanese cuisine. There's an internet bar, tennis, VOD, sauna and clinic.

MINGHU DAJIUDIAN, *398 Beiyuan Road, 250033. Tel. 5956688, Fax 5948888. Three stars. Rooms in this 22-story, 230-room hotel range from Y298 to Y580 but it has been discounting 20%. It accepts credit cards and can change foreign travelers' checks.*

This hotel began renovations in May 2000, and has CNN, billiards, a 24-hour restaurant with Chinese food, a sauna and massage. It will have a pool. It also has poor grouting, no in-room safes but it's okay for budget travelers.

Where to Eat

Exotic local fare are cattails, lotus roots and lotus seeds from Daming Lake, roast duck, winding-thread cakes, and monkey-head mushroom. Good food is in the top hotels. The **Sofitel Hotel's** Southeast Asian set menu costs Y58, and you have a choice for dinner: international buffet Y98, dessert section Y45, cold dish section Y55, cold dish and dessert Y75. Good in its Cantonese restaurant were seafood noodles, beef with onions and oyster sauce, and broccoli.

In addition to the hotels, there are the **Jinsanbei Restaurants**. The most convenient of this chain is across the road from the Qilu Hotel at 5, Qianfoshan Road, *Tel. 2961616, 2961446*. There's also the **Weiwei Juji Wang restaurant** (King of Roast Chicken) which is very close to the Crowne Plaza Hotel and good for seafood too, *Tel. 6021888*.

Seeing the Sights

The **Shandong Provincial Museum** is at 14 Jingshi Yi Road at the foot of Qianfo Hill. It is open 8:30am-11:30pm and closed Mondays. It contains both historical and natural relics. These date from neolithic times and includes Sun Bin's famous treatise on the art of war written on bamboo about 2000 years ago. Also note the frescoes from Sui dynasty tombs, paintings from the tomb of the Prince of Lu (Ming), and musical instruments from the Confucian Family Mansion in Qufu.

The **Qianfo (Thousand-Buddha) Hill,** *Tel. 2951792* and its cableway are open only during daylight hours. It is 2.5 km south of the city. The entrance is beside the Qilu Hotel. Here are Buddhist images carved into the side of a cliff. Much climbing is involved for the Xingguo Si (Revive the Nation Temple), with 60-70 Buddhas from 20 centimeters to over three meters tall, ranging from the Sui to the Tang. On Yangtouyu is a 10-meter-high cave with the head of a Buddha.

If you want to get out into the countryside, the *Lingyan Si Temple*, *Tel. 7463198*, 55 km south of Jinan on the way to Taishan, is one of the "four finest temples" in China. It was founded in 354 A.D. The current temple is from the Tang.

Shopping

Made in the province are silk and human hair embroidery, lace, wool carpets, straw articles, kites, feather or shell pictures (lovely), and dough figurines. The province also produces the popular Tsingtao Beer and Hualong wines. The main shopping area is **Quanchen** and also along **Jin 2-Road**. The **Silver Star Plaza** at 66 Leyuan Avenue is good for general shopping and is open 9am to 9pm.

Nightlife & Entertainment

Foreigners frequently gather at the big bar in the Shandong Sports Centre stadium. There's also the **Lan Gui Fang**, on Wenhua Dong Lu, near Shandong Teachers Univeristy and Shandong Arts College.

Excursions & Day Trips

You really need a couple of days to take in **Tai'an**, 80 km away, and **Qufu**, 160 km south. Both are very worthwhile. Nearby is Linzi, a day trip. In the province also are Qingdao, with excursions to Yantai, Weihai, and Weifang. See separate listings.

*Linzi is one hour's drive east of Jinan and about five km east of Zhandian in Zibo. It was the capital of Qi state that existed from the 11th century B.C to 221 B.C. It has several on-site museums, the most impressive of which is The Ancient Chariots' Museum, built over the actual site of buried chariots and horses. These were uncovered during the building of the expressway and is worth making an hour's stop. Call 533/7080468 for exact directions. It is 8 km from Linzi City at Exit 8, and is open 8am-5:30pm daily. The building is ultra-modern, the most obvious part a pyramid with its top flattened. Part of the museum is under the expressway and can be entered from either side. The toilets are bad but the exhibit is amazing: with about 32 pairs of horse skeletons in two neat lines, buried in the mid-Spring and Autumn period (770 B.C.-476 B.C.). The museum also contains reproductions of ancient camel and elephant carts, and war chariots.

Nearby in **Qidu**, the capital of Qi, Linzu District, 255400, is the **Qi Ancient Capital Museum** with armour belonging to the first king of Qi state (11th century B.C.) and wax figures and dioramas. *Tel. 7030229.* A guide is necessary because the other museums are hard to find.

Food in Zibo is good and cheap at the three-star **Zibo Hotel**, 175 Zhongxin Road, Zhangdian District, *Tel. 533/2180888 or Fax 533/2184800.* It takes Visa and MasterCard. Good and reasonable also is that at the **Century Hotel** (Qidu Dajiudian), *Tel. 2288688 ext. 4483.* **CITS** is at 189 Zhongxin Road, Zhangbian, Zibo, 255037, *Tel. 2133418. 2149900.* The **telephone code** is 533.

Practical Information

China Shandong Tourism Corporation, *180 Quancheng Road, Suite 606A, 250011. Tel. 6025270, Fax 6025290. E-mail:sdotcu@public.jn.sd.cn.* Ask for John Ma (Ma Feng Jian), Deputy Manager, English Department, who has been a great help with information for this book and is one of the best travel agents and guides found. He says the train fare from Jinan to Shanghai is $52(soft berth) and $34(hard berth); from Jinan to Beijing it's $25(soft berth), $17 (hard berth), $15(soft seat); from Jinan to Yantai $12(hard berth). A service charge is additional. For individual guests, CSTC charges for a standard room at the Sofitel: US$80 with breakfast, Zhong Hao $60 with breakfast, Qilu: $65 with breakfast, Hua Neng $50 with breakfast, and Minghu $45 with breakfast.

China Shandong Travel Service, *86 Jingshi Road, 250014. Tel. 2608568, 2607659, Fax 2608558. E-mail: csts@public.jn.sd.cn or csts@sdta.gov.cn. Website: www.csts.sdta.com (English).*

Internet Cafés: A 24-hour internet service is at 3 Qianfoshan Road (near the Qilu Hotel). It has 32 computers and charges about Y2.50 an hour. *Tel. 2910430.*

Fire, *Tel. 119*; **Ambulance**, *Tel. 120;* **Police** *Tel. 110.*

Office Hours: 8:30 or 9 to 11:30am or 12 noon. In summer 2 or 2:30 to 5:30pm or 6pm. In winter from Nov. 1 to end of March, 1pm to 5pm.

Shandong China International Travel Service, *78-8, Wenhua Dong Road, Xulin Hotel Room 212, 250014. Tel. 2929071, Fax 2965651. E-mail: sdcitsaa@public.jn.sd.cn. Website: www.citssd.com. Ask for Joy Zhai Baoping,* Manager of English Department. She says air tickets from Jinan to Shanghai is $88, to Beijing $72, to Yantai is $68, to Urumqi is $273, to Xi'an is $99, to Guangzhou $183 and to Hong Kong $245. She charges $6 for booking flights. CITS also charges for a room in the Sofitel $96, Crowne Plaza $75, and Zhonghai Grand $58.

Shandong Tourism Bureau, *88 Jing Shi Road, 250014. Tel. 2965858 X 6311, Fax 2963201, 2964284. E-mail: sss@sda.gov.cn. Website: www.sdta.gov.cn. (English)*

Telephone Code: 531.

Tourist Complaints: contact Supervisory Bureau of Tourism Quality of Shandong Province, *Tel. 2963423, 2965858, Fax 2964284.*

Tourist Hotline: *Tel. 2963423*

Qufu
(Chufu)

The hometown, and grave, of **Kong Fuzi (Master Kong)**, known to the West as **Confucius**, is a good place to be immersed in old China. Take your time. Meditate in these beautiful, exotic surroundings. Read the Analects of Confucius. The discipline he advocates might be just what your family lacks. Go back in time.

Confucius was born in Nishan, 35 km southeast of his temple. He moved with his mother to Qufu after the death of his father, when he was three. His father was a general of the State of Lu. He preached his social and political theories while traveling around China, and after he died, his disciples, the most famous of whom was Mencius, spread his teachings. The Qin emperor later burned his books, but the succeeding Han dynasty adopted his philosophy officially. Succeeding emperors continued this practise in varying degrees until the early 20th century.

Qufu was the capital of a minor kingdom during the Shang (14th-11th century B.C.). The city is named Winding City Wall after the old wall built 3,000 years ago. The current wall is Ming.

Today, one-fifth of the people in Qufu are surnamed Kong, and those in a direct line of descendants once received state pensions (with no need to earn their living otherwise). Currently living are the 69th to 80th generations. The sage's birthday, September 28, is now celebrated with a festival from September 25 to October 10 and a re-enactment for tourists of the sacrificial ritual and homage by an emperor. This performance is in the hypnotic, slow movements and music of the times. A telephoto lens is necessary for photographers.

The hottest temperature in summer is 39°C; the coldest temperature in winter is a chilly -7°C. About 800 millimeters of rain fall annually mainly in July and August.

Arrivals & Departures

Qufu is about 170 km south of Jinan, the closest major airport. You can get there by expressway from Jinan and from Tai'an (70 km). Public air-conditioned buses take about 2.5 hours, and leave every ten minutes from the Long Distance Bus Station near Jinu Park in Jinan. These arrive a five minute walk from the Queli Hotel. You can go by train from Beijing and from Jinan. From the station in Yanzhou, taxis and buses can take you the remaining 10 km to Qufu, far away because officials didn't want a railway to disturb Confucius' grave and its *feng shui*.

Orientation

Spend at least two days in this small, charming city, one day for the three Kongs (mansion, temple and forest), and one day for the tomb of Mencius, the birthplace cave of Confucius, and the Temple of Shao Hao.

This is a good place for bicycling or hiking. It is relatively flat and has many interesting things to explore. At least a week is necessary for adventurous bicyclists. You can rent bicycles in the Forest of Confucius.

The old city is centered around the Confucian monuments. The business area is south of it. Qufu is in southwestern Shandong province. The urban population is 60,000, the total 600,000.

Where to Stay

The only hotel for tourists is the charming Queli, which has food, but needs work. Its English is poor, it's grubby and badly maintained. It has the best location within walking distance of the Mansion, Temple, and shops, and just a ten-minute taxi ride from the forest.

Fussy tourists should stay in Jinan and take day trips here but part of the experience is absorbing the old atmosphere of this town at leisure.

QUELI HOTEL (Binguan), *1 Queli Street, 273100. Three stars. Tel. 4866400, 4411300, 4866523 (Sales), Fax 4412022. Website: www.sd.cninfo.net/ Queli (Chinese). Almost adjacent to the Temple of Confucius. About Y398 for rooms, Y988-Y3288 for suites. No clear television channels in English.*

First built in 1986, this hotel has exquisite Chinese architecture with courtyards and ponds. It has two-stories and 160 rooms, striking murals and sculptures. It provides concerts of classical Chinese music if enough guests are interested. There's a video of Confucian ceremonies on request. It also has a gym.

Where to Eat

Confucian food is not as salty as Shandong and each dish has a meaning; for example, turtle is a symbol of longevity. A genuine banquet used to have 400 courses! The food at the Queli Hotel is Confucian, interesting and adequate but not exciting. You might want to try the 39 proof Confucian Family liquor.

Seeing the Sights

The Confucian monuments are in and near the old city, and can be seen in a day. The ***Confucian Temple** (Y30), occupying more than 20 hectares (about 50 acres), is the most important one in China and the largest in the world. First built in 478 A.D., it was rebuilt and enlarged to its present size during the Ming and Qing. Its gold-tiled roofs, its arches, red doors, and carved tile dragons are Ming. Live egrets and cranes nest in the gardens here.

The **Dacheng Hall** is the main hall for paying homage. Only an emperor could be carried over the carved dragons up to its door. The hall is over 31-meters tall and 54-meters wide, with a resemblance to some of the buildings in Beijing's Forbidden City (that was copied from this temple, some say). Important are the ten carved stone columns, two dragons with a pearl on each, slithering between clouds and a pearl. Note the set of ritual bronze bells which are played on ceremonial occasions. (See also Provincial Museum, Wuhan.)

The ***Kong Family Mansion** has nine courtyards, over 400 rooms and a garden, on 14 hectares. The gate in front is Ming. The Main Hall, Second Hall, and Third Hall were offices of the Duke of Yansheng, who was made a noble by Emperor Renzong of the Song. These offices, with his desk under a yellow canopy and painted beamed ceiling, give authenticity to opera stage sets of the period. Ancient weapons, banners, and drums line the walls. The mansion was started in 1038 and has been falling apart while a dispute between the local, provincial, and national governments rage over who should pay to fix it.

Gifts to the family from emperors and high-ranking visitors include Zhou and Shang dynasty bronzes. Visitors would do well to read *In the Mansion of Confucius' Descendants* by Kong Demao and Ke Lan before arriving. From it you can feel the human drama that took place here. Kong Demao, who is still living in Beijing, was the daughter of the second wife of the Duke of Yansheng. Her mother was believed to be poisoned by the first wife. Her tale of being confined behind these walls is very sad, but she was also party to great events as well as family misfortunes. Some photographs of the family are on display. The current Duke of Yansheng is living in Taiwan.

The Philosphy of Confucius

Confucius lived from 551 to 479 B.C. during the Spring and Autumn Period, a time of small warring kingdoms and political chaos. He was an itinerant teacher who preached that stability could be achieved by a return to the classics and the old Zhou dynasty rituals. He defined and promoted an already existing system of interpersonal relationships with its emphasis on responsibility and obedience.

The virtuous or benevolent man did not lose his temper; the virtuous man thought ill of people who criticize others in their absence, who talked badly of other people to make themselves look better, or who persisted in promoting deceptions they know are false. He did not concern himself with insignificant things, material gain, fame or ambition. He was moderate in all things.

He was no democrat. People who do not hold office in a state should not discuss its policies, he said. He advocated that subjects be unquestionably subordinated to rulers, sons to fathers, younger brothers to older brothers, wives to husbands, and younger friends to older friends.

His philosophy was the official ideology in China for over 2,000 years, promoted because it supported the oligarchic power structure. Filial piety was essential to the system, and the state enforced this policy. If a child failed to care for his aged parents or was rude to them, the authorities would punish the child. Children owed their lives to their ancestors. They were obligated to respect and worship these people.

The philosophy became a religion where Confucius was worshipped as a god and descendants performed rituals to keep ancestral spirits happy, so the dead would influence the fortunes of the living.

One finds elements of his theories still stifling Chinese people everywhere. Confucius was behind the famous civil service system, based on the memorization of the classics and his analects. The imperial examinations and the arrogant, insular thinking did, however, outlive their usefulness. The civil service examination system was abolished in the early 1900s.

In some family temples, food is still shared with ancestors, heads bowed and incense burned in worship, especially during the Qing Ming Festival in spring, and the autumn equinox. Vestiges of the traditions surrounding the cult remain to this day, in spite of governmental discouragement of things like arranged marriages, marriages between two deceased people, or between one living and one deceased person, etc. This is not, however, as common as it was before 1949. Rote memory is still the basis of much education, but hopefully this is changing soon.

Other Sights in Qufu
The **Confucian Forest** contains 200,000 family tombs and is reputedly the oldest and largest cemetery in the world. The 30,000 trees were collected by disciples from all over the country. It is about three by four km. Elaborately crafted gates, stone lions, and a stone-arched bridge punctuate the lovely greenness. Tall stone nobles and animals guard the gate to the *Tomb of Confucius, a tumulus marked with stone tablets and fancy incense burners.

A small brick house, **Zi Gong's Hut**, stands nearby. One of the master's disciples built it and lived there for six years after Confucius' death, to show respect. Lady Yu's Arch was named after a daughter of Qing Emperor Qianlong, who was married to the then Duke of Yansheng. The title was hereditary until the Nationalists officially stopped the practice.

Also in Qufu is a Sacred Way with stone animals and steles, the Temple of Yan Hui, the Temple of the Duke of Zhou, and the remains of the former capital of the State of Lu.

The Tomb of Shao Hao, one of the five legendary rulers, is about eight km away. The Temple of Mencius is 27 km south of the city. Here is also a small museum, a temple to the mother of Mencius, and a hall for the wife of Mencius.

The Birthplace of Confucius in Nisan is also open as a museum. A tacky theme park based on the Six Confucian Arts is between the Forest and his temple. Tour groups might eat here and watch a 30-minute show.

Shopping
Locally produced are wood carvings, stone rubbings, carpets, and Nishan inkstones. The Antique Store attached to the gate of the Family Mansion, Tel. 4412757, has been selling beautiful carved and gilded wooden beds and can ship them. A market in Ming architecture is one block to the left as you leave the Queli Hotel.

Practical Information
CITS, *1, Jingxuan Xi Road, 273100. Tel. 4412491, Fax 4412492. E-mail: cits@confucius-tour.net. Website: www.confucius-tour.net (English).*
Qufu Tourism Bureau, *1 Kuiquan Road, 273100, Tel. 4497576, Fax 4497576*
Telephone Code: 537
Tourist Complaints, *Tel. 4497673*

Tai'an

Tai'an is where you ascend **Mt. Tai** (Taishan), one of China's **Five Sacred Mountains** and a UNESCO World Heritage site. It is 2.5 billion years old, one of earth's oldest mountains. In ancient times, emperors came here to offer sacrifices to Earth and to Heaven; if they went up the mountain, they were probably carried up, and visitors today have the same choice, but by bus, taxi, or cable car. The summit is 1545 meters above sea level. The city itself is at 150 meters.

The hottest time (37°C) is in July and August; the coldest is December and January, minus 10°C. The annual precipitation is 700 mm, mainly from July to September. It is about 10 degrees cooler at the top of Mt. Tai. The best time to climb is from April to October, but you can climb all year round except in inclement weather. The urban population at the base is over 300,000, the total population six million.

Arrivals & Departures

Tai'an is accessible by road and rail, and is usually combined with a visit to Qufu, 80 km away. It is about 60 km south of Jinan, which has the closest airport. It can be reached by daily overnight train from Beijing. On the expressway, the trip from Jinan is 40 minutes.

Where to Stay

At the foot of the mountain, the best hotel is Taishan Hotel. The Overseas Chinese Hotel is second best for tourists. On the summit, the best is the Shenqi. If your schedule is tight and a strong wind threatens to cancel cable cars, you had better stay down below.

Being built is the three-star, Taishan International Hotel, with seven stories, and 100 rooms. It is in the suburbs, a 15-minute drive from the city and will be open in 2002. CITS can arrange **homestays** in Buyang Zhuang Village, *Tel. 8601579*, 17 km southeast, for about Y100 per day including meals.

Prices listed below are subject to change and 10% surcharge. Hotels here generally have relaxed standards, but have foreign exchange, international direct dial, air-conditioning, etc.

TAISHAN HOTEL, *Daizongfang, 26 Hongmen Road, 271000. Tel. 538/ 8224678, Fax 8223837. 2.5 km from the railway station. Three stars. Y380 for rooms.*

Built in 1980, this 110-room, six-story hotel has Shandong, Sichuan and Cantonese restaurants. It has a gym, clinic, and ticket office, but no CNN, and takes American Express credit cards only.

TAISHAN OVERSEAS CHINESE HOTEL (Huaqiao Dasha), *Dongyue Zhong Avenue, 271000. Four stars, Tel. 8228112, Fax 8228171. Two km from the railway station, close to Daimiao Temple, and across the road from a* *department store. Y480-Y680 for rooms, Y780-Y880 for suites. Credit Cards but no Diners.*

Built in 1995, and renovated 1997, this 19-story, 205-room hotel has Cantonese, Italian and Western food, heated indoor pool, bowling, gym, and night club. It has two television channels in English. Famous Hotel VIP Club.

SHENQI HOTEL (Binguan), *10 Tian Street, Taishan, 271000. Three stars, Tel. 8223866, 8337025, Fax 8207619. Y680.*

About two km upward from the top of the cable car, 20 km from the railway station, this hotel is at 1500 meters. Built in 1991 with two stories, and 102 rooms, it has a sauna, clinic, great view, seven restaurants, and a traditional medicine and wild vegetable banquet. It also has Cantonese and Sichuan food. But note: because of a water shortage, this hotel might be closed, or no baths allowed December through March.

Where to Eat

The hotel restaurants are good; so is Taishan Beer. Tai'an's liquor is 29, 39 and 44 proof. The Chinese restaurant in the **Taishan Hotel**, *Tel. 8225888, Fax 8221432,* is especially good. Its bean curd banquet is famous, Delicious are the deep fried crispy bean curd balls, fried pancakes, and beef with oyster sauce. At the **Overseas Chinese Hotel**, good dishes are the shredded turnip, garlic fried crisp chicken, fried fresh milk, spicy beef with bamboo shoots and oyster sauce, and stir-fried snow peas. The best Western food is also here, but don't expect much. Only the hotels accept credit cards.

Seeing the Sights

An **Information Center for Tourists** is at the Hongmen Hotel, Hongmen Road, 271000, *Tel. 8259899.*

If you have only one day, you can be driven halfway up the mountain to the Zhongtian (Middle Celestial) Gate, the shorter way. Then you can take the 2078-meter-long suspended cable car almost to the top at Nantian (South Gate of Heaven) between 7am and 7 or 8pm. During the summer and autumn, the cable car starts at 4:30am so you can see the sunrise. From the top of the cable car to the peak, at an altitude of 1,545 meters are 500 more steps. Tours usually spend a half day. Avoid holidays. Hotels are full then.

A second 2100-meter cable car from Peach Blossom Ravine on the northwest side also reaches the South Gate of Heaven. This side has no temples but lots of natural scenery. You can lunch at the Shenqi Binguan near the summit and then return to see the Daimiao Temple and a free market.

Ascending Mt. Tai on Foot

The longer, more satisfying way is to climb (at least one way) because the mountain has 30 old temples and 66 well-documented scenic spots, including beautifully carved memorial arches, Han dynasty cypress trees, white water, breathtaking views of forests and crags, and a stone pillar that looks suspiciously like a lingam. If you do it the hard way, you are following in the footsteps of Confucius!

The top can be reached in five or six hours through the **Path of Eighteen Bends**. Note the 7,000-plus stone stairs, each carefully placed by human labor like an almost vertical Great Wall! And they are not narrow! It is difficult to get lost. The stairs are very steep and in some places difficult to climb.

The **Temple of Azure Clouds** on the mountain is over 970 years old (Song). Note the bronze or iron roof ornaments, rafters, bells, and tiles of the main hall, made of metal to endure the severe mountain storms. Inside are nine huge gilt statues. Can you imagine having to carry these and the bronze Ming tablets up here! The top is at **Tianzhu Feng (Heavenly Pillar Peak)**, also known as Yuhuang Ding (Jade Emperor Peak).

The **Tomb and Museum of Feng Yuxiang** (Feng Yu-hsiang) may be of interest to students of modern Chinese history. This was the famous Christian General who fought with the Nationalists against the Japanese and baptized his men with water hoses. He is known more for his eccentricity than his military successes. His tomb is at the east end of Dazhong Bridge, downhill from the Dragon Pool Reservoir. These are on the north part of Puzhou Street.

Seventy-two visiting emperors used to offer sacrifices at the **Daimiao (Temple to the God of Taishan)**, Hong Men Road. This is close to the Taishan Guest House at the base and is open 7:30am-5pm. On special occasions like the Climbing Festival or on request in advance, actors perform a re-enactment of the rituals by Song Emperor Zhengzong at this impressive building. Though slow-moving, this should not be missed. The main hall has a mural 3.3 by 62 meters, painted in the Song, showing the pilgrimage of this emperor here. It includes 570 to 657 figures. (Count them!) This hall was built in 1009 A.D. and is considered one of the three eminent halls of China.

A nunnery with seven nuns is open 8:30am-6pm daily near Tiger Hill.

Festivals: From September 6-8, there is the mountain climbing festival. The third day of the third lunar month is the birthday of the grandmother of the mountain whose shrine is at the Azure Cloud Temple.

Shopping

Carpets and baskets are made locally. Peaches, walnuts, chestnuts, and dates are grown. The **Tai'an Antique Store** is at No. 1 Hongmen Road, near the back of Daimiao Temple, *Tel. 8222416*.

Practical Information

Ambulance, *Tel. 120*

CITS Taishan Branch, *22 Hongmen Road, 271000, above the Dai Temple and the Taishan Arch, Tel. 8223259, 8221183, Fax 8332240, E-mail: tscits@public.taptt.sd.cn. Website: www.taishan-cits.com*

City Center Hospital, *Tel. 8224161 (but no English)*.
Telephone Code, 538

Qingdao
(Tsingtao)

Qingdao lies on a peninsula on the southern coast of Shandong province, 393 km east of the provincial capital Jinan. It is an important manufacturing center, ice-free port and pretty summer resort, famous for its beer, mineral water, wine, and European heritage.

Starting as a fishing village, Qingdao (pronounced Ching Dow) has been an important trading port since the seventh century. During the Ming, it was fortified against pirates. The Germans seized the area in 1897 in retaliation for the assassination of two German missionaries. Here they built a naval base and trading port, and protected them with at least 2000 men. The large number of Germans accounted for its German architecture and its beer recipe.

In 1919, the Versailles Peace Conference confirmed Japan's 1915 capture of the German territories in Shandong. The Japanese stayed long enough to build huge cotton mills before they were forced to withdraw in 1937. During this period, the British built cigarette factories. The Japanese navy regained the city early in 1938, but not before a Chinese mob smashed the breweries, sending rivers of beer into the streets!

Qingdao's breweries were rebuilt, of course, and still produce the most popular Tsingtao Beer. Qingdao also bottles Laoshan mineral water, and now makes Huadong Riesling wine, the product of a recent joint venture.

The climate is temperate: the highest in August an average 25°C; the coldest in January an average -1.2°C. The annual precipitation is 715 mm. Fog in June and July might delay flights. The urban population is 2.2 million, the total seven million.

Olympics Update: Qingdao will host some water sports of the 2008 Olympic Games. The Olympic site will be on Fushan Bay, near May Fourth Square on the south side of Qingdao. Guests in the upper floors of the Holiday Inn have a view but will need telescopes. The local government is planning to build more than 20 hotels in Qingdao before 2008. More than 10 of these will be near Fushan Bay.

Arrivals & Departures

From Qingdao to Beijing the fastest train takes 10 hours, the train from Shanghai takes 20 hours, from Tai'an over five hours, and from Jinan, four hours. It's a one-hour flight south from Beijing or north from Shanghai. There are or will be direct air connections with at least 35 other Chinese cities and Fukuoka, Hong Kong, Tokyo, Germany, Osaka, Seoul and Singapore.

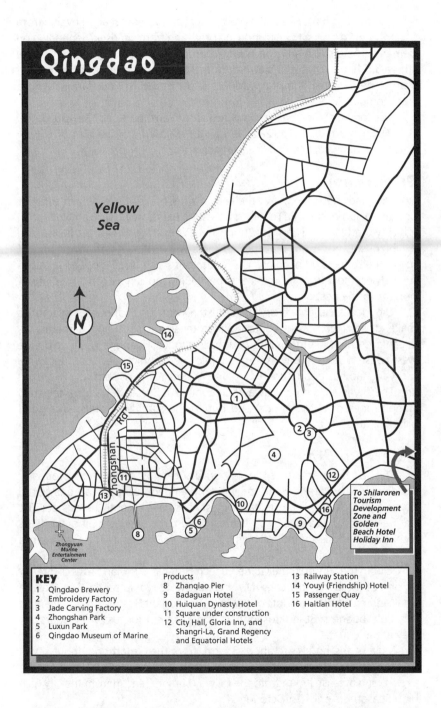

Qingdao

Yellow
Sea

N

To Shilaroren
Tourism
Development
Zone and
Golden
Beach Hotel
Holiday Inn

Zhongyuan
Marine
Entertainment
Center

KEY

1 Qingdao Brewery
2 Embroidery Factory
3 Jade Carving Factory
4 Zhongshan Park
5 Luxun Park
6 Qingdao Museum of Marine

Products

8 Zhanqiao Pier
9 Badaguan Hotel
10 Huiquan Dynasty Hotel
11 Square under construction
12 City Hall, Gloria Inn, and
   Shangri-La, Grand Regency
   and Equatorial Hotels

13 Railway Station
14 Youyi (Friendship) Hotel
15 Passenger Quay
16 Haitian Hotel

Qingdao is on the Huanghai (Yellow Sea) and you can reach it by ship from Shanghai in 24 hours, from Inchon in Korea, and from Simoseki depending on demand. There's also an expressway from Jinan (3.5 hours) and from Yantai (three-3.5 hours). A super-highway under construction now will connect it with Hebei, Shanxi, Shaanxi provinces and eventually Yinchuan in Ningxia Autonomous Region.

The long-distance bus stations are at 7 Wenzhou Road, *Tel. 3833275*, (West) Guantao Road, *Tel. 2825598* and (East) Harbin Road, *Tel. 5615680*. There are many hard-to-find bus stations.

Orientation

Qingdao should be put at the end of a hectic, tight schedule in summer because of its beaches. Full of hills, interesting parks, trees, and red-tiled roofs, it is very pretty for walking. Try Zhongshan Park which sometimes has special exhibitions. Laws insure that the red roofs will continue in the west part of town. It also has 200 buildings in 25 different Asian and European architectural styles, most from its imperialist past. Qingdao is now concerned about preserving the best of them.

Qingdao is the largest city and industrial center in Shandong. Its factories make diesel locomotives, automobiles, television sets, and cameras. Its oceanic research institute is internationally famous. Huangdao District, on the west coast of Jiazhou Bay, is its economic and technical development zone.

Qingdao has good public buses for Y1 and Y2. Taxis start at Y7 for four km. The city is building a subway due about 2005 that starts from the train station, goes near the airport and out to the suburbs. Hotels have good bilingual maps.

Where to Stay

The best five-star hotel is the Shangri-la but almost as good is the four-star Holiday Inn. The Grand Regency is recommended but it has an uninspired downtown location. The Huiquan Dynasty has been recently renovated. The Hai Tian is fine, has a pleasant seaside location, but needed a bit of work. Its recent renovations should solve its maintenance problems. The Gloria Inn is still a three-star with good value.

Out in the suburbs, the Golden Beach Hotel at Old Man Stone is directly on one of the better beaches. My second choice would be the Sea View, a small, intimate hotel with lots of garden. The Student Hostel is for travelers on very tight budgets. Standards in these three are not for fussy foreigners but they are adequate.

Most of the hotels are about 35 km. from the airport and about seven from the railway station. Those near Golden Beach are about 17 km from the airport, and at least 17 km from the railway station, ten km from the city hall. High Season is April 1 to October 31.

Four- and five-star hotels here all accept credit cards, and can change foreign travelers' checks. Hotels here add a 10 or 15% service charge and offer discounts even in high season. Rates are higher during the Beer Festival late August or early September when reservations are needed.

SHANGRI-LA HOTEL (Shang Gorilla Fandian), *9 Xiang Gang Zhong Road, 266071. Five stars. Tel. 3883838, Fax 3886868. E-mail: slq@shangri-la.com. Website: www.Shangri-la.com. $175-$250 for rooms, and $320-$1600 for suites. It has been offering 35-40% discount packages. It is a 40 minutes drive from the airport.*

This 1997 hotel is not as lavish as other Shangri-La's but is very attractive with rooms 37.7 square meters. It has 502 rooms (including 82 offices), two executive floors, and German, Cantonese, and Western food. Buffets are Y90 for breakfast, Y78 for lunch and Y118 for dinner. There's a good gym, 25-meter-long indoor pool, and outdoor tennis court. Rooms have safes, irons, and smoke hoods. They also have voice mail, CNN, CNBC, and HBO, and fax and computer outlets. It has international newspapers in English and high-speed internet access.

HAI TIAN HOTEL (Dajiudian), *48 Xianggang Xi Road, 266071. Five and four stars. Tel. 3871888, Fax 3871777. E-mail: htsales@hai-tian-hotel.com. Website: www.hai-tian-hotel.com. Rooms are $138-$178 and suites $168-$1800. It has been giving 20%-30% discounts. It is seven km from the railway station, 200 meters from No. 3 Swimming Beach, almost beside a three-kilometer waterfront walkway, and 15 minutes walk to a 2008 Olympics site.*

Opened in 1989, this hotel renovated its top 9th to 15th floors in 2001. It has 15 (west building) and 26 (east building) floors, two of them executive. There are 606 rooms, offices and apartments. Rooms have safes, CNN, and satellite television and are 30 square meters. Its executive floor has high speed internet access and video phone service. There's a lighted tennis court, 18-meter indoor heated pool, antique gym, and bowling. Its ballroom, can seat 400 at tables. Its Japanese restaurant has tatami rooms, and teppanyaki. See *Where to Eat* below. China Famous Hotels.

GRAND REGENCY HOTEL (Lijing Dajiudian), *1 Taiwan Road, 266071. Five stars. Tel. 5881818, Fax 5881888. E-mail: regency@public.qd.sd.cn. $138-$158 for rooms and $228- $2888 for suites. It has been discounting about 50%.*

This 352-room hotel has a Kaiser Clock with Snow White and "European Renaissance" relics in its lobby. Rooms are 29 square meters with CNN and safes. It has three executive floors, non-smoking rooms, and 24-hour room service. It has a limited gym, squash, bowling, lighted tennis, and a 15-meter long indoor pool. There's Cantonese, French, and Japanese restaurants, a grill room, and a food court. Its breakfast buffet is Y80. It provides international newspapers in English. Its magnificent ballroom can seat 600 banquet style. Orient Hotel Management Company.

QINGDAO SEAVIEW GARDEN HOTEL (Qingdao Hai Jing Hua Yuan Dajiudian), *2, Zhanghua Road, 266071. Four stars. Tel. 5875777, Fax 5894031. It is on 3500 square meters of land with gardens, a ten-minute drive south of the Golden Beach Hotel. Rooms are 24 square meters and are Y650-Y1230. Suites are Y1980 to Y5130. It has been giving 30 to 40% discounts.*

This charming Chinese hotel has an exceptionally high standard of English. It has a 25-meter long outdoor pool and a small year-round indoor pool, bowling, billiards, and tennis. Its gym has seven machines. Its 198 rooms are about 24 square meters and in four-story buildings, only one of which has an elevator. It has a business building, meeting rooms, Cantonese, Chaozhou, Shandong, Japanese and Korean cuisines. Its breakfast buffet costs Y58. It subscribes to the South China Morning Post.

HOLIDAY INN QINGDAO (Yi Zhong Jia Re Jiu Dian), *76 Xiang Gang Zhong (Hong Kong) Road, 266071. Four stars standards. Tel. 5718888, Fax 5716666, 5763383. E-mail: hiqingdo@public.qd.sd.cn, smhiqd@public.qd.sd.cn (sales). Website: www.holiday-inn.com. It has had a $71 package for a standard room with upgrade. $120 to $200 for rooms; $170 to $1800 for suites. It is almost next door to JUSCO, one of the biggest shopping malls, and near the Bank of China. On warm evenings, people dance nearby and there are lots of local restaurants.*

This 38-story, 2000 hotel has 388 rooms, executive rooms, CNN and European television channels, and in-room safes. Standard rooms range from 26 to 29 square meters. Its business center has American newspapers. The buffet breakfast is very luxurious and there's Cantonese and Italian food. It has offices and service apartments and looks more like a five star. It has 247 seaview rooms.

HUIQUAN DYNASTY HOTEL (Huiquan Wang Chao Dajiudian), *9 Nanhai Road, 266003. Four stars. Tel. 2873366, Fax 2896204, 2871122. E-mail: hqdhtl@qd-public.sd.cninfo.net. Y840-Y1350 for rooms and Y1680 for suites. It has been discounting 20-50%. Reservations through SRS. It is 35 km from the airport; five km from the railway station. Across a busy street with no stoplights from Number One Swimming Beach and close to the Shandong Foreign Trade Centre*

This 1979, 12- and 25-story hotel has over 500 rooms and a non-smoking floor. One of its wings was renovated in 2001. It has two-story penthouse suites, CNN, pay television, Air China office, and a Sichuan, Western, and a revolving restaurant. Its breakfast buffet costs Y58. There's a gym, bowling, 25-meter indoor pool, and tennis.

HUANHAI GLORIA INN (Huanhai Kailai Shangwu Jiudian), *29 Donghai Xi Road, 266071. Three stars. Tel. 3878855, Fax 3864640. E-mail: gloria@giqingdao.com. Website: www.giqingdao.com. It is near the waterfront and Olympic sailing competitions, 30 minutes from the airport. Rooms now range from Y580-Y780 (discounted to Y368-Y528 for example in low* *season), and Y1080 to Y1800 for suites. (low season discounted to Y788-Y1280). Its high season is July 1-August 31, May 1-7, and October 1-7. Prices include service and tax.*

This charming six-story hotel has 227 rooms. Its standard rooms range from 26 to 42 square meters and have continental beds, kettles and refrigerators, but no in-room safes. It has BBC, and a Huaiyang, Sichuan and Cantonese restaurant with hot pot. Its breakfast buffet costs Y38, lunch Y48 and dinner Y55 and its coffee shop has U.S. newspapers. Its business center can issue air tickets. Guests can use pool and sports facilities ten minutes walk away. Gloria Hotels and Resorts.

GOLDEN BEACH HOTEL (Huang Jin Hai An Dajiudian), *Old Stone Man National Tourism Resort, 266101. Three stars aiming for four. Tel. 8897888, 8897052. Rooms range from $70 to $106, and suites $165 to $750. It has been giving up to 40% discounts. It is 17 km from downtown (about Y30 taxi), but a walk to Beer City. It can be reached by buses 104, 125, 301, 304, 312, 313, 317, 321, and 362.*

This simple but adequate 160-room hotel owns a part of one of Qingdao's best beaches, but its carpets don't fit. It also has tennis, Chinese, Western, Japanese and Korean restaurants. Rooms have safes, CNN, moldy grouting, refrigerators and kettles. It has a Y30 Western and Chinese buffet. You need a reservation one week in advance in summer.

FOREIGN STUDENT HOSTEL (Xi Xiao Men), *International Student Centre, Ocean University, 23 Hong Kong Dong Road, Telephone the Foreign Affairs office (Wai ban) at 2032436 or 5901868 between 7:30am-5pm weekdays.*

This good six- or seven- story hostel has no elevator but is air-conditioned and available all year round. It has 25 rooms with private baths for Y180 during peak season. Guests eat with teachers.

Where to Eat

You have to try seafood here, of course, especially abalone and prawns. It is especially good in the top hotels. The Regency has a wonderful seafood restaurant.

For Chinese food, the **Hai Tian's** Chinese restaurant is very good. The appetizers of chicken gizzards were Y14 and bean curd with chili peppers Y14. The main courses, fried beef in black bean sauce was Y28, stir-fried spinach with garlic Y20, baby octopus and onions in XO sauce Y38, and lianyu geng (fish and bean thread soup) Y20 a small bowl. Tsingtao beer was Y6 a bottle. Its XO sauce is wonderful and made of seafood.

The best Western food is in the hotels too and the **Shangri-La's** is authentic and delicious. Expatriates hang out at the **Club Honolulu** in The Dynasty Hotel and **Murano's** restaurant in the Holiday Inn. The Holiday Inn's Italian restaurant has lamb grilled with herb butter and saffron risotto for Y92, ossobuco alla Milanese, braised veal shank cooked in tomato sauce, white wine and vegetables with polenta croutons for Y80, and fruit tart for Y32.

All the restaurants on Yunxiao Road are Chinese. The best for foreigners there is the **Gaoshi Restaurant** with a menu in English. The **Jing Yuan Seafood Restaurant** is at 63 Yun Xiao Road, *Tel. 5711346*. The **Huo Lie Niao Restaurant** is at 28 Yun Xiao Road, *Tel. 5717329* (Seafood and Shandong).

The **Xin Guang Restaurant** on Hong Kong Road has good Cantonese food. Also recommended are the **New Princes Restaurant**, West Building, 6 Xiang Gang Zhong Road, *Tel: 5919999*, and the **Yiqinglou Restaurant**, 90 Xiang Gang Zhong Road, *Tel. 5872018*. The city also has at least four KFC's and two Pizza Huts. JUSCO has a McDonald's. A KFC is on Zhongshan Road.

Seeing the Sights

You can cover all of Qingdao's important urban attractions in a day, including a leisurely walk through this museum of old European architecture and a 45-minute boat ride in the harbor. You need a second day or two for Laoshan Mountain if you enjoy hiking in exotic settings, and a visit to the brewery or winery. In the evening, look for the incredibly beautiful "flame of Qingdao," a huge red-lit sculpture in May 4th Square (Wu Si Guan Chang). Qingdao's four km of city beaches slope gently into the sea and are protected by four large bays east from 440-meter-long **The Pier** (1891). The city's signature landmark is a good place to absorb the sunrise. Southeast of it, and linked with the shore by a 700-meter-long dike, is Xiaoqingdao (Little Qingdao Island) with a lighthouse, another interesting place to walk.

Of its ten hills, **Zhongshan Park** is best seen when its 700 cherry trees bloom in April and it sometimes has special exhibits. Luxun Park has an excellent view of Number One Beach, Xiaoqingdao, and the European buildings. Look for the Christian church on Jiangsu Road and two German churches near Hubei Road.

Travel agents can arrange tours of the **Tsingtao Brewery** (May 4th Square, Xianggang Zhong Road, *Tel. 5711119*), and the **Shell Carving Handicraft Factory** at 106 Yanan San Road, *Tel. 3873162*.

Among China's best wines is Huadong which is produced about 25 km outside of Qingdao. Travel agents can also arrange tours here. Or you can contact the **Qingdao Huadong Winery Co.**, Nanlongkou, Laoshan, Qingdao, 266102. *Tel. 8818989, Fax 8817350. E-mail: hdwinery@public.qd.sd.cn*. It is best to visit the winery during the harvest in October, but tourists are always welcome and charged about Y5 each. It was developed in 1984 with cuttings from France. Australian workers welded the tanks. In 1985, it produced its first bottle and has even exported some to France. Don't expect discount prices but you might get a sample sip.

You should explore the **Badaguan area** by bicycle or on foot. Each street here is lined with a different kind of blossoming tree: cherry, peach, or crape myrtle. Behind the trees are individually-designed houses, a bit of old Europe. The most famous is the 1903 Granite/Stone Castle at 18 Huanghai Road. The entry fee is Y5 and it is open 8am to 5:30pm daily. It also has an intriguing view of the seashore. During the auspicious wedding season (late April to early June, September to mid-November on even days) brides and grooms clamber there on the rocks, the women in full length gowns. They want to be photographed expressing their love "until the sea goes dry," a local custom.

Qingdao now has **five golf courses**. The 18-hole Qingdao International Golf Club near Shaolaoren is good. The Holiday Inn has a golf package with the Huashan International Country Club. The largest and best of the seven city beaches is at the Shilaoren National Tourist and Resort Area, 17 km east of downtown and should be less crowded.

The **Number One Beach** downtown with lifeguards, medical station, shark nets, and changing facilities is too crowded. Beaches are open from early July to the end of September. If you are worried about pollution, **Yangkou Beach** is the cleanest. It is at the foot of Laoshan Mountain 50 km from the city. A taxi should cost about Y400 for the day to take you there. **Qingdao Ocean Park**, China's largest, is in Shilaoren National Holiday Resort, *Tel. 5882373*. It has a dolphin show (April-October), water sports, Aquatic Museum, and hotel. The **Qingdao Museum** is good. Ask about the interesting local **Lunar Market** in Li Cun, a north suburb towards the airport. Unfortunately for visitors, it's only open every fifth day.

Nightlife & Entertainment

The expatriate community is very active here and has a newsletter in English with social events, Bible study, travel tips, and book exchange. If you're staying a while, ask for it at the Holiday Inn business center.

Festivals: The annual International Beer Festival, which begins July 8 and runs for 15 days, has rides, fireworks and is lots of fun. The Ocean Festival is in July.

Shopping

Local products include beautiful feather pictures, carpets, weaving, embroidery, and knitting. Shops are along Zhongshan and Jiaozhou Roads. Foreign resident Elizabeth Stone recommends the Arts and Crafts store on Zhongshan Road and a nearby fabric shop on Beijing Road with silk, suiting, and a good tailor. Look for Parksons department store nearby.

JUSCO's department store on Hong Kong Road near the Holiday Inn is huge. The Cultural Market has curios, handicrafts, stamps and coins and is at Changle Road and Yixian Road. There is the indoor **Jimo Road Daily Use Commodities Market** (a.k.a. Jimo Bargain Market because you have to haggle hard). This is not far from the north end of Zhongshan Road with many pearls on sale. It also has clothes, shoes, watches, mahjong sets, beads, bags, jade articles, CD's, DVD's, video games, baskets, and toys. It can be very crowded, particularly on Sunday.

Excursions & Day Trips

The **Laoshan Mountains** are roughly 40 km east of the city, reached by bus, and said to be the home of the **Eight Taoist Immortals**.

You may have to choose one of three routes to tour Laoshan. The most popular one is the south Taiqinggong route with the Taoist temples, but the most beautiful is the Yangkou route. The waterfalls can be seen only in summer and autumn. A leisurely three-day trip to include them all would be ideal for hikers. There's a 400-meter-long chairlift.

Do not expect fancy, large temples. The meditative Taoists didn't and don't want to be distracted in their search for eternal peace, their communion with nature. Laoshan is famous for the masculine shape of its mountains and its rushing waterfalls. The highest peak, **Mt. Laoding**, is 1,333 meters above sea level. The mountains extend over 386 sq km and are full of granite canyons, grotesque crags, old temples, rivers, streams, and the Laoshan reservoir. The **Taiping (Great Peace) Taoist Temple** was founded in the Song. The home of Qing writer Pu Songling (1640-1715) is open to the public. He lived in a very modest corner of the Taiping Temple. Pu wrote his famous *Strange Tales from a Lonely Studio* here. The trees he described are still standing. The biggest temple, Taiqing Taoist Temple, has over 150 buildings.

An inscription about the visit of the first Qin emperor in 219 B.C. is also on the mountain. The builder of the Xi'an ceramic army searched here too for pills of immortality.

Other day trips can be to Yantai, Weihai, or Weifang. See separate listings below.

Practical Information

Korean Consulate, 7/F, Sino-Korean Business Building, 8 Qinling Road, Laoshan District, 266061, Tel. 8976001-3.

Internet café: Many 24-hour e-mail services are available around town for less than Y10 an hour. An internet bar is on the 4th floor of the Xin Hua book store, almost across the street from the Holiday Inn, open 9am to 9pm. It charges Y7 an hour.

Qingdao Hai Tian International Travel Service, 1F, Mid-Building of Hai Tian Hotel, 48 Xianggang Xi Road, Tel. 3872014, 3871340, Fax 3879574, 3879584. E-mail: hits@qdhits.com or hits@hai-tian-hotel.com. Website: www.qdhits.com (English). Ask for Song Jinlin, General Manager, or Peter Sun, Deputy General Manager. This travel agency gave me a lot of help in Qingdao, and it should be helpful to you too.

Qingdao China International Travel Service, 9 Nanhai Road, 266003. Tel. 2880390, Fax 28602998. E-mail: citsqdm@public.qd.sd.cn. Mitchell

Gong, Manager, North America Dept., Mobile 13906488135. E-business Dept. citsqd@public.qd.sd.cn. Website: www.citsqd.net.

Qingdao Overseas Tourist Company, Room 1603, Fu Tai Plaza, No. 18 Xianggang Zhong Road, 266071, Tel. 5719819, Fax 5722979, 5716506. Ask for Howard Song. E-mail: Howard/QDOTC qdotc@ ns.qd.sd.cn.

Qingdao Hueiho Intercontact, Room 102, Building No. 2, 27th Fushun Road, 266033, Tel. 3743285 or 13070880223 (24 hours), Fax 3736713. E-mail: cntravel@public.qd.sd.cn. Ask for managers, Philip Sue and Helen Wang (Tel.13808961771). They give a free airport transfer in Qingdao for clients who book flight tickets. They can deliver flight tickets.

Qingdao Tourism Administration, 11 Xianggang Zhong Road, 266071, Tel. 5912027, Fax 5912028.

Telephone Code: 532

Tourist Hotline: Tel. 3875345. Websites: www.chinaqingdao.net (Chinese only), www.qdta.gov.cn (English and helpful), and www.sdqd.qdinfo.stlac.cn.

Weifang

Weifang is almost in the center of Shandong province, 180 km from Qingdao and 250 km from Jinan. Weifang is noted for its annual international kite festival (April 20-25), its unique kite museum, and home stays. The urban population is 500,000.

Arrivals & Departures

You can fly here from Beijing, Linyi and Shanghai. The airport is 10 km southeast of the city. The Qingdao airport is one hour's drive and the Jinan airport is two hours away. Express trains between Jinan and Qingdao, and Jinan and Yantai stop here. It is two hours by train from Qingdao and is on the Jinan-Qingdao expressway.

Where to Stay

Prices are about 30% higher during the kite festival, but discounts of about 30% at other times. All rates are subject to 10% surcharge. Room prices quoted here are from CITS Weifang, not the hotel, and are already discounted.

FUHUA HOTEL, No. 168, Fushou Dong Road, 261031. Five, four and three stars. Tel. 8881988, Fax 8880766. Y780-Y1080 for rooms, and Y1380-Y7800 for suites. Located in the hi-tech development zone 15 km northeast of the airport, and seven km from the railway station, it is next door to the Fuhua Amusement Park. Standard rooms in its main building are $50 each for tour groups and $65 for individuals.

This 1996, nine-story, 246-room hotel also has 322 three- and four-star rooms in its adjacent international convention centre where standard rooms are $30 each for groups, and $40 for individuals.

Both sections have CNN and in-room safes, and there are Shanghai, Cantonese, Japanese and Korean restaurants. There is also bowling, gym, heated indoor pool, sauna, steam bath, and tennis. In its lobby, a long-tailed phoenix looking suspiciously like dripping strings of money, hangs from the ceiling, five tons of copper. It has an executive floor.

YUAN FEI HOTEL (Dajiudian), *31 Siping Road, 261041. Three and four stars. Tel. 8236901, Fax 8233840. It is five km from the airport and 2.5 km from the railway station; it is walking distance to the kite museum. It built 368 three-star rooms in 1987 with renovations in 2002. It has 150 four-star standard rooms. $45 for rooms for groups, and $55 for individuals. Only Visa and MasterCard accepted.*

This 21-story hotel has CNN and Star TV, Shandong, Cantonese, French and Japanese restaurants. It has a gym, sauna, bowling, indoor pool, and tennis.

Where to Eat

Your best bet for good food is in the top hotels. One of the food treats here is fried scorpions or cicadas, actually quite tasty. Try celery and macadamia nuts, Beijing duck, crabs, *luo bo dun pai gu* spare ribs, and corn bread.

Seeing the Sights

In Shanwang, southwest of the city, 18-million-year-old prehistoric fossils and unique stones have been found. The **Shanwang Paleontological**

Kite Heaven in Weifang!

Kites are the main draw and they are fun. You can visit the kite and woodblock print-making village of **Yangjiabou** to watch the process. Here professional adult kite fliers test their goods. It's about a 10 minute drive east of the Fuwah Hotel, *Tel. 7252050.* You can buy a kite here or from peddlers on the road, and learn flying techniques from the champions. Did you know that silk kites fly better and last longer, but paper kites fly higher? That China invented kites during the era of Confucius? Explore the **Weifang Kite Museum** with the world's best kites from 350-meter-long centipedes to tiny matchboxes that fly. It's at 66 Xingzheng Street, 261041, *Tel. 8227009.*

The kite festival itself draws 300,000 spectators. You should book early or go on a tour to ensure transportation and hotel. Contestants have come from all over the world and every foreign kite flier gets a prize. The world headquarters of the **International Kite Federation** is in Weifang at the Kite Museum.

Museum there has 10,000 specimens. Tourists can live with farming families in Shijiazhuang village.

Students of modern history might be interested in the **Second Middle School**. This was once the **Weihsien Concentration Camp**. British, Canadian, and American prisoners were held here by the Japanese in the 1940s, including Eric Liddell, the hero of the movie *Chariots of Fire*. A gold medalist in the 1924 Olympics for winning the 400 meters, this Scottish athlete refused to race on Sundays. He later became a Congregational missionary in China and died of a brain tumor in 1945. He was buried near the prison camp six months before the end of the war. Look for the seven-foot-high memorial stone in Chinese and English. Some of the original prison-missionary buildings are still standing.

Practical Information

CITS, *197 Dong Feng Road E., Weifang, 261041, Tel. 8290095, Fax.8887725. E-mail: znlx@public.wfptt.sd.cn* with a copy to *zongqian@hotmail.com* for an answer within 48 hours. Ask for Tony Lee, North America Department. Write to him for a Weifang tourist map in English.

Telephone Code: 536

Weihai

(Wei-hai-wei)

Weihai is a beautiful little open-port city on the Bohai Sea, with small but good beaches and hot springs. Natives are proud of its appearance and cleanliness. There are no fancy resorts. It is 90 km east of Yantai and 307 km northeast of Qingdao with an urban population of about 230,000, total 2,430,000.

Weihai was developed in the Ming because of its excellent harbor. Some of the funds to strengthen the navy base here were squandered by Empress Dowager Cixi on her Summer Palace in Beijing. In 1894, the Japanese won a naval base on a 25-year lease, which was used to monitor the Russians at Port Arthur (now Dalian), 100 km north.

The Sino-Japan Sea War Hall and the Navy Museum are on Liugong Island. The British tutor of the Last Emperor, Reginald Johnson - remember Peter O'Toole in *The Last Emperor* movie? - was the British administrator here. It has a navy museum and factories that produce carpets, leather goods, embroidery, artificial fur, etc. Nearby is the easternmost tip of China at Chengshan Cape, where the Yellow Sea meets the Bohai Sea. A fishing village, Yuanya, five km from Weihai, has been available for overnight home stays.

The hottest temperature is 28°C in August; the coldest is -12°C in January. 700 mm of rain falls mainly in August.

This off-the-beaten-track family vacation city can be reached by road, or soon by rail, flights from five other cities, and a ferry from Dalian and Inchon, Korea.

Hotel prices increase during holidays. The best hotel is the 150-room **Golden Bay Hotel**, which is aiming for 5-star standards. It's at 128 Huanhai Road, Torch High-tech Industry Development Zone, Weihai, 264209. *Tel. 5688777, 5688666, Fax 5687999. E-mail: gbhotel@public.whptt.sd.cn. Website: www.whgoldenbayhotel.com (English).* Shandong CITS charges $70 a room.

The four-star **Weihaiwei Mansion** (Dasha) is at 82 Haigang Road, 264200, *Tel. 5232544, Fax 5232281.* It is 100 meters from the port and 30 km from the airport. It has 17-stories, 153 rooms, hot spring water, and satellite television. It offers French, German, Korean, Sichuan, and Cantonese food. Shandong CITS charges $65 a room here.

CITS is at 96 Guzhai Dong Road, 264200, *Tel.5816148, 5817211, Fax 5817456, 5225850.* The **telephone code** is 631. For **Weihai Tourism Bureau**, *Tel. 5222335.*

Yantai

(Chefoo, Cheefoo or Zhifu)

Yantai is an ice-free port city, primarily of interest to business people. It also hosts international cruise ships. It is about three hours by expressway northeast of Qingdao. Inhabited almost 2,200 years ago, this fishing village was visited by the first Qin emperor early in its existence. In 1398, during the Ming, a military post was set up, and beacon towers built for transmitting messages. Yantai means smoke tower. Yantai was first opened to foreign trade in 1862. It was a summer resort for the US Navy's Yangtze Patrol (with White Russian bar girls). The China Inland Mission operated a school here for missionary children; the buildings now are used by the Chinese Navy. Its seaside Yantai Hill once housed 10 foreign consulates.

The weather is hottest (28.3°C) in July and August; the coldest is -10°C in January. The annual precipitation is about 700 millimeters mostly in June. The urban population is now 1,544,000, the total about six million.

Arrivals & Departures

You can reach Yantai by train from Qingdao in four hours, twice a day, or in four hours by a superhighway (350 km), or from Jinan by road in 5.5 to 6 hours. You can go there by plane from Seoul and Hong Kong and 21 Chinese cities. It can also be reached by ship from Dalian taking three to eight hours. A direct train from Beijing takes about 15 hours, and from Shanghai 23 hours. The airport is about 20 km from town.

Orientation

Yantai is one of China's prettiest little cities, nestled between the sea and, on three sides, gentle hills. Many of its buildings are topped with orange tiles, and some are of rose-colored stone. It has a cheerful atmosphere of vitality and prosperity. Off the main tourist track, it is more for relaxed family sightseeing and swimming than hectic tourism. Its old colonial section is near the Bund waterfront and Yantai Hill.

It farms prawns, abalone, scallops, and jelly fish. It grows peanuts (one fifth of China's crop), cherries, grapes, apples, and white asparagus. It mines one-quarter of China's gold. The closest mine is about 80 km from the city.

Where to Stay

Yantai has poor hotels. The best are the Pacific and Marina which are close together, central, and close to the exhibition center. China Shandong Tourism Corp in Jinan charges $60 a room for the Pacific, and $50 for the Marina.

SHANDONG PACIFIC HOTEL (Taiping Yang Dajiudian), *74 Shifu Street, 264001. Four stars. Tel. 6206888, 6224421. Fax 6224421. E-mail: tpybc@public.ytptt.sd.cn. It is 17 km from the airport. This hotel is conveniently located adjacent to a night market and less than 100 meters from the Yantai Museum. A sign on the roof says "Pacific Ocean."*

The 1999 Pacific has 148 rooms, seafood, Cantonese and Chaozhou food, a bowling alley, pool, and health club. Rooms have CNN, rusty plumbing, and a safe too complicated to use. The food was delicious, the restaurant clean, and the service good. But the area around the swimming pool, and the carpets on the lower floor, were in dire need of refurbishing. Its 25-meter indoor pool and other areas hopefully will be renovated soon. We caught a half-dressed man with large tattoos necking with a fully-clothed young woman in the gym. It appears that the health club is not controlled by the hotel, a bad situation for hotel security. The manager ignored the couple and said it was building a new gym with good equipment soon.

YANTAI MARINA HOTEL (Binhai Jia Ri Jiudian). *Tel. 6669999, Fax 6669770. This hotel has a good location near No. 1 Beach.*

The standard room seen had CNN, kettle, safe, dirty scales, and make-up mirror. We saw a carpet being shampooed. It had no periodicals in English, and its gym had eight antique exercise machines. Its Conference Hall seats 300 banquet-style.

Homestays

Yantai is a pioneer in home stay programs for travelers bored by temples. By Chinese standards, some of the rural villages here are incredibly wealthy, and a visit should explain why. **Xiguan Village**, 23 km away is one of the places where you can spend the night with a family, usually part of a package and not cheap. Contact a travel agency.

Where to Eat

The best restaurants are in the hotels. And what to eat? Fresh seafood, of course! Shandong food is not peppery hot or overly sweet, but it has lots of garlic, onions, and salt. Yantai people say that Beijing duck originated when two indigent Yantai peasants went to Beijing and found a dead duck on the road. Improvising an earthen oven, they cooked the duck. An official happened by, liked the smell, and asked for a taste. Pleased, he presented the dish to the emperor, who rewarded the official and the cooks. If you don't mind noise, the **Haoxianglai**, across the road from the Pacific Hotel, has Western-type food but no menu in English. It serves sizzlers for Y25.

Seeing the Sights

Penglai Pavilion is the most important tourist attraction here and is 83 km northwest of the city, past the Yantai Economic and Technology Development Zone. A visit can take a half day.

It was from Penglai Pavilion that the **Eight Taoists Immortals** flew across the seas. After getting drunk, they tried to compete with each other using his or her own treasure. Guides should indicate the room where the Immortals partied! (See *Attributes of the Eight Taoist Genii* in Chapter 5.) Some people say they flew to Japan. But some people say they achieved immortality or arrived in paradise. Myths vary.

The pavilion was first built in the Northern Song (960-1127) and extended in 1589. Among the other buildings nearby are the Temple of the Sea Goddess Tian Hou, a Taoist temple, and the Wind Protection Hall, where lit matches will not blow out even if the wind is from the north. Important is the room full of calligraphy by a famous Ming calligraphist who lived here for three years waiting unsuccessfully to see a mirage.

The ***Penglai Water Town** or Beiwocheng, immediately to the south of the pavilion, was built as a fortress, particularly against Japanese pirates. The Song and Ming navies trained here. Intriguing is the water gate. In the old days, the Chinese lured in pirates and closed the gate behind them. Then, after the water level rose, the gate was opened and the dead pirates were flushed out. Originally built in 1376, the gate was rebuilt in 1596.

A replica of the Ming town **Dengzhou**, including an old style bazaar, is on the way from the bus stop to the pavilion. Nearby is the **Dengzhou Ancient Ship Museum**. On special occasions, spear-carrying guards in Ming dress, waving dynastic flags, enliven the market along with stilt and boat dancers, and firecrackers.

People have claimed they've seen mirages from the Penglai Pavilion. A recent sighting was on June 28, 2000 and lasted two hours. CITS says it has a video of a mirage which can only be shown in Penglai. Ideal conditions for mirages are summer and autumn, with the east wind blowing shortly after a gentle rain, between 2 and 3pm. The mirage is of a high mountain, an island, or old city, which some people believe to be Dalian or Korea across the Yellow Sea.

Ask your hotel to show videos about the Immortals. These mythical people were each from different periods of history but the Penglai legend puts them together here during the Song! Fairies can do anything!

Also important downtown is the **Yantai Museum**, 2 Yulan Street, *Tel. 6222520*. Open daily, except perhaps Mondays, from 8:30am-5pm with lunch from noon to 1pm. Y5. It is in a flamboyant Fujian-style guild hall with a temple dedicated to the sea goddess. This beautifully restored building was constructed from 1884 to 1906 in Fujian, and brought here in three sections. A statue of the goddess, destroyed during the Cultural Revolution, has been replaced in wax. The museum has a few relics from 8000 B.C. with labels in English and can be seen in 40 minutes. It has 4000-year-old grains of rice and paintings of the life of the Fujian goddess Mazu. It has nine chime bells from the Western Zhou and tomb figures from the Ming.

There isn't much for the average tourist to see at the Zhangyu wine museum. If you have more time, you can enjoy a good view of the harbor from the lighthouse built on top of a Ming dynasty beacon tower on Yantai Hill. I would also visit the old British consulate in the Golden Gulf Hotel at the west end of the Bund. Ask for the Chefoo Club and look at its manual bowling alley and old photos.

Yantai has two bathing beaches in the city proper: Number One Bathing Beach, in central Yantai, and Number Two Bathing Beach farther east. Both have all facilities. The swimming season goes from June to early September.

Shopping

Manufactured here are Riesling wines, vermouth, Gold Medal Brandy, lace, tablecloths, straw weaving, wooden-framed clocks, and woolen needlepoint pieces. Try the factories and department store.

Practical Information

CITS, *181 Jietang Road, 264001, Tel. 6234145, 6234144, Fax 6234147. E-mail: ytcits@public.ytptt.sd.cn*. It has 30 English-speaking guides. Ask for Li Yue Wen.

Telephone Code: 535

Nanjing

(Nanking: Southern Capital)

Located in the southwest part of Jiangsu province of which it is the capital, **Nanjing** lies on the Yangtze River. It is important because of its magnificent wall, gates and relics, many built by Zhu Yuanzhang (Chu Yuan-chang), first emperor of one of China's greatest dynasties who reigned from 1368 to 1399. After his death, his successors moved the capital to Beijing, where they built the Forbidden City and were buried in elaborate tombs north of it.

Nanjing was settled 6,000 years ago and became a walled city 2,400 years ago. From 229 to 1421 A.D., it was intermittently the capital of the Eastern Wu (229-280 A.D.), Eastern Jin (317-420), Song (420-479), Qi (479-502), Liang (502-557), Chen (557-589), Southern Tang (937-975), Ming (1368-1421), and Taiping Heavenly Kingdom (1853-64).

In 1842, England and China signed the Treaty of Nanking, ending the First Opium War, and the city was forced to become an open port. From January 1 to April 5, 1912, it was the capital of the Sun Yat-sen government after which the capital moved to Beijing. After a period of much confusion, Chiang Kai-shek unilaterally declared Nanjing the capital again in 1927.

The Japanese captured Nanjing in 1937, and massacred 300,000 civilians in what is referred to as the Rape of Nanking. A museum was recently opened to commemorate this tragic event. Nationalists' headquarters moved to Chongqing but returned to Nanjing after the Japanese surrender in 1945. Most buildings survived the war. The Communists took the city in 1949, and moved the capital to Beijing. Nanjing is still the provincial capital.

Its 2000 factories make metallurgical and chemical equipment, ships, telecommunication instruments, and synthetic fibers. The Zhong Xin Yuan Silk Factory manufactures brocade, and the Arts and Crafts Carving Factory works in ivory and wood.

For background on Nanjing, read Barry Till's *In Search of Old Nanking*.

Nanjing's hottest temperature is a rare 40°C in August; its coldest is -7°C in January. The annual precipitation is more than 1,000 mm with rain mostly in summer. The humidity can be incredibly high in late spring and summer. The population is 5.5 million (3 million urban). A good time to visit is late October to mid-November when the streets are lined with chrysanthemums.

Arrivals & Departures

Planes arrive from Hong Kong and 39 Chinese cities. Nanjing is a 1 3/4 hour flight by air southeast of Beijing and a 45 minute flight northwest of Shanghai. The airport is about 40 km from the city.

The 300 km Nanjing-Shanghai expressway means about a four-hour direct Y88 air-conditioned bus trip. Buses leave for Shanghai every 30 minutes or so from the Hanzhong bus station near the railway station and the Zhong Yang Hotel, north and east of the Yangtze River bridge. This is a long way from downtown, and buses end up near the Shanghai Railway Station. The bus from the Shanghai Stadium in Shanghai might be more convenient. It connects with the Jinling Hotel downtown. Nanjing is a three hour trip by train (Y86) from Shanghai. A taxi to Wuxi from Nanjing costs about Y500 and to Shanghai about Y1100.

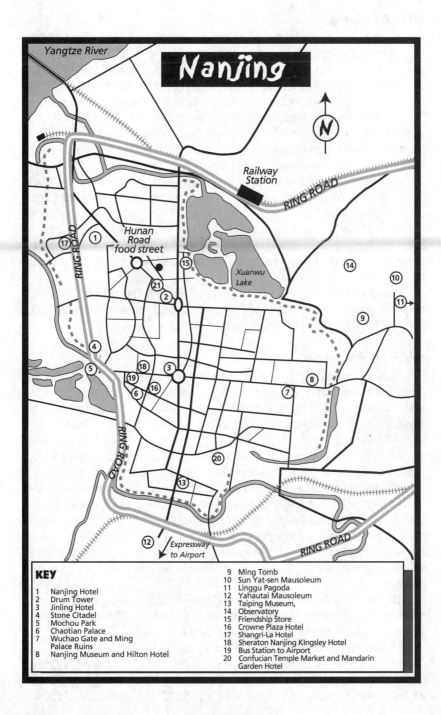

Yangtze River

Nanjing

Railway Station

RING ROAD

N

Hunan Road food street

Xuanwu Lake

RING ROAD

Expressway to Airport

RING ROAD

KEY

1 Nanjing Hotel
2 Drum Tower
3 Jinling Hotel
4 Stone Citadel
5 Mochou Park
6 Chaotian Palace
7 Wuchao Gate and Ming Palace Ruins
8 Nanjing Museum and Hilton Hotel
9 Ming Tomb
10 Sun Yat-sen Mausoleum
11 Linggu Pagoda
12 Yahautai Mausoleum
13 Taiping Museum,
14 Observatory
15 Friendship Store
16 Crowne Plaza Hotel
17 Shangri-La Hotel
18 Sheraton Nanjing Kingsley Hotel
19 Bus Station to Airport
20 Confucian Temple Market and Mandarin Garden Hotel

Orientation

Nanjing is a beautiful city of broad avenues thickly lined with 240,000 sycamore trees. Centrally located is the Drum Tower, with Zhongshan Road, the main shopping street, running south, northwest, and east, intersecting in the center of town. Xuanwu Lake dominates the north-eastern sector. Above it to the east looms 450-meter Zijin (Purple Gold) Mountain. The magnificent Ming city wall snakes around most of the urban area. The Yangtze River borders the western part of the city with two bridges across it. The city is building a 16.4 km south-north subway line from the Zhonghua Gate to the train station. The first phase should operate in 2004.

If you can't book city tours through your hotel, you can try the travel agents below. There are also four cheap city tour bus routes to major tourist site. Among these:

You 1 (Tour Bus 1) is from the railway station to Sun Yat-sen's Mausoleum, stopping (among other stops) at Xuanwu Park, Drum Tower, Jiming Temple, Presidential Palace, Ming Palace, Zhongshan Gate, Meiling Palace, and Sea World.

You 2 (Tour Bus 2) is from the Rain of Flowers Terrace to Sea World, stopping (among other stops) at Zhonghua Gate, Presidential Palace, Ming Palace, Plum Hill, Meiling Palace, and Sea World.

Where to Stay

Hotels here add a 10% service charge and 5% tax, and accept credit cards. The downtown hotels (Crowne Plaza, Jinling, Ramada, and Sheraton) are within a couple of kilometers of each other, about 42 km from the airport, and seven km from the train station. The best price for tour groups seems to be at the Sheraton.

My favorite hotel here is the Shangri-La in spite of its small, strange lobby. It has good service, lots of space and is beautiful. For tourists, the second choice is the Hilton because of its location. For business people there are the downtown hotels. The Jinling is one of the best Chinese-managed hotels in the country with lots of experience hosting North Americans. If you want to sleep more cheaply, there's the four-star Dingshan and then the three-star Nanjing Hotel. For getting closer to things Chinese, the Mandarin Garden is smack in the middle of the Confucian Temple area but standards are not international.

The hotels listed here accept major credit cards, have business centers, minibars, air-conditioning, money exchange, and add a 10%-15% surcharge. Prices are subject to change, negotiation, and discounts.

SHANGRI-LA DINGSHAN (Dingshan Xiang Ge Li La Dajiudian), *90 Chahaer Road, 210003. Four and five stars. Tel. 8802888, Fax 8821729. E-mail: sldn@shangri-la.com. Website: www@shangri-la.com (English). Rooms in the five-star Shangri-La Wing are $200-$320 and suites $350-$2000.*

Rooms in the four-star Dingshan Wing are $120-$160 and suites $200. It has been discounting 30 to 45%. Special room packages can be even better during holidays.

The new ring road expressway now means it's only a 15 minute, 7 to 8 km drive from the downtown center. You can see this Chinese castle from at least a kilometer away, its three towers joined together. It is set on 80,000 square meters of grass, flowers and driveway. The Nanjing International School is on its grounds. Within 10 minutes walk are a Carrefour supermarket, and some interesting restaurants. See *Where to Eat* below.

This 2001 hotel has 689 rooms including serviced apartments and villas. Rooms are 50 to 60 square meters, most with balconies. They have safes, irons, CNN, CNBC, and lots of lights. Bathrooms have a tub and a shower stall with a seat. It has tennis, a golf driving range, and a 25-meter-long pool. It should now have a deli, pool deck, gym and night club. The ballroom seats 700 banquet style and offers simultaneous translation, and digital television walls. The breakfast buffet costs Y98, and dinner Y98. Shangri-La chefs add no MSG even to Chinese food. Its frequent shuttle buses downtown are free for guests.

HILTON NANJING HOTEL (Xi Er Dun), *319 Zhongshan Dong Road, 210016. Five stars. Tel. 4808888, Fax 4809999. E-mail: PR_NANJING@Hilton.com. Website: www.hilton.com. It has 561 rooms, and a non-smoking floor. $180-$280 for rooms; $300-$1800 for suites. It has been discounting 40%.*

The "S" shaped, 42-story Hilton is set on 45 acres, conveniently located close to the city wall, and next to the Nanjing Museum in a residential part of town. You can also walk to the ruins of the Ming Palace. It is 30 minutes by car from the new international airport and ten minutes from the city centre if no traffic jams. It has a big, airy lobby with two grand staircases, a coffee shop and murals of Einstein and Galileo. Its restaurants have Italian, Jiangsu, and Cantonese food. Its ballroom can seat 1200 for a banquet. The business center has padded arm chairs. Rooms are very spacious with stuffed arm chairs and leg rests, safes, and in-house movies. It has a health club with aerobics, indoor pool and a 700-square meter sauna. There's bowling and simulated golf. The Hilton is owned by China Travel Service.

CROWNE PLAZA NANJING HOTEL AND SUITES (Jin Ying Huang Guang Jiudian), *89 Han Zhong Road, 210029, at Wang Fu Street. Tel. 4718888, Fax 4719999. E-mail: crowne@jlonline.com. Website: www.crowneplaza.com/hotels/nkqch. (English). $108 and $118 for rooms, and $185-$1888 for suites. It has been offering a Y598 suite package with breakfast.*

This is the highest hotel in Nanjing. There are 290 rooms, with 60% suites from 55 square meters and rooms from 34 square meters, some non-smoking. It was originally the G.E. Plaza Hotel. The hotel layout is unconventional since its lobby is on the 7th floor. The Chinese restaurant is on the 7th floor and the coffee shop is on the 9th. Guests rooms are on the 37th to the 53rd floors.

Other floors are offices, and the lower ones the Golden Eagle shopping mall and a supermarket. A subway station will be opening nearby.

There are mirror-like marble floors and good standards. Rooms have safes, broadband internet access, and CNN, BBC, Italian, and German channels. Its breakfast buffet costs Y78 and dinner Y98 to Y138 (seafood). It has a night club, karaoke and a Y56 foot-massage service. There's a year-round pool, aerobics and a good 19-piece gym. Its business center charges Y0.50 a minute for e-mail and should have English-language international newspapers on hand.

SHERATON NANJING KINGSLEY HOTEL & TOWERS (Kingsley Binguan), *169 Hanzhong Road, 210029. Five stars. Tel. 6668888, Fax 6669999. E-mail: nanjing.kingsley@sheraton.com. Website: www.sheraton.com/nanjing or www.sheraton-nanjing.com. Rooms are $155-$230. Suites are $215-$980. It has been discounting up to 45%. It is on the edge of the commercial, business, and government area, 500 meters west of the Jinling Hotel, and close to hospitals and CAAC office.*

This 41-story, 350-room hotel opened in 1999 with a big incense burner and fountain in front. Standard rooms are 37 square meters with floor-to-ceiling windows, safes, second modem lines, and irons. It has executive and non-smoking floors, an Irish fun pub, 24-hour room service, and piano bar with high tea. To help you keep fit, there's a 25-meter lap pool, lighted tennis court, gym, and traditional medicine and massage therapy center. It has offices for hire.

JINLING HOTEL (Fandian), *Xinjiekou Square, 210005. Five stars, Tel. 4711888, 4711991, Fax 4711666. E-mail: hotel@jinlinghotel.com. Website: www.jinlinghotel.com (English). $170-$280 for rooms and $300-$2000 for suites. For walk-in guests, there has been a 20%-30% discount.*

Opened in 1983 and renovated in 2001, this 37-story, 600-room hotel is attached to the 17-story World Trade Center. Services include a health club, sauna, steam bath, and tanning machine. It also has a very pretty indoor pool and snooker. There is a grill room, Italian, Japanese, German, American, and Cantonese food, and scheduled shuttles with the airport and train station. Rooms have CNN and CBS, safes, and 24-hour room service. It has an exchange program with the U.S.'s Purdue University whose student interns have been working here. It has bus service to Shanghai. A member of the Leading Hotels of the World.

RAMADA PLAZA NANJING, (Huameida Yihua), *45 Zhongshan Bei Road. Four stars. Tel. 3308888, 3301666, Fax 3309688. E-mail: nkgch@public1.ptt.js.cn. It is downtown close to Xuanwu Lake and about two km from Xinjiekou Square, 35 km from Lukou International Airport and seven km from the railway station. $120-$165 for rooms, $170-$1988 for suites. It has been giving 50% discounts.*

This 34-floor, 272-room hotel started out as a Holiday Inn and became a Ramada Plaza in 2000. It has executive floors, 25 to 35 square-meter rooms and CNN, CNBC, and VOD. There's a 24-hour business center, coffee shop, Italian, Cantonese and Asian restaurants. It has a 13-piece gym, 20-meter-long indoor pool, sauna and steambath. An internet center is almost across the road in the Telecom building.

MANDARIN GARDEN HOTEL (Zhuang Yuan Lou Jiudian), *9 Zhuang Yuanjing, Fuzi Temple, 210001. Three and five stars. Tel. 2202988, Fax 2201876. E-mail: ZYLhotel@public1.ptt.js.cn.*

Standards here are not international and English is almost non-existent, but it's an interesting location for tourists. Published room rates for three-star Y480-Y530, and suites Y1000-Y2600. It has been discounting 30%. I can only recommend the three-star for budget travelers who are not fussy. Its five-star section cannot compare with the hotels above.

NANJING HOTEL (Fandian), *259 Zhongshan Bei Road, Tel. 3411888, Fax 3422261. It is 47 km from the airport, and five km from the railway station, and in a good location northwest of the Holiday Inn. In its Zi Jin block, rooms cost $96-$108 and suites $158-$806. In its Zi Xia Block, rooms cost $32-$52, the quality of course much lower. Breakfast is included.*

This 1936-built hotel has several buildings set in a garden. No safes and CNN in rooms, it is generally clean and okay but don't expect excellence. It has Chinese and Western food, a gym and sauna.

Where to Eat

Nanjing people say the recipe for Beijing roast duck originally came from Nanjing, so you might want to try the Nanjing version. Among the other local specialties are: salted duck, especially August Sweet Osmanthus duck, salted duck gizzard, roast chicken with coriander, salted shrimps, casserole cabbage heart, big flat pork croquette (outside crisp, inside soft), chrysanthemum-shaped herring, long-tailed shrimp, and squirrel-like mandarin fish. Its peaches in July drip with sweet juice.

The best food is in the hotels. The **Hilton** has had a great dinner buffet for about Y98 that included roast beef, sushi, fish, won ton, salads, and brie cheese. For good western food, try also the **Shangri-la**, **Crowne Plaza** and **Sheraton**. The **Jinling** has its **Brauhaus Brewery** where you can hide behind the beer tanks, gorge on German-type sausages, and slurp soup from a bowl made of crispy bread.

The **Shangri-La's** two Chinese restaurants serve half-portions on request, and you can thus sample more variety than usual. Its XO Sauce (scallops, dried shrimp, and chili peppers) is so good, you can eat it straight. With prices subject to change, try the cold, salted Nanjing duck (Y20), stewed pork ribs (Y7 a piece, sweet and succulent with cloves), and shrimp and crab meat in half-pastry for Y22 per piece. There is also date paste cake (Y15 for six pieces) and vegetable dumplings (Y12 for six pieces) and especially good steamed Xiao long tang bao (minced pork dumpling with soup inside) for Y15 for six pieces.

The cooks at the **Shangri-La Dingshan** are very famous for Jiangsu food. There's the related **Dingshan Restaurant** chain, one near the Confucian Temple at 5 Zhanyuan Road, *Tel. 6627555*, and one at 458 Zhongshan Dong Road, *Tel. 4456614*.

Nanjing also has a **food street** now on **Shizi Qiao Lane**, Hunan Road, from which cars are banned. The **Nanjing Da Pai Dang** there has cheap, good, local food and cute little old men greeting you with much enthusiasm at the door. You just point at what you want. I paid Y19 for three small dishes. The barbecued food is good. A couple staffers speak a little English. You get discounts if you arrive after 9pm.

More expensive, better, and less noisy is the **Lion King Restaurant** (Shizi Qiao) almost next door. It has five levels, European décor, and charges about Y100 a dish. *Tel. 3306777, 3300781*. The area even has a Thai restaurant, but don't expect authentic. It's at 2 Shizi Qiao, Hunan Road, *Tel. 3242525*. A Pizza Hut and KFC should be under the Crowne Plaza.

Seeing the Sights

Nanjing takes two days to see, but if you only have one day in the city itself, most important are the Sun Yat-sen Mausoleum, Linggu Temple, and Ming Tomb statues in the eastern part of the city. You can also visit the Observatory (for the view) and the wonderful new provincial museum. The Zhonghua Gate and city wall are important too. If you have more time, see the Confucian Temple, Qinhuai River, and the Taiping Museum which are close together. A tour bus stop is across the street to the left, from the Hilton, and goes to the Sun Mausoleum.

The **Dr. Sun Yixian (Sun Yat-sen) Mausoleum**, *Tel. 4446111*, open daily, is on an 80,000-square-meter site. The building was designed to be more impressive than those of the emperors whom the father of the Chinese republic overthrew. It is eight km from the Jinling Hotel, on the south side of Purple Gold Mountain, its *feng shui* ideal. Dr. Sun (1866-1925) was buried here in 1929 in the rear of the hall. The mausoleum has 392 steps and a five-meter-high statue, and is well worth visiting. But you must leave bags and purses behind.

Sun Yat-sen was born of peasant stock in Guangdong province, near Macau, in what is now called Zhongshan County, renamed after its most distinguished son. Zhongshan was his honorific name. Dr. Sun spent most of his life outside China, leaving home at the age of 12 to study at an Anglican school in Hawaii, where his older brother had settled. He studied medicine in Hong Kong and for a short time set up practice in Macau. He spent much of his life traveling in Europe and America, living in Japan, writing and plotting against the Manchus, and planning a government for China.

An intriguing, complex man, Dr. Sun became a Christian early in life and, although he attacked missionaries as being imperialists, he admitted on his death bed that he was a Christian. He fought the Manchus because they could not rid the country of the foreign imperialists. After becoming president, he formally informed the first Ming emperor of what had happened! Dr. Sun did not remain president for long. Because he wanted to unite the country, he abdicated in 1912. The north was not willing to accept a southerner as head of state, he reasoned. He later accepted a post as director of railways for the country. At the same time, he flirted with socialism, coming under the influence of Russian advisers.

He was married first to a peasant woman and later to Soong Chingling, much against her father's wishes. The second marriage shocked the Christians but not most Chinese. Mme. Sun was the sister of Mme. Chiang Kai-shek. See also Shanghai and Zhongshan.

Linggu (Valley of the Soul) Temple, open daily, is the only survivor of a whole complex of Buddhist structures, its statues destroyed during the Taiping war when the Qing army slept here. Eight km from the Jinling Hotel, a Liang princess built it originally in 513 A.D. in memory of the famous monk Xuan Zhang. The first Ming emperor moved it to its current location at the eastern foot of Zijin Mountain because he wanted the original site for his own tomb. Built without beams, it is reminiscent of medieval Europe because of its arches. Nearby is a nine-story pagoda built in the 1920s to improve the feng shui around the mausoleum, two km to the northeast.

The **Xiaoling Mausoleum (Ming Tomb)** is open daily, *Tel. 6642990.* This mausoleum, for the first Ming emperor, Zhu Yuanzhang, is not as impressive as those north of Beijing, but is worth a visit only for its Sacred Way with over a dozen well-proportioned, larger-than-life mythical animals, generals, and ministers. The exact location of the grave of the emperor, his wife and 46 concubines has been unknown until recently. The tomb was built between 1381 and 1383. Do not expect to visit this very important recent find yet but keep your eyes open for signs of archaeological work when you are visiting the area.

Zhu Yuanzhang was a peasant and former Buddhist monk and beggar who fought his way to the throne and was a brilliant emperor. Most of his Nanjing buildings were destroyed in the early days of the Qing, who overthrew his dynasty. The mausoleum is six km from the Jinling Hotel. The Botanical Garden, with tropical and subtropical plants, is on one side of the Sacred Way.

Zijinshan (Purple or Bell Mountain) dominates the northeastern skyline. The Observatory is on the west side. This major research center of the Chinese Academy of Science, built in 1934, is involved with space research and man-made satellites. You can go there for the view and to see copies of ancient instruments outside.

Chinese astronomers invented the armillary sphere (four dragons and spheres) 2,000 years ago to locate constellations. They invented the abridged armillary sphere (three dragons) in the Yuan for the same purpose. Astronomers used the gnomon column next to the abridged sphere (a 3,000-year-old invention), to survey the seasons and calculate the days of the year. It faces due south and north. In the large column is a small hole through which the sun shines at noon, casting light on the gauge below. Because of this instrument, the Chinese decided very early that there were 365 1/4 days a year.

The new **Nanjing Museum**, Zhongshan Dong Road, *Tel. 4802119*, is in a traditional Chinese-style building and is immediately east of the Hilton Hotel, about the fourth building from the road. It contains exhibits ranging from the era of Peking Man to revolutionary times.

The **Nanjing City Wall** is 12 meters high, 33.4 km in circumference, and from 7.62 to 12 meters thick. Built from 1368 to 1387, it once had 13,616 cannons on top. Roughly 10 km north-south by 5.62 km east-west, it is believed to be the longest city wall in the world. The bricks were made in five provinces, and each is inscribed with the name of the superintendent and the brickmaster, plus the date made. The mortar was lime, tung oil, and glutinous rice paste. Originally built with 13 gates, 11 more were added later. You cannot miss this magnificent wall.

The **Zhonghua Gate**, *Tel. 6625752*, on the south side, is the best gate to see. It has four two-story gates in succession (in case the enemy breaks through one), 12 tunnels, and room to garrison 3,000 soldiers. You can walk along the top of the wall here.

If You Have More Time or Special Interests

The **Confucius Temple (Fuzimiao)**, *Tel. 6628639*, adjacent shopping center, hotel, and free market, has a couple points of interest including Ming and Qing architecture. The Temple was originally built in 1034 A.D. as a place of worship. Wars destroyed it many times and the current building is a post-Liberation reproduction. It has a performance of ancient chime bells and a good exhibit in stone of the life of the sage. Its market is not for serious shoppers. Birds, fish, pearls, and clothes are on sale. Nearby on the other side of the Qinhuai River is the Former Residence of the Wang and Xie families, worth a visit for its slate carvings and a table full of little canals where miniature boats bearing drinks for guests used to float. The mansion was originally built in the Six Dynasties, at least 1,500 years ago.

A relic of the Taipings well worth seeing is the **Tianwang Mansion (The Heavenly King's Mansion)**, 292 Changjiang Road in the eastern part of the city. The mansion was made for Hong Xiuquan (Hung Hsiu-chuan) the head of the Taipings, with materials from the Ming palace. It is now the Taiping Museum. Read *God's Chinese Son* by Jonathan Spence.

Prominently displayed inside the museum is a plaque "in memory of the organizer and leader of the Ever Victorious Army, erected by the Frederick Ward Post, American Legion, May 27, 1923." Frederick Ward was an American mercenary who fought against the Taipings and died in 1862.

You can study the Ming Palace ruins near the Hilton in about five minutes. It was built between 1368 to 1386 for the first Ming emperor. The Forbidden City is about the same size. Qing troops partially destroyed it in 1645 and the Taipings pulled down the remainder. In 1911 only a gate was left standing, but in 1958 the government restored a few pieces.

Also in the city is a memorial hall to **Zheng He**, the Muslim eunuch who became one of China's most famous maritime commanders, making seven voyages to 30 countries of Asia and Africa from 1405 to 1433. His tomb is 10 km south of Nanjing. Read *When China Ruled the Seas*.

From more recent times is the **Memorial of the Nanjing Massacre**, 7 Jiang Dong Gate, *Tel. 6501033*. The **Meiling Palace** is about three km outside the Zhongshan Gate. This 1930s building was the weekend home of Generalissimo Chiang Kai-shek and his wife from 1945 to 1949. They held church services here, sometimes with the American ambassador.

Walks

Great walks include Purple Mountain, and along the top of the city wall. The area around the Sun Yat-sen mausoleum is sylvan and beautiful, and is good for hiking. It is full of tiny museums, including one in the Linggu Temple of Sun Yat-sen's life in wax.

Nightlife & Entertainment

Good **discos** are in the Jinling, Hilton and Sheraton hotels. A favorite watering hole of local foreigners is **Swede & Kraut**, near Nanjing University. On a side street beside the Crowne Plaza, is a little dinky local bar, **77**, a favorite of foreigners trying to escape the world of glitz and business.

Sports & Recreation

The **Nanjing Zhaofu Golf Club** is at 176 Zhuzhu Street, Pukou District, *Tel. 8853333, 8853460*, and the **golf driving range** is at Xuanwu Lake, *Tel. 3609424*.

Shopping

Made in Nanjing are "Yunjin (Figured) Satin" brocade, velvet flowers, tapestry and carpets, imitations of ancient wood and ivory carvings, silver jewelry, and paper cuts. Made in the province are inlaid, red lacquer, purple sand pottery (Yixing), Huishan clay figures, fresh-water pearls, silk underwear, batik (Nantong), and Suzhou embroidery. Prices for double-sided embroidery seem to be the best here. Don't pay more than Y500 for a large one.

A small antique and curio market is around the Confucius Temple. Government shops there say they will accept credit cards. This market had stones and pearls too. Try also the **Co-op Antique Building** upstairs at 99

Gong Yuan Road across from McDonald's and KFC, *Tel. 3226811*. It is open 9am-7pm weekdays or 8pm on weekends. The Chaotian Gong Palace near the Jinling Hotel has a courtyard of shops and vendors, especially good on weekends, open about 9am-5pm. It's on Jianya and Mouchou Roads. (The entrance fee here for the Museum of the Six Dynasties, which has titles in English, is Y5.)

The **Nanjing Arts and Crafts Industry Corp**. at 31 Beijing Dong Road is open 9am-6pm daily. It claims "set prices" and takes credit cards, but prices are steep. Serious shoppers might want to visit its factory instead for a look. Unique here are human hair embroidery, and elegant brocade at Y1800-Y2300 per meter and used for Japanese obis. Prize-winning craftspeople demonstrate on the upper floor. The Golden Eagle Shopping Centre under the Crowne Plaza is open 9 to 9:30 and takes credit cards and travelers checks.

Excursions & Day Trips

You can make day trips from Nanjing to Wuxi, Yangzhou and Zhenjiang but it's better to spend more time in Suzhou and Wuxi. See travel agents below for tours. **Yixing** is due west of Shanghai and Suzhou and on the west side of Lake Taihu. It is the home of the purple clay pottery in Dingsu which you see everywhere in this area. You can visit factories and the huge exhibition hall. It's also known for its limestone caves.

Shanjuan Cave, 25 km southwest of Yixing city, was discovered about 2,000 years ago. The 700-meter walk takes about an hour. It has a 120-meter-long underground river. The **Zhonggong Cave**, 22 km southwest of Yixing was the home of Zhang Daoling (one of the founders of Taoism), and Zhang Guolao (one of the Eight Taoist Immortals). With 72 small, interconnected caves, its one km walk includes 1,500 stone steps.

Practical Information

China Jiangsu Overseas Tourist Corporation and Nanjing China International Travel Service, *202-1 North Zhongshan Bei Road, 210003. Tel. 3421948, Fax 3410271. E-mail: ea01@njview.com. Website: www.njview.com.* Ask for Mr. Zhou Zhi Qin who helped with this book. It has a wide variety of tours, one of which is an eight-day seven-night coach tour largely in the province (if there are at least 10 people). The price is about $350—a cheap and quick introduction. This is for double occupancy in three-star hotels and includes all meals and transportation from and back to Shanghai. Cities include Suzhou, Tongli, Wuxi, Yixing, Nanjing and Hangzhou. CITS says it stops at clean washrooms. See website for details.

CYTS, *160 Hanzhong Road, Tel. 6523345, Fax 6523355. E-mail: CYTSYQ@public1.ptt.js.cn.* Contact Asian & Oceanian Department. Ask for Jessica Chen Yueru. Flight tickets from Nanjing to Beijing cost Y920, to

Guangzhou Y1070, to Tianjin Y810, to Lanzhou Y1250, to Urumqi Y2250, and to Xi'an Y990. Trains take three hours to Shanghai, 12 hours to Beijing, 30 hours to Guangzhou, and 27 hours to Xiamen.

Hours: offices 8:30am-11:30am, 1:30pm-5 or 5:30pm; department stores 9am or 10am-10pm.

Internet Services: **China Telecom**, *268 Hanzhong Road, open 8am-5:30pm. 15 minutes one yuan.*

Jiangsu Provincial Tourism Bureau, *255 Zhongshan Bei Road, 210003. Tel. 3420013, Fax 3437742. E-mail: eunicejs@163.com. Website: www.jstour.com.* Ask for Eunice Gong (Gong Yue).

Medical concerns: **AEA Nanjing Clinic**, *Ground floor, Nanjing Hilton Hotel, Zhong Shan Dong Road, Tel. 4802842, Fax 4802843.*

Telephone Code: 25

Suzhou

(Soochow)

Located on the ancient Grand Canal in Jiangsu province, **Suzhou** is famous for its architecture, gardens, half-moon bridges, canals, and its silks and pearls. UNESCO has listed four of its classical gardens as World Heritage sites. The old city proper is under national government protection as a historic and cultural treasure. Its renovated old buildings, and even new ones, are exquisite and in traditional Huaihai Chinese style. No new construction is allowed to be higher than the North Temple Pagoda. No one can build any new factories downtown, and existing factories that pollute must move to the suburbs.

Suzhou's downtown streets are thickly lined with plane trees and some of its tiny white-washed cottages are original Ming. Unlike other Chinese cities, the Japanese war inflicted little damage here. Suzhou is known primarily as a cultural and scenic city, similar in this respect to Japan's Kyoto.

Choosing between a visit to Suzhou and its rival, the silk resort city of Hangzhou, is not easy. Both are among the best of old China. Suzhou is closer to Shanghai, but you can fly direct to Hangzhou from Hong Kong and Singapore. Hangzhou has West Lake and is especially romantic. The new expressway could mean going to both. It should be open October, 2002 and take two hours.

The hottest temperature is 36°C (usually muggy too, for one or two days in late July, early August); the coldest is -9°C around the end of January, averaging 0°C to 7°C. It snows once or twice a year. 1063 mm of rain fall mainly from May into early September. The population is 5.7 million, of whom over one million live in the city.

He Lu, King of Wu, founded the city as his capital in 514 B.C. Iron was smelted here more than 2,500 years ago and silk weaving was well developed in the Tang and Song. Marco Polo visited in the latter half of the 13th century and proclaimed it another Venice. Textile manufacturing flourished during the Ming. From 1860 to 1863, 40,000 troops of the Taiping Heavenly Kingdom controlled the area. During the Japanese occupation, the Jiangsu provincial puppet government had its headquarters in the Humble Administrator's Garden.

People here speak the Wu dialect, which is similar to that of Shanghai, only with softer tones and more adjectives. Industries include the manufacturing of television sets, wristwatches, chemicals, and electronics. Among its sister cities are Portland, Oregon and Victoria, Canada.

Here you can see the museum where artisans spin and weave silk, and the factories where they make sandalwood and silk fans. Here they create one of the four most famous embroideries in China, and double-sided embroidery. They also make musical instruments. You can visit the villages that raise silkworms, jasmine flowers for tea, shrimp, and tangerines.

But Suzhou has also got its foot in the 21st century. In 2001, the APEC Finance Ministers congress was held here. It has experience in hosting top-level international conferences and its prices are cheaper than Shanghai's. Its two industrial zones have been flourishing.

Arrivals & Departures

The fastest way to Suzhou from Shanghai is by express train from Shanghai's downtown railway station. Trains leave every 30 minutes or so and take less than an hour (86 km). The buses from Shanghai's Hong Qiao airport and from the Shanghai Stadium also take about an hour.

Trains from Hangzhou take 4.5 hours as they have to go through Shanghai. When the expressway is finished in 2002 or 2003, buses from Hangzhou will only take two hours. The Suzhou railway station is in the north outside the city moat. Suzhou has a small military airport 30 km away but it only has a few flights with Beijing and Foshan.

There are three bus terminals in Shanghai with express buses to Suzhou, one of which is at Gong He New Road. The bus station in Suzhou is on Zhong Shan Road. You can also arrive by boat on the Grand Canal from Wuxi for about Y119 each if the boat is full. Contact a travel agent.

Orientation

This old formerly walled city is still surrounded by a rectangular moat. The Shanghai-Nanjing Expressway runs parallel outside and close to its north side. The old city is about 2.5-4.6 km north-south, and about 2.6-3 km east-west. It is criss-crossed by many canals (some in need of cleaning). The western and southern moats are actually branches of the famous Grand Canal (610 A.D). Immediately to the east is the 70-square-kilometer Sino-Singapore-Suzhou Industrial Park, a Singapore joint venture. To the west is the 60-square-km High

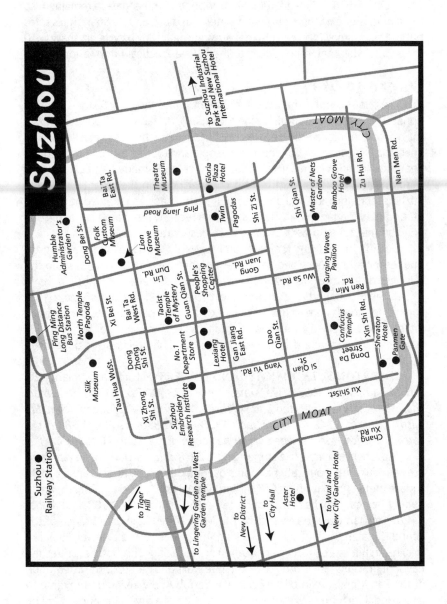

Suzhou

to Suzhou Industrial Park and New Suzhou International Hotel

CITY MOAT

Zu Hui Rd.

Nan Men Rd.

Theatre Museum

Bai Ta East Rd.

Gloria Plaza Hotel

Ping Jiang Road

Shi Qian St.

Master of Nets Garden

Bamboo Grove Hotel

Twin Pagodas

Shi Zi St.

Humble Administrator's Garden

Dong Bei St.

Folk Custom Museum

Lion Grove Museum

Lin Dun Rd.

Gong Juan Rd.

Surging Waves Pavilion

Ping Ming Long Distance Bus Station

North Temple Pagoda

Xi Bei St.

Bai Ta West Rd.

Taoist Temple of Mystery

Guan Qian St.

People's Shopping Center

Wu Sa Rd.

Ren Min Rd.

Tau Hua WuSt.

Dong Zhong Shi St.

No.1 Department Store

Lexiang Hotel

Gan Jiang East Rd.

Dao Qian St.

Confucius Temple

Xin Shi Rd.

Silk Museum

Si Qian St.

Yang Yu Rd.

Dong Da Street

Sheraton Hotel

Panmen Gate

Xi Zhong Shi St.

Suzhou Embroidery Research Institute

Xu ShiSt.

CITY MOAT

Chang Xu Rd.

Suzhou Railway Station

to Tiger Hill

to Lingering Garden and West Garden temple

to New District

to City Hall

Aster Hotel

to Wuxi and New City Garden Hotel

and New Technology Zone. Beyond that is Lake Taihu 20 km east of the old city. The main street, Renmin (People's) Road, runs north-south; Guanqian Street runs east-west, meeting almost in the center of the city. The city wall was built in 514 B.C. and remnants, including three gates, remain. Also remaining is one of the eight water gates. Taxis are double Shanghai's rates but the city is small. You can also get around cheaply by bicycle rickshaw (Y10 for a couple kilometers) or public tour bus (see Practical Information).

Where to Stay

The five-star hotels here are the Sheraton and the New Suzhou International. The latter is beautiful, beside a lake, but too far away from downtown for anyone but business people associated with the Industrial Park. The Sheraton is the best for both business people and tourists and one of the most beautiful hotels in China. The recently renovated Ramada Bamboo Grove is third and the Gloria is fourth. For a cheaper hotel in the old city, I like the Suzhou for its location and garden, but it's been badly maintained. It could be getting new management. There's also the recently renovated Lexiang Hotel in a commercial area near CITS if you're desperate.

Outside the old city, the Aster and New City Garden Hotel are good for budget-mined business people. These two are west of the city moat in the business district close to Suzhou Customs and the trade center.

Prices mentioned below are subject to seasonal discounts, and a 15% surcharge. Hotels here all have money exchange, business centers, mini-bars, international direct dial, and take credit cards. They all add 10% to 15% surcharge. The standard of English in the hotels here is not as good as in Shanghai.

SHERATON SUZHOU HOTEL AND TOWERS (Xi Lai Deng Jiudian), *388 Xin Shi Road, 215007. Five stars. Tel 5103388, Fax 5100888. E-mail: sheraton_suzhou@sheraton.com. Website: www.sheraton-suzhou.com (English). $200 to $242 for rooms and $388 to $1588 for suites. Y888 is the "privilege price" for the weekend. It has been discounting 20 to 40%.*

The Sheraton has five-stories and 328 rooms, including an amazing presidential suite. Four cabana rooms overlook the pool. Rooms are 32 to 34 square meters, and it offers CNN, international newspapers in English, and a good 17-piece gym. Its breakfast buffet is Y115, lunch Y98-Y108, and dinner Y128. You can walk to the ancient Pan Men Water Gate on a branch of the Grand Canal. If Suzhou still had its king, his palace would probably look like this. Its architecture, decor and location are amazing. This hotel captures the flavor of gracious old Suzhou with its white walls and gardens. The integration of the Pan Men Gate into its view is wonderful. And walking up the ramp to its second floor lobby is like walking up to the top of a city wall in ancient China. The service is strictly 21st century however and the food is great.

See Chapter 13, China's Best Places to Stay.

NEW SUZHOU INTERNATIONAL HOTEL (Xin Su Guoji Dajiudian), *Jinji Lake, northeast corner of the Sino-Singapore Suzhou Industrial Park, 215021. Five stars. Tel. 7616688, Fax 7612288. E-mail: nszih@public1.sz.js.cn. Website: www.nszihotel.com. Twenty minutes' drive from the railway station and 60 minutes from Shanghai Hongqiao Airport. $120-$145 for its 20 medium-sized rooms, $200-$300 for suites, and $800-$6000 for apartments in its five villas. It has been discounting 20%.*

Rooms have safes, coffeemakers, and satellite television. It has a heated indoor pool, gym, mini-golf, and squash. It is good for small conferences, has a 100-seat theater, and its ballroom can seat over 200 banquet-style. The business center operates 24 hours. There's a shuttle bus, internet bar and nightclub. Nearby is a pleasant one-kilometer lakeside walkway.

RAMADA PLAZA BAMBOO GROVE SUZHOU, (Zhu Hui Fandian), *168 Zhu Hui Road, 215006. Four stars, Tel. 5205601, Fax 5208778. E-mail: bghsz@public1.sz.js.cn. $120-$170 for rooms. $230-$2200 for suites. This hotel is six km from the railway station and a seven-minute drive to the pier. It is walking distance to Shi Quan tourist street and close to No. 1 Silk Spinning Mill.*

Built in 1990, this hotel became a Ramada in 2000, and has been making major renovations into 2002. It has five stories, three connecting buildings and 356 rooms. Rooms are 28 to 30 square meters. It has an executive floor, Italian, Cantonese and Japanese food. Sports include a gym, tennis, indoor pool, bicycles, and sauna. Rooms have CNN and HBO. Its ballroom seats 250 people banquet-style and its creative chefs have concocted their own Suzhou dishes. It has a garden and a Filipino band, the only one in town.

GLORIA PLAZA HOTEL (Kailai Dajiudian), *535 Ganjiang East Road, 215006. Four stars. Tel. 5218855, Fax 5218533. E-mail: gloria@gphsuzhou.com. Website: www.gphsuzhou.com. This hotel is 1.5km from the Sheraton on the main street of the old city between its newer eastern and western parts. It is a 10-minute walk to Guan Qian Street and is relatively near Suzhou University. Rooms are $118-$178 and suites $239-$492. It has been discounting 40%.*

This 296-room hotel has 24-hour room service, good food, an eight-piece gym, outdoor Jacuzzi, steam bath and a mini-golf putting green. Rooms are 32 square meters. All have fax and internet outlets, safes, CNN, HBO, and voice-mail in four languages. It renovated its executive floor and bar in 2001. Its business center subscribes to international newspapers in English and charges Y0.40 per minute for the internet. Managed by Gloria International Hotels and Resorts.

NEW CITY GARDEN HOTEL (Xin Cheng Hua Yuan Jiu Dian), *Shishan Road, 215011. Four stars. Tel. 8250228, Fax 8250573, 8257179. E-mail: sales@ncghotel.com.cn or mail@ncg.sz.js.cn. Website: www.ncghotel.com. Rooms are $100-$150, suites are $200-$500. It has been discounting 30%.*

This 1997, 182-room hotel is about five km west of the west moat, and has 182 rooms all with safes, CNN but little drawer space. It has an executive floor. There's bowling, gym and squash. It has Japanese, Chinese and Western food. E-mail is relatively cheap.

SUZHOU HOTEL (Fandian), *115 Shi Quan Street, 215006. Four stars, Tel. 5204646, Fax 5204015. E-mail: szhtl@public1.sz.js.cn. $70-$100 for rooms, $150-$1000 for suites. Six km from the railway station. Quiet setting in large garden next to CITS.*

Built in 1958 and renovated in 1996, this hotel has two buildings with a total of 301 rooms, the better ones with kettles, televisions, scales, CNN and CNBC. It also has a sauna and gym. The air could be better, and it's poorly maintained.

ASTER HOTEL (Yadu Dajiudian), *156 Sanxiang Road, 215004. Four stars, Tel. 8291888, Fax 8291838. E-mail: aster@public1.sz.js.cn. Website: www.aster.com.cn. Rooms are $65-$80 and suites are $136-$3000. It has been discounting 30%. Four km from the railway station.*

This 1991, 29-story hotel with a cheerful two-story lobby does not have a reputation for snap-to-it service. But it's okay if you're not fussy. It has 388 rooms, most 28-43 square meters. You might want to aim for its 27th floor with larger rooms renovated in 1998. It has satellite television, a 12.5 meter-long indoor pool, and bowling alley, Cantonese, Chaozhou and Suzhou food, and a revolving restaurant. There's Japanese and Western food, and 24-hour room service. Its ballroom seats 360 at banquet tables.

LEXIANG HOTEL SUZHOU, *18 Dajing Line, 215005. Two stars. Tel. 5222890, Fax 5244165. Rooms range from Y380 to Y580, and suites Y780. It accepts credit cards and travelers' checks.*

Opened in 1985 and close to Guanqian Street and Renmin Road. Rooms offer CNN but no safes.

Where to Eat

Restaurant inspectors here publish their results in the newspapers, a practice that is helping to raise standards. Hotel food is the best. Consider the Sheraton, New Suzhou International, Gloria, and Ramada Plaza Bamboo Grove for Western or Chinese food. For simple coffee shop food, there's the **Mingtien Coffee Language** chain, 211 Jingde Road, *Tel. 5227282*. A good Chinese Restaurant is the **Tian Zhu Jiu Lou** at 800 Gan Jiang Dong Road in the Chang Gu Building, *Tel. 5219495*. There's also **Guibinlou Restaurant** (Cantonese), 888 Gan Jiang Road, *Tel. 5217888 or 5219888*. Take along chapter 25 from this book. This is almost across the street from the Gloria Plaza Hotel. Open 11am-1:30pm and 5pm to 9pm. It takes Visa and American Express cards.

Towards the Qian Tang Cha Ren and across the street from the Suzhou Hotel is **Yang Yang**, a relatively cheap and good café at 144 Shi Quan Street, *Tel. 5192728*. Popular with foreigners, it is named after the grandson of its founder. It offers six pieces of deep-fried won ton for Y5, special marinated chicken for Y15, green beans in garlic sauce for Y25, sweet and sour pork for Y18, Gong Bao chicken for Y18, and half a roast duck for Y28. At these prices, don't expect it to be fancy.

Qian Tang Cha Ren is not a restaurant but an exotic **tea house** at 311 Shi Quan Street, 10 minutes walk from the Suzhou Hotel. Its second floor has *ping tan* (traditional story-telling). It is open 8am to 2am. The manager's office telephone is 530078. It has antique or reproduced old Chinese furnishings, bare wooden floors and curtained cubicles. It has carved wooden pictures, black brick walls and latticed windows. Its decorator has captured the feeling of old China and this tea house should be visited just for a look. Waiters are in Song dynasty costume and the music is Buddhist. Most teas cost Y48 which includes a buffet of noodles, dried fruit, sweet pastries, rice, and nuts.

Seeing the Sights

If you only have one day, you might consider visiting one of the gardens (but not the Master of Nets until the evening), climb the North Temple Pagoda, visit the Silk Museum across the street, and get a peek at the No. 2 Silk Refining and Dyeing Factory machines. Then you can see the Temple of the West Garden and Tiger Hill west of the old city. You can go back into the old city and look around the shops and canals on Shi Quan Street and snack at the nearby Yang Yang Café or Qian Tang Cha Ren tea house, then go to the Master of Nets Garden for its exotic cultural show.

On a second day, there's a morning at Tongli (25 km from the city) or Zhujiajiao both charming ancient water towns. (See Shanghai excursions.) Wander over to the Pan Men, and then have tea or dinner in the Sheraton. If you want to, you can look around the store at the nearby No. 1 Spinning Mill. (See Shopping.)

There is enough to enjoy for three or four days, if you just want to poke around the museums, meditate in temples, look at the embroidery factory, and indulge in shopping for silk or pearls. Visiting the Pearl Market (strands from Y40 to Y400) takes a morning. Taking a boat along the canals is another hour. For transportation see tourist buses below, but if you're in a hurry, you might want to negotiate a taxi for the day.

North inside the moat: the **Beisi Ta (North Temple) Pagoda,** at the north end of Renmin Road inside the old city at 652, is nine-stories and 76 meters high, the tallest pagoda south of the Yangtze River. It was first built in the 10th century. On the grounds are exhibition halls and across the street to the northwest is the excellent Silk Museum at 661 Renmin Road. It should fascinate lovers of textiles. You can see reproductions of ancient brocades, giant looms (with weavers balanced on top), and "stone washing" or stone grinding. Look at the nearby canals and whitewashed cottages.

Suzhou has 70 gardens in traditional Chinese style and more temples. Most gardens are open 7:30am-4:30pm with seasonal variations. The Master of Nets Garden (see below) opens again for its show about 7:30pm. Admission prices are around Y8 to Y12 each for the gardens and about Y60 for the show.

Shizilin Yuan (Lion Forest) Garden, 23 Yulin Road, *Tel. 7272428*, four km from the Suzhou Hotel, was built in 1350 during the Yuan and is so named because the teacher of the monk who built it lived on Lion Rock Mountain. It is a UNESCO heritage site. Some of the rockeries are shaped like lions. It was once owned by the granduncle of American architect I.M. Pei and takes about thirty minutes to see but more to relax in and enjoy.

By the entrance, the maze inside the rockeries is notable, and some of the rocks have clearly been carved and then weathered in Lake Tai for scores or hundreds of years. The rock structure above the stone boat was a waterfall, which in the early days was hand-poured. The Standing-in-Snow Study is exquisite, so named because a student once went to visit his teacher there and, too polite to awaken him, waited patiently in the snow.

Changlang Ting Yuan (Gentle Wave or Surging Wave) Pavilion, 3 Canglang Street, *Tel. 5306148*, is one km from the Suzhou Hotel. About two acres, it is the only garden that is not surrounded completely by a view-blocking wall. A pond lies outside to be enjoyed from a View-Borrowing Pavilion. A hall houses 125 steles with the images of 500 sages, dating from the Kingdom of Wu to the Qing. Carved in relief in 1840, the deeds of each one are confined to 16 poetic characters. The poet Su Tzu-mei founded the garden, one of the oldest in the city, in 1044 (Song). In the Yuan and early Ming, it was a Buddhist nunnery. This garden is not as spectacular as the others, so if you're short on time, skip it. Normally it takes about 30 minutes to see.

Yi Yuan (Joyous) Garden, 340 Renmin Road, *Tel. 5249317*, was built by a Qing official and, at 100 years old, it is the newest. It has taken the best of all the gardens, concentrating them into about an acre. The rockeries are from other older gardens. The dry boat is an imitation of the one in the Humble Administrator's.

*Liu Yuan (Lingering) Garden, 79-80 Liuyuan Road, *Tel. 5337940*, six km from the Suzhou Hotel, was originally built in 1525 (Ming). The eight-acre garden consists of halls and studios in the east sector, ponds and hills in the central, and woods and hills in the western section. In late autumn, these woods are red. Look through some of the 200 different flower windows at the scenes beyond. You are in a living picture gallery. A huge five-ton, six-meter-high rock from Lake Tai stands in the eastern section. This garden takes at least 30 minutes to see.

Wangshi Yuan (Master of Nets) Garden, 11 Kuotao Xiang, *Tel. 5223550*, 0.5 km from the Suzhou Hotel. Originally built in 1140 (Southern Song), it is one of the best, and a UNESCO Heritage site. Usually it take 40 minutes to see. The Metropolitan Museum of Art in New York City has reproduced its Peony courtyard as the Astor Chinese Garden Court. This garden is very pretty, especially when decorated with colorful palace lanterns for the Classical Night Garden in summer when tourists rotate among the pavilions to hear musicians and storytellers. Don't miss this charming experience.

*Zhuozheng Yuan (Humble Administrator's) Garden, 178 Dong Bei Street, *Tel. 77536224*, five km from the Suzhou Hotel, is the largest in Suzhou and a UNESCO heritage site. A humble administrator, a dismissed official, laid it out in 1522 (Ming). Later it was divided into three gardens after an owner lost it gambling. The largest and most open of the gardens, three-fifths water, is typical of the water country south of the Yangtze. Almost all buildings are close to water. If you only have a short time, visit the central part. At Fragrant Island, there is a two-story stone "dry boat" complete with gangplank, "deck," and "cabin." The Mandarin Duck Hall has blue windows and classical furniture, and maybe live ducks in a cage. Note the covered walkway and the Lingering and Listening Hall for listening (of course) to the raindrops on the lotus leaves. A 200-year-old miniature pomegranate tree is included in the excellent collection of *penjing* miniature trees. A museum of gardens with titles in English is near the exit.

Xiyuan (West Garden) Temple, 18 Liuyuan Road, *Tel. 7232911*, open 8:30am-4:30pm. It is also very beautiful and is the largest group of Buddhist buildings in Suzhou. It was originally built in the 16th century but was destroyed by fire, and rebuilt in 1892. Look at the ceilings. The central Buddhas are seven meters tall, including base and mandala. The 500 arhats here are worth studying, each face so real, expressive, profound, individual. Outstanding is the crazy monk, who can look sad, happy, or wry, depending on the angle from which you look at him. Gilded on modeled clay, each statue is larger than life. But can you find any women? Enjoy those incense burners. During the Great Leap Forward (1958-60) they were supposed to be smelted. But the CITS director said no!

Important but not spectacular is the ***Huqiu (Tiger) Hill**, 8 Huqiu Shan, *Tel. 5314921*, nine km from the Suzhou Hotel. The 45-acre site is northwest of the city outside the moat and takes about an hour to see. Named Tiger Hill because a white tiger appeared here at one time. Important here is the site where Fu Chai, King of Wu, is said to have built a tomb for his father, He Lu, in the early fifth century B.C. The workers were slaughtered to keep the location a secret. The tomb of He Lu is believed to be beyond the moon gate. In 1956, unsuccessful attempts were made to enter it. The foundation of the pagoda started to protest. Inside are supposed to be 3,000 iron and steel swords. You can see the cave, blocked by large, cut stones, from the bridge to the pagoda.

Northwest of the park is the **Tiger Hill Pagoda**, known also as the "Leaning Tower of Suzhou." This was built originally in the 10th century A.D.

(Northern Song) but was burned down thrice. The latest repairs were made in 1981, when its foundation was strengthened. At 47.5 meters high, it tends to tilt to the northwest. Pilgrims used to climb the 53 steps here on their knees. Note the Indian arches.

The **Pan Men**, the water gate just behind the Sheraton, is a good place to walk. It is beside a narrow canal and a 300-meter long part of the city wall, two thick 2.7-meter and 5.3- meter-high gates, and Qing dynasty cannons. There's a large garden, signs in English, and people exercising here in the morning. Pan Men is open 8am to 4:45 or 5pm, *Tel. 8267737*, and the entrance fee is Y6, but you can sneak into part of it earlier from the west side. Just follow the taiji people.

For a water town, avoid **Zhouzhuang**, which is too commercial and expensive. Better is Tongli, 25 km from Suzhou which has gardens, bridges, boat trips, and old mansions from the Ming and Qing. It is charming because it hasn't been developed for tourists. Recent visitors have been invited into a kindergarten and people's homes.

There's also 1000-year-old **Zhujiajiao village** in Qingpu County on the way to Shanghai which has well-maintained old houses, shops, 16th century moon bridges, a museum of farm tools, and a 1912 garden you can visit. There are also narrow alleyways and old tea houses. It is just developed enough to be interesting. People are friendly and seem happy to be photographed. The entry fee was Y20. You can get here by taking No. 4 tourist bus from Shanghai Stadium or a tour from Suzhou. The office is 100 Gongyuan Road, Qingpu, 201700. *Tel. 21/59732890 or 59242771. Website: www.zhujiajiao.com (English).*

If You Have More Time

The **Theatre Museum** is near the east moat at 14 Zhangjiaxiang, *Tel. 727-5338*. It is in a fancy old Shaanxi Provincial Guild Hall. The **Folk Arts Museum**, *Tel. 7271478*, is charming. The **Suzhou Museum**, 204 Dongbei Street, *Tel. 7274203*, near the Humble Administrator's Garden was the official residence of a royal Taiping prince, first built in 1860.

The **Han Shan (Cold Mountain) Temple** is at 8 Hanshansi Long, *Tel. 5336317*, and open 8:30am-4:30pm, just 10 km west of the Suzhou Hotel, it was the home of two Tang monks, Han Shan and Shide. To the right of the central, gold Sakyamuni Buddha is Wu Nan, the young disciple who wrote the sutras; the older man is disciple Ja Yeh. Japanese pirates stole the original bell but Japan replaced it with a bell cast about 100 years ago. Originally built in the Liang dynasty (sixth century), the current buildings are Qing and the pagoda was built in 1993. Travel agents organize special excursions to hear the bronze bells here on midnight December 31, New Year's Eve. If you hear the bells chime 108 times on this night, you should have few troubles in life! Monks chant and pray for their guests. Lions and dragons dance. The temple is open 7pm-1am on this occasion.

The **Confucian Temple (Wen Miao)** can take about 40 minutes. It is on Renmin Nan Road with a miniature tree collection, and a small museum with Song dynasty astronomical and city maps. It also has some antiques and reproductions for sale. The **Xuan Miao Guan (Mysterious Wonder Taoist Temple)**, Guanqian Street, *Tel. 7274348*, is in the middle of the city, near the Renmin (People's) Department Store, and car-free shopping. Three giant, gilded sculptures of the founders of Taoism dominate but this looks more like a museum than a functioning temple. Originating in the Jin (265-420 A.D.), the temple's current central Sanqing Hall was built in the Southern Song. The Twin Pagodas, almost in the middle of Suzhou, are known as the big and small "brushes" (used by Confucius for writing). They were built in the Song in honor of the sage.

A visit to the **pearl farm** in the eastern suburbs could be fun for groups. After a 15-minute boat ride, you can choose a living, breathing oyster from the lake, and keep the pearls found within. (Pick a big one.) Contact Suzhou Fishery Industry, Marine Tourism Service, Huangshiqiao, Fengmen, 215006, about 20 minutes from the city. *Tel. 7261987*. Open 8:30am-3pm.

The famous wholesale pearl market is open daily 5am-7pm and is 20 km from Suzhou. See Shopping.

The Suzhou Tourist Bureau is working on a Wellness Centre and will be offering lecturers on gardens, embroidery, Sun Tze and the Art of War, and the places where Marco Polo visited here. Among the new areas open to tourists is hiking along Taihu Lake. You can take a bus to 80-square-kilometer Xishan Island (as big as Hong Kong island with a hiking trail around it). This is especially good in the spring, says Xu Wei Rong of the Suzhou Tourism Bureau, because then you can view a sea of plum blossoms. The four-star Xishan Hotel is near the Hill of Old Stone Man there. You can spend the night and explore a well-preserved **Ming dynasty street** in Moon Bay Village.

Walks

The gardens are good but can be crowded at times, a little difficult if you want fast-moving exercise. Try Tiger Hill and Xishan Island. You can walk around the old city too.

Nightlife & Entertainment

From mid-March to late November, 7:30pm-10pm daily, Chinese artists perform in the Master of Nets Garden, a not-to-be missed experience. See above. Popular bars are in the Aster and Bamboo Grove Hotels. A **night market** is in front of the Taoist temple on Guanqian Street.

There are many bars between the Nanlin and Suzhou Hotels on Shi Quan Street but avoid those that charge high prices for women to drink with you. Avoid most tea houses because of their unsavory side businesses. Better stick with the hotels.

Sports & Recreation

Suzhou has several golf courses. One of the best is the 18-hole Jack Nicklaus-designed **Sun Rise Golf Course** 20 minutes by car west of the Sheraton. Hotels should be able to make arrangements. For the **Hash House Harriers**, ask foreign staff at the Sheraton, Gloria or Ramada. The Hash are the drinking people with a running problem.

Shopping

The main shopping streets are Guanqian Street, Shi Lu Road, and Nanmen. The **Friendship Shopping Center** at 433 Ren Min Road is popular. *Tel. 5237061.* Suzhou is a major tourist city with a great variety of crafts on sale. Available are inkstones, brushes, pearls, jewelry, embroideries, silks, traditional musical instruments, antiques, iron reproductions of ancient relics, excellent woodblock prints, and reproductions of some of the arhats. Onyx vases here have nice colors and patterns. Also on sale are turquoise carvings, fossils (that could or could not be real), and crystals. It is a good place to buy sandalwood fans but they might just be perfumed so buy from the **Sandalwood Fan Factory** and make sure you get a receipt saying they are real. It's at 38 Xibei Street, *Tel. 7537334* and open 8:30am-5pm. The **Jade Carving Factory** is at 33 Baita Road West, *Tel. 7271224.*

Good to buy here is double-sided embroidery because of the variety available and the prices. Some of the embroideries have embroidered signature chopmarks which implies they might be of high quality from well-known artists. They are not necessarily one-of-a-kind. The **Embroidery Research Institute** is at 262 Jingde Road, *Tel. 5222415.* You can watch double-sided embroidery being worked between 8:30am-5pm. It has a small embroidery museum. *Tel. 5222403.*

Good also to buy here are fresh-water pearls especially at the **Pearl Market**. My friends have been successfully buying from the Yadong Pearl Handicraft Factory, 51 Jen Zhu Jie, Hejiawan Weitang town. *Tel. 5404130, 13906200290.* Ask for sisters Gu Qiao Gen and He Jian Fen, who can tell you which of the black pearls are dyed and which are expensively real. Strands start at about Y40-Y60 knotted with clasps. The Y40 pearls weren't flawless nor perfectly matched, but they were real and the store has a clean Western toilet.

There's also the **Dongjia Pearl Handicraft Article Factory**, *Tel. 5403143. E-mail: pearl@dong-jia.com or jw@dong-jia.com.*

There are many small snuff bottles painted on the inside, the crystal ones more expensive than glass. Valuable are the ones with recognizable famous people and fine quality painting.

There's good shopping in the tiny **curio shops** on Shiquan Road near the Nan Lin Hotel and Nanyuan Guest House. This quaint tree-lined street has old facades. Many shops are open during the day but most come to life at night until 10pm. Look for paintings by local farmer artists. A good antique dealer who seems honest is Mr. Xu Zhi Cheng, **Shyuee Lahng Antiques**, 200 Shi Quan Street, *Tel. 5295084.*

There are a few curio and antique shops around the Confucian Temple open at different times of the day, starting from mid-morning. More are there on weekends. The more expensive government **Suzhou Antique Store**, 238 Renmin Road, *Tel. 5220017,* has lots of variety.

Suzhou is one of the best places to buy silk. Tourist stores offer credit card service, have a wide variety of sizes and styles and are expensive. Even group discounts are hard to get, but give it a try. At the **No. 2 Silk Refining and Dyeing Factory** next door to the Silk Museum, you can see the whole process from cocoon to noisy mechanical spinning and weaving, but clothing styles and patterns in its showroom are conservative and meant to appeal to Asians. It's open 9am-5:30pm (Y240 for long johns top, and Y240 for bottoms.) *Tel. 7521812.* The **Silk Spinning Mill No. 1** south of the Ramada Plaza Bamboo Grove Hotel has styles more to Western tastes, but you can't see the process. It's at 94 Nanmen Road, *Tel. 5251047.* Look in the **Silk Museum**, Tel. 7536538 for its reliable store with good quality. Silk stores and stalls are all over, around most tourist attractions.

Many stores sell "washable" silk ("mian tang si chou" in Chinese) which needs no or little ironing. Can you trust clerks to tell the truth? The Spinning Mills and Silk Museum should be reliable. Look at the Silk Markets in Hangzhou and Beijing. They are much cheaper.

Angela's Design is a recommended tailor shop at 164-1 Shi Quan Street, near the Sheraton Hotel, *Tel. 13906134922.* (English-speaking). It should be able to make a good chi pao dress in one day. Open 9am to 8pm except on the second of each month.

Practical Information

Canal boat tours are usually booked through a travel agent. CITS says they cruise from the railway station to Panmen City Gate, and Tiger Hill and take one hour. The whole boat costs about Y300 for ten people, the price split among the group.

CITS, *18 Dajingxiang St., 215005. Tel. 5152401, 5223783, Fax 5159006. E-mail: cits@citssz.com, dragonlu@pub.sw.jsinfo.net. Website: www.citssz.com (Suzhou).* This is near the Lexiang Hotel. Ask for Lu Guangxing (Bruce), Deputy Manager, English Department who helped with this book a lot. *Tel. 13606219715.* He can tell you about the garment factory that exports to the U.S. and has overruns for sale. It charges for a four-passenger car to Wuxi Y400, to Nanjing Y900, to Shanghai Y550, and to Hangzhou Y850. For a guide for one or two visitors a day, it charges Y400.

China Travel Service, *251 Ganjiangxi Road, 215002, Tel. 5225522, Fax 5225931.*

CYTS Tours, *4/F 208 Zhu Hui Road, 215006. Tel. 5205591, Fax 5291929.* Contact person: Mr. Shen Zong Shun.

Hours: 8am-11am and 1pm-5pm for offices, five days a week.

Internet: *Near post office. Suzhou YiYuan Internet Bar, 333 Renmin Road, Tel. 5110115.*

Jobs: The **Suzhou International Foreign Language School**, *Lumu, 215131. Tel. 5760026, Fax 5490201. E-mail: stmao@cmmail.com.* Ask for Mao Songtang, Vice-Principal. It has been looking for teachers of English.

Suzhou Municipal Administration of Tourism, *115 Shiquan St., 215006. Tel. 5268952, Fax 5304615.* Ask for Ms. Yong, fourth floor, Tel. 5223131. This is on the grounds of the Suzhou Hotel, to the right as you enter the gate. For brochures.

Suzhou University has a three week Mandarin class for foreigners. *Contact: Billie Ng, Coordinator, Suzhou Summer Program, 3121 Saddle Lane, Vancouver, V5S 4L4, Canada.*

Telephone code: 512

Tourist buses: The city has five tourist bus routes from the railway station to the main attractions. Tickets are Y2. Suzhou Tourism Administration maps are marked:

• Tourist Bus 1: (East) Railway Station – North Temple Pagoda-Humble Administrator's Garden, Lion Grove Garden, Jinmen Gate, Lingering Garden, West Garden, No. 1 Bridge, and Tiger Hill.

• Tour Bus 1: (West) Railway Station, Lingering Garden, West Garden, Tiger Hill.

• Bus 5: Tiger Hill – West Garden, Lingering Garden, Guanqian Street, Lion Grove Garden, Zoo.

• Bus 27: (Inner Circular Route) Railway Station, Dongda Street, Friendship Hotel, Master-of-Nets Garden, Twin Pagodas, Lion Grove Garden, Humble Administrator's, Qimen Gate, North Bus Station, Railway Station.

Other maps give different routes for the same bus numbers. It is best to show the name of your destination to the drivers outside the station.

Tourist Information *is south of the Railway Station, Tel. 7511125.*

Wuxi

(Wushi)

Wuxi is one of the oldest cities in China, founded over 3000 years ago. After deposits of tin became depleted here, inhabitants changed its name to Wuxi, meaning "no tin." It is worth visiting now because of Taihu Lake, famous for the rocks used in many of China's classical gardens, and its sail-filled image (October only). It is also known for its gardens, silks and pearls, and the ancient

Grand Canal. Wuxi is not as developed for tourists as Suzhou, nor are its gardens as crowded. The population of the great Wuxi area is 5.18 million. The hottest weather is in July at 38°C; the coldest in January, minus 4°C. The annual precipitation is 1056 mm mainly in June.

Arrivals & Departures

Wuxi is 25 minutes by express train from Suzhou on the Beijing-Shanghai railway. It is 130 km west of Shanghai's Hongqiao airport (1.5 hours by expressway and about Y600 by taxi). You can get a bus from the Shanghai Stadium leaving once an hour. It is 180 km or two hours by expressway plus traffic jams from Nanjing, or one hour (58 km) from Suzhou (Y200-Y500 by taxi, and cheaper by frequent buses) via the Nanjing-Shanghai expressway. It will soon be on the new road from Beijing to Guangzhou. It shares a small airport with Suzhou.

Express buses go from the bus terminal near the Wuxi railway station to Nanjing, Shanghai, and Suzhou about every 20 minutes between 6am to 6:40am and 6pm or 7pm. Trains leave for Nanjing about four times a day, for Shanghai nine times a day, and Suzhou five times a day. A taxi to Nanjing could cost from Y500 to Y600, to Suzhou Y150 to Y180, to Shanghai Railway Station Y450 to Y500, and to Shanghai Pudong Airport Y550 to Y600.

Orientation

Wuxi sits on the northeast shore of **Lake Taihu**, south of the Yangtze River in southern Jiangsu province. Its main tourist area is along the lake with its peninsula and islands. To the east about 12 km is its city center with shops, crafts factories, temples, and the Grand Canal. Public tour buses go from the railway station to major tourist attractions. According to the map of the tourist office, No. 1 goes to Turtle-head Park, No. 2 to Plum Garden, and No. 802K and 820 go to the Three Kingdoms.

Where to Stay

In Wuxi's bustling center the best hotels are the Sheraton and the New World Courtyard. The Lakeview Park Resort is best for relaxed vacationing and is a few kilometers closer to the big Buddha and the Three Kingdoms theme park. But don't swim in the lake.

The Taihu International Convention Center Hotel is the current incarnation of the World Trade Center, Taihu and Sunshine Hotels. In 2001, it looked very good, new, and is on a hill overlooking the lake. The old Hubin/Lakeside Hotel has gotten very commercial and crowded but it's still okay for budget travelers.

Hotels here add 10% to 15% service charge. All accept credit cards, have money exchange, business center, air-conditioning, etc. The following prices are subject to change, and discounts.

SHERATON WUXI HOTEL & TOWERS (Shi LaiTun Dafandian), *Garden City Mall, 403 Zhongshan Road, 214001. Almost five stars. Tel. 2721888, Fax 2752781. E-mail: Sheraton_wuxi@sheraton.com. Website: www.sheraton.com. It has 396 rooms and 66 apartments. Rooms are $143 to $163 and suites $224 to $828. It has been giving 20 to 25% discounts.*

Every room has a swivel chair by the desk, voice mail, one-touch service buttons, safes, HBO and CNN. Each also has an iron and broadband internet access. There's a 17-piece gym, a heated, 16-meter, indoor pool with retractable roof, and attached shopping center. It has day care and a marvelous bar, each booth with its own Fosters' tap, a gauge measuring the amount drunk, and a sign giving the table's record. Someplace Else has great fries and good pizza. It also has an outdoor lighted tennis court and a garden. Ask for its handy map. See Where to Eat below.

NEW WORLD COURTYARD BY MARRIOTT WUXI (formerly Ramada and now Xin Shi Jie Wan Yi Jiudian), *335 Zhongshan Road, 214001. Tel. 2762888, Fax 2763388. Website: Marriott.com. Three stars. The 265 rooms here include 22 apartments with kitchenettes. $70 to $90 for rooms, $150 for suites, and $60 to $100 for apartments. It has been giving 30% discounts. It is surrounded by department stores.*

This hotel had a problem with thin walls when it opened, but the staff insist now that padding between all the rooms muffled the noise forever in 2000. Standard rooms are medium-sized with small baths, and all rooms should have safes and HBO now.

WUXI TAIHU INTERNATIONAL CONVENTION CENTER HOTEL (Taihu Fandian), *Yonggu Road, Meiyuan, 214064. Tel. 5517888, Fax 5519964. E-mail: hnhotel@public1.wx.js.cn. Website: www.taihuhotel.com (Chinese). Rooms are Y660-Y1280, and suites Y1500-Y2000. Villas are Y1280-Y22200. It has been giving a 10% discount.*

This five-star, 260-room hotel is 12 km from the railway station, and 10 km from downtown. It is good for conferences, relaxing, and country hiking. The setting is beautiful and green. Guests can also catch up on Time, Fortune and Newsweek, which it has been selling. The outdoor pool is huge and it has an up-to-date gym, bowling alley, tennis, night club, and tennis. It also has a children's play room. The English is better at the Sheraton but some staff here should be able to handle requests. It does not charge guests to book a flight, but charges Y10 to Y30 service charge for a train ticket and Y20 for a bus ticket. You don't need to go downtown until you leave.

WUXI LAKEVIEW PARK RESORT (Taihu hua yuan du jia cun), *Tai Lake Shanshuicheng (Mountain-Water City) Tourism Zone, 214081. Four stars. Tel. 5555888, Fax 5556909. E-mail: lpr@public1.wx.js.cn, sales@wuxiresort.com. Website: www.wuxiresort.com (English). Five km from the Three Kingdoms' theme park, and seven km from downtown. Rooms are Y658-Y888, and suites*

Y1388-Y8888. *It has been giving a 20% walk-in discount and accepts travelers' checks.*

Standard rooms are 26-28 square meters. Its 151 rooms have safes and CNN. There's a small indoor pool, gym, snooker, four tennis courts, bowling, and archery. It also has conference facilities, free shuttle bus and a beer garden. From its 250 meters of lake front, you can see Istanbul (in the theme park across the bay). It is adding 50 villas in 2002 and apartments in 2003. It's a Hong Kong-Shanghai-Wuxi joint-venture.

LAKESIDE HOTEL (Hubin Fandian), *Hubin Road, Li Yuan, 214075. Four stars. Tel. 5101888, Fax 5102637. E-mail: hnhotel@public1.wx.js.cn. Web: www.hubinhotel.com. Rooms are Y480-Y780 and suites Y1080-Y2380 in the main building. In its cheapest Shuixiu Garden section, it's Y200-Y380 for rooms and Y570 for a suite. Villas are Y480-Y28000. If you book by e-mail, there's a 10% discount. Otherwise the assistant manager might give you 30% but don't count on it. It is twenty-three km from the airport, 12 km from the railway station, and 10 km (about Y35 for a taxi) from city center.*

Opened in 1978, this hotel is set in a 30,000-square-meter lake-side garden. Some of its 365 rooms range from 22 to 40 square meters. It has a good looking 25-meter-long indoor pool, CNN, and clinic. It is noted for its good food and floating restaurant and is next to the abandoned hulks of an unfinished theme park.

Where to Eat

Local specialties include ice fish, spareribs, deep-fried eel, crabs, and shrimp. The hotels listed above are your best bets here. The **Sheraton** is very good. The dinner buffet in its Brasserie costs Y108. It serves great double-decker brownies for Y48. Live Chinese classical music is performed in its Chinese restaurant which is open 11am to 2:30pm, and 5:30pm to 10pm. Recommended there are its hot and sour soup with seafood Y22, sweet and sour pork with pineapple Y35, pan-fried beef filet Cantonese style for Y45-Y68, Yangzhou fried rice for Y32 and Y48, and deep-fried spring rolls Y8 each.

WUXI ROAST DUCK RESTAURANT, *a ten-minute walk from the Sheraton, is at 222 Zhong Shan Road, Tel. 2708222.*

It serves Wuxi food and takes no international credit cards. It is open 11am to 2pm, and 5pm to 9pm. The Yangzhou fried rice is Y15, deep-fried duck skewer Y28, and Wuxi roast duck half for Y25, whole for Y45. Its deep-fried pork steak costs Y25, pork chop Y30, and mushrooms Y18. It has white table cloths, and a menu in English with photos of its entrees.

ZHUANG YUAN LOU, *200 Qing Shi Road, Tel. 2612888, 2627878.*

This huge restaurant in a white building has some photos on its menus, but nothing in English. A few staff speak English.

A good Cantonese restaurant the **Yunfu Shaoezai Food Plaza** is near the Sheraton at 278 Zhong Shan Road, but also has no English. Take along Chapter 25 in this book which lists some dishes in English and Chinese.

Seeing the Sights

The three-hour daytime tour boat from Wuxi to Suzhou along the **Grand Canal** gives you a feel for the heavy traffic and life on the water. Book this or shorter trips through a travel agent.

For gardens, there's the Liyuan Garden near the Hubin Hotel. The recently-renovated **Meiyuan (Plum) Garden** with its plum blossoms is best appreciated in the early spring. These are both beside Lake Taihu. On the peninsula, 17 km west of the city, is **Yuantouzhu (Turtle Head) Park** (open 5am-6pm. Y35. *Tel. 5866807*). **Xihui Park** closer to downtown is huge, and includes a nine-dragon wall, and the lovely **Jichang Garden** (open 8:30am to 4:30pm, Y20, Tel. 3708324). It also has a cableway to the top of Huishan Mountain with a great view. Unfortunately no signs are in English. The park is at 2, Huishan Straight Street, *Tel. 3707864, 3708324*.

The best of the theme parks and movie sets is **The Three Kingdoms** (220-265 A.D.) with its 20 reproduced miniature 1800-year-old warships from which flames explode. This theme park also has had a show with real galloping horses and fighting costumed riders. But prepare for no shade, and lots of walking between interesting buildings, the waterfront, and reproductions of famous sites from the book. Better still, make notes from the book and try to identify the sites. (If you don't expect a North American-quality park, this theme park is interesting.) The Three Kingdoms is about 20km from downtown, open about 8am-6pm. Y30.00, *Tel. 5888819*. Don't waste time at any of the other nearby theme parks unless you're interested in historical Chinese movies.

About 20 km southwest of the city on the other side of Taihu Lake is the 101.5- meter-high (including base) cheerful **standing giant Buddha**, 760 tons of bronze. *Tel. 5996166*. Open 7:30am-5:30pm. About Y35. (The Statue of Liberty is 93 meters high including the base.) It's worth the trip if you consider the amazing workmanship going into something that big. But you might get turned off too by the commercialization of a religious symbol.

Wuxi is also a silk-producing center, the hills around the city filled with mulberry bushes. Tourists can learn about **silk**, from silkworm rearing through the printing and dyeing process at a silk factory. You can visit **Huaxi Village**, 1.5 hours away for demonstrations of ancient farming and village life. These can be arranged by travel agents. A good time to visit is the Mid-Autumn Festival, with lots of colored lanterns, moon cakes, and an evening cruise on the lake and, one hopes, a full moon.

Festivals: The week-long Lake Tai Arts Festival features folk dancing and singing; and the Cherry and Pottery festivals are held in April.

Shopping

Good locally-made products include hand-painted clay figurines, silk embroidery, knitted silk clothing like underwear, fresh-water pearls, pearl face cream, and silk. Also made in the province are porcelain, and Yixing purple sand pottery (especially tea pots in collectible shapes and sizes).

The Bird, Fish and Pet Market opposite CITS at the **Nanchan Temple** has the best prices for old coins, pearls, stamps, art work, pearls, antiques and reproductions. Some prices are marked but vendors come down easily. This fascinating market is around a wonderful old temple with huge deities and monks burning incense, and it's open about 9am-5pm. No credit cards are accepted and nothing can be guaranteed authentic.

The **Wuxi Clay Figurine Research Institute** is open 8am-4pm daily. It is at 8-1 Xiahetang, Huishan, in a charming neighborhood of old houses, Tel. 3709594. You should be able to see artists make these cute hand-painted clay figures in the mornings, a folk art from the Ming dynasty. It also produces embroidery and accepts credit cards. Prices, however, are cheaper at the stores just outside and down the block.

Number One Silk Spinning Mill might have a display of silkworms. *Tel. 5012461, 5014649.* A couple of merchants might be outside selling over-runs at good prices. **Parkson's Department Store** is across from the New World Courtyard. Hold off until you get to the Silk Market in Hangzhou, or the pearl market in Suzhou, unless you see something irresistible.

Excursions & Day Trips

You can take excursions to Yixing and the nearby (69 km) Yixing purple sandware ceramic factory, ceramic museum, and tea plantations. There's also the Yixing limestone caves, bamboo forest, and Jiangyin (home of Ming dynasty scientist and traveler Xu Xiake). Jiangyin and Huaxi village can be combined in one day's sightseeing. These are on the west side of Lake Taihu. See also Nanjing, Shanghai and Suzhou.

Practical Information

Hours: 8am-5pm five days a week (offices). Department stores are open 9am-7 or 8pm, daily, and street markets all day or from 7pm-9pm.

Wuxi CITS, *18 Zhong Shan Road, 214002. Tel. 2725190, 2700224.* E-mail: *engdep@public1.wx.js.cn. Website www.citswx.com (Chinese only).* Ask for Lu Xin Yi, Euro-American Department. *Tel/Fax 2700268.*

Wuxi Tourism Bureau, *7 Xinsheng Road, 214002. Tel. 2704314, Fax 2729644 or 2703851. E-mail: wxtour@public1.wx.js.cn.*

Wuxi Overseas Tourist Corporation, *7 Xinsheng Road, 214002, Tel. 2754026, 2762480, Fax 2716780. E-mail: wxotc@public1.wx.js.cn.* Complaints to Xu Jirong or Wang Bosheng.

Telephone Code: 510.

Yangzhou

(Yangchow)

Yangzhou is a charming city 20 km north of the Yangtze on the Grand Canal and 98 km from Nanjing in Jiangsu province. It is almost 2,500 years old and famous for its gardens and classical architecture. It is worth a special trip, its ancient district a nice change from the hectic pace of other cities. It was a very prosperous port after the building of the canal in the seventh century. In the Tang dynasty, it was the residence of over 5,000 foreigners. One of the Prophet Mohammed's descendants is buried here, and from 1282 Marco Polo is said to have spent three years as an inspector or mayor here. Yangzhou's wealth declined with that of the canal, and by the Qing, it was famous only as an imperial resort.

The hottest temperature has been a rare 41°C in July-August; the coldest is 0°C in January-February. The annual rainfall is about 1000 mm, mainly from June to September. Its population is 5 million of whom 500,000 live in the city proper.

Arrivals & Departures

Yangzhou can be reached in less than two hours via the expressway from Nanjing. Buses leave every 10 to 30 minutes during the day. It is also faster to go from Shanghai by bus (3.5 hours) than by train (5 hours and via Zhenjiang). You must cross the Yangtze River either by ferry or bridge. The closest airport is at Nanjing 109 km away. The closest railway station is in Zhenjiang on the other side of the Yangtze 20 km away (after the new four-km bridge is built in 2005).

Orientation

The old section of Yangzhou is one of the 24 historical and cultural cities protected by the State Council. All new buildings must be in traditional Chinese style, and industries must be confined to the suburbs. (It manufactures Mercedes buses.)

Where to Stay

The best located hotels for tourists are the Xi Yuan and Yangzhou, with good gardens and close to the museum, tourist stores, and Slender West Lake in the northwestern suburbs. They are five km from the long-distance bus station. The better Grand Metropole Hotel is only 1.5 km. from Slender West Lake. Hotels here add 10% surcharge, accept credit cards and travelers checks. CITS charges for one standard room at the Yangzhou Hotel Y200, Xiyuan Hotel Y280 and the Grand Metropole Y280 but prices rise in high season 20%-30%.

GRAND METROPOLE HOTEL (Jinhua Dajiudian). *1 Wenchang Xi Road, 225009. Four stars. Tel. 7322888, Fax 7368999. E-mail: yz.jhjd@public.yz.js.cn, yzgmh@pub.yz.jsinfo.net. Website: www.gmhotel.com (English). Its 242 rooms are Y700-Y900, and suites Y1500- Y8000. It has been discounting 30%.*

The breakfast buffet costs Y38. This 242-room hotel has bicycles for rent, BBC and CNBC, and non-smoking and executive floors with data ports. It has a gym, sauna, and night club. A China Travel Service (H.K.) Hotel.

XI YUAN HOTEL (Fandian), *1 Fengle Shang Street, 225002. Four stars, Tel. 7344888, Fax 7233870. Main building Y620-Y630 for rooms, Y1456-Y8728 for suites. It has cheaper, less luxurious rooms for Y256 and up and has been discounting 20-50%.*

Built in 1976 and rebuilt in 1997, this seven-story, 270-room hotel has small bathrooms, CNN, a pool, and lighted tennis court on the roof.

YANGZHOU HOTEL (Binguan), *5 Fengle Shang Street, 225002. Four stars, Tel. 7342611, Fax 7343599. Rooms are Y388-Y480 and suites Y680-Y4400. It has been discounting 25 to 35%.*

Built in 1985 and renovated in 1998, this nine-story, 150-room hotel has a business center, gym, indoor pool and CNN. You can request a safe in your room.

Where to Eat

"Thousand-layer oily cake" (qian chun gao) may sound awful, but it is delicious. People also go to Yangzhou from Nanjing for the dumplings. Both the **Yangzhou** and **Xi Yuan** hotels can reproduce a banquet from the novel *Dream of the Red Mansion;* the author's father lived here.

At the Yangzhou Hotel, delicious dishes include salty goose, sweet Mandarin fish, sliced dried bean curd in chicken soup, and duck's blood with green soy beans. Another good place is the **Ye Chun Restaurant** by the gate of the Xiyuan Hotel.

Seeing the Sights

The highlight is the boat trip on **Slender West Lake**. Both Qing Emperors Qianlong and Kangxi took this two-hour, five-km long cruise about six times each, the buildings paid for by salt merchants. You board near the Yangzhou Hotel and you'll see 24 of Shouxi Hu (Slender West) Lake's relaxing, exquisite scenic spots: curled-roof pavilions, potted landscape garden, and imposing White Dagoba (Qing). You can also follow the river by tricycle for Y30 and visit many of the same places, but a boat is more fun and historical.

The **Five Pavilion Bridge** is best seen on the night of a full moon, when 15 moons are supposed to reflect in the water under the arches, a Chinese puzzle that must be seen to be understood. You'll see the Daming Temple, founded in the fifth century, with its 18 three-meter-high carved Buddhist statues. The beautiful Jian Zhen Memorial Hall here was built in 1973 to commemorate the 1,200th anniversary of the death of Monk Jian Zhen. It is a copy of the Toshodai Temple in Nara, Japan. This abbot of Daming Temple persisted in going to Japan to teach Buddhism in spite of five unsuccessful attempts and his blindness. He succeeded at age 66. Because he and his disciples also introduced Tang literature, medicine, architecture, sculpture, and other arts to Japan, he is highly honored in that country, where he died and is buried. The statue of Jian Zhen is a recent copy of a 1,000-year-old-plus statue, a national Japanese treasure. The original was brought back for a visit in 1980 "because it looked homesick" but was destroyed in a fire in Japan in 1998.

Along the way, you can also look for the bird and fish market, the former city moat, and the 24-Maid Bridge. The four larger-than-life jade Buddhas can only be seen between 7:30am-4:30pm daily and are lovely. There are also a 70-meter-high pagoda and two three-ton iron cauldrons used to feed the dragon king and control floods. Prepaid tours might also visit a lacquerware, jade-carving and paper-cutting factory.

The **Yangzhou Museum** (Yangzhou Bowuguan) next to the Yangzhou Hotel was originally a temple, later turned into a temporary palace. It has a Marco Polo Hall to which modern-day Italians sent a bronze lion, the symbol of Venice. There are two Italian tombstones on display, dated 1342 and 1344. An antique and curio market is here, liveliest on weekends. It is open 8am-4:30pm daily.

The charming **Geyuan Garden** in the east of the city, 10 minutes from the Xiyuan Hotel, started as a private garden, and later became the home of the Ye Chun Poet's Society in the Qing. It is full of gnarled rockeries, moon gates, bamboo, latticed doorways, wavy walls, and real picture windows. It's on Dongguan Zhong Street.

The **Heyuan Garden**, in the southeastern part of the city on Xu Nin Men Street is typical of Yangzhou's gardens. The Islamic-styled **Tomb of Puhaddin** is on the east bank of the Grand Canal, near the Heyuan. Built in the 13th century, it contains the remains of this 16th generation descendant of Mohammed, the founder of Islam. Puhaddin (Burhdn Al-Dan) came to China as a missionary in the Southern Song. The 700-year-old **Xianhe (Crane) Mosque** is one of the four most famous in China, and was built between 1265 and 1275. It is not usually open but CITS can take you there.

Just 50 km east is Gaoyu County where a farmer has been able to summon thousands of **wild ducks** on command. There's also an ancient post office. This trip is available every month except April and May through travel agents.

If you book a visit to the **Moon Culture Festival** in September-October through Mr. Zhou of Nanjing CITS, the local tourist bureau promises free crab, free moon cake, a free boat ride and free entry to events like traditional dancers (and long speeches).

Shopping

Good local products are red lacquer carving, jade carving, velvet flowers, paper cuts, and silk lanterns. Yangzhou also exports potted landscapes. Better quality goods than the museum market but less fun to buy are at the **Yangzhou Cultural Relic and Antique Shop** (Wen Wu Shan Dian), 1 Yanfu Xi Road, Tel. 7349610. It is open 8:30am-6pm. The Yangzhou Jadeware Factory is at 50 Yanhe, 225002, *Tel. 7320222, 7347338 X 8003, Fax 7340265. E-mail: yzqiqi@pub.yz.jsinfo.net. Website: www.yztaojs.com and www.yangzhou-lacquer.com (English).*

Practical Information

CITS, *10 Fengle Shangjie Street, 225002, Tel. 7348925, Fax 7344278. E-mail: yz.c.i.t.s@yeah.net.* Ask for Mr. Gao Bihua, General Manager.

Yangzhou Tourism Bureau, *8 Fengle Shangjie Street, 225002, Tel. 7363909, Fax 7343646. E-mail: yz.lyj@public.yz.js.cn* for brochures. Ask for Zhang Jing who speaks English.

Telephone Code: 514

Zhenjiang

(Chinkiang, Chenchiang, Chenkiang)

Zhenjiang should be visited because of **Pearl S. Buck** and a famous story. It is in central Jiangsu province, where the Grand Canal meets the south bank of the Yangtze and is surrounded on three sides by hills.

Zhenjiang is an historic old city with streets lined with plane trees. Some of its houses are small and whitewashed like Suzhou's, others black brick with courtyards. The city was founded in the Xia. It boasts 3,000 years of history, including seven years as the capital of the Eastern Wu (third century), when it was called Jingko (entrance to Nanjing). In the Qin dynasty (221-206 B.C.), 3,000 prisoners were sent here to build canals and roads. Many battles were fought in the area and the city is mentioned in the novel *The Romance of the Three Kingdoms.*

During the Yuan, Marco Polo visited it and the first British missionaries arrived in the 17th century. Toward the end of the First Opium War, it was the only city that strongly resisted the imperialists. After that failed, however, about 1,000 foreigners, mainly merchants and missionaries from Britain, Germany, and the United States lived here. The foreigners left their mark on some of the architecture and on education.

For seven years Zhenjiang was the capital of Jiangsu province. In 1938, the Communist army fought against the Japanese here. In April 1949, the British warship H.M.S. Amethyst, while rescuing British citizens upriver, was caught in the crossing of the Yangtze by the People's Liberation Army and held for over three months here. The British captain refused to cooperate or admit his ship fired first. Under cover of a passing passenger boat, the Amethyst finally escaped.

Its hottest temperature, in July and August, is 35°C, with breezes from the Yangtze; its coldest is -3°C from the middle to the end of January. The annual precipitation is 1000 mm mainly in July. The urban population is 680,000, the total 2.8 million.

Arrivals & Departures

Zhenjiang is 50 minutes by train east of Nanjing, and about three hours northwest of Shanghai. The closest airport is about 80 km away at Nanjing. It is on State Highway No. 312. Until the new bridge gets finished between Zhenjiang and Yangzhou in 2003 or so, you have to cross the Yangtze by ferry. A taxi from Yangzhou to Zhenjiang costs Y500 to Y600 including tolls. A taxi from Nanjing to Zhenjiang costs about Y300 to Y450.

Where to Stay

The Zhenjiang Hotel is better for business people and Pearl Buck fans. It is downtown near her home. Hotels add 10% surcharge and accept credit cards.

INTERNATIONAL HOTEL ZHENJIANG (Guoji Fandian), *218 Jiefang Road, 212001, Tel. 5021888, Fax 5021777. Four stars. $68-$108 for rooms, and $108-$1558 for suites. It has been giving 20% discounts.*

This 31-story hotel has a pool and revolving restaurant.

ZHENJIANG HOTEL (Binguan), *92 Zhong Shan Xi Road, 212004. Four stars. Tel. 5233888, Fax 5231055. E-mail: zjhotel@public.zj.js.cn. It is 300 meters from the railway station. Y300-Y580 for rooms and Y888-Y2600 for suites including breakfast. It has been discounting 30-40%. It accepts international credit cards and travelers' checks, and has safes in some but not all rooms.*

Built in 1963 and expanded in 1999, this hotel has 20-square-meter rooms. There are 188 rooms and 10 suites, an indoor pool, tennis court, bowling, and a gym.

Where to Eat

The best restaurants are in the hotels. Also good is the **Xin Yan Chan restaurant** close to the Zhenjiang Hotel. A local specialty is crab cream bun, a steamed meat pastry. Make a hole first and slurp out the steaming hot soup inside. Food here is concerned with fragrance, shape, and color, and is neither too sweet nor too salty. You might find your hors d'oeuvres looking like butterflies, peacocks, or fans. Everything can be dipped in vinegar. Ask for crystal pork.

Seeing the Sights

If you only have one day, consider seeing Jinshan Hill, Jiao Shan Island, the museum, Pearl S. Buck's house, and the Thousand-Year-Old Street.

Thousand-year-old tiny Xiao Matai Street has an unusual Song or Yuan stupa built above the sidewalk. Jiao Hill (150 meters high) on Jiao Shan Island is less than half a kilometer from the city. For the **ferry** to Jiao Shan Island, *Tel. 8815502*. It operates 8am-5pm. Up 250 steps is a magnificent view of the Yangtze and you can see the place where the Chinese held the Amethyst. What would you have done if you were captain?

Back at the base of Jiao Hill, you can look at the Battery, which was used against the British in 1842. Also below is a garden with steles of many calligraphers, including that of the father of modern calligraphy, Wang Hsi-chih, who lived 1,500 years ago.

Pearl S. Buck, Friend of China

The American Nobel and Pulitzer Prize-winning author **Pearl S. Buck** (1892-1973) grew up here, studied in what is now the Zhenjiang Second Middle School (founded 1884), and taught here (1914-17), a total of 18 years. She started writing to help pay for the care of her disabled child. Communist China criticized her for being 'imperialist' and ignored her writings. In the 1950s, US Senator Joseph McCarthy accused her of being a Communist. For the 100th anniversary of her birth, Zhenjiang and sister city Tempe, Arizona, renovated one of her homes as the **Zhenjiang Friendship House** (Sino-US Cultural Exchange Center).

The home is also for the study of English, foreign missions and her books: *Good Earth, Imperial Women, Dragon Seed, My Several Worlds,* etc. You can talk with some of her old students. It has photos, copies of her books, and classes in English. If it isn't open and you want to see inside, contact CITS.

Friendship House is at 6 Runzhoushan Road, 212004. *Tel. 5234174.* It is up the hill above the back door of the Zhenjiang Hotel.

The **Pearl S. Buck Foundation**, based outside Philadelphia, has been supporting American-Asian children.

Jinshan (Golden Hill), at 62 Jinshan Road, 212002, *Tel. 5281631,* one km from the Jinshan Hotel, looks better from afar than close up. The temple here was first built 1500 years ago (Jin) and rebuilt several times since, a victim of lightning, fire, and weather. The current pagoda was finished in 1900 with animal carvings, in time for the Empress Dowager Cixi's birthday. It reflects her crude tastes. Seven-stories-tall, 30-meters-high, it is easier climbing up the 119 steps than down because the steps are shallow.

There are some fun caves, all the more interesting because of the presence in one cave of the white, ghostly, life-size figure of the monk Fa Hai, and in another the two beautiful women said to be the **White Snake** and the **Blue** (sometimes Green) **Snake**, both fairies (see sidebar below). The cave is said to reach Hangzhou!

The Snake Story & Chinese Opera

The story of the Snakes is also the plot of a famous Beijing opera. Briefly, the several, thousand-year-old White Snake from Mount Emei (the Blue Snake is the maid) becomes a beautiful woman and goes to Hangzhou. There, she falls in love with a scholar, and eventually the two marry.

The White Snake, using her magic powers, takes money from a government official to build a house, but because the official's seal is still on the money, the young man is arrested and ordered beaten for theft. The White Snake again uses her magic so that whenever her husband is beaten, the official's wife feels the pain. Consequently, the young man is expelled to Zhenjiang.

After his arrival, the monk master Fa Hai, jealous of their happiness, tries to separate the couple, but the White Snake floods the area, including Jin Shan temple. They are reunited in Hangzhou. The unrelenting monk master retaliates by imprisoning the White Snake under the Leifeng pagoda in Hangzhou. There she is rescued by the Blue Snake. The White Snake, her husband, and her son are reunited and live happily ever after.

This is a popular Chinese tale and a study of its symbolism and the psychology of its popularity could keep a folklorist busy for years.

Other Sights & Tours

The **museum** is housed in the former 1890 British consulate building, 85 Boxian Road and Daxi Road, 212002, *Tel. 5277317, 5277143*, open 8am- 5pm daily. It includes the former Southern Baptist mission residences. Its permanent collection includes an anchor from the British ship Amethyst, a land lease referring to the 'former British Concession' lot, and the tomb stone of the famous missionary Hudson Taylor. A tiny silver coffin found under the nearby Iron Pagoda contains two gold coffins and the ashes of a Buddhist saint. Charming is the Song porcelain pillow in the shape of a sleeping child. No titles are in English.

Shopping

Dashikou is Zhenjiang's main shopping area. Factories here make elaborate palace lanterns and are famous for their 'crystal' meat and vinegar. Also made in the city are silk, jade carvings, paper cuttings, and bamboo crafts.

Practical Information

CITS, *Zhenjiang Hotel, 92 Zhong Shan Xi Road, 212004, Tel. 5233888, Fax 5244818.*

CTS, *6 Jiankang Road, 212001, Tel. 5016926, 5017256, Fax 5017911.*

Zhenjiang Travel and Tourism Bureau, *92 Zhongshan Xi Road, 212004, Tel. 5232959, Fax 5236425. Website: www.tour.zj.js.cn (Chinese).*

Telephone code: 511

Chapter 17

Tianjin
(Tientsin)

Tianjin is a port city, the largest commercial seaport in north China. It is one of China's biggest industrial centers and is mainly for business travelers, but in between appointments, there are some interesting things to do in addition to golf and sports. It's a good shopping city (cheaper than Beijing) as well as a museum of 19th century European architecture and history. It has a less commercial section of the Great Wall. Many of Beijing's foreign residents drive to Tianjin on weekends for a change of pace and its antique and curio market.

Tianjin has been inhabited for 2,500 years. It was not until after the Grand Canal opened in the seventh century that inland commerce, and Tianjin's fortunes started to improve. During the Ming (1404), city walls were built and the city was called Tianjinwei by the Duke of Yen, who crossed the Haihe River here on a military expedition.

The British and French invaded Tianjin in 1858. In June of that year they and the Chinese signed the Treaty of Tientsin giving Christian missionaries freedom of movement and protection "because the Christian religion as professed by Protestants and Roman Catholics inculcates the practices of virtue, and teaches man to do as he would be done by." In 1860, British and French troops from Tianjin marched on Beijing and forced the Qing rulers to ratify the Treaty of Tientsin; they then burned down the Summer Palace. The resulting Treaty of Peking opened Tianjin and nine other ports to foreign trade.

Nine countries eventually controlled over 3,500 acres of this city: Britain, France, Germany, Japan, Russia, Italy, Belgium, Austria, and the United States. The concessions lasted from 20 to 80 years and, as in Shanghai, left the Chinese some very interesting old European architecture as well as bitter memories. The Treaty of Peking also forced the Chinese to permit French missionaries to own or rent property in China, and further helped to inflame smoldering anti-Christian and anti-foreign resentment.

Many of these feelings resulted from what the Chinese saw as Christian arrogance, which insisted that the Christian god was the only true god. Added to this were cultural misunderstandings. Quite a few Chinese actually believed that the children in Catholic orphanages were either eaten by nuns or ground up for medicine. The French Catholics did pay money for female babies - to keep them from being killed. By 1870, the atmosphere had grown so tense that after the French consul fired at a minor Chinese official, the consul was immediately hacked to death. Ten nuns, two priests, and another French official were also brutally killed in what is now known as the Tientsin Massacre, or what the Chinese prefer to call the Tientsin Revolt. In 1976, an earthquake centered in nearby Tangshan severely damaged the city.

The weather is hottest in July briefly at 40°C, and coldest in January, -10°C. The annual precipitation averages 600 millimeters, mostly in July and August. It is China's fifth-largest city. The urban population is six million, the total over 10 million.

Arrivals & Departures

Tianjin is 137 km southeast of Beijing and is joined by nine express trains a day with Beijing Railway Station. In Tianjin, you don't need to reserve a train ticket in advance. At the train station, look for the big sign in English that says something like "Train to Beijing." This express train will take you to the main station near Jianguomenwai and avoid traffic jams into the city in a little over an hour for Y35-40.

At Tianjin railway station, some taxis organize shared rides and ask about Y200 a seat to Beijing but you can probably negotiate a taxi of your own for Y350 to Y500. The Hyatt's limos cost about Y600.

The main Tianjin bus station is near the railway station but express buses leave from several terminals. Buses from Beijing leave from the Zhaogongkou bus terminal or the Beijing Railway Station there and take about 100 minutes plus traffic jams with departures during the day every 15 minutes. It costs about Y30 one way. From the Hyatt Hotel it takes 50 minutes (70 km) by road to the port of Tanggu on the expressway. There are four trains a day there, about an hour's trip.

Tianjin has air connections with Hong Kong, Nagoya, and 33 Chinese cities. Some airlines provide buses from Tianjin to connect with their flights at Beijing airport.

Tianjin also has ferry service with Inchon (a 28-hour trip leaving Korea every five days), Kobe (a 48-hour trip leaving Japan every Thursday), Dalian (leaving Tianjin daily), and Yantai (leaving Tianjin six times a month).

Orientation

Tianjin is more of a gateway to elsewhere than a tourist destination in itself. Resident foreigners say it is a good place to live because the people are friendlier and more polite than in Shanghai and Beijing, and the sightseeing is less crowded.

Tianjin is one of the four municipalities directly under the central government. It has eight urban and four rural districts, and five suburban counties. The Dagang Oil Field, for example, is 60 km away, but it's part of Tianjin. Its factories make Flying Pigeon bicycles, Seagull watches, petrochemicals, textiles, and diesel engines. Its counties grow walnuts, chestnuts, dates, rice, and prawns. The city is rather smoggy. You might be interested in seeing its arts and crafts factories.

The city proper sprawls on both sides of the Hai River. The area immediately southwest of the Jiefang (Liberation) Bridge was formerly French. The section south of that, around the Astor Hotel, was formerly British. Liberation Road was Victoria Road. In a couple of years, the 10-hectare former Italian concession should finish its renovations and look like something out of Italy. This area is bounded by Minzu, Tinbu, Boai, and Beian Road.

The four blocks near the Drum Tower are a cultural area with no cars and a theater giving the likes of martial arts, clay figurines and New Year's pictures demonstrations for tourists. In Xiqing District in the west of the city, an ancient town (Gu Zhen) should also have demonstrations and craft sales. This is the area where the New Year's Pictures were first made, and where the Shi Family Mansion is already open as a folk arts museum. You'll also see how old wine and "tou fu" were made, and exhibitions of Chinese medicine, tea ceremony and folk dances. You can expect rides of several kilometers long in old-style boats, graced by the presence of "Emperor Qian Long" who arrived in the same way.

The subway is currently 7.4 km long from the intersection of Nanjing and Xinhua Roads to Tianjin West Railway Station with trains every 15 minutes from 5:30am to 10:30pm. In about 2006, it should extend to 26 km.

Where to Stay

The best hotel is the Sheraton, the second best the Hyatt, and the third the Astor. The latter is one of my favorites because of its history and location. It is almost next door to the Hyatt, both about 20 km from the airport and three km from the railway station. The Sheraton is best for families and is in a quieter residential district within walking distance of the 400-meter-high telecommunications tower. The World Economy Trade and Exhibition Centre, Friendship

Store, and CITS are near by. The Hyatt borders the Haihe River and is more central, closer to government offices and the antique market. The Holiday Inn is good too but far from downtown. A new Renaissance is expected to open in 2002 in city center. (For information, contact the Marriott Regional Office in Hong Kong, *Tel. 852/2192-6057, Fax 852/2192-6030.*)

Hotels in Tianjin take credit cards, book tickets, change money, and have business centers. Hotels here add a 15% surcharge and about Y5 tax.

SHERATON TIANJIN HOTEL (Sher Er Don), *Zi Jin Shan Road, Hexi District, 300074. Five stars. Tel. 23343388, Fax 23358740. E-mail: sheraton@mail.zlnet.com.cn. Website: www.sheraton.com, www.sheratontj.com. It is 27 km from the airport, and nine km from the railway station. $140-190 for rooms and $280 for suites. It has had a temporary promotion rate of $88 for a superior room.*

Built in 1987, this six-story, 235-room hotel also has 65 apartments. It has non-smoking rooms, an executive floor, CNN, HBO and BBC, and Japanese, Western and Chinese restaurants and a bar. Rooms are 32 square meters with safes. It has bicycles for rent, a 20-piece gym with a treadwall, two lighted tennis courts, putting green, and steam bath. There's a lounge with baby sitter and toys, and a supermarket. An ATM (Visa Plus and Cirrus) is in its lobby. Its rooms for women have pink bathrooms, nail files, and makeup mirrors.

HYATT REGENCY TIANJIN (Kai Yue Jiudian), *219 Jiefang Bei Road, 300042. Four stars. Tel. 23301234, Fax 23312757, 23311234. E-mail: information@hyatt-tianjin.com. Website: www.hyatt.com. Rooms are $128 and suites $213 to $1200 and it has been giving a low season $79 promotion. It is well located near restaurants and is on the river.*

Built in 1986, this 19-story, 428-room hotel is in great shape. Its rooms are 28 square meters and have CNN, BBC and HBO, and mini-bars. The river view is best. It has 24-hour room service, a good business center, and Cantonese, Chaozhou, Tianjin, Western and Japanese restaurants. Its two executive club floors have only suites. It has bicycles, a good 10-piece gym with steam bath and sauna, and basketball court. Its ball room seats 300 for banquets. Buffet prices are about Y80 for an excellent breakfast and Y108 for dinner. It has ANA and Air China ticketing offices.

HOLIDAY INN TIANJIN, *288 Zhong Shan Road, Hebei District, 300141. About four-star standard. Tel. 26288888, Fax 26286666. E-mail: hotel@mail.hitianjin.com. Website: www.hitianjin.com. $130-$150 for rooms, $280-$300 for suites. It has been discounting 40% and including one breakfast with a standard room.*

A long block from the Hai River, four km from the railway station, and 18 km from Tianjin international airport, this 1997 hotel is a little bit out of the way. It would make a good conference site. Its ballroom can serve a sit-down dinner for 300. With 263 rooms and suites, executive and non-smoking floors, this 29-story hotel has a handy ATM (Cirrus, Visa Plus) in its spacious soft-beige lobby, 24-hour room service, and a business center. It has a delicatessen, Western, Cantonese and Asian food. The coffee shop is open 24 hours. Its unusual-shaped rooms have CNN, HBO, CNBC, safes, and kettles. There's a good eight-piece gym and 12-meter-long indoor pool. Rooms are 25 square meters.

ASTOR HOTEL (Lixun De Fandian), *33 Taier Zhuang Road, 300040. Four stars. Tel. 23311688, 23311112, Fax 23316282. E-mail: astorsal@mail.zlnet.com.cn or astorbc@mail.zlnet.com.cn. About $130-$180 for rooms; $200-$580 for suites. Discounts have been 20-30%.*

Originally built by the British in 1863, and expanded in 1924 and 1987, it's provided a bed for US President Herbert Hoover. The charming old wing has 94 big rooms and two executive floors. The new wing has 129 rooms. This is the hotel for people who like history, and much of it is in English on plaques and in its stunning lobby mural. Look for "the reproduction of Emperor Guang-Xu's dick," a line from its booklet "The Sightseeing of the Hundred Year's History of Astor Tianjin, China." But it also has modern facilities like CNN and safes in its rooms, and an ATM (Cirrus, MasterCard, Visa Plus) in the lobby. But "The ATM doesn't always have money," said a clerk.

Where to Eat

The Hyatt has a good dumpling restaurant among its several good restaurants. Its Chinese restaurant has a great Sunday brunch. The Sheraton has an outstanding fine dining restaurant with American and European food.

CHENG GUI RESTAURANT, *287 Hebei Road. Tel. 23311702. It is open 11am to 2pm, and 5pm to 9:30pm. It accepts American Express and Visa.*

On its ground floor, salads cost Y6 to Y24, borscht soup with sour cream Y5, deep-fried breaded prawns Y20, chicken Kiev Y15, spaghetti Y12 to Y15, ice cream Y6, and home-made pastry Y6 to Y10. On its classier second and third floors, it offers salads Y18 to Y23, borscht Y12, prawns Y30 to Y55, beef tenderloin Y30 to Y90, chicken Kiev Y25, home-made pastry Y10, and ice cream Y10.

YUE WEI XIAN RESTAURANT, *283 Hebei Road, part of a chain. Tel. 2339888, 23309930. E-mail: ywx@ywxgroup.com. Website: www.ywxgroup.com. It takes credit cards and is open from 10am to the departure of the last guest.*

Good for eating and sightseeing. The restaurant is full of antiques, a painting by the last emperor's younger brother, Ming dynasty swords, an opium bed, live goldfish, and a squat toilet. The service is attentive, and the peanuts are good at Y6. Its menu says live shrimps Y168 for 500 gms, beef dishes Y22-Y32, pork Y20-Y28, vegetables Y12-Y32, rice and noodles Y12-Y28, and steamed garoupa Y68. It serves Canadian ice wine for Y128 a bottle, Dynasty Red for Y88, and beer for Y15 to Y20. Ask for a tour of the place. Waiters bow as guests leave.

COSY CAFÉ, *across from CITS at 21 Youyi Road, Tel. 28372349. E-mail: CozyCafe@eyou.com. It accepts credit cards and is open 11am to 2am.*

Reliable but not outstanding. Ask for Manager Si Yi Zhang. Chicken quesadilla is Y58, 14 oz Dallas T-bone Y128, soup Y10 to Y18, deep-fried onion rings Y30, Buffalo chicken wings Y35, spaghetti Y35 to Y48, BBQ pork ribs Y52, Caesar salad Y38, and country-fried steak Y58.

TIANJIN BAI JIAO YUAN, *43 He Xiou, Ping Shan Dao, Tel. 23016846, 23526120.*

They make dumplings fresh on ordering.

FENG GUANG SEAFOOD RESTAURANT, *across from the Hyatt at 162 Jiefang Bei Road, Tel. 23128888. It is open 11am to 2:30pm, and 5pm to 10pm. It takes credit cards and has a menu in English.*

A Cantonese-style place whose specialty is abalone with brown sauce for Y1088, but you can also get braised fresh asparagus for Y25, garlic spare ribs for Y32, braised abalone with squid for Y28, live-cooked flounder Y88 for 500 gms, crab Y58 for 500 gms, and hairy crab Y68 for 500 gms. Ask for Ms. Pu Xiao Xia who speaks English.

Fun is the northeast (dong bei) restaurant on the street over the bridge from the Hyatt about two kilometers. The **Shang Yang Tun Dong Bei Restaurant** there serves northeastern food as it was served during the Cultural Revolution – in small rooms designed to look dumpy with newspapers as wall paper and service staff in costume, a real bit of nostalgia. One room has an opium bed. It serves fresh seafood including sturgeon, shark, and shellfish as well as meat. It's at 106 Wei Guo Road, and is open 11am to 2pm, and 4pm to 10pm. This restaurant is usually full at mealtimes so it's best to make a reservation, *Tel. 24599888, 24592027, 24349888.* It takes no credit cards and has no menu in English. But it's good and cheap, so bring a Chinese-speaking friend to help you order. It has grilled pork, fried pork spare ribs with preserved bean sauce, braised chicken with bean-and-flour noodles, and beef stew with white turnip.

Nanshi Food Street has shops, restaurants, wine shops, and tea houses – but very little English. The food here is from all over China and abroad, and includes typical Tianjin snacks such as *goubuli* (steamed meat dumpling), *erduoya*n (fried cake), and *shibajie* (deep-fried dough twist). Famous is the **Gubuli Baotze Restaurant**, 17, First Section, *Tel. 27270062,*

The **Ming Liu Tea House** has cross-talk only on Saturday evenings at 107 or 177 Xin Hua Road, *Tel. 27116382, 27116328.*

Seeing the Sights

The standard tour could include Ancient Culture Street, a temple, carpet factory, television tower, the Zhou Enlai Museum, European architecture, Food Street, and the New Year's Picture Factory. There's also the Art Museum, the Catholic Cathedral, and the Theater Museum. Ask about the ostrich farm, dinner in a farm house, and a children's palace. The **Dabei (Grand Mercy) Temple,** 40 Tianwei Road, near the Holiday Inn, *Tel. 26352320,* is the city's biggest Buddhist temple. It was founded in 1656 and houses the bones of famous monk Xuan Zang. It has a vegetarian restaurant.

The **Grand Mosque** is on Xiaohuo Alley, northwest corner of Hongqiao Dist., and was built in 1644 (Qing). *Tel. 27273422.* The **Tianjin History Museum,** 4 Guanghua Road, Tel. 24314660 contains exhibits on the ancient and revolutionary histories of Tianjin, and has some bronzes, jade, paintings, and calligraphy.

The **Tianjin Arts Museum,** 12 Chengde Road, *Tel. 23991127 or 23391127,* has sculptures and other traditional works of art from ancient times, and is highly recommended. The **Catholic Cathedral** is at 9 Xining Road, in Heping District, *Tel. 27301929.* It is next to the International Market and you can talk with staff there.

The **Zhou Enlai Museum** is at 20 Sima Street, Nankai, *Tel. 27371961.* The former premier studied at Nankai Middle School here from 1913 to 1917, and briefly at Nankai University (1919) where he led student uprisings. It has some titles in English.

The 100-room, 1875 **Grand Mansion of the Shi Family** is in a back alley off a park in Yangliuqing Township, Xiqing District. A 50-minute drive from downtown, it is worth seeing for the architecture and its folk arts, life-size models of a wedding sedan, a real wedding bed, and demonstrations of woodblock printing. It houses the **Yangliuqing Folk Museum** of New Year Pictures and clay figurines.

Near Food Street is **Ancient Culture Street** (Men Hui Jie) in Qing dynasty style, and the 1326 A.D. Temple of the Sea Goddess. But the street is nothing like Beijing's Liulichang or Nanjing's Confucian Temple area. I found nothing much to buy except traditional musical instruments. It does have a well-stocked antique shop and a tiny folk museum, *Tel. 22355062, 27357506.*

The **Theater Museum** (Guangdong Hui Guan)**,** 31 Nanmennei Street, Nankai District, Tel. 27273443, is a must for theater lovers. The building itself is a gem in the gaudy south China style, a guild hall for Guangdong merchants built in 1907. The **Television and Radio Tower** is 415.2 meters high and has a revolving restaurant. It's at 1 Jinzi Road, Hexi District, *Tel. 23343557.*

Nightlife & Entertainment

The bars in the hotels here are lively. The beach at Tanggu is "tacky." The **night cruise** on the river leaves from the pier at the Railway Station when there are enough customers around 8pm. It's cheap (Y10) and pleasant enough, if you like loud popular Chinese music and don't mind the occasional mosquito, but can be skipped as there isn't all that much to see. (Longer boat trips go from here during the day to the Shi Family Mansion at Yang Ling Qing town.)

Festivals are expected to be held at the Gulou, the Ancient Building Tower with dragon and stilt dancers and special exhibits for the Mazu Temple Fair which in 2002 falls on May 5. On the first Sunday of April is the International Marathon; the Rose Festival is in May; the Great Wall Mountain Produce Festival is in the autumn; and the New Year Picture Festival is during the Spring Festival. Cultural presentations here sometimes include traditional opera, Tianjin ballet, acrobats, and puppets and visits can be arranged through travel agents.

Sports & Recreation
You can bowl, or rent skates at the **ice rink** on the eleventh floor of Isetan Department Store (Jili Dasha), open 10am to midnight. Y30 an hour. *Tel. 27221086 ext. 166.* You can sip tea in a tea house and converse. See above.

Around Dong Li Lake with its underground hot springs, is a huge 50,000 square meter **swimming** pool with waves. This should open in 2002 along with **go-carting.** The lake itself is currently open for swimming and water sports in warm weather, *Tel. 24880668.* Dong Li Lake is between Tianjin and Tanggu. The Hyatt and Sheraton can arrange golf (maybe with a discount).

Shopping
The main shopping streets are the pedestrian Binjiang Dao and Heping Road, and Nanjing Road. Made in Tianjin are wool carpets, painted clay figurines by Master Zhang, New Year's pictures, porcelain vases, tablecloths, accordions, cloisonne, pens, soccer balls, basketballs, kites, jade, Dynasty wine, pictures painted on feathers, and inlaid lacquered furniture.

Tianjin Friendship Corporation is at 21 Youyi Road, Hexi District, 300201, *Tel. 28353159. E-mail: tjfriend@public.tpt.tj.cn.* It is open 9:30am-8:30pm. This department store sells most of the above and more. It also ships purchases, tailors clothes, and arranges certificates of origin and orders.

Isetan is a Japanese department store on Nanjing Road and an eight-minute taxi ride from the Hyatt. It is open 10am-8:30pm daily, *Tel. 27221111,* and sells major international brands and Japanese merchandise. Tse Sui Luen, the Hong Kong jewelery store is on the top floor. It accepts major credit cards. Packing and shipping service is available. Next door is the International Market Place, a local store with lower prices, services and quality.

The **Sheraton Hotel** has the largest amount of hotel shop space. When the Italian concession gets finished renovating, you should be able to buy things marked "Made in Italy."

The **Antique Market (Shen Yang Dao)** is open daily from about 8:30am-about 2pm with goods spread out for about seven blocks alongside three regular blocks of full-time more expensive antique shops. Individual peddlers let you peek inside their bags at what they hope you think is a genuine Ming vase. There must be over 100 merchants here with Victrolas, old handsewn clothes, jewelry, old silver and clocks. You can see plenty of cricket boxes. Be prepared for some hard haggling and crowds. **Tingbaozhai Antique Shop**, opposite the party school on Shandong Road, had lots of embroidered shoes for bound feet. *Tel. 13602181758* or evenings Ms. Zhang at *27303660*. These are private shops. The Bird and Flower Market is behind the Cathedral.

The Cultural Relics Shops are **Yilinge**, at 161 Liaoning Road, *Tel. 27110308*, **Cuiwenge**, on Ancient Culture Street, *Tel. 27275227* and **Wenyuange** at 191 Heping Road, *Tel. 27301338*.

Visit a Factory

Tianjin is a good place to visit factories. **Yangliuching New Year's Picture Studio,** Sanhe Lane, Tonglou, Hexi District, *Tel. 28351531* should show you how these charming folk prints are made. This company has a store on Ancient Culture Street. The **Number Two Carpet Factory,** Heiniucheng Road, Hexi District, *Tel. 28331920*, is one of the biggest carpet factories here, and has been making Junco-brand carpets for more than 100 years in Tianjin. These include thick carpets of pure wool, with no synthetics. Knots are made by hand, either 70 rows per square foot (ordinary) or 120 rows (refined). Embossing is also done by hand. Washing in a chemical solution adds gloss.

You can also visit and buy from factories making Pierre Cardin clothes, and Italian bicycles. The Sales Manager at the Hyatt should know about these factory outlets and about factory overruns at the Arts and Crafts Centre on Heping Road.

Note: visitors allergic to dust or wool should avoid carpet factories.

Excursions & Day Trips

Beidaihe and Qinhuangdao are 3.5 hours northeast by train. Other nearby excursions could include Beijing, Chengde, and the Qing Tombs.

Jixian City: ***Dule (Temple of Solitary Joy),** 170 km north, about two hours drive from the Hyatt, is in the western part of Jixian city and can be combined with a trip to Panshan Mountain, the Great Wall, and Qing Tombs in two days. It was founded in the Tang. Its Guanyin (Goddess of Mercy) Hall and the Gate to the Temple were rebuilt in 984 A.D. (Liao). The magnificent Guanyin Hall, 23 meters high, is the oldest existing multi-storied wooden structure in China. The 16-meter-high, 11-headed goddess is one of the largest clay sculptures in China. The **Great Wall at Huangyaguan** is 28 km north of Jixian County town. *Tel. 29718106*. It has a museum, and usually is free of peddlers and tourists and can be reached in less time from Beijing. See also Beijing, Great Wall.

The **Panshan (Screen of Green) Mountain** (about 12 km north of Jixian City, *Tel. 29143954*) has been a mountain resort since the Tang. The highest peak is 1000 meters above sea level, on top of which is a pagoda said to contain a tooth of Buddha. Its 70 Buddhist temples were burned by the Japanese during World War II. Some of the buildings have been replaced or renovated. This is an overnight trip, especially good in the autumn. The Hyatt once said it can arrange for you to stay in an old Chinese house. There are two trains a day between Tianjin and Jixian town, taking almost three hours each way.

Zunhua (Tsunhua) is in Hebei province, about 125 km northeast of Tianjin and 135 km east of Beijing. It's a day trip from these two cities. Among the **imperial Qing tombs** (built 1743-1799) at **Dongling (Eastern Tombs)** are those of Emperor Qianlong (Chien Lung) at Yuling. Qianlong was the man who snubbed Britain's envoy. He is buried with his five wives. A devout Buddhist and patron of the arts, his tomb is covered with religious statues and sutras in Indian, Tibetan, Chinese, Manchurian, and Mongolian.

The tombs of **Empress Dowager Cixi (Tzu Hsi)** and **Empress Cian** are together at Dongling, about one km from Qianlong's. Cixi was the fascinating, outrageous, scheming, brilliant, scandalous but short-sighted woman who built the Summer Palace in Beijing. Her tomb, covered with phoenixes deliberately and arrogantly placed above the dragons (symbolizing the emperor), was completed in 1873 and renovated in 1895, with an additional 4,590 taels of gold as decoration. She died in 1908.

Both mausoleums can be entered. The carving is more elaborate than that in the Ming tombs, with Buddhist sutras (in Tibetan and Sanskrit) and figures inside. You can study an exhibition of her clothes, utensils, a coat for her dog, and photos. Her tomb was robbed in 1928 by a Nationalist warlord who used explosives to open it. He stripped over 500 pearls off her clothes.

Like the Ming tombs, there is also an animal-lined Sacred Way, the figures here smaller but more elaborately carved. It seems each dynasty tried to outdo its predecessors, the Ming being more elaborate than the Song (see Zhengzhou). The tombs of the emperors and empresses have glazed yellow roofs. Tombs of lesser importance have green roofs.

The Qing Tombs here are less spread out than the Ming Tombs. At least six of the 15 are open to the public. The atmosphere is quieter, less commercial. In the vicinity live 10,000 Manchu farmers.

The **Xiling (Western Tombs)**, 120 km southwest of Beijing at Yixian are not as illustrious. The 14 mausoleums hold the remains of Emperors Yongzhen (Tailing), Jiaqing (Changling), Daoguang (Muling), and Guangxu (Chongling), plus the usual retinue of wives and children. Visitors can enter Chongling, the last royal tomb in China, but it has no funeral objects as it was robbed.

Practical Information

China Travel Service-Tianjin, *Olympic Tower, 3rd floor, Chengdu Road, 300050, Tel. 23552035, 23552036, Fax 23552032. Mobile: 13902194792. Email: tour@public.tpt.tj.cn. Website: www.tjcts.com. Ask for Louie Liu,*

Manager of Overseas Tourist Dept. It charges $25 a day for an English-speaking guide.

CITS Ticket booking office. *Ground floor, 22 Youyi Road, 300074. Tel. 28350822, 28358866.* Ask for Ms. Li Li.

Tianjin China International Travel Service/Tianjin Overseas Tourism Co., *22 Youyi Road, 300074, Tel. 28350104, 28138231, Fax 28358974. E-mail: citstj@public.tpt.tj.cn.* Ask for Ms. Tang Feng Wei or Mr. Zheng Wei. It has study tours, homestays in farm houses, and traditional medicine tours. It charges Y20 to book one flight and Y200 a day for a guide for one or two English-speaking visitors.

Helpful websites: The *Tianjin Telegraph* has a helpful online newsletter, *www.tianjintelegraph.com,* for expatriates in Tianjin published by Kevin van der Laan. He can be reached at: *summitgraphics@bigfoot.com.* This newsletter gives images of Tianjin, reports of Hash House Harriers events, bus lines, postage prices, supermarkets and schools.

Telephone code: 22

Shijiazhuang

(Shihchiachuang)

This capital of Hebei province has a total population of six million, **Shijiazhuang** is primarily an industrial city manufacturing textiles and pharmaceuticals.

It is of importance to Chinese revolutionary history as the burial place of the Canadian who became a Chinese hero. Dr. Norman Bethune arrived in China in 1938 to help the Communist Eighth Route Army in its fight against the Japanese. Working almost in the front lines, he died of blood poisoning on November 12, 1939, in Huangshikou village, Tangxian county, in Hebei.

That year, Chairman Mao wrote a much publicized article, pointing him out as an example of utter devotion to others without any thought of self. He became known to every school child, and statues were made of him all over the country. Highly recommended is the Canadian feature film, Bethune, the Making of a Hero.

Arrivals & Departures

Shijiazhuang is 282 km/2.5 hours by train south of Beijing, on the main line to Guangzhou, east of the Taihang Mountains on the Hebei Plain. It is also three hours by the 224-km long Jingshi Expressway with Beijing, and now linked by air with 12 Chinese cities and Hong Kong. The airport is 33 km from city center and is one of Beijing's alternatives, should Beijing's airport be unexpectedly closed.

Where to Stay & Eat

The only internationally-managed hotel is the Crowne Plaza. Services in the others are not as good.

CROWNE PLAZA SHIJIAZHUANG, *303 ZhongShan Dong Road, 050011. Tel. 6678888, 6671694. Five stars. Website: www.sixcontinentshotels.com. It is 38 km from the airport and about 3.5km from the train station.*

Opened in 2002, this centrally-located 238-room hotel is opposite the Hebei Museum and Square and close to shopping and the city hall. Rooms have high speed internet access, VOD, safes, and voice mail. It has four executive floors and is the only hotel in town with an expatriate chef and an Italian Food & Beverage Manager.

HEBEI GRAND HOTEL (Binguan), *168 Yucai Road, 050021. Four stars, Tel. 5815961, Fax 5814092. Y480-Y750 for rooms and Y980-Y16800 for suites.*

It has Continental, American, Japanese and Western food. It is two km from city center, 15 km from the airport, and four km from the railway station.

INTERNATIONAL HOTEL, *301 East Zhongshan Road, 050011. Three stars. Tel. 6044321, Fax 6034787. E-mail: gdhotel.sjz@sjz.col.com.cn. This is 25 km from the airport, 2 km from the railway station and in the city center. Y480-Y690 and Y790-Y3880 for suites.*

Seeing the Sights

Among its many temples and pagodas are the Longxing Temple, the Zhaozhou Qiao Bridge, and the Hangying Palace, none of which are internationally famous.

The **Bethune International Peace Hospital**, first set up in 1937 in the Shanxi-Chahar-Hebei Military Area, was moved here in 1948. Dr. Bethune is buried in the western part of the North China Revolutionary Martyrs' Cemetery, where there is also the Bethune Exhibition Hall and the Memorial Hall for Revolutionary Martyrs. The city also has the Hebei Provincial Exhibition Hall and Museum.

Shopping

Locally made are painted-on-the-inside snuff bottles, paper cuts, and ceramics. There are also white marble carvings from Quyang County, and Liuling wine. Elsewhere in the province are made golden-thread tapestry (Zhuoxian), shell crafts (Qinhuangdao), horse saddles (Zhangjiakou), ink slabs (Yishui), woven straw (Chengde), Handan ceramics, and Tangshan porcelain.

Practical Information

Hebei Overseas Tourist Corporation/CITS, *175 Yucai Street, Tel. 5815102, 5821994, Fax 5816047, 5815368. E-mail: otchb2@info.net.*
Telephone code: 311.

Chengde

(Chengteh, Chengte, Jehol, Jehe)

This historic mountain resort is in Hebei province, 250 km northeast of Beijing. It is at an altitude of 340 meters with a total population, including counties, of 764,000 people.

Chengde oozes with history. The Qing court lived here from May to October each year. It was in a yurt here in 1793 that Lord Macartney of Britain refused to kowtow to Qing Emperor Qianlong. The emperor dismissed the Englishman as a bearer of tribute from King George III, and refused his requests for trade.

In 1860, the Manchu court fled to Chengde as Anglo-French forces approached Beijing. The death of Emperor Xianfeng in 1862 led to the rise of Cixi, the Empress Dowager, as regent. Think of the plotting that went on as he lay on his deathbed here. Cixi visited here again, by train, in 1900.

In the 1930s, warlord Tang Yu Liu looted and destroyed many of the buildings. The most important have been repaired. Chengde's coldest temperature is -19 C; the hottest is 35 C for a very short time. Most rain falls in June and July.

Arrivals & Departures

Panda Tours has a two-day, one-night package tour that leaves Beijing Railway Station about 7am. It includes an English-speaking guide, hotel transfers, a tour of the summer resort and sightseeing of the Eight Outer Temples. There are four meals, hotel, and a return early afternoon on the second day. You should be able to stay longer if you pay for other nights in a hotel. *Website: www.chinaonlinetravel.com/pandatours/pandacde.htm.* Contact CITS in Beijing.

You can also do this trip on your own since there are only two places to see. You can go by bus from Beijing in about 2 1/2 hours. You can hire a car and follow the Great Wall past Simatai and Jinshan Ling in one day. (In the last century a one-way trip took the Manchus three to 20 days by horseback, palanquin, or bumpy chariot).

Orientation

The Qing Imperial Summer Resort was built for Emperors Kangxi and Qianlong, not just to relax in, but to curry favor with the Mongolian nobles in the area. To help win them over, Emperor Kangxi (1703-1790) built 12 Buddhist temples also. Chengde is well worth seeing, especially if you don't go to Tibet. It is one of the 24 historical cities protected by the State Council and is a UNESCO heritage site. The Imperial Summer Resort covers an area of 5.6 million square meters, which is larger than the Summer Palace in Beijing.

Most of it is surrounded by a 10-km-long wall. These two places are at the edge of town and quite close together.

Where to Stay & Eat

The best hotel is the four-star, 70-room Qianyang Hotel, built in 1998. Tours stay also at the Yunshan Hotel. The Qiwanlou Hotel beside the Summer Palace has a new building.

QIANYANG HOTEL, *18 Pule Road, Shuang Qiao District, 067000. Four stars. Tel. 2057000, 2057058, Fax 2057777, 2057169.*

YUNSHAN HOTEL, *6 Nanyuan Dong Road, 067000. Three stars. Tel. 2156171, Fax 2154551.*

Seeing the Sights

You can explore the main palace and garden in half a day and five of the outer temples on a second day. If you rush and avoid the climb to the Club Stone, you can cover all the open temples and the summer resort in one full, hurried day. You can get around in an electric cart that holds seven people, with many stops, for Y200.

The **Imperial Summer Resort** has nine courtyards. It is not as palatial as Beijing's Summer Palace, but it is worth seeing. The building to the right inside the second gate has a painting of the Macartney visit and a hunting scene with officials wearing animal head masks and imitating mating calls to attract the animals.

To the left of the entrance is the Hall of No Worldly Lust but True Faith, also called the Nanmu Hall because of the scented wood from which it is made. The emperor received subjects and envoys in this ceremonial hall. On either side are waiting rooms, one for foreign visitors and one for relatives and tribal leaders. Among the exhibits in these and other halls are Manchu robes with sleeves shaped like horses hooves, sedan chairs, an elephant dotted with pearls, and brilliant blue kingfisher feather ornaments. In a hall displaying fine porcelain are Qing imitations of Ming vases.

The Refreshing-at-Mist-Veiled-Waters Pavilion was the imperial bedroom. On either side are the pavilions of the two empresses. The imperial bedroom has a hollow wall (seen from the back) where Cixi listened carefully as the emperor lay dying inside. As a result of her eavesdropping, she was able to seize power. Cixi lived in the Pine Crane Pavilion, which was originally built for the mother of Emperor Qianlong. The emperor used the two-story pavilion beyond to enjoy the moon with his concubines. It has no interior stairs.

The garden is beautiful and great for walks. Visitors should be able to rent ice skates and bicycles. The trees planted by the Qing are tagged with identification numbers. These two influential emperors chose 72 scenic spots and wrote poems about each. Kangxi's poems have four characters; Qianlong's have three. Of these places, thirty are still marked by pavilions from which you can enjoy the view, including one on the top of the hill to view the snow. There is even one to view the Club Stone.

Among the buildings counterclockwise around the lake is the Jinshan Pavilion, copied from one of the same name in Zhenjiang, and the Yanyulou (Misty-Rain Tower), the latter built by Qianlong, a copy of one now destroyed in Zhejiang. It was used to watch the misty rain, of course, and to read.

On the flatland area here, Emperor Qianlong stooped to receive the equally arrogant Lord Macartney, the envoy from Britain. The walled garden on the Changlang Islet is a copy of the Changlang Garden in Suzhou. Some people collect postcards when they travel; the Qianlong emperor collected buildings! Nearby, on a side road, is a herd of spotted deer, started here during the Qing because some of the emperors drank deer's blood as a tonic.

The two-story Imperial Library has a pond in front and a few trees as a precaution against fire. The library is a copy of one in Shaoxing. It is approached through the rockeries. If you notice tourists in front of the library staring into the water, its because they are looking for the reflection of a crescent moon.

As a Chinese garden, this imperial summer resort is one of the best, a microcosm of the whole country with buildings, lake, grasslands, and mountains.

The **Eight Outer Temples** outside the walls are a mixture of Manchu, Mongolian, Tibetan, and Han Chinese architecture with a similar mix of artifacts inside. Once housing 1,000 lamas or monks, they are now primarily museums. The steles usually have Manchu writing in front, Chinese behind, and Mongolian and Tibetan on the sides. If you are short of time, the Putuozongsheng and Puning are the most important to include. Otherwise, start with the ***Pule**, which is also known as the Round Pavilion, as it was built in 1766 to resemble the Temple of Heaven. Inside is a statue of two hard-to-see copulating gods from the tantric sect of Tibetan Buddhism. From this temple you can climb or take a cable car to the Club Stone, the giant, mallet-shaped stone, for a marvelous view.

The small Anyuan Temple is patterned after a temple in Xinjiang that no longer exists. Inside is a statue of Lu Du Mo, a female goddess. The Puren should be open for your visit.

Inside the gate of the ***Puning Temple** is a stele about Qianlong's suppression of a rebellion of the minorities. The Puning Temple contains a copy of the spectacular 1,000-headed and 1,000-armed Guan Yin, Goddess of Mercy, which should not be missed. Actually he/she has only 42 hands and arms, each representing 25. On each palm is an eye. The statue in Mahayana Hall is 22.28 meters high. A warlord stole the original.

The Puning Temple is patterned after the Sumeru temple in Tibet and is known also as the Temple of Universal Peace or Big Buddha Temple. Inside are a drum and a bell tower, a laughing Buddha, and four guardian kings. About 100 larger-than-life-size arhats remain of the original 508; the others were destroyed by fire. Only eight of the saints are Chinese. The mural of the 18 arhats is 230 years old and original, remarkable for its preservation. Look for the big bronze cooking pot that fed 1,000 lamas. The number of buildings and stupas are symbolic. The center of the world was Sumeru Mountain, with four great continents around it.

In the Puning have been live, chanting red-robed monks, probably from Inner Mongolia and Qinghai on a three-year contract. They chant every morning. If you can't go to Tibet, this is the place to come.

The **Xumifushou (Longevity and Happiness) Temple** was inspired by the Tashilhunpo/Zhaxilhunbu Temple in Shigatse, Tibet, and used as a residence for the sixth Panchen Lama. Dragons seem to scamper along the edges of the roof, most unusual for a Han temple. Built in 1780, it is the newest of the temples and commemorates Qianlong's 70th birthday, at which point he started to learn Tibetan. In the main building is a statue of the founder of Lamaism and behind him Sakyamuni. The tent-like pagoda in the back is similar to the one in Fragrant Hill Park in Beijing.

The *Putuozongcheng Temple** is patterned after the Potala Palace, home of the Dalai Lama, in Lhasa. It was built from 1767 to 1771 for the 60th birthday of Qianlong and for the 80th birthday of his mother. The elephant symbolizes the Mahayana sect. (One elephant equals 500 horses.) The five pagodas on several of the buildings symbolize the five schools of Buddhism. Dancers might perform here.

Not to be missed is the **Donggang Zi Dian (East Hall)**. Statues here are from the Red Sect of Tibetan Buddhism, where sex with a person other than one's spouse was part of the religious ritual. In the opposite hall on the same level are other metal Buddhist statues. Another 164 steps lead up to the main building, which is decorated by Buddhas in the niches – the 80 at the top representing Qianlong's life. Some birthday cake! The temple was built to commemorate the birthdays, as well as a visit by tribal leaders. This temple is the largest. Finally, the Yongning Temple, built in 1751, is worth a quick look.

Practical Information

Chengde China Travel Service, *2nd floor, No 1 Government Comprehensive Building, Tel. 2035321, 2030741, Fax 2028930.* It charges Y100 for an English-speaking guide for 1-2 visitors for a day. Ask for Feng Yonghong.

Telephone code: 314.

Qinhuangdao

(Chinwangtao)

The huge city of **Qinhuangdao** at the northeastern tip of Hebei province on the Bohai Sea, and 280 km east of Beijing, encompasses three separate districts and five counties. It has a total population of 2.6 million of whom 600,000 live in its urban areas. With its ice-free harbour, Qinhuangdao is one of China's busiest ports and is joined to a nearby oil field by a pipeline.

Originally a small village, Qinhuangdao was opened as a seaport in 1898 and became a base for foreign shipping. In 1902 the British army built a small pier. The railway was finished in 1916.

The city is named after a legend. The Qin emperor passed through here about 2,200 years ago looking for pills of longevity. Suddenly, he recognized a special tree described by his teacher. Surprised and afraid, he bowed to the tree and a branch bowed back.

Qinhuangdao includes the resort town of **Beidaihe**, the favorite seaside beach of Beijing people, including its political leaders. Some districts are industrial and commercial. There's also the walled city of **Shanhaiguan** where the Great Wall meets the sea, a swimming beach, a chair lift up the mountain following the Great Wall, and a nearby lake.

So where should you relax with your family? The hotels in Beidaihe are larger than Shanhaiguan's, the beaches longer, some with life guards. Both places have very crowded swimming areas with umbrellas and chairs for hire. Beidaihe has more facilities for tourists and is closer to the beaches of Changyi County and Golden Beach.

On the other hand, Shanhaiguan has the Great Wall at one end of its beach. There are no life guards. (The scenery at the other end is pretty industrial with petroleum tanks.) Those who prefer basking in the shadow of history should come here and only look south. The Gloria is the only international hotel this close to the whole of the Great Wall. It is cheaper and less crowded than the Beidaihe hotels, has fewer services, quite a bit of English, and is okay.

Arrivals & Departures

Near Beijing train station, there are buses to Qinhuangdao every day taking three to four hours. During summer time, the buses stop at Beidaihe first. Beidaihe is about 45 km from Shanhaiguan and 25 km south of Qinhuangdao.

Qinhuangdao is a 2.5 hour express train trip from Beijing Railway Station. The closest airport is near Shanhaiguan. Flights arrive from 10 other cities but not daily. Migrating birds also make Qinhuangdao a stop in autumn and winter.

Orientation

From north to south along the coast, minibuses go from Shanhaiguan with a stop at the Great Wall, 25km to downtown Qinhuangdao. There you change buses and go about 25 km to Beidaihe. It costs Y5 for each leg. In between Qinhuangdao and Beidaihe are the Sea Sports Club and the Qin emperor's theme park.

Where to Stay
Shanhaiguan
The best place to stay in Shanhaiguan is the Gloria which is a ten-minute walk to the Great Wall.

GLORIA HOLIDAY VILLAS QINHUANGDAO (Kailai or Haisheng Binguan), *Shanhaiguan Economic Technological Development Zone, Huan Hai Nan Road, 066206. Three stars. Tel. 5081688, or fax 5081919. In Beijing Tel. 10-65158508, Fax 65155273. E-mail: gih.Beijing@gloriahotels.com. Website: www.gloriahotels.com. A tiny taxi from the Qinhuangdao train station costs about Y41. Rooms are Y480-Y528 and suites Y980-Y3888. It has been giving 20% to 40% discounts to walk-ins in low season. It has had a family package of Y360 a room Sundays to Thursdays and there are very good long-stay villas.*

Just don't expect the five-star quality of the Gloria's sister resort in Sanya. This one only has 106 rooms in eight villas and one three-story building. It has a sauna, billiards, and a gym. Gloria took over this resort in 2000 and will be upgrading it with in-room safes. It should get BBC television soon. It accepts credit cards but not travelers' checks and can book tickets. There's a Chinese restaurant and small coffee shop. The public beach across the road in front is very popular and has chairs and umbrellas for rent. It has no life guards and the water is not tested for E. coli. Nearby is an interesting fishing village and modest seafood restaurant where dinner for two can cost Y47. If you're energetic, you can continue on to the shipyard.

Qinhuangdao District City
This is primarily a commercial and industrial city. The hotels here are more for businesspeople. The Great Wall Hotel seems slightly better and more polished. Both have stained carpets.

QINHUANGDAO INTERNATIONAL HOTEL (Guoji Fandian), *330 Wenhua Bei Road, Qinhuangdao, Tel. 3083083, Fax 3604783. E-mail: qhdgjfd@public.qhptt.he.cn. Website: www.qhdih.com. Rooms are Y600 and suites Y960-Y4800. It has been discounting 10 to 30%.*

Twenty of its 175 rooms come with computers and its in-room safes are big. It has non-smoking and executive floors. The English is poor but it has the best food. It also has bowling, a lighted outdoor tennis court, gym, and an 18-meter-long indoor pool. The mold and grouting are bad.

GREAT WALL HOTEL (Changcheng Jiudian), *202 Yanshan St., Qinhuangdao, 066001. Four stars. Tel. 3061666, Fax 3061075. E-mail: qhdgwh@public.qhptt.he.cn. Website: www.gwhotel.com. Rooms with break-*

fast range from Y580 to Y620, and suites Y1000 to Y6800. It has been discounting 20% and accepts credit cards. Six rooms have computers and safes.

This hotel is okay but no one understands English in the business center. It has no pool but it has a gym, Jacuzzi, sauna, tennis court, and billiards.

Beidaihe

While no international-standard luxury resorts exist here, the best, the Jinshan Hotel, is pretty good and is half a block from the best beach. The second best is the Beidaihe International Club Hotel (but it's not on a beach and you have to cross a busy highway to get to it). The Beidaihe Guesthouse for Diplomatic Missions is on a beach and is okay.

Some beach houses on West Beach belong to the Party Central Committee, so during the summer ordinary people are not allowed near.

JINSHAN HOTEL (Binguan), *4, the Third Road of East Beach, 066100. Three stars. Tel. 4041338, Fax 4042478. E-mail: jinshan@public.qhptt.he.cn. It is closed the end of October to April 15. Rooms in high season are Y520-Y620 (low season is Y380), and Y780-Y980 for suites (low Y580-Y780). It takes credit cards and travelers' checks but has no CNN.*

It has 267 rooms in five two-story buildings, a business center and should be doing some renovations in spring 2002.

BEIDAIHE GUESTHOUSE FOR DIPLOMATIC MISSIONS (Wai-jiao-ren-yuan Binguan), *No. 1, Baosan Road, 066100, Tel.4041287, Fax 4041807. Website: www.dphotel.com.cn (Chinese only). Its representative office in Beijing is East Gate, Building No.12, Dongzhimenwai Street, Chao Yang Districts, Tel. 10/65324336, 64175849. This guesthouse is usually open May to mid-October. Rooms range fromY380 to Y780, and a villa apartment Y1580 in high season (July and August). In low season, it's Y200 to Y550 for rooms, Y780 for a suite, and Y1180 for a villa apartment.*

This has 150 rooms in 11 buildings and two villas, placed close together. Rooms have CNN, but no safes. It is on a beach with no life guards. Rooms are air-conditioned. It has tennis, billiards, a gym, massage, and karaoke hall.

Where to Eat

Your best bet is the hotels. In Beidaihe, there's also the simple **Hai Tian Xiang** on Dong Jing Road with a menu in English, about five minutes walk from CITS and near the Jin Sha Hotel. *Tel. 4047159.* It has noodles, seafood, crispy deep-fried prawns or prawns cooked in their shells, chicken and pork, at cheaper prices than the hotels. It has squat toilets. A small bowl of noodles and a plate of shrimp can cost Y45.

The historical **Kiessling Bakery and Restaurant** (Qishilin) is very expensive and has Western-type food. Its at 96 Dongjing Road, Beidaihe, *Tel. 4049220.*

Seeing the Sights

Shanhaiguan

Laolongtou (Old Dragon Head), the place where the Great Wall meets the sea, is four km south of Shanhaiguan city. Chenghai Tower, on the seashore, was originally built in 1579. It has been rebuilt and decorated with "soldiers" in Ming costumes. There is also a recent reconstruction of a 1622 military camp that was used to train the marine corps. This camp was destroyed by the eight foreign powers in 1900. Signs are in English but there's not much to see, and it has a smelly toilet. A small temple to the Sea Goddess is nearby. Fee Y40.

The **Great Wall Festival** in June has races, 18 to 40 km, up and down the Wall. It also has costumed Ming and Qing performances, lantern shows and large scale fireworks at Old Dragon Head.

At Jiao Shan, where the Great Wall rises steeply about five km from the sea, there is an 1,833 meter-long chair lift almost to the top. It operates 7:30am to 7pm, and costs Y20. *Tel. 5052916.* The view is wonderful but some of the paths are unpaved. Old Shanhaiguan is surrounded by a well-maintained wall of its own.

About six km north is the **Meng Jiang-nu Temple,** built in memory of another of China's chaste, almost supernatural heroines. Mme. Meng traveled on foot during the winter in search of her husband, one of the hundreds of thousands of men forced to work on the Wall. Her deep sorrow and tears moved Heaven so much that the Great Wall collapsed to reveal her husband's bones. The temple was originally built in the Song dynasty, but the Red Guards destroyed the statues. The government restored them in the late 1970s in gaudy, crudely-painted clay. But the view of the hills to the north is interesting.

Between Qinhuangdao and Beidaihe, there are two places of interest:

The **Park of the Shrine of Emperor Qin's Quest for Immortality** is about a 15 km/30-minute drive from Beidaihe towards Qinhuangdao. Take buses No. 3 or 4. It is at 56 Nansan Street, Hai Gang District. *Tel/Fax 3410987.* This is a 19-hectare theme park based on the first emperor's search for pills of immortality. The park is full of dioramas and buildings representing historical and mythological events from other dynasties as well. Bring your own guide because there's no English. Bring a flashlight to see some of the archaeological specimens. The place needs fixing up and repainting and takes between 40 minutes to two hours to see – if you want to see it all. It has an amusement park and a restaurant.

The **Sea Sports Club** is at 22 Wenti Road, *Tel. 8051474.* It is about 9 km from Beidaihe towards Qinhuangdao. It is one of the rare places in China where you can rent sail boards. They are over-priced at Y100 an hour here but you don't have much choice. You can also rent sail boats for Y200 an hour, and scuba one hour for Y300. If you can't speak Chinese, ask CITS Beidaihe to help you since no one speaks English. There's also a wildlife park in Qinhuangdao, and an **Underwater World** in nearby Xin-ao.

Beidaihe

Beidaihe is primarily a seaside resort, built after the completion of the Beijing-Shanhaiguan railway in 1893. By 1949, 706 villas and hotel buildings had been completed, many of them for foreign diplomats and missionaries as well as wealthy Chinese. After Liberation, the Chinese government rebuilt some of the old buildings and added new ones as rest and recreation centers for its employees. The urban population is around 20,000.

This resort stretches along 12 km of hard, golden sand sloping gently out into the **Bohai Sea**. Swimming is good, too though there may be a few jellyfish. Rock promontories divide the beaches. At the Pigeons Nest in the east, you can look at Qinhuangdao across the bay and the best sunrise. At the Tiger Stone in the center, crab fishermen sell their catch in the summer.

Several swimming areas are attached to each of the hotels, manned by life guards and protected by nets. Each hotel has changing rooms on the beach with hot and cold fresh-water showers. The swimming season is from May to September, depending on how cold you like your water. The hottest days are in August (maximum 36°C for a few days), but the high is usually 31°C, sometimes dropping to 24° or 25°C at night.

A **Guanyin Temple**, built in 1911, is on the grounds of the West Hill Hotel. The Red Guards destroyed it and the government restored it and two statues and frescoes in 1979. The temple is about 1.5 km behind the hotel's service bureau, a nice walk. The **Xiaobaohezhai Village** is also a good place to visit. It was one of the first in China to have pensions for its older citizens and one of the first with a birth-control program. It grows apples, peaches and pears for export, so an ideal time to visit is late August-September.

Dong Shan (East Mountain) is where the Qin emperor searched for the pills of longevity and boarded his ships. There's a good view of the sea and the sunrise. You can visit a shell-carving factory and the Sea God Temple.

An incredible seaside playground built by Changli County is located less than 60 km south of Beidaihe. It has fake castles, sand-slides, water-slides, cabanas, hotels, amusement parks - none of which appears to be up to North American standards. Only foreigners wanting a do-nothing seaside vacation with something to amuse the children would probably be interested.

The **Great Wall Wine Factory** is located at Changli County which is over one hour's drive from Beidaihe. The Golden Beach (Changli Huang Jin Hai An) here is one of the best in the area.

Shopping

Grown locally are peaches, pears, sea cucumbers, and crabs (biggest in September-October). Made locally are shell pictures, lamps and ashtrays. Also manufactured are mirrors, magnifying glasses, painted eggs, painted stones, butterfly and insect specimens, bird-feather crafts, and necklaces of red beans (symbol of longing between lovers).

Practical Information

Beidaihe CITS has an office in the Qinhuangdao International Hotel, *330 Wenhua Road, 066001. Tel. 3890115, Fax 3890119.*

Qinhuangdao Haiyan International Agency, *4 Apartment Building A Qinxin Garden, Hebei Street, Tel. 3733373, 3044666, Fax 3045558. E-mail: qhyits@heinfo.net , Haiyan001@0335.net, or qhyits@pop.heinfo.net.* It has 10 full time English-speaking guides. It also has walking tours of the Great Wall. Ask for Wenjun Shi.

CITS Beidaihe International Travel Service, *4 Jinshan Zui Road, Beidaihe 066100, Tel. 4041748, Fax 4031890. E-mail: bits@0335.net.* It can arrange boats and sailboarding at the Sea Sports Club. Its one-day tour includes the Great Wall, Yan Sai Lake, and the Grape Village. It has bird-watching tours, especially good in May, September and October for red-crested cranes (autumn only), Saunder's gulls and Relict gulls. It can make arrangements for trekking along the total length of the Great Wall. For a room at the Beidaihe Jinshan Hotel it charges $60, Friendship Hotel $50, Beidaihe International Club $56, Qinhuangdao International Hotel $55, Qinhuangdao Great Wall Hotel $55, Shanhaiguan Gloria Resort $40. Ask for Yuzhen (Jean) Wang, General Manager, who has been very helpful in providing information for this book.

Teaching English: Try the **BFSUBTC**, a branch school of the Beijing Foreign Studies University. It's near the beach. *Telephone 4049907, Fax 4049917.* Contact: Ms Zhang Bao-dan (Dianna) or Miss Lu (Belinda). *Mailing address: Lanlou, Yingliao Rd., Beidaihe, 066100. E-mail: bfsubtc@heinfo.net or Zhangbd@netease.com, or isabelalu@hotmail.com.*

Telephone code: for the whole of Qinhuangdao is 335.

Taiyuan

Taiyuan is in the center of industrial Shanxi province, of which it is the capital. It has several interesting tourist attractions, one certified world class. Best known up to recently for its Jinci Temple and pilgrimages to nearby Wutai Mountain, Taiyuan is now known for its nearby Ancient Pingyao City.

Taiyuan was founded in the Western Zhou (1066-771 B.C.). Because of its strategic location, it was the site of many battles, changing hands five times between 396 and 618 A.D. It was a silk center under the Sui and has been growing grapes for a thousand years.

The hottest temperature is 35°C for a few days in August; the coldest is -14°C in January. The annual precipitation is 400 mm mostly from July to September, and the altitude is 800 meters. The urban population is 2.04 million.

Arrivals & Departures

Taiyuan is over an hour's flight southwest of Beijing, and 2.5 hours north of Guangzhou. It can be reached by air from Hong Kong and 28 other Chinese cities. By train from Beijing, it's about 10 hours, Xi'an 13 hours, Hohhot 12 hours, and Datong 5.5 hours. By express air-conditioned bus, it can be reached in six hours from Beijing 540 km away, ten from Xi'an, eight from Hohhot, and five from Datong. Long distance buses leave for Beijing every 15 to 30 minutes between 7am and 3pm from the Jian Nan Chi Che Zhan bus station in Taiyuan. *Tel. 7074539.* Buses for Pingyao leave from here too. This is a new modern building with orange chairs. Touts tend to grab you and pull you to their buses.

Where to Stay

The friendly Shanxi Grand Hotel is the best in town for English-speaking guests. The Yingze looked good. Hotels add a 10 or 15% service charge.

SHANXI GRAND HOTEL (Shanxi Dajiudian), *5 Xin Jian Nan Road, 030001, Tel. 4043901, Fax 4043525. E-mail: sales@shanxigrandhotel.com. Website: www.shanxigrandhotel.com (English). It accepts credit cards and travelers checks. Rooms range from $75 to $105 (March to December) and $70 to $95 (January and February). Suites range from $190 to $370 (March to December) and $170 to $350 in January and February. It has been giving a 20% discount to walk-in and repeat guests. It is 16 km from the airport.*

Opened in 1989, this hotel has 14 stories, and 168 rooms, CNN, Cantonese and Shanghai restaurants. There's an indoor pool, bowling, and a gym. Safes are in rooms on some floors.

YINGZE HOTEL, *189 Yingze Street, Tel. 4043211, Fax 4043784. It has 294 rooms. Four stars. Rooms range from Y480 to Y580, and suites from Y970 to Y6800. It has been giving a 20% discount and accepts credit cards.*

This hotel has had a Y58 buffet dinner labeled only in Chinese. Its two-star East Building built in 1945 has 163 rooms; its four-star West Building, built in 1976, has 294 rooms. It is putting in central air-conditioning. This hotel needs polishing. Some floors were recently renovated, and some rooms are non-smoking rooms. Rooms have hot and cold drinking water always available. The grouting is moldy.

Where to Eat

Shanxi people love noodles and vinegar-flavored dishes. It is best to eat in the main hotels. Five hundred-meter-long Food Street, in the southern part of the city, has 46 food shops and restaurants. There's the **Xiangjiang**

Restaurant at 155 Fuxi Street, *Tel. 3534518*, and the **Sanqiao Hotel Restaurant**, 4 Hanxi Guan, Xin Jian Bei Road, *Tel. 3045885.*

Seeing the Sights

The **Jinci Temple,** 25 km southwest of the city is at the foot of Xuanweng Mountain. One source says it was initially built in the Northern Wei (386-534) in memory of the second son of King Wu of the Western Zhou. The Jin Temple was renovated, with additions, in 1102 (Northern Song). The temple has female statues, which, aside from goddesses, is very rare in China. Was this second son a lush? A son much pampered by women? Are the women here to continue indulging him in the after-life?

Alas, no! Centuries ago, Shanxi was very short of water. Sea and water deities have usually been female. In Shanxi a spring was found near Jinci, so people started worshipping Shuimu (Mother of Water). The maids-in-waiting and the mermaids were her retinue.

The temple is the oldest wooden structure in the area and is charming. In the Shengmu (Sacred Lay Hall) are 43 dusty, lifesize clay figures, 30 of these court maids-in-waiting, all lithesome, each different in expression, and still retaining much color. They were made in the Song.

The **Chongshan Monastery** in the city itself is believed to have been a Sui palace once. Only part of the original (Tang) monastery is standing, and part of that is the Shanxi Provincial Museum. The monastery is famous for its ancient 1000-handed, 1000-eyed Goddess of Mercy. It, along with the two other bodhisattvas are eight meters tall. The beams and ceiling are quite remarkable. It is three km from the Yingze Hotel.

Next door is the **Shanxi Provincial Museum** with a vast collection of neolithic artifacts. **Provincial Museum Number Two** is considered more important than Museum Number One. Located at the site of the Chunyang Palace on the west side of May 1 Square, the palace itself was built between 1573 and 1619, and renovated in the Qing. It contains 20 exhibition halls with ceramics, bronzes, carvings, lacquer, calligraphy, embroidery, books, and other documents unearthed around the province. There is also a huge coal museum.

The **Shuangta Temple,** also known as the Yongzuo Monastery, has twin pagodas, symbols of Taiyuan, eight km from the Yingze Hotel. The pagodas were built in the Ming and are over 50 meters high. They are octagonal and of carved bricks. Inside the monastery are exhibitions of old coins, pottery, etc., and a corridor with 207 stone tablets of Ming calligraphy.

Shopping

Locally made are fur coats, including rabbit and wild rat(!) skin, gold and lacquer inlaid crafts, reproductions of ancient ironware, black-glazed porcelain, Junco brand carpets, Fen Chiew wines, vinegars, fine glassware, lacquerware, jade carving, and brass and copperware (especially fancy charcoal-burning hot pots). Grown locally are dates, pears, persimmons, walnuts, and wild jujubes.

Excursions & Day Trips
PINGYAO

You can get to **Pingyao** southwest of Taiyuan by bus or train. The train is more comfortable but less fun. These take about 1.25 hours one way. The best time to visit is late autumn. It can be windy and dusty in spring and autumn.

Pingyao is a small walled town full of extremely well preserved Ming and Qing architecture with a population of about 50,000 urban. It was once very wealthy, the home of China's first bank, and is now a UNESCO Heritage site. About 100 km southwest, it can be a day trip from Taiyuan. It does have a lacquer factory, and an hour by bus away, is the fengjiu wine factory.

Pingyao is not as beautiful or as developed for foreign tourists as Lijiang or Yangshuo. But it does have a lot of wonderful ancient buildings, multi-tiered gates, a 10-meter-high wall rebuilt in 1824, and a bank museum. The relics museum is in the Tianjixiang Shanghao, a former silk store, and streets are typically narrow with forbidding walls. Ask about the Wang Family residence and the Hou Family House. If you are not on a hectic tour, I would suggest spending one night, a total of two full days here. This will give you time to walk along the top of its over six-kilometer wall, and explore its streets and Christian churches. There are antique and curios shops. The food and language is only Chinese – which is something in its favor if you want to get away from foreign influences. There are a few signs in English and a lot to photograph.

You can pay Y25 for a pedicab and driver for a half day's tour around town. This would include the charming main business street on the far side of town away from the railway station, time to hike on the city wall, see the Three-Jin Shop Owner Furniture Museum/Bai Chuan Tong, *Tel. 5684212*, and visit Chun Huang Miao Temple. The governor's yamen/office, open 7am to 7pm (Y15), is on Zheng Fu Street. This has crude statues of how prisoners were punished by the authorities. (If a woman married two husbands simulta-neously, they cut her in two. If a merchant cheated while weighing goods, they cut off his face, hands and tongue, and gouged out his eyes. Don't take young children there.) The governor's house also has decent models of scholars passing the official examinations, a model of the old city, and a display of official badges. Cars are generally not allowed inside the wall.

You should be able to pay about Y40 for a taxi to go six kilometers to the **Shuanglin/Zhongdu Temple,** wait half an hour, and return to Pingyao. Y40 entry fee. This temple is well worth a trip. It was founded at least 1500 years ago and has ten halls. It has several hundred Ming and Song Buddhist sculptures of wood and clay with titles in English. Look for the Qing fertility goddess with her babies and the1000-armed Guan Yin.

It's easy to stop at the **Qiao Family Compound** and folk museum, originally the home of a wealthy Qing merchant. This is highly decorated with carvings and should be of interest to those who saw the Oscar-nominated Chinese movie *Raise the Red Lantern*. Built in 1755 in Qixian County, it was used as the main set. The mansion has 313 rooms. It is about 10 km from Pingyao towards Taiyuan.

Pingyao's **telephone code** is 354.

Lodging & Food in Pingyao

Across from the De Ju Yuan Restaurant and at 73 Ming Qing Street, 031100, is the **Tian Yuan Kui Ke Zhan**, *Tel. 5680069, Fax 5683052, E-mail is root@pytyk.com, Website: www.pytyk.com* (in English and has photos and a map of Pingyao and the hotel). This guest house has several old renovated buildings with rooms ranging from Y160 to Y198. It also had dorms without air-conditioning for Y50 a bed. It takes no credit cards. While it's far from Holiday Inn standards, it's charming with lots of old world atmosphere.

Another attractive old guest house is the **Folkway Hotel** (Minzu Binguan), *Tel. 5680285, Fax 5681991*. It has 40 beds.

Credit cards are accepted at the **Xie Shunlong Hotel** at 72 Ming Qing Street, *Tel. 5680824,* where you can get a room with a carved bridal bed and two twins (suitable for four people) for Y268. The **Folk Custom #2 Hotel** has rooms for Y150, tatami for Y60, but no private baths. It was run-down. It's more interesting to stay with a local family. Ask at restaurants or the travel agents below for a home stay.

For food, try the **Zhong Du Guest House** (Binguan) with a Western-type breakfast and is near the train station. It is at 1 Ping Yao Shun Cheng Road, *Tel. 5626618*. This hotel is more of a convenience because you can wait for your train there. The **De Ju Yuan restaurant** at 82 Ming Qing Street, *Tel. (0354) 5681453* had two kinds of noodles (one known as cats' ears). The total cost for two was Y25 including tea and it was good.

FURTHER AFIELD

This escursion requires at least a four-day tour. In the southern tip of Shanxi province is ***Yong Le Palace** in Ruicheng County, with beautiful 400-meter-long Yuan dynasty murals. From it, you can also study social and architectural history. Nearby in Yuncheng County is the **Guan Di Temple**, founded in the Sui and completely renovated in the Qing.

At Hongdong, about 200 km southwest of Taiyuan, is the ***Guangsheng Temple**, listed as Yuan and Ming. It has excellent colored ceramic figures and frescoes. An intricate, stunning collection of about 1,000 lively Buddhist and animal figures over 300 years old is at the Xiaoxitian (Miniature Western Paradise), northwest of Guangsheng Temple and north of Xixian county town. These are also worth a visit. Be prepared to climb and crane your neck. Take a flashlight and binoculars. Recently opened for tourists is a Ming dynasty jail in Hong Dong County. There, a woman, wrongly accused of poisoning her husband, was incarcerated.

*Dingcun paleolithic ruins are in Xianfen county, roughly 25 km southwest of Hongdong. Also in this area is a Han (nationality) folk museum, with 19 Ming and Qing courtyards, the oldest built in 1593. **Houma**, another 50 km southwest of Linfen, is a Jin site from the Eastern Zhou. A low but spectacular (depending on the season) waterfall is at **Hukou** on the Yellow River, northeast of Dingcun. Guesthouses are at Yuncheng City. You could spend a fruitful month exploring this province alone! Much of the Chinese collection in Toronto's Royal Ontario Museum is from southern Shanxi.

See Datong for the Yungang Grottoes, the Great Wall, Wutai Mountain, Sakyamuni Pagoda, the Huayan and Shanhua Monasteries, and the Mid-Air Temple.

Practical Information

Shanxi CITS, *A38 Ping Yang Road, 030012, Tel. 7244126, Fax 7244312. E-mail: sxcits@public.ty.sx.cn.* Ask for Hu Zhong You.

Shanxi China Travel Service, *8 Xinjian Nan Road, 030001, Tel. 4043377, 4035053, Fax 4035024. E-mail: gcjia@public.ty.sx.cn* and ask for George Jia who helped with this book. Its website: *www.sxcts.com.cn* (English) is good and worth visiting. CTS can arrange for foreigners to stay with local families in Pingyao. The cost including meals is about Y100/per night per person. It charges Y30 to help an individual get to the right bus in Taiyuan.

An **Internet Bar** is across from the Kang Da Shopping Center and charges Y6 per hour.

Telephone code: 351.

Datong

(Tatung)

Datong is most famous for the Yungang (Yunkang) Grottoes, said to be the best-preserved, the largest, and the oldest sandstone carvings in China. Founded during the Warring States, about 2,200 years ago, this settlement was a garrison town built between two sections of the Great Wall. The Northern Wei (386-534) declared it their capital and instructed Monk Tanyao to supervise the carving of the caves.

The population is 520,000 urban, 2.7 million total. The highest temperature in summer (July-August) is 37.7°C and the lowest (December-February)

-29.9 °C. Rainfall is a scant 400 mm a year, mainly May-October. The best time to visit is May-October. The altitude is 1000 meters.

Arrivals & Departures

Located in northern Shanxi province, Datong is less than seven hours by train from Beijing. Panda Tours has a two-day package tour. See website: www.chinaonlinetravel.com/pandatours/pandadatong.htm. It leaves about 11:20pm and arrives at 5:50am. It's two nights on trains and one night in a hotel. You can do this on your own too. You can also continue from here by once-a-week train to Ulan Bator, and thence onward to Moscow. Datong also has daily flights with Beijing. By road from Taiyuan it takes about five hours, and from Wutai, it takes about four hours if you go via the Hanging Temple.

Orientation

Datong is basically a coal-mining city, one of the largest open pit coal-producing areas in the world, with a 600-year supply at the current rate of production. The city is industrial and heavily polluted. Outside Datong, you can see the coal deposits with all kinds of coal transport equipment on the roads. Some of the equipment is the most advanced in the world.

The mining may be ugly but it is worth your time. Because the mines have unearthed many old burial grounds, Shanxi has an extremely large number of excavated tombs and neolithic sites.

Where to Stay

At press time, the best hotel is the Hong An Hotel (Dajiudian). Second best is the Yungang Hotel.

DATONG GRAND HOTEL, *1 Yingbin Dong Road, 037008, Tel. 2032476, Fax 2035174. Three stars.*

YUNGANG HOTEL (Fandian), *21 Yingbin Dong Road, 037008. Three stars. Tel. 5021601, Fax 5024927. E-mail: yunganghotel@china.com. Y260 for rooms and Y688 for suites.*

Where to Eat

Look for people preparing Knife-cut Noodles on the street. Ask about the chefs who put noodle dough on their heads and slice the dough with a knife into a cooking pot. The hotels are your best bet.

Seeing the Sights

If you only have two days to spend in the city, good choices are the Yungang caves and Hanging Temple. On your second day, there's the Huayan Monastery, Nine-Dragon Screen, and the Steam Locomotive Museum. Take a flash light for the grottoes and a flash camera. Nine of the caves have wooden protectors in front and many are dark.

You can reach the ***Yungang (Yunkang) Grottoes** by taxi about 20 km west from Datong. They have been open 9am to 5:30pm daily. Fifty-three caves here contain over 51,000 stone carvings of Buddha, bodhisattvas, apsaras (angels), birds, and animals. These statues range from 17 meters to a few centimeters high and some of them still retain their original color. They were restored in 1976. The grottoes are at the southern foot of Wuzhou Hills. They were built between 460 and 494 A.D. after a period of persecution against the Buddhists supposedly led to the illness of Emperor Taiwu. The grottoes extend east-west for a kilometer. The Wei dynasty later moved its capital to Luoyang and built another set of grottoes there.

Although the exposed caves have suffered natural erosion as well as damage by man, they are nicely preserved and well worth visiting. The walking is easy. The best are at the Five Caves of Tanyao (Nos. 5, 6, 16-20), which include the largest statues. The large ears mean deliberate poverty (no earrings). Although Datong was not on the Silk Road, the carvings carry strong Indian, Persian, and even Greek influences. They could take half a day. There are several restaurants.

The ***Huayan Si (Huayan Monastery)** is one of the largest temples in China. You can easily spend from two hours to a half day there, there is so much to absorb. It is in the southwest of the city. The monastery is well preserved and is separated into the Upper Huayan and the Lower Huayan. You pay two entrance fees. In Upper Huayan is the magnificent main hall, Daxiong Bao Dian, built in 1062 and rebuilt in 1140. It is 53.75 meters wide and 29 meters long. The beam structure, murals, five large Ming Buddhas, and 26 guardians are most impressive. In Lower Huayan is the main hall, the Bhagavan Stack Hall, built in 1038. Along its walls are 38 two-story wooden cabinets housing the Buddhist sutras. The temple's exquisite 31 clay statues were made in the Liao. An antique store is at the temple.

The **Nine Dragon Screen** has been reproduced in cities in America but here is one of the originals. It is in the southeast of the old city, is almost 600 years old, and at 45.5 meters, is larger than the two in Beijing. The morning is better for photographs. A nearby Christian church is worth a visit. The **Steam Locomotive Museum** is at 1 Qian Jin Lane, Da Qin Road, *Tel. 5090124*. For information about steam locomotive tours, try *www.dialspace.dial.pipex.com*.

Shopping

Locally made products include porcelain, knitting wool, furs, leather, silk dolls, and carpets.

Excursions & Day Trips

The 67.3-meter-high *Sakyamuni Wooden Pagoda at Foguang Temple should be worth the 1.5 hour drive if you are interested in unusual pagodas. It is the tallest ancient wood-frame structure in China. It was constructed in 1056 (Liao), with eight corners and nine stories. From the outside it looks like five stories. Local folklore says that the pagoda only sits on five of its six vertical beams. One of the beams is always resting, and you can pass a piece of paper underneath it. Each beam takes its turn at being weightless. Bring a piece of paper and test it for yourself. It is 75 km south of Datong in Yingxian county. The Great Wall is 40 km and 150 km away.

You can also visit Hengshan Mountain, 70 km southeast, for the Xuankongsi or **Temple in Mid-Air (or Hanging Temple)**. This is a marvel of cliff-side architecture. The temple literally clings to an almost vertical mountainside. It was first built over 1400 years ago (Northern Wei) and rebuilt in the Tang, Jin, Ming and Qing dynasties. Its clay statues are poor. The bronze and iron castings and stone and wood carvings are better and probably older. Take lunch in Hongyun County town nearby. From here you can go on to Wutai Mountain, 240 km south of Datong.

On **Wutai Shan**, one of the **Four Great Buddhist Mountains of China**, there are about 50 temples from the fifth century. Important are the *Main Hall of the Nanchan Temple (Tang to Qing), *Foguang Temple (Tang to Qing) and the *Xiantong Temple (Eastern Han). The main halls of the Nanchan and Foguang temples are the oldest extant wood-frame buildings in the world. Both have histories of over 1200 years and are worth the white-knuckle trip through the mountains.

Visitors can hike on a paved path to the summit. The liveliest time to visit is during its festival here in July and August. Dr. Norman Bethune's model hospital is also in the area. On Wutai Shan, you can stay at the three-star Youyi (Friendship) Hotel.

Practical Information

China Comfort Travel Service, *28 Yingbin Dong Road, opposite the Yungang Hotel, Tel. 5101107, 5103222, Fax 5103222.*

CITS, *21 Yingbin Dong Road, 037008, Tel. 5102165, 5102164, Fax 5102763. E-mail: dtcts@public.dt.sx.cn.*

Datong CYTS, *108, Jiao Chang Street, 037008, Tel. 2063965, Fax 2063303.*

Telephone code: 352.

Hohhot

(Huhehot, Huhehaote)

Hohhot, the capital of Inner Mongolia (Nei Monggol Autonomous Region), is northwest of Beijing in the south central part of this 1800-km-long region. The urban population is over 800,000.

Genghis Khan united the tribes living here in 1206, and his descendants went on to conquer the rest of China and then parts of Europe. The traditional religion, as reflected now in its monasteries and temples, is a distinctive branch of Buddhism and is related to that practiced in Tibet. Many Mongolians however worship Genghis Khan.

Hohhot dates from the Ming, at least 400 years ago. It was called Guisui under the Nationalists. After Liberation, it was renamed Hohhot, the name preferred by the natives. In the past, Inner Mongolia has been a temporary home for nomads.

The best time to visit is June through September. The highest temperature in Hohhot is 30°C, but the nights are cool. The winters are very cold and windy, with an occasional minus 32°C low in January, and you need long johns even in early May. The spring has a few sandstorms. The annual precipitation is between a scant 50 and 450 mm, mostly late summer and early autumn. The altitude is 1500 meters above sea level and it has from 90 to 160 frost-free days.

Arrivals & Departures

Hohhot can be reached by train from Ulan Bator, Mongolia, or plane from Beijing and 20 other Chinese cities.

Orientation

Today Hohhot's population includes Han, Daur, Ewenki, Oroqen, Hui, Manchu, Korean, and, of course, Mongolian nationalities. The Mongolians are now actually a minority. Hohhot looks like any other Chinese city, except for the horse statues.

Where to Stay

ZHAOJUN HOTEL (Zhaojun Dajiudian), *53 Xinhua Road, 010050. Three stars upgrading to four stars in 2002. Tel. 6962211, Fax 6968825, 6967645. E-mail: zjininte@public.hh.nm.cn. Website: www.zhaojunhotel.com.cn. 15 km from the airport, 0.5 km from the railway station, 200 meters from city hall. It accepts credit cards and travelers checks. Y580-Y680 for rooms and Y680-Y980 for suites. (It has some cheaper rooms.)*

Built in 1987, this hotel has 262 rooms, satellite television and international direct dial. Sichuan, Cantonese, French and Italian food.

PEARL INNER MONGOLIA HOTEL, *2 Xincheng Bei Avenue, 010010. Three stars. Tel. 6280088, Fax 6910499. E-mail: pearl-hotel@pearl-hotel.com.cn. 12 km from the airport and two km from the railway station. Rooms are Y420-Y720 including breakfast.*

This hotel has 112 rooms, satellite television, dim sum, Western and local food, and a business center. There's a gym and sauna.

XIN CHENG (Binguan), *Hu Lun Nan, 010010, Tel. 6963322, Fax 6968561. Rooms start at Y200 and it takes major credit cards.*

Where to Eat

Meat, mainly mutton but also beef, is the big thing here. Notable dishes are barbecued lamb, mutton hot pot, sesame pancakes, braised oxtail, beef kebab, yu mian noodles, ox tendon in egg white, and camel hoof. Mongolian food is better in Hohhot at the hotels than in the grasslands. Outside and to the right of the Zhaojun Hotel you'll find a place for good Mongolian hotpot.

Seeing the Sights

In summer, visitors can travel out from here, if they wish, and sleep in a yurt in the beautiful sparsely-settled grasslands. You can drink tea laced with milk, butter, and grain, said to be very filling and great for cold winter days. (It's too greasy for hot weather.) Visitors can go to one of several rural communities located 90 to 180 km away, on roads cut through the rolling prairie lands.

Mongolian **yurts** or tents are made of compressed sheep's wool with no windows unless you count the roof. They are shaped somewhat like igloos, and can be folded up and carried by horse. Eight people can put up a large one in 40 minutes. Visitors staying in yurts sleep on padded earthen mattresses. Everything smells of sheep. (Put a bag between you and the wall if the smell keeps you awake.)

Up to three people to a yurt is very comfortable, and over six very crowded. Sometimes you can hear bugs eating the felt. A mosquito net might be useful. Most Mongolians now live in houses but keep yurts around because they are cooler in summer.

In some yurt hotels, there is a separate bathhouse with running water and flush toilets (when the pump is working). The people are charming and wear their traditional costumes. The food might be barely edible, with tough fresh-killed mutton, fried millet, boiled millet, rice, boiled eggs, and cake. Do not expect traditional Mongolian hot pot or barbecue except in winter or in the cities. Take some snacks to fill up. Also soap. Each travel agency has a different hostel on the grasslands, some better than others.

You can visit Mongolian homes and an **aobo**, the rock mounds at high points where people worship, gather, and leave messages for each other. Mongolians now ride motorcycles much more than horses.

Hohhot used to have many temples but the Red Guards destroyed them during the Cultural Revolution. Among the survivors is the oldest, **Dazhao Temple** (Ming), with a rare silver Buddha and many musical instruments, and the Xiaozhao Temple. At the Wutasi Temple, the tallest of its five pagodas is 6.26 meters and all are made of glazed bricks carved with Buddhist symbols and inscribed in three languages: Mongolian, Sanskrit, and Tibetan. Behind the pagodas is a Mongolian astrological chart.

The **White Pagoda** on the eastern outskirts of the city at the Xilitu Lamasery (monastery) is from the 10th century and is 40 meters or seven-stories high. Inside are native tapestries. For more on Tibetan Buddhism, see Tibet.

The **Tomb of Wang Zhaojun** is about 10 km southwest of the city. In 33 B.C., she was an imperial Han concubine, married off to a Xiongnu tribal chief to form an important political alliance. The story goes that the Han emperor picked his bed partner from paintings of his many concubines. Consequently, the women bribed the painter to make them look beautiful. Wang Zhaojun refused and he made her look awful. She was continually ignored. In choosing a gift for the tribal leader, the emperor decided on the ugliest of his wives. He never saw Wang Zhaojun until the day of the presentation. She was beautiful, but it was too late. The Xiongnu liked her too. And the peace was kept for 40 years! A Han Chinese, she helped to bridge the two groups.

The **Great Mosque**, built in Chinese style, is worth seeing, as is the **Provincial Museum**, 2 Xin Hua Avenue with a highly recommended exhibition about the Mongolians. For those seriously interested in Mongolians, there is a Mongolia Society in the US. You might also be interested in the Mongolia Art Performing College and the Horse Rodeo School with displays of singing, dancing, and horsemanship. Ask about them at the local tourist office.

Resorts are set up in the grasslands so tourists can visit, stay in a yurt, and ride. Gegentala in Siziwang Banner is 145 km north of Hohhot.

Walks

Out in the rolling grasslands, you can see for miles, and hiking is a pure joy.

Festivals

The dates of the **Nadamu Festival** are now set by the province and depend on the harvest. Some areas celebrate in July, others in August. This annual fair in Hohhot is held around August 15-20th. Tourists then go on to celebrations outside Hohhot.

For example, at **Sitenghuile**, 100 km north of Hohhot on a poor road, there is a demonstration of Mongolian culture with a parade, wrestling, archery, horsemanship, and traditional songs and dances. You eat Mongolian food, sleep in a concrete yurt with cement floor, use flush toilets, and visit

Mongolian homes. You can ride horses and camels. Tourists sometimes outnumber Mongolians.

At **Xilinhot**, 700 km from Hohhot, foreigners might sleep in yurts or in town and commute about 40 minutes to the fair grounds carrying their own food. The 10,000 Mongolians attending Nadamu sleep in yurts, put up booths to sell kitchenware, boots, carpets, and motorcycles, but no native clothes or jewelry. They wear traditional dress, and use muddy open pit toilets with canvas covers. There could be circus acts, wrestling, archery, and horse-riding competitions with lots of chaos and no explanations, no dancers, and no horseback rides. Only a few foreigners attend.

You have to choose. Because of the crowds, I urge you to book a place through a travel agency and expect no star accommodations. These will probably improve as organizers get more experience.

Shopping

Today, in addition to less exotic goods, Inner Mongolia produces woolen textiles, cashmere sweaters, carpets, and tapestries. It also manufactures Mongolian-style boots, daggers with chopsticks, silver bowls, brass hot pots, cheap but fancy tweezers, wrestlers jackets, saddles, stirrups, and felt stockings. Also available are antique jade or agate bottles. Shopping is better in Hohhot than in the grasslands.

Excursions & Day Trips

Baotou in western Inner Mongolia, 20 km north of the Yellow River, is 144 km from Hohhot. It is 800 km from Beijing, about a 12-hour train trip, or a 1 1/2 hour flight. It is connected to eight other cities by air. The average altitude is 1000 meters, its annual rainfall a sparse 312 mm. The city was founded in the 17th century (Qing) on a neolithic site. The urban population is about 1,700,000, of whom the Han are 90%, the Mongolians 2.5%, and the rest 21 other national minorities.

Locally produced in this region are carpets, cashmere knitwear, leather and furs, porcelain, and arts and crafts.

If you only have one day, you might want to visit the **Wudangzhao Lamasery** and take a quick city tour. The Wudangzhao Lamasery is 70 km east of town in Huluntu Mountain, Guyang county. It is a massive 2,500 room complex established in 1794 (Qing), once home to 1,200 monks and covering about 50 acres. The largest monastery in western Inner Mongolia, it contains statues, murals, and tangkas typical of the yellow sect of Tibetan Buddhism. (More about Tibetan Buddhism under Lhasa and Chengde.)

If you have more time, also visit the **Meidaizhao Lamasery**, originally built in the Ming, which is at Tumd You Banner, 80 km east of Baotou. It is also known as the Sanniangzi Temple after Wang Zhaojun. Her husband, the temple's founder, is buried here.

The ***Tomb of Genghis Khan** was moved 170 km south of Baotou to Ejinhoroq (Elinhoro) in 1954. It contains ashes, said to be his. Pilgrims gather here to pay homage for one day in the third, fifth, ninth, and tenth lunar months.

You can also visit the **Great Wall**, 40 km and 70 km north of Baotou. All places of interest are open 8am-6pm daily.

The best hotel here is the three-star **Qingshan Hotel**, 1 Yingbin Road, Qingshan District, 014030, *Tel. 472/3331199, Fax 5156001.*

CITS and **CTS** are at the Baotou Hotel, 33 Gangtie Avenue, 014010. Kundulun District, 014010, *Tel. 5156655, Fax 5154615.*

Practical Information

Business Hours, offices 8:30am-5:30pm. Stores 9am-7pm

China Travel Service, *95 Art Hall South Street, Xincheng District, Hohhot, 010010, Tel. 6281554, Fax 6936487, 6967924. E-mail: imcts@public.hh.nm.cn. Website: www.chinaholiday.com/imcts*

CYTS Tours, *9 Zhong Shan Dong Road, 010020, Tel. 6964968, Fax 6964910. E-mail: cyts@public.hh.nm.cn*

Inner Mongolia Tourism Bureau, *95 Yishuting Nan Street, 010010, Tel. 6914197, 6965978, Fax 6968561*

Police, *Tel. 110*

Telephone code: 471

Changchun

Capital of Jilin province, **Changchun** is noted mostly as an industrial city manufacturing automobiles, trucks, railway carriages, tractors, and textiles. It was also the capital of Japanese Manchuria and it has Emperor Puyi's palace. The total population is 6.5 million; the urban population 2.67 million. Changchun is very cold in winter (lowest -30°C). The average annual rainfall is 600-700 mm., mainly in July and August. There are about 150 frost-free days!

Arrivals & Departures

Changchun is a 90-minute flight northeast of Beijing. It can also be reached by plane from about 27 other Chinese cities, Seoul, Vladivostok, and Hong Kong. From Shenyang, you can take a train or road trip in three to four hours. From Harbin it is a three-hour train or four-hour car ride.

Orientation

Changchun was founded in 1800. Invaded by Tsarist Russia in the 1890s, it became a Japanese concession in 1905 and the capital of Japanese-controlled

Manchukuo from 1931 until 1945. Parts can be very attractive with lovely broad avenues flanked by beautiful hospital and university buildings.

The province of Jilin borders on Korea and Russia. Its 24 million people include Koreans, Manchus, Hui, Mongols and Xibos. Settlements have been recorded since the Qin dynasty.

Where to Stay

The luxurious Shangri-La Hotel is the best place to stay. The Noble is second. The four-star Marcourt is third but opened too late to be reviewed. Most hotels add 15% service charge, and some also add a Y5 tax and Y2 social security fund. All accept major credit cards, have discounts, money exchange, direct dial telephones, and business centers.

SHANGRI-LA HOTEL CHANGCHUN, *9 Xian Road, 130061 at Chongqing Road. Five stars. Tel. 8981818, Fax 8981919. E-mail: slcc@shangri-la.com. $140-$210 for rooms; $340-$1200 for suites. It has been discounting 40% to 50%.*

Located in the diplomatic, financial, business and entertainment district, the Shangri-La is 2.5 km from the railway station, 10 km from the airport, and one km from the city hall. Opened in 1996, it has 458 rooms plus 63 serviced apartments and 84 offices. It also has three executive floors, a Cantonese restaurant, and karaoke lounge. There's a gym, jacuzzi, sauna, steambath, indoor pool, children's playground, and lighted tennis court. Rooms have safes, and five television channels in English. The decor is Western-style, and it has been lacking the antiques, art work, and fancy chandeliers that make its sister hotels in Hong Kong and Beijing so special. But it is attractive with frosted glass accents and comfortable stuffed arm chairs. The service is very good.

NOBLE HOTEL, *135 Renmin Street, 130021. Tel. 5622888, Fax 5665522. Five stars. Y1050-Y1240 for rooms, and Y2481-Y14317 for suites.*

This 25-story, 301 room hotel has narrow halls and low ceilings. It has safes in rooms, bowling, sauna, indoor pool, and CNN, Thai and Singaporean food.

Where to Eat

Changchun has some exotic specialties: houtou (golden orchid monkey head) mushrooms, ginseng chicken, thick deer antler soup (with sea cucumber, prawns, egg white, ham, and chicken), and frog oil soup. Frog oil is said to be very nutritious and tastes better than it sounds. Please, no endangered species! And yes, you can get other dishes too! Ask for the carmelized potatoes.

The best restaurants are in the hotels, but for a change you can try the **Nong Jia Restaurant**, 23 Bei Jing Da Jie, *Tel. 2734137*; or **Papa's Korean Restaurant**, 20 Da Jing Road, *Tel. 8738504*. The Shangri-La's prices have been moderate: silver garlic cod Y80, broccoli Y28 and sizzling beef Y65.

Seeing the Sights

If you have only one day in Changchun, you must see the **Museum of the Former Palaces of the Last Emperor Pu Yi,** 10 km from the Changbaishan Hotel. From 1932 to 1945, Pu Yi lived and worked in this complex. He was made Emperor of Manchukuo by the Japanese. The Ton De Palace was actually used as one of the sets in the movie *The Last Emperor*. (The movie company put in the chandelier). Only one of Pu Yi's wives lived in this palace which was built for Pu Yi by the Japanese and now is a museum. A good guide can tell you which rooms she lived in. Pu Yi himself lived in a neighboring building; he believed the Ton De Palace was bugged and used it only for receptions.

You can see the emperor's throne and his living quarters in the Qian Ming Building. Wax figures, photographs of the emperor, his wedding, wives, and English teacher are on display. The palace was looted after the Japanese surrender and Pu Yi was exiled to the Soviet Union. During the Cultural Revolution, Mao badges were produced here. (Many are still on sale.) A tunnel goes from here to the railway station.

You might want also to include the Changchun Film Studio, one of China's largest. The Changchun Movie City, a theme park, is more for domestic tourists. At the Changchun Number One Motor Vehicle Plant, you can watch a more labor-intensive manufacturing process than in America or Europe. You won't believe the wages! Ice sculptures are at South Lake in winter.

On summer evenings you can find dancers in costume in **People's Square**. And you should be able to relax across from the Shangri-La at Second Home (songs in English), and Friday Bar.

The **Changbaishan Nature Reserve**, with tigers, deer, and sable is in Antu County about 300 km southeast, with its own mythical monster and at least two hotels. The best time to see the red-crested cranes at Xianghai Lake is the end of August.

For fans of steam locomotives, see *www.dialspace.dial.pipex.com* for tours. You can visit Korean, Manchurean and Mongolian villages.

Festivals

A fascinating time can be had at the **Mongolian Festival** in **Baicheng**, 400 km from Changchun, five or six days of horse racing, archery, wrestling, and dances. A **Ginseng Festival** is held for three days, usually in August, in Fusong county at the foot of Changbai Mountain. In August-September is the **Port Wine Festival**. A film festival takes place every two years in August. Check exact dates with travel agents.

Shopping

Changchun manufactures wine, ginseng, sable, deer antlers (aphrodisiacs), and frog oil (tonic). It also produces carpets, embroidery, mushrooms, azalea wood carvings, and bark pictures. Please avoid furs from endangered species. **People's Department Store** near the Shangri-La is open 9am-5:30pm. Good buys are leather coats, fur hats and jackets but check the tanning carefully.

The four-story **antique center** at 75 Qing Ming Street is open 9:30am-4:30pm. It has old cameras, stamps, coins, onyx vases, "Tang" figurines, silver Qing hair ornaments, etc. The **Ginseng and Pilose Antler Market** at 27 Tongzhi Street, *Tel. 5677275*, specializes in ginseng. Valuable are the ones with strings, the longer and most human-like the better. Red and Korean are very popular.

Excursions & Day Trips

Jilin is in the center of Jilin province, 90 km east of Changchun, and about 100 minutes away by highway. You can get a bus every 30 to 60 minutes from the Jilin Bus Station on Renmin Bei Road in Changchun. You can reach it by rail from Beijing, Changchun, Shenyang, Harbin, and Tianjin. You can fly there from Beijing, Guangzhou and Shanghai. The airport is 25 km away. The population of Jilin is nearly one million.

Tourist attractions include the Jilin Exhibition Hall with a 1770-kilogram meteorite, believed to be the largest in the world, and **Songhua Lake**, a 480-square kilometer, man-made lake, 20 km from the city center. The Songhua River runs through the city and beautiful hoarfrost forms on the trees lining its banks in -20°C weather. The Rime Festival celebrates this phenomenon. Ice lanterns are sculpted in the winter.

Jilin has skiing. Jingyuetan and Beida Lake have lifts. The Changbai Mountains have alpine skiing with lifts operating from December to February.

The **Changbai mountains** are 380 km southeast of the city, their highest peak 2,691 meters. The famous crater is beautiful Heavenly Lake with its own mythical monster. The mountains can be reached by road from Jilin and Yanji, and by rail from Tonghua and from Yangji. The other side is Korea.

You can also see Arladi Village, 70 km from Jilin, where Korean customs are still practiced.

Local specialties include venison, frog oil soup, steamed whitefish, raw salmon and carp, and chicken and ginseng in earthenware pots.

Visitors can stay at the four-star **Crystal Hotel**. CITS and CTS are at 4 Jiangwan Road, 132001. The telephone code is 432.

Practical Information

CITS Jilin, *7th floor, Yinmao Dasha Building, 14 Xinmin Street, 130021, Tel. 5609039, mobile 13904302380, Fax 5645069. E-mail:citsjlp@public.cc.jl.cn*. Ask for Zhang Xinsheng, Vice-General Manager. It organizes steam locomotive railway tours.

Hours: 8:30am to 4:30pm Monday through Friday (offices). Stores are open 8 or 9am to 5:30 or 6:30pm.
   Telephone Code: 431

Harbin

(Haerhpin)
   Harbin is the capital of China's northernmost province of Heilongjiang, formerly part of Japan's Manchuria. It produces the likes of helicopters, boilers, and coal. Important for tourists are its Siberian tigers, its colorful morning market, and its ice sculpture festival. Outside the city is a red-crested crane reserve, the best skiing in China, and trips to Siberia.
   Its highest summer temperature is 36°C; its lowest in winter is -38°C with an average daytime temperature in January of -15°C. The July average is 27°C. The winter is six months long, so take your longjohns. Wintertime, however, is brightened by the Ice Sculpture Festival, its major tourist attraction. The annual precipitation is 250-700 mm, mostly June through August.
   Of the cities in the northeast, Harbin is my second favorite.

Arrivals & Departures

   Harbin is a 90-minute flight or 12-hour train ride northeast of Beijing, or a four-hour train ride from Changchun (faster than bus). Flights are with Hong Kong, Khabarovsk, Niigata, Seoul, and Vladivostok and 33 Chinese cities. The airport is about 40 km south of the city.

Orientation

   The area was first settled by people of the Nuzhen nationality in 1097. In the Yuan, the city was renamed Harbin. In 1898 it became a Russian concession with Tsarist police in charge. After the Communist revolution, it became home for thousands of White Russians who built synagogues as well as Russian churches. From 1932, the Japanese occupied it until the war's end in 1945. You will see a lot of imperialist Russian and Japanese architecture, and cobblestone streets (in Dao Li District). The sprawling city has a few convenient expressways but is still subject to traffic jams and air pollution.
   Harbin has a total population of 9.3 million, of whom 3.4 million are urban. Heilongjiang province numbers among its 37 million people Han, Manchu, Korean, Hui, Mongolian, Daur, Orogen, Ewenki, Kirgiz, Hezhen, and other nationalities.

Where to Stay

   The best hotels are the five-star Singapore and Shangri-La hotels. The Singapore has a magnificent water park next door. The Shangri-La is close to the river, not far from the Gloria Inn. The New World Hotel is third best for quality and is close to government buildings, the Trade Exhibition Center, the Russian Market and Museum. The best for group tourists is the Gloria Inn because of its fantastic location near the morning market, and the Holiday Inn (the second best location). Between them is the very pleasant car-free Central Avenue (Zhongyang Dajie), the main shopping area. Nearby are St. Sophia Cathedral, a European-style neighborhood, and city hall. People gather and dance on summer evenings in the square in front of the Gloria.

All hotels listed have money changing, business centers, international direct dialing, minibars, and credit card service. Hotels add a 15% surcharge. You can also get discounts.

SINGAPORE HOTEL (Xingjiapo Dajiudian), *68 Ganshui Road, Xiangfang District, 150090. Five stars. Tel. 2336888, Fax 2331818, 2333720. E-mail: sales@harbinsingaporehtl.com. Website: www.harbinsingaporehtl.com (English). This 338-room hotel is in the Xiangfang Economic Development Zone, with 21-stories and rooms $203-$275. Suites cost $372-$3927. It has been discounting 48% in high season. The presidential suite has nine rooms.*

With its curved staircases, and wood-trimmed, pink and beige marble interior, the lobby here is a joy to see. Rooms are Western-style with safes, and CNN, and the grand ballroom can seat 500 for dinner. The Singapore also has executive floors, a non-smoking floor, 24-hour room service, and indoor pool. Its restaurants serve Cantonese, Chaozhou, Western and local cuisine. Its dinner buffet is Y78. See below. Managed by Ananda Hotel Management Limited.

SHANGRI-LA HOTEL, HARBIN, *555 You Yi Road, Dao Li, Dist. 150018. Five stars. Tel. 4858888, Fax 4621777. E-mail: shar@shangri-la.com. Website: www.shangri-la.com. Rooms are $121-$183 and suites $194-$1022. It has been discounting to $84-$120 on rooms. Breakfast is Y40. On the south bank of the Songhua River near the Honghua Kiang Highway Bridge. 45 minutes from the airport.*

This 346-room hotel has non-smoking rooms, data port, coffee-makers, and in-room safes. It has an executive club and 24-hour room service. There's a gym, indoor pool, outdoor tennis court, steam bath, sauna, and Asian and continental cuisines. Its ballroom can seat 780 at tables.

HOLIDAY INN CITY CENTRE HARBIN, *90 Jingwei Street, Daoli District, 150010. Four stars. Tel. 4226666, Fax 4221661. E-mail: holiday@public.hr.hl.cn. Website: www.holiday-inn.com/harbinchn. Centrally located right across from the pedestrian shopping street Zhong Yang Lu/Central Street, within walking distance of Sophie Church and 10 minutes to the Songhua River. Two km to the railway station and 34 km (40 minutes) to the airport. Standard rooms are $108 which have been discounted 30 to 50% and inclusive of breakfast.*

This 157-room hotel has 14 floors and includes executive club and non-smoking floors. Rooms have safes and BBC, CNBC, HBO, and Cinemax. It has

Western, Cantonese and Northeastern food, an English pub and gym, but no pool or tennis.

SONGHUAJIANG GLORIA INN (Kaili Fandian), *257 Zhongyang Avenue, Daoli District, 150010. Tel. 4638855, Fax 4638533. E-mail: gloria@giharbin.com. Website: www.giharbin.com (English) which says Y408 nett per room with no service charge. There are 304 rooms and duplex apartments.*

This simple, unpretentious hotel functions okay but its location is great and exotic. In the winter, you can enjoy the sunset and river from its front rooms (though the windows are small). In the summer, you can walk along the river or look for onion-domed Orthodox churches nearby and try to visualize the bushy-hatted czarist police patrolling the streets here. We found the hotel's ambience light and airy, the business center very helpful. Don't expect a pool but it does have CNN, in-house movies and room service. It has a seafood restaurant and coffee shop.

Where to Eat

The most exotic dishes are moose nose and hazel grouse. Please, avoid endangered species! For those who want something less questionable, try monkey-head-shaped mushrooms.

The hotels have excellent food. There are also the **Hua Mei Restaurant**, 142 Zhongyang Street, *Tel. 4617368* for Russian food, and the **Harbin Restaurant**, Shang Zhi Street with good northeastern food.

Seeing the Sights

Come for the natural scenery, China's best skiing, and the ice sculpture festival. Come for the red-crested crane sanctuary and the Siberian tigers. Come for the cooler summers and Siberia. How many people can say they've been to Siberia? Get your visa in Beijing or North America first.

The magical **Ice Sculpture Festival**, from early January to February 25, depends on the weather. You can easily spend three hours here. Its twinkling colored lights are best seen at dusk around 5pm, before it gets too cold. Teams compete from all over the world with giant ice pagodas, bridges, lanterns, human figures, and palaces.

If you have a couple of days to spare, you could add **Siberia** to your list of exotic destinations. Heihe on the border is 600 km north and travel agents can arrange a day trip from there. They can also get you bird watching, gold panning, horse riding (Mongolian), and skiing. You can take steam locomotive tours on narrow-gauge mining and logging trains as this province has China's second largest number of still-operating steam locomotives. See website: www.dialspace.dial.pipex.com.

If you only have one day in Harbin, it only takes a couple hours to visit the 100 or so very healthy Siberian tigers and watch them gobble down live chickens, rabbits, deer or calves in their huge home. On the other hand, the gore might turn you off. The animals, however, are beautiful. Take a taxi three km south of the toll booth beyond the Song Wan Jeung Gong Lu Da Qiao Bridge. The bridge is near Sun Island on the Song Hua River. Turn right, a few meters past the huge red mansion and drive about one km to the only "Tiger Park" sign on the way. The Y50 entrance fee gives you a 30-minute ride on a bus with barred windows. Attendants request additional money for the live sacrifices. You can join a tour, a Chinese one if an English-speaking guide is not available. It doesn't take much language to be fascinated by them. A shuttle bus goes from the Flood-Control Monument.

You could visit Sophia church, and the Provincial Museum with its mammoths instead. Be sure to visit the morning market near the Gloria Inn. It is really amazing; it follows the riverside for at least three km west of the Gloria Inn, full of flowers, food, clothing, pets, snakes, antiques, and women hobbling on bound feet.

If You're a Bird Watcher

China's biggest bird sanctuary, the 210,000-hectare **Zhalong Nature Preserve** is near Qiqihar, four hours/250km drive from Harbin. Its cranes, storks, swans, geese, and herons are best seen from April to September. The famous red-crested cranes are considered a symbol of luck.

Nightlife & Entertainment

Ask about the annual **Harbin Summer Music Festival** in July. **Singapore Hotel's Water Paradise** is a great place to swim all year round. Safety standards are high. Waves in its 1000 square meter pool churn for 15 minutes per hour and slides drop you from a height of 15 meters. Open 10am-10pm weekdays, 9am-10pm on weekends, it puts on a 10 minute laser show projected on mist every evening. Credit cards are accepted. *Tel. 2336888 X 7401, or 2336813.*

Shopping

Sable, mink and muskrat hats, jackets, and collars are made here. Handicrafts include straw patchwork, horn-carving, knitting, and ivory, jade, stone, and wood-carving. Good to eat are its pine nuts and good for you, is ginseng. The stalls at the **Chinese-Russian Street Market** near the New World Hotel are worth a look. Open 8am-5pm, daily, it had Y20 fresh water pearls, mink pelts, fur hats (Y150-Y650), Russian dolls and imports, Chinese antiques of ivory, jade and coral, fossils, and petrified wood.

The upmarket **New World Department Store** near the New World Hotel takes major credit cards, and is open 9am-8pm. It has up-to-date styles and imported brands. Central Street (between the Gloria Inn and the Holiday Inn has the popular **Zhong Yang Shang Chang Department Store**, Bossini's and KFC. Stalls here operate after the stores close. The "antique building" is at 62 Hoang Jun Street, Nan Gang District, near many gold stores. It is across the square from the International Hotel and provincial museum, and is open 8:30am-4pm five days a week. Stores here sell porcelain and old jewelery.

Excursions & Day Trips

Heilongjiang has China's biggest ski resort: **Yabuli Ski and Vacation Resort**, *Tel. 451/3455088, Fax 3455138, E-mail: skiyabuli@21cn.com*. It is 195 km by expressway from Harbin, about 1.5 hours from Mudanjiang. Buses leave at 8am and 1:20pm daily from the Longyun Road bus station in Harbin and takes three hours. *Tel. 3634528*. By train it takes four hours.

On 2,255 hectares, with an elevation of 1000 meters, Yabuli is used also for training China's national ski team.

Stay at the **Windmill Inn**, 150631 in the Yabuli Ski and Vacation Resort. *Tel. 3455088, 3455168, Fax 3455138*. This three-star ski lodge has 700 beds, Chinese and Western restaurants, and a conference room seating 500 people. It has international direct dial, business center, and fax service, and was open for the 1996 Asian Games. There's a swimming pool, night club and bowling, a gym and massage.

The skiing season goes from early November to April. The resort has three lifts, three beginners' tows, and night skiing. It offers lessons and has two first-aid stations, 11 runs totalling 30 km for all levels. It also has five km of cross-country trails. Yabuli is open in the summer with a 2680-meter bob-sled run, mini-golf, hot air ballooning and gliding. See also Chapter 10, Sports, Recreation, & Ecotourism.

Closer to Harbin and less challenging is **Yuquan**. In both places you can rent skis and clothes. Lift tickets cost about Y40 per day. For the **Heilongjiang Yabuli International Travel Service**, *Tel. 3678987, Fax 3661785*. The telephone code is 451.

Practical Information

Ambulance, *Tel. 120*

Office Hours, 8am-5pm; stores 9am-7 or 8pm

Heilongjiang Overseas Tourist Corporation/China International Travel Service, *11/F, Hushi Building, No. 2 Tielu St, Nangang, 150001, Tel. 3661159, Fax 362108. E-mail: liguoliu@163.com.cn*. Ask for Liu Liguo. It can sell tickets on the once-a-week train to Moscow.

Police, *Tel. 110*

Telephone Code: 451

Shenyang

(Formerly Mukden)

Shenyang is the capital of Liaoning province which borders on North Korea. In the news recently because of its recently discovered fossils of bird dinosaurs, it was inhabited by apemen 280,000 years ago. It has a history of over 2,700 years. Shenyang was the Manchu capital from 1625 until 1644. Then the Manchus moved to Beijing as the Qing dynasty. Shenyang is the biggest industrial city in this region which was formerly Japanese-held Manchuria. The Mukden Incident on September 18, 1931, a surprise attack on the Chinese army stationed here, marked the beginning of Japanese aggression in China.

The weather is hottest in August, averaging 23.8°C; the coldest in January is -30°C. Rain is mainly from June to August with an annual 760 mm. The urban population is about 6.12 million, total 6.8 million. Shenyang is a sister city of Chicago.

Arrivals & Departures

Shenyang is 75 minutes by air northeast of Beijing. Flights with Hong Kong, Irkutsk, Macau, Osaka, Pyongyang, Sapporo, Seoul and 41 Chinese cities are available. You can also reach it by train and expressway from Dalian about 375 km away. Trains connecting with Beijing and Harbin use the Shenyang North Station at 102, Bei Zan Road, Shen He District; those connecting with Dalian go to the South Station, 2, Sheng Li Nan Street, in He Ping District.

Orientation

Shenyang today is an industrial and cultural center, with many institutions of higher learning and research. It has two ring roads around the city, one 30 km long, and the other 80. You should always add extra time for traffic jams.

Where to Stay & Eat

The top hotel is the Marriott, but it is in the southern part of the city in the high technological zone. An Intercontinental opened too late to be reviewed and should be considered near the top. Traders is considerably better than most four stars anywhere. The next best is the New World Courtyard. The Sheraton Shenyang opened too late to be reviewed in 2002. For U.S. toll-free telephone numbers, see Chapter 12. With all these choices, prices should be soft. Hotels listed here should all have money changing, credit cards, and business center services. Prices are subject to 15% surcharge on all services, and discounts.

SHENYANG MARRIOTT HOTEL (Huang Chao Wan Hao Jiu Dian), *388 Qing Nian Da Street, Heping District, 110003. Tel. 23993931, Fax 23907337. E-mail: mhrs.shemc.dom@marriott.com. Website: www.marriotthotels.com. Rooms are $116-$146, and suites $195-$2168. It has been discounting 14.5%. It is in the Riverside Garden residential area and five minutes' walk to Wu Li He Football Stadium, 15km to the airport, and 20km to the Railway Station.*

This 435-room, 25-story hotel was opened in 1999. It has five executive floors and six non-smoking floors. Rooms are 38 square meters and offer CNN and CNBC. Its breakfast buffet costs Y90. There are Japanese, Chinese and Western restaurants, and a cigar bar. Its grand ballroom seats 500 banquet-style.

TRADERS HOTEL (Shang Mao Fan Dian), *68 Zhong Hua Road, Heping District, 110001. Four stars. Tel. 23412288, Fax 23411988. In North America, Tel. 800/942-5050. $150-$210 for rooms; suites $310-$1300. It has been discounting up to 65%.*

This 595-room hotel has an Irish fun pub, northeastern, Western, and Cantonese food. Its health club has a gym, jacuzzi, sauna, and steambath. Rooms have safes, in-house movies, and 24-hour room service. Executive floor rooms are very spacious with wide twin beds. Shangri-La Hotels and Resorts.

NEW WORLD COURTYARD SHENYANG (Xin Shi Jie Jiu Dian), *2 Nanjing Nan Street, Heping District, 110001. Four stars. Tel. 23869888, Fax 23860018. E-mail: nwsales@online.ln.cn. Website: www.courtyard.com. This is 30 km from the new airport and 10 km from the railway station. $125 to $450 for rooms and suites but it has been charging only $54-$59 including breakfast for a standard single.*

Built in 1994, this 22-story, 263-room hotel is centrally located. It has non-smoking floors, CNN, ESPN, an indoor pool, gym and sauna. A Courtyard by Marriott Hotel.

Seeing the Sights

If you only have one day, consider the not-to-be-missed Imperial Palace and Beiling Tombs. The 19-year reigns of Nurhachi (Nulhachi) and Huangtaiji (Huang Tai Chi) were enough to build the very impressive ***Imperial Palace**, 171 Shenyang Road. The palace dates from 1625 to 1636, and is now restored to its original gaudy splendor. In an area of almost 60,000 square meters, be prepared for lots of walking. Although this palace has much Han influence, look for Mongolian and Manchu-style touches. The most impressive section is the eastern one, with its octagonal Dazheng Dian (Hall of Great Affairs) and Shiwang Ting (Pavilions of Ten Princes). Does the Beijing Palace have such dragons on its pillars and the yurt-like design? The hall was used for important ceremonies and meetings with top officials.

Huangtaiji commanded his military forces and conducted business from the Chongzhen Dian (Hall of Supreme Administration). At the back of this hall is a road to the Fenghuang Lou (Phoenix Tower) and the Qingning Gong (Palace of Pure Tranquility). The families lived in the Qingning Gong, which is the most distinctively Manchu.

In the western section is the Wenshuo Ge (Hall of Literary Source), especially constructed for the Complete Library of the Four Treasures of Qing Emperor Qianlong. Unfortunately, no signs are in English.

The *Beiling (or North) Tombs**, also called the Zhaoling Tombs, are on Beiling Street, in the north of the city. They are of Huangtaiji and his wife Borjigid (Poerchichiteh). Huangtaiji was the son of Nurhachi. Begun in 1643, the tombs were completed in 1651. If you still want to study more Manchu tombs, the Dongling (East) Tombs (or Fuling Tombs), of Nurhachi and his wife Yihnaran, are 20 km from the city. During the Ming, Nurhachi unified the tribes, became Khan in 1616, and made Shenyang his capital in 1625.

Other Sights

Also of interest is the **Shenyang Steam Locomotives Museum**, Sujiatun Jiwuduan, Sujiatun District, open daily 9am-4pm with exhibits from nine countries. The best place to see the real thing is at Chaoyang City. This has more locomotives than Shenyang and the slope is better for taking photos. See also Harbin and Datong for these locomotives.

The **Liaoning Provincial Museum** is located at 26, Shiwei Road, Heping District in the mansion of a former warlord's son. It has had an excellent exhibition of photos of the city taken 1901 to 1912 by a French photographer. It also has exhibits, with a few English titles, starting from 280,000 years ago. Open 9am-4:30pm daily except Mondays from May 1 to October 30; otherwise 9am-3pm. Its store had outrageously high prices, ten times the prices for souvenirs than at the Imperial Palace. It takes credit cards.

Only 26 km outside Shenyang near the airport, is Aerolite Hill Park, the home of a giant 160-meter-long, two million-ton aerolite/meteorite. It is believed to have landed here 1.9 billion years ago.

Nightlife & Entertainment

Warm evenings from 8pm-1am around Chairman Mao Square can be fun. This is where many Chinese people relax and dance. You could also try it at 6am too. Look for the nearby Liaoning Hotel, a relic from its Japanese past. The art deco stained glass windows, dark mahagony woodwork and rattan furniture are worth savoring if they haven't been trashed by now. This hotel used to be the most fashionable in the city.

Shenyang has go-carts, golf and bowling.

Shopping

Produced in the province are diamonds, ginseng, sable and carvings of jade, agate, jet, and amber. Also produced are ceramics, root carvings, the musical instrument *zheng*, shell carvings, feather pictures, and paintings. Ask about the jade factory and the feather picture factory.

The main shopping area is around the **Dong Ya Commercial Square** on 212 Zhongjie Street, around the **Liaoning Department Store**, 63 Zhonghua Road, *Tel. 23863312*, and around the **Zhongxing-Shenyang Department Store**, 86 Taiyuan Bei Street, *Tel. 23838888*. Look for antiques and curios at the **Shenyang Eastern Folk Art Exchange City** (Friendship Street City), 5, You Hao Street, Shenhe District, *Tel. 22525687, 22525689 or Fax 22520485*. Open daily 8:30am-5pm. This building should house four stories of tiny private shops with collectors' teapots, root carvings, black porcelain, serpentine carvings, and jewelry. Unfortunately there's no air-conditioning or elevators.

The Imperial Palace is full of arts and curios stores.

Excursions & Day Trips

Dandong is at the border with North Korea and can be reached by air from seven Chinese cities or by a five-hour train ride from Shenyang. A train goes from Beijing every other day. Shenyang has the closest North Korean consulate and travel agents need two days to a week to process visas. You can't land in Korea without one, but you can boat on the Yalu River. This river is known to those who remember the Korean War. You might want to visit the King of Medicine Temple on Feng Huang (Phoenix) Hill, a visit to which should cure you of all ills.

There are only three-star hotels here. Try the **Dandong International Hotel**, 88 Xinan Street, 118000, *Tel. 2137788 X 3004, Fax 2146644*. It is 30 km from the airport, and five km from the railway station.

CITS is on No. 1 Square, 118000, *Tel. 2137493, Fax 2131853*; and Korea International Travel Company, Room No. 3, 2/F, 25, Xianqian Street, Yuanbao District, Tel.2812542, Fax 2818438. Both offer tours and can help you obtain visas for North Korea.

Practical Information

Hours: most tourist attractions are open 9am-5pm in summer and shorter hours are possible in winter; the large department stores above are open 8:30 or 9am-6 or 7pm in winter, or 9pm in summer.

Japanese Consulate, *50, 14 Wei Road, Heping District, 110003, Tel. 22322749*.

Shenyang Tourism Administration, *Tel. 22848657 or website: www.sytour.com (English)*.

Telephone Code: 24

US Consulate, *52, 14th Weir Road, Heping District, 110003, Tel. 23220848, 23221198. Fax 23222374. Website: www.state.gov/.*

Dalian

(Talien or Luda)

Dalian is worth visiting because it is a beautiful little well-run city. It appears to be more progressive, better organized and more prosperous than Shenyang. For example, you shouldn't have to wait longer than three minutes for a bus, and traffic lights are co-ordinated. Its government has decreed that all new construction be in Western-style architecture, and this uniformity makes it look very attractive, as does its seaside location. Occasionally you hear talk that the provincial capital should be moved here instead of grubby Shenyang.

The area also has lots of fresh seafood, peaches, pears, strawberries, and 100 varieties of apples. It is a sister city of Oakland, California, and Vancouver, Canada.

Dalian has a total population of 5.38 million. While its weather is generally moderate, its hottest temperature (August) has been 34 C, and its lowest -21 C (for one or two days). The annual precipitation is 600-800 mm. The best time to visit is May 1 to October 1. It is an ice-free port near the southern tip of Liaoning province on the Yellow and Bohai Seas and an important industrial center.

Arrivals & Departures

Dalian is south of Shenyang, a forty-minute flight, a 3.5 to four-hour train trip, or a drive (375 km) on the expressway. Taxi prices from Shenyang airport range from Y1000 to Y1200. You can reach Dalian by express train from Beijing in less than 10 hours or by frequent plane in less than an hour. It's two hours from Shanghai. You can also fly here from Hong Kong, Irkutsk, Osaka, Pyongyang, Sapporo, Seoul, and 45 Chinese cities. You could however be delayed by fog.

By ship, you can arrive from Inchon in 18 hours. Ocean cruise ships sometimes stop here. It has one of the two biggest cargo ports in North China.

Orientation

Known during imperialist times as **Port Arthur**, Dalian was seized briefly by the Japanese in 1894, but was leased as a naval base for 25 years to Russia in 1898. Russia was also given the right to build a railroad connecting the base with the Trans-Siberian railroad. As the result of the Russian defeat by Japan in 1905, Japan took over the base until 1945. It left behind a high standard of education.

Dalian has Japanese and old tsarist architecture and a high percentage of first-rate hotels. It has a lot of coastline and its commercial area is on a 8 by 15 kilometer peninsula, easily accessible from the expressway. You can walk to most places downtown and air pollution is minimal. A sightseeing bus 801 that looks like an old tram car goes from Victory Plaza around town from 8am-5:30pm, a nice introduction to the city.

Where to Stay

The top hotel is the Shangri-La followed closely by the new tower of its neighbor the Furama. This is a highly competitive situation you might want to exploit. The service at the Shangri-La is better. Other five stars are the Swiss (Tel. 2303388) and the Hilton (Tel. 2529999, neither of which I've seen). In the four-star category are the Holiday Inn and Ramada. All these hotels are within two km of each other, close to shopping and the harbor, and about 12 to 14 km from the airport to the north.

All hotels listed add an additional 15% service charge and have such services as credit cards, money exchange, business center, etc. All these hotels give discounts and packages during low business season, some as high as 50%. Hotels can arrange golfing.

SHANGRI-LA HOTEL DALIAN (Shang Gorilla), *66 Renmin Road, 116001. Five stars. Tel 2525000, Fax 2525050. E-mail: slda@shangri-la.com. One km from the harbor and two km from the railway station. $190-$260 for rooms; $290-$1200 for suites. Normally 30% off the "value rate" for walk-ins in low and high season.*

This hotel has 562 rooms, each with coffee-maker, big fluffy pillows, CNN, and safe. It also has a health club with gym, indoor pool, two tennis courts, steam bath, Jacuzzi and sauna. Three executive club floors have fax lines in rooms, late checkout, and good friendly service. The club's complimentary breakfast has included dim sum, hash browns, smoked salmon, carrot and other juices, and made-to-order eggs. Its regular Y125 breakfast is even more elaborate.

FURAMA HOTEL DALIAN (Fulihua), *60 Renmin Road, 116001. Five stars. Tel. 2630888, Fax 2639128. E-mail: furama@furama.com.cn. Website: www.furama.com.cn. Main Building, Y980-Y4710; New Tower, Y1640-Y20750. Visit its website for price updates. In North America, Tel. 800/44UTELL.*

The Furama's 1988 Main Building has 22-stories and 445 rooms and should be completely renovated in 2002. Its New Tower, opened in 1996, has an additional 376 larger rooms and chandeliers in its elevators. It offers CNN and HBO, and in-room safes. There are Chaozhou, Chinese, French, Japanese and Korean restaurants. Its huge classy lobby has upscale stores like Hugo Boss, Bally and Cartier, and Ermenegildo Zegna. It has office suites and free shuttle bus. Its health club has an indoor pool (with a sign that says "no swimming when drunk"), a gym, putting green, squash, aerobics, and tennis court.

RAMADA HOTEL, *18 Sheng Li Square, Zhong Shan District, 116001. Four stars. Tel. 2808888, E-mail: ramada.dalian@online.ln.cn. Website: www.ramadahotels.com. Opposite the railway station, Shengli/Victory Plaza, and next to a "walking" street, it is about one kilometer from the harbor. $99-$148 for rooms and $198-$380 for suites. It has been discounting 40-50%.*

This 329 room hotel has CNN and HBO.

GRAND HOTEL (Bolan), *1 Jiefang Street Zhongshan Dist, 116001. Tel. 2806161, Fax 2806980. Three stars. $78-$98 for rooms and $150-$280 for suites.*

It is clean, has room safes, and CNN, and is downtown near Zhongshan Square. For budget travelers only.

Where to Eat

Seafood is the main specialty here. The best food is in the top hotels, especially the **Shang Palace** in the Shangri-La for spicy jelly fish and lemon duck. The **New Orient Seafood City**, at 3 Harbor Square, *Tel. 2713999*, near the port is the most popular but it is more expensive than other restaurants. You can choose from many tanks of swimming fish, 10 kinds of crab, or abalone, squid, turtles, snakes, and lobster. There's also dumplings and sushi, and stir-fried vegetables.

There is also the **Tian-Tian Yu Gang Restauran**t at 72 Tianjin Street, Zhongshan District, *Tel. 2641678*, and its branch at 26 Yanan Street, *Tel. 2816999*. The **Shuang Shengyuan Hotel** has a good restaurant at 27 Qinjian Street, Zhongshan Dist., *Tel. 2727777*.

Seeing the Sights

There are no world-class attractions except the beautiful seashore but enough to keep you busy for a couple of days. Tourists might be interested in its ornamental glass factory, the centrally-located zoo, and the harbor (tour boats from Tiger Beach).

You can visit part of old Port Arthur, the 1900 tsarist-built fort on Jiguanshan Hill and prison. With permission, you can cruise to Snake Island, 25 nautical miles away, northwest of Lushun. With an estimated 13,000 pit vipers, this is a snake sanctuary. It supplies a research center studying the medical benefits of the venom.

You can also hike and raft in the small but exquisite **Bingyu Valley** with its Guilin-like scenery, 90 minutes by expressway northeast from Dalian and 40 km from Zhuanghe city. (You will also be close to North Korea.) It is best to go by taxi because there's only one train a day. Mini-buses do leave from the railway station in Dalian but schedules are not regular. Bingyu has 40 peaks and 20 caves to be explored in a 47-square kilometer park. Here the best hotel is the three-star 104-room branch of the Dalian Furama. The Bingyu Furama has a pool, disco, sauna and two restaurants.

This **national park** is a pleasant day trip, a chance to see the countryside. You do have to bring your own interpreter. Another guest house here has served good fresh-water shrimp, celery and conch, and deep-fried silk worm cocoons. The Tourism Bureau is at 296, Xiang Yang Road, Zhuanghe, Dalian, 116400, *Tel. 8612315*.

Nightlife & Entertainment

Head for the two main squares in the evening for badminton, dancing, games, concerts, and just hanging out. The Kylin stage is a theater for Peking opera that performs upon request. It's at One, West Lane of Kylin, Kunming Street, Zhongshan District, *Tel. 2305411*.

Sports & Recreation

There's a Brunswick Bowling Alley behind the Shangri-La with over 20 lanes. For golf, the Golden Pebble is the best of two courses. The season is nine months long. The Pebble Beach Golf Course telephone is *7900502, 7900137 and fax 7900548, 7900425*. Unfortunately no one speaks English there but hotels and travel agents can arrange for you to play. The best swimming beach is at the Bangchuidao on Binhai Road only a few kilometers from downtown.

Practical Information

CYTS Tours, *94 Shenyang Road, Xi Gang District, 116011, Tel. 3684579, Fax 3685258. E-mail: CYTS@yandex.ru. Ask for Ada.*

Dalian Overseas Tourist Corporation, *One Changtong Street, Xigang District, 116011. Tel. 3680856, 3680938 (European and Asian Department), Fax 3687831, 3680856.* They might not answer within 48 hours and might be difficult to understand.

Hours: the main stores open from 9:30am-9:30pm here, especially in summer. Office hours are 8:30am-5:30pm with a one-hour lunch break at 11:30am. Rush hour is 7am-9am, and 5pm-7pm.

Telephone code: 411.

Chapter 18

Silk Road

The term **Silk Road** was first used by a German author in the 19th century and is still used because it is so apt. Silk was the main commodity carried along the caravan routes between Cathay and Europe. It dazzled the eyes of Marco Polo who traveled here in 1275. Bales of silk were buried in ancient tombs along the way for use in the afterlife, it was that highly valued.

In 138 B.C. (Han), Emperor Wudi sent his emissary Zhang Qian (Chang Ch'ien) on missions westward to get help to fight the Huns. Zhang returned 13 years later, having been imprisoned most of that time by hostile tribes, but he fired the emperor's interest in trade. The Han emperors encouraged trading caravans with imperial protection and the building of beacon signal towers.

From then on, the routes flourished periodically until the 14th century, especially in the Tang. It declined because merchants were able to transport their goods more efficiently by sea, and because of hostilities along the land routes.

Trade was mainly in easily transported goods. The Chinese exchanged silk, tea, and seeds for peach and pear trees. They also exchanged skills, such as iron-, steel-, and paper-making; they received grapes, pomegranate and walnut trees, sesame, coriander, spinach, the Fergana horse, alfalfa, Buddhism, Nestorianism, and Islam.

Goods were exchanged along the Silk Road especially with India and West Asia. Some even reached Rome. The route went west from Xi'an along the Weihe River valley, Hexi Corridor, Tarim Basin, and Parmirs (in Central Asia).

Then it continued through Afghanistan, Iran, Iraq, and Syria. It was about 7000 km long (2,700 kms within China). Northern and southern routes divided at Dunhuang on either side of the Taklamakan Desert. Many Arab and Persian merchants settled in Xi'an and even as far east as Yangzhou.

Foreign visitors can visit most of the Silk Road cities, an exotic world of onion-domed mosques, bazaars, oasis, grapes, central Asian and Turkish faces, embroidered caps, and strange languages. Spontaneous dancing and singing, uncontrolled by Han reserve, make people here delightful. Visitors are frequently asked to join in.

You can find giant rock carvings and murals, some of the best in the world, and explore earthen-walled ghost cities, the western end of the Great Wall, old tombs, and Buddhist temples. You can study 4000 year-old mummies who look European. You can try to figure out how and what the beacon towers communicated and learn how water is channeled to make these deserts flourish. Carpets, jade goblets, jeweled daggers, and musical instruments are good buys here.

But the Silk Road is not Turkey, Pakistan, or Afghanistan. It is China, an ingredient that makes this region of mixed cultures special and worth the occasional hardships like sandstorms. The air is generally clean however. The people are warm and naturally hospitable to foreigners. The history and conflicts are interesting and the Chinese government is now putting a lot of money into developing the area.

Arranging Travel

Travel here has improved in the last three years. You can trek, take a luxury or ordinary train, fly, or drive a vehicle yourself, as well as ride a camel. For a leased luxury train, contact **China Rail Express Travel Service**, (6/F, Building B-23, Second Block of Sanlihe, West District, Beijing, 100045, *Tel. 68530610, 51840990, Fax 68530610. E-mail: crts@public.fhnet.cn.net*. Ask for sales manager, Sun Lianfeng). **Conference World Tours** has a couple China Orient Express luxury train tours too. See Chapter 6 for address.

Several agencies have less elegant land tours. **China Nature Tours** and many of the other Urumqi travel agencies can arrange week-long camel treks. Regular charter flights during the summer serve Dunhuang, Jiayuguan, Lanzhou, and Xi'an. A railway now joins Urumqi, Turfan, Korle, Kuqa and Kashgar. A desert highway goes across the once-feared Taklamakan Desert from Korle to Minfeng in five to six hours. The Taklamakan is the second-largest desert in the world and it used to take 20 to 25 days to cross by camel. July and August are frightfully hot in Turfan, and between there and Kashgar. But up in the mountains and in North Xinjiang, the weather can be much better.

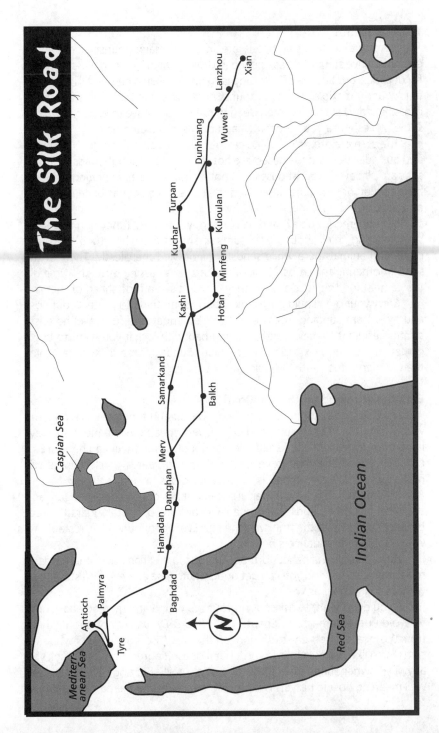

Travel Realities

Comfortable four-star hotels are in some major tourist cities, and a exemplary five-star hotel has opened in Urumqi. Xi'an has had five-star hotels for decades. But outside of Xi'an and Lanzhou, traveling here is still not for the finicky and inflexible. Toilets in tourist hotels are fine but others are pretty gross. Restaurants have gotten cleaner, but you still have to be careful and in some places, rinse your chopsticks and bowls in scalding hot tea.

The area is extremely dry and can be cold on a summer night. Long train and bus rides through the desert are not comfortable though roads to tourist sites are all paved. Tourist buses, but not all trains, are air-conditioned. Buses have broken down in the desert and the coolest retreat has been the shade of a rock or a sand dune, if you're lucky.

Be prepared for delays and be pleasantly surprised if they don't happen. While waiting, think about the peasants and herdsmen who struggled to raise crops and animals here while sandstorms howled mercilessly. Think of the sand smothering the crops. Think of the caravans passing through. What did the camels and traders do when they couldn't see a foot ahead of them?

Carry your own liquid refreshments and something to protect your nose and eyes from stinging grains of sand. Also imperative for travel here is a strong flashlight for caves and a folding bag with lock if you want to buy a carpet. Try to plan your trip for the fabulous Sunday bazaar in Kashgar. Enjoy the wonderful food – the Middle Eastern spices.

Eating & Drinking on the Silk Road

Muslim food is common in Xinjiang, Gansu and Ningxia. It is wonderful with varying degrees of spice and can be very cheap but the meat is always lamb or mutton. A bowl of steaming hot noodles with meat can be Y5-Y8 or a huge ground meat pancake can be Y15. Standards of cleanliness will probably improve even more as the area develops generally.

Muslim Ba Bao tea is wonderful because it has dried jujubes, longan, and tiny red wolf berries, and is sweetened with a chunk of crystal sugar. It's great because you can eat the fruit with the tea. Every community has restaurants where lively Uighur dancers perform.

Large cities like Lanzhou, Urumqi and of course Xi'an have other kinds of restaurants as well and you can get good Cantonese and even Western food with pork and beef as well.

If you don't want to risk spoiling your trip with diarrhea, read about how to avoid upset stomachs in Chapter 11, *Food & Drink*. Do not eat anything from the local markets unless it's right off the fire. Wise is the traveler who says something like "I would love to try it, but it doesn't agree with me. Thank you anyway," when handed a glass of mare's milk buzzing with flies. The well-meaning host in his yurt is not going to appreciate the pain you may go through later. If you drink it because you don't want to hurt his feelings, you are the one who will suffer!

Ethnic Groups
As you travel around, try to pick out the characteristics of the different nationalities. Attempt to identify people from their facial features and their distinctive dress. Among the groups here are the Han, Huns, Huis (Muslims), Kazaks, Kirghiz, Manchus, Mongols, Russians, Tarjiks (Tajiks), Tartars, Turfans, Uzbeks, Uygurs (Uighurs), and Xibos.

Guides leave visitors in minority villages to fend for themselves, with no introductions or suggestions as to what to do. Do some reading beforehand. Prepare some questions about lifestyles, schooling for nomads, number of children allowed, handicrafts and courtship customs. Many guides know nothing about these people. For the archaeology, read Peter Hopkirk's *Foreign Devils on the Silk Road* about archaeological raids here in the early 1900s and Elizabeth W. Barber's *The Mummies of Urumqi*. There are many books on China's national minorities. See Xian, Dunhuang, Kashgar, Lanzhou, Turpan, and Urumqi.

To get a big smile from a Uygur, just say "Rakh mut" meaning "thank you."

China has reacted to recent worldwide terrorist threats by arresting those members of its own national minorities suspected of being secessionists and saboteurs. It has closed its border from time to time with Afghanistan and Pakistan, as a precaution against incursions from outside. Some Chinese minority people were fighting with the Taliban. Suspicious explosions have taken place. Check your government's travel advisories before venturing here or anywhere else in the world.

Lanzhou

(Lanchow)
Lanzhou, the capital of Gansu province, is almost in the center of China. The province was settled 200,000 years ago and the inhabitants started farming 5000 thousand years ago. Founded about 2200 years ago, Lanzhou was called the "Gold City" after gold was found here.

Situated on the Yellow River at an altitude of 1,524-2000 meters, Lanzhou's coldest temperature is -10°C in January; the hottest is a fleeting 30°C in summer. The annual precipitation in the province is 400-800 mm. Sandstorms occur in April and May sometimes in the Hexi Corridor. The best time to visit is April-November.

With an urban population of 2 million, and a total 3 million, Lanzhou is industrial, with petrochemicals, machine-building and smelting. Gansu province today has a population of 25 million, including Han, Hui, Tibetan, Uygur, Dongxiang, Bonan, Mongolian, Kazak, Tu, Salar, and Manchu nationalities.

Arrivals & Departures

Lanzhou can be reached by air from Hong Kong and 34 Chinese cities including Beijing, Dunhuang (1165 km away), and Xi'an (800 km). The airport is about 80 km or one hour from the city by expressway. The CAAC bus (with smelly seat covers) costs Y25 and goes about once an hour. A private taxi should cost Y150 to Y200. A shared taxi shouldn't be more than Y40 per person.

CITS says the fastest trains are Lanzhou to Jiayuguan nine hours, to Urumqi 24 hours, Xining three hours, Xian 11 hours, and Yinchuan 10 hours.

Orientation

Lanzhou is important because of its Silk Road history and as a gateway to two cave temples, the *Bingling Si Grottoes and the *Maijishan Grottoes. The central government is putting $30 million into Gansu's tourism infastructure from 2001-2006. The infamous pollution in its capital has been reduced by the growing use of electricity instead of coal but it's still bad. It is in a valley surrounded by hills rising up to about 500 meters. One of these hills, Daqing Shan in the east, is currently being cut down, partly to allow bad air to be diluted or blown away.

Where to Stay

The best hotel is the Legend and then the new Jin Jiang, the latter too recent to be reviewed. The Gansu International and Xilan International Hotel are okay for budget travelers. Unless it has had a recent renovation, some of the rooms in the Legend have worn carpets especially on the lower floors. Hotels here have air-conditioning, beauty salons, and business centers. Except for that of some managers, English generally is poor to non-existent.

LANZHOU LEGEND HOTEL, *599 Tianshui Road, 730000. Four stars, Tel. 8882876, Fax 8887876. E-mail: llhsm@public.lz.gs.cn. It is 76 km from the airport, and two km from the railway station. Rooms are Y880 to Y9800. Good downtown location near shopping, other hotels, and Lanzhou University.*

This 384-room hotel has two non-smoking floors, a gym, and a Cantonese restaurant. It has Singapore management.

GANSU INTERNATIONAL HOTEL, *260 Qing Yang Road, 730030. Three stars. Tel. 8457188, Fax 8457288.*

Opened in 1998-99 near China Post and in the downtown financial district, this 20-story hotel has 305 rooms with in-house videos, non-smoking rooms, pub, night club, gym, sauna and Jacuzzi. Finechain Hotels Management.

XILAN INTERNATIONAL HOTEL (Xilan Guoji Dajiudian), *133 Tuan Jie Xin Cun Dingxi Road, 730000, Tel. 8628998, Fax 8612396. Rooms are Y428 and Y588, and suites Y888 to Y8888. It has been discounting 20%. It can change foreign cash, and should take credit cards now. In the eastern downtown section, it is over a kilometer from the railway station.*

This hotel has 30 stories topped by a revolving restaurant with Hong Kong-type Western food. It serves a good Cantonese dim sum breakfast buffet and offers American hamburgers and what clerk Charley Zhang insisted was roast suckling duck. If you have language problems, ask for Charley at the front desk. There's a six-piece gym with mostly China-made machines and its 15-meter pool looked okay. Rooms have television in Chinese only, and safes. Across the road is an internet bar.

Where to Eat

Local specialities include roast piglet (delicious), sweet and sour Yellow River carp, steamed chicken, fried camel hoof (ugh), and fried sheep's tail. Hotel restaurants are best. Downtown across the street from the Tourism Building is one of Lanzhou's specialty noodle shops.

The **Xin Yuan Beef Noodle Restaurant** is at the back door of the Lanzhou Legend Hotel at 33 Nong Min Xiang Road, *Tel. 8416321 ext. 8668, 8688.* Chili oil is like ketchup on the table. It is open 6am to 9pm and charges Y5 for either a big or small bowl. The **Chao Shan Cantonese restaurant** is at 12 Nong Min Xiang Road, *Tel. 8889494* and has a good reputation. Many restaurants that stay open until 2-3am are on Nong Min Xiang Lane, between the Legend and Jincheng Hotels. The largest of these is the **Ya Ou Shang Chang** with Asian and European food. Locals say Lanzhou makes the best Ba Bao Cha – the Muslim or Eight Treasure tea.

Seeing the Sights

In Lanzhou itself, of mild interest is the **Baita (White Pagoda Park)** on the north bank of the Yellow River. First built in the Yuan, then rebuilt and expanded in the Ming and Qing, the Baita has seven stories and eight sides and is about 17 meters high. On the opposite shore is a functioning water wheel that's worth a stop if you've never seen one before.

Five km from downtown is the **Wuquan (Five-Spring) Hill** with genuine temples, the oldest, the spooky Ming dynasty Chung Wen. Legend credits General Huo Qubing (Huo Chu-ping), in 120 B.C., with stabbing the ground with his sword after finding no water for his horses. Five streams of water appeared and have been flowing ever since. Other important relics to see here are the Taihe Iron Bell, three meters high, weighing five tons, and cast in 1202; and the Tongjieyinfo Buddha, cast in bronze in 1370, and weighing nearly five tons. It's open 8:30am-5pm.

The **Yellow River cruise** is not special, but the **Provincial Museum** at 3 Xijin Xi Road (opposite the Friendship Hotel and five km from the Legend Hotel) is worth a visit. It costs Y15, and is open to 5:30pm but closed from 12 noon to 2:30pm Saturday-Monday. *Tel. 2334106.* Here is the famous 1,800-year-old Galloping Horse of Gansu that toured the US and Canada. It was found in Wuwei in the middle of the province. Also important are the 2000-year-old-wooden "slips" (documents of history and medicine) from north and west Gansu, and 8,120-year-old painted pottery.

You can take a cable car to the top of Gaolan Mountain to look at the city. It costs about Y10 return and runs 8am-10pm.

Shopping

Lanzhou produces many kinds of melons, red dates, carved ink slabs, luminous "jade" cups, and bottle gourds. It also manufactures silk carpets, lanterns, and reproductions of ancient paintings based on the Silk Road murals. Beautiful are the Buddha head reproductions from the Maiji Grottoes and some of the replicas of the famous Flying Horse made from molds directly from the original. There are also whimsical cloth animals. See the **Gansu Cultural Relics Shop**, 3 Xijinxi Road, and the good shop in the **Gansu Provincial Museum**.

For reproductions of Buddha heads, the **Le Seine Culture and Art World** is at 45 Qinan Road, 730000, *Tel. 8828987, 8828989*. It is opposite the Huadu Hotel and you can haggle there too. The **Huangmiao Market**, five minutes by taxi from the Jingcheng Hotel, is especially good on weekends. It has curios, stamps, coins, and some reproductions.

Excursions & Day Trips

The fifth century ***Binglingsi Grottoes** has some dramatic natural scenery nearby but the statues and murals are not well preserved. It is 35 km west of Lanzhou on the Yellow River but the road is not good and you have to go over 129 km to get there. Boats are readily available to take you across a reservoir. The fastest takes 40 minutes. Binglingsi has 800 stone statues ranging from 25cm to 27 meters. The best cave is number 169 to the left of the big Buddha at the entrance. The statues range from Northern Wei to Ming, the youngest, at least 350 years old. If you want to take photos, it costs you Y300 per photo in some of the caves. Prepare for many stairs. Some impressive looking resorts are in the reservoir area.

In better shape and worth a tedious trip with a stunning view of the countryside is the ***Maiji Grottoes**, also Northern Wei to Ming. These are 45 km southeast of Tianshui, itself about 380 km southeast of Lanzhou. Tianshui can be reached by expressway from Lanzhou in four hours. This is faster than by train. By expressway from Xi'an, it's nine hours; by train it's eight hours overnight or five hours by day. Then it's a one-hour road trip for the last 45 km from Tianshui or Beidao railway station to the base of the small mountain There are once-a-week flights in the summer from Lanzhou and Xi'an.

At Maiji are 194 caves with over 7,200 **stone and clay Buddhist statues**, and 1300 square meters of murals dating from the end of the fourth century to the 19th, a period of 1500 years. These caves are in a 142-meter, high mountain, which rises almost vertically, and are reached by wooden staircases. Some of the statues are completely unsheltered; others are protected by doors and windows. The work on the mountain was done by craftsmen who piled blocks of wood up to the top and started carving while standing on them. As the artisans worked their way down, they gradually removed the blocks. Tourists are charged a prohibitive Y500 each if they take interior photos and no video cameras are allowed. Leave your bags in your bus.

The largest statue, in number 13 cave, is 15.8 meters high. The best is considered number 133. The most important are 127, 115, and 165. 44 and 135 are very special and from 386-534 A.D. You have to pay an additional Y500 to enter. All are protected by wire mesh and you need a full day to see them. A museum is near the parking lot. No titles are in English anywhere and no English-speaking guides are available on site You can get a guide from Tianshui or Lanzhou CITS. The grottoes are open 9am-4pm daily, all year round with an entrance fee of Y51. *Tel. 2816023 or 2816024.*

Tianshui was a trade distributing center on the Silk Road. Its altitude is 1000 to 2000 meters.

The **Fuxi Temple** is 20 km west of Tianshui in **Xiguan**. This is worth a trip if you are interested in Chinese mythology. Fuxi was China's Adam and is considered the human ancestor of the Chinese people. Titles are not in English. Five minutes away by car is the Jade Emperor Temple on National Highway 316. It is open 8am-6 or 7pm. This functioning Taoist temple is home to about 40 monks and two nuns. It's a lot easier to visit these two temples by taxi. One of the best hotels is the three-star Tianshui Guest House (Binguan) at 5 Yingbin Road, Qincheng District, *Tel. 938/8212611, Fax 8212823*. It has a fancy VIP section with 38 rooms. Rooms cost about $60 but Silk Road International can give you a 20% discount. It takes credit cards, changes money, has a business center, and pool.

The Tourism Bureau's telephone is *2729661, Fax 2731407*. CITS can be reached by telephone *8214463 and Fax 8213621*. I would recommend our guide, Sheldon Chen Lin, *Tel. 8299433*. The telephone code is 938.

Xiahe is a six to seven hour, 280 km taxi ride from Lanzhou. It is one of my favorite towns because of its Tibetan monastery, the Labrang/Labuleng, the largest outside of Tibet, built in 1709. It is in a Tibetan town with 30,000 people.

Buses leave early in the morning from the West Bus Station in Lanzhou (8 or 9 hours); a taxi costs about Y800. By taxi, you can lunch at the Linxia Guest House (Binguan) in Linxia, *Tel. 621132*. It puts on a good Muslim or Chinese lunch and you can enjoy Linxia's beautiful new mosques.

At Xiahe, you find yourself in Tibetan Buddhist rather than Muslim country. The altitude is over 2500 meters, so bring warm clothes even in late August and read about altitude sickness in Chapter 19. Labuleng is most exotic during the twice yearly festivals during which a giant 60-meter-long tangka is put out to sun. Another colorful time to go is the Sanko Tajuk Tibetan Horse Races. On that occasion, we found ourselves the only foreigners surrounded by several hundred Tibetans on horses in a snow storm in the nearby mountains in August. The best time to visit is July-August when the highs are 28C.

Lin Hua of the Gansu Silk Road International Tours in Lanzhou has figured out dates on the Western calendar as Feb.13, 2003 (Feb.03, 2004) for the Tangka Sunning Festival, Feb.14, 2003 (Feb.04, 2004) for special Buddhist ceremonies, and Feb.15, 2003 (Feb.05, 2004) for the butter exhibition. Every summer, the Tibetans also hold a big harvest festival for six days with dancing and horse racing. It's July 14-20, 2003 and July 31 to Aug.05, 2004.

For festivals, you should book hotels and transportation through a travel agent because of the crowds and the shortage of hotel rooms.

My favorite hotel is the grubby, poorly-run two-star 220-bed **Labuleng Hotel** at Laizhou Cun, Xiahe, 747100, *Tel. 941/7121849, Fax 7121328*. It costs $56 a room and reservations should be made from July to September a month in advance. Its bathroom floor was continuously wet and hot tap water only arrived five hours a day. We had to order and pay for meals in advance, and could only use US or Chinese cash. The location, however, makes up for everything. It is on the edge of town about a kilometer from the monastery, surrounded by barley fields and three Tibetan villages. The area is wonderful for hiking, and horseback riding.

There's also the 33-room **Jinlong** on Renmin Street, 747100, *Tel. 941/ 7122305, Fax 7122305 ext. 8118*. This is in the middle of town and has good food but no English. Rooms there are about $40, less a discount which Silk Road International can get you. This also has four-bed dormitories for about Y40 a bed. It has no money exchange, takes no credit cards, and has no elevator. It has been across the road from a cheap e-mail service. The **Tara Guesthouse** and the **Overseas Tibetan Hotel** are popular with backpackers.

Of its nearly 80,000 urban and rural inhabitants, about 40% are Tibetan and 40% Han. Around 1800 monks of the Yellow Sect live around the monastery, and you can see their maroon robes everywhere. Monk guides speaking English give tours, and buildings are open to visitors 9am-12noon and 2:30-5:30pm for a fee. But we entered at noon hour and wandered around on our own without paying. The monastery is full of wonderful murals, brocade prayer ladders, and tangkas. The monks are friendly. You can watch the three-hour noon-time catechismal debates and the serving of lunch, both fascinating. Evening chants are best heard and seen from the mountain above the temple around 7pm.

Near the monastery are several small restaurants with menus in English aimed at tourists though the toilets are terrible. These have names like the Snowland (among the cleanest), Everest Restaurant, and Tibet Restaurant. Some organize tours and treks.

The shopping for Tibetan items is wonderful and ranges from proletarian to a few good quality antiques. Prices are geared to local Tibetans. You can also find for sale what looks like genuine human skulls. Internet service is at the Shang Cheng Yintewang Julebu, *Tel. 941/7121744*. It is open 9:30am-9pm.

Wuwei is where archaeologists believe 2,000 Roman troops settled after losing their way 2000 years ago. Descendants of these soldiers live in Zhelai Village, Yongchang County, 100 km from Wuwei town. Jennifer at CITS Gansu can put you in touch with scholars. It's also where the famous flying horse of Gansu was found. Wuwei has the three-star Tianma Hotel, Xixiaoshizi, *Tel. 935/2215170, Fax 2212356*.

Zhangye has the Tian Tishan and Matisi Grottoes, and is the home of the Yugu Nationality who are unique to Gansu. Also in the province are Dunhuang and Jiayuguan. See separate listings.

Practical Information

Ambulance, *Tel. 120*.

Business hours: Bank of China, 9am-5pm daily. Travel agents 8:30am-12 noon; 2:30pm-6pm.

China Lanzhou Railway International Travel Service sponsors a luxury express train tour. *Tel. 8886124*. Mr. Wang Bo.

CITS Gansu, *10 Ningmin Xiang Lane, 730000. Tel. 8416164, 8826181, Fax 8416163, 8418556. E-mail: citsgsmd@public.lz.gs.cn. Website: www.silkroadtour.com.cn (English) or www.citsgs.myetang.com (English)*. It has Yellow River rafting tours and self-drive tours through the Hexi Corridor to Tibet. It can arrange tours to Tibetan sites in Gansu, Tibetan festivals, desert expeditions, treks, and archaeological tours. Ask for Jennifer Qin Li Juan, Sales Manager, American and Pacific Department who helped this book a lot. *E-mail: jannyqlj@public.lz.gs.cn.*

Gansu Silk Road International Tours, *Euro-American Department, 10 Nongmin Road, 730000, Tel. 8414368, 8416638 ext. 6587, Fax 8866068. E-mail: hualin@public.lz.gs.cn.Mobile: 13609320332*. Contact Ms. Lin Hua who helped this book a lot. She can arrange home stays with local families too.

Gansu Tourism Administration (brochures and complaints) are both at *10 Ningmin Xiang Lane, 730000, Tel. 8418443, Fax 8418443*. Ask for Mr. He Xiaozu who helped this book a lot. *Tel. 8416638. Website: www.chinasilkroad.com.*

Internet Service: The **Lanzhou Dianxin Zhong Duan** is at Er Lou, Wang Luo, Jiu Le bu (hau de shang chang dui mian). *Tel. 8851551*. This is in the corner building of China Telecom downtown and it's cheap.

Police, *Tel. 110*
Telephone code: 931

Dunhuang

(Tunhuang, Tunhwang)

In isolated western Gansu province lies one of the world's greatest art treasures, now a UNESCO Heritage Site: the Thousand Buddha Mogao Grottoes. It is well worth the effort to get here.

Arrivals & Departures

The fastest train to Dunhuang from Lanzhou takes 14 hours, from Turpan 10 hours, and from Urumqi 12 hours. These are overnight trains. Public minibuses and taxis are at the Dunhuang train station in Liuyuan which is 128 km northeast of Dunhuang. It costs about Y500 for a taxi or Y30 a person in a bus or mini-bus to town.

From April 1 to October 31, flights to Dunhuang leave almost daily from Beijing, Chengdu, Jiayuguan, Lanzhou, Urumqi, Xi'an, Xining, and Yinchuan. From November 1 to March 30, flights are fewer and only from Beijing, Lanzhou, Urumqi, Xi'an, Xining, and Yinchuan. Dunhuang is 12 km from the airport.

Many public buses ply between Dunhuang and Jiayuguan, about a 400 km trip on a two-lane highway.

Orientation

Dunhuang was an important cultural exchange center, military post, and oasis on the Silk Road. It was founded in 121 B.C. during the Western Han. From here, the Silk Road west splits into northern and southern routes, ending at the Mediterranean Sea. Dunhuang was a military outpost under the Tang. In 400 A.D., it became the capital of the Xiliang kingdom. In 1227, Genghis Khan seized it. You can see the ruins of the Han walls and a 16-meter-high tower in the old part of town, 250 meters west of the current one. The population now is 60,000 in the city, 150,800 urban and rural.

Between the fourth and 14th centuries, more than 492 caves were cut out of the cliffs. They were 25 km southeast of the city. These were filled with Buddhist carvings, sculptures, gilded and colored frescoes, and murals–the now famous caves.

Summers are hot, the highest about 40 C in July and early August, the coldest has been briefly -21 C in December, but it can be -15 C in April. The annual rainfall is only 39 mm. The best time weather-wise to visit is May, June, September or October. The altitude is 1,000 to 1,200 meters. Apricots, jujubes, pears, melons, peaches, and wine grapes are grown locally and are juicy and wonderful.

Where to Stay

The top hotels have air-conditioning and business centers. They add about 13% service charge and tax. There is no CNN. The best hotel downtown should be the Grand Sun's five-star section. The Dunhuang Guangyuan (Silk Road) Hotel on the outskirts is wonderful with a wide range of prices. In town for budget travelers is the Guangyuan Dajiudian with Y380 rooms and Y80 a bed in a dorm. (It has been discounting 20-40%.) The Liyuan is a small, very clean and cheap, three-star hotel behind the Feitian Hotel.

THE GRAND SUN HOTEL (Dunhuang Tai Yang Dajiudian), *No.5 North Road Shazhou, Tel. 8829998, Fax 8822019, E-mail: dhtyn@public.lz.gs.cn. Website: www.dhsuntravel.com (Chinese). This 220-room hotel accepts credit cards, changes travelers' checks and is in the center of the city. Rooms in its 2001 five-star Sun Village are Y688-Y1188 with a low season 15% discount. This hotel has cheaper, scruffy Y240 rooms too.*

SILK ROAD DUNHUANG HOTEL (Dunhuang Shan Zhuang), *Dungyuet Road, 736200, Tel. 8882088, Fax 8882086. Three stars. E-mail: srdsales@sina.com. Website: www.the-silk-road.com. This 200-room hotel between the Ming Sha Hills and the city is in imposing Dunhuang-Jiayuguan fortress-style. From it you can watch the sunset on the desert. The town is three kilometers away. Rooms are $43-$100, suites are $75-$1000, and dormitories Y80 a bed. It has been discounting 20%.*

There are non-smoking rooms, a sauna, and steam bath. It takes credit cards and travelers checks. The banquet hall can seat 1200 guests at tables. It has Asian and international food, and its own camels – for riding. Silk Road Hotel Management Co. Hong Kong.

Where to Eat

It's best to eat in the hotels especially for Dunhuang and Sichuan food, and in the winter, there's good hot pot. A couple of tiny, shabby local restaurants right downtown cater to foreign backpackers: **Charley Johng's Café** has three tables and a book exchange. It rents bicycles, and has e-mail service. *Tel. 8825113 or 8833039. E-mail: jqdhzch@public.lz.gs.cn.* It's at 21 Ming Shan Road. **John's Café**, *Tel. 8827000*, is part of a chain. *E-mail: johncafe@hotmail.com.* It has Western and Chinese food, tickets, tours, internet, and photocopying. For Muslim food, the **Xin Yue Can Ting Qing Zheng** on South Street is okay.

And for something to do after you eat, The Grand Sun Hotel's dance show is at 8pm for Y50.

Seeing the Sights

You can get to the Grottoes by taxi that will wait for you for a negotiable fee. You can now take a mini-bus 25 km to the ***Magao Grottoes** from the Long-Distance Bus Terminal on South Street in front of the Feitian Hotel. These leave between 6:30am and 8pm and return from Magao between 11:30am to 12 noon. In the afternoon, they go between 2pm and 2:30pm, and return at 4-30pm to 5pm. The fare is Y15. Don't linger. There are no hotels at the Grottoes. You can not take purses inside, nor can you photograph interiors. You can leave these valuables at a kiosk outside.

About 492 caves remain today in three or four rows on a 1.6 km-long cliff. They are open about 8am-5pm with time off for lunch. Hours depend on the season. The last admissions are about 3:30pm. *Tel. 937/8869060*. The entrance fee of Y100 includes the Exhibition Centre but only allows one entry a day. If you leave for lunch, you have to pay another Y100 to get back in. Knowledgeable guides are available on the site to show you around, and some speak English.

The State Council has renovated murals like the Feitian (Flying Apsaras) Fresco (Tang) and repainted over 2,400 statues. Some of the statues, in about 20 caves, were repainted in the Qing. Note the intricately painted ceilings.

The most important cave is the **Cangjing (Preserving Buddhist Scriptures) Cave**, now Number 17. They date from the Jin to Song (or late Tang to Western Xia, depending on sources), a span of over 800 years. In the Cangjing, 50,000 important old documents were found, including the Diamond Sutra (868 A.D.) This book is the oldest existing printed book and is now in the British Museum in London.

Other important caves include number 45 (clay figures); number 158 (the 15.6- meter-long Sleeping Buddha), and number 96. The art depicts Buddhist stories. One of the most famous is about a woman who is badly treated by her husband. A wolf kills her two children. After becoming a nun, she learns that her miseries are punishment for mistreating her step-sister in a previous incarnation.

Some of the statues are damaged, many by Muslims and a few by the Red Guards. Signs indicate which museums abroad have the pieces originally here. Some of the colors are still original and vivid. The red might be from pig's blood or cinnabar. One can get a real mystical feeling of history here. Caves were used as temples because they were conducive to meditation, like a mother's womb.

You can rent a flashlight here so you don't have to depend on that of a guide. Do not expect to observe an entire mural as you would in a spacious museum. You have to piece each section together in your own mind. A heavy metal door protects each cave.

Entry to specific caves on request cost an additional fee and photography needs special permission in advance. Tourists cannot wander around the site without a guide. Only 30 caves are open at a time and these are rotated every year. Most visitors only spend a half day there and see less than 10 caves because of the queues. It is best therefore to go in November-December when prices are lower and queues are shorter. The days in winter have highs of about 10°C, but avoid March which has sand storms.

Restaurants nearby are open for lunch. Stores sell locally-made stuffed camels, luminous cups of green jade, batik wall hangings, books in English, reproductions, videos and paintings. There are also carpets based on designs from the murals. Clerks are very aggressive but there are Western toilets.

Eight or nine reproduced caves are in the **Exhibition Centre**. Not to be missed are the ancient Tibetan artifacts on the second floor said to have been made at the Labuleng Monastery in Xiahe and meant for Tibet. Zhou En-lai kept them from being destroyed during the Cultural Revolution.

About 12 km. from Dunhuang on the way to the caves, and six kilometers off on a side road are two third-to-fifth century tombs you can enter, The **Western Jin Tombs**, *Tel. 8829998, 8822464*. They are open 9am to 6:30pm daily. Y30. One tomb has brick paintings of Fuxi and Nuwa, the Adam and Eve of China, and mythical fish. The nearby Han tomb has a flying horse, elephant, and a man holding up a mountain. No signs are in English.

The Yumen Gate and the nearby earthen remains of the Han Great Wall are only for those interested in earthen ruins. They are a 95 km, 4.5-hour, day trip by road northwest of Dunhuang city. The one- and two-lane road is paved. The tower and garrison here were built in 137 A.D. to protect the merchants. They are near a once-wider river that nourished the reeds and hemp for building the walls. You can see a stack of almost 2000-year-old petrified reeds stored for fuel for the beacon fires. From the Pass to the remains of the Great Wall is a 10 minute, 5 km drive. Look for rabbits and four-feet snakes and visualize the hardships of the camel caravans supplying the wealthy homes of Europe, and the envoys bringing tribute to the emperor.

Mingsha (Singing Sands) Hills is 6 km south of Dunhuang. You can ride one of its 200 camels from the gate to the top of the dunes, to Crescent Spring, and return, for Y60 per person. A shorter trip is Y30. This is in addition to the Y50 entry fee. You can get here by mini-bus from the Long Distance Bus Station for Y5 between 7am and 7:30am. Buses leave the dunes for the return to Dunhuang from 9:30pm to 10pm. Most people go in the evening when it's cooler.

Mingsha is open from 5am to 11pm daily. It charges Y10 to climb about 200 meters on stairs placed against one of the dunes for a wonderful view from the top. Here you can rest and listen for the drums and horses of the army that was buried by a sandstorm here. These hills are part of a 20 X 40 kilometers of classic sand dunes.

The **Dunhuang Museum** is open 8am to 6:30pm in summer (April 1 to Oct. 31), and 8:30am to 12, 2:30pm to 6pm in winter. It is at Yangguan Dong,

Tel. 8822884. Three exhibition rooms display hemp paper from 206 B.C., hemp shoes, socks and rope, bronze arrowheads, and an animal trap. It has a piece of 2000-year-old silk. Only one of the rooms has titles in English. There's also a map of the route that Buddhist missionary Xuan Zhang took to today's Pakistan. The museum has a store.

Shopping

The **night market** is on Nanjie Street. The **Silk Carpet, Handicrafts and Batik Factory** is at 35 Minsha Road, 736200, *Tel. 8822778.* The **Jewellery and Luminous Cup Factory** is at 12 Yangguan Dong Road, 736200, *Tel. 8822736.*

Practical Information

Dunhuang Sun International Travel Service, *5 Shazhou Bei Avenue, 736200, Tel. 8841285, Fax 8841259. E-mail: dhtyn@public.lz.gs.cn. Website: www.dhsuntravel.com.* Ask for George Ji who helped a lot with this book. It has self-drive tours on the Silk Road, study tours of the Mogao Grottoes, and three-hour camel rides to the Magao Caves from the Mingsha dunes at sunrise with picnic breakfast at the caves.

Dunhuang Tourist Bureau, *13 Yangguan Dong Road, 736200, Tel. 8822403, Fax 8822234. Website: www.dunhuangtour.com (No English).*

Fire, *Tel. 119*
Police, *Tel. 110*
Telephone code: 937

Jiayuguan

Jiayuguan is at the western end of the Great Wall in the Hexi Corridor in the western part of Gansu province. It is in the eastern Gobi Desert. The altitude is 1500-1800 meters, the population 170,000. The hottest weather in August is 34°C. The coldest, in January, is -21°C. The best time to visit is May-October. Sandstorms sometimes occur March to May, especially around Anxi, and strong winds in November and December could make for an unpleasant trip then.

Arrivals & Departures

Jiayuguan can be reached by daily summer flights from Lanzhou and Xi'an, and five times a week from Dunhuang. Fewer flights in winter. The airport is 13 km away. The train from Wuwei takes five hours, from Lanzhou nine hours, and from Urumqi about 12 hours. Trains also arrive from Beijing, Shanghai, Xi'an, and Chengdu.

A mini-bus on the 383-km paved road takes five or six hours from Dunhuang, more if you lunch at the Yumen Guest House or Anxi Hotel on the way. Some stop in Qiao Wuan town to see the 300-year-old earthen ruins of an imperial scam, 85 km east of Anxi.

Where to Stay

The Jiayuguan Hotel is the best in town. Then comes the Great Wall. Even better is the three-star Jiuquan Hotel in Jiuquan, but besides the springs and a factory, there isn't much else to see in that town. Hotels are open all year round here.

JIAYUGUAN HOTEL (Binguan), *1 Xinhua Bei Road, 735100. Three stars. Tel. 6226983, 6226321, Fax 6225406. 6227174. It is 14 km from the airport and five km from the railway station. Standard rooms are Y380 (lower in winter). It accepts credit cards.*

This five-story, 179-room hotel was renovated in 2001. It has IDD, air-conditioned cars, foreign currency exchange, store, sauna and gym.

CHANGCHENG BINGUAN/GREAT WALL HOTEL, *6 Jianshe Xi Road, 735100. Three stars. Tel. 6225288, 6225213, Fax 6226016. Y280-Y380 for rooms and Y780 for suites. It has been giving a 20% discount. This is 14 km from the airport and two km from the railway station. It accepts American Express credit cards.*

Built in 1990-91 like a fort with a view of the snowcapped Qilian Mountains, this five-story, 159-room hotel has 24-hour hot water, international direct dial (IDD) telephones, a gym, sauna, steam bath, and pool.

Seeing the Sights

The **western end of the Great Wall** is marked by **Jiayuguan Fortress,** seven km from town. It was originally built in 1372 when the first Ming emperor ordered the Wall repaired to keep out the defeated Mongols. He sent government and military officers to develop the region and to protect commerce on the Silk Road. The fort covers over 33,500 square meters and has three imposing gates with fancy 17-meter-high towers. In addition to military structures, it has a theater built in 1502, a reading room for officials, and a temple to the God of War. The god did co-operate. No army ever captured it. The end of the Great Wall here is a mere trickle of its eastern magnificence but it still fascinates. It continues from here south for 7.5 km to the first beacon tower. The **Great Wall Museum** is at the Fortress. *Tel. 6396218, Fax 6399614.*

The **Wei and Jin Tombs** (220 to 420 A.D.) are 20 km northeast of the city and open 24 hours. You can enter them to study the famous bricks with their delightful paintings of old lifestyles and mythology. The modest museum is worth seeing. *Tel. 6385393.*

Jiayuguan also has a glacier (136 km away and a one-day trip). You can go gliding at the gliding base of the civil airport 10 km northeast of the city which claims one of the three best airflows in the world. Contact a travel agency in advance. A gliding festival takes place mid-July.

Jiuquan is 22 km away, with a **Bell and Drum Tower** originally built in 346 A.D. and renovated in the Qing, an Eastern Jin tower, and a carpet factory. The **Wine Spring Park,** the Western Han relic after which the city is named, should be seen. The other city attraction is the **Luminous Jade Cup Factory** (open 9am-6pm) which makes almost egg-shell-thin goblets of "jade." There is also the **Jiuquan City Museum,** open 9am-5:30pm.

For shopping, there's the **Jiuyu Arts and Handicraft Souvenir Shop**, 6-2 Mid Xinhua Street, Tel: 6266516. There's also the **Guancheng Tourist Souvenir Shop** at the Fortress, *Tel. 6396244, Fax: 6396914. E-mail: jyggch@public.lz.gs.cn.*

Practical Information

Jiayuguan City Tourist Bureau of Gansu Province, *Mid-Xinhua Street No. 25, Jiayuguan City. Tel. 6226183, 6260751, Fax 6226068. E-mail: gsjygslyj@163.com.* Ask for Mr. Li Yong and Meng Yaqi who helped this book a lot.

CITS Jiayuguan, *Tel. 6281826, 6222582, Fax 6280471, 6226931. E-mail: jits02@pubilc.lz.gs.cn. Website: www.greatwalltour.com.cn (Chinese)*

Jiayuguan International Tourist Service, *2 North Shengli Street No.2. 735100. Tel. 6281826. E-mail: jits02@public.lz.gs.cn or coldorb@sina.com.Website: www.greatwalltour.com.cn (Chinese).* It can arrange for people to go gliding, and charges Y380 a room for the Jiayuguan Hotel and for the Great Wall Hotel. Ask for helpful Zhou Haihong.

Police, *Tel. 110*
Telephone code: 937

Urumqi

(Wulumuqi, pronounced Oo-roo-MOO-chi)

Urumqi is the capital of Xinjiang (Sinkiang) Uygur Autonomous Region, an area one-sixth of China's total, with 5,700 kilometers of borders with Mongolia, Russia, Kazakhstan, Kyrghzstan, Tajikistan, Afghanistan, Pakistan, and India. The region has 17 million people and is four times the size of France. It has 24,000 mosques and more than eight million Muslims. It produces petroleum, ketchup, sheep, pears, grapes, and grain.

Urumqi is at an altitude of 650-910 meters and is surrounded on three sides by mountains. Its hottest weather is in August, 40.9˚C. Its coldest month, January, averages minus 16.3˚C. In May and June, the coldest has been -8.9 C. Consider yourself warned. The annual precipitation is 200 to 800 mm with snow between November and March. The best time to visit this amazing region is late April-May and late-August to the end of September. South Xinjiang is very hot in summer with temperatures well over 40 C. Urumqi and North Xinjiang have more rain and are comparatively cooler, especially in the mountains.

The urban population is 1.6 million. The people are mainly Uygurs, but also Han, Kazaks, Mongolians, and Huis. The city has 13 nationalities, the region 47.

Note: It is especially here that the government has been arresting "religious radicals, separatists and terrorists" following September 11, 2001. The official *Legal Daily*, mentioning government statistics and quoted by Hong Kong's *South China Morning Post*, has said that police have dealt with over 1,000 violent incidents in the past decade. Separatists want an independent East Turkestan.

I visited Turpan, Kashgar, Korla and Urumqi in mid-2001 and enjoyed nothing but friendly hospitality. After September 11, some of the border areas were closed temporarily, but Xinjiang was still giving foreign visitors a good time. Again, please check with your country's mission in China for advice before you go there. Check with travel agents there too.

Arrivals & Departures

You can reach Urumqi by plane from Beijing (2,631 km in 3.5-4.5 hours), Lanzhou (three hours), and Shanghai (4.5 hours). Direct flights have been arriving from Almaty, Bishkek, Hong Kong, Islamabad, Moscow, Novosibirsk, Tashkent and 37 other Chinese cities. Flights with Hong Kong have been only on Saturdays. Flights to and from Almaty are Mondays and Fridays, and Tashkent Wednesdays and Saturdays.

The Beijing-Urumqi express train covers almost 4,000 km in 48 hours, and the Shanghai-Urumqi train takes 51-52 hours, the longest train ride in China. From Lanzhou it's 19 hours and Dunhuang 10 hours. Passenger and freight trains arrive from Kazakhstan and beyond that from Moscow and Rotterdam.

The border with Kazakhstan is open all year round.

Note: A limited number of seats on night flights are sold at 20 to 50% discounts from Beijing, Shanghai and Guangzhou, if booked 12 days in advance. Urumqi travel agents say planes are normally full in August and September. Book at least 10 days ahead then. In low season, book two to three days ahead. For trains, it is best to start booking two weeks in advance.

Orientation

Urumqi dates from the Tang, 618 to 907 A.D., but its attractions are its people and nearby scenery and rich archaeology. It is a bustling city, at least 25 years behind eastern China but starting to catch up commercially. Xinjiang is important for business people now because the central government is pouring in resources to develop it. You can expect the infastructure to improve in the next few years. Tourists usually go here on the way to somewhere else.

Where to Stay

The Holiday Inn and Hoi Tak Hotels are both international quality and are the best for people who don't speak Chinese. The Hoi Tak is on People's Square close to the Tian Shan Department Store (shang chang), provincial government offices, and city hall, and is the most luxurious of the two. The Holiday Inn has been established longer with good service.

The City Hotel is an okay three-star. The Overseas Chinese Hotel is currently being seriously renovated so should be beautiful when it reopens who knows when. Prices listed below are subject to 15% surcharge and 3% tax, change, discounts, and negotiation. They can change travelers' checks, and accept credit cards. A taxi from the airport costs about Y60 and takes about 40 minutes.

HOI TAK HOTEL (Hai De Jiudian), *1 Dong Feng Road, 830002. Five stars. Tel. 2322828, Fax 2321818. E-mail: xjbc@mail.hoitakhotel.com. Rooms range from $145 to $169, and suites are $250 and include breakfast. It has been discounting 35 to 55%.*

This 1997, 318-room hotel is renovated yearly and it shows. It is good-looking and inviting. Rooms have CNN, high-speed internet access, and safes, and are 30 to 36 square meters. Its breakfast buffet is Y90, lunch Y100, and dinner Y110. You have a choice of Western, Chinese, and Muslim restaurants and a food court. Its ballroom can seat 320 banquet-style. There's a cigar bar, a 14-piece gym, heated indoor 15-meter-long pool, sauna and bowling. Hoi Tak (H.K.) International Management.

HOLIDAY INN URUMQI (Xinjiang Jia Ri Da Jiudian), *168 Xinhua Bei Road, 830002. Four stars, Tel. 2818788, Fax 2817422. E-mail: hiusales@mail.xj.cninfo.net, Website: www.holiday-inn.com/hotels/urcch. $135 for rooms. It has been discounting 40-55% off. Six km from the railway station.*

With a good central location, this 1992 hotel has 24 stories and 360 rooms. It has CNN, non-smoking and executive floors, Muslim, Sichuan and Cantonese food. It has a deli, pub, and rooms that are 26 square meters with safes. There's an 11-piece gym, sauna, jacuzzi, and steam bath. It is building an annex probably with 40 suites, a pool, restaurant and offices due in 2003.

XIN JIANG CITY HOTEL (Cheng Shi Dajiudian), *119 Hongqi Road, 830000. Three stars. Tel. 2309911, Fax 2305321. E-mail: Xjcityhotel@163.com. It is 15 km from the airport, four km from the railway station and one kilometer from the Holiday Inn. Rooms range from Y280 to Y500, and suites are Y1880. It has been giving a 50% discount.*

This 1996 hotel has 220 rooms with in-house movies, satellite television, and poor English. It has conference rooms, a Ladies Club, tea house, and 24-

hour room service. There is also a gym and sauna. You could be awakened by noisy guests. Breakfast is Y20 and you get a 20% discount off your use of recreation facilities.

Where to Eat

Local specialties include roast whole goat or sheep, *kebabs*, thin-skinned steamed buns with stuffing, fried rice (eaten with bare hands), deep-fried *nan* bread, mare's milk, and dried sour cheese. The food can be chili hot. Local fruits include seedless white grapes, pears, Hami melons, apples, and raisins. See Chapter 11 on Muslim food.

Restaurants in the hotels are best. The **Holiday Inn** has a great Muslim restaurant. Prices are higher than in restaurants outside, but it's only in the top hotels that you're sure the food is safe and the ingredients are good. Among its delicious dishes were braised lamb in pancake Y45; deep fried lamb chops Y45; fried barbeque fish Xinjiang style Y40; Xinjiang rice (pilaf) with lamb and carrots Y8; baked lamb buns (four small pieces) for Y8; and Xinjiang noodles with meat and vegetables Y16.

Cecelia He of the Holiday Inn recommends the **Tai-Bai-Song Restaurant** with performing dancers at 9:30pm every evening. It's at 15 Cang Fang Gou Road, *Tel. 5818777*. Then there's **John's Café** on the same street as the Holiday Inn and across the street from the old Hongshan Hotel in a small park. Telephone John Hu at *13678875206, E-mail: johncafe@hotmail.com*. This is one of the scruffy John's Café chain catering to backpackers with menus in Chinese and English. (It has restaurants also in Turpan and Kashgar.) It offers tours as well as simple Western food.

Seeing the Sights

The Hoi Tak Hotel charges Y160 per person to join a one-day tour to Tianzi Heavenly Lake (120 km. from Urumqi), Y130 per person half day to Nanshan Pasture; and Y260 to Turfan. These include transportation, guide, tickets and in some cases, lunch. Turfan deserves more than a quick trip.

Tianshan (Heaven Mountain) and **Lake Tianzi (Heavenly Lake)** is about 1,980 meters above sea level and cooler than Urumqi. They've had snow in early May. Take something extra for warmth, especially if you want to climb. Tianzi has beautiful scenery but the boat trip on the lake can be missed. You get the same scenery while walking. The lake is five square kilometers and 100 meters deep. An ancient glacier, about 100 meters thick and two by five km wide, sprawls near ice caves and valleys close by, but visitors are frequently too cold to explore. Your visit to a yurt (tent) is usually not well planned as guides explain very little. So bring questions.

This area might look like the Rockies or Switzerland. But did you ever find yurts and herds of cashmere goats near Lake Louise?

The Uygurs

The different minority groups make this an interesting region. The **Uygurs** (or Uighurs) are Xinjiang's largest group. They controlled northwest China during the Tang. In 788 A.D., a Tang princess married a Uygur khan, by no means a love match. In subsequent years, Chinese silk and sugar were exchanged for Uygur horses and furs. Uygur cavalry often helped the Tang emperors. Strangely enough, the Uygurs were the main supporters of the Manichaean religion (see Quanzhou).

The power of the Uygurs declined after their capital was sacked by the Kirghiz of western Siberia. In 842, a food shortage turned them into very aggressive raiders and China retaliated with force and the execution of Uygurs in Xi'an. The Uygurs also supported Genghis Khan but because they had a written language, they were the bookkeepers and administrators, not the warriors.

On another day you can drive about 75 km south of Urumqi to the **Nanshan Pasture** for more mountains, valleys, fountains, waterfalls, and cypress and pine trees. Horseback riding, mountaineering, and digging for valuable *ginseng* roots are among the attractions.

Here, if you are lucky, or unlucky, you might find a game of polo played with an initially live goat instead of a ball! Shades of Afghanistan! Or you might cheer on women chasing and beating men on horseback, a courtship ritual. You might also be able to dine and sleep in a *yurt*. Barbecued mutton drowned by tea with mare's milk has been offered to some groups. The **Kazaks** are nomadic herdsmen, whose ancestors rode and plundered with Genghis Khan.

Xinjiang is building a new museum in Urumqi to open in 2004. In the meantime, twelve of its famous **mummies** are on display and worth seeing on the same grounds. The entrance fee is Y25 and it's open 9:30am to 6:30pm. The **Museum of Xinjiang Uygur Autonomous Region** is at *132 Northwest Road, Tel. 4816436.* The 3000 to 5800 year old mummies are from tombs in the region including Loulan. Many of these mummies have been in this museum for years, but they are much better displayed now with English titles and signs indicating Acoustiguides. Read about mummies in Kashgar, Turpan, and Korla/Kuerla, and if interested, Dr. Elizabeth W. Barber's book, *The Mummies of Urumchi.*

The **Russian market** is interesting because it has goods from Central Asia and Russia like cameras, shoes, and appliances. But the trade is more from China to Kazakstan.

In Urumqi itself, you can visit the nine-story **Hong Ding Shan Ta (Red Pagoda Hill)**, *Tel. 2828416.* Founded in the Tang, the current building was finished in 1788. There is a good view of the city from the pagoda.

Shopping

Urumqi and Kashgar are just about the best places on the Silk Road to shop for minority handicrafts. These include carpets, cashmere sweaters, decorated Yengisar daggers, jewelry, embroidered caps, red copperware, jade carving, embroidery, musical instruments, and fur and leather articles. Hand-knotted wool carpets in Persian designs are especially good buys but are probably cheaper in Pakistan. The **Holiday Inn** has books in English and some unusual crafts.

Other outlets of interest are the **Urumqi General Carpet Rug Factory**, 40 Jinger Road, *Tel. 5813297*; **Xinjiang Antique Store**, 325 Jiefang Nan Road, *Tel.2825161;* and the **Urumqi Foreign Trade Carpets Factory**, 14 Li Yu Shan Road, *Tel. 2863687*. The **Tian Shan Department Store** is one of the biggest in Northwest China. It's near People's Square and has fashionable items.

Excursions & Day Trips

See also separate sections on Turpan and Kashgar.

Xinjiang is a huge region, the largest in China. It is much less populated than other parts of China as most is desert and mountains.

Kuqa/Kuche/Kucha is an important archaeological city, the home of the Kizil/Kerzil/Qiucil **Thousand Buddha Grotto Temples** which are 76 km away. These are one of the four largest such temples in the country and are said to be better preserved than those in Turpan. It has 236 grottoes from the Wei to the Jin dynasties, about 2000 years old. Kuqa should have an airport soon. The train from Urumqi takes 14 hours to Kuqa. The train from Kashgar takes about 10 hours. For more information, see my website: *www.china-travel-guide.com.*

Relatively near Kuqa on the railway line is **Korla/Kuerla,** about 285 km away. It is well worth visiting for the five 3-4000 year-old well-preserved mummies which some scholars believe to be Celtic. You can also reach Korla by air daily from Qiemo and Urumqi. The new desert highway goes from here across the Taklamakan.

Korla is a new city built by petroleum. The four-star 168-room **Tazhi (Petroleum) Hotel** is best. It takes credit cards and travelers checks, and charges Y480 to Y880 for rooms. It is on Shi Hua Street, 410000, *Tel. 996/2173170, Fax 2173167*. The only international travel agency here is the **CBITS,** G/F, Tourism Administration Building (Lu Yiu Ju Dalou), Bayin Dong Road, 841000, *Tel. 996/2024341, Fax 2036477. E-mail: cits-bz@163.net. Or loulan@neteasy.com .* Ask for Mr. Liu Heping who helped a lot with this book.

If you can afford the Y40,000 and are desperate to see it, **Loulan** is the source of many of the European mummies. It is about 400 km from Korla and the roads are not good. There are ruins of Buddhist buildings, three rooms, dwellings, and a 10.5-meter-high stupa. Travel agent Liu Heping of CBITS has been there at least 15 times. Groups pay at least Y64,000 to visit the site which was abandoned in the fourth century. Liu can also arrange guides, tickets and desert camping.

Practical Information

Urumqi travel agents below can arrange horse and camel trips, desert camping, mountain climbing and ecological expeditions.

Business Hours, 10am-12am, 3:30pm-7:30pm (winter), and 9:30am-1:30pm and 4pm-8pm (summer) for offices, five days a week. 10am-7pm (summer) and 11am-8pm (winter) for stores.

China Xinjiang Nature International Travel Service, *A2-17th floor-Tianji Mansion, 128 Jiefang Bei Road, 830002. Tel. 2333891, Fax 2332174. E-mail: xjnature@ns.xj.cei.gov.cn.* Ask for manager, Song Yong who says it costs Y30,000 to get a group permit to look for wild donkeys, antelopes and yaks in the Artun Nature Reserve. You have to trek in. Unlike other agencies here, this one does own a toilet tent. It carries drinking water, but you wash in streams. It has other exciting itineraries too.

Xinjiang China Travel Service, *51 South Xinhua Road, Tel. 2861735, 2865410, Fax 2872178. E-mail: lixinlh@sina.com Ask for Li Xin.*

CYTS Xinjiang International Tour Co., *9 Jianshe Road, 830002, Tel. 2818451, Fax 2817078. Europe and America Dept., Tel. 2832331, 2845182(OMB), Fax 2832331. E-mail: 246581@163.net or linmu321@sina.com.cn. Website: www.cytsonline.com (English.)* This agency is also knowledgeable about dinosaur fossils, mountain grasslands, Junggar Basin, Samarkand, Almaty, and Kizil Caves. It has partner contacts with a travel agent in Almaty.

Xinjiang China International Travel Service, *51 North Xinhua Road. I highly recommend Mr. Wang Wanping, who arranged an inexpensive trip for me with two nights on trains. Tel. 2821428, Fax 2810689. E-mail wangwanping@xinjiangtour.com or citsxj@mail.wl.xj.cn. Website: www.xinjiangtour.com*

Xinjiang Tourism Administration, *Marketing and Promotion Dept., 16 Hetan Nan Road, 830002, Tel. 2846342, 2831907. Fax 2824449. E-mail: xjta@xj.cei.gov.cn. Website: www.xinjiangtour.gov.cn (English but out of date).* It should be able to provide brochures and information.

Telephone code: 991

Kashgar/Kashi

At the far western tip of Xinjiang province, 164 km from the former Soviet republic of Kyrgyzstan, **Kashgar** is one of the highlights of a Silk Road trip because of its Central Asian ambience, Uygur flavor, architecture, and extraordinary Sunday market.

Urban Kashgar has about 330,000 people, and greater Kashgar 3,300,000. Uygurs are about 70-80%. The altitude is 1,289 meters. The annual rainfall is below 100 millimeters. The highest temperature in summer is 40C (with 20C summer evenings), and the lowest in winter is -24 C. June to early September is fine to visit if you can take the heat. The end of September can be cold and sand storms blow in May. If you're going up into the mountains it can be 0 C even on a summer evening.

Arrivals & Departures

From Urumqi, you can get to Kashgar by air (1,085 km in 1.5 hours for Y980) at least once a day. Flights are frequently late. You can also go by express train in less than 24 hours. A regular train goes between Kashgar and Urumqi every other day. It is not air-conditioned, has hard- and soft-sleepers, and stops in Aksu, Kuqa, Korla, and Turpan.

Long-distance buses take 36 hours non-stop. You can rent a Land-Rover and do it leisurely in four days and three nights. There's not much to see between Kuqa and Kashgar however.

Kashgar has also been accessible by road from Pakistan (520 km), or by public bus from Bishkek in Kyrghyzstan. Going in the other direction, you need visas for these two countries, not obtainable in Kashgar or Urumqi. The border with Pakistan was closed after September 11, 2001 for three days and is usually closed from November to the end April every year. For more information on this area, see my website *www.china-travel-guide.com and sitara@sitara.com.*

Orientation

Kashgar is over 2,000 years old. In the mid-10th century, a Uygur-Turkish coalition, the Karahanid (Qurakhanid) Dynasty took over the area. Its leaders later converted to Islam and made Kashgar their capital. Today it grows rice, wheat, fruit, and cotton. It exports tomato sauce. Government officials, hotels and tour guides operate on Beijing time, but some shops keep "Kashgar time," and others keep "Pakistan time," which could be a three-hour difference.

The city is relatively small and taxis are cheap, about Y5 most places. It's Y20 for a taxi from the airport. You can walk from the hotels to the Grand Mosque, the center of town. The famous market however is a little too far.

Where to Stay

No hotels here have non-smoking rooms. English is very poor except for some managers. Rooms are hard to get in August and September, so book ahead. The best hotel for North Americans with the best service and big garden is the Seman. Hotels here add a 10 or 15% service charge. Some hotels offer Uygur dances in the evening. The Friendship and Qiniwak are together in one compound. High season is mid-May to mid-October. No hotel has CNN.

FRIENDSHIP GUEST HOUSE (You Yi Binguan), *144 Seman Road, Tel. 2833235, Fax 2823087. Two stars going on three. Pakistan joint venture. Just 500 meters to Idkah Mosque. Eleven stories and 72 rooms. Rooms are 40- to 50- square meters, the biggest in the city, and cost Y240, while suites are Y600.*

This hotel should be air-conditioned and renovated in winter 2002, after which it should be a three star. It has 24-hour hot water, accepts travelers' checks, and currently takes no credit cards. It has no pool. When it is air-conditioned and if the service improves, this should be the best hotel in town. Check-out is at 2pm.

QINIWAK HOTEL (Qinibagh Binguan), *144 Seman Road, 844000. Two stars. Tel. 2822103, Fax 2823087. It is in a residential neighborhood, and takes travelers' checks but no credit cards. Rooms with breakfast are Y200 to Y260, and suites Y480 to Y580. A bed in a dorm costs Y25 to Y30. It has been discounting 10 to 20% with no breakfast.*

Rooms should be renovated soon. Air-conditioning is in suites only. The old British Consulate building is still here.

KASHGAR WHITE DOVE/SEMAN HOTEL, *337 Seman Road, 844000. Two stars. Tel. 2552129, 2552001, Fax 2552861. E-mail: whitedove19@hotmail.com. Rooms are Y280 and suites Y1200 in high season including breakfast. Dorms are Y15 a bed. It has been discounting 30-35% with no breakfast in low season.*

This 1956, 161-room hotel includes the 1890 Russian consulate but it's not air-conditioned. The food is good though its restaurants tend to be grubby. The most comfortable is the semi-outdoor coffee shop Grape Vineyard. The Seman is generally, but not completely, air-conditioned. It has 24-hour hot water, CITS is on the grounds, and it is across the street from more restaurants. The staff is friendly but rooms are badly maintained. If you have a problem communicating, look for a manager in the internet bar and travel agency off the lobby. It charges Y10 an hour for e-mail. Check-out is at 4pm because of the late flight to Urumqi. This hotel is a favorite of motor tours because of the parking.

TUMAN RIVER HOTEL, *5 Airport Road at North Bridge Arch. Tel. 2822912, Fax 2822952. Rooms cost Y120 to Y160 and it has been giving 30% discounts.*

This two star hotel is attached to the long-distance bus station, is run-down but very handy for budget travelers. It has 24-hour hot water, morning calls, and sells bus tickets, but has no English. It is probably not good for single women traveling alone.

Where to Eat

The best is in the hotels, and the Caravan Café.

JOHN'S CAFÉ, *across the street from the Seman Hotel. Tel/Fax 2551186. E-mail: johncafe@hotmail.com. It's open 8:30am to 1am and takes no credit cards.*

Favorite of backpackers, there's a menu in English and a semblance of Western food, the décor rustic and open. Prices are cheap: a Western breakfast costs Y11, toast and jam Y4, pilaf yogurt Y2, fried eggs and ham Y5, coffee Y6 to Y16, and sirloin steak Y22. John's also sells travel tickets, rents jeeps with drivers, rents sleeping bags and tents, and charges Y15 an hour for the Internet. It has a book exchange and bulletin board.

1001 NIGHTS RESTAURANT OF DELICIOUS DELIGHTS, *near John's Café.*

Good Muslim food.

RED FLOWER BAKE SHOP, *near the Idkah Mosque is the 57 Renmin Bi Road, Tel. 2820567.*

Gorge on a huge Uygur pizza full of meat for Y25. You could go just to see its ceiling that looks like marshmallow frosting. The food is good and cheap and the place clean.

CARAVAN CAFÉ, *next to the Qiniwak/Friendship Hotels at 120 Seman Road, 844000. Tel. 2841864, or E-mail: torgunmusa@yahoo.com.*

This is an American-owned coffee shop with a menu in English serving good Western food in an international-quality setting with a Western toilet. A pizza costs Y20, a croissant Y6, cinnamon rolls Y7, granola (muesli) with yogurt Y10, carrot cake muffin Y5, coffee Y5, and espresso coffee drinks start from Y15 (i.e. latte, cappuccino, frappaccino). It's an oasis.

Seeing the Sights

You can get around locally by taxi, but if you want to try something different, go for the bumpy donkey cart experience. Just wave one down near the Market. They are not allowed on main streets.

The **Sunday market** is a medieval crush of 100,000 Uygurs, Pakistanis, Kyrgyz, Tajiks, and Mongols, blacksmiths, barbers, and "dentists." Bought and sold here are peppercorns, pomegranates, grapes, flashy silks, bright felt carpets, jeweled knives, fur hats, and boots, donkeys, horses, and goats. Camels are rare. Tinkerers repair kettles and bicycles. This market is for photographing rather than for buying, and needs at least three hours. Most residents don't mind cameras. Go early to avoid the heat. It opens at 6am Beijing time. It's great but not as great from the end of June to mid-July when farmers are busy harvesting and attendance is down to only 50,000. A permanent market with dry goods is nearby and also colorful.

Like other cities of Xinjiang, Kashgar gives you a feeling more of Central Asia than of China. It is one of the few places in China where women veil their faces by choice. The city center is around the peaceful **Idkah Mosque**, *Tel. 2823235*, (1442 A.D.) which holds 7,000 people. The prayer hall was built in the 1690s by Zopia Han who wanted to go on a pilgrimage to Mecca but couldn't because of war in Afghanistan. He put the money instead in this building. The mosque is open from 10am to 2pm to tourists except on Fridays when it closes at 1pm. It is open again at 4pm. Female tourists can visit if properly dressed, arms and legs covered but Muslim women pray at home.

Behind the mosque are streets with old buildings, wrought-iron balconies, and alleyways with mud townhouses more typical of north Africa than China. The local people are friendly. The area has 9,500 mosques. You can rent bicycles from some of the hotels.

The **Kashgar Silk Road Museum** is at 19 Tarboguz Road, and is open 9:30am to 2pm, and 4pm to 7:30pm daily. It charges Y6. Among the relics are 4000-year-old bronzes, 3000-year-old wooden tomb figures, one 3200-year-old mummy, and one mummy with a fur-lined jacket. It has titles in English.

Important to visit is the huge **Abakhojia Tomb**, *Tel. 2822638* (Ming and Qing), the final resting place of 70 descendents of Muhatum Ajam, an Islamic missionary. It is five km from the Kashgar Hotel. Recent visitors have seen the snow-covered Kunlun Mountains from **Scholar Mohamed Kashgari's Tomb** 45 km southwest of Kashgar on the road to Pakistan.

Thirty km north of Kashgar is the town of **Hanoi**, abandoned after the 11th century and now just a ruin. South of the city and west of the Sino-Pakistan Highway towards Afghanistan are the 7,719-meter-high Mt. Kongur and 7,546-meter-high Mt. Muztagta, part of the Pamirs. If you keep in mind that Hunza in Pakistan and Kashmir in India are also to the south, you will get an idea of the magnificence and isolation of the area here. Think Himalayas!

Shopping

Kashgar produces gold and silver ornaments, leather boots, bronzeware, jewelry, rugs, jade carving, embroidered caps, textiles, daggers, and musical instruments made of apricot wood. The **Gold Jewelry Bazaar** is on Zhiren Street, out the Idkah Mosque and across the main street. It is a narrow alley on the left.

The **Odali Bazaar** on Jiefang Bei Road sells Uyger clothes and caps. Try the **Ying Yi Bazaar** for knives but be sure to put them in your checked luggage if you're flying. At the **Kashgar City Traditional Minority Handicraft and Souvenir Shop,** you can see silk carpets, and musical instruments being made. This shop accepts credit cards and can ship. It's at 237 Renmin Xi Road, near the Idkah Mosque. Open 9:30am to 1:30pm, and 4am to 8pm. It is closed on Tuesdays.

Practical Information

CITS Kashgar, *in the Seman Hotel, at 337 Seman Road, 844000, Tel. 2551688, 2553153, Fax 2553159. E-mail: j.cninfo.net"* cits-ks@mail.xj.cninfo.net. Contact general manager Kamil Zunun, *E-mail: kamil-ks@mail.xj.cninfo.net; mobile is 13909989088.* He and guide Adil Tura Hun were really good, charming and resourceful. Adil's e-mail is: *ktbadil@yahoo.com.*

Telephone code: 998

Turpan

(Turfan, Tulufan)

Turpan is located in a desert in northeast Xinjiang province. With so many Chinese cities clogged with traffic and frentic with activity, it is refreshing to find this relatively sleepy, charming, exotic little town with so much history. No cars are allowed under the grape arbors that line the downtown streets between the Oasis and Turfan Hotels. The arbors are in turn bordered by canals of rushing glacier water. But things are changing. Its donkey carts have been banned to the suburbs.

The weather here is the hottest in China! Turpan is in the Turpan Basin and known as "the oven." From late June to early August, it gets up around 45°C and outdoor activity after 9am is very uncomfortable and exhausting. Local women assured me that walking outside alone after dark is safe too but yes, it's better to come May to mid-June, and mid-September-October. Rainfall averages 16.6 mm. a year. Strong winds blow more than 30 days a year. The hot air from the basin and cold air from the north create violent storms.

The temperature has fallen to minus 17°C in January. A few sandstorms blow in April and early May. An old Chinese saying goes: In winter, Turpan people wear fur coats in the morning, light silk clothes at noon, and dine on watermelon in the evenings around hot stoves.

The lowest point of the basin is Aydingkol Lake, its water surface 154 meters below sea level and almost extinct. It is second only to the Dead Sea as the world's lowest body of water. It is not usually included on tours because of the poor road and lack of water. The population is 250,000, 80% Uygurs.

But wait! Don't stop reading! Those of us who have been there say the dust and plumbing are worth it!

Arrivals & Departures

The fastest train from Dunhuang takes ten hours. From Kashgar, it's 22 hours and from Urumqi two hours but the Turfan station is about 50 km away at Daheyan so add another hour. By road from Urumqi an express bus goes every 30 minutes for Y25 and travel is faster, but locals warn about accidents. Choose a big Volvo bus. Turpan has no airport and that's good and bad.

Roughly 200 km southeast of Urumqi, Turpan is best as a three-day tour. Urumqi travel agents offer one-day tours, but that's not enough to truly enjoy this place. Your tour should include visits to Gaochang, Jiaohe, the Baziklic Caves, Astana Tombs, Imin Minaret, a vineyard and the Karez wells. There are also opportunities to stay overnight in Uyger homes, or in the desert. If you're seriously interested in the archaeology, CITS can supply scholars to talk about it for about Y800.

Orientation

Turpan was once an oasis on the Silk Road. It existed then and now because of subterranean water from Karez wells, some dug 2,400 years ago. The Western Han emperors (206 B.C.-24 A.D.), sent soldiers to develop agriculture here. Some historians say the technology arrived from farther west since *karez* is a Persian word. In any case, the wells are most common in Turpan and nearby Hami, to the east.

In spring, snow from the Tianshan Mountains melts, and this water flows into the Turpan Basin and gets stored in vast natural underground reservoirs reached by sloping channels tapped in turn by the wells. You can see the desert dotted with lines of wells.

Visit the Karez Well Museum which explains with diagrams just how those 40- km-long irrigation tunnels were dug. There are 5,000 km of these tunnels.

Modern irrigation methods based on these wells have transformed Turpan into an agricultural area. Grain and cotton are grown here. Look for Hami melons which have a sweet perfume. The wooden huts with the holes are for drying grapes which have grown here for 2,000 years. Turpan's grapes are very sweet with a 15-20% sugar content.

Turpan is also a good place to study Uygur culture.

Where to Stay

The Oasis and Turfan Hotels have only a bit of English but they have had years of experience dealing with foreigners. The Oasis Hotel is still the best here but the yet-to-be opened three-star Turpan International Hotel nearby might be better. No hotels have CNN or newspapers in English.

OASIS HOTEL (Liuzhou Binguan), *41 Qinian, 838000. Three stars. Tel. 8522491, Fax 8523348. Website: www.the-silk-road.com. Rooms are Y280 to Y680, and suites are Y980. It has been giving a 40% discount and has beds for backpackers. It is close to the main city square, shopping and the museum.*

This 156-room hotel has a garden and several buildings with different interior themes, one of which is American wild west. It has a gym, beauty salon, and internet bar at Y30 an hour. There's Western, Chinese, Asian and Xinjiang food. It will be expanding in 2002. It has had a Canadian manager. Silk Road Hotel Management Co. Hong Kong.

TURFAN HOTEL (Tulufan Binguan), *2 Youth Road, 838000. Three stars. Tel. 8522301, 8522642, Fax 8523262. E-mail: billyturpan@hotmail.com. It is also walking distance to the main shopping street, the Oasis Hotel, and a colorful morning market at Laocheng Road and Xincheng Road. Its 2000-built building (No. 3) to the left of Reception as you enter the courtyard is the newest and best. Rooms are Y380 and suites Y680 and it's been giving a 20% to 40% discount. Its dorms cost Y27 per bed and have air-conditioning but no telephone. It accepts credit cards and travelers checks.*

This five-story, 200-room hotel has money exchange and not-too-bad service. Hot water is on from 7:30am to 2am. It has a 50-meter indoor pool and charges Y10 an hour for e-mail. Its buffet breakfast costs Y15, lunch Y45 and dinner Y45.

FOLKWAY HOTEL (Folk Custom Garden of Turpan Karez or Minzu Binguan), *888 Xincheng Road, Ximen Cun Village, 838000. Three stars. Tel. 8534681.*

This 2001 hotel looks beautiful, but alas, no one speaks English. Rooms are 28 to 36 square meters and are Y260 to Y340 a room, no discount. This Japanese joint venture is a hotel for people who want to immerse themselves in the interesting Ugyur culture: the food, dances, Karez wells, and grape growing. But you need to know some Chinese and it's only open in the high season.

Where to Eat

The hotels are still best. The cheaper **John's Information Café** is on Qingnian Road across from the Turfan Hotel, *Tel. 8524237,* is a hangout for foreign backpackers and okay for Western-type food. It has good yogurt, sweet and sour meatballs for Y20, Sichuan chicken for Y15, Kashgar pizza on Uygur nan Y10, beer Y4.50 and Y8. It also has a travel agency, bike rentals, and can book discounted rooms at the hotels.

Seeing the Sights

The 37-meter-high **Imam Minaret** (1778) stands two km east of Turpan, its geometric patterns in the Uygur style. However, its smooth inverted-cone shape with rounded top is reminiscent of towers south of New Delhi on the road to Agra. The **Turpan Museum** is open 9am to 8pm daily, *Tel. 8522619.* It has 12 mummies, a couple of Manichaean pictures, and lots of ethnic boots. The entrance fee is Y20. No explanations are in English, alas, but there's a helpful brochure in English with some photos. The Grape Festival is on August 20 and there's an interesting morning market.

The ghost city of *****Gaochang,** 40 km southeast of Turpan, was capital of the State of Gaochang (500-640 A.D.) and reached its peak in the ninth century, with a population of 50,000. It was on the Silk Road and flourished from the first century B.C. until the Mongols ravaged it in the 14th century A.D.

Here were once 30 to 40 monasteries! The buildings were made of mud bricks and are now only ruins. Take a donkey cart if it's too hot to walk.

The equally ancient city of **Jiaohe,** on the other hand, shows the effect of its UNESCO and Japanese help: a scale model, signs in English saying the likes of "five minutes to the temple," or "Do not enter." The paths are paved and it is hard to get lost.

*Jiaohe (also known as Yarkhoto, and possibly Yaerhu), 10 km west of Turpan, existed from the second century B.C. to the 14th century A.D. Its mud brick buildings are better preserved than Gaochang's and are in an area 1.65 km x 0.3 km. It also had a population of 50,000. In the northwestern part are temple ruins with the remains of Buddhist images. There is also a rare brick Buddhist temple. Jiaohe was carved rather than built. One source says it was abandoned in the Ming for lack of water; another says it was destroyed by fire during fighting in the Yuan dynasty.

Located eight km from Gaochang and 40 km southeast of Turfan are the **Astana Tombs** dating from the third century to about the eighth. This is where 500 mummies, plus their belongings, were found. Take a flashlight. Visitors routinely see only a couple of Tang mummies in a dark room. The well-preserved bodies still have discernible eye lashes and eyeballs.

The ***Pazikelik** (or Baziklic, Bazeklik) **Thousand-Buddha Caves** are 16 km northeast of Turpan by dusty road, and are on a cliff on the Flaming Mountains. About 80 of the grottoes are still intact but in poor condition, destroyed by looters, earthquakes, and archaeologists. Many of the murals were taken to the Berlin Museum in Germany and destroyed by bombs during World War II. (Read *Foreign Devils on the Silk Road* by Peter Hopkirk.) Faces were mutilated by Muslims. They were built over a period of 1,400 years, starting in the Southern and Northern Dynasties (420-550 A.D.). Dunhuang's are more interesting and younger, but it is good to compare the two and are worth a visit.

The **Flaming Mountains** themselves are literary, so named because the incessant sun is supposed to make the red rocks seem on fire from a distance. Perhaps this happens at sunset only in the classic fairy tale *Pilgrimage to the West*. In that story, the monkey king helps put out the fire so that Monk Xuan Zang can go to India. The mountains are 100 km long and 10 km wide, their highest peak 800 meters above sea level. Unless you know the story, this could be another set of hills except that they look like one of the settings of the movie *Crouching Tiger, Hidden Dragon*. They are between the Caves and Turpan in the hottest part of the depression.

There's also a five-hour trip to **Yuyoq (Tuyugou),** an old village of earthen houses with Muslim and Buddhist relics on the other side of the Flaming Mountains. Guides said its mosque has a story of the faithful men who slept in a cave and emerged years later, This story is mentioned in the Koran, but is the Chinese connection correct?

Travel agents can arrange a **night in the desert** where you can see the sun set and rise. It's a two hour drive on a bumpy road. In the summer the temperature goes down to 20C at night. CITS provides sleeping bags and tents for about $10 per person. It can also arrange visits to a **vineyard** from August to October where you can pick your own grapes and bottle wine or mineral water from a karez well with your own label. You can also eat with a local family.

Practical Information

Freelance tour guides hang out at **John's Information Café** on Qing Nan Road, opposite the Turpan Guesthouse. *Tel. 8524237.* It's a good place to assess their competence and negotiate a price. CITS guides generally are better qualified and cost Y100 a day for a small group, but if price is a consideration, you might want a cheaper freelancer. However, if something bad happens, they are answerable to no one.

One arranged a small air-conditioned taxi to Bazelik for three people for Y400. He also arranged a meal in his family home but never answered e-mails so cannot be recommended. More reliable and more expensive are guides through established travel agencies.

CITS Turpan, *41 Qinnian Road, 838000, Tel. 8523215, 8531311, Fax 8526878.* Look for its sign beside the main gate of the Oasis Hotel. Ask for Ms. Li Qin (Merry) who speaks English and helped with this book. *Her cell phone is 13999690909 and e-mail citslq-tl@mail.xj.cninfo.net.*

Telephone code: 995

Xi'an

(Sian, Chang An)

Xi'an, the capital of Shaanxi province on the Guanzhong Plain, borders on the Loess Plateau to the north and the Qinling Mountains to the south. It was the center of China's world from the 11th century B.C. to the early 10th A.D.

Xi'an was the capital intermittently for 1,183 years of 11 imperial dynasties, including the Western Zhou (of the ritual bronzes), the Qin (of the Great Wall and terracotta army), the Western Han (of the jade burial suits), the Sui (of the Grand Canal), and the Tang - ah, the Tang! Commerce on the Silk Road thrived west of here to the Mediterranean and beyond then. (See Silk Road.)

In spite of the occasional invasions and sackings by rebels and tribesmen, Xi'an, then named Chang'an (Everlasting Peace), reached its peak in the Tang, when the population was nearly two million. It was one of the world's largest cities, with walls measuring 36 km in circumference. It declined because of late Tang debauchery and corruption, the eunuchs ruling the court, and increasingly powerful governors-general controlling the provinces. In 906, one of the last Tang emperors allowed one of his generals to take complete charge while he enjoyed his lady love. Xi'an rolled downhill from there on, following the fortunes, also, of the Silk Road. Read Cooney and Alteri's marvelous novel about this period, *The Court of the Lion.*

A short-lived peasant regime made Xi'an a capital again in the 17th century, but it never regained its past glory. Xi'an did, however, continue to be a tourist resort and destination for religious pilgrimages because of its Buddhist roots. In 1900, when the Empress Dowager fled Beijing, she went to Xi'an.

In 1936, one of his top officers, known as the Young Marshall, kidnapped Generalissimo Chiang Kai-shek here in what is known as the Xi'an Incident. They forced him to cooperate with the Communists against the Japanese. The Communists subsequently set up a liaison office here which is now the *Museum of the Eighth Route Army. On May 20, 1949, the Communists took over the city.

The altitude is 400 meters. The hottest weather is 40°C in July; the coldest is -14°C in January. Rain falls all year round, but especially July through early September with an annual precipitation of 550-770 mm. The best weather is May-June when the pomegranates are in bloom, and September-October. The air can be badly polluted at times but the government is taking measures to improve it. The total population is over six million, 3.6 million urban.

Arrivals & Departures

Xi'an is a 1.75 hour, 1,165 km flight southwest of Beijing. Air routes with 42 cities now include Fukuoka, Hiroshima, Hong Kong, Macau and Nagoya. Check with travel agents about summer flights with Tianshui and Dunhuang.

The airport at Xianyang is 38-53 km from the city's hotels. The one-hour CAAC airport bus costs about Y40 to take you into the city and operates frequently between 5am-6pm. Taxis cost about Y180. On the way, look for the 2,200-year old Qin imperial burial tumuli (pointed tops) and almost as old Han imperial burial mounds (rounded top). Try to see the Han Yang Tomb on the way to or from the airport to avoid a special trip.

Early morning taxis to the airport from hotels might charge less (about Y100) since they have to go there anyway, but do forbid your driver from stopping for other passengers; otherwise the trip will be much longer. CAAC buses go from its office outside the West City Gate.

Be warned that Xi'an airport is notorious for charging for overweight luggage.

Xi'an is about a seven-hour train ride west of Luoyang and 17 hours west of Shanghai.

Orientation

Next to Beijing, Xi'an is the best city to visit in China, especially if you are interested in ancient Chinese history, traditional culture, and archaeology. It is one of the 24 historical cities protected by the State Council and, unfortunately, it has been sinking due to lack of water.

Just to glimpse what it has to offer takes a full week. To savor Xi'an slowly, to study it deeply, to read about Empress Wu and her lover-protector-henchman while sitting in the shadow of a Tang pagoda - or to read about that crafty fictional Tang detective Judge Dee, two giant silk-flower petals sticking sideways out of the back of his magisterial cap - that kind of depth could take months.

Ancient Xi'an is the setting for many Chinese operas, their sweet young heroines waving flowing ribbon sleeves, and their flag-pierced generals galloping away to battle amid the clash of cymbals. Here the foreign caravans, the traders on camels exchanged silver, furs, horses, and sesame for Chinese silk and porcelain with Europe. It is here that the egomaniac Qin emperor ordered the burning of all books except those he liked, and demanded that his subjects create an army of life-size soldiers to maintain his empire forever.

Xi'an today is a textile and manufacturing center. It also produces Chinese and Western medicines, and airplanes. It is an educational center, with about 40 colleges, universities, and research institutes. Xi'an Jiaotung (Communications) University is the best known, and one of the 11 'super-key' universities in the country. The municipal government has embarked on a program to bring Xi'an up to international standards between now and 2010. It plans to make the city more green and develop its high-tech industries. All residents inside the walled city are supposed to have switched to gas for cooking.

Xi'an's farms grow cotton, maize, wheat, vegetables, pomegranates, and persimmons. Many rural houses and walls have been made of loess soil mixed with straw. If cared for properly and protected with bricks on top, mud walls can last 100 years. Cheap too!

Getting Around Town

You can book tours and cars through the hotels or travel agents. The YMCA seems to have the cheapest tour. Public tourist buses from the east side of the railway station in front of the Jie Fang Hotel go to the Terracotta Warriors, Banpo and Hot Springs for $5. They also go to Qian Ling for $6, and to Famen for $6. City buses are Y2. A car from the New World Hotel to the airport with a stop at the Hanyang Museum costs Y200, and to the Terracotta Warriors, etc. Y480 return. To go to Qian Ling it costs Y700, Famen Y850 and the Huxian peasant painters Y400 return. It would be cheaper negotiating with a taxi.

The walled city is a grid, a rectangle. The downtown commercial area is on Dongda Jie or East Street. North (Bei), South (Nan) and West (Xi) Streets meet it at the Bell Tower. The Railway Station is at the north end of Jiefang Road. West Street ends at the very impressive West City Gate. Xi'an has a 34 km expressway circling the walled city called Second Ring Road (Er Huan Lu).

Tourist Sights in Xi'an by Location

In Xi'an and immediate vicinity: Wild Goose Pagodas, Bell Tower, Drum Tower, City Wall, Great Mosque, Xi'an Stele Museum, Shaanxi Provincial History Museum, Xingqing Palace Park, Banpo Museum, Memorial Museum of the Eighth Route Army, and Xi'an Film Studio.

West and South of Xi'an: Chariot and Horse Pits, Xingjiao Temple, Xiangji Temple, Qinglong Temple, Temple of Du Fu, Cao Tang Temple, and Peasant Painters of Hu County.

East of Xi'an: Huaqing Hot Springs, Qinshihuang's Tomb and Terracotta Army, and Bronze Chariots.

North and Northwest of Xi'an: Xianyang Museum, Maoling, Zhaoling, and Qianling tombs, Famen Temple, Han Yang Tomb, and the international airport.

Where to Stay

The best hotels are the Shangri-La Golden Flower, Hyatt and Sheraton, all modern-day world class palaces with grand and beautiful lobbies. The Hyatt has the smallest standard rooms, but the best furniture. The Golden Flower seems to be the busiest, its lobby crowded. The Sheraton makes note of the taxis that pick up its guests, in case you leave something behind.

Also of international luxury quality are the Grand Castle, the Xi'an Garden and the Grand New World. Of the three-star hotels, the modest Bell Tower is best for location and service.

The best location for business people and individual tourists is inside the city wall but traffic jams are common and the air is not as fresh as outside. The Bell Tower Hotel is the most convenient. The other hotels inside the wall are the Hyatt, Royal Xi'an (recently renovated), Grand New World, Longhai, the YMCA, and May First Hotels.

The Xian Grand Castle is closest to the South Gate, and Stele Museum.

Romantic travelers should consider the lovely Chinese architecture of the Xi'an Garden Hotel. Backpackers should stay at the May First Hotel or the YMCA, right on Dongda Street. The four- and five-star hotels here are all international quality unless noted, with money exchange, credit card service, business centers, international direct dial, etc. They can change travelers' checks. The prices here are subject to change, discounts from 10%-60%, and 10%-15% surcharge. Some hotels charge for local as well as long distance telephone calls.

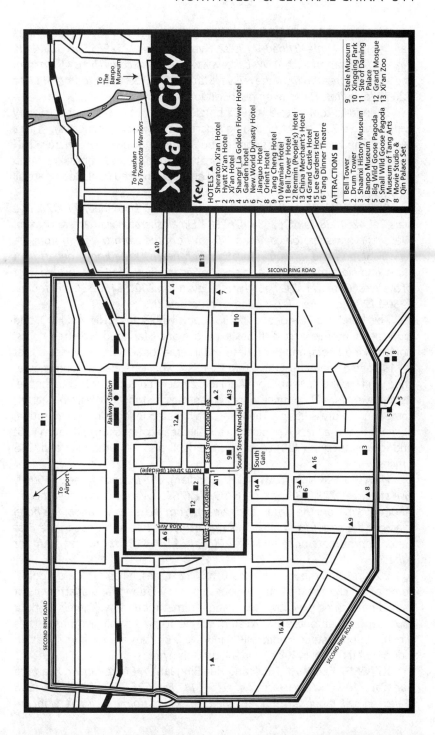

Xi'an City

Key

HOTELS ▲
1 Sheraton Xi'an Hotel
2 Hyatt Xi'an Hotel
3 Xi'an Hotel
4 Shangri-La Golden Flower Hotel
5 Garden hotel
6 New World Dynasty Hotel
7 Jianguo Hotel
8 Orient Hotel
9 Tang Cheng Hotel
10 Wannian Hotel
11 Bell Tower Hotel
12 Renmin (People's) Hotel
13 China Merchant's Hotel
14 Grand Castle Hotel
15 Lee Gardens Hotel
16 Tang Dinner Theatre

ATTRACTIONS ■
1 Bell Tower
2 Drum Tower
3 Shaanxi History Museum
4 Banpo Museum
5 Big Wild Goose Pagoda
6 Small Wild Goose Pagoda
7 Museum of Tang Arts
8 Movie Studio & Qin Palace Set
9 Stele Museum
10 Xingqing Park
11 Site of Daming Palace
12 Grand Mosque
13 Xi'an Zoo

To The Banpo Museum

To Huashan
To Terracotta Warriors

SECOND RING ROAD

Railway Station

To Airport

North Street (Beidajie)
East Street (Dongdajie)
South Street (Nandajie)
West Street (Xidajie)
XIDA LU

South Gate

SECOND RING ROAD

SHANGRI-LA GOLDEN FLOWER HOTEL (Shang Gorilla or Jinhua Fandian), *8 Changle Xi Road, 710032. Five stars, Tel. 3232981, Fax 3232888. E-mail: slx@shangri-la.com. Website: www.shangri-la.com. This is 45 km from the airport, three km from the railway station. $150-$240 for rooms; $260 to $2000 for suites. It has been discounting 15%-40%.*

Shangri-La took over this 1985 hotel in 1993. It has seven and 10-story wings with 423 rooms (including apartments with kitchenettes). It has executive and non-smoking floors, in-room safes and voice mail. There's CNN and HBO, 24-hour room service, a superb bake shop, great $12 breakfast, and good coffee, a gym, jacuzzi, sauna, and an indoor heated pool. Rooms are all 42 square meters.

SHERATON XIAN (Xilaidun Jiudian), *12 Feng Hao Road, 710077. Five stars, Tel. 4261888, Fax 4262188, 4262983. E-mail: sheraton.xian@sheraton.com. Website: www.sheraton.com/xian. 45 km from the airport, 4.5 km from the railway station and in a quiet location with nearby restaurants, department store, and night market. It is also close to Second Ring Road and two km west of the West Gate. This 1991 hotel was renovated in 2001. $150-$200 for rooms, $280-$1280 for suites. It has been discounting 20%.*

This hotel has 16 stories and 438 rooms with safes, CNN and HBO, and high-speed internet access. It has executive and Starwood Preferred floors, non-smoking floors, and Cantonese and international food. The lunch buffet is Y138 and dinner buffet the same. There's a cyber café, games room, flower shop, and bicycles to rent. From April to October, it has an outdoor barbecue. Its relatively formal continental restaurant has a stringed Western quartet, something to dress up for. There's a small heated indoor pool, gym, sauna, steambath and jacuzzi. A popular, relatively cheap coffee shop with latte (Y25) and ice cappuccino (Y20) is on its grounds. It also has Dragonair and CITS offices.

HYATT REGENCY XIAN (Kaiyue Fandian), *158 Dongda Street, 710001. Five stars, Tel. 7231234, Fax 7216799, 7277650. Website: www.hyatt.com. About 45 km from the airport and two km from the railway station, this hotel is across the street from Parkson's Department Store and close to the East Gate. Approximate prices in May, 2002 are $144-$184 for rooms, $274 for suites.*

Built in 1990, the Hyatt has 8, 10, and 12 stories. It has 315 classy rooms, some of which have attractive Japanese paper windows, and apartments. It should have three executive floors and internet room now. There's 24-hour room service, Cantonese and Western cuisine. Its pizzeria has live music. It has a gym, aerobic, steam room, HBO and CNN. Bicycles are for hire. It has an indoor heated pool in Xi'an, and a high-tech gym.

XI'AN GARDEN HOTEL (Tang Hua Binguan), *4 Dong Yan Yin Road, Da Yan Ta, 710061. Four stars, Tel. 5261111, Fax 5261778 (B.C.), 5261998 (Sales). E-mail: tanghua@pub.xaonline.com. 53 km from the airport, eight km* *from the railway station. Convenient public bus #610 goes from here past the Big Wild Goose Pagoda, provincial museum, and then to the Bell Tower for Y2. Some rooms have a view of the exotic Big Wild Goose Pagoda beyond the weeping willow trees and gold Tang roofs. $100-$140 for rooms, $300 for suites. It has been discounting 10%.*

This garden-style hotel on the southern edge of the city is also within walking distance of the Xi'an Film Studio (theme park). It has a small Tang dynasty museum (Y5) titled in English, and its own theater restaurant. Built in 1988 in Tang courtyard style, it has four stories, 292 rooms, and non-smoking floors. Its twin rooms, televisions and bathrooms are small, and you might have to walk a long way between the lobby and your room. It has Star TV but no CNN or in-room safe. Its good breakfast buffet is $13. It has Japanese, Chinese and fast food restaurants and a gym. Member Prima Hotels. Managed by Mitsui.

ANA GRAND CASTLE HOTEL XIAN (Chang'an Cheng Bao Dajiudian), *12 Xi Duan Huan, Cheng Nan Road, 710068. Five stars, Tel. 7231800, Fax 7231500. E-mail: anasales@pub.xaonline.com. Just outside the South Gate. $120-$180 for rooms and $180-$800 for suites. It has been discounting up to 40%.*

Built in 1993 and renovated in 2000, this 10-story, 340-room hotel looks like a castle and has a huge atrium lobby with a life-size camel and driver. It has Japanese, Cantonese, and Western cuisines, and health foods. There's 24-hour room service, Star TV and CNN, kettles and a five-piece gym, in-room safes, and no pool. Rooms are 26-42 square meters. The breakfast buffet is $11 and dinner buffet $18. Managed by ANA Hotels.

GRAND NEW WORLD HOTEL (Gu Du Dajiudian), *48 Lian Hu Road, 710002. Four stars, Tel. 7216868, Fax 7214222, 7317043. E-mail: gnwhxian@sein.sxgb.com.cn or nwsales@public.xa.sn.cn. Website: www.gnwhxian.com (English). It is within walking distance of a park and the Muslim section of the city with its interesting restaurants and shops. Immediately behind is a new Buddhist temple you can also visit. It is 45 km from the airport and four km from the railway station. Near West Gate in the northwest part of the old city. $100 for rooms and $180 for suites. It has been discounting 10%-50%.*

Built in 1989, this 14-story hotel has 491 attractive rooms with unusual color schemes, two business floors, and one executive floor. Rooms are 28 square meters. It has a Cantonese restaurant and a more casual and cheaper food street, a large heated indoor pool, gym, sauna, steam bath and lighted tennis court. Its rooms have CNN, two telephone jacks, electronic keys, and room safes. Managed by New World Hotels, a Marriott brand.

See also Chapter 13, *Best Places to Stay.*

JIANGUO HOTEL XIAN (Fandian), *2 Hu Zhu Road, 710048. Four stars, Tel. 3238888, Fax 3235145, 3237180. E-mail: jgsale@pub.xaonline.com or* *jianguo@pub.xaonline.com. Website: www.jianguohotels.com.cn. 50 km from the airport, five km from the railway station, and in a residential area outside the east wall about one km south of the Golden Flower Hotel. $68-$120 for rooms and $180-$800 for suites. It has economy rooms for $68 and has been discounting about 30%.*

Built in 1989 with renovations 2001, this six- and 14-story hotel has 800 rooms, most with big beds, televisions in beautiful cabinets, CNN, and no safes. It has 24-hour room service and a coffee shop, Sichuan and Cantonese food. Its breakfast buffet is $8. There's an executive floor, gym, indoor pool and casual standards. It's a little grubby but okay if you're not fussy. Economy rooms are 18-22 square meters, most standard rooms are 30 square meters and garden rooms 35-40 square meters.

HOTEL ROYAL XI'AN (Huang Cheng Binguan), *334 Dongda Jie (East Street), 710001. Four stars, Tel. 7235311, Fax 7235887. E-mail: rsvn@royalxa.com.cn. Good downtown location across the street from a marvelous produce market, near good shopping and Bank of China. $90 and $100 for rooms. $180-$500 for suites. It has been discounting 30%.*

Built in 1992 and renovated in 2001 and 2002, this 12-story, 439-room hotel has kitchenettes in all suites. It has CNN, Cantonese food and 24-hour room service. There's also un-inspired architecture, almost non-existent English, and dirty hall carpets. It has no health club, no pool and no in-room safes. Its breakfast buffet is $10. Nikko Hotels International (JAL).

BELL TOWER HOTEL (Zhong Lou Fandian), *110 Nan Da Jie, 710001, southwest corner of Bell Tower. Three stars aiming for four stars in 2002. Tel. 7279200, Fax 7218767. E-mail: bth@sein.sxgb.com.cn. 45 km from the airport, three km from the railway station. Overlooking both Drum Tower and Hua Jue Xiang (with its modern underground Ginwa shopping center). You can walk to the Drum Tower, Bell Tower, internet café, South Gate, and Grand Mosque. $80-$110 for rooms, $120-$160 for suites. It has been discounting 20-30%.*

Built in 1982, this hotel has seven stories and 321 rooms. The best view is from odd-numbered rooms. It has CNN and HBO, a Cantonese restaurant, small old gym and bicycles for rent. Rooms are 21, 38 and 40 square meters. Some rooms have safes.

LONG HAI HOTEL, *306 Jiefang Road, 710004. Three stars. Tel. 7416090, 7420093, Fax 7416580, 7420093. $70 and $80 for rooms. $115-$260 for suites. It has been discounting 40% and is 400 meters from the railway station.*

This 308-room hotel run by the railways has Chinese and Western food and standard rooms 18 to 22 square meters. It has a wonderful, bigger than life size Warring States rhinoceros in front.

WAN NIAN HOTEL XI'AN (Fandian), *93 Chang Le Zhong Road, 710032. Three and soon four stars, Tel. 3231932, Fax 3210896. E-mail:*

wnhotel@pub.xaonline.com. Website: www.wnhotel.com. Y488-Y688 for rooms, and Y888 for suites in three-star section. It has been discounting from 20%-55%. It is outside the east wall about one km east of the Golden Flower. It is building a 300-plus-room four-star building with pool, mini-golf, gym and outdoor tennis that should be open late 2002.

This is a good basic hotel with very good food and non-smoking rooms but no CNN nor in-room safes.

YMCA, *339 Dongda Street, Tel. 7262288, Fax 7235479. E-mail: YMCAHOTEL@SINA.com. Three stars. This hostel has a great downtown location east of the Bell Tower and west of the Hyatt. Opened in 1998, it has 60 rooms at $32, and four suites at $60. No discounts.*

The Y has a health club, Chinese and Western food, foreign exchange, and tour desk. This is a basic seven-story hotel with safes in rooms and air-conditioning. Carpets are stained but the manager promised to have them cleaned during the winter. Light bulbs are 25 watts. The bathroom floors look dirty. If English is a problem, ask for G.M. Johnson Zhai. A two-day tour to Yanan costs Y500 per person, and a tour to the Terracotta Warriors is Y35 plus Y9 plus Y80 (entry ticket). The YMCA also has accommodations for travelers now in Beijing, Shanghai and Guangzhou.

MAY FIRST HOTEL (Wuyi Binguan), *351 Dongda Street, 710001. Tel. 7210804, 7215932, Fax 7213824. Y280 for rooms and Y618 for suites. The entrance to this well-located 110-room hotel is through a Chinese cafeteria with open kitchen serving Qin dynasty snacks.*

The hotel has dirty carpets, dim lights and a musty smell, no CNN and no in-room safes. Otherwise it's fine for low-budget travelers. It offers tours to the Warriors for Y340, and to Hua Shan for Y240 including bus, cable car, and entrance fee.

Where to Eat

Xi'an food is similar to that of Beijing and somewhat bland. Its famous local dishes are crisp fried chicken or duck, and dried fish shaped like grapes. Much of its food has been inspired by imperial tastes.

Two celebrated wines are made here: one is thick and sweet with the appearance of milk. Served hot, Chou Jiu wine inspired Tang poet Li Po, who drank 1000 cups and wrote more than 100 poems. The other wine is Xifeng Jiu (55% alcohol), one of the Eight Most Famous Wines in China.

Most hotels have excellent Chinese food – the best and most expensive in the top hotels – but joint ventures have the best Western food and Western wines. For Chinese food, The **Cantonese Restaurant** at the **Garden Hotel** has great frogs and hot peppers, celery and macadamia nuts, steamed Gui fish, mushrooms and cabbage, and lots more. Try the **Shangri-La**, **Hyatt** and **Sheraton**.

SMALL WORLD RESTAURANT, *just outside and to the west of the South Gate, 1 Nan Men Wei Huan Cheng Nan Road, Xi Duan, 710061. Tel. 7817618. E-mail: swrfood@pub.xaonline.com. It is open 8:30am to 11:30pm.*
Casual Western dining not in a hotel. A set breakfast with eggs, sausage, hash browns, toast and coffee costs about Y26. Sandwiches have been 20-30. Burgers Y20. Beef steak is Y36; pizza Y20 with Y3 toppings. Pasta Y32. Ice cream is Y18.

A **Kenny Rogers Roasters** and a **deli** are in the mall below the Bell and Drum Tower (Hua Jue Xiang) Square. Both are reasonably priced and good.

TANG DYNASTY THEATER RESTAURANT, *39 Changan Road, Tel. 7211633, 7211655, across from the Xi'an Hotel.*
This has an international menu with good food. The dinner and show costs about $49. The show only costs $19, and the buffet lunch $14. There's a discount if you book through Xian CITS.

DE FACHANG *on the other side of Drum and Bell Tower Square from the Bell Tower Hotel. Tel. 7214065. On the upper floors, there's more choice, and higher prices. Tel. 7269010 or 7218260. No credit cards. Open 11am-2pm and 5pm-9pm.*
This famous jiaotze dumpling restaurant serves over a hundred different kinds of dumplings. The ground floor offers a limited but cheap menu of dumplings (about Y8 a bowl). You can also choose cold dishes from a trolley.

WANNIAN HOTEL, *1 Changle Zhong Road, Tel. 3231932.*
Good dumplings, and a well-served hot pot banquet (Y50). Its food generally is good and moderately priced.

Muslim food is important here and a typical Muslim dish is Yang Rou Pao Mutton Soup. A good place is the **Tong Sheng Xiang Restaurant** with its pancake-in-mutton soup. It's on Xi Dong Street near the Bell Tower, *Tel. 7214636, and 2482828.* The **Lao Sun restaurant** outside the wall to the southeast is fine. It is close to a sign that says "West China National Food Centre." It serves Muslim food on mother-of-pearl inlaid tables. The downstairs has a limited menu, mainly greasy beef or mutton soup poured over bread crumbs which you break up yourself for Y13. You can choose from a trolley of cold dishes (Y8 or so each). The staff speaks a bit of English. Look for the travel agent in the west of the building and the bright red lanterns outside 78 Dong Guan Nan Street, *Tel. 2483388.* Upper floors are fancier and more expensive with a wider selection of food that you can point to.

Food at the **Muslim Markets** is cheap and quite good, but of questionable hygiene. One such market is on **Dai Mai Shi Street**. You can get good Cantonese snacks and dim sum (best in the morning) at the Grand New World Hotel's Food Street. Its fried rice and noodles range from Y12-Y20 and congee is Y5-Y14.

Seeing the Sights

Very special guests or tours arranged in advance with travel agents, can be greeted at one of the ancient gates with an elaborate welcoming ceremony, the lowering of the draw bridge, and the gift of an ancient passport with an official seal. Officials, dancers and singers in Tang-dynasty costumes, camels and horses can be on hand – as in the old days.

If you only have one day, you must see the Terracotta Warriors, then Banpo Village, the Big or Small Wild Goose Pagoda, the Provincial Museum, the Bell Tower, and the City Wall. If you've never experienced a Chinese-style mosque, try to fit in the Great Mosque, too. This is a very rushed itinerary, better done in two days. On the way to or from the airport, you must stop to see the 2100-year-old Han Yang Tomb. The admission fee is Y60. Most tourist attractions are open 8:30am-5pm.

*The Museum of Emperor Qin's Terracotta Army (Qin Yung Bo Wu Guan) is a 40-minute drive northeast of the city. The entrance fee is Y65-Y80 including the movie. *Tel. 3911961. Website: www.bmy.com.cn (Chinese).* You can go by a group tour, or a Y80 taxi (one way). You can negotiate for the taxi to wait for you, or take public bus 306/307 from the railway station for about Y10. This bus goes past the hot springs.

This is one of the most spectacular and important places to visit in the world. It has a 2,200-year-old painted-ceramic army of more than 8000 soldiers buried to "protect" the tomb of the first Qin emperor. Upon entry you are given a "smart card" which you use later to get into other buildings. You can purchase slides, photos and books of reasonable quality in souvenir shops.

The terracotta army is a puzzle because the emperor left no record of its existence. Excavation started in 1976. Permanent buildings protect the army and tourists from most of the elements, and you are able to walk around the periphery of these once-buried relics. If you look carefully, you should see bits of the original colors, most lost once exposed to air.

Local peasants digging a well discovered the relics in 1974. Some of these men now spend their time signing autographs on books you buy inside for Y180, and outside for Y95. Look for them in the Cinema building. Also in the Cinema is a not-to-be missed 19-minute, 360 degree movie. It makes the history come alive and shows you the costumes, the war, the making of the ceramic army, and its burning. Groups might have to request a showing in English, but you don't need any language to understand it.

There are three pits. **Vault Number One**, opened to the public in 1979, is 62 X 230 X 5 meters deep. Most of the army was found facing east, toward the tomb, 1.5 km away. The soldiers were in lines of roughly 70 across and 150 deep, separated by 10 walls and 11 corridors.

The men are hollow from the thigh up and made in two parts; they are 1.78-1.87 meters tall. The soldiers in front hold crossbows; also in front were

Terracotta Army Museum Tips

Do not allow guides to hurry you through this exhibit. Take your time. They have to wait for you. When it first opened, photography inside the buildings was forbidden. In the last couple of years, it has been allowed, even in front of signs that say "No Photography."

Guides do not take you to all the exhibits. If you are seriously interested, look around **pit Number Two** beyond the balconies for more to see.

bells and drums. Charioteers hold their hands out before them as if still clutching reins. The horses originally wore harnesses with brass ornaments and are a breed native to Hechu in Gansu. You can distinguish the officers from the soldiers by their clothing and armor. Is every one of the 600 faces here different? Judge for yourself. This pit actually had 6000 warriors but only 600 are visible. The rest will be replaced when repaired. Researchers believe that kilns were built around the molded figures (probably two horses at a time) and destroyed after firing. An exhibit explains this on the second floor of Vault Number Two. There are remains of 30 wooden chariots.

Vault Number Two is in a separate building, 124 X 98 meters, holding 1,400 cavalrymen, archers, charioteers and infantrymen, some kneeling and shooting. There's also Vault Number Three which has 68 officers and was probably the "command post." You pay extra to visit these two unless you have your card. In Vault Number Two, look carefully for the charred remains of the ceiling, believed burnt by farmers angry at the emperor. Near the main museum is the Bronze Chariots and Horses Exhibition Room with two of the 20 tiny bronze chariots found. These are also outstanding and you should see them at close range.

There are seven human skeletons, believed to be of noble family, on display. Were they competitors for the throne killed by the second emperor as some people believe?

Shopping here at the Warriors is almost fun. Peddlers are sometimes controlled now though they still might pull you to their stalls. You have to haggle to get the bargains.

You pass the Tomb of Emperor Qinshihuang (Chin Shih Huang-ti) on the way to and from the Terracotta Warriors. The first emperor of the Qin Dynasty, the builder of the Great Wall, and first unifier of China, lived from 259 to 210 B.C., and became King of Qin State at age 13. What he achieved in so short a reign is incredible, and it is no wonder that he searched his empire for pills of longevity. Over 700,000 people worked on his magnificent underground palace tomb, begun in 246 B.C. when he was 14 years old.

Archaeologists have made preliminary excavations at this site and so far believe that the tomb has not been robbed, and that the ancient records are

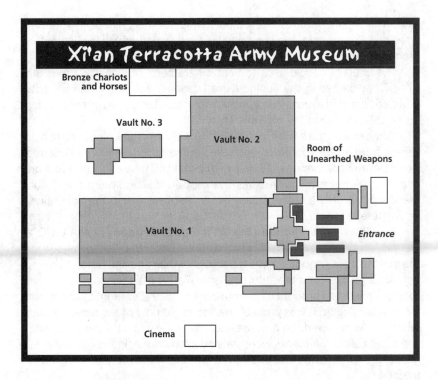

correct. "Rivers of mercury" probably flow through it. Lack of money and technology have postponed its excavation. All you can see is a grave mound six km in circumference, covered with pomegranate trees and a small pavilion. Ask about the nearby recent excavation of warriors in jade suits which might be open during your visit.

Many tourists eat at the Li Shan Hotel restaurant which is quite good and about one km away. We liked the chicken there, the sweet potatoes, cauliflower and bean sprouts, carmelized potatoes, and the noodle soup.

The *Huaqing Hot Spring, the site of the Xi'an Incident, is open 7:30am-7pm daily in summer, shorter in winter. It has been so overshadowed by modern events that its ancient history is frequently overlooked. It is at the base of Lishan Hill, 30 km northeast of Xi'an, and a visit here is usually combined with the Terracotta Warriors and lunch. If time is short, don't spend more than five minutes here. Other sites are more important as little that is original is left.

Huaqing has been an imperial resort since the mid-Tang, about 1,200 years ago. Its most famous tenants were Emperor Xuanzong (Hsuan-tsung) of the Tang, and the woman blamed for his downfall, his favorite concubine Yang Guifei (Kuei-fei). The influence of Concubine Yang and her relatives caused much dissatisfaction at court. In 755, an adopted son of hers rebelled, and the emperor's troops refused to move against him as long as she remained alive. The Japanese say she escaped to Japan. The Chinese say she was strangled. The emperor lived on even though they had vowed to die together. Promises! Promises!

The imperial couple used to winter here because it was warmer than Xi'an. They bathed in the Jiulong (Nine Dragons) Hot Spring and the Lotus Bath. You can find a reconstruction of her personal bath. The current buildings are post-Liberation in the old Tang style.

You can also trace the flight of Chiang Kai-shek, the Chinese Nationalist leader, from his bedroom as he panicked at the sound of gunfire at 5am on a cold December morning in 1936. He left behind his false teeth and wore only one shoe. A pavilion today marks the spot up the hill where the "Young Marshall" captured him and forced him to co-operate with the Communists against the Japanese.

The ***Dayan Ta Pagoda (Big Wild Goose Pagoda)** of the Da Ci'en Temple (south of the city wall), along with the Little Wild Goose Pagoda, are the most famous pagodas in China because of their age and history. They are not, however, the most beautiful or spectacular. The bigger pagoda was built to house the sutras brought back from India in 652 A.D. (Tang) by the famous monk Xuan Zhang. It was probably named in memory of the temple in India where the monk lived, on a goose-shaped hill. Or it could have acquired its name because some monks were starving and Buddha, in the form of a wild goose, dropped down close to them. The monks, being vegetarians, refused to eat it.

The pagoda has seven stories, 248 steps, and a great view from the top. In the adjoining Da Ci'en Temple (647 A.D.) are painted-clay statues of 18 lohan (Ming), most with strong Indian rather than Chinese features. These buildings are usually full of tourists.

The ***Little Wild Goose Pagoda (Xiao Yan Ta)**, south of the wall, is 45 meters high and was constructed of brick in 684 A.D. At thirteen stories high, it is missing two of its original stories, which were destroyed during earthquakes in 1444. This is all that remains of the great Da Jianfu Temple, so important in the Tang.

While both pagodas are state-protected historical monuments, only a stop at one is really necessary. The little one is in a park, no longer a temple. It is a pleasant place to rest and enjoy because there are fewer people.

The **Shaanxi Provincial History Museum (Shaanxi Li Shi Bo Wu Guan)**, 91 Yanta Zhong Road, 710061, is south of the walled city and is open 9am-5:30pm daily, with the last entry at 3:30pm, *Tel.5254727*. The fee includes a locker for your purse. This separate entrance for foreigners has a shopping area, clean toilets, and a snack bar. This is one of China's best museums and is worth seeing with some explanations in English. It requires a minimum of one hour, more if you want to savor it. It covers prehistory 1.5

millions years ago to the end of the Qing and has original Tang frescoes. Look for the tiny gold Tang dragons and the great but tiny Han tomb figures.

The 36-meter-high ***Bell Tower (Zhong Lou)** in city center was first built in 1384 (Ming) in another location, and moved to its current site here 200 years later. Three sets of eaves weaken 'the force of the rainfall,' and actually only two stories are here. The furniture is gorgeous (Qing) and the very fancy traditional ceiling is Ming. From the second story you can look at all four gates of Xi'an. Parking is impossible. Park inside the Bell Tower Hotel compound, pretend you're eating there, and take the tunnel.

The nearby **Drum Tower (Gu Lou)**, within walking distance to the west, is also impressive. The tower was built in 1384 and is original. Drums used to be beaten about 800 times in 10 minutes before the city gates closed for the night. You don't need to go inside.

The ***Great Mosque (Qing Zhen Si)**, *Tel. 7271504, 7272541*, the largest in Xi'an, is on a back street north past the Drum Tower. It was founded as a mosque in 742 (Tang) by Moslems from Xinjiang and Guangzhou with the permission and help of the Tang emperors. The present buildings are mainly Ming. The buildings are a good example of the sinofication of foreign religious buildings right down to the bats, dragons, unicorns, and mother-of-pearl-inlaid furniture–contrary to Muslim practice. The Great Hall (Ming) is, however, west Asian, the writing Arabic, the arches and flowers more like Istanbul or Baghdad. You remove your shoes if allowed to enter. Prayers are said five times a day. Its gilded wooden Koran, the largest in the world, was carved here. Today in Xi'an, 14 other mosques and this one serve at least 60,000 Moslems.

Banpo Neolithic Museum (Banpo Wu Guan), *Tel. 3279240, 3279248*, open 8am-6pm daily, is in the eastern suburbs of the city. It is the actual archaeological site of a 6,000-year-old neolithic village. The site covers 50,000 square meters, of which the museum encloses 3,000. There you see living quarters, one of the oldest pottery kilns in the country, and a graveyard.

The museum encompasses a communal storage area, moat, graveyard (skeletons under glass), and fireplaces. In the museum are a bow drill, barbed fish hook, clay pots, and pottery whistle believed to be the earliest musical instrument in China. Among its other artifacts are hairpins, stone axes, and a pot with holes in the bottom, probably used as a steamer. Its narrow-necked, narrow-based water jugs, with two handles, look surprisingly like amphoras also used by the ancient Greeks and Romans! Is there a connection? The exhibits are labeled in English.

This culture is believed to be matrilineal because:
• the burial customs; most of the 174 graves had one skeleton each, and the few graves that contained more than one skeleton had no male-female couples; scientists concluded that there were no fixed marriages.
• the women gathered wild food at first while the men hunted. After the

women discovered how to plant seeds, land became valuable and it was passed on from mother to daughter.
• the village consisted of one big house in the center for old and young, and smaller houses for visiting males. The men kept their belongings in their native villages, where the men were later buried.

As agriculture developed, men started pursuing it too. As surpluses grew (and probably the basic principles of physiology were discovered), fixed families started. In later neolithic gravesites in Gansu, male skeletons were found lying straight, females leaning toward them. Since the women were bound, they were probably buried alive. So much for early women's lib! Now, what is your theory?

The *City Wall was built from 1374 to 1378 (Ming), probably with material from the old Tang wall. It is 3.4 km (north-south) by 2.6 km (east-west), and 12 meters high. The walls follow the boundaries of the Tang imperial city. The gates open to the public are on each of the four sides. From these you can climb the wall. Six new gates have been recently added to the original four. You can see a small section of the south wall in its original Tang dynasty state. You can walk on top of most of the wall and an electric car can take you to the East or West Gate for Y10 one way. But it's a good place to walk and watch people go about their lives down below. The entry fee is about Y8.

The new **Han Yang Museum** is an essential. You must see it! The site is between the Wei River and the airport, and is convenient if you are near the airport anyway, as it's only a few hundred meters from the main road. This exhibition is not on the grand scale of the Terracotta Warriors, but it's wonderful because the faces are so real, so eerily like those of people in Xi'an today, and most are smiling. To see the museum costs Y30. In a nearby building, you can look down into an actual archaeological site and if you're lucky, watch archaeologists at work. If you want to see more, you pay an additional Y30, but there's not much more to see. Titles are in English and Chinese and no photos are allowed indoors.

The museum features the tomb of **Emperor Jing Di** of the Han, the dynasty that succeeded the Qin dynasty. Jing Di was the fourth emperor of the Western Han who reigned from 157 to 141 B.C. and was the father of the more famous Emperor Wu Di. The museum is full of pottery figures, chariots and houses, weapons, tools and household utensils, warriors, eunuchs and animals. It has dancing women in long graceful gowns. The ceramic figures originally wore silk and had wooden arms but these have since disintegrated. The bodies are nude. The National Geographic says there are 24 pits with a minimum of 700 figures, and that about 10,000 prisoners probably died building this tomb. The figures are about two feet tall.

This tomb was featured in the *National Geographic*, August 1992 ("A Chinese Emperor's Army for Eternity"). It was discovered in March 1990 when the road to the airport was being constructed. You can just drive in, pay the fee, or make arrangements with a travel agency. If it's not listed on your tour, do ask if you can make a stop there. It's worth paying an additional Y30.

If You Have More Time or Interest

It is possible to hire a small taxi for the day for about Y360 to go to the tombs of Princess Yantai, Empress Wu and Emperor Gaozong, and Famen Temple. On the way shortly out of Xi'an we came across the very imposing 1993 Roman Catholic church in East Dongpu and met Franciscan Father Li Jiang Ping. He was very welcoming, so if you see this church just off the main road, stop in for a look.

*Qianling is the Tomb of Tang Emperor Gaozong (Kao-tsung), and the Empress Wu, 79 km northwest of Xi'an. She was as ruthless and outrageous as Qing Empress Dowager Cixi, but a more successful ruler. He died in 683 A.D. and she in 705 A.D. This unexcavated tomb is a worthwhile full day's excursion that can include other area tombs as well. While earlier tombs were built to create their own artificial hills on the plains, the Tang tombs were built into existing hills. This one is 400 meters high and you climb steps or take a horse. At the base are some cave homes you can visit.

Approaching the highest hill, you pass statues of horses and ostriches, and three to four-meter high guardian figures holding swords. Then on the left are the life-size statues of guards, tribal heads, and foreign diplomats who paid their respects at the funeral. The 61 statues are now without heads, alas; look for names on their backs. One is labeled "Afghanistan." The wall around the tomb is 4470 meters long. There are plans to open the actual tomb to the public. Although many of the structures at Qianling were destroyed in the war at the end of the Tang, the museum here contains about 4000 pieces.

Some of the minor tombs in the neighborhood are excavated, and you can also go underground to find the coffin and fine murals of court scenes in the tombs of Princess Yong-tai and Prince Yide three km away. Titles are in English. Yong-tai, the granddaughter of Gaozong, was 17 at her death, and some believed she was murdered because she found out that Empress Wu was having an affair. The cause of death was officially a liver ailment.

Famen Temple, 130 km from Xi'an, should be included in a one-day trip along with the Qianling Tomb. The entrance fee is about Y18 and it's open 9am-6pm daily. The temple was founded in the Han Dynasty, 2000 years ago. It is extremely important because it houses a finger bone of Prince Gautama, the founder of Buddhism whose statue is in every Buddhist temple in China and who lived in the fifth century B.C. Unfortunately a tourist town has been built around this shrine.

While tourists will not normally be shown the rare relic, you can see some of the 900 treasures that were buried with it: well-preserved gold-inlaid ceremonial vessels, ancient glass and jade, gilt Buddhas, jewelry, gold walking stick, gold chain basket, fake "bones" of jade - the largest group of Tang artifacts found since 1950. They were gifts from Tang Emperors Yi Zong and Xi Zong. Empress Wu donated gilded embroidery with threads finer than those made today. Titles are in English and the museum air-conditioned.

Fans of ancient bronzes might ask to see a fantastic Zhou dynasty museum nearby.

More Tombs?

*Maoling on a plateau north of the Wei River, 40 km northwest of Xi'an, has more than ten tombs, small grassy pyramids, about 46.5 meters high. The main tomb is that of the fifth Han emperor, built 139-87 B.C. According to records, it contains a jade suit with gold threads (seems to be a Han fad), and, in a gold box, more than 190 different birds and animals, jade, gold, silver, pearls, and rubies.

Near Maoling is the **Xianyang Museum**, containing 3,000 painted terracotta warriors and horse figures from the Western Han (206 B.C. to 24 A.D.). They are each between 55 and 68 cm high, and artistically better than the Qin Army. Also near Maoling is the **Tomb of Yang Guifei**, the beautiful, tragic imperial concubine. Women have taken earth from here to put on their faces, hoping it will make them equally alluring.

*Zhaoling, 70 km northwest of Xi'an near Liquan, is the tomb of the second Tang Emperor Taizong. You can visit its small museum with Tang pottery, stone tablets, and murals. This tomb is not worth visiting unless you can read classical Chinese. The famous bas-reliefs of the emperor's favorite horses in the Stele Museum are from here. (One of these is in Philadelphia.)

Tired of Tombs?

In town, the **Xian Film Studio** is worth a visit if only for the magnificent reproduced Qin palace used for the strongly recommended Sino-Canadian movie (and book), *The First Emperor*. There are other exhibits as well. It is near the Garden Hotel.

The **Kaiyuan Men Gate**, in the western part of the city, was the starting point of the Silk Road and is now marked with a huge recent photogenic statue of a caravan. The ruins of *Daming Palace, built in 634 A.D. (Tang) are about two km north of the railway station. Now partially reconstructed, it should be furnished in the Tang style.

Head southwest of Xi'an about 40 km to **Huxian County Town**. Here you can visit the **Huxian Peasant Painting Exhibition Hall**, *Tel. 4812871*. This is open daily 8am-12 noon and 2:30pm-6:30pm. The entry fee has been Y20. Some of the 2,000 painters in the county have also exhibited abroad these recordings in gay colors of their everyday lives and achievements. While you can buy these paintings everywhere in Xi'an and many of them are now mass-produced, you might want an opportunity to meet the artists. There's

Ms. Pan Xiao Ling who lives nearby in Dong Han village, Guang Ming Xang, Tel. *29/481-3544.*

A good restaurant is in nearby Huxian County town. The **Wang Long Food Restaurant** is at 383 Dong Da Jie, *Tel. 728-6755.* This is another of those point-and-order places, and we had red beans, peanuts on black rice; seafood with glass noodles, and beef and lamb shishkebobs.

The **Horse and Chariot Pit**, Zhangjiapo, Chang'an county, can be combined with Huxian county for a half-day tour. It is the burial site of two chariots, six real horses, and one slave (11th century B.C. to Western Zhou) and is the best of seven such pits found. It is of special interest to archaeologists.

About 25 km away from the city is the thatched-cottage **Caotang Temple** (Tang), where Indian monk Kumarajiva Jiumoluosi translated the Buddhist sutras into Chinese. He died in 413 A.D.

*Xingjiao Temple, about 25 km east of the city wall, is on a sylvan hillside, which, with a little mist, could look like the lonely setting of the famous Japanese movie Rashomon. The place oozes with atmosphere although the buildings are recent. It was founded by Tang Emperor Gaozong in 669 A.D., but destroyed and rebuilt several times. The remains (at least some of them) of monk Xuan Zhang, who brought back the sutras from India, are buried in the small, five-story pagoda here. About 20 monks are in residence. It is peaceful with few tourists.

The **Louguan Taoist Temple** has now been restored. It is beyond Huxian, about 70 km west of Xi'an. It is said to be the place where Lao Tzu, founder of Taoism, taught. The temple has resident monks and makes traditional medicines. The setting and especially the entrance gate are very fine. A big yearly fair is held here.

Nightlife & Entertainment

There's not much aside from the theater restaurants or their shows. The **Tang Dynasty Theater Restaurant** has an international-quality show of Tang-inspired dances and music. It's at 33 Chang'an Road, *Tel. 5261633, Fax 5261619,* nightly at 6:30pm-8pm for dinner; 8:30pm for the show. The food is very good. See Where to Eat above for prices. A second newer dinner theater is the **Shaanxi Grand Opera House**, Song and Dance Theatre, at 165 Wenyi Road, *Tel. 7853295, Fax 7853299,* Attention Ms. Wang Hong. Tours get 20 different kinds of dumplings for Y80. The show only is Y118. It is also very pleasing. The dinner is at 7pm, the show at 8:30pm. For lunch, it's 11am-2pm.

The **Tanghua Garden Hotel's dinner theater** includes a French dinner at 6:30pm for $35. Just the show at 8pm costs $15. It's mainly for men, but the performance at the Tang Dynasty Theater Restaurant has more variety.

Some visitors feel that these shows are tourist traps. Of course they are. But they are entertaining, they make a good attempt to give you the flavor of ancient times, and the food is delicious.

Parkson Department Store across from the Hyatt has a many-splendored entertainment center on its 12/F with a bar, lounge, karaoke, and night club. Its international show had good costumes, fancy lighting, billowing smoke, loudly played popular Hong Kong songs, Korean folk songs, a passo doble, and even a scene from a revolutionary opera. It was worth Y100 plus drinks to watch it from a comfortable arm chair.

Hotels have the usual discos and karaoke, the best at the Hyatt and Sheraton. Unfortunately there are lots of prostitutes frequenting locally-run bars, but fewer if any in these good hotels.

The **City Wall** has some drink stands on summer evenings. You can probably see some local outdoor dance halls from the top of the South Gate. The Wall is lighted and decorated with huge lanterns during festivals and is very pleasant up on top especially at dusk. Groups can arrange a fireworks display. Ask about the powerful Shaanxi waist drum dancers. A **night food market** is near the Drum Tower, and other places around town.

The annual Cultural Arts Festival in September is highly recommended. **Defu Street** has many coffee houses and tea houses.

Sports & Recreation

The 18-hole **Ya Jian Golf Club** is 31 km from Xi'an at Cao Tang Village, *Tel. 4955235*; the **New Century Golf Driving Range** is at New Century Square, Gao Xin Road, *Tel. 8226699*.

Shopping

The main shopping area is east of the Bell Tower on **Dongda Dong Street**. Made locally or in the province are rubbings, reproductions of three-color Tang camels and horses, and murals. Also made are inlaid lacquer, cloisonné, stone and jade carvings, gold and silver jewelry, peasant paintings, silk embroidery, and celadon. Cloisonné seems cheaper in Shanghai and Beijing than here. You should haggle with everyone, especially in the over-priced factories, and during low tourist season when some have settled for 50%-60% off on carpets and silk scarves.

You will also find cheap reproductions of the Terracotta Warriors. Some of these are not kiln-fired and are easily broken. The better quality is usually found in government-approved stores like the **Xi'an Pottery Art Factory**. It's on the way to the Terracotta Warriors at 5, Dian Chang Dong Road, Bu Zi or Puzi Village, 710038, *Tel. 3519063*.

A 200-meter-long Tang Dynasty-style street, with food, souvenirs and actually good-quality modern paintings is near the Big Wild Goose Pagoda. At stalls outside many tourist attractions, you will find cheap tiger slippers for children and red cotton vests with appliquéd snakes, scorpions, lizards, and pandas. These are the cheapest in China here. The yucky bugs are to frighten away the evil spirits. But do you think they will survive a washing machine?

Among the factories you could visit are the **Jade Carving factory** near the Provincial Museum where you can see a demonstration and its big showroom full of beautiful stones. It is open 9am-6pm and is at 9 Yan Ta Road, Tel. 5523421. The **Phoenix Embroidery Factory** and the **Cloisonné Factory** are at 33 Dong Road, 710005, *Tel. 7277689, 7271437.*

The best shopping for curios has been in the alley between the Drum Tower and Grand Mosque, open 9am-6pm. Towards closing time prices might fall from Y180 to Y60 for antique hand scales. The first asking price for a brass reproduction of a dragon is Y180, but try for Y50.

At the South Gate behind the head of the gold dragon is **Shu Yuan Men Street** in ancient architecture where some traditional arts like writing brushes are made and curios and antiques sold. The **Xi'an Antique Store** is here near the Stele Museum, *Tel. 7213672.* **Shaanxi Cultural Relics Store** is in the Shaanxi Provincial Museum, *Tel. 7213691* and the **Xi'an Cultural Relics Shop** is at 375 Dongda Street, *Tel. 7215874,7441572.* An antique store is in the Drum Tower.

Below Drum and Bell Tower Square is the modern underground **Ginwa shopping center** with a supermarket, open 9am-10pm, *Tel.7212166.* It takes only MasterCard. The **Minsheng Department Store** has arts and crafts of medium quality and reasonable prices. It's at 103 Jiefang Road, near the railway station, and is open 9:30am-9pm, Saturday and Sunday 9am-9pm. **Parkson Department Store** is across from the Hyatt Regency Hotel.

Excursions & Day Trips

*Huangling County is almost halfway between Xi'an and Yan'an, about four hours by road. Important there is the *Tomb of the Yellow Emperor Xuan Yuan. This is 3.6 meters high and 50 meters in circumference, originally built in the Han but moved here to its present site in the Song. The Yellow Emperor is the legendary ancestor of the Chinese people believed to have lived about 2,000 B.C. The tomb is at the top of Qiaoshan Hill, one km north of Huangling town. At the base is Xuan Yuan Temple built in the Han. The throne stands in the middle with information about Xuan's life on both sides. In ancient times, travelers had to dismount from their horses and pay their respects to their First Ancestor as they passed by. His memorial day is the 5th day of the fourth lunar month.

Of its 63,000 cypress trees, the Yellow Emperor himself is supposed to have planted one. It is the largest known ancient cypress in China.

Huashan Mountain is 120 km east of Xi'an, two to three hours drive each way. It has one of the most thrilling cableway rides in China, 80-degree cliffs with iron chains to hang on to, and a "1000-foot-long Flight of Stone Steps." Famous as one of the Five Sacred Mountains, it has Taoist temples at its base, and tiny old temples on its slopes. Peaks rise up to 2,100 meters. It can be visited in one day. Renting a van and driver is about $90. If you want to stay overnight, the best hotel here is the three-star Financial Hotel at the base. A cheap hostel is at the top of the cable car, one of the few comfortable places to sit. The 1550-meter-long cable car is a Sino-Singapore joint venture using Austrian hardware. It is otherwise a nine-hour climb and no porters are available.

Practical Information

Business Hours, 8:30am-5:30pm, five days a week for offices; 9am-8 or 8:30pm for stores. About 5pm-about 11pm depending on weather for night food and clothing markets.

CITS, *Xi'an Branch, 48 Chang'an Bei Road, 710061, Tel. 5263697, 5262066, Fax 5261453. E-mail: xacitswl@public.xa.sn.cn.* Ask for Ma Ya He, Manager, FIT Department, Fifth floor, *Tel. 5263697*, who gave a lot of information for this book. Branches in Sheraton and Bell Tower Hotels open 8am-8pm. Ask about join-in Panda Tours.

Internet Cafe, *2/F China Telecommunications Office across the square north from the Bell Tower Hotel. Open daily 9am-8:30pm. Y10 for 30 minutes, Y18 an hour;* **Internet Relaxation Club**, *254 Dong Da St. (between Royal and Hyatt Hotels), Tel. 7276098. E-mail: wangzhan@163.ent.com. Open 24 hours. Y3-Y9 an hour. 103 computers.*

Panda Tours, *48 Chang'an Bei Road, 710061. Tel. and Fax 5263697, 5261454. E-mail: fit@citsxa.com or xacitssk@public.xa.sn.cn for tour prices and group discount. Website: www.citsxa.com (some English).* The Terra Cotta Army tour is a guaranteed daily departure for $41 per person, inclusive of admission fee, lunch and English-speaking guide.

Shaanxi Far East Travel Service Co., *5/F, Jianshe Xilu, 710054. Tel. 7888695, 7819263, Fax 7892360.* Ask for Mr. Wang Jun, a reliable agent, who has helped with this book, and my own travel arrangements. *E-mail: jwang9998@sina.com.*

Xi'an China Travel Service, *5/F, No. 103 Chang'an Bei Road, 710061, Tel. 5397116, 5261802, Fax 5393137.* For a self-drive vehicle tour on the Silk Road from Europe to Beijing, contact Tian Xiaopeng, Assistant Manager of Sales, Marketing, and Reception Center of Xi'an CTS, *Tel. 5259537, 5397115 or 13909280885, Fax 5253433, 5225244. E-mail: xactstxp@263.net.* Few travel agencies in China know first hand how to get permits to drive your own car here, especially on the Silk Road. The Germans I met with Mr. Tian were happy with his arrangements.

Shaanxi Provincial Tourism Administration, *15 Chang'an Bei Road, 710061, Tel. 5251437, 5261337, 5261179, Fax 5250151, 5261483.* For brochures. Ask for Mr. Gao Jia Fu, Director, Promotion Department, who has helped this book a lot.

Telephone code: 29.

Xian Sun International Travel Service, *7/F Hong Yang Building No. B-18, East Tao Yuan South, Second Ring Road (west), Tel. 4257597 (24 hours) or 4236089. Fax 4249146 or 4257981. E-mail: SSITWQ@public.xa.sn.cn.* This is a small privately-owned, share-holding travel agency. Ask for Dorothy Wang (Wang Qian) who is very enthusiastic, charming, and eager to be of service. Her English is excellent. This agency should be able to make travel arrangements, and also sell tickets for the Song and Dance Grand Theatre Shaanxi which it manages. The show is good. Do let me know your experience with this agency if you use it.

Yinchuan

Yinchuan is the capital of Ningxia Hui Autonomous Region, which lies between Inner Mongolia and Gansu on the north central border of China. This region has some little-known world class tourist attractions: relics and tombs from the Western Xia dynasty that ruled this area when the Song was in charge of the rest of China. The Xia had a highly developed culture. The area already had an incredible irrigation system based on the Yellow River on which it is dependant even today. There's the Great Wall and a well-preserved Buddhist grotto, (unfortunately a long way from Yinchuan).

The tourism infastructure is currently being developed by the central government with a new highway from Yinchuan to Zhongwei. Its regional weather is coldest in January at -22°C; its hottest is 33°C in May to September. It has very little rain, but a few sandstorms blow hard in spring and autumn. The altitude is 1017 meters in Yinchuan, and 3200 meters on the top of Helan Mountain. The annual precipitation is 200-700 mm mainly from July to September.

Arrivals & Departures

Yinchuan is linked by air mainly with Beijing (1.5 hours), Xi'an (1.3 hours) and 25 other Chinese cities. The airport is 15 km from downtown. It is also reached by train from Beijing (fastest 20 hours), Lanzhou (9 hours), and Xi'an (15 hours). It is on the Lanzhou-Baotou-Hohhot railway line. A taxi from Lanzhou could cost at least Y1200.

Orientation

Yinchuan is not as far from Beijing as the Silk Road, but the weather is more severe, and it is still being developed. Today the population in urban Yinchuan is 1 million and in Ningxia region 5.62 million.

Ningxia was inhabited 30,000 years ago, and archaeologists have collected 8000-year-old neolithic relics here. It was home to the Yong and Di tribes in the Western Zhou dynasty. The first Qin emperor conquered the tribes and connected parts of the Great Wall. He sent thousands of men to settle and defend this area but the Xiongnu tribal federation took it over in the fifth century. Yinchuan became capital of the Western Xia, a tribal dynasty during the early part of the Song (1038). The Xia kings reigned until Genghis Khan defeated them. Very little has been known about them until recently.

Ningxia was close enough to the trade routes for Persian coins to be buried in its Northern Wei tombs. A great deal of the region is covered by the Liupan Mountains, through which the Long March passed in 1935.

Ningxia Hui Autonomous Region was founded in 1958, and the Cultural Revolution sent many people here from urban China in the 1960s to "learn from the peasants." Today, it has many national minorities, including the Huis (31.7%), Mongolians, Manchus, and Turfans. The region exports coal and also produces petroleum, mica, asbestos, and lime.

Where to Stay

Until the International Hotel reopens in 2002 or so, the best hotel is the downtown Rainbow Hotel. Hotels add a 6% surcharge.

RAINBOW BRIDGE HOTEL, *16 Jiefang Xi Street, 750001. Four stars. Tel. 6918888, Fax 6918788. E-mail: Hongqiao@public.yc.nx.cn. CTS charges $42 a room.*

INTERNATIONAL HOTEL, *Bei Huan Dong Road, 750004. Applying for four stars. Tel. 6728688, Fax 6711808. It's 27km from the airport (Y80 taxi) and 13km from the railway station. It accepts credit cards.*

This 159-room hotel has been the top hotel in town. It has had CNN, Star Plus and non-smoking rooms. Prices will be determined later when it reopens, so check first.

NINGXIA CHANGXIANGYI HOTEL, *No. 88, Yuhuangge North Street, Tel. 6710668, Fax 6710658. Three stars. You can walk to downtown.*

Some foreigners have been staying happily here.

Where to Eat

The hotels are the best places to eat, but there are lots of clean looking and very cheap restaurants with great Muslim food and Eight Treasure Tea. Unfortunately, few had toilets and guests have to go outside to public (ugh) facilities.

BAI LE JI FAN ZHANG, *133 Jiefang Xi Street, Tel. 5035586.*

I've had great mutton noodle soup here.

YANG ZHOU SHI FU RESTAURANT, *178 Jie Fang Xi Street, Tel. 5028797.*

Good mutton hot pot, lamb, and beef noodles.

Seeing the Sights

Yinchuan has tiny taxis, which cost Y150-Y180 a day negotiable for out-of-town trips. It is otherwise hard to get around. Most important to see is the **Ningxia Provincial Museum** (Y10) with some of the Western Xia relics. Hours are 9am-12 noon and 2pm-5pm. Tickets cost Y5. The **Chengtian Pagoda** (Y10) is on the same grounds, was built in 1050 A.D.(Western Xia), and renovated in the Qing. Lots of antique and arts stores are in the neighborhood around Xin Hua Xi and Jinning Street.

The Western Xia had 12 emperors from 1038 to 1227. It had its own writing with about 6000 words based on the Song characters, and the oldest example of moveable type printing found so far of Buddhist culture. Look for the wonderful gilded copper statues and white porcelain. And the sculptured column bases that look like women with breasts but guides say are male slaves. These are beautiful and incredibly well-made. The museum also has an exhibit about the Hui people.

Next in importance are the **Western Xia Mausoleums** (Y30) which are 40 km due west from Yinchuan. These are in an area five km by 10 km and look like giant old-fashioned, earthen beehives, some as tall as 26 meters. You can look into one of these to the left of the entrance. The Mongols burned down the wooden structures originally over the tombs.

The **Western Xia Museum** with relics found in the tombs is nearby and is worth a visit. Unfortunately there are no English-speaking guides nor titles.

Also important, 67 km south of Yinchuan, is a reproduction of the **108 Dagobas** on a hillside in Qing Tong Xian county. These have been arranged in the shape of a triangle in 12 rows from one to 19 across in odd numbers. The smallest is about two meters tall and the Buddhist originals are from the 13th and 14th centuries, apparently built to ward off the "108 human frustrations."

You have to take a small boat across to the western bank of the Yellow River five minutes to the site. It is open 8am-6pm and charges Y10 per person plus Y10 for the boat. The originals were flooded by a new dam and reproduced in 1983. Snack restaurants only. You might not think it worth the trouble to see reproductions but these do give some idea of the vast scope of the originals.

You can see the irrigation system as you drive around, and the many wonderful mosques. In town, the Drum Tower and Jade Emperor's Pavilion are impressive but worth only a photo stop. **Helan Mountain** is 60 km northwest across the desert. The road is lined with shade trees, the only vegetation there. About 100 of the famous 2000-year-old **rock paintings** can be seen in the vicinity. A taxi costs about Y150.

Excursions & Day Trips

Zhongwei is about 200 km. and 2.5-3 hours by road south of Yinchuan. It has the unusual and multi-tiered 15th century **Gao Temple** with statues of the Jade Emperor, the Holy Mother and Guan Yu, the God of War. It is only 300 meters from the three-star **Yi Xing Hote**L, near the fancy Drum Tower. Rooms here are Y168-Y388, with a three-bed dorm going for Y150. It's at 2 Gulou Bei Road, *Tel. 953/7017666, Fax 7019993.* CTS in Yinchuan charges $24 a room.

Zhongwei, on the border of the A La Shan Grasslands and the Tenge Li desert, has camel and horse **treks in the desert.** You can also float 50 km on a **sheepskin raft** for three hours down the Yellow River, but get a look at it first because it could be an uncomfortable experience.

Guyuan is well worth the effort though there's hardly any English in the town. Buses take eight hours from the South Gate of Yinchuan. You can also go by train and onward from there to Xi'an or vice versa. An overnight bus costs about Y60 to Xi'an.

Guyuan is a wonderful 2000-year-old town of 50,000 people with ties to the Western Xia dynasty and Silk Road. From downtown, you can walk to the countryside in 15 minutes if the 2000-meter-high altitude doesn't bother you. Guyuan has the **Buddhist grottoes** at Xumi Mountain (Xishan Wen Guan Suo), and for those who like Buddhist art, these are world class. You can hire a taxi for the 55 km drive past beautiful fields of corn and barley and mountain passes topped with the ruins of old castles.

Few tourists go to Xumi because of the difficulty getting there and the lack of decent hotels. Like the great grottoes in Datong and Luoyang, these were also started in the Northern Wei and continued on through the Tang. They are also superb.

The only grotto you can photograph is the 20.6-meter-high Tang-dynasty **Maitreya** which is out-of-doors. The rest of the 349 Buddhas are in over 151 caves, many of which you can visit. Originally there were 900 statues, but some were destroyed in a 20th century earthquake. All are carved red sandstone with especially good drapery. Statues in numbers 45 and 46 still show traces of gold. Some faces or just eyes have been destroyed. Cave 51 is worth the climb. It is the biggest with several large amazing statues. The entrance fee is Y10. *Tel. 954/2695706.* Take your own flashlight. There are no restaurants, no nothing here except for some friendly officials who said to "come any time" and not just between the posted 8am-12 noon and 2:30pm-6:30pm.

Earthen ruins of the **Great Wall** are four km west of Guyuan. You can see fired mud bricks of equal thickness but not the big stones of the wall north of Beijing.

There are several cheap, modest hotels here. Not bad was the new section of the three-star **Youdian (Binguan) Hotel** which is a short walk to stores, restaurants and the museum. The postal code is 756000, *Tel. 954/2031856.* CTS in Yinchuan charges $30 a room. This hotel has a Muslim Restaurant but no Western food and no credit card service. It did have wonderful minced beef or lamb buns for Y4 for breakfast. Rooms are clean with limited hot water, no English, and no air-conditioning.

The local **museum** exhibits relics found in the vicinity. It ranges from the Stone Age through Han and Tang but has no titles in English. It has a model of Guyuan as it looked in the Qing. Its most valuable relic is a Persian ewer from 569 A.D. The museum is open 8:30am-11:30am and 2:30pm-5:30pm, closed on Mondays. It is at 133 Xi Cheng Road.

Ms. Guo Xiping of the Foreign Affairs Office in Guyuan, *Tel. 2032971*, should be able to arrange for guides and transportation to Xumi Mountain for about Y120. Her address is 51 Zhengfu Street. Our driver Mr. Zhang Wen Xue is wonderful but cannot speak English. He knew more about the sites than anyone else we met in Guyuan. If you have an interpreter, look for him. We paid Y150 for transportation which included the Great Wall, grottoes, and museum. *Tel. 954/2040273, BP 126-8202176.*

Shopping

The region produces sheepskin garments, licorice root, Helan inkstone carvings, rugs, and blankets. Its Eight Treasure Tea (Babao Cha) is well-known. Try the **Shopping Center** on Gulou Nan Street, *Tel. 6023046.*

Individuals might try to sell you relics stolen from the many ancient tombs in this area. Possession of cultural relics is a crime sometimes punishable by execution. Ancient artifacts cannot be taken legally out of the country without a certificate from the Antiquities Bureau.

Practical Information

Business Hours, for offices, 8am-12noon, 2:30pm-6 or 6:30pm; 9am-9pm for stores.

China Travel Service Ningxia, *122 Gulou St., 750004. Tel. 5047460, Fax 5044025. E-mail: nxcts@public.yc.nx.cn or Frank-ctsnx@sohu.com. Mobile Phone: 13995102152 or 8278024.* Ask for Frank Chen, Manager, Inbound Department, who helped a lot with this book.

E-mail service: the **Internet Café**, *China Telecom, Zhongshan Bei Street, Tel. 6092050, 6041235, Y9 an hour and Y50 deposit.*

Ningxia CITS, *4/F, 116 Jiefang Xi Street, 750001, Tel. 5045555. Fax 5043466.* Ask for Chen Xiaodong, Marketing Manager for Europe and the Americas, who also helped with this book. *E-mail:nxcits@126.com.*

Telephone code: 951

Xining
(Siling)

Xining is the capital of Qinghai (Tsinghai) province. It is important because of Taer Lamasary and the bird sanctuary in Qinghai Lake. It is the main land gateway to Tibet, and the birthplace of both the Dalai Lama and the Panchen Lama, an important province for those interested in Tibetan Buddhism.

The Qinghai region covers one-thirteenth of China. It has less than four million people, Han (60%), the rest Tibetan, Hui, Mongolian, Kazak, Salan, and Tu. Many of these are nomadic herders. Roughly 96% of its land is pasture for 22 million horses, yak, dzos, oxen and sheep. Livestock breeding has been practiced here for 4000 years. Half of China's yak, and one-third of all the world's yak, are in Qinghai.

Times are changing however. The national government has been focusing its economic development in the northwest region. Pasture land is now contracted to herdspeople for 30 years, hopefully encouraging wise management. Counties give bonuses to families who send their children to school, not an easy task for nomads. The government is building railways and highways and trying to move tens of thousands of Han people into Tibetan areas. These are rich in petroleum, gas, potash, zinc, copper, and lead.

Qinghai is the source of both the Yellow and Yangtze rivers and has a lot of hydro-electric power. It is rich in aluminum, coal, and oil. Its hottest weather is about 30 C in July and August, but thermometers could hit 50°C or more out in the desert sun in its northwest. Its coldest temperature is -20°C in January and December. The annual precipitation is 450 mm mainly in July and August. The urban population of Xining is about 1,180,000, the total 2180,000.

Do consider altitude. Xining is at 2261 meters, Golmud 2800 meters, and Qinghai Lake 3200 meters. See Altitude Sickness under Lhasa.

The region is also known as the Gulag of China. Here criminals who have served their sentences continue to live because they cannot get residence permits elsewhere. Some stores in Xining are stocked with products made from prison labor.

Arrivals & Departures

Xining is a two-hour flight from Beijing and has four flights a week with Lhasa. (Y1390). It also has direct flights with 18 other Chinese cities. The fastest train takes 2.59 hours from Lanzhou (leaving at 4pm), 13 hours from Golmud, and 18 hours from Xi'an.

Where to Stay

Most foreigners stay in the Qinghai Hotel. The Tsonkha Hotel is about 25 km from Xining, across from the Kumbum/Taer Monastery and is a great place to stay if you want to spend more time at the monastery than the usual tour allows.

SILK ROAD TSONGKHA HOTEL IN QINGHAI (Zong Ka Binguan), *57 Ying Bin Road, Lu Sha er Town, Huang Zhong County, 811600. Tel 972/236 761, Fax 972/233900. Email: webmaster@the-silk-road.com or tsongkhahotel@sina.com. Sixty km from the airport and 15 km from the railway station. It is located on one of the eight-petalled hills of sacred Lotus Mountain at over 3400 meters, and faces the spot where Tsongkhapa, founder of Tibetan Buddhism was born. A taxi from downtown could cost Y80 to Y120. Standard rooms are $70 and Tibetan rooms $100. It has been discounting 20%-40% depending on the season. No international credit cards nor travelers checks.*

This hotel has 32 rooms, of which 16 are in Tibetan-style, the rest Western-style. It will be adding another 100 rooms by 2003. There are Tibetan, Muslim and Han restaurants and conference facilities for up to 300 people. It has a meditation room, prayer chamber, study room, and travel service.

QINGHAI HOTEL (Binguan), *158 Huang He Road, 810001. Four stars. Tel. 6144888, Fax 6144145. E-mail: qhbg@public.xn.qh.cn. Website: www.qhtravel.com. 407 rooms. 32 km from the airport, 10 km from the railway station, and 30 km from Taer Monastery. It is near government trade offices. Rooms are Y268-Y438 and suites Y498-Y6800 and include breakfast. It accepts credit cards.*

Built in 1989, this 21-story hotel has European food, a gym and a travel agency.

Where to Eat

Hotels are best but there are a couple restaurants. CITS suggests the **Xiao Yuan Men** at 126 Dong Da Jie Road, *Tel. 8125529.* There's also the **Yun Feng Ge**, 158 Huanghe Road, *Tel. 6144888 ext. 2411.*

Seeing the Sights

A one-day visit to Xining can include the Taer Monastery, Dongguan Mosque, and North Mountain Temple. The Dongguan Mosque, one of the biggest in northwest China, was built in 1380 and is two km from the Qinghai Hotel. It has Tibetan touches. The North Mountain Temple is also two km from the hotel.

The ***Kumbum/Taer Monastery** (Ming), the center of the Yellow Hat sect of Tibetan Buddhism, is at Huangzhong, about 25 km south of the city. Built in 1379, it is worth a visit if you are interested in Tibetan culture and Tsong Khapa. Its kitchen has three bronze cauldrons that are said to cook 13 cattle at one time to serve 3,600 people. Ask why meat is served in this Buddhist monastery! In the winter, frozen butter, two-meters high by 26-meters-long, is sculptured into Buddhist scenes and displayed on the 15th day of the lunar new year. It also has 20,000 religious paintings and embroideries. See Silk Road Hotel above.

You can visit the birthplaces of the current Dalai Lama in Sarkok, 50 km from Xining. There's also the birthplace of the 10th Panchen Lama and the Windo Monastery, 150 km by good road west of Xining in Dowei. About 60 km east of Xining in Lu Du county is the ***Qutan Monastery** (Ming). Also in the vicinity is the 6282-meter-high **Ma Qing Gang Re (Anyemaqen) Mountain** (two to 10-day trip). Ask about the Regong Tibetan artists with their 300-year-old tradition.

Qinghai is also for mountaineers. Its has several peaks up to 6860 meters and trekking between April and November. There is white-water rafting.

Shopping

Good buys are handicrafts made by the minorities like wooden bowls inlaid with silver.

Excursions & Day Trips

Golmud is the place to get a bus to Lhasa. It is a new industrial city in the desert in the western part of the province. It has a population of 200,000, is 800 km from Xining by train, and is a trans-shipment point for Tibet. The highway to Lhasa from here is now asphalt, the highest highway in the world. Currently being built is an 1100-1200-km rail line from Golmud to Lhasa. When it is finished about 2007, it should be one of the most spectacular train rides in the world.

Foreigners stay in the **Golmud Salt Lake Hotel**, *Tel. 979/448668*, the **Golmud Jin Long Hotel**, *Tel. 979/420876*, or the **Golmud Hotel**, *Tel. 979/412061*. The **Yanhu Hotel** is a four star.

Golmud C I T S is at 160 Kunlun Road, *Tel. 979/413003, Fax 979/418849*. Ask for Mrs.Xi Ming Ru, *Tel. 412764*, or Mr. Ma Wen Qing, *Tel. 413003* who speak English.

Qinghai Lake, China's largest saltwater lake, is 3,196 meters above sea level and 151 km from the capital. It has no train service. CITS has a daily tour bus there during peak tourist season. A bird sanctuary, Bird Island, is about 300 km away from Xining in the northwest section of the lake and is best seen April to July. The small island attracts 100,000 migrating geese, black-neck cranes, gulls, Griffon vultures, Mongolian larks, minivets and skylarks. The island has bird-watching pavilions and Tibetan-style hotels. This trip can be a two-day tour from Xining. Foreigners usually stay in the **Qinghai Lake Tent-styled Hotel**, *Tel. 974/519660*.

Birders should ask also about the Longbao Black-necked Crane Sanctuary. The province has wild antelope, yak, donkeys, camels, lynx, deer, snow leopards, and pheasant, all protected.

Practical Information

Qinghai CITS, *156 Huanghe Road, 810001, Tel. 6101686, 3992299 (24 hours), Fax 6131080. E-mail: qhcits@public.xn.qh.cn or ask for Yang Cheng Cai at wildyak@21cn.com. Website: www.citsqh.com (to be updated soon).* Yang gave lots of information for this book.

Qinghai Provincial Tourism Administration, *156 Huanghe Road, 810001, Tel. 6157011, Fax 6131080.* Brochures and information.

Qinghai-Tibet International Travel Service, *4/F Guoyuan Mansion, 23# Huanghe Road, 810000, Tel. 6106919 (General Manager), 6106939 (Vice-Manager,* Japanese and Western Departments). *Fax 6105133, 6123622. E-mail: qtit@263.net.* Ask for Tashi Phuntsok, *E-mail: Phuntsoktashi@hotmail.com or Lhungrik@yahoo.com.* This agency specializes in tours to Tibetan areas of Qinghai, Sichuan, and Yunnan as well as Tibet. It has native-speaking Tibetan guides and takes 15 days to get a Tibet permit. Tours include trekking, visits to monasteries, nomadic families, shamen festivals, masked dancers, and horse racing, This agency gave this book a lot of help.

Telephone code: 971

Tourist Complaints, contact Supervisory Bureau of Tourism Quality of Qinghai Province, *57 Xida Street, 810000, Tel. 8239630, Fax 8239515.*

Central China

Zhengzhou

(Chengchow)

Zhengzhou is the capital of Henan, a province considered one of the cradles of China's civilization with much to offer visitors. Zhengzhou was established during the Shang dynasty 3,500 years ago, one of China's first cities. It is close to Shaolin Monastery kung fu martial arts, the former capital of the Song dynasty, and the earliest Buddhist temples. Zhengzhou is a good place to start a week's driving tour.

For historians and archaeologists, there's nearby Anyang where the oracle bones with the first Chinese writings were found. The capitals of the Eastern Zhou, Han, Wei, Jin, Northern Song, Tang, and Liang were in Luoyang. At least one of the capitals and possibly four of the five other capitals of the Xia dynasty were also here. The Xia was China's first dynasty, and until recently its history was clouded in legend, traditionally dating from the 16th century

B.C. The Longmen Grottoes and the earliest astronomical observatory are also in the province.

More recently, Zhengzhou was the site of the February 7th Beijing-Hankou Railway Workers' General Strike of 1923, part of a larger workers' movement for better wages and conditions. Over 100 railroad workers were killed. The strike is commemorated with a modern 14-story double pagoda-like clock tower in February 7th Square, built in 1971.

The coldest average temperature is -10°C in January; the hottest can be 40°C briefly in July. The annual rainfall is 500-900 mm especially July through September. The urban population is two million, the total six million.

Arrivals & Departures

On both the Beijing-Guangzhou and the Shanghai-Xi'an railway lines, Zhengzhou is about 20 km south of the Yellow River. By train it's between Luoyang (two hours away), and Kaifeng (one hour). Zhengzhou-Guangzhou by the fastest train is about 18 hours, Zhengzhou-Kowloon about 20 hours, Xi'an 8 hours, and Zhengzhou-Beijing about 7 hours.

It is a two-hour flight south of Beijing and can be reached by air from 38 other Chinese cities and Hong Kong. The airport is 35 km from the main hotels.

The city is on the North-South China freeway 700 km south of Beijing. Every day and every hour from 7am to 6pm, an express bus leaves the Zhengzhou Railway Station for Luoyang and takes about 2 hours.

Orientation

Zhengzhou itself doesn't have much to offer tourists unless you can get excited by a seven km stretch of 3500-year-old wall. A half-day is enough for its marvelous provincial museum and sightseeing along the Yellow River at Mangshan Mountain. If you are interested in ancient relics, there are the Shang ruins and the old city wall. Better head further out of town.

Where to Stay

This city of almost no tourist attractions has three five-star hotels. Other high class hotels are being built, most notably a Shangri-la due in 2003. Travelers should take advantage of this situation and haggle. There's also a good four-star Holiday Inn.

The proximity of four good hotels close to each other makes for great conference possibilities. In addition, because the hotels are not as good in Luoyang, Anyang, Kaifeng, and Dengfeng, fussy tourists should consider spending their nights in Zhengzhou. New expressways can get you to these cities for day trips.

Three of the international hotels are almost adjacent so you can get a quick look at each before you make up your mind. Also adjacent is the three-star International Hotel which is adequate though a little grubby; however, the Holiday Inn's prices are so low, you might as well stay there. These four are 34 km from the airport in the eastern part of the city, eight kilometers from Liu Cheng Huangchang (Grand City Square), and four km from the railway station.

These three five-stars are very good (but not perfect) and the problem is choosing. All are international standard and beautiful. The Yuda is the most luxurious. The Crowne Plaza has the best service. The Sofitel is also comfortable and recommended but third best. All hotels here take credit cards, have money exchange, ticketing services, and business centers. Prices below are subject to change, 15-20% surcharge, and discounts.

YUDA PALACE HOTEL (Yuda Guomao Dajiudian), *220 Zhongyuan Zhong Road, 450007. Tel. 7438888, Fax 7422539. E-mail: yudaeo@public2.zz.ha.cn It is in the same building as the Central China International Exhibition Center in the western part of the city near the city hall and city museum. Rooms range from $150 to $220 but it has been discounting about 50%. Suites range from $250 to $1500. The Yuda Palace adds no service charge for guests who make a reservation in advance.*

The lobby of this 1999, 29-story hotel is on the 8th floor. The Yuda has a basketball court and a gym. A pool should open soon. It is in the tallest building in the province and has 388 guest rooms. Rooms range from 48 to 56 square meters and some are non-smoking.They have safes, data ports, voice mail, and BBC, CNN, and HBO among its 42 television channels. There's continental, Asian, Japanese, and Chinese cuisine, an old English style bar, and a lounge. Its biggest banquet room accommodates 280 people at tables.

CROWNE PLAZA ZHENGZHOU, *115 Jinshui Road, 450003. Five stars. Tel. 5950055, Fax 5953851, 5990770. E-mail: hicpzz@public.zz.ha.cn. Website: www.crowneplaza.com/hotels/cgoch. $126-$141 for rooms, and $160-$700 for suites. It has been offering a room special of $79 to $118.*

This 222-room, five-story hotel has a few duplex rooms, non-smoking and executive floors. All rooms have a safe, two telephones lines, ADSL fast internet connection, HBO, CNBC, CNN, and BBC. Rooms are 35 to 38 square meters. The $12 breakfast at the Crowne Plaza is lavish. Its ball room can seat 500 people at banquet tables, and it has Western, Asian, and Chinese food, a pizza restaurant and 24-hour room service. There's a 25-meter long indoor pool, gym, steam bath, and outdoor tennis court and complimentary airport shuttle service for major flights.

HOTEL SOFITEL ZHENGZHOU, *289 Cheng Dong Road, 450003. Five-stars. Tel. 5950088, Fax 5950080. E-mail: Sofitel@public2.zz.ha.cn. Website: www.accorhotels-china.com. Y996 to Y1245 for rooms and Y1660 to Y5810 for suites but it has been discounting 30%.*

This 222-room, five-story hotel has executive floors and a few duplex rooms. Rooms are 35 to 38 square meters and all have a safe and two telephones lines, HBO, CINEMAX, CNBC, CNN, and BBC. Some are non-smoking. The service is eager. The gym has 12 good machines and its year-round indoor pool is 18 meters long. There's free scheduled airport shuttle.

HOLIDAY INN ZHENGZHOU, *115 Jinshui Road, 450003. Four stars. Tel. 5950055, Fax 5990770. E-mail: hicpzz@public.zz.ha.cn. Website: www.holiday-inn/com/hotels/cgcch. $98-$123 for rooms, and $160-$620 for suites and apartments. It has been giving a 30-40% special promotion.*

This 1997 hotel has 224 rooms, seven floors, with two-bedroom apartments, offices, and non-smoking rooms. Rooms are 28 square meters with HBO, Cinemax, CNBC, CNN, and BBC, and ADSL internet connection. It has 24-hour room service and its own coffee shop but guests can use all facilities at the Crowne Plaza. Rooms have safes and irons. It has a complimentary airport shuttle.

Where to Eat

The best food is in the above hotels but there are also some good restaurants nearby. The modest **Yue Xiu** (Cantonese) is 100 meters west of the Holiday Inn. The **Hai Xian Chen Restaurant** is close. The **International Hotel** has fried milk, chicken with peanuts, steamed fish, fried or steamed buns with sweetened condensed milk, all good. The **Guangdong Kaibao Restaurant** (Cantonese) is on Shunhe Road near the Crowne Plaza, *Tel. 13017652235.* Low to moderate prices. Ask your hotel's concierge for directions.

Baixing Renjia Restaurant is 100 meters from the intersection of Hanghai Road and Xinmi Road on the road to Dengfeng. *Tel. 8979818 or 8972779.* This has an exhibition of rural life as well as good food.

Seeing the Sights

You can't miss the **Henan Museum**, considered almostthird best after Shanghai. It's on 8 Nongye Road, *Tel. 3511063, 3511066,* open 8:30am-5:30pm. It has a dinosaur exhibit, a jade burial suit held together with gold wire, tortoise divination shells with the earliest Chinese writing, gold and silver inlaid in bronze, some unusual ancient bronzes, and tomb figures. It has signs in English, a display of the lost-wax process of putting designs in bronze, and it gives a daily free performance of ancient chime bells because "The Chu Kingdom was partly in Henan province." (See Wuhan.)

You can miss the **Dahecun Village**, a 5,000-year-old site of the Yangshao and Longshan neolithic cultures, especially if you're going to see the better organized Banpo Museum in Xi'an. This one is poorly presented and boring.

The **Mangshan/Yellow River Scenic Area** is a park on the south shore, about 40 km north of the city, an opportunity to get out into the countryside. On the way a market at Laoyacun village sometimes blocks the road, a good chance to mingle with people. At Mangshan, you can take a lift parallel to the river for a good view of China's second longest river. The Yellow River is 5646 km long. Note the dikes and the water level (if there's water), sometimes three to ten meters higher than ground level.

The 45-minute cruise (Y60) of the Yellow River 8am-6pm daily (from the pier a couple of kilometers away from the mountain) not only gives a view of the impressive 5.5-km-long bridge (a train goes over every five minutes) but you can actually bounce (and maybe ride ponies) on a mud flat on the most heavily silted river in the world. Riding a hovercraft on mud is a unique experience.

The water has become so low through sedimentation, diminished rainfall, and overuse recently that plans have been made to divert water from the Yangtze River to this one, and onward to Beijing. The Yellow River has not even been able to reach the sea at times. The Xiaolongdi Dam near Luoyang is almost as big as the controversial Three Gorges Dam, but no one has made a fuss about it.

Where to Stay

Made here are reproductions of three-color Tang porcelain figures, jade and lacquerware, calligraphy and paintings. It's a good place to buy Chinese writing brushes, paper, inkstones, and inkbars. Made in the province are also Jun porcelain, and embroidery from Kaifeng. The **Zhengzhou Jade Carving Factory** cuts sapphires, jades, rose quartz, and cat's eyes. The **Friendship Store** is at 96 Erqi Bei Road, north of People's Park. The **#Henan Cultural Relics Shop** is at 4 Jinshui Dadao, *Tel. 5955347*. The largest department stores are the Dennis on Renmin Road and the King Bird on Erqi Road.

Excursions & Day Trips

An interesting itinerary by road could be Zhengzhou, Kaifeng and Anyang (with three nights in Zhengzhou), Gongxian, Dengfeng (overnight), and Luoyang (with two overnights in Luoyang). After that, there are flights between Hong Kong and Zhengzhou, and Beijing, Shanghai and Luoyang. A train goes from Luoyang to Xi'an.

For destinations close to Zhengzhou in Shanxi province see Taiyuan.

ANYANG

In the northern part of Henan province, **Anyang** lies about 200 km north of Zhengzhou by express highway or via the Beijing-Guangzhou railway line. A quick visit can be made by car in one day from Zhengzhou. The urban population is 700,000.

Anyang is one of the oldest cities in China, inhabited at least 4,000 years ago. It was a capital of the State of Yin during the Shang dynasty for 273 years. It was here that the oracle bones, an ancient means of divination were found. The earliest writings were inscribed on tortoise shells and the shoulder blades of oxen and then cracked with heat. The direction of the crack foretold the future.

Visitors can see a reproduced Shang palace and tomb, a Shang museum, the mausoleum of the man who proclaimed himself emperor after the republican revolution, some temples, jade carving and carpet-weaving. There is also the birthplace of the I Ching. Anyang is primarily of interest to people who like history, archaeology, fortune-telling, and air sports.

Important sights are the 24-square-kilometer ***Yin Ruins** on the edge of town, *Tel. 331689*. These include the palace foundations, 11 royal tombs, bronze and jade artifacts, and a small but good museum. There are reproductions of the palace, tombs and the largest bronze vessel found anywhere in the world, the 875-kilogram Simuwu Tripod. (The real relics are in museums in Beijing and Zhengzhou.) You can also see the Tomb of Fu Hao, concubine of King Wuding. She was the first woman general in Chinese history. Many of the pits hold reproductions of human sacrifices. One pit has 16,000 oracle bones. The annual Shang dynasty festival takes place September 16 to 25.

Elsewhere, the five-story 40-meter high **Wen Feng Pagoda** is unusual. It is wider above than below and is crowned with a tiny white stupa. Built in 952 A.D., it can be climbed if you don't mind high steps. The **City Museum**, 2.5 km from the Anyang Hotel, is in the Mausoleum of Yuan Shi Kai, *Tel. 425959*. Yuan was the warlord, an overly ambitious, brilliant official of the Qing court who took over the presidency of republican China from Dr. Sun Yat-sen in 1913. He declared himself emperor in 1915 and died of a heart attack in 1916. He reigned for 83 days.

Among other historical monuments is the **temple of Yue Fei** which is surrounded by a street reproduced in Song Dynasty architecture. For those interested in the Book of Changes divination, there's **Youli Zhou Yi Museum**, *Tel. 6231399*, where a Western Zhou king and nobleman was imprisoned for seven years and developed the 64 hexagrams used for fortune telling even today. Local people claim these inspired the binary system of computers.

The **Anyang Aerial Sports School** is the main place for aerial sports in China and is 3.5 km north of Feng Leyuan Hotel. This is the only place where foreigners can rent planes to fly themselves (at about $300 an hour). It has AN-2s, Astir-Jarus-Cessna 172Rs, Yun-5s, and Robinson helicopters in its fleet of over 50 aircraft. If you have a pilot's license, you still need to take a test here before you can fly on your own. (The easiest way around this is to have a licensed Chinese pilot fly with you.) It has 30 instructors in Anyang.

As for gliding, you have to have a US or Chinese glider's license. "A Chinese glider's license," said Qin Jianmin, who is involved with the school, "takes about 15 days to get, and costs $4000, and is valid all over the world." The sports school also has "motor-parachuting," sky-diving, and hot air ballooning. Skydiving requires a certificate. Diving from 1000 meters costs $10, from 2000 meters $18, and 3000 meters $25. Diving piggy back costs

$80 to $100. You can go hot air ballooning alone, but it is better to take a recovery truck and crew which costs about $300.

You should bring your own paragliding equipment. You have to apply to CAAC for permission to import your own plane. If you can communicate in Chinese, you can contact Zhang Jie, President, Anyang Air Sports School, Shengli Road, Middle Section, 455001. *Tel. 2298218, 2930455, or Fax 2924686. E-mail: gjtzah@public.ayptt.ha.cn. Website: http://hx.ayinfo.ha.cn (in English and Chinese).* See also below.

If you have the Chinese surname Lin or Lim (as in "forest"), you might be interested in the temple of the first Lin, a Shang dynasty prime minister. At **Bigan Miao Temple**, a short way off the expressway halfway between Zhengzhou and Anyang, you can learn about the maligned Bigan who had to take out his own heart to prove his honesty. His son changed the family name to Lin.

The three-star **Feng Leyuan Hotel** is in the Hua Shan Road Development Area, 455000, *Tel. 372/3901888, Fax 3901777.* Rooms range from Y398 to Y438, and suites from Y688 to Y1888. Add 10% service charge, but try to get a discount. It even has a small gym, business center, and foreign exchange.

For more information about the Aerial Sports School, Anyang, tours and guides, contact Qin Jianmin, Deputy Director of the Anyang Municipal Tourism Bureau who helped a lot with this book. His address is 129 Renmin Road, 455000, *Tel. 372/5929735, 5925859 (office) or 5929102 (home). Fax 5929734.* The telephone code is 372.

ZHENGZHOU-GONGXIAN

If you have your own transport and are looking to get well off the beaten path, go to **Gongxian County** between Zhengzhou and Dengfeng. The ***Gongxian County Cave Temple** has 7,743 small Buddhist figures dating from 517 A.D. (Northern Wei) to the Song dynasty. Some are very well preserved. They are not as big or as impressive as Luoyang's, but they are certainly worth a look.

There are also eight groups of imperial ***Northern Song Tombs** here, at least one with 60 impressive giant stone statues, among them foreign envoys wearing turbans. The tombs themselves are less spectacular than those of the later Ming and Qing emperors and are spread over an area 15 km long. They were built in a much shorter time without the personal supervision of the emperors who were going to reside there. These are 65 km west of Zhengzhou. The Tomb of Song Emperor Hengzong is the easiest to visit because of its location in Gongxian County town. That of Emperor Yong Ding is in the suburbs.

DENGFENG

Buses leave downtown Zhengzhou for Dengfeng every 20 minutes for Y12-Y15. If you drive here from Zhengzhou, there's a pit stop at a huge

souvenir shop where we bargained down to a quarter of the first asking price. This shop has a carving workshop at the back which was working on water agates and jade. It's at 5 Xi Street, Xinmi City, *Tel. 371/9889068.* Manager Gao Chao, *Tel. 13938298568.*

Mixian (now renamed **Xinmi City**) is worth a stop because you can enter the Han Tombs at Dahuting (Tiger-hunting) Pavilion. The paintings and stone carvings there are lively. They are about a 15-minute drive from Dengfeng.

Dengfeng County with Shaolin Temple and bare, rugged **Songshan Mountain** is about 80 km southwest of Zhengzhou (its closest airport and railway station), and 180 km from Luoyang (about 1 1/2 hours by road). The mountain stretches more than 60 km east to west. The highest peak is 1,512 meters above sea level. It is one of China's Five Sacred Mountains, and emperors used to come here to worship. During the Southern and Northern Dynasties (420-589 A.D.), 72 temples and monasteries flourished here. It is well worth visiting also for the lovely Chinese countryside, and air so clean you might want to stay an extra day.

From your hotel in Dengfeng County town (population 50,000), you can bicycle or drive to China's largest Taoist temple, China's most famous temple, and a pagoda from 520 A.D. Thirteen km northwest of Dengfeng County town is **Shaolin Temple**, *Tel. 2749305,* the home of kung fu martial arts. Shaolin Temple was first built in 495-496 A.D. and became famous in 728 A.D. because 13 fighting monks from here supported the prince who became the first Tang emperor. Here you can see 48 depressions in the floor worn by generations of monks practicing martial arts. Shaolin has a Wushu (martial arts) Festival around September 10.

Among the murals and frescoes are some of the 500 arhats (Ming), and some depicting fighting monks. At its peak in the 15th century, 2,000 to 3,000 monks lived here. In the seventh century there were 500, and now there are about 80-100. All monks take the surname Su.

The ***Ta Lin (Forest of Pagodas)** is the largest group of memorial pagodas in China. A cemetery for abbots, it has over 240 miniature pagodas, two to seven levels high, dating from 791 A.D. to 1995. Clean toilets are here and outside the main temple. Prepare yourself for this visit by seeing the movie *The Fugitive Boys of Shaolin* starring Li Lianjin, China's Bruce Lee. It was shot here.

Northwest of the temple is a cave where the sixth century Indian missionary Bodhidharma, was reputed to have spent nine years in meditation before achieving Nirvana. He was the founder of Chan Buddhism, more popularly known as Zen, and is frequently depicted in art in his robes, crossing the Yangtze River standing on a reed.

You can also stay and eat at the **Shaolin International Kung Fu Training Center** (Wu Shu Guan), Shaolin, 452479. *Tel. 2749120, 2749018, Fax 2749017.* No credit cards. Book through CITS. The accommodations and food are basic with both meat and vegetables.

This training center gives **demonstrations** to tourists almost continuously during the day for Y50 each between 10am and 4pm daily. Athletes jump on a bed of nails, break bricks with a head, and invite visitors to smash a midriff. The kung fu here is somewhat different in style from that in North America. Foreigners can also study and live at the school, but foreigners cannot become monks. The 20-room hostel at the school is spartan and you can stay there too. It is the only state-run school.

Dengfeng has at least 43 private kung fu schools, the largest of which has 7000 students. Private schools are cheaper (but six to a room). The state school has two to a room. These schools have grown in popularity lately because the skills learned are valuable for future teachers, policemen and body guards.

If You're Staying Overnight

It's great to bicycle around this area. From Shaolin Temple you can see a cable car to a small nunnery at the peak of Song Mountain. The scenery is magnificent. There has been only one nun living on the top.

This mountain is full of temples. The 43-meter-high ***Songyue Pagoda** at Fawang Temple is the oldest proven extant pagoda in China, and is four km from Dengfeng. Built of brick about 520 A.D. (Northern Wei), it is also unusual because it has 12 sides and is curved like an Indian sikhara tower. It is important to those studying pagoda architecture. The Songyang Shuyuan (Songyang Academy of Classical Learning) at the foot of the mountain has two cypress trees said to be over 3,000 years old, each measuring 12 meters in circumference. The school was one of the four imperial academies preparing students for the imperial examinations.

Zhongyue Miao (Central Mountain Temple) at the base of Taishi Peak and four km east of Dengfeng town, was founded in the Qin and moved here in the Tang. It has four feisty 3.5-meter-high iron figures (Northern Song)

Searching for China's Oldest Dynasty

A search for the first Xia capital has been centered in Dengfeng County, half a kilometer west of the town of Gaocheng at Wangcheng Gang (Royal City Mound). This site is not usually included in a tour, but people interested in archaeology might ask about it. City walls, skeletons (probably of slaves buried alive in foundation pits), wine vessels, bronze fragments, and ceramic pots have been uncovered. However, Wangcheng Gang was found to be of a later date.

Across the river and half a kilometer northwest of Gaocheng is another site where the earlierst bronze vessels in the province were found and carbon-dated to 2000 B.C.

guarding it. Children pat these "to gain strength." This is one of the earliest Taoist temples (it's huge) and the largest extant monastery in the province. It was enlarged during the Qing, along the lines of the Forbidden City in Beijing. The *Taishi Tower is from the Eastern Han. You can climb to the top of Huanggai Peak for an overall view of the 400 or so buildings and the 300 2,000-year-old cypresses. Some 10-day temple fairs take place during the third and tenth lunar months.

The *Shaoshi Tower and the *Qimu Tower also on the mountain, are from the Eastern Han too. The *Astronomical Observatory, 14 km from Dengfeng town, was built early in the Yuan, based on a Zhou dynasty concept. It is the oldest in China. Ancient astronomers here proved that the earth revolved around the sun once every 365.2425 days, 300 years before the Gregorian calendar. China's first astrological museum is nearby.

The best hotel here is the three-going-on-four star **Tianzhong Hotel** (Jiudian), 6, Zhongyue Dong Street, 452470. *Tel. 2891688, 2861688, Fax 2861560. Website: www.tzjd.com.* Rooms are $40-$50 a night and it has been giving 20% discounts in low season. It accepts no travelers checks or credit cards. It is in town, has 129 rooms, and is 13 km from Shaolin Temple. Henan Tourism Group in Zhengzhou charges $35 a room.

CITS is at 48 Zhongyue Street, 452470, *Tel. 2872137, 2877038, Fax 2873137. E-mail: qgl@dfintertour.com or yuminking@sohu.com.* Ask for Wang Yu Min who speaks English and helped with this book. It has a map in English of the area and charges Y200 for a guide for a day for one or two people. **Dengfeng Tourism Bureau** is at 177 Zhongyue Street, 452470, *Tel. 2873043, Fax 2873137.*

Hours are 8am-6pm for tourist attractions. The telephone code for Dengfeng is 371.

Practical Information

Henan CITS, *8F, Haitong Building, No. 50 Jingqi Road, 450003, Tel. 3927758, 3927768, Fax 3811753, 3927768. E-mail: lhm@public.zz.ha.cn. Website: www.citshn.com.* Ask for Li Shengjiang, Manager, European & American Department. *E-mail: lishengjiang@371.net.* It can arrange for visitors to plant trees. It charges $120 for a car from Zhengzhou to Anyang, $75 for a car from Zhengzhou to Kaifeng, $100 for a car from Zhengzhou to Dengfeng.

Henan Tourism Administration, *1 Zhengsan Street, 450003, Tel. 5957880, Fax 5909345, for information. For tourist complaints, contact the Supervisory Bureau of Tourism Quality of Henan Province, Tel. 5955913, Fax 5955656.*

Henan Tourism Group Company Limited (HTC), *288 Chengdong Road, 450003, Tel. 5961133 est. 5775, 5944797, Fax 5952273. E-mail: hntc@public.zz.ha.cn. Website: www.hntg.net (English and good).* Ask for

Miss Chris Zhang, European, North American and Oceanic Department, who along with Lucy and their colleagues helped a lot with this book. *E-mail: zhangy@hntg.net*. It has a branch in Luoyang. It can organize tree planting for student groups.

Hours: People in this small city go home for lunch so offices open 8am-12 noon, 2pm-6pm in winter, or 3pm-6:30pm in summer.

Telephone code: 371

Website: *www.travelchannel.com.cn (English on Henan).*

Kaifeng

The former imperial capital of **Kaifeng** is in northern Henan province. It is 10 km from the southern bank of the Yellow River, and is highly recommended for its history, and its quiet, exotic charm. It has a new economic zone in its west suburbs and it seems to be moving towards the Suzhou model of architectural development. No new high buildings have been constructed inside the wall since 1995. Factories have moved out of the city and roads have widened. But it doesn't have Suzhou's financial resources so don't expect too much.

With a history of 2,600 years, Kaifeng was the capital of several imperial dynasties, including the Wei, Liang, Later Jin, Han, Later Zhou, Northern Song, and Jin. During the Song it was an important commercial and communications center, producing textiles, porcelain, and printing. It was sacked by Jurched tribesmen in 1126 and never recovered.

With 120 recorded Yellow River floods due to damaged dikes between 1194 and 1948, you might wonder why Kaifeng exists at all. In 1642, during a peasant uprising, Ming forces destroyed an embankment and completely inundated the city killing 372,000 people. In 1938, the Nationalists destroyed the dam upriver near Zhengzhou to stop the Japanese, and 840,000 people died. Today, the river bed, raised by centuries of silt deposits, is about 10 meters higher than ground level near Kaifeng. Since Liberation, the Chinese have given top priority to controlling the Yellow River here.

The total population of Kaifeng today is 4.6 million. The urban population is around 700,000. The hottest weather in July to early August is 38°C; the coldest in January is -9°C. Its annual rainfall is about 600 mm mainly in July and August. Spring is dry, dusty, and windy.

Arrivals & Departures

On the Shanghai-Urumqi railway line, Kaifeng is accessible from Zhengzhou to the east, its closest airport, about a 90 km expressway trip away. You can take a taxi from the airport, or more cheaply, go into Zhengzhou to the long distance bus station and hop a bus there–if you arrive early enough. Kaifeng is on National Highway 106 (Beijing-Guangzhou) and Highway 310 (Tianshui-Lianyungang).

Orientation

Kaifeng is one of the 24 historical cities protected by the State Council. It is laid out in classic Chinese grid style, and has a well-preserved but decaying earthen Song city wall. It is easy to get around because it is small. It has a downtown shopping area built in Song architecture. Except for the Yellow River, all important sites are inside or near its four by eight km-long wall. It has already restored many old buildings and is planning to renovate the office of Lord Bao, the most important mayor in the Northern Song Dynasty. This should be ready in 2004 and become another theme park. Lord Bao was a very upright official and a symbol of justice. There are plans to link the lakes with canals and boats to Dragon Pavilion in the northwest and to the Iron Pagoda in the northeast of the walled city.

The best time to visit is the spring, or September-October. The annual Song Dynasty Culture Festival in Kaifeng is celebrated every April. The annual Chrysanthemum Festival is in early October. There's a good map in English with bus routes.

Where to Stay & Eat

TIAN ZHONG HOTEL, *41 Gulou Street, 475000, Tel. 5958888, Sales 5988568, Fax 5952185. Three stars. Its 108 rooms are air-conditioned and are Y238-Y338 for rooms and Y518-Y1188 for suites. Only Chinese credit cards are accepted and there's no CNN. An interesting night food market is outside. Unfortunately, there's no English.*

This is the best hotel and also has the best location downtown.

DONGJING HOTEL (Dongjing Dafandian), *99 Ying Bin Road, Tel. 3989388.*

This hote is dirty and stuffy but it's okay for lunch. The fried chicken, shao bing sesame buns, stir fried celery, onions and garlic were all good. So were the steamed dumplings, and carp with the strangest most wonderful noodles I've ever seen. Other local dishes include fried bean jelly, spiced dried bean curd, and peanut cake.

Seeing the Sights

Kaifeng has 22 historic and cultural sites, a large number for such a small city. You need two days to see the most important: temples, museum, guild hall, Jewish relics, and iron pagoda. Pedicabs cost Y5 or Y10 to carry you between monuments inside the walled city.

The 13-story, 55.6-meter-high ***Tie Ta ('Iron Pagoda')** in the northeast corner inside the wall was built in 1049. It is actually made of glazed brick The entrance fee is Y15. The Xiangguo Temple in its south-center, built in 555 A.D.,

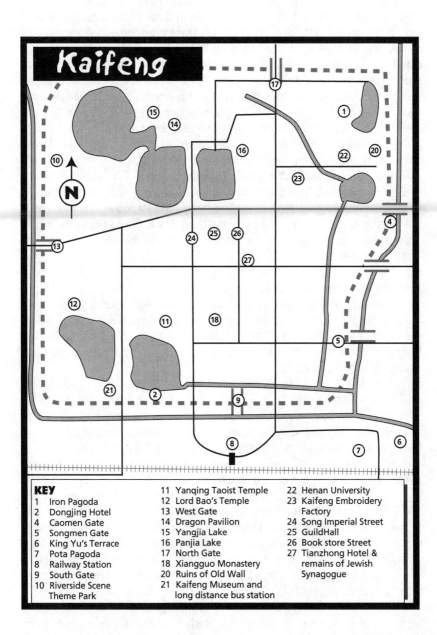

Kaifeng

KEY

1 Iron Pagoda
2 Dongjing Hotel
4 Caomen Gate
5 Songmen Gate
6 King Yu's Terrace
7 Pota Pagoda
8 Railway Station
9 South Gate
10 Riverside Scene
    Theme Park
11 Yanqing Taoist Temple
12 Lord Bao's Temple
13 West Gate
14 Dragon Pavilion
15 Yangjia Lake
16 Panjia Lake
17 North Gate
18 Xiangguo Monastery
20 Ruins of Old Wall
21 Kaifeng Museum and
    long distance bus station
22 Henan University
23 Kaifeng Embroidery
    Factory
24 Song Imperial Street
25 GuildHall
26 Book store Street
27 Tianzhong Hotel &
    remains of Jewish
    Synagogue

was rebuilt in 1766 after a flood. It has a famous thousand-armed, thousand-eyed Buddha of gingko wood. The Longting (Dragon Pavilion, 1734, Y25) in the north-center is at the site of the Northern Song palace. The existing buildings here are from the Qing, the stone lions in front from the Song.

Also worth seeing are the **Yanqing Taoist Temple, Lord Bao's Memorial Hall** (Y20, wax figures) on Baogong Lake, and the very fancy **Shanshangan Guild Hall** (of Three Provinces, Y10). These three are all within walking distance of the Dongjing Hotel. The Guild Hall is worth a 20 to 30 minute stop. Worshipped there was Guan Yu, the god of merchants as well as war. Tourists can play reproductions of the chime bells and an exhibition here soon should include photographs of Jewish history. Built in 1776, it's on Xufu Street downtown, and is open 8am to 6:30pm. It costs Y10.

The **Yuwang Miao (King Yu's Temple)** was built in the Ming in honor of Emperor Yu, who tried to control the floods; it is outside and to the south of the east wall. Near the Yuwang Miao is the **Pota Pagoda**, its bottom built in 977, and its top section replaced in the Qing. The **Kaifeng Museum** is now open 9:30am to 11:30am and 2:30pm to 5:30pm, *Tel. 3933624*. It's small but worthwhile (see below).

The Jewish Community of Kaifeng

Jews first arrived here at least 2,000 years ago. Most came as silk merchants and migrants from Persia. In the Song dynasty, thousands of Jewish merchants arrived from India. Most left in the Ming because of the floods. Marco Polo came across groups of Jews in Beijing, Hangzhou, Suzhou, Guangzhou, and Kunming.

In the late 13th century, there were about 2,000 Jews in Kaifeng. The original 1163 synagogue was built by Jews who passed the imperial examination. Jews from other communities, such as Hangzhou, contributed to the rebuilding of the Kaifeng synagogue each time it was destroyed by flood or fire. The last synagogue was destroyed between 1850 and 1866.

About 200 Jews still live in Kaifeng today although they don't practice Jewish traditions. The **Kaifeng Museum** has a third floor room with a reproduction of a seventh century drawing of the synagogue, and steles dated 1469, 1512, and 1679 describing the history of the community, etc. You have to give advance notice to the museum and your travel agent to see these. A photographic exhibit donated by the Sino-Judaic Institute of Palo Alto, California has been located in the nearby Riverside Scene theme park but you have to look for someone with a key. (Contact Professor Al Dien, president of the Institute at: *aldien@leland.stanford.edu*.)

Tourists can still visit the house of **Zhao Pingyu**, at #21 South Teaching Scripture Lane (Nan Jiao Jing Hutong), which is in back of the original site of the synagogue. Zhao was the major spokesperson for the descendants until his death. Several artifacts from the original synagogue can also be seen in the local Great East Mosque (Dong Da Si). These include the stone lotus bowl and the original blue roof tiles from the synagogue.

There is some local interest in the city's Jewish roots. One of the younger generation of Jewish descendants studied in Israel in 2001-2002. For more information and tours from the US, contact Dr. Wendy Abraham, **Jewish Historical Tours of China**, P.O. Box 9480, Stanford, CA 94309, Tel. 888/731-3388, E-mail: wabraham@leland.stanford.edu, Website: www.jewishchinatours.com.

Canadians might be interested in the grave of Canadian Dr. Tillson Lever Harrison, who died in Changqiu in 1947 after delivering three boxcars of medical supplies under horrendous conditions through Nationalist areas to the Communists. It is in the Revolutionary Martyrs Cemetery with a stone almost two meters high. There is also a Tillson Lever Harrison Memorial School in the city.

A **theme park**, the Riverside Scene during the Qing Ming Festival (Qing Ming Shang He Yuan) is based on the famous painting of the 11th century Song city. It's at 5 Longtinxi Road, Tel. 5663586 and is open 9am-6pm. "Lord Bao" greets all early visitors. There's stilt walking, drum dance acrobats and puppet shows 9am-11am, and 2pm-4pm. Do not expect Hong Kong's version of the same thing. The buildings and costumed people here do give you a feeling of the era, but it's only a pale attempt at that marvelous old painting with its beautiful wooden buildings, hundreds of people playing ball, shopping, driving animals, worshipping, selling, buying, wrestling, and carrying things by shoulder poles.

This park should be of particular interest to children and to people who have just arrived in China. It has English, German and French-speaking guides for hire, and an evening show on weekends and holidays. Look for goat and camel rides. Avoid the cock fights. It has a wonderful "sugar blower" named Ma Qian Tang who makes figures of mainly animals like oxen, horses, goats, monkeys and snakes. We found him at the foot of the bridge in a little stall by himself. Many other novelties are also for sale.

Shopping

Kaifeng is famous for its embroidery and fighting kites. Shopping is extensive at the theme park and on **Song Du Yu**, Imperial Dynasty Street in the north of the city. Also made locally are porcelains and New Year's pictures from Zhuxian Township printed from wood blocks. Department stores are on Madao Street.

Practical Information

Kaifeng CITS, 98 Yingbin Road, Tel. 3980084. E-mail: kfcits@public.kfptt.ha.cn. Ask for Liu Wenqing.

Kaifeng Foreign Affairs Office, 98 Yingbin Road, 475000. Tel. 3934819, Fax 3934818. E-mail: davidliu @371.net. Contact Liu Wei who helped a lot with this book for complaints and information.

Kaifeng Tourism Administration, 98 Yingbin Road, 475000, Tel. 3924810, Fax 5956662. Contact Xia Feng for complaints and information.
Telephone code: 378

Luoyang

(North bank of the Luo River)

Luoyang, about 25 km south of the Yellow River, is important because of the Longmen Grottoes, the White Horse Temple, and Mrs. Yang. Because it was an imperial capital for many centuries and the site of many battles, many valuables were buried here for safe-keeping – almost as many as in Xi'an. It is one of the 24 cities of historical importance protected by the State Council.

Luoyang was built in the 11th century B.C. From 770 B.C. it was the capital at one time or another of the Eastern Zhou, Eastern Han, Wei, Western Jin, Northern Wei, Sui, Tang, Later Liang, and Later Tang dynasties. The imperials moved here frequently because of drought in Xi'an, a city they preferred.

Because there are hills on three sides, it was relatively easy to defend, and whoever wanted to control western Henan had to take Luoyang. Consequently, many battles were fought in this area and many treasures were buried to save them from the soldiers.

Luoyang was one of the earliest centers of Buddhism, dating from the first century A.D. During the Tang, it was the biggest city in China. It declined later because the capital moved away. Luoyang people will proudly tell you that the Silk Road actually started from here and not from Xi'an, as is commonly supposed. "Knowledgeable merchants always came here for silks," they say. "It was cheaper."

The hottest temperature is 39˚C in July and August; the coldest in January and February -12˚C. The weather is usually mild. The altitude is 145 meters above sea level. The population is at least 1,290,000 in the city, between five and six million including the suburbs. The city has had a quiet, provincial atmosphere, but is starting to get lively.

Arrivals & Departures

Luoyang is two hours by train or expressway west of Zhengzhou, a 160 km trip. The fastest train from Xi'an is about six hours and from Beijing about eight hours. There are infrequent air connections with seven Chinese cities. Highway buses go between the Zhengzhou Railway Station and downtown bus stations, and the Luoyang Jinyuan Bus Station every 20 minutes between 7am and 6pm for about Y15.

Orientation

Luoyang has over 400 factories manufacturing everything from truck cranes to ball bearings. It has one of the biggest free markets in China, serving 50,000 people a day. This is near the Guan Yu Temple and Longmen Grottoes. Visitors might be interested in its arts and crafts factory which makes palace lanterns and reproductions of three-color Tang porcelains and Shang bronzes.

Area farms grow cotton, corn, winter wheat, a little rice, sesame, sorghum, sweet potatoes, apples, pears, and grapes. They also raise yellow oxen, goats, and donkeys. The city is noted for its peonies, first grown 1400 years ago in the Sui! Flower lovers should aim for the Royal City (Wangcheng Park) between April 15 and 25.

Where to Stay & Eat

The best hotel for North Americans in Luoyang is Luoyang Grand Hotel. The second best is the Luoyang Peony. I've stayed on four different occasions at the Peony Plaza, the last time October 2000. It has a great location for tourists at one end of Peony Square where people dance in the morning and evening and peddlers put up stalls. But the management here is bad and I would avoid it unless it has improved since.

Hotels add a surcharge of 15% and prices are subject to change and discounts.

LUOYANG GRAND HOTEL, *South Section of Nanchang Road. Four stars. Tel. 4327000, Fax 4310784. E-mail: sale@ly-grandhotel.com. Website: www.ly-grandhotel. $55 per room including continental breakfast.*

LUOYANG PEONY HOTEL (Mudan Dajiudian), *15 Zhong Zhou Xi Road, 471003. Three stars, Tel. 4856699, Fax 4857999. About Y480-Y580 for rooms and Y1200 for suites. It is 15 km from the airport, four km from the railway station, and in the center of the city.*

Built in 1990, this 15-story hotel has 196 rooms, a gym, in-room safes, CNN, and business center. CITS in Zhengzhou charges $52 for a room.

Where to Eat

This is a small provincial city so don't expect much. Good restaurants have been behind the Friendship Hotels, like the Ya Xiang Lou restaurant.

YA XIANG LOU, *Anhui Road, No. 4, Tel. 4911993. Second floor.*

Good dishes here include curried beef, chicken with fruit (#2515), stir fried bean curd (#2536), and flat noodles and fried rice. Noodles are made by hand in the dining room. Prices are moderate.

GODDESS HOTEL RESTAURANT (Luo Shen Da Jiudian), *Luoyang Glass Factory Nan Road. Tel. 3944878.*

Food here has been good with interesting spices. Parrots are painted on the ceiling and a grand piano is in the lobby bar. We liked the eggplant with fish flavor, chicken with mushrooms, sweet and sour pork, dried soy bean string and stringed potatoes. It is a 25-minute drive east of the Peony Plaza Hotel, and 15 km from the White Horse Temple.

LUOYANG PEONY HOTEL, *15 Zhong Zhou Xi Road. Tel. 4013699.*
Food is good here; try the banana fritters.

Seeing the Sights

The following can be covered in one day if you don't dawdle. The ***Baima Si (White Horse) Temple**, *Tel. 3789053*, 25 km from the Friendship Hotel, was founded in 68 A.D. after the second Han Emperor Mingdi dreamed that a spirit with a halo entered his palace. His ministers convinced him that the spirit was the Buddha, so he sent scholars to India to bring back the sutras. After three years, the famous Indian monks Shemeteng and Zhufalan arrived here with the scriptures, having made the last part of the trip on a white horse. Here they translated the scriptures into Chinese. Both monks died in China and were buried in the east and west corners of the grounds beyond the moon gates. This was the first Buddhist temple in China.

None of the buildings here are original: the red brick foundation of the Cold Terrace is Han, and none of the others are earlier than Ming. The State Council lists them as Jin to Qing. The abbot here was one of Tang Empress Wu's boyfriends.

In the main hall to the right of Sakyamuni is Manjusri, the Bodhisattva of Wisdom carrying the sutras, and at Sakyamuni's left, Samantabhara, Bodhisattva of Universal Benevolence. In the next hall are 18 clay arhats, each with a magic weapon. These are the oldest statues here (Yuan). One is Ceylonese, one Chinese (the Tang monk Xuan Zhang who went to India), and the rest Indian. Inside the back halls are statues of the two Indian monks, the Pilu Buddha (Sakyamuni), and the drawers where the scriptures are kept.

The 13-story **Qiyun (Cloud Touching) Pagoda** nearby is in the Tang style, first built in 1175. You get a strange echo effect if you stand either north or south of it and clap your hands. This temple is a good place for meditation, for enjoying the peonies and fresh air. There are, however, some very deformed beggars waiting outside, giving you an opportunity to gain some merit.

The **Luoyang Municipal Museum**, *Tel. 3937107*, has a special exhibit on the second floor with English titles and it's worth a stop. The museum has 2,000 pieces on display and roughly 50,000 pieces in its collection. Relics include historical maps of the city that show the imperial cities. Other items include a meter-wide bronze tripod incense burner, a sandalwood pagoda, and two mammoth tusks found right in town. There's a double boiler used 3,700 years ago, a crossbow with a trigger (476-221 B.C.), and iron farming tools (Han). Look for figures from the tomb of a Northern Wei prince, including a band with one musician falling asleep; and original three-color Tang horses and camels from which copies are made. Study these carefully for comparison if you want to buy reproductions. It is open 8:30am-5:30pm daily in summer, winter to 5pm, and has a shop.

Longmen Grottoes
The parking lot is half a kilometer from the entrance and it cost Y2 each for a ride on an eight-passenger electric cart there. The toilets near the entrance are very clean and even had hooks to hang purses!

China has 19 important cave temples and the ***Longmen (Lungmen) Grottoes**, *Tel. 5981650*, is among the top three. They have titles in English. Predating these caves and built also by the Wei, those at Datong are better preserved, more elaborately colored, and bigger. The stone at Longmen, however, is better. The grottoes are about 18 km south of the Peony Plaza Hotel and extends north along the Yi River for about 1000 meters. They were not touched by the Red Guards, but the heads and hands of some were damaged by farmers wanting the stone for fertilizer. Look for the 303-meter copy of a famous Sui bridge. Peddlers here are among the most persistent. Just say "Boo yow!" (I don't want) and they should go away. There's lots of climbing of stairs to look into caves.

Work on the caves began about 494 A.D., when Emperor Hsaio Wen of the Northern Wei moved his capital here from Datong. Work continued at a great pace from then until the Tang, financed also by people who wanted to gain merit. A few statues were added during the Five Dynasties and Northern Song. There are 1352 grottoes, over 750 niches, and about 40 pagodas of various sizes. They contain more than 100,000 Buddhist images, ranging in size from two centimeters to 17.14 meters. The most important have signs in English.

The **Wan Fo (10,000 Buddhas) Cave** actually has 15,000 Buddhas on the north and south walls. It was completed in 680 A.D. (Tang). Note the musicians and dancers at the base. The back wall has 54 bodhisattvas, each sitting on a lotus flower. Outside the cave is a Guanyin with a water vessel in her left hand and a whisk in her right. There used to be two lions here, but they are now said to be in the Boston Museum of Fine Arts. The Guyang Cave was the earliest, built around 494 A.D.(Northern Wei). The corn-like design represents a string of pearls. The ceiling is covered with Buddhas, lions, and tablets.

Fengxian Temple, the largest and most spectacular, was completed in 675 A.D. The main statue (17.14 meters) is the Vairocana Buddha (i.e. Sakyamuni), the face said to be modelled after Empress Wu. The square holes around the statues were used to hold the roof structure that was taken down when it was found that sunlight was good for limestone. Behind the smaller disciple to Sakyamuni's right is an imperceptible cave large enough to hold 400 people and from which climbers used to negotiate the top of the head. This is now blocked. On Sakyamuni's far left is Dvarapala, whose ankles are worn black and smooth by individuals trying to embrace them in return for happiness. A Western toilet is at ground level in the store at the base of these statues.

Compare the dress of the statues. Some are clothed in the plain robes of Indian holy men. Others wear female Chinese court dress, sometimes with jewelry, a later development. You can understand that wealthy, devout worshippers wanted to clothe their gods in the best fashions of the day. This practice is much like that of medieval European religious art. The narrow, regular pleats are characteristic of the Northern Wei. The Tang statues tend to have rounder faces. While it is said that gods could change their sex at will, the feminine faces are because, as one adherent said, 'We want people to look at the face of Buddha. Since women's faces are more attractive than men's, the statues are made to look more feminine." It seems that Guanyin changed from male to female in the third century Wei dynasty.

A highlight of many tours is a visit to charming Mrs. Yang Xiu Hua in her late 80s. Her feet were bound at age six and her once wealthy family lost its money to opium. She will let you photograph her feet and ask questions. She lives by preference in a 200-year old cave hollowed out of the ground and sells a few cheap souvenirs. Arrangements have to be made through travel agencies as she is not always there. A nearby masseur might entice you into some treatment, but don't pay more than Y20 negotiated beforehand. The place is not clean.

Other Sites

The **Tomb of Guan Yu**, *Tel. 5975746, 5962018* or at least that of his head is near the Grottoes. Guan Yu was one of the heroes of The Three Kingdoms period, and he is also known as the Chinese god of war. His tomb, between the grottoes and the city, was built in the Ming. He was beheaded about 219 A.D.

Outside of the city is the **Tomb of Liu Xiu**. He was first emperor of the Eastern Han 1,900 years ago. A visit could be combined with a trip to see the Yellow River. The **Luoyang Ancient Tombs Museum** is seven km from the city near the airport and is worth a visit if tombs interest you. These 22 are from the Han, Tang, Ming and Qing dynasties, some genuine, some reproductions. Mainly in one building and underground, this museum is cool in summer, dark and spooky. Take a flashlight. Children would love it. An imperial Wei tomb is next door.

The **Folk Customs Museum**, *Tel. 3957064*, is charming if you have a good guide explaining the symbols on tiny women's shoes, embroidered headbands, and children's clothes. It has a special display of birthday and wedding customs and religious influences. The tombs and folk customs museums are not on the regular tour and you must ask for them. It is in an old guild hall and for Y20 extra each, you can see a 10-minute puppet show with music and explanations.

The **Yellow River Theme Park** has recently opened here, a Singapore joint venture. Let me know if you like it. You can visit the 154-meter-high Xiaolongdi Dam project on the Yellow River, 40 km north of Luoyang.

Shopping

We found prices at the **Luoyang Artistic and Ceramic Corporation** excessively expensive, especially compared to stores outside. But it had a good selection and you can see the process. It's on 503 Zhongzhou Road, No. 503, *Tel. 3935387.*

Practical Information

CITS Luoyang, *Tourism Mansion, Jiudu Xi Road, 471003, Tel. 5944797, Fax 5952273. E-mail: citsly@public2.lyptt.ha.cn or zhangy@hntg.net.* This is a branch of **Henan Tourism Group Company**, Zhengzhou, *Tel. 371/ 5944797. Fax 371/5952273. E-mail: zhangy@hntg.net*

CTS, *6/F, Zhangfang Mansion, 26, Zhong Zhou Xi Road, 471003, Tel/Fax 4856504.*

t
i
b
e
t

Chapter 19

Lhasa

Lhasa, the capital of **Tibet**, is your main point of entry to the "roof of the world." Lhasa is situated north of Bhutan and Bangladesh and almost due south of Urumqi.

Tibet is generally safe for visitors, except those who get involved in local politics or can't take the altitude. Avoid getting close to the many stray dogs here.

Tibet is one of the more exotic places in the world to visit, almost a country in itself, with an area about the size of France, Spain, and Greece combined. It is isolated by the highest mountains on earth. It is important to see because of its unique culture, its celebrated monasteries, and its stark, spectacular scenery. You should go so you can make up your own mind about its controversial situation.

Good books to read before your trip here include Pratapaditya Pal's *The Art of Tibet*, which gives some history and explains the religion and its symbols. There's Heinrich Harrer's *Seven Years in Tibet*, about his adventures here in the 1940s, a good picture to compare with today's Tibet. Harrer, a German, taught the Dalai Lama English and was his cameraman. See the movie too but believe the original source, the book. A sequel relates Harrer's return trip. The movie *Kundun* tells about choosing the current Dalai Lama. An excellent movie is *Caravan (Himalaya)* about a Tibetan group in Nepal, and the slow-moving *Saltmen of Tibet*. Also recommended are the classic books *Tibet and Its History* by Hugh E. Richardson and Peter Fleming's *Bayonets to Lhasa*. More recent are *Dalai Lama, My Son* by Diki Tsering, and Tom Grunfeld's *The Making of Modern Tibet* (1999). Look also at literature from China's point of view obtained from its embassy websites. Consider the positions of the different factions within the Tibetan community.

Arrivals & Departures

You need a permit to go to Tibet, obtained by prepaying a tour. See Chengdu. Lhasa is reached by two daily two-hour flights from Chengdu early in the morning. It also has flights from Beijing (Y1940), Chongqing (Y1300), Guangzhou (Y2000), Kathmandu, Kunming, Shanghai, Xi'an (Y1320), Xining (Y1290) and Zhongdian – but not daily. The Kathmandu flights operate only on Saturdays in winter (October 31-April 1), and Tuesdays and Saturdays in summer. (See also Chapter 6.) Kathmandu to Lhasa is 650 kilometers, about one hour's flight, and China Southwest Airlines is better and more reliable than Royal Nepal. Ask to sit on the Everest side of the plane which is on the left as you go toward Lhasa.

Lhasa's **Gonggar Airport**, the third highest in the world at 3,542 meters, can now accommodate 747s. There is talk of direct flights from Hong Kong. The airport is about 100 km from Lhasa and the road follows the Yarlung Tsangpo River, the highest river in the world, which becomes the Brahmaputra in India. A bus from the airport to downtown Lhasa costs about Y35. You can share taxis with other passengers.

You can also go between Lhasa and Golmud (about 1,100 km) in Qinghai by daily bus. It costs about Y700 for a non-stop bus with sleeping berths, and Y500 for a budget bus with an overnight stop in Nagchu. Tibet CITS says a car from Lhasa to Golmud costs Y7000-Y8000, no permits needed going down. It's about 30 hours driving-time with the possibility of snow in the high passes, even in June. Take warm clothing, boots, motion sickness pills, and your own food. Buses might not have toilets and heat.

Travelers have also been going overland from Kathmandu; you can travel from the Nepal border to Lhasa in one long day if you don't stop to sightsee or sleep, but some people have gotten very sick this way. You have to make a fast ascent. You also might have to walk around the landslides. Three days is better for this route. Some guides feel it is better to get used to the altitude by flying to Lhasa first before attempting this rough route to the border.

You could also go by land from Chengdu via Chamdo to Lhasa, from Kashgar, and via Zhongdian in Yunnan province. Most of these roads are very poor, however, and you should expect delays due to landslides in summer. In Zhongdian, it could take a week to get permits, but a lot of travel agents there can help you with Land Rovers and Tibetan-speaking guides. The trips from Chengdu and Kashgar are very difficult and not recommended. Two roads go between Lhasa and Chengdu, but travel agents warn of robbers. "It's too dangerous." If you're going by land, it is better to go through Golmud in Qinghai, they said. See also Xining for tours in Tibetan areas outside Tibet.

Officials are now talking again about the highest railway line in the world between Golmud and Lhasa, due if all goes well, about 2007. They have been talking about this for years, perhaps decades, but now the difficult railway project is on again.

Arranging Travel to Tibet
Tibet has been officially open (except during times of civil unrest) only for prepaid tours with a guide, even for one person. You need authorization from the Tibet Tourism Bureau sent to the Chinese mission where you are applying for a visa. You can also arrange tours after you arrive in China. If you wait until you get to China, do not mark "Tibet" on your visa application form. If you mention Tibet, the Chinese consulate will need to see your permit from the Tibet Tourism Bureau first. See Chengdu OTC on Lhasa.

Waiting until after your arrival in China to get a permit can mean a cheaper trip. You can start discussions with a travel agency in China before you leave home, its location depending on your itinerary. It can take one to three days to get permission, but better give yourself a week. Chinese Travel agents anywhere can help you but Chengdu is fastest.

For diplomats assigned to countries other than China and traveling as tourists, legal entry to Tibet is decided on a case-by-case basis which could take three weeks to a month once authorities receive your name and passport number. As for journalists, what is a journalist? As long as you call yourself something else, and behave like any other tourist, journalists should have no problems. Just don't put "journalist" on any form and leave your press card at home.

From time to time, these official restrictions have not been enforced and a few people have entered without a permit. You do risk a fine and deportation if authorities decide to enforce the law.

If you want an ethnic Tibetan rather than Chinese guide, make your request when you book your tour. A Tibetan guide might not speak English as well as a Chinese one. A Tibetan guide will be able to communicate better with other Tibetans. Tibetans can be hostile to Chinese guides. You could also request a guide with good English but you might not get one.

Bring Cash to Tibet
Recent travelers have found a stronger demand for US cash than for travelers' checks. Only the Lhasa Hotel, and maybe the Shangbala by now, will change money for its own guests. The main Potala branch of the Bank of China will cash travelers' checks. It is open weekdays and also on Saturday morning. Don't count on changing money easily after arrival, and don't count on credit cards, especially outside of Lhasa.

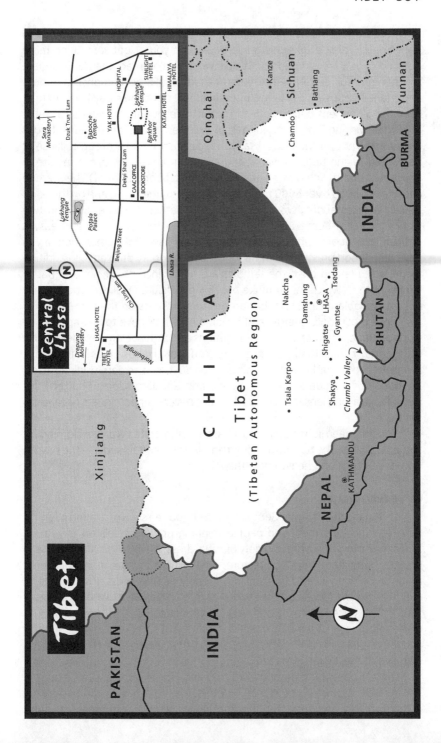

Because tourists have complained of guides with little knowledge and poor English, please take this guide book with you or get something more detailed. If you are worried about political unrest, contact the US Consulate in Chengdu for current information. There could be demonstrations on important Tibetan anniversaries, but guides will steer you away from them. If something happens before your trip, your travel agent can always cancel it.

While visiting Tibet is no longer an experience just for the adventurous few, it is still not for the weak. I saw one member of a tour group collapse as he waited in line upon arrival at the airport in Lhasa. (Within a minute, a uniformed doctor and oxygen arrived so it must happen often!) The average altitude in Tibet is **over 5000 meters** (very hard on the lungs, and on the skin). Usually it takes about two days to decide whether you'll be sick, and two weeks to feel at home. Just don't push yourself too hard. Taking it easy is difficult, as a lot of climbing is involved just to sightsee. Take precautions if you have high blood pressure, asthma, or other pulmonary problems. In addition to the altitude and dust, the temples are full of incense smoke and butter lamps, both of which might make breathing difficult. Qualified doctors may not be available. See the sidebar on *Altitude Sickness* on the next page.

Since most food, energy, and building materials have to be imported by truck or plane, the cost of accommodations and sightseeing is higher than in other parts of China for the same quality. You should take serious hiking boots, flashlight, nose masks and sun glasses for dust, sun screen, drinking flask, medicine for altitude sickness, aspirins, and an alarm clock. Shutter bugs should take a long lens for people who have never seen foreigners or cameras before.

You only need light clothing for Lhasa in summer, but warmer clothing for higher altitudes. The bus from Golmud in June encounters snow in the passes. You need boots and heavy coats then.

Orientation

This is colorful National Geographic land: you can see prostrating pilgrims, fierce-looking tribesmen, and people spinning prayer wheels on the street. You can photograph a great variety of tribal dress, maroon-robed monks, and unusual handicrafts and architecture. You will thrill at great snow-covered mountains. You will also find smiling, friendly people, most of whom don't mind having their picture taken when asked, and some of whom obviously take baths once a year. Feel lucky if you encounter groups of monks challenging each other with questions catechism-style amid much laughter and the clapping of hands. And there are yak or at least dzos – crossbred oxen who live at these high altitudes.

Lhasa's population is about 175,000 and Tibet's population 2.3 million. The altitude in Lhasa is about 3,607 meters. Most of the year can be very dry with lots of blowing dust. Only light clothing is needed in summer for Lhasa,

Altitude Sickness

If you only have two days, it is not worth going because it takes so much time to acclimatize. In Lhasa you get about two-thirds the amount of oxygen at sea-level. In Shigatse, you get 50%!! In summer you get more than in winter. Jogging or any physical exertion makes matters worse. About 60% of new arrivals get a headache. If you are one of the small minority afflicted with severe altitude sickness, you could spend much of your time in bed.

You won't know you are susceptible until you get to about 3,000 meters. You can travel successfully in high altitudes 20 times and get it on the 21st. It seems to hit the young and strong more than the old and weak. Young people have passed out checking into hotels. You should not jump onto a bicycle or jog upon arrival, even though you feel fine.

The symptoms are severe headache, dizziness, insomnia, nausea, vomiting, and difficulty in breathing. People who make a gradual ascent by road rarely get it, if at all. People who fly in are prone. So are people with colds, breathing difficulties, poor health, and heart disease. High blood pressure can be made even higher by altitude. In spite of headache remedies, my companion's headaches started a day after we reached 2500 meters and didn't stop until we went below 2500 meters.

Pregnant women should stay below 3,600 meters, says the Himalayan Rescue Association in Hints on High Altitude.

It is better to let your body adjust naturally. Avoid smoking, alcohol, and sleeping pills. Move about in slow motion. Drink over three liters of liquid a day. Get plenty of bed rest especially if you feel any of the symptoms. Open your windows. Breathe deeply. Relax. Do not panic.

Some hotels have oxygen in the rooms. This will give relief but will retard the time it takes the body to adjust. Some people have found aspirins helpful. Some have successfully taken the diuretic Diamox available in North America by prescription only. Many doctors will not prescribe it because they don't know its effect at high altitudes. With a few people Diamox has caused vomiting, confusion, and, of course, urination. Discuss it with a mountaineering club or travel agency doctor before you go. You have to start taking it a day before you arrive.

In very severe cases of altitude sickness, the only recourse is evacuation to a lower altitude – but you may not get a plane out for days.

but warmer clothes are needed for higher altitudes. Winter days can be warm with highs of 20˚C and you can get a sunburn. But the nights can be freezing. The best weather is May, and September to November. The hottest temperature in Lhasa is 27˚C in July and August; the coldest, -15˚C in December to

February. The annual precipitation is about 500 mm, mainly in June, July and August.

Lhasa has an old Tibetan city and a new Chinese city. These two areas are connected by #3 mini-bus for Y2, and Y10 taxis—only about a 15-minute ride. The Tibetan city is much more interesting, with old architecture. Aside from the Potala and the Johkang and central square, the monasteries are on the edge of town. The Norbulinka, the summer palace, is on the edge of the new city near the Lhasa Hotel.

When to Visit

The busiest tourist months are April, May, and July through October. In Lhasa, sometimes tourists outnumber costumed locals then. But from November to March, Lhasa Valley is full of colorful nomads going on pilgrimages from monastery to monastery, and living in tents. My favorite time to go is when fewer tourists are about, especially March, with lots of sunny 15 C days. At night the temperature then dips to near freezing but there's nothing to do outside anyways. Be warned however that there may not be any decent heat and hot water in hotels except in Lhasa, Gyantze or Shigatse. There may not be adequate heat in mini-buses.

At New Year's in the spring, houses and mountains look glorious with fresh prayer flags. Monasteries have special ceremonies, but markets are only partially open, and stores and factories are closed for two weeks. This is the best time for photography and tourist market haggling. Just take a hot-water bottle. You can also visit Zetang year round.

Tibetan History

Tibetans were nomadic herdspeople or farmers who raised barley, yak, and sheep. In 233, King Tho-tho-ri-Nyantsen received a book of Buddhist doctrine from India as a gift, but it was written in Sanskrit and no one in Tibet could read it. The king did nothing about it, nor did his successors for hundreds of years; it was finally translated in the mid-600's, by officials working for King Songtsen Gampo.

In the seventh century, this king of Tubo conquered the other tribes and made Lhasa his capital. He also invaded neighboring Sichuan, and although he was repulsed, his request for a Chinese wife was granted. His marriage with Tang princess Wen Cheng and his interest in Tang culture introduced much Chinese culture into Tibet. Among the innovations were silk, paper, and the architecture of the palace he built for her. His marriage to a Nepalese princess also meant Nepalese-Indian influences. Tibetan script is derived from Sanskrit, which was developed in India.

The Tibetan kingdom subsequently expanded to include parts of Yunnan and northern India. The Mongols invaded Tibet in 1252. They adopted Tibetan Buddhism for themselves and propagated it to help control their subject tribes in other parts of China. Some Tibetan lamas, or high priests, became very powerful during the Yuan. Kublai Khan appointed a lama as king, to maintain overall power himself. This system has continued with varying degrees of Chinese enforcement ever since. Qing Emperor Qianlong (Chien Lung) especially asserted his authority in Tibet.

In 1624, the Jesuits were the first Western missionaries here. During the lifetime of the fifth Dalai Lama, the office of Dalai Lama became political as well as religious. The first British mission arrived in 1774 and a British military expedition (Younghusband's) forced the Dalai Lama to flee to Mongolia from 1904 until 1909. In 1910, the Chinese again asserted their control and the Dalai Lama retreated for a time to India.

In 1911, the Tibetans repelled the Chinese. The British tried to maintain some control, but the Tibetans pretty much ruled themselves until the Chinese People's Liberation Army invaded in 1950-1951. The 1950s saw periods of turmoil as well as calm as the Chinese strengthened their hold.

An uprising by many Tibetans and a fierce Chinese crackdown in 1959 caused the current **Dalai Lama** (the 14th) to fear for his life; he and a large number of Tibetans fled to India. He has been living in Dharamsala, India, ever since, and over a hundred thousand Tibetans live today in exile in India, Nepal, and to a lesser extent Bhutan. Some live in North America.

In 1964, China made Tibet an "autonomous region" within China. During the Cultural Revolution, the Red Guards destroyed many of the monasteries. In 1980, the government agreed to rebuild a number of monasteries, which it has been doing. The Tibetan and Chinese governments maintain and regulate the monasteries. Today, Chinese sources say there are 1400 monasteries open, and 46,000 monks and nuns. Before the Chinese army took over, Tibet had 2770 monasteries.

Look for Tibetan policemen, Tibetan managers and officials. Ask about the percentage of Tibetans in Tibet and is this growing or decreasing? And does this percentage include the Chinese military? Due to government incentives, many Han Chinese are moving into Tibet, especially Lhasa. Some estimates put the number of Chinese soldiers and security forces in Tibet at 300,000.

In 1987, again in 1989, and sporadically in the past few years, a number of Tibetans (led by monks) have demonstrated for independence. Several dozen people have been killed and hundreds imprisoned.

The current Dalai Lama was awarded the Nobel Peace Prize in 1989, for his nonviolent resistance in exile to the Chinese occupation of his country, and for a peace plan offering the Chinese sovereignty of sorts in exchange for genuine autonomy in everyday life, with guarantees of political and religious freedom. China accused the United States and other countries then (and still does) of interfering in its internal affairs.

Not all Tibetans agree with or follow the Dalai Lama. Look up the followers of the deity Dorje Shugden and the young people who are impatient with his non-violence. See the Dalai Lama's website: *www.tibet.com*.

Tibetan Buddhism

Tibet's Buddhism is different from that of the rest of Asia, aside from Mongolia and a few parts of China. It believes in reincarnation—the apparently wrathful side includes a torturous hell for sinners, which is reflected in its art, full of demons and human skulls, witchcraft and magic, much influenced by the pre-Buddhist polytheism of the Tibetans. Tibetans explain that the demon masks are to scare away the bad spirits and are actually benevolent.

The peaceful side of the religion is largely from Buddhism and also reflected in Tibetan art. It has also many pre-Hindu influences and much recitation of spells. You might hear the chant 'Om Mani Padme Hum,' which means 'Hail to the Jewel in the Lotus,' a mantra that helps the individual communicate with the eternal. Buddhism also has many mystical elements, and a highly developed theology. The goal of Buddhism is the end of continuous reincarnations.

At one time, a quarter of the male population of Tibet were monks, and the theocracy was such that no matter how cold it was, on whatever day spring was proclaimed by the Dalai Lama, everybody had to change into summer clothes!

Like other religions, Buddhism is divided into sects: the two main ones in Tibet are often referred to as the Red Sect, where sex is an expression of the

Wanted - Dalai Lama Photos

As you move around the region, be sensitive to the feelings of people. I have been appalled by the loud talking of my Chinese guide during Tibetan prayers. Walk clockwise around temples and cairns. The left hand is consided dirty and should be kept away from sacred places. If you hand a picture of the Dalai Lama to a Tibetan, make sure no Han Chinese is around because you and your Tibetan friend could get in trouble. Hold the photo in both hands, put it to your forehead and then bow your head as you hand it over.

The Dalai Lama is considered by Tibetans to be an incarnation of the God of Compassion, and they might ask you for a "Dalai Lama picture" in every monastery. You probably could give out 40 in the Potala alone. However, if you have pictures of the Dalai Lama in your possession, the police could conclude that you support Tibetan independence. They have arrested some foreigners for getting involved in this dispute.

universal life force, and the Yellow Sect, (the **Gelukpa** sect), which practises celibacy and other Buddhist monastic traditions. The Dalai Lama is head of the Gelukpa sect.

The title Dalai Lama comes from combining Dalai, which is a Mongolian word meaning "ocean," and Lama, which means "revered one," "teacher," or, in this case, "wisdom." So Dalai Lama means Ocean of Wisdom.

Determining Reincarnated Lamas

How successive Dalai Lamas are chosen is fascinating. Toddlers recognizing objects used by themselves in their previous incarnation and answering questions correctly is the usual way it's determined. The current incumbent is from a peasant family from Amdo (northeastern Tibet, now in Qinghai province). The Dalai Lamas are believed to be earthly incarnations of the four-armed god Chenrezi, the God of Compassion or Mercy. When each incarnation dies, his spirit takes on the body of another Tibetan child at birth.

Disputes have arisen over who is the real reincarnated Dalai Lama or any other lama, and the issue is politically sensitive. To the chagrin of his followers, the current Dalai Lama has said there should be "no more Dalai Lamas," and "there is no need to preserve this institution."

Lamas are very learned monks or recognized reincarnations of previous lamas or monks, and their identities are determined in a similiar way. One American woman has recently borne the reincarnation of a high lama. In 1995, the Dalai Lama proclaimed one child as the reincarnation of the Panchen Lama while the Chinese government proclaimed another. The Chinese pointed to a Qing dynasty agreement that said it had to approve the appointment.

Tibetan Customs

"Tashi delek" is the Tibetan greeting. It means "good fortune." Hello is "Wei." Among traditional Tibetan customs is the giving of a "kata," a long silk scarf, as a token of esteem and good luck. The sticking out of the tongue is a sign of respect. At one time, Tibetans practiced polyandry, brothers sharing one wife because of poverty. Every summer a festival celebrates the annual washing and cleaning.

Funeral workers cut up the remains of the deceased at dawn to feed vultures, a 1,000-year-old tradition. Tibetans believe these birds take the spirits to heaven. Tourists are forbidden from seeing the birds at work, because the families fear strangers will scare the birds away. Those who cannot afford this expensive rite, like beggars or victims of serious illnesses, are fed to fish, which is why Tibetans don't eat fish. Burial in the ground is for the very poor and unfortunate, such as criminals or victims of murder. Some high lamas are covered in butter and cremated. The highest lamas are interred in monasteries; the previous Dalai Lamas are in the Potala Palace (see below).

Look for the "tangkas" hung on monastery walls. These are the scrolls used by preachers to illustrate the teachings of the Buddha and the best are valued by art collectors. You'll also see prayer wheels, with a written prayer inside, which adherents spin clockwise in the belief that each rotation sends a prayer to Buddha. Monasteries have giant prayer wheels. Prayer flags are blue symbolizing the sky, white for clouds, red for fire, green for water and yellow for earth. They are for protection.

Religious institutions usually decide the time and date of ceremonies and special events at the last moment. You have to telephone each morning for the time if you want to see these. No one really knows what is going on when, and you could find many changes to your itinerary.

Tibetan-Chinese Place Names

In this chapter, I've attempted to use the Tibetan name, but please forgive any errors. Guides might know only the Chinese name, here in parenthesis. With many thanks to Steve Powers: Chonggye (Qonggyai), Drepung (Daipung) Monastery, Ganden (Gandan), Gyantse (Gyangze, Chiang-tze, Jiangxi), Jokhang (Juglakang, Tsuglag Khang, Dazhaosi) Temple, Lhasa (Lasa), Lhoka (Shannan), Norbulingka (Norpulinkha, Luobulinka) Summer Palace, Potala (Budalagong) Palace, Sera (Sela) Monastery, Shammo (Zhangmu), Shigatse (Xigaze, Xigatse, Rikaze), Tashilhunpo (Zhaxilhunbu), Tibet (Xizang), Tingri Shegar (Xegar), Tsedang (Zedang), and Yarlung Tsangpo (Yarlung Zangbo) River. Mount Everest in Chinese is Qomolangma.

Where to Stay

Most hotels have problems with English but the Lhasa and the Shangbala have the highest standards. Some hotels here add 10% service charge and do not have CNN. The Lhasa Hotel said it occasionally gets CNN but not always. Many hotels have bulletin boards with notices from other travelers, especially helpful if you want to share rides outside of Lhasa or look for friends.

The best hotel in the new city is the Lhasa Hotel, then the Lhasa Tibet Hotel. The Lhasa and Tibet are within walking distance of each other and the Norbulinka. The best location for tourists is in the old city where the best here is the three-star Shangbala. This hotel is not as good as the Lhasa, though better than the Tibet. It is only 1.5 blocks from the Jokhang, interesting shops and restaurants. You feel you have truly arrived in Tibet if you stay in this area.

My favorite is the Yak Hotel because it looks Tibetan, is next door to the good Dunya Restaurant, two blocks from the Jokhang, and is clean and cheap. Service is not as good as the Shangbala and there's no elevator. The third best here is the Hotel Kyichu only a few steps further. In the old city, there are also the Kirey and Banok Shol. Aside from Lhasa and Shangbala, few hotels in Tibet honor reservations. You might have to send a scout a day ahead to secure rooms in high tourist season. Hotels outside of Lhasa's top three can be downright crude.

LHASA HOTEL (Lhasa Fandian), *One Minzu Road, 850001. Four stars. Tel. 6832221, (Sales office) Fax 6835796, 6834117. E-mail: sales@public.ls.xz.cn. Y1020 and Y1328 nett for rooms and Y2056-Y8888 nett for suites April 2002 – October 31 2002. It has been discounting 20%. It is 95 km from the airport in the western suburbs and it accepts international credit cards and travelers' checks.*

Built in 1986 with renovations 1998-99, this 468-room former Holiday Inn is in five and six story buildings with exotic Tibetan-style suites, and non-smoking floors. Heated in winter, it has satellite television, Sichuan, Western, dim sum, Huaiyang and Tibetan food. Its Western buffet costs Y130, lunch and dinner Y160. Its outdoor pool is open June to September. It has its own airport bus. Individual safes are in some but not all rooms. And there are elevators. The hall carpets needed replacing even though management told me the whole hotel had been renovated in 1998 and 1999. And its economy room was musty with cheap furniture and poor grouting. Its Tibetan suite was charming, with a Tibetan tent ceiling, carved wooden furniture, and tangkas.

LHASA TIBET HOTEL (Xizang Binguan), *221 Beijing Xi Road, 850001. Three stars. Tel. 6833677, Fax 6836787. Renovations in 1998.*

Located behind the Lhasa Hotel, this 1986 hotel has a clinic. Room are Y880-Y2800. It has been discounting its cheapest rooms to Y680 and accepts credit cards. It is aiming at four stars and has 24-hour money exchange. Its Western buffet breakfast costs Y68. Lunch and dinner buffets cost Y85 each. Rooms are good but its carpets fit badly and there's no gym, no pool, and no CNN. Rooms are generally Western style with kettles, mini-bar, hair drier, and make-up mirror. It has an elevator. CITS has been charging $69 for rooms here. And I did find staff sleeping in its coffee shop at 3pm.

SHAMBALA/SHANGBALA HOTEL (Jiudian), *1 Danjielin Road, 850000. Tel. 6323888 and Fax 6323577. With 61 rooms in a four-story building, it has the only elevator in the old city. Its standard rooms are small. It was open in April, 1999 and is aiming at three stars. Prices range from Y400-Y480 for rooms, and Y1200 for suites, and it has been giving 10-20% discounts to walk-in guests. It currently does not accept credit cards like Visa, American Express and MasterCard but hopes to do so in the future.*

It has 24-hour hot water and can change foreign cash but no travelers' checks. It has no e-mail, no CNN, no in-room safes, and shallow closets. But it has a sauna, and business center. It should have a travel agent in the future. Its simple breakfast buffet costs Y40, but if you're a guest, then it's only Y20. I did find chipped cups in its Chinese restaurant. Sales Manager Leon Lee was extremely helpful and he speaks excellent English. Shangbala means Shangri-La in Tibetan. Yak International has been charging Y320 for a room here. It is a sister hotel of the five-star Jinjiang in Chengdu.

YAK HOTEL, *100 Beijing Dong Road, 850000. Trying for two stars. Tel. 6833496, 6323496, 6323496. About Y260 for rooms with shower, Y110 for no private bath, and Y25-Y50 for beds in a dormitory.*

This bright and friendly hotel was built in 1985, renovated and expanded since. It has a new wing with about 40 rooms, and remote-controlled heaters. Bicycles are for rent. A Y260 a night, third floor room has a fancy ceiling, brightly colored murals of the Tibetan countryside, and brightly colored carved wooden furniture—like an upper class Tibetan home. Its newer wing has three stories and a roof-top dormitory. Having no elevators might be a problem for people not yet used to the altitude so ask for a lower floor. The Yak was first opened in 1986, has 62 rooms and hot water 24 hours a day. It has bicycles for rent, a business center with IDD and Fax, and changes only foreign cash. It has no coffee shop.

HOTEL KYICHU (Kechu), *149 Beijing Dong Road, 850000, Tel. 6338824, Fax 6320234. Near the Yak Hotel. Y230 and Y420 for rooms, and it has been discounting 20%.*

This 22-room hotel has 24-hour room service and has no stars. It has Chinese, continental, Indian and Nepalese food, and a safe deposit box on the ground floor. It looked relatively fine, had laundry, postal, and air ticketing services, but the grouting in the bathroom was bad. Rooms have no carpets. Breakfast costs Y45-Y50. It has 24-hour hot water and room service. It has been adding 35 more rooms. Avoid its older front section which might have no views. Some of its staff speak English.

Where to Eat

Tibetan tea is drunk with yak butter and salt, and tastes more like an overly rich beef broth. It does tend to give much needed energy and is said to be good for colds. The proper way to drink it is to lightly blow the top cream away from you and allow it to settle on the sides of your cup. The thicker the cream, the more generous the host. Fresh, hot yak milk is sweet and "heavenly" and has a higher fat content than cow's milk. Barley-like flour is often added to the milk or tea to form a dough. Chang, a barley wine, is another favorite drink offered to guests. Most foreigners do not like yak butter and yak-butter flavored Tibetan food – it's too rich.

You can get Tibetan food (yak meat and cheese), Moslem (mutton or lamb), and Chinese food in Lhasa. If you are going outside of Lhasa, stock up on snacks before you leave for Tibet.

The **Lhasa Hotel** has good food, but it's extremely expensive. The **Shangbala Hotel** should be good too. Open now are many restaurants in the old city obviously aimed at foreigners with signs and menus in English and much cheaper than the hotels. None of them will take credit cards however. While prices are reasonable for foreigners, they are too high for local people.

DUNYA, *right next to the Yak Hotel (but independent of it), 100 Beijing Dong Road, Tel. 6333364, Fax 6330482. E-mail: dunya@public.ls.xz.cn. Website: www.dunyarestaurant.com.*

This is the best restaurant for foreigners, run by an American-Dutch-Tibetan partnership. Ask for Kris or Jannette. They are aiming to provide "hygienic Tibetan food and a variety of dishes from around the world using local ingredients." They are succeeding very well, though they do import their pasta and cheeses now. The food is surprisingly international. Meals range from Y15 for some local dishes to Y45 for certain speciality items like chicken cordon bleu. The yak steak (fresh daily) is Y35. The wine is Y90 per bottle and up. They cook their mo-mo dumplings fresh which are worth the 25 minute wait (Y20). It has been opening 8am-10pm from the beginning of April to the first of November. Its second floor bar with balcony has longer hours.

BARKHOR CAFÉ, *at the far end of the square in front of the Jokhang Temple. From the Jokhang, bear left.*

If you have problems with English, ask for the manager Mr. Zhang Ke Qiang. It has an art gallery and internet service. A yak sizzler sells for Y30, yak burger for Y20, yak curry for Y38, banana lassi for Y7, and roast chicken for Y30. It is open 7am-12 midnight.

SNOWLAND RESTAURANT, *next to the Snowland Hotel, only half a block from the Barkhor towards the Yak Hotel, on Tibet Hospital Road. Tel. 6337323. It is usually open at 7am but on Saturday and Tuesday because of early flights, it has been open at 5:30am. It closes about midnight.*

A little grubby with an American greasy-spoon atmosphere, it is okay if you don't want New Delhi standards. It offers American breakfast for Y25, Y6-Y8 for eggs, Y8 for a pot of coffee, and Y10 for fruit juice. At dinner time, a Tandoori chicken leg cost Y30, vegetable korma cost Y25, butter chicken Y25, Tibetan mo-mos Y15-Y20, lamb ribs Y25, plain yogurt Y5, and banana fritters Y10. Its Indian food is considered by some the best in town.

MAKYE-AME RESTAURANT, *"Yellow Building," Barkor Road, Southeast Corner, Tel. 6324455. E-mail: makyeame_1999@yahoo.com.*

You pass this restaurant as you circumambulate the Jokhang. Facing the front door of the temple, it's at about 2 o'clock. We had a good meal - potato curry for Y12, vegetable mo-mos for Y10, meat mo-mos for Y10, pakoras for Y8, and ginger tea. This restaurant has simple Tibetan décor, e-mail service, and a book exchange.

KANDSHIPO RESTAURANT, *out the front door of the Lhasa Hotel, turn left and cross the street on the same side. It's at the corner.*

In the new city, this place serves very cheap Sichuan food, is quite clean, but has no menu or signs in English. (See Chapter 25 for Sichuan dishes in Chinese and English.) An ample dinner for three cost us Y50. Yes Y50. Recommended by staff at the Lhasa Hotel, the Kandshipo was a little grubby but the food was delicious. And the atmosphere busy, noisy and lively.

Seeing the Sights

The best time for seeing the area around the Jokhang (if you don't want to shop) is from about 6pm to 8pm (hopefully before it gets too dark to take photos.) This is the time when thousands of Tibetans do their circumambulating around the temple, many in costume. Groups of a half dozen monks, each in the unique robes and hats of their own monasteries are seated here and there chanting, beating drums, and hoping for donations. Merchants sing out advertisements as they close up for the night. Men with long hair braided with red ribbons swagger with their heavy robes hanging off one shoulder. You'll see the latest in Tibetan fashions. A couple years ago floppy sun hats were in style on the women. Everyone swings a prayer wheel. The view from the roof of the Makye Ame Restaurant is great, but spoiled for photos by electric wires.

I asked four different Lhasa-based guides the same questions and got four different answers. What are the hours for the monasteries in Lhasa? You still have to check these yourself, but roughly, the monasteries are open for tour groups every day but only Monday, Wednesday and Friday mornings for pilgrims. If you want to photograph local people, best go on those three days. If you want to avoid crowds, choose accordingly. The Norbulingkha is open both morning and afternoon with a break for lunch. Ask your hotel to telephone for the exact time if you don't have a guide to take you. You don't want to climb all the Potala's exterior steps to find it closed.

The most important buildings to see in Lhasa are the Jokhang Temple, Potala Palace, Sera Monastery, and Drepung Monastery. You should also see the Barkhor or bazaar, and Norbulingka Palace. You might want to visit a carpet factory or traditional medicine hospital.

In your spare time you may want to go out on your own. The Yak Hotel has bicycles. Taxis cost about Y10 within the city. To travel to other parts of Tibet, ask your hotel, travel agents, or other travelers. You may need permits. The Yak, Kirey, and Sunlight Hotels have notice boards with messages.

You can see the temples and palaces of Lhasa in two days if you are in good shape. You must not miss the **Potala Palace**. It costs at least Y40 to enter and incredible amounts to photograph. The Potala is 3.5 km from the Lhasa Hotel and one km from the Jokhang. It dominates the city from its lofty cliff. Groups get driven up to the entrance, but individual travelers have to climb the 300 meters to the door. In spite of its 13 stories, there are no elevators. If you follow the crowds and go into every open doorway, you should be able to take in everything worthwhile in three hours. Unless things have changed since my last visit, there are no signs in English or arrows. There are a lot of stairs, and a toilet is near the east entrance.

Originally built in the seventh century by Songsten Gampo, the Potala was the official residence of the Dalai Lama, the religious and secular head of Tibet. The first Dalai Lama lived from 1391 to 1474. The Potala has 1,000 rooms, 10,000 chapels, and the tombs of eight Dalai Lamas, some gold-plated and studded with diamonds, turquoises, corals, and pearls. The largest tomb is 14.85 meters high. More than 200,000 pearls cover the Pearl Pagoda. The tombs are not always open so ask about them. Additional payment is worth it. Every room has a helpful monk-guide.

The building was destroyed and rebuilt several times, the latest structure dating from 1642. Among its 200,000 statues are those of King Songsten Gampo and his Chinese wife. Every wall is covered with murals. Noteworthy are those in the Sishiphuntsok Hall. In the West Grand Hall, the murals record the life of the Fifth Dalai Lama, including his meeting with Qing Emperor Shunzhi in Beijing in 1652.

The palace is 400 meters by 350 meters, and is made of stone and wood, its brightly colored walls between three and five meters thick, yellow for living quarters, and red for chapels. Black around doors is good luck. The White Palace was built during the time of the Fifth Dalai Lama (1617-1682) and the Red Palace afterward. From the 18th century, with the construction of the Norbulinka Summer Palace, the Potala was used only in winter. Can you imagine a child growing up here? The current Dalai Lama was brought here at the age of four. Think of him flying his kite from the Potala's roof and exploring the city and its people with a telescope!

The *Jokhang Temple (Juglakang) is the most important Buddhist temple in Tibet. It is here that most pilgrims prostrate themselves and you can take a great photo of them from its second floor. It is in the square in front that China's largest concentration of policemen seem to be, ready to show up whenever a crowd gathers. The Jokhang is 4.5 km from the Lhasa Hotel and is the heart of the old city. It was built in the mid-seventh century, also during King Songsten Gampo's time. It has been expanded several times since. Note the Nepalese and Chinese features. Princess Wen Cheng brought with her from China the seated statue of the child Sakyamuni. Some Tibetans believe that the statue was made by the Buddha himself. The Great Prayer Festival is held annually here from the third to 25th of the first month of the Tibetan calendar.

The *Sera Monastery, in the northern suburbs 10 km from the Lhasa Hotel and four km from downtown, was built in 1419. It was extended in the early 18th century, and is one of the four major monasteries in Tibet, at its height housing 10,000 lamas and monks. Today it has about 500. The 18 sandalwood arhats and four heavenly kings here were gifts from a Ming emperor. Look also for a gold statue of an 11-faced Guan Yin, the Goddess of Mercy.

The *Drepung Monastery, Tel. 6323149, is in the western suburbs six km from the Lhasa Hotel and 10 km from the Jokhang. You can climb to the roof for a view of the valley. Financed by the same nobleman who built the Sera, the Drepung was founded in 1416 and extended several times. Among its treasures is a white conch and a gilded Buddha. Inside the abdomen of the statue in the main hall are the remains of a master translator named Dorjidak.

At one time, this monastery also had a population of over 10,000 monks and lamas; today it has about 600.

If you have more time, the **Norbulingka**, *Tel. 6322157*, was the summer residence of the Dalai Lamas. With 370 rooms, it is four km from the Potala and set in this 100-acre garden. Kalsang Podang, the first building, was originally erected in 1755. The New Palace for the 14th Dalai Lama was built in 1954 and 1956. It is also full of statues and murals. The murals are of Princess Wen Cheng and her marriage to the king, the three worlds, and Buddha preaching under a banyan tree. The bedroom is as the current Dalai Lama left it when he fled to India. In the 1940s, the German mountain climber Heinrich Harrer set up a movie theater for the Dalai Lama here.

An exhibition of tangkas is usually in one of the temples in the back. Study it so you'll know what good quality is. Some tangkas look like paint-by-number products. If you don't like the toilets, go over to the Lhasa Hotel nearby.

One of the temples in Lhasa has a bronze bell with Latin inscriptions. It should be from 17th century Catholic missionaries. Ask about it if you're interested. Also of interest is the Sunday market, down the hill and across the street in front of the Potala, a delightful innovation with rides for children, market stalls, and food to eat. At the **Tibetan Medicine Hospital**, you can also learn about Tibetan medicine. This is open 9am to 6pm daily. It's at the same end of Barkhor Square as the Barkhor Restaurant. Go out the door of the restaurant and go left. Look across the street for a red cross. My friends walked in without an appointment and asked to see an English-speaking doctor who arranged for her to tour the hospital next day.

If you want to ride a yak-skin raft, that should be possible too. Inquire at your hotel or a travel agent. Ask about the Nechung oracle monastery. It's small, less crowded, with very interesting chapels.

Festivals

Dates are hard to pin down and some festivals have been canceled at the last minute.
• October-November: the Gods Descending Festival
• November-December: the Fairy Maiden Festival (Jokhang Temple)
• December: Tsong Khapa's Festival
• January-February-March: Tibetan New Year
• February-March: Great Prayer Festival (Jokhang)
• February-March: Butter Lamp Festival
• July: Giant Tangka Festival (Shigatse)
• August: Shoton (Tibetan Opera) Festival

Shopping

Tibetan boots, rugs, saddle blankets, jewelry, temple bells, prayer wheels, and wool blankets on sale. Shops in the Lhasa and Tibet Hotels have tangkas, religious statues, and books in English. The **Lhasa Hotel** has the best selection, but the highest prices. A book store and some souvenir shops are at the southeast base of the Potala. Merchants in Nepal say the best antique Tibetan carpets are found in Tibet; the best new Tibetan carpets are found in Nepal.

It is fun shopping in **Barkhor Square** and around the **Jokhang Temple** where shops are open 9am to 6pm. Fancy necklaces sell for Y30 though peddlers might first ask Y80. Much of the same jewelry is also found in the markets of Jordan. Necklaces with turquoise and coral are typical Tibetan designs however. Very cheap tangkas and boots are probably made here. Metal religious statues and ringing bowls could be Tibetan but are probably made in Nepal and cheaper there.

The **Pentoc Hotel Gift Shop** is across from the Snowland Hotel at 5 Tibetan Hospital East Road (Zang Yi Yuan Dong Road), 850000, Te*l/Fax 6330700. E-mail: pentoc@public.ls.xz.cn*. It has better quality souvenirs for tourists than the market. It has tiny stones carved with "Om Mani Padme Hum" and "Lhasa" in Tibetan fitted as refrigerator magnets, a great idea - and not too heavy. They were about Y12 each. It is open from 9am to around 9.30pm in summer and 9:30am to 8pm in winter. Closed Mondays. It also has a café on the reception level of the Pentoc Guesthouse, in the same building as the shop. It specializes in breakfasts and light meals, home-made pastries and ice cream, coffee and teas from China, Tibet, Nepal and India. The café is open from 7.30am to 11pm daily except Monday. Ask for Christian Bossy.

You can watch carpets being woven in Lhasa of Tibetan highland sheep wool with traditional Tibetan-inspired designs. The **Khawachen Carpet Factory**, a US joint venture, will also sell carpets at prices considerably lower than in the US. It is a 20-minute drive from the Jokhang and 10 minutes form the Lhasa Hotel at 103 Jinzhu Xi Road, *Tel. 6836916, Fax 6833250*. For a preview of what to expect before you go, contact **InnerAsia Trading Company**, 236 Fifth Avenue, New York, NY 10001, *Tel. 212/532-5230*. E-mail: *tashi@innerasiarugs.com*.

Excursions & Day Trips

From Lhasa are public buses to Tsedang (Y25), Shigatse, Nyingchi, Nagqu, Gyantse, and Gormu which leave the Long Distance Bus Terminal about 8am daily.

SHIGATSE & GYANTSE

Hotels in **Shigatse** and **Gyantse** are decent three-star quality and no real hardships. The most important town outside of Lhasa is Shigatse because of the ***Tashilhunpo Monastery**. On the new highway, this is about a five-hour, 260 km journey west of Lhasa. It can be combined in a two-night, three-day trip with Gyantse. You can return on the older, longer and more spectacular road that includes the monastery in Gyantse, a climb up to a 5,000-meter pass full of stone cairns, and thousands of prayer flags, vibrating in gale-force winds. You can leave a cairn there yourself if you're not too cold. You also get spectacular views of snow-covered **Najun Gsancy Glacier and Mountain** (7,220 meters high). This is a journey of about 10 hours, including a picnic lunch and a drive around sacred Lake Zambok.

Shigatse is at an altitude of over 3,900 meters. The Tashilhunpo was founded in 1447 and was the home of the Panchen Lamas, the reincarnations of the Buddha of Eternal Light. The Chinese consider the Panchen Lama a political equal to the Dalai Lama, but this is also a very sensitive and controversial point.

At one time, the Tashilhunpo had a population of 3,800 monks. Today there are less than one thousand. This monastery also has many halls and chapels, and statues of the 18 arhats. The Hall of the Buddha Maitreya Champa/Qiangba was built from 1914-18 with a 26.7-meter statue of the Buddha in gold and copper. The gold-plated reliquary of the fourth Panchen Lama is 11 meters high and is decorated with precious stones. The tenth Panchen Lama died here in 1989. Look for the photos of British Prime Minister Major and US President George Bush on a stupa. There are also 15th century paintings. You can probably hear the lamas chanting in the Grand Chanting Hall three times a day. A good market for Tibetan handicrafts and unique boots is nearby.

Shigatse is a good place for walking around, except for the vendors who grab you, hoping for a sale. It is flat and interesting especially around the market. Shigatse also has a traditional Tibetan medicine hospital to visit and the **Gang-Gyen Carpet Factory**, 9 Mount Everest Road, 857000, with traditional Tibetan designs. This factory is owned by Tashilhunbo monastery. It makes carpets, bags and jackets with sheep's wool and natural Tibetan-grown dyes and is open 9:30am-12:30 noon then 3:30pm-6:30pm.

The **Xigatze Hotel** (Binguan) at 13 Beijing Zhong Road, 857000, *Tel. 892/8822550, Fax 8821900*, has at least 123 rooms and growing. It has heat and hot water. It's less than one km to the monastery and almost next door to the Bank of China, and bars I can't recommend. There's also the **Manasarova Hotel**, *www.hotelmanasarovartibet.com*.

Gyantse is almost a two-hour drive from Shigatse, and 205 km from the airport outside Lhasa. It is worth a stop, unless you're tired of monasteries by now. Gyantse's is the spookiest of the lot and has about 85 monks, but few visitors because of its isolation. The town itself looks positively medieval with the remains of an impressive old fort above it. Gyantse has a carpet factory and the two-star, 1988 **Gyantse Hotel**, 8 Yingxiong Nan Road, Gyangtze, *Tel. 892/8172222, Fax 8172366*. It's within walking distance of the Balkhor Chen monastery and the ruins on Mt. Tzong.

ELSEWHERE IN TIBET

Hotels outside of Lhasa, Gyantse and Shigatse are frontier quality and you take your chances. There are also bed-and-breakfasts in private homes. Just don't expect flush toilets.

*Ganden Monastery, 45-60km east of Lhasa, is listed as early Ming to Qing. At least 10 buildings have been restored. Less than 100 monks live there now. At one time, it had over 8,000 monks and was one of the largest monasteries of the Gelukpa sect.

Guge Kingdom is a difficult eight-day drive west of Lhasa, just north of Dehra Dun in India (and impossible to go from there). Its alternate capitals were at Toling and Tsaparang. This was founded in the 9th century and was an important centre of Buddhist art whose original painters were from Kashmir. It reached its height in the 15th century and is well-preserved. It is sometimes combined with a trip to Kailas.

Kailas/Kailash is a sacred mountain of Buddhists, Hindus and Jains which pilgrims walk around in one to three days at an altitude of 5700 meters. In planning my own trip to Mount Kailas, I would seriously consider **Royal Mountain Trekking**. Its 17-day trip is deliberately long so travelers can get used to the high altitude. It involves only three days of walking. Land costs are $1924 per person including all transportation by landcruiser, truck for Nepali staff and food, guide, permits, sightseeing in Lhasa, Gyantse and Shigatse, accommodations, camping fees, yak and yak man. It also includes 12 days food on the trail, transportation from Kodari to Kathmandu, full kitchen equipment and flight ticket from Kathmandu to Lhasa. See Nepalese companies below. One of the guides of **Dharma Adventures** below has been to Kailas 35 times. **Tibet International Travel Service** at the Lhasa Hotel says it takes a week to get permits and access there is only by Land Cruiser. **Intrepid Tours** is operating tours from Kathmandu to Kailash; visit their website at *www.intrepidtravels.com.*

Quangtang grasslands is a 200,000 square km nature reserve with 60 kinds of rare wild animals like yak, argali, bear, and wild donkeys.

Rombuk Monastery at 5050 meters has one of the best views of Everest and is close to **Everest Base Camp**. Royal Mountain Trekking in Kathmandu has fixed departures.

Tsedang, about 200 km southeast of Lhasa, is the capital town of Shannan area with a relatively mild climate, the Yarlung River valley, and the first capital of the Tibetans. The altitude in Tsedang is 3600 meters.

On the way is **Samye**, where the first monastery was founded in 779 A.D. Samye has the oldest remaining monastery of the Red Sect (8th century). From Tsedang you can visit the ***Royal Tibetan Tombs** from the 7th century. The Yumbulakang Palace built in 228 B.C. by the first Tibetan king, is 15 km from town and is open daily in summer 9am-6:30pm and winter 9:30am-6pm for Y25. The three-star 190-room **Tsedang Hotel** has a good reputation. It is two km from old Tsedang at 21 Nedong Road, 856000, *Tel. 893/7821668, Fax 7821688. E-mail: tsedang@public.ls.xz.cn.* Tsedang **CITS** is in the Tsedang Hotel, *Tel. 893/7825555, 7821899, Fax 7821855. Email: tsedang8@public.ls.xz.cn.*

Tsurpu is two hours' drive from Lhasa and has the newly rebuilt 9th century Tsurpu Monastery, the seat of the Karmapa, the head of the 'Black Hat' sect. He is the 17th reincarnation, discovered in 1992 at the age of eight years, but an old soul. The lineage is older than the Dalai Lama's. In 2000, the Karmapa fled to India but you can still visit his monastery. There is still a handfull of monks. It charges Y25 entrance fee, Y20 for shooting photos and Y40 for videos. Travel agents suggest combining a trip to this monastery with a farm village visit on the way back. While its statues are new, it is a sacred place still visited by pilgrims.

Tingri has a good basic hotel. (Y300). It's clean with 25 rooms and electricity. From Tingri to Shigatse, the road is bumpy and dusty. This is near Everest Base Camp and the Nepal border.

Yamdrok Yamsto Lake is a one-day excursion from Lhasa, a large undeveloped lake, but an opportunity to enjoy the stark countryside.

Zhangmu, on the Tibet side of the Nepal border has three tourist hotels: the Zhangmu Hotel, Gang Gyen Hotel, and Pema Hotel. It is not worth staying there as the town is the pits. Zhangmu is between 840 km and 900 km from Lhasa. Routes differ.

The **China-Nepal border** is only open 9:30am-6:00 or 6:30pm. If you are late, you have to spend the night in Zhangmu. See also **Zhongdian** under Kunming, Taer Monastery and the Dalai Lama's birthplace in **Xining**, Labuleng Monastery in **Xiahe**/Lanzhou, and **Chengdu** for other Tibetan regions of China.

Treks

Several tour agencies now offer treks in Tibet, and prices for these are higher than similar treks in other countries. Mountaineering can be organized through the **Chinese Mountaineering Association**.

The best trekking months are June-July and September-October. August has the most rain and landslides. I would personally go with a Nepalese company because they are better equipped (toilet tents), are used to cooking for fussy foreigners, are more careful about hygiene and the environment, and know more about altitude sickness than the Chinese.

For women trekking in areas with no bushes or in overnight buses, carry an umbrella and open it to protect your modesty when nature calls. There may not be bushes.

Practical Information

Bank of China, main office, *between the Lhasa Hotel and the Potala.* A sign there says it is open from 9:30am to 1pm, and 3:30pm to 6pm, Monday to Friday. On Saturday and Sunday, it is open 10:30am to 3pm. There's also a branch where you can change money between the Kirey and Banok Shol Hotels, down the street from the Yak Hotel on Beijing Road.

Hours: for offices, 9am-9pm in summer; 10am-6pm in winter. Lunch break is 1pm-3:30pm. Stores are open sometime between 8am and 10am, and closed between 7pm and 10pm.

Internet bars: the **Yak Hotel** has a small internet bar but the better one in the old town is on the *2nd floor of the Kirey Hotel, Room 203, at 12 Beijing Dong Road, Tel. 6339847, 6342576.* The mobile telephone number for manager Tashi Tsering is *13908908994*, and it's open 8am to 11:30pm. About Y20 an hour.

Medical Emergencies, contact your hotel.

Nepalese Consulate, *13 Norbulingka Road, Tel. 6822880*

Tibet Tourism Bureau, *208-218 Beijing Xi Road, 850001, Tel. 6826793, 6832980, Fax 6835277, 6833241. For permits and complaints, Tel. 6824584. Offices in Tibet Hotel, Chengdu and 149 West Gulou Street, Beijing 100009, Tel. Beijing 64018822 ext. 1601, Fax 64015883 or 64019831. Office also in the US, Tel. 909/629-8888, Fax 909/629-8889*

Travel Agents/Tour Operators:

• **Shigatse Travels,** *Yak Hotel/Dunya Restaurant, 100 Beijing Dong Road, 850000, Tel. 6330489, 6330483, Fax 6330482. Website: www.shigatsetravels.com (to be open soon).* Genden Gyamtso, Sales Manager, *Tel. 13908906626. E-mail: amdo@public.ls.xz.cn or gendengyamtso@hotmail.com.* Group department, *Tel.* Rene Schrama, or Dorjee Tashi (Travel Agency Manager, *mobile 13908918808). E-mail: stsad@public.ls.xz.cn.* This agency offers custommade itineraries for small groups and expects to have a trekking department. It gave this book a lot of help.

• **Tibet CITS, CTS, and Tibet Tourism Corporation**, *208 Beijing Xi Road, 850001, Tel. and Fax 6343854, Tel. 6349239, 6331327 (res.), Fax 6321845.* Mobile for Lhakpa Tsering, Sales Manager, who helped this book a lot, *Tel. 13908913347. E-mail: ttccits@public.ls.xz.cn or ttbfit@fm.365.com.* Contact also Rinzin or Samdup. CITS charges individual travelers Y200 a day for a guide. *Tel. 6836626/6835046, Fax 6835277.* For the CITS office near the Lhasa Hotel, *Tel 6836626 or 6835046, Fax 891-6835277.*

• **Tibet International Travel Service**, *Lhasa Hotel, One Minzu Road, 850001. Tel. 6824305, Fax 6834957. E-mail: thits@public.ls.xz.cn.* Ask for Mr. Yugyal Wangchuk who suggests Eastern Tibet for travelers who have already seen Shigatse and Gyantse; i.e. Basum Tso Lake and Mountain, Ba Yi, Nangxian, and Tsedang, a seven day trip from Lhasa. It charges Y200 for an English-speaking guide for a group. Cash and bank transfer only.

• **Tibet Mountaineering Association,** *No.10 East Linkhor Road, Lhasa, Tel. 333720.* Travel agents can reach them.

- **Tibet Yak International Travel Service** (no connection with the Yak Hotel), *41-3 Beijing Zhong Road, 8500000. Tel. 6871061, 6871062, Mobile: 13908918464, Fax 6871060. Website: www.tibetwin.com.cn (Chinese only). E-mail: yak@public.ls.xz.cn.* Ask for Ms. Cui Xiaoyan, general manager, who speaks English and helped this book a lot. Address also: B-21, The National City of Zhonghe, Lhasa, *Tel. 6871061,6871062, Fax 6871060.* Yak International says you can ride yaks on its Kailash-Guge treks. It has one toilet tent 1.5 m. tall. It has one chemical toilet and will be buying another. It has no shower tent and trekkers wash in rivers. Its guides speak English. If the tour is from Kathmandu, Sherpas will cook and you'll get better service and food. Camp food and water are cheaper in Nepal than in Tibet.

- **Tsedang China International Travel Service** and **China Travel Service**, *1 Minzu Road, 850000, Tel. 6829364, 6834324, Fax 6832603, 6832346. E-mail: tsedang@public.ls.xz.cn or phubu@public.ls.xz.cn.* See also Tsedang. Ask for Tsering Nima, Sales and Marketing Manager, who helped this book a lot. For information and bookings in Shannon or Tsedang. Chinese treks are cheaper with simple facilities, he says. If the group starts from Nepal, then they can take a Nepalese cook. If the group starts from Lhasa, then they have to buy supplies in Lhasa and take a Tibetan cook.

- **Travel Agents in Nepal for Tibet: Royal Mountain Trekking** is at: *P.O. Box 10798, Durbar Marg, Kathmandu, Tel. 977-1-241452 or 258236, Fax 245318. E-mail: Royalmt@mos.com.np or Website: www.royal-mt-trek.com.* For Tibet visit www.royaltibet.com. E-mail Sandra Korver directly for information. This company also has mini-tours to Lhasa from Kathmandu which are cheaper than any others I've seen. You pay for a bed in a dorm but you can upgrade on your own to anything else.

- **Dharma Adventures, Shiva Kailash Tours**, *Gairidhara, GPO Box 5385, Kathmandu, Tel. 977-1-430499, Fax 421053. E-mail: info@shivatours.com. Website: www.shivatours.com.* Every trip over 3500 meters has a pressure bag and oxygen. All water is filtered and boiled. Its camp beds have foam pads. It travels with a shower tent, biodegradable chemical toilets, and tents you can stand in. Its guides speak Tibetan and English. Ask for Pawan Tuladhar.

- **Travel Agents in North America or Europe for Tibet:** An American, Steve Powers of **Hidden Treasure Tours** organizes Tibet trips led by local staff and Nepal-based Western guides. Steve helped this book a lot. For his address, see Chapter 6.

Websites: for more details and updates, see my website: *www.china-travel-guide.com*
Telephone code: 891

Chapter 20

Changsha

Located south of the Yangtze River, **Changsha** is the capital of Hunan province. It is partly famous because Chairman Mao was born in nearby Shaoshan. He studied for about five years at the First Hunan Normal School (1912-18) in Changsha. Yale University started a mission here about 1904 and eventually established a medical school, hospital, and middle school. The Americans left shortly after 1949.

Changsha is also known for its important 2100-year-old Han excavation. Its embroidery is one of the four most famous in China. It is also the gateway to Zhangjiajie, a UNESCO World Heritage site.

Changsha, in one of China's main rice-growing areas, was a small town 3,000 years ago. It became a city 2000 years ago and is one of the 24 historical and cultural cities protected by the State Council. It was almost completely destroyed during the Japanese War. The coldest temperature is about -8°C in January; the hottest about 30°C in July. The rainfall is from 1250 to 1750 mm, mostly April to June. The population is about five million, with 1.5 million in the city proper.

Arrivals & Departures

The city is a 95-minute flight southwest of Shanghai, one hour northeast of Guilin, and 100 minutes south of Beijing. It has direct flights with Hong Kong, and 38 other cities. It is on the main Beijing-Guangzhou railway line and on National Road 107 from Guangzhou to Beijing, about 894 km by road from Guangzhou.

Orientation

The novel and movie The Sand Pebbles was set partly in Changsha during the Northern Expedition in the late 1920s. The hero was an engineer on an American gun boat, which sailed up the Yangtze through Lake Dongting and along the Xiang River. Changsha is also the setting of a more recent book, Liang Heng and Judith Shapiro's autobiographical *Son of the Revolution*, a refreshing look at growing up in Communist China, and beating the system. The excellent but sad novel *A Small Town Called Hibiscus* is set in the southern part of this province during the Cultural Revolution.

In addition to Han, Hunan province has many national minorities, including Tujia, Miao, Dong, Yao, Hui, Uygur and Zhuang.

Downtown Changsha, with its hotels, lies mainly on the east bank of the Xiang River. Three bridges link its downtown area with the suburban Mt. Yuelu, its universities, and a couple of tourist attractions like the Yuelu Academy of Classical Learning, which was established in 976 A.D. and now offers a concert of chime bells. This is near the south gate of Mount Yuelu and Hunan University. Nearby is a museum with ancient tomb figures. Nearby also is the Aiwan pavilion (Y18) which was first built in 1792, and the 1700-year-old Lu Shan Temple. These have a few descriptions in English and are worth the time if you have nothing else to do. See below for tourist buses.

Where to Stay & Eat

The best for English-speakers is the Dolton and the Huatian, both downtown. The Huatian opened its new extension too late to be reviewed but it sounds good. A good four- star is the Gold Source. The Holiday Inn Donghan is expected to open late in 2002.

Hotels here add 10% or 15% service charge. All take credit cards, change money, and offer majiang (mah jong) rooms. All have mini-bars and business centers with internet services.

Hunan food is spicy, hot, and salty. Aim for the hotels.

DOLTON HOTEL (Tong Cheng Dajiudian), *149 Shaoshan Bei Road, 410011, Tel. 4168888, Fax 4169999. E-mail: dolton@doltonhotel.com. Website: www.dolton-hotel.com. Rooms are 29 to 38 square meters. Y918-Y1118 for rooms, and Y1380-Y26888 for suites and it has been giving 35% discounts. It is 300 meters from the Apollo and Friendship Stores, and next to a small square with neighborhood dances.*

This 51-story, 1998 hotel has fancy name-brand stores, and 450 rooms and duplex suites. Rooms are 30 to 41 square meters with HBO, CNN, and in-room safes. Desks are 43 inches wide. Its business center subscribes to the SCMP and Time. Its breakfast buffet costs about Y78. There's a 24-hour Food Street and its ballroom can seat 960 banquet-style. It has a 30-meter long pool, billiards, and bowling.

HUATIAN HOTEL (Dajiudian), *380 Jiefang Dong Road, 410001, Tel. 4442888, Fax 4442270. Five stars.Website: www.reservation@huatian-hotel.com. $88-$158 for rooms, and $188-$2380 for suites. It is 23 km from the airport and 1.5 km from the railway station.*

Built in 1990, this 17-story, 288-room hotel has an eight-story recreation building, executive floor, Chaozhou and Thai food. It also has a pool, bowling, gym and disco.

GOLD SOURCE HOTEL, *465-457 Fu Rong Road, 410007. Tel. 5558888, Fax 5164677. E-mail: gsbusn@public.cs.hn.cn. Four stars. Rooms are Y688-Y1018, and suites Y1380-Y3888. It has been giving a 45% discount.*

This good-looking 341-room hotel has a white marble lobby with a gilded picture of children at a money tree. English is poor here. Rooms are 28 square meters with a large safe. Hall carpets were dirty but some floors should be renovated by now. It has a non-smoking floor. Some rooms have three beds and no carpet. It has a pool with limited hours and a small gym.

XIANG JIANG HOTEL (Binguan), *36 Zhongshan Road, 410005. Three stars. Tel. 64974451, 64974452, Fax 64974872. E-mail: csxjhtl1@public.cs.hn.cn and roger@21cn.com. Website: www.cbw.com/ hotel/xiangjiang / (English). Rooms cost Y288 to Y320, (discounted about 15%). Its suites are Y580 to Y1880.*

This 289-room hotel will respond to e-mail requests.

Seeing the Sights

If you only have one day, the Hunan Provincial Museum, the embroidery factory, the Yue Lu Academy, and a walk on Orange Island are good choices. Tourist bus Number One goes from the railway station to the Provincial Museum, Changsha Museum, and finally to the Yuelu Academy. It costs Y3, and you can get off and on with the same ticket twice. It operates from 7am to 7pm. Other routes are being added.

The **Hunan Provincial Museum (Hunan Bo Guan)**, 28 Dongfeng Road, *Tel. 4514630*, open 8am-12 noon and 2:30pm-5:30pm. Hours are longer in summer and weekends. Y25. This is the main tourist attraction. Skip everything else if you are short on time. You must see the relics from these three 2,100-year-old Han tombs because of their excellent state of preservation and vast numbers. It takes about one hour.

The three tombs were of Li Tsang, chancellor to the Prince of Changsha and Marquis of Dai, his wife, and his son. The son died in 168 B.C. The body of the woman, 1.52 meters long and weighing 34.3 kilograms, is incredibly well preserved, with flesh, 16 teeth, and internal organs. The lungs, intestines, and stomach were removed and preserved in formaldehyde. They are all on display in the basement. An autopsy revealed arteriosclerosis, gallstones, tuberculosis, and parasites. Death came to her suddenly at age 50; there were undigested melon seeds in her stomach. The body was wrapped in hemp and nine silk ribbons, and sealed from oxygen and water in three coffins surrounded by 5,000 kilograms of charcoal and sticky white clay. She died after her husband and her tomb is the largest.

The 5,000 relics include 1,800 pieces of lacquerware, many of which needed only cleaning to appear new. Look for the ear cups for wine and soup, and a make-up box with comb, mirror, powder, and lipstick. For her after-death use, she also had incense burners, clothes, silk fabrics, medicinal herbs, and nine musical instruments. Maybe she did play them! An inventory of the relics was written on bamboo strips, paper still being rare then.

The Han tomb site, only four km away in Mawangdui, is now just a large hole in the ground under a roof. Geomancy students can figure out the feng shui. Did the tomb face south?

The **Hunan Art Gallery** is in the same compound as the museum.

The **Hunan Provincial Research Institute**, 70 Bayi Xi Road, *Tel. 2291061, 2291952* is open 8:30am-12 and 2:30pm-5pm. It is a worthwhile visit if you're interested in embroidery. You can see this ancient craft being practiced and be amazed at the number of workers not wearing eyeglasses. Look for embroidery so fine it can be displayed from either side. Admission has been free.

At five km long, **Juzi (Orange) Island** is in the middle of the Xiang River, the "long sand" after which Changsha is named. It is just a pretty walk among fruit trees.

The **First Hunan Normal School**, Shuyuan Road, outside the south gate of the city, has a small museum. Mao studied and taught here in 1913-18 and 1920-21. The current structure, built in 1968, is a copy of the 1912 school and reflects its European connections.

The **Changsha Museum (Changsha Bo Wu Guan)**, 81 Bayi Road, *Tel. 2257307*. Open 9am to 5:30pm. Most important are the 1700-year-old bamboo slips or records of taxation, census registration, and economic and military affairs of the State of Wu. They were found in 1996 and are of great historical importance. There are also Western Zhou bronzes, the earliest musical instrument, and Tang ceramics from Changsha's famous kilns.

Nightlife & Entertainment

Local **Huagu opera** originated from provincial folk songs and ditties. The **Hunan Provincial Puppet Show Troupe** is well known. Performances can be arranged through travel agents if booked in advance. **Windows of the World Theme Park** has international song and dance performances at 7pm. It's at Liuyang River Dong Bridge, *Tel. 4256737, 4256763*.

Shopping

Made in the province are embroideries, brocade, batik, porcelain and pottery, peach stone and bamboo carvings, fans, firecrackers, lacquer reproductions, and chrysanthemum stone, smoky quartz and bloodstone carvings. There's also minority handicrafts and duck-down clothing. Look for these items at the **Friendship Store** and **Apollo Store**, on Shaoshan Road near the Hua Tian Hotel. **Qing Shui Tang Road** has lots of antique shops.

Excursions & Day Trips
ZHANGJIAJIE

Zhangjiajie is 385 km northwest of Changsha, nine hours by bus, about 12 hours by train leaving at 7:30am. There's also a 30-minute flight, three times a day in summer, once in winter. It has flight connections also with seven other cities.

This is a 369-square kilometer national forest, 35 km from Zhangjiajie in the western part of Hunan province. This well-maintained park has lots of guides and sedan chair porters eager to help you and it's full of beautiful hills, stone pillars, flowers, wild boar, monkeys, and leopards. Thirteen different ethnic groups live here including the Miao, Zhuang, and Tujia in Jishou City. There are karst caves in Longshan county and white-water rafting on the Mongdong River in Yongshun County. A Forest Protecting Festival takes place the end of October. Visitors can walk to their hearts content.

Recently, UNESCO has threatened to withdraw its heritage status because too many commercial buildings and over five million tourists a year are affecting the ecology. Restaurants, for example, have been dumping sewage into its streams.

The best hotels in the town are the four-star Dragon International and the 227-room Zhangjiajie International Hotel. The latter is new and travel agents charge $40 a day. The Pipaxi Guest House and the new three-star Wulingyuan Hotel ($30) are in the National Forest Park. Hotels add a 14% surcharge.

DRAGON INTERNATIONAL HOTEL (Xianglong Guoji Dajiudian), *46 Jiefang Road, Zhangjiajie, 416680. Four stars, Tel. 8226888 or Fax 8222935. Credit cards. Some travel agents charge $40 for a standard room.*

Built in 1994, this 260-room hotel is a 30-minute drive from the park, and six km from the airport.

PIPAXI GUEST HOUSE, *Zhang Jia Jie National Forest Park, 427401, Tel. 5718888, Fax 5712257. Three stars. Y200-Y480 for rooms, Y1280 for suites, plus 14% surcharge. It is 32 km. from the airport, and 35 km. from the railway station.*

Built in Tujia style, the 189-room Pipaxi was renovated in 1999. It has CNN and BBC, Y12 buffet breakfast, and takes credit cards. If you stay inside the park here, you only need to pay one entry fee.

Zhangjiajie China Comfort Travel has an office. *Tel. 8262222, 8263333, Fax 8267777, 8233333.* Contact Mr.He Binrui, *Tel. mobile 013807449255* or Ms Liu, *Tel. 13974487188. E-mail: khdb@mail.china.com.*

SHAOSHAN

Shaoshan is 100 km southwest of Changsha, a worthwhile 1.5 hour trip by road, 90 km by train. The countryside is lovely with tea plantations, orange groves and rice fields. This is the ***Birthplace of Chairman Mao**, a simple mud-brick farmhouse where the founder of the People's Republic was born on December 26, 1893.

He lived in this charming, and apparently peaceful village until 1910, when he left to study in Changsha. He returned briefly several times, holding meetings and conducting revolutionary activities. The Nationalists confiscated and destroyed the original house in 1929, but after 1949, the Communists rebuilt it along the original lines. Two families shared the house, the section on the left as you enter being Mao's. It is very sparsely furnished. The dining room still has the original small table, typical even for large families. The master bedroom has portraits of the parents and the bed in which he was born. Another room holds original farm tools.

The museum, with ten large galleries, is a ten-minute walk from the farmhouse. It is full of exhibits depicting his life. Also open is the Water-Dropping Cave where Mao Zedong stayed hidden for 11 days in 1966 and planned the Cultural Revolution. It is three km from Shaoshan. You can also visit the family temple and eat at the three-star Telecom Bureau Hotel (Dian Li Binguan).

YUEYANG

Yueyang, 2,000 years old, is on the north shore of Lake Dongting, just south of the Yangtze River, and is sometimes a stop on a Yangtze River cruise. It is 160 km north of Changsha and is close to the mother of all dragon boat races. The 19-meter-high Yueyang Tower was first built in 716 A.D. to train the navy. It was rebuilt in 1867 in the original Tang style. One of the eight Taoist genii, Lu Tung-pin with the supernatural sword, is credited with saving the tower from collapsing.

You can also visit **Junshan Island,** which grows Junshan Silver Needles tea and a tree with red leaves on one side and green on the other. It is a bird watcher's paradise. Try to imagine the Song dynasty when 10,000 troops were stationed here.

As for the **dragon boats**, in 278 B.C. in the nearby Miluo River, Qu Yuan, the great patriotic poet, drowned himself in protest against the destruction of the State of Chu by the first emperor of China. Ever since, this tragic event has been commemorated with races, usually held in June to feed the fish before the fish can feed on Qu Yuan! The races are on Nan Lake north east of Yueyang. Travel agents can arrange the best place to watch, which is the east watchtower.

The best hotel in town is the three-star **China Bank Hotel** (Zhong Yin Dajiudian), 1 Front Road at the train station, Yueyang, *Tel. 8270666, Fax*

8270111, 8262119. Y348. For **CITS***, Tel. 8265298, Fax 8275125.* The telephone code is 730.

Practical Information

Changsha China International Travel Service, *38 Zhanlanguan Road, Changsha, 410005, Tel. 4434935, Fax 4441275. E-mail: hntravel@public.cs.hn.cn.*

Hunan China International Travel Service and Overseas Tourist Corporation, *11/F Xiaoyuan Mansion, Wuyi Dong Road, 410001. E-mail: citsgaow@public.cs.hn.cn.* For the Euro-American Department, *Tel. 2280439, Fax 2280455. E-mail: citsamer@public.cs.hn.cn. Website: www.hncits.com (English).* It can arrange white-water rafting, trips in Japanese jeeps, and wild pig hunting. It has a tour for Buddhist pilgrims and is a member of China International Travel Service Group.

Telephone Code: 731

Nanning

The capital of Guangxi Zhuang Autonomous Region, **Nanning**, is in the southwestern part of Guangxi near the northeastern border of Vietnam. It has a subtropical climate, resulting in great fruit, flowering trees, and mild, humid weather. Its hottest is 38°C; its coldest is 5°C. The annual precipitation of about 1300 mm falls mainly May to September. Nanning is worth visiting because of its minorities, its karst caves, medicinal herb garden, and its location as a gateway to Vietnam.

Founded in 214 B.C., Nanning was the provincial capital from 1912 to 1936, and after 1949. It has light industries like pearl farming, arts and crafts, sugar refining, soft drinks, beer and food processing. The population is now 1.2 million urban, and three million rural.

This capital of Guangxi province is booming and modern. At the same time, it has an interesting anachronistic feature in the official writing used for the Zhuang majority. In 1958, the government invited some Russians to create an alphabet for the Zhuang people, who up to then had no written language. You can see it still only on government buildings, but "Guangxi", the region, is spelled "CVANGJSIH" and "Minzu" (nationalities) is spelled "MINCZU." Ah, those Russians!

Arrivals & Departures

You can reach Nanning from Guilin in four or five hours by bus but it takes about seven hours by train. Guangxi CTS in Nanning says the fastest train to Kunming is No. 2005 departing at 15:43, and arriving in Kunming at 08:01 next morning. Currently the once-a-day long distance bus takes 12 hours. You can also get to Nanning by air from 27 cities, Bangkok, Hanoi and Hong Kong.

It is about a 33-km, 40-minute drive now from the airport, but it should be about 20 minutes soon with the opening of the new expressway.

Where to Stay

The top hotels are the Mingyuan and Nanning International Hotel, but the latter is far from the city. A new five-star, the Jin Hua Hotel (Dajiudian) should open soon. Hotels add an 11% surcharge.

MINGYUAN XINDU HOTEL (Da Fandian), *38 Xin Min Road, 530012. Five stars with a four-star section. Tel. 2118988, Fax 2830811. It is 1.8 km from the railway station, 35 km from the airport, and in Nanning's commercial district. Rooms are Y858-Y968 and suites Y1858-Y11880. It has been giving 20% discounts including breakfast.*

Built in 1995, this 298-room hotel has in-room safes, lots of closet space, in-house movies, and CNN. It has executive floors, non-smoking floor, and a deli. It serves Cantonese, Asian and American food, and has a fun, point-to-order food street outside its front door. There's a gym, outdoor pool, jacuzzi, and tennis. Its four-star section was renovated in 2000.

NANNING INTERNATIONAL HOTEL (Guoji Dajiudian), *88 Minzu Dong Avenue, 530022. Five stars. Tel. 5851818, Fax 5886789. E-mail: nnihps@public.nn.gx.cn. Website: www.gxnnih.com (English). Rooms cost Y768-Y968; suites cost Y1388-Y13888. It has been giving a 20% discount. It's near the Guangxi Customs Building and South Lake, the closest hotel to the airport. It is five km from the railway station, five km from a bus station, and one km from bars, shopping and banking.*

This 318-room hotel has CNN and pay TV, but no pool and no in-room safes. It does have two lighted tennis courts, Food Street, and sauna. It has an executive floor.

YONGJIANG HOTEL (Binguan), *41 Jiangbin Dong Road, 530012. Four stars. Tel. 2808123, Fax 2800535. E-mail: yihng@public.nn.gx.cn. Its spacious rooms are Y480-Y780, and Y1880-Y8880 for suites. It has been giving 40% discounts.*

Where to Eat

The food here is much like Cantonese. Please avoid eating endangered species. The **Sun City Restaurant** in the Yongjiang Hotel above is good. It's at 41 Jiangbin Dong Road, *Tel. 2808123 ext. 5085.*

Cantonese food at the **Yu Xiang Ge Restaurant**, on the 11th floor of the three-star Jin Yue Hotel, was delicious and reasonably priced, *Tel. 2802338.* It's at 59 Xin Min Road. Otherwise, the restaurants in the top hotels are where you should eat. **McDonald's** is at 39 Chaoyang Road (first floor of the Nanning Department Store), *Tel. 2810908, Fax 2820141.*

Seeing the Sights

Twelve different nationalities live in the region, of whom the Zhuang form over one-third. They are related to the hill tribes of northern Thailand. The colorful Miao and Yao live here also. This makes Nanning a good place to look for handicrafts to study and buy.

The **Guangxi Provincial Museum**, 27 Minzu Road, *Tel. 2806602* has botanical and zoological specimens, historical relics, and Taiping history. It also boasts the largest collection of bronze drums (over 500) in China. It is open Tuesday to Friday, 9am to 12 noon, and 3pm to 6pm. On weekends it's 9am to 4pm and it's closed on Monday. On the same grounds as the museum is the Ethnic Garden, with typical minority houses, and an 1883 German cannon used against the French.

The **Guangxi Botanical Garden of Medicinal Plants**, eight km from the city in the eastern suburbs, has 2100 kinds on 200 hectares. It also raises animals for medicinal purposes.

Yiling Cave, the largest cave in Guangxi is 16 km from Nanning. It is in the Wuming Yilingyan Sightseeing District, 530103, *Tel. 771/6020420*. It is open 8am-5pm with a Y6 entrance fee to the park; and an additional Y15 for the cave. Visitors walk 1.1km and climb lots of stairs. On Saturday and Sunday, about 11am, its mainly Zhuang ethnic folk dances include invitations to the audience to join in the bamboo dance, and a wedding ceremony. The antics of wild monkeys rival the dancers for your attention. There's a basic but decent restaurant.

Shopping

Locally made are Zhuang brocade, ethnic embroidery, bamboo, and pottery ware. The province also sells its artistic shell, horn, and feather products, and stone carvings, Xishan tea and Milky Spring Wine. You can visit the silk factory. Locally grown are jack fruit, mangos, almonds, and longan fruit.

Excursions & Day Trips

The most important tourist destination is of course Guilin (see separate entry below), but there's also Beihai for its beach.

BEIHAI

Beihai is Guangxi's sea port. A tourist train connects it with Guilin, Nanning and Liuzhou but by bus it is only five hours from Guilin and over three hours from Nanning. It has a splendid ten km beach and clean air. It grows pearls and seafood. There are connections by sea with Vietnam, but bus via Dongxing by land is more reliable though roads in Vietnam are bad. Daewoo buses take 2.5 hours to the border. In Vietnam, it's a total of about 10 hours from Beihai to Halong Bay.

Hotels here add 10-15% to hotel prices including food. The Shangri-la and Furama Hotels are side-by-side, the five-star Shangri-la much better than the three-star Furama. They are both about one kilometer from the bus station, 24 km from the airport, 3.8 km from the railway station, and only a 20-minute taxi ride to Silver Beach. Both have waterfronts but you definitely shouldn't swim there. CITS in Nanning recommends the Jiatianxia International Hotel.

SHANGRI-LA HOTEL, *33 Chating Road, 536007. Five stars. Tel. 2062288, Fax 2050085. E-mail: sbhi@shangri-la.com. Website: www.Shangri-la.com. $100-$160 for rooms, and $500-$1600 for suites. It has been discounting 30-45%. It is 20 km from the airport, nine km from the railway station and 12 km from Silver Beach, the main tourist attraction.*

This classy, 1996 hotel is the best in town. It has 364 rooms, an outdoor pool, two lighted tennis courts, gym and sauna, HBO and ESPN. Its ballroom can accommodate up to 1800 guests theater style. Computer ports and in-room safes are only in its executive floor and suites.

FURAMA (Fuli Hua), *31 Beibu Gulf Chating Road, 536007. Three stars. Tel. 2055588, 2050088, Fax 2051210. Y680-Y720 for rooms and Y1445-Y10880 for suites. It has been giving 20-40% discounts.*

This 318-room hotel has a better, newer eight-story 1993 building. It has e-mail service for Y20 an hour and a problem with English. It is clean but needs refurbishing. It has no in-room safes.

Going to Vietnam

You need a valid **Vietnam visa**, available in China only in Guangzhou and Beijing. Travel agents here can get one for you in 10 days. You can fly from Nanning to Hanoi any Monday or Thursday (40 minutes for about Y860). The fastest train leaving from Nanning to Hanoi has been No. T905 (departing from Nanning at 7:20pm, and arriving in Hanoi about 9:01am Vietnamese time next morning). There are two stops at the borders that take about three hours. The train only operates on Tuesday and Saturday but check all these times with a travel agent.

An overnight boat cruises from Beihai in China and arrives next day in Haiphong in Vietnam, but is not recommended.

Air-conditioned buses go from Nanning to Dongxing on the Vietnamese coastal border almost hourly from the General Bus Station and No. 2 Bus Station. CTS can arrange a car to meet travelers and take them from the border to Halong Bay (five hours) and on to Hanoi in another three. The Vietnamese portion costs about Y950.

An expressway between Nanning and Pingxiang is being planned. And there's talk of a Guilin-Haiphong-Ho Chi Minh City route in two or three years.

Beihai China Travel Service, *2/F, Huangdu Hotel, Guizhou Road, 536000, Tel. 3033935, Fax 3035256. E-mail: bhctsnet@ppp.nn.gx.cn and sharonxi@21cn.com. Website: www.bhtour.com*
Beihai China International Travel Service, *6 East Beibu Gulf Road, 536000, Fax 2062525. Mobile: Deputy G.M. Li Hao Cheng, Tel. 1397790806. E-mail: bh-cits@ppp.nn.gx.cn.*
The **telephone code** is 779.

Practical Information

Business hours: offices 8am-12 noon, 2:30pm-5:30pm; stores, 9am-10pm
Internet Service, *third floor of the Hua Mei Building, 44 Xing Ming Road, Tel. 2627730.* This is to the right less than a block outside the side gate of the Majestic Hotel. It is open 8:30am to 4am and charges Y10 an hour.
Nanning Municipal Tourism Bureau, *No. 1 Jiabin Road, Tel. 5530413, Fax 5530492. E-mail: nntb@public.nn.gx.cn. Web: www.nn-tourism.gov.cn .* Ask for Mrs.Maixu. For complaints and a list of interesting tour possibilities including forest preserves, Zhuang traditional medicine, hot sand treatment, and dates of festivals.
Travel Agents:
• **China Youth Travel Service**, *No.6—1 Gu Cheng Road, Tel 5853657, 5851920, Fax 5860175.*
• **Guangxi China International Travel Service,** *40 Xinmin Street, 530012. Tel. 2804960, Fax 2806025. E-mail: citsgx@public.nn.gx.com* and Zhou Run Ling promises to answer within 24 hours. Ms. Tan Hong should be able to help individual travelers go to Vietnam. CITS charges $66 for a room at the Mingyuan Hotel, including surcharge but no breakfast, plus a $3 booking charge.
• **Guangxi China Travel Service,** *10/F, Diamond Plaza (across from the Nanning Department Store), 66 Chaoyang Road, 530012. Tel. 2616008, Fax 2619975. E-mail: ctsguangxi@163.com with a copy to rogerlin@263.net.* Ask for Roger Lin (Dongqing), Manager International Tour Center. CTS charges Y680 for a room at the Mingyuan with breakfast. It can get a Vietnam visa in 10 days. It promises to answer within 48 hours.
• **Nanning OTC,** 4 Minzu, Tel. 2624854, 2837509, Fax 2837509.
• **Telephone Code**: 771

Guilin

(Kweilin: City of Cassia Trees)
In northeast Guangxi, west of Guangdong, **Guilin** was founded as a prefecture in 214 B.C. It is famous for its vertical limestone mountains rising

above flat tree-lined streets, rice and water chestnut fields, and the meandering Li and Taohua (Peach Blossom) Rivers. It is also known for its caves. The Li River cruise is the main reason tourists flock here.

Guilin developed with the opening of the Ling Canal over 2200 years ago. It was the provincial capital until 1014 A.D., and a command post for the Northern Expedition in 1928. The Japanese war destroyed much of the city during which the Seven Star Cave alone sheltered 5,000 refugees from bombs.

The weather is subtropical, the hottest a rare 36°C in August; the coldest -3°C. The rainy season is February to May, the annual precipitation 1900 mm. The best time to visit is October through December (but not Christmas or the October 1 holiday) or late spring, when it is warm enough to ignore the rain.

The mountains are best seen in the mist, an inspiration to centuries of landscape painters. From November until the February rains, the water in the river may be low. It has been recently dredged, and with a reservoir controlling the flow, boats should be able to use it year-round.

Arrivals & Departures

Guilin is a 55-minute flight northwest of Guangzhou with air links with 34 other cities, and direct flights with Fukuoka, Hong Kong, Macau, and Seoul. Travel agents can tell you about regular charter flights from Bangkok and discount flights. Prices have been Guilin to Beijing Y1580, Shanghai Y1190, Guangzhou Y610, Huangshan Y760, Xi'an Y990, and Chongqing Y660.

The fastest train from Beijing takes 24 hours, from Shanghai 25 hours, from Nanjing 28 hours, and from Guangzhou 13.5 hours. Guilin has two railway stations. Guilin OTC below says No. 182/181 Kunming-Shanghai trains stop only at North Railway Station. No. 152/151 or 155/156 Kunming-Fuzhou trains stop only at the south or Guilin Railway Station. All other trains stop at both and most tourists should get off at Guilin South.

Guilin has bus connections with Wuzhou (the port for the boat from Guangzhou and Hong Kong). Liuzhou is one hour away by express bus. The Liangjiang airport is 40 km from the city and a taxi could cost about Y120. From here south, buses are faster than trains.

Warning from OTC: Unlike most other airports in China, Guilin airport has been strict about overweight luggage, even for one kilo excess.

Orientation

Guilin is a small and beautiful city with a relaxing pace, clean air, and fun tourist shopping. The land here is generally flat so bicycling and walking are great in between the peaks. There are other things to do too.

Guilin has a total population of 4,750,000 of whom only about 580,000 live in the city proper. It doesn't feel big because the main tourist sites, the hotels, restaurants, shopping, Li River, and downtown mountains are rela-

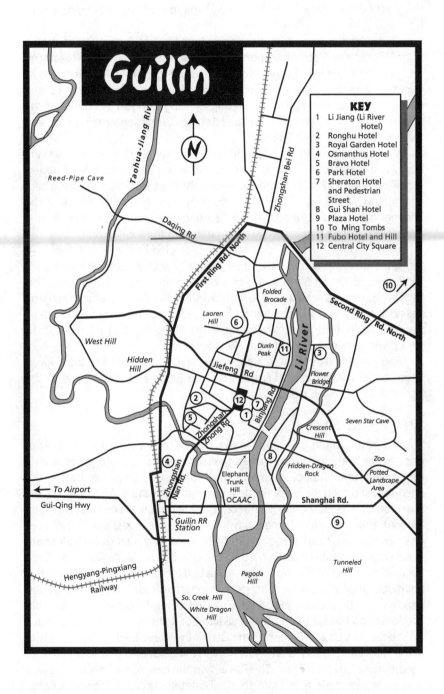

Guilin

N

KEY

1. Li Jiang (Li River Hotel)
2. Ronghu Hotel
3. Royal Garden Hotel
4. Osmanthus Hotel
5. Bravo Hotel
6. Park Hotel
7. Sheraton Hotel and Pedestrian Street
8. Gui Shan Hotel
9. Plaza Hotel
10. To Ming Tombs
11. Fubo Hotel and Hill
12. Central City Square

Taohua-Jiang Riv

Reed-Pipe Cave

Zhongshan Bei Rd

Daqing Rd

First Ring Rd North

Folded Brocade

Laoren Hill

West Hill

Hidden Hill

Duxin Peak

Jiefeng Rd

Li River

Second Ring Rd. North

Flower Bridge

Seven Star Cave

Zhongshan Zhong Rd

Binjiang Rd

Crescent Hill

Zoo

Potted Landscape Area

Zhongshan Nan Rd.

Elephant Trunk Hill

OCAAC

Hidden-Dragon Rock

To Airport

Gui-Qing Hwy

Shanghai Rd.

Guilin RR Station

Hengyang-Pingxiang Railway

So. Creek Hill

White Dragon Hill

Pagoda Hill

Tunneled Hill

tively close to each other. You don't need to pay more than Y10 to most places by taxi.

Guilin used to be a quiet, sleepy city. In the last few years, it has started to get livelier with better transportation, more restaurants, better roads and bridges. The standard of English in the hotels is higher than in other cities its size. You can spend a week here poking into alleys, climbing rice terraces, and hiking in the countryside. From even quieter Yangshuo you can canoe on the Li River, walk, and bicycle. You can take day trips to investigate minorities, and the rice terraces in Long Sheng.

While many tourists see the sights in Guilin in a fairly hectic two days, the city is wonderful for the resourceful individual traveler, a favorite of honeymooners. Best of all, prices here are among the cheapest in China. Living here is tempting. One-third of the 10 million people living in Guangxi are of the Zhuang nationality, Guangxi is an "autonomous region" rather than a "province." National guides may not understand the local dialect.

Guilin is one of the 24 historical cities protected by the State Council. At the same time, it has recently made a big city square, and widened eight kilometers of Zhong Shan Road, one of its main commercial streets. This Central Square extends a couple of blocks behind the Sheraton Hotel and beside the Lijiang Hotel to Zhong Shan Road. Under the square is a mall, appropriately called Xiao Xianggang (Little Hong Kong) Mall. Pedestrian streets are beside and behind the Sheraton.

The five old lakes of the city are being cleaned and joined to the Li River. Soon, boats will be able to cruise from the Bravo and Park Hotels to the Sheraton and Li Jiang Hotels.

Where to Stay

The best location for tourists in Guilin is still the west bank of the Li River close to the evening tourist market, the night cormorant tour, good restaurants, pedestrian shopping streets, and the new square. The best is the Sheraton, and then the Royal Garden, both rated five stars. After that, it's the four-star Bravo even though it's not on the river but on a lake. Next would be the Park now that city planners have made it more accessible. If these are unattainable, the next choice would be the relatively new Golden Elephant Hotel with its genuine Korean food and riverside location. A quick look there however revealed next to no English and a bad attitude at the reception desk, not much different from the Universal. The staff attitude is better at the Fubo which is right beside lovely Fubo Hill. The Guishan Hotel is architecturally cold and looks too much like an office building but it should be otherwise okay.

So far, service and English at the Osmanthus have been better than that of the Plaza which is too far away from everything but the huge new Jiatianxia Square, now Guilin's largest. The Plaza is on the east side of the Li River and is now across the street from the Guilin International Exhibition Centre.

Backpackers with a Chinese phrase book should consider the International Youth Hostel near the Sheraton, a first-rate location. The **Lijiang Hotel** is being rebuilt and upgraded, its future quality unknown, but its location is ideal at 1 Shanhu Bei Road, 541001. It is expected to be reopened in late 2002 with four- and five-star wings. English could be a stressful problem at all but the top hotels.

Hotels add a 15%-18% surcharge. You might be able to book these hotels for even better discounts through Chinese travel agents. Most of the Guilin hotels here have money exchange, business centers, Western coffee shops, and gyms. All are air-conditioned. Most of these hotels take credit cards and are listed in order of most expensive to cheapest. The hostels and the Yangshuo hotels have fewer services. The airport is about 35 to 40 km from the hotels.

SHERATON GUILIN (Da Yu Da Fandian), *Bing Jiang Nan Road, 541001. Five stars. Tel. 2825588, Fax 2825598. E-mail: shr483@public.glptt.gx.cn. Website: www.sheraton.com/guilin (English). $140-$190 for rooms, $270-$480 for suites. It is five km from the railway station and 30 km from the airport.*

This 1988 hotel has six stories and 430 large rooms, some non-smoking. It has CNN, 24-hour room service, and four restaurants with international, local, Cantonese and Sichuan food. To keep you in good shape, it has a 20-metre outdoor pool, sauna, 14-piece gym, and bicycles for hire. Its beautiful atrium lobby has a pianist playing mornings and evenings. It has a China Southwest and Zhong Xing Airline offices, sightseeing and golf packages.

GUILIN ROYAL GARDEN HOTEL (Di Yuan Jiudian), *Yanjiang Road, 541004. Five stars. Tel. 5812411, 5813611, Fax 5815051. E-mail: dyxsb@public.glptt.gx.cx. Website: www.c-b-w.com/hotel/royalgarden. It is three km from the railway station. $110-$120 for rooms; $230-$1500 for suites. It has been giving 20% discounts but check its website.*

Built in 1987, this beautiful hotel has eight stories, 335 spacious rooms with safes, wide beds, but smallish bathrooms. It has good furniture and decor but rooms could be a long walk from its elevators. There's CNN, Australian TV and Star TV. It has a huge atrium garden coffee shop, Japanese and continental restaurants, and 24-hour room service. There's also a clinic, small outdoor pool and tennis, and it has mountain bikes for rent.

GUILIN BRAVO HOTEL (Jia Ru Binguan), *14 Ronghu Nan Road, 541002. Four stars, Tel. 2823950, Fax 2822101. E-mail: glhi@public.glptt.gx.cn. Website: www.placestostay.com (English) or: www.glbravohtl.com (English). $110-$120 for rooms, $230 for suites. It is 3.5 km to the railway station.*

Built in 1987, this nine-story, 268-room hotel has a nice intimate atmosphere, and in-room safes. It has Cantonese, Sichuan, Japanese and Asian food, satellite television, health club and bicycles. There's a six-piece gym, steambath and outdoor pool. It should have a new tennis court soon.

GUI SHAN HOTEL (Guishan Dajiudian), *Chuan Shan Road, 541004. Four stars. Tel. 5813388, Fax 5813856, 5814851. E-mail: guishan@public.glptt.gx.cn or sales@public.glptt.gx.cn. Website: www.guishanhotel.com. Rooms are $90-$250 and it's been discounting 20%. Suburban setting between two rivers near Seven Star Park.*

This hotel was built in 1988, and renovated in 2001. It has five stories, four connecting buildings, and it could be a long walk to your room. Its 607 rooms include some for non-smokers and some designed for Muslims. It has Western, Cantonese and Muslim restaurants, and a good room service menu. There's an outdoor pool, gym, steam room, jacuzzi and bowling. It also has bicycles to rent, CNN and Star Plus, and lots of shops.

GUILIN PARK HOTEL (Gui Hu Fandian), *1, Luosi Hill, Laoren Shan Qian, 541001. Four stars. Tel. 2828899, Fax 2822296. E-mail: glpark@public.glptt.gx.cn. Rooms are $90-$100 and suites $180-$300. It has been giving 20% discounts to individuals if rooms are available and booked a month in advance. It is close to the Princely Mansion, is now ten minutes walk to the main square, and 5.5 km from the railway station.*

This 1990 hotel has five stories, 268 rooms, non-smoking rooms, CNN, Cantonese and Zhejiang food. It was renovated in 2000. The breakfast buffet costs Y60. It has a steam bath and sauna, and outdoor pool. Its gym is small and poor but its e-mail is only Y20 an hour and some rooms have safes. It is a bit run down. Managed by Merit International Hotels. It has a very pretty suburban setting in the northwest of town next to the Laoren Hill and thought to have good feng-shui.

FUBO HOTEL (Fubo Shan Dajiudian), *121 Binjiang Road, 541001. Three stars applying for four. Tel. 2829988, Fax 2822328. E-mail: fubo@public.glptt.gx.cn. Website: www.fubohotel.yahtour.com. $80-$90 for rooms and $120-$150 for suites. It has been discounting 20 to 50%. It is next to Fubo Hill and has a great view of the mountains and river.*

This 1992 hotel was renovated in 2001. It has four stories, 150 rooms, some non-smoking, and good Cantonese and Sichuan food. It has generally friendly and thoughtful service, but it has been a bit scruffy. English and Western food might be problems.

OSMANTHUS HOTEL (Dangui Fandian), *451 Zhong Shan Nan Road, 541002. Three stars. Tel. 3834300, 3832261, Fax 3835316. E-mail: glosmh@public.glptt.gx.cn. It is one km from the railway station and off a six-lane boulevard beside the Peach Blossom River. Three-star west wing $70-$90 for rooms, and $160 for suites. It has been giving 20% discounts. Its east wing is not as good.*

Built in 1986, this hotel has 14 stories and 214 rooms, its even-numbered rooms with river view. It is somewhat rundown and has soft beds, health center with outdoor pool, and Cantonese dim sum. Its rooms are stuffy but they should be okay after the air-conditioning is turned on. It has a disco, bicycles for rent, and problems with carpets and English. Vista International Hotels management.

GUILIN PLAZA HOTEL (Guan Guang Jiudian), *20 Li Jiang Road, 541004. Three stars. Tel. 5812488, Fax 5813328. $70-$400 for rooms. It has been discounting 20%. Five km from the railway station and one km from Zhishan Bridge. In the eastern suburbs near the International Exhibition Center, nowhere near good shopping.*

Opened in 1990 this hotel has 13 stories, 287 rooms, European, Cantonese and Sichuan restaurants. It has bicycles, Star TV, an outdoor pool, gym, and sauna. It is primarily for tour groups, the service is not exemplary, and English is a problem. It should be used only as a last resort. Macau CTS Management.

GOLDEN ELEPHANT HOTEL, *36 Binjiang Road, Tel. 2808888, Fax 2809999. E-mail: gehotel@public.glptt.gx.cn. $50-$70 for rooms, and $120 for suites. It has been giving 20% discounts and still might do so if booked at least two weeks in advance.*

Opened in 2000, the Golden Elephant has an American and good Korean restaurant. The buffet breakfast is $4-$5. It has an Asiana Airlines office. The reception desk was not helpful and the English poor.

GUILIN INTERNATIONAL YOUTH HOSTEL, *46 Bin Jiang Road, 541001. Tel. 2809217, 2819936X8103, Mobile 13005958171, Fax 2827116. Website: www.iyhf.org. Ask for Tang Yufang who speaks English. Standard rooms Y300-Y458. Y80 a bed in a dorm. Accepts credit cards but no travelers' checks. Chinese breakfast only Y6. Coffee Y5. No menu in English.*

Where to Eat

The top hotels have very good food, especially the Sheraton and **Royal Garden** for both Western and Chinese. Many restaurants have opened around huge Central Square. Western-type food is available there at **Mingtien/ Coffee Language** (with a Western toilet and patio) next to the Lijiang Hotel. The **Sheraton** has its Studio Café (for hamburgers) and Food Street (noodles and won ton) on the southwest side of the hotel. Chinese food in Guilin is usually Guangxi or Cantonese. It is served with chili sauce and fermented bean curd. You should like this bean curd if you like blue cheese. Mix a bit with your rice. The local rice wine, Sanhua, is made from a 200-year-old recipe.

UILIN REN JUFULOU RESTAURANT, *behind the Sheraton Hotel at No 10, Zhengyang Road, Tel. 2829542, 2808749.*

The food is local, very tasty, and highly recommended but there's no English. Take Chapter 25 from this book.

AUNT (BA SHI GUI), *the name in English is up on a wall outside a big building on the far side of the new square away from the Sheraton Hotel and towards Niko Niko Do. Tel. 2861111, 2863333. Open 11am-2pm; 5:30-9pm, Monday to Friday. Weekends: 10:30am-3pm; 4:30-11:30pm.*

This restaurant takes no credit cards. It is more interesting than it is gourmet and romantic. The food ranges from very good to mediocre. You're the one who takes a look and chooses, an interesting guessing game. In spite of its 500-plus guest capacity, you might have to queue at meal times. It's best to go there before noon. First you get a table and a card. Then you inspect the rows of stalls, each with a cook inside. When you see something you want, you point and hand the card to the attendant who makes a note on it. Then you cruise on to the next stall. The prices are good; many are in the Y5 range so you end up with a lot of interesting-looking dishes. It has sushi, pizza, French toast, and all kinds of local dishes. By the time you get back to your table, they have all magically appeared ready to eat.

LONG ZHE TEA HOUSE, *close to Liberation Bridge at 2 Huaqiao Street, Tel. 5812852, or 5831663. It is open 11am to 2pm, and 5pm to 8pm and accepts no credit cards yet.*

This is special and worth a trip to the east bank. It has no menu and at first the manager wouldn't let my friends in. He assumed they were drinking-smoking government officials who would mess up his restaurant and make lots of noise. There are two set menus, one meat and one vegetarian, both Chinese. Manager Zhang Jie Jie designed the dishes. "Xiang Shan Shui Yue" came sculptured with food in the shape of nearby Elephant Hill. It consisted of pork, quail egg, and stir-fried chicken or beef. The egg was the moon. "Cha Nong Chun Run" had dumplings in the form of tea bags, on a raft of cucumbers. "Ju Hua Si Bao Shan" or Four Treasures Fan was made of mushrooms in the shape of a fan. The food here had no MSG, and is beautiful and delicious.

Seeing the Sights

For those in a hurry, one morning could be spent at Fubo Hill and Seven Star Park, and the afternoon at Reed Flute Cave, Diecai Hill and Elephant Hill. Tourist attractions usually open 8am-5pm. The Li River boat trip could be enjoyed on a second day. The Ming Tomb Museum, the Guilin Museum at Xishan Park, *Tel. 2822892*, Gao Shan for the view, a handicraft factory, shopping, just walking or cycling could be the third. Then there's lovely Yangshuo, and the Longshen rice terraces.

Diecai (Folded Brocade) Hill, *Tel. 2822326*, 3.6 km from the Sheraton Hotel, is the tallest hill in town at 73 meters. The peaks are named Bright Moon, Crane, and Seeing Around the Hill. Partway up, past the ornamental arch, is the Wind Cave with Ming and Song poems and memorials on its walls. You can get a good view of the area from the top.

Fubo (Whirlpool) Hill, *Tel. 2823620*, a short walk north of the Sheraton Hotel, named after famous Han Marshal Ma Fubo, is 60 meters high. At the base is a 7.5-ton iron Qing bell belonging to the temple originally here. To the right is the Cave of the Returned Pearl, where guides used to tell you a dragon left a gift of a pearl for a poor family, who returned it. "This illustrates the honesty of working people." Partway up on the east side is a pavilion with a view of the river.

Qixing (Seven Star) Park, *Tel. 5813652*, 2.7 km from the Sheraton Hotel, is about 10 square kilometers. It contains a zoo, Camel Hill (with nearby miniature garden), and Seven Star Hill whose seven peaks are positioned like the stars in the Big Dipper. Seven Star Cave on the west side of Potaraka Hill has three levels; visitors enter the middle one. It is bigger than Reed Flute Cave, one km long, 43 meters at its widest, and 27 meters at its highest. Colored lights, lasers, and sound effects highlight the grotesque limestone formations. Just think, you will be following in the footsteps of tourists from the Sui (581-618) dynasty!

A forest of cassia trees blossom in spring and a 700-year-old stone replica of the Flower Bridge (Song) spans a stream. The bridge was designed so that the water below reflects its arches to form a complete circle.

The "Cave for Hiding a Dragon" looks like it could snugly fit a dinosaur. The most famous of the stone Song steles nearby lists people doomed for execution. The emperor sent copies around China (although paper was invented by then), and when the verdict was reversed, all but the stele in Guilin were destroyed.

Ludi (Reed Flute) Cave, *Tel. 2602241*, is eight or nine km from the Sheraton Hotel. One km long, this cave takes about 40 minutes to explore. The temperature inside is a cool 20°C. The lighting is cleverly placed so that with a bit of imagination the limestone resembles a giant goldfish, a Buddha, a wall of assorted vegetables, etc. The reeds that grow at the entrance gave this cave its name.

Xiangbi (Elephant Trunk) Hill, *Tel. 3850544*, Y15. This is one km from the Sheraton Hotel, at the junction of the Li and Taohua Rivers and really does look like an elephant drinking. Shuiyue (Moon-in-Water) Cave is between its trunk and front legs. Elephant Eye Cave is where you would expect. The Samantabhadra Pagoda tops the hill.

Duxiu (Unique Beauty) Peak is at the back of the mansion of Zhu Shouqian, grandson of Emperor Hongwu of the Ming, which dates from 1393. Destroyed during the Qing, and again during the Japanese war, it is now the teachers' university. Today, only the original wall, its gates and steps remain but you can visit its museum inside *Tel. 2809217*.

The **Jingjiang Ming Tombs** are a good place to bicycle to. You pass old villages, water buffalo herds, mountains, and several intriguing Ming cemeteries, a total of 320 tombs in 100 sq km. All persons buried here in relatively simple graves are descendants of the Ming emperor's family. A museum, Tel. 5827276, and several guardian statues of animals, servants and officials are at the unexcavated tumulus of Zhu Shou Qian Chi, grandson of the dynasty founder's older brother. He died in 1370 A.D. Much smaller and less elaborate than the Ming tombs near Beijing, they are worth a visit if you have the time. The museum is open daily about 9am-5pm.

There's also **Yao Shan (Broadcast Mountain)**, which is 300 meters high with a road to the top. A chair lift should be operating 9am-4pm.

Engineers and history buffs could visit the **Lingqu (Ling Canal)**, *Tel. 6221913*, dug in 214 B.C. to connect the Chang (Yangtze) and the Zhu (Pearl) rivers. It was an inland route to Guangzhou, used as such until the 1930s. It is still important for irrigation. It has 18 locks and sections, and starts about 57 km north of Guilin in Xing'an County. You can ride a small bamboo raft and enjoy its tranquillity and ancient bridge.

Travel agents can arrange visits to the highly recommended rice terraces at Longji and nearby minority villages, a one or two-day visit. The terraces are 2.5-3 hours by car from Guilin by road, and one hour from Longsheng where OTC puts its foreign guests in the Longsheng Hotel. A hotel is being built at Longji.

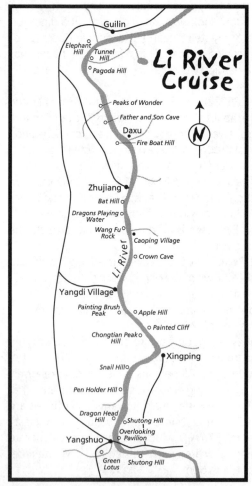

You can book the **Li River boat trip** with a travel agent or your hotel. Travel agents could pick you up at your hotel. Not including transportation to the pier, this famous cruise costs: Y180 from Mo Panshan Pier (only a squat toilet); Y320 from Zhujiang Pier about 20 km from Guilin (mostly Western-style toilets); Y450 from Zhujiang Pier, super-luxurious three-decker boats with Western-style toilets; Y130-Y150 for 16-60 seat boat with air-conditioning Yangshuo-Fuli-Liugong village. (See Yangshuo below).

The ride from Zhu Jiang to Yangshuo is 59 km and takes about four hours. Prices usually include lunch and the bus back to Guilin from Yangshuo about mid-afternoon on any day.

The Li River, normally 50 to 100 meters wide, winds its way between some incredible stone peaks, the highest about 80 meters.

Pollution control has been upgraded, but you still notice dishes being washed in the river.

Look for **Crown Cave** (shaped like the British imperial crown), a cock with tail up bending down to pick up rice, followed shortly by the U-shaped Ram's Hoof Mountain on the right. On the right is **Conch Shell Hill**, then a temple on a cliff. If you're trying to save on camera film, the most beautiful area is between Yangdi Village and Snail Hill, that is, between Number Nine and Number 16 on the map they might give you.

On the way, look for large cormorants (real birds, not stone), usually seen sitting on fishing boats. If you're lucky you might even watch them at work, fishing on behalf of humans.

Nightlife & Entertainment

The night boats to watch the **cormorants** go from the 4th pier of Binjiang Road, eight minutes walk from the Fubo Hotel. The tour begins about 7pm and if you haven't seen it before, do go. It costs about Y100. Cormorant fishing is traditionally done at night by men so their wives can take the catch to market the next morning. The process is fascinating with the light on the fisherman's bamboo raft attracting tiny fish. The birds swim underwater and jump back on board the raft with fish tails sticking out of their beaks. Birds are trained as soon as hatched to work for humans.

"Ethnic" dance and song performances at the **Gui Shan** and **Royal Garden hotels**. Both are entertaining, the same quality, and start at 8pm every evening. The acrobatic and minority show at the **Spring Theatre** near Ronghu Lake has a good reputation and Sheraton can arrange for tickets and transportation. If you want a real minority show, go on the trip to Longsheng, where performances are sometimes held. Better still, go to a minority festival.

Travel agent Wei Wu says "a good place for watching Guilin's lively nightlife is **Cheng's Local Food Restaurant**. It is next to the Souper Restaurant (meaning they have great soup) on Zhengyang Pedestrian Road back of the Sheraton Hotel. Beer in Cheng's Local Food only costs Y3 a bottle. Zhengyang Pedestrian Road swarms with small shops, selling everything from clothes to Italian ice creams. Every evening until 10 o'clock, there's a local auction. Although the goods are just little trinkets like toys and razors, it's a chance to see the reaction of amused local people."

Be forewarned of bars that overcharge for the drinks of hostesses who invite themselves to sit with you. The 18-hole Twin Peaks and 18-hole Golden Fortune golf course are both good. The latter is near the pier where you board the Li River cruise.

Shopping

You can buy locally-grown oranges, pomelo, and mangosteens (luohan guo) in season. Guilin also produces artistic pottery, bamboo, new and old-style wood carvings, redwood chopsticks, woven and plated bamboo, dough figures, stone exercise balls, tablecloths, embroidery, and less exotic items like bicycle bells and down jackets.

The main shopping area is along Zhongshan Zhong Road where you can find the best department store, **Nikko Nikko Do**, open 9am-9:30pm, *Tel. 2819856.*

The **night tourist market** between the Universal and Sheraton hotels has at least 100 stalls and is full of jewelry, tea pots, old gilded wood carvings, silk shirts, table cloths, porcelain, "opium pipes" etc. Occasionally you can find something really valuable like 12 inch long, old, gilded wood carvings for Y100 a pair, circular crocheted table cloths six feet in diameter for Y80, and a fine child's silver necklace with bells (they first asked Y600 but gave in at Y140). Avoid ethnic earrings because they have big stems requiring big ear holes.

Yangshuo's riverside market is huge and has the same sort of curios for sale but day trippers only have about 20 minutes between the boat and the bus to shop. An overnight here can give you more time. Serious shoppers should look at the **Wa Yiao Tourist Wholesale Market,** which supplies both these markets. It is also open to the public, and is 15 minutes by car southeast of the Sheraton on the way to the river cruise.

Excursions & Day Trips

Caoping Village is 29 km south of Guilin. This is a two-day Li River tour with stops at Daxu village and a minority cultural center. There is overnight camping at Crown Cave in tents, or in the crude Misty Hotel, Caoping Village, *Tel. 3848899, Fax 3858139.* Crown Cave has several levels and a cable car. It also has a subterranean river on which you can boat for three km.

After caving, people can also swim, rent boats, sauna, get a massage and visit nearby villages. The only access seems to be by boat. The setting is beautiful and gives photographers a chance to capture the river in a variety of different lights. For information, contact a travel agent.

Festivals include the Cassia Festival in March, and the annual Mountain and River Festival in October or November (three days). One night is spent in the mountains with the minorities. See also Nanning above for Liuzhou, 140 km by highway from Guilin.

See also Yangshuo.

Practical Information

Ambulance, *Tel. 120*

Guilin CITS, *North American Department, 41 Binjiang Road, 541002, Tel. 2810927, 2828304, 2828314, Fax: 2827424, 2805303. E-mail: cits@chinahighlights.com, christine@chinahighlights.com or victor@chinahighlights.com. Website: www.chinahighlights.com.* Ask for Victor Shu or Christine Gong who helped a lot with this book. As you leave the

Sheraton, the office is to the right about three blocks. CITS has a four-day tour that includes a visit to Dong villages. Its website is the best in China. It has a calendar of Yangtze River trips and it can accept orders paid by credit card.

Guilin Overseas Tourist Corporation, *No. 8 Zhishan Rd., Guilin, 541002. Tel. 3810555, 3810888, Fax 3810333. Email: easytour@public.glptt.gx.cn. Website: www.easytourchina.com.* Ask for Thomas Lu or Wei Wu who helped a lot with this book. They are at the Europe & the Americas Department, *Tel. 3810555, 3811461. Beijing Office: E-mail: etpek@163bj.com.* This agency can issue transportation tickets and specializes in off-the-beaten-track tours in Beijing and Guilin (rice terraces and Dong villages).

Police, Tel. 110

Telephone code: 773

Websites: *www.chinaonlinetravel.com/pandatours/pandakwl.htm (English)*. Guilin Tourism Corp. Ltd.: *www.guilintravel.com (Chinese only)*.

Yangshuo

Yangshuo is even better for hiking and bicycling than hectic sightseeing. This tiny town at the end of the Li River boat ride, has a park, art museum, good curio shopping, and an old guild hall. If time allows, you can walk along the main street to the right after you land. The main tourist area is West Street (Xi Jie) which is only open to pedestrians. You can hire a bicycle rickshaw to carry your luggage if necessary. You can walk to the hotels from the bus station which is almost at one end of West Street. The Li River is at the other end.

Yangshuo is the place to revel in rural China, to hire bicycles, to take boats and hike, and soak in the amazing scenery. Its tourist street is interesting, full of schools of English, travel agencies, souvenir shops, cyber cafés, and relatively cheap bars and restaurants with menus in English and Chinese.

Arrivals & Departures

You can take the tourist boat from Guilin to Yangshuo and go back to Guilin a day or so later by the same tourist bus at no additional cost. You can also get to Yangshuo by frequent mini-bus from the Guilin railway station in 90 minutes for about Y5 (Y10 on holidays) if you don't mind bumpy, crowded buses. OTC charges Y220 for a car. Haggling with a taxi should be cheaper.

Where to Stay

The most exotic is the Hong Fu Hotel which is attached to Le Votre French Restaurant on West Street. The hotel with the most services is the Paradise. The inexpensive guest houses have small rooms with no shower curtains. Your toilet seat and bathroom floor can get pretty wet. They also do not have international television channels in English. With that in mind, there's the Hotel

Explorer (Y100 a night with a good view of the river from the roof), and the West Street Hotel. Both are clean and adequate with 24-hour hot running water. You don't need a hotel restaurant. West Street is nearby and full of cheap tourist restaurants. The international youth hostel is good. There's also Country Cottage below for a real Chinese experience. Hotels here charge 15% surcharge.

Except for the Paradise, hotels here can only change U.S. cash, but the Bank of China can change travelers' checks at its branch near the river. No other hotel has CNN.

PARADISE HOTEL (a.k.a. Yangzhou Resort Hotel), *in a garden at 116 West Street, 541900, Tel. 8822109, Fax 8822106. E-mail: glpysr@public.glptt.gx.cn. Website: www.paradiseyangshuo.com. $48-$110 for rooms, and $120-$300 for suites. These prices include service charge and tax. It has been giving 10-50% discounts off some rooms.*

This 145-room hotel has an outdoor pool, small gym, golf-driving range, fishing, rock-climbing wall, CNN, IDD, 24-hour hot water and restaurants. Its banquet hall seats 220. Rooms are 31 square meters and the air could be fresher. Assistant Manager Helen Huang speaks English.

HONG FU HOTEL, *79 West Street, Tel. 8828040, Fax 8828070, E-mail: levotre@hotmail.com. Aiming for three stars. Opened in 2002, this charming 26-room Qing-style hotel charges $22-$80 for rooms and $200 for its presidential suite including breakfast. A group discount depends on the season. It accepts credit cards.*

Rooms are 25 square meters and its suite 80 square meters. Guests get one hour free e-mail per day.

WEST STREET HOTEL (Xi Jie Binguan), *108 West Street, 541900. Tel.8828659, Fax 8828658. E-mail: WSHotel@yeah.net. Rooms cost $30 to $66 and suites $75. Discounts have been 20%.*

This hotel was opened in April 2000 and is a few meters on a side street off West Street bordering onto a canal. Ask for General Manager Linda Tao who speaks English if you have a problem. It has 40 rooms, air-conditioning, television, and a good mountain view. There is 24-hour hot water and a restaurant.

HOTEL EXPLORER, *40 Xian Qian Street, Tel. 8828116, Fax 8827816. E-mail: JimmyQin@hotmail.com. Y150-Y200 for rooms in high season, Y100 in low season. This 27-room air-conditioned hotel is one block from the river and has IDD, television, and 24-hour hot water. It should have an inner garden and restaurant soon. It accepts credit cards.*

GUILIN INTERNATIONAL YOUTH HOSTEL WEST STREET BRANCH, *102 West Street, Tel. 8820933, 8820988 or fax 8820988. Website: www.iyhf.org. Rooms with baths are Y80 and dormitory beds Y18. It accepts only cash. It gives a discount of 10-20% to members according to the season.*

Do not confuse this good hostel with the crappy hostel across from the bus station at 85 Pantao Road. This one is affiliated with the IYHF. Four of the rooms have balconies. All have 24-hour solar powered hot water but no telephones. This is a good deal.

COUNTRY COTTAGE, *Li Cun Village, Moon Hill, Gao Tian, Tel. 773/ 8902389, 13977351911, E-mail: FengPing99@Yahoo.com. Y60 to Y100 a room. For large groups,meals cost Y10 per person. For small groups, it's Y15 per person.*

A wonderful place even though the rooms were the size of four-star bathrooms, windows didn't fit, and it had no closets and no sinks. We put our clothes on a wire strung across the room. We spat our tooth paste water into the squat toilet. We had 24-hour hot water and managed just fine. Our three days at Country Cottage was one of the highlights of a two-week China visit.

Li, our hostess, spoke English. We watched her as she went out to her garden to pick the evening meal of stuffed pumpkin flowers with green peppers and bean curd. Her husband and brothers-in-law are farmers. To get the compulsory water-buffalo-ploughing photo, we just had to ask. Li's brother-in-law was already out working and her sister-in-law told him where to go so we could get the best light. She also showed us the new calf in the shed.

We ate Li's tasty cooking on the terrace outside the house, under the shadow of one of the area's lovely vertical limestone mountains. We were near the entrance to one of the caves and within sight of famous Moon Hill. When one of the guests had a problem walking on uneven ground, Li's husband put a stool on a bicycle cart and pushed her to the road. When he learned she could not cope with squat toilets, he made a seat she could use. We played with the puppy and learned some family secrets.

Every morning, we awoke to the quacking of ducks and exercised on the roof as the sun came up and reflected gold on the paddies in front of the house. When sister-in-law Feng Ping took guests bicycling, the Americans were very happy. They didn't see any other tourists – just mountains and rice, bamboo, streams, and thatched roof farm houses. As a bicycle guide, LI charges Y50 per person per day for three people or more. For one or two people, it's Y100 per day. Add a bicycle rental fee of Y10 a day per bike, and food, at Li's of course. At Country Cottage, we felt we were in the "real China," a village of 600 people.

From the three-story "cottage" we walked 300 meters to the highway to get a passing mini-bus for the 10-minute ride to downtown Yangshuo or 1 1/2 hours to Guilin. On the way, we tried to make friends with the smiling villagers. Feng Ping arranged for a van to pick us up at the airport, and another to take us back. She arranged for the boat trip on the Li River. She was wonderful.

Where to Eat

New restaurants are opening and old ones are closing. But you have lots of choice after you get there.

LE VOTRE, *French restaurant is in the old Jiangxi Guild Hall at 79 West Street, Tel. 8828040, Fax 8828070, E-mail: levotre@hotmail.com. Website: www.yangshuo.com.cn/LeVotreTour. It is open 7:30am for a French breakfast (Y25-Y35) and a Chinese breakfast. It closes whenever.*

Ask for French manager Vincent Christophe (whose Chinese partner is the brother of Wild Swans author Jung Chang). The Western food should taste genuine. It offers at least eight different French wines. Sandwiches are Y8-Y25, and a two-course lunch costs Y48. An appetizer and entrée cost Y40; a salad, hot dish and dessert cost Y60 or Y80. It can cater a party on a boat and organize tours. Behind is its exotic-looking guest house, and Annie can take you to a 500–year-old village for an overnight stay, swim and boating.

Just down the road is the **Mei You Café** offering Chinese and Western food with attractive prices, English and good service. The sign outside says "Mei You (don't have) warm beer, mei you lousy food, mei you rip offs...." Good also is **Drifters** at 58 West Street, *Tel, 7721615.*

RED STAR EXPRESS, *66 West Street, Tel. 8822699, e-mail: lizhaoke@hotmail.com.*

Noted for its pizza.

Karst Café, *Tel. 8828482. E-mail: karstcafe@hotmail.com.*

New, and across from Hotel Explorer, and claims the best ham and sausage, and pizza in town.

CAFÉ UNDER THE MOON, *83 West Street, Tel. 8825000, Fax 8825525. E-mail: unrmoon@gl.gx.cninfo.net.*

This is open from 7am to midnight, and offers an American breakfast for Y19, a high fiber breakfast with muesli for Y25, and a club sandwich for Y16. Its latte and Irish coffee sell for Y6 to Y18, and beer for Y7 to Y15. Its roast duck with pancakes cost Y25, *mapo* bean curd Y13, sweet and sour pork on rice Y18, and dumplings Y8 to Y14. Its homemade ice cream is Y5 and up. It offers copies of China Daily. The only fault found was a crack in a honey pot.

Seeing the Sights

The **museum** has copies of famous paintings of galloping horses and Li River scenes by Xu Beihong who lived here between 1935 and 1938. His residence is at No.5 Xianqian Street and is open weekdays 8:30am-12:00 and 2:30-5pm. It is closed on weekends.

You can take a mini-bus or bicycle about eight km to the base of **Moon Hill**, and start climbing. The first 250 meters up is okay. Above that, it's slippery and muddy in wet weather. The view of the countryside is great. Some people visit the mud baths for a soak, and go to watch the cormorant fishing. Nearby is the **Buddha Water Cave**.

Guilin recently stopped boats operating on the Yangshuo-Xing Ping–Yangti-Yangshuo route, thus depriving tourists of this cheaper cruise. Who knows if this will change again. If these boats are operating when you get to Yangshuo, tour boats could go to the same best area of the **Li River** about 45 km upstream from here. It's better to carry your own snacks. These boats have been smaller and nosier than those from Guilin and didn't have air-conditioning. Only bicycles were allowed on the roof. They had no English-speaking guides.

Many visitors used to put bicycles on these boats and cycle back to Yangshuo from Xing Ping. A word of warning however. If you cycle back, do not take the main road that goes through a narrow unlit 500-meter-long tunnel. This is used by wide trucks which do not turn on their headlights. The New Zealander who barely survived it said it was the scariest experience of his life. Non-bikers can also take crowded mini-buses back too. Xing Ping should have a four-star riverside hotel soon. If you can't get bicycle guide Xu Feng Ping, try to get a guide at the bicycle rental shop or through a travel agency.

Note: There have been no boats recently from Yangshuo to the Crowne caves.

For **Xingping** and **Yangti**, travel agents will know if they are available again. From Yangshuo you can only take a boat to Fuli a few kilometers away whenever these ferries have enough passengers (Y60 each person). It is possible to rent a canoe for Y100 or an innertube for Y5-Y10.

Shopping

Stores open between 9am and 10am and stay open in the evening. At 104 West Street, you can buy tee-shirts that say, "Go Away" or "I'm not a big nose foreigner." There's a book exchange and places to leave messages on the street. You can cash travelers' checks at the Bank of China which has a branch near the boat pier. Travel agencies, freelance guides, and internet cafés are everywhere. So are some local people who say they are collecting coins of different countries. It seems to be a local industry.

Practical Information

Rosemary Deng at **CITS** should be helpful, *118, West Street, Tel. 8822975 or 8828733 (home). E-mail: rosemary@gl.gx.cninfo.com.* CITS has a one-hour tour to the Buddha Water Cave for Y40, and a two-hour tour to the mud baths for Y60. She charges Y25 a person for the cormorant fishing in the evening, a fascinating experience.

Telephone code: 773.

Guangzhou

(Kwangchow, Canton)

Guangzhou is the bustling capital of Guangdong province, which has been one of the fastest developing areas in the world. It is important for business people, and those who have ancestral roots in the area. While it is not a major tourist city, there is enough to do here for about four days. It is 165 km to the northwest of Hong Kong on the Zhujiang (Pearl River).

Guangzhou is known as the Goat City because five fairies came here supposedly in 1256 B.C, riding goats from whose mouths the fairies drew the first rice seeds. In 214 B.C., the first Qin emperor set up the Prefecture of Nanhai here. It has been south China's largest trading city since at least the Tang dynasty when Arab traders started arriving. The Portuguese settled in Macau, 150 km away, in 1557, and foreign traders moved here seasonally after that. More recently, it was the site of the Canton Trade Fair (China Export Commodities Fair), for 23 years China's main foreign trade institution.

Being far from the political center of China, the people here developed an independent spirit. Guangzhou was the starting point or site of many important historical events, including the fight against the importation of opium. Chinese officials destroyed 20,000 chests of it near here in 1839. The Taiping Heavenly Kingdom's Leader Hong Xiuquan (Hung Hsiu-ch'uan) was born about 66 km north and was given the Christian tract that changed his life, and China's history in Guangzhou. Dr. Sun Yat-sen was born south of the city in Zhongshan county. He led the Republican campaign in the early 1900s. The officers of the Northern Expedition were trained at the nearby Huangpu (Whampoa) Military Academy. Chiang Kai-shek was director and Chou En-lai was in charge of political indoctrination.

Many foreign missionaries established schools and churches here after the Treaty of Nanking in 1842 opened the city to foreigners. From 1938 to 1945, the Japanese occupied Guangzhou. The Communists took over in 1949. Guangdong has 11 institutions of higher learning, including Zhong Shan University, which is on the site of the missionary-founded Ling Nam University.

In recent years, Guangdong has been one of the main suppliers of food, water, and electricity for neighboring Hong Kong. It is rich in livestock, fruits, and vegetables and is a major manufacturing center.

Guangzhou is at the same latitude as Cuba. The weather here is subtropical, the coldest about 0°C in January and February; the hottest and most humid about 38°C in July and August. The average rainfall is 1680 mm. The best time to visit is October to February before the rains. The urban population is 3.85 million, the total about six million. While Mandarin is understood by almost everyone, the language in most homes is Cantonese. People who haven't been here in the last three years will not recognize the city with all its new, modern buildings. It is cleaner now, no longer drab and as interesting. People here say crime has increased but I saw no evidence of it and felt quite safe.

Arrivals & Departures

Note: China Travel Service's website has flight, train, bus, and boat schedules between Hong Kong and Guangzhou at: *www.chinatravelone.com*

(English). It is best to send a message asking specific questions to: *enquiry@chinatravel1.com or Fax 852/2789 3498.*

By Air

The easiest way to fly from the U.S. southwest coast to Guangzhou is direct from Los Angeles on China Southern Airlines. It has a Premium Economy Class for which a client pays an economy fare but gets a business class seat. Except for the food, this airline is just as comfortable as U.S. airlines. In addition, every seat, even in Economy, has its own video screen and recent American and Chinese movies. Its top Premium Business class has a washroom big enough for people in wheelchairs, and almost full bed-type seats and fax service. It has special fares for new parents adopting children in China.

From Los Angeles, China Southern takes less than fifteen hours westward (thirteen hours eastward), and flies three times a week each way. Its website: *www.et-china.com* offers on-line China and international air travel booking and ticketing, travel and hotel reservations, in English. This website also gives individual seat and meal selections on flights. You can also book connecting flights in China. It is China's largest airline.

Guangzhou also has air links with 77 Chinese cities, and Amsterdam, Bangkok, Ho Chi Minh City, Hong Kong, Jakarta, Kuala Lumpur, Melbourne, Osaka, Penang, Phnom Penh, Seoul, Singapore, and Sydney. The Hong Kong flight takes about 20 minutes. Guangzhou's new airport should open in late 2003. This airport is 30 km north of the current Baiyun airport and joined to the city by an expressway.

Airlines that service Guangzhou include:
- **Air China**, *Tel. 86681399.*
- **China Northern**, *Tel. 86682488.*
- **China Southern**, *next to the main railway station, Tel. 86661818. 86662749, 86661830, 86681803 (international); Tel. 86662969. 86671583 (domestic); Airport Service Desk, Departure Lounge, Tel. 86666123, 86678901.*
- **China Southwest**, *Tel. 86673747.*
- **JAS**, *Tel. 86696688, Fax 8666-5603.*
- **Malaysian Airlines**, *Tel. 83358828.*
- **Shanghai Airlines**, *Tel. 86681149.*
- **Singapore Airlines**, *Tel. 83358999, 83338898 X 1056.*
- **Xiamen Airlines**, *Tel. 81340984.*
- **Vietnam Airlines**, *Tel. 83827187.*

By Train

From Shenzhen and Hong Kong use the East Guangzhou train station at Tianhe. Trains from elsewhere use the main railway station near the Liuhua and China Hotels. A total of seven pairs of through train trips have been made daily between Hong Kong and Guangzhou East. These take about two hours each way.

These services are jointly operated by Hong Kong and Chinese railway companies. For schedules and ticketing information, you can visit website: *www.kcrc.com* (via Sitemap>Intercity Passenger Services>Through Train Schedules & Fares). Or telephone Intercity Passenger Services Hotline on *852/ 2947-7888, or Fax 852/2690-3705.* The 8:25am train leaving Hong Kong is especially comfortable, clean and good with an English-speaking attendant.

At least 23 express trains now go between Guangzhou and Shenzhen daily. If you walk across the border and catch a train on the other side, it's much cheaper than taking the through train. And it could be faster.

By Bus

These are frequent, air-conditioned, comfortable and take about three to four hours (depending on traffic) direct to Guangzhou's Garden Hotel or China Hotel, at least 20 trips a day each for about HK$160-$190. Hong Kong buses arrive at other hotels as well.

China Travel Service buses leave from Hong Kong's international airport daily for hotels in Guangzhou at least five times a day. The Customer Service Counter No.2A in the Meeters and Greeters Hall, Level 5, can book tickets for HK$230-$250. Buses from other Guangdong cities arrive at the teminal across from the China Hotel. For schedules see: *www.chinatravel1.com/english/bus/zhonglv-jch.htm.*

You should ask about your bus the day before departure, but only need to arrive at your terminal fifteen minutes before it leaves The trip means shorter queues but struggles with luggage at the two border points. Avoid arriving in Hong Kong during rush hours.

From Guangzhou to Hong Kong, make sure you know if your bus terminates on the Hong Kong-side, the Kowloon-side, or the airport. You could end up carrying your luggage onto a ferry or taking an expensive taxi.

By Boat

There are overnight boats, fast catamarans and hovercraft leaving several times a day from Hong Kong China City at 35 Canton Road in Hong Kong. Ferries arrive at Zhoutouzui or

Holidays & Hong Kong Crowds

Every time there is a long holiday, over 150,000 visitors a day go through Guangzhou railway station, so avoid traveling then. The lunar new year holiday in late January or early February is the worst. There's also May 1 and October 1. Don't even think about it. Christmas and New Year week and sometimes Easter are very stressful too, with long line-ups, pushing and shoving, and not enough tickets.

Dashatou south of the Pearl River in Guangzhou. On an over-night boat you can save money on a hotel room. On a day boat, you can see the scenery, bridges, and old forts.

Note: If you join a tour group through a company like CITS and CTS, you can visit some cities in Guangdong province for up to 144 hours without a visa. These cities are Guangzhou, Zhuhai, Jiangmen, Shenzhen, Foshan, Dongguan, Zhongshan, Zhaoqing and Huizhou. You have to enter from Hong Kong or Macao in a group of three or more. You need a name list with passport numbers, sex, date of birth, and addresses.

No photos are required and no journalists or diplomats are allowed into China this way. You can also get visas at some border ports. See Zhuhai, Zhongshan and Shenzhen.

Guangdong's Gift to the World

Guangdong province is the provincial "home" of many **Chinese immigrants** to Australia, the United States, Canada, and Southeast Asia since the 1850s. These people have contributed to the economic development of their adopted lands and have also brought or sent back expertise as well as money to their ancestral home. Many are playing a leading role in China's modernization program, and are largely responsible for Guangdong's economic boom.

Orientation

Guangzhou is divided by the Pearl River, which is crossed by seven bridges, a tunnel and innumerable ferries. These are to be avoided at rush hours (roughly 7:30am-9am and 4:30pm-7pm). Even though the city has tried to alleviate its traffic jams with elevated highways, wider roads and bridges, traffic congestion is still bad. The city has also banned motorcycles, and cars from out of town. It has forbidden bicycles on some streets, opened multi-storied car parks and created one-way streets. Guangzhou is also trying hard to clean up its air. Leaded gasoline is forbidden downtown, and trees are being planted.

The tourist sites, train stations and airports are all on the north side of the river. The trade fair will move to the south side soon. Tianhe is seven km east of the Holiday Inn. An 18 km-long metro line goes from the Guangzhou Steel Plant to Tianhe's East Railway station with 16 stations. A second line should be finished in 2002.

The metro is well air-conditioned and frequent, with signs in English or pin yin. You get change from an attendant and go to a machine for a ticket. Prices range from Y2 to Y5; the logo looks like the letter "Y" split down the middle.

Air-conditioned taxis with uniformed drivers and clean vehicles cost Y2.60 per kilometer with a Y7 flag-fall. Taxis without air-conditioning cost Y2.20 per kilometer. Taxi fares can be high because of the one-way streets.

Where to Stay

All hotels here give discounts especially on weekends, and if you book in advance. Ask about packages. Guangzhou's hotels, however, do not give discounts during the first week of the Export Commodities Trade Fair. Instead, prices double or triple and reservations must be secured by a deposit for at least the first week. See Festivals below.

The top five-star hotels are the White Swan, then the China and the Garden. The best four star is the Holiday Inn, Ramada Pearl, and Landmark in that order. The most convenient three star is the Bai Yun Hotel which has had much experience with foreigners but hardly any English. If you want to pay less, try the International Youth Hostel.

All hotels listed here of three stars and more have TV reception from Hong Kong in English. The higher-rated hotels also have CNN. Most hotels add 10% service, 5% tax and 5% subway tax, and rates are in US dollars or Chinese yuan. Distances from the old Baiyun airport, not the new airport, are mentioned.

China & Dong Fang Hotels area

The China and Dong Fang Hotels have been the best located for the Trade Fair (until it moves). They are still within walking distance of big parks, the Orchid Garden, the Han Museum, the Six Banyan Tree Temple, Zhenhai Tower (museum), China Southern Airlines/CAAC, CITS, and the main railway station. They are also close to some good restaurants.

CHINA HOTEL BY MARRIOTT (Zhong Guo Dajiudian), *Liu Hua Road, 510015. Five stars. Tel. 86666888, Fax 86677014, 86677288. E-mail: gzchinaa@public.guangzhou.gd.cn. Website: www.marriotthotels.com. Five km from the airport and close to the soon-to-open Yue Xiu Park subway station. $148-$225 for rooms, $225-$2500 for suites. It has been discounting 15-25%.*

Built in 1983, this international class property has 19 stories and 1013 rooms including 85 suites. It has executive floors, a separate check-in for commercial guests in the lobby, a Bank of China, and up-scale stores. Rooms are 38-45 square meters. There's a children's playground, one of the best gyms in town, and an aerobics room. It offers tennis, bowling, a golf simulator, and a 25-meter outdoor pool. It has a deli, good coffee shop, Asian and Japanese restaurants. The buffets costs Y98 for breakfast. A Marriott hotel. See also *Where to Eat.*

DONG FANG HOTEL (Dong Fang Binguan), *120 Liu Hua Road, 510016. Five stars, Tel. 86669900, 86662946 (reservations), Fax 86662775. E-mail: dfhtlbc@public.guangzhou.gd.cn. Five km from the airport. $90-$120 for rooms; $145-$1930 for suites. This used to be a charming hotel with a large beautiful courtyard garden until it added a busy shopping mall.*

Built in 1961, the Dong Fang has eight- and 11-story buildings with 1300 rooms, some very spacious. CNN is available and some rooms have safes. It has

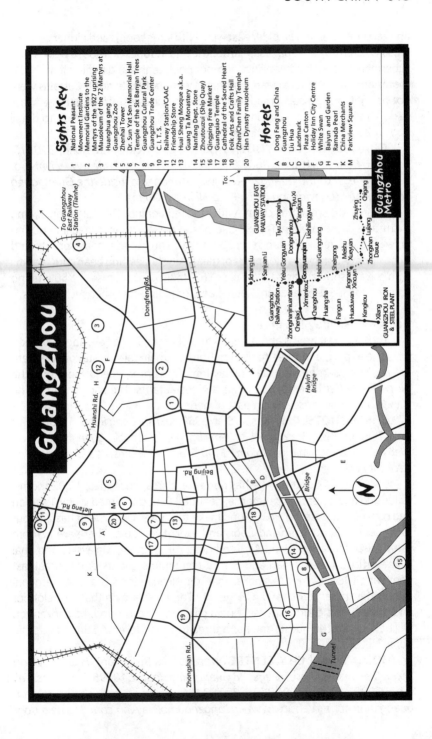

Guangzhou

Sights Key

1 National Peasant Movement Institute
2 Memorial Gardens to the Martyrs of the 1927 uprising
3 Mausoleum of the 72 Martyrs at Huanghua gang
4 Guangzhou Zoo
5 Zhenhai Tower
6 Dr. Sun Yat Sen Memorial Hall
7 Temple of the Six Banyan Trees
8 Guangzhou Cultural Park
9 Guangzhou Trade Center
10 C. I. T. S.
11 Railway Station/CAAC
12 Friendship Store
13 Huai Sheng Mosque a.k.a. Guang Ta Monastery
14 Nanfang Dept. Store
15 Zhoutouzui (Ship Quay)
16 Qingping Free Market
17 Guangxiao Temple
18 Cathedral of the Sacred Heart
19 Folk Arts and Crafts Hall (Zhen/Chen Family Temple
20 Han Dynasty mausoleum

Hotels

A Dong Fang and China
B Guangzhou
C Liu Hua
D Landmark
E Plaza Canton
F Holiday Inn City Centre
G White Swan
H Baiyun and Garden
J Ramada Pearl
K China Merchants
M Parkview Square

Guangzhou Metro

GUANGZHOU EAST RAILWAY STATION

Tiyu Zhongxin
Tiyu Xi
Yangjiang
Dongshankou
Lieshilingyuan
Haizhu Guangchang

Sanjiaru Lu
Yuexiu Gongyuan
Gongyuangian
Ximenkou

Guangzhou Railway Station
Zhongshan Jinkuantang
Chenliaji
Changshou

Huangsha
Fangcun
Huaduwan
Kengkou
Xilang

GUANGZHOU IRON & STEEL PLANT

Zhujiang
Chigang
Zhuying
Zhongshan Lujiang
Daxue

Meishu
Shergong

Jingnan
Xiancun
Xueyuan

To:
J

To Guangzhou East Railway Station (Tianhe)

Dongfeng Rd.
Huanshi Rd.
Beijing Rd.
Jiefang Rd.
Zhongshan Rd.

Haiyin Bridge
Bridge
Tunnel

N

an executive floor and an older east wing with large rooms and higher ceilings. It has Western, Thai, Japanese, Cantonese and Indonesian food, a book store, supermarket, four-lane bowling, outdoor pool, tennis and mini-golf. In 2001, rooms and carpets were clean, but things were not quite right. Curtains were not straight and the bedspreads did not fit. The air was stuffy and the hallways dark. This hotel is okay if you're not fussy, but the lack of attention to detail does raise questions about the services.

GUANGZHOU CITY YOUTH HOSTEL, *179 Huanshi Xi Road, 510010. Tel. 8666-6889 X 3812. Fax 8667-0787 or 8667-9787. Website: www.iyhf.org. It is to the east of the Guangzhou railway station and inside the Guangdong Tourist Hotel (Guangzhou Guoji Qing Nian Liu Guan).*

Rooms are small but clean, with air-conditioning, IDD telephones, and thermoses of hot water. This 81-bed hostel has a washing machine but no dryer. A good deal is the lunch for about Y10. You get rice, bean sprouts, and a choice of two generous toppings of meat, vegetables, and bean curd. Rooms with private showers and toilets cost Y60. It also has rooms for Y50 with no private baths. See Shenzhen, Zhuhai and Zhaoqing for other such hostels.

Garden & Holiday Inn area

The next best area is about three km east of the Trade Fair, about nine km from the airport, and three to five km from the main railway station. Here are the Bai Yun, Garden and the Holiday Inn City Center, Friendship Store, the World Trade Center and lots of bars and restaurants. The zoo is nearby. The Tianhe area is six or seven km east of here.

GARDEN HOTEL (Huayuan Jiu Dian), *368 Huanshi Dong Road, 510064. Five stars. Tel. 83338989, Fax 83324534. E-mail: gzgarden@public.guangzhou.gd.cn. Website: www.summithotels.com. $140-$250 for rooms. It's been offering discount packages.*

Built in 1984-85, this hotel has good standards, 30 stories, 1,002 rooms, suites and apartments. Its immense, beautiful, wood-trimmed lobby, location and convenient buses to Hong Kong make this hotel a favorite. It has 24-hour room service, a non-smoking floor, and executive floors. There are in-room safes, HBO, Star World, and Air Cambodia, Air Vietnam, Malaysian and Thai airline offices. It has Italian and French restaurants and its buffet breakfast goes for Y108. Rooms are smaller than the Holiday Inn's but it has large in-room safes. It has tennis and a bigger pool and better gym than its neighbor and it has tennis courts, squash, and a children's playground. Its convention hall banquets 1200 guests and has a three-ton chandelier. A Summit International Hotel.

HOLIDAY INN CITY CENTRE (Wen Hua Jia Ri Jiudian), *Huanshi Dong Road, Overseas Chinese Village, 28 Guangming Road, 510095. Four stars. Tel. 87766999, Fax 87602063, 87753126. E-mail: resvn@holidayinn-guangzhou.com. Website: www.guangzhou.holiday-inn.com. It is next door* to the Dong Shan Plaza and Electronic Building. $130-$180 for rooms; $230-$1000 for suites. It provides free shuttle buses with the railway station and airport.

This 1989-90, 24-story, 383-room hotel has a gym, outdoor pool, and 500-seat cinema. It has three executive floors, a clinic, in-room safes and renovations to several floors in 2002. The breakfast buffet is Y95. Its ball room seats 230 people banquet-style.

BAI YUN HOTEL (Binguan), *367 Huanshi Dong Road, 510060. Three stars. Tel. 83333998, Fax 83336498. Six km from the airport and next to the Friendship Store. Y398-Y548 for rooms, and Y658-Y9888 for suites. In its East building, Y300-Y430 for rooms.*

Built in 1975, the Bai Yun has 34 stories with wide hallways and over 700 large rooms and suites, some with poor grouting. There's a real post office and some television in English from Hong Kong. The 28th floor is best but don't be surprised by worn carpets or poor English.

Other areas

The White Swan Hotel is relatively isolated on historic Shamian Island, but an elevated highway means only a 15-minute drive to the Trade Fair Building. It is next to the US Consulate, and you can walk to the interesting but grubby Qingping Market. Also on the island are some decent restaurants. Within steps of the Pearl River Bridge downtown is the Landmark Hotel, close to CTS and shopping. The Ramada is in a less crowded area to the east, far from anything but the river. The White Swan has the most beautiful lobby, its bar and coffee shop the best view of the busy Pearl River, but the Ramada's river view includes a genuine pagoda.

WHITE SWAN HOTEL (Baitian'e Binguan), *1 Southern Street, Shamian Island, 510133. Tel. 81886968, Fax 81861188, 81882288. E-mail: swan@whiteswanhotel.com. Website: www.white-swan-hotel.com. It is 11 km from the airport and seven km from the railway station. It has direct buses with Hong Kong. Rooms are $148-$180, and suites $240-$550. It has been discounting 20% for walk-in guests.*

Opened in 1983, this charming, 28-story hotel has 843 spacious rooms with polished white marble bathrooms It has non-smoking and executive floors. It has a fine grill room with French food, Japanese food, and a marvelous Chinese restaurant. In summer from April to November, it offers a daily riverside barbecue. There's a gym, tennis, squash, and two beautiful outdoor pools. You can practise on its golf-driving range and enjoy its Rolls Royces. It has a convention center and banquet hall. Member Leading Hotels of the World.

RAMADA PEARL HOTEL (Hua Mei Da), *9 Ming Yue Yi Lu, Dong Shan District, 510600. Four stars. Tel. 87372988, Fax 87377481. E-mail: gzramada@public.guangzhou.gd.cn. Website: www.ramadahotels.com/*

canpe. *$139-$190 for rooms; $190-$220 for suites. On 150 meters of waterfront, the Ramada is generally too far to walk to anywhere else of importance. It is the closest international hotel to Tianhe five km away and is 15 km from the airport.*

Opened in 1991, this 25-story, 339-room hotel has non-smoking rooms and apartments. All rooms are 30-60 square meters. It has a California café, in-room safes, and 24-hour room service. For getting into shape, there's a gym, squash, tennis, 19-meter-long indoor pool, an outdoor pool, and a golf-driving range. It has lots of space for children. It receives CNN, HBO and Australian television.

HOTEL LANDMARK CANTON (Huaxia Dajiudian), *8 Qiao Guang Road, Haizhu Square, 510115. Four stars. Tel. 83355988, Fax 83336197, 83331564. E-mail: gzhuaxia@public.guangzhou.gd.cn. Website: www.hotel-landmark.com.cn. Y420-Y600 for rooms and Y650-Y1200 for suites except during the Trade Fair. It is seven km from the airport, six km from the Guangzhou railway station, and 13 km from the Guangzhou East Railway Station in Tianhe. It is on the Pearl River.*

Built in 1991-94, this 39-story, 672-room hotel has business studios and three executive floors. It has CNN, in-room safes, in-house movies, a gym, indoor pool, Western, Cantonese, and Chaozhou food. Its buffet lunch is Y48, and buffet dinner Y108.

Where to Eat

Look for tourist handouts like "City Talk," and "That's Guangzhou" for lists of restaurants and bars. Your best bets for both Chinese and Western food are the top hotels – the Garden, China, and White Swan. The Holiday Inn's Italian restaurant has a good reputation. It has been offering a set menu for Y168 per person plus 15% and is open 6pm-10:30pm, Tuesday to Sunday.

Prices may not be as high as you think. The China Hotel's Food Street offers an order of barbecued suckling pig for Y38, sweet and sour pork with pineapple for Y30, double boiled crocodile meat soup for Y42 per person, and wonton noodles for Y20. It's been giving a free dim sum breakfast for a child below one meter for each paying adult. It's half price on all its food after 9:30pm. From 7am-11am daily, its dim sum starts at Y3.5 a basket. Its Super Deli has sandwiches for Y10 and Y15 and pastries for Y5 and Y6.

The White Swan has a deli where prices are relatively cheap. At the Holiday Inn City Centre's Dai Pai Dong restaurant, the daily morning all-you-can-eat tea buffet costs Y25 net per person. Look for similar bargains.

Dim sum

Dim sum are small steamed or fried pastries and dumplings served frequently from trolleys in small baskets. See Chapters 11 and 25. Dim sum originated in this province so while you're here, you could try the mother lode.

Most people just take the old favorites "har gau" and "shui mai" but there are many varieties the adventurous can try.

FOUR SEASONS' RESTAURANT, at *the China Hotel, Liu Hua Road, Tel. 86666888.*

Here dim sum is a fine art and you have to order by name. Chef Chen Ling Xian offers deep-fried shrimp paste rolled with bean curd skin for Y15 a basket. Delicious also were the baked lily bulb barbecue balls made of barbecued pork, lily bulb, and sesame seeds. The egg tarts were unbelievable and yummy, because they had a few dabs of "birds' nest" on top and cost Y20 a basket for three small tarts. The carrot dim sum was in the shape of a carrot but made of sticky rice, mushrooms, pork and pineapple. It was especially good but almost a dessert. The most popular is the baked chestnut puffs which are round balls of chestnut paste for Y12. Chef Chen has created 30 new varieties of dim sum in his 16 years at the China Hotel.

PAN XI (Ban Xi) RESTAURANT, *151, Long Jin Xi Road, Tel. 81815955 or 81817038. E-mail address: gzpanxi@public.guangzhou.gd.cn. Website: www.gzcater.com/panxi. (Chinese only). No international credit cards.*

This 1949 restaurant is famous for the 300 different varieties of dim sum it serves daily. It's set in a classical garden but it has chandeliers and frosted glass screens. Its English is almost non-existent but you only need sign language. The "da bow" are almost like western-style donuts and the prices are proletarian. Two small egg tarts cost Y4 (no birds' nest). Its famous rabbit-shaped dumplings costs Y33 for 10, its cute hedgehog-shaped buns of pork, dried mushroom, and bamboo shoots cost Y50 for ten pieces. Tea costs Y2 a pot. The Panxi serves dim sum between 6:30am and 11:30am. It closes at midnight. Aside from the dumplings, worth trying are fried noodles for Y15; 500 gm barbecued suckling pig Y55; fried green vegetables Y18; baked prawns Y55; crispy crab claws Y40; and crispy deep-fried chicken Y88. Reservations are mandatory for its fancy function rooms. It has clean Western toilets too.

GUANGZHOU RESTAURANT, *112 Tiyudong Road. Visa and American Express accepted.*

There are seven branches and this is the most convenient. One of the best Cantonese restaurant chains in town, it has great dim sum and has been inventing new dishes. A whole Wenchang chicken costs Y140. Beef in oyster sauce is Y20, sweet and sour pork ribs Y20, roast suckling pig Y30, and noodles and shrimp soup Y28. Dim sum goes for Y2.50-Y9.50 a basket. The telephone for the branch at 2 Wenchang Nan Road is *8139-2285;* in Tian He, it's *3880-9228.* They're open 7am-3pm; 5pm-10pm.

Near the Garden Hotel & Holiday Inn

The area around the Garden Hotel and Holiday Inn has many good restaurants and bars.

BANANA LEAF CURRY HOUSE, *8 Luhu Road, Tel. 83591288 X 3119, 3123, 3118. North of the Friendship Store in the Broadcasting and Television Hotel. It is open daily 11am-midnight and accepts credit cards. Some foreigners get a 15% discount.*

It cooks moderately-priced Singaporean and South Asian food from an illustrated menu. Try the curried crab, chicken and cashews, Vietnamese spring roll, and satay.

Near the China Hotel

PEACE RESTAURANT, *Shanghai cuisine. 2/F Parkview Hotel, 960 Jiefang Bei Road, Parkview Square, around the corner south and east of the China Hotel. Tel. 86671731 and 86671732. Open 6:15am-11pm. No credit cards. It has Shanghai food and old Shanghai decor.*

This restaurant has a menu with appetizing photographs. Cooks wearing nose masks inspire confidence about the hygiene. Popular here are the braised meat balls for Y18, sautéed eel for Y28, braised pork for Y16, toasted fried beans for Y14, and braised Tientsin cabbage with dried black mushrooms for Y18. The menu is in English.

DONG BEI REN RESTAURANTS, *Northeastern Chinese cuisine. Open daily 9:30am to 11:30pm. The easiest branch to find is around the corner to the west and south of the Dong Fang Hotel about 300 meters. Cheap. Menu in English on request.*

These restaurants frequently have line-ups that extend outside. Those seated inside waiting get free watermelon seeds. This is not the place for a romantic dinner. It is, however, amusing and fascinating with snakes in bottles, strings of red chili peppers, and giant red paper cuts on the windows. The food is interesting and good. Dumplings cost Y8-Y10 a plate, royal-style braised donkey, yes, donkey Y35, Harbin fragrant chicken Y48, deep-fried pork shashlik with onion Y35, and stir-fried potato noodles with pork Y15. There's also northeast wines for Y8-Y10 a glass and juices for Y6. Ribs or backbone arrive with disposable plastic gloves. Another branch of Dong Bei Ren is in Tianhe at South Second Tianhe Road, *Tel. 87571507.* No one speaks English but you can point. Bright, noisy and almost manic.

THE HARD ROCK CAFE, *in the China Hotel, open Sunday through Thursday from 10:30am-2am, and Friday and Saturday from 10:30am-3am. E-mail: randyjia@hardrock.com. Website: www.hardrock.com.*

The ribs are good (Y90), a Caesar salad costs Y75, and fajitas are Y105. Add a Y100 charge for home delivery. Happy hour is from 2pm-7pm.

McDONALDS, *in front of the Dong Fang Hotel.*

A Big Mac costs Y9.90 and a Double Cheeseburger costs Y9.90. It is open 7am-11pm.

Shamian Island

WHITE SWAN'S DELICATESSEN, *outside of this hotel's VIP entrance.* It has green tea ice cream, pastries and yogurt at prices considerably cheaper than inside. In addition, restaurants, curio shops and parks make Shamian a good place now to spend a few relaxing hours.

Favorites among foreigners are the **Jade Café** and **Garden Restaurant** at 7 South Street. Cheaper is **Lucy's** at 3 Shamian Nan Street, *Tel. 81874106.* It's open 11am-2am and only takes cash.

Seeing the Sights

If you only have one day, do visit the Chen Family Hall, the Han Dynasty Mausoleum Museum, the Temple of the Six Banyan Trees (for exotic Chinese architecture), and the Qing Ping Free Market (for genuine local color). You could also decide on a garden (if you like plants), or an arts and crafts factory.

Be sure to have a drink in the riverside coffee shop or bar at the White Swan Hotel. If you have more time (at least a day), go to Foshan for the ancestral temple, 61.9-meter- high sitting Buddha, and ceramic factory.

The **Chen (Zhen) Family Hall,** Liwan Bei Road, *Tel. 81814559,* is open 8:30am-5pm daily. It was built in the 1890s with nine halls and six courtyards. Its windows, door frames, and pavilions are all lavishly decorated with carvings and sculptures, almost too much to absorb at once. Take it in small doses. Because the army occupied these buildings during the Cultural Revolution, the artwork suffered very little damage. Look at the ceramic opera scenes on the roofs and the charming carved mice eating the lichees on the pillars.

The **Liu Rong (Six Banyan Trees) Temple,** Liu Rong Road, *Tel. 83357754,* open 8am-5pm daily, was founded 1,400 years ago. It was so named because the famous Song poet Su Dong Po found six luxuriant banyan trees here in 1100. The present buildings are recent. Its nine-story Flower Pagoda is 57.6 meters high and originally built in 537. It can be climbed for a good view and the exercise.

The **Qing Ping Free Market (Qing Ping Ziyou Shi Chang),** is the largest herb and vegetable market in the city (about five blocks). Here you can find dehydrated lizards, snakes, plants, and weird-looking roots. It has some live fish and animals, too, for pets or food, including pangolins (an endangered species) and civet cat. This market is not for children nor the squeamish as it has skinned barbecued dogs dangling in the stalls.

It can be filthy especially in the rainy season, always crowded, but fascinating even if you don't want to buy anything. It is within a 20-minute walk of the White Swan Hotel, across the north bridge to the mainland, and runs about three blocks in each direction. It is open 6am-6pm daily except Sundays when it opens at 8am. As in all crowded places anywhere beware of pickpockets!

Guangzhou has a 2100-year-old "royal" tomb officially known as the **Museum of the Western Han Dynasty Mausoleum of the Nanyue King**, about half a block behind the China Hotel on 867 Jiefang Bei Road towards the river, *Tel. 86664920, 86678030*, open daily 9:30am-4:45pm. You need at least 1.5 hours here. The Nanyue Kingdom was founded by one of the ruling generals of the first emperor Qin. After Qinshihuang's death in 210 B.C., his son and successor who lacked his father's fanatical drive, let loose the reins of empire. Zhao Tuo, the surviving general in charge of south China declared himself Emperor of Nanyue in 204 B.C.

The Han dynasty took over China in 206 B.C. Five years later, the Nanyue Emperor was given the choice of renewing his allegiance to the Chinese empire, or bringing suffering on his people. Zhao Tuo chose the former, and died at age 93 in 137 B.C. The tomb here is of his successor, the second Nanyue King. Included in the find of over 1000 burial objects are the oldest jade burial suit so far found in China, a chariot, ritual bronzes, gold and silver vessels, ivory and lacquerware, musical instruments, weapons, and tools. Also buried with him were human sacrifices, concubines, and servants. The relics are beautifully displayed, with English titles, at the actual site. Don't miss the video, in English, of the excavation.

If You Have More Time or Interest

Shamian (Shamien, Shameen) Island, in the Pearl River in central Guangzhou, became a British and French concession in 1859-60. It was then an 80-acre sandbank, later built into a European ghetto. The architecture is European and efforts have recently been made to preserve eight of the buildings. Signs are up giving dates and the likes of "former Germany consulate." Many were built between 1865 and 1908. At 6am, stay out of the way of little old ladies wielding swords. At the western tip is the White Swan Hotel, built on reclaimed land, one of the top hotels in China. See *Where to Eat* above.

The **Guangzhou Museum**, *Tel. 83832195*, open 9am-5pm daily, is in the Zhenhai (Sea-dominating) Tower in Yuexiu Park. The original tower itself was built in 1380 to assert the power of the Ming dynasty. It has been rebuilt several times since then. Located at one of the highest points in the city, it starts with prehistory on the second floor. Look for the original clock from the Catholic Cathedral.

The **Mausoleum of the Seventy-two Martyrs at Huanghuagang** (Yellow Flower) Hill on Xianlie Road is east of the Garden Hotel on the road to the zoo. This commemorates Dr. Sun Yat-sen's unsuccessful attempt to overthrow the Qing in 1911. Of special interest to visitors of Chinese ancestry, this 260,000 square-meter park was financed by Chinese Nationalists' Leagues around the world. The stones are inscribed in English with the names of the donors, among these Chicago, Moose Jaw and Lima, Peru.

The **Dr. Sun Yat-sen Memorial Hall,** *Tel. 83332430,* is a theater seating over 4,500, built in 1931 and expanded in 1975. This building is architecturally important because its huge hall is supported by four vertical concrete beams. The modern technique and pure Chinese style, with its bright blue circus-tent-shaped ceramic octagonal roof, is unique. (For more on the life of Dr. Sun, see Nanjing.)

The ***Guangxiao Temple,*** 109 Sheshi Road at Guangxiao Road, *Tel. 81087421,* has the longest history in the city. It was founded on the site of the Nanyue King's residence. The temple was built in 397 A.D. to commemorate the visit of the Indian monk Dharmayasas, and is the largest temple in south China. The present buildings are from the Five Dynasties to the Ming. The attractive Sixth Patriarch's Hair-burying Pagoda is a miniature of the Flower Pagoda.

The **Huaisheng Mosque and Guangta Minaret,** 56 Guangta Road, Jiubuqian, Yide, *Tel. 83336737,* are of historical value. Considered the oldest mosque in China, it was built in 627 A.D. by Arab traders and is open daily.

The **Shishi (Cathedral of the Sacred Heart),** Yide Road, *Tel. 83336737,* was constructed in 1863-88. Its 57.95-meter Gothic spire was probably designed deliberately to be taller than the pagoda nearby. Shishi means Stone House. During the Cultural Revolution, it was used as a storehouse. Mass has been celebrated weekdays at 6am and Sundays and festivals at 6, 7:30, and 8:30am.

In the summer, a **Pearl River boat trip** leaves Tianzi Wharf a few hundred meters east of the Landmark Hotel at 6:45pm and 8:45pm, *Tel. 81888932, 81908190,* and ask for Ms. Pan Li Li who speaks English, or book through your hotel. The earlier trip includes dinner at the same price as the later trip with only peanuts. The commentary is in Chinese so bring your own map. The boat goes by the White Swan Hotel, then east past Tianzi wharf and Zhongshan University to the Guangzhou Bridge at Ershatou Island, and back again. It is interesting and pleasant but Guangzhou doesn't have the lights of Shanghai.

Gardens, Parks, & Zoos

Depending on the season, don't forget to bring your own insect repellent. The **Orchid Garden**, Dabei Road, at the foot of Yuexiu Hill, *Tel. 86677255,* is a delight for orchid lovers. It has over 300 species on five hectares. The **Xi Yuan (West Garden)**, next to Dongfeng 1-Road, *Tel. 81885867,* specializes in penjing, miniature trees, and landscapes. The **Guangzhou Zoo and Ocean Park**, Xianli Zhong Road, *Tel. 87752702,* are in the northeastern suburbs. They have 200 species, including pandas.

Further Afield

Worth a stop on the way to Shenzhen is the **Humen Fort** on the north shore of the Pearl River, under the Humen Bridge, south of Dongguan County city, *Tel. 750/6288551*. This is about a 90-minute drive towards western Shenzhen on the coastal road. The fort was built against the foreign invaders during the Qing and is quite impressive. At Humen, Minister Lin Zexu destroyed the opium in 1839.

The **Huangpu Military Academy** (1924) should be of interest to modern history buffs. It's on Changzhou Island, Huangpu, *Tel. 82201082* and can be reached by boat from the Xidy Wharf, Yanjiang Xi Road, or Tianzi Wharf, Yanjiang Zhong Road, *Tel. 81888932, 81908191, Fax 8188932*. The **Taiping Museum** at leader Hong Xiuquan's Former Residence is in Guanglubu Village, Huaxian County. Read *God's Chinese Son* by Jonathan Spence.

Another escape from crowds is a nearby village, many of which grow and preserve fruit for export. Guests are frequently given samples. Lucky are those who go during the lichee season! It is in June.

The Happy Festival with performing arts groups is in the autumn. A fine food festival takes place during the autumn Trade Fair. The **Export Commodities Trade Fair** goes from April 15-26 or 27 and October 15-26 or 27 and the closest hotels are the China and Dong Fang. Starting with the April 2003 fair, unless there's another change, it will be at Pazhou Island, 45 minutes south of the Pearl River by road. The closest international hotel will then be the Ramada Pearl, 20 minutes by taxi away. North Americans can get an invitation through China Travel Service (USA), Inc. San Francisco Main Office or its Los Angeles branch. See Chapter 6. The Fair's address is 117 Liuhua Road, 510014, *Tel. 86678000 ext. 88791, Fax 86671722*.

See also Foshan, Taishan, Zhaoqing, Zhongshan, and Zhuhai below.

Nightlife & Entertainment

The bars in the top hotels are popular with foreigners. The Garden Hotel's **Lotus Bar** has a multi-colored lighted floor. Across the street to the west of the Garden Hotel at the base of the overpass is the **Cave**. It is in the basement of the Zhujiang Building, 360 Huanshi Dong Road, *Tel. 83863660*. Beer is Y15-Y36 and it doesn't take credit cards.

The **Concert Hall** can be reached by buses 277, 194, 89 and 248 from downtown. The Performing Arts Center's telephone is *87375869 or 87375986*, *website: www.concerthall.com.cn (in English)*.

Sports & Recreation

The best golf is at the **Nansha Golf Club** an hour away in Panyu. Closer to town is the small but beautiful **Nan Hu golf course**.

You can rent bicycles near the back door of the White Swan Hotel, and from some other hotels. They are not allowed on main streets. Ask your consulate or hotel about the Hash House Harriers ("a drinking club with a running problem.") You'll probably be able to join them for a run on weekends.

Shopping

Locally-made are carvings of ivory, jade, bamboo, and wood, and gold and silver jewelry. Shantou (Swatow) drawnworks and embroidery and Foshan's ceramics are famous, and should be cheaper here than outside the province.

The main shopping area is around Zhongshan 5-Road and Beijing Road. Ask for the Guangzhou Department Store at 12 Xihu Road (and Beijing Road). Also proletarian is the Nan Fang Da Sha department store at 49 Yan Jiang Xi Road.

The Friendship Store is at 369 Huanshi Dong Road. It is expensive with imported name brands and locally manufactured goods and is next to the Baiyun Hotel. Lots of fun is the curio and antique **Da He Lu Market** area. It's partly a wholesale area for tourist products – expandable stone bracelets and manufactured amber, real pearls, beads, gems, and interior painted balls. It looks like a good place to buy souvenirs wholesale. Ask for Wen Chang Road. Unfortunately this market is spread all over – and the antique stores are not together in one place. You go through narrow alley ways and get lost easily.

The stores at the White Swan Hotel have good quality and variety for silks, crafts and antiques. The #**Guangdong Cultural Relics Store**, is at 696 Renmin Bei Road, Tel. 86678608. Books in English are at the White Swan and Dong Feng Hotels.

The **Xihu Road Night Market** (open from 7-10pm) has over 900 stalls with casual clothes, factory overruns and seconds. For Computer, VCDs, and software, try the He Run Electronics Plaza, 2/F, corner of Jiefang Road and Zhongshan 6 Road or Computer City, NEC Building, Ti Yu Dong Road, Tian He.

Excursions & Day Trips

Most of these places in Guangdong province are mainly for business people and for people trying to connect with their Chinese roots. They are, however, worth seeing. The countryside is lush and beautiful except for the hills carved bare to fill in Hong Kong's harbor. It is full of villages with black brick buildings and watchtowers built against tigers and bandits. Hong Kong has short tours. This is a quickly developing area that is losing much of its distinctive architecture and way of life. But it still has many charming aspects.

FOSHAN

Foshan (Fatshan) is about 25 km southwest of Guangzhou by expressway. It is important because of its Ancestral Temple, and its handicrafts. It is usually reached by road from Guangzhou, a one-day excursion. Named 'Hill of Buddhas' because a mound of Buddhist statues was excavated here, Foshan is one of the Four Ancient Towns of China. The city is over 1,300 years old and has a population of 3,292,400 of whom 474,400 are urban.

Hotels here add a 10% surcharge plus Y5 per person tax on rooms.

FOSHAN HOTEL (Binguan), *75 Fenjiang Nan Road, 528000. Four stars. Tel.2986881. Fax 3352347. E-mail: gzfshl@pub.foshan.gd.cn. Website: www.foshanhotel.com.cn. $82-$95 for rooms, and $110-$1783 for suites. You should be able to get at least a 30% discount. It accepts credit cards but not travelers' checks.*

This attractive downtown garden hotel was opened in 1981, has 19 stories, and 395 rooms with safes, CNN and broadband internet service. It has executive and non-smoking floors, an outdoor pool, gym, and French and Chaozhou food. It's the best hotel in town.

OVERSEAS CHINESE HOTEL *(Huaqiao Da Sha), 14 Zumiao Road. Tel. 2223828, Fax 2220291. Three stars.*

This hotel has a decent restaurant.

The **Ancestral Temple**, now the Foshan Municipal Museum, was founded in the 11th century, expanded and rebuilt after Liberation. It is at 21 Zumiao Road. Open 8:30am-7pm. Y20. *Tel. 2293723.* It contains sculptures, ancient relics, and a 2,500-kilogram bronze figure named Northern Emperor. Note the decorations on the bases of the arches, and the stone, wood, and brick carvings. Four of the statues are made of paper, the others of wood or clay. The roof, decorated with Shiwan pottery figures, is one of the most elaborate in the country, quite gaudy, but artistically and culturally important.

Locally made are cuttlebone sculptures, brick carvings, silk, lanterns, paper-cuts, and of course the famous Shiwan ceramics. The **Foshan Folk Art Institute** also produces palace lanterns, T-shirts, and paper cuts. It is on Zumiao road, open 8am-5pm. *Tel. 2242556.* Bus 1, 5 or 11.

The **Shiwan Artistic Ceramic Factory** is one of the most famous ceramic factories in China and is worth a visit, not only for its temple-top figures, but also for its maroon-robed lohan saints, with expressive, bulging eyes and unglazed faces. Its exhibition hall has works by master artisans. It is at Dongfeng Road, Shiwan. Open 9am-4:30pm. *Tel. 2272992,* buses 1, 19 or 15. Tours usually visit a silk factory too. The 19th century **Langyuan Garden** is good and close by, if you have time to spare. *Tel. 2241279.* Open 8:30am-5:30pm. Bus 5 or 18. Y10. You can also drive to **Xijiao Mountain** which has a cable car to good hiking places, big statues, and old villages.

CITS, *Tel. 2981048, 2981053, 2980108, Fax 2981054, 2980308. E-mail: fscits@pub.foshan.gd.cn.* It charges $45 for an English-speaking guide per day. The **telephone code** is 757.

JIANGMEN

Jiangmen (Kiangmen or Kongmoon in Cantonese) is about 100 km south of Guangzhou, the closest airport. You can reach this old port city by road or ship from Guangzhou, or by daily non-stop four-hour ferry from Hong Kong and Macau. Jiangman City is made up of five counties: Xinhui, Heshan,

Kaiping, Enping, and Taishan. The best hotel is the Crystal/Celeste Palace. The East Lake is a good garden-style hotel. Both are close together in the suburbs, take credit cards, and are five km from the port and two km from the bus station.

CELESTE PALACE (Yin Jing Jiudian), *22 Kong Kou Road, 529051. Four stars. Tel. 3183288, Fax 3183001. E-mail: jmcph@pub.jiangmen.gd.cn. Website: celeste-palace-hotel.com. It has been giving 20-25% discounts and accepts credit cards but not travelers' checks.*

Opened in 1990 with renovations in 1999, this hotel has 216 spacious rooms, some of them non-smoking. It has a large outdoor pool, CNN, a gym, bowling and tennis.

EAST LAKE HOTEL (Dong Hu Binguan), *15 Guang Hou Road, 529051. Three stars. Tel. 3100888, 3363611, Fax 3361010, 3351010. Built in 1973, this three-story hotel has 208 small rooms, suites and a pool.*

SHANTOU

Shantou (Swatow), an industrial seaport city and Special Economic Zone in northeastern Guangdong province, is laid back, charming and famous for its handicrafts. It is 350 km by air north of Guangzhou. By the end of 2002, it should be a two hour express bus ride from Xiamen. It is four hours by bus from Shenzhen and 5.5 hours from Guangzhou. It is reached by train from only Guangzhou. It has air connections with 35 other Chinese cities and Hong Kong, Bangkok, and Kuala Lumpur.

Shantou is the ancestral home of innumerable Chinese emigrants to Southeast Asia, Japan, and Africa. Some were kidnapped from here and sent to Cuba in the late 1800s. Today about 15% of the population receive remittances from overseas. The Shantou urban population is now 1.08 million; the urban population of nearby Chaozhou is less than 200,000. The weather is mild, with an annual rainfall of 1,400 to 2,000 mm mainly in the summer.

Shantou is a 2,000-year-old town to which disgraced officers of the Tang were exiled.

2000 years ago, Shantou belonged to the Yue Kingdom (see Guangzhou). Europeans used its port to import opium. In addition to its famous lace and embroidery, it produces carpets, painted porcelain, jewelry, bamboo carvings, lacquer, and stone, shell, and gilded wood carvings.

This city has several centers, one of which is around Renmin Square in the old city and used for National Day celebrations. The old city of Shantou is full of low-rise houses with pleasant, interesting walks. You can take the nearby ferry which is two km from the International Hotel at the Square Pier across the harbor to Queshi and start climbing for a pleasant walk. To the left is Bai Hua Jian monastery.

The **Chen Chi Hong Gu Ju** or **"Little Imperial Palace"** Qian Mei in Longdu, Chenghai city *Tel. 5786955*, is 20 km northeast of Shantou and said to be a beautifully-restored 506-room Teochew family mansion. It is full of gilded wooden carvings, glass and stone sculptures. **Maya Islet** close to the Regency has a tiny temple to the sea goddess, and the former British Customs House and can be reached by taxi. A globe at Shantou University marks the **Tropic of Cancer**.

Chaozhou is 30 km north of Shantou, and is one of the traditional Four Famous Ancient Towns. The main attractions are the Kaiyuan Temple from the Tang dynasty, West Lake Park, and a huge porcelain market. None of these are world class. Chaozhou used to be more important than Shantou, so that's where the main temples are. Buses go every 20 minutes to an hour between the two cities during the day for about Y10. The porcelain market is in Feng Xi Town on Anjie Road about four kilometers from the west bus station, about a Y10 taxi ride.

One hears of Chaozhou but not Shantou food. The cuisine is a branch of Cantonese, with lots of seafood, and was so named because Chaozhou used to be the name of the whole area. Now Shantou has become more prosperous and famous, but the name of the cuisine remained.

Shantou has at least three five-star hotels and a good four-star. They are all relatively downtown and close to the Special Economic Zone. The Regency is in the east side of town in a newly developed residential area surrounded by grass.All add a 15% surcharge, and have foreign exchange and credit card services. Prices are subject to change and discounts.

The best has been the Regency. The 318-room Meritus Shantou Hotel (Junhua Dajiudian) opened too late to be reviewed. Based on the reputation of its Singapore management company, it should be considered. It is on Jin Sha Dong Road, 515041, *Tel. 8191188, Fax 8192288. E-mail: shantou.msc@meritusa-hotels.com. Website: www.meritusshantou.com.*

The English in all of them is relatively good (for China). The International and Golden Gulf are downtown near shops.

REGENCY HOTEL SHANTOU (Di Hao Jiudian), *Jinsha Dong Road, 515041. Five stars. Tel. 8199888, Fax 8800000. E-mail: stdhint@pub.shantou.gd.cn. Website: www.regencyhotelshantou.com (in English). Y1280-1680 for rooms, and Y2680 to 19800 for suites. It has been giving 35% discounts. This 1999, 33-story, 542-room hotel is a five-minute walk to the Shantou Railway Station and close to the airport expressway. It is 12 km from the airport.*

The Regency has executive and non-smoking floors. Rooms are 40 square meters, have safes, CNN, HBO, and VOD movies. It has two tennis courts and about a 20-meter- long, year-round outdoor pool. Its gym has nine good machines. (One was broken.). There's bowling, billiards, and tennis. Its banquet hall can seat 1040 at tables. There's Japanese, Chinese and Western food and a 5600-square-meter International Exhibition and Conference Centre. Regency Hotel Management (Hong Kong).

GOLDEN GULF HOTEL (Jin Hai Wan Da Jiudian), *Jinsha Dong Road, Shantou, 515041. Five stars. Tel. 8263263, Fax 8265162. E-mail: "mailto:stgghotl@pub.shantou.gd.cn"stgghotl@pub.shantou.gd.cn. Website: www.goldengulfhotel.com (English soon). Y1100-Y1300 for rooms and Y2200-Y11200 for suites. Apartments available. It has been giving at least 40% discounts, and is located 12 km from the airport, near Ying Bin Square and next to Bank of China. Walmart and McDonalds are 200 meters away.*

Built in 1991 with renovations 2001, this hotel has 28 stories and 380 rooms, CNN, executive floor, and some non-smoking rooms. There's hot pot, Chaozhou and western food. Rooms are 30 square meters. It has a 17-meter-long outdoor pool, sauna, tennis, and gym. Orient (Dong Fang) Hotel Management Group.

SHANTOU INTERNATIONAL HOTEL (Guoji Da Jiudian), *Jin Sha Dong Road, 515041. Four stars, Tel. 8251212, Fax 8252250. E-mail: stih@pub.shantou.gd.cn. Website: www.stih.com (English). It is 15 km from the airport. Y980-Y1380 for rooms; Y2200-Y9800 for suites. It has been discounting 40% on rooms and 60% on suites. This hotel is in the Special Economic Zone, around the corner from a pedestrian shopping street and close to the old city.*

Built in 1988, this 26-story property has 353 rooms, a gym, revolving restaurant, and 24-hour room service. It has CNN and CNBC, VOD with pay movies, and in-room safes. It has some stained carpets, non-smoking floors, and rooms for single women. Rooms are 31 square meters. It has a revolving restaurant with a great view of the whole city. The English and service are above average for a four-star in a city with so few English-speaking visitors. Sunpride International Management Group (Hong Kong).

An **internet bar** is to the left as you leave the International Hotel. Cross Jin Sha Road at McDonald's. It's on the second floor of the corner building. Look for a sign with a computer and a tell-tale "e" on its screen. Open 9am to 2am.

Travel agents: best go through your hotel. It can organize sightseeing, help with ticketing and guides. There's **Shantou China Travel Service,** 42 Shan Zhang Road, 515041, *Tel. 8610689, Fax 8328879.*

The **telephone code** is 754.

TAISHAN

Taishan (Cantonese, Toishan; Toishan, Hoishan) is important as the ancestral county of the descendants of those who left China for the Chinatowns of North America, Southeast Asia and Australia in the early 1900s. For tourists, the attractions here are rural, a restful exposure to south China, towns that still retain old over-the-sidewalk architecture and villages with watchtowers (protection from bandits and tigers). But things are changing so get there soon. The population of the main city Taicheng is about 980,000 and it makes good billiard tables.

This Taishan should not be confused with the mountain in Shandong farther north, also called Taishan. This Taishan is a county on the southern coast of Guangdong province, 70 minutes by expressway southwest of Guangzhou, 1.5 hours west of Macau and Zhuhai and 2.5 hours southwest of Shenzhen. Its county town is Taicheng.

A 3.5 hour ferry to Gongyi links it with Hong Kong. The ferry is a pleasant introduction to the area and a public bus or a hotel car can take you 20 km to Taicheng. The ferry leaves Hong Kong-China City once a day in the morning and leaves Gongyi about 1:30pm to go back. Weisheng Bus Limited has buses between Hong Kong and Taicheng. *(Tel. in Hong Kong 2391-8090 or 9367-2824; in Taishan, Tel. 5622255 or 5525890.)* The trip takes less than four hours and costs HK$200 except on holidays when the price goes up. Please consult a travel agency or the Garden Hotel for the best buses to Shenzhen, Guangzhou, Zhongshan, and Zhuhai. There are also buses to ferry ports at nearby Kaiping, Xinhui and Jiangmen.

You can get around Taishan by taxi, public bus or motorcyle rickshaw.

Where to Stay

The Garden Hotel can be a little run-down and too relaxed, but this is the best place in town. The food has been superb but the management has changed since my visit in 2001. Hotels here add a 10% surcharge.

GARDEN HOTEL (Yuanlin Jiu Dian), *Nanmenxi Road, 529200. Four stars. Tel. 5525890 or Fax 5518015. Y380-Y700 for rooms; Y880-Y2800 for suites. Villas with 5-13 rooms cost Y4800-Y9800. It has been discounting 20 to 30%. Less than one km south of the Overseas Chinese Hotel bus station and McDonald's, its central location is ideal for walkers who want to see both the old town and the tourist attractions.*

This is an attractive garden-style hotel on the edge of a man-made lake. It has hot spring water in all 148 rooms but no CNN. Rooms including balcony are 29 to 33.5 square meters. It can't accept travelers' checks, only cash and credit cards. It has a golf driving range and pool. The staff is friendly and helpful, but the English still needs work.

SUNRISE HOT SPRING HOTEL, *about six km from the Garden, in the Hot Spring Developing Zone, 529252. Tel. 5843888, Fax 5843822. It is isolated in the countryside. Rooms cost Y338, and suites Y438 and Y798.*

It has five good-looking natural mineral water swimming pools open from 9am. to 1am daily (Y38). The hotel itself is air-conditioned, basic, and clean; however, its restaurant has chipped dishes.

OVERSEAS CHINESE HOTEL (Huaqiao Dasha), *1 Tong Ji Road, 529405, Tel. 5524768, Fax 5529405. Rooms cost Y218-Y278 and suites Y308.*

This hotel is dumpy, old, across from McDonald's and no one speaks English. It is only for the financially desperate.

Where to Eat

Taishan food is basically the same as Cantonese, but there are some dishes that are unique, like mud fish, steamed minced pork with salted egg (yuk beng), peanuts fried with water chestnuts, and double boiled soup. The **Garden Hotel** has the best restaurant here. A line of at least 10 seafood restaurants on Huan Shi Road is less than a 10-minute drive from the Garden Hotel and open from 10am to 3am. None have menus in English and the hygiene is questionable. See Chapter 25. My local friends like the **Tian Tian Hai Siam**, *Tel. 5571129*. This is third from the right as you face the restaurants. You can pick from fish swimming in tanks. Expect to be entertained or bothered by strolling musicians, depending on your mood.

A glitzy, five-star hotel has opened about a 35-minute drive away which has had an excellent Chinese restaurant. **Ever Joint Peninsula Hotel** is at 2 Zhong Yin Road in Kai Ping, 529300, *Tel. 750/233333, Fax 2338333*.

Seeing the Sights

Stone Flower Mountain (Sek Fa Shan), one of the major tourist attractions, is about 10 minutes by taxi from the Garden Hotel in the northeast of town. One-way costs about Y10. There's a small temple to the Goddess of Mercy and a low but interesting mountain to climb.

The **Tongji Sightseeing Tower** is 20-30 minutes walk from the Garden Hotel. From there you can see all of Taishan city. You cross the bridge on Tongji Road from the Overseas Chinese Hotel, and take the second left onto Tai Hai Lu. The tower with its elevator is open 8am to 12:30 midnight (Y5). *Tel. 5671245 and 5671511.*

If you don't have an **ancestral village** to visit, travel agents can arrange for you to see one. Near the Bank of China is a statue of **Chen Yu Hi,** a Chinese-American who in 1906 started the first railway line by a private company in China. The 100 km-long track was used from 1912 to 1942 when it was destroyed by the Japanese.

The town has a tiny **museum** at Huan Bei Da Dao Shi Shan, 529200. It gives a history of the overseas emigrations and has some ancient relics. Some titles are in English. Call *5529446 or 5524045* to make sure there's someone there to let you in. It's on the second floor at Shi Hill, Huan Bei Avenue.

A **Protestant Church** is at 186 Tai Xi Road, *Tel. 5525709*. It is open 8am-11:30am and 2pm- 5:30 pm daily. It has fellowship and services Fridays and Saturdays 7:30pm-8:30pm, and Sundays 12 noon to 1pm. Visitors are welcome.

Shang Chuan Island's Fei Sa Beach is about 40 km south of Taicheng, plus a 30-minute jetfoil ride. It has four km of beach and clear water but Taicheng people say it's overpriced. The Sam Xing Kip is the best hotel with villas but no English. Locals say it is badly managed. Nearby is the **St. Francis Xavier Church** where the Jesuit died in 1552. (His body is in Goa in India.) To the east of Taicheng is **Zhongshan** county, birthplace of Dr. Sun Yixian (Sun Yat-sen).

A **summer youth program** affords young people with at least one parent from the area an opportunity to learn about their ancestral land. Canadians should contact Mr. Lee, Secretary of the Taishan Association of Ontario preferably in March or April of each year, *Tel. 416/971-8887 or 482-4070*. The address is 42 Huron St., Toronto, Ontario, M5T 2A4, Canada. Americans should look for the Taishan Association in major Chinatowns.

Those interested in the U.S. program **"In Search of Roots"** should contact Albert Cheng in San Francisco, *Tel. 415/9861822, Fax 415/9862825, E-mail: alcheng888@aol.com*. This program sponsored by the Chinese Culture Foundation of San Francisco is for ages 16 to 26, and applications should be received in November for the following summer's 14-18 day trip of Taishan. The program actually starts in February with classes and assignments. The Chinese government provides lodging and meals.

Also of interest: Marlon Hom, Department Chair, Asian American Studies Department, San Francisco State University, *E-mail:mhom@sfsu.edu*, teaches a summer course. (AAS629: Selected Topics in Chinese American Studies—Travel Study in China). It is a 30-day study of Cantonese migration history and Chinese-American emigration regions along the Pearl River Delta.

The **Taishan Bureau of Travel and Tourism** and **Taishan Tourist Company** are at 19 Stone Flower Overseas Chinese Village, Huan Bei Street, 529200, *Tel. 5534714, 5525847, Fax 5529999*. They are friendly but only Echo Chan speaks English.

The **Overseas Chinese Affairs Office,** is at 38 Huan Nan Street, Back Building, *Tel. 5523864, Fax 5522567*. This office should be able to help people of Chinese ancestry find their ancestral villages. Ask for Steve Liu at the **Foreign Affairs Office,** 19 Huan Bei Avenue, Shihua Huaqiao Xincun, *Tel. 5503379, 5501286*. **China Travel Service** is at the Overseas Chinese Hotel, 1 Tong Ji Road, 529200, *Tel. 5524768, Fax 5529405*.

Websites: The county has one in English: *www.taishan.com*, a good introduction. The government's website is: *www.tsonline.com.cn*, currently only in Chinese, but English is planned. For more details, see my website: *www.china-travel-guide.com*.

The **telephone code** is 750.

ZHAOQING

This little town is famous for its Seven Star Crags, and its relatively tranquil atmosphere, a good place for walkers and bicycles. It is also known for Mt. Dinghu. It can be reached by bus or train from Hong Kong, Shenzhen and Guangzhou and is about 100 km/two hours by road west of Guangzhou, and 263 km/three hours from Shenzhen. Zhaoqing is on the Guangzhou-Chongqing, Guangzhou-Kunming, and Hong Kong-Zhaoqing train lines. It has two long-distance bus stations: one is downtown near the Star Lake Hotel; the other, the Qiaoxi, is in the west part of town. It's a pity there is so little English spoken here; Zhaoqing is a wonderful place for a few days away from big cities. I found only one person in the CTS office who spoke English, and no one at the Overseas Chinese Hotel, or in the Tourism Committee office. Accommodations and restaurants are adequate but not great.

The total population is 3.7 million, the urban population is closer to 200,000. The weather is subtropical, with an annual precipitation of 1599 mm mainly from April to August.

Where to Stay & Eat

No international class hotel exists in this resort city. The best, by the lake in the center of town, is the Star Lake Hotel but don't expect much. Second is the Overseas Hotel close by. English is a problem. If you want to be away from town beside the lake, there's the International Youth Hostel, but it isn't very good. If you want to be up in Dinghu Mountain, there's another international Youth Hostel with some basic rooms that are better if you're not fussy. Hotels add a surcharge of 13%.

STAR LAKE HOTEL (Xing Hu Sing Dajiudian), *37 4th Duan Zhou Road, Four stars. Tel. 2261188, Fax 2236688. E-mail: bc@ZQ.Col.com.cn. Rooms are Y500-Y600, and suites Y880 to Y8888. It has been giving 20-30% discounts but not on holidays, and it accepts credit cards. It's near Star Lake, and well located for the night market.*

There are 31-stories, a revolving restaurant and 400 rooms. There's a 25-meter-long outdoor pool, and gym.

OVERSEAS CHINESE HOTEL, *90 Tian Ning Bei Road, 526040, Tel. 2232952, Fax 2231197. E-mail: zchcdc88@pub.zhaoqing.gd.cn. Rooms are Y330-Y440, and suites Y660-Y3888, and it has been discounting 30% off "sometimes."*

There has been peeling wallpaper and some carpet stains but it has a nice garden and a good view of the lake from the top floors. CTS is on the premises. This 1987 hotel has 239 rooms.

SEVEN STAR CRAGS INTERNATIONAL YOUTH HOSTEL (Chut Sing Yen Lu Guan), *Seven Star Crags Scenic Spot, 526040, Tel. 2226688, Fax 2224155. Website: www.iyhf.org. It is on the east side of the lake near the crags, and marked on the map as "Xingyan Hotel." Beds in a dorm cost Y30. Standard rooms cost Y168. You can take #19 bus and then walk into the park. A taxi costs about Y15 from the main bus or train station.*

This hostel has 85 rooms. If you have a problem, ask for Chen Xin Yong or Lin Qi Le who speak English. Lin is at extension 2618. I would recommend spending one night in town and then move to Mt. Dinghu to take advantage of its wonderful air, anions, and greenery.

MT. DINGHU INTERNATIONAL YOUTH HOSTEL (Dinghu be shu shan zhang), *Dinghu Shan, 526070, Tel. 2621668, Fax 2621665. E-mail: gdzqyha@pub.zhaoqing.gd.cn. Take number 21 bus between 6:30am and 11pm from the bus terminal on the lake across from the Star Lake Hotel.*

To enter the nature reserve, you pay a Y30 entry fee the first time you go. Show your receipt on other occasions. Then hike up the hill to the left a couple hundred meters. On the way, get a map of the mountain at the Tourist Information Office (open 8am to 5:30pm). Look for the IYH sign. It has 100 beds. Ask for wonderful Liang Bing Qiang (Ivan) who seems to be the only person around who speaks English, and is the hiking guide and hotel manager.

The hostel is in two buildings and charges about Y38 per bed in a dorm with private bath. This hostel is part of a very modest two-star hotel with rooms for Y308, but it takes no credit cards, cannot change money, and needs work. There are nearby grubby but adequate restaurants, one open for breakfast. The rain is heaviest in April, May and June.

Seeing the Sights

Zhaoqing was the home for six years of the Italian Jesuit missionary **Matteo Ricci**. He lived in "Shuihing" in the 1580s. While no one knows exactly where Ricci's house was, an educated guess places it between the boat landing and the Ming pagoda in the old city by the river. The district here has a Song dynasty gate with houses that look like they haven't changed since Ricci's time. An earthen wall circles the old city. For good background, read *The Wise Man from the West – Matteo Ricci and His Mission to China* by Vincent Cronin.

Zhaoqing was developed as a resort in 1955. It was named Seven Star Crags because its mountains appear placed like the seven stars of the Big Dipper. It is like a potted miniature garden, like Guilin. You can climb 130-meter **Heavenly Pillar** for the view.

The **seven crags** are named Langfeng (Lofty Wind), Yuping (Jade Screen), Shishi (Stone Chamber), Tianzhu (Heavenly Pillar), Chanchu (Toad), Shinzhang (Stone Palm), and Apo (Hill Slope). The biggest cave is at the foot of Apo Crag and you can enter it by boat. If you hit the rocks at Musical Instrument Rock, you get different musical notes.

The **museum** is in Yuejiang Tower (Y5) by the river. It has a good display of Duan ink stones, and a few bronzes, tomb figures, and porcelains. This area was part of the Yue Kingdom (see Guangzhou) during the Warring states period. Its name became Zhaoqing in 1118.

Also very pleasant is 11.33 square kilometer **Dinghu (Tripod) Mountain,** 18 km northeast of the city and reached cheaply by bus from the station in front of the Star Lake Hotel. The mountain, which is a UNESCO Man and Biosphere Research Centre, is a nature preserve. Fascinating is the walk down the mountainside 700 meters through the sprawling, functioning Qing Yun

Temple (Buddhist and 17th century) down to the youth hostel; another trail goes across a lake, and up into the mountains along a paved meter-wide path with railing, to the giant "ding" tripod.

Made in the area, in addition to famous inkstones, are ivory and bone carvings, sandalwood fans, paintings, straw products, umbrellas, and jewelry. Ginseng Beer is made here too. The night market with some clothes, curios, and crafts is between the Overseas Chinese Hotel and the Star Lake Hotel.

China Travel Service is behind the Overseas Chinese Hotel at 90 Tianning Bei Road, 526040. *Tel. 2229908. Fax 2229983.* Ask for Miss Xu who speaks English.

The **tourist information offices** are in the Railway Station (*Tel. 2835114*), Paifang Square on the lake near the Overseas Chinese Hotel, as well as at Mt. Ding Hu. At least you should be able to get a local map in English. For more details, visit my website: *www.china-travel-guide.com/updates19.htm#ZHAOQING.*

The **telephone code** is 758.

ZHONGSHAN CITY

Zhongshan is important because of the former residence of Dr. Sun Yat-sen (Sun Yixian) in Cuiheng village, 26 km from Shiqi (the main city). The father of the Chinese republic designed the house himself, a blend of Spanish and local styles. The prestigeous Sun Yixian Memorial Middle School and an interesting folk culture museum are nearby. For more about Dr. Sun see Nanjing and Shanghai. There is also a riverside village to explore.

Close to Macau, and across the Pearl River delta south of Hong Kong, Zhongshan can be reached directly by 1 1/2 hour hovercraft from Hong Kong at least five times a day, or via road from Macau and Zhuhai in about 45 minutes. It is about 1 1/2hours by four-lane expressway, southwest of Guangzhou and Shenzhen.

Shiqi (Shekki, Shekket) is the cultural, economic, and political center of Zhongshan City. Its urban population is 350,000. It is full of intriguing waterways begging to be explored. It has a lot of activity and new buildings,

Special Visa Arrangements

Tourists (except those from UK) arriving from Hong Kong can get an **express visa** for one month at the **Zhongshan City Customs Post** for HK$180 each (HK$40 extra for photo). They can leave China any place. Tourists entering from Hong Kong for less than 144 hours can get a free **"144-hour Easy Visa"** through any designated travel agencies in Hong Kong and Macau.

yet the canals and the age-old river boats, might remind you of a much smaller, older Bangkok.

The top hotels in Shiqi are the Zhongshan International and the Fu Hua, both about 15 km from Zhongshan port and 56 km from the closest airport in Zhuhai. They are almost together near the bridge in the center of Shiqi, night market and shops. They are about even in quality. All hotels here receive Hong Kong television programs. Most add a 15% service charge to the following prices (which should be discounted) and some add an additional 10% surcharge on weekends and Hong Kong holidays. A five-star, 400 room Shangri-La Hotel is due to open mid-2003 and should be the best hotel.

FU HUA HOTEL (Jiudian), *1 Fuhua Road, Shiqi, 528401. Four stars. Tel. 8638888, Fax 8611862. E-mail: htl@fuhuahotel.com.cn. Web: www.fuhuahotel.com.cn. Built in 1986, this 19-story, 242- room hotel is set in a garden. Rooms are Y580-Y1200 depending on executive and standard, weekdays (lowest), weekends and holidays (highest). Economy rooms are Y320-Y572. Suites Y880-Y9800. You can still get a discount.*

This hotel has smoke hoods and emergency flashlights, a revolving restaurant, and satellite TV. A separate building for sports has a nightclub, 30-piece gym, and sauna. It has Western (of sorts), Cantonese and Chaozhou food.

ZHONGSHAN INTERNATIONAL HOTEL (Guoji Jiudian), *142 Zhongshan Road Section Number One, Shiqi 528401. Four stars aiming for five. Tel. 8633388, Fax 8633368. E-mail: zsih@pub.zhongshan.gd.cn. Website: www.zsih.com.cn. Rooms are Y580-Y730 and suites Y1100-Y7800.*

This 1986, 22-story, 369-room hotel has a revolving restaurant and good quality stores, four bowling lanes, a sauna and a year-round outdoor pool.

For the **Chungshan/Zhongshan Hot Spring Golf Club**, *Tel. 6683888, Fax 6683990.* A visit can be arranged in Hong Kong, *Tel. 852/25210377, Fax 28684642.* The Arnold Palmer Course Design Company planned the 18-hole, par-72 course which now has 36 holes and is one of the best in China.

The **Gu Hok (Gu He) Old Furniture Market** with about 200 stores is just this side of the border from Zhuhai in Tanzhou Town, Zhongshan county. It has more to see than any furniture museum. The first asking price for one of those fancy carved beds was Y18,000 and the choice is vast. Beds can be taken apart and shipped. They have other antiques and reproductions too. Most of the stores do not take credit cards, and are open 9:30am to 7pm daily. Sam at the **Yong Chang Furniture Plant**, *Tel. 760-6650502* speaks English and can give directions. He's at 1-3 Building, Shuntai Industrial Area, Fourteenth Hamlet, Tanzhou Town, *Mobile Tel. 013703039481. Web: www.yc-furniture.com (English with photos).*

Practical Information
China International Travel Service of Zhongshan, *142, Zhongshan Rd.1, Tel. 8611888, Fax 8623890.*

China Travel Service of Zhongshan, *No.1 Fuhua Road, Tel. 8638888, Fax 8611650, E-mail: cts@ctszs.com.*
Zhongshan Overseas Travel Corporation, *38 Zhongshan Road, 2, Tel. 8807493, Fax 8923376. E-mail: zsotit@hotmail.com.* It charges HK$250 per day for a guide for one or two people, and HK$450 per day for a small car in the Zhongshan area.
Zhongshan Tourism Bureau, *38 Zhongshan Road, 2, Zhongshan City, 528400. Tel. 3326473, 3326468, Fax 8806615. E-mail: zstbcyb@pub.zhongshan.gd.cn or zsot@pub.zhongshan.gd.cn. Website: www.zhongshantour.com.cn.* Ask for Che Wei, Deputy Director.
Zhongshan CYTS, *Tel. 8822263, Fax 3322670.* Use this if you can't get anyone else.
The **telephone code** is 760.

Practical Information for Guangzhou

Ambulance, *Tel. 120*
Bank of China in China Hotel is open 9am-6pm weekdays and 9am-5pm on Saturdays and Sundays.
Consulates: usual hours Mondays-Fridays 8:30am-12pm or 12:30pm, and 1 or 1:30pm-5 or 5:30pm. Some close Fridays at 2pm.
• **Australia,** *Tel. 83350909. Fax 83350718*
• **Britain,** *Tel. 83351354. Fax 83336485. E-mail: guangbcg@gitic.com.cn*
• **Cambodia,** *Tel. 83338999 X 809, 810 or 811. Fax 83879006. E-mail: cambodia@public.guangzhou.gd.cn*
• **Canada,** *China Hotel Office Tower, Suite 801, Liu Hua Lu, 510015. Tel.86660569. Fax 86670267. E-mail ganzu@dfait-maeci.gc.ca and ganzu@dfait-maeci.gc.ca. Website: www.canada.org.cn. Closed 12:30-2pm*
• **Denmark,** *Suite 1578, Office Tower, China Hotel, Liu Hua Road, 510015. Tel. 86660353, Fax 86670315. E-mail: gkldan@public.guangzhou.gd.cn*
• **France,** *Tel. 83303405, Fax 83303437*
• **Germany,** *Tel. 83306533, Fax 83317033. E-mail: gkkanton@gitic.com.cn . (shorter hours). Website: www.deguangzhou.org/*
• **Italy,** *Tel. 38770556, Fax 38770270. E-mail: itconsgz@gitic.com.cn.*
• **Japan,** *Tel. 83343009, Fax 83338972. E-mail: ryojikan@public.guangzhou.gd.cn*
• **Malaysia,** *Tel. 87395660, Fax 87395669*
• **Netherlands,** *Tel. 83302067, Fax 83303601. E-mail: nedcons@gitic.com.cn*
• **Philippines,** *Tel. 81886968 ext. 421, Fax 81862041. E-mail: gzphcggz@public.guangzhou.gd.cn or gzphcggz@public1.guangzhou.gd.cn*
• **Thailand,** *Tel. 81886968 X 3313, Fax 81879451*
• **U.S.,** *White Swan Hotel, 1 Shamian Nan St., 510133. Tel. 81888911 ext. 256, 81862441, Fax 81862341, 81862341. American Citizen Services Unit, Tel. 81862418. Adopted Children Immigrant Visa Unit, Tel. 81888911, Fax 81883000. E-mail: GuangzhouA@state.gov*

• **Vietnam**, *Tel. 83305911, Fax 83305915. E-mail: tlsqvn@mx2.gd.cei.gov.cn*

Tourist Handouts: "That's *Guangzhou.* "*Website:www.thatsGuangzhou.com*" *www.thatsGuangzhou.com.* There's also "City Talk." Both have lists of restaurants, bars, and events. Available from hotels, bars and restaurants.

Travel agents:

• **China International Travel Services Guangzhou** (CITS Canton), *185 Huanshi Xi Road. Tel. 86675371, 86666279, 86666275, Fax 86678048, 86678356, 86671459. E-mail: itd@citsgd.com.cn and citsgea@public.guangzhou.gd.cn.*

• **GZL International Travel Service**, *13/F, Globe Plaza, 829-832, Renmin Bei Road. Tel. 81073466 or 81080265* and ask for Manager of Inbound Tour Dept. Frank Fang. E-*mail: gztcrjy@public1.guangzhou.gd.cn or gztcrjy@21cn.com.* Frank helped me buy a mobile telephone for Y800, as well as plane tickets. This is one of the largest travel agencies in Guangzhou with tour buses, guides, and ticketing.

• **Guangzhou Merchants' International Travel Agency,** *Room 425, 426, Baiyun Hotel, 510065. Tel. 83312839, 13609796061. Fax 83311782. E-mail: sales@tour2000.com.cn, jeromezh@public.guangzhou.gd.cn. Website: www.tour2000.com.cn.* Ask for Jerome (Zhihong) Zhang, Business Travel Department.

Internet services: **Meet Internet Coffee House**, *first floor, Guangfa Bank Building, No. 83, Nang Lin Xin Road, Tel. 87679932.* It has 18 machines for Y15 an hour and is open from 11am to 2am. Here are booths, privacy, and food. **Qing Shui Ju** has about 10 computers. You pay Y12 an hour and you get tea too. It has three branches, one of which is at 12 Bao An Qian Street, Yan Dun Rd. Both are relatively close to the Garden Hotel.

The **Zhongshan Public Library** (Tu Shu Guan) on Wen Ming Road has internet service for Y3 an hour, but it's closed at noon.

Medical emergencies: Consult your hotel or consulate above. There's also **Guangzhou International SOS Clinic**, *2/F, Guangdong Provincial Hospital of TCM, Da Tong Lu, Er Sha Island, 510105. Clinic Tel. 87351051/1240/1843, Clinic Fax 87352045.*

Telephone code: 20

Tourist Information Center, *Tel. 86696882, 86687051*

Shenzhen

(Shumchun)

On the Hong Kong border, this Special Economic Zone has been the wealthiest and the fastest growing in China. In 1979, **Shenzhen** had 20,000 people. Today, urban and rural, it has at least 3,580,000 and growing.

Aspiring to become the next Hong Kong by the year 2010, it has its own stock exchange and a tightly-packed garden of skyscrapers. At least 50% of all "foreign" arrivals into China pass through its Customs Houses. Most are Hong Kong commuters. Shenzhen has the highest cost of living in China, but it is still cheaper than Hong Kong.

Shenzhen is Hong Kong's weekend playground. It has some of China's best theme parks, amusement parks and resorts. Its golfing is among China's best. Prostitution seems to be out of control.

Arrivals & Departures

China Travel Service's website has train, bus, and ferry schedules between Hong Kong and Shenzhen at www.chinatravelOne.com (English). You can also send an e-mail asking specific questions to: *enquiry@chinatravel1.com* or *Fax 852/27893498.*

Airport Chinalink has been operating a bus service between the Hong Kong airport and several hotels in Shenzhen including the Landmark and Nanhai (Shekou) for HK$150. For schedules telephone in Hong Kong *952/ 97471202 or 97471202.* In Shenzhen, telephone the Landmark Hotel, *3372546 or 3751805, Fax 3751805.* This bus doesn't usually encounter traffic jams as it doesn't go to downtown Hong Kong.

Warning: See Guangzhou above for travel here on holidays. Don't even think about it.

Trains are the fastest and most convenient way to get to downtown Shenzhen from downtown Kowloon because of sluggish road traffic. With buses, you have to drag out your luggage twice at borders, but some buses go direct to hotels here. No Hong Kong taxis are allowed into Shenzhen.

Ferries go from China Hong Kong City to Shenzhen's Shekou and to the Shenzhen airport. (You go to Fuyong and take a connecting bus).

Shenzhen is reached by air from at least 57 Chinese cities, and Anchorage, Chicago, and Subic Bay. Huangtian Airport is 40 km west of the city and has luggage storage open from 6am-8:30pm, and four restaurants. *Tel. 7776156.* The Landmark and Shangri-La Hotels have downtown check-in counters for China Southern flights.

Note: A **five-day visa** can be purchased at the Shenzhen Customs House or Shekou Ferry Terminal for Y100 (but no British passport holder). Once over the border, you are not required to spend one night in Shenzhen, but you are required to leave China through Shenzhen. You enter from Hong Kong by train between 7:30am and 10pm. The border is currently open from 6:30am-11:30pm on weekdays and to midnight on weekends. There is talk of extending these hours. For entry with no visa, see Guangzhou.

Orientation

Shenzhen is about 7 by 10 kilometers, spreading mainly east and west from the railway station. A 39.5 km east-west subway should be finished soon from the main railway station to Shenzhen airport.

The main resorts are in the suburbs, or toward Shekou, which is 29 km west. At least two resorts have amusement park rides, the biggest at the Honey Lake Country Club (eight km from the train station), boasting the longest roller coaster ride (two km) in the world. Its monorail is 4.5 km long.

Where to Stay

Hotels and food here are cheaper than in Hong Kong for the same quality. The English is generally not as good as Hong Kong's. The best hotel for English-speaking foreigners is the Shangri-La. Near the theme parks, the best should be the Crowne Plaza. There's a four-star Holiday Inn. For budget travelers there's the International Youth Hostel. In Shekou, the best is the Nan Hai Hotel but there's the cheaper Ming Wah.

Hotels here add a 10%-15% service charge. Hotels might quote their prices in Hong Kong dollars **(one US dollar = about HK$7.80).** The hotels listed here receive television in English from Hong Kong and take credit cards. They have foreign exchange and business centers. All except the youth hostel have services expected of international standard hotels.

Downtown hotels

SHANGRI-LA SHENZHEN HOTEL (Shang Gorilla), *East Side, Railway Station, Jianshe Road, 518001. Five stars, Tel. 2330888, Fax 2339878, 2330470. E-mail: slz@shangri-la.com. Y1865-Y2875 for rooms and Y3355-Y17050 for suites. Direct buses from Admiralty MTR station and China Hong Kong City in Hong Kong should arrive several times a day. It has a shuttle bus north of the Customs House, but if you climb up to the second floor level outside, you should be able to see this hotel.*

Opened in 1992 and refurbished in 2000, this hotel has 31 stories, 553 large rooms and CNN, NBC and inhouse movies, in-room safes, and voice-messaging system. There are executive and non-smoking floors, revolving restaurant and 24-hour room service. There's a clinic, good 20-piece gym, jacuzzi, sauna, steambath, outdoor pool and excellent security. A China Southern Airline service counter is in its business center for downtown check-ins and tickets.

LANDMARK HOTEL SHENZHEN (Fuyuan Jiudian), *3018 Nanhu Road, 518001. Five stars. Tel. 2172288, Fax 2290473, 2290479. E-mail: landmark@szlandmark.com.. Website: www.szlandmark.com.cn. English is good. Y1500-Y2650 for rooms and Y2500-Y4500 for suites. It has been discounting up to 40%. There's a five-minute complimentary shuttle to/from*

Lowu Immigration Station for hotel guests and it is a three-minute walk from the Dongmen shopping area.

Built in 1994, this hotel has 27 stories, 351 rooms, CNN, and an executive floor. It has a night club, gym, 20-meter outdoor pool, golf driving range, cyber bar, and children's play corner. There are Brazilian, Chaozhou, Cantonese, steak, and seafood restaurants. A Cathay International Hotel.

Near the Theme Parks

The **Crowne Plaza** opened too late to be reviewed, but it should be the best here. It is across the road from Window of the World at 9026 Shennan Road, Overseas Chinese Town, 518053, *Tel. 755/693-6888, Fax 6936999. E-mail: cpsz@szemail.com. Website: www.crowneplaza.com.* The Shenzhen Bay Hotel is most convenient to the parks. Many of its rooms overlook the Folk Culture Village. You can sometimes see flocks of egrets in nearby mangroves, and the skyscrapers of Hong Kong's New Territories across the bay.

SHENZHEN BAY HOTEL (Shenzhen Wan Dajiudian), *Overseas Chinese Town, 518053. Four stars, Tel. 6600111, Fax 6600139. E-mail: hksbhtvl@vol.net. Website: www.shenzhenbayhotel.com.hk. About Y860-Y1030 for rooms and Y1300-Y9780 for suites. There are 308 rooms with narrow twin beds and some with balconies. Renovations are due in 2002.*

It has a beautiful outdoor pool, tennis, gym, and night club. There's a grill room, and dim sum (7am-11am). A CTS Hotel.

HAPPY VALLEY YOUTH HOSTEL, *Overseas Chinese Town. Tel. 6949443, Fax 6949445. Website: www.iyhf.org This pleasant hostel is behind the Crowne Plaza and close to the Happy Valley theme park.*

It has washing machines and internet service. Beds for $5-$10.

Towards the Shekou Ferry

Shekou is 30 km from downtown Shenzhen, about 25 km from the airport. It has 50-minute hovercraft service with Hong Kong and ferries to Zhuhai and Haikou. It is near the science park with its many factories, and is about 10 km from Splendid China. Here is the lovely five-star waterfront Nanhai and the cheaper but adequate Ming Wah International on a mountain.

NAN HAI HOTEL (Da Jiudian), *1 Gong Ye First Road, Shekou Industrial Zone, Shenzhen, 518069. Five stars. Tel. 6692888, Fax 6692440, 6679476. E-mail: sznanhai@public.szptt.net.cn. Website: www.nanhai-hotel.com. In a residential area next door to the ferry to Hong Kong. It charges Y1250-Y1950 for rooms and Y1950-Y14800 for suites. It has been discounting 40%.*

This hotel was built in 1985 and has non-smoking rooms. There are 11 stories and 396 rooms with safes, smoke hoods, 24-hour room service and CNN. It has lighted tennis courts, disco, a small gym, outdoor year-round pool, and foot reflexology. A bus goes to Splendid China, the Shenzhen railway station and Hong Kong airport. Managed by Miramar International Hotels Management Group (H.K.).

HOLIDAY INN DONGHUA SHENZHEN, *Donghua Park, Nanyou Road, 518054. Tel. 6416688, Fax 6645282. E-mail: hiszhen@public.szptt.net.cn. Website: www.holiday-inn.com. Rooms are Y996 and suites Y1495. It has been discounting 50%. It is 5 km from the Shekou Ferry, 26 km from the Railway Station, and 9 km from the Folk Culture Village.*

MING WAH INTERNATIONAL, *8 Gui Shan Road, Shekou Industrial Zone, 518067. Three-star standard applying for four. Tel. 6689968, Fax 6687356, 6679615. Website: www.mhctr.com. Rooms are Y900-Y1000 and suites and apartments Y1500-Y2800. It has been discounting 30%. It has a shuttle bus going to the Hong Kong ferry.*

This six-story, 113-room hotel has small bathrooms, CNN and BBC, and a pleasant college dormitory atmosphere with relaxed standards and dirty hall carpets. It also has a heated indoor pool, squash, bowling, steam room, gym, and golf-simulator. In the complex are a conference center, service apartments and offices. Operated by China Merchants Holding Co.

Where to Eat

Vegetables here are fresher than Hong Kong's. The hotel restaurants are best especially for Western food, but these restaurants are good too. Shekou has a lot of restaurants catering to Western tastes.

SEAFOOD MARKET RESTAURANT (Hao-shi-jie) *3/F, Neptunus Mansion, Nanyou Rd., Tel. 6647788, 6405566. Website: www.goodworldseafood.com. It's open 11am-midnight. Reservations suggested.*

This is one of four in the city. Ask for Johnny Cheung, Manager. Accepts credit cards. Korean, Japanese and Cantonese seafood, live from tanks. Sauteed fresh shrimps Szechuan style Y85. Baked spare ribs with pepper and salt Y38. Complimentary dessert table.

CASABLANCA BAR AND WESTERN RESTAURANT, *Ground Floor, Yin Bun Building, Taizi Road, Shekou, Tel. 6676968.*

Popular with foreigners.

The Chinese restaurants in the nearby **Shenzhen Bay Hotel** are fine. Across the street are several local restaurants and the **Crowne Plaza Hotel.**

You can also eat at the theme parks. At the **Tujia Pavilion** in the Folk Culture Village, you can buy sticky rice wrapped in lotus leaves. **McDonald's**, open 7am-11pm, is outside Windows on the World.

Seeing the Sights

The day trippers can see the reservoir that supplies half of Hong Kong's water supply and its skyscrapers. Shenzhen has no historical monuments save the modest grave in Shekou of the last Song emperor, who fled here to escape the Mongols.

Four theme parks are together around the Shenzhen Bay Hotel, about a 25-minute drive from the railway station towards Shekou. Takes buses 101, 204 or 223. They should be linked together now by monorail and are worth one or two days if you like theme parks and have children with you. If you visit more than one, you get a special rate. Folk Cultures Village has a place to leave luggage. For all parks, *E-mail: szocthv@public.szptt.net.cn. Web: www.chinaoct.com (Chinese).* They are all run by the same company.

Splendid China (Jinxiu Zhong Hua) is on 29 hectares with over 80 of China's top tourist attractions in 15:1 miniature. It is highly recommended (but not in the rain). Take a guide as no explanations are in English. Thousands of tiny ceramic people, each different, in period or ethnic dress, and in scale, add liveliness. They include Mongolian wrestlers in their leather vests and baggy pants, and emperors paying homage at the Temple of Confucius. Open 8:30am-5:30pm daily. Y50.

The **Folk Culture Village** is next to the miniatures. This is a 180,000 square meter exhibition with demonstrations of handicrafts, cooking, and three shows a day of dances and songs by genuine Miao, Mongolians, etc. It is more interesting than Splendid China because it has real people. With samples of full-scale Tujia, Uygur and Wa architecture, and of course real Miao, Jinuo and Tibetan people in ethnic dress, you can really get a good introduction to China's 55 minorities.

If you want to do more than just shoot photos, take an interpreter so you can ask questions. There is only one small sign with a limited amount of information in English beside each exhibit.

You can spend two to six hours at Folk Culture Village, plus the parade. It is open 11:30am-9pm weekdays, and 10am-9pm weekends and holidays. The 50-minute 7:30pm dance show is in the Central Theatre. The daily 8:30pm Carnival Parade is outside, lively and professional, with permanent floats and show-biz adaptions of minority dances and costumes. In case you missed it the first time, the parade goes around twice. Its happy-happy atmosphere with 500 performers should not be missed. Seats cost Y15 and Y20 extra.

Photo opportunities abound and attendants willingly pose. No one runs shyly away nor asks for money. While the dirt and poverty of the real villages are missing, and the variety within cultures are absent in each exhibit, there are enough farm implements, hanging husks of corn, and looms to show how these people differ from the Han majority. In some cases, you can sample ethnic food. And the toilets are clean! For lazy tourists, this is the next best thing to reality.

You can go there even as late as 4pm, snack on the grounds, and explore until the parade. Y50.

On the other side of the Shenzhen Bay Hotel is **Windows of the World,** a 480,000 square meter theme park with miniatures of world monuments like the Golden Gate Bridge and Eiffel Tower (which you can climb for the view).

Its Alps Indoor Ski Dome has a 12-meter-high ski hill and 114-meter run. You can rent skis. Shows are all day but the big one is 7:30-8:45pm with galloping "British" horsemen, lavish costumes, and international performers. Avoid the front seats. You'll have to turn around. *Tel. 6608000, Fax 6602590.* Y110.

Nearby is **Happy Valley** with water sports, rides and inter-active exhibits aimed at children. *Tel. 6949168, 6608088, 6908866.* Y90.

Safari Park, a wild animal park with 15,000 animals, is in another part of the city, at Xili Lake, 518055, Tel. 6622888. It takes at least two hours to tour and at 4pm has a parade of animals and clowns. You take buses through the various habitats but there's lots of walking. Among the 150 species are pandas, golden monkeys, Asian elephants, red-crested cranes, and Asian tigers. It is all right if you have time and haven't been to such a park elsewhere, but if you have to choose, go to Splendid China and Folk Culture Village because they are uniquely Chinese and better done.

Festivals

During the summertime lichee season, tourists come here to pick this sweet fruit. The tour price usually includes all-you-can eat and 2.5 kilograms to take home. A Lichee and Fine Food Festival takes place the end of June and early July.

Nightlife & Entertainment

In Shekou, the expat hangouts are the **China Beach** and **Red Rooster bars**, near Sea World. A **night market** is at Nanguo Square near the Sunshine Hotel from 8:30pm-midnight.

Sports & Recreation

One of China's best courses is the beautiful, world-class **Mission Hills Golf Club**, about 30 minutes drive north of Shenzhen, used for the 1995 World Cup. This 72-hole course was designed by Jack Nicklaus, Nick Faldo, and Masashi Ozaki and is open 6am-11:30pm. It also has 50 lighted tennis courts and a 3000-seat stadium, an outdoor pool and a 64-bay driving range, squash court, gym, and children's play area. Its 228-room hotel is a real oasis from the cities. Its restaurants offer about 65 mainly French wines. Rates are Y1210-Y2420 for rooms, Y1925-Y13068 for suites. It's very beautiful.

The **Mission Hills Golf Club** is at Mission Hills Road, Guanlan Town, 518110. *Tel. 82020888, Fax 8010713.* Its office in Hong Kong can make arrangements, *Tel. 852/29730303, Fax 28699632,* and it takes credit cards.

The 27-hole **Xili Golf Course** is exclusive and good, about 45 minutes from downtown. Book through any Shangri-La Hotel.

Shopping

The **Lowu Commercial Centre** is north of the Shenzhen Customs House right at the Hong Kong border and is the favorite shopping place of foreign and Hong Kong people. It is usually full of name-brand clothes, watches, jewelry, sun glasses, and purses. You have to haggle hard. From time to time, the Chinese government cracks down on these fakes, overruns, and seconds but if you ask, clerks will pull out "Gucci" bags from under their counters. Please don't go into the women's washroom in the large third floor restaurant. Trust me.

Dongmen is the street for bargains and crowds. It has many buildings. Tell your driver "Dongmen, Mao Ye." For computers and software, there's the **SEG Building** (Sai Ge Dian Zi) on Shen Nan Road. These are all in the same general area. The Landmark has a map with the main shopping areas. You don't have to stay there to get it. It is beside the Oriental New World Department Store.

Warning: Some counterfeits can be dangerous. Sun glasses tagged "UV protection," might not be so. Cosmetics might have poisonous ingredients. Do not believe labels.

Practical Information

Business Hours, 8:30 or 9am-5:30pm, mostly five days a week for offices; 9am or 10am-10pm for stores daily.

China Comfort Shenzhen Travel Service, *Flat C, 5/F, Shenzhen Textile Building, 3 Huaqiang Bei Road, 518031, Tel. 3218064, Fax 3219049.*

CTS-OTC Shenzhen, *Tel. 6949987, 6911395, Fax 755/6606039. E-mail: chinats@public.szonline.net.* It is near the theme parks.

Shekou International SOS Clinic, *Villa 3, Jing Shan, Shekou, 518067. Tel. 6693667, Fax. 6674780.*

Telephone code: 755

Zhuhai

Zhuhai is adjacent to the Special Administrative Zone of Macau and across the Pearl River delta southwest of Hong Kong. It produces electronics, and trains airplane pilots. It is one of the most pleasant cities in China and it does have one international class tourist attraction. It also has an air show every two years from November 2002. Its Formula One Grand Prix car races are in October-November, and will probably be held every other year after 2003.

There are also two golf courses and an international trade and exhibition center. See Zhongshan above for a better golf course. The urban population is about 160,000, but its total population is 1.15 million. It was founded in

1979, and became a Special Economic Zone in 1980. It has 75 km of coastline and is building a 142 km Guangzhou-Zhuhai Railway Line.

Arrivals & Departures

You can reach Zhuhai SEZ directly by ferry from Hong Kong, or by bus from elsewhere. China Travel Service's website has bus and ferry schedules between Hong Kong and Zhuhai: www.chinatravelOne.com(English) and then click on "Tours." You can also send an e-mail asking specific questions to: *enquiry@chinatravelOne.com or Fax 852/27893498.*

You can go by road or foot from Macau via Gongbei in Zhuhai. You can also enter Macau at Hengqing, an island off Zhuhai, but buses and taxis there are rare for pedestrians. Zhuhai is a two-hour drive from Guangzhou plus traffic jams. Its small but very modern airport 35-40 minutes from town has links with 29 other Chinese cities. Shenzhen airport, one of the busiest in China, is only about two hours away by road.

Frequent mini-buses and air-conditioned highway buses go from two bus stations near the Gongbei Customs House to Guangzhou, Shenzhen, Zhongshan (30 minutes) and Taishan. You can also go from the Zhuhai Hotel to Guangzhou non-stop for Y55 in about two hours.

Visa Note: Most Western passport holders (except U.K.) can get a three-month tourist visa at the Zhuhai border for HK$180 and one ID photo. This visa is good for the whole of China and visitors can leave China from any exit point. In Shenzhen, visitors can get five day visas that allow exits only from Shenzhen and nowhere else.

Where to Stay & Eat

The best hotel for English-speakers is the beautiful Harbour View Hotel because of its good service, and sunset ocean views. The best four-star should be the Holiday Inn. A Youth Hostel is at the Zhuhai Holiday Resort, on the ocean. Reservations are needed weekends, July-August and Hong Kong holidays. A language school here can arrange home stays for free in exchange for English lessons. Hotels add a 10%-15% surcharge.

HARBOUR VIEW HOTEL & RESORT, *47 Middle Lover's Avenue, 519015. Five stars. Tel. 332 2888, Fax 337 1385. E-mail: hvhbc@pub.zhuhai.gd.cn or resvn@zenithhotels.com. Website: www.zenithhotels.com. Rooms are Y880-Y980, and suites Y1380-Y28880. It has been discounting about 40% off some of these. It is in a residential-resort area adjacent to the sea, about ten minutes by car from the Macau border crossing and five minutes by shuttle bus from the ferry port.*

This 383-room hotel has good guest rooms with broadband data ports, and CNN, BBC and HBO. It has a helpful business center and a Conference Center suitable for mid-size meetings and seminars. It also has four restaurants, gym, pool and snooker, outdoor pool, and a four-lane bowling center.

HOLIDAY INN ZHUHAI, *188 Jingshan Road, 519015, Tel. 3228888, Fax 3228899. E-mail: E-mail@holidayinn-zhuhai.com. Website: www.holiday-inn.com. Y800 to Y1100 for rooms, and Y1300 to Y30000 for suites. Ask about discounts. This 30-story complex is five-minute drive from the Macau border, three minutes drive from the Jiuzhou Pier, and 40 minutes drive from Zhuhai Airport.*

It has a complimentary shuttle from the pier and 268 rooms with kettle, mini-bar, safe, and data port. It has two executive floors and non-smoking rooms, an outdoor pool, gym, and Chinese and Italian restaurants, a deli, internet lounge, and 24-hour room service. Its ballroom can seat 200 people at banquet tables.

ZHUHAI HOLIDAY RESORT HOTEL RESORT (Dujiachun Jiu Dian), *9 Shi Hua Dong Road, Ji Da, 519015. Five stars. Tel. 3333838, Fax 3333311. E-mail: rsv@zhuhai-holitel.com. Website: www.zhuhai-holitel.com. Rooms are Y680-Y1180, suites Y980-Y1680, and villas Y2280-Y4980. Discounts have been 30% except on weekends and holidays when they are 10%. Regular guests with a VIP card get a 60% discount. It is 1.5 km from the Jiuzhou ferry port to Hong Kong and Shenzhen. It is on 350,000 square meters of land, you can get around by golf cart, and it has 468 rooms.*

Rooms in the main Holiday Resort building are 26 to 38 square meters with CNN, green marble desks, data ports, sprinklers, and in-room safes. It has two Western and two Cantonese restaurants. Its western buffet breakfast costs Y38 and its dinner buffet Y88. You can get a medical massage and play in its four outdoor tennis courts. It has bowling, outdoor pool, roller skating, archery, shooting gallery, go-karts, and water sports. It has a golf shop. Alas, only a few staff speak English. Guests are mainly domestic or Asian so the standards are local rather than international.

ZHUHAI INTERNATIONAL YOUTH HOSTEL, *located in a building of the vast Zhuhai Holiday Resort Hotel.*

This 84-bed hostel is a good deal for backpackers. It has dormitories with beds at Y60 each and is clean. Guests can also swim in its huge pool. Hostellers pay Y5 for a simple breakfast with the staff. They can use a washing machine for free. To book the Youth Hostel, go to the website: *www.iyhf.org* or the e-mail address for the Zhuhai Holiday Resort, above.

Seeing the Sights

A **sightseeing bus** leaves the Zhuhai Hotel every 20 minutes and stops at the major tourist attractions but has no English-speaking guide. It is cheap. Unfortunately, its map is only in Chinese, but it has a few photos of its stops which include the home of Afong. Tel. 3320696, or 3357055.

This beautiful little city is worth a visit for its own sake. It is an ideal place to escape the cold of winter. The only tourist attraction worth stopping for is the **New Yuanmingyuan** (see Beijing chapter, Seeing the Sights (Day Three), for information about the real summer palace). The park is open 9:30am-10:30pm and costs Y80-Y90 for adults, less for seniors and kids. It's at Lanpu Jiu Zhou Road, *Tel. 8610388*. This is a theme park based on the favorite palace of several emperors that was built in 1709 with the help of Italian missionaries and destroyed by foreign troops in 1860. You could spend two hours walking around here, and another two hours at the evening show. This reproduction is quite good, and enlivened by "soldiers" and "court ladies," dancers, musicians and storytellers in Manchu costume. Unfortunately there are no signs in English but you can hire an English-speaking guide.

A food court with stalls from various provinces and countries will keep you from going hungry. Wine is available in the second floor restaurant which serves imperial Qing food. It is open 11am-9pm daily.

The evening show is at a 5000-seat outdoor theatre behind the Lama Temple and only the front seats require an additional Y10 payment. The lighting of the park is very good and you should visit just before dusk. The show however has only a few good moments, like 16 real galloping horses, and an impressive fire scene; it has too many slow arty dances. Hopefully it will improve.

Hawaiians should be interested in the home of Afong who made his fortune from sugarcane in Hawaii, and married a Hawaiian princess. Unfortunately there are only a few titles in English, so ask for the director who studied at Harvard. Look for the Hawaiian influences in this home. Y30 entrance fee. *Tel. 8635652, E-mail: zhmeixi@sohu.com*.

Teaching English & Learning Chinese

Gateway Language Village (Zhuhai) is a total immersion language school which hires native-English speakers to teach English. Teachers need ELT training or experience and a strong commitment to teaching. They receive an above average salary by Chinese standards, food, accommodation, etc. Non-qualified native speakers are also hired to help with informal teaching and social activities. GLV also offers an internationally accredited TESOL certificate program for native speakers. The four-week course runs ten times a year. Short-term intensive Chinese language courses for visitors are also held in the summer.

GLV also offers international travelers free food and accommodation in the school hostel or private Chinese homes, in exchange for volunteer work. I visited one of these homes and found it very modern, clean, and the family friendly and eager to learn English. The Gateway Language Village's address is: P.O. Box 935, Ningxi, Zhuhai, 519001. *Tel. 2291934 and 2291935. Fax 2294934. E-mail: info@glvchina.com . Website: www.glvchina.com.*

You can also visit the Sun Yat-sen home in neighboring Zhongshan, and the home of many overseas Chinese in Taishan where the old architecture remains.

Practical Information

A 2001 **Zhuhai Guide for Foreign Residents and Visitors** is available from author Susan Andert Hansen, of Connect China Consulting, Zhuhai, 519070, *Tel. 8630820, Fax 8630821. E-mail: zhsah@pub.zhuhai.gd.cn.* This lists stores, restaurants, hotels, visas, and attractions in Chinese and English. Y75 includes postage.

Zhuhai CITS, *Tel. 3321833. Fax 3321235*

Telephone code: 756

Haikou, Hainan Island

Haikou is the capital of Hainan, China's second largest island and its 31st and smallest province. Hainan is 30 km off China's southern coast, and includes the Xisha, Nansha, and Zhongsha Islands. It is important because it is China's tropical playground and agricultural area, wonderful in winter. Though it has no heavy industries, it is a major stop for business people. Its air is among China's cleanest.

The weather is tropical, with 2000 mm of rain a year. Summer has high temperatures but is usually cool at night. Typhoons could hit from March to October. The high tourist season is Christmas to the end of March, but could start earlier. The island is at the same latitude as the southern tip of Hawaii.

Arrivals & Departures

Haikou has flight links with Bangkok, Hong Kong, Kuala Lumpur, Macau, Singapore and 46 Chinese cities. The airport is 26 km from downtown. It has been reached by regular weekly cruise ship from Hong Kong. *E-mail: sales@starcruises.com.hk or Website: www.starcruises.com.hk.*

Note: members of tour groups organized by authorized Chinese travel agencies do not need a visa to visit Hainan Province for less than 15 days. Members can be from 21 countries, including Australia, Britain, Canada, Germany, the Netherlands, New Zealand, Singapore, and the US. Tourist groups and individuals from any country with diplomatic relations with China are allowed to apply for a visa upon arrival at Hainan. CITS in Haikou says these visas are good for one month and you can leave from other Chinese ports.

Orientation

Han dynasty troops first colonized Hainan. From the Tang dynasty, disfavored scholars and officials were exiled here, a tropical Siberia. During the

Health Situation on Hainan Island

Doctors at the People's Hospital in Haikou where ambulances are international standard, provided by AEA, insist they haven't had any **malaria** cases in "many years." The World Health Organization suggests that visitors to this island get protection for malaria (larium). "Malaria is found only in the deep forests," said Dr. Liu Shu Yong. I met no one who lives here taking any precautions, not even foreigners.

The decision is up to you. I found only two mosquitos during my stay in November, and only a few in April. The winter should have less. Bring long sleeves and trousers for the evening.

1930s and 1940s, a Communist army detachment fought here, and after Mao's victory in 1949 part of the island became an autonomous region because a large percentage of the population are national minorities: mainly Li and Miao, but also Hui.

Hainan Island is 34,000 square kilometers and just about as big as Taiwan. The Chinese government is developing it as a very special economic zone with more flexibility and openness than other such zones. The island has a 1528 km coastline, 60% of this sand beaches. The government has targeted Sanya and Yalong Bay in the south as major resorts areas.

The island produces tea, coffee, rubber, fish, sugar, coconut and rice. The population is over seven million. Haikou itself has an urban population of 300,000 and who knows how many transients. Its road traffic does jam up in spots and it has a frontier attitude. People are out to make a fast yuan.

Getting Around

Haikou has three sections – the north (old Haikou), north tip with the university and Golden Coast Hotel, and the financial section. The architecture in old Haikou is much like Hong Kong's in the early 1960s–a charming mix of old buildings hanging over the sidewalks, and huge palatial hotels. English could be a problem except in the top hotels.

Where to Stay

The best hotel for English-speaking business people is the Mandarin. The Huandao Tide has a little. A Holiday Inn Crowne Plaza should be opening soon. The University Hostel is for budget travelers. Hotels add a 15% service charge. Prices listed are subject to change, discounts and a surcharge.

Note: Standards of morality in Hainan are more "flexible" than in other parts of China. While prostitution is illegal, it is pretty obvious. You might get a call at night about "special services." Five-star hotels at least monitor all telephone calls so guests won't be disturbed.

HAINAN MANDARIN HOTEL, *18 Wen Hua Road, 570105. Five stars. Tel. 68548888, Fax 68540453. E-mail: hmh@meritus-hotels.com. Website: www.meritus-hotels.com. (English) The airport is 26 km away and the Mandarin meets all international flights with free transportation. It is in the financial district, close to the harbor, a main shopping area and a beach. Rooms are $190-$215 and suites are $290-$770. It's been giving 50% discounts.*

This hotel has executive club rooms, a gym, steam bath, nightclub, indoor pool, and Haikou's largest outdoor pools. Its business center has international newspapers, and its 318 rooms are located on the 9th to 23rd floors, each with a safe and computer port, and some with ocean view.

HUANDAO TIDE HOTEL (Dajiudian), *18 Heping Road, 570208. Five stars. Tel. 66268888, Fax 662655588. E-mail: hotel@huandaotide.com. Website: www.huandaotide.com (English). $165-$185 for rooms and $360-$2118 for suites including breakfast. It has been discounting 30% to 50%. It is in an area of restaurants and shops popular with foreigners and is a 20-25 minute drive from the Mandarin Hotel.*

Opened in 1994, this hotel has 23 stories and 408 rooms with safes. Standard rooms are 36 square meters. The lobby is covered by a giant glass pyramid (sometimes with dirty glass) giving it a feeling of openness neverthe-less. It also has garden suites, one non-smoking floor, some narrow halls, and an executive lounge. There's also a Chaozhou restaurant, Korean barbecue, Italian Restaurant, and a 24-hour Western coffee shop. There's a small gym. It is related to the Asiana hotel group.

HAINAN UNIVERSITY GUEST HOUSE (Hainan Da Xue Shao Yi Fu Xue Shu Zhong Xin), *570228, Tel. Foreign Affairs (Wai Ban) office, 66187636, 66258112 or Fax 66258369. Ask for Belle or "wai ban." Y120 per room and about Y50 a day for food. 56 clean, air-conditioned rooms with television, private bath, and basic services.*

This is a beautiful spacious campus with friendly staff, palm and flame trees, but little English.

Where to Eat

The province produces all kinds of fruit: pineapples, mangosteens, mangoes, lichees, watermelons, jackfruits, and rambutans. It also has fresh, fresh seafood. Other famous dishes are Wenchang Chicken (known elsewhere as Hainan chicken, poached with ginger), Jiaji duck, Hele crab, and Dongshan mutton. Some restaurants serve dog meat too, so beware.

One of Hainan's specialties is steamboat, where you cook your own food in a pot of steaming hot water. You can get a pot divided in two with one soup bland, and one soup spicy hot; you can share one pot with friends who have different tastes.

Jin Long Road, relatively close to the Mandarin Hotel, has several good restaurants almost side by side. Among them are the **Aiwan Ting, Beijing Kao Rou**, and **Xinjiang Restaurant** (Muslim). Food in the hotels is very good but expensive. The **Huandao Tide Hotel** serves crocodile, yes crocodile, among other delights.

Seeing the Sights

In Haikou, you can visit the restored **Five Officials Memorial Temple**, originally built in 1889 in honor of its banished officials. A butterfly museum is adjacent. Near this is the **Su Temple**, a memorial to the famous Song poet, Su Dong Po, who was exiled to Hainan in 1097. Travel agents will also send you to the **Hai Rui Tomb**. While mildly interesting, you can ignore all these if you want. The only important tourist attraction in Hainan are the southern beaches and resorts.

Not worth a special trip, but good for people just wanting to see some countryside, is a drive to the mangrove forest at Haikor, 30 km northeast of Haikou. You can take a small boat for an hour's tour.

The **Dong Jiao Peninsula** is a little further south. There you have to take a short ride in a small noisy motor boat past fish farms to a string of dumpy open-air beachside restaurants. The better ones have signs "Designated Tourist Unit," and you can gorge cheaply on coconut rice, and fresh crab, squid, abalone, and mackerel.

Swimming is better elsewhere. Sad however are the stalls selling stuffed endangered sea turtles. Nearby, within 10 minutes walk, is a statue of the three Soong sisters, a remarkable family. Wenchang was the home of Charlie Soong, the father of these three influential women. (See Shanghai).

Sports & Recreation

The island has 17 golf courses completed or in construction in a variety of beach and mountain settings. Sanya and Yalong Bay are one of the country's best places for water sports. Hainan also has six hot spring resorts.

Shopping

Local goods include saltwater pearls, rubies, rose quartz, coconut and ox horn carvings, hand weaves and embroidered ethnic textiles. Pictures are made of butterfly wings. Department stores are on Haixiu Road.

Excursions & Day Trips

Three roads go from Haikou south toward Sanya. If you take the 296 km central road through the mountains, you can stop at the Feng Mu Deer Farm (arrangements in advance), and then visit a Miao village. There's a modest hotel and the Museum of Nationalities in Tongzha but this road is not great. If you go via the eastern expressway route, you can also visit Kangle Garden Resort at Xinlong, and stop at the Chao Yin Si Temple on Mount Dongshan. The 405 km western road is longest and non-stop it would be a 3.5 hour drive to Sanya.

The best resort on the east coast of Hainan Island is the 42-acre Kangle Garden Resort and it's well worth a stop. It is 140 km (less than two-hours drive and about Y200 taxi) from the airport at Sanya. It is 170 km (about Y300 taxi) from the Haikou airport. Buses from the East Bus Station in Haikou go to Xinglong's Pearl Resort, less than one km away.

KANGLE GARDEN RESORT (Kangle Dajiudian), *Xinglong, Wanning, 571533. Five stars. Y900-Y1400 for rooms; Y2000-Y30000 for suites, plus 10% tax. It has been giving 40% discounts, and takes credit cards and travelers checks. It is eight km off the Eastern Expressway at Exit 14 Shimei. Tel. 898/62552008, Fax 62554140, 62552038. E-mail: Kangle@public.hk.hi.cn. Website: www.kangleresort.com (English).*

This 499-room resort was built in 1989 and expanded in 2001. All rooms have CNN, ceiling fans and air-conditioners. Its convention center accommodates 500 people. The Asian, Cantonese, French, Western, Korean, and Sichuan food and service here are good, the surroundings beautiful. Its largest outdoor swimming pool is 120 meters long (24 C). It also has outdoor jacuzzis. The staff makes a good attempt at speaking English.

This resort is primarily for people who want to soak in natural hot spring water, swim, and play golf and tennis. It also has bowling, billiards, karaoke and a disco. It is not for those who want to be on the ocean. The nearby Riyue Beach is an eight km, nine-minute drive away. The Resort can drive groups there for free but it only has showers, umbrellas, and a small hotel. Beach people had better head for the more developed Yalong Bay.

From here you can also make day trips to Sanya, to Li and Miao villages, and hike in the mountains. Hiring taxis by the day costs between Y300 and Y500. The town and tropical botanical garden are close by. You can rent bicycles. Nearby are two golf courses, one of which is the 18-hole Haiwang Nanyanwan Golf Club designed by American Bob MacFarlane.

Xisha (Paracel) Islands

While the government has given permission for tourists to visit this controversial group of islands about 400 km southeast of Haikou, arrangements to do so on a regular basis might not be ready yet. Do contact travel agents for the latest information. Recent visitors have arrived there by a very unstable ship in 20 hours, too long a trip just to be able to say you've been there. There's not much to see, but the water and air are clean.

These islands are very sensitive, the source of conflict between China and its neighbors. Known also as the Spratly Islands, this archipelago is situated on a strategic shipping route thought to be rich in oil. The islands are claimed wholly or partly by China, Malaysia, the Philippines, Brunei, Taiwan and Vietnam.

See Sanya below for a full descriptionof what to see and do there.

Practical Information

Ambulance, Tel. 120.

For **ticketing service**, it's better to try your hotel first.

CITS, *Tel 65357999, Fax 65378816. Website: www.citsdonghu.com (Chinese).* It charges Y50-Y100 a day for a guide per guest. Ask for Fu De, Tel. 13807592345 but don't expect the best English. *E-mail: fudee@public.hk.hi.cn.*

CTS, *Tel. 66766523, 6772652, Fax 66782183, 6772095*

CYTS Hainan Co., Ltd., *Tel. 5375158, 5337793, Fax 5337004. Website: www.hncyts.com (Chinese only).*

Hainan Tourist Corporation, *HNTC Building, 2# Long-She Road, Tel. 5350264, Fax 5351647.* Contact Yang Wen Bo, Hainan Tourist Corporation, *8-1 Hailu Building, Airport Road East, 570203, Tel. 5352431, Fax 5351647.*

Hainan Provincial Tourism Administration, *Jichang Road, 570203, Tel. 5358526, Fax 5353074. E-mail: slyjgh@public.hk.hi.cn. Website: www.ctrs.com.cn (English).* You can make hotel and flight reservations through this website. Tourist complaints and requests for brochures should go to Mr. Chen Chuan Min, Director.

Hours: government offices: 8am-12 noon; 3pm-6pm; travel agents 8:30 or 9am-11:30; 3-5:30pm. Department stores: Monday-Friday 8 or 8:30am-9:30 or 10pm. On Saturday and Sunday open to 10:30pm. Smaller shops close at 12 noon, reopen about 3pm.

Internet bar, *third floor of the Hua Bao Bldg., Tel. 6754802 at 356 Da Ying Road,* with thirty computers at Y8 an hour. It is open 24 hours, but clerks said it was best for foreigners to arrive after 8am when there were people to help in English. This is behind the First Department Store at 8 Haixiu Road, *Tel. 6787624* (open 9am-10:30pm).

Telephone Code: 898

Sanya, Hainan Island

Sanya is at the southern tip of Hainan Island. Here no one will get you up at 7am and onto a tour bus at 8:30 for 12 hours of sightseeing and eating – unless you want to, of course. Sanya is for relaxing, for sun and sand, for water sports, hiking, and golf. Of course you can visit a Muslim fishing village, a pearl farm, and the rocky "Ends of the Earth."

Arrivals & Departures

See Haikou above for special visa regulations.

You can fly direct to Sanya from Haikou but you can fly from 25 other Chinese cities and Hong Kong. The international airport is 15 km north west of Sanya City.

You can take air-conditioned buses from Haikou to Sanya from the East Bus station in Haikou. Buses leave every 20 minutes during the day. It takes about three hours and costs about Y90. Hiring a car for the same trip can cost about Y700-Y800. Star Cruises stop here seasonally from Hong Kong. *E-mail: sales@starcruises.com.hk. Website: www.starcruises.com.hk.*

Orientation

Sanya has 16 sea ports, 10 islands, and 180 kilometers of coastline. The urban population is about 120,000, the total 380,000. The high tourist season is October to February. Sanya City has an urban area with stores, restaurants and hotels. Yalong Bay is part of Sanya but is primarily a beach resort.

Where to Stay

The best hotel in Sanya City is the Mountain Sea Sky. The best four-star is the Pearl River Garden Hotel. For the best three-star and resorts in Yalong Bay, see below.

MOUNTAIN SEA SKY (Shanhaitian Da Jiudian), *Luling Road, 572021. Five stars. Tel. 88211688, Fax 88210230. E-mail: market@shthotel.com. Website: www.shthotel.com. (English). Y1098 to Y1398 for rooms, and Y1588 to Y5988 for suites. This hotel has been discounting 20% and accepts credit cards and travelers' checks.*

This eight-story, 203-room hotel isolated on the west side of Dadonghai Bay has a stunning view of the bay. There's an ATM, two outdoor pools, and its own beach front. Its gym is very good. Rooms have computer ports, CNN, fancy shower heads, and mini-clothes dryer. It has a Western, Chinese, and teppanyaki and sushi restaurants, beach bar and nightclub.

PEARL RIVER GARDEN HOTEL (Zhujiang Huayuan), *Dadonghai, 572021. Four stars. Tel. 8211888, 6302280, Fax 8212955, 8211999. E-mail: prgarde n@public.syptt.hi.cn. Website: www.prgardenhotel.com.cn. Y980-Y1580 for rooms, Y1918-Y2818 for suites. It has been discounting 50%. It accepts credit cards and travelers' checks.*

Built in 1995, this 239-room hotel has some rooms with large balconies and jacuzzis. All rooms have safes and CNN. The hallways have badly-fitting carpets. Covered walkways are between the buildings and the beach. There is 24-hour room service, an outdoor pool with a mountain view and a decent gym. It has Chinese and Western restaurants, good service, and higher than average standard of English.

Where to Eat

Seafood is great but outside of the hotels, restaurants have no menus in English. See Chapter 25 for help with Chinese characters. There's the reasonably priced **Jiulong Ge Restaurant** on the road to the Mountain Sea Sky Hotel. At the **Aiwan Ting**, a quality upscale Hunan restaurant, Manager Chau Chi Sun ordered us a banquet that included Ba Bao Cha tea, 1000-year-old egg pudding, Hunan smoked duck, and the sweetest crab ever tasted. Ask for stir-fried chili crab. Hostesses speak English and they can tone down the fiery chilis if you ask. It's in the Yulin Hotel in Da Dong Hai, Tel. 8213278.

The **Shenyang Jin Niu Jiao Zi Guan (Golden Cow Dumpling) Restaurant** on Yu Hai Road, *Tel. 8211152,* is a modest little northeastern flavor restaurant with good dumplings. It is open 7:30am-10:30pm and takes no credit cards. You can get good mutton and beef dumplings, good stir-fried spare ribs, Chinese turnip soup, stir-fried sliced potato salad, corn and pine nuts, and deep-fried egg plant, all highly recommended. Ms. Meng, the friendly manager, speaks a few words of English. Prices are very reasonable.

An adventurous place to eat fresh seafood are the restaurant stalls on **Lu Hui To Beach,** at the west side of downtown Sanya, two km west of Da Dong Hai beach.

Seeing the Sights

Ends of the Earth is so named because Hainan was the end of the political career of high ranking officials from the Song and Tang dynasties. It is about 30 km west of downtown Sanya City and is a pleasant rocky place to explore. There's also a Pearl Farm. At *Monkey Island*, the monkeys can be vicious, and a visit is not recommended. The local tourist attractions are not special. But from the Ends of the Earth, you might want to hire a glass-bottom boat (Y180) to go look for coral.

The **Nanshan Cultural and Tourist Zone** which is thirty minutes by road southwest of downtown Sanya is based on an actual historic event — the one-year stay by Tang Buddhist monk Jianzhen after his fifth failure to take Buddhism to Japan. (See Yangzhou.) This 60-square kilometer theme park is not worth a Y150 taxi ride and Y46 entrance fee. You might want to wait until 2004 when the **108-meter-high bronze three-headed Guan Yin** is finished. It should be 16 meters higher than the Statue of Liberty and spectacular at that height. The gardens are beautiful and the feng shui said to be superb. There's a vegetarian restaurant with a buffet. You might enjoy studying the curious ambiotic relationship of the 30 real Buddhist monks, the government, and the developers. *Tel. 8831878 or fax 8831899. Website: www.nanshan.com (Chinese).*

The **boat people** living on the Sanya River on both sides of the Sanya International Hotel on Yu Ya Road are fascinating. This was Hong Kong's Aberdeen 30 years ago. You can get good photos from the bridges here.

Number two minibus (Y1), as well as taxis, can get you there and to the Internet bar near the railway station

About 3-4000 Muslims live in **Yanlan village** near the Ends of the Earth, and many wear a distinctive dress. During the Ming and Yuan dynasties, the emperors sent Muslim soldiers to secure the borders. Some are also descendants of traders from Central Asia. The temperature is about 26-32°C in summer and 21-25°C in winter.

See also **Yalong Bay** below, only a few kilometers away.

Nightlife & Entertainment

November 18 every year is the Wedding Festival. Chinese and foreign couples getting married or celebrating 5th, 25th, and 50th anniversaries get special treatment. Contact travel agents.

Hotels have sports and shows. You can hike to the top of Lu Huitou Garden for a view of the city, or do a night dive. Bars in the better hotels shouldn't have annoying girls pestering customers.

Excursions & Day Trips
YALONG BAY

Yalong Bay is about 20-25 km (about a Y40 taxi ride) southeast of Sanya City, and 30 km from the Sanya airport (by taxi Y100 to Y150). It is located between the beach and mountains. The main Yalong Road, follows the beach and passes the golf course and most of the hotels which are all within two km of the town square. Yalong Bay is much more open than Sanya City and its beach is cleaner and safer for swimming. In 1990, it was just beach. The water is clear and usually peaceful. Today it is a nationally-protected marine reserve. No commercial fishermen are allowed to fish there nor harvest or destroy coral. Yalong Bay Development Company has built a water treatment plant.

Where to Stay

From west to east, the resorts are Gloria, Resort Horizon, Yalong Square, Huandao Beach Hotel, Cactus, Golden Palm, and Holiday Inn. The best resorts are the Gloria, the Resort Horizon and probably the Holiday Inn which opened too late to be reviewed here, but is expected

Lovely Yalong Bay

Yalong Bay is my favorite tropical resort in China, even though its original ecological restrictions on the number of resorts have been altered. It was supposed to only have six, ranging from two-to-five-star ratings. Its goal was "fewer people spending more to maintain a good environment." No resort was supposed to be closer than 100 meters from the 7.5 km-long beach but that's no longer the case. Still, it is the only **beach** in Sanya where I would swim.

to be good as well. A Sheraton should open in 2003. These are world class resorts.

The Gloria and Resort Horizon both are beautiful with gardens, freshwater pools and beach fronts. The Gloria is better, has carpets, and better quality furniture. The Resort Horizon has bare floors. Food in both is great. The differences in facilities between the Gloria and Resort Horizon aren't that important because foreigners who don't look Chinese can easily use the facilities of either resort. However, if you do look Chinese, you might be sent away from the beach, unless you pay something like Y300 for day use. This is a policy that is necessary, says management, especially during high season, when hundreds of vacationing locals want to camp out in the cabanas meant for paying guests. In effect, obvious foreigners can usually get away without paying this fee.

For budget travelers, there's the Cactus, the three-star sister hotel of the Gloria. The English is almost non-existent there but you can always telephone big sister for help. Without carpets, the Cactus tends to be noisy. It is one block from the beach but it has a wonderful huge pool.

Hotels listed here accept credit cards and have money exchange. They have travel agents, and sports facilities. They add a 10% surcharge plus Y11 per person per day tax.

GLORIA RESORT, (Kai Lai Du Jiajiudian), *Yalong Bay National Resort District, Sanya City, 572000. Five stars. Tel.88568855, Fax 88568533. E-mail: gloria@gloriaresort.com. Website: www.gloriaresort.com. $158 to $208 for rooms, and $348 to $3133 for suites. It currently gives a discounted price of about $135 for rooms. Ask about packages.*

This sprawling eight-story 1996 hotel has a main building and beautifully-furnished villas. The lobby is open to sea breezes which blow most of the year. (July to September is hot.) The coffee shop staff, dressed in Hawaiian shirts, set an informal tone. There's an excellent Chinese restaurant.

Rooms are comfortable with rattan furniture, and HBO, CNN, and CBS. Guests can scuba, sailboard, sea kayak, waterski, hobie cat, waterskoot (but not within 200 feet of the beach), or boat. It also has a disco, all-weather tennis courts, archery and billiards. It should have mountain bikes to rent with a map of the area. The future should also bring a convention and exhibition center. Its three-bedroom presidential villa is the closest building to the beach, has its own swimming pool and costs about $3133 a night.

RESORT HORIZON (Tian Yu Du Jia Jiudian), *Yalong Bay National Resort District, 572000. Five stars. Tel. 88567888, Fax 88567890. E-mail: welcome@horizon.com.cn. China Website: www.horizon.com.cn (English), US website: www.resort-horizon.com. In Hong Kong Tel. 852/25251923. $161-$218 for rooms, and $266-$350 for suites. It charges 62% more during spring festival.*

This hotel has 360 rooms, four restaurants with Cantonese, Western/

Asian and Korean cuisine, jet-skiing, kayak, scuba diving, water-skiing, tennis courts, bicycles, pool, and night club. All rooms have a computer with broadband internet access.

HOLIDAY INN RESORT YALONG BAY SANYA, *Yalong Bay National Resort District, 572000. Five stars. Tel. 88565666, Fax 88565688. E-mail: hotel@holiday-inn-sanya.com. Website: www.hotel@holiday-inn-sanya.com. Rooms are Y1088-Y1288. Suites are Y2300-Y3800. It has been discounting a maximum of 20%. These rates do not apply during Chinese New Year, May Labour and October National Day holidays.*

This 2001, 358-room resort has seven stories, an executive floor, CNN, CNBC, Star World, and in-room safes. It has banquet facilities for 600 people theater seating, Chinese restaurant, noodle bar, and coffee shop. It has a disco. Sports facilities include gym, tennis, and swimming pools. Rooms have CNN, CNBC, Star World, and safes. Its travel agent can book flights and boat tickets.

CACTUS RESORT SANYA, (Xian Ren Zhang), *Yalong Bay National Resort District, 572016, Tel. 88568866, Fax 88568867. Three stars. E-mail: cactus@cactusresort.com. Website: www.cactusresort.com. Reservations can be made through gloriahl@hkstar.com About Y480-Y560 for rooms, Y780 for suites. It is across the street from Butterfly Park and is about 300 meters from the beach and the Underwater World kiosk*

Opened in 1998, the Cactus has 600 Spartan rooms with safes, satellite television and in-house movies. It claims China's largest swimming pool (1600 square meters), and has beach volley-ball, tennis, water sports, and a children's playground. It has a lobby lounge and pool bar, and a tour desk. There's a "mud" tennis court and pool-side restaurant, menus in English and Chinese, one fluent English speaker on call, and the use of the Gloria's free shuttle service.

Where to Eat

The only restaurants in Yalong Bay are at the hotels, except for the Food Court below the monument in Yalong Bay Square. This cheaper restaurant is open primarily for lunch for groups from 11:30am to 2pm. Individuals can get a set lunch there for about Y30. *Tel. 8568899 X 8012.*

For inexpensive food try the **Huandao Beach Hotel** (Haidi Shi Jie), near the Cactus and Holiday Inn. *Tel. 8565588, Fax 8567788.* Food is not bad at the **Cactus Hotel**. Downtown Sanya City has many more places to eat.

Sights & Sports

Yalong Bay's disadvantage is the lack of things to do outside of the beach and resorts. It is a work in progress. It expects to develop its hot spring resources and also open a magnolia garden and factory making Magnolia products. It hopes to build more golf courses.

Yalong Square has a public beach, showers, beach umbrellas to rent and life guards daily from 8am-7pm all year round. The shell museum there has exhibits that are displayed like fine jewelry and worth a visit.

One of the worthwhile attractions is the charming **Butterfly Park** (hu die yuan, jia yuan hai xuan fang) within sight of the Cactus Hotel. It has a mountain hiking trail and stream and is worth an hour's visit. It's on Nan Bian Hai Road, *Tel. 8215526, 8568720.* This is the 1500 square-meter home of 500 varieties of live, fluttering butterflies. Trees and some butterflies are labelled. Specimens and products are for sale. It is best seen from 9am-11am when butterflies are flying. It is open 7:30am-6pm and costs about Y18.

The 18-hole **Yalong Golf Club** operates 7am-6pm and is beautiful. It was designed by Robert Trent Jones, Jr. on 68 hectares, and has rentals. Green fees are about Y700 but if you book through nearby Gloria Resort, it's cheaper. Underwater World near the Holiday Inn arranges visits to the Submersible, snorkeling, parachuting, fishing and speed boating. You can also rent fishing gear and a boat.

You can go to downtown Sanya. Some hotels have shuttle buses. There are many more restaurants there and a few tourist attractions. There's also shopping for cultured pearls and there's a showroom for crystal and other gem products on the road to Nanshan.

The **Tiandu Outlet Center** sells namebrand bathing suits, sports shoes, and sun glasses. It claims that its prices are 10% cheaper than elsewhere and accepts credit cards. It also has toys, snack foods, and jewelry. It is 20 km from the Shanhaitian and 8 km from the Gloria. It's in Tiandu Zhen, on Yu Hai Road about a kilometer west of Yalong Bay's big white entrance sign. *Tel. 8710818 or fax 8710792.*

Scuba Diving

Scuba diving can be a dangerous sport and should not be attempted without at least eight hours of training. If a store wants to rent you gear without asking for proof of training, do be suspicious about its other standards. The gear may not be carefully maintained or cleaned between customers.

The **South Sea International Ocean Club** (SSIOC) has shops in several hotels here. Its general manager Edward Chan speaks English, *Tel. 13826231801, 88277320 or 88277251, E-mail: sales@ssholiday.com or ssdiver@netvigator.com.* There is also **West Island Marine World**, *Tel. 88262007, Fax 88262801, E-mail: xiisland@xiisland.com.* I have not tried either yet so I cannot give recommendations.

The navy hospital in Sanya has a decompression chamber.

Practical Information

Sanya Tourism Bureau, *7/F, No. Second Building West River Government, 572000. Tel. 88268452, Fax 88268450.* Contact Cai Shi Dong. *Website: www.hainanisland.com.*

Cheap e-mail service, *in the lobby of the Ji Ya Hotel, next to China Telecom, at No. 8, Third Jiefang Road in downtown Sanya.* Y10 an hour.

southwest china

Chapter 21

Chengdu
(Chengtu)

Chengdu is important because of its pandas, its marvelous new Sanxingdui Shu Museum, the Dujiangyan Dam, and the Divine Light Monastery. It is the main gateway to Tibet, Zigong, Emei Shan, and the giant Buddha in Leshan. Eco-tourists should aim for Jiuzhaigou, and people interested in China's satellite projects should go to Xichang. Adventure tours have started from Chengdu through Yunnan to Lhasa. Sichuan of course is the home of Sichuan cuisine.

Located in central Sichuan province of which it is the capital, Chengdu has a history of over 2,000 years. In the fourth century B.C., the King of Shu moved his capital here and named it Chengdu ('Becoming a Capital'). In the Han, after brocade weaving became successfully established, it was called the Brocade City. During the Three Kingdoms, it was the capital of Shu. Many American, Canadian, and British missionaries and teachers lived here in the late 19th and early 20th centuries.

With an altitude of 500 meters, its hottest temperature is 38°C in July and its coldest minus 3°C in January. The tourist season is April to November, with July and August uncomfortably hot. Annual precipitation is about 1000 mm. mainly in July and August. The population is over two million urban. Minorities in the province include Naxi, Qiang, Yi, Jingpo, Miao, Lili, Tujia, and Tibetan.

Arrivals & Departures

Chengdu is slightly over two hours by air southwest of Beijing. There are direct flights from 63 other cities in China,

Bangkok, Hong Kong, Macau, and Singapore. The airport is about 40 minutes from downtown. The airport bus goes by the Jinjiang and Minshan Hotels before getting to the CAAC office downtown.

Chengdu can also be reached in 19 hours by the fastest train from Kunming through 250 km of tunnels, less than 30 hours from Beijing, and 16 hours from Xi'an. Express buses from Chongqing are faster than train. From there, it is a 3.5-4 hour, 340 km trip on a super highway for about Y98.

For buses to Leshan, use the Xinnanmen Bus Station; to Chongqing and Dazu (four hours), use the Wuguiqiao Bus Station; to Jiuzhaigou and Wolong, use the Ximeng bus station.

Orientation

Chengdu is an educational and an industrial center with metallurgy, electronics, and textiles. The area grows rice, wheat, canola, chilis, and sweet potatoes. It also grows medicinal plants and herbs that are sold all over the country. It has so much to offer, you need at least two days to cover it, and more for nearby excursions.

Its notorious traffic jams have been relieved somewhat by three ring roads around the city, but its downtown areas are crowded especially around the Jin Jiang and Minshan Hotels and north towards one of the few remaining statues of Chairman Mao, the big department stores, the Crowne Plaza, and Inter-Continental Hotels. A 46-km subway is being built.

Where to Stay

The top hotels are the Crowne Plaza and the Sheraton. The Amara is a good four-star. In the three-star category, the Tibet and Traffic Hotels are popular with foreign low budget travelers who are not fussy. A youth hostel should be opened near People's Park that should be better than the Traffic Hotel. Details will be announced later in my website.

Prices here are subject to 10%-15% service charge. Some hotels have been giving 20%-50% discounts, free breakfasts, and free airport pickups. The railway station is about seven km to downtown. Hotels here have business centers, Western coffee shops, and money change. Top hotels accept credit cards.

HOLIDAY INN CROWNE PLAZA (Zong Fu Huang Guan Jia Ri Jiudian), *31 Zong Fu Street, 610016. Five stars. Tel. 6786666, Fax 6789789. Website: www.sixcontinentshotels.com. It is 18 km from the airport and 0.5 km from the Provincial Exhibition Centre. Y1411-Y1909 for rooms, Y2158-Y6640 for suites. It has been giving 40% discounts.*

This 33-story, 434-room hotel has in-room safes, bathroom safety bars, data ports, and high-speed internet access. There are non-smoking floors and a 24-hour business center, a grill room, Japanese, Sichuan and Cantonese restaurants. Its lobby is decorated with a Sistine Chapel-like ceiling, sort of. It has floor-to-ceiling windows, a Clark Hatch gym, 17-meter-long year-round indoor pool, and tennis court. There are CNN, CNBC, HBO and Star movies. Look by the elevator in the top floor lounge for one of my favorite modern Chinese paintings: the child emperor Puyi approaching his destiny.

SHERATON CHENGDU LIDO (Xi Lai Deng Fandian), *15, Section 1, Renmin Zhong Road, 610015. Five stars. Tel. 6768999, Fax 6768267, 6768888. E-mail: reservations@sheraton-chengdu.com.cn. Website: www.sheraton.com/chengdu (English). It is on a side street next to the Sports Centre about one kilometer from the Crowne Plaza and on the northern edge of the central business and entertainment district. Rates start from $170 with discounts from 40-50%.*

This 2000 hotel has 402 rooms, 35 stories, and an impressive four-story atrium lobby. It has a coffee shop, two Chinese restaurants, two bars and a deli café. It has an indoor pool and health club, and 28 to 33 square meter guest rooms. There are executive floors Its ballroom can fit 300 sit-down banquet guests. The nearby Sports Center has a golf-driving range which charges Y20 for a bucket of balls.

AMARA CHENGDU, *2 Tai Sheng Bei Road, 610017. Four stars. Tel. 692-2233, Fax 692-2323. E-mail: amaractu@mail.sc.cninfo.net. Rooms are about Y800-Y880 plus 10% and suites are $290-$390. It has been giving discounts. It is downtown near the Crowne Plaza. E-mail: amanactu@mail.sc.cnifo.*

Partially opened November, 1999, this pretty 14-story hotel has 237 rooms plus service apartments. It is a Singapore joint venture. Because of its less convenient location on a side street, prices are softer. It is okay for tour groups with their own transportation and is much more modern and newer than other four-stars. It has a gym, sauna and pool. Rooms have safes and CNN. It offers Thai, Chaozhou and Sichuan food, a Wall Street Pub, and a ballroom that fits 30 banquet tables.

TIBET HOTEL (Xizang Fandian), *10 Renmin Road, 610081. Three stars. Tel. 3333988, Fax 3333526. About Y368-Y780 for rooms, and Y938-Y1188 for suites. Travel agents in lobby charge Y170 for standard rooms with bath, air-conditioning, and no CNN. It's Y40 a bed with breakfast in a dormitory.*

In the north part of the city, four km from the center, this modest, dumpy, unpolished 359-room hotel has Sichuan, Cantonese and Western food. Its advantage is its Tibet Travel Bureau office, convenient for arranging trips to Tibet. Rooms are small, and don't expect CNN or in-room safes. But it does take credit cards and rents bicycles.

TRAFFIC HOTEL (Jiaotong Fandian), *6 Lingjiang Road, Xin Nan Men, 610041. Three stars. Tel. 5551017, Fax 5434699, 5531877. E-mail: traffic@public.cd.sc.cn. Near the Xinnanmen Bus Station. Air-conditioned rooms are about Y200-Y210, and beds in a dorm Y40 with breakfast. It's been giving 60% discounts. Travel agents in its lobby give good discounts.*

This hotel has Star TV and dirty carpets, but no CNN.

Where to Eat

This is one of the best cities for Sichuan food. Flower petals and herbs are used in such specialties as fried lotus flower, governor's chicken, diced chicken with hot peppers and peanuts, and smoked duck with tea fragrance. Try also the dan dan noodles. See Chapter 25.

If you don't like hot spices, ask the restaurant to tone them down. The food is still good without chilis. If you want more hot spices, ask for "la jiao." Local snacks are lai tang yuan dumplings or long chao dumplings.

Restaurants in hotels are very good. But try any of the following:

GINGKO RESTAURANT, *Cantonese food. One of the best and very expensive. 16 Section 1, Binjiang Rd. Tel. 6666688 for directions.*

For Sichuan food and seafood, there's another of the same chain at Yong Lin Road. Same telephone. Confirm the address. They take Visa and American Express and have menus in English

BOYAYUAN RESTAURANT, *Sichuan cuisine. 109 Renmin Nan Road, Tel. 5577288, near the Sichuan Provincial Museum. The Boyayuan is used to tourist groups, so if you're with a group, the spices will be mild. Medium priced.*

MAPO DOUFU RESTAURANT, *Sichuan cuisine. 197 Xi Yu Long Street, Tel. 6754512, 6627005.*

This restaurant was opened about 1862 and is downtown. It is open 10:30am-9pm daily, and takes no credit cards. It is a simple restaurant where the tea-smoked duck with camphor leaves costs Y12 or Y30, and chicken with peanuts is Y12. It has mixed reviews. It originated the well-known spicy hot bean-curd dish and still offers 30 other variations of bean-curd. The food is especially spicy hot and medium priced.

TANDOOR, *Indian cuisine. No. 34, Section 4, Ren Min Nan Road, Tel. 5551958, 5563388 ext. 2156.*

ZHONG DUMPLING RESTAURANT, *7 Tidu Street, Tel. 6753402.*

Not a bad place, and prices are cheap.

Wen Shu Temple has very cheap and good vegetarian food and a nice temple atmosphere. But don't expect luxury or good staff attitude; this is not the place to celebrate an anniversary.

For Western food, try the hotels. For Western-type food, there are several little inexpensive restaurants around the Traffic Hotel.

Seeing the Sights

Entrance fees range from Y2 to Y41. The Green City cable car costs Y35 extra.

West

*Du Fu's (Tu Fu) Thatched Roof Cottage is a 20-hectare park with a replica of the modest residence of the famous Tang poet who lived here and wrote 240 poems in four years from 759 A.D. A temple and garden memorial were first built in the Song. The pavilions here are from the Qing era. Among the exhibitions are some translations of his poems in 15 foreign languages which might help you understand his importance. It is open daily.

South & Southwest

The **Sichuan Provincial Museum** is about two km south of the Jin Jiang Hotel. It has an amazing display of bronzes from the Ba Culture that developed in the Yangtze valley to the east. These are the people whose coffins you look for in the hills along the Yangtze River. Unique to the Ba/Shu culture are these incredible humanoid figures. It's at 3, Section 4, Renmin Nan Road, and open daily. A good tourist restaurant is on the grounds. For more about these mysterious people, see the Sanxingdui Museum.

The **Temple of Marquis Wu**, at 231 Wuhouci Avenue was originally built in the sixth century in memory of Zhuge Liang, a famous strategist and prime minister of Shu during the Three Kingdoms (220-265 A.D.). Here are tablets written during the Tang, larger than life-size statues, and the still unexcavated Tomb of Liu Bei, the King of Shu. The current buildings are Qing. The *Zhuge Liang Memorial Hall is a national historical site.

The **Guanyin Temple**, Bao Qiao village, Xingjin county, 32 km from Chengdu on Dajian Road (the old road to Leshan), is 500 years old and has original murals and painted clay sculptures. This small temple off the main tourist route is a gem for art-lovers. As yet undeveloped for tourists, it is home for 10 nuns. Open daily 8am-9pm, *Tel. 2450282*. No photos allowed.

North

The best place for giant pandas is the **Chengdu Giant Panda Breeding and Research Base**. Open 8am to 6pm. Entrance fee Y10. *Tel. 3505513, 3516970*. You can get there by bus 302 on Saturdays and Sundays. The stop is called Xiong Mao Ji Di and it's almost at the gate. The "Motorola Feeding and Activity Area of Cub Giant Panda" frequently has cubs on display. This park is huge so it's best to take someone who speaks Chinese. Or ask for "Xiao Xiong Mao." The animals there live in habitats, not cages. Sichuan is the home of 80% of the world's pandas, and reserves are under the control of Chengdu.

The 25-hectare **Chengdu Zoo** is six km north of the city and boasts five giant pandas. The zoo also has rare golden-hair monkeys among 2,000 animals of over 200 varieties. Open daily. The ultra-modern **Sanxingdui Museum** was built on the 3000-year-old, 12 sq km site of the Shu (also known as Ba) culture. It is one of the most exciting new museums in China, beautifully displayed with magnified pictures above tiny artifacts, creative lighting, and titles in English. It has sacrificial pits, gold-leaf masks, huge bronzes, and one of the earliest dragons, not bad for people with no written language. The relics are unique to this area, never before seen anywhere in the world. The museum is open daily from 9am-4:30pm or 5:30pm, with entrance fee Y20 and is worth a special trip to see. It's 38 km from downtown Chengdu in Guanghan, 618300, *Tel. 5222917, 5240907, Fax 5227645.* An exhibit from this museum recently toured the U.S.

The **Baoguangsi (Divine Light Monastery)** should not be missed. It is 18 km north of the city at Xindu, and famous. Originally founded about 2000 years ago, it became the site of a palace ordered built by Tang Emperor Li Huan. During the Ming, war destroyed the monastery but it was reconstructed on its original foundation during the Qing in 1671. Pagodas, five halls, and 16 courtyards make it most impressive. The Tang Pagoda is 30 meters high, 13 stories with a glazed gold top. The 500 arhats are from the Qing in 1851, each about two meters high, unique and vivid. Look for the 175-centimeters-high stone Thousand Buddha Tablet, carved on four sides in 450 A.D., and for the Buddhist scriptures written on palm leaves from India. Open daily.

Northwest

The *****Dujiangyan Irrigation System**, a one-hour drive (57 km) out in Guanxian county, usually takes a full day when combined with Green City Mountain. It was originally built in 256 B.C., the oldest such project in the country. Impressive because of its age and scope, it controlled floods and diverted half of the Minjiang River to irrigate the fertile Sichuan plain. Here are also old temples with murals. It has a 240-meter-long swinging bridge first built before the Song, but most recently rebuilt in 1974, so don't be afraid to walk on it. The Fu Long Kuan (Dragon Subduing Temple) houses a statue of Li Bing, the project's mastermind. The Erwang (Two Kings) Temple is a memorial to Li Bing and his son.

Also near Dujiangyan and 90 km from Chengdu is **Qingcheng (Green City) Mountain**, one of the birthplaces of Taoism and still a Taoist center, with 38 left of its original 70 temples, shrines, and grottoes. There's a 15-minute cable car almost to the top, but you have to hike a way first.

With some of its cliffs shaped like city walls, this strikingly beautiful mountain rises up to 1,600 meters. It was a base for a peasant insurgency led by Zhang Xianzhong, who captured Chongqing in 1644 and occupied Chengdu. Visitors can reach the **Jian Fu Temple** (Tang dynasty) by road. There are guesthouses midway up and on top.

The **Cavern of Taoist Master Temple** was founded in 617 to 605 B.C. The building is from the Tang and contains a portrait of Master Zhang Daolin, stone carvings of the Three Emperors, and murals of the Eight Taoist Fairies. The mountain is full of legends.

Nightlife & Entertainment

Bars in the top hotels are classiest. "Everybody" goes to the **Sentosa Tea House** for entertainment, says Valerie Tan of the Crowne Plaza. It's at 175 Fu

Qin Xi Street, *Tel. 7714113*. Y30 cover. She says young people like the **Golden Era** with its Filipino band, *Tel. 5199583*. The **Golden Time Brewhouse** is at 88 Ti Du Street, *Tel. 6766770*.

The city has several cultural shows. **Sichuan Opera** in the Cultural Park (next to Qing Yang Gong, *Tel. 7326189*) is set up for tourists. It costs Y80 each. This is a 1 1/2 hour show, at 8pm.

For the price of tea at the museum-like **Shunxing Tea House**, you can watch a show in a charming Qing dynasty setting. The show includes the usual acrobats and lion dance, but it also has an unusual macabre dance performed by a man with masks which is worth seeing. (The masks get replaced in the fraction of a second.) The show is completely in Chinese. Eight Treasure Tea costs Y48 a pot, chrysanthemum tea costs Y28, Lipton's Y28, and soft drinks Y8 a can. This is on the third floor of the Chengdu International Convention and Exhibition Center Mall (CIERCC), Fashion Plaza, *Tel. 7649999 X 3201, 3238*. E-mail: cdiech@Mail.sc.cninfo.net.

Shopping

The main shopping is on Renmin Road, Yanshikou, and Chunxi Road with many big department stores, including the huge **Pacific**, open 10am-10:30pm daily. Prices at the Pacific are higher generally than other stores for local products, but not as high as in North America. In the evening, the street market beside the Jin Jiang and Minshan Hotels is a half-km-long sidewalk art gallery of ethnic crafts and paintings, stuffed animals, and "antiques." Tibetan relics and ethnic textiles are beside the Minshan Hotel. On the Jin Jiang Hotel side is a line of antique and craft shops that sell tourist junk but also some genuine antiques from Tibet that look like human skulls, ceremonial daggers, scriptures and tangkas.

Sichuan Provincial Antique Store is the biggest and government operated, *Tel. 6120233*.

There is an open air antique market in Songxianqiao.

Excursions & Day Trips

Baoxing County, 350 km west of Chengdu, has a wildlife preserve that is bigger than Wolong with 100 pandas, but park officials cannot guarantee you'll see any. **Baoxing** also has Tibetan minorities, with traditions stronger than at Jiuzhaigou. It is best to go here in a tour.

See separate entries for Chongqing and Dazu, below.

EMEI SHAN

Emei Shan is 140 km southwest of Chengdu and 31 km (50 minutes) from Leshan by train or frequent bus. Either can be a quick one-day or overnight trip if you take the cableway up the mountain. Travel agents offer a two-day tour of both Emei Shan and Leshan but you can make it longer if you want.

Emei Shan is one of China's **four great Buddhist mountains** and a UNESCO Heritage Site. You can reach its base by tourist train from the North Railway Station in Chengdu in less than two hours. The climb to the summit and back can be done on foot in one day if you're energetic, or two days for the less agile. Along the 60-km of stone paths are 23 monasteries, intriguing caves, gushing waterfalls, magnificent views, and birds. Be careful of monkeys; they can be vicious.

A cable car can take you from Jingshui to Wannian Temple; Land Rovers drive within six km of the peak at Jieyin Hall, at 2,670 meters. From there another cable car can take you from Jieyin Hall to the Golden Summit. At that height, it can be very chilly, about - 20 C at the top in January. Hostels are at the base and on the 3,100-meter-high summit, and there are snack bars along the way. Guides are available.

The best time to climb is from April to June, and September to November. It may be hazardous December to March, but the mountain is beautiful. The rainy season is July and August.

Baoguo Temple, at the base, has a scale-model map of the mountain with lights. The temple originates from the Ming. Wannian (Samantabhadra) Monastery on the slope dates from the fourth century. Its bronze and iron Buddhas are Song to Ming. The bronze Samantabhadra on a white elephant is 7.4 meters high and weighs 62 tons. How did they carry it up here? The beamless brick hall, its roof, and square walls, are said to be typically Ming.

The Red Spider Mountain Hotel (see below) is the best. Some hardy visitors prefer the two-star **Golden Top Hotel** at the top of the mountain, *Fax 5098015*. Okay is the **Phenix Lake Hotel**, *Tel. 5527888. Fax 5529666*.

RED SPIDER MOUNTAIN (Hong Zhu Shan Binguan), *614201. Number Five Building is four stars. Number Eight is three stars. Tel. 5525888, 5525727, Fax 5525666. E-mail: hzshotel@email.com.cn. Website: www.hongzhushan-hotel.com. (Chinese). It is 130 km from the airport, 10 km from the railway station. Tourist groups pay Y380 a room. It takes credit cards and travelers checks and is near the Baoguo Temple.*

Built in 1935, this hotel has three stories, 180 rooms and 10 buildings. It is the largest hotel in town.

The **telephone code** for Emei Shan is 833.

JIUZHAIGOU

Jiuzhaigou is a **nature preserve** about 450 km north of Chengdu, a UNESCO Heritage site. It comprises 60,000 hectares of primitive forest with species earlier thought to be extinct. Expect exotic animals, forested hills, carpets of flowers, lakes and waterfalls. Jiuzhaigou means Nine Stockades Canyon, three of which are about 2500 meters above sea level. Tibetan and

Qiang minorities live in the area. The best time to visit is September and early October but be sure to book your hotel well in advance then. In the vicinity is the renovated Nyingma Longchen Nyingtik (Maiwa) Tibetan Temple in Hong Yuan County, originally built in 1646. The Long March passed through here in the mid-1930s.

For Jiuzhaigou, you'll need at least three days from Chengdu but that will only give you one day for hiking around this beautiful wilderness area. You can go by long-distance bus from the West Bus Station. Chengdu ITS says it's an 8-10 hour drive from Chengdu and it charges $400 for a four-passenger Landcruiser. Billy Zhao at Traffic Travel in Chengdu says it's best to bring cash as credit cards and travelers' checks are difficult to use here.

The best hotel is the new section of the **Jiuzhaigou Hotel** (Y800), now four stars with 120 rooms. The three-star **Jiulong Hotel**, *Tel. 837/7734567*, on a 3000-meter high mountain has 100 rooms for Y300. No credit cards.

Jiuzhaigou is open all year round but nearby Huang Long is closed around October 20th because of the snow. Normally the better hotels stay open in winter and are heated. Zhao also says, "Our four-day tour costs about Y850 per person with Chinese-speaking guide. You don't need a guide very much in Jiuzhaigou but a guide will take care of all arrangements." Sichuan CITS charges $400-$500 for a small car to go to Jiuzhaigou for two nights.

LESHAN

Leshan is about 150 km southwest of Chengdu (the closest airport) and less than two hours by expressway, the fastest way to go. Buses are more frequent and leave from the station near the Traffic Hotel. Its train station is 31 km from Leshan. It is 40 km from Emei Mountain. Traffic Travel Service charges about Y550 yuan for a six passenger car from Chengdu.

Warm rains from April to June add to the mystical atmosphere. It is a small 1,300-year-old town of 200,000 people, a good place for pedicab rides. On the ***Dafu (Great Buddha) Temple** grounds sits a Buddha (either 58.7 or 70 meters in height, depending on sources) started in 713 A.D. and completed 90 years later. It is now the largest ancient Buddha in the world (after the Taliban destroyed the one in Afghanistan) and is a UNESCO Heritage Site. From Leshan city across the river, visitors can take a public bus to the front gate or arrive by ferry. The view from the water is better; otherwise, you can't see the temple guardians. From the water, you should see an even bigger, more virile, reclining Buddha, head to the right, formed accidentally by the shape of the hills and a pagoda. At the confluence of three rivers (Min, Dadu, and Qingyi), the monastery buildings stand at Buddha's eye level.

This huge statue was built to offset the large number of serious accidents on the river. Since statistics were probably kept before and after, it would be enlightening to know if the statue fulfilled its purpose. You can reach the **Wuyou (Black) Temple** in 15 minutes by footpath from the Dafu Temple. It has a good museum for its tiny size. There is also an **Eastern Han Dynasty Museum** at Mahao Cliff Tomb, south foot of Lingyun Mountain.

The best hotel is the Jia Zhou (see below). The second best is the **Shanwan Hotel**, *Tel. 2350888, Fax 2350009, 2350158*

JIA ZHOU HOTEL (Binguan), *19 Bai Ta Road, 614000. Three stars, Tel. 2139888, Fax 2133233. About Y450. Credit cards. This hotel has a good location on a main street across the river from the Great Buddha.*

Built in 1956 with a second building in 1987, this 13-story, 200-room hotel has an outdoor pool and bicycles for rent. It is on the site of a former Canadian mission, near shopping, a park, and boat to the Great Buddha Temple.

Leshan CITS is at 129 Renmin Nan Road, Changchen Building, 614000. *Tel. 2124570, 2133198, Fax 2132154.* The **tourist hotline** is *Tel. 2124570.* Contact the Leshan Tourist Bureau, 23 Boshui Street, Leshan, 614000, *Tel. 2131968*, if you have any complaints. The city's **telephone code** is 833.

ELSEWHERE NEAR CHENGDU

Lhasa in Tibet is most easily reached from Chengdu with at least twice-a-day flights leaving about 6:40am and 6:50am. You can book flights and tours easily here because Chengdu's travel agents have close ties with travel agencies in Tibet, and in town is the Tibet Travel Bureau where permits are obtained.

The **Overseas Tourism Corporation Chengdu** here explains the regulations about travel to Tibet. It is at No.130 Shanxijie Street, Rongcheng Hotel, *Tel. 6154179, Fax 6099022. E-mail: samtour@yahoo.com.* Says Samuel Yue: "To go to Lhasa, a foreign tourist has to pay for a basic tour of Y2800 which includes airport transfer, one-way flight ticket, three nights in a hotel dorm, two-days' city tour in Lhasa and the permit. Food and entrance tickets are extra. It takes one day to arrange. You can stay as long as your Chinese visa is valid. If you want to go to other areas in Tibet, you have to get another permit from a travel agency there. (Some tourists go by themselves without a new permit after they get to Lhasa. It seems there's no problem.)

"If you stay for a week in Lhasa, all additional expenses will cost about Y1000 minimum plus the one-way Y1270 flight back to Chengdu. To get the permit, travel agents need a copy of your passport and Chinese visa with its entrance stamp. It has been difficult to get a permit if your Chinese visa has less than 10 days of validity left. If you do not have an "L" tourist visa, you will need a Chinese student card, Chinese residential permit, or a letter from the Chinese company you work for." See also Chapter 19, *Tibet*.

Wolong Nature Preserve is about a 150 km, three-to-four hour trip on a bumpy, narrow road from Chengdu. Public buses go from the Ximen West Bus Station to Dujiangyan (1.5 hours). Then you get another bus from there to Wolong (2.5 hours), a total cost of Y12 but a difficult and uncomfortable trip. Better take a tour or taxi. The scenery is great and there should be hiking trails with maps. It gets cold at night because of the altitude. There are many pandas in the wild, but you might not see any except in cages; there are usually about six around. Some can be seen only on video monitors. Recent visitors found they had to pay to take photos. Some refused the offer to pat these wild creatures not wishing to disturb them.

There's a **panda museum** here. Read *The Last Panda* by George B. Schaller. Naturalists estimate that there are now about 1,000 pandas in the wild. Ask about the September Panda Festival.

The better and more convenient hotel is the **Panda Shangzhuang**, *Tel. 837/6243050.* There is also the 150-room **Wolong Shanzhuang**. Both are about Y200-Y300 and near the Panda Breeding Centre inside the reserve.

Xichang is China's **satellite-launching center** and tourists are welcome. From Chengdu, it is an overnight train ride on the Chengdu-Kunming railway line. Xichang has an airport with flights twice a day from Chengdu. Be sure you get permission through a travel agent before you go if you want to see a launch. Xichang also has the Museum of Liangshan Yi Slave Society on Qionghai Lake in a southeast suburb. It was a stop on the southern Silk Road and claims a visit by Marco Polo. It is the home of the largest Yi community in China. Sichuan CITS says the best hotel here is the four-star **Conily Inn**, *Tel. 834/3200888.* It's at 88 Shengli Nan Rd.

The **telephone code** for the area is 834.

Zigong, 190 km from Chengdu and 200 km from Chongqing by road, is noted for its locally-found dinosaurs and giant lanterns. There's a daily train from Chengdu. It has a **Dinosaur Museum** (built at the site with over 100 specimens) and a dinosaur festival, a **Salt Museum** (showing 2,000 years of the industry), and a Chinese lantern museum. The city makes huge spectacular lanterns and a good time to visit is the Lantern Festival every three years from 2003. This lasts for about 20 days before and after the Spring Festival in January or February. The very fancy ***Shaanxi Guild Hall** houses the salt museum. The hall was first built in 1736 A.D. and has lots of gilded wood and stone carvings. It is at 107 Jiefang Road, Ziliujing, 643000, *Tel. 222746, 222083.*

The best hotel is the three-star **Shawan Hote**L, 3 Binjiang Road, 643000, *Tel. 2208888, Fax 2201168.* Y363-Y418 for rooms, Y748-Y935 for suites.

CITS Zigong is at 2 Tangkan Shang Road, Zigong, 643000, *Tel. 2203569.* **Internet "web bar" services** are on the second floor of the Telecom Building at 155 Tai Shun Nan Road, a main street full of stores selling mobile phones. Open 10am to 11pm daily. Y10 an hour. 35 computers. If that's too expensive, the Internet & Cafe's service is Y4 an hour. It's at 13 Binjiang Zhong Road, *Tel. 6660053.* E-mail: *bar@path123.21cn.com. Website: www.path123.com.cn. (Chinese).* The **telephone code** is 0813.

Practical Information

Business Hours: stores open 9am-9 or 10pm; offices 8am-12 noon, 2pm-5:30pm.

Chengdu International Travel Company, *Room 610, My Hotel Office Building, 6 Yandao Jie (beside the Minshan Hotel). Tel. 6723528, 6723568, 6722928, 6722938. Fax 6723628. E-mail: tibettvl@mail.sc.cninfo.net. Website: www.tibettravelling.com.* It accepts payment by credit card and specializes in Tibet travel.

Chengdu Overseas Tourism Corp., *Domestic Tour Dept., 80 Zhen Fu Street, Tel. 6780739, 6742508, Fax 6780192.* Contact Robinson Zhang (Zhang Jin Chuan), who helped this book a lot. *Mobile: 13708072860. E-mail: jinchuan@hotmail.com.* It charges Y150 for an English-speaking guide for one day. See also Lhasa above.

China International Travel Service, *65 Section 2, Renmin Nan Road, 610021. Tel. 6659708, 6659726. Fax 6661975. E-mail: shieying@hotmail.com. Website: www.heatour.com (English and worth a visit).* Ask for Peter Xie, senior manager, Marketing Center who helped a lot with this book. This agency accepts Visa and MasterCard and says it answers e-mails within 48 hours. It charges $20-$30 per person per day for an English-speaking guide.

The **English Corner** for high school students is at Bin Jiang River Park at Renmin Road. Tuesdays and Fridays at 7 pm.

Global Doctor Clinic, *Holiday Inn Crowne Plaza, Room 402, 31 Zong Fu Street, Tel/Fax 678-6746. E-mail: gmc@chengdunet.com.* It advertises English-speaking doctors and nurses.

Sichuan China International Travel Service, *65 Section 2, Renmin Nan Road, 620021, Tel. 6659474, Fax 6655042. E-mail: Shieying@hotmail.com*

Sichuan Tourism Administration, *65 Section 2, Renmin Nan Road, 610021, Tel. 6659653, 6622065, Fax 6671042, 6674460.* For brochures.

Tibet Tourism Office, *Room 229, Tibet Hotel, 10 Renmin Bei Road, 610081, Tel. 3333988 ext. 38.* For Tibet travel permits.

Telephone code: 28

Traffic Travel Service, *6 Lin Jing Zhong Road, 610041. Tel. 5441877, 5451017 X 2803, Fax 5441877, 5434699. E-mail: traffic@public.cd.sc.cn.* Ask for manager Billy Zhao who helped a lot with this book. *E-mail: billyzhao@yahoo.com. Mobile: 13908176330.* TTS is open 8am-10pm and can also book horse treks in Sichuan and tours to Tibet. If you book a tour, you get one hour free internet service.

US Consulate General, *4 Lingshiguan Road, Tel. 5583992, 5589642, Fax 5583520.* American Citizen Services, *E-mail: acs@chengdub.us-state.gov. Consular information: consinfo@public.cd.sc.cn. Website: travel.state.gov.*

Chongqing

(Chungking)

For tourists, **Chongqing** has been only a gateway to the Yangtze Gorges. With the opening of an expressway, it now has day trips to a UNESCO World Heritage Site. Before 2009, it should be changing its landscape, acquiring a lake and a harbor for ocean-going ships even though it's about 2500 km from the sea. This sister city of Toronto and Seattle should become an even more important economic center for Southwest China.

Urban Chongqing is located between the Yangtze and Jialing Rivers and their immediate surroundings, and is at an altitude of 168-400 meters. The urban population is about six million, the total about 30.2 million.

Chongqing is over 3,000 years old. It was the capital of the Kingdom of Ba in the 12th century B.C. During the Song, it was named Chongqing, which means double celebration. During the Qing, a 10-meter-high, seven-km wall was built around the city. In the 19th century, Chongqing was one of the treaty ports open to foreigners, and foreign missionaries and teachers worked here before 1949. Innumerable books have been written in English about this area.

World's Largest City?

In 1997, with the stroke of a pen, Chongqing became China's and probably the world's largest city. Because of the Three Gorges Dam, it has joined Beijing, Shanghai and Tianjin as municipalities directly under the central government. It is no longer in Sichuan province and at 82,304 square kilometers, it is **bigger than Belgium**. Its borders extend to the provinces of Hubei, Shaanxi, Hunan, and Guizhou as well as Sichuan, and includes Wanxian/Wanzhou and two of the three Yangtze Gorges.

In the late 1930s, during the Sino-Japanese War, the Nationalist government moved its capital here, and Han Suyin's book *Destination Chungking* reflects that period. Unfortunately, Japanese bombs destroyed much of the city, and few ancient relics survived the war. Zhou Enlai (Chou En-lai) lived here as he tried to work with the Nationalists against the Japanese. American missions (Stilwell, Hurley, Marshall and Wedmeyer) attempted to get the Nationalists to work with the Communists. Read Theodore H. White's *In Search of History* for more information on that period in the 1940s.

The highest temperature in summer has been a rare 43°C, the lowest in winter, 6-8°C. The annual precipitation is 1000 mm. Chongqing is one of the "three furnaces of China." You can see clear skies only in summer, and fog between November and March might affect flight and ship schedules. The best weather is April, May, September and October.

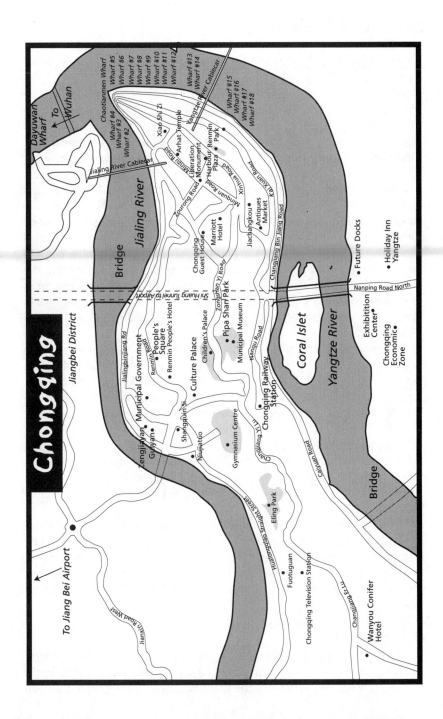

Chongqing

Jiangbei District

To Jiang Bei Airport

Jianxin Road West

To Wuhan

Dayuwan Wharf

Chaotianmen Wharf
Wharf #5
Wharf #6
Wharf #7
Wharf #8
Wharf #10
Wharf #9
Wharf #11
Wharf #12
Wharf #4
Wharf #3
Wharf #2
Wharf #13
Wharf #14
Wharf #15
Wharf #16
Wharf #17
Wharf #18

Jialing River Cablecar
Yangtze River Cablecar

Jialing River

Bridge

Xiao Shi Zi
Arhat Temple
Liberation Monument
Zourong Road
Minquan Road
Xinhua Road
Harbour Renmin Plaza Park
Ya Xuan Road
Changjiang Bin Jiang Road

Marriott Hotel
Chongqing Guest House
Jiachangkou
Antiques Market

Future Docks
Holiday Inn Yangtze

Nanping Road North

Shi Huang Tunnel to Airport

Coral Islet

Yangtze River

Zhongshan Yi Road
Zhongshan Yi Road
Nanqu Road

Pipa Shan Park
Municipal Museum
Children's Palace

Exhibition Center
Chongqing Economic Zone

Bridge

Jialingbinjiang Rd
Renmin Road
People's Square
Renmin People's Hotel
Culture Palace

Chongqing Railway Station

Zenjiayan Municipal Government
Guiyan
Shangqinsi
Niujiaotuo
Gymnasium Centre

Qiaijiang Yi

Huatongzhao Industry Street

Eling Park

Futuguan

Chongqing Television Station

Cajuan Road

Changjiang Er Lu

Wanyou Conifer Hotel

Arrivals & Departures

Chongqing is a little more than a two-hour flight southwest of Beijing, or a 7-9 hour train ride from Chengdu. It's much faster to take a bus. Flights arrive from Bangkok, Hong Kong, Macau, Nagoya, Seoul, and 49 Chinese cities including Lhasa. A regular charter flight from May to October arrives on Mondays from Munich, Germany. Jiangbei Airport is 30 km from downtown. When departing by air, give yourself at least 45 minutes to get there from Liberation Monument (Jiefang Bei). The CAAC shuttle bus terminal is at Meizhuanxiao Street. It leaves for the airport every 30 minutes and costs about Y15. It also stops at the Southwest Airline ticket office next to Cygnet Plaza.

An expressway from Chongqing to Yichang and eventually to Changsha and Shanghai should be finished about 2004. Parts are already in use. Big air-conditioned highway buses leave at least every 30 minutes or so for Chengdu for about Y110 and take 3.5-4 hours plus traffic jams. The countryside is beautiful, hilly and full of sorghum and Tudor-like farm houses. The bus and railway stations in Chongqing are both together about one km west of the bridge to the Holiday Inn at Caiyuanba Square. CITS says air tickets from Chongqing to Bangkok cost about Y2881, Beijing Y1350, Guangzhou Y1020, Hong Kong Y2341, Lhasa Y1400, Shanghai Y1290, Wuhan Y680, and Urumqi Y1580.

Arrangements for cruise ships are in transition. Up to now, many cruise ships have been leaving from Quay No. 3 at Chaotianmen Wharf which has very dirty elevators (Y2). At least you don't have to climb the stairs there. Sometime soon, cruise ships should be docking on the south side of the Yangtze near the Holiday Inn. When that happens, only ferries and hovercraft should be using the Chaotianmen Wharves. For these cheaper craft, you can get tickets from travel agents or at the counter inside the Navigation Office Building at Chaotianmen, under the Chaotianmen Hotel. Ignore the other so-called government-run tour agencies which charge you higher prices than inside, or promise you all meals and shore excursions, unrecognized later by your ship.

You can get tickets and information from cruise ship offices and travel agents here. They will tell you where your ship is. Tips for porters should be no more than Y10 per reasonable load. If porters are obnoxiously aggressive, try to wait at the top of the stairs and hope a member of your ship's crew sees you. Learn to say, "Wo bu yao," meaning, "I don't want." See also Yangtze Gorges.

Orientation

Today, Chongqing is crowded. Downtown is a hilly peninsula, its ferry wharves and main commercial area at its eastern tip, the airport to the north, and an economic development zone to the west. The Three Gorges Dam will raise the water level four or five meters and ships over 10,000 tons will be able to reach here after 2009. There are four bridges across the Jialing River and one more to come. A total of five bridges should cross the Yangtze River. Cable cars span the Jialing and Yangtze Rivers.

The government is developing a diplomatic area north of the Jialing River. The city has no bicycles because of its hilly roads. It does have electric buses, and a light rail system is due to operate in 2002 or 2003 from the Liberation Monument area between Jiao Chang Kou and Da Du Kou.

As part of the mayor's attempt to make this the cleanest city in China, trucks and buses cannot go into the city during the day without a permit. (They can only enter after 11pm and before 7am). Be sure to ask about this if you hire a vehicle. Once known as a badly polluted city, Chongqing has been cleaning itself up. It has moved factories away from downtown. People are using natural gas instead of coal for cooking. Unleaded gasoline is now on sale. It is testing car emissions and building a big waste water treatment plant.

Where to Stay

Hotels three-stars and up accept major credit cards. These four- and five-star hotels have business centers, coffee shops with Western food, and international direct dial telephone service, foreign exchange, and business centers. The airport is about 30 km from downtown, the train station about 3-5 km. Hotels here add a 10%-15% surcharge, and have been giving discounts of 20%-40%.

The Marriott is the best hotel. It and the Harbour Plaza are within walking distance of Liberation Monument and thus have the same basic good downtown location. The Harbour Plaza's location is slightly better because it is next door to offices, ice skating, and malls with restaurants, drug store and department stores, but the difference is minor.

HILTON CHONGQING, *10 minutes (three or four kilometers) from the new pier. Tel. 69039999, Fax 6903 8600. E-mail: prcqhilton@online.cq.cn. It will be the closest five-star hotel to the airport,*

This new five-star opened in 2002 too late to be reviewed here, and is the other serious competitor for top hotel. It is five kilometers from Liberation Monument towards the airport and closer to the new cruise ship docks than the Marriott. This 443-room hotel is east of the Stadium at the corner of Laodong Da Dao, and Zhong Shan San Lu.

The **Hyatt Regency** and **Hotel Inter-Continental** are expected in late 2002 or 2003. The five-star, 485-room Inter-Continental is on Minzu Avenue near Liberation Square, *Tel. 63999999. Fax 63666666.* It claims the largest deluxe guestrooms and suites and the largest ballroom in the city.

The Holiday Inn has had exceptionally good service for a four-star and its location near the soon-to-be opened cruise ship docks is super.

CHONGQING MARRIOTT HOTEL (Wan Hao Jiudian), *77 Qing Nian Road, Yu Zhong Dist., 400010. Five stars. Tel. 63888888, Fax 63888777. E-mail: hkres@marriott.com.Website: www.marriott.com. Rooms range from $180-$215 and suites from $260 to $4675. It has been discounting over 50%. One kilometer from new light rail system.*

Opened in 1999, this 505-room hotel has in-room safes, and bathrooms with huge tubs and separate showers. Rooms have a data port, call-waiting and voice mail, and range from 38 to 50 square meters. They offer CNN, CNBC and HBO, etc. There's an indoor pool, steam bath, and its gym has machines with heart monitors. At its business center you can read international newspapers in English.

The Marriott also has a steakhouse, a Japanese restaurant, cigar bar, and 24-hour room service where the American breakfast costs Y88, continental costs Y58, hamburger Y58, sourdough club sandwich Y46, wonton noodles Y25, ice cream Y25 and hot dog Y46. Its dinner buffet is Y108-Y128. Its ballroom holds 450 banquet-style.

HARBOUR PLAZA CHONGQING (Hai Yi Jiudian), *Wuyi Road, 400010, Tel. 63700888, Fax 63700778, 63726304. E-mail: hpcq@public.chongqing.cngb.com. Reservations in North America Tel. 1-800-44UTELL. Five stars. Y1330-Y1600 for rooms, and Y1750-Y9960 for suites. Discounts have been up to 60%.*

This 1997 downtown hotel with 391 spacious rooms, 34 suites, and 3.5-meter-high ceilings, is near offices and banks, the Metropolitan Plaza Mall and Sunshine Building. It has wood-panelled halls, CNN and Star TV, medium-sized bathrooms, and big closets. Standard rooms are 34 square meters. There's a coffee shop, summertime weekend barbecue, restaurants serving Cantonese and Sichuan food, and 24-hour room service. Its ballroom can seat 350 guests at a banquet. It also has a good 18-piece gym, 25-meter- long heated indoor lap pool, lighted tennis court, sauna, and steam bath. It has an airport shuttle. At the back of the Harbour Plaza and down the stairs is a fascinating bridal salon through which you have to walk to get to the department store. Here couples get ready for photographs in a dream world of good fortune and beauty. It is a wonderful opportunity to glimpse the new China. A Cheung Kong and Hutchison Whampoa Hotel.

HOLIDAY INN YANGTZE (Yangzi Jiang Jia Ri Fandian), *15 Nan Ping Bei Road, 400060. Four stars. Tel. 62803380, Fax 62800884. E-mail: hickg@public.cta.cq.cn. Website: www.holiday-inn.com/hotels/chgch (English). $135-$140 for rooms, $185-$998 for suites. See website for promotions.*

Built in 1989, the Holiday Inn offers CNN, HBO, and CNBC. It has 21 stories, 379 rooms and 66 long-stay apartments with irons and ironing boards. Rooms are 29 square meters. There are non-smoking and executive floors, a local snack restaurant, grill restaurant, German beer house, coffee house, Japanese restaurant, disco, and 24-hour room service. There's a summertime weekend barbecue. Its ballroom holds 350 banquet style. It has an outdoor pool, an up-to-date gym, steam bath, lighted tennis court, and putting green. Its business center offers the South China Morning Post and there's ISDN teleconferencing facilities. It has a 24-hour clinic.

This hotel is relatively isolated on a hill overlooking the Yangtze, but within walking distance of department stores, an amusement center, and supermarket. With the Huang Shi Tunnel now open through the peninsula, it takes only 25 to 30 minutes to the airport. It is the closest hotel to the currently-being-constructed International Exhibition Center and cruise ship wharves.

HOI TAK HOTEL (Hoi Tak Dajiudian), *318 Nanping Nan Road, Nanping Economic Development Zone. Four stars. Tel. 62838888, Fax 62805747, 62906241. E-mail: hthcq@public.cta.cq.cn or gtmaie@public.cta.cq.cn. Website: www.hoitak.com. This hotel is about 10 minutes south of the Holiday Inn and better located for tourists than the Wanyou but not as good. Rooms range from Y560 to Y730 and suites from Y900 to 1560. It has been giving a 50% discount.*

Opened in 1996, this good-looking, 15-story, 243-room hotel offers CNN, in-room safes and free local calls. It has a seafood restaurant, a pub, and 24-hour room service. There are non-smoking rooms, rooms for wheel-chair travelers, and an executive floor. It has a heated indoor pool, steam bath, lighted tennis courts, ping pong, bowling and gym. Its convention center, equipped with simultaneous translation, can seat 250 banquet-style. Managed by Hoi Tak International (HK) Limited.

CHAO TIAN MEN HOTEL (Dajiudian), *18 Chao Tian Men Xinyi Road, 400011. Three star standard. Tel. 63712600, Fax 63713035. Rooms range from Y288 to Y378 and suites are Y628. It has been discounting 20%. The price includes breakfast but it has no coffee so bring your own.*

This 26-story, 135-room hotel is walking distance to No. 3 quay and a new garden between the two rivers. It accepts credit cards and changes money. Some rooms have safes. Little to no English. Recommended for budget travelers only who are taking ferries.

HUIXIANLOU HOTEL, *186 Minzu Road, 630010. Two stars. Tel. 3837495, Fax 3844034. Rooms range from Y200 to Y550 and suites Y580. Discounts have been about 35%. Dorm beds are Y50-Y60 each.*

There are 168 rooms and a great downtown location but generally grubby with no apparent English. Recommended only for the desperate.

Where to Eat

The international hotel chains have the best Western and Sichuan food. Not all Sichuan food is chili hot. See Sichuan Dishes in chapter 11 and 25.

CYGNET HOT POT RESTAURANT (Xiao Tian E Bayusifu), *Chang Bai Road next to the Carrefour Department Store (Mian Hua Jie) down the hill towards the wharves. Tel. 63730111. No credit cards.*

The most famous hot pot restaurant in town, meals at this huge restaurant cost about Y100 each, including soft drink and show. It has a hour and a half show of primarily female dancers daily at 7pm. We had beef, liver, spinach and other kinds of greens, mushrooms, garlic, and soup base with one mild and one industrial strength chili seasoning. We also had sticky rice cake and dumplings.

AMERICAN COWBOY RESTAURANT, *178 Renmin Road (south of and down the hill from the Renmin Hotel), Tel. 63620045.*

Its buffet has uncooked dishes which you or staff can stir-fry at your own table. It also has cooked dishes. A fun place.

PICOLLO PIZZA, *in the Liberation Monument area, Tel. 63730022.*

It charges Y20 to Y40 for a 21 cm (about 9 inch) pizza and you can choose from the likes of calzone, tutti fruiti, meat lovers (mainly sausage), bacon and pineapple, honey and jam. You can use its computer for free. It is open 10am to 11:30 pm daily.

Seeing the Sights

For art lovers, **Painters' Village** in Huang Kuo Ping District is worth a visit. The institute is one of the best in China for traditional styles, wood block prints, oils and water colors, good technique but not much creativity. The government has supported most of these 17 artists for 40 years and you can watch some of them work. Some have exhibited abroad. It has a three-story gallery with art for sale. Open daily, it is at 24 Huacun, Hualongqiao, *Tel. 63862177.*

For modern history and especially Americans, there's the tiny **Stilwell Center**, open daily 9am-6pm but closed December-May. *Tel. 63850085.* It is good for people who want to remember the Sino-Japanese War and it has videos to see. Nanshan Park on the south bank of the river was the home of General George C. Marshall, the American mediator, and Chiang Kai-shek. The Nationalist leader lived in Yun Xiu, now renovated and open to tourists.

You can learn a bit about China's version of modern history at the Hong-yan Cun Revolutionary Memorial Hall (**Red Crag Village**) at 13 Hongyang Village. This was the office of the Communist Party and the Eighth Route Army between 1939 and 1946. It was also the residence for Chou En-lai and other revolutionary leaders including, briefly, Mao Tse-tung. This office was opened as a result of the kidnapping of Nationalist leader Chiang Kai-shek in Xi'an in 1936.

For older history, the **Chongqing Museum**, Pipashan Zheng Street, near Loquat Park, is open daily, with a display of Ba relics and ship coffins. You strain your neck looking for Ba coffins in Yangtze River caves. Here they are! This museum is dirty, dark, with no English nor air-conditioning. If you want to go back farther than that, try the **Chongqing Museum of Natural History,** Beibei District, 43 km northwest of the city. Dinosaur bones were found in this region and some are on view here. Open daily. See also Zigong under Chengdu.

There is a rundown zoo here, with half a dozen **pandas**. Better wait until you get to Chengdu where conditions are better. You can pet a panda for a fee, but please don't do it. These are wild, endangered creatures.

A 800-meter-long **cableway** goes across the Jialing River from Cangbailu Station in Jiangbei District to Jinshajie Station near Liberation Monument for a bird's-eye view of the area. Another cableway goes across the Yangtze at Xinhua Road to the south side close to Yikeshu. It costs Y1.50 one way and closes at 10pm.

Ciqikou or Lao Gai (Old Street) is 17 km from Liberation Monument past the busts of Einstein and Galileo in the high tech zone. Take No. 402 trolley bus to Shapingba and then a taxi (Y5). Telephone 9868242. This is an attempt to preserve and present to tourists the flavor of old Qing dynasty Chongqing. What you get is a rundown town founded a 1000 years ago with several highlights. Expect lots of stairs, flagstones, old archways and mah jong players. A temple called Yau Si Fu Miao is at the top of the stairs and a make-shift tea-house is by the Jialing River. Don't expect a smoothly-run theme park. This is a real town with real people who don't speak English and stare at you. When I saw it, there were no signs in English. It is best to take a knowledgeable guide.

Nightlife & Entertainment

China Travel Service has had **dinner cruises** with performances on two ships, the Jia and the Yang for Y68. In Eling Park, at 350 meters up, you can see both the Yangtze and Jialing Rivers and all the lights. Pipashan is a good place for an evening stroll. If you want bright lights, head for Liberation Monument. The Metropolitan Plaza there has ice skating (skates need sharpening) and bowling.

On warm evenings, people dance and taiji at People's Congress Hall (below the Renmin People's Hotel). Its square has a musical fountain. Every Saturday and Sunday at 7:30pm, there have been opera performances in the **Sichuan Opera Theatre** at Jintang Street. It costs Y5-Y10 and you can watch the actors put on make-up. A nine-hole golf course should be open soon.

Shopping

Chongqing makes umbrellas, silk, satin, bambooware, glassware, jewelry, knitting wool, carpets, and motorcycles. See Painters Village above. Going to stores around Liberation Monument (Jiefeng Bei) and the Harbour Plaza Hotel is now actually very pleasant. Cars are banned. A big mall is in the Metropolitan Plaza (open 10am-10pm) where the Pacific Department Store is uncluttered and reasonably-priced. A Watson's drug store is next door.

You can buy antiques, curios, stamps and old coins down the hill behind the **Antique Building** (Jiu Huo Jiao Yi Shi Chang) on Zhong Xin Road. It is open at 9 am.

The **Chongqing Museum** has an overpriced third floor gift and antique shop where one clerk easily came down 50%, and would probably come down more if pressed. Serpentine rollers (for cooling the face) cost Y600 at the museum but Y10 to Y20 in the markets, and Y160 to Y180 in local department stores. Down the hill to the right as you leave the museum are about eight other antique shops, where you can haggle too. "Purple jade" stone carvings are considerably cheaper from peddlers around the Dazu grottoes than in town. Try for less than Y200.

Excursions & Day Trips

Dazu County is the home of the **Dazu Stone Buddhist Sculptures** and is about 105 km northwest of Chongqing, about 95 minutes away mainly by expressway. It can also be about a 2.5 hour drive from Chengdu, or reached by train. The railway station is 15 km from Dazu town. This is an outstanding historical and artistic site recognized by UNESCO. Please try to visit it. You need almost a full day.

You can go by public air-conditioned tourist buses from Chongqing that leave every 30 minutes from 10am to 1pm from the main bus station. You can also go through travel agents. CITS' one-day trip to the highlights at Baodingshan and Beishan ranges down from Y780 per person and includes transportation, lunch, and entrance tickets – cheaper if there are more than two people. For just a car and driver, it's Y1000. Taxis are probably cheaper.

It is best to have your own transportation because there are several groups of sculptures too far apart to walk to and taxis may be hard to get there.

These original outdoor sculptures are better preserved and of finer quality than those in Luoyang, Datong, or Dunhuang. They were started in the Tang, and added to in the Song. A few were carved in the Ming and Qing. Because there were no roads then, they were untouched by the Red Guards but many are weather damaged. About 50,000 sculptures are located in 76 places in Dazu County, most still not readily accessible. Roads are currently being improved.

Under State Council protection are *Guangdashan, *Longtan, and *Linsongpo. Easiest to reach are those at **Baodingshan** (about Y30), 15 km northeast of the Dazu Guest House in a horseshoe-shaped mountainside with one or two levels of carvings. It takes about half an hour to take in the most famous: a mother sleeping next to a bed-wetting child, a village girl tending ducks, the 31-meter long Reclining Buddha, and the beautiful bodhisattvas, one with 1000 arms. Some of the standing figures are seven meters high. Only still cameras and photos of selected relics are allowed. There's hardly anyone around to enforce this rule in the other groupings however.

The sculptures here were mostly made by one monk, Zhou Zhifeng, from 1179 to 1249, and centered on the theme Life is Vanity. No signs are in English. It is essential that you obtain a tour guide if you want explanations.

*Beishan has about 400 stairs to climb in total. It gets fewer visitors than the more famous Baodingshan but has the largest concentration of statues and pagodas. It takes about 30 minutes and is two km north of the Dazu Guest House. Look for the elegant Goddesses of Mercy.

Another group of sculptures, carved in the Song dynasty, is at **Shimenshan**, 20 km southeast of the Dazu Guest House. These are Buddhist, Taoist and Confucian (smooth and simple). The **Nanshan Carvings** are 1.5 km south of Dazu town and are Taoist from the Southern Song dynasty. Look for the flying stone dragon.

Peddlers at the sites can be a real pain, but they can also save you money. A one-foot-high, carved "purple-jade" stone statue here (Y200) costs twenty times as much at hotels in Chongqing.

Dazu county is a relaxing, pleasant place to spend a couple of days. You can hike, explore Longshui Lake, and wonder how many of its locally-made switchblades will be used by gangs abroad.

DAZU HOTEL (Binguan), *47 Gongnong Street, Longganzhen, 402360, Tel. 43722476, 43721888, Fax 43722967, 43722827. Two and three stars. Rooms range from $30 to $50.*

This is the best place to stay or eat. It has 133 attractive rooms with small bathrooms and is far from luxurious. You might get a 10%-40% discount. The high season is August to October.

Dazu's **telephone code** is 23.

For other places of interest within Chongqing, like two of the Three Gorges, Wushan, Shibaozhai, Fengdu and Wanzhou/Wanxian, read the Yangtze Gorges section below.

Diaoyu Castle

At **Hochou/Hechuan**, about 100 km north of Chongqing is a fortress which changed the history of Europe. At **Diaoyu Castle** in 1259, five km southeast of Hochou, the Mongolian King Mangu/ Mongke, elder brother of Kublai Khan, was killed while personally trying to take this castle with an army of 70,000. His death stopped the invasion of Europe as Mongol leaders in the field withdrew to war among themselves for the leadership of the Mongol empire. Only the walls and a few structures remain. There is no museum and the road will not improve until 2002.

Practical Information

Ambulance, *Tel. 120*

China International Travel Service, *Chongqing Branch (CITSCQ), 120 Zaozi Lanya Street, Yu Zhong District, 400015, Tel. 63850693, 63851362,*

63850196, 63879724. E-mail: citscq@cta.cq.cn. Website: www.netour.net. It has a liaison office for information about cruise ship movements. Ask for Zhou Shizhi who has helped this book a lot.

Chongqing Dayou International Cruise Travel Co., *3/F, Jingdao Business Building A, No. 58 Songshi Bei Road, Yubei District, 401147. Tel. 67912575, Fax 67906969.* Star Dipper. Contact: Leon Lee. *E-mail: dylcgs@public.cta.cq.cn. Website: www.yangtze-river-travel.com (English).* Cabins are 18 square meters, with bathtubs. It has a business center, fitness center and casino. In 2002, its ship goes between Chongqing and Shashi. In 2003, it will go between Chongqing and Maoping, which is in front of the Three Gorges Dam.

Consulates:

• **Consulate of Britain**, *28/F, No. 68, Zourong Road, Metropolitan Tower, 400010, Tel. 63810321. Fax 63810322. E-mail: bcgchq@public.cta.cq.cn*
• **Consulate of Canada**, *Room 1705, Metropolitan Tower, Wuyi Road, Yu Zhong District, 400010, Tel. 63738007, Fax 63738026. E-mail: chonq@dfait-maeci.gc.ca. Website: www.canada.org.cn*
• **Consulate of Japan**, *Tel. 63733585, Fax 63733589*

CYTS Tours, *No 125 Renmin Road, Yuzhong District, Tel. 63868108, Fax 63850951. E-mail: cqcyts@public.cta.cq.cn.*

E-mail services. See Picollo Pizza above. The China Telecom e-mail office is very hard to find. It is down the hill from Liberation Monument on the road to the Chaotianmen piers, left side, with no sign.

Holiday Inn travel agent. *Tel. 62803380, Fax 62800884. E-mail: hickg@public.cta.cq.cn.* Overseas and Tibet travel. Trips to Beishan in Dazu cost Y1450 for one, and Y1620 for two people (each Y810). Ferry and cruise ship bookings.

Hours: most tourist attractions are open 8 or 9am-6pm. Business hours: 8:30am-12:00 noon, 2pm-5:30pm, Monday-Friday.

Orient Royal Cruises (East King and East Queen), *Suite 1205, Metropolitan Plaza, 68 Zourong Rd., Yuzhong District, 400010, Tel. 8576-9988. Fax 8576-6688. E-mail: orcruise@public.wh.hb.cn.* To reach the East King directly, *Tel. 13972600817 or Fax 27/90988610.* To reach the East Queen directly, *Tel. 86/13972600837 or Fax 27/90988612.*

Regal Cruises, *28 Xinyi Street, Chaotianmen, 400001. Tel. 63712662, Fax 63818551. E-mail: rcccqcom@public.cta.cq.cn.*

Telephone code: 23

Guiyang

(Kweiyang)

Guiyang, the capital of Guizhou (Kweichow) province, is 463 km due south of Chongqing and 786 km northwest of Guilin.

Guizhou is a landlocked region known for its minorities, many of whom still wear their unique costumes even to work in the fields. It has some of the best ethnic embroidery and batik in China, and cultures that are still relatively intact. It also has beautiful mountains, and China's largest waterfall. This is National Geographic-land, the frontier, truly exotic and amazing. But it's changing so don't wait too long before coming.

The province is rich in minerals like aluminum, coal, iron, lead, gold, silver, and zinc. It has China's largest mercury deposit. It grows rice, corn, tobacco, cork, raw lacquer, and timber. And many of its people are very poor.

Arrivals & Departures

Guiyang has direct flights with Bangkok, Hong Kong, and 36 other Chinese cities. Its Long Dong Bao Airport is ten km from downtown. Guiyang is at the hub of railway lines with Chengdu (967 km), Nanning (865 km), Kunming (639 km), and Changsha.

Orientation

Guiyang is a big, lively, modern city with dirty air and not much unusual to see. The urban population is about 800,000, the total 1,600,000. It is a gateway to the rest of this extraordinary region.

Guizhou province on the other hand is one of my favorites. Its high percentage of ethnic groups is due to its hard-to-cultivate land and karst mountains. China's dominant Han people did not want it and the minorities had no choice. Today, out of a total population of 30 million, 36.5% are minorities: Miao, Bouyei, Dong, Yi, Shi, Hui, Gelo, Zhuang, and Yao. They have fascinating architecture and more than 100 lively unique festivals a year with bullfights, horse races, and lusheng (bamboo pipes) dancing.

Because this province has only recently been opened to tourists, people will find the exotic here but don't expect private baths and hot water outside of Huangguoshu, Guiyang and Kaili. You'll be lucky to get a clean, functioning hotel room. Think of your accommodations as camping, and you'll be okay. New hotels are being built however, but with more tourists, do not expect the minorities to remain unchanged. High tourist season is April to October. August is hottest and it can go up to 34°C for several days.

You can still find villages effusive with genuine hospitality, and a brilliant bouquet of ethnic clothing. You will experience elaborate welcoming ceremonies, totem worship, a coffin on a back porch to make its future inhabitants happy, and unusual music. It is, in places, a time warp. Some women's

Miao Song

Welcome,
Today is not a festival but
Since you have come,
Today should be a festival.
The vegetables were planted by me,
The rice was planted by me,
The chickens were fed by me,
And the wine was made by me.
The more you drink the happier I will be.
I don't know which wind brought you here.
If I knew which wind brought you today,
I hope every day that kind of wind will come.
– translated by Pan Xin Xiong

hairstyles are from the time the group arrived in the area, each village different. You can actually see real Tang and Song hair-dressing!

Contact the tourism offices and travel agencies for festival dates. Some are on my website. They are mainly in the spring and subject to many last-minute changes. The dragon boat races are around July and the weather is best in September and October (but no festivals).

Where to Stay

The best hotel in Guizhou is the Holiday Inn, then the Park, and the Trade Point (Bai Dun). All are in downtown Guiyang. These hotels take major credit cards, have money change, business center, IDD, etc. and are subject to 10-15% surcharge and discounts. For budget travelers, look for Guizhou University guest house.

HOLIDAY INN GUIYANG (Shen Qi Jia Ri), *1 Beijing Road, 550004. Four stars. Tel. 6771888, Fax 6771688. E-mail: higybc@public.gz.cn. Website: www.sixcontinentshotels.com/holiday-inn (English). It is 12 km from the airport, seven km from the railway station and near the Qianlin Park in a commercial shopping area. Y800-Y960 for rooms, and Y1200-Y6000 for suites. It will be giving 40% discounts.*

This 230-room 1998 hotel has 24-hour room service and a 24-hour coffee shop. It has non-smoking rooms, a floor with computer ports in its rooms, an indoor pool, and is wheel-chair accessible. It has a tour desk and 47 television channels including BBC. An elevated highway is almost next door and tends to spoil the look of its entrance and the views from some of its rooms.

PARK HOTEL (Guizhou Fandian), *66 Beijing Road, 550004. Four stars. Tel. 6823888, Fax 6824397. Website: www.gzhotel.com Ten km from the airport, six km from the railway station. Y320-Y680 for rooms, Y1380-Y4800 for suites. It has been giving 20-30% discounts.*

The Park has 410 rooms, CNN, bowling, billiards, and a piano bar. It has 24-hour money changing, in-room safes, and cleaner rooms on upper floors but a few dirty carpets and poor grouting. Its location, off a main street, is convenient to restaurants and a food market.

TRADE-POINT HOTEL (BAI DUN JIUDIAN), *18 Yan An Dong Road, 550001. Four stars. Tel. 5827888, Fax 5875755. E-mail: smtph@public.gz.cn.*

It is on a main street and has 254 rooms with 29 executive rooms/suites offering CNN, in-room safes, and kettles. It has a ticketing office and its business center had recent copies of USA Today, Time, and Newsweek—a real plus.

Where to Eat

The best and safest food is in the four-star hotels listed here. The **Holiday Inn** is good for Western food. Local food is frequently chili hot, but you can get cook-it-yourself hot pot spiced to your own liking. Restaurants in Guiyang do not yet take credit cards and tend to look grubby. Guizhou wine is 35% alcohol – check contents before drinking. This is maotai country. Guiyang is not famous in gourmet circles for good reason. Food here is not great.

JIA XIU YAN RESTAURANT, *19 Xi Fu Road, across from the Jia Xiu Pavilion. Tel. 5935328. It is open 9am-9pm and takes credit cards.*

It has a dinner show with ethnic songs and dances. The interior looks like a cave with stalactites. It serves Guizhou family dishes but it has no menu in English. Qin Yan Do Foo is fried dried bean curd for Y15, good but tough; sour fish soup was made with a sauce of ginger and chilies, and aged. The manager thought Americans wouldn't like it but it was edible and interesting. It also served wild fungus and vegetables in soup or fried for Y20 and fish-flavored meat for Y18. You can ask your hotel to order for you and tone down the chilies. No one here speaks English. Take Chapter 25.

Jonathan at CITS says the **Jinxing Restaurant** is okay too, *Tel. 6851999.*

Seeing the Sights

Guiyang itself has little to see beyond karst caves, wild monkeys, some temples, and visits to Sinocized Bouyei and Miao villages. It does have the **Guizhou Provincial Museum**, a good introduction to the region. This is open 9am-about 5pm daily except Mondays at 47 Beijing Road, *Tel. 6825674.* It is worth a stop for its collection of minority costumes, especially if you are looking to buy good embroidery and genuine textiles. Look also at the fossilized fish and plants, and relics of the 2000-year-old Yelang culture found in the province. This is half a block from the Park Hotel.

Together there's the **Jia Xiu Pavilion** (in old architecture with dragons), a Buddhist temple first built in 1592 and the **Cui Wei Yuan Garden**. **Qianling Park** is a good green place to walk. It has a cable car that takes you up to 1600 meters.

Outside of town, however, it's wonderful. Among the day trips available is **Xiangzhigou**, 32 km from Guiyang where you can see paper-making for

Festivals in Guizhou

Guizhou's **ethnic festivals** are wonderfully unorganized. They are genuine, an opportunity for young people to find spouses, for everyone to see friends, and a chance to relax from farming. Like county fairs everywhere, it's a place to have fun - some have circuses. Some have competitions and buffalo fights. And some even have libraries so kids can catch up on the latest comic books.

Animal lovers should avoid the fights because the buffaloes are motivated by a kick in the genitals. They are separated if the going gets too rough. Buffaloes can lock horns and throw each other like human wrestlers. The loser usually runs away.

For tourists, it is a wonderful place to take photos because many people dress up in their best costumes and amazing silver headdresses. Women spend hours preparing their hair. But festivals don't always start on time, and sometimes there are last-minute changes in dates. Tourists must not expect to be entertained. You should be prepared to be flexible and wander around on your own, and ask questions. Guides don't volunteer much information. Look at my website for festival dates.

funerals, and have a meal with a family. You can see the highlights of Anshun in a day trip, though it's best to stay longer. Kaili needs at least two nights, preferably more. See below.

Shopping

The main shopping streets are Yan'an Zhong Road, Yan'an Dong Road, and Zhong Hua Road – around two traffic circles. The **Guiyang Department Store** is at No.2 Zhonghua Zhong Road. Guiyang has stores with embroidery but the place to buy is in the countryside where women will sell their grandmother's baby-carrier to you.

Excursions & Day Trips

Note: Toilets in this province are especially gross. The best seem to be in gasoline stations, government guest houses, specific restaurants, or behind a bush. Food however is available everywhere, and hot pot is hygienic and good. (You can sterilize chopsticks in the hot pot's boiling soup.) The area has the infamous five-step snake (before you die after being bitten), the cobra, golden pheasant and wild pig.

HUANGGUOSHU FALLS

China's **biggest waterfalls** are 150 km west of Guiyang and 40 km south of Anshun. It is most convenient to take a taxi from Guiyang, especially if you want to see more than the falls and Dragon Cave. Taxis and rickety, dangerous, motorcycle rickshaws are available in Huangguoshu. The rickshaws are big enough for one big foreigner or two small ones.

You should be able to join a day tour from Guiyang. Check to see if you can get an English-speaking guide, and whether you stop at a village. Cheaper public tour buses also leave early morning from the railway station, definitely without English.

A day trip by taxi to the falls from Guiyang could cost you about Y700. For two days, it's Y800. If you want to stay longer, there are public buses, or you can pick up the tour bus on subsequent days back to Guiyang, or get public transport to the train station in Anshun or wherever. Public buses park on the east side of the Huangguoshu Hotel. Public mini-buses stop briefly at major sightseeing spots and drivers try to tell you what time they are leaving in Chinese. Buses leave irregularly for Anshun between 8:30am and 11am from the hotel. I feel there is enough hiking and sightseeing to do in this area for at least three days, and it's beautiful.

Huangguoshu Falls is best seen after the rains, from June to early October, when they are 74 meters wide and 81 meters high. In November, they could be one-third this maximum; in April, they can be just a trickle. You can walk behind them any time and later enjoy world-class views of the countryside nearby. Don't expect Niagara Falls. This area is still undeveloped for tourism, thank goodness.

The daytime entry fee of about Y50 includes a cable car ride which operates daily, year round 7:30am-6pm, when full. You could spend two hours exploring. Colored lights shine on the falls weekend evenings all year round, and ethnic dances are performed here during high season from about 9:15pm to 10pm on weekends at Y400-Y500 for tour groups.

The Huangguoshu Hotel and waterfall are at an altitude of 1000 meters, across the road from each other. Mosquitos are pests from July through September. From December to mid-March, the temperature averages 7 or 8°C, going down below zero for a couple of days in January.

If you want to stay overnight the best hotel is:

HUANGGUOSHU HOTEL, *Huangguoshu Scenic Sports Area, Anshun, 561208. Three stars. Tel. 853/3592110, Fax 3592111. It accepts no credit cards but it can change money. It has 3000 square meters of grounds, and good and bad rooms. The best is in its three-star 60-room Courtyard Number Three with a Chinese and Western restaurant. Its cheapest rooms are in its Fan-Shaped House with big bathrooms, small beds, and no heat, a total of 300 rooms. All rooms however have poor bedside reading lights.*

The Huangguoshu Hotel has CNN and 24-hour hot water. It has a sign in English at the gate. The food is good but not great, some dishes greasy and chili hot: deep fried beef, lily with Yunnan beef, steamed Lu fish, fried dumpling and hot sesame cake. Women in minority dress tour tables and offer drinks and toasts in the traditional style. The hotel's travel desk should have maps in English, and hopefully English-speaking guides for over Y100 a day. Hopefully too, services have improved since my inspection.

On your second day, you could hike five km or hitch a ride from the hotel, downhill to the **Garden of Stone Bamboo Shoots**. You can follow the green Bai Shui River below the waterfall on a parallel road. At the bottom is the **Tenxing Qiao** (Y40), a wooded area with lots of little waterfalls and paved pathways where you can look for wild monkeys, parrots, and other birds. This whole area is full of old banyan trees with their roots clinging to 200 million year old limestone.

In the Tenxing parking lot Number Three, you should be able to see an incredible pair of human **tight-rope walkers** performing daily on a 200 meter-long cable, 300 meters above you. They do their stuff hourly from 9am to 5pm for twenty minutes at a time with a bicycle, but no safety net. When you hear music, look up.

Here also is a decent fast-food snack bar and a regular restaurant with moderate prices. At the snack bar you might get a tray with bony fried fish, pork dumpling soup, and some raw medicinal root. Nearby is the tiny 16-room **Yin Lian Dui Tan Inn** with no screens, but CNN and karaoke. It is in a pretty sylvan setting by a waterfall. Rooms there cost Y200-Y300 but you can haggle.

In this 115 sq km scenic area, you can also spend two or three more days climbing mountain roads, finding a 300-meter-high waterfall, and dropping in to visit Bouyei villages at leisure. People are friendly, but none speak English. In some villages you may be attacked by swarms of women trying to sell you batik and embroidery. Don't expect the pleated skirts to stay pleated after washing. They're originally pressed by finger nail. You can get small embroidery pieces for as low as Y20.

When in Rome

• A local custom is hitting the table instead of clicking glasses while toasting.

• A Dong custom is to single out the poorest person in a village, one day a year, dress him up, and invite him to eat.

• When a baby is one month old, the parents place the child outside on the ground at an intersection. The first man to pass by is asked to be the godfather.

• When a couple gets married, the woman gives more gifts to the man's family and pays for most of the wedding.

• Kissing is unknown in Miao culture. "He bit me!" exclaimed an old woman after an Italian tourist thanked her with a kiss for a delicious dinner.

• Villagers experiencing their first flash from a camera thought it was lightening, and covered their ears expecting thunder.

The **Long Gong Dragon Palace Cave** is open 8:30am-6pm daily. *Tel. 853/3223969.* Transportation could be as cheap as Y5 by mini-bus (47 km) from the waterfall, but none of the drivers speak English. The entrance fee is Y50 which includes the 40-minute rowboat ride in a 1.6-km-long cave. It's peaceful if other tourists are quiet and your guide is not singing folk songs.

On the other side of Anshun is **Chaiguan village**, a 20-minute drive (nine km) northeast of the city, and about 60 km north of the waterfall. The masked **peasant opera** here glorifies the soldiers sent by the Tang emperor to quell a rebellion. One story is of Mu Gui Ying, a woman, who successfully led an attack against the minorities and became a famous general.

For about Y500, the farmers, some of whom have performed in France, will put on an opera for tourists if you contact the village chief. Otherwise all you might see is a small mask museum (about 100 masks, some with 13th century designs). You might also see families carving masks which they sell for about Y100 to Y200 each. Travel agencies can make arrangements if given 24 hours notice. *Tel. 412/5534403 or Fax 5534403.* CTS is at *Tel. 3223173, Fax 8224537.* The Tourist Office telephone in Huangguoshu is *853/3224747.*

Chaiguan people are **Old Han.** To this day, some of them and the other 100,000 Old Han in Anshun area wear clothing styles unchanged since their ancestors first arrived here from Nanjing. Look for women wearing a white headband in mourning for the soldiers who died then. Also in Anshun is a batik factory.

KAILI

This is a small city of 150,000. The air in town is cleaner than Guiyang's, but black smoke belches from its factories. Its hotels are basic, badly managed and maintained. From here you can make day trips to villages by taxi or public bus. Or if you're adventurous enough, you can try even dumpier hotels further out, or spend the night in a village.

This area has a large percentage of people below the poverty line. Roads are generally paved but bumpy. Side roads to individual villages can be muddy after rain.

Kaili is 196 km east of Guiyang, the closest airport. It is on several main train lines: Beijing-Kunming, Shanghai-Chongqing, and Guangzhou-Chengdu. You can take the once-a-day express train which leaves Guiyang in the morning and arrives less than 3.5 hours later. Buses should take about three hours on the new expressway.

The scenery is not as dramatic as Huangguoshu's but the rice fields and architecture are marvelous. In the spring, the fields are gold with canola blossoms, and in November, the leaves of poplar trees turn yellow.

No hotels take credit cards yet, and IDD calls are made only from the front desks. You can change money only at the Bank of China. The hotels here are really crude and worn with badly stained carpets. Foreigners are now put in the three-star standard **Honyan Hotel**. New and better hotels should be opened in 2002.

The best restaurants are in the hotels but I've had no problems with tiny road-side stalls, especially with hot pot. If it's still there, there's the **Flying Dragon Teng Long Restaurant**, Shao Shan Nan Road in Kaili near the Wuyi Binguan and close to the Big Cross (Da Shi Zi), *Tel. 8233120, 8226424*. This has been the best restaurant in town, and is air-conditioned. The service is good, and they have the highest prices (relative to the rest of Kaili). It serves Cantonese, Sichuan and sea food.

Dog is a favorite food around here, especially in Pan Jiang town, 60 km from Guiyang towards Kaili on the old road. In front of over a hundred dog restaurants you'll see naked, cooked rumps and tails.

The **Museum of National Minorities** in Kaili is worth visiting, though it lacks titles in English. It has been open Monday to Friday, 10am-5:30pm for a Y15 entry fee. It is best to telephone the day before at *8223557*. Get a guide to explain. It is full of good exhibits of minority life and crafts.

The huge **Sunday Market** is for local people to shop and is good to see but not many people are in costume. It's open 11am-4pm, and near the Ying Pang Po Nationalities Hotel. It's better to get out to the villages.

Outside of Kaili

If you're eager to really rough it outside of town, look at the family-run no-star Xiao Kiang Nan Inn. For about Y50 a room, it has a good location for hikers, is clean, has air-conditioning, heaters, and a tiny museum of local embroidery and batik. Beside a river, it has its own boat. Hot water is in thermoses only and its menu is limited. It only has 10 double rooms but from here you can hike in all directions. **Xiao Jiang Nan Inn** is in Chonganjiang town (between Kaili and Huangping). *Tel. 855/2451208*. Ask for owner Gong Ming Yu in Chinese.

I used to recommend an overnight stay in **Lande Village** but it has become too touristy.

For day trips close to Kaili, there are many Gejia and Miao villages. You can arrange a village visit through CITS or drop in on your own. If the visit is arranged, be prepared for a traditional welcome drink from a buffalo horn, during which your hands should be behind your back. Some women should be in costume for you to photograph and music played. Miao music is sung high and loud, as if from mountain to mountain. Do take a tape recorder as well as lots of film.

If you drop into a village unexpectedly, you can ask any woman to put on a costume and a 15 kilogram silver head dress. You might want to give a tip for their trouble.

The **Gejia village of Matang,** 23 km from Kaili, has been extremely well-organized for tourists and the dances are good. The official costume of Gejia women is of male military origins because of the bravery of the women who fought Han soldiers during the Qing dynasty. The skirt is short for riding horses. Though the Gejia say they are a separate group, the government classifies them as Miao. Their founder, General Da Sa, is said to have been a Manchu general who married a Miao woman and was later forced to flee to the mountains.

The town of **Taijiang**, 75 km from Kaili, is the center of Miao culture with a 97% Miao population. It has a silver factory and an embroidery factory (seeded by UNICEF) at 444 Heping Street. Both are within a few hours drive of Kaili.

Huangping County, east of Kaili, has a **Museum of Minority Festivals** in the Feiyun Temple. Zhenyuan, about 140 km east of Kaili, is near the **Black Dragon Cave.** The Miao and Dong believe they are descendants of dragons or water buffaloes who in turn were born of butterflies. The **Zhenyuan Binguan Guest House** is not too bad. There has been a tiny one-man silver jewelry factory in the village of **Tang Bai** near Zhenyuan (Shidong), but not much silver is on sale.

The **Museum on Marriage Customs** is in Xinyi, a bird sanctuary at Grassy Lake in Weining County, its black neck swans seen in winter and early spring. From Kaili, you can actually drive to Guilin.

Visiting areas where Dong people live with their elaborate multi-gabled bridges and drum towers, is still difficult. The road from Kaili to **Rongjiang** is currently being improved however, and a five-hour road trip should be possible in the future.

Trekking trips are great here if you don't mind the lack of decent hotels and coffee shops. There is also a problem of getting an English-speaking guide willing to sleep in uncomfortable villages. You are lucky if you can get Mr. Pan Xin Xiong of the Guizhou Tourism Administration in Guiyang who speaks Miao, and is known to most of the people in the area. This remarkable Shanghai native, who owes his life to Miao people, can also keep you entertained for hours with games, demonstrations of Chinese opera, and local folklore, some of which he makes up himself. Travel agencies here do have tents and rubber boats to rent for white-water.

Shopping: In Kaili peddlers wait at the gate of the hotels. The museum has a shop. Stores on the street and inside the hotels have antique pieces. You are expected to haggle. A reasonable price for an embroidered fanny pack is Y25, for a good, embroidered fancy baby hat Y30, and fine small embroidery pieces Y30-Y60. You can frame the pieces or sew them on your own clothing. You can hang baby-carriers and aprons on walls. Be careful of the jackets. They are not tailored and tend to slip back when worn. The indigo dye might come off. The brown color is made from pig's blood. The shine could be from egg white.

Each village sells only its own unique styles. Expect to be surrounded by a lot of competing women peddlers. Also look for silk funeral boots, caps, purses and sleeve pieces. Be aware that handicrafts are also getting mass-produced and commercial now. If you want the real thing, look for old pieces, quality, fine workmanship, and muted natural dyes. Please note that some of the costumes on sale are worn only for weddings, funerals, and religious ceremonies. If you grow tired of them later, offer them to a museum in your own country, especially if you've kept a record of its purpose, the name of the village, and the woman from whom you bought it.

China International Travel Service of South Guizhou, 53 Yinpan Dong Road, Tel. 8229441, Fax 8222506. Website: www.qdncits.com. E-mail: leemqing@hotmail.com. Ask for Lee Mao Qing who can also answer questions about the region. It does not accept credit cards.

Kaili Tourism Bureau, Kaili Hotel, Tel. 8222547. For brochures and complaints. Festival dates should be posted on my website: www.china-travel-guide.com. This office covers the whole Southeast Guizhou region. Taxis will take you most places in town from the railway station for Y10. Taxis cost about Y2.50 per kilometer.

Telephone code 855.

Practical Information

China International Travel Service. Try Ms. Zhang Penghua, General Manager. *E-mail: gzcits@public1.gy.gz.cn*, or Jonathan Jiang Huihua, Sales Manager, Europe and America, *E-mail: jianghuihua1010@yahoo.com*.

Guizhou Overseas Travel Corp., *Da Hen House, 11th Floor, 7, He Qun Road, 550001, Tel. 6576162, 6573214, Fax 6576053, 6576675. Mobile: 13608552274*. Ask for Wang Tai Lin, English Interpreter or Zhou Zu Xin, Manager, Ecotour Department. GOTC has five English-speaking guides.

Guizhou Provincial Tourism Bureau, Promotion Department, 346 Zhonghua Bei Road, 550004, *Tel. 6838257, Fax 3836309*. For information and brochures. Ask for Ms. Song Xiao Ping.

Internet Bar, Telecom Building (You Dian Da Lou), Zhong Hua Zhong Road. It is open 8am-12noon and 2pm-6pm and charges Y10 an hour. *Tel. 5850534*. Across the street on the fourth floor is a better internet bar charging Y8 an hour, *Tel. 5814899 or 5814999*. Ask for Guo Xing Wang Ba.

Office hours: 8:30am to 5:30pm with lunch about 12 noon to 1pm.

For **tourist complaints**, it's *Tel. 6818436, Fax 6836309*.

Telephone code 851

Kunming

(Kunnanfu)

Kunming is the capital of Yunnan province, which borders Vietnam, Laos, and Myanmar. It is beautifully situated on 330 sq km Dianchi Lake, China's sixth largest. Because of its altitude (1600-1894 meters) and its subtropical location, it is blessed with the best weather in China, spring all year round. (It occasionally gets snow.) The hottest temperature is 29°C in May and the coldest is -1°C in January. Precipitation is 1,500 mm mainly from May to August. Kunming is a good place to go in the summer. Dali, Lijiang and Zhongdian are even better, especially if you go in that order so your body can adjust to the altitude. Kunming's altitude is 1891 meters. Zhongdian's is 3300 meters.

One of the loveliest times to visit is February when the camellias are in bloom. The best times to visit are February to May, and August to November. The urban population is 1,800,000 and the total four million. The total provincial population is over 40 million.

Arrivals & Departures

You can reach Kunming by the fastest train from Beijing in about 44 hours, Chengdu in 19 hours, Guiyang in 12.5 hours and Hanoi in 30 hours. It has flight links with 58 Chinese cities, Yangon/Rangoon, Bangkok, Kuala Lumpur, Macau, Singapore, Hong Kong, Vientiane and Seoul. The flights from Kunming to Lhasa with stops in Zhongdian have been Wednesday and Saturday afternoon. (Y1770). The airport is five km from the city.

Buses to Dali and Lijiang leave from the Long Distance Bus Station.

Orientation

Yunnan province is the third most desirable tourist destination in China, another of my favorites. You could easily spend two weeks here. It is important because of its mountain scenery, its national minorities, the artistry and history of its temples, architecture, the Burma Road, Shangri-La, and the Stone Forest. From here you can travel to Laos, Myanmar, and Thailand.

In the province are several unusual sights. These range from almost year-round snow-capped mountains to tropical jungles where elephants and monkeys roam freely. Yunnan is aiming to get 1.5 million overseas tourists by the year 2005. To do this, it is pouring money into upgrading its infrastructure and opening new areas. The population is now 43 million of whom one-third belong to 25 national minorities.

Kunming is completely surrounded by mountains. Sightseeing here can be a little rugged. The Dragon Gate has a cable way so you don't need to climb so much.

Where to Stay

The best hotels listed here are the Courtyard by Marriott (more American) and the Harbour Plaza (more Asian). The Harbour Plaza and Green Lake Hotel are close together within walking distance of interesting Green Lake, Western-oriented restaurants and bars, and the bird and flower market (open 10am to 5pm). Walmart is a short taxi ride away. The Green Lake Hotel is good value for money. The Holiday Inn is a good four-star. The Holiday Inn, Camellia, and the Courtyard by Marriot are closer to downtown and People's Square.

Hotels here add a 10%-15% surcharge, but offer discounts. All hotels here have foreign exchange, private baths, and take credit cards unless stated.

HOLIDAY INN KUNMING (Yinghua Binguan), *25 Dong Feng Dong Road, 650011. Four stars. Tel. 3165888, Fax 3135189. E-mail: hikmgm@public.km.yn.cn. Website: www.holiday-inn.com. $68-$86 for rooms and $120-$268 for suites. It has been giving 25% discounts. Seven km from the airport and two km from the railway station and close to consulates.*

Built in 1993, this hotel has 18 stories and 235 rooms with small bathrooms. Rooms are 25-38 square meters with CNN, CNBC, and HBO. It has a cluttered lobby, executive and non-smoking floors, and 24-hour room service. To keep you healthy, it has a gym, 18-meter-long, year-round indoor pool, 16-lane bowling alley and clinic. It offers Thai and Yunnan food and genuine U.S. beef steaks.

COURTYARD BY MARRIOTT KUNMING (Wan Yi Jiudian), *300 Huan Cheng Xi Road, 650032. Four stars. Tel. 4158888, Fax 4153282. E-mail: cyhotel@public.km.yn.cn. Website: www.courtyard.com. It is in a residential area just west of city center, three kilometers from the railway station.*

This beautiful 1999, 255-room hotel has 30-34-square meter rooms, in-room safes, non-smoking floors and almost looks like an American five-star. It has a 22-meter, year-round indoor pool, hot spring water, gym, tennis, and Jacuzzi. There is no executive floor but there's CNN, BBC, data ports, coffee shop, steak house, and Chinese restaurants.

GREEN LAKE HOTEL (Cuihu Binguan), *No 6 Cui Hu Nan Road, 650031. About four star standard. Tel. 5158888, 5155788, Fax 5157867. E-mail: glhsales@public.km.yn.cn. Y588 to Y788 for rooms, and Y1000 to Y6999 for suites. This 15-story, 254-room hotel has been discounting 20%, but in summer, rooms on its lower floors were going for Y288 including breakfast.*

This is a great deal when the summer discounts kick in, despite the stained carpets, no safe, and stuffy air. It is otherwise clean. Its location by the lake and 33-44 square meter rooms make up for it. It is 15 km from the airport, and eight km from the railway station. Its old front section by the lake has been torn down and should be replaced with a new one, maybe in 2003, with lighted tennis courts, ball room, gym, restaurant, and amusement center.

HARBOUR PLAZA KUNMING (Hai Yi Jiudian), *20 Hong Hua Qiao, 650031. Five stars. Tel. 5386688, Fax 5378717. E-mail: sales.kunming@harbour-plaza.com. Website: www.harbour-plaza.com/hpkm. Rooms are $125-$160, and suites $215-$1380. It has been discounting to $78 on a standard room and is a Y40 taxi-ride from the airport. The Harbour Plaza is at the south end of the lake, closer to town, and near the museum.*

This 1999, 315-room hotel, has executive and non-smoking floors, and a 25-meter year-round pool. Rooms are 32-37 square meters, have three telephones, ATV, CNN and CNBC but no electrical outlet in the bathroom for a shaver. Its in-room safe fits a standard laptop snugly. There's Western, Japanese and Chinese restaurants. Its American breakfast is Y98 and is very good. The lunch is Y68, and dinner Y98 and Y118. A children's playground is in the coffee shop.

CAMELLIA HOTEL (Cha Huan Binguan), *96 Dongfeng Dong Road, 650041. Two stars. Tel. 3163000, 3162918, Fax 3147033. E-mail: chbg@public.km.yn.cn. Rooms are about Y140-Y360, and suites are Y270. No credit cards.*

A favorite of budget travelers, the Camellia was built in 1985. The staff speaks some English and a message board is up for travelers. It has some television in English. It has 192 rooms, and 24-hour hot water, a business center, bicycle rentals, and foreign exchange.

Where to Eat

Specialties include Rice Noodles Crossing the Bridge, Yunnan ham, and crispy, deep-fried goat's cheese. The adventurous could try snake, deep-fried bees, dog, or congealed blood. Dai food includes grasshoppers. Try the cook-it-yourself hot pot. The best local food and minority dance restaurant is the Jixing Yunnan Flavor Food City, see *Nightlife* section below.

The international hotels are best for Western food.

BLUE BIRD RESTAURANT, *in House 1, 127 Dongfeng Xi Road (near Xinwen Road), Tel. 3610478.*

This Western-Eastern restaurant is relatively close to the Harbour Plaza Hotel.

MA MA FU'S NO. 2 RESTAURANT, *diagonally across the road from the Holiday Inn at 219 Baita Road, Tel. 3111015.*

It has Western and Chinese food and is open 8am to midnight, and its pizza ranges from Y15 to Y38. It is casual and relatively cheap.

ROMANCE RESTAURANT, *opposite the Golden Dragon Hotel on the second floor of 158 Beijing Road.*

SENDITOSA, *near the Green Lake Hotel, Tel. 5768199. Website: www.coffeecn.com*

A good family bar.

Seeing the Sights

If you only have one day, you have to choose between a tour of the city or going to the Stone Forest. It is better that you stay at least two days, preferably more. Important in the city are the Western Hills, Golden Temple, Black Dragon Pool, Bamboo Temple, Yuantong Temple, Daguan Park, and Green Lake.

Xishan (Western Hills), *Tel. 8182211*, is about 26 km from the Holiday Inn. The 14th-century Huating Temple is the largest in the city. South of here is the Taihua Temple (Yuan) with the best view of the sunrise over the lake. The Sanqing Tower, two km farther south, was the summer resort of Emperor Liang of the Yuan. It has nine tiers, each about 30 meters above the other. On the top is the Long Men (Dragon Gate) with another great view of the lake. The stone corridors, chambers, paths, and intricate carving of the Dragon Gate were cut from 1609 to 1681.

The coppercast ***Golden Temple**, *Tel. 5154306*, 11 km northeast of the city, is 300 years old, 6.5 meters high and weighs 200 tons. The Qiong Zhu (Bamboo) Temple, 18 km northwest of the Holiday Inn has 500 life-size arhats carved in the Qing. These are very expressive and well worth a visit. The temple was founded in 1280.

The **Daguan Lou Pavilion**, *Tel. 4142335*, across the lake from Xishan Hill (seven km from the Holiday Inn), has a 180-character couplet at its entrance, the longest ever found in China. Composed by a Qing scholar, the first half praises the landscape while the second deals with Yunnan history. Also important is the **Black Dragon Pool**, *Tel. 5150395*, with its Ming temple and tomb. The Heishui Shrine here may be from the Han. Nearby are the Botanical Gardens. Yuan Tong Si, the only Tang temple in town, is a little over one km from the Green Lake Hotel.

The **Yunnan Ethnic Group Village** on Dian Chi Road is worth a visit for the architecture (Bai, Dai), and an introduction to Yunnan's minorities. It is 12 km from the Holiday Inn. There are dance demonstrations and a sampling of the water-splashing. But unless you are there during these demonstrations, you can find very few people in minority costume to photograph. If you are going to real minority villages, skip this. But if you are shopping for minority crafts, go for a look.

The **Stone Forest** is 80 km (about two hours by bus) southeast of the city. It can be a day trip or an overnight in the adjacent two-star **Stone Forest Hotel** (Shilin Binguan), Lunan County, 652211, *Tel. 7795401, Fax 7795414*. Many tour groups eat at this hotel. Hardly any stay here.

On the way to the Stone Forest is a new golf course and a lake, which is usually a pit stop for tourists. Singapore money is developing a 34-sq-km tourist resort with casino and villas. Many tourist buses now stop at a huge store owned by a collective under the Yunnan Provincial Tourism Administration, so it should be okay. It sells jade and other stones, and all manner of tourist goods. You can watch them carve jadeite from nearby Myanmar.

About 270 million years ago the Stone Forest was covered with water. The sea receded and rain continued to corrode the limestone into these artistic pinacles. One-fifth of its 64,000 acres is open to visitors. Here too are many steps. The shortest of the two routes is 2.5 hours long, but you can get the picture in much less time and spend your time elsewhere.

Near the Stone Forest Hotel is a Sani ethnic village with minority-type handicrafts for sale. If you want to visit a real Sani village, this is not the place; this one is too touristy. Peddlers can be a real nuisance. Groups of local dancers in ethnic costume have entertained hotel guests in the evening. The blandness of the Stone Forest makes it difficult to photograph. You can hire a local guide in Sani costume to take you around and be your model.

The trip between Kunming and the Stone Forest is remarkable because of the hilly scenery and the eucalyptus trees. A fascinating cave, 100 meters straight down, is located 93 km from Kunming and 24 km from the Stone Forest at Jiuxiang in Yiliang county. A word of warning: one of our group was overcome by the humidity, particularly towards the bottom. He spent an hour negotiating the stairs back up, a few at a time. The waterfall there was pretty however, but not worth that experience.

The Stone Forest (Y88) is one of the highlights of a Kunming visit but it's become very crowded and you can see a cheaper (Y25), similar geological formation at **Naigu** five km away.

The **Expo Garden** with many exhibits left from Expo '99 is still there for flower lovers to see. The entrance fee is about Y80. It is at the Jindian (Golden Hall) Scenic Resort, four km from downtown. There are rare plants, tea gardens, bamboo gardens, miniature gardens, and vegetable-and-fruit gardens.

Other Attractions

If you have more time, the **Provincial Museum**, is towards the Green Lake Hotel. Open daily except Sundays from 9am-4:30pm, it has a worthwhile exhibit of minority costumes and local history. The **Institute for Nationalities** also has a good exhibit of minority costumes but you have to make arrangements through a travel agent well in advance as it is not generally open.

Along the west shore of the lake is Sleeping Beauty Hill and a series of swordlike peaks. On the southern tip of the lake is Jinning county town, the birthplace of the famous Ming navigator **Zheng He**, who sailed to East Africa half a century before Vasco da Gama. The Memorial Hall to Zheng He is on a hill above the town. Read *When China Ruled the Seas*.

Festivals & Markets

Festivals and markets are worth experiencing and too numerous to mention. There are many more than the famous Water-splashing Festival in Jinghong in mid-April, the Yi Torch Festival (in late July or early August), the Third Moon Market (usually April, sometimes May) in Dali, and the Horse and Mule Market (about early April in Li,iang). Write to local travel agents for exact dates and arrangements.

Ask about regular minority markets. An arts festival with performances by most of China's national minorities has been held mid-February to early March.

Nightlife & Entertainment

The best dinner and minority dance restaurant is the **Jixing Yunnan Flavor Food City**, inside the gate of the Camellia Hotel. The show is daily about 7pm, *Tel. 3178508*. The liveliest action is at the **Holiday Inn**, the top floor of the **King World**, and **Kundu Entertainment** near the Harbour Plaza. Be wary of bars outside of hotels because you might have to buy drinks at high prices for the girls who sit with you. At least one of these bars has been known to give a guest an incredibly high bill at the end of an evening and threatened him with violence unless paid.

Shopping

Look for batik, feather products, minority handicrafts, embroidery (especially shoulder bags and clothes), tin and spotted copperware. You can get minority crafts at the **Yunnan Ethnic Group Village**, though the cheapest handicrafts have been from peddlers. The cross-stitching is an excellent buy.

Try the **Bird and Flower Market** about five blocks behind the Green Lake Hotel where antique jewelry and porcelain, real and fake, share space with live goldfish and budgies. In this area too are a growing number of real antique stores. Department stores are on both sides of the Holiday Inn.

Excursions & Day Trips
JINGHONG

This is a town where you visit minorities and their villages. It is southwest of Kunming in Xishuang Banna region (pronounced She-Schwan-Ban-NA), about a 740-km, 14-hour drive on paved roads with an overnight in Simao. Planes fly there daily in 50-minutes. There are also flights from Dali. The city is 10 km from the airport.

At an altitude of 550 meters, Jinghong is humid but not overly hot in May, and can get pretty steamy in July and August. The area rises up to 2,300 meters, and grows rubber and tea. There are 1,200 to 2,000 mm. of rain annually. Take precautions against malaria. Jinghong's urban population is about 30,000 people.

Thirteen minorities inhabit this region. The ethnic people here are related to those of northern Thai and Laos, but the standard of living is higher.

The best hotel in Jinghong is the four-star **Dai Garden** (Daiyuan Jiudian), at 8 Nonglin Nan Road, 666100, *Tel. 2123888, 2130558, Fax 2126060*. Rooms are Y670 discounted to Y300. The second best is the three-star **Prosperity Hotel** (Cai Xin), 666100. *Tel. 2139888, Fax 2133721*. Rooms are Y500-Y580.

The hostels in the Dai village (Manjinglan) are just barely recommended for backpackers. But many backpackers stay there and like them. No hostel has IDD.

Just outside the Dai Village is a park with a replica of a beautiful white stupa or pagoda next to a genuine Buddhist monastery with a friendly abbot. A museum of Dai costumes should open in Jinghong soon.

David Huang of OTC in Kunming says you can go by chartered boat from Jinghong to Laos down the Lancang River which becomes the Mekong 30 km south of Jinghong, but it's very expensive. This river is 293 km long in China. In Yunnan it falls 1,780 meters, and 14 power stations will eventually harness it for electrical power.

You can visit **Hani** and **Jinuo** villages in the mountains. Guides tend to just drop you off at villages allowing you to wander around on your own. Don't be afraid to knock on doors. You can even ask them to don their costumes for photos. They understand sign language. (Tip them five yuan or buy something.) Interested visitors should go armed with questions about life-styles, unique customs, technology, child-rearing, courtship rituals, and the percentage of women on village councils.

A visit to a Dai village could include songs, dances and a demonstration of the Water-Splashing Festival (below) any time of the year if you're expected. Some of these villages can also provide good meals in a Dai home. Some of the temples are similar to those in neighboring Laos. You can take an organized tour, or rent a bicycle or car and go off on your own. You could also take public buses, but they are infrequent.

The **Menglun Botanical Garden**, 75 km west of Jinghong has been badly maintained. Hopefully it is better now but the drive there through intensely exotic and lovely countryside is worth the trip. **Simao** (with an airport) is the mother of all the world's tea; 23 kinds of tea still grow wild there. Simao is 540 km from Kunming (a 40-minute flight) and 160 km from Jinghong. There is also the wildlife reserve at **Sanchahe**, 47 km north of Jinghong. Few wild Asian elephants live there now, decimated by poachers. Visitors can see only a small part of the reserve, ride tame elephants, and visit Dai and Jinuo villages. There are tree-top hotels to see the animals but no guarantees you will spot any.

Travel to Southeast Asia

The easiest way to go to neighboring Laos, Myanmar, Vietnam and nearby Thailand is to fly from Kunming. The second easiest for Vietnam is train from Nanning or Kunming. From Jinghong, you have to charter a boat and arrangements could take three weeks. In all cases, you have to obtain visas for these countries. Lao, Thai, and Myanmar consulates are in Kunming. A Vietnamese consulate is in Guangzhou. All have embassies in Beijing. To save time, it's better to get your visa in your home country. See Nanning for Vietnam.

CTS says you can catch the train to Hanoi in Kunming, and in Hekou on the border. It is a narrow gauge railway built by the French in 1904 and goes 30-40kmh, taking 30 hours to Hanoi. Two trains a week have soft-sleepers on Friday and on Sunday.

Shopping is best at the various tourist attractions or factories: silver jewelry, embroidered purses, natural marble pictures, and tie-dyed cotton. You can buy handicrafts directly from villagers. In Jinghong, there's the early morning food market to see and craft stores outside the gate of the Xishuangbanna Hotel.

The Water-Splashing Festival marks the Dai New Year. If it's well-organized, there will be minority dances and demonstrations, dance dramas, and bamboo rocket competitions. Wa tribesmen, former headhunters, may sacrifice a bull. CITS has a boat for you to watch the dragon boat races. The water-splashing is confined to certain areas between 10am and 4pm on one designated day. Take a water pistol and shower cap. Guides loan you basins. Local youths attack foreigners gleefully. It is a lot of fun, but keep your mouth closed and keep your valuables at the hotel and your camera in a plastic bag. You can be splashed at the Local Customs Garden of National Minorities, Chunhuan Park too.

For help with travel, contact travel agents in Kunming if you need a travel agent in Jinghong. The **telephone code** is 691.

XIAGUAN & DALI

You can take a daily overnight train from Kunming to Dali. Buses (Y103) leave Kunming for Dali from the Long Distance Bus Station on Beijing Road near the railway station. Local Dali bus Number 8 goes from the Xiaguan/Dali railway station to Yu Er Road in Old Dali for Y1.50.

Flights leave daily from Kunming and take about 30 minutes. The airport is a few kilometers south of Xiaguan which is 15 km south of old Dali. The taxi from the airport to Dali costs between Y50 and Y80 and goes by the Xiaguan railway station, past the Three Pagodas and the four-star Asia Star and on to the old city. Many of the plane passengers tend to go directly to the pier in Xiaguan where they take a Y100-Y180 cruise on Erhai Lake to see a couple of islands and 4092-meter-high Cangshan Mountain, snow-capped most of the year. Boats leave between 8:30am and 9am and might offer you a demonstration of cormorant fishing.

If you have a choice, don't go on these crowded boats. You can take a smaller boat later, booked at one of the restaurants, Edward Adventures, or No. 4 Guest House. Edward can lay on your own cormorant demonstration.

Buses go from Xiaguan to Lijiang for about Y50/540 km, and in the other direction along the Burma Road to Tengchong, and to Ruili/Dehong twice a day. The Burma Road should take about six hours after the new road is open late 2002. See below.

Be aware that there is a tendency to confuse the names Dali and Xiaguan. **Xiaguan** is capital of Dali Bai Autonomous Prefecture and a good hotel here is the three-star **Man Wan** at Canglang Street, 671000, *Tel. 2188188, 2181739, Fax 2181742*. There's also the **Xiaguan Hotel**, *Tel. 2125579. Fax 2124463*.

CITS here can arrange **village homestays** for Y100 a night and has join-in tours of Old Dali for Y180/person, Lijiang Y200/person and Zhongdian Y250/person. It's at 9th Floor, Building B of YI-LE, 48th Cangshan Rd, Xiaguan, 671000, *Tel. 2191980, Fax 2124902. E-mail: ptcitsdl@ynmail.com. Website: www.dalicits.com*. Ask for Peter Chen, who also helped with this book.

Xiaguan is at an altitude of 1,980 meters. The highest temperature here is 29°C in June. The coldest is -3°C in December. The annual rainfall is 1,200 mm mainly May to August. It's windy all year round but the strongest winds are from November to March. Xiaguan is at the southern tip of 41-km-long Lake Erhai. There is a tea brick factory and a temple to the Tang general who failed to conquer Xiaguan.

Tourists should head for **old Dali**, about 14 km north of Xiaguan, a walled town that was the capital of the Nanzhao and Dali Kingdoms. The Tang emperors never conquered the Nanzhou empire but Kublai Khan's Mongols subdued it in 1253, and Marco Polo visited.

For hotels, the four-star Asia Star is the best. The Santayuan is better than the Jinhua, but these two are in the suburbs. The Jinhua is right on the pedestrian tourist street, convenient to restaurants and travel agents but has little English and is spartan. The No. 4 Guest House is okay for backpackers.

The **Asia Star Hotel** is in the Holiday Distict, South Suburbs of Gucheng, 671003, *Tel. 2670009, Fax 2672299*. It is one km from old Dali. It costs $88 for a room but $56 including breakfast if booked through Edward Adventures below. Check with other travel agents too. The 62-room two-star **Golden Flower (Jinhua Dajiudian Hotel** is at the intersection of the two main streets, Yiang Ren/Huguo Street and Fuxing Road, 671003. *Tel. 2673343, 2673344, Fax 2670573, 2673846*. Rooms are small with air-conditioning, hot and cold drinking water dispensers, and clean carpets. Beds are good, but it has no CNN. Rooms are about $24, but Edward charges $18.

Number Four Guesthouse/Yuan Garden Hotel (Di si zhao dai shou) is for backpackers. It's at 4 Huguo Road, 671003, *Tel. 2672093. E-mail: yuangarden@hotmail.com*. Its location at one end of Foreigner Street and close to the main highway is good. The English is exceptional for a hostel. It charges Y10-Y15 for a bed in a dorm and rooms are about 120Y a day. At that price, don't expect much.

Food is very cheap and adequate here. Bai food is much like Sichuan's with chilis, vinegar, soy sauce and sesame seeds. The **Wooden House** has sandwiches, salads, soup, and pizza. Beer costs Y5-Y10. Its music is Bai. Every Sunday afternoon from 2 to 4pm, performers rehearse Tang dynasty music here. It's at 51 Hugou Road, *Tel. 2672166, 2670508*.

Marley's Café on the corner of Hugou Road at 105 Bo Ai Road is convenient, and the food good. Regular Number Four buses pick up passengers outside. Its American breakfast costs Y9, cappuccino Y6, and beer Y19 (Guinness). It is open 6:30am to 11pm, and offers a Sunday evening Bai banquet for Y25 plus drinks. (It wasn't spicy enough to be authentic but unknowing foreigners liked it.) *Tel. 2676651. E-mail: Marleydali@hotmail.com.* No credit cards.

Also interesting with e-mail service and Bai food is **Mr. China's Son Café**, 67-5 Bo Ai Road, 671003. The owner He Li Yi is the author of two books in English, including his autobiography *Mr. China's Son* published in the US. Mr. He complained that a guide book had mentioned that he was dead. His website is: *www.homestead.com/yndali/homepage2.html*. He can reserve a hotel room for you without a service charge.

Dali is very small. The traditional women's dress is basically white with red or black vests and a colorful bonnet. Foreigner's Street/Yiang Ren/Hugou Street is only about two blocks long, cars are forbidden and signs are in English. You can also walk everywhere inside the wall of this tiny town and along the top of the wall from the South Gate. The City Wall originally circled the town, but was damaged during the Cultural Revolution. The 790 meters of the southwestern part was rebuilt in 1999. The **Tower of Five Glories** (East, South, West, North and Center) was first built elsewhere during the time of the Nanzhao Kingdom. It was the royal reception hall and residence until 1253 and was rebuilt a couple of time in Dali from 1383. The current smaller version north of the South Gate was rebuilt in 1999 and does not resemble the original.

The **San Ta Si (Three Pagoda Temple)** on the west shore of Lake Erhai, was first built in the Nanzhao period. The view of the lake, the three towers (70 and 43 meters tall), and the mountains behind are famous. So is its marble. (At the factories, don't stand too close to the saws.) Dali is a good place for hiking, generally flat in the valley, with inviting mountains. Taxis start at Y5.

Butterfly Pool on the northern tip of the lake is a natural spring with one huge tree covering it. In May, strings of different kinds of butterflies appear. **Xizhou**, just north of Dali, has especially remarkable Bai architecture, incorporating marble, white-washed walls, and black trim. The much-decorated houses are courtyard style. The Tian Zhuan Hotel (Binguan) is built in the Bai style, is charming but not good enough to stay in.

Wase Market, every fifth day, is across the lake and better than the Monday Shaping Market in Jiangwei 45 minutes by road from Dali. Wase is more remote and just for the local Bai people. Most people still wear traditional clothes. Shaping has more tourists.

Better still is the **Sanyuejie (Third-Moon) Market**, the 15th to 20th day of the third lunar month, with caravans of horses and mules, and containers of traditional medicines arriving to be traded. About 30,000 people take part in the market which is enlivened by dances, horse and boat races, and probably gambling. The site west of Dali at the foot of the mountain is a former Nationalist execution grounds.

You can take a taxi to the cable way (shou dao) on **Cangshan Mountain**. Travel agents charge Y35 round trip for the Cangshan Cable Car (to Zhonghe Temple) or Y80 round trip for the Cangshan Gantong Cable Car (to Qingbi Stream). The view of the lake at 2540 meters is beautiful and you can do some hiking to a tiny waterfall overlooking the three pagodas.

Shopping: Circular tie-dyed table cloths cost about Y50. The dye will run with the first couple of washings, but then it's okay. The batik you see here is from Guizhou. You can see the tie-dyeing process in Zhouchong Village, forty minutes from Dali by road.

From Dali, you can travel on to **Shizhong Si** near Jianchuan, which has a unique **Buddhist grotto** reached by a steep 45-minute climb or drive. Women there rub a one-meter-high natural stone female genitalia for fertility and boys rub it for courage. You can decide if its natural or carved. It also has some of the earliest Buddhist carvings in China, several styles, including some humans with long curly hair, foreigners perhaps. Shibao Shan nearby also has temples and an annual singing contest in late August or early September by young people of many minorities. Courtship here also is by song.

You can stop here also on your way to Lijiang which takes about five hours on the 200 km old road plus time for lunch and the 66 km detour to the grottoes. CITS charges Y600 for a car to Lijiang including a stop at the grottos. It is 150 km from Dali to Shizhong Si.

From Dali to Lijiang non-stop takes 3.5km for the 180km trip on the new road. CITS charges Y500 for a car direct to Lijiang. You can also pay Y40 or Y50 by public bus. These have been leaving at 8:50am, 2:20pm and 7:20pm. Long-distance buses have also left Dali for Zhongdian at 6:40am and 10am. Sleeping buses go overnight.

Contact CITS in Xiaguan above, *Tel. 2191980*. Clerks in the Dali branch don't speak English.

You can reach Edward He at **Edward Adventures**, 94 Yincang Road, Dali, 671003, *Tel. 2679218. Fax 2670222, Mobile:13908726121, E-mail: edad@public.km.yn.cn*. He can arrange trekking in Tibet and Southwest China too. Locally born and a Bai himself, Edward knows this area and can take you hiking on Cangshan Mountains and trekking in Tibet. (He is well equipped, even with a toilet tent.) He has bicycle tours around Erhai Lake and can also arrange meals in fishermen's houses. Much of the information here about Dali is from Edward and like other travel agents, he can book hotels at a discount. Write for his beautifully illustrated brochure. Edward charges $2.00 for booking a hotel room.

The **telephone code** is 872. For more detailed information, see *www.china-travel-guide.com*.

LIJIANG

To get here from Dali, the tourist town to the south, see above. To get here from Kunming, you can take a 40-minute flight, some of which originate in Shanghai. Flights also arrive from Jing Hong in Xishuang Banna. Lijiang is about 27 km from the airport and the CAAC bus costs about Y10 per person. A small taxi to and from the airport is Y60 to Y70. By express bus, Kunming is about 544 km from Lijiang via Dali and takes eight hours. There are nine-hour sleeper buses but you miss the scenery.

Lijiang has the UNESCO World Heritage, 800-year-old Dayan Ancient Town, and the 5596-meter high Yu Long (Jade Dragon) Mountain. 15 km north is Yulong Mountain where you can take a 2968-meter long cableway up to 4500 meters above sea level. This can be very, very cold.

Dayan Ancient Town is charming with tiny cottages, winding streets and old bridges. It was completely rebuilt in its original style after a 1996 earthquake destroyed it. Dayan Ancient Town was given by the emperor to a Mr. Mu, a Naxi, 800 years ago. It has developed into a very interesting little community where mainly ethnic Naxi people live (over 6600 households) and tend to go about their lives in Naxi costume oblivious of the many visitors. Fortunately for us, some locals have opened antique and crafts stores, internet cafés, and guest houses. They have also provided bicycles for rent. The attempts at English are welcoming and we could have spent two to three days wandering around the place on foot and climbing up the surrounding hills.

At 8pm every evening, you can hear 15th century imperial Tang court music, preserved in Lijiang. It is not "Naxi" music as advertised and there are several competing orchestras. Music students will want the most authentic group, which is the one directed by Xuan Ke, and is in the **theater** at 74 Mishi Lane, Xinyi Street, *Tel/Fax 5127971*. Lijiang is also a place to learn about the Dong Ba shaman religion, which pre-dated Buddhism.

You can take a lot of memorable day trips from here. One CITS tour goes to the Meadow, the temple with the King of Camellia trees, the Fresco Naxi Village, Pine Tree Forest, and the White Sand River for Y180. The price pays for transportation, Chinese-speaking guide, entrance fees and lunch. You pay Y40 extra for the cable car.

With a tour you might miss the spartan **Joseph F. Rock House**. You could also negotiate with Santana taxis for about Y150-Y200 a half day. Rock's house is on a side road off the main road to the Camellia tree and there's a sign in English. Take the left fork. The American botanist lived here from 1922 to 1933 collecting specimens and writing for the National Geographic Society. No photos are allowed, said Mr. Niuzhen Lin, who is in charge of this exhibition hall. It's at Yu Hu Village, Baisha, *Tel. 888/5190205*. Telephone Mr. Lin, at *5165105 or at 1398883580*. With few other tourists you might find it otherwise locked. The scenery is lovely and you can understand why Rock lived here so long.

Lijiang is cooler than Kunming and padded jackets are needed in spring and autumn. In Lijiang the Naxi people still use hieroglyphic writing and wear sheepskin capes on their backs for warmth and to cushion heavy baskets. On the sheepskin are seven small embroidered moons to show how hard they work (until the moon and stars appear).

The Mosuo people are a branch of the Naxi. Some who live near Lugou Lake to the north are matriarchal with walk-in marriages. At age 14, the boys are put out of their homes and have to find girlfriends to sleep with. Without a girlfriend, a male sleeps with the dogs. There are no marriages. Men eat breakfast with their mothers. Children are supported by all the males in the community.

The **Tiger Leaping Gorge (Hu Tiao Xia)** can be a Y180 day trip from Lijiang, a couple of days trek, or a stop on the way to Zhongdian. It is 90 km. north of Lijiang, and you can go there if you have a vehicle. A side road (and lunch at the Backpackers Café) in QiaoTou follows the river for 10 km to the deepest part of the gorge at a parking lot and souvenir stores. The Tiger-Leaping Gorge is 3100 meters deep from the top of the mountain to the surface of the water and another 800 meters to the bottom. It is very popular with tourists. The gorge is only 30 meters wide at this slenderest point. You can also continue on the river road for another 10 km or so. This part is not paved and you need a four-wheel drive vehicle if it has rained in the last week. Landslides are endemic. Signs at the tunnel at the end of the pavement point to guest houses. Trekking is safer than it used to be and could take 4.5 hours. There's **Half-way Guest House** and **Tina's Guest House**, *Tel. 887/8806079*.

From Lijiang to Zhongdian non-stop, a taxi can cost Y400-Y800. It is now a four to five hour, 200 km drive. From Qiao Tou to Zhongdian is three hours.

Where to Stay & Eat

The best hotel in Lijiang is the Guanfeng. The Grand Lijiang and Jade Dragon Garden Hotels have the best hotel location and are at the edge of the old town. The Grand Lijiang is the second best in town. The Jade Dragon Garden is the third. Hotel services are not very good inside the old city, but the ancient atmosphere and location is better. Some of the inns have thin walls and no hot water. Hotels here charge a 15% service charge and inns charge a Y20 fee.

GUAN FANG HOTEL, *Shangri-La Road, 674100. Five stars. Tel. 5188888, Fax 5181889. E-mail: ebooking@china.com or gfhotel@ynmail.com. Website: www.gfhotel-lijiang.com.cn. $120-$180 for a room, and $250-$1000 for a suite. In low season, it offers a 20% discount.*

It has 23 stories, 288 rooms, and also has CNN and in-room safes, a large indoor pool, and tennis. It accepts credit cards.

GRAND LIJIANG (Lijiang Dajiudian), *Xingyi Street. Three stars. Tel. 5128888, Fax 5127878. E-mail: lih@21cn.com. $60-$80 for rooms and $120-$300 for suites but discounts should come easily.*

It has 127 rooms, CNN and CNBC, and accepts credit cards. It is a Thai hotel.

JADE DRAGON GARDEN HOTEL (Yu Long Dajiudian), *62 Jishan Lane, Xinyi Street, Dayan Town, 674100, Tel. 888-5182888, Fax 5187999. E-mail: yigarden@lj.yn.cninfo.net. Ask for Ms. He Yu, Sales and Marketing Supervisor.*

Opened in 2000, this 148-room hotel should be a four-star by now. Rooms range from Y680 to Y740 and suites Y1480 and Y2680. It has been giving a 40% discount and accepts credit cards. It is in Naxi architecture with a charming little garden. Rooms have safes, CNN and HBO.

THE FIRST BEND INN, *43 Mishi Alley, Xinyi Street, Old Town. Tel/Fax 5181688. It does not take credit cards but can change money.*

Good for backpackers. It has public showers and toilets. $10 for twin rooms, and $11 for rooms with three beds. There's also the SAN HE HOTEL at 4 Jishangxia, Xingyijie, Old Town, Tel. 5120891, 5120892, Fax 5120891. Private rooms were Y80, and dorms with three beds were Y90, and with four beds Y100. The food here is excellent. Try the deep-fried bees.

ANCIENT TOWN YOUTH HOSTEL, *Mishi Alley No. 44, Xinyi Street, Old Town, Tel. 5102345, 5105403, Fax 5129610. E-mail: lj_hostel@163.net or Xaliy@hotmail.com. Website: www.lijiangYH.com/ or www.iyhf.org/.*

Affiliated with the IYHF, looks good, rents bicycles. Beds in dormitories range from Y15, Y60 and Y100. Discount for IYHF members. Some rooms have private bath and television. It has a washing machine and 24-hour hot water. It charges Y3 for 30 minutes for internet services. Opened in 2001, it has no air-conditioning.

CITS can arrange **homestays** in Bai Hun Village for Y100 for one night, plus Y20 for food. Guests can do farm work and learn to do local cooking if they want to.

Good food can be had at the **Tibet Café** and the **Well Bistro** at 32 Yi Jie Mishi Xiang (for pizza.) There's also the **Red Mansions (Hong Lou) Restaurant**.

Lijiang International Travel Service, Red Sun Hotel, New Street, Dayan Town, Dayan, 674100, *Tel. 5125559, 5125232, Fax 5182948. Email: hezhijian@hotmail.com.* Ask for He Zhijian (Dennis) who helped with this book. For a one-day Snow Mountain trip, it charges Y180 per person. For an additional Y40, you can tour Yun Shan Meadow.

The Nature Conservancy is working in part of Lijiang and in Zhongdian. For more detailed information, see my website: *www.china-travel-guide.com.*

The **telephone code** is 888.

ZHONGDIAN TO TIBET

Zhongdian or Zhongxin town is also known as Shangri-La. It has an old and a new section. The old has a frontier atmosphere because in some places roads are unpaved and there are no street lights. It has no decent restaurants except in the hotels and the Tibet Café. Pigs get driven down the main street to market. Fortunately, this city is not as developed as Lijiang and Dali. Its beauty is in its remoteness, its mountains, its wonderful monastery, and Tibetans. Hiking in the countryside amidst herds of yaks, alpine flowers, tiny villages, and exotic temples is wonderful.

Zhongdian is 315 km north of Lijiang, about five hours by road. See Lijiang above. It is over an eight-hour drive from Dali. It is toward the Tibet border at an altitude of 3,300 meters, almost the same as Lhasa, so read about altitude sickness in Chapter 19. It is a 45-minute, 659 km flight from Kunming and less than two hours from Lhasa. Flights also arrive from Chengdu and there's talk of direct flights from Hong Kong and Beijing in 2002. The airport is about a 10-minute drive from town.

Zhongdian is the capital of the Diqing/Deqen Tibetan Nationality Autonomous Prefecture and Zhongdian County. This county has 470 mountains over 4000 meters high, 41 percent of its people are Tibetan, and 18 percent are Naxi. It is now promoted as the "real" Shangri-la, the inspiration for James Hilton's novel *Lost Horizon* and the 1937 movie.

You can take Bus #3 from the Tibet Hotel five kilometers to the **Ganden Songzanlin/Sumtseling (Gukhua Si) Tibetan Buddhist Temple** for Y1. This Gelukpa (yellow) Sect Temple is open from 7am to 7pm daily and charges Y10. Be sure to take a flashlight so you can see its darker rooms. A good time to visit is at 7am when prayers are chanted for about an hour. This monastery was first built on this hilltop in 1679. During the Cultural Revolution, the Red Guards totally trashed it. The main hall has been reconstructed and today it has about 800 monks.

Fancy hotels have started to appear but the family-run easy-going Tibet Hotel is still there, charming because it isn't very professional. The Gyalthang Dzong Hotel is nicely rustic, ecological and friendly, a good family place to get away from the heat. The best hardware is at the Pacific Rim Hotel (Huangtai Dajiudian.)

I prefer the Gyanthong Dazong even though it is less comfortable. It has cultural programs and its standard of English is the best in town.

PACIFIC RIM HOTEL (Huangtai Dajiudian), *Jiantang Dong Road, 784400. Three stars. Tel. 8229999, Fax 8228586. Rooms are $52 and $62, and suites $72 and $128. No menus or signs in English.*

GYALTHANG DAZONG HOTEL (Jentan Binguan), *peacefully isolated by fields of canola on the edge of town. E-mail: gylhotel@chengdunet.com or directly to Uttara at uttara@chengdunet.com. Its website www.shangrila.com is still under construction.*

It has ponies to ride and a mountain to climb. Taxis are available but it's only a 20- minute walk to town. Rooms have bare floors and electric heaters and blankets. They have IDD telephone service, but no CNN nor room safes.

Its maintenance needs work and it could be cleaner. Its Tibetan, Chinese and Western food is good. It gives classes in wild alpine flowers, the Tibetan language, handicrafts, traditional medicine, and Tibetan Buddhism.

Renovations to its 46 rooms should take place in 2002. It is planning a "Well Being Center" and arts and crafts center. Rooms are $40 and it has been discounting 20 to 30% in winter for walk-ins. Rates will change after renovations and an official three-star rating. It accepts credit cards and cash, but cannot change travelers' checks. It can book flights and arrange trips, even to Lhasa by land. It is looking for teachers of English. This is an American-owned hotel.

TIBET HOTEL (Yongsheng Binguan), *28 Changfang Street, Fax 8223863, Tel. 8222448. E-mail: tibethotel@hotmail.com but don't expect an answer. Double rooms are Y240-Y280 (discounted at times to Y180-Y200). Triple rooms are Y330 (or Y270 with discount). Beds in dormitories are Y20 to Y50. It accepts credit cards but can't change travelers' checks or foreign cash.*

Backpacking tourists are the mainstay at this 230-bed two-star. Rooms have electric heaters, and its coffee shop has internet service. The gravel road outside should be paved in 2002. It has a travel agency that books road trips to Lhasa.

TIBET CAFÉ, *beside Martyrs' Park, on Changzheng Road, Tel/Fax 8230282. E-mail: kangbareng@21cn.com It is open 7:30am to 12 midnight.*

It has a breakfast of three scrambled eggs, hash browns, cheese, bacon and ham for about Y16. Its pizza is good, and its stuffed eggplant is wonderful. It takes no credit cards. Staff speak English. It also is a travel agency and says it takes four to five days to get a permit to Tibet, and that it takes seven to nine days to go overland from here to Lhasa.

The US Nature Conservancy and the Yunnan government have signed an agreement to set up a national forest park here in the northwest of Yunnan.

For more detailed information, visit my website *www.china-travel-guide.com* under "Zhongdian." The **telephone code** is 0887.

Note: You need a permit to go on to Tibet by road or air. It could take several working days. Hotels, some restaurants and CITS can make arrangements. Don't expect to enter from Zhongdian immediately. From Zhongdian to Lhasa by land can be a grueling seven to eleven days by land cruiser, camping overnight in snowy mountain passes or in the gorges of the upper Lancang River. **CITS** is at Jiantang Dong Road, 674400, Zhongdian, *Tel. 887/8222364.* See also Tibet Café, Tibet Hotel and the Gyalthang Dazong Hotel. See Tibet and Chengdu.

THE BURMA ROAD

The **Burma Road** goes from Kunming as far as Xiaguan, and instead of going north to Lijiang, it runs south to the Myanmar (Burmese) border. From Xiaguan onward, don't expect luxury hotels. Take cash and don't count on credit cards or travelers checks. **Dali/Xiaguan** is usually an overnight stop on the Burma Road, first used as part of the southern silk route from Sichuan to India in the fourth and fifth century B.C.

The Burma Road was built 1937-1939 by 160,000 Chinese and Burmese laborers. The United States financed it to supply China in her fight against the Japanese. It was used by the Allies until 1942 when the Japanese captured Burma. It was extended and reopened between India and Kunming in 1945 and renamed the Stilwell Road after the American general.

Unfortunately, there is nothing in Yunnan to mark this Sino-US achievement except for a small, hard-to-find pillar in Kunming. Local people seem to know nothing about it. There is a monument to the Chinese soldiers who fought in the Japanese war (near historic Tengchong).

Along the road live Yi, Dai, Bai, Lisu, Deang, and Achang minorities. Ask about the famous bronze drums. There are also neolithic sites, and takins, pheasants, camphor trees, coffee and pepper, all indigenous to this area.

The drive south from Dali is an expressway that should be finished in 2002 and takes about six hours through the mountains, the highest elevation reaching 4,000 meters. Many World War II battles took place here. Tengchong also sits near 97 dormant volcanoes and hot springs with geysers. It has a huge rhododendron forest, with the biggest tree 16 meters high. You can get a lovely room with balcony at the Tengchong Guest House for about Y30 a night.

Luxi/Mangshi has an airport and its best hotel is the three-star **Zhou Binguan**, *Tel. 692/2236122.* Rooms cost about Y150.

Just 88 km southwest is **Ruili** on the Myanmar border. It has China's largest diamond market and of course you can buy Burmese jadeite, rubies and sapphires. You can take an eight km rafting tour on the Ruili River or rent a bicycle from the Jue Jue Cold Drinks' shop and explore the Burmese-style temples. Here the best hotel is the three-star **Kai Tong International Hotel**, on Bian Cheng Street at Y360 a room, *Tel. 692/4149528.* The **Nan Yang Hotel** charges Y25 a room, Y50 a suite. The city itself is the pits but renting a bicycle and exploring the countryside is marvelous. The people here are mainly Jingpo and Dai.

Flights go between Kunming and Baoshan City, 176 km from the Myanmar border, and between Kunming and Dehong at the border. At Baoshan (571 km drive from Kunming or 45 minutes flight), you can stay at the Yindou Hotel for Y40 a night in a big room. Baoshan was on the southwest Silk Road, 160 km east of Tengchong County. A museum is in Yuhuang Pavilion. The Temple of the Sleeping Buddha is 16 km north of Baoshan and was founded in 716 A.D.

At Dehong, you should be able to see the barter trade between the two countries, and pigs sniffing for heroin. The urban population is 920,000. Manshi, also close to the Burmese border, has an airport.

Practical Information for Kunming

Office hours are 8:30am to 12noon, 2pm to 6pm.

Consulates: The Thai Consulate is in the Kunming Hotel. The Laotian and Myanmar Consulates are in the Camellia Hotel.

Cyber café: **Yunnan Jixle Keji**, diagonally across from the Holiday Inn is at 221 Baita Road (next to Ma Ma Fu's), *Tel. 3112134*. It charges Y6 an hour.

English Corner: contact Thomas Nixon, *mobile-6676879 6731263. Automatic pager-959610928879, Mobile-13888662263. E-mail: thomasnixon@km169.net or thomasnixon@163.com.*

Travel Agents:

• **China Travel Service of Yunnan**, *6th floor, Zhong Ming Plaza, 152 Beijing Road, 650011. Tel. 3174366, 3515208. Fax 3179878, 3174086. E-mail: ctsyn@public.km.yn.cn.* Ask for Ms. Zhong Chen, Sales and Marketing Dept. Manager or Carolyn Gao. It says it usually answers e-mails within 24 hours and accepts credit cards.

• **Kunming China International Travel Service**, *285 Huan Chen Nan Road, 650011, Tel. 3535448, 3536641, 3552511, Fax. 3169240, 3535448. E-mail: yncits@public.km.yn.cn.* Euro-American Center. Contact Mr. Ma Xiaowei, Manager, who helped with this book. His e-mail: *maxiaowei@kmcits.com.cn.* He should be able to arrange home stays in Dali, and in Lijiang for Y100 a night.

• **Yunnan CITS and Panda International Co.**, *15/F, Commercial Center, Green Land Hotel, 80 Tuo Dong Road, 650041. Tel: 3151708, 3151518, Fax 3151498, 3151408.* Ask for Cai Guan Jie (Charlie Tsai Guangjie), Sales Director and Assistant to the general manager. *E-mail: ynpanda@public.km.yn.cn. Website: www.panda-tour.com (English).*

• **Yunnan Overseas Travel Corporation**, *96 Dong Feng Dong Road, 650041, Tel. 3330821 (office), 3830379 (home), Fax 3330674.* Ask for **David Huang,** (Huang Jian Yong) who has been extremely helpful in providing information and opportunities for the author. *Mobile: 13908854822. E-mail: davidtour@163.net.* David can book tickets, hotels, and guides, especially along the Burma Road where he grew up. He is also experienced in the Chengdu-Emei-Wolong-Jiuzhaigou areas. He says flights from Kunming to Bangkok cost $225, to Beijing $198, to Chongqing $81, and to Dali $50. His service charge for booking a flight is $ 4/per person.

The **International Marketing and Promotion Division of the Yunnan Provincial Tourism Administration**, *285 Huancheng Nan Road, 650011, Tel. 3557861, 3546339, Fax 3545973.* Ask for Oliver Huang. *E-mail: oliver@public.km.yn.cn. Website: www.traveloyunnan.com (English with map of Yunnan).*

Telephone code: 871

Wuhan

Wuhan, the capital of Hubei province, is really three cities: Hankou, Hanyang, and Wuchang. These are separated from each other by the Yangtze and Han Rivers, and joined by bridges and expressways. You might find yourself there because of business or a Yangtze River cruise. You should go there because of its ancient chime bells. Students of modern history might be interested in the beginning of the Sun Yat-sen republican revolution and Chairman Mao's house there. Fans of the Oscar-winning Crouching Tiger, Hidden Dragon and Taoists would be interested in the Wudang Mountains. There are no other international class attractions.

Wuhan has been an important port for at least 2,000 years. The city itself dates from the 11th century B.C. (Shang). The city wall in Hanyang, no longer standing, was first built almost 2000 years ago. The Wuchang wall was constructed during the Three Kingdoms (220-265 A.D.), by Sun Quan, King of Wu, and can still be seen at the Small East Gate. Hankou and Hanyang were originally one city, but in the 15th century, the Han River changed its course.

Several foreign nations forced concessions here after the Opium War, and some of Hankou's architecture still reflects old Europe. Wuchang is especially famous because on October 10, 1911, the first victory of the Sun Yat-sen revolution against the Manchus took place here. It was an accidental explosion of a bomb on Shouyi Road in Wuchang in what is now the 1911 Revolution Memorial Hall. Wuhan later became the headquarters of the left wing of the Nationalist party. In 1923, the Communists led a successful railway workers' strike.

The Communists took the city in May 1949. The three cities merged administratively shortly afterward. During the Cultural Revolution, it experienced some of the heaviest fighting among factions. Today it is the home of the huge modern Wuhan Iron and Steel Works (which you can visit). Other industries include Citroen automobiles, electronics, textiles, and computer software. It is developing quickly, largely because of the Three Gorges Dam.

The weather is hottest in July and August at 42°C, and coldest in January and February at 5°C. The annual precipitation is 1,200 mm, mainly February to May. The population is seven million, of whom 3.8 million are urban.

Arrivals & Departures

Wuhan is 12 hours by train south of Beijing, north of Guangzhou, and east of Shanghai. The capital of Hubei province can also be reached by air from 59 Chinese cities, Hong Kong and Fukuoka. It is a 70-minute flight west of Shanghai. The main Tian He International Airport is 20 km north of the city. Only the Wuhan Air Company uses the downtown airport. Both are in Hankou.

Buses leave about once an hour from the Hankou and Wuchang bus stations for Yichang (3.5 hours) and Jingzhou (three hours). Cruise ships and ferries arrive from Nanjing, Chongqing, and other points upstream. A hovercraft arrives at least once a day from Jiujiang in 3 1/2 to four hours.

Orientation

Hankou is the main downtown area with department stores and some ship piers. This was the old European section. It and Hanyang are on the northwest bank of the Yangtze. The main tourist attractions, the provincial museum, East Lake and the Yellow Crane Tower are in Wuchang on the south bank.

Wuhan has recently opened a circular beltway around the city, alleviating somewhat the traffic jams downtown. It is working on a light rail system due around 2003 which will run behind the Holiday Inn Tian. Not all taxis may go between the various parts– so don't feel offended if a driver refuses to take you.

Where to Stay

The best hotels are the Shangri-La and then the four-star Holiday Inn Tian An. The Holiday Inn Riverside is still my favorite four-star hotel here because it is convenient to downtown Hankou, beside the Yangtze, and is great for morning walks.

The Holiday Inn Tian An and the Shangri-La are close to the main Wuhan Pier, good locations for business people and close to municipal government offices. The Holiday Inn Riverside is convenient if you're cruising on Splendid China, President, Yangtze, Yangtze Paradise or Star Dipper, as these ships dock at its pier. In Hankou, Victoria Cruises ties up at Pier 16, and the Blue Whale, Yangtze Angel, and the Regal princesses berth at Pier 19 across from the Metropolitan Hotel. The East King and East Queen are at Pier 14. These are closer to the Hankou hotels.

The high tourist season is April to June, September and October. Prices listed below are subject to change, negotiations, and 15% surcharge. Hotels below all have business centers, foreign exchange facilities, ticketing offices, etc.

SHANGRI-LA HOTEL (Shang Gorilla), *700 Jianshe Avenue, Hankou, 430015, Tel. 85806868, Fax 85776868. Rooms are Y1245 to Y1700 and suites Y2240 to Y14940. It is located in a business district near a shopping mall, tax bureau and municipal government offices. About 25 km from Tianhe Airport and eight km from Wuhan Port.*

This 1999, 21-story hotel has 507 spacious rooms, executive floors, 13 long-stay apartments and 17 serviced offices. Rooms have data ports, safes, and full executive-size desks. It has valet parking, 24-hour room service, a Cantonese restaurant, delicatessen, sports bar and restaurant, and coffee shop with open kitchen. Its ballroom can seat 1,200-1,350 for banquets, and is equipped for conferences. It has a good gym, jacuzzi, steam room, 12-meter indoor pool and outdoor tennis court, and its own garden and playground.

HOLIDAY INN TIAN AN (Tianan Jiu Dian), *868 Jie Fang Da Dao Avenue, 430022. Four stars. Tel. 85867888, 85845484, Fax 85845353. E-mail: wuhchsal@public.wh.hb.cn. $120-$160 for rooms; $290-$1600 for suites. In a good downtown location near stores and the pedestrian street, and two km from the Port. It's 37 km from the international airport, five km from the railway station, and 10 minutes drive from the convention center.*

Built in 1996 with major renovations in 2002, this pleasant 394-room, 27-story hotel has five executive floors, non-smoking rooms, Cantonese and Asian cuisine. It has a revolving restaurant, 24-hour room service, gym, 18-meter outdoor pool and tennis court. There's a night club, offices, rooms for the physically challenged, and Dragonair office. Most rooms are 33 to 38 square meters. It gives free 15-minute internet service per day to its guests.

HOLIDAY INN RIVERSIDE, *88 Xi Ma Chang Street, Hanyang, 430050. Four stars. Tel. 84716688, Fax 84716181. E-mail: hirwsale@public.wh.hb.cn. Website: www.sixcontinentshotels.com. $62-$85 for rooms; $138 for suites. It has seasonal packages as well. 29 km from Tian He International Airport, eight km from the railway station, and five km from the port. Within one kilometer is a McDonald's, the Sogo Department Store, and Carrefour Supermarket. The Holiday Inn Riverside has a fantastic location for tourists across the Yangtze River Bridge from the main tourist attractions but also next to the TV Tower, the Qingchuan Pagoda, Guishan Hill, and the Han River. The Three Kingdoms Museum across the road is open 8am to 5:30pm. It is the closest of these hotels to the provincial government in Wuchang.*

This 336-room hotel was originally built in 1984 and extensively renovated in 1998-99. It has a gym, tennis, CNN and ESPN sports. There are non-smoking rooms and a ballroom that can seat 300 guests banquet style. It has an international buffet, Italian restaurant, Cantonese and Hubei food, and a Filipino band. There are free buffet meals for one child under 12 when accompanied by one adult per child. Its outside catering can include a buffet at the exotic Qingchuan Pavilion next door. It has two executive floors with their own workout room.

LIJIANG HOTEL, *No. 1 Ti Yu Guan Road, Wuchang, 430071, Tel. 87813666, Fax 87320638. Rooms are Y298-Y508, and suites Y1180 with no discount. It's on the other side of a big square from the White Rose Hotel and closer than other hotels to the provincial museum.*

This 1990, 126-room hotel has almost no English. The staff however is friendly. Rooms are spacious. It has internet service and an uninspiring Chinese breakfast. No western breakfast. Recommended for desperate budget travelers only.

Where to Eat

Among the well-known Hubei dishes are: steamed Wuchang fish, three steamings of fish, pork and vegetables, stir-fried boneless eel, and lotus root soup. Western and Chinese food are good in the top hotels. The Holiday Inn Tian An and Shangri-La have good buffets.

555 RESTAURANT, *8 Jiang Han Bei (Pedestrian) Road, Tel. 85788508, 85710717. E-mail: qhb555@public.wh.hb.cn. Website: www.555hotel.com. (Chinese only).*

This place has a variety of Chinese cuisines and is open 9am to 9pm.No menu in English. 70 cooks. Its kitchen was well organized and clean.

QIAO KOU STREET (Qiao Kou Yi Tou Jie Dai Pai Dong), near the Asia Hotel has many different kinds of restaurants. The **Xiao Nan Jing (Blue Whale)** is the biggest one there. The **Da Jia Le Sea Food Restaurant** is the most expensive one. Both are good.

TAIZI RESTAURANT, *226 Shengli St., Jiangan Dist., Tel. 82716668, and 82717778.*

Recommended and reasonably priced.

White Rose Hotel (Bai Mei Gui), *Tel. 87893366 X 7205. E-mail: wrhssx@public.wh.hb.cn. Website: www.wrhotel.com.cn. Hours: 10:00am - 2:30pm and 5:00pm-9:30pm.*

Has a Korean Restaurant on its second floor. Y28/per order for kimchi and Y58 for bulgogi. It accepts American Express and Visa cards. Its menu has pictures of dishes at which you can point.

MR. XIE'S RESTAURANT, *in the same block as the Holiday Inn Tian An, at 910 Jiefang Da Dao, Tel. 85813580.*

Everybody recommends this place for Cantonese food and its reasonable prices. Mr. Xie himself speaks English and he charges Y20 for pork stew, Y20 for sizzling beef, and Y68 for a whole Peking duck, skin and pancakes. It is open 11am-2pm, and 4:30pm to 9pm. (Sorry no credit cards.)

CHU TOUR PALACE RESTAURANT, *20 Shouyi Park Road, Wuchang is near the Yellow Crane Tower, Tel. 88874155.*

This restaurant has had a modern show from 6:40pm to 8:00pm; a male singer in shining, tight trousers, a magician, clown, acrobats, and a lovely female singer in a long white gown who must have been famous as fans kept giving her flowers. The show is free if you order from the a la carte menu. Otherwise it costs Y20. Lunch time has live music. The food is generally okay though we found very tough meat in one of the cold dishes. Beef and mushrooms cost Y30. Pork hock, which is one of its specialties, was Y24 and very good with just enough hot chilis to make it interesting.

Seeing the Sights

You cannot miss the **ancient chime bells** next to the **Hubei Provincial Museum**, 188 Dong Hu Road, Wuchang, *Tel. 86783683, 86783685.* It is open daily from 9am-4:30pm with two hours closed for lunch from 11:30am or 12. In 1978, 7,000-20,000 articles were excavated from the Zenghouyi Tomb, just outside nearby Suizhou city. Dating from the Warring States period 2,400 years ago, the tomb of Marquis Yi of Zeng contained bronzes, weapons, lacquer, musical instruments, gold, and jade. The contents were found in water in which oxidized copper was accidentally dissolved. This saved most of the pieces from decay. Some of the lacquer is still preserved in water and shows the original brilliant red at its best. 30 of his concubines took poison and died with him.

Most important in the find is a complete set of 64 ritual bells of different sizes, a total of 2,500 kilograms, the heaviest musical instrument in the world. When struck, they emit a perfect 12-tone system covering five octaves. Each bell also has two tones depending on where it is struck, a quality that has not yet been found in any other bell anywhere else in the world. In addition, the name of the tone and the date were inscribed on each bell in both the Zeng and Chu scripts. The two languages side by side are as valuable as the Rosetta stone.

The bells were a gift from the King of Chu. Since the reigns of the donor and the recipient overlapped by only a few years, the technology to produce them must have been at an astoundingly high level. Not only are their tones precise, they were probably cast in a short length of time. The heaviest is 203.6 kilograms and 1.5 meters high. Imagine pouring hot metal into a mold that size! And of the exact amount to produce the prescribed tone!

Ritual bells were only played for ceremonies, not for pleasure. Only aristocrats and royalty were allowed to possess them, and only in certain numbers. Musicians can give you a concert on reproductions of the bells for an additional fee. Foreigners are usually deeply moved by a rendition of Ode to Joy. The original bells are played on very special occasions like the return of Hong Kong in 1997. Some cities like Jingzhou and Zhengzhou also have concerts of reproductions but Wuhan has the original bells.

The five-story, 51 meter-high, **Huang He Lou (Yellow Crane Tower)**, Y30, in Wuchang is a symbol of the city and has a good view. Open 7:30am-5:30pm. It was first built in 223 A.D. and inspired many famous poets, including Li Bai. It was destroyed and rebuilt several times, the latest in 1981. The current design is based largely on the Qing version (1768-1884). Pictures of previous versions are inside. There are 70 steps to climb to the base and more stairs inside. Two elevators are inside for an additional Y2.

The legend of the wine shop on the original site has inspired poets. The owner used to give free wine to an old man who drew a picture of a yellow crane on the wall in gratitude. After the old man left, the crane came to life and danced for the customers, and the owner became rich. When the old man returned decades later, he mounted the crane and flew off into the sky.

If you're looking for other things to do while you wait for your ship, there's the 45-meter-high, seven-story **Hongshan Pagoda**, Wuluo Road, Wuchang, Tel. 87884539, that dates from the Yuan (1279) and is open 7am-5pm. The **Guiyuan Temple**, 20 Cuiwei Heng Road, Hanyang, *Tel. 84841367*, open 8am-4pm, was founded over 300 years ago. It is the most important Buddhist temple in the city, and is one of the 10 biggest in China. It contains 500 clay arhats, each life-size, distinctive, and 250 years old. The Guiyuan is relatively close to the Holiday Inn Riverside.

The house where Chairman Mao stayed when he took his famous Yangtze River swims is one block from the provincial museum. It's an opportunity to see how he lived, a big house with a four-meter high ceiling at 56 Dong Hu Road, *Tel. 86796106*, open 8am-5pm daily. Y20 entrance fee. Tours also go to pleasant East Lake which is bigger than West Lake in Hangzhou.

A **river dolphin research center** is at the Institute of Hydrobiology, Chinese Academy of Sciences, Luojiashan, Wuchang, 430072, next to Wuhan University. *Tel. 87801331*. Only one dolphin is there. Fee Y50. The Bonzai/ Penjing Garden where guides might take you (instead of to the Yellow Crane Tower) is opposite the Guiyuan Temple. It has a fascinating collection of natural picture stones and a huge chrysanthemum stone.

The **Wuhan Zoo** has one panda. The Aviary is worth a visit for the birds. Children should avoid the "live food" show at the Wild Animal Park which charges Y65 and feeds terrified animals to bigger ones. There's a free shuttle from the Wang Jia Wan bus station in Hanyang. Tel. 69741116.

Engineers and scientists should be interested in the museum at the ***Ancient Copper Mine** in Huang Shi City, 80km east of Wuhan. It is now an open pit with mining tools, shaft, ropes, and baskets, started in the Zhou about 3,000 years ago. Nowhere else in the world at the time was mining technology so far advanced. Toby Lee of OTC arranged for us to see the dramatic, flaming **Iron and Steel Works**.

The **Three Kingdoms Museum** across the road from the Holiday Inn Riverside should prepare you for some of the history along the Yangtze.

Note: Be aware that some guides in Wuhan have convinced their groups to substitute some cheaper (Y5) tourist attraction for the more expensive (Y30) Yellow Crane Tower ("because it has a lot of steps," or "it's too hot"). The savings were not passed on to the group who should have gotten extra drinks, a meal upgrade, another stop, or reimbursement. Do make enquiries if this happens, unless you want the agency to pocket the money.

Nightlife & Entertainment

Check with your hotel or travel agent about acrobatic shows or opera. **Chu Tour Palace Restaurant** noted above for its food has a different show each month. It could be acrobatics, a performing panda or Beijing opera. It's at 20 Shouyi Park Road, Wuchang, 430060, *Tel. 88874155*.

For fun, there's **J.J.'s Disco**. The **night food market** at Ji Qing Street near the Lao Tong Cheng Building is open from 7:30pm to 4am and is relatively close to the Holiday Inn Tian An. It has aggressive waiters who grab you by the arm and try to pull you to their table. It also has strolling musicians, begging children, and pickpockets. Until this place gets some kind of order, avoid it.

Sports & Recreation
The 18-hole **Wuhan International Golf Club** is out towards Tian He airport and open all year round.

Shopping
Local products are gold and silver jewelry, lacquerware, carpets, shell carvings, carved turquoise, boxwood carving, feather fans, colored pottery, jadeware, and paintings. The main shopping area is the pedestrian street Jiang Han Bei Road. Antique stores are near the provincial museum.

Hubei Antique Store is at 68 Donghu Road, Wuchang, 430077, *Tel. 86783678*. Other stores and markets are in this area. The **Wuhan Antique Store** is at 999 Zhongshan Avenue, Hankou, 430017, *Tel. 82836243* and 167 Zhongshan Avenue, Hankou. Antique stores are located in Sangyang Road with peddlers' stalls at the back. Near the Holiday Inn Tian An at the 3rd junction of Jianghan Road is a "silk alley" for cheap clothes.

Excursions & Day Trips
Wudangshan Mountain is a UNESCO World Heritage site about 500 km northwest of Wuhan. It's best to get there by overnight train from Wuhan and you need two full days (plus two nights on the train) to see everything. You need much more time if you want to learn about monastic life, "cultivation," Daoism, qigong, martial arts, breatharians and immortalization. In the movie *Crouching Tiger, Hidden Dragon*, the older heroine was always telling the rebellious younger one to go the Wudang Shan to improve herself.

A Martial Arts school is at the foot of the mountain near the railway station. The telephone number is *719/5666355 or 5666982*, and the mobile telephone of administrator Tang Li Long, is *13508670829*.

A 120 year old nun, Li Cheng Yu, has been living in the back of **Yu Xu Palace**, an old temple near the railway station. You can visit her. Ten yuan seems an appropriate gift.

Foreigners are not allowed to stay in the monasteries. No one speaks English in the hotels, the temples, or the town.

Wudanshan the mountain is about 25 km from the railway station. You really need a car to get around. The train station is at an altitude of 400 meters, the Tian Lu Hotel at 800 meters, and Tianxi/Tianzhufeng (Heavenly Peak) at 1600 meters. Wudangshan is the sacred home of southern Daoism or Dragon

Door Daoists. Its kung fu is different from Shaolin Temple's. The best hotel on the mountain is the **Tian Lu** (Du Jia Cun) which charges about Y280 a night. *Tel. 719/5665653, 5667113*. It is the only hotel with heat and air-conditioning and is closed January to March. It takes no credit cards and cannot change money. Hotels near the railway station aren't much better.

Important to visit are the temples: the **Zixiao Palace** (Y33) on Qing Long Shan up the hill from the hotel. *Tel. 719/5689190*. There's also **Nanyan Palace** (Y10), and **Bai Hu Ya (White Tiger Hill)** three kilometers uphill from the hotel. *Tel. 719/5666355*. Don't miss the 500-year old Tianyi Zhen Qing, the Stone Palace and the cable car ride up to the Golden Hall from the middle level.

Wudangshan China Travel Service, can provide a guide. It's at 94 Shatuoying Road, Danjiangkou City. *Tel. 719/5223354, 5224707, Fax 5239100. E-mail: hxy5053@sina.com.* Ask for Ms. Huang Xue Ying.

The **Qigong Dharma Society** organizes tours to Taoist and Buddhist monasteries and goes to Wudangshan. It is at 53 Continental Ave., Forest Hills, NY 11375, *Tel. 718/268-3153. E-mail: qigong@earthlink.net.* See also Taoism in Chapter 4. For more details on Wudangshan, look up *www.china-travel-guide.com*.

Zhangjiajie is a national scenic spot in the south of the province, about 300 km southwest of Wuhan and accessible by air. See Changsha.

For the Yangtze Gorges and other important destinations along the river, keep reading. From Wuhan, you can take a regular ferry or one of the luxury cruise ships through the Yangtze Gorges to Chongqing.

Practical Information

Business hours: 8:30 or 9am-5 or 5:30pm for offices, five days a week. 9am-12 noon and 1:30pm-4:30pm for the Bank of China. 8:30am or 9am-7 or 8:30pm for stores.

China Hubei CITS and Hubei Overseas Travel Group, *7/F, Xiaonanhu Building, 26 Taibei Yi Road, 430015, Tel. 85784100, 85762651, Fax 85784089, 85784109. E-mail: citswuh@public.wh.hb.cn. Website: www.citshubei.com.*

Cruise Ship Companies:

Changjiang Cruise Overseas Tourist Corporation, *55 Yanjiang Avenue, 430014, Tel. 85701021, 85668414, Fax 85701043. E-mail: ccotchw@public.wh.hb.cn. Website: www.ccotc.com.* Contact: Ai Yong Hong (Grace Ai). Its ships are the M.S. Yangtze Angel, MS.Yangtze Star, and MS.Sunshine, and they cruise Chongqing-Shashi-Chongqing. Its MS Isabella Series goes Chongqing-Yichang-Chongqing.

East King and East Queen, *Orient Royal Cruiser Limited, Suite E, 14/F, Liangyou Bldg., #316 Xinhua Rd., Hankou, 430022, Tel. 8576-9988. Fax: 8576-6688, 8549-6106 (direct). E-mail orcruise@public.wh.hb.cn. Website: www.orientroyalcruise.com.* Ask for Ms. Lesley Yu, Deputy Director, Sales and Marketing Dept., *Tel. 8576 9988* who helped this book a lot.

Hubei Yangtze International Travel Service, *3 Dandong Road, B-21/ F, Hankou, 430022, (next to Holiday Inn Tian An), Tel. 1380-8680323. Fax 85824549. E-mail: yangtze@126.com. Web: www.yangtzetour.com.* Contact Ben Chen. The Cruise Department should know about ship movements. It says it answers e-mails within 24 hours.

Telephone Code: 27.

Wuhan Overseas Tourist Corporation, *No 1. Baofeng Road, Wuhan Commercial Building, 18th floor, Wuhan, 430030. Tel. 8360-2712, Fax 8360-2715. E-mail: toby_lee18@hotmail.com.* Ask for Toby Lee Xiang Bin who helped this book alot.

Yangtze Gorges

(also known as Yangzi or Changjiang River Gorges)

The boat trip through the **Yangtze Gorges** and on the great river itself is highly recommended, not just for its spectacular scenery but also for its ancient history, its history in the making, and its changing life style. Bring binoculars, a telephoto lens if you're a camera bug, and some books about the river.

The scenery includes sheer cliffs and mountains rising up to 1,000 meters on both sides of narrow, rushing water, old towns cut by slender lines of stone steps, and a hill almost lined from top to bottom with a pagoda. You can hear reproductions of ancient chime bells, and meet a 2,000-year old gentleman. You might race a dragon boat and look for wild monkeys and hanging coffins. You will see signs on hills showing the new water levels after 2009, towns and temples that will be flooded, and the building of the largest dam in the world.

There's living social history: ships still loaded by strings of men carrying coal in baskets on their backs. If you go up Shennongjia Stream, you will see Tujia men pulling boats upstream with shoulder harnesses and chanting in the old way.

The Yangtze Gorges were created 30-50 million years ago as a result of collisions between the Indian and the Eurasian continental plates. These formed the Himalayas and its foothills. They are primarily made of limestone, except for the site of the Three Gorges Dam which is granite. The Yangtze River is a busy highway. Aside from a few short sections, there has been no road along the river between Yichang and Chongqing. (There is one being built now and due in 2004.)

Guides should tell you stories of the Three Kingdoms, but bring your own books along because the ships' information is sketchy: Most important is John A. Hersey's novel *A Single Pebble*. This is about a U.S. engineer going up river to build a dam many decades ago.

Richard McKenna's novel *The Sand Pebbles* and Van Slyke's *Yangtze, Nature, History and the River* also describe the foreigners who lived here. *River*

Town by Peter Hessler is about his two years teaching English in Fuling in 1996. The *Romance of the Three Kingdoms*, a historical-mythological war novel, has been translated into English, and you will encounter the names, statues and temples of its heroes in many places in the Yangtze valley: Liu Bei, Zhang Fei, Guan Yu, and Zhuge Liang – and their arch enemy, Cao Cao. But it's heavy. Let's hope your ship has a copy.

Note: The government's Three Gorges Project Committee said in 2001 "...the Yangtze River cruise trip would really be affected only 15 days, June 01-15, 2003. If we make good preparations...we can still welcome travelers then." So bear this in mind when planning your trip. See my website for updates.

Warning: In 2002, reservations in high season on the main cruise ships were booked up the year before. If you want to go, start making enquiries now. Don't delay.

When To Go

The best time is September and October. The rainy season is May to August. There are landslides due to heavy rains and floods in July and August which could disrupt land excursions. The winter is cold, the hotels and ferries inadequately heated. A sweater and windbreaker is necessary for the wind in the gorges even in mid-October and mid-April. Expect delays by fog from early November and March. Also expect delays waiting for berths in Chongqing and Wuhan.

For **cruise ship schedules**, ask a travel agent in Wuhan or Chongqing, the cruise companies or consult the handy cruise ship calendar organized by CITS Guilin on its website: *www.chinahighlights.com/yangtzecruise/months/2002schedule.htm.*

In spring, if the water level is low in Chongqing, you may have to board or disembark in Fuling, Fengdu or Wanxian. It can be an ironical end to a luxury voyage as Fuling has been squalid. (We couldn't find any clean toilets.) The government will be building new facilities but who knows when.

History

Among the highlights of the archaeology and history in this area are relics of the Ba, a little known group who lived here from about the 16th century B.C. to the third century B.C., their capitals in Chongqing and Chengdu. They were worshippers of white tigers and left behind some very distinctive and impressive bronzes in humanoid forms. See museums in Chengdu (better) and Chongqing. These are the people whose coffins you look for in the cliffs above the Yangtze.

The Kingdom of Chu dominated what is now Hubei from about 770 B.C. until it was taken over by the King of Qin, the first emperor of China in 221 B.C. This was the period of the poet-statesman Quyuan, whose death inspired the first dragon boat races.

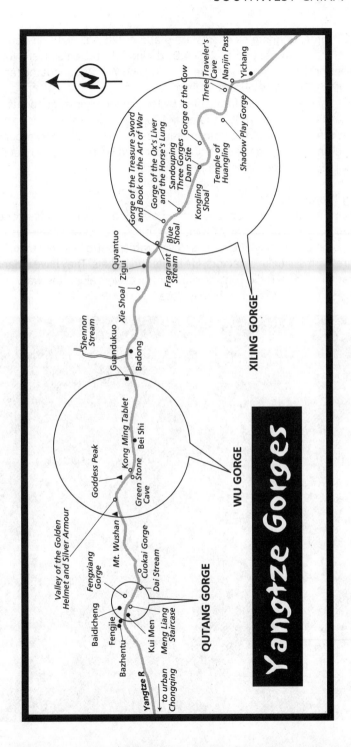

Yangtze Gorges

The Three Kingdom's period started about 220 A.D. with an oath in a peach orchard, and ended in 265 A.D. during which battles were fought between contending kingdoms, the Wei, Shu and Wu. Ask about the famous Battle of the Red Cliffs west of Wuhan.

The Yangtze was also frequented by foreign merchants, gunboats, and missionaries in the late 1800s and early 1900s, but guides will not give you much information about this embarrassing period. This is the background of the novel and movie, *The Sand Pebbles*. Nobel and Pulitzer prize winner Pearl S. Buck lived and worked in Zhenjiang downstream.

Sailing the Gorges

I have never heard of anyone getting seasick on this river and accidents are rare. Between Wuhan and Chongqing, it is under three kilometers wide and in some places only 100 meters. River traffic controllers are strict. Ships have fire alarms, smoke detectors, life boats and jackets. They have radar and their captains are in radio contact with control towers along the way. Traffic is heavy so if there is trouble, help is close by.

The Dam Controversy

A **controversial dam** is currently being built that will displace over a million people, raise the water level upstream, and decrease the dramatic effect of the gorges by over 100 meters at the site, and less elsewhere. The dam should help control floods, provide irrigation and 84 million kwhs of hydroelectric power, and enable ocean-going ships to reach Chongqing. You should be able to see the furious construction activities in Sandouping, day and night. It is lit at night but not well enough for photos or to satisfy people who want a good look. Let's hope you get there during the day.

Some but not all cruise ships stop for a visit at the site. Buses take them to the highest point, a look-out tower called Jar Hill and nearby exhibition room with a scale model. Plans for the largest civil engineering project in the world call for submerging 632 square kilometers of land, and creating a lake at Chongqing. The project includes new bridges, more flights, airports, easier navigation and better hotels.

Critics argue that sedimentation will destroy the dam's turbines in less than 10 years, that it will affect the ecology, and destroy archeological sites. They say that the costs far outweigh the benefits, especially in terms of disrupted lives. If you get the chance, ask local people how they feel about it.

The government website, *www.china3gorgesdam.com*, says it will answer your questions.

The Cheap Way

The cheapest ships are the **passenger ferries**. But if you don't speak Chinese, how will you make your wishes known? How will you buy a ticket? And get a berth assignment once on board? How long will it be before you see the Gorges? How long will the ship stop in each port? Don't go this way unless you're very short of money, love adventure, and speak some Chinese. You also have to be healthy and flexible and know some Chinese.

Warning: on passenger ferries and Tianzi cruise ships, you usually pay only for the fare and bed ahead of time. Some unscrupulous travel agents will try to get you to pay for a package, food included. The ships don't recognize these packages and make you pay for food. Book a package through one of the travel agents listed here or directly at the ticket office at the Pier. With it, you eat after everyone else has lined up and eaten. But you do eat with fewer hassles.

Passenger ferries operate all year round and are decreasing in numbers because of the faster hovercrafts and the new roads. They are crowded with little privacy. Though a few now have first class cabins with air-conditioning and private bath for two people, the top second-class has a lounge, bunks for four people to a cabin, and soap, toothbrushes, towels and tea. The public bathrooms might have a tub, shower, western toilet and lots of water all over the floor. Try for an outside cabin. The inside ones can get stuffy in summer, and you might find other passengers gambling noisily on the floor outside your room all night.

In second, third, fourth, or fifth class, you share a room with an increasing number of people, get suffocated by cigarette smoke, and worry about thieves. Aim for a cabin with a window. In "No Class," you rent a blanket and sleep on the floor.

Below second class, you have to bring your own towel, mug, soap, etc. Steaming hot water is available. These ferries leave Chongqing in the morning. If you want your choice of cabin, you could pay extra (not much) and check in the night before, also saving yourself a hotel room.

Stops on ferries are short and not necessarily at tourist sites: Badong, Zigui, Wanxian, Fengjie and Fengdu. By ferry you can get closer to Chinese people and experience with them the loudspeakers blaring announcements at 6am and queues for showers. After all, didn't you come here to meet the people?

The food is usually edible but with little variety. Conditions are basic.

Tianzi Cruise Ships for Chinese tourists or sightseeing ferries cost a little more than regular ferries. These stop at tourist attractions for a couple of hours and you pay extra for shore excursions and food (breakfast Y10). You can book these through travel agents.

These ships leave Chongqing in the late afternoon daily and arrive about 7am in Wuhan after four nights on board with stops in Fengdu, Shibaozhai,

Wanxian, the Lesser Three Gorges, and Yueyang. Conditions are in no way modern. Expect the worst. These are so bad that CITS Chongqing suggests you pay a little more and take one of the low-class cruise ships instead.

Hovercrafts leave Chongqing and also make stops along the way. They arrive in Yichang in one or two days and sometimes you have to pay extra for a hotel in Wanzhou/Wanxian. They are meant for speed, not sightseeing, and they are bouncy, noisy and in summer, hot. Jetfoils also service Badong, Zigui, Wanxian, Fengjie and Fengdu. It is best to avoid the noisy back end. Travel agents can ticket these for you. If you have more than your own weight in luggage, you pay for a second ticket.

More Expensive, Tourist Cruises

Currently most foreign tourists take one of the 80 much more expensive air-conditioned tourist cruise ships that ply the Yangtze from mid-March to late November or early December. About 10 of these meet standards suitable for the average middle-class North American tourist but don't expect the services of bigger, more luxurious cruise ships elsewhere in the world, not even soft comfortable lounge chairs.

You can book the top ships through travel agents in North America or China to ensure your dates during high season, or at the last minute on the spot at other times. You are isolated from all but rich Chinese people or bureaucrats on junkets, and crews. But you can expect more comfort than the cheaper ships, and some English.

The government has tried to regulate these ships and their safety, and rates them with stars the same way it rates hotels. Five stars should be the best, but not necessarily.

On **one-star ships** half the cabins should have private baths, and all get heat and air-conditioning, and twelve hours of hot water a day. They should also have money-changing services, stamps for sale, and English-speaking guides. (The quality of the English will not be very good.)

On **two star ships** and up, cabins should have televisions, toilets, and telephones, and the ship should have a karaoke dance hall, reading room, clinic and massage. Linens should be changed every other day and managers speak English.

On **three stars** and up, you get color televisions, satellite telephone service, a gym, and 24 hours a day hot and cold water in your cabin. Linens get changed daily, and you have a card room, business center and a library. On **four stars** and up you get credit card service, Star television satellite reception with news in English, and background music. On **five stars**, you could have a swimming pool, jacuzzi, and bathrobes.

The top ships should have same-day laundry service, refrigerators, currency exchange, postal and safe deposit services, beauty salons, lounge, pool (rarely working), bars, and a small store. Television news in English is hard to find. Some of these ships have dancing, mah-jong and taiji classes, cooking and medical demonstrations, and karaoke. In the evening, they could have fashion shows (of goods available in the store), and variety shows. Service staff double as performers and it's good to see them in another role.

Cruise Warnings

• Shipboard satellite telephone service costs about $12-$15 or so a minute plus 15% starting from the time you dial! You should wait until you get on shore to phone, or ask for someone's mobile. Zigui and Fengdu CITS have long-distance telephone service near the quay.

• Porters in Chongqing have been so obnoxious, I've had to call the police once. They will grab your bag. I've seen two seize a tiny woman tourist and carry her and her bags protesting down the stairs. You might want to wave at your ship and hope it will send its own bell man. Officers there will tell you what a fair tip is (Y10). But before that, learn to say, "Wo bu yao," or "I don't want to."

• Stops usually necessitate climbing a lot of stairs, part of the Yangtze lifestyle. Chongqing has a filthy elevator at Chaotianmen from the ship to the street above (Y2). Ship personnel should be able to arrange for a sedan chair to take wheelchair-confined travelers up and down stairs and through the streets in some but not all places on shore. Ships themselves also require climbing. Most ships have four or five storys and none have elevators. Wheelchair travelers have difficulties unless they travel with help or make some arrangements beforehand.

What to Wear

Dress is generally casual but the top ships have a captain's banquet or cocktail party and your crew could be dressed in white. You might want to take something dressy (but not too dressy) for that occasion. Definitely take good walking shoes or boots for shore excursions. Take warm jackets but not in summer. For the Lesser Three Gorges and Shennongjia excursions, it is best to take life jackets from your own cabins. The ones available outside have been smelly.

Prices

Check with travel agents for prices and discounts which could range upwards from $840 upstream and $910 downstream (MV President) between Chongqing and Wuhan. The Victorias charge a minimum of $920 upstream in shoulder season plus $75 each for shore excursions. It seems to be the only one where excursions are not included in the package price.

In 2002, the East King and East Queen charged per person on a twin-sharing basis for the shorter Yichang-Chongqing trip upstream, four days and three nights, Shoulder Season, from $530-$830 for cabins, and $1575-$2500 for suites. For Chongqing to Yichang downstream (four days and three nights), they charged Shoulder Season from $580-$880 for cabins, and suites $1625-$2550.

If space is available, you can upgrade to more spacious suites on all ships. If stops are canceled and you've paid in advance, you might want to ask for a refund. You should get something back.

Which ship to choose?

CITS Chongqing says: "In our opinion: the best cruise ships are the East Queen, East King, and Regals. The second best is the President and Splendid China. For the Victoria Cruises, some are good and some are not. So we would say they are between second and third. The third best are the Yellow Crane and Yangtze Garden."

In effect, the choice may not be yours. It all depends on your schedule, and their schedules and availability. Aim for any of CITS' choices, ask for a ship with good English, and don't let anyone tell you the Pinghu is good. It isn't. The quality of the ships differ; they are owned by different companies. Avoid ships that cater primarily to Chinese passengers; their staffs don't know how to serve foreigners adequately and the English is usually poor.

Be aware that none of the cruise ships is perfect. They age quickly and are not well maintained. They range in size from 130 to 270 passengers. Food on some is better than on others. Guides on some are better than others of the same line. Food depends on which chef is working.

The five-star **East King** and **East Queen** will be cruising in 2002 between Yichang and Chongqing from March until late November. In winter, a Three Gorges highlight tour will be operated between Yichang and Fengjie (White King Town). Guides, entertainment, and food have been better on some of the Victorias. The cabins are bigger (166 square feet) than the Victorias and the Regals, and they have room safes and larger television, but not much cupboard space. All cabins are "outside," and you can leave your curtains open to enjoy the view in almost total privacy. The only outside decks are on the top with little shade or protection from rain.

The **Victorias (I, II, III, and Pearl)** have been among the best but it depends on the staff. Again, some are good and some are not, according to CITS.

Cabins on the **Regals (Princesses Sheena, Jeannie**, and **Elaine)** are the smallest, and the food has needed work. If the ship is full, buffet line-ups can be long and people at the end get short-changed. The Regals were built in Germany and are the best made, but they were designed for the Volga River. They have no private balconies. They go upstream in five nights and six days from Wuhan to Chongqing, and downstream in three nights and four days.

S/S President I seems to be the most popular of the **Presidential Line** which sails between Chongqing and Jingzhou, and Chongqing and Wuhan.

The top ships usually have small televisions, and good Chinese movies with subtitles. The exercise equipment even on the five stars might be outdated. Some ships have smelly toilets, even the top ones. Some have mold. I haven't found any with working swimming pools. Most have thin walls.

Sometimes excellent American cruise staff have been on board the Regals and the Victorias but you can't count on it. Shore excursions are usually well organized, but being on a five-star does not guarantee a guide with good English on shore excursions. The English of the management staff is usually good, but that of service staff, quite poor. Doctors don't usually speak English.

Do not expect the Love Boat but there's usually a captain's dinner or reception, and a final dance (to ancient music, so bring your own cassettes). There might even be a farewell banquet. There's drinking water in each cabin. (You can buy bottled water on the ship or on shore.) Merchandise in stores on board can cost ten times the price on shore. Discounts are better towards the end of the trip. Avoid the cabins over the engines, and cabins near bars and night clubs. Get on the higher floors for the best views.

Cruise staff give life jacket briefings and passengers should check window exits in cabins and locations of life jackets early on.

No ships announce points of interest along the way in English unless you ask. They do give you a blow-by-blow description as you go through the Gorges and past the Three Gorges Dam.

Itineraries

Between Chongqing and Wuhan, you travel 1286 km, between Chongqing and Yichang it's 660 km, and Jingzhou and Chongqing it's 808 km. Itineraries differ depending on which direction you are going, up or down river, and which ship you book. Upstream is cheaper and longer with fewer passengers and it's fine if you have the time.

If you have a particular site you must visit, you take a ship that will stop there. If you are going upstream, ask if your ship will stop for all announced sightseeing spots. They don't always. And there could be last minute changes.

All ships are regulated through the gorges by the navigation authorities and some have no choice but to pass through after dark or during meal times. You might have to get up at four in the morning to see the dam or take your food out on deck.

The highlight for many tourists is the day trip on the **Lesser Three Gorges** on the **Daning River**, or the similar **Shennongjia Stream** at **Badong**. Ships only stop at one. These are on smaller boats through narrower canyons with hanging coffins, wild monkeys (rarely seen), and Tujia villages. The water is crystal clear when not white and bubbly. The better trip is the Shennongjia Stream, more like rafting, and glory be, with no diesel fumes, no engine vibrations, or noise.

You may want to ride only between Chongqing, and Jingzhou or Yichang. Between Yichang and Wuhan by ship isn't all that interesting and you can do it by bus in three hours. On the other hand you might prefer to relax on a ship than bounce in a bus.

It might be possible to board the ship the night before you sail.

Cruise ships go between Chongqing and Wuhan, Jingzhou, or Yichang. Some cruise companies have a Shanghai-Chongqing service with additional stops in Mt. Lushan, Mt. Huangshan, Nanjing and Yangzhou, 11 days upstream and eight days downstream. The East King and East Queen have two-day and three-night Yichang-Chongqing schedules. The Regal takes longer and has a Shanghai-Chongqing run too.

Downstream Schedule

These differ with the speed of the ship, of course, but the following should give you an idea of what to expect:

Leave Chongqing early and note white pagoda and Buddha on the north bank. At about three hours out, you pass Fuling; at 8 1/2 hours out, Zhongxian. At about 10 hours out, you reach Shibaozhai. At 12 1/2 hours, you're at 2,000-year-old Wanxian/Wanzhou.

About 4 1/2 hours from Wanxian, you pass Fengjie and Baidicheng and arrive at the first gorge, the **Qutang**. Near the entrance of the gorge on the north bank is a two-story pavilion with red lacquer columns, which marks the beginning of the gorges. On the south side of Kui Men Gate are two stone towers and five Chinese characters, which mean "The Kui Men Gate is an unmatched pass."

The Qutang Gorge is eight km long. It is the most imposing and shortest of the gorges, only 100-150 meters wide. Prepare for a very windy passage, as the wind as well as the water, is funneled between the cliffs. Canadian and Chinese tight-rope walkers once crossed here and you can still see their parallel wires.

The **Wuxia** or **Wu Gorge** starts 30 minutes after you leave the Qutang. It is 44 km long and takes about 1 1/2 hours (upsteam 3 1/2 hours) to pass through. Look for the "Twelve Peaks Enshrouded in Rain and Mist," of which you can see six on the north bank and three on the south. Of these **Goddess Peak** is the highest, at over 1,000 meters. It has a tall stone column on top that looks like an anorexic young woman. Look for a table-shaped rock with six Chinese characters meaning "The Wu Gorge boasts craggy cliffs," said to be written by a prime minister of the Shu Kingdom in the third century. Look for coffins in caves here.

The town of **Wushan** is between the Wu and the Qutang Gorges. From here cruise ships might stop for a shore excursion on the Daning River through the Lesser Three Gorges. Continuing on, twenty minutes after leaving the Wu Gorge is the town of Badong on the south shore. You have left Chongqing and are now in Hubei province.

About one hour after Badong you see Zigui on the north shore. This is the birthplace of Quyuan and some ships stop for a dragon boat race or show at the pier.

Five or so minutes after Zigui is **Xiang Xi (Fragrant Stream)** on the north side, where the lovely imperial concubine Wang Zhaojun accidentally dropped her pearls 2,000 years ago. A white statue marks the spot. The water here is said to be limpid and fragrant as a result. There's more about this woman, who is considered one of the four famous beauties of China in Hohhot, Chapter 17. Ship guides say this is where the waterway between the Yangtze and Yellow Rivers will be built after 2009 to alleviate water shortages there and in Beijing.

Shortly after Xiang Xi is the 75 km-long **Xiling Gorge**, which takes about 1 1/2 hours (upstream two hours) to pass through. It is the longest and has been the most treacherous of the three. Thirty minutes beyond the entrance, on the south side, is Kuang Ming village, with a large temple, Huang Ling Miao. Then comes Five Sisters Peaks, Three Brothers Rocks, and the Needle. While still in the Xiling Gorge, you'll see Zhongbao Island and Sandouping, the site of the new dam. You can't avoid it.

The end of the Xiling Gorge about 37 km later is marked by a large Buddha, and a statue of Zhang Fei of the Three Kingdoms on the north side. Then you reach the east part of Yichang, and go through the locks of the 1988-built 70-meter-high Gezhouba Dam. If you stay on board you pass hundreds of kilometers of levees and you might stop at Jingzhou 148 km later on the north side, or Yueyang on the south 247 km beyond that. Wuhan is 231 km beyond Yueyang.

Important Stops on the Yangtze Gorges Trip

Badong is where you get off for a boat trip on Shennongjia Stream. One trip takes about six-hours by bus and boat. The village in the Gaolin Scenic Area where you get an 18-passenger boat is about 47 km from the ferry pier on the north side of the Yangtze, about two km west of Badong. Gaolin has made a good attempt at clean toilets compared to toilets in other rural area. You drift 3.5 hours downstream from there helped by three boatmen on each boat. You might have a lunch stop and look for 1400 year old coffins. The scenery here is very beautiful, the air clear and it is wonderful.

Most cruise ships however prefer to send their passengers on three-hour tours to better fit their schedules. This is another aspect of history. Trackers actually pull you upstream for two hours with ropes and harnesses, as they did in the old days. No toilets are available on this trip and you end up surrounded by peddlers.

I prefer the six-hour trip up into the mountains, seeing a village, and many more people – even though they might be sticking things into your face to buy.

Fengjie, at the western end of the Qutang Gorge, was the capital of the state of Wei during the Spring and Autumn Period (722-481 B.C.), the time of

Confucius. It has the tomb of Liu Bei's wife. Here on a hill top, reached by a ferry and 300 steps, is Baidicheng or White King City with its great view of the river. Wax statues show you how Liu Bei entrusted his son to Zhuge Liang.

Fengdu (170 km east of downtown Chongqing on the north bank) has been regarded as hell, **a gathering place for ghosts** since the seventh century. This is because two men lived here whose combined names Yu and Huang meant King of the Underworld. Here believers built 48 Taoist and Buddhist temples, all destroyed in the 1960s by the Red Guards. Rebuilt recently by Fengdu townspeople, it now has tacky statues of demons and hell, of no artistic merit, probably no different from the originals. These will give you an idea of the folk concept of the after-life, and the role of religion in their lives.

Guides here make you go through various tests of agility and strength, most of which you can probably pass, and make it to heaven (instead of hell). Don't bother with the fortune sticks. Y18 is too much to throw away on a one-line "fortune." But the Qing Ming Festival celebrated here is special.

The ghost city is on a 288-meter-high hill reached by stairs or a cable car (Y15 return). It often remains open after hours (7am-5:30pm) to accommodate cruise ships. While well lit, you should take a flash light after dark. CITS puts on an acrobatic show at its store in town which can be missed. This lowland town will be moved across the river to a new site. The ghost city will remain high and dry where you see it.

Many tourists don't like the Fengdu stop, but it is a historical folk tradition and belief, crudeness and all. You might prefer to wander around the town instead. Terribly disfigured beggars wait on the stairs at the pier. But a marvelous little Catholic church is across from the pier with Sinofied statues of Jesus and Mary, and very friendly clerics.

Jingzhou/Shashi, at 3000 years of age, is one of the famous 24 cultural cities, and is about ten hours east of Yichang by ship. It is a recent union of the cities of Jingzhou (the capital of the State of Chu), and Shashi (a 2000-year old transshipment port), opened to foreign trade in 1895. It was known as Jinsha for a year or so. It is one of the best places to stop because of its good museum where, if you're lucky, you can hear reproductions of the ancient chime bells played (See Wuhan.) They were found in this county. This museum is also the home of 2150-year-old Mr. Sui, a county governor who died of a bleeding ulcer, his silks and hemp shoes on the second floor, lacquerware and bronzes on the ground floor. You can photograph his remarkably well-preserved remains. The museum is open from 8:30am-5pm daily or until the last boatload leaves, and is protected by vicious dogs at night.

In another part of the city is a 300-year old gate and 10.9 km long wall, first built 1700 years ago. The present one is at least 300 years old, so well preserved that costume movies are made here. Jingzhou is a well-governed city with no beggars and annoying peddlers (so far)! Shashi has an airport and air links with Guangzhou, Haikou and Wuhan. The telephone code is 716. The flood of 1998 crested here 46 meters above normal.

To visit the **Lesser Three Gorges**, see Wushan.

Lushan is 40 km south of the port of Jiujiang. This 1,094-1,400 meter-high mountain-top plateau has been a summer resort since the mid-1800s. Its tourist belt is about eight by four km and it has been a stop on some Yangtze River cruises. There are great views of Poyang Lake and the Yangtze River and its sites relate to the Taoist Immortals and the first Ming emperor. It has an alpine botanical garden.

About 9,000 people live in Gulin. The three-star Lushan Hotel is best. It's at 446 Hexi Road, 332900, Tel. 792/8282060, Fax 8282843. The hottest weather is a rare 32 C at noon in July; the coldest, -16 degrees in January with snow from the end of November through February. The best time to visit is June through October.

For **Shennongjia,** see Badong above.

The 300-year-old **Shibaozhai** (Precious Stone Village), or Shibao Block on the north bank about 10 hours downstream from Chongqing, has an 11-story Qing pagoda. It is built on a limestone rock hill that rises to 160 meters above the river. Smaller ships can stop here but the Regals and Victorias are too big.

In the main temple here are statues of Liu Bei, Zhuge Liang, Guan Yu, and Zhang Fei. Three of these swore oaths in a peach orchard to support each other. They are immortalized in *The Romance of the Three Kingdoms* novel. Emperor Liu Bei, who led an unsuccessful army to avenge the death of Guan Yu, retreated here and died in sorrow.

It is a climb of at least 300 steps, but you can hire a sedan chair for only Y20 round trip from the pier to the entrance of what looks like a fancy staircase up a hill. Shibaozhai's urban population is 4,000, the entire area 70,000. This area will be flooded and a dike will be built to protect the temple.

Wanzhou/Wanxian, is a district of Chongqing. It became a treaty port in the 1890s when its biggest crop was opium. It is the largest town between Chongqing and Yichang. In 1926, the British accused the Chinese of interfering with a foreign steamship company here. Two British gunboats started shooting and over 3000 people were killed. Some historians consider this one of the first successful assertions of Chinese power against the imperialists.

You have to climb about 85 steps to get to this town of 300,000 for the Zhang Fei Temple (to be relocated because of the dam). There's the tiny but worthwhile **Three Gorges Museum**, and an airport. The top hotel is the three-star **Wanzhou International Hotel**, *Tel. 58222602, 5810888.* The two-star **Taibai Hotel** has been alright in the past, at 30 Baiyan Road, Wanzhou, Chongqing, 404000, *Tel. 58223976.* About 80 rooms. No money change, but it is near the Bank of China (closed Sundays). The **telephone code** is 23.

Wushan is where you change to a small boat for about 3.5 hours on the Daning River through the 50 km Lesser Three Gorges. This is between the Wu and Qutang Gorges. If water conditions prevent you from getting onto your motor boats right from your ship, be prepared for aggressive peddlers. This excursion should not be attempted if diesel fumes bother you. The boatmen push with poles to help their straining engines climb up the foamy white rapids. You might have to queue up behind other such boats or get out and walk for a few meters around the most difficult parts.

Look for the square holes made in rock walls for horizontal posts for the plank roads. If you're lucky, you can go past the restaurant in Shuanglong/Double Dragon village to an attempted reproduction of such a plank road. We found monkeys there. Downstream of Double Dragon village where groups have lunch, look up near the sky in two narrow horizontal caves for the old coffins of the Ba people. Enjoy the clarity of the water, and the vertical cliffs. The lower end will disappear with the completion of the Dam. If it is raining hard, trips here will probably be canceled.

Yichang is a 2,400-year old settlement which became a treaty port in 1876 and was almost leveled by Japanese bombs during World War II. It grew dramatically with the building of the 2,605 meter-wide Gezhouba Dam in the late 1980s. Your ship will probably take a 12 minute, 30-meter water-borne elevator ride in its locks. In Yichang itself, you can visit this dam by land and the eastern end of Xiling Gorge at Nanjin Pass with its statue of Zhang Fei of The Three Kingdoms, a giant welcoming Buddha, and the Three Travelers Cave. These are worth a visit for the scenery high above the river.

In the city also, the **Sturgeon Research Institute**, *Tel. 6713213,* is open 8am to 6pm. It has a couple of live specimens of this huge, ugly fish from the dinosaur era, an endangered species. It also has four alligators. (For alligator information see the National Geographic Society site: *http://ngnews.com/news/2000/02/02292000/chinesedragon_10530.asp.)* No one seems to know if the millions of sturgeon fingerlings put into the river each year are surviving. It is obvious from the poor quality of the exhibit that a large infusion of money is needed here if these fish are to survive.

Yichang has the closest airport to the Three Gorges Dam with flights from 22 other Chinese cities. Local travel agents say a few flights get cancelled because they do not have enough passengers. Flying here and out is not 100% reliable. The train from Wuhan takes 11 hours, but the bus is only four hours. From Yichang also, you can go by road to Wudangshan, Changsha, Yueyang and Shennongxia, soon if not already.

From Chongqing by hovercraft it's 10 1/2 hours or overnight, and there are daily flights. A road is currently being constructed.

Yichang's hotels are air-conditioned and add a 10 to 20% surcharge. They should have IDD, ticketing services, and accept credit cards. The Tao Hua Ling Fandian is the best four star but the three-star Hui Feng Yuan has the best service.

The **Peach Flower Hotel** (Tao Hua Lin Fandian) is at 29 Yunji Road, 443000, *Tel. 6442244*. Ms. Zhu Lin, Sales Manager, speaks a little English. Rooms are Y498-Y698 and suites Y998-Y8900. It has been discounting about 35%.

The **Hui Feng Yuan Hotel** (Fandian) is at 18 Shenzhen Road, Yichang Development Zone, 443000. Three stars. *Tel. 6330999. Fax 6330888. Web: www.ychfy.com*. Y260-Y368 for rooms, Y588-Y1188 for suites. It has been giving 20% discounts. It is in the suburbs 500 meters from the Expressway to Wuhan, 30 km from the airport, and 10 minutes drive from downtown. This 22 story, 160-room hotel has non-smoking floors, some rooms with safes, an indoor pool, bowling, gym and tennis.

The **Three Gorges Hotel** is at Bahekou, Three Gorges, Yichang. Number One Construction Street, Yichang , 443133, 443002. *Tel. 6613666 ext. 68307, 68802, 68800, 6745618. Fax 6613071, 6613072, 6762351. E-mail: tgph@china3gorgesdam.com*. This is at the Three Gorges dam site.

For travel assistance, try the **Great Three Gorges International Travel Service,** *80 Dongshan Avenue, Yichang, Hubei, P.R.China, Tel. 6735519,6756273,6756271, Fax 6730008. E-mail: bert@china3gorgesdam.com. Website: www.china3gorgesdam.com*.

Yichang's **telephone code** is 717.

For **Yueyang**, see separate listing in Chapter 20, *South China*.

Zigui, west of Yichang, can be reached from Yichang in about one hour by ship or six hours by bus, unless the new road is finished. The Quyuan Temple here will be moved again. The original ninth century Tang site was flooded by the Gezhouba dam. Quyuan (see sidebar below) was the poet/statesman who drowned himself in the third century B.C. because the King of Chu did not heed his warning about the ambitions of the King of Qin. You can pay respects at his tomb which contains some of his clothes. The temple has 1976-made slate tablets of his poetry based on Qing designs, a painting of Quyuan by Yang Chu, and a 400-year old statue of Quyang. He was born in this county.

Cruise ship passengers have raced fellow tourists in dragon boats here. This is the traditional way to honor Quyuan (and save him from the fish). Boat men have also performed a powerful boat dance at a dockside theatre right beside your ship in the evening and CITS provides a convenient store.

Practical Information

Tipping: you don't have to give any tips but if you want, each guest could give Y10 to your guide on shore excursions, and Y20 for the whole crew pushing your little boat upstream. You might want to give more after you see how hard they work. Cruise ships have boxes for tips to be shared by the whole crew with a suggested $6 per day per passenger.

Some **ship companies** include:

• **Orient Royal Cruise Ltd. (East King and East Queen),** Representative Office in New Jersey. *Toll free Tel. 888/565-4088, Tel. 973/334-4080. Fax*

973/334-8819. E-mail: usa@orientroyalcruise.com. Ask for Lesley Yu who helped this book a lot.

- **Presidential Cruises**: S/S President I seems to be the most popular of this line for westerners. It is 90 meters long. There're also 2 (Yellow Crane), 3 (Splendid China), 4 (Yangtze Prince), and 5 (Snow Mountain.). They can be booked through CITS Head Office in Beijing: *E-mail zhuhb@cits.com.cn (for North America and South Pacific guests), E-mail: yingm@cits.com.cn (for Europe), E-mail: zhanggc@cits.com.cn for Japan, or E-mail yangwx@cits.com.cn for Southeast Asia. Tel. 10/66053747. Fax 66012046.*
- **Regal China Cruises,** *57 West 38th Street, New York, NY 10018, Tel. 212/ 768-3388, or 800/808-3388, Fax 212/768-4939. Web: regalchinacruises.com. E-mail: info@regalchinacruises.com or rccny@aol.com.* Its three ships Princess Elaine, Princess Jeannie and Princess Sheena, all have the same design and specifications.

They are all rated five stars but the cabins are very small and don't have private balconies.

See also Chongqing and Wuhan.

Li Sao

This is the poem "**Li Sao**," by the poet/statesman **Quyuan**, in whose memory dragon boats are raced in June all over the world. Quyuan tried unsuccessfully to save the Kingdom of Chu from the first emperor of China:

"The conspirators steal their heedless pleasures;
Their road is dark and leads to danger.
What do I care of the peril to myself?
I fear only the wreck of my lord's carriage.
I hastened to his side in attendance
To lead him in the steps of the ancient kings,
But the Fragrant One would not look into my heart;
Instead, heeding slander, he turned on me in rage."
–Reprinted from China Tourism, translator unknown.

Chapter 22

hong kong

Hong Kong is unique in the world – the partnership, at times reluctant, of British law and capitalism, combined with an 1100-square kilometer Chinese territory, Chinese labor, and Chinese entrepreneurship. The official relationship lasted from 1840 to 1997 but the spirit continues. It has been one of the most vibrant cities in the world.

It is now the Hong Kong Special Administrative Region (HKSAR) of China, but with its own flag and currency. It is allowed to keep its own social and economic systems for 50 years after the handover, but China is in charge of its foreign affairs and defense.

You should visit also to see what changes have been made by the Chinese, and the effects of September 11. In 2002, like much of Asia, it has been having economic problems.

Judges may still wear their powdered British wigs and Christmas is an official holiday. But is Falun Gong outlawed here too? Is there self-censorship of newspapers? Read the Hong Kong newspaper *South China Morning Post* before you go. On the web it's at *www.scmp.com*.

Hong Kong is an exciting mix of life styles and architecture, of exotic religions and customs that flourished and developed while those on the China mainland were periodically suppressed. Here amid the money-making are the world's largest seated bronze Buddha,

NOTE: prices listed in this chapter are in Hong Kong dollars unless otherwise specified.

and the world center of feng-shui, the belief that the placement of buildings and furniture affects one's fortunes. Here are bustling stock and vegetable markets, huge skyscrapers, and beautiful ocean, beaches, gentle mountains and vast parks. Enjoy its world-class hotels and the best Chinese food in Asia. Explore its air-conditioned shopping malls, its cheap street markets and factory outlets.

And don't worry. English is still an official language; street signs are in both languages. Rugby and cricket are still played. It is the easiest place in China for foreign tourists to visit on your own. There's a lot to see and do, much of it cheaply.

Hong Kong, which means Fragrant Harbor, was a remote, unpopulated part of China to which the last emperor of the Song dynasty escaped temporarily – he was then only ten – in the 13th century.

In the 19th century, the British needed China's trade to pay for its passion for tea and silk; the Chinese wanted only gold in exchange. Britain forced the Chinese to take opium. The Chinese fought back and lost. In 1841, Britain got a "barren island with hardly a house upon it," today's Hong Kong Island.

This center of British trade flourished, and with subsequent wars the British acquired the Kowloon peninsula up to Boundary Street in 1860 and then leased the much larger New Territories and islands in 1898 – a lease that expired in 1997 with all of Hong Kong reverting to Chinese rule.

The Japanese occupied Hong Kong from 1941 to 1945. In 1945 it had about 600,000 inhabitants. It has been growing ever since, first with refugees from China's communism, and since 1997 with 150 legal Chinese immigrants a day eager for bright lights and better-paying jobs. Today its population is 6.8

US$-Hong Kong$ Exchange Rates

You have to shop around even for money. There has been talk of un-pegging the Hong Kong dollar from the U.S. dollar. Price quotes in this section are in Hong Kong dollars. **One US dollar has been worth about HK$7.80**, but exchange rates and service charges vary considerably. You usually get a better rate through banks, but most banks add upward from $30 each time you change money. American Express charges no service fee for its travelers' checks and has been a good deal. Sometimes better rates have been at one of the money changers in the back of the crowded Chungking Mansions on Nathan Road near Middle Road but be careful of pickpockets and counterfeits.

For a link to a currency converter, visit the home page of my website: *www.china-travel-guide.com*. The current economic downturn means prices in Hong Kong are soft. It's a great time to visit.

million. Tung Chee-hwa is Chief Executive, and 98% of its people from 20 to 29 years of age own a mobile telephone.

The development continues. Disneyland is due in 2005 and bridges are being built to the site. In 2006, Hong Kong is hoping to host the Asian Games. Hong Kong is also building a cable car system between the airport and Po Lin Monastery, and more roads and mass transit. In the works is a market, similiar to Fisherman's Wharf in San Francisco, in Aberdeen and the redevelopment of west Kowloon.

When you're thinking of a visit, first contact the **Hong Kong Tourism Board** (HKTB). Its website is great for up-to-date information like special hotel bargains, and the latest visa requirements. You can make reservations for hotels. It will send you a lot of helpful information. See *Practical Information* below.

Business people especially should check the date of their visit to avoid a holiday. From the American Chamber of Commerce of Hong Kong, at *www.amcham.org.hk/hongkong/public_holidays.html*, in 2002, holidays are January first, the Lunar New Year Feb. 12-14, Good Friday March 29, the day following Good Friday March 30, Easter Monday April 1, Ching Ming April 5, Labour Day May 1, Buddhas's Birthday, May 20, Tuen Ng Festival June 15, SAR Establishment Day July 1, the day after the mid-autumn festival September 21, National Day October 1, Chung Yeung Festival October 14, Christmas December 25, and the first weekday after Christmas December 26.

Dates for the lunar new year are Feb. 1, 2003, Jan. 22, 2004, and Feb. 9, 2005.

Arrivals & Departures

Visa requirements are different here than in the rest of China. Citizens of the US and 20 other countries can enter with a valid passport, without a visa, and stay for one month. Citizens of Canada, Australia and other Commonwealth countries need a valid passport, no visa, and can stay three months.

Visitors are allowed to import duty-free only one-liter of alcohol, 200 cigarettes, 60 ml of perfume, and 250 ml of toilet water.

Bus, train, ferry and plane schedules between Hong Kong and China are on the China Travel Service website: *www.chinatravelOne.com (English)*. You can also send a message asking specific questions to: *enquiry@chinatravel1.com or Fax 852/27893498*.

By Air

Hong Kong has international flight connections with about 110 countries, and at least 41 Chinese cities. You can fly from New York on **Cathay Pacific** in 15 1/2 hours *(www.cathay-usa.com)*.

The airport is open 24 hours a day. The **airport express train** to Central (34 km in 23 minutes) is $90 and to Kowloon $80. You get tickets from a kiosk in the arrival area. Carts await you at each station. The train is the fastest way downtown aside from a helicopter. This train leaves every four to eight minutes between 6am and 1am. *Tel. 2881-8888. Website: www.mtr.com.hk.* Cheaper airbuses also go downtown from 6am to 11pm every 20 minutes, and less frequent public buses all night. For a list of hotels serviced, city buses from the airport into town, or times of facilities like the left luggage at the airport, an airbus costs a maximum $45 to Causeway Bay.

Taxis are about $350 to Hong Kong Island. The MTR offers a $200 package that includes one journey on the Airport Express, and three days of unlimited rides on the MTR. This is a good deal if you're going to do a lot of subway journeys.

You pay your airport tax of $80 when you buy your ticket.

For about $250, you can get a shower, massage, watch in-house movies, and access your e-mail without leaving the transit area. To get to the **Plaza Premium Transit Lounge**, just go to the restricted airside area on the 7th floor of the West Hall Concourse (via T4 to the Departure Level, follow signs to gate 40 and Airline Lounges. Then take the escalator just before gate 40). You can shop at the airport's 140 shops and restaurants which advertise "downtown" prices. Or just hire a taxi and sightsee. See also Regal Airport Hotel.

By Bus

Dozens of public buses go between Hong Kong airport and Guangzhou, Dongguan and Shenzhen. Buses also arrive at China Hong Kong City. Bus travel is often delayed by rush hour traffic jams. You have to lug all your bags out at two border posts, and struggle with them back onto the bus or even some trains for inspections. *Tel. 2261-2472.*

By Ship

Ferries between Hong Kong and Macau run every 15 minutes during the day and take less than an hour. The main terminal is west of the Star Ferry on the Hong Kong side, close to the Sheung Wan MTR station. **China Hong Kong City** is the terminal for all China-linked ships and some buses. It is on Canton Road a few hundred meters north of the Star Ferry in Kowloon. Here ferries arrive from such Chinese cities as Guangzhou, Haikou, Shekou, Shantou, and Taishan.

You can also arrive by cruise ship on such lines as Cunard, Holland America, P & O Cruises, and Princess Cruises. These berth at Ocean Terminal in Tsim Sha Tsui next to the Star Ferry in Kowloon. For **Star Cruises** with ships from Haikou, Halong Bay (Vietnam), and Zhanjiang, *Tel. 2378-2057, E-mail: sales@starcruises.com.hk, Website: www.starcruises.com.hk.*

You pay a small marine departure tax when you leave Hong Kong by ship.

By Train

Five trains go each way between Hong Kong and Guangzhou a day, a 102-minute trip. One train a day connects with Zhaoqing. Between Beijing and Hong Kong is a super high-speed train that takes about 28 hours every other day with stops in Zhengzhou, Wuchang, Changsha, Shaoguan, Guangzhou and Dongguan. Another high-speed train connects with Shanghai in over 15 hours with stops in Hangzhou, Shaoguan, Guangzhou East, and Dongguan. *Tel. 2947-7888, Fax 2690-3705.* The train station is in Hung Hom in Kowloon.

Departures

All passengers taking the Airport Express rail service can check-in downtown at its terminals and then go to the airport. You don't have to pay the airport departure tax here; the marine ferry terminal passenger fee is $18. It is cheaper to go by ferry to the Shenzhen airport, and then fly from there to anywhere in China, than to fly directly from Hong Kong.

Orientation

Hong Kong is on the South China Sea on the north shore of the Pearl River estuary across from Macau. In a sub-tropical zone, it rarely experiences frost. Summers, especially in August, can be extremely humid and hot (33°C), and most people then find themselves drawn by 70% discounts to air-conditioned malls. The best time to visit is cool, dry, sunny October to early December with an average temperature of 22.6°C. January and February is usually the coolest time but not intolerable. Rain falls mainly from March to mid-May, but it's not sunny enough for good photos. Typhoons do hit from July to September, so look at weather maps for circles near the Philippines. They could affect your travel plans a few days later.

Hong Kong has three distinctly different areas: 14 km-wide Hong Kong Island, tiny Kowloon including Tsim Sha Tsui, and the vast New Territories and outlying islands. Historic Hong Kong Island is a short five-minute ferry ride south of Kowloon.

Hong Kong Island and the mainland are joined together by four tunnels and numerous ferry, bus and subway train routes. The 235 islands range in size from Lantau which is much bigger than Hong Kong Island, down to a few rocks. 40% of Hong Kong is green country parks.

Note: Hong Kong uses the British system of numbering floors. The first floor is the American second floor. The Chinese system is the same as the American but is written in Chinese.

Getting Around Hong Kong

Get a good map and booklets from the HKTB. Kiosks are in the buffer hall of the airport (open 8am-10:30pm daily) as well as downtown. You should be

Senior Discounts

Generally, people over 60 or 65 and children under 11 get a discount on public transportation including the Macau ferry. Seniors 65 and older are **free on the Star Ferry** (wave your passport), and HKTB can give you a pass, discounts on tours, and a "Mature Traveller's Guide." Seniors also pay only $1 on weekends and holidays in some periods on some City Bus routes. *See website: www.citybus.com.hk*. Some coffee shops give discounts. Always ask.

able to get a bus map from Citybus, Booth 2D, Arrival Hall, at the airport, or call *2873-0818, Website: www.citybus.com.hk (English)*. Hong Kong is easy to get around but avoid rush hours 8am-10am and 4pm-7pm, especially through the Cross-Harbour Tunnel. Other tunnels usually have less traffic.

Do not be shy about asking for directions. Policemen with a red shoulder patch speak English. All train stations have neighborhood maps and signs in English.

If you are using a lot of public transport, do buy a stored-value Octobus Card for use in most buses, trains, and the MTR. (See By Air above.) You can buy these at any MTR station. It is the most convenient, quickest. and cheapest way to get around.

If you walk west of the Star Ferry and metro on Queen's Road Central, you'll find Central Market, the starting point for the free Central-Midlevels or Hill **Escalator**. It is the longest in the world at 800 meters. Please note that it runs downhill from 6am-10am and uphill 10:20am-midnight. You will pass Hollywood Road and the green and white Jamia Mosque. The Ohel Leal Synagogue, built in 1902 is at 70 Robinson Road. The escalator ends at Conduit Road. To return to Central, you can catch a taxi, a #3 mini-bus going downhill, or walk down the stairs.

Look for special tourist deals. Kowloon has had a Hop-on, Hop-off **tourist bus service** for $30 a day or $9.40 single journey between 10am and 8pm every 20 minutes from the Star Ferry. Its circular route stopped at the Jade Market, Flower Market, bird garden, Museum of History, and Chi Lin Nunnery—but alas no more.

You can get a one-week pass for unlimited entry to five museums (History, Science, Heritage in Shatin, Space, and Art), a good deal for museum lovers.

Buses: Fares range from $1.20-$34.20 which you deposit on entry. There are regular buses, express buses, and mini-buses (where you are assured of a seat). Buses with red signs on top go between Kowloon and Hong Kong Island.

Ferries: The famous Star Ferry is a five-minute hop between Central on Hong Kong Island, and Tsim Sha Tsui in Kowloon. It costs $1.70 to $2.20 and leaves every 3-10 minutes between 6:30am and 11:30pm. You can take a cheap tour of the harbor just by taking a ferry to Silvermine Bay (Mui Wo) or

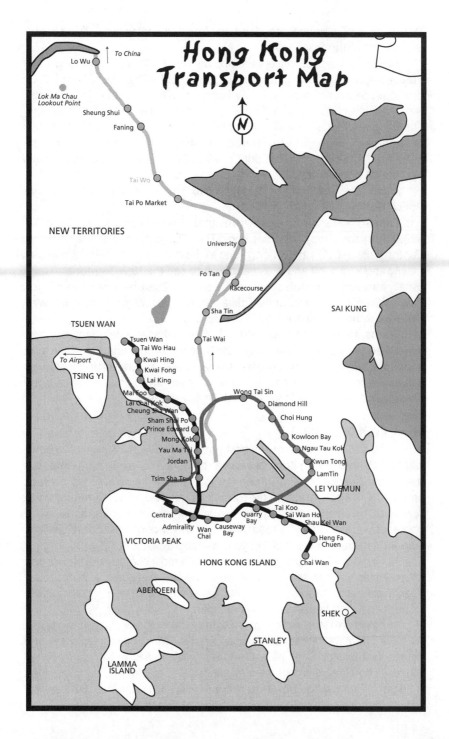

Discovery Bay. On Hong Kong Island, the ferry terminal to the outlying islands is just west of the Star Ferry.

Taxis: I always feel drivers are ripping me off. To get from Hong Kong Station in Central to Chong Hom Kok beyond Repulse Bay costs about HK$100 or about US$14. You can wave down taxis anywhere but not at yellow curbs. Most taxi drivers do not speak English but can call on a radio for a translation. The charge at flagfall is usually $15 for two km plus $1.40 for every 200 meters thereafter. If you use the Cross-Harbour Tunnel, you must pay $20 extra, and $45 extra for the Western Harbour Crossing. Other tunnels are cheaper. Taxis operate 24 hours a day.

If you have any complaints, get the taxi's number and call the 24-hour **Police Hotline**, *Tel. 2527-7177.*

Trains: Trains run every five minutes 6:00am-1am. Fares range $4-$23.00. Ask for a free MTR Guide Book. The MTR connects with the Kowloon-Canton Railway (KCR) at Kowloon Tong MTR station, exit B. The KCR operates mainly above ground and is a cheap way to see the New Territories. Trains usually run every 4-6 minutes between 5:30am-12:25am between the Kowloon Railway Station and Lowu at the Chinese border. The **Mass Transit Railway (MTR) Enquiry Hotline** is *Tel. 2993-8880.*

Trams: These are the cheapest ($2.00) and slowest rides in town. Trams leave their terminals every 45 seconds. They run from about 6am-1am from Kennedy Town to Western-Central-Wanchai-Causeway Bay-North Point-Quarry Bay and then Shau Kei Wan. They operates only on the north side of Hong Kong Island and some detour through Happy Valley.

Where to Stay

Hong Kong has some of the best hotels in the world. Unfortunately we can't list them all. Hong Kong has had a reputation for overly high prices but these have been dropping. During low occupancy times, hotels have been giving 10%-50% discounts off the following published prices, sometimes with breakfast. HKTB and travel agents can tell you about specials. Some travel packages were including six room nights for the price of a discounted airfare. So don't let these prices frighten you. Ask about discounts.

All hotels here take major credit cards and most charge 10% service and 3% room tax. The low seasons are around the January-February Chinese New Year, and June to early September. But low season could be any time riots are in Indonesia, or if banks are failing in Japan.

All hotels are listed in order of price, the most expensive first, in each area. All have international standards unless noted. Most have peep-holes and double- or triple-locks. All have Cantonese restaurants and Western coffee shops. All hotels here accept major credit cards. They have television channels in English. The Kowloon Hotel has computers in each room free. But beware: Local telephone calls can range from free to $6 each.

For more about my favorite hotels, see Chapter 13, China's Best Places to Stay.

Hong Kong Island

The best place for business people is Central and Wan Chai, and for history, Central. The Shangri-La is my personal favorite. The Rosedale's high-tech capabilities are ideal for people doing business in Hong Kong and fun for tourists. The hostels are good for budget travelers. The Grand Hyatt and Renaissance are both attached to the Hong Kong Convention and Exhibition Centre and share the same lovely roof garden and pool.

GRAND HYATT HONG KONG (Guan yut chow deem), *1 Harbour Road, Wan Chai, Tel. 2588-1234, Fax 2802-0677. E-mail: info@grandhyatt.com.hk.*

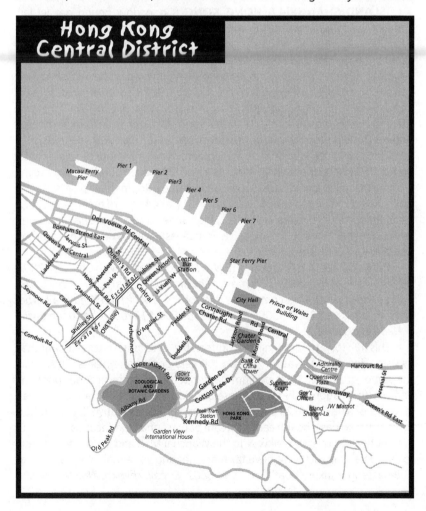

Website: www.hongkong.hyatt.com. 572 rooms of which over 70% have harbor views. $3600-$4400. Suites $6400-$25400. Extra bed $350.

This magnificent, 36-story hotel is indeed grand with curving staircases swirling down to its impressive black marble lobby. It has an elegant disco with a champagne bar, a coffee shop with a good harbor view, and some of Hong Kong's best restaurants. Try the Milanese, Japanese, or Cantonese. The breakfast buffet has been Y195 and dinner Y350. Its outdoor recreational facilities on an 11,000-square meter, roof-top terrace include a 335-meter jogging trail, golf-driving range, two flood-lit tennis courts, and a sizeable gym. Its 47-meter year-round pool is downtown Hong Kong's longest. It has broadband internet access, cordless keyboards, and shuttle service in a London taxi.

ISLAND SHANGRI-LA HONG KONG (Gong dow heung gat lei lai), *Pacific Place, Supreme Court Road, Central. Floors 5-8 and 39-56, Tel. 2877-3838, Fax 2521-8742. Website: www.shangri-la.com. E-mail: isl@shangri-la.com. 565 rooms. $2500-$3650. Suites $5800-$26000. It has been discounting 10% to 30%. Like other Shangri-La's, if you pay the published rate, you get a lot of perks. It's handy to the Admiralty MTR, shopping, restaurants, and wonderful Hong Kong Park. It's a pleasant walk to Lan Kwai Fong and the Star Ferry, and high on a hill with a much broader view than harborside hotels. The bus from the Airport Express terminal drops you at the door.*

This 1991 hotel is very classy and opulent. It has a 24-hour business center and a 28.5-meter pool. It also has a good 28-piece round-the-clock gym, tanning machine, steam bath, sauna, and Jacuzzis. Rooms have bidets, double sinks, two desks, three telephones and are 41 to 44 square meters. They also have chandeliers, wireless keyboards, high speed internet access, and safes. Its banquet hall seats 600 at tables. Its French restaurant is one of my favorites. See below.

RENAISSANCE HARBOUR VIEW, *1 Harbour Road, Wan Chai, Tel. 2802-8888, Fax 2802-8833. E-mail: rhvhksal@hkstar.com. Website: www.renaissancehotels.com. It has 860 rooms of which 65% have a harbor view. Rooms are $2300-$3000 and suites $3600-$18800. It has been giving a 10-50% discount.*

This 42-story, modern, glitzy, comfortable 1989 hotel is less elegant than its sister, the Grand Hyatt next door. It is very good nonetheless. They share the same, great 11th floor podium garden, children's playground, pool and harborside location. It has Cantonese and continental restaurants, and well-lit rooms of an average 25-31 square meters. Its four executive floors have CD players. It also has a health center, steam bath, sauna, and Jacuzzis. It is about 300 meters by covered walkway to the Wanchai MTR and is close to the ferry to Tsim Sha Tsui. All rooms have fax machines and voice mail. You can rent its 100-passenger luxury boat, *Tel. 2584-6862. E-mail: rhvhksc@hkstar.com.*

ROSEDALE ON THE PARK, *8 Shelter St., Causeway Bay, Tel. 2127-8888, Fax 2127-3333. E-mail hotel@rosedale.com.hk. Website: www.rosedale.com.hk. $1180 to $1480 for rooms, and $1880 to $6880 for suites. This 274-room hotel has been offering a summer package of $780 net. It is near the Causeway Bay MTR stop and is a Best Western. It is across from Victoria Park in a crowded commercial area, close to Hong Kong Stadium and the Jockey Club.*

Rooms in this 2001 high-tech hotel are 22 square meters. Suites have open kitchens with refrigerator, microwave and free mini bar. They have broadband access, an Internet Web Phone, and Digital Enhanced Cordless telephone service that can be used inside the hotel only. Rooms also have safes, in-house movies, kettles, voice mail, and fan heaters. Its SkyZone Lounge has a "computer cyber-corner" and its business center operates 24 hours. It has a wide variety of interesting food including Halal and vegetarian.

BISHOP LEI INTERNATIONAL HOUSE, *4 Robinson Road, Mid-Levels, Tel. 2868-0828, Fax 2868-1551. E-mail: resvtion@bishopleihtl.com.hk. Website:*

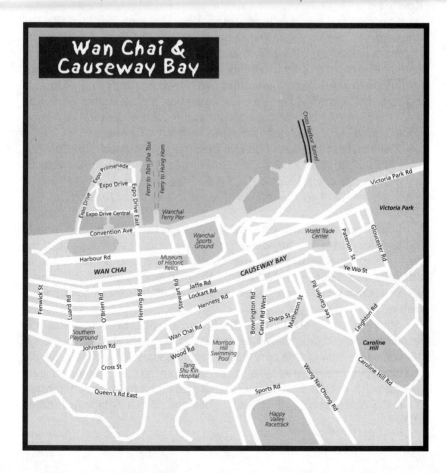

www.bishopleihtl.com.hk (English). Free shuttle from Admiralty, Central and Wanchai. 10 minutes by Mid-levels Escalator from Central. Rooms range from Y1080 to Y2080, and suites Y3800 and Y4800. No tax. It has been giving 20% discounts.

It changes travelers' checks and accepts credit cards. 205 rooms. Gym and outdoor pool. Managed by the Catholic Diocese of Hong Kong.

TWO MACDONNELL ROAD (Mut-don-no do yee ho), *2 Macdonnell Road above Central, Tel. 2132-2132, Fax 2131-1000. 220-rooms and 32 stories. $1050-$1200 for rooms; $1750-$2450 for suites. Discount depending on season. No tax. Accepts credit cards and changes travelers' checks.*

This St. John's Ambulance Society hotel has CNN and microwaves, but no bar nor room service. It is across from the lush Botanical and Zoological Gardens and a 20-minute walk up from Central and the MTR. Public mini-buses 12A and 1A from the Star Ferry make access easier.

Kowloon

Shoppers and tourists should aim for Kowloon, especially Tsim Sha Tsui where my favorite hotels are The Salisbury and The Peninsula, the latter with history as well as class. These two and The Kowloon are together and close to a wide range of shops, restaurants, and night clubs. (You must take a look at the Felix in The Peninsula). Another plus is their proximity to the Museum of Art, the MTR, the Star Ferry, the railway station, and pleasant walks beside the harbor. Free lunch-time concerts are at the Cultural Centre. The budget Booth Lodge and the Kowloon Shangri-La are not far away.

THE PENINSULA (Boon Doe Zow Deem), *Salisbury Road, Tsim Sha Tsui, Tel. 2366-6251, Fax 2722-4170. E-mail: pen@peninsula.com. Website: www.peninsula.com. 300 rooms. $3000-$4900; suites $5600-$39000. It gives packages, not discounts. Book through its website or Leading Hotels of the World.*

This, the oldest and most beautiful hotel in Hong Kong, is in a great location with top service except for its small in-room safes. It has some of the best and most expensive restaurants in town. It is also a historic tourist attraction and deserves at least a look. The high lobby ceiling in the original wing has carved gold trim and rams' head pillars. Rooms are 41 to 46 square meters.

For the Peninsula's restaurants, see below. It also has dim sum, a Japanese restaurant and 500 different wines. Its health spa has a waterfall, year-round 18-meter-long Roman-style pool with retractable screen, steam bath, sauna, Jacuzzi, gym, and massage. Its shops are upmarket and it has its own helicopter which costs $7500 for up to four passengers for an airport transfer. It has the world's largest all-Rolls-Royce fleet including a vintage Rolls dated 1934.

KOWLOON SHANGRI-LA, *64 Mody Road, East Tsim Sha Tsui, Tel. 2721-2111, Fax 2723-8686, 2366-0961. E-mail: ksl@shangri-la.com. Website: www.shangri-la.com. Rooms cost $2100-$3550. It has been discounting 10% but ask about packages. It is 12 minutes from the Star Ferry, five minutes from the ferry directly to Central, and five minutes walk from the metro. It is within walking distance of the train station and is across the street from the harbor.*

This is a beautiful, magnificent-looking hotel with very good standards and recommended Japanese, Continental and California restaurants (a choice

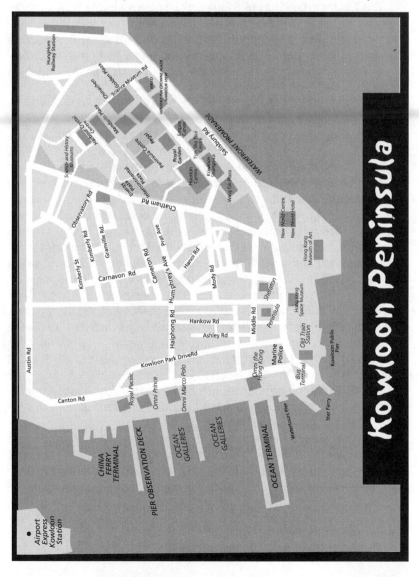

of butter or olive oil on your bread). It has 24-hour room service, 24-hour business center, executive floors and 725 rooms averaging 45 square meters. You can enjoy its small indoor pool, spa, and beauty salon. Rooms have three telephones, data ports, and soon broadband internet access.

THE KOWLOON HOTEL, *19-21 Nathan Road, Tel. 2929-2888, 2734-3777 (reservations), Fax 2301-2668 (reservations), 2739-9811 (enquiry). E-mail: khh@peninsula.com. Website: www.peninsula.com. Rooms are $1300-$2650 and suites $3600 to $5100. It has been giving discounts.*

This 736-room hotel has 18.6 square meter rooms with plastic sinks, safes, CNN and Australian TV, computers with spreadsheets, fax capability, and free internet service. The Kowloon is a four-star version of its sister, The Peninsula next door. It has a pizzeria, Cantonese seafood, and a 30-shop arcade. While it has no gym, guests can use the facilities at a nearby fitness center. Its breakfast buffet costs $140. Bus tours meet in its lobby.

THE SALISBURY YMCA, *41 Salisbury Road, Tel. 2268-7000, Fax 2739-9315. E-mail: sales@ymcahk.org.hk or room@ywcahk.org.hk. Website: www.ymcahk.org.hk. Rooms are $600-$940 and suites $1100-$1400. Extra bed $175. Dorm bunk bed $210. No tax. It has been giving 10%-15% discounts during low season and 20% discounts on its buffet meals which cost $110 for breakfast, $98 for lunch and $218 for dinner. The set American breakfast is $40 and $50.*

Everybody knows this 363-room hotel is the best deal in town. It is next door to The Peninsula Hotel and has 14 television channels in English. It has room service, two restaurants of mainly Western food, in-room safes, a 50-meter-long pool, and a good pay-for-use gym and indoor climbing wall. It provides squash, laundromat, secretarial and fax services, and piano studios. YMCA membership is not necessary. It first opened in 1924 with major renovations in 2000. Local calls are $3 each. E-mail costs $100 for five days. (See Practical Information below for a cheaper alternative within a five minute walk.)

BOOTH LODGE (Bo Wei Lim), *11 Wing Sing Lane, at Yau Ma Tei MTR station just north of Tsim Sha Tsui, Tel. 2771-9266, Fax 2385-1140. E-mail: boothlodge@salvation.org.hk. Website: http://boothlodge.salvation.org.hk. Rooms are $420-$1500. Extra bed $180. No tax. To reserve space in this 53-room hotel, fax, e-mail or call with credit card number.*

This hotel close to the Jade and night markets is another great deal, run by the Salvation Army, which does an excellent job. Its 14-square meter rooms are spotless, quiet, and offer 12 television channels in English. Major renovations were made in 2000. The staff is friendly and it has a coffee shop. The lunch buffet is $48, the dinner barbecue $84. It accepts travelers checks, Visa, MasterCard and American Express but not Diners. Alcohol is not allowed. Free internet service is at a library nearby.

HONG KONG YOUTH HOSTEL, *head office is at Rm 225-226, Block 19, Shek Kip Mei Estate, Shamshuipo, Kowloon, Tel. 2788-1638, Fax 2788-3105. Website: www.iyhf.org.*

They run six hostels throughout the city.

The Islands

If you only have one night between planes in Hong Kong, and especially if you have an early flight, I'd recommend you spend it at the Regal Airport Hotel to save on time and transportation downtown.

REGAL AIRPORT HOTEL (Fu ho ki cheung tsau dim), *9 Cheong Tat Road, Chek Lap Kok, Lantau Island, Tel. 2286-8888, Fax 2286-8686. E-mail: rah.info@regalhotel.com. Website: http://RegalHotel.com. $1700-$3200 for rooms and $6800-$25000 for suites. It is attached to the airport 100 meters away by a walkway.*

This 1103-room hotel has executive and non-smoking floors, in-room safes, CNN, BBC, pay movie channels, and televisions with games and internet functions. Rooms are 28 and 34 square meters. It has flight monitors, a business center, and baby-sitting. There's also Japanese, Shanghai and continental restaurants and 24-hour room service. It has a 12-meter indoor pool, and a pay-for-use 23-piece gym, sauna and steam room. Its banquet hall seats 960. The breakfast buffet costs $138 and a play room for children is open lunch and dinner time. It is ideal for conferences and you can get to the big Buddha directly by bus, and in 2005 or 2006, by cable car from here. It has a China visa service, saving you two trips downtown.

For transit passengers, a day-use room costs $300 for three hours between 6:00am and 9:00pm. $600 gives you six-hours sleep and $100 per hour thereafter. It has a branch of the HSBC bank, open 9am-4:30pm Monday to Friday, and 9am-12:30pm on Saturdays. This bank is closed on Sundays and public holidays.

Holiday Homes rent out rooms in two- or three-story houses but they don't take credit cards. Many are in Cheung Chau, Lantau (at Mui Wo), and Lamma Islands. On weekdays, you can get a relatively decent room cheaply. Booths with photos are near the ferry exits on the islands. Look at the real thing before you commit yourself to staying. The Hong Kong Tourism Board also has a list.

Where to Eat

Hong Kong has the world's highest ratio of restaurants and cafes. The city has one eating place for every 700 people!

It has a wide cosmopolitan variety of superb restaurants, the best offering in China. Some are in expensive hotels while others are in grubby pigeonholes. Reservations are necessary at popular, fancy restaurants, especially for harbor-view tables. The best wine lists are at the top hotels, as are the best high teas.

Dim Sum & Tea

You must try **dim sum** (See chapters 11 and 25) at the Luk Yu, Jade Garden, Serenade, City Hall, or any of the restaurants in the top hotels. You must have goose at the Yung Kee. For traditional **British tea**, try the Grand Hyatt, the Peninsula, the Island Shangri-La or the Regent. Expect to pay about Y165 each.

Generally, restaurants are open only for lunch and dinner between 11am-3pm and 6pm-11pm. A few stay open all day. Some are closed on Sunday. Try to get there no later than 11:45am for lunch. The top restaurants have dress codes. "Smart casual" generally means no shorts, sandals, collarless shirts and ripped clothing. Petrus wants a tie. Rules are less strict for women. Telephone if in doubt. Most accept major credit cards (Visa, American Express, MasterCard and sometimes Diners Club). The website: *www.discoverhongkong.com/eng/gourmet/tips/sp_rest.jsp* has restaurant specials like free desserts or two for one entrees.

Food in Hong Kong is generally more expensive than in North America, sometimes two or three times so. Moderate here means expensive in North America. For a range of prices, you can go cruising in Lan Kwai Fong (the trendy upscale hangout for yuppies on Hong Kong Island). Take the MTR to Central, exit on Peddar and go up the hill above Queen's Road. There's also Soho up the Escalator where the food is cheaper. In both places you can look at menus, conveniently posted outside. The restaurants below go roughly from expensive to cheaper.

The Hotels

Among the best and most expensive are restaurants in the top hotels. In addition to the ones below, there's also One Harbour Road at the Grand Hyatt for Cantonese, and Margaux the continental restaurant at the Kowloon Shangri-La. The Peninsula also operates the Repulse Bay restaurants, Spices and Veranda.

GADDI'S, *European. The Peninsula Hotel, Salisbury Road, Tsim Sha Tsui, Tel. 2366-6251. E-mail: dining.pen@peninsula.com. It accepts credit cards and is relaxing, cozy and historic. Ask about its incredibly delicious raw-marinated goose liver, eggplant in a red bell pepper reduction (a work of finely detailed art), and the sea bass fillets. Its hot chocolate soufflé is heavenly. Its average meal price here is $800 without wine.*

Gaddi's has one of the most sought-after and exclusive dining tables in Hong Kong. Its Chefs' Table only seats six and is made of stainless steel, but it's right in this famous kitchen. Here you can watch the cooking, and hobnob with affable British chef Philip Sedgwick who consults with guests about the menu. You should book this special table at least three months in advance. At its sister restaurant, CHESA, an average price is $350 without wine, but the three-course set lunch is only about $195.

SPRING MOON, *Cantonese. The Peninsula Hotel, Salisbury Road, Tsim Sha Tsui. Tel. 2366-6251, 2315-3142. E-mail: dining.pen@peninsula.com.*

Students at The Peninsula Academy sometimes help dim sum chefs prepare the first course at The Peninsula's fine Chinese restaurant. They can watch chefs make birds' nest, abalone, and sharks' fin dishes. Classes are available once a week. The Academy charges $10,000 for one to four people and six courses. Ask for Katherine Kam. None of the Peninsula's restaurants use MSG.

PETRUS, *Contemporary French with less butter and more olive oil. 56th floor, Island Shangri-La, Pacific Place, Tel. 2877-3838.*

The harbor view is stunning. The restaurant is relaxing, with understated European décor and Venetian chandeliers. Service is very, very attentive. It has 500 different international wines, some dating from 1900. Its most popular appetizer is pan-fried goose liver. Among the most popular main courses are Bresse chicken with rosemary, and pigeon stuffed with herbs, bread and liver, thyme, rosemary, chervil and chives. The most popular desserts are mango souffle, and chocolate millea. A two-course set lunch costs $290, three-courses $340. A five-course set dinner is $750, and six-course $900. Add wine and 10% service charge.

Hong Kong Island

YUNG KEE RESTAURANT, *Cantonese. Moderate. 32-40 Wellington Street Central, Tel. 2522-1624. Website: www.yungkee.com.hk. From Central MTR Peddar Street exit, head south uphill along D'Aguilar or Wyndham Streets. Make a right on Wellington. This restaurant is open daily 11am-11:30pm and serves dim sum Monday to Saturday all day. Reservations are recommended and it accept credit cards.*

Started over 50 years ago with a small shop and a great recipe for juicy goose with crispy skin, the Yung Kee now charges $380 for a whole bird, $190 for half. You can also get minced pigeon with lettuce for $120, and braised spinach for $52. Avoid the deep-fried garoupa fillets and fried rice. Tables come with preserved egg (pei dan) which cost $25 if you touch it. Its *foo yu* or fermented bean curd is special, if you like that kind of thing. The service is relatively fast and friendly and the head waiter speaks English.

INDOCHINE 1929, *Retro Vietnamese Expensive, 2/F California Tower, Lan Kwai Fong. Tel. 28697399. Accepts credit cards. Open weekdays noon to 3pm, and 6:30pm to midnight and Friday, Saturday and holiday's eve noon to 3pm, and 6:30pm to 12:30pm. Sundays and public holidays it serves only dinners.*

Specialties are fried fish Hanoi style $190, soft shell crab $180, hot and sour fish soup $52, and beef tenderloin with tomato $180. It has over 100 French wine labels.

JUMBO FLOATING RESTAURANT, *Cantonese. Seafood. Expensive. Shum Wan Pier Drive, Wong Chuk Hang, Aberdeen. Tel. 25539111.*

Many tours go to this garish, brightly lit, floating restaurants in Aberdeen harbor. The food at the Jumbo is good but not great. See Aberdeen below.

STAUNTON'S WINE BAR AND CAFÉ, *Western. Expensive. 10-12 Staunton Street, Tel. 2973-6611. Soho. Accepts credit cards.*

A good starter is grilled smoked mozzarella and Swiss chard $75. A recommended main course is teriyaki "Angus" tenderloin fillet for $168. If you still have room, there's cheesecake with Tia Maria Sauce and mixed berry compote for $68. It's open 5:30pm to 4am.

LUK YU TEA HOUSE, *Cantonese/dimsum. Moderate. 24-26 Stanley Street Central, Tel. 2523-5464, 2523-5463. Open 7am-10pm with dim sum 7am-5:30pm for $25-$55 a plate. Avoid 12:45 noon to 1:45pm when regulars take over. No credit cards.*

This is one of my favorites because all old Hong Kong tea houses used to have surly waiters and spittoons like this. It has no menus in English but public relations man John speaks English. The décor, a reproduction of the original 1920s building, is a lot brighter and cleaner than it originally was. Oh yes, the food is good too. Try the fried milk $120, and sweet and sour pork $100.

JADE GARDEN RESTAURANT, *Cantonese. Moderate. Dim sum. 25-31 Carnarvon Road in Tsim Sha Tsui, on the ground floor of the BCC Bank Building. Tel. 23698311, Fax 23673576. Accepts credit cards.*

Manager Simon Wong speaks good English, and it has a menu in English with photos. You can choose from the trolleys, or ask for gow choi (vegetarian dumplings), or sweet pineapple bun with barbecued pork inside. I liked the boiled sea whelk stuffed in its shell with dried abalone and broccoli for $30 each. The egg rolls stuffed with fish, and the asparagus dumpling with shrimp and pork were good. Dim sum ranges from Y16-Y26 a basket and fried noodles from Y55-Y75 a dish. Jade Garden has 26 Cantonese restaurants in the city.

M AT THE FRINGE, *Continental food, Moderate. 1/F, 2 Lower Albert Road, Central, Tel. 2877-4000. A menu is on its website: www.m-atthefringe.com. Open noon to 2:30pm and 7pm-10:30pm.*

Recently the soup of the day was $68, house salad with Parmesan shavings $72.00, spiced salad of Dungeness crab, $96.00, and roasted duck neck sausage sliced over salad greens, dressed with date and pomegranate molasses $96.00.

FAT ANGELO'S, *Italian and American, G/F 414 Jaffe Road, Causeway Bay, Tel. 25746263 or G/F 33 Ashley Road, Tsim Sha Tsui, Kowloon, Tel. 27304788. Website: www.fatangelos.com.*

Salads, $25 and $30, Chicago pizza bread meat deluxe $130, spaghetti marinara $65 or $88, lasagna $125, rosemary roasted chicken $125 and lamb osso buco $170.

HOUSE OF TANG RESTAURANT, *Szechuan. Moderate. Metropole Hotel, 75 Waterloo Road, Kowloon, Tel. 2761-1711. E-mail: hotel@metropole.com.hk. Website: www.metropole.com.hk. Open 11:00am-3:30pm; 5:30pm-11pm. All credit cards.*

The personal chef of Deng Xiao Ping has been coming here twice a year as a consultant. Ma Po dow foo is $88, half a smoked duck costs $130; chili hot pot is $198, dan dan noodles $28; steamed vegetarian bun Y28; sauteed chicken with chili and peanuts $88.

BISTRO MANCHU, *Northeast China. Moderate. G/F, 33 Elgin Street, Tel. 2536-9218, 2536-9996. Open noon to 2:30pm and 6pm to 11pm daily. Menu in English.*

Popular are cucumber in garlic sauce for $48; lapi salad with sesame dressing and minced pork $78; sautéed potato shrimps with green peppers $68, and cumin sautéed lamb for $98. It has straight back chairs, Chinese lanterns and fake corn cob decorations.

JEWISH COMMUNITY CENTRE, *Mediterranean and Kosher. Moderate. One Robinson Place, 70 Robinson Road, Mid-Levels above Central, Tel. 2801-5440. Coffee shop 25892650. E-mail: ngm@jcc.org.hk. You have to apply for a temporary membership.*

The coffee shop at lunch time has a mezze platter for $48, Israeli steak sandwich Y64, felafel $30, and chicken noodle soup for $65. The Club can deliver food to hotels.

SERENADE, *Dim sum. Moderate. 1/F, Hong Kong Cultural Centre, across from the Peninsula Hotel. Moderate. Tel. 2722-0932.*

Good for Cantonese, especially dim sum. Its downtown location is convenient.

CHUEN KEE RESTAURANT, *Live seafood. Far-off Saikung.*

This market is the ultimate in live-cooked seafood, with the largest variety and the largest and freshest fish. Fishmongers climb on top of the tanks with nets as they fill your order. Then it all gets put into plastic bags at your restaurant to be picked up by your cook. There's no menu of course. Price is by weight, and varies by season. We've had steamed shrimp, garoupa that melted in our mouths, scallops with ginger, garlic and rice noodles. We had tender baby abalone in soy sauce and deep-fried squid in pepper garlic (some tough, some tender). It was seafood heaven. The only disappointment were the scallops with noodles on a shell. They were over-cooked and tough. This restaurant is Spartan, and the service hectic and fast.

COCO CURRY HOUSE, *Indian. Moderate. G/F 8 Wing Wah Lane, Lan Kwai Fong. Tel. 25236911. Open noon to 3pm, 6pm to 1am. Monday to Saturday. It takes some credit cards.*

Mutton korma is $55, chicken vindaloo $48, spicy prawns $70 and naan $18. This is on a side street east of D'Aguilar St., up the hill towards but not connecting with Wyndham Street. It is next to the Good Luck Thai Food restaurant and is usually full at 9 pm.

The Islands
The simple open-air island restaurants on Lamma and Cheung Chow islands near the ferry pier are good for fresh seafood. The **Rainbow** in Sokkuwan on Lamma is best and moderately priced, *Tel. 2982-8100*. Make sure the food is thoroughly cooked and piping hot. English is generally not spoken.

Inexpensive
The cheapest places to eat are fast food restaurants like McDonald's and Chinese food stalls. Many of these are in the basements of large shopping malls. The **Pacific Place Food Fair** is always packed and has stalls that serve Thai, Singapore, Shanghai, Cantonese and American food. Try the ground-floor Mall café in **The Salisbury** (YMCA, 41 Salisbury Road, Tsim Sha Tsui). **Oliver's Super Sandwiches** sells good, deli-style sandwiches (about $39), baked potatoes ($12-$26), soup $12, salads $20-$30, breakfasts ($14-$23), and $10 and up for coffee. About 23 Oliver's dot the city, including The Landmark in Central (basement, *Tel. 2877-6631*) and Ocean Centre (*Tel. 2735-0068*).

Delifrance has several restaurants. Get an address list from its branch at 1/F, Worldwide House, 19 Des Voeux Road, *Tel. 2868-1355* or the basement of the Hyatt Regency, 67 Nathan Road, *Tel. 2316-2805*. The chicken tikka pizza tasted like any other pizza but it offers soups, baguette sandwiches and rich cheese pasteries.

Look for interesting deals like the Hungry Hour at the **Oasis Bar** in the **Renaissance Harbourview Hotel**, which costs $80 for a cocktail buffet and one standard drink. It is available 5 to 7:30pm, Monday to Saturday, *Tel. 2802-8888 ext. 6353*. The **Park Hotel** at 61-65 Chatham Road South in Kowloon has an all-you-can-eat **tea buffet** at 3pm-5:30pm with sushi and noodles, *Tel. 2366-1371*.

Seeing the Sights
Tours
Hong Kong has more to do than any other Chinese city. The easiest way to see it is by a tour which **HKTB** (Hong Kong Tourism Board) can book, *Tel. 2508-1234, 2807-6177*. These are generally good with knowledgeable guides. They save you a lot of time. Tours with meals give you a chance to try a wider variety of food. A list of available tours with prices is on the HKTB website (see *Practical Information* below) but you don't need to book any until you arrive. A half-day tour, for example, to the Peak, Aberdeen, Stanley and Repulse Bay costs $280. A full day tour to the Peak, Repulse Bay, Aberdeen, Stanley with lunch at the Jumbo Restaurant is $380.

On **The Land Between tour** you might glimpse a People's Liberation Army uniform, Hong Kong's highest mountain, and trees full of birds. From September to mid-June you can go to the horse races ($530), a British tradition dating from the 1840s, now a local passion. Guides give lessons on how to gamble and the food is superb. Shatin is a bigger, less-crowded club. Happy Valley has instant replays on the biggest race-course screen in the world.

The **Feng/Fung Shui tour** is for those who have an interest in how the placement of furniture, doors, and grave sites, affect the fortunes of the living. Many Hong Kong people believe in such things as the right placement of the lions in front of the Hong Kong Bank.

Seeing Hong Kong On Your Own

Aberdeen harbor and floating restaurant. This former fishing village with a well-protected harbor, moors fishing boats and pleasure craft. A fresh seafood market operates after 9am all day. You can smell fish everywhere. Look for drying squid and air-conditioned family junks. Five thousand boat people still live in this typhoon shelter.

Take bus No. 70 from Exchange Square near the Star Ferry in Central. Get off at the first stop after the Aberdeen Tunnel and walk about 20 minutes to the pier (ma tow) at the main seawall opposite Aberdeen Center. Here you can get a 20-minute sampan ride for about $70. For a short free trip on the harbor, take Jumbo Restaurant's ferry. The Jumbo Restaurant also has a tour boat. As part of a package that includes dim sum, you can take it to Stanley and back to Aberdeen.

Dolphins and bird watching. You book this half-day tour with Hong Kong Dolphinwatch Ltd. Some of these dolphins are actually a rare deep pink. The marine sanctuary is near the airport. If none of the 120 dolphins are seen, you can go again on any scheduled trip (subject to availability) free of charge. The sighting record is better than 96% overall, however. Adults pay $320, children half-price. The boats don't chase these animals. The water might be choppy so if you're prone to motion sickness, do take precautions. The best time is September-December. Spring has bad weather. See website: *http://home.pacific.net.hk/~dolphins*. GPO Box 4102, 1528A Star House, Tsim Sha Tsui, *Tel. 2984-1414, Fax 2984-7799, E-mail: dolphins@pacific.net.hk.*

At the **Mai Po Nature Reserve**, you should be able to see the rare blackface spoonbill and other exotic species. The reserve has three floating tower hides, and eight fixed hides. In addition to birds, it also has mudskippers, toads, otters, leopard cats, and mongooses. Contact: Peter Scott Field Studies Centre, Mai Po Nature Reserve, Mai Po, Yuen Long, N.T., *Tel. 2471 6306, Fax 2482 0369, E-mail Rebecca at: rchoi@wwf.org.hk, Website: www.wwf.org.hk.*

Giant Buddha. Lantau Island is twice the size of Hong Kong Island. At least 21 ferries leave Hong Kong island every day for Mui Wo (Silvermine Bay) 7am-12:20am midnight for about $17. The trip takes 35 minutes to an hour.

Before you leave Mui Wo, note the bus schedule back from Taipo or the monastery–unless you want to spend the night there. Buses and taxis meet the ferries and the ride to Po Lin Monastery is about 25 minutes. Some tours to the giant Buddha also go by land, about 45 minutes from Kowloon via the airport.

Access to the Buddha is 10am-6pm daily, but you can see it any time from a distance. It is 34 meters high and weighs 250 metric tons. You need to buy a ticket first for Po Lin's vegetarian lunch, about Y100. You can sightsee around this impressive temple while you wait. From here you can walk downhill to Taipo fishing village by paved path in an hour or so, or take a bus.

Hiking on the mountain ridges. HKTB can book three different hiking trips with experienced guides. You can also hike on your own with a good map but be sure to tell someone where you're going. Its three-hour, 8.5 km Shek-O hike, for example, starts near Shek-O Beach and ends at Big Wave Bay not far from Stanley. Having transportation and a guide with a cell phone has its advantages. Public buses are not that frequent. Trails are well marked in Chinese and English with distances, and numbered "Distance Posts" every 500 meters tell you exactly where you are if you need to telephone for help. We found only one emergency telephone during our hike, and very little shelter in case of rain.

Trail quality ranges from stone or concrete stairs, to stony and uneven, dirt paths that could be slippery if wet. Good sturdy hiking footwear is a must. The paths are part of the Hong Kong Trail which stretches about 50 km from the Peak. The scenery is green and great, an amazing contrast with urban Hong Kong, a few kilometers away.

History Museum. The History Museum is really worth visiting. It should have good Acoustiguide commentaries and historical dioramas. It's at 100 Chatham Road South in Tsim Sha Tsui and open 10am-6pm daily, except Sunday when it closes at 7pm. It is closed on Tuesday and some holidays. Free on Wednesdays, *Tel. 27249042, Email: hkmh@lcsd.gov.hk, Website: www.lcsd.gov.hk/hkmh.*

Hong Kong Harbor The **Star Ferry** is one of the most famous ferry rides in the world, spectacular day or night. It started in 1898. First class is cleaner, more comfortable and has a better view. Second class has more interesting people but also diesel fumes. In recent years, land reclamation has decreased the size of the harbor and there is now a moratorium on new projects. From the ferry wharf west of the Star Ferry pier in Central, you can take the Mui Wo Ferry for a cheap ride through the harbor and out to beautiful Lantau Island (and bus connections to the Giant Buddha). See "Ferries" above.

Hong Kong's People Social welfare agencies offer two tours, ideal for visitors who are more keen on meeting people than in seeing places. The Family Insight Tour lets you visit a real family in a government housing estate, and real children at a day-care center where they learn English. The Hong Kong

Christian Service tour asks for a donation. Its office is at 33 Granville Road, 9/ F, in Tsim Sha Tsui, *Tel. 2731-6316, E-mail: hkcs@hkcs.org, Website: www.hkcs.org.*

The People-to-People Hosts Programme is a continuing free daily lecture series on Hong Kong festivals and gods, antiques, tai chi, tea history and lore, contemporary Chinese art, Cheung Chau Island, and feng shui. Each day has a different subject. Presenters are interesting locals such as historian and former high-ranking civil servant, S.J. Chan who has been a volunteer for Caritas and an expert on Jewish history in China. HKTB can arrange any of these.

Noon Day Gun. The Noon Day Gun is an old British institution. Take the Metro to the Causeway Bay MTR stop. Walk towards the harbor. Go through a tunnel door in the west side of the World Trade Centre on Gloucester Road. The gun is across the road from the Excelsior Hotel and it goes off at noon.

Ocean Park is on a peninsula in Aberdeen, *Tel. 2552-0291, Fax 2873-5584, E-mail: webmaster@oceanpark.com.hk, Website: www.oceanpark.com.hk.* This is especially good for children but also for adults. The park is open 10am-6pm. A special Citybus No. 629 leaves Admiralty MTR station and Central Star Ferry between 10am and 6pm. Ocean Park's admission is $165, child $85. Seniors over 65 with identification are free. In the lower part, near the main entrance, are a pavilion with free-flying butterflies and other live exhibits. Then you take the cable car to see the dolphin, whale and high diving shows, a shark tunnel and an aviary. The shows are in an incredibly beautiful setting by the South China Sea. Don't miss Atoll Reef, a three-story salt-water aquarium full of fish, sea turtles, etc. with different species at different levels.

Peak Tram. You can take the 15C bus from the Hong Kong Star Ferry to the lower Peak Tram station on Garden Road. Leaving the ferry you go left to the buses. The tram station is across the road from St. John's Cathedral and the Botanical Gardens. Go only if you can see the peak clearly from below. Clouds could obscure your view. Avoid 10-10:30am when all tour groups seem to arrive at once. My favorite time is just before sunset. The tram operates 7am to midnight, every 10-15 minutes and costs $18 one way. For the best view, sit on the right side or by the very back window on the way up. The Peak Tram takes five to eight minutes to go up to 334 meters above sea level, about 200 meters below the top of Victoria Peak.

The modern, three-story **Peak Galleria** building beyond the terminal has restaurants and tourist stores. Harlech and Lugard Roads circle the peak for views of the entire island, the harbor and Kowloon, a very pleasant one hour walk.

You can return downhill by bus, another beautiful ride. No. 1 mini-bus connects with the Star Ferry, No. 15 double-decker bus with Exchange Square, and No. 15B bus with Causeway Bay. The bus station is down Peak Road from the Peak terminal.

Tram after dark. Hop on any relatively empty tram that says Western or Shau Kei Wan after dark and head for a window seat on the top floor. The lights inside buildings illuminate a fascinating world of flats and shops, and the neon is bright and cheerful. See "Trams" above.

Wong Tai Sin Temple is unique to Hong Kong, and three million worshippers a year come offering food and incense to this unusual Taoist god. It has a free herbal medicine clinic, and over 100 fortune tellers (some of whom speak English). It is right at Wong Tai Sin MTR in Kowloon and is open 7am-5pm. Donations are expected.

Nightlife & Entertainment

You can go on a night cruise tour, or the night races. Read the lists of current sports and cultural events from the HKTB and totallyHK.com websites below. You should book tickets in advance. The main orchestras are the **Hong Kong Philharmonic** and the 85-piece **Hong Kong Chinese Orchestra**. The latter uses traditional Chinese and Western instruments. There's live theater and movies in English. A good concierge should also be able to help you.

At sunset, go for a walk beside the harbor in Tsim Sha Tsui, take a ferry or watch the lights come on from the Peak. Ride the Hong Kong island tram. Go shopping in Tsim Sha Tsui or Causeway Bay where the stores close late.

There's tennis, squash, bowling, ice-skating or rollerskating. Or just relax in one of Hong Kong's many lounges, pubs and discos.

Recommended are the bars in the top hotels, especially the **Regent's Lobby Lounge**, **J.J.'s** in the Grand Hyatt, or the Peninsula's unusual **Felix** where you can look into the women's washroom from the men's. Bar hop in Lan Kwai Fong and Soho from about 10pm onwards–see *Where to Eat* above. Saturday nights are the busiest. Most places are open on public holidays, but telephone ahead to be sure. Most bars take credit cards. The action starts after work at the pubs and after 10 or 11pm at the discos. And yes, most have happy hours. Beware of bars that charge you outrageous fees or drinks for conversing with the staff. You can get beer at convenience stores and supermarkets too if you want.

I liked the following bars and TotallyHK.com has reviews of others:

DELANEY'S WANCHAI, *Irish pub. 2/F One Capital Place, 18 Luard Road, Wanchai, Tel. 2804-2880. All cards.*

It serves Delaney's ale, its own brew, as well as Guinness, Harp and Caffrey. It has live Irish music and jam sessions. Set meals can be $98 and $99 and reservations for dinner are recommended.

DELANEY'S KOWLOON, *Irish pub. Basement, Mary Building, 71-77 Peking Road, Tsim Sha Tsui, Tel. 2301-3980.*

MAD DOGS, *British pub. Century Square, 1 D'Aguilar Street, Central, Tel. 2810-1000. Accepts credit cards. Open 11:30am-3am. Beer Y51-$61.*

STAUNTON'S WINE BAR AND CAFÉ, *10-12 Staunton Street, Soho, Tel. 2973-6611.*
The food here is also good.

Shopping

Hong Kong has the latest and best variety of everything. It has year-round fashions, bikinis and down jackets. Prices for many goods are better abroad. Chinese goods are cheaper in China, but the China Arts and Crafts Stores sell the best of China. They can save you a lot of time.

China Products Stores sell more than products from China. They are essentially department stores. They take credit cards and you can usually get a 10% discount. **China Arts & Crafts Stores** have higher quality and prices than China products stores. Both sell silk, embroidered table cloths, jewelry, stone carvings, etc. from China. Among these are the China Arts & Crafts, at 24-28 Queen's Road Central. Another is in Star House at the Star Ferry in Tsim Sha Tsui. Yue Hwa Chinese Products, is at 301-309 Nathan Road, Yau Ma Tei.

The best buys are in good-quality or casual clothes from factory outlets, jewelry, eye glass frames, watches, gems, jewelry, silk, and Chinese crafts. Stores have incredible sales usually before the Chinese New Year and in August, but also whenever tourism is down. For cheaper goods and seconds, look in the Temple Street night market. For better quality, try Stanley. Prices are good for only Hong Kong-published books.

HKTB has a list of sole distributors and authorized dealers so you can be sure you're not getting counterfeits.

Many **antique stores** are above Central. Take the Hill Escalator up to Hollywood Road. You will see many as you walk west to the Man Mo Temple, about five or six blocks, and then downhill on Cat Street or Lascar Row. Nearby are the **Cat Street Galleries**, a collection of antique stores at 38 Lok Ku Road and Upper Lascar Row. Antiques here older than Qing dynasty can be legally exported.

Computers have been cheaper but the Hong Kong government has been cracking down on illegal clones and pirated software. However if you want to see what's available try: **Golden Shopping Arcade**, 156 Fuk Wah Street, Shamshuipo, Kowloon. Take the MTR to Shamshuipo, north of Tsim Sha Tsui, and leave by the Golden Shopping Arcade exit. Walk one block and look for a sign. The arcade is a dirty, crowded, three-story building on the first corner.

Groups of computer shops are also in the **Computer Mall**, 11/12/F, Windsor House, 311 Gloucester Road, Causeway Bay. Again, HKTB has the addresses of sole distributors whom you can telephone for reliable outlets. Make sure you buy 110 volts and NTSC videos for North America.

But be forewarned: you could be fined $7000 for possessing pirated software and CD's.

Department Stores: should be able to cash travelers' cheques at good rates with no service charge. These carry big international name brands like Lanvin and Chanel at higher than North American prices. The main department stores are the middle-priced **Sincere**, 173 Des Voeux Road, Central. Cheaper prices are at **Shui Hing**, 23-25 Nathan Road, Tsim Sha Tsui. **Lane Crawford** is the best and most expensive. Its main store is at 70 Queen's Road, Central, *Tel. 2526-6121*. **Marks & Spencer** is British with branches in Quarry Bay, Excelsior Plaza (Causeway Bay), Pacific Place (Admiralty MTR station) and the Landmark in Central. It has larger clothing sizes.

Factory outlets: give you the best deals on brand-name clothing. HKTB has a list. Among the most convenient are those in the **Pedder Building** across from the Landmark on Pedder Street in Central (though not all the stores here are factory outlets). The **Esprit Outlet Shop** has been at B01-03, the Sheraton Hotel. Open 11am-8:45pm. A **Leather Jacket Outlet** is at 403 Block C, Hong Kong Industrial Centre, Cheung Sha Wan Road, Lai Chi Kok MTR. Monday-Saturday 9am-8pm. **Adidas** and **Nike** are at Unit G, 8/F, Yip Fat Factory Building, Phase II, 73-75 Hoi Yuen Road, Kwun Tong, *Tel. 2172- 7938*.

Gems & Jewelry: It is illegal to take out new elephant ivory, unless you have an import permit from your own country and an export permit from Hong Kong. Call the Hong Kong Agriculture and Fisheries Department, *Tel. 2733-2283*. If you can prove that you have an antique, there should be no problem.

Hong Kong is a great place to buy locally-made jewelry and carved gems, especially diamonds, jade, opals, pearls, rubies, sapphires and emeralds, all free of sales taxes. Synthetics and imitations are available but if you buy from a HKTB or Diamond Importers' Association store, you have some protection. Just make sure you get a detailed receipt. For jewelry and gems, try **Sunny Tsui**, shop no. B, 117A, Basement, Golden Mile Holiday Inn, 46-52 Nathan Road, Kowloon, Tel. 2723-4775. Open 9:30am-7pm; Sundays 9:30am-5:30pm.

Most gold in Hong Kong is 24-carat or 99.9% pure, too soft for jewelry, and with a different color than that used in North America. You can also buy other gold alloys like 22, 18, 14 and 10 carats. See Jade in chapter on Shopping before you buy any jade. The Jade Market is fun to browse in.

Malls: By the harbor near the Star Ferry in Tsim Sha Tsui is the huge 600-store **Harbour City Mall**. The upscale **Pacific Mall** is across the street from Admiralty MTR station which is also surrounded by malls.

Markets: Stanley Market on Hong Kong Island is open 10am-5:30pm, depending on the season. It is the best market for fashionable casual clothes, jeans, sneakers, arts and crafts, factory over-runs, seconds, silks, and larger sizes. Non-shoppers can look for the old foreign cemetary, good restaurants and bars, and Stanley village nearby. The British-built **Stanley Fort** now houses the People's Liberation Army. Take buses 6, 6A, and 260 from Central. **Temple Street night market** is Hong Kong's biggest and about one km long. It is as cheap as it gets. Don't expect quality unless you're lucky. It is open about

6pm daily, is busiest 9pm-11pm, and closes around 1am. Go to Jordan MTR in Kowloon, exit A. Walk west on Jordan two and a half blocks, turn right onto Temple Street. The first couple of blocks are mainly clothes and food stalls. Temple Street continues slightly to the right for fortune tellers, sidewalk medicine men, and Cantonese street opera, mainly on weekends. Beyond this are more clothes, the Tin Hau temple (closed at night), household goods, mahjong halls, and more food stalls. The market ends at Man Ming Lane, so turn right. Yau Ma Tei MTR is only a block or two away.

Photography: hundreds of camera shops are in Tsim Sha Tsui, Central and shopping malls. Camera film and processing are reasonable here and you pay only for prints that are good.

Tsim Sha Tsui. The area around the Hyatt Regency, Beijing Road, the Holiday Inn Golden Mile, and Kowloon Park is set for tourists. It has fantastic bargains, but also bait-and-switch. It is very crowded so take precautions against pick-pockets and slight-of-hand money exchangers. You can find bargains here in belts, jeans, name-brand jackets, export quality silks, linens, souvenirs, watches, folding scooters, and embroidered cases for mobile telephones. Lipstick cases and glasses cases are better and cheaper than in China. Look around grubby, fascinating Chungking Mansions on Nathan Road but be careful.

Excursions & Day Trips

To go into other parts of China, you need a **China visa** which you can get through any travel agent, or directly through China's Ministry of Foreign Affairs, *Tel. 2835-3657*. The office is in the southwest corner of the China Resources Building, 27 Harbour Road, Wanchai and is open Monday to Friday 9:30am-12:20pm; and 2pm-5:30pm. Visas take one working day to process, and it's been $100 for a one-month stay, and no multiple entries. It has express service at a higher price. Photo service is available. CITS and CTS (see below under *Practical Information*) are the major travel agents for China.

Consider these travel agencies for visas and trips to China:

The **Hung Shing Travel Service**, Room 711, 7/F, New East Ocean Centre, 9 Science Museum Road in Tsim Sha Tsui, *Tel. 23693188, Fax 23693293, E-mail: hsing@hkstar.com*. This agency can get three-month visas, and six-month multiple entry visas if you've been to China before.

Japan Travel Agency Ltd., Room 507, 5/F East Ocean Centre, 98 Granville Road, Tsim Sha Tsui East, Kowloon, *Tel. 23689151*. This charges $200 for a double entry visa and $400 for a six-month multible entry visa (if you've been in China before). It has express same-day service too.

Shoe String Travel, Flat A, 4th Floor Alpha House, 27-33 Nathan Road, Tsim Sha Tsui, *Tel. 27232306*. This one can get you a visa on a Sunday under certain conditions.

You can get individual visas in Haikou, Sanya, Shenzhen, Zhongshan, and Zhuhai on arrival in those cities, but these may or may not be good for the rest of China or for more than 72 hours. If you book a tour through an authorized travel agent like CTS or CITS, you don't need a visa at all for some cities in Guangdong.

Travel to the rest of China from here is easy and you have lots of choices. There are day tours to Macau, Shenzhen, Zhongshan, and to Guangzhou. If you have more time there's the rest of China. How about the Silk Road, Tibet, Guilin and Beijing? The main travel agents for China are China Travel Service and China International Travel Service. Other agents might buy from these.

The Chinese border at Lowu has been open from 6.30am to midnight daily and at Lok Ma Chau from 7am to midnight. Trains from Hung Hom go to Lowu. There has been talk of opening the border here 24 hours. A very comfortable train from Hong Kong to Beijing operates on alternate days and takes about 28 hours. It is cheaper than flying. It departs at Hung Hom Station at 3pm and arrives at Beijing West at 6:58pm the following day. In case of train delay, you should take a mobile telephone. Look at its website: *www.kcrc.com* for prices and schedule.

See also *Arrivals & Departures* above.

Practical Information

Your best friend in Hong Kong is the **Hong Kong Tourism Board** (HKTB); see below under Tourist Help. Keep picture-identification, like a driver's license, with you at all times. Foreigners are rarely asked for their documents, but it's better to be safe. In emergencies, you can get help from your consulate.

Consulates & Trade Commissions:
- **Australia**, *Tel. 2827-8881*
- **Britain**, *Tel. 2901-3000*
- **Canada**, *14th Floor, One Exchange Square, G.P.O. Box 11142 Central, Tel. 2810-4321. Fax: 2810-6736. E-mail: hkong-cs@dfait-maeci.gc.ca/. Website: http://www.hongkong.gc.ca)*
- **India**, *Tel. 2528-4028*
- **New Zealand**, *Tel. 2877-4488*
- **Philippines**, *Tel. 2823-8500*
- **United States**, *Tel. 2523-9011, 2841-2211, Fax 2845-4845. E-mail: acshnk@netvigator.com. Website: www.usconsulate.org.hk or www.travel.state.gov*

Cyber cafes: the **Pacific Coffee Company** has at least one computer terminal in each of its 21 or so branches on which you can surf for a quarter-hour or so for the price of a muffin. Get a list of addresses from the one in the Star Ferry Pier, Tsim Sha Tsui, *Tel. 2367-1750*, or Peak Tower, *Tel. 2849-6608*. **Shadowman Cyber Café**, *ground floor, 7 Lock Road across from the Hyatt Regency, Tel. 23665262,   Website: www.shadowman.com.hk,* has five computers and is open 8:30am to midnight. You buy a lasanya for $38, or noodles for $20. This gives you 20 minutes free after which it's 15 minutes for $10.

Emergencies: *Tel. 999* for ambulance, police and fire.

Golf. You can golf, play tennis or swim at the beautiful **Clearwater Bay Golf and Country Club** on a tour, or just golf at the **Jockey Club Kau Sai Chan**, Sai Kung Island. There's a tour for that too. (If you have more time, it's better to go to the cheaper, larger and less crowded courses in Shenzhen and Zhongshan across the border. The Shangri-La Hotels manage the Xili course in Shenzhen and can make arrangements. Beautiful Mission Hills in Shenzhen has an office in Wan Chai, *Tel. 25202711, Fax 28613634.*

Helicopters: *Tel. 2108-4838*

Hours: Offices, 9am-5:30 or 6pm, lunch 1pm-2pm. Saturdays 9am-1pm. Closed Sundays; Banks: 9 or 9:30am-4:30pm, Saturday 9 or 9:30am-12:30pm, closed Sundays; Stores: in Central 9, 9:30 or 10am-6 or 7pm. In Causeway Bay and Tsim Sha Tsui 10am-9 or 10pm. Some open past midnight.

Luggage Storage: storage at the Hong Kong airport is expensive. It is free if you store luggage at your hotel.

Mail: The general post office is next to the Star Ferry in Central and is open weekdays 8am-6pm, Saturdays 8am-2pm, and closed Sundays. There is also a branch at 10 Middle Road in Tsim Sha Tsui near the Sheraton Hotel.

Medical: Many hotels have doctors on call. **Anderson & Partners** have an office in Central. The **D.L. Clinic** in Kowloon is at *Tel. 2721-2111 ext. 8342.* Hong Kong has cheap, public hospitals with emergency rooms and good English-speaking doctors, but you may be in a ward with 20 or more people. **Queen Elizabeth Hospital**, Kowloon, *Tel. 2958-8888*; **Queen Mary Hospital**, Hong Kong Island, *Tel. 2855-4111.*

Money Matters: Hongkong Bank and Guangdong Bank ATMs give out cash for a fee if you have Global Access, ETC, Electron, Visa and Plus System cards. You should be able to access Cirrus cards at Citibanks. American Express has offices here. Many shops, restaurants, and most hotels accept credit cards (Visa, American Express, MasterCard and less so Diners). Credit card fraud is common in Asia, so please be careful. Listen carefully when impressions are made. One or two?

Saving Money: Fly to and from other cities of China via Shenzhen not Hong Kong. Flights from Hong Kong are more expensive. Look for hotel packages that include airport transfers. Buy food at grocery stores, fast food outlets or markets. Use public transport. Take advantage of free cultural programs like concerts, and free tai chi lessons from HKTB.

Banks, some stores, apartment blocks, restaurants and hotels have free telephones. While hotels might charge a lot for local calls, a public phone is usually nearby which only costs $1. The hour of long distance calls makes no difference to the US and Canada now. It's cheaper to telephone overseas from Hong Kong than from China.

You have to pay a $5000 fine if caught in a no-smoking area and $7000 if you buy a pirated CD. But if you are also going to China, wait until you get there to get a haircut or shop for China-made goods.

Telecommunications: Telephone code is 852. A 24-hour Telecom office is at *10 Middle Road, Tsim Sha Tsui, behind the Sheraton Hotel*. To call the U.S. via AT&T dial *800-96-1111*. **AT&T's websites:** *www.att.com/traveler*.

Tourist Information: See the Hong Kong Tourism Board below, and the SCMP website: *www.totallyhk.com*. Totallyhk.com rates restaurants and bars, and lists stores, markets, and entertainment dates. It is relatively easy to navigate. Free tourist giveaways like "Where Hong Kong" have lists of stores, restaurants, bars, galleries, museums, and helpful articles.

Tourist Help: Hong Kong Tourism Board has offices and booths where you can obtain lots of useful, free information. There's the Ground Floor of 99 Queen's Road Central, to the right after you get off the Star Ferry, about a ten-minute walk. Open weekdays 9am-6pm. Saturday 9am-1pm. Closed Sundays. There's the Ground Floor of the Star Ferry in Tsim Sha Tsui. *Tel. 2508-1234* for information between 8am and 6pm daily, weekends and holidays to 5pm. A booth is at the airport.

See their website, *www.discoverhongkong.com*, for tour schedules and prices, showtime-interactive calendar, booking hotels, etc. For emergency translations and help for tourists, *Tel. 2807-6177*, 8am-6pm, Monday-Friday, 9am-5pm Saturday, Sunday and holidays. Qualified stores and restaurants should prominently display a gold "Q" encircling the Chinese character for Quality and Excellence. (*www.qtshk.com*) and be listed in HKTB literature.

For HKTB's offices in North America, *E-mail: hktalax@hkta.org, Tel. 310/ 208-4582 (Los Angeles). For Chicago, Tel. 312/329-1828. For New York, Tel. 212/869-5008. For Canada, E-mail: www.hktayyz@hkta.org or Tel. 800/563-HKTA or 416/366-2389*. Offices are also in other countries like Australia and New Zealand, and cities like Beijing and London. The HKTB head office is *9/ F-11/F, Citicorp Centre, 18 Whitfield Road, North Point, Hong Kong, Tel. 2807-6543, Fax 2806-0303*.

Travel Agents: You can buy train tickets at the train station in Hung Hom, Macau ferry tickets in the MTR, or boat tickets at Hong Kong China City ferry terminal on Canton Road. You can also use the services of the following travel agencies who have been in business a long time.

- **Abercrombie & Kent**, *19/F, GITIC Centre, 28 Queen's Road East, Wan Chai, Tel. 2865-7818, Fax 2866-0556, E-mail: co@abercrombiekent.com.hk. Website: www.abercrombiekent.com*
- **American Express**, *1/F China Insurance Building, 48 Cameron Road, Tel. 23159188, 22771010 (exchange rates), 28082828*

- **Arrow Travel**, *Tel. 2523-7171, E-mail: arrow_on_line@arrowtravel.com.hk. Website: www.arrowtravel.com.hk.*
- **China International Travel Service**, *13/F, Tower A, New Mandarin Plaza, 14 Science Museum Road opposite the Regal Kowloon Hotel.* Inbound Travel Dept., contact Leonard Yu or Linda Kwok. *Hotline Tel. 2732-5854, Fax 2367-6785, E-mail: citsint@cits.com.hk, Website: www.cits.com.hk.*
- **China Travel Service**, *4/F, CTS House, 78-83 Connaught Road, Central, Tel. 2853-3888, Fax 2541-9777, E-mail:ctsdmd@ctshk.com or ctsdmd@hkstar.com. Bran*ch at Alpha House, 27-33 Nathan Road, (entrance on Peking Road), *Tel. 23157188, Fax 23157292.* It has a helpful website: *www.chinatravelOne.com.* E-mail your travel questions to *enquiry@chinatravel1.com.*
- **Moon Skystar Ltd.** can book the trans-Siberian train and tours. *Chung King Mansion, Nathan Road 36-44, E-block, 4th floor, Flat 6, Kowloon. Tel. 2723-1376, Fax 2723-6653. E-mail: MonkeyHK@compuserve.com. Website: www.monkeyshrine.com.* Open: Mon to Sat from 10am to 6pm. Closed: Sunday & holidays
- **Travel Advisers**, *Tel. 2312-7138, Fax 2312-7231. E-mail: general@traveladvisers.com.hk*

Voltage: 220V. Note that most VCRs, video tapes and electric appliances available here cannot be used in North America. If you buy, make sure your purchases are compatible with systems in your home country.

Macau

Chapter 23

Less than an hour south by ferry from Hong Kong is beautiful, little **Macau**, one of my favorite places because of its beauty, hybrid history and culture, and lower prices. Then there's the fantastic food. Try to spend at least two weekdays here. It's cheaper and more relaxing than Hong Kong, but not on weekends.

Settled by the Portuguese in 1557, this, the oldest European settlement on the China coast, returned to China in December 1999 as a Special Administrative Zone. Pastel-colored Portuguese colonial buildings, hills and sea coast, give it a Mediterranean feel. The Chinese majority add their own lively flavor. It's been a city built largely on gambling and trading.

China gave Portugual land for a colony to keep pirates away. After the handback, China should maintain existing economic and cultural traditions for 50 years, including gambling and the pataca as well as Hong Kong money. Both are accepted at par here but no one wants patacas in Hong Kong. At press time, the exchange rate was HK$1=MOP$1.03 patacas or **US$1=MOP$7.94 patacas**. For a currency conversion chart, visit: *www.china-travel-guide.com*.

Arrivals & Departures

You can walk from Zhuhai in China past two Customs posts to Macau beside historic Barrier Gate in the north part of the city. You can also walk from Zhuhai to two Customs posts at Lotus Bridge which is between the islands of Coloane and Taipa but I don't recommended this. Public transportation is infrequent on the Macau side.

Buses arrive frequently from Zhuhai, Guangzhou, Shenzhen, Zhongshan and Shantou. The Macau bus terminal is next to the Peninsula Hotel. Contact China Travel Service for information and tickets. The land border is open from 7:30am to midnight. You can obtain visas only up to 10pm.

Macau is also within commuting distance of the Hong Kong-Macau Ferry Terminal near Hong Kong's Sheung Wan MTR stop. You can get a ferry ticket there at the last minute during the week but not Friday evenings and weekends. The ferry from Hong Kong costs HK$131-$176. Jetfoils take 45-60 minutes, are the most comfortable, most frequent and most expensive. *Tel. in Hong Kong 2859-3333; in Macau Tel. 7907039; www.nwff.com.hk and www.turbojet.com.hk.* The departure tax by ferry is MOP$19.

There are helicopter rides from Hong Kong for HK$1206-$1310 every 15 minutes from 9:30am to 11pm. *In Hong Kong Tel. 2108-4838 or in Macau Tel. 727288.* They accept credit cards.

Flights have been arriving from Bangkok, Kaohsiung, Pyongyang, Taipei, and nine Chinese cities. The Macau airport is only eight km from downtown. The airport tax is MOP$80 to China, and MOP$130 to elsewhere. No tax is charged for visitors in transit, 24 hours or less.

In any case, you can get your Macau visa upon arrival, but no visas are required for up to 20 day stays for citizens of Australia, Canada, India, New Zealand, United Kingdom, the U.S., etc.

Orientation

The population is 430,000. The Macau mainland is only 7.5 square kilometers so getting around is cheap and easy. The whole territory is 23.8 sq km. The island of Taipa with its airport and Hyatt is joined to the mainland by two long bridges and to the island of Coloane by a causeway. The mainland has the ferry terminal, the downtown and government area, and most of the stores. Coloane has the golf course, Westin Resort and beaches. The Macao Tower is the world's tenth tallest in the world at 338 meters and is on the southwest tip of the peninsula.

Getting Around Macau

AP1 bus service from the airport downtown to the ferry terminal and Barrier Gate costs about MOP$6 and is available 6:15am-1:20am. You can rent an electric self-drive Moke at Level One of the ferry terminal, *Tel. 726888 or 726868.* Taxis and public buses are plentiful. Taxis are metered and start at MOP$10 for the first 1.5 km, and one MOP for each subsequent 250 meters. Taxis do however add a surcharge from the airport. Few drivers speak English.

Hotels have shuttle buses. If you catch the Westin Resort bus or the Hyatt bus at the ferry, you can get a quick, free tour out to the islands.

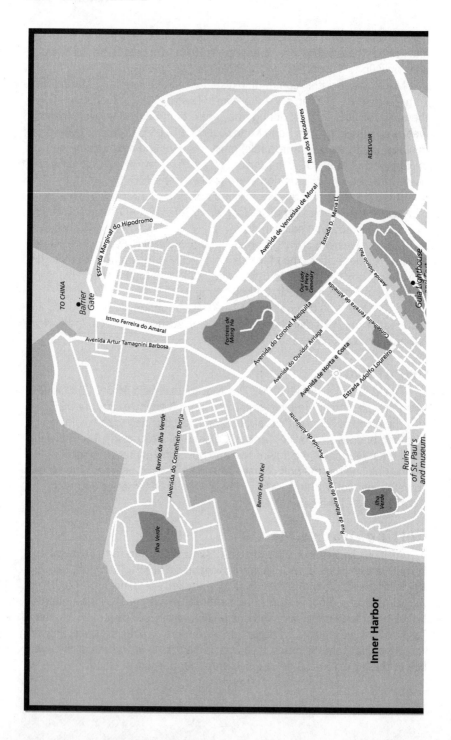

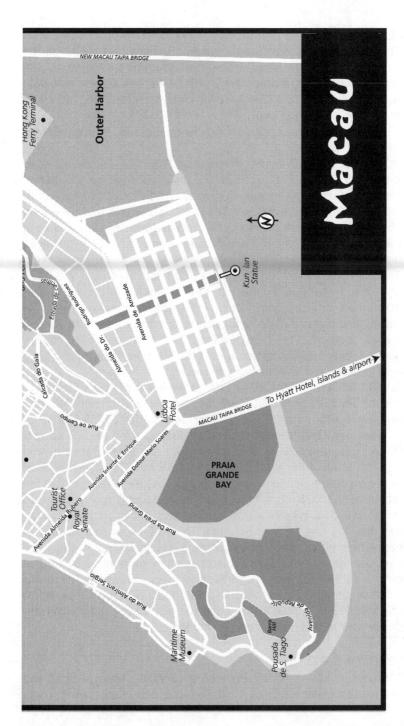

Macau

NEW MACAU TAIPA BRIDGE

Outer Harbor

Hong Kong Ferry Terminal

Kun Iam Statue

N

Estrada de Cacilhas

Rodrigo Rodriguez

Avenida do Dr.

Avenida de Amizade

Calçada do Gaia

Rue oe Campo

Lisboa Hotel

MACAU TAIPA BRIDGE

To Hyatt Hotel, islands & airport ▶

PRAIA GRANDE BAY

Avenida Infante d. Enrique

Avenida Dotour Mario Soares

Rue Da Praia Grand

Tourist Office

Avenida Rubero

Royal Senate

Avenida Almeida

Rua do Afmirant Sergio

Maritime Museum

Barra Hill

Pousada de S. Tiago

Avenida de Republic

Where to Stay

The Hyatt Regency is the closest major hotel to the airport, aside from the airport hotel. The most romantic and interesting hotel is the Pousada de São Tiago but it has fewer services. The famous Hotel Bela Vista is no longer available. Hotels add a 10% service charge and 5% tax. Travel agents might give a 50% discount on rooms.

Hotel rates go up on weekends and Chinese holidays. Both hotels here accept credit cards.

POUSADA DE SÃO TIAGO, *Avenida da Republica, Fortaleza de São Tiago da Barra, Tel. 378111, Fax 552170. E-mail: saotiago@macau.ctm.net. Website: www.saotiago.com.mo. 24 rooms. MOP$1620-$1960 for rooms, and MOP$2300-$3950 for suites. It has been discounting 10%. Free ferry transfers are on request. It accepts credit cards and you need reservations in summer, New Year's, Christmas, and Grand Prix time. It has CNN, but no in-room safes.*

This cozy 1981 inn is unique. It was built into the ruins of a 1629 Portuguese fort, chapel and garden. It is full of antique Portuguese leather furniture, short carved wooden beds and chests. It has fancy, old-style telephones, and blue and white Portuguese tiles. It does have a television and mini-bar in each room but with no elevators, you might have to climb three or four levels. It overlooks the harbor, is near the Maritime Museum and good restaurants, and has a tiny outdoor pool, restaurants and bar.

HYATT REGENCY MACAU, *2 Estrada Almirante Marques Esparteiro, Taipa Island, Tel. 831234, Fax 830195. E-mail:hyatt@macau.ctm.net. Website: www.macau.hyatt.com. HK$750-$1600 for rooms and HK$1750-$16000 for suites. See: www.greatdeal.hyatt.com for discount packages. It accepts credit cards. Rooms are 28-35 square meters. It has a 11am check-out, non-smoking rooms, and free shuttle buses. Take public bus 30 from Barrier Gate.*

A five km drive from the ferry terminal or three kilometer drive from the airport, this 1983, 326-room, hotel offers team-building programs. It has lighted tennis and squash courts, gym, and aerobics. It has a program for older children and day care for younger ones. There's 24-hour room service, a business center, plastic sinks, CNN, and a small casino. Its heated pool has a swim-up bar. Its romantic Flamingo restaurant is surrounded by tropical greenery and you find cheerful Portuguese ceramics everywhere. The food is unique; its chef creative. Try the delicious baked duck rice or cod. The breakfast buffet is MOP$133. Outside, there's a good view of Macau, and you can rent bicycles or walk to two nearby temples and stores.

Where to Eat

Macanese cuisine is Portuguese with spicy Indian, Malay, African and South American influences. Enjoy it with Portuguese wine and no dress code.

The service is slower than Hong Kong's, and that's what Macau is all about. Restaurants here add a 15% service charge.

Macanese specialties are African chicken, curried crab, grilled prawns with garlic and chili, cod fish, grilled sardines, caldo verde soup (potatoes and sausage) and Brazilian feijoados (stews). Cruise along the waterfront by the big statue. There are many interesting restaurants there.

A LORCHA, *Macanese/Portuguese. Moderate. 289 Rua do Almirante Sergio, south near the Maritime museum on the mainland. Tel. 313195. E-mail: alorcha@macau.ctm.net. It is open 12:30 noon-3pm, and 6:30pm-11pm and is closed Tuesdays. It accepts credit cards.*

You get big portions here. Famous are its charcoal-grilled codfish about MOP$75, seafood rice $70, stuffed squid $58, roast Portuguese sausage $24 and clams $50.

FERNANDO'S, *Portuguese. Moderate. 9 Hac Sa Beach, on Coloane Island. Tel. 882531. No cards. Open noon-9:30pm daily.*

This cute, little place with checkered table cloths is one of Macau's most popular restaurants. It offers big portions and good country cooking. You have to try the delicious house-style clams (ameijos a casa) MOP$98, or garlic prawns at MOP$148 a catty.

PIZZERIA TOSCANA, *Italian. Moderate. 1/F, Edificio de Apoio Ao, Grande Premio de Macau sito na Avenida da Amizade. Across from the ferry pier to the left. Tel. 726637. It accepts credit cards.*

This unpretentious and casual restaurant has especially good seafood spaghetti MOP$68 and ravioli di spinaci e ricotta ai quattro formaggi MOP$66. The staff is friendly and efficient.

CHIU CHOW RESTAURANT, *3/F, Hotel Lisboa, 2-4 Avenida de Lisboa. Tel. 377666. E-mail: lisboa@macau.ctm.net. Website:www.hotelisboa.com.*

This has great dim sum with moderate prices from 11am-4pm. It accepts credit cards.

RESTAURANT PLATAO COFFEE SHOP, *north and east of the tourist office, ground floor, Block B, 3 Travessa, Sao Domingos, Tel. 331818, E-mail: tangnco@macao.ctm.net.*

Recommended primarily for its fantastic "serradura" egg–white pastry.

Seeing the Sights

You can squeeze in all of the major historical sights in one day. If you have two days or more, it has a lot of interesting museums charging adults MOP$10-15, less for children and seniors. It's also a wonderful place to explore on foot. It's even nicer to spend a relaxing week here.

Downtown, you'll find the heart of Macau, along **Avenida de Almeida Ribeiro**. Here is the senate, its most beautiful church and other historic buildings. (The Lisboa and Floating Casinos are nearby in opposite directions along this road. Here you will also find the post office and telecommunications bureau.)

Leal Senado is the Royal Senate, currently the Municipal Council. Built in 1784, this yellow and white building is across the street from the main square. The **Largo do Senado (Senate Square)** is actually L-shaped and bordered by restored colonial buildings and a street market. The yellow and white building is the **Macau Tourist Office** where you can get free maps and brochures. At the north end of the square is St. Dominic Church, built 300 years ago in baroque style and open 10am- 6pm. Don't miss its **Museum of Sacred Art**.

Behind the Leal Senado, southwest up the hill on Calcada Tronco Velho is **São Augustino Church** from the early 1800s. Beyond is the Dom Pedro V Teatro built in 1872. Then down towards Rua da Praia Grande are more churches and Government House. To the right on the hill is the famous Bela Vista, which is now the Portuguese consul's home.

To the south and east of the Lisboa Hotel is reclaimed land where you can see the 20-meter-high Kun Iam (Guan Yin) statue, but it's not worth a visit except for the restaurants and bars nearby, and the **Museum of Art and Cultural Centre** on Avenida Dr. Sun Yat-sen.

South

Take a taxi from Government House to the **Maritime Museum** which displays lots of historic boats. It has a few hands-on displays, fish tanks, and a model of Macau in the 17th century. The museum is open 10am-5:30pm daily but not on Tuesdays, and has a snack bar. It's on Largo do Pagode da Barra, No.1, *Tel. 595481.*

A-Ma Temple (Ma Kok Miu), 400 years old, is the oldest and most famous in Macau. It is across the street from the Maritime Museum. As you enter, spin the ball inside the lion's mouth three times to get rid of bad luck. Three of the temples here are dedicated to A-ma the sea goddess and one to the Buddhist Goddess of Mercy. It is open dawn to dusk and sometimes has beggars giving you a chance to earn merit. Look for mourners burning paper cars and money for the deceased. The recommended A Lorcha restaurant is across the street.

West

It would be best to take a taxi from the A-Ma Temple to Monte Forte where the museum is open 10am-6pm and closed on Monday. The **Citadel de São Paulo do Monte** was built by Jesuits in the 1600s. The Jesuits invited the first Spanish governor to dinner. After the meal, the governor kicked his hosts out and took over the building.

You can then walk 5 to 10 minutes down to Macau's most famous attraction, the fascinating facade of **St. Paul's/São Paulo Church**. This handsome ruin dates from 1602. Italian Jesuits designed it and exiled Japanese

Christians helped build it. The huge wooden church burned down in a typhoon in 1835 and now there's an important museum of sacred art here open 9am-6pm. Free.

East

Guia Fortress, Macau's highest point, built in the 1630s, is open 9am-5:30pm. It has the best view of the outer harbor and Taipa. The 1865 **Guia Lighthouse** is the oldest on the China coast. A cable car should help people who don't want to climb. Its base is at the Jardim da Flora and operates 9am-6pm.

The **Macau Grand Prix Museum** is in the basement of the Tourism Activities Centre, next to the Forum and the Kingsway Hotel on 431 Rua Luis Gonzaga Gomes, *Tel. 7984108*. The museum is open daily 10am-6pm and has a racing car simulator, and memorabilia from these annual November races. For information about the races, contact the Tourist Office.

In the same building is the **Macau Wine Museum** with similiar hours, *Tel. 7984188*. This museum is charming, and focused on wine-making in Portugal, and is well worth a visit.

The Islands: Taipa & Coloane

It's fun to rent a car or moke to explore Macau's islands for a couple of hours. Traffic is light apart from rush hours. **Taipa Island** was once home to pirates, but now makes firecrackers. On the north side of Taipa are the university, the **Pou Tai Un Buddhist Temple** and the Hyatt Hotel. Further south is the Jockey Club. On Macau's most beautiful street is the **Taipa House Museum** (1920s). You must see this area of former summer homes of wealthy Macanese. The museum is open 10am-8pm. **Taipa village** itself is full of cute little restaurants, shops and bakeries.

Coloane Island still builds junks and fishing boats and has nature trails and Macau's only beaches. Follow the coastal road to pleasant Coloane Village in the southwest corner. The small **Chapel of St. Francis Xavier** here was built in 1928. It houses the arm bone of the famous Jesuit missionary who died in 1552, close to Macau. A 20-meter-tall statue of the sea goddess A-Ma can be seen on top of 170-meter-high Coloane Peak.

From here head to **Cheoc Van Beach**, Macau's nicest. This small beach has white sand and silt-laden water. It has an outdoor pool and changing rooms. On the other side of the parking lot at Hac Sa Beach is **Fernando's restaurant**. See also "Zhuhai," "Zhongshan" and "Taishan" for nearby cities in China.

Nightlife & Entertainment

The main entertainment here is **gambling**. Macau has ten casinos with the same games known in the West, but sometimes with minor differences in rules. None of the casinos are as family-oriented or as big as in Las Vegas, though the **Lisboa** and the **New Century hotels** bear some similarities. All are open 24 hours with an 18-year-old age limit.

In 2002, two Las Vegas casinos were given concessions to operate casinos here. Stanley Ho who has held the monopoly, was granted the third concession. You should expect Las Vegas style casinos here within a couple of years.

The British East India Company held the first horse race on Hac Sa Beach in the 1790s. The **Macau Jockey Club** is on Taipa Island, *Tel. 336802*. The racing season is from September to June, sometimes at night. A free shuttle bus goes from the Lisboa Hotel.

The **Crazy Paris Show** is in the Mona Lisa Hall, Hotel Lisboa, *Tel. 577666*. About fourteen nude and semi-nude European women dance a burlesque-style show. The admission is about MOP$300. Shows are 8pm and 9:30pm nightly. The Lisboa's concierge has the best tickets for sale.

Practical Information

Cyber Café, *555 Avenida de Amizade, Tel. 786988*. Open 11am-10pm. Free with drink.

China Travel Service, *1 andar, Edif. Xin Hua, Rua de Nagasaki, ZAPE, E-mail: cts@cts.com.mo. Website: www.cts.com.mo. (Chinese)*

Estoril Tours Travel Agency, *Rua de Luis Gonzaga Gomes, No. 192 Centre Comercial Kingsway, R/C A&B, Tel. 710360, Fax 710353. E-mail: estoril@macau.ctm.net. Website: www.macau.ctm.net/~estoril (English)*.

Hours: government offices, 9am to 1pm, 2:30pm to 5:45pm Monday-Friday; banks Monday-Friday 9am-4:30 or 5pm, Saturday 9am to 1pm.

Macau Government Tourist Office, *No. 9, Largo do Senado, Macau, Tel. 315566, Fax 510104. E-mail:mgto@macautourism.gov.mo. Website: www.macautourism.gov.mo*. A kiosk is in the Hong Kong airport buffer hall or you can telephone *852/2549-8884 or Fax 852/2559-6513*. In the US: *5757 West Century Boulevard, Suite 660, Los Angeles, CA 90045-6407, Tel. 877/MACAU-00, 310/670-2234, Fax 310/338-0708. E-mail: mgto@itr-aps.com*.

Telephone code: 853

Chapter 24

If you know nothing about China, read Chapters 4 and 5 of this book. To get deeper, start out with Brian Catchpole's *A Map History of Modern China*, an easy high-school level read with half maps and diagrams. You can graduate from that to Ann Paludan's *Chronicle of the Chinese Emperors*, with lots of illustrations and spicy gossip from the third century B.C. to the early 20th century. For more recent history, there's Jonathan D. Spence's *The Search for Modern China*.

For US involvement with China, there's John Fairbank's *The United States and China*. If you're interested in missionaries, try Pat Barr's *To China with Love*.

Edgar Snow's *Red Star Over China* not only relates the history of the 1934 Long March but has the only autobiography dictated by Mao. For selective periods of relatively recent history and good bedside reading, try the very informative *Wise Man from the West*, about Matteo Ricci's unsuccessful attempts to convert China to Christianity 400 years ago.

For Tibetans, read Heinrich Harrer's classic *Seven Years in Tibet* and *Dalai Lama, My Son* by Diki Tsering about the current Dalai Lama's early life and family.

For the Cultural Revolution, the classic is Jean Daubier's *A History of the Chinese Cultural Revolution* and Roxanne Witke's *Comrade Chiang Ching*, one of the best books about Chairman Mao's widow. (See Sasha's restaurant in Shanghai.) A bestseller in the late 1980s was Nien Cheng's *Life and Death in Shanghai* that includes a personal experience of the Cultural Revolution. There's also Jung Chang's *Wild Swans*, an excellent story of three generations of women in one family in China and the U.S.

The authority on foot binding is Howard S. Levy's *The Lotus Lovers*.

If you are concerned about human rights, get reports from Amnesty International. For background on the Tiananmen tragedy, read the Chinese versions obtained from Chinese missions abroad and *June 4—the Tiananmen Papers*, as well as Western sources like Simmie and Nixon's *Tiananmen Square*, or Gargan's *China's Fate*. For a possible future scenario, you might want to look at Bernstein and Munro's *The Coming Conflict with China*.

Among the most important books is Gao Xingjian's *Soul Mountain* by the winner of the 2000 Nobel Prize for Literature. This is an account of a ten-month walking tour along the Yangtze River in the late 1980s after one of the author's plays was banned in China.

Of the novels, I highly recommend *Bones of the Master: A Journey into Secret Mongolia*, by George Crane. This is a delightful account of a 1996 trip by a hedonistic American poet and a Chan Buddhist monk to find and properly bury the bones of the monk's master.

Ha Jin's *Waiting* is an important book that tells of a doctor and his woman friend who wait 18 years for his divorce. This very intimate portrayal of yearnings and restrictions is set in an army hospital in Heilongjiang province near the Russian border in the 1960s and 70s.

A favorite especially if you're going to Xi'an is Coonay and Alteri's *The Court of the Lion*, that brings the Tang dynasty court to life and understanding.

A lot of old China flavor is in Pearl S. Buck's *The Good Earth* and *Pavilion of Women*. There's also Gu Hua's *A Small Town Called Hibiscus* set during the Cultural Revolution.

Chinese periodicals can usually be found in bookstores in many Chinatowns. The best-stocked store for China books is **China Books and Periodicals**, 2929 24th Streeet, San Francisco, CA 94110, *www.chinabooks.com*. For current events, read the periodicals or websites of the *South China Morning Post*, *Observer*, *The New York Times*, *Far Eastern Economic Review*, and *Asian Wall Street Journal*. See also books listed under individual destinations throughout this book.

Reading List

Barr, Pat. *To China with Love-The Lives and Times of Protestant Missionaries in China, 1860-1900*. New York: Doubleday & Co., Inc., 1973.

Bernstein, Richard, and Munro, Ross H. *The Coming Conflict with China*. New York and Toronto: Alfred A. Knopf, Inc., 1997.

Coonay, Eleanor and Alteri, Daniel. *The Court of the Lion*. New York: Avon Books, 1989.

Crane, George. *Bones of the Master: A Journey into Secret Mongolia*. Bantam Books. 2000.

Daubier, Jean. *A History of the Chinese Cultural Revolution*. New York, Toronto: Vintage Books, 1974.

Fairbank, John K. *The United States and China*. Cambridge: Harvard University Press, 1983.

Gao Xingjian. *Soul Mountain*. Translator Mabel Lee. Harper Collins, 1999.

Gargan, Edward A. *China's Fate-A People's Turbulent Struggle with Reform and Repression, 1980-1990.*

Gu Hua. *A Small Town Called Hibiscus*. Beijing: Panda Books, 1983.

Ha Jin, *Waiting*. Pantheon Books.

Hopkirk, Peter. *Foreign Devils on the Silk Road*. New York: Oxford University Press, 1989.

Levathes, Louise. *When China Ruled the Seas*. Oxford University Press, 1996.

Levy, Howard S. *The Lotus Lovers, The Complete History of the Curious Erotic Custom of Footbinding in China*. Prometheus Books, Buffalo, N.Y. 1992.

Lo Kuan-chung. *Three Kingdoms*. Robert Moss, translator and editor. New York: Pantheon, 1976.

McCawley, James D. *The Eater's Guide to Chinese Characters*. Chicago and London: The University of Chicago Press, 1984.

Nathan, Andrew and Link, Perry, Editors. *June 4, Tiananmen Papers*. Public Affairs, 2001.

Paludan, Ann. *Chronicle of the Chinese Emperors*. Thames and Hudson, 1998.

Richardson, Hugh E. *Tibet and Its History*, Boston and London: Shambala, 1984.

Ryder, G., ed. *Damming the Three Gorges*, Toronto: Probe International, 1990.

Snow, Edgar. *Red Star Over China*. New York: Penguin, 1977 (first published 1937).

Spence, Jonathan. *God's Chinese Son, The Taiping Heavenly Kingdom of Hong Xiuquan*. London: Harper Collins, 1996.

Spence, Jonathan. *To Change China: Western Advisers in China, 1620-1960*. Boston, Toronto: Little, Brown, 1969.

Tsao Hsueh-Chin. *The Dream of the Red Chamber* (Hung Lou Meng), New York: The Universal Library, Grosset & Dunlop, 1973.

Van Slyke, Lyman P. *Yangtze: Nature, History and the River*. Reading, MA: Addison-Wesley: 1989.

Wong, Jan. *Jan Wong's China – Reports from a Not-so-Foreign Correspondent*. Doubleday 1999. Also see her *Red China Blues*. 1996.

Chapter 25

chinese characters

I have listed below as many Chinese characters or pinyin romanization as I could get for the names of restaurants, stores, and tourist attractions. You can communicate by pointing to them so non-English speakers will know where you want to go.

Each city is arranged alphabetically within its region. Within each area itself, I've alphabetized the listings for easy reference.

SOME IMPORTANT AGENCY LISTINGS

CITS 国际旅行社
CTS 中旅社
CAAC 中国民航

REGIONAL & SPECIAL FOOD

BEIJING DISHES (aka Peking or Northern) 北京
- Smoked chicken/duck 熏鸡/鸭
- Crispy duck 香酥鸭
- Peking duck 北京烤鸭
- Sweet-sour fish/pork 糖醋鱼/肉
- Stir-fried pork with bean sprouts (served with pancakes) 京酱肉丝
- Chinese cabbage with black mushrooms 冬菇白菜
- Pan-fried onion cake 葱油饼
- Hot and sour soup 酸辣汤
- Pan-fried dumplings with minced pork 生煎小包子
- Steamed bread rolls 银丝卷
- Assorted meat soup in casserole 什锦砂锅
- Shrimp with popped rice 虾仁锅巴
- Apple/banana fritter 拔丝苹果/香蕉

CANTONESE DISHES (aka Guangdong or Southern) 粤菜
- Deep-fried shrimp toast 炸虾托
- Crisp-skinned roasted goose/pork 烤鹅/烤乳猪
- Steamed chicken with green onion 葱油鸡
- Stir-fried diced fish/filet 松子鱼/炒鱼片
- Shark's fin soup 鱼翅羹
- Steamed live fish 清蒸鱼
- Quick-boiled fresh shrimp 白灼虾
- Stir-fried beef in oyster sauce 蚝油牛肉
- Cantonese stuffed bean curd 酿豆腐
- Sautéed fresh Chinese vegetable 炒新鲜蔬菜
- Assorted meats in winter melon 冬瓜盅
- Bird's nest in coconut milk 椰奶燕窝羹

DIM SUM DISHES 点心
- *Har gau*: smoothly wrapped shrimp dumpling 虾饺
- *Shui mai*: minced pork and shrimp dumpling 烧卖
- *Cha shiu bau*: barbecued pork buns 叉烧包
- *Tsun guen*: deep-fried spring roll with pork, mushrooms, chicken, bamboo shoots, and bean sprouts 春卷
- *Ho yip fan*: steamed fried rice wrapped in lotus leaf 荷叶饭
- *Pai gwat*: steamed pork spareribs 排骨
- *Gai chuk*: steamed chicken in bean curd wrapping 腐竹包鸡
- *Daan tart*: egg custard tart 蛋挞

FUJIAN DISHES 福建菜
- Five spices roll 五香卷
- Fried fish slices 炒鱼片
- Fried pig's kidneys 炒腰片
- Spareribs in sweet-sour sauce 糖醋排骨
- Fish with brown sauce 红烧全鱼
- Buddha Climbs the Wall 佛跳墙
- Shellfish in chicken soup 鸡汤海蚌
- Fried straw mushrooms with pork 草菇肉片
- Fried shrimps in sweet-sour sauce 糖醋虾
- Fried razor clams in sweet-sour sauce 糖醋鲜蚌

SHANDONG DISHES 山东菜
- Abalone with green vegetables on shell 鲍鱼青菜
- Fresh scallops with shell 鲜带壳干贝
- Roast prawns 烤大虾
- Conch with fire 火螺
- Steamed bread 馒头
- Sweet and sour croaker 糖醋黄花鱼
- Three delicacies soup 三鲜汤
- Toffee apples 拔丝苹果

SHANGHAI DISHES 沪菜
- Smoked fish 熏鱼
- Deep-fried shrimp balls 炸虾球
- Vegetarian vegetables 素什锦
- Sautéed fresh bamboo shoots 红烧冬笋
- West Lake fish 西湖醋鱼
- Chicken with cashew nuts 腰果鸡丁
- Scallops with turnip balls 干贝罗卜球
- Won-ton (dumplings) in soup 虾仁馄饨
- Beggar's chicken 叫化鸡
- Sautéed egg plant 红烧茄子
- Lion's head casserole 红烧狮子头
- Sweet sesame dumplings 芝麻汤圆

SICHUAN (SZECHUN) DISHES 川菜
- Smoked duck with camphor and tea flavor (not spicy hot) 樟茶鸭
- Stir-fried chicken with hot pepper 宫爆鸡丁
- Spicy stir-fried prawns 干烧明虾
- Stir-fried shrimp with peas 豌豆烧虾仁
- Stir-fried squid with/without hot pepper 金钓鱿鱼
- Bon-bon chicken 棒棒鸡

- Dry-fried string beans 干煸四季豆
- Steamed spareribs (or pork) coated with rice powder 粉蒸排骨
- Steamed fish with fermented black beans 豆豉鱼
- Ma-po bean curd 麻婆豆腐

SUZHOU DISHES 苏州菜
- Sautéed shrimp meat 清炒虾仁
- Squirrel mandarin fish 松鼠桂鱼
- Stewed turtle 清蒸元鱼
- Stir-fried eel 生炒鳝贝
- Fried crisp duck 香酥肥鸡
- Water-shield soup with floating Mandarin duck 鸳鸯炖菜汤
- Snow-white crab in shell 白雪蟹斗
- Pickled duck 苏州酱鸭

BEIJING 北京
Airport 北京机场
Baita shan (White Dagoba Hill) 白塔山
Baiyunguan (Temple of White Clouds) 白云观
Baohedian (Hall of Preserving Harmony) 保和殿
Beihai (North Sea) Park 北海公园
Beijing Arts and Crafts Co. 北京工艺美术公司
Beijing Department Store 北京百货大楼
Beijing Gu Tianwentai (ancient astronomical observatory) 古天文台
Biyunsi (Temple of Azure Clouds) 白云寺
Capital Museum 首都博物馆
Chairman Mao Memorial Hall 毛主席纪念堂
Chang Ling 长陵
China Art Gallery 中国美术馆
Confucian Temple 孔庙
Cultural Palace of the Nationalities 民族文化宫
Dazhongsi (Temple of Awareness of Life) aka Great Bell Temple 大钟寺
Diamond (Vajra) Throne Pagoda 金钢宝座塔
Ding Ling 定陵
Dragon King Temple 龙王庙
Fangshan Restaurant 仿膳
Fire 火警
Friendship Store 友谊商店
Gu Gong (Imperial Palace) 故宫
Hall of Dispelling Clouds 排云殿
Hall of Five Hundred Arhats 五百罗汉堂
Hall of Jade Ripples 玉栏堂
Jiaotaidian (Hall of Union) 交泰殿

Jingshan (Coal Hill) 景山
Kunninggong (Palace of Earthly Tranquility) 坤宁宫
Liulichang Cultural Street 琉璃厂
Lugouqiao (Reed Valley Bridge) aka Marco Polo Bridge 芦沟桥
Maolong Shop 懋隆商店
Monument to the People's Heroes 人民英雄纪念碑
Museum of the Chinese History 中国历史博物馆
Museum of the Chinese Revolution 中国革命博物馆
Niujie Mosque 牛街清真寺
Overseas Chinese Hotel 华侨饭店
Peking Roast-Duck Restaurant 北京烤鸭店
Police 警察
Qianmen Gate 前门城门
Qianqinggong (Hall of Heavenly Purity) 乾清宫
Quanjude Roast Duck Restaurant 全聚德烤鸭店
Railway Station 火车站
Renshoudian (Hall of Longevity and Benevolence) 仁寿殿
Shisan Ling (Ming Tombs) 十三陵
Sichuan Hotel 四川饭店
Summer Palace 颐和园
Taihedian (Tai Ho Tien; Hall of Supreme Harmony) 太和殿
Tan Zhe Si 潭柘寺
Temple of the Sea of Wisdom 智慧海
Tian'anmen Square 天安门广场
Tiantan (Temple of Heaven) 天坛
Tingliguan (Pavilion for Listening to Orioles) 听鹂馆
Tower of Buddhist Incense 佛香阁
Wangfujing Ave. 王府井
White Dagoba Monastery 白塔寺
Wofo Temple (Temple of Universal Spiritual Awakening) 卧佛寺
Xiangshan (Fragrant Hill) Hotel 香山饭店
Xiangshan (Fragrant Hill) Park 香山公园
Xiequyuan (Garden of Harmonious Interests) 谐趣园
Xinhua Book Store 新华书店
Yonghegong (Lama Temple) 雍和宫
Yuanmingyuan Ruins 圆明园
Zhonghedian (Hall of Complete Harmony) 中和殿
Zhongnanhai 中南海
Zhoukoudian 周口店

Embassies
Australia 澳大利亚大使馆
Britain 英国大使馆

Canada 加拿大大使馆
France 法国大使馆
Japan 日本大使馆
Mongolia 蒙古共和国大使馆
New Zealand 新西兰大使馆
Philippines 菲利宾大使馆
Poland 波兰大使馆
United States 美国大使馆

EAST CHINA

FUZHOU 福州
Baita (White Pagoda) 白塔
Friendship Store 友谊商店
Fujian General Antique Store 省文物总店
Gushan (Drum Hill) 鼓山
Hualin Temple 化林寺
Lingyuan Dong (Spirit Source Cave) 灵源洞
Memorial Hall of Lin Zexu 林则徐祠堂
Qianfo Taota (Thousand-Buddha Pottery Pagoda) 千佛陶塔
Shuiyun Ting (Water and Cloud Pavilion) 水云亭
Wuta (Black Pagoda) 乌塔
Wuyi Mountain 武夷山
Yongquan (Surging Spring) Temple 涌泉寺

HANGZHOU 杭州
Baidi Causeway 白堤
Beigao (North) Peak 北高峰
Cable car 缆车
Feilaifeng (Peak that Flew from Afar) 飞来峰
Gu Shan (Solitary Hill) 孤山
Hangzhou Botanical Garden 杭州植物园
Hangzhou Silk Printing and Dyeing Complex 杭州丝织厂
Hupao (Tiger) Spring 虎跑泉
Huagang Park 花岗公园
Jade Spring 玉泉
Liuhe Ta (Pagoda of Six Harmonies) 六和塔
Longjing (Dragon Well) 龙井
Longjingcun (Dragon Well Village) 龙井村
Meijiawu Tea Garden 梅家坞茶园
Mogan Mountain 莫干山
Pavilion for Storing Imperial Books 御书楼
Pinghu Qiuyue (Autumn Moon on Calm Lake Pavilion) 平湖秋月

Tidal Bore of the Qiantang River 钱塘江观潮
Tomb and Temple of Yue Fei 岳飞庙/岳坟
Wuling Guest House 武陵宾馆
Xihu (West Lake) 西湖
Xiaoyingzhou (Three Pools Mirroring the Moon) 小瀛州（三潭映月）
Yan'an Road 延安路
Yaolin Cave 瑶琳仙洞
Zhang Xiaoquan Scissors Shop 张小泉剪刀店
Zhejiang Hospital 浙江医院

HEFEI (HOFEI) 合肥
Cured Mandarin Fish 腌鲜桂鱼
Fuliji Braised Chicken 符离集烧鸡
Huangshan (Mt. Huangshan) 黄山
Jiuhuashan (Mount Jiuhua) 九华山
Lecturing Rostrum/Archery Training Terrace 教弩台
Ma'anshan (Horse Saddle Mountain) 马鞍山
Stewed Turtle 清炖马蹄
Temple of Lord Bao Zheng 包公祠
Wenzhengshan bamboo shoots and sesame cakes 问政山笋和芝麻糕
Wuhu 芜湖
Xiaoyaojin 逍遥津

HUANGSHAN MOUNTAIN 黄山
Cable car 缆车
Jade Screen Tower 玉屏楼
Lianhua (Lotus) Peak 莲花峰
Tiandu (Heavenly Capital) Peak 天都峰

NANJING 南京
Arts & Crafts Service 工艺美术服务部
Bamboo Garden 竹海
Botanical Garden 植物园
Dasanyuan Restaurant 大三元
Drum Tower 鼓楼
Foreign Languages Book Store 外文书店
Friendship Store 友谊商店
Jiangsu (aka Nanjing) Museum 江苏省博物馆
Linggu (Valley of the Soul) Temple 灵谷寺
Maxiangxing Moslem Restaurant 马祥兴菜馆
Meiyuan Xincun (Plum Blossom Villa) 梅园新村
Ming Palace 明宫遗址
Mochou (Sorrow-Free) Lake Park 莫愁湖

Nanjing City Wall 南京城墙
Nanjing Museum 南京市博物馆
Shanjuan Cave 善卷洞
Shitoucheng (Stone City) 石头城
Sichuan Restaurant 四川饭店
Southern Tang Tombs 南唐二陵
Stone Engravings of the Southern Dynasties 南朝石刻
Taiping Museum 太平天国历史博物馆
Tea Plantation 阳羡茶园
Xiaoling Mausoleum (Ming Tomb) 明陵
Xuzhou 徐州
Xuanwu Lake 玄武湖
Yuhuatai (Rain-Flower) People's Revolutionary Martyr's Memorial Park
Zhanggong Cave 张公洞   雨花台烈士陵园
Zhonghua Gate 中华门
Zhongshan (Sun Yat-sen) Mausoleum 中山陵
Zijinshan (Purple Mountain) aka Bell Mountain 紫金山

NINGBO 宁波
Ayuwang (King Asoka) Temple 育王寺
Baoguo Temple 保国寺
Putuo Mountain 普陀山
Tiantong Temple 天童寺
Tianyige Library 天一阁

QUANZHOU 泉州
Heavenly Princess Palace 天妃宫
Islamic Tombs 圣墓
Old God Rock 老君岩
Overseas Chinese University 华侨大学
Qingjing (Grand Mosque) 清静寺
Tomb of Zheng Chenggong 郑成功墓
Tower of the Two Sisters-in-law 姑嫂塔
Wind-Shaking Rock 风动石

SHANGHAI 上海
Antique Branch of the Friendship Store 友谊商店古玩部
Antique Store 上海古玩商店
Arts and Crafts Store 上海工艺美术商店
Arts and Crafts Trading Corp. 上海工艺美术交易所
Botanical Garden 植物园
Confucian Temple 孔庙
Consulate of Australia 澳大利亚领事馆

Consulate of the United States 美国领事馆
Foreign Languages Book Store 外文书店
Former Residence of Zhou Enlai 周恩来故居
Friendship Store 友谊商店
Hongqiao Airport 虹桥机场
Huangpu Park 黄浦公园
Huangpu River boat trip 黄浦江游船
Industrial Exhibition Hall 工业展览馆
Jade Buddha Temple 玉佛寺
Jiading County 嘉定县
Longhua Pagoda and Temple 龙华塔/寺
Railway Station 火车站
Renmin (People's) Square 人民广场
Shanghai Museum 上海博物馆
Shanghai Tourism Administration 上海旅游局
Shanghai Zoo 上海动物园
Site of the First National Congress of the Communist Party of China
中国共产党第一次全国代表大会会址
Songjiang County 松江县
Square Pagoda 方塔
Statue and tomb of Soong Ching-ling 宋庆龄墓
Tang stone pillar 唐朝石柱
Yuyuan Garden 豫园
Zuibai Chi (Pond for Enjoying Bai's Drunkenness) Garden 醉白池

SHAOXING 绍兴
East Lake 东湖
Jianhu Lake 鉴湖
Lu Xun Memorial Hall 鲁迅纪念馆
Orchid Pavilion 兰亭
No. 2 Hospital 第二医院
Shen's Family Garden 沈园

SUZHOU 苏州
Canglang (Gentle Wave or Surging Wave) Pavilion 沧浪亭
Confucian Temple 孔庙
Hanshan (Cold Mountain) Temple 寒山寺
Huqiu (Tiger Hill) Garden 虎丘
Lingyan (Divine Cliff) Hill 灵岩
Liuyuan (Lingering-in) Garden 留园
Shizilin (Lion Forest) Garden 狮子林
Traveling along the Grand Canal by boat 大运河游船
Twin Pagodas 双塔寺

Wangshi (Fisherman's) Garden 网师园
Xiyuan (West Garden) Temple 西园
Yiyuan (Joyous) Garden 怡园
Zhuozheng (Humble Administrator's) Garden 拙政园

WUXI 无锡
Grand Canal 大运河
Huzhou 湖州
Huishan Clay Figures Factory 惠山泥人厂
Jichang (Entrust One's Happiness) Garden 寄畅园
Jiangyin 江阴
Liyuan Garden 蠡园
Longguang (Dragon Light) Pagoda 龙光塔
Meiyuan (Plum) Garden 梅园
No. 2 Spring under Heaven 天下第二泉
Taihu Lake 太湖
Xihui Park 锡惠公园
Yuantou Zhu (Turtle-Head Islet) 鼋头渚

XIAMEN 厦门
Arts and Crafts Factory 工艺美术厂
Anthropology Museum 人类博物馆
Botanical Garden 万石植物园
Ferry Quay 轮渡码头
Friendship Store 友谊商店
Gulang (Drum Wave) Island 鼓浪屿
International Airport 厦门国际机场
Lacquer Thread Sculpture Factory 漆绒雕厂
Overseas Chinese Museum 华侨博物馆
Railway Station 火车站
South Putuo Temple 南普院
Sunlight Rock 日光岩
Turtle Garden 鳖园
Xiamen Antique Store 厦门文物店
Xiamen No. 1 Hospital 厦门第一医院
Xiamen University 厦门大学
Zheng Chenggong Memorial Hall 郑成功纪念馆

YANGZHOU 扬州
Daming Temple 大明寺
Geyuan Garden 个园
Heyuan Garden 何园
Jian Zhen Memorial Hall 鉴真纪念堂

Shouxi (Slender West) Lake 瘦西湖
Yangzhou Museum 扬州博物馆

ZHANJIANG 湛江
Dashikou 大市口
Jiaoshan Hill 焦山
Jinshan (Golden Hill) 金山
Tongxing Restaurant 同兴楼饭店

NORTH CHINA

BAOTOU 包头
Carpet Factory 包头地毯厂
Kundulun Reservoir 昆都仑水库风景区
Nanhaizi Water Park 南海子水上公园
Tomb of Genghis Khan 成吉思汗陵墓
Wudang Temple 五当召

BEIDAIHE 北戴河
Pigeon's Nest 鹰角石
Temple of Goddess of Mercy 观音祠
Tiger Stone 老虎石

CHENGDE 承德
Anyuan Temple 安远庙
Canglang Islet 沧浪屿
Club Stone 磬锤峰
Friendship Store 友谊商点店
Hall of No Worldly Lust but True Faith aka Nanmu Hall 楠木殿
Imperial Library 文津阁
Imperial Summer Resort 避暑山庄
Jinshan Pavilion 金山亭
Mahayana Hall 大乘之阁
Outer Eight Temples 外八庙
Pule Temple 普乐寺
Puning Temple 普宁寺
Putuo Zongcheng Temple 普陀宗乘之庙
Qing Dynasty-style street 清朝一条街
Xumi Fushou (Longevity and Happiness) Temple 须弥福寿
Yanyu (Misty-Rain) Tower 烟雨楼

DATONG 大同
Brass Products Factory 铜器工厂

Foguang Temple 佛光寺
Friendship Store 友谊商店
Great Wall 长城
Huayan Monastery 华严寺
Nanchan Temple 南禅寺
Nine-Dragon Screen 九龙壁
Sakyamuni Wooden Pagoda at Fogong Temple 佛宫寺释迦塔
Shanhua Monastery 善化寺
Wutai Mountain 五台山

HOHHOT 呼和浩特
Dazhao Temple 大召庙
Great Mosque 清真大寺
Inner Mongolia Museum 内蒙古博物馆
Lingyin Temple 灵隐寺
Tomb of Princess Wang Zhaojun 王昭君坟
White Pagoda 白塔
Wuta (Five-Dagoba) Temple 五塔寺

JINAN 济南
Baotu Spring 豹突泉
Five-Dragon Pool 五龙潭
Heihu (Black Tiger) Spring Park 黑虎泉
Jiuding (Nine-Pagoda) Temple 九鼎寺
Lingyan Temple 灵岩寺
Liubu 柳埠
Pearl Spring 珍珠泉
Shandong Museum 山东博物馆
Simen (Four-Door) Tower 四门塔
Thousand-Buddha Hill 千佛山
Xingguo (Revive the Nation) Temple 兴国寺
Yellow Stone Cliff 黄茅岗
Yilan (Panoramic View) Pavilion 一览亭

QINGDAO 青岛
Antique Store 青岛文物商店
Arts and Crafts Shop 工艺美术商店
Badaguan Area 八大关
Former Residence of Pu Songling 蒲松龄故居
Huiquan No. 1 Bathing Beach 汇泉第一海水浴场
Jimo Hot Spring 即墨温泉
Laoshan Mountains 崂山
Lesser Qingdao Island 小青岛

Lu Xun Park 鲁迅公园
Marine Museum 青岛水族馆
Passenger Quay 客运码头
Pier 栈桥
Qingdao Museum 青岛博物馆
Railway Station 火车站
Shilaoren Beach 石老人海滩
Taiping (Great Peace) Taoist Temple 太平宫
Taiqing Taoist Temple 太清宫
Xiaoyu (Little Fish) Hill 小鱼山
Zhongshan Park 中山公园

QINHUANGDAO 秦皇岛
East Mountain 东山

QUFU 曲阜
Confucian Temple 孔庙
Confucian Mansion 孔府

SHIJIAZHUANG 石家庄
Cangyan Hill 苍岩山
Hebei Exhibition Hall 省展览馆
Longxing Monastery 隆兴寺
North China Revolutionary Martyrs' Cemetery 华北军区烈士陵园
Xibaipo Village 西柏坡
Zhaozhou Anji Bridge 赵州安济桥

TAI'AN 泰安
Daimiao (Temple of the God of Mt. Taishan) 岱庙
Nantian (Southern Celestial) Gate 南天门
Taishan Mountain 泰山
Tiankuang Hall 天贶殿
Tianzhu (Heavenly Pillar) Peak 天柱峰
Tomb of Feng Yuxiang (Feng Yu-hisang) 冯玉祥墓
Zhongtian (Middle Celestial) Gate 中天门

TAIYUAN 太原
Chongshan Monastery 崇善寺
Dingcun Village 丁村
Jinci Temple 晋祠
Pingyao 平遥
Shanxi Museum 山西省博物馆
Shengmu (Sacred Lady) Hall 圣母殿

Yongle Palace 永乐宫

TIANJIN 天津
Ancient Culture Street 古文化街
Dule (Solitary Joy) Temple 独乐寺
Friendship Club 友谊俱乐部
History Museum 天津历史博物馆
Panshan Mountain 盘山
Tianjin Museum of Natural History 自然博物馆
Zhou Enlai Memorial Hall 周恩来纪念馆

YANTAI 烟台
Bathing beach 海水浴场
Dengzhou 登州
Kongtong Isle 空峒岛
Penglai Pavilion 蓬莱阁
Xiguan Village 西关村
Yantai Museum 烟台博物馆
Zhangyu Wine Company 张裕葡萄酒厂

NORTHEAST CHINA

ANSHAN 鞍山
Qianshan Mountain 千山风景区
Tanggangzi Hot Spring Sanatorium 汤岗子温泉

CHANGCHUN 长春
Changchun Film Studio 长春电影制片厂
Chicken with ginseng 人参鸡
Chunyi Hotel 春谊饭店
Friendship Store 友谊商店
Frog oil soup 哈什蚂油汤
Fur Factory 长春市皮毛厂
Houtou (golden orchid monkey head) mushrooms 猴头菇
Jilin Antique Store 吉林省文物店
Nanhu Park 南湖公园
No. 1 Automobile Manufacturing Factory 长春第一汽车制造厂
Songhua Lake 松花湖
Thick deer antler soup 鹿茸羹
Wood Carving Factory 长春木雕工艺厂
Xinlicheng Reservoir 新立城水库

DALIAN 大连
Dalian Museum of Natural History 自然博物馆
Glass Factory 玻璃制品厂
Passenger Quay 客运码头
Railway Station 火车站
Tiger Beach Park 老虎滩公园
White-Cloud Mountain Park 白云山公园

HARBIN 哈尔滨
Ice Sculpture Festival 冰灯游园会
Miniature Railway 儿童铁路
Zhalong Nature Preserve 扎龙自然保护区

JINLIN 吉林
Jilin Exhibition Hall 吉林展览馆
Songhua Lake 松花湖

SHENYANG 沈阳
Beiling, North Tombs (aka Zhaoling) 北陵
Dongling, East Tombs (aka Fuling) 东陵
Imperial palace 沈阳故宫
Laobian Dumpling Restaurant 老边饺子
Qianshan Mountain Park 千山公园
Shenyang Steam Locomotives Museum 沈阳火车博物馆

NORTHWEST CHINA

ANYANG 安阳
Azure-Cloud Palace Temple 碧霞宫和大石佛
Linggu Temple 灵谷寺
Mausoleum of Yuan Shikai 袁林
Red-Flag Canal 红旗渠
Yin Ruins 殷墟
Yue Fei Temple 岳飞庙

DUNHUANG 敦煌
Cangjing (Preserving Buddhist Scriptures) Cave 藏经洞
Carpet Factory 地毯厂
Mingsha (Ringing Sand) Hill 鸣沙山
Mogao Grottoes 莫高窟
White Horse Pagoda 白马塔
Yangguan Pass 阳关
Yumen (Jade Gate) Pass 玉门关

JIAYUGUAN 嘉玉关
Bell and Drum Tower 鼓楼
Jiuquan 酒泉
Jiuquan County Museum 酒泉博物馆
Luminous Jade Cup Factory 玉杯厂
Wei and Jin Tombs 魏晋墓群

KAIFENG 开封
Guild Hall of Three Provinces 山陕甘会馆
Longting (Dragon Pavilion) 龙亭
Pota Pagoda 繁塔
Tie Ta (Iron Pagoda) 铁塔
Xiangguo Temple 相国寺
Yanqing Taoist Temple 延庆观
Yuwang (King Yu) Temple 禹王庙

KASHI 喀什（喀什噶尔）
Abakhojia Tomb 阿巴克和加麻扎
Hanoi 罕诺依
Kongur Mountain 公格尔冰山
Muztagtz Mountain 穆士塔格山
Sanxian (Three Immortals) Buddhist Caves 三仙洞
South Lake 南湖

LANZHOU 兰州
Baita (White Pagoda) park 白塔
Bingling Temple Caves 炳灵寺石窟
Maiji Grottoes 麦积山石窟
Tianshui 天水
Wuquan (Five-Fountain) Hill 五泉山

LUOYANG 洛阳
Arts and Crafts Store 工艺美术商店
Baima (White Horse) Temple 白马寺
Fengxian Temple 奉仙寺
Longmen (Lungmen) Grottoes 龙门石窟
Luoyang Museum 洛阳博物馆
Qiyun (Cloud Touching) Pagoda 齐云塔
Tomb of Lord Guan (Kuan Yu) 关林庙

TURPAN 吐鲁番
Astana Tombs 阿斯塔娜古墓
Flaming Mountains 火焰山

Gaochang 高昌故城
Hui 回族
Imim Minaret 额敏塔
Jiahoe (yarkhoto, Yaerhu) 交河故城
Karez wells 坎儿井
Pazikelik (Baziklic, Bazeklik) Thousand-Buddha Caves 柏孜克里克千佛洞
Uygur (Uighur) 维吾尔族

URUMQI 乌鲁木齐
Baicheng 拜城
Free Market/Bazaar 自由市场
Glacier 冰山
Hongdingshan (Red-topped Hill) Pagoda 红顶山塔
Nanshan Pasture 南山草原
National Minorities Palace 少数民族宫
Tianchi (Heaven) Lake 天池
Tianshan (Heaven) Mountain 天山
Urumqi General Carpet Factory 乌鲁木齐地毯厂
Xinjiang Museum 新疆博物馆

XI'AN 西安
Banpo (Panpo) Museum 半坡博物馆
Binxian County 彬县
Caotang Temple 草堂室
Famen Temple 法门寺
Great Mosque 大清真寺
Greater Wild Goose Pagoda 大雁塔
Horse and Chariot Pit 车马坑
Huxian County 户县
Huaqing Pool 华清池
Huashan Mountain 华山
Lesser Wild Goose Pagoda 小雁塔
Mausoleum of Emperor Qin Shihuang 秦陵
Museum of the Eighth Route Army 八路军西安办事处博物馆
Pits of Terra-cotta Warriors and Horses of the Qin Dynasty 秦俑坑博物馆
Qianling 乾陵
Tomb of Concubine Yang Yuhuan 杨贵妃墓
Ximen (West Gate) 西城门
Zhaoling 昭陵

XINING 西宁
Bird Island 鸟岛
Dongguan Mosque 东关清真寺

Golmud 格尔木市
North Mountain Temple 北禅寺
Qinghai Lake 青海湖
Taer Monastery 塔尔寺

YAN'AN 延安
10,000-Buddha Cave 万佛洞
Baota (Precious Pagoda) 宝塔（延安宝塔）
Former Residence of Chairman Mao 毛主席旧居
Huangling County 黄陵
Yan'an Revolutionary Memorial Hall 延安革命纪念馆

YINCHUAN 银川
Chengtian Monastery Pagoda 承天寺宝塔
Drum and Bell Tower 钟鼓楼
Great Wall 长城
Haibao (Sea Treasure) Pagoda (aka North Pagoda) 海宝塔
Hanyan Canal 汗延古渠
Helan Mountain 贺兰山
Jade Emperor Pavilion 玉皇阁
Mausoleum of the Emperor of the Western Xia Dynasty 西夏王陵
Qingtong Gorge 青铜峡
South Gate Mosque 南关清真寺
Tanglai Canal 唐徕古渠
Tongxin Mosque 同心清真寺
Twin Pagodas at Baizi Pass on Helan Mountain 拜寺口双塔
Xumi Mountain 须弥山
Yinchuan Museum 博物馆
Zhongda Mosque 中大寺

ZHENGZHOU 郑州
Astronomical Observatory 观星台
Dahe Village 大河村
Dengfeng county 登封县
Fawang Temple 法王寺
Gaocheng 告城
Han Tombs at Dahu (Tiger-hunting) Pavilion 打虎亭村汉墓
Huangcheng (Royal City) Mound 皇城岗
Mangshan Mountain 邙山
Mixian County 密县
Qimu Tower 启母阙
Shaolin Temple 少林寺
Shaoshi Tower 少室阙

Songshan Mountain 嵩山
Songyang Academy of Classical Learning 嵩阳书院
Songyue Pagoda 嵩岳寺塔
Talin (Dagobas) 塔林
Taishi Tower 太室阙
Zhongyue (Central Mountain) Temple 中岳庙

TIBET

Drepung Monastery 哲蚌寺
Jokhang Monastery 大昭寺
Norbulingka Park 罗布林卡
Potala Palace 布达拉宫
Sera Monastery 色拉寺
Tashilhunpo (Zhasilhunbu) Monastery 扎什伦布寺

SOUTHWEST

CHENGDU 成都
Arts and Crafts Shop 工艺美术商店
Chengdu Zoo 成都动物园
Cultural park 文化公园
Deer Farm 养鹿厂
Divine Light Monastery 宝光寺
Du Fu's (Tu Fu) Thatched Hut 杜甫草堂
Dujiang Dam Irrigation System 都江堰灌溉系统（灌溉工程）
Erwang (Two Kings) Temple 二王庙
Fulong (Dragon Subduing) Temple 伏龙观
Guanxian County 灌县
Meishan County 梅山县
Qingcheng (Green City) Mountain 青城山
Renmin Road 人民路
Sansu Shrine 三苏祠
Sichuan Museum 四川省博物馆
River-Viewing Pavilion 望江楼
The Institute of Wisdom 文殊院
The Temple of Marquis Wu 武侯祠
Tomb of Liu Bei 刘备墓
Tomb of Wang Jian 王建墓
Wolong Nature Preserve 卧龙自然保护区
Xindu 新都
Yanshikou 盐市口
Zhuge Liang Memorial Hall 诸葛亮殿

CHONGQING 重庆
Arts and Crafts Service 重庆二艺美术服务部
Cable Car 缆车
Chongqing Art Gallery 重庆美术馆
Chongqing Department Store 重庆百货公司
Chongqing Museum of Natural History 重庆自然博物馆
Eling (Goose Neck) Park 鹅岭公园
Friendship Store 友谊商店
Hongyan (Red-Crag) Revolutionary Museum 红岩村革命纪念馆
Sino-American Special Technical Cooperation (Concentration Camp)
中美合作所集中营

DAZU 大足
Baoding Mountain 宝顶山
Greater Buddha Bay 大佛湾
Lesser Buddha Bay 小佛湾
Thousand-armed Goddess of Mercy 千手观音

MT. EMEI 峨眉山
Anshun 安顺
Baoguo Temple 报国寺
Chaiguan Village 柴官村
Dragon Cave 龙宫
Guiyang 贵阳
Huangguoshu Waterfalls 黄果树瀑布
Huangping County 黄平
Jieyin Hall 接引殿
Kaili 凯里
Langde 郎德
Leishan 雷山
Rongjiang 榕江
Taijiang 台江
Tianxing No. 3 Parking Lot 天星三号停车场
Wannian Monastery 万年寺
Whirlpool 漩塘

KUNMING 昆明
Black Dragon Pool 黑龙潭
Butterfly Pool 蝴蝶泉
Daguan pavilion 大观楼
Golden Temple 金殿
Huating Temple 华亭寺

Institute of Nationalities 少数民族学院
Lijiang River 丽江
Longmen (Dragon Gate) 龙门
Qiongzhu (Bamboo) Temple 筇竹寺
Rice Noodles Crossing the Bridge 过桥米线
Sani 撒尼族
Santa (Three-pagoda) Temple 三塔寺
Sanyue (Third-month) Market 三月街
Shibao Mountain 石宝山
Shizhong Mountain 石钟山
Stone Forest of Lunan 路南石林
Taihua Temple 太华寺
Xishan (West Hills) 西山
Yulong (Jade Dragon) Mountain 玉龙山
Yuantong Temple 圆通寺
Yunnan Museum 博物馆
Zheng He Memorial Hall 郑和纪念馆

LESHAN 乐山
Giant Buddha 大佛
Wulong (Black Dragon) Temple 乌龙寺

WUHAN 武汉
Ancient Copper Mine in Tonglushan 铜禄山古铜矿
Antique Store 武汉古玩店
Arts and Crafts Store 工艺美术店
Friendship Store 友谊商店
Guiyang Temple (of Original Purity) 归元禅寺
Hankou (Hankow) 汉口
Hanyang 汉阳
Hongshan Pagoda 洪山宝塔
Hubei Antique Store 湖北古玩店
Hubei Military Government Building 武昌起义军政府旧址（红楼）
Hubei Museum 湖北省博物馆
Lesser East Gate 小东门
No. 1 Hospital, Wuhan Medical College 武汉医学院附一院
No. 2 Hospital, Wuhan Medical College 武汉医学院附二院
Port Passenger Transport Station 武汉港客运站
Uprising Gate 起义门
Wuchang 武昌
Wudang Mountain 武当山
Yellow Crane Tower 黄鹤楼

SOUTH CHINA

CHANGSHA 长沙
Aiwan Pavilion 爱晚亭
Fire 火警
Han Tombs 墓址
Hunan Antique Store 湖南省文物店
Hunan Arts and Crafts Shop 湖南工艺品商店
Hunan Embroidery Factory 湖南省湘绣厂
Hunan Museum 湖南省博物馆
Juzi (Orange) Island 橘子岛
Lushan Temple 麓山寺
Police 警察
Yuelu Academy 岳麓书院
Yuelu Hill 岳麓山
Shaoshan Road Department Store 韶山路百货商店

FOSHAN 佛山
Foshan Museum 祖庙博物馆
Institute of Folk Arts 佛山民间艺术研究社
Shiwan Ceramic Factory 石湾美术陶瓷厂
Silk Weaving and Spinning Mill 丝织厂

GUANGZHOU 广州
Air Australia 澳洲航空公司
Bank of China 中国银行
Banxi (Pan His) Restaurant 泮溪酒家
Beijing Road 北京路
Daxin Ivory Carving Factory 大新象牙工艺厂
Dr. Sun Yat-sen Memorial Hall 中山纪念堂
Foreign Trade Center 外贸中心
Friendship Store 友谊商店
Guangzhou Antique Store 广州文物店
Guangdong Arts and Crafts Service 广东工艺美述服务部
Guangdong Museum 广东省博物馆
Guangdong People's Hospital 广东人民医院
Guangta Smooth Minaret 光塔寺
Guangxiao Temple 光孝寺
Guangzhou Cultural Park 广州文化公园
Guangzhou Jewelry Center 广州市金银首饰总汇
Guangzhou Museum 广州市博物馆
Guangzhou No. 1 People's Hospital 广州第一人民医院
Guangzhou Porcelain and Pottery Shop 广州陶瓷商店

Guangzhou Restaurant 广州酒家
Guangzhou Zoo 广州动物园
Liuhua Park 流花公园
Liurong (Six-Banyan-Tree) Temple 六榕寺
Mausoleum of the Seventy-two Martyrs 黄花岗七十二烈士墓
Nanfang Department Store 南方大厦商店
Nanyuan Restaurant 南园酒家
National Peasant Movement Institute 广州农民运动讲习所
No. 1 Hospital, Zhongshan Medical College 中山医学院第一附属医院
No. 2 Hospital, Zhongshan Medical College 中山医学院第二附属医院
Orchid Garden 兰圃
Painted Porcelain Factory 广州金彩瓷工厂
Passenger Pier for Hong Kong 洲头咀客运码头（往香港）
Qingping Free Market 清平路自由市场
Railway Station 火车站
Shamian (Shamien, Shameen) Island 沙面岛
Shishi (Cathedral of the Sacred Heart) 石室
South China Botanical Garden 华南植物园
Traveling along the Pear River by boat 珠江游船
Xiyuan (West) Garden 西园
Yuexiu Park 越秀公园
Zhen (Chen) Family Temple 陈氏书院（陈家祠）
Zhongshan 5-Road 中山五路

GUILIN 桂林
Cave of Hiding Dragons 龙隐洞
Diecai (Folded Brocade) Hill 叠彩山
Fubo (Whirlpool) Hill 洑波山
Guilin Airport 桂林机场
Ludi (Reed Flute) Cave 芦笛岩
Qixing (Seven-Star) Park 七星岩
Xiangbi (Elephant Trunk) Hill 象鼻山
Yangshuo 阳朔

HAINAN ISLAND 海南岛
Dongshan Mutton 东山羊肉
Five Officials Memorial Temple 五公祠
Haikou 海口
Hele Crab 和乐蟹
Jiaji Duck 加积鸭
Monkey Peninsula 猴岛
Overseas Chinese Farm, Xinglong 兴隆华侨农场
Pearl Farm 珍珠场

Sanya 三亚
The End of the Earth and the Corner of the Sea 天涯海角
Tomb of Hai Rui 海瑞墓
Wenchang Chicken 文昌鸡
Yalong Bay 亚龙湾

JIUJIANG 九江
Causeway between Gantang and Nanmen lakes
甘棠湖和南门湖之间的长堤
Dasheng Pagoda 大胜塔
Yanshui Pavilion 烟水亭

MT. LUSHAN 庐山
Big Heavenly Pond 大天池
Grottoes of the Taoist Immortals 仙人洞
Guling Ridges 牯岭
Hanpokou (the Mouth that Holds Poyang Lake) 含鄱口
Mt. Lushan Botanical Garden 庐山植物园
Pavilion for Viewing the Yangtze 望江亭

NANNING 南宁
Arts and Crafts Service 工艺美术服务部
Foreign Languages Book Store 外文书店
Friendship Store 友谊商店
Guangxi Art College 广西艺术学院
Guangxi Botanical Garden of Medicinal Plants 广西药用植物园
Guangxi Museum 广西博物馆
Institute of Nationalities 广西民族学院
Nanhu (South Lake) Park 南湖公园
Nanning Antique Store 南宁古物店
Yiling Cave 伊岭洞

SHANTOU 汕头
Arts and Crafts Exhibition Hall 工艺展览馆
Chaoyang County 潮阳县
Chaozhou City 潮州市
Embroidery Factory 潮绣厂
Gourd Hill 葫芦山
Han Wengong Temple 韩祠
Jiaoshi Scenic Spot 石风景区
Kaiyuan Temple 开元寺
Lingshan Temple 灵山寺
Maya Bathing Beach 妈屿海滨浴场

Shantou City 汕头市
Wenguang Tower 文广塔
West Lake Park 西湖公园
Zhongshan Park 中山公园

TAISHAN 台山
Feisha Beach 飞沙里
St. Francis Xavier Church 沙勿略墓
Stone Flower Mountain 石花山

ZHAOQING 肇庆
Mateo Ricci Home 利玛窦
Seven-Star Crags 七星岩

ZHONGSHAN 中山
Cuiheng Village 翠亨村
Former Residence of Sun Yat-sen 孙中山故居
Shiqi 石歧
Zhongshan (Chung Shan) Hot Spring Golf Club 中山温泉高尔夫球会

ZHUHAI 珠海
Jiuzhou Islet 九洲岛
Pearl Land Amusement Park 明珠游乐场
Zhuhai International Golf Club 珠海国际高尔夫球场

China Guide

Note: *All places are listed under "Destinations" beginning on page 806*

Things Change!

Phone numbers, prices, addresses, quality of food, etc, all change. If you come across any new information, we'd appreciate hearing from you. No item is too small! Drop us an email note at: Jopenroad@aol.com, or write us at:

China Guide
Open Road Publishing, P.O. Box 284
Cold Spring Harbor, NY 11724

travel notes

travel notes

travel notes

If you're traveling elsewhere in the region beyond China, check out these other Open Road travel guides to Asia & the Pacific Islands:

$14.95

$21.95

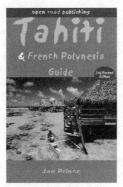

$18.95

$18.95

$18.95